3e

Auditing Assurance & Risk

W . R O B E R T K N E C H E L

UNIVERSITY OF FLORIDA

S T E V E N E . S A L T E R I O

QUEEN'S UNIVERSITY

B R I A N B A L L O U

MIAMI UNIVERSITY

THOMSON
™
SOUTH-WESTERN

Australia · Brazil · Canada · Mexico · Singapore · Spain · United Kingdom · United States

Auditing: Assurance and Risk, 3e
W. Robert Knechel, Steven E. Salterio, Brian Ballou

VP/Editorial Director:
Jack W. Calhoun

Publisher:
Rob Dewey

Acquisitions Editor:
Matt Filimonov

Developmental Editor:
Craig Avery

Marketing Manager:
Kristen Bloomstrom

Content Project Manager:
Tamborah E. Moore

Manager of Technology, Editorial:
Vicky True

Manufacturing Coordinator:
Doug Wilke

Production House:
Interactive Composition Corporation

Printer:
Transcontinental – Louiseville
Louiseville, Quebec

Art Director:
Linda Helcher

Internal and Cover Designer:
Jennifer Lambert, Jen2Design LLC

Cover Images:
© Getty Images

Library of Congress Control Number:
2006906043

For more information about our
products, contact us at:

Thomson Learning Academic
Resource Center

1-800-423-0563

Thomson Higher Education
5191 Natorp Boulevard
Mason, OH 45040
USA

DEDICATIONS

To my wife, Anna, and children, Abigail, Martina, and Andrew, collectively an ongoing source of encouragement and toleration of my efforts.

—W. Robert Knechel

To my spouse, Leslie, and my son, Alexander, who do double duty as my research and teaching assistants in addition to their familial roles. With their active support I have learned that anything is possible.

—Steve Salterio

For my wife, Maria, and sons, Alex and Grant, for all of their love, patience, and support during my career.

—Brian Ballou

Brief Contents

Contents

1 ASSURANCE AND AUDITING   1

2 MANAGING RISK: THE ROLE OF AUDITING AND ASSURANCE   27

3   THE BUILDING BLOCKS OF AUDITING   58

4   THE INTEGRATED AUDIT PROCESS   104

5   UNDERSTANDING THE CLIENT'S INDUSTRY AND BUSINESS: STRATEGIC ANALYSIS   144

6   BUSINESS PROCESSES AND INTERNAL RISKS   190

7   RISK MANAGEMENT AND INTERNAL CONTROL   226

8   EVALUATING INTERNAL CONTROL OVER FINANCIAL REPORTING   271

13   AUDITING RESOURCE MANAGEMENT PROCESSES   567

14   COMPLETING THE INTEGRATED AUDIT I: BUSINESS MEASUREMENT
ANALYSIS   612

Preface

AN AUDITING TEXTBOOK FOR A CHANGING WORLD

The period 2000 through 2006 has been a very turbulent time for the auditing profession, a period that witnessed numerous scandals and their aftermath (Enron, WorldCom, Parmalat), strident calls for changes in the way that auditors practice their profession, and regulatory initiatives that significantly change the way the profession is governed. Long-held attitudes and customary practices have been challenged and found to be deficient by the media, the investing public, and those charged with regulating financial reporting and auditing. Issues of auditor independence, the role of corporate governance, the responsibilities of management, the appropriateness of consulting services, and the overall professional obligations of auditors have all been discussed and debated by a broad array of interested groups and individuals. The theme linking these debates has often been "what is wrong with the auditing profession?" and its close relative, "what can be done to improve the auditing profession?" As a result, this period has probably resulted in more substantive changes to the auditing profession than any other period in modern business history.

The past decade has also seen an increase in the complexity of auditing as business organizations have had to adapt to an evolving international, real-time, technology-dependent economy. Increasingly, organizations form strategic alliances and expand operations to meet the needs of an international, interconnected marketplace. The rapid growth in India and Asia; continued development of the European Union; increased availability of information; reduced barriers to communication; and increased costs and scrutiny of financial reporting in the United States are examples of forces that have increased competition and increased the costs organizations incur to react to changes or correct problems encountered in their business. As a result, organizations are more concerned about managing risk, and stakeholders demand timely information about performance in a broad range of areas. Auditors must keep these issues in mind when evaluating whether financial statements are fairly stated.

OUR PHILOSOPHY: AUDITING AS A JUDGMENT PROCESS

Given the ebb and flow of the auditing profession in the period leading up to 2006, the challenge of a book on auditing is to adequately nurture the long-term effect of these changes while maintaining the best traditions of auditing. The profession is at the cusp of a new world of auditing, and auditing educators face an environment that is no less challenging. *In writing the third edition of this book, the author team has strived to maintain the balance between the new world of auditing increasingly complex organizations and the proven methods of tradition.* To facilitate this balancing act, we have chosen to focus on *auditing as a judgment process* rather than as a process driven by regulations. This philosophy permeates the book and influences the way various topics are presented and discussed. We believe this approach allows instructors a great deal of flexibility in using the book in undergraduate or graduate auditing courses.

AUDITING AND REGULATION

Prior to 2002, the Auditing Standards Board (which is part of the American Institute of Certified Public Accountants) was the only source of authoritative auditing standards in the United States. However, following Enron and WorldCom, the U.S. Congress passed the Sarbanes-Oxley Act of 2002, stripping the profession of the ability to regulate itself and to monitor its own practices as they relate to the audit of publicly listed companies. This authority is now assigned to the Public Company Accounting Oversight Board (PCAOB), and any firm that audits a publicly listed company in the United States must register with the PCAOB and is subject to inspection by the PCAOB no matter where in the world that audit firm is located.

In many other countries, public accounting firms perform audits in accordance with standards established by the International Accounting and Auditing Standards Board (IAASB) of the International Federation of Accountants (IFAC). In some cases, the standards of the IAASB are supplemented with oversight by a local authority—for example, the Auditing and Assurance Standards Board of the Canadian Institute of Chartered Accountants (CICA). The IAASB has also been recognized as an authoritative source of auditing standards in the United States, as evidenced by the decision of the Auditing Standards Board of the AICPA to issue standards consistent with those of the IAASB whenever possible and practical.

In this spirit, we provide coverage of promulgations by both the IAASB and the PCAOB (which include many pre-2002 ASB standards as an interim measure). Although the audit process described in this book is not dependent on either set of standards, we believe that auditors worldwide need to be familiar with both because most auditors will work in international settings throughout their careers. For example, many non-U.S. public companies are registered with the U.S. SEC, or are subsidiaries of U.S. companies, so auditors around the world need to understand PCAOB standards. In turn, auditors in the United States need to understand international standards, as many non-publicly traded clients are audited under the standards of the AICPA, which are being harmonized with the standards of the IAASB. As a result, the largest international audit firms have pushed to have a single audit methodology on a worldwide basis that facilitates compliance with both sets of standards.

Authoritative Guidance & Standards
Throughout the textbook, authoritative guidance that enhances descriptions of standards in the text are included in **Authoritative Guidance and Standards** boxes. Because this book may be used in auditing courses taught from a variety of pedagogical approaches and in a variety of contexts, these boxes help illustrate that *each topic in the text is consistent with generally accepted auditing standards (GAAS) and those standards issued by the PCAOB.* However, these standards are not embedded within the text each time the topic is mentioned; this reinforces the idea that *an audit complies with standards but is not driven by the standards.*

KNOWLEDGE AND SKILLS NEEDED BY AUDITORS IN THE 21ST CENTURY

This textbook describes auditing within the context of current economic, regulatory, and global conditions. The conduct of a financial statement audit has become increasingly complex, and the skill set necessary to perform effective and efficient audits has expanded greatly in recent years. The critical skills and knowledge needed by auditors are far ranging, and the chapters, problems, and cases in the book are developed to provide exposure to a wide range of issues in auditing. More specifically, this book will help students to

- Develop an understanding of the role of auditing and corporate governance in ensuring reliable financial reporting and appropriate behavior by stakeholders.
- Understand how organizations design and carry out corporate strategies that affect financial reporting.
- Evaluate how business processes and strategic alliances that affect financial reporting are designed and implemented.
- Assess the effect of external forces on organizations in an international marketplace.
- Assess how internal forces create risk within an organization.
- Evaluate control responses to organizational risks.
- Integrate business knowledge about an organization with accounting knowledge to develop expectations about its financial reporting.
- Understand the design and effectiveness of internal control over financial reporting.
- Link an understanding of an organization's business risks to concerns about its financial reporting and the need for audit testing.
- Develop critical thinking, ethical reasoning, and problem-solving skills to enable careful, objective analysis of audit issues.

UNIQUE FEATURES OF THIS BOOK

Emphasis on auditing as a judgment-driven, rather than a standards-driven, process: The audit is a complex judgment and decision process. Although there are many standards that affect how an audit is conducted—standards referred to in each chapter and emphasized by the **Authoritative Guidance and Standards** boxes throughout the book—the conceptual structure and execution of an audit involves a series of challenging professional judgments. We present the audit process in this light rather than as a standards-driven process. The foundation for the audit process is presented in Chapter 3, where the key elements (assertions, procedures, and evidence) and concepts (risk, materiality, and evidence) are presented and illustrated. In virtually every chapter, key decisions are presented conditional on factors that must be evaluated using professional judgment.

Auditing as an enterprise-wide, risk-based activity: A common theme of this book is that audit risk is inextricably entwined with client business risk. Risks that threaten an organization are also the source of risks that will affect an audit. Consequently, an effective audit requires an in-depth understanding of the client's industry, strategic goals and plans, critical internal processes, and residual risks that are most likely to threaten its success. This perspective is much broader than the risk perspective underlying the traditional audit risk model with its focus on financial statement results and related assertions. Auditors have come to realize that the risk of misstatements in financial reports is the by-product of a complex risk-management process within an organization. To fully understand audit risks, the auditor must also understand how the organization identifies and responds to its external and internal risks.

Presents a global perspective on auditing: The auditing profession has become increasingly global as clients increase their far-flung operations, public accounting firms become internationally integrated, and standards are harmonized across national boundaries. In this text, we recognize these forces toward a global view of auditing and incorporate examples and practices that are relevant to virtually all countries and governments.

Integration of fraud considerations as a pervasive part of the audit: The audit failures of the past decade have elevated the responsibilities of auditors for detecting and addressing fraudulent financial reporting. The increased focus on fraudulent behavior by management is integrated throughout the book and is the particular emphasis of an innovative chapter on business reporting that brings together the latest thoughts in how to detect potential fraud at the final review stage of the audit (Chapter 14).

Integration of ethical considerations as a pervasive part of the audit: Another recognition that came out of the financial scandals of the past decade was the need to focus on the ethics of decision making, whether by management or by the auditor. Consequently, we have woven ethical considerations throughout the text to illustrate how various aspects of the audit may be affected by ethical reasoning in addition to our integrative treatment of this topic in Chapter 17.

Comprehensive coverage of the audit process: This book provides comprehensive coverage of the audit process, including some topics that are not well developed in most other textbooks, without becoming overwhelming. We accomplish this by emphasizing the conceptual and judgmental nature of the audit process. Key concepts and aspects of the audit are presented with realistic and practical illustrations.

Detailed illustration of business risk analysis: A primary feature of the book is the emphasis on analyzing business risk in order to assess the effect on the conduct of the audit. The effectiveness of management in reducing or controlling significant risks is relevant for the auditor because management actions that mitigate business risks have the potential to reduce the residual risks that the auditor should consider in the conduct of the audit. In this text, we present a number of techniques for analyzing strategic and process risks that are used in practice but do not appear in other auditing textbooks.

Integration of financial reporting and business process controls as a pervasive part of the audit: Auditors have become extremely sensitive to the need for good internal control in all organizations, as well as the impact of internal control on the audit. The PCAOB now requires the auditor to provide a report on the effectiveness of a client's internal control as it pertains to financial reporting. Although this requirement does not apply to non-listed companies in the United States, or to public companies not registered with the U.S. SEC, it has heightened the interest in internal control on most audits. This book adopts the broad approach to internal control that is embodied in the two COSO reports and is fully consistent with the new COSO Enterprise Risk Management—Integrated Framework.

We use the context of risk management to introduce concepts of internal control and then apply them directly to internal control over financial reporting. The topic of internal control over financial reporting (as required by the PCAOB) flows naturally from the broader discussion of internal control and risk management. The discussion of internal control and its effect on the audit is pervasive to the book. Chapter 7 specifically addresses internal control in a risk management framework, whereas Chapter 8 discusses internal control over financial reporting specifically.

Use of the balanced scorecard. The audit process presented in this book presumes that auditors will utilize analytical procedures as a significant source of audit evidence whenever possible. Chapters 9 and 14 are devoted to analytical procedures and performance measurement as used in the audit. We utilize a well-known technique, the balanced scorecard, to facilitate the development of analytical evidence during the course of the audit. This allows us to illustrate how both financial and nonfinancial analytical evidence can be used to provide evidence to the auditor.

Assurance services linked tightly to current practice. We tightly integrate the current "menu" of assurance services offered by practitioners of many different sized firms with the core competencies of auditing and accounting. We focus on financial information related services such as reviews, compilations, and agreed-upon procedures engagements that often form the basis of the assurance practices of many mid-sized regional and local public accounting firms, not to mention the Big 4 firms in some of their individual country practices. We focus on "newer" assurance services to the extent that they have become widely integrated into public accounting firms (such as Trust Services in large international firms and *PrimePlus* in regional and local firms) or have a great potential for future growth (such as enterprise risk management services).

Integration of evidence collected from years of audit research into the appropriate text chapters: The results of various investigations of auditing by many auditing scholars has resulted in a broad base of evidence to judge the effectiveness of certain areas of audit practice. This evidence has been integrated into the text in a non-technical fashion. The authors believe an evidence-based book that incorporates the best audit thinking without emphasis on arcane matters of research methods ensures a sound theoretical foundation for a practice-based learning experience.

ORGANIZATION

The organization of the topics in the book reflects the logical flow of the audit process; thus, the book is divided into four main sections:

1. **Chapters 1–4:** Introduction to auditing, risk management, and the concept of the integrated audit.
2. **Chapters 5–9:** An integrated approach for evaluating client risks and controls and identifying residual risks affecting the conduct of the audit.
3. **Chapters 10–15:** Testing residual risks and financial statement assertions.
4. **Chapters 16–18:** Elaborations on pervasive themes including how to develop and interpret sample-based evidence; an integrative chapter on ethics, judgment, and legal aspects of audit practice; and expanded coverage of both financial information related assurance services and newer assurance services.

Chapters 1 and **2** introduce the concepts of auditing and risk management and present an economic explanation of the role of the financial statement audit in a global business environment. **Chapter 3** discusses the auditor's responsibilities and presents the conceptual structure of the audit process. This chapter introduces the significant elements of the audit process: assertions, audit procedures, and audit evidence. It also defines and illustrates the *three key concepts of audit judgment* that influence all auditor decisions: *risk*, *materiality*, and *evidence*. **Chapter 4** introduces the integrated audit, which combines the auditor's evaluation of internal control over financial reporting and the audit of the information in the financial statements.

Chapters 5 through **9** cover the knowledge acquisition portion of the audit process, culminating in the assessment of residual risks that may affect the audit in general and financial statement assertions and disclosures specifically. **Chapter 5** illustrates techniques for obtaining an understanding of the client's industry and operations and performing an analysis of strategic risks confronting the organization. **Chapter 6** introduces the concepts of process analysis and analysis of internal risks. **Chapter 7** discusses the role of internal control in risk management, followed by a specific discussion of internal control over financial reporting in **Chapter 8.** Finally, **Chapter 9** introduces analytical techniques for assessing audit risks.

Chapter 10 provides the link between the evaluation of risks and the testing of financial statement assertions and disclosures. This chapter covers the topics of the audit risk model and materiality as they relate to the substantive testing of financial statement assertions. **Chapters 11, 12,** and **13** discuss specific areas in detail, including in-depth coverage of substantive audit tests. **Chapters 14** and **15** discuss issues related to completing the audit including evaluating the overall reliability of financial information and preparing the auditor's report.

The final section of the book covers a number of auditing topics in greater depth. In **Chapter 16,** we discuss issues related to developing and interpreting the many different types of samples used in the course of an audit. **Chapter 17** emphasizes the nature of the audit as an ethical judgment process and specifically addresses the role of personal ethics, the professional code of conduct, and responsibilities imposed by the legal system. The final chapter, **Chapter 18,** addresses the both traditional financial information related assurance services such as reviews, compilations, and agreed upon procedures as well as "newer" assurance services such as Enterprise Risk Management and Trust Services.

CHANGES FROM THE SECOND EDITION

Sharing the judgment-based philosophy of the first two editions of this book, the third edition has been totally rewritten to reflect the dramatic developments in auditing since the second edition and advances in state-of-the-art audit practice and theory. With the addition of two new co-authors, the entire team wrote and rewrote chapters, classroom-tested chapters and sequences of materials within and between chapters, obtained student feedback, and revised again. The book continues its emphasis on auditing as a judgment process with extensive use of problems and cases supplemented with **new** short-answer questions at the end of each chapter.

Of particular importance are the following changes:

- **New Co-authors.** With the addition of Steve Salterio (Queen's University) and Brian Ballou (Miami University), the third edition taps a unique wellspring of expertise and vision in the future direction of auditing.

- **Increased Focus on the Integrated Audit.** The third edition introduces the integrated audit as consistent with the standards of the PCAOB but generally applicable to audits not under the auspices of the SEC.
- **Increased Coverage of Ethics.** The third edition integrates fraud, ethical considerations, and corporate governance into topical coverage, examples, and homework throughout the book.
- **New Management Assertions Coverage.** Chapter 3 integrates the revised structure of management assertions that comprise the financial statements consistent with recently issued standards by the AICPA and IFAC.
- **Improved Organization.** The third edition reorganizes the risk and control discussion to provide improved flow of topics. In the current edition, risk analysis (Chapters 5 and 6) is presented prior to control analysis.
- **New and Improved Integration of COSO Framework.** The discussion of internal control is fully consistent with the new COSO *Enterprise Risk Management—Integrated Framework*. In Chapters 7 and 8, the topic of internal control over financial reporting (as required by the PCAOB) flows naturally from the broader discussion of internal control and risk management.
- **New Coverage of Evidence from Client Inquiries.** Chapter 9 includes new material on conducting client inquiries and evaluating evidence obtained from inquiry procedures.
- **New Guidance on Linking Business Risk and Testing.** Chapter 10 contains improved and expanded discussion of how to link the consideration of a client's business risk to the conduct of substantive testing.
- **More Internal Control Examples.** Chapters 11, 12, and 13 include numerous specific examples of internal control over financial reporting as it pertains to specific areas of the audit.
- **New Coverage of Financial Statement Preparation.** Chapter 14 includes an in-depth discussion of the process by which financial statements are aggregated and prepared.
- **New Analytical Approaches for the Final Review of Financial Statements.** Chapter 14 expands on the material in Chapter 9 of the previous edition by employing the balanced scorecard both as a planning analytical tool in Chapter 9 and as an integrative final review tool in Chapter 14.
- **New Coverage of Reporting Requirements.** Chapter 15 adds complete coverage of new reporting requirements under *Auditing Standard 2* of the PCAOB.
- **Sampling Coverage Revised.** Chapter 16 approaches sampling from the viewpoint of what do you need to know to interpret sample-based evidence, and then incorporates the details of sampling based on that framework.
- **Assurance Services Linked Tightly to Current Practice.** Chapter 18 tightly integrates the current menu of assurance services offered by practitioners of many different sized firms to the core competencies of auditing and accounting. We focus on financial information related services such as reviews, compilations, and agreed-upon procedures engagements that often form the basis of the assurance practices of many mid-sized regional and local public accounting firms, not to mention the Big 4 firms in some of their individual country practices. We focus on "newer" assurance services to the extent that they have become widely integrated into public accounting firms (such as Trust Services in large international firms and *PrimePlus* in regional and local firms) or have a great potential for future growth (such as enterprise risk management services).

- **New Guidance and Standards Boxes.** As shown on p. xiv, this new box helps document how topics in each chapter are fully consistent with U.S. and international auditing standard-setting bodies.
- **New and Revised Homework.** Short-answer questions at the end of each chapter have been added, many of which are designed to improve critical thinking skills of auditing students. New and revised homework throughout the text conforms both to the content of the chapters and to the balance of audit judgment and audit skills that is at the heart of the third edition.

SUPPLEMENTS

The following supplements support instructors in planning and managing their course:

Instructor's Resource CD-ROM (ISBN 0-324-37821-1). The Instructor's Resource CD-ROM includes the following supplements:

- **Instructor's Manual with Solutions (**ISBN 0-324-37818-1). Written by the authors with the help of Chrislynn Freed (University of Southern California) and Robert Tucker (University of Florida), this supplement contains suggested solutions for every homework item in the text, along with instructor tips and additional instructor materials.
- **Test Bank** (ISBN 0-324-37820-3). Written by Amelia Baldwin (University of Alabama, Huntsville), this complete bank of test items in Word is fully correlated with the content in the text.
- **PowerPoint Slides.** These PowerPoint slides, by the authors, support instructors as they plan and present lectures and classroom activities. The slides are downloadable from the product support web site and available on the Instructor's Resource CD-ROM.

Product Web Site. This web site (www.thomsonedu.com/accounting/knechel) contains downloads of the Instructor's Manual with Solutions, the Test Bank files in Word, the PowerPoint slides, and periodic updates and additional instructor material.

ACKNOWLEDGMENTS

A project of this size and scope requires input from a large number of individuals and can only succeed with their full faith and support. We have benefited from assistance and discussions with a large broad range of professionals. We especially wish to thank Timothy Bell (KPMG) and Jim Sylph (IFAC) for their generous remarks in the forewords to the text.

Discussions with our academic colleagues have influenced the way in which we observe audit practice. Our gratitude extends to our colleagues at the University of Florida, Queen's University, and Miami University. Individuals who have had a direct effect on the ideas expressed in this book include Stuart Turley and Chris Humphrey (University of Manchester); Emir Curtis (University of Galway); Steven Maijoor, Caren Schelleman, Roger Meuwissen, Rogier Deumes, and Ann Vanstraelen (all of Maastricht University); David Hay (University of Auckland); Morley Lemon, Efrim Boritz, and Natalia Kotchetova (all of University of Waterloo); Ira Solomon and Mark Peecher (both of the University of Illinois); William Kinney

(University of Texas); Kevan Jensen (University of Oklahoma); Mike Stein (Old Dominion University); Michael Bamber (University of Georgia); Philip Wallage (University of Amsterdam); Christine Earley (Bentley College); Jay Rich (Illinois State University); Dan Heitger (Miami University); Mike Gibbins (University of Alberta); Susan McCracken (University of Toronto); Richard Tabor (Auburn University); Vaughan Radcliffe (University of Western Ontario); Dan Simunic (University of British Columbia); Roger Simmett and Ken Trotman (both of the University of New South Wales); Hun-Tong Tan (Nanyang Technological University); Aasmund Eilifsen (Norwegian School of Economics and Business Administration); Marleen Willekens (Tilburg University); and Anna Noteberg (Rotterdam University).

Numerous reviewers have provided feedback on the revisions of the text and many of their excellent suggestions have been incorporated in the new edition:

James Bierstaker (Villanova University)

Allen Blay (University of California, Riverside)

Jan Colbert (Eastern Kentucky University)

Diana Franz (University of Toledo)

David Hay (University of Auckland)

Aretha Hill (Florida A&M University)

Venkat Iyer (University of North Carolina at Greensboro)

Steve Kachelmeier (University of Texas)

Roger Martin (University of Virginia)

Thomas C. Pearson (University of Hawaii at Manoa)

Mark Peecher (University of Illinois)

Joel Pike (University of Illinois, Urbana-Champaign)

John D. Rossi, III, CPA (Moravian College)

Pamela Roush (University of Central Florida)

Hannu J. Schadewitz (Turku School of Economics and Business Administration)

Caren Schelleman (Universiteit Maastricht)

Bahram Soltani (University of Paris 1 Sorbonne)

Robert R. Tucker (University of Florida)

We thank the publishing team at Thomson Business & Economics Publishing (South-Western) for their help: Rob Dewey, Matt Filimonov, Craig Avery, Tamborah Moore, and Linda Helcher.

We are grateful to Chrislynn Freed (University of Southern California) and Robert Tucker (University of Florida) for preparing solutions to the end-of-chapter material in this edition.

Finally, Brian would like to thank the many recruiters at KPMG working under Blane Ruschak who have enabled him to teach two-day seminars consistent with the ideas conveyed in this book to more than 2,000 audit interns from over 125 universities over the past eight years. The insights received from the partners, managers, and staff while interacting with the interns has been invaluable in identifying research issues and better conveying many of the ideas expressed by him within this book.

Steve would like to thank the students in his auditing classes at Queen's University (Canada) from 2003 to 2006 who provided detailed feedback each and every term as the rewrite of the book continued on a chapter-by-chapter basis.

Their frequent and detailed feedback has resulted in greater clarity. Steve's view of auditing has benefited from close contact with audit professionals at PricewaterhouseCoopers, KMPG, and Grant Thornton who have provided literally hundreds of hours of partner, principal, and manager time to aid in his research, upon which many of the book's new ideas are based.

Robert would again like to thank the students and colleagues at the University of Florida and University of Auckland who were often the first audience for many of the ideas in the book. Robert's approach to auditing and auditing education has been influenced by a large number of professionals and academics in auditing who have taken the time to share their ideas and experiences over the many years since the first edition of the book was begun. Robert is particularly grateful to the professionals at Ernst & Young, KPMG, PricewaterhouseCoopers, and BDO Spicers who have devoted a tremendous amount of time to facilitate the investigation, education, and research on which this book is based.

About the Authors

W. ROBERT KNECHEL

W. Robert Knechel is the Ernst & Young LLP Professor of Accounting in the Fisher School of Accounting at the University of Florida. He is also the Director of the Center for Accounting Research at the University of Florida. Professor Knechel holds a B.B.A. from the University of Delaware and a Ph.D. from the University of North Carolina at Chapel Hill. He has served as the resident auditing research fellow at KPMG Peat Marwick LLP. He holds a CPA in the state of Florida and is an active member of the American Institute of CPAs, the Florida Institute of CPAs, and the Institute of Internal Auditors. Professor Knechel has served as the Chairman of the Auditing Section of the American Accounting Association and was responsible for initiating the Biannual Auditing Education Conference and the Auditing Section Mid-Year Meeting. He also served as the Director of Education for the Auditing Section. Professor Knechel has written extensively on auditing issues in research and education for over 25 years, having published over 50 articles during that time in respected academic journals. He has actively pursued the development of case materials for auditing classes. He has also made presentations on auditing research, practice, and education at numerous forums in the United States, New Zealand, Australia, Europe, and China.

STEVE SALTERIO

Steve Salterio (B. Comm. Mt. A. '82, Ph.D. Michigan '93, FCA) is a professor and the PricewaterhouseCoopers/Tom O'Neill Faculty Research Fellow of Accounting at the Queen's School of Business (Canada). The Institute of Chartered Accountants recently awarded Steve the designation of "Fellow" that is given for outstanding contribution to the accounting profession and is awarded to fewer than 3% of all Chartered Accountants in Canada. His research investigates negotiations between auditor and client management on financial reporting issues and the effects of enhanced disclosure on the quality of corporate governance; corporate governance with special attention to the role of the audit committee and external auditor; and judgmental effects of performance measurement systems. Steve has recently been cited in Canadian Accounting Perspectives as among the most productive accounting researchers in Canada in the decade ending in 2000 and among the top North American accounting researchers by *Advances in Accounting*. He is an associate editor at *Contemporary Accounting Research* and an editorial board member at *Auditing: A Journal of Practice and Theory, Journal of Management Accounting Research*, and *Behavioral Research in Accounting*, among others. He has published articles in *Journal of Accounting Research, The Accounting Review, Contemporary Accounting Research, Accounting Organizations and Society,* and *Auditing: A Journal of Practice and Theory,* among other journals, and authored several book chapters. He is the co-author (along with Royston Greenwood) of one of the three most used cases in business risk auditing, Loblaws Inc. Recently two of his professional articles published in *CMA Management* (co-authored with Tony Atkinson) were recognized by the International Federation of Accountants' PAIB as Articles of Merit. He is a chartered accountant who is active in professional accounting organizations in Canada, acts as a consultant to large and mid-size public accounting firms on audit methodology, and presents workshops to directors on governance and control.

Brian Ballou

Brian Ballou is an associate professor of accounting at Miami University in Oxford, Ohio, and co-director of its Center for Governance, Risk Management, and Reporting. Professor Ballou holds a BS/BA from The Ohio State University and a Ph.D. from Michigan State University. He was a CPA in the state of Indiana and an active member of the American Institute of CPAs, where he has served on the Risk Assessment and Risk Assessment Audit Guide Task Forces. He is also an active member of the American Accounting Association, where he has chaired the Auditing Section's Auditing Standards Committee and Communications Committee. Professor Ballou's teaching and research emphasis is on business-risk-based auditing approaches, enterprise risk management, and corporate sustainability reporting. He has taught these topics extensively at the undergraduate, graduate, professional, and executive level over the past 10 years. He has conducted more than 50 case workshops on business risk auditing approaches for more than 2,000 KPMG interns (from more than 125 universities) throughout the United States since 1999. Professor Ballou has actively published over 20 academic research, educational cases, and practitioner articles in leading journals during the past 10 years. He has received more that $200,000 in research and case development grants from The KPMG Foundation and the Economic Development Administration of the United States.

Foreword

From the Director, Academic Research, KPMG LLP

Recent business improprieties aided by materially misstated financial statements have revitalized society's demand for high-quality financial statement audits. Relevant and reliable business information fosters the flow of capital toward its most productive uses. When information is misleading, or users perceive that it is not credible, capital may flow to less productive uses and thus hinder an economy's adaptive efficiency. The resulting cost is borne not just by those who are invested in a given security at a given time, but by society at large. High-quality financial statement audits, therefore, serve the public interest by reducing uncertainty about the reliability of financial information.

The quality of audits and the quality of auditing education are inextricably linked. *Auditing: Risk and Assurance,* Third Edition, by Robert Knechel, Steven Salterio, and Brian Ballou, has several distinctive features that will help auditing educators instill in their students the footprint of a high-quality 21st-century audit. For example, the book presents the contemporary integrated audit as a process of professional judgment and decision making. In my view, one of the most important lessons that faculty can provide to students of auditing is that they are beginning a journey toward becoming *professional judges*. By presenting overarching concepts that illuminate the nature, role, and importance of professional judgment in auditing, this book will help students perceive more clearly and fully the fundamental drivers of audit quality. Students using this book will learn the difference between a professional judgment process and the judgment of a layperson.

Another distinctive feature of *Auditing: Risk and Assurance* is its extensive coverage of concepts and tools for risk identification, assessment, and management. Today's complex financial reporting frameworks require management's exercise of judgment to measure past, present, and expected future economic conditions and events. In turn, the auditor exercises professional judgment to make inferences and form opinions about matters that are inherently uncertain. For this and other reasons, the 21st-century audit is a risk-assessment process. Audit teams successively assess and respond to risks of material misstatement in management's assertions until they conclude that their latest revised assessments rest on valid reasoning from an accumulation of sufficient and appropriate audit evidence.

This book introduces students to risk assessment frameworks, techniques, and tools useful for attaining the high level of quality expected of today's audit. These include, among others, strategic risk analysis, process risk analysis, techniques for evaluating the operating effectiveness of internal control over financial reporting, and substantive testing techniques. The book provides more extensive coverage than other auditing textbooks of the role and importance of the auditors' assessments of entity business risks and controls. And it presents realistic examples that illustrate how and why evidence gathered by auditors to make assessments of entity business risks *is audit evidence*. That is, it shows how these assessments influence conclusions on which the final audit opinion is based.

Building on the introduction of these fundamental auditing concepts, the book defines the components of audit risk and discusses why it is important for students to understand the difference between *risk of material misstatement* in the financial statements and *detection risk*. This discussion helps to develop in students an in-depth understanding of what it really means to be a *professional judge*. The professional auditor not only identifies, assesses, and responds to conditions and events that may affect the entity's achievement of its financial reporting objectives (risks of material misstatement), but also assesses and manages the quality of his or her (or subordinates') own reasoning processes (detection risk). This discussion sets the stage for faculty to provide students with lessons on the fundamental causes of auditors' judgment errors, such as the failure to amass sufficient, appropriate audit evidence and invalid reasoning from evidence.

Other noteworthy features of the book include (1) incorporation of both PCAOB standards and IAASB standards (which is consistent with the audit methodologies of the Big 4 international accounting firms and should meet the needs of audit educators around the world); (2) in-depth discussion of the process of client inquiry; and (3) integration of ethical decision making and how it is affected by cognitive, ethical, professional conduct and legal influences.

The third edition of *Auditing: Risk and Assurance* is a coherent, conceptual, and practical introduction to the 21st-century audit process. In light of the increasing use of judgment and estimates in the preparation of financial statements, the 21st-century audit starts and ends with audit risk assessments. In order to add value to society in the 21st century, auditors must assess the risk that management's judgments and estimates may rest on invalid reasoning—assessments that require a sufficient understanding of the entity's business, including its significant business risks and controls. This book provides the auditing educator with a rich and unique source of material that is essential for students' understanding of the modern process of auditing and the attainment of a high level of quality in auditing education. Effective use of this material in the classroom will help ensure that students are well on their way to becoming the professional judges that society needs in today's demanding audit environment.

Timothy B. Bell, Ph.D., CPA
Director, Academic Research
KPMG LLP
Montvale, New Jersey

June 2006

Timothy B. Bell, Ph.D., CPA, is director, academic research at KPMG International's Audit & Advisory Services Center (AASC) in Montvale, New Jersey. Prior to joining KPMG LLP, Dr. Bell was a member of the accounting faculty at the University of Texas at Austin. Dr. Bell served as vice president-academic and president of the Auditing Section of the American Accounting Association. He was the section's director of research and a member of the editorial board for *Auditing: A Journal of Practice and Theory*. He is co-founder, executive director, and managing director-practice of the KPMG/University of Illinois (UIUC) Business Measurement Case Development and Research Program and its successor, the KPMG and UIUC Business Measurement Research Program. Dr. Bell has authored numerous articles published in journals including *Journal of Accounting Research*, *The Accounting Review*, *Management Science*, and *Auditing: A Journal of Practice & Theory*, as well as in *Accounting Horizons*, *Journal of Accountancy*, *Management Accounting*, and the National Association of Corporate Directors' Governance Series: *Ethics in the Boardroom*. He was co-editor of the AICPA monograph *Auditing Practice, Research, and Education: A Productive Collaboration* (1995) and co-author of the KPMG monographs *Auditing Organizations Through a Strategic-Systems Lens* (1997), *Cases in Strategic-Systems Auditing* (2002), and *The 21st Century Public Company Audit* (2005). Both the 1995 and 1997 monographs received the Joint AICPA/AAA Collaboration Award. In 2003, the 1995 monograph received the Auditing Section's Notable Contributions to the Auditing Literature Award. In 2005, Dr. Bell received the section's Distinguished Service in Auditing Award and the Innovation in Auditing and Assurance Education Award.

Foreword

From the Technical Director,
International Federation of Accountants

The International Auditing Standards Board (IAASB) is a standard-setting body designated by and operating under the auspices of the International Federation of Accountants (IFAC), and subject to the oversight of an international Public Interest Oversight Board. The objective of the IAASB is to serve the public interest by setting, independently and under its own authority, high-quality standards for quality control and auditing, review, other assurance, and related services engagements, and by facilitating worldwide convergence with them. These activities enhance the quality and uniformity of audit practice throughout the world, strengthen public confidence in the global auditing and assurance profession, and contribute to economic development worldwide. Jurisdictions throughout the world recognize the value of a core set of high-quality international auditing standards (ISAs) that are developed with substantial public interest input. For these reasons, they increasingly use or rely on IAASB standards.

An important aspect of the implementation of ISAs is the proper application of the standards by practitioners. This application requires education. Authors Robert Knechel, Steve Salterio, and Brian Ballou have created a text that not only leads the student to a thorough understanding of the audit process, but does so in a way that creates a comprehensive global understanding of the core IAASB and ASB/PCAOB standards. Each chapter of their book contains real examples from around the world, references to authoritative literature from IAASB and ASB/PCAOB, detailed end-of-chapter cross-referencing to both sets of standards, and a bibliography of current audit research that underlies the practical material in each chapter. The authors integrate ethics into numerous text chapters including references to both IFAC's *Code of Ethics for Professional Accountants* as well as U.S. regulations and *Code of Conduct*. The authors also integrate fraud awareness throughout the book and cap their discussion of fraud considerations with an integrated business measurement chapter that is fully compliant with current standards yet shows a way forward that goes beyond current standards to illustrate state of-the-art practice.

The need for an integrated understanding of IAASB and ASB/PCAOB standards by all auditors is demonstrated by the remarkable recent changes in auditing that include

- The International Standards on Auditing (ISAs) are currently adopted by, or incorporated in, the national standards of more than 70 countries, including Australia, New Zealand, South Africa, and the United Kingdom.
- The revised Eighth Company Law Directive, recently finalized within the European Union, specifies that international standards on auditing will be

used for all audits in all Member States, with ISAs being the most likely standards to be adopted.

- The American Institute of Certified Public Accountants (AICPA) has established a policy of making its standards for private company and not-for-profit audits consistent with those of the IAASB. In its first major set of new standards since 2002, the AICPA's Auditing Standards Board (ASB) issued six new Statements on Auditing Standards that are fully consistent with recent ISAs.
- China has established a policy of converging its national auditing standards with the ISAs, reformed its standards system, and planned a schedule for international convergence.

I commend the authors for their efforts to enhance the understanding of all auditors and auditing students at this decisive stage in the development of worldwide auditing standards.

James M. Sylph, FCA
Technical Director
International Federation of Accountants
New York, New York

July 2006

James M. Sylph is technical director of IFAC. He manages the work of the International Auditing and Assurance Standards Board (IAASB), the International Ethics Standards Board (IESBA), and the International Accounting Education Standards Board (IAESB). He was director of Audit Standards and then director of Strategic Programs for the Canadian Institute of Chartered Accountants (CICA), and is former chairman of the Canadian Auditing and Assurance Standards Board and a retired partner at Moores Rowland, Canada, and at Ernst & Young.

IFAC is comprised of approximately 160 professional accountancy bodies in 120 countries. It is committed to achieving global convergence of national standards with international standards as part of its mission to protect the public interest. Its Statements of Membership Obligations (SMOs), published in April 2004, formally capture IFAC's longstanding requirement that its member bodies support the work of the IAASB by using their best endeavors to incorporate the respective international standards in their national requirements and to assist in implementing the international standards, or national standards that incorporate them. The IAASB consists of a full-time chairman and 17 volunteer members from around the world. Meetings are open to the public, and agenda papers and meeting summaries are posted on the IAASB web site. Visitors can also view project histories and may download audio recordings of the IAASB meetings. They can also download IAASB exposure drafts and view all comments made on those drafts. To download the IAASB standards or for more information about the IAASB and the IFAC, see their web sites at www.ifac.org.

Assurance and Auditing

Outline

INTRODUCTION

Knowledge in the form of an informational commodity indispensable to productive power is already, and will continue to be, a major—perhaps the major—stake in the worldwide competition for power.

> *Jean François Lyotard (b. 1924), French philosopher.*

The truth is not simply what you think it is; it is also the circumstances in which it is said, and to whom, why, and how it is said.

> *Václav Havel (b. 1936), Czech playwright, past president.*

To live is to make decisions. Informed decisions should be based on information that is objective, relevant, reliable, and understandable. But how does an individual making a decision know that he or she has reliable information? In a nutshell, this question captures the nature of the problem which justifies the study of auditing. In today's global business environment in which all sorts of data is transmitted on a real-time basis, decision makers worry that the information they have available will *not* be objective, relevant, reliable, or understandable. Indeed, information can be incorrect because someone makes an accidental mistake, or it can be intentionally manipulated for the benefit of others. Individuals who rely on information that is misleading, incomplete, or confusing may make decisions that lead to unexpected and/or unacceptable outcomes, such as investments that result in significant losses.

People rarely accept information at face value when a critical decision depends on it, especially when the information comes from a source that may have questionable motivations (e.g., a salesperson). Information provided by an unreliable or self-serving source will be skeptically received. To compensate for potentially inaccurate data, people often seek information from multiple sources with adequate expertise and objectivity to be considered "reliable." Buyers read consumer reports before making a major purchase, patients get second opinions before undertaking medical procedures, shoppers compare prices online or on foot, and employers obtain multiple references about a job candidate. Regardless of the decision being made, people need useful information about their options and would like some assurance that they will make their decision based on information that is, in fact, objective, relevant, reliable, and understandable. For accounting information alternative public sources are often not available, hence the need arises for assurance over the information's quality.

INFORMATION, BUSINESS, AND GLOBAL CAPITAL MARKETS

Investors in today's international marketplace have more choices than ever for how to invest capital. A multitude of options elevates the importance of high quality information used to make investing decisions. An important source of information to all investors is the periodic financial statement prepared by publicly listed companies. Furthermore, the availability of real-time information about competitive pressures and environmental forces that threaten the value of an investment provides investors with a better understanding of the risks surrounding their investments. Consider a few of the information risks that investors face when making decisions based on financial reports:

- Information may be *biased* to entice an investor to purchase shares in a company that is intentionally overvalued. Accounting procedures that accelerate revenues and slow down expenses are common tricks for pushing earnings to high levels.
- Information may be *irrelevant*, emphasizing facts that appear important but are unrelated to the future prospects of the company. The marketing of new stock issues may involve claims about future prospects that are hard to evaluate and tangential to the operations of the organization.
- Information may be *inaccurate*. There could be many reasons why information might be incorrect, whether by accident or through intentional manipulation by the management of a company.
- Information may be thought to be "*sensitive*" so a company may decide to hide it from outsiders, especially if the information will have a negative impact on the company's market valuation. For example, a company may not want to disclose that much of its profits come from transactions with affiliated companies.

- Information may be *complex* hence difficult to understand or decipher. Some companies may deliberately report complex transactions, such a derivatives, hedges, and pension accounting in ways that confuse investors.

Any of these conditions may lead to poor decisions if the investor is unaware of the low quality of the information being used. The role of the auditor is to reduce these risks for people who use the information.

Virtually any information provided by one party to another can be subject to an "audit" if the recipient of the information is concerned about its objectivity, relevance, or reliability. In this book, we focus on situations where an independent third party evaluates financial statements to ensure that they are prepared in accordance with established criteria known as generally accepted accounting principles (GAAP). So why is an audit of financial statements important to the stakeholders of an organization? At least four general reasons explain the natural demand for auditing:

- Managers of an enterprise may get sloppy or behave in inappropriate ways if they are not subject to independent scrutiny. An audit helps keep management honest and motivated since they know that they are being examined.
- Many stakeholders (employees, casual investors, politicians, etc.) might not have sufficient expertise to evaluate the quality of financial statements. An audit serves the role of providing this review in an efficient and effective manner.
- Reliable financial reports reduce an organization's cost of capital. Because potential investors use audited information to help make their investment decisions, reducing the risk of unreliable information reduces the risk of surprises and improves investment decisions.
- Investors and creditors want insurance against significant errors or fraud associated with financial statements. Auditors provide a reasonable level of assurance that information received by capital providers is reliable. However, on rare occasions when fraud is uncovered, investors and creditors typically take legal actions against auditors because they believe that the level of assurance provided constitutes a virtual guarantee about the quality of information.

The combination of the risks of unreliable information and the benefits of an audit create a natural demand for auditing and related services that arises as a result of economic forces, human nature, and the need to make informed decisions. In this book, we specifically examine the audits of financial statements and the role of auditors in maintaining fair and active capital markets as well as providing assurance over the financial statements of important non-public entities such as private companies and not-for-profit entities.

THE ROLE OF AUDITING IN AN INTERNATIONAL ECONOMIC SYSTEM

The demand for auditing is not a new development dependent on modern economic conditions. In ancient times, auditors worked for the government and also doubled as tax collectors. The auditing profession as we know it today dates from the 1800s and developed as a result of the economic forces of the time. England was a major economic power as a result of its industrial prowess, far-flung colonial empire, and strong navy. Consequently, the economic base of the country's wealth was scattered all over the world. At the same time, wealth was typically controlled by individuals, families, or family-run banks, who hired local caretakers to run the day-to-day operations of their widespread interests. A major concern of these wealthy and powerful individuals was that their distant assets were properly maintained and utilized by local caretakers. The early emphasis of auditing was on asset stewardship, meaning verification of the existence and proper handling of assets. As a result, auditing professionals tended to follow the assets, often to some ports-of-call that, at the time, were considered very exotic.

This model of auditing thrived until the early 1900s when companies began to outgrow the capital base that could be controlled within a family or close-knit group of individuals. Equity markets were developing and large corporations were beginning to sell shares to outsiders and small investors. At this point, the role of both accounting and auditing began to change. Because outside investors were more concerned with future profitability than stewardship of specific assets, new approaches to accrual accounting were developed, along with refocusing auditing on the results of accrual accounting (i.e., earnings). Profitability became the basis for assessing and predicting share values, and measuring and verifying financial results became the dominant concern of accountants and auditors.

Modern business enterprises have a great deal in common whether they manufacture cars, sell food, dispense health care, or loan money. These similarities include the need to procure capital, acquire productive assets, sell products or services, collect payment from customers and, eventually, provide adequate returns to investors. The specifics of operations, however, may vary dramatically from business to business. For example, capital may be obtained by borrowing money from a bank or by selling stock in a public offering; products may be manufactured or purchased from another vendor; and sales may be made through retail outlets, catalogs, telemarketing, or the Internet.

Another commonality across businesses is the need to generate and report reliable information about the activities of the business. Large and small business enterprises, not-for-profit entities, and governmental organizations all need relevant and reliable information because the quality of decision making at all levels is directly affected by the quality of information used to make decisions. All organizations have some type of accounting and information system. In some organizations, the accounting system is highly sophisticated and complex. In these cases, computerized databases may be used to capture desired information which can then be sorted, aggregated, and reported in different ways depending on the needs of the audience. In other organizations, the accounting system may be rather informal, going down to the most basic level of a checkbook and shoe box of receipts. The need for reliable information is equally important in both instances.

Furthermore, businesses operate in a global, real-time marketplace in which developing and maintaining a competitive advantage has become increasingly difficult. The cycle of reporting and using information has become increasingly dynamic, almost fluid, to the extent that users of information are looking for ways to understand not only how well an organization is performing now but also how well it can be expected to perform in the future. This task is made more complex by the reduction in barriers between countries, industries, and market participants. As companies become more and more innovative in their production and distribution processes, boundaries between organizations become blurred. For example, just-in-time inventory systems necessitate an extensive degree of integration between the information systems of two or more companies. In fact, technology has the power to make traditional boundaries virtually invisible.

Example

> When a customer logs on to Amazon's website or any of its country-specific affili-
> ated sites to shop for books, music and movies, they are accessing the computer-
> ized information system of Amazon. That is, the customers are effectively inside the
> information system of Amazon. This creates both opportunities and challenges for
> the Internet retailer. First, such access serves to improve customer service and re-
> duce administrative costs as customers can place orders, check on order status,
> store items for future purchase, process returns and provide feedback, all without
> the intervention of a human employee. However, Amazon would not want cus-
> tomers electronically roaming around the entire system so electronic boundaries
> must be put in place (e.g., customers should not be allowed to change posted price
> lists). Given the power of technology, those boundaries can be placed at various lo-
> cations within the electronic world of Amazon and are not relegated to the front
> door or checkout counter as would be the case in a traditional retailer.

Adding further complexity to technology developments are changes in the ways businesses conduct some of their basic operations. Many independent organizations are linked with strategic partners such that the performance and actions by one party will impact the performance of other parties. These relationships often are complex and involve organizations in different countries and/or industries. To illustrate, consider a Japanese automotive company that manufactures vehicles in Canada for sale in North America. Some of the parts and components will be manufactured by suppliers in Canada while others will be manufactured in Japan, the United States, or Mexico and shipped to Canada. The information needs for this company are highly complex. First, the company must design vehicles based on projected consumer preferences, technological developments, and regulatory requirements. The company must forecast sales to make decisions related to facility location, production planning, coordination with suppliers, labor management, and distribution. Furthermore, given the degree of integration with suppliers, unforeseen disruptions anywhere in the supply chain can result in an expensive factory shutdown. Finally, the company must know where to move completed vehicles to maximize the efficiency of product sales and distribution.

In short, access to good information can be used to acquire wealth and power; lack of good information may lead to failure. Accountants who oversee the company's information systems, and auditors who audit the financial statements, are uniquely positioned to increase the usefulness of information which ultimately contributes to the economic growth of a society.

THE DEMAND FOR ASSURANCE: INTEGRITY, TRUST, AND RISK

As discussed in the last section, the history of auditing suggests that it arises naturally from economic activity and is not solely a by-product of government regulation. To illustrate this view more concretely, consider a company that wishes to obtain a bank loan in order to purchase equipment. Normally the company will have to provide financial statements to the bank as well as other information about its assets. The bank may be willing to loan money to the company but will protect itself against the risk of being misled by charging a risk premium in the form of higher interest rates. The bank will forgo some of this risk premium if the company agrees to submit audited financial statements that report the results of operations and the financial status at the end of the year. Some accounting academics have reported that this interest rate reduction may be as great as 50 basis points (1/2 percent).[1]

Consider another typical business story: In the early stages of a start-up business, the founder may supervise everything and perform the most critical tasks. If the business is successful, two things happen. First, it gets bigger so that more help is needed and some management responsibility must be turned over to others. Second, the transactions of the company become more numerous and more complicated. For example, the company may lease some of its locations using long-term leases or extend employee benefits to include health insurance and retirement benefits. The natural result of growth means the owner can no longer directly observe all actions and decisions and give them his personal approval. Furthermore, he may not have the expertise to evaluate the handling of complicated transactions such as long-term leases and employee benefits. As this continues, he will become more dependent on performance reports prepared by managers and accountants. Hence, the owner must be concerned with the accuracy of those reports. The managers preparing the reports may accidentally make mistakes, or may intentionally misstate the results to show their own performance in a positive light.

These illustrations highlight the need for integrity and trust in economic activities. A lack of trust may cause potential market participants to avoid getting involved in situations where integrity may be lacking. A bank won't loan to a person it does not trust and an owner will not employ individuals of questionable character. A used car dealer may *say* that a specific car is reliable and free from problems, but in the absence of an independent confirmation that it has not been in a past accident or that its parts are not defective or worn out, a buyer is unlikely to trust the dealer completely. At best, the buyer will offer a low price for the car; at worst, the buyer will go somewhere else.

Management reports their performance in the annual financial statement. However, managers are subject to two competing forces that will influence the likelihood that they will misstate financial results for their own benefit: (1) incentives and (2) ethical principles. *Incentives* refer to motivational forces such as bonuses or contingent compensation that may push a manager to work hard to achieve goals and objectives, but may also motivate an individual to lie or employ accounting "tricks" when the goals are not met. *Ethical principles* provide a counterweight to perverse incentives by defining norms of behavior or conduct for individuals and organizations that define inappropriate actions and activities.

INCENTIVES

Why do organizations create incentives? Normally the goal is to increase the individual manager's commitment to achieving the broad goals of the organization. Monetary and non-monetary incentives have been found to lead to greater productivity and better responses to changes in the environment. However, an uneven distribution of information among individuals may make it difficult for

---

1 Blackwell, D. W., T. R. Noland, and D. B. Winters. 1998. The Value of Auditor Assurance: Evidence from Loan Pricing. *Journal of Accounting Research.* 36 (1): 57–70.

stakeholders to observe the behavior of managers. *Information asymmetry* occurs when one party (e.g., the supplier of information) knows more about the quality of the information provided (i.e., reliability) than another party (e.g., the user of the information). Because stakeholders are aware of the possibility that others may misrepresent information or take advantage of circumstances for personal gain, a certain degree of distrust will arise among parties in an economic relationship. Economists have identified two situations where incentives and information asymmetry may create potentially dysfunctional distrust: (1) adverse selection and (2) moral hazard.

Adverse selection exists when a buyer of products or services cannot distinguish between good and bad alternatives. Is that car really reliable? Is that restaurant really as good as they advertise? Can I believe the information on the job candidate's resume? Are these financial statements really prepared in accordance with GAAP? In all these examples, the seller (management) knows more about the product/service (financial statements) then the buyer (investor/creditor) does. If the buyer or investor or creditor is uncomfortable enough with this information asymmetry, he or she may walk away from any association with the seller—no car sales, no dinners, no jobs, no loans, no investment.

Furthermore, even if a company is a valuable investment with excellent future prospects, potential investors may only be willing to offer a low price for the company's shares if they cannot discriminate it from a poor quality investment. In the extreme, the market for the company's shares may collapse if there are no buyers willing to trust management. To avoid this possibility, management has an incentive to provide trustworthy information about the company so that prospective buyers can sort out good investments from bad. This need creates an economic role for assurance about the reliability of information, thus the need for an auditor. Adverse selection in the financial reporting context usually refers to whether investors have credible information on which to determine if an investment is "good" or "bad." Absent such information, investors will reduce the price they are willing to pay for a company's stock, avoid a company's securities altogether, or even avoid an entire market (e.g., stock exchanges in countries infamous for their level of corruption).

The second problem related to information asymmetry is *moral hazard*, which refers to how individuals (managers) behave when their actions cannot be observed by other stakeholders, or when they are not held accountable for their decisions by those who provide them the resources that they manage. To illustrate, if a manager knows that his or her actions cannot be directly observed by the owners of the company, he or she may have an inclination to goof off a bit or to consume corporate resources for his or her own personal benefit (e.g., expensive and unnecessary travel, fancy meals, corporate funded transportation, club memberships, or low interest personal loans). The less likely the owner is to observe this behavior, the more likely it is to be a problem. In general, this type of inappropriate behavior—at least from the owner's perspective—is referred to as *shirking*. Moral hazard in financial reporting refers to situations where owners do not have enough information to evaluate whether management is doing a good job or not.

The owner is not without recourse, however. Knowing full well that the manager cannot be observed at all times, the owner will then be inclined to pay the manager less for his or her services. The cost of inappropriate behavior by the manager and the manager's loss of earnings attributable to the owner's distrust are often referred to as *agency costs*. Accurate and trustworthy information about the manager's actions provides a way in which to avoid agency costs.

ETHICAL PRINCIPLES

Ethical principles influence the willingness of individuals, particularly managers, to take part in inappropriate activities that can arise as a result of information asymmetry. To determine if a decision has an ethical dimension, an individual can simply ask: "If this action were to appear on the front page of the local paper, would I be ashamed or concerned?" Ethical behavior by individuals comes from their own internalization of what is ethical, based in part on the behavioral norms of society. Consequently, ethical principles can vary widely from person to person. There are a variety of philosophical perspectives that expound on the nature and value of societal norms:

> **Utilitarianism** involves making decisions that will provide the maximum benefit to a well defined group of people.
>
> **Golden Rule** involves making decisions that result in treating others in a manner in which the individual making the decision would like to be treated.
>
> **Theory of Rights** suggests that the rights of a decision maker and other parties should be equally balanced in making a decision.
>
> **Theory of Justice** suggests that decisions should treat all stakeholders fairly, impartially, and equitably.
>
> **Enlightened Self-Interest** involves pursuing long term self-interests and avoiding a short-term focus that might harm others.

Although these perspectives differ in what they emphasize, the norms that follow from each perspective facilitate ethical decision making. Individual norms may be further affected by the organizational context of a decision. Consequently, it is important for stakeholders to understand how an organization approaches the ethical dimension of its decisions, communicates the need for ethical considerations throughout the organization and implements decisions that are consistent with reasonable standards of ethical behavior. Again, however, the priority that individuals will give to ethical norms depends on many factors and can lead to a wide range of behaviors given the circumstances of an organization.

Individuals can react in one of three ways when they encounter a situation in which decisions may be ethically questionable. One easy reaction is to do nothing, that is, to *remain loyal* to those making unethical decision by choosing to actively or passively collude in the unethical practices (e.g., many employees at Enron participated in the company's unethical practices, often enriching themselves, or knew about them and did nothing). Indeed, some individuals exhibit a level of organizational or interpersonal loyalty that disguises the fact that they have been complicit in unethical behavior. Another response would be to *exit from the situation*, that is, to quit because of unethical decisions but without informing others who have a legitimate stake in the practices of the organization (as when Jeffrey Skilling quit as Enron's CEO without revealing the unethical lapses at the company). Finally, the response that is often the most difficult to pursue is to *voice concern* or to warn others about unethical practices (e.g., a whistleblower who informs others in authority of unethical practices). In other words, the individual actively tries to rectify the unethical organizational practices without considering the personal cost.

Example

To encourage employees to voice their concerns, which exposes an employee as a whistleblower, laws have been enacted in the United States to protect individuals from being punished for this action. Further, public companies must implement anonymous hotlines which can be used by individuals to voice concerns that they might not wish to discuss publicly.

Full and complete disclosure of information about the performance of an organization goes a long way to discourage unethical decisions because few people are willing to undertake actions that will make them look bad (or worse, guilty) if the public were to find out. Hence, managers who have ethical norms that enable them to recognize ethical dilemmas are less likely to take advantage of information asymmetry and are more likely to do the "right" thing when confronted with an ethical dilemma.

THE ROLE OF CORPORATE GOVERNANCE

The problems related to adverse selection, moral hazard and ethical breakdowns are so important to the stakeholders of most organizations that a system for dealing with these risks has developed over time, referred to as *corporate governance*. Corporate governance involves oversight of management's activities, including establishing strategy, conducting operations to achieve strategic objectives and manage risks, and communicating effectively with key stakeholders. A system of corporate governance usually includes the Board of Directors, committees of the Board such as the Audit Committee and Compensation Committee, the internal auditor, and the external auditor.

Most organizations elect those charged with corporate governance using a process in which shareholders vote on who will serve on the Board of Directors. Ideally, most Board members will be from outside the company but some members may have executive positions within the company (called insiders) or other economic links with the organization. For example, directors who also serve as the external legal counsel or attorney, or are senior executives with a significant supplier of the company, are referred to as "grey directors" because they are neither insiders nor outsiders in the strictest sense.

An important board subcommittee, which all U.S. public companies must have by law, is the audit committee, which monitors management's financial reporting process. The audit committee consists of at least three members, all of whom should be outsiders. Other countries have similar rules embedded in laws or stock exchange regulations, but these may only call for the majority of the audit committee members to be outsiders. A common responsibility of the audit committee is to hire and terminate the external auditor. This is now a legal requirement for publicly traded companies in the United States. Typically, the audit committee is briefed on the audit plans of both the external and internal auditors, receives all correspondence from auditors during the engagement and assists in resolving accounting or other disagreements between auditors and management.

Given the importance of the audit committee for fostering reliable financial reporting, the criteria for being a member may be higher than for simply being a member of the Board of Directors. In the United States, each member of the committee must be financially literate, with one member being a financial expert. To be *financially literate*, a committee member must be able to read and understand financial statements of the complexity normally associated with the organization. To be a *financial expert*, a committee member must have served an accounting role or supervised accountants in a previous or current position such that it can be expected that he or she would have an in-depth understanding of the organization's financial statements. Ultimately, the ability of the external auditor to communicate with the audit committee is critical to conducting an effective audit because the interests of the auditor and the audit committee are likely to be the same—that is, to produce reliable financial reports.[2]

Example

> In 2004, Deloitte & Touche LLP became concerned by accounting policies established by the CFO of Molex, Inc. Further, the CEO admitted to having signed the letter of representations (relating to the audit) without having first read the document. Based on these and other issues, Deloitte demanded that the Board of Directors of Molex terminate both the CEO and the CFO. When the Board decided against such action, Deloitte & Touche resigned as auditors. Only after the Board yielded and demoted both the CEO and CFO was the audit committee able to retain a new auditing firm, Ernst & Young LLP.

Another element of corporate governance is the Compensation Committee of the Board which is responsible for overseeing the awarding of compensation to the management team. This committee is charged with overseeing executive compensation and to provide reports to the shareholders about the amount and nature of compensation given to individuals. These committees have been under scrutiny in the United States because of the excessive compensation packages offered to senior executives in the form of salary, bonuses, and stock-based compensation.

Internal auditors are also a key component of corporate governance and are primarily responsible for monitoring the effectiveness and efficiency of operations, including the reliability of processes that handle information within the organization. The existence, extent and quality of internal auditing activities directly affect the extent of control within the organization. For example, publicly-owned companies in the United States are required to have an internal audit function that reports to the audit committee of the board of directors.

Although all of these mechanisms are helpful in reducing problems related to adverse selection and moral hazard, there are limitations on their effectiveness. Internal auditors work for the managers they audit and the effectiveness of board oversight is dependent on the quality of information they have for evaluating management. Thus, external auditors play a critical role in the system of corporate governance because they are independent and provide assurance about the quality of information available to the Board and investors.

The Role of the External Auditor

Because incentives may push managers into actions or decisions that are undesirable to other stakeholders, and because personal and organizational ethical principles are an incomplete or uneven brake on undesirable practices, a role develops naturally for an auditor to reduce the effects of information asymmetry and questionable ethics. More specifically, providers and users of information may agree to

---

2 It is also the auditor's responsibility for companies selling securities on U.S. stock exchanges to evaluate the effectiveness of the audit committee in carrying out its responsibilities, which can be challenging given the role of the audit committee in hiring and terminating the auditor.

bring in a third-party to evaluate the extent to which information is objective, relevant, reliable, and understandable. The *auditor* is considered a trusted arbiter of the information. To be useful, however, an auditor must be free of conflicts of interest with the supplier and user of the information, possess adequate expertise, be able to evaluate the reliability of the information, and understand the context in which the information is being conveyed. Traditionally, this situation is best exemplified by the reporting relationship between company management and investors and other market participants (e.g., lenders). Thus, auditors help to preserve the necessary level of trust that investors have in the capital markets.

However, auditors are people too, and they face incentives that may cause them to act in an unethical fashion. External auditors are paid by the organization they audit and face cost constraints and time pressure to finish an audit on time and at a profit, while maintaining the perception that they are competent professionals. These incentives may tempt auditors to act in ways that are unethical. Pressures on the auditing profession in the 1990s led to an unprecedented level of competition among accounting firms. The resulting downward pressure on audit fees led to two potentially devastating developments: (1) reduced audit effort on individual engagements and (2) increased emphasis on non-assurance services for generating fee growth (consulting).

One firm that went too far in both directions was Arthur Andersen, which faced crippling lawsuits arising from audit failures associated with its audits of Waste Management, Sunbeam, Global Crossing, WorldCom, and Enron. In the latter case, Andersen was indicted for failing to follow up on questionable accounting practices at the energy company, known for its high level of intangible assets and complex transactions. Making matters worse, the partner on the engagement pleaded guilty to obstruction of justice for his role in encouraging the shredding of documents that were likely to be subpoenaed in connection with the Enron engagement. The loss of confidence in Andersen that followed the firm's conviction on felony charges led to dissolution of the firm during 2002. The reversal of that conviction in 2005 was a pyrrhic victory given that the firm itself had ceased to exist.

The audit of Enron and the resulting tragedy of Andersen taught the profession a powerful lesson—*no amount of revenue can justify abdicating or appearing to abdicate an auditor's professional responsibilities.* Considerable emphasis throughout this book will be placed on the need for the auditor to recognize ethical dilemmas and deal with them properly when they arise. Because of the importance of ethical decision making by auditors, both the accounting profession and society have rules and regulations to help auditors to recognize ethical problems and to react appropriately.

DIFFERENTIATING ASSURANCE, ATTESTATION, AUDITING, AND ACCOUNTING

Succinctly stated, investors want *assurance*. That is, they want to be confident that the information they use for decisions is reliable. The role of the auditor is to provide assurance about financial statements.

FUNDAMENTAL AUDIT CONCEPTS

Before going further, we need to define some terms more precisely. Assurance and auditing are very broad concepts, and go beyond the basic audit of financial statements. Although the concept of assurance is fundamental to auditing, not all accountants agree as to what constitutes an engagement to provide assurance. For example, evaluating the reliability of corporate performance reports or the effectiveness of management in complying with legal regulations could both be considered assurance services. Currently, the most general and succinct definition of *assurance services* is suggested by the American Institute of Certified Public Accountants (AICPA):

"Independent professional services that improve the quality of information, or its context, for decision makers."

Although this definition is not an official standard of the profession, it suggests a broad range of professional services that an accountant/auditor can provide to a variety of clients and clearly pertains to the reliability of information.

Assurance services can also apply to a large set of general decision making issues. For example, assurance providers can address questions about the relevance of information used in making decisions, the viability of a company's business plan, the appropriateness of its business processes, the effectiveness of its attempts to reduce risks, and the quality of its decision processes. Although the boundary is not well defined, assurance services do not include engagements to provide advice aimed at directly improving the profitability of the organization (e.g., consulting).

Example

Public accounting firms may be hired to design and implement an information system or to help value a potential merger target. These services would constitute consulting. However, if an accountant is hired to verify the reliability of the system or the accounting treatment of a merger transaction, that would constitute an assurance engagement.

The International Federation of Accountants (IFAC) addressed the issue of assurance services in a more narrow fashion than the United States or Canada. The *International Standard on Assurance Engagements* defines an assurance engagement as

". . . an engagement in which a practitioner expresses a conclusion designed to enhance the degree of confidence of the intended users other than the responsible party about the outcome of the evaluation or measurement of a subject matter against criteria."

International Standards make the distinction between (1) a direct reporting engagement and (2) an attest engagement. In a *direct reporting engagement*, the practitioner measures and evaluates information directly.[3] The nature of the measurement or evaluation is provided to the intended users in an assurance report. For example, the audit firm PricewaterhouseCoopers counts and reports the votes for the Academy Awards. The process of counting votes represents a direct reporting engagement.

Attestation is the process of providing assurance about the reliability of specific information provided by one party to another. Attestation focuses on a specified assertion that is made in writing. The professional who is providing an

---

3 Alternatively, the auditor might obtain a representation from a responsible party that has measured and evaluated the relevant information but which cannot be communicated directly to the intended users.

Figure 1–1   Relationship Among Assurance, Attestation, and Financial Statement Auditing

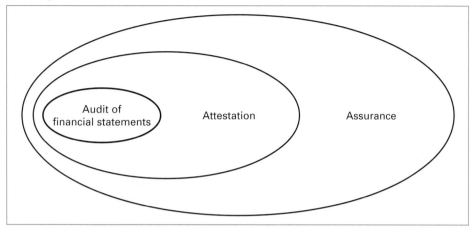

attestation does not usually generate original information since that is the responsibility of the party reporting the information. The attester is simply adding his or her opinion about the reliability of the information. Figure 1–1 shows attestation as a subset of assurance engagements. An attest service cannot be a direct reporting engagement.

Example

In 1998, members of the United Auto Workers Union went on strike at Delphi Automotive, a key supplier of General Motors, over the issue of overseas outsourcing of certain manufacturing processes and parts. As part of the agreement that resolved the strike, GM agreed to hire a public accounting firm to provide assurance on the reliability of the metrics included in the contract that would be used in future periods to determine the nature and extent of outsourcing of manufacturing to other countries.

The most common form of attestation pertains to the verification of financial reports. As a result, auditing and "accounting" are integrally entwined. More specifically, *accounting* is the process by which information about an activity or enterprise is identified, recorded, classified, aggregated, and reported. Most often, the information of interest relates to the monetary effects of economic events that have an impact upon the enterprise. *Financial accounting* refers to the specific process of identifying, recording, classifying, aggregating, and reporting the information that is required for external purposes by *generally accepted accounting principles* (GAAP). Financial accounting is a subset of the total information that is generated by a business enterprise. In the United States, the Financial Accounting Standards Board (FASB) issues standards for financial reporting. Most countries in the European Union follow GAAP as defined by the International Accounting Standards Board (IASB). Other countries (such as Australia and Canada) follow rules set by their local accounting profession, often based on a variant of FASB or IASB standards.

Financial statement auditing is the process of providing assurance about the reliability of the information contained in a financial report prepared by management in accordance with GAAP. Management generates the financial reports based on its interpretation of GAAP. The external auditor examines them in accordance with *generally accepted auditing standards* (GAAS), suggests changes to client management where the auditor believes GAAP has not been applied correctly, and reports to the shareholders the results of the audit. This book focuses on the audits of financial statements.

THE NATURE OF ASSURANCE AND ATTESTATION ENGAGEMENTS

Although the range of potential assurance services that an accountant can provide is very broad, there are some general guidelines as to when an accountant should or should not provide specific services. In general, an auditor or public accountant should only undertake an *assurance engagement* when three conditions are met:

1. He or she has adequate knowledge of the context in which assurance is to be given.
2. The subject matter of the assurance can be examined with an objective evaluation process.
3. The assurance provider must be independent and objective in regards to the information and its context.

For example, public accountants have developed a service related to Internet-based electronic commerce that provides assurance to customers that web sites are legitimate and that transactions will be properly executed with appropriate security and confidentiality (in one case, the American Institute of Certified Public Accountants [AICPA] and partners worldwide marketed these services under the names *WebTrust* and *SysTrust*). Given the existing expertise that many public accountants possess regarding information systems, such an assurance service is a logical extension of their knowledge domain and satisfies the three conditions above.

Other examples of assurance services that are commonly provided by auditors and public accountants include

*   *Environmental audits* to test compliance with environmental laws and regulations.
*   *Ethics audits* to evaluate management's compliance with the norms of ethical decision making.
*   *Software audits* to test the reliability of commercial software.
*   *Royalty audits* to determine proper amounts for licensing fees or royalty payments.
*   *Utilization audits* to verify key operating data such as occupancy rates or attendance levels.
*   *Investment performance audits* to verify yields on managed portfolios and mutual funds.
*   *Cost audits* to verify data used in computing reimbursements under cost-sharing contracts.

The general criteria for offering *attestation services* are somewhat more specific than an assurance engagement. In an attest engagement, a public accountant is engaged to issue a written communication that expresses a conclusion about the

Figure 1–2   Three parties involved in an attest engagement

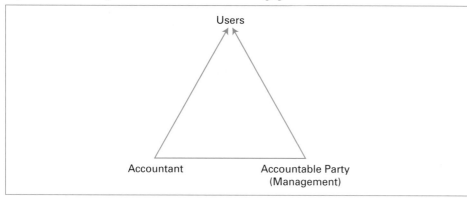

reliability of a written assertion made by one party to another (as illustrated in Figure 1–2). To offer such services, the accountant should meet four basic conditions:

1.   There must be an assertion being made by one party, the accuracy of which is of interest to another party. This assertion may be quantitative or qualitative in nature.
2.   There must exist agreed-upon and objective criteria which can be utilized to assess the accuracy of the assertion. All parties must agree as to how the assertion is to be evaluated using a common unit of measure and measurement technology.
3.   The assertion must be amenable to verification by an independent party. That is, the accountant must be able to obtain adequate, diagnostic evidence to support or refute the assertion being made.
4.   The accountant should prepare a written conclusion about the accuracy of the assertion(s).

These conditions clearly apply to the audit of financial statements, which can be considered a special form of attestation engagement. Indeed, we will be spending most of the rest of this book seeing how these conditions apply to the audit of finanical statements.

Beyond these general guidelines, specific legal and regulatory constraints may limit the assurance and attestation services that an accountant can offer, or limit to whom some services may be offered. One very important limitation is on the provision of consulting services to audit clients. Drawing the line between assurance and consulting services can be problematic, but the general trend in practice and regulation is to severely limit the types of services than can be provided to an audit client, although the same service might be offered to non-audit clients without restriction.

THE AUDITING PROFESSION AND REGULATION

Society, government, business, and the profession all wish to avoid future massive auditing failures such as Enron. Consequently, a wide variety of rules govern the public accountant. The accounting profession regulates itself to some extent but it is also subject to extensive government regulation, either directly in national/state/province laws or via regulatory bodies that receive their mandate from the state. The nature and form of self- and government regulation varies from country to country but is generally focused on the need to maintain the integrity of the profession and the trust society has in auditors. Areas affected by regulation include requirements for entering the profession, the organization of accounting firms, and the process for updating and modifying the rules under which professionals are governed. Each of these is discussed in turn below.

ENTERING THE PROFESSION: EDUCATION, TRAINING, AND CERTIFICATION

The process for becoming a licensed public accountant varies by country. Almost all countries require (1) a minimum level of education, (2) testing of applicants, (3) work experience, and (4) continuing education. Generally, to be a public accountant one needs to be technically competent, independent, and have good judgment. There is also a need for deep understanding of financial statements and generally accepted accounting principles. To practice public accounting and conduct an audit, an auditor needs to be a licensed certified public accountant (CPA), a chartered accountant (CA), or hold the appropriate level of certification consistent with the rules of a country. Adequate knowledge of GAAP is implicit for anyone holding a professional accounting certification (e.g., CA or CPA). Some countries have a single professional body of accountants who can do audits (e.g., CPAs in the United States), whereas others have competing professional groups that can legally conduct an audit (e.g., in Australia both CPAs and CAs can perform audits).

In the United States, each state has a licensing board that administers CPA licenses. In most states, CPAs need a degree in accounting that includes 150 semester-hours of credit, including a specified number of hours in accounting. Each state varies on the specific components of the degree, but to meet the requirements many CPA candidates opt to pursue a graduate degree, often a Masters of Accountancy. A candidate possessing the appropriate educational requirements must successfully complete the CPA exam, which is nationally administered by the AICPA. The exam is taken in four separate modules: auditing and attestation, business environment and concepts, financial accounting and reporting, and regulation. A candidate must pass all four parts of the exam within an 18-month period, meaning that the candidate has 18 months to pass the other three parts once one part of the exam is successfully completed. The exam consists of multiple choice questions and audit simulations involving research and essay answers.

The remainder of the licensing process in the United States involves work experience and continuing education. States vary on the specific amount of work experience required, but two years in public accounting is commonly required for licensing. Upon receiving a CPA license, a CPA must participate in continuing education in accounting, auditing, and professional ethics. Continuing professional education may include internal firm training, industry conferences, and educational workshops.

Other countries vary the type of examination given to candidates and may include integrative case questions with essay style answers. Some countries include taxation as a core knowledge requirement for professionals, whereas others focus solely on examining audit skills. In some countries an individual can conduct an audit upon receipt of a professional accounting designation that is accepted by law, whereas in some countries (relatively few) anyone can conduct an audit. Some countries have uniform national standards for how one obtains a public accounting license, while others like the United States are regulated at the state/province level.

ORGANIZATIONAL FORMS OF PUBLIC ACCOUNTING FIRMS

The accounting and auditing profession is organized into self-selected groups of professionals that form professional services firms. Although audits require extensive work by individual professionals, most are performed by teams of licensed public accountants working within larger accounting firms. In general, there are four types of accounting firms in most countries:

1. *Local:* Sole practitioners or small accounting firms that mostly serve small businesses and not-for-profit organizations in local communities. These firms perform relatively few full-scale audits. They often provide basic accounting services (bookkeeping) and may have a heavy emphasis on tax services.
2. *Regional:* Regional accounting firms usually consist of multiple offices of the same firm in one region of a country. These firms typically serve mid-size clients, including publicly-owned companies, but on a relatively limited basis. These firms tend to offer a full array of accounting services.
3. *Emergent international:* Emergent international accounting firms are generally comprised of loose federations of national accounting firms. They often start as federations of regional firms in one country and gradually became integrated national firms. They may have some international integration as well. They tend to compete for small-to-medium size public company audits and medium-to-large private company audits. The largest firms in this category are BDO (with various local affiliates such as BDO Seidman in the United States and BDO Spicers in New Zealand) and Grant Thornton.
4. *International:* International accounting firms perform a wide range of services for organizations of many sizes; however, these firms specialize in publicly-owned organizations, many of which are multinational. The dominant four firms in this category are Deloitte, Ernst & Young, KPMG, and PricewaterhouseCoopers—commonly referred to as the **Big Four.** The number of these firms has been reduced from twelve to four over the last 25 years.

The hierarchy within an accounting firm is usually based on relative levels of experience among the professional staff. At the top of a firm are the partners. Newly hired employees are referred to as associates or staff and are closely supervised as they learn to apply their academic knowledge in a practical setting. Staff accountants typically perform basic auditing tests, with senior staff assigned more complex audit tests and limited supervisory responsibilities for junior staff. Individuals will usually be promoted to manager in four to six years, taking on many key responsibilities for running the day-to-day operations of an engagement, planning the audit, supervising and reviewing the work of associates, and resolving routine audit issues. Senior managers perform activities that may lead to promotion to partner such as client development, resolution of complex audit issues, and collection of fees. Managers deemed qualified are voted as partners by the existing partners of the firm. Partners have a claim to net revenues of the accounting firm but also are liable for partnership losses. Some firms also have a permanent position called "principal" or "associate partner" for people that are more skilled and experienced than managers but who will not be admitted to the partnership of the firm.

One effect of structuring accounting firms as partnerships is the potential legal liability that may arise if professionals within the firm do not provide services that meet reasonable standards of quality. The most visible and unfortunate form of a breakdown in audit quality occurs when an auditor certifies a company's financial statements that turn out to be misleading or fraudulent. In such circumstances, the individual auditor and the firm may be held accountable by the legal system. Sometimes, the partners in the firm must pay large settlements to stakeholders who relied on misleading financial statements. To protect against high levels of personal liability, many firms form a *limited liability partnership* (LLP) or *limited liability corporation* (LLC), which provide some protection for individual partners against the mistakes made by others.

REGULATING THE AUDITING PROFESSION

Following Enron and other audit failures in the United States, the U.S. Congress passed the Sarbanes-Oxley Act of 2002, which regulated the auditing profession for public companies by stripping the profession of its ability to self-regulate and self-assess its quality control. Most of the authority to regulate the external audit of public companies in the United States is now assigned to the Public Company Accounting Oversight Board (PCAOB), which is charged with supervising and regulating audit firms and their practices. Additionally, Sarbanes-Oxley changed some of the common practices of the profession. For example, firms were prohibited from performing certain non-audit related services for their audit clients. As a result, at most public companies, those charged with corporate governance reacted by limiting auditors to the audit engagement only, regardless of whether other services were allowable under the law.

The PCAOB also regulates who can conduct audits of publicly traded companies in the United States. A firm that wishes to audit publicly traded companies must register with the PCAOB and be subject to inspection by PCAOB review teams. Inspections are performed on an annual basis if the firm audits 100 or more clients, or every third year if it audits fewer than 100 clients. Most regional, all emergent international, and all international firms are registered firms, whereas most local firms are not registered.

The audit of non-listed companies in the United States is governed by standards of the Auditing Standards Board (ASB), which is part of the AICPA. Prior to the PCAOB, the ASB was the only source of authoritative auditing standards in the United States. Many of the standards of the ASB are still in effect for all audits in the United States, including listed company audits, at least until the PCAOB gets around to superseding those standards with their own.

In many other countries, accounting firms perform audits in accordance with GAAS as established by the International Accounting and Auditing Standards Board (IAASB) of the International Federation of Accountants (IFAC). In some cases, the standards of the IAASB are supplemented with oversight by a local authority, such as the CICA's Auditing and Assurance Standards Board. Recent regulatory changes in the United States are in contrast to the global movement towards global harmonization of auditing standards. However, fraud and audit failures around the world (such as Parmalat in Italy and Barclay's in the United

Kingdom) suggest that enhanced scrutiny of the auditor is likely to continue. Most countries to date have resisted the level of government regulation that is now the hallmark of the U.S. audit profession. Even in the United States, the IAASB has been recognized as an authoritative source of auditing standards as evidenced by the decision of the ASB of the American Institute of Public Accountants (AICPA) to issue standards consistent with IAASB standards whenever possible, only deviating when there are justifiable reasons given business practices in the United States.

Example

As the first example of the ASB responding to auditing standards issued by the IAASB, a series of standards relating to assessing risk during the auditing process were issued in early 2006 that are very similar to a series of standards issued by the IAASB during 2004. These standards initially were prepared with the help of a joint task force of the IAASB and AICPA. However, upon the formation of the PCAOB, the AICPA delayed issuing its standards for several years while the auditing standards-setting process in the United States was reorganized. In the future, the ASB will continue to issue standards similar to IAASB standards.

The move toward two major bodies of auditing standards on a worldwide basis is particularly lauded by international auditing firms who have previously had to comply with rules from many jurisdictions (such as PCAOB standards for publicly owned companies, ASB standards for privately held U.S. companies, IAASB standards for many non-U.S. companies, and local standards for companies in some countries). Furthermore, by concentrating standard setting in fewer organizations, more resources can be devoted to developing the best possible auditing standards, with a significant reduction in the redundancy of standard setting across multiple jurisdictions.

In this spirit, we provide coverage of promulgations by both the IAASB and the PCAOB/ASB. Although the audit process described in this book is not dependent on either set of standards, we believe that auditors worldwide need to be familiar with both sets of standards. Many non-U.S. public companies are registered with the U.S. SEC so non-U.S. auditors need an understanding of PCAOB standards. U.S. auditors need to understand international standards since many non-publicly traded clients are audited under the standards of the AICPA which are being harmonized with the standards of the IAASB. As a result, the largest international audit firms have pushed to have single audit methodology on a worldwide basis that facilitates compliance with both sets of standards.

Authoritative Guidance & Standards
Throughout the remainder of the textbook, authoritative guidance that enhances descriptions of standards in the text will be included in text boxes in this format. Because this book is written to be applicable for auditing courses taught in a variety of pedagogical approaches in a variety of contexts, these boxes help illustrate that each topic in the text is consistent with generally accepted auditing standards and those standards issued by the PCAOB. However, these standards are not embedded within the text each time the topic is mentioned. This approach reinforces the idea that an audit complies with standards but is not driven by the standards.

KNOWLEDGE AND SKILLS NEEDED BY AUDITORS IN THE 21ST CENTURY

During the past decade, the auditing profession underwent an unprecedented number of rapid changes, particularly in the United States. The 1990s started with many of the largest global accounting firms implementing new audit approaches that emphasized a deep understanding of business risks relating to a company's strategies and processes in order to facilitate the assessment of risks related to financial reporting. This shift occurred partially in response to frauds that occurred in the late 1980s and early 1990s that were not detected by auditors because of an insufficient understanding of how organizations operated within their respective industries. Furthermore, the technology boom of the 1990s that accompanied the shift to an information age changed the way information is created, processed, and communicated. Also complicating matters was the increase in highly complex transactions such as financial derivatives. Taken together, these developments increased the challenges facing auditors in verifying financial reports.

This textbook describes auditing within the context of current economic, regulatory, and global conditions. The conduct of a financial statement audit has become increasingly complex and the skill set necessary to perform effective and efficient audits has expanded greatly in recent years. The critical skills and knowledge needed by auditors are far ranging and the chapters, problems, and cases in the book are developed to provide exposure to a wide range of issues in auditing. More specifically, this book will help students to

- Develop an understanding of the role of auditing and corporate governance in ensuring reliable financial reporting and appropriate behavior by stakeholders
- Understand how organizations design and carry out corporate strategies that affect financial reporting
- Evaluate how business processes and strategic alliances that affect financial reporting are designed and implemented
- Assess the effect of external forces on organizations in an international marketplace
- Assess how internal forces create risk within an organization
- Evaluate control responses to organizational risks
- Integrate business knowledge about an organization with accounting knowledge to develop expectations about financial reporting
- Link an understanding of an organization's business risks to concerns about financial reporting and the need for audit testing
- Develop critical thinking, ethical reasoning and problem solving skills to enable careful, objective analysis of audit issues

SUMMARY AND CONCLUSION

As a result of the Sarbanes-Oxley Act in the United States and regulatory changes in other parts of the world, the role of those charged with corporate governance has been increasingly emphasized. To focus the attention of management more directly on the quality of financial reporting, executives determined to be culpable in the production of fraudulent reports will now receive mandatory prison sentences in certain situations. These events have helped the accounting profession in several ways. First, those charged with governance are paying higher fees to auditors to ensure that situations such as Enron do not happen again. Second, the scope of auditing is expanding to accommodate new regulations and, more importantly, to reduce the likelihood of issuing the wrong opinion. Consequently, accounting firms have seen increases in revenues and demand for personnel that are unprecedented. Third, it is unlikely that in the foreseeable future the audit will be perceived as a commodity or unessential service to be given to the lowest bidder without consideration of audit quality as it often was in the 1990s. Fourth, the assertion that historical cost–based financial statements are irrelevant and auditors are an anachronism is unlikely to be made again soon!

All of this indicates that the need for assurance is more important than ever for decision makers, particularly for users of financial information in today's complex, real-time global marketplace. Organizations that provide information that is accompanied by independent assurance help maintain stable international capital markets. To provide such assurance, auditors should possess a set of skills that will facilitate the decision processes needed to properly conduct an engagement. For the most part, we will focus on the audit of financial statements, and the remainder of this book is designed to introduce and illustrate the most critical of those skills as well as the institutional and regulatory aspects that determine how audits are performed. The next chapter will further discuss the nature of assurance and auditing in a global market economy with specific analysis of the various roles assurance can play in mitigating various risks to the stakeholders of an organization. Later chapters will focus specifically on the audit of financial statements and deal with specific aspects and skills of the audit process in more detail.

BIBLIOGRAPHY OF RELATED PROFESSIONAL LITERATURE

Research

Beasley, M. and S. Salterio. 2001. The Relationship between Board Characteristics and Voluntary Improvements in Audit Committee Composition and Experience. *Contemporary Accounting Research.* (4) 539–570.

Blackwell, D. W., T. R. Noland, and D. B. Winters. 1998. The Value of Auditor Assurance: Evidence from Loan Pricing. *Journal of Accounting Research.* 36(1): 57–70.

Chaney, P. K. and K. L. Philipich. 2002. Shredded Reputation: The Cost of Audit Failure. *Journal of Accounting Research.* 40(4): 1221–1245.

Copeland Jr., J. E. 2005. Ethics as an Imperative. *Accounting Horizons.* 19(1): 35–43.

DeZoort, T. and S. Salterio. 2001. The Effects of Corporate Governance Experience and Financial Reporting And Audit Knowledge On Audit Committee Members' Judgments. *Auditing: A Journal of Practice & Theory.* (2): 31–48.

Elliott, R. K. 1995. The Future of Assurance Services: Implications for Academia. *Accounting Horizons.* 9(4): 118–127.

Frankel, R., M. Johnson, and K. Nelson. 2002. The Relation between Auditors' Fees for Nonaudit Services and Earnings Management. *The Accounting Review.* 77(Supplement): 71–105.

Hodge, F. D. 2003. Investors' Perceptions of Earnings Quality, Auditor Independence, and The Usefulness of Financial Information. *Accounting Horizons Quality of Earnings.* 17: 37–48.

Kinney Jr., W. R., Z-V Palmrose, and S. Scholz. 2004. Auditor Independence, Non-audit Services, and Restatements: Was the US Government Right? *Journal of Accounting Research.* 42(3): 561–588.

Larcker, D. F. and S. A. Richardson. 2004. Fees Paid to Audit Firms, Accrual Choices and Corporate Governance. *Journal of Accounting Research.* 42(3): 625–658.

Mautz, R. K. and H. A. Sharaf, 1961. *The Philosophy of Auditing.* American Accounting Association Monograph No. 6, Sarasota, FL: American Accounting Association.

Senkow, D., M. D. Rennie, R. D. Rennie, and J. W. Wong. 2001. The Audit Retention Decision in the Face of Deregulation: Evidence from Large Private Canadian Corporations. *Auditing: A Journal of Practice & Theory.* (2) 101–114.

Zeff, S. A. 2003. How the US Accounting Profession Got Where it is Today: Part I. *Accounting Horizons.* 17(3): 189–205.

Zeff, S. A. 2003. How the US Accounting Profession Got Where it is Today: Part II. *Accounting Horizons.* 17(4): 267–286.

Weber, J. and M. Willenborg. 2003. Do Expert Informational Intermediaries Add Value? Evidence from Auditors of Mircocap IPOs. *Journal of Accounting Research.* 41(4): 681–720.

Professional Reports and Guidance

American Institute of Certified Public Accountants. 1994. *Improving Business Reporting— A Customer Focus: Report of the AICPA Special Committee on Financial Reporting (Jenkins Committee).* New York: AICPA.

American Institute of Certified Public Accountants. 1996. *Report of the AICPA Special Committee on Assurance Services (Elliott Committee).* New York: AICPA.

Auditing Standards

International Audit and Assurance Standards Board. 2003. *International Framework for Assurance Engagements.*

International Ethics Standards Board for Accountants. 2005. *Code of Conduct for Professional Accountants.* New York: International Federation of Accountants.

International Accounting Education Standards Board. 2003. *International Education Standards 1–6: International Education Standards for Professional Accountants.* New York: International Federation of Accountants.

International Auditing and Assurance Standards Board. 2005. *International Standards on Auditing.* New York: International Federation of Accountants.

QUESTIONS

1. Why should auditors view auditing from a global, risk-based perspective? Specifically, what benefits are realized from viewing organizations as global entities and analyzing organizations from a risk-management perspective?

2. Define *assurance, attestation, auditing,* and *accounting,* including the interrelationships among them.

3. Compare and contrast the different ethical frameworks that can be used in organizations and by assurance providers. Which of the frameworks do you believe is easiest for you to employ and which is most difficult? Justify your answer.

4. Why do you believe understanding and assessing corporate governance mechanisms at clients is so important for auditors? Offer arguments for why you believe that auditors should or should not agree to provide assurance services when corporate governance mechanisms for a client are not deemed effective.

5. Describe the role of the audit committee in performing corporate governance. As part of your answer, describe the criteria for inclusion on audit committees for public companies in the United States and describe why you agree or disagree with such requirements. In addition, contrast them with the criteria employed by a major U.S. trading partner such as Canada, China, any of the European Union countries, or Japan.

6. Previously auditors and accountants were allowed to establish their own procedural guidelines e.g., generally accepted auditing standards in the United States were established by the AICPA. However, the Sarbanes-Oxley Act of 2002 (SOX) regulated the

auditing profession for U.S. public registrants by stripping the profession of its ability to self-regulate and self-assess its quality control. Accordingly, the Public Company Accounting Oversight Board (PCAOB) has now been assigned the authority to regulate external audit practices for U.S. registered public companies. Based on these events, what are some international implications to the accounting or auditing profession?

7. Discuss economic explanations for why audits arose before any government or governmental agency required them.

8. Two situations where information asymmetry may create distrust between shareholders and managers:
   a. Adverse selection
   b. Moral hazard
   First, explain these two situations in a general context and then how these two situations could apply to the context of financial reporting and auditing.

9. How are financial statement audits and other attestation services (e.g., environmental and cost audits) similar and different?

10. Consider each of the four types of professional accounting firms—local, regional, emergent international, and international—mentioned in the chapter. Discuss what you believe are the most significant competitive advantages and challenges associated with each type of firm.

PROBLEMS

1. The United States has a federal income tax system that relies significantly on the honesty of its taxpayers in that the Internal Revenue Service (IRS) can't audit everyone who files a tax return. In fact, the IRS has conducted as few as 1.3 million audits in a given year. On the other hand, many studies show that the average citizen substantially complies with the tax code.
   a. How does the IRS attain such a high rate of compliance from the U.S. taxpayer while auditing so few returns?
   b. What strategies do you think the IRS employs to maximize the return to its auditing effort?

2. Which of the following claims is amenable to attestation? Discuss the problems with attesting to each assertion (e.g., measurement issues).
   a. "PFD's net income for the second quarter of 2005 rose 10 percent compared to the same quarter last year."
   b. "HOC's market share as of the end of 2005 stands at 17 percent."
   c. "RGS's new product will be significantly cheaper than its competitors' products."
   d. "WRK's products are the best in the business."
   e. "We, The Union of Non-Capitalistic People, are substantially in compliance with the terms of the anti-ballistic missile treaty."
   f. "My personal travel expenses for the Phoenix trip were $64.88."
   g. "The Bendit Corporation meets or exceeds all standards contained in the Equal Opportunity Employment Act."
   h. "Chris' National Bank has sufficient capital to withstand a downturn in the economy of its lending area."

3. Advances in information technology have made the timely receipt of information more and more valuable. Today, real-time information can be extracted externally from company databases through secured web sites. Analysts representing institutional investors are able to receive this type of information in real time. Similarly, press releases and quarterly information can be posted to web sites for instant access by the public.
   a. Analyze the effect that this technology may have on the value of stock market information to market participants, paying special attention to the value of information in the market.

     b.   Explain the problems that less sophisticated investors face when they trade in a stock market where such technology is widely used.

     c.   Explain why stock market regulators might limit restricted access to real-time company information under some circumstances.

4. For each of the following industries and situations, discuss and give examples of the ways that information technology has improved the reliability and efficiency of decision making and made the timely receipt of information more valuable.

     a.   Health care (such as a local hospital's equipment purchasing decisions)

     b.   Entertainment delivery (such as a cable company's channel expansion plans)

     c.   Agriculture (such as a farmer's decisions on where to sell his or her crops)

     d.   Politics (such as a candidate's campaign strategy)

     e.   General retailing (such as Wal-Mart)

     f.   Utilities (such as water and electric)

5. Consider a local pizzeria and IBM. It should be obvious that their information needs will differ. However, their information needs will also be alike in some areas.

     a.   Discuss the similarities and the differences. Specifically, how are the environments in which they operate and the publics they serve different, and how are they similar?

     b.   Discuss the manner in which each collects and processes that information.

6. Imagine that you are interested in buying a car. Contrast the difference between buying a new car from a licensed Hyundai dealer and buying a used car from an individual through an online intermediary.

     a.   Describe how information asymmetry presents similar challenges under both scenarios.

     b.   Describe how you are able to reduce the risks associated with information asymmetry under each condition.

     c.   How could an independent, third party reduce the risk associated with information asymmetry?

7. Auditors face some unique circumstances in auditing financial statements. Two that suggest themselves immediately follow.

     a.   The parties paying their bill are the ones whose financial statements are being audited.

     b.   Of the two types of errors auditors can make (accepting misstated financial statements or rejecting fairly stated financial statements), accepting misstatements are of much greater concern.

How do these circumstances affect the audit process, and how might they differ under different regulatory jurisdictions? Specifically, how do they affect the process of identifying and obtaining relevant audit information, evaluating alternatives, and selecting the best action from among those available to an auditor?

8. Cynthia Cooper was the heralded Director of Internal Audit who exposed the largest fraud in U.S. history at WorldCom in Mississipi. Explain how she might have reacted upon discovering the fraudulent capitalization of maintenance expenses—would she have selected a loyalty strategy, voice strategy, or exit strategy? As a whistleblower, she chose the voice strategy. What are the personal ramifications, both good and bad, of selecting a voice strategy (in other words, why do many believe that the voice strategy takes much courage)?

9. The directors of High-Class Brands Limited are choosing an audit firm. They decide to appoint a major firm, at an expected fee of $200,000, instead of an alternative audit firm costing $100,000. Suggest reasons for and against making such a decision.

10. Access the web site for Microsoft. Link to the company's Corporate Governance section.

     a.   Who is the Chair of the Board of Directors and what is his or her background?

     b.   Briefly describe each of the Committees of the Board of Directors.

     c.   Briefly describe each member of the Audit Committee. Who do you believe is the financial expert?

d. Based on the composition of the Audit Committee and the Chair of the Board of Directors, what recommendations do you have for the partner on the audit engagement when he or she meets with the Audit Committee or Chair of the Board of Directors?

11. After Enron's debacle, the importance of corporate governance has heightened and received considerable attention. In general, a system of corporate governance usually consists of the Board of Directors, committees of the Board such as the Audit Committee, external auditing, and internal auditing. Research each of the following functions and discuss how each can be used as a mechanism to support high-quality financial reporting:

a. Board of Directors
b. Audit Committee
c. Internal Auditing

12. Describe how information asymmetry creates the demand for an external assurance service when fulfilling contractual obligations between an auto manufacturer (e.g., DaimlerChrysler) and one of its unions (e.g., the United Auto Workers). As an example, consider a critical issue facing automotive manufacturers and unions today, the partial outsourcing of the assembly process to key suppliers. Global competition has placed a significant amount of pressure on companies to reduce production and assembly costs. To reduce costs, manufacturers are outsourcing more of a vehicle's production to suppliers, many of which are located in emerging economies. As a result, companies are reducing labor forces in the high-cost countries of North American, Europe, and Australia, most of which are unionized. Most negotiated contracts with the unions allow for outsourcing decisions to occur; however, the contracts stipulate specific conditions that must exist before these decisions are allowable.

13. Perform research to identify what is meant by the expectations gap and discuss recent developments in auditing practice that are intended to reduce the expectations gap.

Case 1–1: Anthony's Pizzeria

Anthony is a recent graduate from State University. Anthony spent five years at State U earning a baccalaureate degree in philosophy. Since the economic prospects of philosophers are not very good these days, Anthony realizes that he needs to find a way to support himself. His friends have often told him that he makes an excellent pizza, so he decides to open a pizza parlor at the local mall. The mall has a "food court" where vendors sell many different varieties of food. Anthony has the only pizza parlor in the mall. In fact, he doesn't really have a "parlor" since all the food is sold over the counter and the mall provides centralized seating arrangements for the customers. Anthony has signed a one-month lease for his "counter" and will pay the owners of the mall 10 percent of his gross revenue.

The business situation described in this scenario is relatively simple. Nevertheless, Anthony has a great deal to do to get the business started. He must arrange for suitable equipment to be set up (e.g., ovens, soft-drink dispensers, coolers, etc.), hire employees, obtain a ready supply of ingredients, and advertise. Millions of businesses operate in similar ways. What is slightly unusual about Anthony's pizza business is that his rent is dependent upon how well his business does. At the end of the month, Anthony will tabulate his gross sales, report to the owner of the mall and pay the owner 10 percent of gross sales.

The difficulty that arises in this scenario is that the owner of the mall does not know Anthony very well and is uncertain about his truthfulness. As a philosophy student who specialized in ethics, Anthony would not cheat the owner by intentionally understating his sales. The owner is not so sure. On the other hand, Anthony is a bit absentminded and he may accidentally fail to keep track of some of the pizzas that he sells during the month. Therefore, whether one doubts Anthony's honesty or simply worries about his commitment to precision, the reliability of Anthony's reported gross sales becomes an open question.

Requirements

1. The business arrangement between Anthony and the mall owner can be acceptable only when both parties are reasonably assured that the available information related to gross sales is reliable. In this way, a fair and mutually agreeable amount of rent can be determined. To accomplish this, the parties have three choices: (1) accept Anthony's word at face value, (2) let the mall owner verify Anthony's sales directly, or (3) find an alternative solution. Describe the issues associated with each choice and suggest the proper solution.
2. Suppose that an independent public accountant was hired by Anthony to provide assurance about the accuracy of his sales. What makes a public accountant qualified to perform this service? How might the public accountant approach Anthony's assertion about sales?

Managing Risk: The Role of Auditing and Assurance

2

Outline

INTRODUCTION

The financial statement has been the primary focus of auditors for most of the last 100 years. Accounting standards and auditing technology have become increasingly complex, but the purpose of the audit has not changed much—to provide an opinion about the fairness of periodic financial reports. The need for a financial statement audit arises naturally from the needs of external stakeholders, especially investors and creditors, for reliable information about an organization's financial status and performance. Although organizations are able to release this information through various channels (such as corporate web sites or press releases), formal financial statements continue to be the most effective and efficient mechanism for communicating corporate performance to a wide range of stakeholders. Furthermore, stakeholders want to know if the financial information they receive is reliable. Reliable financial reporting is facilitated by the use of established accounting rules as verified by an external auditor and described in the auditor's report.

Stated generally, the auditor's overall objective is to determine if the financial statements of an organization are fairly and consistently reported in accordance with generally accepted accounting principles (GAAP). To reach that conclusion, the auditor must obtain sufficient information to support the conclusion that the financial results and position are reported appropriately. In general, a traditional audit conducted under generally accepted auditing standards (GAAS) has three broad objectives:

- Evaluate whether financial statements are presented in accordance with GAAP.
- Evaluate the possibility of fraudulent financial reporting.
- Evaluate the likelihood that the organization will continue as a going concern.

Authoritative Guidance & Standards

In general, audits in the United States are conducted under the guidance of *Generally Accepted Auditing Standards* promulgated by the American Institute of CPAs (AICPA). Audits of publicly-listed companies in the United States are conducted under *Auditing Standards* issued by the Public Company Accounting Oversight Board (PCAOB). *International Standards on Auditing* are established by the International Auditing and Assurance Standards Board (IAASB). In addition, much of the discussion of enterprise risk management presented in this chapter is based on *Enterprise Risk Management–Integrated Framework* by the Committee of Sponsoring Organizations of the Treadway Committee (COSO).

Although not an explicit objective of the audit, information gathered during the conduct of an audit may also provide guidance to an organization for improving its business processes, information systems and competitive position. In addition, a fourth objective now exists for audits of public companies in the United States registered with the SEC:

- Evaluate the internal process by which financial reports are generated.[1]

Overall, financial statements are the result of a complex process of capturing, classifying, aggregating, and reporting information. This complexity makes the apparently straightforward objectives of the auditor quite complex in practice. Furthermore, in many countries auditors are subject to extensive regulation that affects the conduct of the audit. The purpose of this chapter is to introduce the related concepts of risk and risk management as they pertain to stakeholders with an interest in an organization. An organization faces a variety of different risks and adopts different strategies to mitigate the potential impact they may have on operations, performance, compliance with legal mandates, and the quality of financial reporting. Given their unique focus on the reliability of financial statements, auditors have a special regard for managing financial reporting risks. However, auditors are also concerned with risk management in its

Example

Most companies face some form of competition and are under constant threat that a competitor will introduce a better or cheaper product or service. This type of risk goes directly to the heart of a company's competitive position. However, it may also have implications for information contained in the financial statements. If competition is severe, a company may need to record a decrease in inventory valuation to lower-of-cost-or-market, or even take a write-off for impaired assets dedicated to producing products that are no longer competitive.

1 As we discuss in detail, this objective refers to the evaluation of what is referred to as "internal control over financial reporting." We will define this terminology in a later section.

broadest sense because any risk that can negatively impact an organization has the potential to influence the results reported in the financial statements and the auditor's planning and conduct of the audit.

RISK MANAGEMENT IN A BUSINESS ENTERPRISE

THE NATURE OF RISK

To understand the role of auditing and assurance, it is first necessary to understand the nature of risk in a business enterprise and how an organization can mitigate or reduce risks. For the moment, we will adopt a general definition of risk:

> *Risk:* A threat to an organization that reduces the likelihood that the organization will achieve one or more of its objectives.

Threats from the competitive environment may prevent an organization from achieving its growth and profitability objectives. Serious problems can occur when employees or management take improper or incompetent actions that adversely affect the organization. Management can make bad decisions or employees can squander or steal corporate assets. Problems can also arise from ineffective efforts to deal with risk, such as management's failure to identify and properly react to changes in the business. From an auditor's perspective, problems within the organization may result in inaccurate information processing, lead to noncompliance with regulatory constraints, allow fraudulent activities to occur, or suggest a risk of failure for the business. Furthermore, inaccurate processing of information can lead to poor decisions, increased operating costs, diminished asset values, and unreliable reports to significant stakeholders.

Risk comes in many forms, and we will discuss numerous types of risk in great detail throughout this text. However, one risk that is particularly relevant to auditors and will be mentioned frequently is *information risk*, which is defined as the risk that information used in decision making is inaccurate or insufficient. Financial statements represent a sizeable category of information used by a clearly identified group of decision makers, in other words, investors. Misstatements in financial statements can occur in a number of ways, but an important distinction is made between errors, mistakes or unintentional inaccuracies and fraud, dishonesty or intentional manipulation. One purpose of the audit is to reduce the information risk associated with financial statements by reducing the likelihood that the financial statements include either type of misstatement.

ENTERPRISE RISK MANAGEMENT

Efforts to manage risk are becoming increasingly proactive in many organizations, with a focus on avoiding problems before they occur, and minimizing their impact when they are unable to prevent them. To better ensure that risk is addressed by senior management and the board of directors, organizations are adopting *enterprise risk management* (ERM) as a formal process that affects all levels of an organization. In 2004, the Committee of Sponsoring Organizations of the Treadway Commission (COSO) issued a framework for enterprise risk management which includes the following definition:

> Enterprise Risk Management (ERM): A process, enacted by an entity's board of directors, management, and other personnel, applied in a strategy setting and across the enterprise, designed to identify potential events that may affect

the entity, to manage risks to be within its risk appetite, and to provide reasonable assurance regarding the achievement of entity objectives.

ERM is an iterative, continuous process that involves identifying, assessing, and managing key risks that threaten an organization's strategic, operational, compliance, and reporting objectives at all levels of an organization. Effective risk management recognizes that

- Risks affect organizations in various ways (e.g., achieving strategy, performing effectively, reporting faithfully, and complying with regulations fully).
- Risks are interrelated (e.g., one risk event may trigger other risk events).
- Risks can only be managed through intervention by management or other stakeholders.

Furthermore, the more serious the risk, the more strenuous the intervention will need to be in order to achieve the desired results. However, intervention in the case of one risk may create unintended consequences, often in the form of new or increased risks in other areas. For example, management can reduce the risk of customers defaulting on their obligations by refusing to grant credit. However, if all credit sales are banned by the company, it may find that its risk of going out of business has been increased dramatically as it loses customers to competitors. This cause and effect necessitates that management adopt a cost/benefit view of their response to risk and balance the direct and indirect consequences of intervening to manage a specific set of risks.

Figure 2–1 illustrates the COSO view of enterprise risk management. The side of the cube represents the different levels at which risk management can be applied: entity, division, unit, or subsidiary. Enterprise risk management is considered to have eight components:

- *Internal environment:* The organization's general philosophy and approach to risk management.

Authoritative & Guidance & Standards

COSO's *Enterprise Risk Management—Integrated Framework* presents an excellent opportunity for organizations to organize and implement an effective enterprise risk management framework. Many aspects of the *Framework* are relevant to the conduct of the audit. However, adopting it is not required under any authoritative guidance.

Figure 2–1   COSO's 2004 Enterprise Risk Management—Integrated Framework

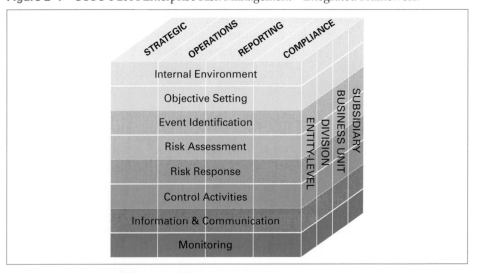

Source: *Enterprise Risk Management—Integrated Framework,* Committee of Sponsoring Organizations of the Treadway Commission. 2004, AICPA, Jersey City, NJ. Reprinted by permission of COSO.

- *Objective setting:* The set of organizational objectives to be supported through risk management. The top of the cube represents the four types of objectives that might be relevant to risk management: strategic, operations, reporting, and compliance.
- *Event identification:* The circumstances and events that represent potential risks that are relevant to the organization's objectives. Identifying situations and events that may negatively affect an organization is the first step in dealing with potential problems.
- *Risk assessment:* The identification and evaluation of potential risks that emanate from the identified events. Management must prioritize risks in order to determine which ones are most critical at any point in time.
- *Risk response:* The organization's basic plan for avoiding, accepting, reducing, or sharing risks.
- *Control activities:* Specific activities undertaken by an organization to reduce risk. Examples of control activities are discussed in detail below.
- *Information and communication:* An organization needs information to effectively respond to risk, and the production and distribution of relevant and timely information will determine the effectiveness of risk management.
- *Monitoring:* Because circumstances change for any organization, the continuous evaluation of risk management efforts is necessary to assure its effectiveness over time.

Although all components of risk management are important, the *internal environment* is critical because it lays the foundation for all other elements of risk management. Specifically, the internal environment reflects the attitudes, approach, and competence of management towards enterprise risk management. If owners can hire competent and honest management whose personal goals are aligned with the owners, many other forms of control may be reduced. However, control is inherently limited by the quality and integrity of people working within the organization. Undue reliance on management to "do the right thing" often creates incentives and opportunities to act contrary to the objectives of the owners, even if management had no initial intent to do so. Furthermore, even the best run company can occasionally stumble with bad decisions. Consequently, elements of control implemented only through management are rarely adequate for reducing risks to an acceptable level.

Because there may be different ways to deal with a specific risk, management must design a portfolio of risk responses that is consistent with their appetite for risk. In general, risks to an organization can be dealt with in one or more of the following ways, depending on the nature of the risk and the resources available:

- *Avoidance:* The organization may attempt to avoid some risks by carefully circumscribing its activities (e.g., avoiding certain markets or products).

Example

A bank may decide to not issue loans in certain countries due to problems with currency volatility and political stability.

- *Acceptance:* Some risks may be accepted as an inevitable, unavoidable result of business decisions.

Example

A company which manufactures trendy clothing recognizes that tastes and styles can change quickly and accept that as an inherent element of its product market.

- *Sharing:* Risk sharing involves transferring, at a cost, all or part of a set of risks to another party. Examples of the ways in which risks may be shared with other organizations include insurance (paying premiums), strategic alliances (dividing profits), and/or hedging transactions (incurring financial fees).

Example

Strategic Alliance: An organization that produces motion pictures might reduce the risks associated with costs of producing, marketing, and distributing a motion picture by partnering with another studio. In exchange, both studios agree to share the revenues from the project.

Example

Financial Hedging: An organization sells its product in various overseas markets, usually getting paid in the local currency. Given that the company is not an expert in foreign currency speculation, it may wish to protect itself against unfavorable swings in currency exchange rates. This can usually be accomplished through the use of financial derivatives linked to currency trading markets.

- *Reduction:* An organization may attempt to reduce many risks by designing and implementing proactive policies, procedures, and processes.

Example

A bank may protect itself against default by formally reviewing loan applications from prospective borrowers (a process), obtaining a credit report on the borrower (a procedure), and/or requiring borrowers to pledge collateral for a loan (a policy).

Example

An organization's Board of Directors engages an auditor to examine financial statements to reduce the risk that they (and shareholders) will receive inaccurate information about a company's activities and results.

In general, it is management's job to decide which approach to adopt for any specific risk. The approaches are not mutually exclusive and can be used in combination to reduce risks to an acceptable level. *Control activities* refer to any actions taken by a company or individual to reduce the likelihood or significance of risk. However, very few risks can be reduced to zero, no matter what approaches or combination of approaches are selected.

Different control responses have different degrees of effectiveness and costs to implement. Two key attributes influence the effectiveness of a control mechanism: diagnosticity and objectivity. *Diagnosticity* refers to the ability of a control activity to provide a reliable and timely warning of potential problems (e.g., signaling when a bad decision may have occurred or there may be errors within a business process). *Objectivity* refers to potential bias inherent in the execution of a control. For example, control activities may be influenced by individuals that have an

Figure 2–2   Relationship Between the Control Attributes of Diagnosticity and Objectivity

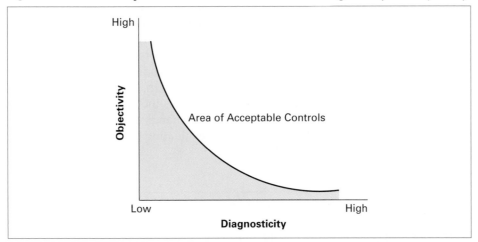

interest in the outcome of a process, potentially undermining the quality of a control activity. An objective control is desirable because it is less likely to be influenced by the process itself (or constituents within the process). Unfortunately, there may be a trade-off between diagnosticity and objectivity—the farther removed a control is from the source of risk, the less likely it is to identify problems on a timely basis. This relationship is depicted in Figure 2–2 which highlights that there may be minimum levels of both diagnosticity and objectivity that are necessary for a control to be effective.

An important point to keep in mind related to auditing and assurance services is that many stakeholders are interested in the ways in which management deals with risk. These stakeholders usually have their own interests and objectives that may or may not be affected by management's efforts to manage risk. Unfortunately, the objectives and risk appetites of various stakeholders may be in conflict. The combination of business risks and conflicting objectives can lead to breakdowns that cause unacceptable results, unreliable information, potentially illegal activity, and/or other adverse conditions.

CONTROL ACTIVITIES FOR BUSINESS RISKS

In the broadest sense, enterprise risk management focuses on reducing risks that confront an organization regardless of the source of the risk and the area of the organization that might be affected. *Business risk* refers specifically to potential risks arising from the company's external environment and internal activities that may have a negative impact on its operations and overall performance. Management has a variety of approaches available for reducing its most critical business risks. An important consideration for the auditor is that control activities for one risk might impact other risks as well.

Controlling Strategic Risks

Management controls reflect the efforts to reduce risk that are the responsibility of senior management. Many of these controls deal with establishing corporate objectives and strategies, and then evaluating the financial performance of the organization and progress towards those objectives. These controls can motivate employees to strive for goals and behave within established boundaries of conduct and activities (for example, corporate policies on discrimination and sexual harassment), or provide feedback about potential problems or risks that the organization may need to address (for example, periodic internal reports may highlight products, regions, or locations of operations that are not performing as well as expected). Examples of management controls include assessing strategic risks, monitoring business processes, reacting to changing circumstances, establishing codes of conduct, setting budgets, and evaluating performance of personnel or business units.

Example

Senior management receives weekly sales reports by product line and location to identify slow moving inventory. They also periodically prepare and evaluate performance reviews of subordinates to improve employee performance.

Controlling Operational Risks

Business process controls encompass the activities designed to assure that the activities within a process are performed efficiently and effectively, for example, designating the specific procedures for handling cash receipts from customer sales so as to avoid employee theft. Business process controls define how tasks are performed within an organization and comprise the policies and procedures that determine how internal processes operate on a day-to-day basis. They dictate who has the authority to execute transactions or other activities, how documents are to be processed, how information is to be collected and reported, and how problems are to be handled.

Example

To update the master price list for its products, a company may conduct periodic market research to discover what the competition is doing. Based on this information, the marketing manager authorizes changes in prices for specific items in the company's inventory. The prices are then input into the sales system by a data entry clerk. To assure the accuracy of the revised prices, the marketing manager receives and reviews a report which lists the actual price changes entered into the system. Errors are referred back to data entry for correction.

Example

In order to obtain new office equipment, a department head prepares a purchase request (requisition) that is submitted to central administration. Senior management reviews the request and determines if it is acceptable based on the needs of the department and available funds. If approved, the purchasing department then solicits prices from possible suppliers and evaluates their ability to deliver and service the equipment. The placement of an order is authorized by a responsible level of management and the equipment is delivered to the company. If the items that are delivered are incorrect or defective, they are returned to the supplier for a refund or replacement.

In planning management and process controls, an organization should consider both the likelihood that a risk occurs and the impact the risk will have on the organization if something bad happens. Controls that reduce the probability of a problem occurring may be different from controls that reduce the impact of the potential problem. For example, providing driver training to delivery personnel may improve their skills and reduce the chance that they have an accident. Purchasing insurance for the drivers is a way to share the cost of an accident if one occurs, thus minimizing the impact the incident would have on the company's financial position. In a similar manner, generating reliable information for decision making reduces the chance of bad decisions on the part of management, while using financial planning budgets put a limit on the extent of corporate assets that may be put at risk by a specific manager.

CONTROL ACTIVITIES FOR COMPLIANCE RISKS

Organizations must also manage compliance and regulatory reporting risks associated with government regulations or oversight. Regulatory reporting risks are managed by identifying internal decision makers who are responsible for significant regulatory mandates, and then providing them with relevant and reliable information so that they can monitor conditions related to those mandates. Most organizations have a process in place to focus on the core regulatory requirements they face (e.g., regulations of the U.S. Food and Drug Administration related to the development of new pharmaceutical products).

One emerging area of reporting and compliance risks for organizations that can involve the auditor is *corporate responsibility reporting (CRR)*. Under CRR, organizations follow established criteria for reporting information about the sustainability of the organization and its impact on the environment. For example, as of 2006, over 850 international organizations are issuing reports in accordance with the Global Reporting Initiative (GRI) on risk management activities and performance across key areas that impact investors, employees, customers, suppliers, communities, governments, and the environment. Some firms audit these reports, and there is a growing demand by stakeholders for audits to increase in number and scope.[2]

CONTROL ACTIVITIES OVER FINANCIAL REPORTING RISKS

Auditors typically are interested in an organization's overall ERM framework, but they are explicitly responsible for the portion of it that directly impacts the financial statements upon which the auditors are issuing an opinion. Thus, auditors are responsible for understanding risk-management activities related to the information that is included in the financial statements. These activities are referred to as *internal control over financial reporting*. Determining which parts of ERM comprise internal control over financial reporting can be challenging because many information systems integrate controls relating to operations and compliance with controls that relate to information processing and reporting. In general, internal controls over financial reporting are the subset of controls that

2 For more information, see Ballou, Heitger, and Landes (2006).

Figure 2–3   COSO's 1992 Internal Control—Integrated Framework Used as Basis for Addressing Internal Control over Financial Reporting

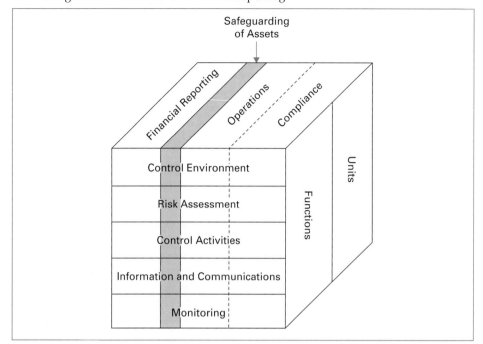

Source: *Internal Control—Integrated Framework,* Committee of Sponsoring Organizations of the Treadway Commission. 1992, AICPA, Jersey City, NJ. Reprinted by permission of COSO.

help ensure accurate and reliable processing, storing, and reporting of information relating to transactions, accounts, and financial statement aggregation.

Currently, most organizations are using COSO's 1992 report, *Internal Control— An Integrated Framework*, which is a forerunner of the 2004 ERM framework, as the basis for evaluating internal control over financial reporting. Figure 2–3 illustrates the five components of internal control over financial reporting:

- *Control environment:* The general environment in which internal control will operate, including the attitudes and competence of management and employees of the organization.
- *Risk assessment:* The activities the organization performs to identify, assess, and prioritize risks. A breakdown in identifying or prioritizing risk will probably have a negative impact on the performance of the organization.
- *Control activities:* The activities the organization performs to reduce the effect of risk on its performance. The range of possible control activities in any organization is extremely broad and depends on the nature of the environment and risks that are of concern.
- *Information and communications:* The production and distribution of information necessary for effective internal control.
- *Monitoring:* The oversight of internal control to determine if it is effective.

The drafters of COSO's ERM report clearly meant their framework to be consistent with the narrower framework for internal control. Other countries have internal control frameworks that the SEC has stated might also be acceptable, such as the United Kingdoms' Turnbull Combined Code or Canada's Criteria of Control (COCO) Framework. However, as most available professional guidance centers on COSO, it is likely that the 1992 document will be followed internationally as well as in the United States, adapted for local conditions as needed.[3]

As was the case for controlling risk in general, internal controls over financial reporting may be imposed at different levels within an organization. First, the basic attitude towards reliable financial reporting is set at the management level. The *control environment* is the component of the organization's internal environment that reflects management's attitude about internal control over financial reporting, including both intentional and unintentional misstatements or misleading disclosures. The control environment is a necessary condition for effective internal control over financial reporting in the long term. The control environment is particularly important in times of organizational stress because errors or fraud are more likely to occur when conditions are difficult (e.g., rapid growth, pressure to meet earnings forecasts, industry downturns, shortages of competent employees).

> **Authoritative Guidance & Standards**
>
> Understanding control activities over financial reporting risks is an important job of all auditors and is covered under standards established by the PCAOB for U.S. public companies in AS 2, for private U.S. companies in SAS 109, and international companies in ISA 315. These standards will be discussed throughout the book.

Example

Senior management establishes separate codes of conduct for its employees and international supplier network to ensure that unacceptable behaviors are avoided and risks are not taken outside of pre-established guidelines. For example, a company may establish rules against offering or accepting bribes in order to facilitate transactions.

Example

Management is responsible for establishing a reliable system of financial reporting within a company. Management needs good information on a timely basis in order to make the myriad of decisions that are necessary to keep an organization operating and successful. The need for good information is shared by external investors. However, this alignment of interests may be undermined when results are poor and the information reveals management to be weak or incompetent. In such a case, the interests of the two groups are in potential conflict—management wants to look good to retain its position, compensation and perquisites, whereas investors want to know if they should make changes to the organization before problems become severe.

The second level of internal control is within the internal business processes that include embedded controls over financial reporting. In general, these controls encompass the activities designed to assure that transactions occurring in a business process are properly recorded, classified, and maintained. Controls help address the risk that transactions are misstated, as well as help ensure that accounting

---

3 To help smaller public companies in the United States better comply with the requirements of COSO's 1992 internal control framework, COSO issued an exposure draft in late 2005 titled *Guidance for Smaller Public Companies Reporting on Internal Control over Financial Reporting,* which was intended to help companies with fewer resources than larger organizations implement effective internal control over financial reporting. The final document is scheduled for released during 2006.

accruals are reasonable. Many process controls are embedded in automated information systems. Other process controls include authorization, the division of responsibilities among different employees, and reviews of transactions. In the past, auditors have frequently considered these controls in detail when planning an audit of financial statements.

Example

A sales system automatically inserts current prices, discounts and taxes into a customer's bill to prevent computation errors or unauthorized prices.

Credit sales are subject to maximum credit limits and are authorized by a credit manager to reduce the risk of bad debts.

Checks received from customers are restrictively endorsed "for deposit only" and deposited amounts are compared to amounts recorded in the cash receipts journal to reduce the risk of employee theft.

IMPLICATIONS OF RISK MANAGEMENT FOR FINANCIAL PERFORMANCE

Risk management should be approached as a systematic and continuous process, whether in the context of an enterprise risk-management framework or internal control over financial reporting. Risk management is iterative—control is a temporary state, not a permanent condition, depending on current circumstances. Consider the sequence of steps in risk management as depicted in Figure 2–4. The critical starting point for effective risk management is identifying and understanding the important risks of the organization (I). A risk that is not identified can not be reduced or controlled. Once the risk is identified and analyzed, then management can decide how to best cope with the potential problem: avoid, accept, share, or reduce (II). Monitoring of risk and the effectiveness of management's response often requires an information system (III) that provides reliable performance results for subsequent evaluation (IV). If the performance results are acceptable, management may not need to take any further action; however, if results indicate current or future problems, management may want to step in and undertake other actions, in other words, continuous improvement (V).

To illustrate, consider a community bank based in south Florida in 1990. A major risk of all banks is that they will make loans to individuals who will not be able to make the payments in the future (I). In order to reduce the risk of bad debts, most banks implement a number of formal processes and policies to screen potential borrowers before making a loan, and for monitoring a borrower's condition after a loan has been approved. For example, the bank may require that all loans to individuals be secured by collateral such as real estate or similar property. With such a policy in place, the bank may feel that it has adequately reduced the risk of a loss occurring in the event of default—the bank will then foreclose on the property and recover the loan balance (II).

Consider how events that occurred in Florida in 1994 may have affected a bank: Hurricane Andrew ripped a path of destruction through south Florida, the first hurricane to do so in 50 years, and a distressingly large number of people lost their homes and businesses, many of whom had mortgages at the bank. Many borrowers were unable to make the payments on their loans, and most of the collateral that was pledged to support the loans had been destroyed in the storm.

Figure 2–4   The Elements of the Risk Management Process Relevant to the Auditor

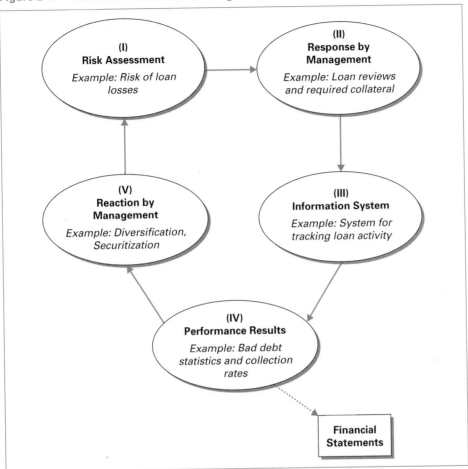

Although some insurance proceeds were available to homeowners, most home-owner's policies provide for little or no coverage of flood damage. As a result of these events, the bank's financial performance suffered greatly, with a large increase in delinquent and defaulted loans (III, IV). The bank may have been unlucky, or it may have failed to adequately consider the risk of a hurricane hitting Florida, effectively adopting the strategy of *accepting* this risk.

Assuming the bank survived the economic wreckage, management had to give serious thought about how to mitigate this type of risk in the future. One reaction was to *reduce* the risk by changing the loan approval policy so as to get assurance that homes pledged as collateral were built to survive a hurricane or were located a safe distance from the ocean. Another reaction was to *insure* the risk by transferring some mortgage loans to other investors. For example, mortgage loans in Florida could be swapped for agricultural loans in Iowa and/or consumer product loans in New York (V). This allowed the bank to diversify its loan portfolio and reduce its risk from any single catastrophic event like a hurricane (after all, what are the odds of a hurricane in Florida, a drought in Iowa, and aliens blowing up New York in the same fiscal year?).

In fact, this form of risk reduction was so successful that new markets evolved for banks (and individuals) to buy and sell investments derived from pools of loans. These types of investments are called loan securitizations and have been developed for mortgages, consumer loans, and credit cards. However, as is the case with all attempts to control one risk, another risk increased. In this case, the banks were committing to financial derivative contracts for which the underlying economics were occasionally misunderstood, sometimes creating unexpected losses when derivative positions were closed.

In the bank, we see how the identification of a risk leads to mitigation of the risk, and performance measurement provides feedback that allows management to react to changes in risks. An organization that is effective at implementing risk management is likely to be successful in the long run. Our Florida bank certainly would have been better off if it had understood its hurricane risk. When a quartet of hurricanes again hit Florida in 2004, the impact on banks and their loan portfolios was much less severe than experienced in 1994. The ability of management to effectively manage risk is of direct concern to the owners of the organization, because it is their investment that is ultimately at risk. Furthermore, the entire risk-management process is relevant to the conduct of the audit because it can inform the auditor's judgments about the collectibility of loans that are recorded in the financial records. Even in the absence of such a direct link to the financial statements, the extent of risk may also be of interest to the auditor because it has a pervasive influence of the culture and activities of the organization.

THE NEED FOR EXTERNAL ASSURANCE AS A COMPONENT OF RISK MANAGEMENT

At the most mundane level, the external audit examines the information in the financial statements in accordance with established professional standards. Depending on the country and/or type of company audited, these standards are either mandated or generally accepted by regulators in the relevant jurisdiction. The primary attribute that makes external auditing valuable is that it is designed to provide an *objective* check on the reliability and fairness of financial information. However, external auditors can and do provide assurance over other aspects of an organization. For example, assurance about the effectiveness of internal control over financial reporting is valuable to both owners and managers. Owners benefit because they obtain corroborative evidence that control is operating effectively, and managers benefit because they obtain feedback on how to improve internal control over financial reporting for their own purposes. Auditors are uniquely qualified to provide such assurance because they possess the professional skills to provide highly diagnostic services, while maintaining objectivity.[4]

The auditor's interest in risk management arises for a number of reasons. First, and most typically, the auditor provides assurance about information generated from processes within the organization. Financial statements contain feedback about the strategic decisions and results of an organization. Consequently, to evaluate such information the auditor needs to understand the strategic position of the organization, its threats and plans, and the reliability of information systems. It is

---

4 In the United States, the external auditor is now required by the Public Company Accounting Oversight Board (PCAOB) to report on management's assessment of the effectiveness of internal control over financial reporting. We will discuss this in depth in Chapter 8.

the auditor's task to evaluate whether reported financial statement results reflect economic reality in accordance with generally accepted accounting principles. Therefore, understanding the economic reality surrounding the information in the financial statements, including management's approach to risk management, is directly within the responsibilities of the auditor.

Second, an auditor may participate in some elements of the risk management process (i.e., the front of the cube in Figure 2–1). For example, many companies outsource some of the monitoring activities related to internal control and internal auditing. From the owner's perspective, replacement of internal sources of monitoring with external auditing may increase the objectivity of the control process without reducing the diagnosticity of the control. In fact, to the extent that outside auditors may be better trained or can afford to be specialists, outsourced monitoring may be more effective than in-sourced monitoring. However, to avoid a loss of objectivity, the auditor of the external financial statements should not perform internal auditing activities.

Third, the auditor may be engaged to provide assurance that one or more components of the risk management process are operating efficiently and effectively. At the same time, the auditor may provide guidance when the risk management process is weak or flawed.

Example

The success of a biotech company in the United States depends on its ability to develop new products in compliance with Food and Drug Administration (FDA) regulations. Although the company may have very strong research capabilities, it cannot bring a product to market unless it complies with FDA rules. To assure proper management of the compliance process (and compliance risk), the company may hire an external auditor to assist in designing, implementing and/or testing the process for assuring compliance with FDA regulations.

Figure 2–5 illustrates how the risk management process parallels the audit process. The audit process begins with an evaluation of the goals and risks of the organization, which requires a deep understanding of the industry and the strategic positioning of others in the industry. This is followed by an evaluation of management's responses to those risks including the design and implementation of internal processes. Execution of management's plans and processes requires reliable performance measurement and reporting that can be used to evaluate the performance of key processes and management activities, along with tests of the effectiveness of control activities. Finally, performance information is used as feedback to assist management to reduce reporting and compliance risks. Overall, effective risk management processes and feedback enable long-term improvement of the organization.

This process is iterative and continuous. Traditionally, auditors have focused on the question of information reliability, primarily constrained by the objectives of financial reporting. However, to develop a sufficient understanding of the risks related to financial reporting, it is important that an auditor understand aspects of the organization's enterprise risk management that go beyond financial reporting. Since effective management requires the effective execution of *all* components of risk management, the auditor should consider the overall effectiveness of management's actions and responses to risk.

Figure 2–5   Relationship Between Risk Management and the Audit

Process Step	Management Perspective	Auditor Perspective
Risk Assessment	Management identifies and evaluates risks that can have a negative impact on the organization. Each risk is evaluated based on the likelihood of occurring and the significance of its impact.	The auditor is concerned that management has identified all potentially critical risks and assessed their significance accurately. Missing or under-appreciated risks will not be effectively managed.
Response by Management (Risk Control and Mitigation)	Management makes choices about how to respond to specific risks. Choices include avoidance, acceptance, insurance, or reduction. Risk reduction involves designing business processes to address groups of related risks. Internal policies and procedures are designed to guide the actions of individuals within the organization.	The auditor assesses whether management's responses to risks are likely to be effective. The more effectively management exercises control, the fewer problems the auditor will expect to observe during the course of the engagement.
Information Reliability	Information systems are designed to provide appropriate performance measurement data to assess the past, present, and future likelihood or significance of various risks.	The auditor assesses the reliability of information processing and reporting. Much of the information that an auditor needs comes from internal processes. The more reliable the information, the fewer problems the auditor can expect during the engagement.
Performance Results	Information is generated on a periodic basis for management review. Performance measures should indicate how the organization has performed as well as provide early warning for potential problems.	Performance measurement information gives the auditor a basis for judging management's control of risks. Data measured over a period of time will indicate when conditions change or risks arise that may lead to problems during the engagement.
Reaction by Management	Management reacts to performance data and decides whether adjustments are needed in strategic decisions, business plans, or business processes as a result of existing circumstances or potential future problems.	The auditor judges management's willingness and ability to react to changes in conditions or risks. If reactions are inadequate, the auditor may expect problems to be revealed by the audit and may offer assistance.

A general rule of thumb is that any business risk that is not effectively controlled has potential implications for the conduct of the audit. A company with weak operations or ineffective risk management is unlikely to be successful in the long run and can present difficult challenges for the conduct of the audit. Indications of ineffective risk management include

- Lack of a formal enterprise risk management process
- Failure to monitor strategic risks
- Failure to adequately respond to identified risks
- Lack of reliable performance measurement data
- Inadequate information for monitoring processes
- Failure to respond to signs of problems and visible threats

These are signs of potential risk from the point of view of the auditor. Consequently, the auditor needs to monitor the action/measurement/reaction cycle described in Figure 2–5 and assess the likelihood, significance, and potential impact of specific risks within the client.

ENTERPRISE RISK MANAGEMENT AND THE INTEGRATED AUDIT

The audit of financial statements is a key component of risk management, especially as it pertains to information risk. Traditionally, a financial statement audit focused almost entirely on whether the numbers and disclosures in a financial report were accurate and trustworthy ("fairly presented" in auditing parlance). However, as modern commerce has become increasingly global and complex, and businesses larger and more sophisticated, the traditional approach to auditing has needed to evolve. The auditing scandals of recent years (e.g., Enron, WorldCom, and Parmalat) have made change a necessity rather than an option.

These developments have increased the levels of both operational risk and information risk such that the auditor is being asked to expand their responsibilities beyond the traditional view of an audit. One specific aspect of these changes is greater external auditor involvement with the client's internal controls over financial reporting. This added level of auditor involvement, beyond just the fairness of the financial statements, is seen as a means of enhancing the likelihood that the auditor will detect potential risks and ensure that they are appropriately reflected in the financial statements. It also reflects the belief that large public companies have a duty to have strong systems of internal control as part of their responsibility to outside stakeholders. Further, it builds on the skill set of the external auditor and his/her knowledge of risk management and control effectiveness.

All audits involve an examination of the information included in the financial statements. The focus of this part of the audit is on the numbers and disclosures included in the financial report, which are evaluated against generally accepted accounting principles and other guidelines for appropriate financial reporting. Regardless of how the numbers are generated, and how sophisticated the client's accounting system, the auditor must do his or her best to verify that the financial statements are accurate, complete, and reasonable given the circumstances of the company. The examination covers all accounting activity for the fiscal period (usually one year).

All audits also involve some level of evaluation of the quality of the internal accounting system that generates financial information. Internal control over financial reporting is the subset of enterprise risk management that pertains to the processes and procedures that management has established to

- Maintain records that accurately reflect the company's transactions
- Prepare financial statements and footnote disclosures for external purposes and provide reasonable assurance that receipts and expenditures are appropriately authorized
- Prevent or promptly detect unauthorized acquisition, use, or disposition of the company's assets that could have a material effect on the financial statements.

These activities are the focus of the auditor when evaluating internal control over financial reporting. The extent to which an auditor is expected to examine internal control over financial reporting depends on whether the audit is being performed under the rules of a traditional GAAS audit or the PCAOB rules for an Integrated Audit. The effort required to evaluate internal control is much more extensive in an Integrated Audit; hence an Integrated Audit can be segmented into three separate phases to be addressed in the following sections:

1. Examination of management's assessment of internal control over financial reporting
2. Examination of the actual effectiveness of internal control over financial reporting
3. Examination of the financial statements (similar to a GAAS audit)

PHASE ONE: AUDITING MANAGEMENT'S ASSESSMENT OF INTERNAL CONTROL OVER FINANCIAL REPORTING

Given the responsibility to provide reliable financial information to investors and the public, management must develop and implement an effective process for maintaining control over financial reporting such that material misstatements can be prevented, or detected and corrected, prior to issuing financial statements. To successfully fulfill its responsibilities, management must

- Formally accept the responsibility for the effectiveness of the company's internal control over financial reporting
- Evaluate the effectiveness of the company's internal control over financial reporting using suitable criteria
- Support its evaluation with sufficient evidence, including documentation
- Provide a written assessment about the effectiveness of the company's internal control over financial reporting as of the end of the fiscal year

An auditor's evaluation of management's assessment of internal control involves understanding the process undertaken by management to assess control effectiveness, including the results of tests of controls for all significant transactions, accounts, and disclosures. To this end, the auditor assesses whether management has identified and tested appropriate controls. These controls include

- Controls over financial reporting processes, from initialization of transactions to financial statement presentation
- Controls over accounting policies, from selection to evaluation of how they were applied
- Fraud prevention and detection controls
- Controls over nonroutine transactions and estimates that typically are associated with errors or fraud

- Company-level controls (management's attitude about misstatements, management's risk assessment process, centralized processing and controls, and monitoring controls such as the audit committee, internal audit, etc.).
- Controls over period-end financial reporting process.

As part of the evaluation, the auditor must evaluate how management tested these controls, including the process for communicating and rectifying problems. Furthermore, the auditor evaluates the documentation provided by management in determining whether management's assessment is adequately supported. Lack of adequate documentation is considered a limitation of the company's internal control over financial reporting.

PHASE TWO: AUDITING ACTUAL EFFECTIVENESS OF INTERNAL CONTROL OVER FINANCIAL REPORTING

The auditor's responsibility is to evaluate and test the effectiveness of internal control over financial reporting as of the end of the fiscal year. The auditor's primary concern is whether ineffective controls could lead to material misstatements in the financial statements. The auditor's understanding of internal control over financial reporting should include the design of controls and whether they have been placed in operation. Procedures the auditor should perform include

- Evaluating the effectiveness of the audit committee
- Identifying significant accounts and disclosures
- Identifying significant processes and major classes of transactions
- Identifying relevant assertions for transactions, accounts, and disclosures
- Understanding the period-end financial reporting process
- Performing walkthroughs for significant classes of transactions

A **walkthrough** involves tracing the steps of an actual transaction, or small set of transactions, through the accounting system from start to finish, including the completion of documentation and updating of computer records. They may include discussions with multiple employees who are responsible for different parts of the process. Walkthroughs should be performed for all significant classes of transactions and are particularly important because they may reveal possible weaknesses in the way transactions are handled or processed.

The auditor should test controls that are important for significant transactions, accounts, and disclosures. The nature and extent of control tests depends on the nature of the controls that management has implemented and should focus on the most sensitive areas of the financial reporting system. For example, the auditor can perform various tests of controls that directly relate to

- Prevention of fraud or errors
- Reliability of significant accounting numbers and disclosures
- Potential sources of breakdowns in controls

Although tests of controls have been an integral part of the audit process for decades, recent emphasis on internal control over financial reporting by the PCAOB has greatly increased the amount of audit effort in this area, resulting in large increases in audit fees. *USA Today* reported that for fiscal year 2004, audit fees for the U.S. companies listed on the Standard & Poor's 500 index were approximately 40 percent higher than in 2003 (up from $2.5 billion to $3.5 billion). Although such increases are attributed in part to the first year start up costs of compliance with new regulations, the increased sensitivity by auditors to internal control over financial reporting suggests that they will continue to expend significant effort on this phase of the integrated audit.

PHASE THREE: AUDITING THE FAIRNESS OF THE FINANCIAL STATEMENTS

The final phase of the audit process is similar for a traditional GAAS audit and an Integrated Audit, although the extent of the examination will vary because of the deep understanding of internal control over financial reporting an auditor develops in an Integrated Audit. One difference is that the auditor may be able to perform more focused tests of transactions, accounts, and disclosures in an Integrated Audit, concentrating on areas of the financial statements where the risk of error is highest, and reducing tests in areas considered to have a low risk of error. However, regardless of how good internal control over financial reporting is, and how low the risk of error may be, all significant classes of transactions, accounts, and disclosures should be subject to some level of examination in all audits. The remainder of this text is devoted to explaining the process by which an auditor examines the reliability of the internal processes for generating financial reports and the accuracy of the information in the financial statements.

OTHER TYPES OF ASSURANCE ENGAGEMENTS

Authoritative Guidance & Standards
Standards associated with other assurance engagements fall under the *Audit and Attestation Standards* of the AICPA, *Statements on Standards for Attestation Engagements* (SSAEs), and the IAASB *International Standards on Assurance Services* (ISAEs).

Risk management creates other opportunities for assurance by independent third parties in addition to the audit of financial statements discussed above. Common types of assurance services provided by public accountants and audit firms include

- Assurance about compliance with laws, regulations, and contractual obligations
- Assurance about the reliability of information and control systems
- Assurance about the effectiveness and efficiency of operations

ASSURANCE ABOUT COMPLIANCE WITH LAWS, REGULATIONS, AND CONTRACTUAL OBLIGATIONS

Most organizations are subject to a wide variety of government laws and regulations which may be imposed by different levels of government. These rules usually have a significant impact on an organization's operations. Assurance about compliance with laws and regulations is often referred to as *compliance auditing*. Possible areas for assurance include compliance with securities laws, consumer protection laws, product quality rules, equal opportunity laws, environmental laws, and worker safety guidelines. Financial institutions such as banks and insurance companies are often subject to regulations dictating the minimum amount of capital they must maintain and the types of investments they may make. Compliance with these rules is also amenable to independent assurance.

An organization may also be concerned about compliance with contractual obligations. For example, entities with outstanding debt may be subject to bond covenants restricting their ability to pay dividends, make investments, borrow additional money, or requiring them to maintain a minimum level of working capital or equity. Union contracts may stipulate that a certain amount of money be spent on specific employee benefits (e.g., pensions, insurance premiums, training, and education). Finally, contracts with customers may require the organization to undertake specific actions such as subcontracting some work with minority-owned enterprises, using materials of specified quality, or using "environmentally friendly" manufacturing processes. Independent assurance may be appropriate for any of these situations.

Assurance about the Reliability of Information and Control Systems

A second area of assurance is the reliability of information and control systems beyond the internal controls over financial reporting. This type of assurance is receiving greater attention from many organizations. As information systems become more complex and computer-dependent, management must be concerned that an organization's systems are designed properly and operating as designed. The increase in electronic commerce and just-in-time inventory systems means that organizations are ever more intertwined electronically and susceptible to problems in system alterations, information processing, system security, and data reliability. Often, transactions between companies are executed through direct electronic links between their respective information systems (so-called business-to-business computing, or B2B). Thus, problems with information technology at one company may have an adverse effect on the other.

Example

In a just-in-time inventory system, a manufacturer allows key suppliers to monitor inventory levels through the manufacturer's own inventory control system. When a supplier's system detects that inventory levels are low, the system will automatically trigger an order on behalf of the manufacturer and ship additional supplies. An electronic payment may be triggered at the same time. Since these transactions are completely automated, any problems or errors may be hard to detect within the system.

Assurance about information and control system reliability usually involves examining the system and identifying possible weaknesses in internal control. A weakness is considered to be any condition that would allow undesirable behavior to occur without detection. Examples of weaknesses include conditions that allow unauthorized modifications to systems, inappropriate access to systems and data, fraudulent transaction processing (especially in an e-commerce environment), and/or misuse or destruction of data. Assurance providers may express an opinion about the reliability of a system in its entirety but, more importantly, they will also provide a list of specific weaknesses that they have noted within the system that should be corrected by the company.

Assurance about the Effectiveness and Efficiency of Operations

A final area for assurance is the evaluation of effectiveness and efficiency of an organization's activities. Most organizations wish to know if they are performing well. Almost any process or system within an organization can be evaluated by an assurance provider. Assurance about the efficiency and effectiveness of an organization when compared to established company policy or industry benchmarks is often referred to as *operational auditing*. In government and not-for-profit organizations, operational auditing is sometimes known as value-for-money auditing or comprehensive auditing. The purpose of these audits is similar to operational audits in the private sector, but in the public sector the goal is to make the most economical and effective use of legislated resources to achieve the mandate given the entity. This is a step beyond compliance auditing, as value-for-money seeks to determine not only that the funds were authorized by the appropriate legislative body and paid to appropriate parties but also that value to the taxpayers was received in return.

To determine if a process or system is effective and efficient (or economical), an accountant can examine actual performance and report on situations or circumstances where effectiveness and efficiency are less than desired. The biggest challenge to the assurance provider is to develop quantitative measures and criteria for measuring effectiveness and efficiency. Various organizations around the world attempt to do this, including the Institute of Internal Auditors, the Organization of Supreme Audit Institutions for governmental audits (including the General Accountability Office of the U.S. Congress), and various foundations set up by these bodies to carry out research on subjects related to operational or value for money auditing.

SUMMARY AND CONCLUSION

Public accountants can perform a wide range of assurance services that would be relevant to the management of risks in an organization. In essence, the value of assurance is directly proportional to the extent of risk reduction that can be achieved relative to a set of objectives for individual stakeholders. The audit of financial statements is the most common form of assurance engagement performed by auditors, and the service subject to the largest portion of professional standards and regulations. The objective of an audit of financial statements is to provide an opinion about the fairness of reported financial position and results based on generally accepted accounting principles. This traditional GAAS audit of financial statements has now been supplemented, at least for publicly listed companies in the United States, with a more extensive integrated audit that, in addition to the opinion on the financial statements, also reflects the auditor's assessment of management's report on the effectiveness of its internal controls over financial reporting, as well as the auditor's own report on the effectiveness of these controls. Assurance/attestation engagements can also be performed for any subject matter for which the public accountant can define generally accepted criteria and assemble a team that has the requisite knowledge about the subject matter. These engagements build on the skill set that the auditor has developed in carrying out the audit of financial statements.

BIBLIOGRAPHY OF RELATED PROFESSIONAL LITERATURE

Research

Ballou, B. and D. Heitger. 2005. Practical Enterprise Risk Management: A Building Block Approach to Implementing COSO 2004. *Management Accounting Quarterly.* 6(Winter): 1–10.

Ballou, B., D. Heitger, and C. Landes. 2006. The rise of corporate sustainability reporting: A rapidly-growing assurance opportunity. *The Journal of Accountancy* (forthcoming).

Beasley, M., J. Carcello and D. Hermanson. 1999. *Fraudulent Financial Reporting: 1987–1997. Committee of Sponsoring Organizations of the Treadway Commission.* http://www.coso.org.

Blackwell, D., T. Nolan, and D. Winters. 1998. The Value of Auditor Assurance: Evidence from Loan Pricing. *Journal of Accounting Research.* 36(Spring): 57–70.

Dlfgaauw, T. 2000. Reporting on Sustainable Development: A Preparer's View. *Auditing: A Journal of Practice and Theory.* 19(Supplement): 67–74.

Gendron, Y. and M. Barrett. 2004. Professionalization in Action: Accountants Attempt at Building a Network of Support for the WebTrust Seal of Assurance. *Contemporary Accounting Research.* 21(3): 563–602.

Hunton, J. E., T. Benford, V. Arnold, and S. G. Sutton. 2000. The Impact of Electronic Commerce Assurance on Financial Analysts' Earnings Forecasts and Stock Price Estimates. *Auditing: A Journal of Practice and Theory.* 19(Supplement): 23–36.

Kinney, W. R., Jr., and R. D. Martin. 1994. Does auditing reduce bias in financial reporting? A review of audit adjustment studies. *Auditing: A Journal of Practice and Theory.* Spring: 149–156.

Mayhew, B. W. and J. E. Pike. 2004. Does Investor Selection of Auditors Enhance Auditor Independence? *The Accounting Review.* 79(3): 797–822.

Newman, D. P., E. R. Patterson, and J. R. Smith. 2005. The Role of Auditing in Investor Protection. *The Accounting Review.* 80(1): 289–314.

O'Donnell, E. and J. J. Schultz, Jr. 2005. The Halo Effect in Business Risk Audits: Can Strategic Risk Assessment Bias Auditor Judgment about Accounting Details. *The Accounting Review.* 80(3): 921–940.

Simons, R. 1995. *Levers of Control: How Managers Use Innovative Control Systems to Drive Strategic Renewal.* Boston: Harvard Business School Press.

Vera-Munoz, S. C., W. R. Kinney Jr., and S. E. Bonner. 2001. The Effects of Domain Experience and Task Presentation Format on Accountants' Information Relevance Assurance. *The Accounting Review.* 76(3): 405–429.

Wallage, P. 2000. Assurance on Sustainability Reporting: An Auditor's View. *Auditing: A Journal of Practice and Theory,* 19(Supplement): 53–66.

Professional Accounting Reports

American Institute of Certified Public Accountants. 1994. *Improving Business Reporting–A Customer Focus: Report of the AICPA Special Committee on Financial Reporting (Jenkins Committee).* New York: AICPA.

American Institute of Certified Public Accountants. 1996. *Report of the AICPA Special Committee on Assurance Services (Elliott Committee).* New York: AICPA.

Sundem, G. L., R. E. Dukes, and J. A. Elliott. *The Value of Information and Audits.* (Coopers & Lybrand, 1996).

Professional Standards

AICPA *Statements on Auditing Standard* (SAS) No. 109, "Understanding the Entity and Its Environment and Assessing the Risks of Material Misstatement."

Committee of Sponsoring Organizations of the Treadway Commissions (COSO). 1992. *Internal Control-Integrated Framework,* Vol. 1–4. New York: COSO.

Committee of Sponsoring Organizations of the Treadway Commissions (COSO). 2004. *Enterprise Risk Management-Integrated Framework.* New York: COSO.

Criteria of Control Committee. 1995. *Guidance on Control.* Toronto: Canadian Institute of Chartered Accountants.

Criteria of Control Committee. 1995. *Guidance for Directors – Governance Processes for Control.* Toronto: Canadian Institute of Chartered Accountants.

International Ethics Standards Board for Accountants. 2005. *Code of Conduct for Professional Accountants.* New York: International Federation of Accountants.

International Accounting Education Standards Board. 2003. *International Education Standards 1-6: International Education Standards for Professional Accountants.* New York: International Federation of Accountants.

International Auditing and Assurance Standards Board. 2005. *International Standards on Auditing.* New York: International Federation of Accountants.

IAASB *International Standards on Auditing* (ISA) No. 315, "Understanding the Entity and Its Environment and Assessing the Risks of Material Misstatement."

International Auditing and Assurance Standards Board. 2005. *International Standards on Quality Control.* New York: International Federation of Accountants.

PCAOB. *Auditing Standard No. 2*, "An Audit of Internal Control Over Financial Reporting Performed in Conjunction with an Audit of Financial Statements."

Turnbull Committee. 1999. *Internal Control – Guidance for Directors on the Combined Code.* London: Institute of Chartered Accountants in England and Wales.

QUESTIONS

1. How do enterprise risk management (ERM) and corporate governance relate? Use the components of the COSO ERM framework to illustrate your answer.

2. What are the five elements of COSO's 1992 Internal Control framework over financial reporting? Provide a definition for each element and give a brief example of how this function can be applied to a community bank.

3. Compare and contrast auditing and monitoring (using the COSO definition of monitoring).

4. Explain the audit implications of the dynamic relationship between strategy and internal control.

5. Control environment is a component of internal control according to the COSO framework. Describe how the control environment may also affect the audit.

6. This chapter described corporate responsibility reporting (CRR) as a growing mechanism for reporting on compliance risks. Access the CRR and Annual Reports for Royal Dutch Shell on its web site. The CRR Report for Shell is called *The Shell Report*. Compare and contrast the types of information contained in each report, including the auditors' reports for each report. Describe why other stakeholder interests in Shell should be of concern to the company's investors.

7. A study on fraud by Beasley et al. (1999), which was commissioned by the Committee of Sponsoring Organizations of the Treadway Commission (COSO), found that in 84 percent of the frauds investigated, either the president, chief financial officer, or both were aware of or actively contributed to the fraud. Discuss how auditors should use this information when designing audit procedures to examine the control environment of an organization. How might auditors better assure themselves that they are not involved with a client where an executive fraud is occurring?

8. Describe the differences between a traditional audit and an integrated audit (i.e., an audit of a company registered in the United States).

9. How are the integrated audit and operational audit related?

10. What is internal control over financial reporting? How does it differ from the concept of internal control as discussed in the COSO's Enterprise Risk Management—Integrated Framework mentioned in Chapter 2?

PROBLEMS

1. Consider an Internet dating service database that charges clients $50 to enter a database and have access to information about other clients. Advertising fees are the primary source of revenue in addition to client payments.
   a. What do you believe are the most critical business risks facing this organization?
   b. What are some examples of external sources of control and internal controls that can help manage these risks?

2. The most common forms of assurance are as follows:
   - Compliance with laws, regulations, and contractual obligations
   - Relevance and context of business risk management process
   - Effectiveness and efficiency of operations
   - Reliability of information and control systems
   - Financial statements

   For each of the following examples, classify the type of assurance that will likely be provided.
   a. A company hopes to secure a bank loan.
   b. An auditor for a large public accounting firm is preparing plans to audit the sales order/receivables process of a mail-order clothing operation.
   c. A company is preparing to "go public" for the first time.
   d. A company prepares to bid on government defense contracts for the first time.
   e. A union questions the integrity of sales volume statistics presented by corporate management used as the basis for laying off employees.
   f. A vice president of operations is charged with improving her division's profits.
   g. Congress calls for a review of the IRS's automated "help lines" in response to taxpayers' complaints of incorrect tax advice.
   h. A bank is considering loaning money to a firm whose primary source of income is making industrial solvents having manufacturing by-products that are considered toxic.
   i. A major airline is losing money on some of its most competitive routes. It believes, however, that it cannot abandon the routes and still maintain its marketing presence.
   j. An Internet portal company has a committee designated to identify threats to its long-term viability as a going concern. Part of its mission is to design and implement mechanisms to mitigate such threats.

3. Using Figure 2–1, give specific examples of each of the four risk elements (Strategic, Operations, Reporting, and Compliance) mentioned under COSO's Enterprise Risk Management—Integrated Framework for a public accounting firm.

4. The basic steps of the risk management process are as follows:
   - Risk Assessment
   - Response by Management
   - Information Reliability
   - Performance Results
   - Reaction by Management

   Suppose you are the auditor of a company that sells jewelry using the Internet. First, consider **one** business risk that may be of critical importance. Then, with reference to this business risk, give an example of how this risk can be mitigated or minimized through the remaining risk assessment process so that the Company can develop competitive advantage over its competitors.

5. To better understand the basic steps of identifying and assessing business risks, research the mission statements available on company web sites. Based on the mission statements, (1) infer two strategic business objectives that likely exist, (2) identify a strategic risk associated with each objective, and (3) assess the significance of each risk.

  a. IBM
  b. YUM! Brands (Pizza Hut/Taco Bell/KFC)
  c. Philips
  d. Procter & Gamble
  e. The Walt Disney Company

6. Recall the four ways that risk can be addressed in a business environment, including avoidance, acceptance, sharing, and reduction. For each company, identify how the risks that are provided can be addressed by one of the four options.
  a. McDonald's:
      • Customers might not want to buy roast beef products.
      • Lawsuits might be brought upon the company should spoiled food be served.
      • Franchised locations might not follow specified guidelines.
      • Food preparation might differ from location to location.
  b. Nike:
      • Individuals might be injured from the production or sale of its sporting equipment.
      • Employees at plants in underdeveloped countries might not be working under conditions acceptable to the customers of Nike products.
      • Nike's alliance agreements with athletes expose the company to negative publicity when the athlete is involved in unacceptable conduct on or off of the field.
      • Nike is unsure whether company recreation centers (batting cages, basketball courts, and so forth) would be successful ventures.
  c. The Home Depot:
      • The strategy of building stores close to each other could reduce the growth rate of sales per store from year-to-year, which is a critical performance measure in the retail industry.
      • Each store is very large, containing a significant amount of inventory; hence, loss due to natural disaster or theft could be material.
      • Customer volume at stores might not be high enough to cover facilities and inventory holding costs.
      • With 40,000 to 50,000 different products in a store, stock outs can easily occur.

7. For each of the following controls, describe the type of control (strategic or business process) being utilized and strengths and weaknesses associated with the control.
  a. The controller of the organization carefully examines the qualifications of each prospective internal auditor to make sure that those responsible for monitoring the accounting and operations control activities are qualified.
  b. Information technology systems designers embed a reasonableness check into the sales system that flags any sale over $50,000 and automatically sends an e-mail message to the chief financial officer of the company and the manager of the auditing firm responsible for conducting the annual audit.
  c. The company forms a risk committee, which includes members from the Board of Directors and Audit Committee. The committee performs annual evaluation and revision of the company's risk management plan.
  d. The vice president of operations inspects the budget variance reports prepared by each plant manager on a monthly basis.
  e. The vice president of information technology has engaged an international assurance services firm to act as an intermediary during the implementation of an enterprise resource planning system. The firm will help ensure that the ERP system provider is carefully setting up and testing the system prior to switching from a file-based system.

8. Examine Figure 2–3, which depicts a generalized overview of the risk management process observed in practice. Using the figure for guidance, beginning with "risk assessment," describe how you believe this process operates for Amazon when addressing the

risk that Barnes and Noble will be able to utilize its retail stores to gain a competitive advantage in marketing its web site.

9. Access BASF's Corporate Report from its web site. Included in this CRR is an exhibit containing its goals, one of which is a reduction of chemical emissions for various chemicals by varying percentages by 2012 (for example, this exhibit is found on page 13 of its 2004 report). Based on the stated goals and progress made toward its goals, compare and contrast management's and the auditor's perspectives as it applies to each risk management step for the risk of chemical emissions at BASF (use Figure 2–4 as a guide).

Case 2–1: Equiticorp Holdings Ltd.

Equiticorp was formed by a small group of experienced financiers in early 1984. The company is primarily a merchant bank but has also established a strong equity base by its investment in Feltex, Rainbow Corporation, and Omnicorp. It is unusual in that all but two of its nine directors are executive directors with major shareholdings. They are a lean organization with a high level of competence. Staff shareholdings provide a considerable incentive to succeed. The company has three main levels of activity: Merchant Banking, Financial Services, and Equity Investments.

Equiticorp has a flat, simple corporate structure; it has no personnel or marketing departments on the basis that managers are expected to manage all of the functions required.

Equiticorp started as a big venture and has had spectacular growth aided by a very high public profile focused on the leadership of Allan Hawkins, the founder, chairman, and CEO. The philosophy is to create history and live by the bottom line on a deal-by-deal basis.

Requirements

Discuss the ramifications of Equiticorp Holdings Ltd.'s corporate structure on internal control using COSO's 1992 Internal Control Framework.

Source: Inkson, K., Henshall, B., Marsh, N., and Ellis, G. 1986. *Theory K; The key to excellence in New Zealand management*. Auckland: David Bateman Ltd.

Case 2–2: Insignia Textiles Limited

Insignia Textiles Limited has recently issued a document to all employees entitled "Our Code of Conduct." It sets out standards of ethical behavior towards other employees, suppliers, and customers. Each employee also has a contract including a formal job description. All new employees are given aptitude tests appropriate for the area they will work in. As a result, the company does not consider it necessary to obtain references or conduct other background checks.

The board includes ten directors, two of whom are independent (being former executives of the company). The directors have an audit committee, which includes both independent directors, and which meets once a year to discuss internal control with the company's accounting and finance staff. The audit committee also meets with the company's auditors twice a year, to discuss audit planning issues and to review the outcome of the audit. The full board meets twice a year and evaluates top management's performance (as well as considering other issues).

Requirements

a. List and briefly explain four strengths of the control environment at Insignia Textiles.
b. List and briefly explain four ways in which the control environment of Insignia Textiles can be improved.
c. What further information would you require to evaluate the control environment of Insignia Textiles?

Case 2–3: Ucantrustus Builders Inc.

In 1992, Hurricane Andrew hit South Florida causing extensive destruction and damage to homes and commercial buildings. Investigations conducted after the hurricane indicated that a great deal of the damage could be attributed to shoddy construction, often in violation of state and local building codes, and certainly inconsistent with best practices for building in a hurricane zone. These inferior construction practices were apparently allowed to thrive because of lax enforcement of building codes by government building inspectors.

In the aftermath of the storm, government officials and homeowners had many things to say and questions to ask about building practices in South Florida. Reporters at the time quoted Mr. Malcolm Teixeira of Modello Florida, "Those hurricane straps should've been more secure. Some of the nails missed the trusses. What I want to know is where were the building inspectors when this happened?" Hurricane straps are strips of metal that are supposed to hold the roof of a house onto the side walls when there is a strong wind. Improper placement will cause a weakness in the overall structure. Many houses were found to be missing the required straps or had straps that were improperly or incompletely installed. The use of nail guns and particle board were also considered prime culprits because they led to rushed jobs and sloppy work.

Law enforcement officials asked similar questions, probing into reports of shoddy construction and improper building inspections. When questioned by journalists, Janet Reno, Dade County State Attorney stated that, "We are investigating what damage could have been averted and if anyone is criminally responsible." After the storm, the U.S. attorney in Dade County listed hurricane fraud as his office's number one priority.

In the face of widespread destruction, afflicted homeowners instigated a large wave of lawsuits against builders and developers, alleging that poor and shoddy construction practices made their homes excessively vulnerable to such storms. Furthermore, changes to the building codes in Dade County were also debated even though the existing laws were already considered to be very tough, requiring that buildings withstand 120-mile-an-hour wind. Unfortunately, Hurricane Andrew exceeded that in many locations.

Many experts feel that the problems were not due to the building code but due to lax enforcement of the codes and even outright payoffs to building inspectors. Homestead, directly in the path of the hurricane, lost approximately 90 percent of its housing stock. Inspectors either did not inspect individual houses or closed their eyes to obvious noncompliance. Just five years before the storm, 15 developers pled guilty to bribing building inspectors and the problems may have been more pervasive than originally believed.

Floridians are now much more concerned about the safety and durability of their homes. As damaged and destroyed homes are rebuilt, homeowners are demanding that shoddy construction practices be prevented and that homes be built to withstand future storms. Insurance companies, which lost billions of dollars as a result of the hurricane, are also much more concerned about the quality of construction of repaired and new homes: they do not want a repeat of Hurricane Andrew either. For example, a Miami Herald article cited that USF&G would begin inspecting every home it insures for hurricanes. Other insurance companies have stopped writing hurricane policies altogether. The industry lost $16.5 billion on Hurricane Andrew. Thus, hurricane insurance is now a riskier business. Premiums will be higher and there will be more obstacles associated with obtaining it.

As a CPA you are continually looking for ways to expand the scope or your practice and to take advantage of your skills at attestation and professional standing as an independent provider of attestation services. A friend suggests to you that the massive rebuilding of homes and buildings, combined with the history of lax code enforcement, may provide an opportunity to enter a new market for attestation services.

Ucantrustus Builders is a reputable building construction company in South Florida. They specialize in large-tract residential housing. Many of their previous construction projects suffered severe damage from the hurricane. Ucantrustus is now concerned that the public perceives their projects as substandard and unable to withstand severe weather problems. If they do not respond to this image and have success regaining their reputation, they will probably go out of business. On the other hand, they also feel that construction services that are of demonstrably high quality will be in high demand at a premium price. The problem is convincing potential buyers that Ucantrustus delivers high-quality construction and repairs.

Requirements

Assume that Ucantrustus Builders has approached you about providing attestation services related to rebuilding homes destroyed by Hurricane Andrew:

a. What conditions must be satisfied for an attestation engagement to be feasible?
b. What would be the overall objective of an attestation engagement related to the above facts?
c. Identify the stakeholders relevant to the attestation engagement. What is the role of each stakeholder and what would be your responsibility to each?
d. Describe the nature of the assertions being tested and the attestation objectives that are pertinent to the engagement. What measures and criteria would you use to test these assertions?
e. What difficulties do you foresee in gathering enough evidence on which to base an opinion that your objectives have been fulfilled?
f. What types of procedures would you apply and what types of evidence would you gather in order to satisfy your engagement objectives? Draft a preliminary program for attesting to building code compliance. Be sure to consider all types of procedures and the role of specialized knowledge that might be needed to obtain sufficient, competent evidence that the objectives have been met.

3

The Building Blocks of Auditing

Outline

INTRODUCTION

Management and auditors have separate, but complementary, responsibilities related to the production and release of audited financial statements. Management is responsible for preparing the financial statements, meaning that it decides what information will be included. Management also has the responsibility to implement and maintain an adequate system of documents and records that enable the preparation of the financial statements. As part of this system, management should implement controls that provide assurance that information (especially financial reporting information) is being properly captured, recorded, and reported.

The auditor's primary professional responsibility is to plan the audit so as to provide reasonable assurance that there are no significant misstatements in the financial statements. The auditor can never know with certainty whether financial statements are fairly presented. Consequently, the engagement is planned to obtain enough evidence to support the auditor's conclusions. Based on all available evidence, auditors evaluate whether the financial statements conform to the appropriate criteria (e.g., GAAP) and issue a report stating their conclusions. If the information does not conform to the established criteria, the auditor will ask the client to address the problems discovered. If the client refuses, the auditor's recourse is to issue an audit report that indicates the nature of the missing or inaccurate information or, where legally permitted, to resign from the engagement.[1] However, in most cases, client management and the auditor discuss the differences and reach a mutual agreement. Hence, although management "owns" the financial statements, the auditor can heavily influence what management will report.

In order to fulfill these responsibilities, auditors follow a structured approach to the audit. Identifying the facts that must be examined, assessing the risk that information may be erroneous, obtaining evidence about the accuracy of information, and reaching an overall conclusion involves a very complex and time consuming process that must be carefully planned if the auditor is to avoid making mistakes. The purpose of this chapter is to introduce and describe the basic building blocks of the auditor's analytical process which, when completed, will support the auditor's conclusion about the fairness of the financial statements.

> **Authoritative Guidance & Standards**
>
> This chapter provides an overview of the fundamental concepts of an audit. Important topics covered in this chapter are included in standards that apply to a wide range of topics including the nature of assertions (SAS 110, ISA 500); the risk of material misstatement and the quality of internal control over financial reporting (SAS 109, ISA 315, AS 2), fraud (SAS 99, ISA 240); materiality (SAS 107, ISA 320), and audit evidence (SAS 110, ISA 500).

MANAGEMENT'S ASSERTIONS

Auditors design an audit to provide a basis for issuing a report on the financial statements. In addition, the auditor of any public company registered with the SEC in the United States, which includes thousands of companies in a wide variety of countries around the world, must design the audit to provide a basis for issuing three reports: (1) the auditor's report on the financial statements, (2) the auditor's report on management's assessment of the effectiveness of internal controls over financial reporting, and (3) the auditor's own assessment of the effectiveness of internal controls over financial reporting. The starting point for making these evaluations are assertions made by management about its financial results and internal control system. The auditor's task is to determine whether the assertions can be believed.

FINANCIAL REPORTING ASSERTIONS

A financial statement audit is designed to assess the fairness of management assertions about financial results. Figure 3–1 depicts the key conceptual elements of

---

1 For public companies registered in the United States and in many other countries, auditors would next involve the audit committee in an effort to have them convince management make necessary changes before issuing an opinion identifying the misstatement or resigning from the engagement.

Figure 3–1 Concepts Underlying the Audit Process

MANAGEMENT ASSERTIONS*		
Transactions	*Accounts*	*Presentation and Disclosure*
Occurrence Completeness Accuracy Cutoff Classification	Existence Completeness Valuation and Allocation Rights and Obligations	Occurrence and Rights/ Obligations Completeness Classification and Understandability Accuracy and Valuation

⬇

AUDIT PROCEDURES	
Risk Evaluation	*Tests of Accounting Information*
Procedures to understand environment Evaluation of information system reliability Tests of controls, including over financial reporting Preliminary analytical procedures	Substantive analytical procedures Tests of transactions Tests of accounts Tests of Presentation and Disclosure

⬇

AUDIT EVIDENCE
Inspection of Records or Documents Inspection of Tangible Assets Observation Inquiry Confirmation Recalculation Reperformance Analytical Evidence

⬇

AUDITOR'S REPORTS
To be discussed as part of the ***Integrated Audit*** (see Chapter 4)

* These categories of assertions, types of tests, and classifications of audit evidence were approved by the ASB in October 2005 as part of the Risk Assessment standards. The forthcoming SAS will be titled *Audit Evidence*.

the audit process. Each of these elements will be defined in turn. The key point to note is that Figure 3–1 represents the thought process that the auditor undertakes in each and every audit. The context, details, and requirements may change, but the logical process is essentially the same.

In the context of an audit, assertions represent the set of information that the preparer of information (management) is providing to another party. Financial statements represent a very complex and interrelated set of assertions. At the most aggregate level, the financial statements include assertions such as "total assets as of December 31 are $30 billion," "net income for the year is $125,000,000," and "gross margin is 35 percent." Each of these assertions is interesting in its own right, but each can also be decomposed into a more refined assertion. For example, the statement about total assets can be decomposed into separate statements about cash, receivables, inventory, and so forth. Similarly, an assertion about net income can be broken into more detailed statements about revenues and expenses.

Although readers of financial statements tend to focus on highly aggregated assertions about margins, income, and assets, financial statements implicitly reflect a number of specific assertions made by management. For example, management implicitly asserts that recorded assets and liabilities exist and transactions occurred; there are no unrecorded assets, liabilities, or transactions; the organization actually owns the assets; and the valuation, presentation, and disclosure of assets, liabilities, and transactions is in accordance with GAAP. Auditors decompose broad assertions into a detailed set of statements referred to as *management assertions* (or *financial statement assertions*), separated into three categories: (1) transactions, (2) accounts, and (3) presentation and disclosure. These categories have been adopted both by the IAASB and by the ASB in their standards.[2] Each category corresponds to the following set of detailed assertions that management makes about transactions, accounts and disclosures:

Management Assertions about Transactions

- *Occurrence*—Transactions and events that have been recorded have occurred and pertain to the entity.
- *Completeness*—All transactions and events that should have been recorded have been recorded.
- *Accuracy*—Amounts and other data relating to recorded transactions and events have been recorded appropriately.
- *Cutoff*—Transactions and events have been recorded in the correct accounting period.
- *Classification*—Transactions and events have been recorded in the proper accounts

Management Assertions about Accounts

- *Existence*—Assets, liabilities, and equity interests exist.
- *Rights and obligations*—The entity holds or controls the rights to assets, and liabilities are the obligations of the entity.
- *Completeness*—All assets, liabilities, and equity interests that should have been recorded have been recorded.
- *Valuation and allocation*—Assets, liabilities, and equity interests are included in the financial statements at appropriate amounts and any resulting valuation or allocation adjustments are appropriately recorded.

Management Assertions about Presentation and Disclosure

- *Occurrence and rights and obligations*—Disclosed events and transactions have occurred and pertain to the entity.

---

2 Previously, IFAC and the AICPA utilized only five management assertions to be applied across classes of transactions and accounts. Accordingly, auditing textbooks and accounting firms incorporated the notion of audit objectives to more easily apply management assertions to audit evidence gathering. With the expansion and clarification of management assertions across three categories (transactions, accounts, and presentation and disclosure), there is no longer a need for an additional layer of audit objectives—the objectives of the audit are to ensure that appropriate evidence is gathered to support management assertions for all three categories of financial reporting.

- *Completeness*—All disclosures that should have been included in the financial statements have been included.
- *Classification and understandability*—Financial information is appropriately presented and described, and information in disclosures is clearly expressed.
- *Accuracy and valuation*—Financial and other information is disclosed fairly and at appropriate amounts.[3]

These assertions are considered to be the basic building blocks of accounting information and can be used to decompose specific transactions, account balances, or presentation and disclosure items. Furthermore, they are generally susceptible to examination by an auditor. The auditor is responsible for verifying that all important management assertions related to transactions, accounts, and line items and disclosures in the financial statements are reasonable, that is, free of significant misstatement.[4] A key point to keep in mind is that these assertions do not necessarily correspond directly with a specific statement made by the provider of information and some may only be implied by the information provided.

Authoritative Guidance & Standards

Recent standards by the AICPA (SAS 110) and IAASB (ISA 500) group management assertions according to the three components of financial reporting—classes of transactions, accounts, and presentation and disclosure. Standards also suggest that auditors should consider assertions made by the auditor for the financial statements taken as a whole (e.g., SAS 109 and ISA 315). Auditors are not precluded from considering management assertions from a different perspective as long as the alternative approach addresses all assertions described in the standard.

To illustrate, consider the financial statements of a manufacturing company. The process of acquiring materials is critical to most manufacturers. Figure 3–2 illustrates the nature of management's assertions related to purchases and inventory. For transactions, management asserts that all inventory purchases *occurred*, the recorded transactions are *complete* (none were overlooked), recorded amounts are *accurate*, purchases occurred before the period-end *cutoff* date, and all journal entries were recorded in the proper account *classifications*. For inventory accounts, management asserts that inventory actually *exists* and is *complete* (no amounts omitted). Potential problems arise when inventory is out on consignment or when shipments are in transit. In these cases, the company may include inventory for which it has no *rights* because title belongs to another party. The *valuation* assertion for inventory must take into account the pricing method being used (e.g., FIFO) and current market conditions affecting the lower-of-cost-or-market. Finally, management also makes assertions related to the disclosures about purchases and inventory in the financial statements, including that they are *understandable*.

INTERNAL CONTROL ASSERTIONS

Management is responsible for establishing effective internal control over financial reporting. Formally, internal control over financial reporting is defined as:[5]

A process designed by, or under the supervision of, the company's principal executive and principal financial officers . . . and effected by the company's board of directors, management, and other personnel, to provide reasonable assurance regarding the reliability of financial reporting . . . for external purposes in accordance with generally accepted accounting principles and includes those policies and procedures that:

1. *Pertain to the maintenance of records that, in reasonable detail, accurately and fairly reflect the transactions and dispositions of the assets of the company;*

---

3 Sources: ISA 500 *Audit Evidence*, IFAC 2004 and SAS 106, *Audit Evidence*, 2005. AICPA: New York.

4 The term material means that the assertion must be significant enough to affect the decisions of a reasonable user (materiality is discussed in more detail later in this chapter).

5 The COSO report from 1992, *Internal Control—Integrated Framework*, provides this definition.

Figure 3–2   Management Assertions for Purchases and Inventory

Assertions	Example
Transactions Assertions	
Occurrence	Recorded purchases of inventory actually took place.
Completeness	All actual purchases of inventory were recorded.
Accuracy	Purchases were recorded at the appropriate amounts (e.g., all prices and quantities were accurately computed).
Cutoff	All recorded purchases occurred in the current period.
Classification	All purchases of inventory were recorded in the proper accounts (e.g., inventory debited and accounts payable credited).
Account Assertions	
Existence	All items included in the list of inventory exist in the quantities indicated.
Completeness	All existing inventory has been included in inventory counts.
Rights and Obligations	Items that have been included in inventory are owned by the client firm who has the right to sell or pledge the items.
Valuation and Allocation	Inventory is properly priced using an acceptable method and considering the application of the lower-of-cost-or-market rule. Inventory transactions, as affected by sales and purchases, have been recorded in the proper period. Inventory has been accurately compiled and summarized and agrees with the recorded account balance.
Presentation and Disclosure Assertions	
Occurrence and rights and obligations	The line item of merchandise inventory includes only valid inventory accounts that reflect actual purchased and produced inventory, all of which is owned by the client.
Completeness	The line item of merchandise inventory includes all inventory accounts.
Classification and understandability	The significant accounting policies footnote clearly describes the inventory method used (e.g., FIFO adjusted for lower of cost or market), and the inventory footnote properly segregates raw materials inventory, work-in-process inventory, and finished goods inventory.
Accuracy and Valuation	The merchandise inventory line item properly sums all inventory accounts net of reserves for obsolescence.

2. *Provide reasonable assurance that transactions are recorded as necessary to permit preparation of financial statements in accordance with generally accepted accounting principles, and that receipts and expenditures of the company are being made only in accordance with authorizations of management and directors of the company; and*

3. *Provide reasonable assurance regarding prevention or timely detection of unauthorized acquisition, use or disposition of the company's assets that could have a material effect on the financial statements.*

Unfortunately, there is no standard approach for evaluating the effectiveness of internal control over financial reporting. Rather, management must choose and employ an appropriate control framework. To be suitable, an internal control framework should be (1) unbiased, (2) subject to consistent measurement, (3) comprehensive, and (4) relevant.

There are three primary frameworks for evaluating internal control over financial reporting that are generally accepted in practice and recognized by the PCAOB. The first framework, *Internal Control–Integrated Framework*, was developed by the Committee of Sponsoring Organizations (COSO).[6] As this framework is specifically endorsed in the United States by the PCAOB, we will discuss it further when we discuss internal control in depth.[7] Other frameworks that the SEC mentions include *Guidance on Control*, developed by the Canadian Institute of Chartered Accountants' (CICA) Criteria of Control Committee (COCO), and the *Turnbull Combined Code*, developed in the United Kingdom. The COCO and Turnbull approaches have a broader view of control than the COSO framework and incorporate elements of enterprise risk management. Whereas the COCO and Turnbull frameworks focus on monitoring and improving control, the COSO framework is oriented toward evaluating internal control. However, improving internal control necessitates using a framework for detecting control weaknesses; therefore, the different approaches have a great deal of overlap.

In addition to adopting a framework, management must accept responsibility for the effectiveness of the company's internal control over financial reporting; evaluate the effectiveness of the internal control over financial reporting using the chosen framework; support its evaluation with sufficient evidence, including documentation; and present a written assessment of the effectiveness of internal control over financial reporting as of the end of the company's most recent fiscal year. Furthermore, the control system must be comprehensive enough to provide reasonable assurance that the management assertions in the financial statements are reliable.

AUDITOR RESPONSIBILITIES

The auditor has four primary responsibilities related to the conduct of the audit: (1) to plan the audit so as to have reasonable assurance that errors and fraudulent misstatements will be detected and corrected, (2) to evaluate the effectiveness of internal control over financial reporting,[8] (3) to evaluate the potential for illegal acts on the part of the client, and (4) to evaluate the likelihood that the company will continue as a going concern.

REASONABLE ASSURANCE ABOUT ERRORS AND FRAUDULENT MISSTATEMENTS

Auditors gather evidence sufficient in amount and competent in content to provide financial statement users with *reasonable assurance* that financial statements are free of significant misstatements. Reasonable assurance for an audit engagement is

6 COSO is part of the Treadway Commission on Fraudulent Financial Reporting formed in response to major frauds in the United States in the late 1980s. The "organizations" are the primary organizations in the United States representing public accountants, financial executives, managerial accountants, internal auditors, and academics.

7 COSO issued a document on enterprise risk management in 2004 that expands the 1992 framework on internal control. However, organizations are likely to continue to use the 1992 framework as a basis for internal control over financial reporting because of its restrictiveness, making it easier to utilize when only responsible for internal control over financial reporting, and not other aspects of enterprise risk management (e.g., strategic and operations risks).

8 Currently, although many auditors consider the evaluation of internal control over financial reporting to be an important aspect of the audit process, it is primarily required for the audits of companies registered with the U.S. SEC.

defined as "a high, but not absolute, level of assurance, expressed positively in the auditor's report as reasonable assurance, that the information subject to audit is free of material misstatement."[9] This concept suggests that the auditor conducts the audit in a manner that other qualified auditors would agree satisfies established criteria for auditing. Auditors are not providing a guarantee that all significant misstatements will be discovered because auditors are not able to evaluate every transaction or account balance detail. Furthermore, management can collude with employees to conceal misstatements or instruct subordinates to override otherwise effective control systems such that auditors might fail to find existing misstatements.

> **Authoritative Guidance & Standards**
> The concept of reasonable assurance is critical to conducting an effective audit. Standards on planning (SAS 108, ISA 300) and assessing risk and materiality (SAS 107, ISA 320) both stress the importance of planning an audit to attain reasonable assurance. These standards imply that reasonable assurance should be a high level of assurance.

Auditors distinguish between different types of possible financial misstatements. *Errors* are unintentional misstatements or omissions of financial information. Errors may be caused by incorrect processing of information, incorrect estimates, mistakes in the application of accounting principles, or incomplete disclosure. *Fraudulent misstatements* are intentional misstatements or omissions of amounts or disclosures in financial statements to deceive users. Fraudulent misstatements can result from the alteration or forgery of documents and records, omission or misrepresentation of key facts, or misuse of accounting principles. The difference between an error and a fraudulent misstatement is the existence or absence of "intent." All organizations and all accounting systems are subject to mistakes. On the other hand, fraudulent misstatements occur when one or more persons try to achieve personal or organizational goals at the expense of other stakeholders of the organization.

Fraud is further distinguished by the nature of the misstatement or omission. *Fraudulent financial reporting* involves management or other parties intentionally manipulating information in the financial statements (sometimes called *management fraud*). If the fraud involves employee theft of entity assets, it is referred to as *misappropriation of assets* (sometimes called *employee fraud*). Typical examples of minor employee fraud are theft of petty cash funds or small tools. *Embezzlement* occurs when an executive steals corporate assets on a large scale and leaves others to absorb the loss. This type of problem is more common in small companies in which owners or managers obtain funds from customers or investors and then disappear before delivering the goods or developing the business.

Example

Fraudulent Financial Reporting: An overstatement in ending inventory usually results in an understatement of cost of goods sold and an overstatement of net income. Due to this relationship, the artificial inflation of inventory balances is a common technique to boost reported income artificially.

Example

Misappropriation of Assets: Lapping is a situation where incoming cash receipts from customers are appropriated by an employee. This theft is then hidden by posting the customer's account as being paid at a later date using cash receipts from other customers. The net result is that today's receipts are stolen and tomorrow's receipts are posted to today's customers. This process must continue indefinitely or until the funds are returned.

9 This definition is taken from the IAASB *Glossary of Terms*.

In some cases, the distinction between the two types of fraud is minimal. For example, if a manager's annual bonus is based on the sales for the period, he or she might intentionally accelerate January sales into December so that they can be counted in the current year (even though the earnings process is not complete and the goods are not delivered until January). This clearly represents fraudulent financial reporting because the financial statements are being intentionally misstated. What may be less obvious is that this also reflects misappropriation of assets because the manager is acquiring corporate assets (in the form of a bonus) to which he or she is not entitled.

The public generally expects that an auditor will ferret out all errors and fraud in a client. The reality of auditing is a bit different, however. As a practical matter, an auditor focuses on errors and fraudulent financial reporting because they directly affect the financial statements and are often highly significant. Auditors are less concerned with misappropriation of assets because the amounts involved tend to be small and often have little direct impact on the financial statements unless the culprit tries to hide the theft by manipulating the accounting records. Professional standards require that the audit be planned so as to provide reasonable assurance that significant errors or fraudulent misstatements will be detected, regardless of their cause. Professional standards also acknowledge that a well-planned audit may not detect all fraudulent misstatements, especially those involving collusion among multiple persons or forgery of documents.

An auditor would have to plan and conduct an engagement differently if the detection of all fraud was the primary goal. Such an audit is called a *forensic audit* and requires an extensive body of evidence that is cost prohibitive in the absence of strong suspicions of the occurrence of fraud.[10] For example, all documents are considered to be potentially fraudulent until proven otherwise. However, to direct auditors' attention to the possibility of fraud on each audit engagement, team members are required to discuss the potential ways fraud could occur at the client during the planning phase of the engagement. This meeting, called a *brainstorming session*, results in the development of an audit plan that adequately accounts for potential fraud. Thus, the auditor's standard of due care in planning the audit is based on a healthy dose of professional skepticism combined with procedures that provide reasonable assurance of detecting significant errors and fraud. Given the seriousness of fraud, auditors may use more forensic audit procedures in the future.

The responsibilities of the auditor regarding potential frauds are summarized in Figure 3–3. If an auditor expects that fraud has occurred at a client, he or she should investigate and obtain evidence about the facts of the situation. If the auditor concludes that fraud has occurred, the facts should be presented to management at a level that is high enough in the organization to intervene. Any financial statement effects should also be corrected. If management refuses to rectify the fraud, or is itself involved in the fraud, the auditor should inform the audit committee and consider issuing a negative audit report or resign from the engagement. The auditor should also consider whether there is a legal responsibility to report the fraud to appropriate government authorities.

---

10 The potential problem of forged documents is particularly troublesome to auditors because the authentication of documents is usually beyond the scope of an audit. At a minimum, an auditor should be careful to examine whether documents have been improperly altered. Also, auditors should always examine original copies if possible, and be careful when examining photocopies/faxes that can be easily altered.

Figure 3–3   Auditor Responsibility for Detecting and Reporting Error and Fraud

The auditor's responsibility is to plan the audit to provide reasonable assurance that material errors and fraudulent misstatements will be detected including
- Exercising adequate professional skepticism
- Investigating whether risk factors are present that indicate a higher than average risk of material misstatement
- Discussing with the audit team explicitly how fraud or other material misstatement might occur in a specific client, how earnings management attempts might lead to fraud, and how the audit team would uncover indications of fraud or other material misstatement

If sufficient risk factors are present to indicate a higher than average risk of material misstatement due to errors and fraudulent misstatements, the auditor should
1. Assign more senior staff to the audit and review all audit work more carefully.
2. Reduce the predictability of audit by changing the nature or timing of audit procedures. Some examples include
   - Increase the extent of testing of large and unusual transactions
   - Follow up on significant unexpected account fluctuations
   - Investigate significant discrepancies in transactions with outsiders
   - Examine transactions with missing or inadequate documentation
3. Heighten professional skepticism in areas where there can be material managerial judgments. Some examples include
   - Examine transactions involving senior management in detail
   - Question whether accounting principles are being misused
   - Inquire about errors known to the client but not rectified
   - Investigate unauthorized transactions

If an error or fraudulent misstatement is detected during the course of the audit, the auditor should
- Document the nature of the problem
- Determine if the misstatements are errors or fraudulent transactions.
  - Consider implications for other aspects of the audit, including possible withdrawal.
  - Discuss the matter with management at the appropriate level for action
  - Refer matters to auditor's legal counsel and suggest the client involve their legal counsel
- Have the client adjust the statements for all material errors and fraudulent misstatements
- If the client will not adjust the statements, issue a qualified or adverse report
- Inform the audit committee

Based on requirements of SAS 99 and ISA 240.

INTERNAL CONTROL OVER FINANCIAL REPORTING

If an auditor is auditing a publicly owned company registered with the SEC, another of the auditor's objectives is to obtain reasonable assurance that no significant limitations exist related to internal control over financial reporting. Although auditors have always paid attention to internal control to some degree, it was up to the auditor to decide how much reliance to place on internal control during the course of the audit. Recent rules promulgated by the PCAOB have made the evaluation of internal control a responsibility that is the equal of the audit of the financial results for public companies in the United States. Consequently, auditors now devote a great deal of time and energy to the audit of internal control over financial reporting and are required to issue two reports on the topic: (1) an opinion on management's reported assessment of the effectiveness of the company's internal control over financial reporting and (2) an opinion on the effectiveness of internal control over financial reporting at the date specified in management's report. These reports are issued in conjunction with the audit of the financial statements as of the end of the fiscal year and comprise the *Integrated Audit.*

ILLEGAL ACTS BY CLIENTS

Another situation that an auditor occasionally encounters is when a company commits an *illegal act*—a violation of laws or government regulations committed by individuals on behalf of the company. For example, if a manager orders toxic waste from the production process to be dumped in a nearby river, he is probably committing an illegal act. Illegal acts that the auditor looks for do not include personal misconduct by the entity's personnel. Furthermore, illegal acts carried out by employees can be distinguished from employee fraud (that is, misappropriation of assets) by noting that illegal acts are actions on behalf of the company at the expense of "society," whereas employee fraud represents actions on behalf of an individual at the expense of the company. This distinction may become hazy in some situations, particularly those involving securities laws and fraudulent financial reporting. For example, if a company intentionally misstates earnings prior to "going public," it may have committed fraud and other illegal acts.

Illegal acts can be further classified by the impact they have on accounting and financial reporting. Violations of tax or financial reporting laws can have a *direct and material* impact on financial reports. Many other laws and regulations apply primarily to the operations of an organization rather than financial or accounting functions, such as environmental regulations. Such laws may be far from the purview of the auditor but can have an indirect and potentially significant impact on the financial statements since violations may lead to fines and penalties.

What are the auditors' responsibilities for detecting illegal acts that have been committed by client personnel? In general, the auditor has a greater responsibility for illegal acts that are direct and material to the financial statements. However, an auditor is not considered to be a legal expert, and thus determination of whether an action is legal may be beyond his or her professional judgment. If the auditor knows that certain laws are important to the operations of a client firm and that significant violations may have occurred, the audit should be planned to provide reasonable assurance that these violations are appropriately reported in the financial statements. Auditors are also expected to obtain the advice of a qualified legal expert when necessary.

Example

Government rules define the attributes of a safe and healthy work environment. Evaluating possible violations of those laws is outside the expertise of most auditors and generally such violations would not be important to the financial statements. Other laws outside the auditor's range of expertise include laws related to environmental protection, food and drug safety, and equal opportunity hiring. However, violations of these laws may lead to sizeable fines for an offending company.

Figure 3–4   Auditor's Responsibility for Detecting Illegal Acts by Clients

---

Procedures Performed in Normal Course of the Audit MAY reveal the following
- Unauthorized transactions
- Improperly recorded transactions
- Lack of transaction documentation
- Unusual year-end transactions
- Ongoing regulatory investigation
- Large unexplained disbursements
- Unusual transfer of funds
- Payments to government officials
- Failure to file tax returns

Procedures Performed When Illegal Acts MAY Exist
- Obtain explanation from management
- Consult legal counsel
- Document facts

Procedures Performed When an Illegal Act is Deemed to Have Occurred
- Consider impact on financial statements
- Reconsider ongoing relationship with client
- Communicate facts to audit committee
- Consider withdrawing from engagement
- Consider whether to contact authorities with legal counsel

Based on requirements in SAS 54 and ISA 250.

If evidence comes to the attention of the auditor that an illegal act may have occurred, the auditor is required to investigate the situation further. Once the auditor understands the facts, the matter should be referred to management at a level high enough to allow corrective action. If the client fails to undertake corrective action, the auditor should consider resigning from the engagement. As a practical matter, the auditor is most concerned with circumstances that may necessitate recognition of a contingent liability for fines and penalties. The auditor would typically not refer the matter to legal authorities unless required by law. In any case, the auditor would be foolish not to discuss the matter with legal counsel. A summary of the auditor's responsibility regarding illegal acts is presented in Figure 3–4.

ASSESSMENT OF GOING CONCERN

As part of the engagement, the auditor evaluates the ability of the organization to continue as a going concern over the next year. Generally, auditors focus on several key issues when evaluating whether there is substantial doubt about the entity's ability to continue as a going concern. Auditors consider the ability of an organization to generate sufficient cash flows to meet obligations by evaluating liquidity ratios and cash flow projections. Further, auditors evaluate trends relating to sales, expenses, and asset management to develop an understanding about the organization's financial stability. Consistent failure in attaining realistic business objectives are also an indicator of possible problems. Finally, litigation issues should be evaluated since significant legal exposures could bring the going concern assumption into doubt.

If the weight of evidence is such that the auditor has substantial doubts that the company can survive the next twelve months, an explanatory paragraph is added to the auditor's opinion describing the conditions leading to this determination. Auditors are supposed to be conservative in making this assessment. As a result, organizations that receive an explanatory paragraph for substantial doubt about being a going concern often do not actually fail. Auditors face a trade-off in making this determination because such conditions can strain relations between an auditor and client management; however, the auditor's responsibility to users of the financial statements necessitates such conservativeness whenever substantial doubt exists.

Example

The following is an excerpt from Ernst & Young's 2003 Auditor's Report for US Airways, which describes an example of substantial doubt about going concern:

The accompanying consolidated financial statements have been prepared assuming that the Company will continue as a going concern. As discussed in Note 2 to the consolidated financial statements, the Company's significant recurring losses and other matters regarding, among other things, the Company's ability to maintain compliance with covenants contained in various financing agreements as well as its ability to finance and operate regional jet aircraft and reduce its operating costs in order to successfully compete with low cost airlines, raise substantial doubt about its ability to continue as a going concern. Management's plans in regard to these matters are described in Note 2 to the consolidated financial statements. The accompanying consolidated financial statements do not include any adjustments that might result from the outcome of this uncertainty.

The Company subsequently filed for bankruptcy protection and was later acquired by AmericaWest Airlines and then renamed US Airways Group.

Most countries, but not all (e.g., Canada), require auditors to alert readers of the financial statements that there is a going concern issue disclosed in the notes to the financial statements.

COMMUNICATING THE RESULTS OF THE AUDIT

The output of any audit is some form of written report. The actual form of the report will depend on whether the audit is done under the rules of a traditional GAAS audit or in accordance with the rules of the PCAOB for an Integrated Audit. In general, a traditional audit produces a single report about the information contained in the financial statements. In an Integrated Audit, the auditor issues a report on the financial statements but also presents reports on (1) management's assertions about the effectiveness of internal control over financial reporting and (2) the auditor's own assessment of the same controls. The reports for an Integrated Audit may be presented separately or together in a single document.

AUDIT REPORTS RELATED TO INTERNAL CONTROL OVER FINANCIAL REPORTING

As noted above, management should test the design and operations of its system of internal control over financial reporting. This testing may reveal one or more

Figure 3–5   Control Deficiencies in Internal Control over Financial Reporting

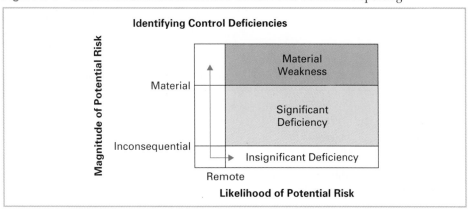

control deficiencies, which arise when the design or operation of the system does not prevent or detect misstatements on a timely basis. If management identifies a deficiency, the next step is to evaluate the significance of the deficiency. The PCAOB defines *significant deficiency* in Auditing Standard 2 (AS 2) as a deficiency, or combination of deficiencies, that "adversely affects the company's ability to initiate, authorize, record, process, or report external financial data reliably in accordance with generally accepted accounting principles such that there is more than a remote likelihood that a misstatement of the company's annual or interim financial statements that is more than inconsequential will not be prevented or detected." In some cases, a deficiency may constitute a *material weakness*, which AS 2 defines as a significant deficiency, or combination of deficiencies, whose impact on the financial statements is potentially material. The differences between insignificant deficiencies, significant deficiencies and material weaknesses are illustrated in Figure 3–5 based on the likelihood of an error occurring and the impact on financial reports.

Auditors issue opinions on (1) management's assessment of the effectiveness of internal control over financial reporting and (2) the actual effectiveness of internal control over financial reporting based on their own testing of controls. Based on the evidence that is available about the effectiveness of internal control, an auditor can issue either an unqualified opinion or an adverse opinion. Separate opinions are issued for management's assertions and the auditor's own conclusions about the effectiveness of internal control over financial reporting. For management's assessment, an *unqualified opinion* may be issued when the auditor feels that management assertions about internal control over financial reporting are fairly stated in all material respects, otherwise the auditor will issue an *adverse opinion*. The auditor's own opinion of internal control may be either unqualified, if he or she concludes that internal control over financial reporting is effective in all material respects, or adverse, if the auditor concludes that internal control over financial reporting is not effective due to one or more material weaknesses.

Figure 3–6 illustrates the possible combinations of reports that might be issued by the auditor given what is contained in the management assessment. For

Figure 3–6   Possible Auditor Reports on Internal Control over Financial Reporting

Management's Assessment of Controls	Auditor's test of effectiveness show	Report to be issued on management's assertions about the effectiveness of internal control	Report to be issued concerning auditor's opinion of actual effectiveness of internal control
No Material Weakness	No Material Weakness	Unqualified	Unqualified
No Material Weakness	Material Weakness	Adverse	Adverse
Material Weakness	Material Weakness	Unqualified	Adverse

example, the auditor may agree that management has reached the correct conclusion about control effectiveness and reported any material weaknesses; hence, the auditor can issue an unqualified opinion on management's evaluation of internal control. However, if a material weakness exists, the auditor's only option is an adverse opinion on internal control effectiveness. The logic here is that material weaknesses in internal control might impact financial statements, but the extent to which they do so is not known.[11] Figure 3–7 provides an example of a joint unqualified opinion over both management's assessment and the auditor's test of the design and operations of the internal control system over financial reporting.

THE AUDITOR'S REPORT RELATED TO FINANCIAL STATEMENT ASSERTIONS

After gathering all the evidence needed to determine if management's assertions about financial results are fairly stated, the auditor issues a formal report stating the nature of his or her conclusions. Auditing standards are very specific about the form of the report that should be used under different circumstances. If all management assertions associated with material amounts are reasonable, the auditor can conclude that the financial statements are fairly presented. If any management assertion associated with a material amount is not supported to the auditor's satisfaction, the auditor cannot conclude that the financial statements are fairly presented in accordance with GAAP. There are five general types of reports used by auditors, and the format that is used in a specific situation depends on the conclusions the auditor has reached. The hierarchy of these reports is illustrated in Figure 3–8 and described in detail below.

Standard Unqualified Report

The most common report is the *standard (unqualified) auditor's report*, which is used when the auditor concludes that the evidence obtained supports the fairness and completeness of all management assertions. An example of the standard

---

11 Under certain conditions in which the scope of the audit is restricted by conditions surrounding the audit of internal control over financial reporting, auditors may issue a qualified opinion or disclaimer of opinion. Those conditions will be explained in more detail in Chapter 8.

Figure 3–7   Report Expressing an Unqualified Opinion on Management's Assessment of the Effectiveness of Internal Control over Financial Reporting and an Unqualified Opinion on the Effectiveness of Internal Control over Financial Reporting Employing PCAOB Audit Standard #2

Report of Independent Registered Public Accounting Firm

[Introductory paragraph]
We have audited management's assessment, included in the accompanying [title of management's report], that W Company maintained effective internal control over financial reporting as of December 31, 20X3, based on [Identify control criteria, for example, "criteria established in *Internal Control— Integrated Framework* issued by the Committee of Sponsoring Organizations of the Treadway Commission (COSO)."]. W Company's management is responsible for maintaining effective internal control over financial reporting and for its assessment of the effectiveness of internal control over financial reporting. Our responsibility is to express an opinion on management's assessment and an opinion on the effectiveness of the company's internal control over financial reporting based on our audit.

[Scope paragraph]
We conducted our audit in accordance with the standards of the Public Company Accounting Oversight Board (United States). Those standards require that we plan and perform the audit to obtain reasonable assurance about whether effective internal control over financial reporting was maintained in all material respects. Our audit included obtaining an understanding of internal control over financial reporting, evaluating management's assessment, testing and evaluating the design and operating effectiveness of internal control, and performing such other procedures as we considered necessary in the circumstances. We believe that our audit provides a reasonable basis for our opinion.

[Definition paragraph]
A company's internal control over financial reporting is a process designed to provide reasonable assurance regarding the reliability of financial reporting and the preparation of financial statements for external purposes in accordance with generally accepted accounting principles. A company's internal control over financial reporting includes those policies and procedures that (1) pertain to the maintenance of records that, in reasonable detail, accurately and fairly reflect the transactions and dispositions of the assets of the company; (2) provide reasonable assurance that transactions are recorded as necessary to permit preparation of financial statements in accordance with generally accepted accounting principles, and that receipts and expenditures of the company are being made only in accordance with authorizations of management and directors of the company; and (3) provide reasonable assurance regarding prevention or timely detection of unauthorized acquisition, use, or disposition of the company's assets that could have a material effect on the financial statements.

[Inherent limitations paragraph]
Because of its inherent limitations, internal control over financial reporting may not prevent or detect misstatements. Also, projections of any evaluation of effectiveness to future periods are subject to the risk that controls may become inadequate because of changes in conditions, or that the degree of compliance with the policies or procedures may deteriorate.

[Opinion paragraph]
In our opinion, management's assessment that W Company maintained effective internal control over financial reporting as of December 31, 20X3, is fairly stated, in all material respects, based on [Identify control criteria, for example, "criteria established in *Internal Control—Integrated Framework* issued by the Committee of Sponsoring Organizations of the Treadway Commission (COSO)."]. Also in our opinion, W Company maintained, in all material respects, effective internal control over financial reporting as of December 31, 20X3, based on [Identify control criteria, for example, "criteria established in *Internal Control—Integrated Framework* issued by the Committee of Sponsoring Organizations of the Treadway Commission (COSO)."].

[Explanatory paragraph]
We have also audited, in accordance with the standards of the Public Company Accounting Oversight Board (United States), the [identify financial statements] of W Company and our report dated [date of report, which should be the same as the date of the report on the effectiveness of internal control over financial reporting] expressed [include nature of opinion].

[Signature]
[City and Country]
[Date]

Figure 3–8   Hierarchy of the Auditor's Reporting Options

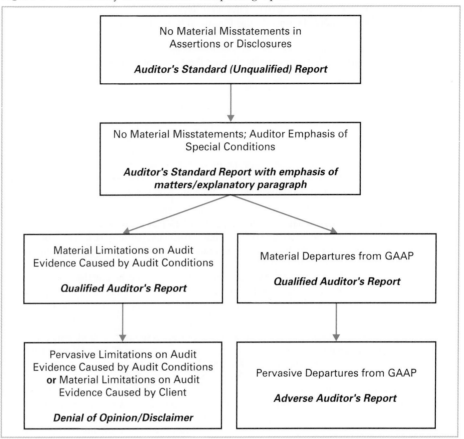

unqualified report is provided in Figure 3–9. A standard unqualified report has seven parts: a title, a date, an addressee, an introductory paragraph, a scope paragraph, an opinion paragraph, and a sign-off. The title of the report is specific to the country in which the report is issued; for example, in the United States the report is entitled "Independent Public Accountant's Report," whereas internationally it is often called the "Auditor's Report." The date of the report is the date on which the auditor completes testing also known as the date fieldwork ends. The addressee is usually the shareholders or the company's board of directors. The introductory paragraph specifies the assertions being attested to (i.e., the financial statements) and the relative responsibilities of the auditor and management. The scope paragraph provides a brief description of what the auditor has done. The opinion paragraph indicates the auditor's conclusion. Finally, the report is "signed" by the firm.

The opinion paragraph is arguably the most important part of the report. It is so important that the entire report is often referred to as the auditor's "opinion." The key words in the opinion are "present fairly" and "reasonable assurance." The report does not say that the financial statements are absolutely correct. Such a conclusion would be unwarranted since total correctness can never be verified due to the inherent uncertainty underlying the audit process. The criteria used for reaching a conclusion about fairness are clearly stated to be generally accepted

Figure 3–9   Standard (Unqualified) Auditor's Report

Title	Auditor's Report
Addressee	To the Shareholders of Pizzeria Inc.
Intro	We have audited the accompanying balance sheet of Pizzeria Inc. as of December 31, 20xx, and the related statements of income, retained earnings, and cash flows for the year then ended. These financial statements are the responsibility of the company's management. Our responsibility is to express an opinion on these financial statements based on our audit.
Scope	We conducted our audit in accordance with Canadian generally accepted auditing standards. Those standards require that we plan and perform the audit to obtain reasonable assurance whether the financial statements are free of material misstatement. An audit includes examining, on a test basis, evidence supporting the amounts and disclosures in the financial statements. An audit also includes assessing the accounting principles used and significant estimates made by management, as well as evaluating the overall financial statement presentation.
Opinion	In our opinion, the financial statements present fairly, in all material respects, the financial position of Pizzeria Inc. as of December 31, 20xx, and the results of its operations and its cash flows for the year then ended in accordance with Canadian generally accepted accounting principles.
Signer	[Name of the accounting firm]
Date	[Date]

accounting principles. If the auditor does not feel that he or she can issue a standard unqualified report, one of the following four alternative reports will be used.

Standard Auditor's Report with Explanatory Paragraph

A *standard auditor's report with an explanatory paragraph* (also known as a *modified unqualified report*) is used when the auditor concludes that management's assertions are correct and complete but, for some reason, the auditor wishes to bring some specific information to the attention of the reader. An example is when a company changes the method of accounting, for example, accounting for inventory is changed from FIFO to weighted average. Another example is when a company is faced with a significant uncertainty (e.g., a lawsuit) that, when resolved, may have a dramatic impact on the future viability of the company. In both these examples, the auditor concludes that the company's financial statements are in compliance with GAAP, but certain facts are so important that the auditor wishes to draw the reader's attention to them.

Qualified Auditor's Report

A *qualified report* is issued when the auditor feels that he or she is unable to conclude that the assertions are completely reliable or fair. This can typically occur for two reasons: (1) scope limitations and (2) departures from GAAP. For scope limitations, the auditor is unable to obtain enough evidence to form an opinion. One example where this might occur is if the auditor is unable to observe the quantity of inventory on hand at the end of the year.[12] In the case of departures from GAAP, the auditor concludes that the company has violated GAAP for some significant assertion or set of assertions included in the financial statements. Such a violation may occur because the company fails to correct material misstatements uncovered by the auditor, omits a required disclosure, or uses an unacceptable accounting method (e.g., capitalizing research expenditures).

Denial of Opinion (or Disclaimer)

In a *denial of opinion* or *disclaimer*, the auditor states that no opinion can be expressed. A denial of opinion may be issued in the case of a scope limitation that has a pervasive impact on the financial statements. In such a situation, the auditor is unable to obtain convincing evidence about the reliability of the assertions and/or disclosures in the statements. For scope limitations, the auditor can issue either a qualified opinion or a disclaimer, depending on how important he or she perceives the missing evidence to be and whether the scope limitation was caused by conditions beyond the control of the client and auditor, or was arbitrarily imposed by the client (e.g., management prohibits the auditor from observing inventory). A disclaimer can also be issued if the there is a conflict of interest between the auditor and client such that he or she cannot render an independent professional opinion (e.g., the auditor's brother is the president).

Adverse Auditor's Report

An *adverse report* is issued when the auditor concludes that the financial statement assertions are largely incorrect or misleading. The auditor has a choice of issuing either a qualified or adverse report depending on the importance of the violation. If the violation is pervasive (e.g., the company does not make year-end adjusting entries), an adverse report could be issued, in which case the auditor clearly states that the financial statements "do not present fairly" the financial status of the organization. Such reports are extremely rare, however, because the auditor will usually resign (or be fired) in situations that are so extreme as to justify an adverse opinion. However, when an auditor resigns under these conditions, the auditor may be perceived as "allowing" the action to continue by not requiring a client to correct a GAAP violation or issuing an adverse opinion.

THE PERVASIVE CONCEPTS OF AUDITING: RISK, MATERIALITY, AND EVIDENCE

Management assertions reflect the start of the audit process, and audit reports the end. How does the auditor determine whether management's assertions are accurate? How does the auditor determine which form of report to issue? We start our discussion of the intervening audit process by focusing on a key phrase that occurs frequently in the discussion of the audit process—*reasonable assurance*. Subjectivity is inherent in the audit process as evidenced by commonly encountered terminology such as "significant," "important," "sizeable," "likely," and "probable." Although aggravatingly imprecise, these terms reflect that the auditor must deal with uncertainty in many different forms. The notion of reasonable assurance

---

12 This situation could arise if the engagement was not obtained until after the end of the fiscal year. Being hired after year end does not automatically lead to issuance of a qualified report, however, because the auditor may have other ways to gather the necessary evidence about inventory.

comprises three concepts that are pervasive to the conduct of an audit: risk, materiality, and evidence.

Risk is fundamental to all auditing because it reflects the reality that an auditor can never be completely certain that the assertions he or she is auditing—regardless of whether they pertain to single accounts, the overall financial statements, or internal control over financial reporting—are free of omissions or misstatements. That condition is why much of the previous discussion used terms such as "reasonable" and "likely." Auditors define many different sources of risk that will be discussed in this text. Misstatements may or may not be present, but the audit must be planned to enable the auditor to provide reasonable—not absolute—assurance that any existing misstatements that would matter to outside users of the financial statements are discovered and removed from the assertions and disclosures that comprise the financial statements.

Materiality is the term used to describe the significance of financial statement information to decision makers. Information is material if it is probable that its omission or misstatement would influence or change a decision. More formally, materiality is defined in FASB Statement No. 2 as "the magnitude of an omission or misstatement of accounting information that, in light of surrounding circumstances, makes it probable that the judgment of a reasonable person relying on the information would have been changed or influenced by the omission or misstatement."[13] Materiality is a matter of professional judgment as to what is significant or important in the context of the financial statements being audited. Unfortunately, the definition of materiality is open to interpretation and there are no regulatory or generally accepted standards for determining what is, or is not, material in a given engagement. Consequently, the implementation of materiality rests firmly with the professional judgment of the practitioner conducting an audit.

Audit evidence is any information that gives the auditor an indication whether an assertion is reasonable or not. Evidence comes in many forms and can provide strong or weak support for the fairness of assertions, depending on the circumstances of an engagement. A key goal of the audit is to obtain sufficient appropriate evidence on which to base an opinion about the financial statements. Unfortunately, evidence is often incomplete or subject to interpretation. The auditor must make explicit decisions about how to obtain sufficient evidence that provides reasonable assurance that there are no material misstatements in the financial statements, and that satisfies generally accepted auditing standards. The general rule that most auditors adopt is that they will concentrate their efforts looking at conditions that are most likely to lead to problems and/or misstatements.

The three concepts of risk, evidence, and materiality interact during the course of the audit to guide the appropriate conduct of the audit. An auditor will gather more evidence for a client who is considered to be high risk than for a client who is considered to be low risk. At the same time, the auditor's perception of materiality will affect the risk of the client. If the materiality threshold is low (that is, small errors are important) the auditor will have to gather more evidence because it is harder to find small errors than large errors. In short,

the auditor gathers evidence to determine the risk that a material misstatement exists in one or more assertions made by the client's management. The more evidence the auditor obtains, the lower the risk that there are undetected material errors in the assertions being examined.

13 FASB SFAC No. 2. Qualitative Characteristics of Accounting Information.

RISK CONCEPTS IN AUDITING

Although auditors deal with many forms of risk during the course of an engagement, three broad types of risk are of paramount interest to the auditor: client business risk, engagement risk, and audit risk.

CLIENT BUSINESS RISK

<table>
<tr>
<td>

Authoritative
Guidance & Standards
The concepts of risk are referenced in many standards; however, the standards most focused on risk considerations during a financial statement audit are those focused on defining risks (SAS 107, ISA 320), assessing risk of material misstatement (SAS 109, ISA 315), performing procedures in response to assessed risks (SAS 110, ISA 330, AS 2).

</td>
<td>

Client business risk reflects the possibility that an organization will experience adverse outcomes as a result of economic conditions, events, circumstances, or management action/inaction. As noted in Chapter 2, business risks are identified, analyzed, and mitigated through enterprise risk management. Auditors are also concerned with client business risks because such risks shed light on the effectiveness of the client's ERM framework, and they may eventually have an impact on the company's financial statements. Business risks may arise from the complexity of the environment and/or changes in the organization, though a failure to recognize the need for change may also give rise to risk. For example, organizations

</td>
</tr>
</table>

may suffer adverse outcomes from the failure of new products, inadequate market development, or from flaws in execution that lead to economic losses or impairment of reputation.

Most client business risks will eventually have an effect on the results reported in the financial statements. However, some business risks can have an immediate effect on a class of transactions, account balance, or disclosure. For example, risk arising from a shrinking customer base due to industry consolidation may lead to questions about the valuation of receivables (which may not be collected) and/or inventory (which may not be sold).

Example

> Some risk may result in the need for significant adjustments to the financial statements. When a tsunami in the Indian Ocean struck two luxury Le Méridien resorts in Thailand in December 2004, both resorts closed for an extended period. This event was a great human tragedy and also had a severe economic impact on many businesses, including the hotel. An auditor would assess whether the insurance on the properties was sufficient to cover the losses associated with the property, as well as the lost business at the damaged properties. The issue is whether any losses sustained are large enough to be material to the hotel chain and, if so, whether the company has fairly reflected such actual and expected losses in its financial statements.

ENGAGEMENT RISK

Auditors are also susceptible to their own form of business risk since they choose which organizations to take on as clients. *Engagement Risk* refers to the risk the audit firm is exposed to due to loss or injury from litigation, adverse publicity, or other events arising in connection with the audited financial statements (SAS 106, ISA 200). Such risk may exist even if the audit is conducted according to professional standards. The concept of engagement risk recognizes the possibility that the firm may suffer a loss from association with a client even though the firm complies with all relevant professional standards and issues the appropriate audit report based on the evidence available at the time of the audit. Possible manifestations of engagement risk include

1. Litigation. If the audit firm is sued because the client goes bankrupt or has committed fraud or an illegal act, the firm will suffer a loss even if it wins the case. The cost of litigation, even in a successful defense, can more than wipe out any profit earned by the firm on the original engagement.
2. Regulatory penalties. Audit firms may be subject to fines or other penalties if they are associated with a failed client or a client involved in fraud or intense regulatory scrutiny (e.g., material restatements of financial statements).

Example

In response to alleged improprieties and lack of professionalism in the conduct of some audits, the SEC prohibited Ernst & Young from accepting any new clients for a six-month period. Ernst & Young did not perceive that the actions in question warranted this punishment. Nevertheless, in an effort to minimize its losses, the firm accepted the ruling while protesting their innocence.

3. Loss of professional reputation. If the firm becomes associated with an enterprise that has a poor reputation, it may lose future clients because more reputable organizations do not want to associate with the firm—that is, they do not want to suffer guilt by association.

Example

In the 1950s, large auditing firms would not accept casinos as clients due to their unsavory links with organized crime. Now that casinos are often owned by large, public companies, auditors are willing to take them on as clients.

4. Lack of profitability. After an auditing firm completes an engagement, it may discover that the fee that a client is willing to pay is inadequate to cover the costs of providing services. Unless there is a good reason for continuing the association, the firm would prefer not to undertake engagements that are not profitable.[14]

AUDIT RISK

Audit risk is considered at both the overall engagement level and the account balance level. It is defined as the likelihood that an auditor will render an incorrect opinion on the financial statements in spite of the effort expended to conduct the audit effectively (e.g., ISA 200, SAS 106). More formally, audit risk is defined as the likelihood or probability that the auditor will conclude that all material assertions made by management are true when, in fact, at least one material assertion is

---

14 Firms will occasionally undertake an engagement knowing that they will not earn their normal profit margin. This can occur in the case of charitable organizations, such as the audit of United Way. It can also occur when the firm is using the audit as a "loss leader" in order to gain entry into a specific audit market (e.g., a geographic region or specialized industry) where significant spin-off work in tax and permitted management consulting is expected, or where the possibility exists that future fees will grow enough to justify the near-term losses. This practice is not recommended for most public company audits as regulatory scrutiny would increase substantially if or when it becomes known to regulators.

incorrect. Audit risk can be decomposed into two component risks: (1) risk of material misstatement and (2) detection risk.

Risk of Material Misstatement

Accounting misstatements—whether unintentional errors or intentional frauds—arise from many sources. Transaction processing can be inaccurate, transactions can be lost or omitted from the accounting system, results can be falsified, assets can be stolen or lost, inappropriate accounting policies may be selected, or accounting estimates may be manipulated. Hence, the auditor must consider the *risk of material misstatement*, which is defined as "the risk that the financial statements are misstated prior to audit."[15] At the financial statement level, the risk of material misstatement pertains to the financial statements as a whole and reflects the joint effect misstatements may have across a number of assertions. The risk of material misstatement also applies to classes of transactions, specific accounts, and individual disclosures and is a function of

- Business risks associated with the client's industry, strategy, business model, and business processes
- Susceptibility of assets to theft
- Ease with which information can be manipulated
- Information processing risks associated with high-volume, routine transactions
- Challenges associated with accounting for nonroutine or complex transactions
- Risks associated with judgments utilized for accounting estimates
- Limitations (e.g., cost, competence, and so forth) that prevent internal controls over financial reporting from preventing or detecting all material misstatements

The auditor cannot directly influence the risk of material misstatement in the current period because it is considered an attribute of the accounting system and internal control over financial reporting that the company has currently in place. In future years, auditors may influence the risk of misstatement by encouraging management to strengthen areas of the accounting system that are considered to be at risk. If management responds to the auditor's advice and implements effective controls, the risk of material misstatement is likely to be reduced for future audits.

Example

> A credit manager is responsible for reviewing credit applications from new customers in order to reduce the risk of bad debts. If the credit manager does not get credit reports on new customers, credit may be granted to customers that have previously defaulted on obligations and eventually leading to the write off the customer's balance. This weakness in internal control may lead to a material misstatement in the current financial statements (such as an inadequate allowance for bad debts). Also, the auditor may provide advice on how to rectify this problem in the future, reducing the risk of material misstatement in future audits.

The risk of material misstatement can be further decomposed into two components that have traditionally been considered by auditors: inherent risk and control risk. *Inherent risk* is defined as the risk that misstatements might occur *if there were no internal controls*. However, this risk only exists in theory because we also know that existing internal controls will prevent and/or detect misstatements.

15 ISA 200 "Audit Evidence" and SAS 106 "Audit Evidence."

Control risk reflects the likelihood that the controls present in the system will not prevent or detect a material error in the financial statements. Past experience has demonstrated that auditors have difficulty separating inherent risk from control risk so the broader concept of risk of material misstatement has become more commonly used in practice (although some firms continue to split the concepts as part of their formal audit approaches).

Detection Risk

The primary task of an auditor is to search for and uncover misstatements in the financial records. The risk that an auditor may fail to discover an existing misstatement is *detection risk*, more formally defined in ISA 200 as "The risk that the auditor will not detect a material misstatement that exists in an assertion." Detection risk is a function of the effectiveness of the audit procedures performed and the interpretation of the resulting evidence. Detection risk cannot be reduced to zero because the auditor usually does not examine all transactions, account balances, or disclosures. Furthermore, the auditor may not perform the appropriate audit procedure, misapply an audit procedure, or misinterpret the results.

Example

Auditors typically test the existence of inventory by examining and counting the items in the client's warehouse. However, the auditor is rarely able to count or observe everything, so he or she may not notice that some inventory listed on the financial statements does not exist. This is an example of detection risk because the auditor can never be totally certain that the procedures will detect an existing problem.

MATERIALITY

The question "does it matter?" reflects the essence of materiality. When an auditor encounters potential problems during the course of the audit, he or she has to anticipate whether other stakeholders will consider the impact of the problem on the financial statements to be important. Judgments about materiality are often about "scale." For example, if a cash drawer is $5.00 short, an error or theft may have occurred, but the auditor is unlikely to be concerned since the amount is small. At the other extreme, an account such as inventory usually represents a large portion of total assets for a manufacturing or merchandising company, as well as the largest expense on the income statement (i.e., cost of goods sold). Therefore, if inventory is misstated by 50 percent, most auditors would agree that the impact on both the balance sheet and income statement would be "material." For other accounts, such as prepaid insurance, an error of 50 percent of the balance may be immaterial, unless management has intentionally misstated the balance.

Authoritative Guidance & Standards
Materiality is one of the most important judgments that an auditor must make, and standards discuss important considerations regarding the concept (SAS 107, ISA 320), although they do not stipulate a preferred method of determining materiality. For publicly traded U.S. companies, the SEC issued Staff Accounting Bulletin (SAB) No. 99 that essentially prohibits any consideration of materiality for known misstatements, meaning that auditors must require clients to correct any known misstatements.

Quantitative Materiality

When planning the audit, the auditor considers the magnitude of an error that would make the financial statements materially misstated. If a company is going to round off its financial results to the nearest million dollars, then it is easy to see that materiality must be at least $1 million—anything smaller would not even show up in the reported results. How large the materiality threshold should be is subject to a great deal of judgment and auditors have developed numerous rules of thumb for setting an initial materiality level. Generally, a reasonable guideline for materiality is 5 to 10 percent of net income for a business making a profit (not showing losses) or 1 to 3 percent of net assets for a not-for-profit organization. However, auditors may select other bases or percentages for establishing materiality if a justifiable reason can be established. For example, an auditor who believes that readers emphasize revenues or gross margin as the basis for evaluating an organization may use something along the lines of 3 percent of revenues or 10 percent of gross margin for materiality.

The auditor should also consider the possibility that numerous small misstatements could have a material effect on the financial statements when aggregated. For example, an error in a month-end procedure could lead to a material misstatement if it is repeated each month. The auditor considers materiality at both the overall financial statement level and in relation to individual account balances, classes of transactions, and disclosures. Auditors should consider materiality both for current period misstatements in isolation, and for prior misstatements that were uncorrected because they were not deemed to be material but might be material when combined with current year misstatements.

Qualitative Materiality

The auditor should also consider qualitative aspects of materiality, that is, the nature of a misstatement may be more important than its size. Some subjective reasons why an auditor might consider a small misstatement to be material include

- Fraud: The discovery of fraud is always considered to be important because it indicates that management's integrity may be impaired.
- Violations of debt covenants: Misstatements that allow a company to avoid technical default may be important since violating a debt covenant may mean renegotiating the entire debt agreement.
- Missing earnings targets: Failing to achieve earnings equal to or superior to analysts' forecasts, even by a penny a share, may cause an extreme drop in the market capitalization of a company.
- Hitting incentive goals: If management and/or employees have incentive-based contracts, misstatements that allow them to achieve their goals can be material.

In some situations, the concept of materiality may not be quantifiable at all. For example, incomplete or improper disclosures may be considered to be "material" if they have the potential to mislead users of the financial statements. Similarly, failure to disclose a breach of regulatory requirements might be considered a material disclosure "error."

The concept of materiality has been greatly abused in recent years. In some cases, auditors have relied on an arbitrary level of materiality to allow revenue and associated profits to be intentionally shifted between time periods in order to meet analysts' forecasts of earnings per share. Typically, this behavior has been rationalized by keeping intentional misstatements small, that is, below materiality. Because the behavior is presumed to affect the decisions of stakeholders interested in the company—otherwise, why do it—it is difficult to argue that such misstatements "don't matter." Some regulatory bodies have taken steps to remove an auditor's ability to use materiality as justification for actions that are taken simply to appease management. The SEC specifically prohibits the use of materiality as a basis for not following generally accepted accounting principles—they require that all known errors in the financial statements be corrected.

EVIDENCE COLLECTION IN AUDITING

An auditor's conclusions about the fairness of financial statements must be based on a convincing body of evidence. In terms of auditing standards, the auditor must gather sufficient competent evidence on which to base an opinion. An auditor follows a well-understood process for obtaining the requisite evidence, conditional on the environment, circumstances, and risks of the client. The process of gathering information and evidence about the client's activities, risks, and results is divided into two main phrases: (1) risk assessment and (2) tests of accounting information (refer to Figure 3–10).

RISK ASSESSMENT

To inform the auditor about the various types of risks related to the audit engagement and to aid in developing criteria for what is to be considered material, auditors assess current conditions within an organization. Information that is necessary for understanding the context of the audit is gathered by means of the following procedures:

- Understanding an organization's environment, objectives, strategies, and risks
- Understanding the design, reliability, and effectiveness of enterprise risk management and internal control over financial reporting
- Performing preliminary analytical procedures

These procedures will be discussed in much more detail in later chapters, but it is important to understand how they influence the conduct of the audit.

Understanding an Organization's Environment and Risks

One of the first tasks during an engagement is to develop an understanding of the client's environment, including the external forces influencing the organization (e.g., regulation, competition); its business objectives and strategies for achieving them; the design of its internal activities and processes; the nature of its information system; and the types of transactions that occur. This information is critical for understanding the risks that threaten the organization, and it provides a framework for interpreting the organization's financial results. Additionally, the auditor tries to develop a comprehensive understanding of the risks that are most critical to the organization, paying careful attention to how these risks likely impact the financial statements.

Example

Knowledge that a company's primary competitor has introduced a technologically superior and less costly alternative to its own products would influence an auditor's expectations about the company's results, may suggest potential impairments to tangible or intangible assets, and may raise concerns about the client's ability to continue in operation.

Figure 3–10   Collection of Audit Evidence

Type of Procedure	Resulting Audit Evidence	Relationship with Financial Statement Errors
Procedures to Assess Risk		
Understanding an organization's environment, strategies, and plans	Inquiry Observation/inspection Documentation Analytical evidence	Indication of errors is very indirect. The procedures indicate the risks from the environment that can adversely affect the organization and the reliability of management and information systems in general, but does not indicate whether specific transactions or accounts are correct.
Understanding information system design, reliability, and effectiveness	Inquiry Observation/inspection Documentation Analytical evidence	Indication of errors is indirect. Breakdowns in the information system and controls over transaction flows may or may not result in an error in a transaction or account. Frequent breakdowns increase the likelihood that errors occur and go undetected by the organization.
Preliminary analytical procedures	Analytical evidence Inquiry	Indication of errors is indirect. The procedures indicate circumstances that appear to be unusual and could lead to misstatements or errors.
Procedures to Test Accounting Information		
Substantive analytical procedures	Analytical evidence	Indication of errors or fraud is indirect. The procedures indicate accounts that appear to have unusual balances which may be due to a misstatement.
Tests of transactions	Documentation Recalculation and reperformance Inquiry	Indication of errors or fraud in a *transaction* is direct; indication of an error or fraud in an *account* is indirect since the problem may have been detected and corrected at a later date or may have reversed by the end of the year.
Tests of accounts	Inspection of tangible assets Documentation Recalculation Confirmation Inquiry	Indication of errors or fraud is direct based on auditor inspection of assets, documentation of specific items, recalculation of numerical values, and/or confirmation of information provided by third parties.
Tests of presentation and disclosure	Documentation Confirmation Inquiry Recalculation	Indication of errors or fraud is direct based on a review of the disclosures or may be indirect in the case of the examination of related documents from which disclosures are derived.

Understanding Enterprise Risk Management and Internal Control over Financial Reporting

Every organization devotes substantial resources to managing risks and safe-guarding itself from errors and fraud in the accounting system. The more effective management is at reducing its risk, the fewer problems the auditor can expect to encounter during the engagement. Of most interest to the auditor is the effectiveness of the internal controls over financial reporting. For example, the auditor might want to know that inventory purchases are being properly authorized, that sales clerks are checking the price of merchandise being sold, and that credit card charges are being properly validated. If these control activities are systematically and rigorously followed, there is less of a chance that sales will be processed incorrectly. Auditors use tests of system reliability, often called *tests of controls*, to assess the quality of transaction processing and measure the risk that transactions may be processed incorrectly.

Example

An auditor may be concerned that a company is charging a noncompetitive price for its product that could lead to a significant reduction in sales revenue and result in unsold inventory. To assess the potential significance of this risk, the auditor would examine the process the company uses for setting prices, for monitoring actions of competitors, and for assigning prices to individual transactions. The auditor may also test to see whether the process is consistently followed.

Preliminary Analytical Procedures

Auditors usually have a great deal of quantitative data available to help assess the significance of risks facing an organization. This data may be financial or non-financial in nature and can be used to develop a greater understanding of the company and expectations about its economic condition. Auditors are required to look at the preliminary financial results during the course of the year, or right after the end of the fiscal year, in order to identify potential problem areas where the results are inconsistent with the known circumstances of the company, or where they just don't make sense given the risk profile of the company. In short, the auditor looks for initial warning signals that results may be out of line, or possibly misstated.

Example

An auditor may examine the sales growth statistics based on product line, location, or region in order to identify unusual activity that needs to be investigated. If the industry is in a recession and the company is threatened by extensive competition, the auditor might expect to see slowing growth and tightening margins. If the preliminary performance results suggest something else, the auditor will be concerned that the results are misstated.

TESTS OF ACCOUNTING INFORMATION

Once an auditor has assessed the risk of material misstatements, the next step is to perform specific tests of reported results. Auditors may perform a broad range of tests at this point dependent on their risk assessments, the assertions at risk, and the type of evidence that is available. In general, there are four different types of tests applicable to accounting information:

- **Substantive analytical procedures:** The comparison of quantitative relationships among account balances and other indicators to an auditor's expectations.

If an auditor's expectations are not met (e.g., the relationships exhibit unusual patterns), additional evidence is gathered to identify whether misstatements exist.

Example

> The revenue for a hotel can be estimated by multiplying the number of rooms in the hotel by the average occupancy rate and the average cost per night. If the result is reasonably close to the recorded amount for revenue, the auditor might conclude that the account is free of material error.

- **Tests of transactions:** The verification of the details of specific transactions.

Example

> To ensure the occurrence of sales, an auditor selects a sample of recorded sales transactions and tests them by examining the supporting sales invoice, shipping documentation, and customer purchase order.

- **Tests of accounts:** The examination of the details that comprise a year-end balance.

Example

> To test the existence and valuation of the construction in progress account for new retail locations (i.e., the percentage of completion), the auditor can visit construction sites to inspect the progress made on projects that in process.

- **Tests of presentation and disclosure:** Review and examination of the disclosures in the financial statements for clarity and completeness.

Example

> To test the understandability of an organization's disclosures about long-term debt, the auditor can inspect the footnotes to ensure they are clear, concise, and does not use complex terminology to mislead users.

Numerous specific examples of these types of procedures are identified and described in later chapters. It is important to keep in mind that the design of these tests depends on the nature of the assertion or account being examined and the level of detection risk the auditor wishes to achieve.

TYPES OF AUDIT EVIDENCE

All audit procedures create audit evidence which facilitates the auditor's evaluation of the accuracy and completeness of management assertions that comprise the financial statements. Auditors should be aware that many of these forms of evidence are now collected with the assistance of information technology. When utilizing information generated from client automated systems, auditors should ensure that data used as evidence is reliable prior to accepting it as evidence. This normally requires that an engagement team member have special expertise in information technology controls. Regardless of the underlying procedure that generates the evidence, there are seven general categories of evidence used by auditors:

- **Inspection (or examination) of Tangible Assets:** Evidence obtained from the firsthand inspection of tangible assets by the auditor. This type of evidence is very reliable but can be used only for assets that are available for inspection. This type of evidence is particularly good for verifying the existence of assets.

Example

> The existence of tangible assets such as inventory, plant and equipment, investment securities, and cash can be physically verified.

- **Confirmation:** Written or oral evidence received from third parties who are independent of the client. This type of evidence is considered to be highly reliable and is particularly useful for verifying the existence or completeness assertions.

Example

> Typical confirmation evidence comes from customers who confirm receivable balances, banks who confirm deposit balances (and loans), attorneys who confirm details of litigation (possible contingent losses), and suppliers who confirm balances owed (accounts payable).

- **Inspection of Records or Documents:** Evidence obtained from the examination of the client's written records or documents in the client's possession. This type of evidence is easy to obtain and can support all assertions in the financial statements. However, because it is obtained from the client, its reliability must be established through other procedures.

Example

> Evidence to test the existence and valuation of sales transactions may be obtained by examining shipping documents, sales invoices, and cash receipts.

- **Observation:** Visual evidence obtained by the auditor by witnessing client activities while they are in progress. This type of evidence can be used in the absence of a "paper trail" for processing transactions, and is often used for tests of controls.[16]

Example

> Companies typically restrict access to computer facilities to avoid unauthorized use and modification of computer records. The auditor might observe the physical security over computer equipment to determine if access is actually restricted and observe authorized personnel performing the necessary procedures to gain access.

---

16 The distinction between inspection and observation can sometimes be confusing. Examination focuses on evaluating tangible assets, records, or documents, whereas observation focuses on witnessing activities or processes.

- **Recalculation and/or reperformance:** Computational evidence obtained by verifying summary totals (e.g., adding up individual transaction amounts to arrive at the total account balance) or reperforming client procedures. Traditionally, auditors referred to recalculation as "footing" or "running a tape." Today, the mechanical steps of adding accounts are normally performed through the use of computer software that can check the accuracy of account activity.

Example

The accuracy of an invoice can be checked by reperforming the procedures that the client follows such as entering the price and quantity of a sale and then recalculating taxes, discounts, and transaction totals. The total of the transaction can then be traced to the proper accounting records such as a sales journal and/or customer receivable ledger.

- **Analytical Evidence (or Analysis):** Auditor comparison of expected balances or relationships to actual financial and nonfinancial data. Unexpected relationships often are based on unusual circumstances that are inconsistent with the auditor's expectations for an account or class of transactions. Evidence based on analysis often involves examining the relationships among important account balances, percentages or ratios for unexplained variations that might indicate that an error has occurred. Another form of analytical procedures is *scanning* client records for the existence of any unusual amounts or entries.

Example

Depreciation expense can be estimated from other facts known to an auditor. The auditor could divide depreciation expense by the average balance in plant assets (buildings and equipment). If this percentage seemed reasonable based on the auditor's prior expectation, the auditor might conclude that depreciation expense is reasonably accurate.[17] If the computed value seems out of line, it may be due to the use of an imprecise estimate, a change in asset mix, a change in accounting principle, or an accounting error.

- **Client Enquiry:** Evidence obtained from written and oral representations made by management or other client personnel. This evidence is usually obtained in response to questions raised by the auditor. Client enquiry is often a starting point for gathering further evidence. Client enquiries are very important for assessing current conditions within an organization but will usually need to be corroborated with other types of evidence. In evaluating the strength of the evidence, the auditor must assess the credibility of the source.

Example

An auditor might ask the credit manager why a specific receivable was written off as a bad debt, ask the marketing manager to explain why sales results are down from prior years, or ask the plant foreman what procedures the company uses to approve the purchase of equipment.

---

17 The reasonableness of the percentage could be evaluated against a benchmark which considered the average useful life of the assets and the depreciation method being used. For example, if a company uses straight-line depreciation and has an average asset life of 10 years, the computed percentage should be close to 10 percent.

COMPETENCE OF AUDIT EVIDENCE

When selecting procedures to address specific management assertions, the auditor will consider the risk assessments related to the assertion and the materiality of the assertion relative to the overall financial statements. With this in mind, the auditor will then determine how competent the evidence needs to be in order to satisfy the auditor's goal for detection risk. If the desired detection risk is low, the auditor will want a great deal of competent substantive evidence; if desired detection risk is high, the auditor may make due with less effective procedures that are easier to perform or that use smaller sample sizes.

> **Authoritative Guidance & Standards**
> The types and competence of evidence are discussed in auditing standards on audit evidence (SAS 106, ISA 500). These standards do not require that the auditor gather specific types of evidence, however, except in very narrow circumstances (e.g. receivables confirmations SAS 67, ISA 505).

How does an auditor know the competence or quality of the evidence from a specific audit procedure? There are a number of characteristics that the auditor can consider in order to understand the competence of audit evidence.

- **Degree of relevance:** Is the evidence obtained from a procedure relevant to the assertion being examined? If the auditor wishes to know if inventory exists, the best way to find out is to physically observe the inventory on hand and count the items. Of course, physical observation will not tell the auditor whether or not the items in the warehouse are actually owned by the client.
- **Independence of the provider:** Is the source of the evidence independent of the company, or is it subject to possible manipulation by the company? Information obtained from a person outside the client's company is usually considered to be superior to that received from an insider. An outsider is assumed to have no vested interest in the outcome of the audit, whereas an insider may try to sway the auditor's opinion in order to advance his or her own goals.
- **Degree of auditor's direct knowledge:** Is the evidence directly observable at its source by the auditor? "Seeing is believing" is an adage that clearly applies to auditors. Again, the best way to determine if inventory is present is to look at it. Supplier invoices may indicate how many items of inventory the client acquired, but this type of documentary evidence is only second-best to direct physical examination of the inventory.

Example

A famous audit fraud was perpetrated by a manufacturer of disk drives for personal computers who was able to fool the auditors into thinking that the warehouse was full of inventory by placing bricks into disk drive boxes, shrink-wrapping the boxes, and stacking them in the warehouse. The auditor failed to realize the charade when physically examining the inventory. "Seeing is believing" only when the auditor knows what he or she is looking at!

- **Qualifications of the provider:** Is the source of the evidence qualified to provide evidence that is accurate? When receiving evidence from another person, the auditor must consider the competence of the provider. For example, the best person to provide information to the auditor about a pension plan is probably an actuary. Similarly, the best person to provide information about the value of real estate is an appraiser.

- **Degree of objectivity:** Is the evidence ambiguous or open to interpretation? Audit evidence is rarely clear-cut in its support of an assertion. This is especially true for the valuation assertion. For example, a company may provide extensive evidence concerning sales debits and cash credits to a customer's account. However, how does the auditor determine if the net balance is actually collectible? Does the evidence that a customer has paid his or her bill in the past imply that he or she will continue to pay the bill? The evaluation of such evidence bears directly on the recorded value of receivables but is potentially ambiguous.

- **Quality of internal recordkeeping:** How reliable is evidence generated from the company's accounting system? Auditors make great use of the client's internal recordkeeping system. In every audit, transaction vouching is a common audit procedure performed in many account areas, especially as related to the existence and completeness assertions. However, the use of internal company documents to support audit conclusions presumes that those documents are accurate. If the system is weak and internal documents are potentially inaccurate, the auditor may need to obtain other forms of evidence for some assertions.

Figure 3–11 illustrates the typical hierarchy of evidence based on the above attributes. In general, the auditor will try to obtain more competent evidence (the "best" evidence) when desired detection risk is low for an assertion. When

Figure 3–11   Hierarchy of Audit Evidence

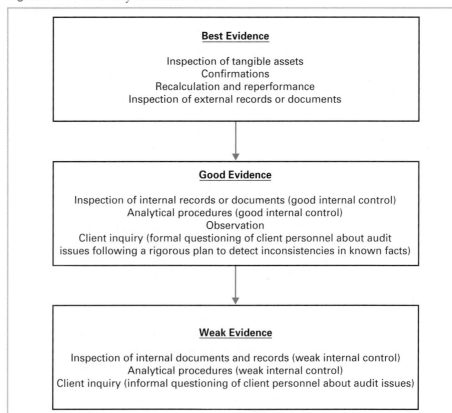

Best Evidence

Inspection of tangible assets
Confirmations
Recalculation and reperformance
Inspection of external records or documents

Good Evidence

Inspection of internal records or documents (good internal control)
Analytical procedures (good internal control)
Observation
Client inquiry (formal questioning of client personnel about audit
issues following a rigorous plan to detect inconsistencies in known facts)

Weak Evidence

Inspection of internal documents and records (weak internal control)
Analytical procedures (weak internal control)
Client inquiry (informal questioning of client personnel about audit issues)

Figure 3–12   Trade-Off of Detection Risk and Audit Evidence

Low Detection Risk/High Audit Effort	*High Detection Risk/Low Audit Effort*
Aged trial balance for receivables prepared by the auditor.	Aged trial balance for receivables prepared by the client's personnel.
100 customer accounts randomly selected and confirmed.	25 customer accounts randomly selected and confirmed.
No client restrictions placed on population of accounts to confirm.	A few accounts omitted from confirmation by request of the client.
Accounts to be confirmed pertain to other businesses.	Accounts to be confirmed pertain to retail consumers.
Customer accounts confirmed as of 12/31 (for fiscal year end of 12/31).	Customer accounts confirmed as of 11/1 (for fiscal year end of 12/31).

detection risk is moderate or high, the auditor will usually be satisfied with evidence considered "good." However, the auditor will rarely be totally satisfied with evidence classified as "weak" unless the account or assertion in question is immaterial or has very low residual risk.

To illustrate the trade-off of the quality of evidence and risk, consider the procedures to test assertions related to accounts receivable for two different levels of risk as described in Figure 3–12. The preparation of the aged trial balance by the client is more risky because the preparer is not independent. Selecting 100 accounts to confirm is better than selecting 25 accounts because the larger sample provides more extensive evidence. Client restrictions on the selection of customer accounts interferes with the independence of the evidence and reduces its competence. Confirmations sent to businesses will usually be more reliable than those sent to retail customers because other businesses are more likely to have accounting systems that allow them to respond accurately to the confirmation request. Finally, confirming accounts before year end provides less competent evidence because the connection between the confirmation results and the year-end balance is less objective than direct year-end confirmation would provide.

THE INTERRELATIONSHIP OF RISK, MATERIALITY, AND EVIDENCE

There is an association between the level of materiality and the level of audit risk, and together, risk and materiality influence the amount of evidence that an auditor may need to collect on an engagement. This relationship leads to two general, but important, observations:

1. **High risk of material misstatement implies the need for high levels of audit effort.** Since risk of material misstatement is not under the control of the auditor and can only be estimated based on the auditor's experience and knowledge of the client, an auditor will gather more evidence in situations where the risk of material misstatement is deemed to be high.
2. **Low audit risk and detection risk is achieved through high levels of audit effort.** The more confident that an auditor wants to be that all material misstatements have been detected and corrected in a financial report, the more evidence the auditor will gather during the course of the audit.

Example

Inventory is usually a critical component of the financial statements of a manufacturing company. It is also a complex area to audit given the nature of cost accounting and allocation and the continual movement of inventory assets. As a result, an auditor will usually consider the processes and activities surrounding inventory to be important to the audit and potentially high risk. This perspective leads the auditor to devote significant resources to the audit of transactions, accounts, or disclosures related to inventory.

The auditor's assessment of materiality and audit risk may be different at the time of initially planning the engagement and at the time of evaluating the results of audit procedures. This could be because of a change in circumstances or because of a change in the auditor's knowledge. For example, if the audit is planned prior to period end, the auditor will anticipate the results of operations and the financial position. If actual results of operations and financial position are substantially different, the assessment of materiality and audit risk may also change. Additionally, the auditor may, in planning the audit work, intentionally set the acceptable materiality level at a lower level than is necessary so as to reduce detection risk and to provide a margin of safety when evaluating the effect of misstatements discovered during the audit. In general, almost everything the auditor does during the course of the audit is designed to provide the appropriate balance between audit risk, materiality and audit evidence.

SUMMARY AND CONCLUSION

In this chapter we have introduced the critical building blocks of auditing. Management assertions about the financial statements and internal controls provide the basis for the auditor's examination. We described the auditor's responsibilities for examining those assertions and the communications whereby the auditor acknowledges his or her responsibilities and communicates the results of his or her examinations. Next, we introduced the critical concepts of audit risk, materiality, and audit evidence. Finally, we illustrated how an auditor uses audit procedures to assess risk and obtain evidence as to the fairness of the overall financial statements. Proper understanding and development of these building blocks of auditing are necessary for an auditing firm to be effective and to minimize the possibility of performing a substandard audit or rendering the wrong opinion on the financial statements. In the subsequent chapters, the building blocks of the audit are applied in detail to the integrated audit once we have set the professional and regulatory context in which the audit occurs.

BIBLIOGRAPHY OF RELATED PROFESSIONAL LITERATURE

Research

Beasley, M. 1996. An Empirical Analysis of the Relation between the Board of Director's Composition and Financial Statement Fraud. *The Accounting Review* 71(3): 443–465.

Bedard, J. C. and K. M. Johnstone. 2004. Earnings Manipulation Risk, Corporate Governance Risk and Auditors' Planning and Pricing Decisions. *The Accounting Review* 79(2): 277–304.

Blokodijk, H., F. Drieenhuizen, D. A. Simunic, and M. T. Stein. 2003. Factors Affecting Auditors' Assessments of Planning Materiality. *Auditing: A Journal of Practice & Theory.* 22(2): 297–307.

Brody, R. G., D. J. Lowe, and K. Pany. 2003. Could $51 million be immaterial when Enron Reports Income of $105 million? *Accounting Horizons.* 17(2): 153–160.

Carcello, J. V. and T. L. Neal. 2003. Audit Committee Characteristics and Auditor Dismissals Following "New" Going-Concern Reports. *The Accounting Review.* 78(1): 95–118.

Cho, S-Y., R. L. Hagerman, S. Nabar, and E. R. Patterson. 2003. Measuring Stockholder Materiality. *Accounting Horizons* 17 (Quality of Earnings): 63–76.

Glover, S. M., D. F. Prawitt, J. J. Schultz, Jr., and M. F. Zimbleman. 2003. A Test of Changes in Auditors' Fraud-Related Planning Judgments since the Issuance of SAS No. 82. *Auditing: A Journal of Practice & Theory.* 22(2): 237–252.

Kinney, W. R., Jr., and R. D. Martin. 1994. Does Auditing Reduce Bias in Financial Reporting? A Review of Audit Adjustment Studies. *Auditing: A Journal of Practice and Theory.* Spring: 149–156.

Khurana, I. K. and K. K. Raman. 2004. Litigation Risk and Financial Reporting Credibility of Big 4 versus non-Big 4 Audits: Evidence from Anglo-American Countries. *The Accounting Review.* 79(2): 473–496.

Krishnan, J. 2005. Audit Committee Quality and Internal Control: An Empirical Analysis. *The Accounting Review.* 80(2): 649–676.

Mautz, R. K. and H. A. Sharaf. 1961. *The Philosophy of Auditing.* American Accounting Association Monograph No. 6, Sarasota, FL: American Accounting Association.

Messier, W. F. Jr., N. Matinov-Bennie, and A. Eilifsen. 2005. A Review and Integration of Empirical Research on Materiality: Two Decades Later. *Auditing: A Journal of Practice & Theory.* 24(2): 153–187.

Moreno, K. and S. Bhattacharjee. 2003. The Impact of Pressure from Potential Client Business Opportunities on the Judgments of Auditors across Professional Ranks. *Auditing: A Journal of Practice & Theory.* 22(1): 13–29.

Nelson, M. W., S. D. Smith, and Z.-V. Palmrose. 2005. The Effect of Quantitative Materiality Approach on Auditors' Adjustment Decisions. *The Accounting Review.* 80(3): 897–921.

Newman, D. P., E. Patterson, and R. Smith. 2001. The Influence of Potentially Fraudulent Reports on Audit Risk Assessment and Planning. *The Accounting Review* 76(1): 59–80.

Tuttle, B. M. Coller and R. D. Plumlee. 2002. The Effect of Misstatements on Decisions of Financial Statement Users: An Experimental Investigation of Auditor Materiality Thresholds. *Auditing: A Journal of Practice & Theory.* 21(1): 11–28.

Waller, W. 1993. Auditors' Assessments of Inherent and Control Risk in Field Settings. *Accounting Review.* 68(October): 783–803.

Professional Accounting Reports

Bell, T. B., F. O. Marrs, I. Solomon, and H. Thomas. 1997. *Auditing Organizations Through a Strategic-Systems Lens: The KPMG Business Measurement Process.* Montvale NJ: KPMG Peat Marwick.

Bell, T. B., M. E. Peecher, and I. Solomon. 2005. *The 21st Century Public Company Audit: Conceptual Elements of KPMG's Global Audit Methodology.* Montvale NJ: KPMG International.

Auditing Standards

AICPA *Statements on Auditing Standard (SAS)* No. 54, "Illegal Acts by Clients."

AICPA *Statements on Auditing Standard (SAS)* No. 99, "Consideration of Fraud in a Financial Statement Audit."

AICPA *Statements on Auditing Standard (SAS)* No. 106, "Audit Evidence."

AICPA *Statements on Auditing Standard (SAS)* No. 107, "Audit Risk and Materiality in Conducting an Audit."

AICPA *Statements on Auditing Standard (SAS)* No. 108, "Planning and Supervision."

AICPA *Statements on Auditing Standard (SAS)* No. 109, "Understanding the Entity and Its Environment and Assessing the Risks of Material Misstatement."

AICPA *Statements on Auditing Standard (SAS)* No. 110, "Performing Procedures in Response to Assessed Risks and Evaluating the Audit Evidence Obtained."

Committee of Sponsoring Organizations of the Treadway Commission (COSO). *Internal Control—Integrated Framework.* AICPA, 1992.

IAASB *International Framework for Assurance Engagements.*

IAASB *International Standards on Auditing (ISA)* No. 200, "Objectives and Principles Governing an Audit of Financial Statements."

IAASB *International Standards on Auditing (ISA)* No. 240, "The Auditor's Responsibility to Consider Fraud in a Financial Statement Audit."

IAASB *International Standards on Auditing (ISA)* No. 250, "Consideration of Laws and Regulations in an Audit of Financial Statements."

IAASB *International Standards on Auditing (ISA)* No. 300, "Planning an Audit of Financial Statements."

IAASB *International Standards on Auditing (ISA)* No. 315, "Understanding the Entity and Its Environment and Assessing the Risks of Material Misstatement."

IAASB *International Standards on Auditing (ISA)* No. 320, "Audit Materiality."

IAASB *International Standards on Auditing (ISA)* No. 330, "The Auditor's Procedures in Response to Assessed Risks."

IAASB *International Standards on Auditing (ISA)* No. 500, "Audit Evidence."

PCAOB. *Auditing Standard* No. 2, "An Audit of Internal Control Over Financial Reporting Performed in Conjunction with an Audit of Financial Statements."

SEC, *Staff Accounting Bulletin* No. 99, "Materiality."

QUESTIONS

1. Why are professional skepticism and ethical behavior on the part of the auditor necessary conditions for an audit?

2. Explain what is meant by the term "management assertions." With respect to the accounts receivable account, briefly explain how the management assertions apply.

3. Provide specific examples for each type of management assertions mentioned in the text:
   - Assertions about transactions
   - Assertions about accounts
   - Assertions about presentation and disclosure

4. Describe the relationships among the following:
   - Management assertions
   - Audit procedures
   - Audit evidence
   - Auditor's reports

5. One of the auditor's responsibilities is to plan an audit in such a way that reasonable assurance can be provided that errors and fraudulent misstatements will be detected and corrected. What is the difference between an error and a fraudulent misstatement? Why do auditors distinguish between the two?

6. Auditors further classify fraud as either fraudulent financial reporting or misappropriation of assets. Describe these types of fraud. Why do auditors make this distinction? How is this distinction likely to affect the audit?

7. Explain each of the three building blocks of auditing—risk, materiality, and evidence—and describe the relationship between the three. Why can these three concepts not be considered in isolation but only in conjunction?

8. Describe the three broad types of risk that the auditor should consider during the course of an audit engagement. Why should the auditor take each of these risks into account during the audit? Indicate how these risks are related and discuss factors that are likely to increase each type of risk.

9. What is audit risk? Describe the components of audit risk (risk of material misstatement and detection risk) and how they are related.

10. Engagement risk is defined as "the risks to the auditor's reputation that comes from being associated with a client firm that goes bankrupt, is found to have misstated previous financial statements, or has any other problems that would reduce the public's confidence in the auditor." Explain the possible manifestations of engagement risk.

11. What is materiality? Why is it such an important concept in auditing? How do auditors determine materiality?

12. An auditor can use a number of procedures to collect audit evidence. Two main categories that are distinguished are risk assessment and tests of accounting information. Discuss how these two categories are related.

13. Discuss the difference between preliminary and substantive analytical procedures and discuss the role of each for an audit engagement.

14. An auditor may collect several types of audit evidence during the course of an audit. Not every type of evidence is equally strong. Discuss criteria that may determine the strength (i.e., competence) of audit evidence.

15. List the types of audit evidence available for an auditor. For each type, provide an example for when the evidence might provide an auditor with persuasive evidence.

16. Describe the reports contained in the integrated audit:
    - A report on the financial statements
    - A report on management's assertions about the effectiveness of internal control over financial reporting
    - A report detailing the auditor's own assessment of internal control over financial reporting

    Describe how each report relates to each phase of the integrated audit.

17. Contrast the difference between a material weakness and a significant deficiency in internal control over financial reporting.

18. Depending on the outcome of the auditor's work, a number of combinations of opinions (the auditor's opinion of management's assessment of internal control, the auditor's opinion on internal control effectiveness, and the auditor's opinion on the financial statements) issued by the auditor are possible for companies publicly traded in the United States. Identify and describe these combinations and indicate which combination is likely to be most difficult to understand for a financial statement user.

19. To perform an integrated audit, an auditor must evaluate management's assessment of internal control over financial reporting. To accomplish this task, auditors evaluate management's process of identifying, documenting, and testing controls, including communication and remediation of identified deficiencies. Why do you believe that auditors should be required to make this evaluation if they also are required to assess the effectiveness of internal controls based on their own tests and assessments?

PROBLEMS

1. Management of the Miles Davis Co. reports that sales transactions for the year were $150 million; the allowance for doubtful accounts was $1 million; and net, unrestricted accounts receivable on the balance sheet is $11.5 million. Discuss how all assertions for transactions, accounts, and presentation (explicitly or implicitly) are represented in these reported numbers.

2. For each of the following situations, state the category (transaction, account, presentation, and disclosure) *and* management assertion that is most likely violated.
   a. Inventory en route at the close of the accounting period and marked FOB destination is included in ending inventory.
   b. The purchase of an office building for the corporate headquarters is placed in the land account.
   c. A clerk drops a box of mail full of incoming sales transactions and does not find all of them.
   d. Management fails to make an allowance for doubtful accounts receivable in its period-ending adjusting entries.
   e. The president of a large organization has his company pay for the new roof on his house as a building improvement.
   f. A maker of rotary-dial telephones reports a 10 percent increase in sales.
   g. A company includes some art on loan from a museum in its Furniture and Fixtures account.
   h. A glitch in a company's software incorrectly posts all sales transactions for the day to the "Other Revenue" account.
   i. A large oil company fails to mention the potential liability for an oil spill that happened shortly before the end of the fiscal year.

3. Identify the type of audit procedure employed (test of control, analytical procedure, or substantive test of accounts, transactions, or disclosure), the type of evidence obtained, and management assertion addressed in each of the following situations.
   a. The auditor uses a sophisticated regression analysis package to determine whether the decrease in accounts payable is out of line with the activity in the cash and inventory account in order to know where to look for potential misstatements.
   b. The auditor sends a questionnaire on the order entry process via e-mail to all the members of the sales business process.
   c. The auditor sets up a dummy customer account on the client's automated sales information system and attempts to input some sales under its name.
   d. During the audit of the automated purchases/payables/receiving system, the auditor queries the system for a sample of purchase invoice numbers indicating that electronic fund transfers (payments) have not occurred for purchases unless the goods have been ordered, received, and approved online by the individual who requisitioned the goods.
   e. The auditor compares the depreciation expense to the level of fixed assets for the past several years.
   f. The auditor accounts for each of the assets listed in the ledger for the Furniture and Fixtures account.
   g. An information systems specialist that works for the auditing firm quizzes the vice president of information system regarding controls that she expects management to have in place for its competitor and customer databases, which are used for pricing and production decisions.
   h. The auditor sends letters to a sample of the client's customers asking them to confirm the amount indicated as owed.

4. For each of the following situations, choose the type(s) of audit evidence that would give the auditor the most assurance that the management assertion provided (in parentheses at end of each item) is reasonably accurate.

   a.   The cash balance of a retail auto parts store (existence).

   b.   The accounts receivable balance of a large manufacturer who sells primarily to a few dozen distributors (valuation).

   c.   The cost of goods sold balance for a manufacturer of chemicals (completeness).

   d.   The balance in allowance for doubtful accounts for a company in the wholesale clothing industry (valuation).

   e.   The ending inventory account balance for a retail consumer electronics store (rights).

   f.   Total purchases for a retail grocery store (cutoff).

   g.   The long-term debt balance for a multinational construction company (completeness).

5. George Auditor is choosing the best audit procedures for several of his clients. He notes two alternatives for several situations. For each of the following situations

- identify the type of evidence for each of the two alternatives
- indicate which of the two alternatives is likely to provide the most persuasive evidence for the given situation

Procedures:

   a.   Inspecting inventory items versus calculating inventory turnover when testing the ending inventory account balance

   b.   Reviewing the client's payments to suppliers after year end to check accounts payable versus obtaining supplier statements as of year end when testing the ending accounts payable account balance

   c.   Confirming a year-end bank balance with the bank versus checking it with the bank statement when testing the ending cash account balance

   d.   Observing inventory counting procedures versus requesting confirmation of inventory held by an independently-run warehouse when testing the ending inventory balance

   e.   Asking about the process for making price changes to the computer system versus observing the process of updating prices when understanding the inventory pricing process

6. Professional skepticism is an important necessary condition to perform an effective audit. For each of the following two conditions, describe steps that the auditor should take to help better establish a state of mind consistent with professional skepticism.

   a.   You are a new auditor for a firm, having just graduated from a local university. Your first client is in the pharmaceutical industry. You remember attending several on-campus demonstrations by students groups accusing the industry of unethical practices. Accordingly, you decide that you will work extra hard to uncover unethical acts by the client.

   b.   You are beginning your third consecutive year on an audit engagement of a large manufacturing conglomerate. During your three years on the engagement, you have become impressed by the apparent integrity of the accounting managers and the controller. You have never encountered a situation where their responses to your questions were not truthful or transparent. You believe that you can conduct an efficient audit this year based on being able to trust their assertions.

7. Suppose you are auditing the financial statements of a large publicly traded firm when you discover some material misstatements that result from error.

   a.   Discuss the most likely scenario that would unfold when you brought these misstatements to the attention of management.

   b.   How would that scenario likely differ if the misstatements resulted from fraud?

8. For each of the following situations: (1) determine whether an employee fraud or a management fraud has likely been committed, (2) discuss the likelihood that the auditor will discover the fraud under ordinary circumstances, and (3) discuss the implications for the audit if the fraud is not found.

   a.   A part-time employee of a grocery store sneaks top-graded meats to his friends through the back door.

b. In an attempt to win a sales contest based on submitted applications, an insurance salesman enters an application for life insurance for significantly more coverage than the customer requested. When the contest ends in a few days, he will tell the underwriting department he made a mistake and will lower the request.

c. To avoid breaking a debt covenant based on net income figures, the CFO changes from the LIFO to the FIFO inventory method and does not disclose this change of accounting policy.

d. Managers of a copier service operation are using the company's fleet of cars for personal use.

e. Right before the end of the year, management of a prerecorded music distribution operation authorizes a large shipment of CDs to its retail outlet customers under terms that allow the outlets to return any unsold recordings. The distributor books the entire shipment as revenue at the normal selling price.

f. Although there is some evidence that some inventory on the books has decreased in net realizable value so that it ought to be written down, management defers the decision until after the next reporting period.

g. The plant manager of a manufacturing operation regularly takes tools home for his personal use. He has not returned many of them.

h. The vice president of finance convinces the CEO not to disclose to the board of directors the details of the deteriorating position of a bond portfolio held for investment.

9. Suppose that you are on an audit engagement when you come across evidence that the CEO has been diverting significant amounts of corporate resources for his own purposes. In other words, he is embezzling.

a. What should you do?

b. Why do you think an auditor does not immediately report fraudulent activities, especially those involving large-scale employee theft, to the appropriate law enforcement officials as soon as they are discovered?

c. What does your answer tell you about the nature of the client management-auditor relationship?

10. Consider two cases of fraud your audit firm came across in the course of its audit of Marsalis & Associates, an Internet service provider.

• A few employees are bootlegging some of the Internet software to their friends. None of the employees is in a management position and the operations of the firm are not seriously affected.

• Management is creating dummy customers on the master file to inflate the company's financial position in an attempt to secure more favorable financing terms for the company's line of credit.

For each of these two cases, contrast the procedures you should follow upon learning of them. How do these procedures protect your interests while attempting to serve the best interests of the client's stakeholders?

11. You are auditing the financial statements of a regional medical center that serves a metropolitan area and the surrounding suburban areas. You identify the following situations that could lead to potentially material misstatements in their financial statements:

a. Property, Plant, and Equipment is misstated by about 3 percent.

b. Prepaid Assets is misstated by 20 percent.

c. The Premium on Bonds Payable account has not been amortized in two years.

d. Some year-end transactions were not posted to Accounts Receivable until after the first of the new fiscal year.

e. Accrued Compensation (relating to some bonus compensation plans to the top administrators) has not been adjusted this year to reflect the new liability.

f. Allowance for Uncollectible Accounts has remained steady for the past few years even as revenues have increased 25 percent.

Discuss the quantitative and qualitative materiality issues associated with each of these items. Specifically, do you expect these items to be considered potential material misstatements in the financial statements? Why or why not?

12. A recent graduate tells you, "I normally set materiality at 5 percent of net profit. However, I set it at negative $50 million for a company that made a huge loss, and at $5 for a non-profit organization that has an objective of breaking even. But then the partner in charge changed my materiality figures totally!" Explain how materiality is defined in accounting and auditing standards, and why the recent graduate made a mistake in judgment.

13. What effect does the acceptable level of audit risk have on the materiality threshold? For example, when auditing the inventory of a well-respected company that has never been subjected to a financial statement audit, would you set the materiality threshold any lower than if this was a repeat engagement? Why?

14. Many countries require auditors to alert users of financial statements when there is substantial doubt about an entity's ability to continue as a going concern. Given that this is the only forward-looking opinion offered by auditors, describe why you believe that this requirement is in place? Provide arguments for and against requiring it, and conclude by taking a position regarding whether this requirement should persist.

15. In late 2005, the airline industry in the United States had an unprecedented situation in which four of the five largest airlines had filed bankruptcy and were undergoing reorganization processes to try to recover. Describe how this type of economic environment affects client business risk, engagement risk, and audit risk for firm that audits one of these airlines.

16. For each of the following scenarios, indicate whether the auditor would issue (1) an unqualified or adverse opinion on management's assessment of ICOFR effectiveness and (2) an unqualified or adverse opinion on actual ICOFR effectiveness. Explain.

    a. Management identifies a less than material but more than inconsequential problem with its general ledger system that happens about once a quarter. The auditor concurs with management's assessment.

    b. Management failed to identify a less than material but more than inconsequential problem in recording commission expenses throughout the year. The auditor identifies the problem during its control testing.

    c. Management identifies a problem with its crisis management controls that could materially impact its financials but assesses that probability that the crisis will occur as remote. The auditor concurs with management's assessment.

    d. Management fails to identify a control problem associated with the process for properly capitalizing or expensing building improvements. The likelihood of failure is only about 15 percent, but the impact would be material. The auditor identifies the problem during its control testing.

    e. Management identifies that its CEO could easily override controls associated with preventing improper accounting for reserves associated with a material restructuring transaction. The auditor concurs with management's assessment.

Case 3–1: Rocky Mountain Electric

Rocky Mountain Electric is an electrical wholesaler with two locations—one in Edmonton, and another in Calgary that just recently opened. The audit senior stayed in Edmonton to do the audit at the main store, and a staff accountant was sent to Calgary.

The staff accountant returned after a week and said that everything was fine at the Calgary store, which was good, thought the senior, because the audit fee had been cut from the previous year, and the audit team was under time pressure to finish the job.

One of the first things the senior did was look at the working paper containing a listing of the audit differences (that is, proposed audit adjustments that the auditors had not yet required the client to address), and she noticed an adjustment in excess of $100,000—a debit to sales and a credit to accounts receivable. "To adjust the general ledger (GL) to the accounts receivable trial balance at the cross-province store" is how the description read. She asked the staff accountant how an error that large could occur, and he told her the store manager said they'd had some problems installing the accounting system at the new store.

The senior thought the adjustment was proper, since the general ledger balance was now in agreement with the subsidiary ledger. A little while later, she was looking at the analytical procedures and noted that the gross margin percentages at the cross-province store were quite a bit lower than the margins at the main store. In the workpapers was the explanation, "Per store manager, prices were reduced at cross-province store to attract new customers in a new location."

The next day, the senior was talking to the controller at the main store, and she mentioned how it looked like there were a few problems at the Calgary store, but they were working out. "I guess those price reductions you had earlier in the year really worked to attract new customers," she said.

"Price reductions?" said the controller. "What price reductions?"

The company was a wholesale distributor, meaning it did not generate sales like one might find in a retail store. The senior asked the controller about problems the company encountered when installing the accounts receivable system at the Calgary store. The controller said that the senior must have been mistaken because no problems had ever been reported by the store manager.

The senior realized something wasn't right, and after consulting with the manager and partner, the auditors discussed their concerns with the controller and company owner. The client and auditors agreed to investigate the situation further, so the auditors expanded their tests tracing customer payments for the Calgary store back and forth from the subledger to the GL.

That expanded testwork led to the discovery that the manager at the Calgary store was stealing payments the customers made on account. That's why the

Source: Adapted with permission of AICPA by S. Salterio Ph.D, CA.

subledger was out of balance with the GL. To cover it up, the manager debited the sales account, which was why the gross margins didn't make sense.

Requirements

1. What should the staff accountant have done in order the find the fraud?
2. Was the senior lucky or skillful in finding out there was the potential for fraud?
3. What parts of the examination standards were not carried out as effectively as might be on this audit?

Case 3–2: New Zealand Refining Co., Ltd.

The New Zealand Refining Co., Ltd. operates an oil refinery at Marsden Point, near Whangarei. It processes crude oil into gasoline, diesel, and other petroleum products on behalf of the major oil companies, and charges a fee based on petroleum refining margins in the Asia-Pacific region for each barrel of oil processed.

Information compiled from the company's announcements to the NZ Stock Exchange and annual reports and announcements shows the following production and sales results:

Production: Barrels in thousands				
	1998	*1999*	*2000*	*2001*
Jan/Feb	5,969	6,604	6,458	6,465
Mar/Apr	7,034	5,703	6,231	6,600
May/Jun	6,858	6,424	6,486	5,829
Jul/Aug	6,494	6,225	6,711	6,623
Sept/Oct	6,621	6,508	6,034	6,496
Nov/Dec	6,722	5,962	6,502	6,068
Total	39,698	37,426	38,422	38,081
Reported in Annual report	39,088	37,062	38,422	38,082

Sales: Fee in $ thousands				
	1998	*1999*	*2000*	*2001*
Jan/Feb	18,195	20,204	23,442	26,471
Mar/Apr	27,763	11,035	26,448	30,391
May/Jun	24,755	12,634	8,117	9,308
Jul/Aug	18,011	13,709	45,071	17,766
Sept/Oct	19,848	12,433	37,805	40,797
Nov/Dec	14,588	246	28,372	17,158
Total	123,160	70,261	169,255	141,891
Reported in Annual report	125,143	85,368	174,931	144,554

Average fee per barrel				
	1998	*1999*	*2000*	*2001*
Jan/Feb	3.05	3.06	3.63	4.09
Mar/Apr	3.95	1.93	4.24	4.60
May/Jun	3.61	1.97	1.25	1.60
Jul/Aug	2.77	2.20	6.72	2.68
Sept/Oct	3.00	1.91	6.27	6.28
Nov/Dec	2.17	0.04	4.36	2.83

Requirements

1. Assuming that the figures were generated from well-controlled systems and processes, conduct preliminary analytical procedures using the sales figures shown.
2. List the major questions you will ask management when you are auditing any of the four years for which data is shown.

4

The Integrated Audit Process

INTRODUCTION

An audit is a complex but systematic process. Although the overall audit process can follow a general methodology, every client is unique and the process must be tailored to fit the circumstances of each individual client. Given the potential variation in the audit process from client to client, auditors and other stakeholders want to be confident that the quality of an audit does not also vary. If an audit is done well, information risk is minimized, the efficiency of capital allocations and investment decisions is improved, and the economy benefits. If done poorly, stakeholders will be subject to an excessive level of information risk and may suffer economic losses as a result of decisions made while relying on inaccurate or incomplete financial information. Given the public nature of the audit report and the sizeable number of stakeholders who have an interest in the quality of auditing, the profession has undertaken extensive effort to assure that audits are, on the whole, done well.

Furthermore, many of the services that can be provided by public accountants are subject to governmental regulation. This is particularly true of the audit of financial statements because the government grants a monopoly to the accounting profession to provide this service. Consequently, public accountants who provide audit services must be familiar with the extensive set of professional rules and regulations designed to ensure that individuals meet their professional obligations and maintain minimum standards of quality. Issues covered by auditing standards and regulations include: Who can do an audit? How should an audit firm operate so as to maintain the quality of its services? How should an audit be conducted? How should the results of an audit be reported?

The purpose of this chapter is to introduce the professional and regulatory requirements that guide the behavior of the auditing profession and the conduct of audits. We will first discuss three basic sets of standards under which an auditor must operate. We will then discuss how these standards influence the acquisition of clients and the initial start of the audit process. In general, the topics discussed in this chapter pertain to all audits, be they traditional audits based on generally accepted auditing standards (GAAS), non-U.S. companies, government organizations, not-for-profit entities, or U.S.-based public companies that are subject to an integrated audit under the rules of the PCAOB. As previously noted, the primary difference between these two types of audits is the extent to which the auditor evaluates internal control over financial reporting. We first discuss the rules of a traditional audit and will introduce issues related to the integrated audit towards the end of the chapter.

> **Authoritative Guidance & Standards**
> The auditing profession is heavily regulated and subject to numerous standards that affect many aspects of the practice of auditing. An auditor practicing in the United States could be subject to standards issued by three different authoritative bodies: (1) the Auditing Standards Board of the AICPA, (2) the Public Company Accounting Oversight Board of the SEC, and (3) the International Audit and Assurance Standards Board. Only time will tell if these standards are reconciled and harmonized, but as of 2006 the appropriate standards to follow depend on the nature of the client being audited.

REGULATION AND THE AUDIT OF FINANCIAL STATEMENTS

Given the long history of the profession, it should not be surprising that the largest body of professional standards pertains to the audit of financial statements. Auditing standards are established for specific countries by national organizations (for example, the AICPA and PCAOB in the United States), as well as internationally by the International Audit and Assurance Standards Board (IAASB). There are three distinct sets of standards that apply to auditors and the conduct of an audit: (1) *generally accepted auditing standards* (GAAS), which are divided into general standards, examination standards (also known as the standards of fieldwork), and reporting standards; (2) ethical standards; and (3) quality control standards. GAAS is probably the most important of the three because the standards cover the conduct of the audit and the form of the report. Ethical standards address who can perform an audit and how auditors should behave. Finally, quality control standards pertain to procedures and practices within an accounting firm.

Generally Accepted Auditing Standards

Generally accepted auditing standards are summarized in Figure 4–1. The *general standards* dictate basic guidelines for conducting an individual audit. An auditor

Figure 4–1   Generally Accepted Auditing Standards*

General Standards (general qualifications and conduct)
- An audit must be performed by persons having adequate training and proficiency
- Auditors must maintain independence in mental attitude
- Auditors must exercise due professional care

Fieldwork or Examination Standards (audit fieldwork)
- The audit must be properly planned and supervised
- Auditor must gain a sufficient understanding of the entity, including internal control
- Auditor must obtain sufficient, competent evidence

Reporting Standards (reporting results)
- Auditor must express an opinion on the financial statements as a whole
- Auditor must indicate those situations where GAAP is not consistently applied
- Auditor must evaluate the adequacy of informative disclosures
- Auditor must state whether statements were prepared in accordance with GAAP

*See SAS 43. ISA 200 outlines the general principles of auditing, which generally are consistent with the generally accepted auditing standards. However, ISA 200 provides more explicit explanation about certain aspects of what the SAS lists as generally accepted auditing standards (for example, descriptions about risks, materiality, and assurance). The guidance throughout this text is consistent with the general principles contained in ISA 200.

should have adequate expertise and training to perform the audit of a specific client consistent with the circumstances of the engagement. This may include industry knowledge that is relevant to the specific client. Furthermore, an auditor should maintain an independent attitude about the client and not be biased in favor or against a particular client. Finally, the audit should be executed with a degree of care that is appropriate for a professional. These standards are rather broad but are expanded under the ethical standards discussed below.

The *standards of fieldwork*[1] dictate how an engagement should be performed. The key requirements are adequate planning and supervision of the engagement as well as acquisition of sufficient evidence to support the conclusions reached by the auditor. The standards of fieldwork require that the auditor adequately plan the audit so that it can be conducted in an efficient and effective manner. The standards of fieldwork also require that an auditor obtains sufficient, competent evidence on which to base his or her professional conclusions. Essentially, these standards suggest that a certain level of due diligence is expected in the execution of an audit.

The standards of fieldwork also require the auditor to obtain an understanding of a client's environment and internal control system that is adequate for planning the audit. This standard deals with understanding the risks facing the organization that can impact the likelihood of material misstatements. Also of specific concern is the quality of the information system used by the company and the attitude of management towards truthful and accurate financial reporting. This latter emphasis is particularly important given current attention directed at the ethical management practices and the behavior of businesspersons. PCAOB rules pertinent to the audit of public companies in the United States are much more extensive than this standard, as will be discussed in later chapters.

---

1 Also known as examination standards in some countries.

The reporting standards provide guidelines for communicating the auditor's findings to interested parties. Audit reports should include the following information:

- Assertions examined: The assertions being examined in an audit of financial statements are understood to be the information contained in the financial statements. The audit report specifically notes what statements the auditor has examined.
- Measurement and reporting criteria: For an audit of financial statements, the basis for evaluating financial statement information is understood to be generally accepted accounting principles (GAAP). These standards may vary by country or type of company (e.g., business reporting vs. not-for-profit or governmental reporting).
- Overall conclusions: In general, an auditor can provide a "positive" report on an engagement when the general and fieldwork standards have been met and the auditor is convinced that the assertions are accurately and fairly presented.

> **Authoritative Guidance & Standards**
> There are several auditing standards dedicated to ensuring that fieldwork standards are properly performed. For example, the AICPA and IAASB recently issued SASs (106–111) and ISAs (300, 315, 320, and 330), respectively, that cover all three fieldwork components of GAAS.

ETHICAL STANDARDS

A great deal of individual judgment goes into the conduct of an audit so it is important that auditors make choices and decisions that are consistent with the professional and ethical principles of the profession. Ethical standards have been developed to guide auditors in their decision making so as to avoid many common sources of bias or ethical breakdowns. The International Federation of Accountants requires that all member bodies (e.g., the AICPA in the United States) have a professional code of conduct that defines the standards of ethical behavior for a professional accountant. These standards cover topics such as the responsibilities to clients and the public, professional integrity, and the nature of professional independence and objectivity. Some of the key provisions that are found in the AICPA's *Code of Professional Conduct* and IFAC's *Code of Ethics for Professional Accountants* are summarized in Figure 4–2. For now, we will emphasize two important areas that have a direct affect on the conduct of the audit: (1) objectivity and independence and (2) professional skepticism.[2]

Objectivity and Independence

One of the core ethical principles of a professional auditor is to be objective, which the IFAC *Code of Ethics* defines as "A combination of impartiality, intellectual honesty and a freedom from conflicts of interest." Rule 101 of the AICPA *Code of Professional Conduct* adds that "a member in public practice shall be independent in the performance of professional standards as required by standards promulgated by bodies designated by the council." If public accountants are perceived as biased, nonobjective, or self-serving, their value as potential assurance providers is essentially eliminated.

Auditors cannot perform audits for clients where they are perceived to have a vested interest in the outcome of the audit. If auditors are perceived to be biased, they are said to lack *independence in appearance*. Whether auditors are actually

2 The AICPA *Code of Professional Conduct* and IFAC *Code of Ethics for Professional Accountants* are discussed in more detail in Chapter 17.

Figure 4–2   An Overview of Issues Addressed in a Code of Professional Conduct or Ethics

Elements of Code of Conduct*	General Requirements
Objectivity and Independence (Rule 101)	Auditors cannot invest in their clients; close relatives of auditors cannot hold executive or audit sensitive positions at clients; auditors cannot enter in business transactions in which a conflict of interest is created with client (e.g., consult with a client and then audit areas covered by the consulting service)
Integrity (Rule 102)	Auditors cannot violate laws or regulatory requirements, knowingly mislead clients or users, or make intentionally biased decisions. In particular, auditors cannot knowingly misstate facts.
Standards and Technical Pronouncements (Rules 201, 202, and 203)	Auditors must follow all standards and technical pronouncements issued by regulatory bodies.
Confidential Client Information (Rule 301)	Auditors must protect the confidentiality of client information. Auditors may disclose client information only after receiving permission from the client, unless directed by a court official, peer review or PCAOB inspection, or ethics investigation.
Contingent Fees (Rule 302)	Auditors may not accept fees that are conditional upon outcome of the engagement. [Note: In some countries contingent fees may be accepted for nonaudit services provided the firm does not also perform the audit and discloses the arrangement.]
Acts Discreditable to the Profession (Rule 501)	Certain acts that are considered serious enough to warrant loss of license include discrimination, harassment, criminal convictions, and cheating or failing to file tax returns.
Commissions and Referral Fees (Rule 503)	Auditors may not accept a percentage or flat fee from a client for recommending that client's services to another organization. [Note: In some countries, commissions and referral fees may be accepted for nonaudit services providing the firm does not also perform the audit and discloses the arrangement.]
Advertising and Solicitation (Rule 502)	Advertising and solicitation by auditors may not be false or misleading, and in many countries it may not be persistent after being told by the potential client that they are not interested in the firm's services.
Form of Practice and Name (Rule 505)	Acceptable forms of practice for auditors include sole proprietorships, partnerships, and certain forms of corporations, depending on statutory regulations. A common form of ownership is the limited liability partnership, which provides limited liability for partners for engagements that are not served by the partner but unlimited liability for engagements directly served by the partner.

* The Rule numbers indicated in parentheses refer to the applicable section of the AICPA Code of Professional Conduct.

independent or not is referred to as *independence in fact*. In general, independence in fact is a state of mind for the auditor that is closely related to the ethical concept of objectivity.

Some countries view objectivity as requiring that the public accountant be independent in appearance, whereas other countries view a public accountant's independence in appearance as demonstrating he or she is objective. In any case, a lack of independence can undermine not only an auditor's professional stature but also the value of the audit in general. As a result, many regulations have been developed to foster the appearance of independence among auditors. These rules dictate conditions under which an auditor would *not* be considered to be independent and thus potentially biased. There are five general conditions that undermine independence in appearance:

- *Having a financial interest in the client:* An auditor (or his or her immediate family) cannot own shares in a client or have a significant investment in a mutual fund owning shares of a client's stock.
- *Having a family relationship with employees, management or owners of the client:* Auditors are not independent of clients where a relative is on the board of directors or holds an executive position with the client.
- *Performing work that is the responsibility of management:* Auditors cannot authorize transactions, approve journal entries to correct the financial statements, or perform accounting procedures to support journal entries.
- *Auditing work that was originally completed by the auditor or the firm:* Auditors cannot assess the effectiveness of internal control over financial reporting for an information system designed or installed by the same accounting firm.
- *Providing services to a client that are incompatible to the objectives of the external audit:* Auditors cannot serve as the legal counsel for an audit client, recommend client products or services to other audit clients, or recruit executives for a client.

Professional Skepticism

An "auditing mind-set" requires that an auditor maintain an attitude of *professional skepticism* if he or she is to fulfill his or her responsibility to external users of financial statements, especially to investors in public companies. Professional skepticism requires that the auditor base judgments on solid evidence and avoid being misled by casual appearances or the personality of management. Professional skepticism is a state of mind that helps auditors remain objective, and requires a questioning mind and a critical assessment of evidence. While working closely with management and other corporate employees, auditors must maintain an attitude of professional skepticism when they evaluate information from and about the people they deal with on a daily basis. Professional skepticism requires a balanced view of people and organizations and is based on the assumption that management is neither honest nor dishonest until evidence proves otherwise; in other words, the auditor remains neutral.

Auditors are often subject to subtle influences that may undermine professional skepticism without the auditor realizing it. Client personnel are often friendly and pleasant, so it becomes difficult for the auditor to look at them as potentially incompetent or fraudulent. Even documentary evidence that has been forged or altered will look good on its face. Thus, auditors may be unknowingly influenced by what they see or hear during the course of the audit in ways that undermine their ability to be skeptical. Ultimately, failure to live up to the professional and ethical standards expected of the auditing profession will damage the reputation of the individual auditor, their firm, and the profession.

QUALITY CONTROL STANDARDS

The final area of professional regulation and standards relates to how an accounting firm operates. Although not directly related to the conduct of a single engagement, policies and procedures within an accounting firm determine the circumstances under which audits are conducted. For example, the way that professionals are compensated, auditors are assigned to engagements, and the quality of audits is monitored could all influence how a specific engagement is conducted. Thus, the profession provides guidance to accounting firms about the appropriate way to run their audit practice. These standards are referred to as quality control standards. The AICPA's *Quality Control Standards* are summarized in Figure 4–3. The IAASB (ISA 220 and International Standards on Quality Control No. 1) and

Figure 4–3   Quality Control Standards: Basic Elements*

Elements of Quality Control	Requirements
Independence	Policies and procedures should be established to provide the firm with reasonable assurance that persons at all organizational levels maintain independence and perform all professional responsibilities with integrity and objectivity.
Personnel management	Policies and procedures for assigning personnel to engagements should be established to provide the firm with reasonable assurance that the firm hires personnel with the appropriate skills, that work is performed by persons having the technical training and proficiency required by the circumstances, that personnel receive adequate continuing training, and that the advancement of personnel reflect appropriate qualifications.
Acceptance and continuance of clients	Policies and procedures should be established for deciding whether to accept or continue a client in order to provide reasonable assurance that the firm will not associate with a client whose management lacks integrity, that the required professional services can be competently provided, that the risks of the engagement are appropriately considered, and that a full understanding of the services to be provided is agreed to with the client.
Engagement performance	Policies and procedures should be established to provide reasonable assurance that the work performed meets all appropriate professional standards, including reference to authoritative literature and consultations with experts.
Monitoring	Policies and procedures for inspection should be established to provide the firm with reasonable assurance that the procedures relating to the other elements of quality control are being effectively applied.

* Established by the AICPA Quality Control Standards Committee and adopted by PCAOB as an interim standard. Similar guidance is provided in ISA 220 and ISQC No. 1.

various countries' legislative bodies also have standards or rules for quality control in public accounting firms.

Quality control standards require that the firm have procedures in place to monitor and maintain independence, manage professional personnel appropriately, review client relationships, and support and monitor engagement quality. Many firms have dedicated personnel to monitor new authoritative guidance in accounting and auditing to ensure that firms adapt to new standards that affect the conduct of the audit. A firm should implement monitoring processes to ensure that its personnel follow professional standards and firm policies when accepting and conducting an audit. An important element of quality control is the process by which individual actions and decisions are reviewed by others. A typical audit involves several layers of review:

- Detailed review of all working papers prepared by subordinates by a superior on the engagement
- General review of critical working papers by senior managers or partners on the engagement
- A general review of working papers by a second partner, who is not otherwise involved in the engagement
- Detailed review of a sample of engagements on an annual basis as part of an overall quality review

Firms should follow up identified quality weaknesses and take steps to rectify these weakness with procedural changes, training, and communications with personnel throughout the firm.

CLIENT ACCEPTANCE AND RETENTION

An area specifically addressed by the quality control standards is the process by which clients are obtained and retained. Auditors provide services to clients in return for fees. Therefore, to succeed and grow, auditors need to obtain a client base that generates fees adequate to cover the costs of professional services and office overhead. Auditors rarely wish to turn away prospective clients or to discontinue auditing current clients but involvement with dishonest clients can have dire consequences for the auditor. One way to think about this trade-off is that clients produce revenues for an auditor, but business failures or accounting problems not discovered by an auditor can lead to very high costs to the auditor in the form of litigation expenses, regulatory fines, or revenue losses due to a decline in professional reputation. In other words, partners in an audit firm weigh the revenues earned from desirable clients against the potential problems that may occur if the auditor becomes involved with a bad client (e.g., engagement risk).

Consequently, auditors screen prospective clients and reevaluate current clients as a matter of professional survival. Client integrity is by far the most important aspect of screening new and current clients. An auditor wants to know a great deal about a client before agreeing to undertake an audit engagement or to renew an existing engagement. The auditor's main concern is avoiding prospective clients and continuing with current clients that could cause the firm to suffer a loss. There are a number of steps that an auditor should perform when deciding whether to accept or retain an entity. These steps fall into four broad categories:

1. Obtain background information about the client.
2. Evaluate the risk factors or changes in risk factors associated with the client.

Figure 4–4   Factors Affecting the Acceptability and Retention of Clients

---

A. Factors within the control of the auditor
 1. Expertise and staffing: Does the firm have the requisite staff available that possesses or can obtain the needed expertise for completing the engagement on a timely basis in accordance with professional standards?
 2. Independence: Is the firm independent of the client so as to be able to provide an opinion that is perceived to be unbiased?

B. Factors which must be evaluated by the auditor
 3. Integrity: Does the management of the company possess adequate integrity so that the firm can be reasonably assured that management is not knowingly committing material fraud and/or illegal acts?
 4. Reputation and image: Does the company have a poor reputation such that the firm's association with the client could be embarrassing or detrimental to the firm?
 5. Accounting practices: Does the company have a positive attitude about complying with professional accounting standards so as to present a full and accurate portrait of the company's financial performance and status in their financial statements?
 6. Financial status: Is the company in danger of ceasing operations in the near-term due to extremely poor performance or other negative factors?
 7. Profitability: Can the audit firm earn a reasonable profit as a result of accepting and completing the audit engagement?

---

3. Decide on the acceptability or retention of the client as part of the firm-wide risk portfolio.
4. Obtain an engagement letter.

FACTORS AFFECTING CLIENT ACCEPTABILITY

Figure 4–4 identifies seven issues to be considered when evaluating a client. The first two factors are under the control of the auditor and, given enough time, can often be resolved. The availability of appropriate expertise will depend on the size of the firm and the experience and training of the professional staff. Firms are often able to shift personnel, hire new staff, and work overtime to service a new client. A lack of independence may be more troublesome but can also be resolved in most situations. A common situation in which an auditor may lack independence is when the auditor has a financial interest in the prospective client (e.g., the auditor owns stock in the company). If the financial interest can be removed, the independence concern will be resolved.

Two of the characteristics of the client that should be evaluated by the auditor prior to accepting an engagement are of special concern. There is little argument among auditors that the most important issue that must be addressed for each client is management integrity. In most circumstances, if management lacks integrity, an audit cannot be performed that will provide reasonable assurance that the financial statements are fairly presented. If the client management is not actively and openly cooperating with the auditor, the auditor has a high risk that incorrect conclusions will be reached about the accuracy of the financial statements and the effectiveness of internal control over financial reporting.

E x a m p l e

For many years, large public accounting firms avoided clients in the mining exploration industry listed on the Canadian Venture Exchange because of a pervasive perception that such firms lacked integrity.

The other point of particular interest is financial status. Public accounting firms prefer to avoid clients that are on the verge of bankruptcy. An incidence of bankruptcy often leads to litigation against the auditor because (1) investors believe that the auditor should have informed them of the impending bankruptcy and (2) the bankrupt firm has few assets left but the auditing firm has the resources to finance a settlement (the so-called "deep pockets" effect). Another reason relates to the profitability of the engagement because audit firms make most of their profits from repeat engagements. The initial audit of a company entails a large start-up cost on the part of the auditors as they gain familiarity with the client. As a result of this start-up cost, the firm may not realize a profit in the first year of the engagement. Therefore, a short-term relationship (i.e., one or two engagements) may not be justified on the basis of the fee relative to the initial engagement cost.

How does an auditor obtain the information needed to assess the factors identified in Figure 4–4? In many cases, the starting point is based on the auditor's existing knowledge of a company, as well as the reputation of management, via accounts in the popular press and the business media or prior experience with the client. The firm will also conduct discussions with the management of the client that may provide suggestions for other sources of information. Typically, the auditor will contact the client's bankers and attorneys for information about the client's business dealings. The firm may also contact stockbrokers, other business acquaintances, employees of the firm, and mutual friends. For new clients, the firm may also undertake more formal investigations by conducting media research for accounts related to the company, obtaining Dun & Bradstreet and other forms of credit reports, and hiring a professional investigator to delve into the background of key executives and shareholders.

Example

With the development of the Internet and technology for finding information on the World Wide Web, investigating a company and its executives is getting easier and easier. Without leaving the office, an auditor can usually explore the company's web site, its regulatory filings, media reports about the company, market performance and analyst ratings, the nature of its products and competition, quality reviews of its products, outside activities of its executives (through links to other organizations), and current issues affecting the industry. Such data searches are now considered standard procedures by large accounting firms.

COMMUNICATION WITH THE PREDECESSOR AUDITOR

An auditor that is new to an engagement is required to contact the predecessor auditor when one exists. The incoming auditor should first get permission from the prospective client to talk to the predecessor auditor; otherwise, client confidentiality restrictions will preclude the old auditor from discussing the client. Once permission is obtained, the predecessor is required by professional standards to respond to reasonable inquiries from the successor. If the prospective client refuses permission in whole or in part, the auditor should consider the ramifications of this refusal, particularly as they relate to the issue of management integrity. Some of the issues that should be discussed with the predecessor are

- The reasons for the auditor change
- The nature of any disagreements the predecessor had with management

Authoritative Guidance & Standards
Communication with a predecessor auditor is required under SAS 84 and by ISA 510 and Section 13 of IFAC *Code of Ethics*. This guidance is intended to prevent clients from replacing one audit firm with another that is likely to be more cooperative in allowing accounting practices that the first auditor rejected.

- The identification of important risk areas, including any internal control weaknesses
- Any prior experience with fraud or illegal acts
- Arrangements for gaining access to the workpapers from the prior-year audit[3]

TO ACCEPT OR NOT?

In the majority of situations, the auditor is going to eventually reach the conclusion that a prospective client is acceptable or decide to retain an existing client—but only if the anticipated revenues over the length of the engagement exceed the foreseeable costs. In most cases, if a major multinational company, such as General Motors, Royal Dutch Shell, AIG, or ING, requests an auditor's services, it is highly unlikely that many auditors would refuse the engagement. However, today's auditor examines even these types of organizations carefully. For example, Royal Dutch Shell changed CEOs in 2004 after revealing that its estimates of oil reserves were significantly overstated, necessitating a restatement of prior financial statements.

Even a company with a long and successful history is not immune to accounting and other problems that can have an adverse impact on the auditor; for example, KPMG was sued by its former client Xerox over alleged problems that occurred during the conduct of its audit. To avoid such problems, the auditor needs to carefully develop an understanding of the client. In most cases, there will be no worrisome circumstances so the auditor will find the prospective client acceptable or will retain a current client. However, in the rare situations where serious conditions are revealed by the preliminary analysis and cannot be resolved, the auditor should forgo the engagement, declining to audit a new client or resigning from the audit of an existing client. The latter, though rare 20 years ago, is now much more prevalent in practice.

ENGAGEMENT LETTERS

Upon determining that a client is acceptable to or will be retained by the firm, both parties should agree to the terms of an engagement. At this point, the firm prepares an engagement letter to be signed by the client. This letter serves as a contract between the public accounting firm and the company and explicitly states the terms of the engagement. The primary advantage of using an engagement letter is to avoid future misunderstandings between the client and the firm. This can minimize the chance that the client is unhappy about the services rendered or that the firm will not be able to recover amounts billed for services rendered.

An example of an engagement letter is included in Figure 4–5. The key elements of a typical engagement letter include the following:

1. Addressee: Typically the Board of Directors, the Audit Committee, or the Shareholders of the company. For U.S. SEC registrants, the PCAOB requires that the engagement letter must be signed by the chair of the audit committee.
2. Identification of the service to be rendered: The service in this case would be a financial statement audit and a brief description of the nature of that service.

---

3 The predecessor's responses to successor inquiries may be less than complete in unusual circumstances, such as if litigation is pending between the company and the predecessor auditor. In this case, the predecessor should indicate that the responses are limited.

Figure 4–5   Example of an Engagement Letter for an Audit*

Smith & Brown
Chartered Accountants

(Date)

Mr. George Jones, Chair
Board of Directors
Johnson Pharmaceuticals, Inc.
2345 North Main Street
Winnipeg Manitoba

Dear Mr. Jones:

This letter will confirm our arrangements for the audit of Johnson Pharmaceuticals, Inc., for the fiscal year ended December 31, 20x5. The purpose of our audit is to examine the financial statements of the company for the year ended December 31, 20x5 and evaluate the fairness of the presentation of the statements in accordance with generally accepted accounting principles.

We will conduct our examination according to generally accepted auditing standards. We will review the internal control of the company and conduct such tests of controls as we deem necessary. Our examination will not be detailed enough to assure the detection of all defalcations or fraud that may have occurred and that are not material to the financial statements, although discovery of such conditions may occur as the result of our examination.

The fair presentation of the financial statements is the responsibility of the management of the company. This responsibility includes the recording of transactions in the records and documents of the company as well as the selection of accounting principles to be used. Management is also responsible for developing, implementing, and maintaining a system of accounting and internal control and safeguarding assets.

We expect to conduct our examination according to the following time table:

	Start	Finish
Preliminary tests	9/11/20x4	9/30/20x4
Management letter on internal control		10/10/20x4
Year-end testing	2/1/20x5	3/3/20x5
Final audit report and financial statements		3/15/20x5

During the examination, assistance will be supplied by your personnel including the preparation of detailed account schedules, preparation of such reconciliations as are needed, and provision of needed documents and records. Timely assistance with these matters will help us complete the engagement on time and reduce the audit fee.

Our fees are based on hourly rates for various personnel that we will assign to the engagement. The total fee will be based on the amount of time needed to complete the tests and procedures that we deem necessary. You will also be billed for out-of-pocket costs such as travel, typing, copying, and so forth, which are necessary for us to satisfactorily complete the engagement. We expect that our total fees will not exceed $20,000, and we will bring to your attention any circumstances that would cause our fees to exceed that amount.

Please indicate your agreement with these arrangements by signing and returning one copy of this letter.

Respectfully,

Roberta Smith, Partner

Accepted by: _____   Date: _____

*Assuming no need for assurance over management's assessment of effectiveness of internal controls. Guidance on content of such letters is found in ISA 210.

Other services that are intended in conjunction with the audit (e.g., preparation of regulatory reports) should also be identified.

3. Specification of the respective responsibilities of the auditor and management.
4. Constraints on the audit firm, such as timing of access to client facilities and accounting records.
5. Deadlines: The dates when reports are due should be explicitly stated along with general guidelines for the timing of the audit work.
6. Description of any assistance to be provided by the client staff: the client's personnel typically prepare some schedules (such as bank reconciliations) and retrieve documents from the files. This assistance should be described in the letter. If the assistance is not provided and the auditors must complete the work themselves, this section of the letter would provide justification for additional billings to the client.
7. Interactions with specialists, internal auditors, and the predecessor auditor needed to conduct the audit.
8. Disclaimer that an audit is not designed to detect all forms of fraud or illegal acts.
9. A description of the basis for fees: This may include a fixed fee or an estimate of fees based on expected completion time and billing rates of personnel assigned to the engagement.
10. Ownership and accessibility of the auditor's files to outsiders.

Authoritative Guidance & Standards
Standards addressing communications between the auditor and client (SAS 83, ISA 210) do not expressly require engagement letters be prepared—although ISA 210 states that an engagement letter or other suitable contract be utilized.

The auditor should always obtain an engagement letter or an acknowledgement that the terms and conditions of a previous year's engagement letter continue. In the past, public accounting firms have faced a number of landmark lawsuits that arose from misunderstandings over the level of service being provided by the firm. In those cases, an engagement letter may have helped avoid such unfortunate situations.

PRELIMINARY PLANNING

The term "preliminary planning" pertains to that period of time immediately following the acceptance/retention of the client and refers to the auditor's actions that comprise the preliminary stages of the engagement. The auditor's preliminary planning has two broad purposes: (1) to obtain background information about the client that will assist in the efficient and effective planning of the engagement and (2) to identify potential problem areas that will require special attention during the engagement.

OBTAIN AN UNDERSTANDING OF THE CLIENT

The logical starting place for preliminary planning is obtaining an understanding of the client and its business. The nature of the information that the auditor should accumulate at this point is summarized in Figure 4–6. A great deal of the information for understanding the client will have been gathered as part of the client acceptance process. This can be supplemented with research utilizing firm databases, industry Internet sites, and other available sources (e.g., Moody's reports). Additionally, the auditor can review the corporate web site, marketing and investment literature,

Figure 4–6   Analyzing a New Client: 10 Questions

1. What are the company's products? Who are the company's customers? What are its markets?
2. What is the company's strategy for developing and maintaining a sustainable competitive advantage over its competition?
3. What is the nature of the company's operating cycle, i.e., how do they produce, market and deliver the product?
4. What are the key processes and activities of the operating cycle?
5. What is the nature and composition of the company's asset base and sources of financing?
6. What is the nature of the company's strategic relationships with outside organizations or companies?
7. How sophisticated is the company's information system(s) that is used to record the activities of each of the elements of the operating cycle?
8. What is the company's attitude and strategy for generating reliable accounting information?
9. What financial reporting information needs to be generated and reported by the information system(s)?
10. What are the critical risks that the auditor should be aware of that reported information will not fairly present results?

analyst reports, and corporate documents (e.g., the company charter). This information can be supplemented with discussions with company personnel who deal with various aspects of the business, particularly areas outside of the accounting department. Further information can be obtained through discussions with industry specialists within the accounting firm. Other procedures for obtaining a sufficient understanding of the client and its environment include

- Reviewing the regulatory environment of the client
- Obtaining or developing a business model of the client that includes such components as the products, markets, customers, resource suppliers, alliance partners, processes, and external forces of the client (to be discussed in Chapter 5)
- Touring key plants and facilities of the client
- Obtaining and reviewing company policies and procedures, particularly mission statements and codes of conduct
- Obtaining and reviewing significant contracts and other legal documents
- Identifying related parties
- Evaluating the need for assistance from specialists
- Considering the appropriate role of the internal audit department, if one exists

ANALYZE THE ORGANIZATION'S STRATEGIC PLAN

Early in the engagement the auditor should determine the organization's strategic plan and its source of sustainable competitive advantage. Every organization has a strategy for attaining its goals, although the strategy may not always be formally stated or the result of a rigorous strategic planning process. A company has two basic strategic decisions to make: (1) Do they want their products to be low cost or highly differentiated and/or (2) do they want to target a broad or narrow group of consumers? The better an organization understands and articulates its strategy, the more likely it is to be successful as it undertakes actions to advance the selected strategy. An organization that lacks a coherent strategy is unlikely to be successful in the long run and may present some difficult challenges to the auditor.

Example

A company with an incoherent or inappropriate strategy for product development is likely to encounter failures in introducing new products. A famous example of a new product failure based on an inappropriate strategy was the introduction of a new formula for Coca-Cola in the 1980s. The new formulation was designed to make the soda sweeter and superior to Pepsi in direct taste tests. A funny thing happened though—hardcore Coke drinkers hated the new formula and exercised their market power. The company quickly reintroduced the original formula under the label Coke Classic and eventually discontinued "New Coke." A similar product failure occurred at Pepsi when it introduced Crystal Pepsi in the 1990s because it believed customers would find clear cola more refreshing—they did not. Such failures generally result in low margins or losses and often lead to accounting problems arising from impairments to plant assets and inventory.

With regard to accounting and the financial statements, the auditor will need to consider the organization's strategic decisions when planning and conducting the audit. As a general rule, organizations in the growth or decline phase of their life cycle tend to have more challenging business risks and also create comparable challenges for the auditor. For example, a rapidly growing company will strain the capacity of its systems and abilities of its personnel, increasing the likelihood of problems within the organization. The auditor will need to assess whether the organization's strategy is likely to lead to success and whether it is being executed effectively. A poor strategy or weak execution will impact on the financial results, either in the current or future periods. We discuss the issue of strategy in detail in Chapter 5.

OBTAIN AN UNDERSTANDING OF INFORMATION PROCESSING

Another important area for the auditor to address is management's overall attitude and approach for obtaining reliable information and financial reporting. As previously noted, management is responsible for establishing a reliable information system. The auditor should identify the key information systems used within the organization. Eventually, critical systems will have to be evaluated by the auditor. Systems that are weak or informal may increase the risk of material misstatement associated with the processing of transactions or stored master records. Furthermore, such problems may indicate potentially severe weaknesses in internal control over financial reporting. Finally, weaknesses in information processing may make it difficult for the auditor to obtain evidence that is needed to verify some management assertions (e.g., documents may be inaccurate), causing the auditor to increase the effort needed to complete the audit.

IDENTIFY PROBLEM AREAS THAT MAY AFFECT AUDIT PLANNING

An important purpose of preliminary planning is to highlight potential problem areas or risk factors in the audit. Some of these risk factors will have a broad impact on the reliability of the financial statements whereas others will be more isolated, having an impact on individual transactions or accounts. Some of the procedures that are helpful to the auditor at this point include:

- Discuss prior-year problems with the predecessor auditor and management.
- Review minutes of significant management meetings (e.g., meetings of the board of directors).
- Obtain and review preliminary financial statements.
- Brainstorm possible fraud situations that might occur and assess the risk of fraud.
- Identify key accounting policies.

We discussed communications with predecessor auditor earlier. Further details about the other procedures are presented below.

Review Board Minutes

An important part of an audit engagement is the review of the board of director minutes for all meetings conducted during the year. The board often discusses significant events and transactions that impact the organization, including major acquisitions and disposals, serious litigation matters, strategic risks, executive performance, and strategic initiatives. Furthermore, only the board can declare dividends, making the board minutes the primary source of audit evidence for testing dividends declared and payable. For publicly held U.S. companies, the audit committee of the board of directors is directly responsible for the audit, so issues discussed among the board should be easy to access. However, for other audit engagements, the auditors might have limited contact with Board members, making access to the board minutes critical. Because of the importance of the issues discussed in the board minutes, a restriction on the client's ability to access board records should be considered a scope limitation.

Review Preliminary Financial Statements

A review of the pre-audit preliminary financial statements will give the auditor a quick picture of the company's situation. Is it making money? Is the company growing? What is its asset base? How does it finance its operations? Are there any unusual circumstances or results that suggest a heightened risk level? Although the auditor cannot obtain a complete understanding of the client based on this type of cursory review, it will provide some insight into what to expect as the audit is planned and executed.

Discuss and Assess Fraud Risk and the Risk of Material Misstatement

An important objective of preliminary planning is to assess the risk of material misstatement associated with fraud. A key procedure for the audit team is to hold a brainstorming session involving all engagement personnel likely to be a significant part of the audit team. This discussion of potential ways that fraud could occur is required under IAASB (ISA 240) and AICPA (SAS 99) standards, and likely will be required by the PCAOB under any modified fraud or risk assessment standards.

Figure 4–7 outlines the issues that should be considered and discussed by the audit team related to the possibility of fraudulent financial reporting. Although quite detailed, the basic structure of the discussion reflects three elements that are necessary for fraud to be a concern in a given engagement. First, management must have some incentive to commit fraud. The incentive may be in the form of desires or needs on the part of senior management (e.g., greed), or it may arise

Figure 4–7   Fraud Risk Factors for Management Fraud/Financial Reporting Fraud: Incentives/Pressures, Opportunities, and Attitudes/Rationalizations*

Incentives/pressures

(a) Financial *stability or profitability* is *threatened* by economic, industry, or entity operating conditions as indicated by:
- a high degree of competition or market saturation, accompanied by declining margins
- high vulnerability to rapid changes, such as changes in technology, product obsolescence, or interest rates
- significant declines in customer demand and increasing business failures in either the industry or overall economy
- operating losses making the threat of bankruptcy, foreclosure, or hostile takeover imminent
- recurring negative cash flows from operations or an inability to generate cash flows from operations while reporting earnings and earnings growth
- rapid growth or unusual profitability especially compared to that of other companies in the same industry.

(b) *Excessive pressure* exists for management to meet the requirements or expectations of third parties due to the following:
- profitability or trend level expectations of investment analysts, institutional investors, significant creditors, or other external parties (particularly expectations that are unduly aggressive or unrealistic), including expectations created by management in overly optimistic press releases or annual report messages
- the need to obtain additional debt or equity financing to stay competitive (including financing of major research and development or capital expenditures)
- marginal ability to meet exchange listing requirements or debt repayment or other debt covenant requirements
- perceived or real adverse effects of reporting poor financial results on significant pending transactions, such as business combinations or contract awards

(c) Information available indicates that the *personal financial situation* of management or those charged with governance is threatened by the entity's financial performance arising from the following
- significant financial interests in the entity
- significant portions of its compensation (for example, bonuses, stock options, and earn-out arrangements) being contingent upon achieving aggressive targets for stock price, operating results, financial position, or cash flow
- personal guarantees of debts of the entity

(d) There is *excessive pressure* on management or operating personnel to *meet financial targets* established by those charged with governance, including sales or profitability incentive goals.

Opportunities

(a) The *nature of the industry* or the *entity's operations* provides opportunities to engage in fraudulent financial reporting that can arise from the following
- significant related party transactions not in the ordinary course of business or with related entities not audited or audited by another firm
- a strong financial presence or ability to dominate a certain industry sector that allows the entity to dictate terms or conditions to suppliers or customers that may result in inappropriate or non–arm's-length transactions
- assets, liabilities, revenues, or expenses based on significant estimates that involve subjective judgments or uncertainties that are difficult to corroborate

*Based on SAS 99 and ISA 240.

Figure 4–7 *(continued)*

- significant, unusual, or highly complex transactions, especially those close to period end that pose difficult "substance over form" questions
- significant operations located or conducted across international borders in jurisdictions where differing business environments and cultures exist
- use of business intermediaries for which there appears to be no clear business justification
- significant bank accounts or subsidiary or branch operations in tax-haven jurisdictions for which there appears to be no clear business justification

(b) There is *ineffective monitoring* of management as a result of the following:
- domination of management by a single person or small group without compensating controls
- ineffective oversight by those charged with governance over the financial reporting process and internal control

(c) There is a *complex or unstable organizational structure*, as evidenced by the following
- difficulty in determining the organization or individuals that have controlling interest in the entity
- overly complex organizational structure involving unusual legal entities or managerial lines of authority; and management incentive plans may be contingent upon achieving targets relating only to certain accounts or selected activities of the entity
- high turnover of senior management, legal counsel, or those charged with governance

(d) *Internal control* components are *deficient* as a result of the following
- inadequate monitoring of controls, including automated controls and controls over interim financial reporting
- high turnover rates or employment of ineffective accounting, internal audit, or information technology staff
- ineffective accounting and information systems, including significant weaknesses in internal control

Attitudes/rationalizations

(a) ineffective communication, implementation, support, or enforcement of the entity's *values or ethical* standards by management or the communication of inappropriate values or ethical standards

(b) *non-financial management's excessive participation* in or preoccupation with the selection of accounting principles or the determination of significant estimates

(c) known *history of violations* of securities laws or other laws and regulations, or claims against the entity, its senior management, or those charged with governance alleging fraud or violations of laws and regulations

(d) *excessive interest* by management in maintaining or increasing the entity's *stock price or earnings trend*

(e) a practice by management of committing to analysts, creditors, and other third parties to achieve *aggressive or unrealistic forecasts*

(f) management *failing to correct* known significant *weaknesses in internal control* on a timely basis

(g) an interest by management in employing *inappropriate* means to *minimize reported earnings* for tax-motivated reasons

(h) *low morale* among senior management

(i) the owner-manager makes *no distinction* between *personal and business transactions*

(j) recurring attempts by management to justify *marginal or inappropriate accounting* on the basis of *materiality*

(continued)

Figure 4–7 *(continued)*

> (k) the *relationship* between management and the current or predecessor *auditor is strained*, as exhibited by the following
>   - frequent disputes with the current or predecessor auditor on accounting, auditing, or reporting matters
>   - unreasonable demands on the auditor, such as unreasonable time constraints regarding the completion of the audit or the issuance of the auditor's report
>   - formal or informal restrictions on the auditor that inappropriately limit access to people or information or the ability to communicate effectively with those charged with governance
>   - domineering management behavior in dealing with the auditor, especially involving attempts to influence the scope of the auditor's work or the selection or continuance of personnel assigned to or consulted on the audit engagement

from pressures to improve the performance of the organization. Second, there must be an opportunity to commit fraud. Opportunities usually arise when an organization has ineffective or incomplete internal controls, weak monitoring, poorly designed and executed processes, or a rapidly changing environment. Finally, an attitude must exist that fraudulent behavior is acceptable, maybe even necessary, in a given situation. Such an attitude usually means that the perpetrator believes what he or she is doing is all right or will never be discovered. The issues identified in Figure 4–7 provide many concrete illustrations of incentives, opportunities, and attitudes that may lead to fraudulent financial reporting.

Example

> In 2002, the SEC indicted John Rigas and several members of his family for committing fraud at Adelphia, the cable company started by Rigas. The fraud involved several facets, including the diversion of company funds for personal expenditures such as open market stock purchases by the Rigas family, purchases of timber rights to land in Pennsylvania, construction of a golf club for $12.8 million, repayments of personal margin loans and other Rigas family debts, and purchases of luxury condominiums in Colorado, Mexico, and New York City for the Rigas family. Rigas and his sons had the opportunity to divert these funds through collusion and the ability to override controls. The incentive likely was driven by the need to pay for their high level of personal spending. The attitude associated with the fraud likely was that all of the Adelphia funds were essentially the Rigas' to spend because they founded and developed the Company.

Identify Key Accounting Policies

Evaluating significant accounting policies used by the client is also quite important. Management's accounting choices can reveal much about its attitudes towards financial reporting and internal control. Although aggressive accounting by itself does not indicate problems with management, consistently aggressive choices that maximize or accelerate revenue and minimize or defer expenses suggests the possibility that management is more interested in "looking good" than in providing realistic information about financial results. Aggressive accounting choices combined with other risk factors such as contingent compensation or fiscal pressure could indicate high risk of material misstatement. Ultimately, the auditor must evaluate whether the accounting choices made by management are appropriate and adjust the audit process accordingly.

Example

> Percentage-of-completion accounting for construction projects is both aggressive (accelerates income) and difficult for an auditor to evaluate. The choice of percentage-of-completion is perfectly acceptable under GAAP, but creates opportunities for management to massage the financial results by manipulating the percentage applied to a specific project. The auditor's challenge is to determine if the choice of accounting method is appropriate, that is, if it reflects underlying economic reality and is not selected simply because it can be manipulated. If acceptable, the auditor also needs to determine if it is applied appropriately given the existing economic circumstances of the client.

Auditing standards also require the auditor to evaluate the reasonableness of accounting estimates made by management. The *IFAC Handbook* (Glossary of Terms) defines an *accounting estimate* as "an approximation of a financial statement element, item or account." Such estimates include reserves for uncollectible receivables or loan losses, net realizable value of assets, contingent liabilities, and the stage of completion of inventory-related assets. These estimates can have a pervasive impact on the financial statements, and the auditor must identify potential issues associated with estimates early in the engagement. Management is responsible for developing these estimates, including determining when estimates are needed, designing a system to gather information needed to make the estimate, making assumptions about likely future events, and calculating the estimate. Furthermore, management is responsible for evaluating the reasonableness of prior estimates, including any adjustments to reflect new information that renders such assessments inaccurate. The auditor's objective is to evaluate whether all needed estimates have been made, whether they are reasonable, and whether they are presented in accordance with generally accepted accounting principles.

CONSIDER SPECIAL CIRCUMSTANCES THAT MAY AFFECT AUDIT PLANNING

Some special circumstances can have a significant impact on the planning of the audit engagement and should be addressed as part of the preliminary planning process. These circumstances are singled out for the auditor's attention because they have the potential to pervasively affect the conduct of the engagement. We will discuss three areas of concern at this point: (1) the existence of related parties, (2) the need for specialists, and (3) the use of internal auditors.

Related Party Transactions

Related party transactions are defined as transactions between two parties who share some common interest. Related party transactions are common for many organizations and, in most cases, reflect legitimate business decisions by the company. However, they are a prime area for accounting manipulations and should be looked at carefully by the auditor. For example, much of the fraud at Enron was perpetrated through related party transactions.

Accounting standard setters have specified reporting standards applicable to related party transactions (such as ISA 550, SAS 45). These standards give numerous examples of related parties, including

(a) a parent company and its subsidiaries
(b) subsidiaries of a common parent

(c) trusts for the benefit of employees, such as pensions and profit-sharing trusts that are managed by or under the trusteeship of the enterprise's management

(d) principal owners, management, or members of their immediate families

(e) affiliates

The accounting standards require specific disclosures when a company has related party transactions. The auditor's primary concern for related party transactions is that they are not represented as being arm's-length in nature since the amounts of such transactions may or may not represent a fair market value for the underlying transaction. The accounting standards presume that the readers of the financial statements will make that judgment for themselves, as long as the transaction is fully disclosed.

The auditor's first step is to determine the identity of related parties in a particular engagement, which is the primary reason that this task must occur during preliminary planning. The entire audit team should be familiar with the identity of related parties so that it will recognize a related party transaction if one comes to its attention. If a related party transaction is detected, the auditor must investigate the transaction, examine supporting documentation, and verify the accuracy of required disclosures. If disclosure is in conformity with GAAP, the auditor need perform no further work on the matter. If disclosure is not adequate or is misleading (e.g., by implying that the transaction is actually arm's-length), the auditor should take remedial action or adapt the auditor's report to reflect the situation.

> **Authoritative Guidance & Standards**
> The auditor's responsibilities when a client has related party transactions are discussed in SAS 45 and ISA 550. The essence of these requirements is that related party transactions not be presented in a misleading manner.

Need for Specialists

The auditor may need to consult with specialists to verify the accuracy of some financial statement assertions. Examples of specialists who may be needed on an engagement include

- Engineer: To verify the stage of completion of electronic components
- Real Estate Appraiser: To appraise realizable value of real estate used as collateral for loans
- Actuary: To evaluate the funding requirements and future cash flows associated with pensions or post-retirement health costs
- Attorney: To evaluate the likely disposition of contingent losses from litigation
- Geologist: To verify the existence of natural resources being held for future extraction, such as oil and metals

It is important that auditors identify the situations where such specialists may be needed on an engagement as early as possible. In some cases, the specialist may need to perform certain activities on specific dates, such as examine the inventory on hand as of year end. In all cases, the specialist should be called in as soon as possible to allow adequate time to complete the necessary work.

Auditing standards specify that once a need is identified, the auditor should arrange for the services of an appropriate specialist (e.g., ISA 620, SAS 73). The specialist should be competent, as evidenced by appropriate professional certification and an upstanding reputation, and be independent of the client (if possible).[4] The

---

4 Auditing standards indicate that independence is not required but is preferred (e.g., SAS 73, ISA 620). If a non-independent specialist is used, the auditor needs to perform additional procedures.

auditor should have a clear understanding with the specialist as to the specific information needed by the auditor and the form of report that the specialist will issue. The auditor should also strive to understand the assumptions, the computational approach, and the data utilized by the specialist in his or her decision process. In many cases, the auditor will test the accuracy of the input data that the specialist uses for his or her calculations. If the specialist's findings provide support for the financial statement assertions being addressed (e.g., valuation of pension obligations), the auditor can accept these findings as competent evidence in support of the related management assertions.

> **Authoritative Guidance & Standards**
> Standards provide specific guidance when auditors use others outside of the engagement team to help conduct the audit. Standards for the work of specialists (SAS 73, ISA 620) and internal auditors (AS 2, ISA 610) generally allow for auditors to rely on their work when performed by qualified individuals and properly supervised and reviewed by auditors on the engagement team.

Use of Internal Auditors

Another condition that may pervasively affect the auditor's engagement planning is the existence of an internal audit department within the company. Some internal auditors perform many of the same tests and procedures that an external auditor performs. If an internal audit staff exists, the external auditor may be able to utilize the personnel and the efforts of that group. The key concerns that the external auditor should address are whether the internal auditors are knowledgeable, objective, and sufficiently independent of management to generate unbiased evidence (e.g., ISA 610). Knowledge can be evaluated by reviewing the company's hiring and training practices as evidenced by the level of education, experience, and certification of the internal audit staff. The auditor will also wish to review the work performed by the internal auditors and evaluate its quality, especially if it is to be used as part of the evidence in support of the financial statement assertions. Objectivity usually depends on the level of management to whom the internal auditors report. Ideally, the internal auditors should report to the audit committee (and are required to for U.S. SEC registrants). In some organizations, the internal auditors may report to lower level management such as the controller, in which case the objectivity and independence of the internal auditors may be open to question.

When the internal auditors are found to be knowledgeable and objective, their work can be relied upon by the external auditor when planning his or her own tests. Specifically, internal auditors can be used to assist in obtaining an understanding of the client's system, to make various risk assessments, and to perform some tests. Many of these tests may be directly related to the internal auditor's own audit plans or may be specifically requested, planned, and directed by the external auditor. All such work performed by internal auditors should be thoroughly reviewed by the external auditor. Rules of the PCAOB allow internal auditors to perform some of the procedures required to test internal controls, as long as the external auditors' work provides the principal evidence for the auditor's opinion.

AN OVERVIEW OF THE INTEGRATED AUDIT PROCESS

Having discussed the *logical* process of performing an audit in Chapter 3 and the regulatory and professional context in this chapter, we now introduce the *sequential* activities that comprise the audit. This sequential process will serve as the organizing structure of the remainder of the text and is illustrated in Figure 4–8.

Figure 4–8   Overview of the Audit Process

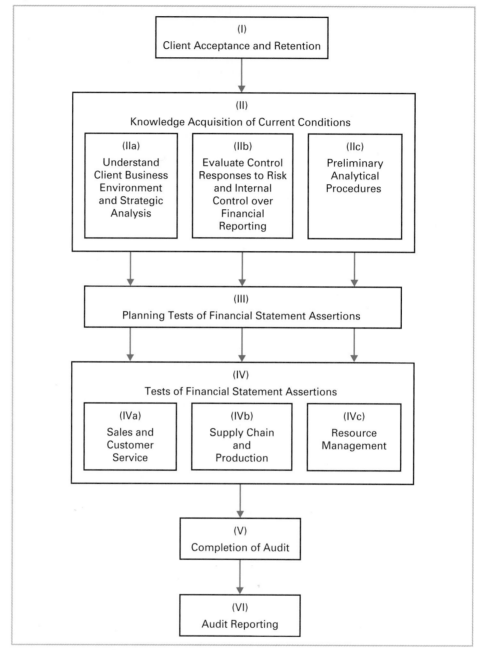

Initially, as we have just discussed, an auditor must reach the decision to accept or retain a client (I). The remainder of the engagement can then be loosely divided into two phases: risk assessment and evidence gathering. The risk-assessment phase involves obtaining evidence about current conditions and assessing the risks facing the organization (II). Some of these risks may suggest that the financial statements may be materially misstated. The auditor performs three types of activities to assess and measure these risks:

- Understand a client's business and industry and conduct a strategic analysis to identify potential risk areas in the engagement (IIa discussed in Chapters 5 and 6).
- Evaluate the effectiveness of internal control to determine the likelihood that risks will be mitigated. The procedures performed during this phase of the audit provide much of the evidence necessary to evaluate internal control over financial reporting as part of an integrated audit (IIb discussed in Chapters 7 and 8).
- Perform preliminary analytical procedures to identify unusual conditions that have arisen that may indicate significant risk conditions and/or the potential for errors in the financial statements (IIc discussed in Chapter 9).

After evaluating current conditions and risks, the auditor reaches some preliminary conclusions about internal control over financial reporting and the financial statement assertions made by management. Based on these conclusions, the auditor can prepare a plan for gathering the remaining evidence necessary to evaluate the financial statement assertions (III discussed in Chapter 10). Following the audit plan, the auditor gathers and interprets evidence in all of the important areas of the audit (IV). The audit is loosely decomposed into key business processes to be examined using the planned audit procedures. The major business processes to be discussed in this text are

- Sales and customer service (IVa discussed in Chapter 11)
- Supply chain and production process (IVb discussed in Chapter 12)
- Resource management processes (IVc discussed in Chapter 13)

Other processes or areas of an organization, such as research and development, brand management, or mergers and acquisitions , can be subject to similar analyses. The processes that require the attention of the auditor depend on the circumstances of the client and the risk assessments made during the earlier phase of the audit.

The final aspects of the audit involve completing the documentation and interpretation of evidence, finalizing conclusions about financial information, and preparing the appropriate report to be issued (V, VI discussed in Chapters 14 and 15).

An important point to remember is that the process depicted in Figure 4–8 is iterative, meaning that information obtained at any stage in the process may necessitate a return to an earlier phase for reconsideration of previous conclusions. For example, if an examination of sales and customer service and related tests of sales transactions reveals a higher risk of material misstatement than was expected, the auditor may need to readdress his or her risk assessments for revenue accounts, reconsider internal control over financial reporting for sales transactions, and consider the impact on additional evidence needed to complete the audit of customer service activity.

The phases of the integrated audit help ensure that auditors develop a sufficient understanding of the entity and its environment, including internal control over financial reporting, such that a plan for gathering sufficient, competent evidence to support transactions, accounts, and financial statements (including disclosures) can be developed. The nature, extent, and timing of the procedures utilized in an audit are based to a large extent on the results of strategic and business process analyses performed by the auditor. These detailed analyses enable the auditor to focus audit effort on transactions, accounts, and aspects of the financial statements most at risk of being materially misstated. Although the auditor will not ignore any aspect of the financial statements, the auditor is unable to perform an unlimited amount of evidence gathering and analysis. This limitation necessitates the auditor to exert more (less) audit effort in areas deemed to be most (least) at risk.

SUMMARY AND CONCLUSION

In this chapter we have consolidated our understanding of the professional and regulatory context within which the integrated audit is carried out. We have considered the auditor as a regulated professional and the audit firm as a regulated business. We have considered the professional responsibilities that go with the business analyses that accompany the client acquisition and retention decision. After acquiring a new client, or deciding to retain an existing client, the auditor undertakes preliminary planning of the audit. This involves consideration of a client's strategy, information processing and related parties, as well as the possible need for specialist assistance or reliance on internal auditors. Preliminary planning mostly involves gathering basic factual information about the client as a precursor to more detailed analysis during the remainder of the audit. The following chapters discuss the nature of the steps of the audit as summarized in Figure 4–8.

BIBLIOGRAPHY OF RELATED PROFESSIONAL LITERATURE

Research

Ayers, S. and S. E. Kaplan. 2003. Review Partners' Reactions to Contact Partner Risk Judgments of Prospective Clients. *Auditing: A Journal of Practice & Theory.* 22(1): 29–46.

Ayers, S. and S. E. Kaplan. 1998. Potential Differences Between Engagement and Risk Review Partners and their Effect on Client Acceptance Judgments. *Accounting Horizons.* 12 (2): 139–153.

Barton, J. 2005. Who Cares About Auditor Reputation? *Contemporary Accounting Research.* 22(3): 549–586.

Beaulieu, P. R. 2001. The Effects of Judgments of New Clients' Integrity Upon Risk Judgments, Audit Evidence and Fees. *Auditing: A Journal of Practice & Theory.* 20(2): 85–100.

Bell, T. B., J. C. Bedard, K. M. Johnstone, and E. F. Smith. KRisk[sm]: A Computerized Decision Aid for Client Acceptance and Continuance Risk Assessments. *Auditing: A Journal of Practice & Theory.* 21(2): 97–113.

Dezoort, F. T., R. W. Houston, and M. F. Peters. 2001. The Impact of Internal Auditor Compensation and Role on External Auditors' Planning Judgments and Decisions. *Contemporary Accounting Research.* 18(2): 257–281.

Dopuch, N., R. King, and R. Schwartz. 2001. An Experimental Investigation of Retention and Rotation Requirements. *Journal of Accounting Research.* 39(1): 93–117.

Gendron, Y. 2002. On the Role of the Organization in Auditors' Client-Acceptance Decisions. *Accounting Organizations and Society.* 27(7): 659–684.

Gendron, Y. 2001. The Difficult Client-Acceptance Decision in Canadian Audit Firms: A Field Investigation. *Contemporary Accounting Research.* 18(2): 283–310.

Godfrey, J. M. and J. Hamilton. 2005. The Impact of R&D Intensity on Demand for Specialist Auditor Services. *Contemporary Accounting Research.* 22(1): 56–93.

Johnstone, K. M. 2000. Client Acceptance Decisions: Simultaneous Effects of Client Business Risk, Audit Risk, Auditor Business Risk, and Risk Adaptation. *Auditing: A Journal of Practice & Theory.* 19(1): 1–26.

Johnstone, K. M. and J. C. Bedard. 2001. Engagement Planning, Bid Pricing and Client Response in the Market for Initial Attest Engagements. *The Accounting Review.* 76(2): 199–220.

Johnstone, K. M. and J. C. Bedard. 2003. Risk Management in Client Acceptance Decision. *The Accounting Review.* 78(4): 1003–1025.

Johnstone, K. M. and J. C. Bedard. 2004. Audit Firm Portfolio Management Decisions. *Journal of Accounting Research.* 42(4): 659–690.

Krishnamoorthy, G. 2002. A Multistage Approach to External Auditors' Evaluation of the Internal Audit Function. *Auditing: A Journal of Practice & Theory.* 21(1): 95–122.

Patterson, E. and J. Noel. 2003. Audit Strategies and Multiple Fraud Opportunities of Misreporting and Defalcation. *Contemporary Accounting Research.* 20(3): 519–549.

Wilks, T. J. and M. F. Zimbelman. 2004. Decomposition of Fraud-Risk Assessments and Auditors' Sensitivity to Fraud Cues. *Contemporary Accounting Research.* 22(3): 719–745.

Auditing Standards

AICPA *Code of Professional Conduct*

AICPA *Statements on Quality Control Standards.*

AICPA *Statements on Auditing Standards (SAS)* No. 45, "Related Parties"

AICPA *Statements on Auditing Standard (SAS)* No. 73, "Using the Work of a Specialist."

AICPA *Statements on Auditing Standard (SAS)* No. 84, "Communications between Predecessor and Successor Auditors."

AICPA *Statements on Auditing Standard (SAS)* No. 99, "Consideration of Fraud in a Financial Statement Audit."

AICPA *Statements on Auditing Standard (SAS)* No. 106, "Audit Evidence."

AICPA *Statements on Auditing Standard (SAS)* No. 107, "Audit Risk and Materiality in Conducting an Audit."

AICPA *Statements on Auditing Standard (SAS)* No. 108, "Planning and Supervision."

AICPA *Statements on Auditing Standard (SAS)* No. 109, "Understanding the Entity and Its Environment and Assessing the Risks of Material Misstatement."

AICPA *Statements on Auditing Standard (SAS)* No. 110, "Performing Procedures in Response to Assessed Risks and Evaluating the Audit Evidence Obtained."

AICPA *Statements on Auditing Standard (SAS)* No. 111, "Amendment to Statement on Auditing Standards No. 39, *Audit Sampling*"

Committee of Sponsoring Organizations of the Treadway Commission (COSO). *Internal Control—Integrated Framework.* AICPA, 1992.

IAASB *International Standards on Auditing (ISA)* No. 200, "Objectives and Principles Governing an Audit of Financial Statements."

IAASB *International Standards on Auditing (ISA)* No. 210, "Terms of Audit Engagements."

IAASB *International Standards on Auditing (ISA)* No. 220R, "Quality Controls for Audits of Historical Financial Information."

IAASB *International Standards on Auditing (ISA)* No. 240, "The Auditor's Responsibility to Consider Fraud in a Financial Statement Audit."

IAASB *International Standards on Auditing (ISA)* No. 300, "Planning an Audit of Financial Statements."

IAASB *International Standards on Auditing (ISA)* No. 315, "Understanding the Entity and Its Environment and Assessing the Risks of Material Misstatement."

IAASB *International Standards on Auditing (ISA)* No. 320, "Audit Materiality."

IAASB *International Standards on Auditing (ISA)* No. 330, "The Auditor's Procedures in Response to Assessed Risks."

IAASB *International Standards on Auditing (ISA)* No. 500, "Audit Evidence."

IAASB *International Standards on Auditing (ISA)* No. 610, "Considering the Work of Internal Auditing."

IAASB *International Standards on Auditing (ISA)* No. 620, "Using the Work of an Expert."

IAASB International Framework for Assurance Engagements.

IAASB *International Standards on Quality Control (ISQC).* No. 1 Quality Control for Firms That Perform Audits and Reviews of Historical Financial Information and Other Assurance and Related Service Engagements.

IFAC *Code of Ethics for Professional Accountants.*

IFAC *Handbook Glossary of Terms*

PCAOB. *Auditing Standard No. 2,* "An Audit of Internal Control Over Financial Reporting Performed in Conjunction with an Audit of Financial Statements."

Securities and Exchange Commission (SEC). 1999. Staff Accounting Bulletin No. 99, "Materiality."

QUESTIONS

1. When testing for the fairness of the financial statements, auditors can reduce the extent of testing if they have assessed the risk of misstatements to be low and found that the internal controls in place to be effective. Argue why the auditor is justified to reduce substantive testing under this condition.

2. When deciding to accept a new client (or retain an existing client) the auditor faces a trade-off. Describe this trade-off and discuss how auditors can and should deal with this trade-off.

3. Reviewing accounting estimates is a critical part of the audit engagement. List concerns that you would have when auditing an organization that consistently fails to meet its earnings targets when not incorporating two accounting estimates—allowance for doubtful accounts and estimated warranty expense—yet consistently meets its earning targets after incorporating accounting estimates.

4. What is the purpose of an engagement letter? What elements should be contained within an engagement letter?

5. When an auditor disagrees with the accounting treatment selected by management for a material item, and management or those charged with governance refuses to change, what types of audit opinion are able to be issued? Why will the threat of issuing such an opinion generally result in the client changing its accounting treatment to be in line with the auditor's preference? Would your answer be different if the client was other than a public company?

6. In his audit planning, why should an auditor pay specific attention to the following?
   - Related party transactions
   - Use of specialists
   - Use of internal auditors

7. Discuss the risks auditors face by not following professional auditing standards and how those risks are expected to change in the near future as a result of changes in business conditions, technology, and regulation.

PROBLEMS

1. Your audit firm is considering taking on as a client an Australian firm that has operated as a closely held company for its entire history. Because it is a leading exporter of wines to the United States, it is going public for the first time by registering as a public

company in the United States. In addition to producing fine wines and spirits, the company has begun to expand into other beverage markets such as niche-brand soft drinks and juices. Its primary customers are grocery stores and restaurants. Management has built the business over the past several years to the point that it will require large investments in warehousing and distribution channels to meet its plans.

Discuss considerations about the potential client that you should consider before accepting the engagement and discuss what measures you might take to satisfy yourself that the potential client meets your firm's standards on each one of them (use Figure 4–4 as a guide).

2. As described in this chapter, auditors are required to communicate certain issues with the predecessor auditor before accepting a new engagement. These issues include the reason for the change, the nature of any disagreements with management, identification of any important risk areas or control weaknesses, and prior experience with fraud or illegal acts. Describe why you believe that this requirement is important for both the protection of the subsequent auditor and the capital market in general.

3. Discuss the errors and omissions in the following sample engagement letter.

May 16, 2006

Hunkabobo Accounting Firm, LLP
1000 High Street
Oxford, OH 45056

Ms. Felice Trackman
Trackman & Associates, P.A.
2000 N. 13th St.
Oxford, OH 45056

Dear Ms. Trackman:

This letter will confirm our agreement to examine the financial statements of Trackman & Associates P.A. with a view toward determining how accurate they are and whether they were prepared in accordance with GAAP.

We will study your company thoroughly. Included in our audit will be a study of the company's internal control structure and any other test we deem necessary. Pursuant to our recent conversation, we will be keeping an especially sharp eye out for employee theft in our detailed tests of the financial statements.

We expect to conduct our examination according to the following timetable:

Time Frame

Preliminary tests of controls	Late 4th quarter
Auditing	Middle of 1st quarter of next year
Final report	Late 1st quarter

We appreciate your assistance in securing all the company's paperwork we will need for this engagement and your staff's assistance.

Our fee is fixed at $10,000 for the engagement plus additional items such as copying, travel, and the like. Of course, we would be willing to negotiate that fee as circumstances warrant.

Unless you have any questions, we will see you late 4th quarter.

Yours sincerely,

Jeff Awseola, Partner

4. You have recently been hired to perform the year-end audit for Coleman Co., a manufacturer of inexpensive jewelry items for sale at mall kiosks and costume jewelry outlets. Among the results of your preliminary planning are the following:
   a. Management is compensated based on an aggressive, earnings-based plan.
   b. Coleman's markets are concentrated primarily in Midwestern U.S. states, particularly Michigan.
   c. Coleman's most valuable asset is a warehouse full of costume jewelry.
   d. The board of directors has no audit committee.
   e. Gross margins in this industry are usually small, and Coleman is no exception.
   f. Many of the sales contracts with Coleman's distributors allow for return of unsold items in exchange for credit.
   g. Although the senior management is mostly experienced, the CFO is new on the job. She is the third CFO in the past two years.

   Discuss the ramifications for your audit plan of the preceding items. Specifically, address the effects of these items on your assessments of client, engagement, and audit risks and the business processes within Coleman from which more evidence should be gathered, paying special attention to the interactions among these items.

5. You have been contracted to audit the financial statements of Ben Webster & Associates, a privately held real estate investing firm. Ben has been in the business for several years and has built up a sizable portfolio of properties, mostly commercial office buildings, but has never issued audited, GAAP-based financial statements. He now seeks to do so since his bank told him they would consider better terms on his line of credit if he provided audited financial statements.

   Ben has a sister, Martha, who is in the construction business. Many, but not all, of Ben's projects are constructed by Martha's firm. The arrangement on a typical project is for Martha's firm to build a commercial office building "on spec" so that Ben's firm can attempt to lease it. Although the normal arrangement in this industry calls for the construction company to be paid off as the construction is completed with the proceeds from the investment company's construction loan, the informal terms between Martha and Ben allow for Martha to share some of the market risk (i.e., that the building doesn't quickly lease up) by her accepting payments from Ben's firm on an as-leased basis. Ben's firm has taken advantage of this several times within the past several years, to the point that Ben considers the arrangement an alternative, but reliable, source of financing. As for her part, Martha knows that by extending the payment terms on occasion she will gain preferential status on Ben's construction business even when her bid is not the lowest.

   Discuss the ramifications of this arrangement for your audit of Ben's firm. Specifically:
   a. What risk is inherently associated with this related party transaction?
   b. How would you identify the related party transactions (e.g., what documentation would you study)?
   c. What accounts and compliance with what accounting methods would require more careful study for those transactions identified as related party transactions?
   d. What disclosures in the financial statements would be necessary as a result of the material related party transactions?

6. In your year-end audit of The Joshua Redman Co., a defense contractor specializing in building sophisticated tracking systems for missile defense systems, you bring in a specialist, Mal Waldron, to assist your valuation of work-in-process and finished goods inventory. Mal has conducted the same function for your audit of The Joshua Redman Co. for several years and is independent of the company. His reputation in the industry is excellent.

   As long as Mal has performed this service for your audit firm, you have kept track of the inputs to the inventory account and you now believe you have built a statistical model of the inventory process of such quality that you can compare its results to those of Mal. Upon comparison, you notice that Mal's estimate of the amount in finished goods inventory is considerably higher than that of your model's. After some attempt at reconciling the two amounts, Mal holds firm on his estimate, claiming that a great deal of judgment goes into some of the lower-of-cost-or-market calculations and that the company's costing scheme is not necessarily accurate for the purposes of assigning overhead to individual products. Further complicating the matter is management's insistence that *its* finished goods inventory number—the highest of the three estimates—is accurate.

Discuss your responsibilities as this point. Specifically, determine what factors may be contributing to the difference between your estimate and Mal's, and discuss your options. Make a judgment and defend it.

7. Consider the internal audit staffs of the following two companies:

Carl Company's internal auditors are college graduates who have been hired mostly from the ranks of marketing personnel who did not make sales quotas. They report to the controller of Carl Company. Their tasks include reconciling all cash accounts to the general ledger, reviewing all major contracts for compliance with relevant regulations, and reviewing control procedures for check-writing and other high-risk activities at the business-process level. Most of the auditors have been on the job for 2 years or fewer.

Ashley Company employs students from major accounting programs in its internal audit department. The manager of the internal audit group reports to the chairman of the audit committee of the board of directors. The auditors' tasks include the design, implementation and periodic review of major internal control systems; the frequent sampling and investigation of high-risk expenditures such as employee travel expense reports; and the reconciling of all cash accounts to the general ledger.

For each of these two companies, discuss the following:

a.   How do the organizational positions and the competencies of the respective internal auditor staffs affect their reliability?

b.   How relevant are the activities of the respective internal audit staffs to the external financial statement audit?

c.   What roles could the internal auditors of these companies play in the financial statement audit?

8. Specialists may be required to perform audit tasks that require knowledge or skills outside the auditor's abilities. Examples from the text include an engineer (to verify the stage of completion of electronic components) and an actuary (to evaluate pension liabilities and expenses). For each of the following specialists, discuss how his or her services may be useful to an audit.

a.   Building contractor/architect

b.   Trial attorney

c.   Geologist

d.   Insurance risk analyst

e.   Forester

f.   Computer/software engineer

9. Client-acceptance decisions have become increasingly important. This is mainly due to the increased risk of litigation against audit firms in some countries as a result of being associated with failed business, unethical organizations, or perceived problems with independence. Hence, it is essential for audit firms to carefully consider the potential benefits and costs of association with prospective clients.

- How do risk evaluation and risk management affect client acceptance decisions?
- Are there situations in which risk-management strategies may cost-effectively moderate each client's unique risks?
- Does the application of these risk-management strategies increase the likelihood of accepting clients?

Based on your understanding of client acceptance, answer these questions. Consider using the results in the following study as evidence to support your arguments: Gendron, Y. 2002. On the Role of the Organization in Auditors' Client-Acceptance Decisions. *Accounting Organizations and Society.* 27(7): 659–684.

10. For each scenario below, describe which of the five general conditions that undermine independence in appearance is most relevant.

    a.   An auditor recommends its audit clients' services to other clients based on her understanding of the quality of such services.

    b.   A partner serves an audit client even though her grandmother has 40 percent of her investments in the client.

    c.   An auditor helps his audit clients by making adjusting entries to correct financial statements for any amount below a pre-established threshold.

    d.   A partner audits the income tax expense for a client, which is based on the taxable income computed for the client by the taxation division of partner's firm.

    e.   A partner serves a client for which his brother-in-law serves as the chief information officer.

11. Bard Carver, an auditor with a philosophy degree from Mims Polytechnic, begins the financial statement audit of Lisa's Grocery, a medium-sized, privately held regional grocery store chain. He enters the store one day and begins to count the inventory. His inventory count completed, he then proceeds to reconcile the bank statements. Finally, he examines some of the documentation supporting the subsidiary accounts payable balances.

Lisa's Grocery's financial statements do not contain any material misstatements, but its investments in marketable securities are accounted for using the cost method as opposed to the mark-to-market method.

Getting back to his office later that week, Bard issues the following report on his audit:

> Bard Carver,
> Auditor
>
> January 30, 2007
>
> Having extensively audited the financial statements of Lisa's Grocery for the year ended December 31, 2006, I can attest to the quality of the assertions therein and conclude that they are fairly presented and comply substantially with GAAP.

Assuming that the description above covers virtually all the work Bard did for the Lisa's Grocery engagement, discuss the sections of the generally accepted auditing standards that Carver likely violated and why.

Case 4–1: Prefab Sprout Company

You have been approached about auditing Prefab Sprout Construction Company, a family-run general contracting company which is publicly traded on the New York Stock Exchange. The president of Prefab is Jack Warner. His wife, Joan, is the vice president, and his son, John, is the treasurer. The Warner family owns about 40 percent of all outstanding shares and no other investor owns more than 1 percent. The company has been previously audited (receiving standard unqualified opinions) by a sole practitioner who closed his practice and is now the controller of Prefab. The company has an audit committee that consists of Joan, John, and a local college professor. The company also has a compensation committee that consists of Jack, the company's lawyer, and an employee selected on a rotating basis.

Prefab specializes in modular home developments located in areas of South Florida that are densely populated by retirees and recent immigrants from the Caribbean basin. Prefab acquires land, builds streets and other land improvements, builds modular homes on the land, and then sells the entire development to limited partnerships that are set up as tax shelters. Prefab finances most of its construction costs through the Sun Atlantic Bank in Fort Lauderdale.

Prefab's condensed financial statements for 2006 (audited) and 2007 (unaudited) are presented below.

	2006	2007
Cash	$ 12,000	$ 10,000
Receivables	300,000	750,000
Projects in Progress	1,200,000	1,000,000
Total Assets	$1,512,000	$1,760,000
Bank Loans Payable	$ 800,000	$1,050,000
Advance from JRW Realty	150,000	200,000
Stockholders' Equity	562,000	510,000
Total Liabilities and Equity	$1,512,000	$1,760,000
Profits on Construction Projects*	400,000	450,000
General and Administrative Costs	275,000	300,000
Net Income	$ 125,000	$ 150,000

* Recognized using the percentage of completion method of accounting for revenues

Approximately 60 percent of Prefab's sales are to JRW Realty, which organizes limited partnerships (or "syndicates") to fund the acquisitions. That is, investors put up the money and JRW Realty uses it to purchase the developments. JRW Realty is privately owned by Jeff Warner (Jack's younger brother). JRW Realty advertises the developments, obtains funds from investors and serves as the buying agent on behalf of the limited partnerships. JRW Realty is a general partner in these arrangements and collects a fee to serve as consultant to the partnerships. JRW Realty currently owes Prefab $500,000 for purchases made during the current year. The financial statements of JRW Realty and the limited partnerships are not released to the public and have never been audited.

Once the partnerships take over a development, JRW Realty transfers control (but not ownership) to a wholly-owned subsidiary call JRW Property Management, which is run by Jim Warner (Jeff's son). JRW Property is paid a fee by the partnership to obtain tenants for the units and to serve as the property manager. JRW Property collects rents from tenants, deducts its fees and costs, and remits the net rental to JRW Realty, which in turn deducts its fees before distributing the net proceeds to the limited partners. The partners have the option of reinvesting their share of these distributions into the limited partnership. Approximately 75 percent of the partners choose this option.

Other facts that may be relevant to the situation include: Jim Warner is a leading shareholder and on the board of directors of Sun Atlantic Bank. During 2007, Prefab paid salaries to the Warner family totaling $350,000. The salaries were recorded as part of the costs of construction for individual projects. JRW Realty periodically advances funds to the construction company to help meet required paydown provisions of Prefab's bank loans. These advances are at market interest and have always been paid back within four months (often by obtaining bank loans for new projects).

Requirements

1. Discuss the business risks of accepting the audit of Prefab Sprout Construction Company.
2. Would you accept the engagement? Explain.
3. Discuss the audit risk related to Prefab Sprout Construction Company. Identify specific circumstances that would be of concern to an auditor. For each risk that you identify:
    a. Describe the potential financial statement impact of the risk.
    b. Describe how you would plan the audit in response to the risk.

Case 4–2: Murphy Tymshare Inc.

Jake Murphy has approached you about auditing the financial statements of his company, Murphy Tymshare Inc., for the fiscal year ended June 30, 2007. Murphy Tymshare (MTS) builds and sells resort time-share condominiums in South Florida. MTS has been in business for five years and recently bought out a competing and floundering time-share development located north of Fort Lauderdale.

Jake owns 51 percent of the stock of MTS. The remaining stock is owned by various officers of MTS, family members, and friends of Jake. No other individual owns more than 8 percent of the stock. The board of directors has the following members:

Jake Murphy	51%	Chairman, MTS
Sally Murphy	8	Real estate agent
John Booth	6	Bank president
Carol Murphy-Jones	4	Housewife
Robert McCallum	3	College professor
Steven Polmikala	2	Shareholder, Murphy Insurance
Christopher Murphy	1	Artist
Harold Bauser	1	Lawyer

There is also an audit committee consisting of the four board members with the smallest ownership interests (McCallum, Polmikala, C. Murphy, and Bauser). The company is considering issuing additional common stock to the public sometime in the near future. Senior management holds stock options that expire in three years and whose exercise price exceeds the current market price of the stock.

The company finances their projects in one of two ways. During construction or when holding periods for time-share units are expected to be short (generally, less than one year), the company draws needed funds against a revolving line of credit with a major bank in South Florida. This line has a maximum available amount of $27.5 million. The interest rate on the line of credit is equal to prime plus 3 percent and the terms are subject to annual review and modification. Funds borrowed under the line of credit are collateralized by the real estate assets of the company subject to superior claims under existing mortgages. For funds that are needed on a longer term, the company enters into mortgages with the same bank using the properties as collateral. In fiscal 2006, the company financed the acquisition of a competing time-share development by issuing mortgages on the acquired property.

Jake also is a majority shareholder in Murphy Insurance Company (MIC). MIC is a privately held company that writes life, health, and liability insurance. Buyers of time shares from MTS are encouraged to purchase credit life insurance from Murphy Insurance. A quick check with the state Insurance Commissioner's office reveals that in the past three years the insurance company has been disciplined for misrepresenting its policies to consumers, violating reserve requirements[5] and failing to file required reports on time. The insurance company is audited by a small CPA firm.

Initial discussion with some of your business acquaintances leads you to the impression that Jake is a flamboyant character who is accustomed to getting his own way, has been party to many lawsuits (both defending and suing), and likes to spend his money in conspicuous ways. A banker friend of yours has described Jake as a "sleazebag," an opinion you don't quite share. However, you did notice Jake's affinity for "loud" Hawaiian shirts, excessive jewelry, and polyester pants. Another business acquaintance tells you that Jake is known to frequent famous "strip joints," although he wouldn't divulge how he knew this fact. On the other hand, Jake's prior experiences include a successful time-share project in Arizona that he sold for a substantial profit.

Your firm already does tax work for Jake. Your tax department tells you that Jake is very aggressive on his tax return and is audited on a regular basis by the IRS, but never balks about the firm's bills as long as they win more than they lose against the IRS. The fee for the audit work will be substantially larger than the fees for the tax work and could be done during the summer months, which is normally a slow time for the audit staff.

MTS was previously audited by a small local practitioner who has retired. You have heard through the grapevine that MTS has contacted other accounting firms about their interest in the engagement. One of your golfing buddies has heard a rumor that a large national firm has already turned down the engagement, but he knows another firm which is seriously considering making a proposal to obtain the audit engagement.

The controller and most of the senior management have been with the company since its inception, but historically there has been a high turnover in the lower ranks of the company, especially in the marketing area. Part of this is because Jake has been known to fire people in a very dramatic fashion when he is unhappy. Many of the personnel from the acquired time-share company have been hired by MTS. The in-house legal counsel was in private practice until six months ago and handled most of the company's real estate transactions at that time. The company changed outside counsel shortly after hiring the in-house counsel.

Some preliminary questions to the controller reveals that the company's accounting system and software is relatively simple. It was designed and installed by the predecessor accountant and is based on a currently available commercial accounting package. The current financial statements of MTS are shown in Exhibit 2–1. All amounts are in 000s.

As a final step in your evaluation of MTS, you call the prior auditor, Joseph Bandano, who is now living in comfortable retirement in Arizona. Mr. Bandano returns your initial telephone call when he gets your message at his country club. In response to your questions, he tells you that MTS is generally aggressive when selecting accounting methods and procedures and determining accounting estimates. This means that the company tends to favor accounting methods that increase/accelerate revenue recognition and decrease/defer expense recognition. Mr. Bandano is proud of the accounting system he helped the company implement

---

5 Insurance company "reserves" represent the amount of claims on policies in force that the company expects to pay out of the assets in its possession. State regulations dictate a minimum level of reserves for an insurance company based on the types of policies issued and the claims that have not been settled.

Exhibit 2–1   Murphy Tymshare Inc. Financial Statements

Murphy Tymshare Inc.
Balance Sheet
as of June 30, 2007

	June 30, 2007 (unaudited)	June 30, 2006 (audited)	June 30, 2005 (audited)
Cash	$ 78	$ 1,247	$ 902
Accounts Receivable (net)	7,968	9,060	5,168
Real Estate Under Development	34,538	26,359	23,346
Real Estate Held for Investment	6,538	5,524	5,744
Income-Producing Property	27,381	13,241	11,045
Property and Equipment (net)	10,977	9,077	9,357
Deferred Charges	4,033	3,429	3,506
Total Assets	$91,513	$67,937	$59,068
Accounts Payable	$ 9,957	$ 7,881	$ 7,098
Amounts Owed Under Lines of Credit	24,653	20,396	15,455
Mortgage Payable	40,088	18,717	13,612
Deferred Income Taxes	2,866	1,947	1,780
Customer Deposits	1,077	903	1,411
Capital Stock	6,103	6,103	6,103
Retained Earnings	7,334	11,990	13,609
Treasury Stock	(565)	0	0
Total Liabilities and Equity	$91,513	$67,937	$59,068

Income Statement
for the year ended June 30, 2007

	June 30, 2007 (unaudited)	June 30, 2006 (audited)
Sales of real estate	$20,226	$26,235
Rental and other income	9,351	7,276
Total revenue	29,577	33,511
Cost of real estate sold	15,538	18,393
Operating expenses	6,045	5,852
Administrative expenses	3,004	3,270
Real estate taxes	1,452	1,256
Depreciation and amortization	3,989	3,966
Interest expense (net of capitalization)	3,705	1,893
Total expenses	33,733	34,630
Net income (loss)	(4,156)	(1,119)
Beginning retained earnings	11,990	13,609
Dividends declared	(500)	(500)
Ending retained earnings	$ 7,334	$11,990

but states that he hasn't really reviewed the system since it was first developed three years ago. Finally, he indicates that, although Jake is reasonable about fees, Jake does like to have the "top guy" available on a regular basis and doesn't like to deal with staff "flunkies" that do most of the fieldwork.

Requirements

1. Identify factors that indicate potential problems with the audit of Murphy Tymshare Inc. that would cause you to assess the overall business risk of the engagement to be higher than usual.
2. Identify factors that would offset some of the negative risk factors identified in part 1.
3. What other information would you try to obtain about the company, people, or industry before making a decision whether to accept the client? Consider the need for additional information from sources that you have already contacted as well as sources that have not yet been considered.
4. Based on the information, would you accept Murphy Tymshare as an audit client? Explain.
5. Assuming that you have decided to accept the client, what specific audit risks are of most importance to you as you begin planning the audit? For each identified risk, indicate:
    a. The accounts or area of the financial statements affected by the risk.
    b. The general audit approach that you would adopt to obtain adequate competent evidence that the accounts are not materially misstated.

Case 4–3: Appetizing Alligator Farms Inc.

Appetizing Alligator Farms Inc. (AAF) raises alligators for slaughter and sale to restaurants throughout the nation. The company is located in Homestead, Florida. The main "ranch" consists of approximately 30 acres of swampland that have been cleared of unnecessary brush and trees and divided into fenced pens of one-half acre (0.2 hectares) each. Elevated ridges of gravel and sand separate each of the pens. Each pen contains alligators that are approximately the same age and size. Each pen can accommodate up to 250 alligators, although those pens with very young animals may contain as many as 500. Alligators are periodically harvested from the pens containing mature alligators. Older alligators are also occasionally culled from the herd since their meat gets too tough to market. The alligators are slaughtered, butchered, frozen, and shipped around the country based on orders received. The farm has very little "frozen" inventory and usually only harvests the animals when orders are received.

All alligators have bands permanently attached to their tails six weeks after birth. A nine-digit number ("xxxxx-yyyy") is put on the band. The first five digits are sequentially assigned based on the order of birth. The company assigned numbers from 11247 to 11698 during 2007. The last four digits indicate the animal's birth date by month and year, for example, 0406 would indicate the animal was born in April 2006.

Your firm has been engaged to audit the financial statements of AAF as of December 31, 2007. As part of that audit, one of the audit staff has been assigned the task of observing the physical count of inventory on hand as of December 31, 2007. The staff person, Joe Canuck, has been with the firm for about six months. He was born and raised in Toronto and moved to Florida when he heard that starting salaries for auditors would allow him to live on the beach near his favorite Spring Break resort.

After observing the physical inventory, Joe prepared a memo to be included in the audit files (see Exhibit 3–1).

Requirements

1. Has Joe performed his procedures in accordance with generally accepted auditing standards? Explain.
2. How does Joe justify his conclusions about the inventory observation? Explain.
3. What potential problems can you identify that Joe may have overlooked?

141

Exhibit 3–1   Memo and Supporting Schedules

Appetizing Alligator Farms
Inventory Observation Memo
Audit Year: 12/31/07

Prepared by: Joe Canuck, 1/6/08

Reviewed by:

The process of observing the physical inventory began at 8:00 a.m. on December 30. I arrived at AAF at 7:45 a.m. and met with the farm foreman for a few minutes before the count was started. Four employees of AAF were assigned to count the animals and assist me with the inventory process. We commenced by randomly selecting one of the pens to count. The employees then used special contraptions to capture twenty of the alligators in the pen. This was a messy and arduous process because the alligators did not seem to like having their jaws pinched shut and being wrestled onto their backs. The AAF workers then read off the identifying numbers that each alligator had been given. I noted these identification numbers on the attached schedule for subsequent tracing to the summary listing of inventory. After noting the ten ID numbers, these alligators were then released.

Next, the four employees took up positions on each of the four sides of the pen. They then counted how many alligators were in each bunch. Upon completing the count they returned to my position (sitting on the fence) and compared their counts. I have entered each of their counts on a separate schedule and computed the average of the four to estimate the number of alligators in each pen.

This process was repeated for nine pens by the time we quit at 6:00 p.m. The remaining six pens were counted in the same way on the next day between 8:00 a.m. and 4:00 p.m. I also noted that four pens were empty.

Finally, it should be noted that the employees of AAF were extremely helpful to me in performing my verifications of the inventory counts. They were courteous, willing to work hard, and relieved me of the need to crawl around in the muck. They exhibited a knowledge of their operations that convince me that the final results of the inventory were reliable, adequate, accurate, and complete.

Appetizing Alligator Farms
Summary Listing of Inventory Observed
Audit Year: 12/31/07

Prepared by: Joe Canuck, 1/6/08

Reviewed by:

Item Number	ID Number Observed	Item Number	ID Number Observed
1	11431-0907	11	11278-0207
2	11315-0207	12	11394-0607
3	11432-0907	13	11346-0307
4	11462-0907	14	11333-0307
5	11422-0907	15	11446-0907
6	11254-0107	16	11312-0207
7	11412-0807	17	11294-0207
8	11349-0307	18	11415-0807
9	11402-0707	19	11265-0107
10	11389-0507	20	11375-0407

NOTE: These identification numbers were taken from pen 3. I noticed that all identification numbers observed start with 11 and end with 07. I asked the employees about this, and they indicated that the number has something to do with the date the alligator was born.

Exhibit 3–1   *(continued)*

Appetizing Alligator Farms
Count Results by Pen
Audit Year: 12/31/07

Prepared by: Joe Canuck, 1/6/08

Reviewed by:

Pen No.	CT1	CT2	CT3	CT4	AvgCT	Notes
1	425	412	365	475	419.3	Newborn gators, <3mths
2	375	390	426	455	411.5	Newborn gators, <3mths
3	200	195	215	179	197.3	Juvenile gators, <12mths
4	156	134	153	156	149.8	Ready for harvesting
5	0	0	0	0	0.0	Pen is empty
6	198	185	215	213	202.8	Juvenile gators, <12mths
7	222	256	286	247	252.8	Juvenile gators, <12mths
8	174	165	180	175	173.5	Breeding stock, female
9	0	0	0	0	0.0	Pen is empty
10	290	234	305	266	273.8	Newborn gators, <3mths
11	237	222	214	209	220.5	Juvenile gators, <12mths
12	105	111	121	96	108.3	Ready for harvesting
13	88	95	88	79	87.5	Ready for harvesting
14	175	171	183	190	179.8	Ready for harvesting
15	222	264	229	253	242.0	Juvenile gators, <12mths
16	35	35	38	37	36.3	Breeding stock, male
17	324	295	333	310	315.5	Newborn gators, <3mths
18	0	0	0	0	0.0	Pen is empty
19	486	475	444	465	467.5	Newborn gators, <3mths
20	0	0	0	0	0.0	Pen is empty

5

Understanding the Client's Industry and Business: Strategic Analysis

INTRODUCTION

In Chapter 4, we discussed procedures for determining client acceptance and preliminary planning and introduced Figure 5–1, which provides an overview of the audit process that will be followed in this text. This chapter focuses on the procedures to develop an understanding of a client's industry and business (IIa). Although a basic investigation of a client and its industry is included as part of preliminary planning, this chapter delves deeper using strategic analysis and evaluation of client business risks. This is a critical step for developing an understanding of the client and the expected financial results of the company. Although the evaluation of a client's industry and business will vary, the depth of the analysis

Figure 5–1   Overview of the Audit Process

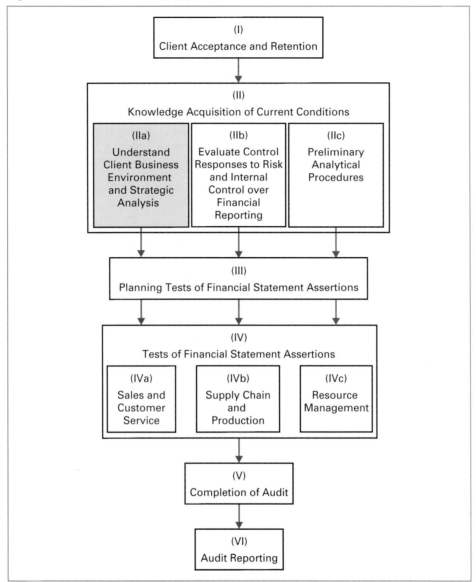

depends on the size of the organization, the complexity of its industry and business, and the heterogeneity of its business units.

This phase of the audit process is critical for most organizations since virtually all auditing and financial reporting problems that an auditor encounters have a basis in unique aspects, operations, or circumstances affecting the client. Failure to obtain an adequate understanding of the client and its business risks may cause the auditor to plan or conduct the audit in an ineffective manner, and to reach inappropriate conclusions about the financial reports being examined.

This chapter is the first of a series that will discuss techniques for acquiring knowledge of current conditions of the client and its industry. Given the complexity, globalization, technology, and speed of change in today's interconnected world

E x a m p l e

> In the late 1980s, Ernst & Young was implicated in a multimillion dollar lawsuit for its failure to understand the nature of the business of one of its clients, ZZZZ Best, in Los Angeles. The client had shifted its business from carpet cleaning to restoring damaged property. The entire business was a sham that the owner, Barry Minkow, supported using an elaborate fraud scheme. For example, he hired fake employees and rented a building that was under construction and passed it off to the auditors as a restoration project. Although Ernst & Young was able to argue fairly effectively that the elaborate collusion scheme would have fooled most auditors, it had trouble arguing that its valuations of revenue for restorations were reasonable given that the level of insurance restoration projects that ZZZZ Best claimed to have under contract exceeded the total number of available insurance restoration projects in the entire country!

of business, it is critical that an auditor develop a thorough understanding of a client's economic environment and strategic management process. Risks can arise from a multitude of sources, and success or failure depends on how the organization responds to the forces impacting its industry or business. Failure to understand the dynamic, complex environment in which a client exists could lead the auditor to develop inaccurate expectations relating to financial reporting or to misunderstand the economic reality underlying the financial statements.

The purpose of this chapter is to introduce an approach for understanding the client's business, its strategy, its position within the industry, the source of threats to its success, and resulting audit concerns. Chapter 6 focuses on internal activities and related risks. Chapter 7 introduces concepts of internal control for mitigating risk while Chapter 8 addresses internal control as it applies to financial reporting in detail. Finally, Chapter 9 introduces analytical techniques for measuring risks and assessing the significance of those risks relative to the ongoing activities and success of the organization. Throughout this discussion we emphasize how such techniques provide assurance to the auditor.

One tool that we will introduce in this chapter is the "business model." A business model of a client provides an auditor with a snapshot of the business, emphasizing how the client adds value to its economic environment, utilizes business processes to achieve its strategic objectives, and identifies and reacts to external threats to the organization. The business model also provides a structure for identifying key audit issues that will need significant attention during the audit. The overall purpose of using these models is to obtain appropriate knowledge about a client, its risks and responses, and the implications for the auditor. Upon completion of the strategic analysis, the auditor will have obtained an extensive set of evidence about the organization's current risks.

> **Authoritative Guidance & Standards**
>
> This chapter is unique in that it is not designed to help auditors meet any specific standard; rather, it is designed to help ensure that auditors place themselves in the best position to accept appropriate clients and allocate resources to conduct effective audits. However, performing strategic analyses for clients helps address the standards for understanding an entity and its environment (SAS 109, ISA 315).

KNOWLEDGE ACQUISITION FOR STRATEGIC AND PROCESS ANALYSIS

All organizations exist to create value for their stakeholders, be they customers, employees, shareholders, or managers. The ability of an organization to create and sustain its value depends on its interactions with a vast network of individuals, entities,and external forces. Every organization exists in a complex network of relationships that affect the markets in which it operates, the alternatives it might pursue, the risks it faces, and the likelihood of achieving its objectives. In order to understand the risks an organization faces, it is first important to understand the nature of this network and the way an organization creates value within the network.

Every organization has an internal environment that interfaces with the external environment that is outside of its control. The internal environment represents the activities within the organization. These activities are generally referred to as processes, and we will be discussing business processes in great detail throughout this book. Serving as a buffer or interface between the internal environment and the external environment is the company's strategic management activities. *Strategic management* comprises the activities of senior management related to developing, communicating, and revising the goals and plans of the organization. In general, strategic management reflects the decisions that an organization makes regarding how it will interact with the external environment, for example, monitoring competitors, negotiating with suppliers, targeting customers, and searching for market opportunities. In effect, strategic management reflects the overall guidance and control of the organization. Also part of strategic management are the efforts to foster desired behavior of personnel, monitor key performance measurements, and control interactions with the external environment.

The external environment consists of local and global economic links that can impact the organization. Local links may be regional or national depending on the industry. Local economic links may include dealings with utilities, employees, raw material suppliers, construction companies, facility suppliers, and taxing authorities. The global environment reflects more distant, often international, economic links. The difference between local and global environments can be blurry. In general, the local environment may be defined by physical vicinity, or may be more broadly considered to be the region in which economic forces and rules of behavior are considered to be "typical" for the enterprise. The global environment reflects the region of economic activity in which different rules, norms, culture, or approaches to business may apply.

Example

The markets for capital and technology are global. Companies may raise funds by selling stock through the New York Stock Exchange or can choose to list on markets such as London or Frankfurt. They may borrow money from money center banks based in New York, London, Tokyo, or Hong Kong. In a similar manner, technology is global because computers are universally dependent on Windows from Microsoft and the three biggest suppliers of enterprise resource planning (ERP) systems are Baan (the Netherlands), Oracle (the United States), and SAP (Germany).

All economic events occur within these environments, but the pattern of economic activity for many organizations is changing rapidly as new technology and business models are developed. Labor has historically been a part of the local environment; witness the historical "company" towns that sprang up near mines, factories, and agricultural areas. With advances in technology, it has becoming easier for employees to telecommute or work in an interconnected "virtual" office. This means that a company's workforce could be anywhere in the world. The cleaning staff may need to be local, but much of the intellectual capital that generates the primary value of an organization may be widely dispersed. For example, many software companies use programmers located around the world, each of whom works in his or her own time zone and forwards the code he or she has written to other programmers at the end of the day. India is rapidly becoming an attractive location for service centers as many companies establish call centers there (facilitated by the increasing quality and declining cost of global telecommunications).

Customers are also becoming more global. Having a grocery store nearby for fresh meat and produce may be important to most people, but most consumer products can be shipped great distances. Mail order sales (such as through Sears) and telemarketing (such as for insurance policies) have existed for many years, but the Internet has created the opportunity to link thin demand across a very wide area.

Example

Business analysts have raised the question of whether companies with new business models like Amazon (or Dell Computer) will come to dominate their market niche. Amazon can capture orders over a large area for the essentially fixed cost of maintaining its web site. The cost of reaching an additional potential customer is trivial. However, other factors may work against Amazon because goods must be delivered using relatively low-tech methods and companies such as Barnes & Noble may be able to turn their physical bookstores into a source of competitive advantage. Amazon must deliver orders over long distances using a delivery service with a commensurate high cost, but, if properly planned, Barnes & Noble only needs to make local deliveries by utilizing its existing network of stores. If Barnes & Noble stores are obsolete, what should auditors do about their reported asset values? If Amazon's business model is not competitive (it did not generate a profit prior to 2003), what should auditors be telling investors who bid the company's shares to unheard of levels in 2000 only to see it crash in 2001-2002? In the mean time, neither Amazon nor Barnes & Noble have stood still: Amazon has attempted to leverage its technological advantages across many product categories, partnering with other brick-and-mortar companies (such as HMV, Virgin, Target, Toys R Us). Meanwhile, Barnes & Noble formed its own e-commerce business.

To fully understand a client's industry and business, it is useful to take a top-down view that helps the auditor to understand how an organization creates value and the nature of the risks that the organization faces. This top-down perspective is reflected in Figure 5–2, which illustrates the approach that we will adopt in this book. We will start with a very broad perspective of an organization and the risks that it faces and filter the analysis down to a few residual risks that are considered significant to the audit. The acquisition of knowledge about a client has three broad phases: (1) strategic analysis with a focus on external concerns, (2) process analysis with a focus on internal concerns, and (3) audit analysis which links client business risks to the objectives of the audit. The latter step is critical because it provides the basis for assessing the risk of material misstatement and planning the testing of management assertions.

Figure 5–2   A Top-Down Perspective for Understanding a Client's Business

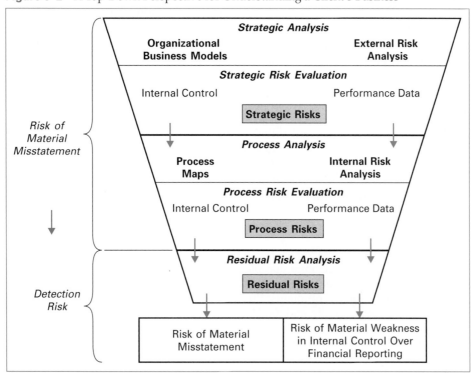

STRATEGIC RISK ANALYSIS

The first component of Figure 5–2 is strategic analysis, which helps the auditor identify the position of the organization relative to external agents and stakeholders. We will use a tool referred to as an *Organizational Business Model* to capture our factual understanding of the strategic conditions of the organization. Strategic analysis helps the auditor to identify the threats to the organization's success that emanate from the external environment. Many, if not all, of these risks will have an impact on the way the auditor conducts the engagement. We use a technique referred to as *external risk analysis* to identify and categorize external risks. We will refer to *client business risk* as any external (strategic) or internal (process) threat that could affect the ability of an organization to achieve its objectives. Once strategic risks are identified, we further evaluate those risks by considering management's efforts to mitigate these risks through the use of controls and business processes.

PROCESS RISK ANALYSIS

The second level of analysis in Figure 5–2 involves the examination of internal processes, which represent the allocation of resources (such as personnel, capital, technology) used by the organization to conduct its business. Business processes represent the internal efforts of the organization to advance its goals and respond to strategic risks. We will use a *process map* to capture information about the operations and information flows of internal business processes. Processes are also a potential source of internal risk. *Internal risk analysis* will facilitate the identification and categorization of process risks. Once process risks have been identified, the auditor can then evaluate the risks by considering mitigating internal controls and quantifying the extent of the risks. Of particular interest to the auditor is the risk of a material misstatement occurring in a process and the related internal controls over financial reporting designed to minimize such risks.

RESIDUAL RISK ANALYSIS

The final step of our analysis of current conditions is to assess the nature of residual risks that pose a significant threat to the organization. Not all risks represent immediate problems—either because they are adequately controlled and mitigated or conditions are not currently conducive for the risk to cause damage to the organization. A *residual risk* is a strategic or process risk that is either uncontrolled by the organization or exhibits quantifiable warning signals that the risk is an imminent problem.

Example

A sudden increase in customer complaints may indicate that product quality has deteriorated, even though the production process has not changed and there are no internal indications of problems. Such a signal may indicate a residual risk that needs consideration by the auditor. Why? It may indicate an inventory valuation issue or that allowances for sales returns may not follow historic patterns—both of which might have material effects on the financial statements if realized.

Auditors are concerned with residual business risks because they represent the most likely source of problems for the company and the most likely source of problems for the conduct of the audit. Significant residual risks reflect conditions where the auditor will need to focus more attention in the audit. When an organization is effectively managed and highly controlled, it is less likely to exhibit the types of problems that result in audit problems, such as misstated financial reports, fraud, or bankruptcy. Under these circumstances, an auditor is justified in using less extensive audit procedures for areas where there are no significant residual risks, or using focused tests in areas where residual risks are localized. However, low residual business risk does not automatically translate into a low risk of material misstatement across all accounts and disclosures because management incentives or unreliable accounting systems may still result in errors or fraudulent financial reporting.

UNDERSTANDING A CLIENT'S OBJECTIVES AND STRATEGIES TO ACHIEVE OBJECTIVES

ANALYZE THE ORGANIZATION'S STRATEGIC PLAN

One very important question that an auditor should address early in the audit is the nature of the organization's overall objectives, strategies for achieving those objectives, and its source of sustainable competitive advantage. Every organization has a strategy for attaining its objectives, although the strategy may not always be formally stated. The better an organization understands and articulates its objectives and strategies, the more likely it is to be successful. An organization that lacks a coherent strategic management process is less likely to be successful in the long run.

A company has two basic strategic positioning decisions to make: (1) Does it want its products to be low cost or highly differentiated and (2) does it want its products to appeal to a broad or narrow group of consumers? These two considerations define four basic positioning strategies for any company:

> **Authoritative Guidance & Standards**
>
> SAS 109 and ISA 315 require auditors to understand objectives and strategies and the business risks that may result in a misstatement of the financial statements.

1. Low Cost Strategy: This business strategy focuses on producing at the lowest possible price for a large market. The product or service will be mass-produced with few special features ("no frills"). Demand for the product is likely to be price sensitive.[1] Success often depends on efficient production and generating economies of scale where unit costs are reduced as production increases. Distribution costs need to be tightly managed and there will be minimal advertising or R&D.

Example

Wal-Mart's strategy is to be the lowest cost, broad market retailer in every market in which it competes. The company achieves its cost advantage with tight cost controls, superior inventory selection and management, and world-class distribution. Although companies such as Zellers in Canada and K-Mart in the United States have attempted the same strategy, they have not been able to keep pace with Wal-Mart and have suffered serious setback (bankruptcy, in the case of K-Mart).

2. Low-Cost Niche Strategy: This business strategy focuses on being a low-cost producer but for a product that has a small market. Many of these companies are small and have limited opportunities to develop brand recognition.
3. Differentiation Strategy: This business strategy focuses on producing unique or high quality products for different segments of a broad market. Competition tends to focus on quality and product features. Price is usually not a primary factor to the company's target market. Differentiation can also be achieved through superior customer service, flexible delivery, and extensive warranties. Research and innovation is often important for staying ahead of the competition.

Example

Holt Renfrew in Canada and Nordstrom in the United States are retailers that provide unparalleled customer service while charging a premium price. The companies are legendary for the lengths their employees will go to meet the desires of customers. Such service comes at a higher cost than many comparable retailers but also generates superior margins.

4. Differentiation Niche Strategy: This business strategy focuses on producing unique products but for small markets. While many of these organizations are small, as in the case of low-cost niche, some companies develop well-known brands because of the exclusivity of what are often high-priced products.

---

1 Economists use the term *price elasticity* to describe how price sensitive a product is. *Elastic* demand suggests that consumers are price sensitive; *inelastic* demand suggests customers do not care very much about price. Obviously, the more elastic demand is, the less ability a company has to raise prices without losing significant revenue.

Example

Aston Martin, now part of Ford Motor Company, continues to produce a small number of vehicles each year in its plant located in England.

A company could also choose a Low Cost–Differentiation strategy, essentially a hybrid approach in which the company tries to minimize costs while serving separate market niches. This strategy is probably the most challenging for most organizations to adopt. If such a strategy is successful, the company may become dominant in the market (at least for awhile).

Example

Amazon.com developed its business model by using the Internet to become a low-cost provider to different market niches. Its rapid growth in the late 1990s and early 2000s was driven by continually adding niches (or forming alliances) in which its distribution technology could be utilized to become a low-cost provider of retail products across different retail niches such as books, music, toys, and electronics.

THE IMPACT OF STRATEGIC POSITIONING DECISIONS

A company's strategic decisions will have a direct affect on the characteristics of the organization. Decisions about markets to enter, products to produce, technology to develop, operating processes to implement, and resources needed are all affected by the basic strategic choices made by the organization. A major challenge for management is to develop business processes that are consistent with the strategy and that effectively advance the organization's goals. Some examples of how internal processes may be affected by strategic decisions are presented in Figure 5–3. An allocation of personnel and resources that is inconsistent with overall objectives or strategies employed is unlikely to lead to success.

The activities, risks, and, thus, financial statements associated with different strategic choices will be quite different. Management in the low-cost company will focus on making processes more efficient whereas management in a differentiated company will search for new and better ways to provide value to the customer. More specifically, a low-cost strategy suggests that operations are critical because the control of costs is vital to the organization's success. Under a differentiation strategy, however, cost of production is less significant and the ability to create innovative new products and features is critical, suggesting that the product development process is crucial. As we will see, these differences would lead the auditor to focus on different aspects of these organizations.

To illustrate, consider the impact of strategy on human resources. A low-cost producer will encounter competitive problems if labor costs increase. Therefore, the critical challenge for a low cost company is to keep the cost of human resources as low as possible. This may be accomplished by outsourcing activities, substituting technology for labor, simplifying tasks so that unskilled labor can be used, and minimizing benefits through the use of non-union, seasonal, or temporary employees. In contrast, the company with a differentiated product may be more at risk if it is unable to meet its unique labor needs. In that case, the cost of labor and benefits is less critical than making sure that adequate human capital and talent is

Figure 5–3   The Impact of Strategic Positioning on Selected Internal Processes

Operational Area	Low Cost Strategy	Differentiation Strategy
Acquisition of Materials	• Resources acquired at the lowest possible cost • Order large quantities to obtain volume discounts • Purchases may be delayed until desired prices can be achieved. • Maximize the efficiency of distribution and storage	• Purchase the best quality materials, at higher cost if necessary • Storage and distribution designed to maintain quality of materials and products regardless of incremental cost
Production	• Emphasis on achieving operating efficiencies • Strive for economies of scale • Optimize labor/capital trade-offs	• Emphasize product quality, even at the cost of high rates of wastage, rejects, and rework
New Product Development	• Research and development to focus on process efficiency • Little effort at product innovation	• Continual research to develop better products with more features
Human Resources	• Minimize costs by avoiding unions, using temporary employees, structuring tasks for unskilled labor • Outsource less critical tasks • Tightly control benefits	• Hire the best employees given the quality demands of the organization • Superior pay scales and benefits
Information Technology	• Information system used to minimize costs	• Information system used to maximize revenue by identifying market opportunities
Branding and Marketing	• Minimal or low-cost mass advertising and promotions	• Extensive, focused, and expensive advertising

available. Given the difference of the two strategies, the auditor would expect that processes dealing with recruiting, compensating, and training employees would be quite different, suggesting different risks and different audit issues. Furthermore, the financial measures related to labor costs should appear quite different for the two strategies.

EVALUATING STRATEGIC POSITIONING

Auditors should evaluate the risks associated with an organization's strategic positioning. In general, auditors look for evidence that managers have made bad or uninformed decisions, misused or misallocated resources, or poorly communicated or utilized information, which can all reduce the likelihood that the organization will succeed in the long term. A long-term lack of success will ultimately be reflected in a loss of shareholder value. Regardless of the strategic position adopted, each of the options available to an organization has potential risks. Some

Figure 5–4   Risks Associated with Strategic Positioning Choices

Risks of Adopting a Cost Leadership Position	Risks of Adopting a Differentiation Position	Risks of Adopting a Broad or Narrow Market Focus
Cost leadership may not be sustainable due to • Imitation by competitors • Changes in technology that allow competitors to reduce costs	Differentiation may not be sustainable due to • Imitation by competitors • Changing customer tastes that put less value on the attributes of differentiation	The target market becomes unattractive due to • Imitation by competitors • A target segment that shrinks or is too small to be feasible
Customers demand more features while expecting low prices.	The cost of providing differentiated features exceeds the price point customers are willing to pay, effectively limiting the extent of differentiation that can be offered.	Competitors with a broad market focus threaten a narrow market because • The differences between segments narrow or disappear • The quality/performance of broad market products and services improve.
Multiple competitors approach the limits of cost minimization, leaving no room for a broad cost leader	Differentiation becomes segment-specific, leaving no room for a broad differentiator	Narrow markets are segmented into even smaller markets by competitors who have an advantage in the smaller segments

of these risks are described in Figure 5–4. These risks will be heightened when the strategic management of an organization is weak.

An auditor will evaluate the quality of a company's strategic choices because they may indicate potential problems the company faces that will affect the financial statements now or in the future. Potential indications of weak strategic management include

- Poor strategic choices or design of overall strategy
- Management's failure to articulate strategy so as to align the goals and activities of various segments of the organization
- Failure to identify and act on potential market opportunities
- Failure to anticipate and react to potential threats
- Poor execution of strategy
- Inflexibility and lack of organizational nimbleness in dealing with diverse objectives and activities
- Inadequate planning for carrying out strategic decisions
- Inadequate resources to carry out strategic plans or mismatching resources and objectives

A great deal of information is needed to support the types of decisions that are made as part of strategic management. Unreliable or unavailable information can cause significant problems in strategic management, especially if poor information leads to missed opportunities, unidentified threats, and poor coordination.

THE IMPACT OF STRATEGIC POSITIONING ON FINANCIAL STATEMENTS AND THE AUDIT

With regard to accounting and the financial statements, the auditor will need to consider the organization's life cycle and strategic decisions when planning and conducting the audit. As a general rule, organizations in the growth or decline phase of their life cycle tend to have more challenging business risks and also create comparable challenges for the auditor. For example, a rapidly growing company will strain the capacity of its systems, increasing the likelihood of problems within the organization, whereas a declining company might incur impairments to underutilized assets that were heavily used during the mature phase of a company's life cycle.

Example

Virtek Vision, a precision laser company based in Waterloo, Ontario, Canada expanded rapidly in the late 1990s, going from being a focused niche supplier of laser marking systems for the manufactured-home industry to being a laser driven company with products in the aviation and biotechnology industry (in addition to its traditional business). During this transformation, it increased its employee base by 200 percent and severely strained its management systems. In 2004, it shed the biotechnology division and downsized its workforce substantially (including terminating both the president and the chief financial officer). Its stock peaked at $7.50 in 2001 and recently was trading at $0.90.

Strategic positioning decisions (such as low cost or differentiation) related to the various resources and processes of the company will also have a direct impact on the audit. For example, a manufacturer adopting a differentiation strategy is likely to have more expensive inventory, larger margins, greater costs of spoilage, more expensive equipment to be amortized, greater rates of quality rejects, and more comprehensive warranties—all of which will affect the results reported in the financial statements. These differences will also influence the client's business risk. Furthermore, the strategic differences need to be considered by the auditor when making decisions about how to conduct the audit. Weak strategic management and questionable strategic decisions will ultimately have an impact on reported financial results and may affect the risk of material misstatements in the financial statements.

Example

Many retailers offer in-house credit cards to customers (such as Target and Futureshop). Customers who would normally use Visa or MasterCard are encouraged to sign up for the store card by the offer of a one-time discount on merchandise. On one hand, if the retailer can get customers to use the store credit card, the retailer saves the fees that would be paid to other credit card companies, and may also generate incremental interest income on customers' unpaid balances. On the other hand, the company is also accepting a certain amount of credit risk for delinquent customers. In planning the engagement of a retailer with its own credit card operations, the auditor would need to evaluate the process of issuing credit cards, recording and accruing interest income and recognizing bad debts. Another strategy for a retailer is to form an alliance with Visa or MasterCard in which customers earn rewards by using the company's exclusive version of the card (an example is Starbucks' Visa Duetto card, which earns customers 1 percent in-store credit). The company avoids the financial risks associated with the card but encourages repeat customers and enhances its brand name.

ORGANIZATIONAL BUSINESS MODELS

The manifestation of a company's strategic decisions is evident in the various interactions it has with external parties such as suppliers, customers, employees, and banks. Consequently, to further evaluate the business risks that the company faces, the auditor identifies and describes the key external links between the company and other companies, individuals, entities, and organizations. This factual description of the company's environment can be organized into an *Organizational Business Model*.

Authoritative Guidance & Standards
SAS 109 and ISA 315 require auditors to understand the nature of the entity, including (as described in the standards' appendices) the nature of revenue sources; products or services and markets; conduct of operations; alliances; suppliers of goods, services, and labor; and industry, regulations, and other external factors.

COMPONENTS OF THE ORGANIZATIONAL BUSINESS MODEL

The components of an Organizational Business Model are depicted in Figure 5–5, which reflects the basic approach we will take for analyzing the strategic environment of a client. There are six basic components which will be discussed in detail in the following sections:

- Markets, customers, and products
- Competitors
- Resources and suppliers
- Internal processes
- External agents
- Strategic partners

Figure 5–5   An Organizational Business Model

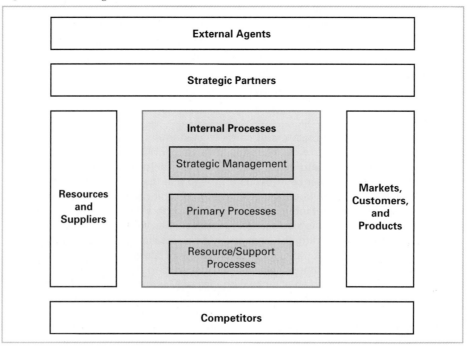

Markets, Customers, and Products

All businesses are formed to market specific products (or services) to targeted customers. Markets represent the discernible economic segments in which an organization chooses to compete. They can be defined by geographic region, nature of product, or level of service provided. Each market includes a targeted set of potential customers. Customers may be undifferentiated or identified by individual traits (such as wealth, level of education, and other demographics). Products (or services) are the source of revenues and represent the source of exchange transactions between customers and the company. The number of markets, products (or services), and customers making up the different business lines of an organization are a key source of complexity in a business model.

Competitors

An external organization that is targeting a similar set of markets, customers, and products is a direct competitor. Such competitors are usually easy to identify and often involve head-to-head competition in the form of price, quality, or service. Obviously, Pepsi/Coke, Qantas/Singapore Air, Cadbury/Nestlé, Philips/Sony, and BMW/Toyota represent direct competitors. Competition may also be indirect in that relevant competitors that appear to be in different industries are often chasing the same customer resources (usually time and money, often described as "wallet share"). For example, movie theaters compete with video rentals, satellite television, and cable television because these activities may be considered substitutes. Stretching the analysis further, movie theaters are also competitors with bookstores, fitness clubs, professional sports, and live performing arts because many of the same potential consumers have limited time and budget for "leisure" activities.

Resources and Suppliers

Every organization needs resources to advance its objectives. Obvious resources include tangible assets such as facilities and inventory. However, resources of many types can affect the organization. Labor, capital, and technology are all important to an organization and each is obtained from a different set of suppliers, involves different processes within an organization, and generates a different set of risks.

Internal Processes

Resources within an organization are allocated to business processes that perform important tasks and activities to achieve corporate objectives and minimize strategic risks. We will consider three types of internal processes in our discussions: (1) strategic management, (2) primary processes, and (3) support processes. *Strategic management* involves setting the direction of the organization; making key decisions about products, markets, and internal activities; monitoring the external environment for threats; reacting to performance results; instilling management controls to dictate behaviors; and guiding continuous improvement. *Primary processes* are the set of activities that are most directly associated with the creation of value within the organization. Manufacturing, marketing, and delivering a product or service are common examples of primary processes, although activities like research and development and customer service can also be part of the primary processes if they lead directly to the creation of customer value. *Support processes* reflect activities that have an indirect relationship to the creation of value within the organization. For example, quality inspection, procurement, and accounting are often considered support processes because their execution does not immediately create value. However, few organizations could succeed without effective and efficient support processes.

External Agents

Various influences outside an organization have a direct impact on its ability to succeed even though they do not have direct economic links or dealings with the organization. For example, the government is responsible for regulation and taxation. Lifestyle trends and other seasonal factors might influence demand. Financial analysts may closely follow the performance of the organization. Local communities care about how the organization affects the environment. Media may draw attention to business practices that are controversial (such as animal testing in the cosmetics industry or price gouging in the used car business). The economy as a whole may impact the expectations and behavior of customers and consumers. To the extent external forces have an impact on the organization, they should be considered part of the economic network even though the linkages may be indirect and subtle. Effective enterprise risk management necessitates that management monitor these external forces and evaluate how they affect the ability of the organization to achieve its objectives.

Strategic Partners

Strategic partners are the final element of the organizational business model. Strategic partners represent external entities with which the company has a formal relationship in order to advance joint objectives. Although the partners are independent and may represent potential adversaries, they agree to work together in order to obtain mutually beneficial results or to reduce the threat from a shared risk. Industry competitors often work together to lobby for or against specific laws and regulations (banks are a good example). Other organizations may undertake shared marketing efforts (Disney and McDonald's are particularly effective at this). Some strategic partnerships are established to extend products and services to markets that would otherwise be inaccessible to the partners on their own (for example, airlines frequently establish such partnerships to provide global routing for their passengers). Finally, elements of the supply chain of an organization can work together to better coordinate the ordering and movement of materials. A key identifying characteristic of a strategic partner is the interconnectedness of organizations such that if one is successful, the other is successful. Accordingly, auditors should pay careful attention to the process for selecting, monitoring, and terminating strategic partner relationships.

Example

With current technology, it is common for customers and suppliers to link computer systems. For example, most car manufacturers have sophisticated systems that allow parts suppliers to monitor production and inventory levels at the manufacturer. This process helps the parts supplier deliver materials on a just-in-time basis. Both the supplier and the manufacturer benefit from lower levels of inventory, more predictable flows of material, and reduced transaction processing costs. Such links may also create potential risks, however, since computer linkages (referred to as an electronic data interface, or EDI) are expensive, difficult to establish, and tend to be exclusive. If a supplier has a work stoppage, the manufacturer may not be able to obtain an alternative supply for a reasonable cost or within a reasonable time. From an auditor's perspective, the presence of such linkages has a direct impact on shared risks as well as inventory levels, costs, and margins.

ANALYZING THE ORGANIZATIONAL BUSINESS MODEL

The term *value* in a business model refers to the results of an organization's efforts that are considered to be of benefit to its customers. The more value that an organization creates, the more revenue it can command from the market and, all other things being equal, the more likely the organization is to achieve its business objectives. It is important that the auditor understand why the organization does (or does not) have a competitive advantage for producing value. The organizational business model facilitates analyzing the links among the economic parties that are relevant to a client. There are three primary reasons why some links may be critical:

- They directly relate to core competencies of the organization.
- They represent unfulfilled opportunities.
- They represent critical vulnerabilities.

Links to Core Competencies

Economic links between the organization and outsiders that have a direct impact on its core processes and value proposition can be extremely important. In the automotive industry, parts suppliers have evolved to providing full-scale components such as seat or dashboard assemblies. The supply of these components, and their quality, is critical to the core manufacturing activity of the company.

Example

Many pharmaceutical companies establish partnerships with small research and biotech companies for the purpose of jointly developing and testing new drugs. Such relationships are critical to the pharmaceutical company's core competencies. Because new drugs are subject to extensive regulation, the links to external agents responsible for drug approval are also extremely important to the small research and biotech companies; hence, the motivation for partnership exists on both sides based on each company's core competency.

Links of Opportunity

Some economic links may represent potential opportunities that have not yet been fully developed. Organizations scan their environment to identify opportunities for new markets, cost savings, increased revenues, and new products. For example, a Canadian oil company could join with a local company to develop energy resources in a country where foreign investment is limited by law. The ability to identify and develop these links can be very important for an organization's success.

Example

The introduction of frequent flyer programs by airlines helped them to increase the switching costs of passengers so as to make it easier to extract incremental revenue from existing customers. If successful, this strategy would have allowed the airlines to increase prices. There appears to be mixed results associated with this strategy. Airline customer loyalty has increased, yet airlines have not performed well overall. Airlines now owe more free flights to frequent fliers than they have available seats!

Links with Significant Vulnerabilities

Some economic links may represent particularly vulnerable sources of risk. Competitors are an important source of risk. A competitor who decreases price or improves the value of its products can cause significant harm to an organization.

For example, Dell, Gateway, and IBM waged a continuous battle to win customers by reducing prices and improving features of their machines. This battle contributed to IBM's decision to sell its personal computer operations to China's Lesovo in late 2004. Strategic partners can also be a sensitive source of risks. For example, airlines may form an alliance to improve their route coverage but such arrangements also make the airline vulnerable to problems experienced by its partners, such as lost luggage or a poor safety record.

The relationship among suppliers, competitors, and customers is particularly interesting because of the complex ways in which organizations can be integrated across markets. In the past, such integration was usually achieved through ownership interests. Increasingly, integration is being achieved through strategic partnerships and the use of technology. There are four types of integration that can be encountered relative to an organization's market position:

- Integrated supplier and competitor: This type of organization supplies *and* competes with the client organization. For example, Sobeys in Canada has supermarkets under various brand names (such as IGA and Sobeys) but also supplies independent food stores through its wholesale operations.
- Integrated competitor and customer: This type of organization competes with *and* buys from the client organization. Sky Chefs is a subsidiary of Germany's Lufthansa airlines and supplies about a third of the food served on planes around the world. Consequently, an airline may be a competitor of Lufthansa while also purchasing food service from Sky Chefs.
- Integrated supplier and customer: This type of organization supplies *and* buys from the client organization. For example, Electronic Arts manufactures game cartridges for use in Nintendo game machines. Therefore, Electronic Arts can be considered a supplier of Nintendo. However, Electronic Arts is also a customer because it must license its game technology from Nintendo.
- Integrated supplier, competitor, and customer: This situation reflects full vertical integration. For example, car manufacturers make components used in upstream manufacturing as well as separately sold in the after market, produce final consumer products, and provide after-market service. In this type of a situation, the fully integrated manufacturer may be someone else's supplier, competitor, and customer, all at the same time.

An Example of an Organizational Business Model

A simplified example of an organizational business model for a publishing company is presented in Figure 5–6. Although a publisher will have many direct competitors, indirect competition can have a significant impact on the likelihood of an organization achieving its goals. An important external element is the media, which can push or pan a book and have a significant impact on the title's sales (consider, for example, the impact of Oprah's book club). The most significant strategic partners are authors, who can also be considered suppliers, and bookstores (and book clubs), which can also be considered customers. Obviously, the absence of respected, successful authors or lack of promotion of titles by bookstores will have an adverse effect on a publisher. In fact, author development and marketing are probably the most critical internal processes. Relationships with printers and successful authors are probably the most critical supplier links.

By identifying the key market participants and their relationship to the client, the auditor is able to make a first step toward understanding the source and nature

Figure 5–6   Organizational Business Model for Publishing Company

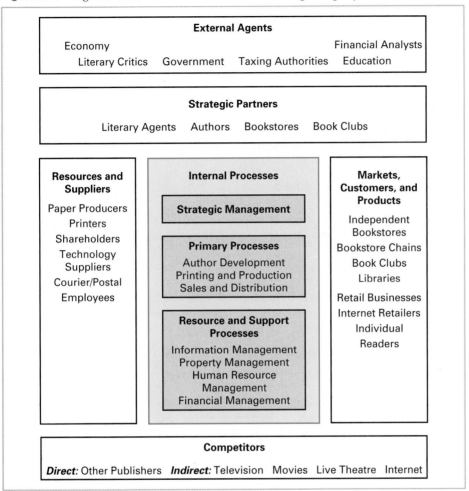

of potential risks affecting the organization and the audit of the financial statements. Much of the information and transaction flows within an organization involve one or more of the elements depicted in the organizational business model. For example, sales, receivables, cost of goods sold, inventory, cash collections, and bad debts involve transactions with customers, whereas fixed assets, accounts payable, accrued liabilities, and expenses involve transactions with suppliers. Continuing with the publishing example, a number of transactions that might be of interest to the auditor can be identified:

- *Transactions with printers:* The nature of long-term printing contracts creates risks related to quality, timeliness, and confidentiality. The auditor may need to analyze the exposure to potential losses on long-term purchase commitments and related disclosures. This analysis requires an understanding of the reasons for the relationship, the relative power of the parties, and the terms of the contract.
- *Sales arrangements with bookstores:* Bookstores typically have the right to return unsold books, which can create potential problems of revenue recognition.

- *Contracts with authors:* Contracts with authors need to be examined to determine the proper recognition of unpaid royalties. Calculation of royalties is complicated by the right of return that bookstores can exercise long after the end of a fiscal period. Furthermore, the process of negotiating author contracts raises risks of overpaying or missing out on the next Stephen King. Large author advances need to be analyzed for recoverability.

Although accounting issues are always important to the auditor, the impact of strategic risks may be much more pervasive and important to the auditor than a narrow consideration of accounting issues admits. We now turn to techniques for analyzing strategic risks in this broader context.

ANALYZING STRATEGIC RISKS

The next step in the process of understanding a client's business is to perform *external risk analysis*. This involves identifying and assessing the possible threats to success that confront an organization. Potential risks are typically classified as coming from industry or macroenvironmental forces. Industry forces include suppliers, customers, competitors, substitutes, and new entrants (also known as Porter's Five Forces).[2] Macroenvironmental forces include political, economic, social, and technological pressures (also known as PEST factors). Figure 5–7 depicts a generic structure for performing risk analysis.

Figure 5–7   External Threats to Business Organizations

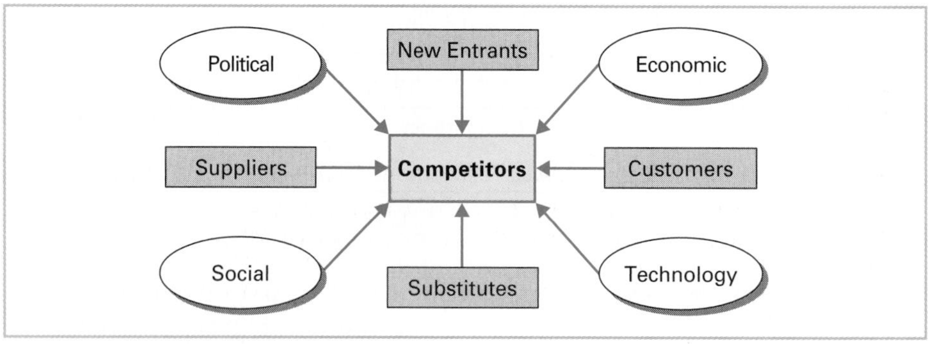

MACROENVIRONMENTAL FORCES (PEST FACTORS)

Macroenvironmental forces will rarely have a direct economic link to the organization but, nevertheless, can present a serious threat since they have a direct effect on the environment in which the company must operate.

Political-Legal

Political threats arise from regulatory or legal constraints on an organization. Employment, worker safety, anti-discrimination, and environmental laws can all have a significant impact on an organization. Compliance with laws may be complex and expensive, but noncompliance may be even more costly to an organization.

2 M. Porter. *Competitive Strategy*. New York, Free Press. 1980.

Many laws and regulations are industry-specific and compliance may be quite challenging when an organization has international activities. Political threats can lead to behaviors by organizations that might be counterintuitive. For example, antitrust concerns may make an industry leader hesitant to merge or acquire a competitor, even though the combination would increase shareholder value. See Figure 5–8 for more examples of the issues an auditor might consider related to political and legal risk (as well as the other categories of risk).

Example

Many countries have trade barriers related to agricultural products. When a potato fungus infected potatoes from a Canadian agricultural company, the United States refused to admit *any* Canadian potatoes until it was shown that the disease was limited to the single company. Similarly, when "mad cow" disease afflicted cattle in the United Kingdom, other countries refused to admit beef shipments from British farmers, many of whom were driven to the verge of bankruptcy.

Example

In early 2005, consumer products conglomerate Procter & Gamble acquired Gillette to create the world's largest company of consumer brands. The acquisition was viewed by most analysts as a good move, particularly when considering the pressures being placed on these manufacturers by customers such as Wal-Mart. However, the deal was heavily scrutinized for antitrust concerns prior to approval and likely resulted in additional political scrutiny for the organization in the future.

Economic

Economic threats relate to general or regional trends in economic conditions that can have an adverse affect on an organization. Risks can arise from a change in interest rates, unemployment, energy prices, inflation, foreign currency fluctuations, and the general economic cycle. Industries such as banking, real estate, and automobiles are sensitive to small increases in interest rates that affect consumer spending. The Canadian economy is particularly vulnerable to changes in the U.S. economy (as evidenced by the old saying "when the U.S. economy sneezes, Canada's economy catches a cold"). As much of what Canada produces is exported, changes in foreign exchange rates are critical for many Canadian industries. Low unemployment makes it harder for an organization to find adequate labor resources, possibly resulting in upward pressure on wages. The cost of energy tends to affect virtually all organizations in some way.

Example

Fast food franchises are often dependent on a ready supply of unskilled, minimum wage labor. When overall unemployment is low, individuals are able to choose from multiple job offers. Working as a fry cook in a burger stand may not seem attractive under such conditions and restaurants may suffer shortages of personnel.

Social

There are a multitude of cultural attitudes, opinions, lifestyles, and social pressures that can have an impact on an organization. For example, protests at the 2001

Figure 5–8   Potential Indicators of External Threats to a Business Organization

Category of Risk	Potential Indicators of Risk
Competition	Does a competitor have a superior product or service? Does a competitor have a cost advantage? Does a competitor have superior brand identification? Does a competitor possess proprietary technology? Does a competitor have favorable access to resources? Does a competitor have a legal or regulatory advantage? Are switching costs low? Does a competitor get preferential treatment in distribution channels? Are competitors nimble and flexible? Can competitors adjust volume levels easily? Can competitors get new products and services to market quickly? Does a competitor have other advantages?
Suppliers	Are inputs differentiated? Do suppliers have significant bargaining power? Are inputs subject to disruption? Are there few potential suppliers? Are inputs of adequate quality? Can inputs be substituted? Is the input a specialized market niche for the supplier? Are switching costs high? Can suppliers integrate downstream? Is the transaction volume significant to the supplier? Does the input influence the differentiability of resulting products and services? Is adequate skilled labor available at a reasonable cost? Is adequate capital available at a reasonable cost?
Customers	Do buyers have significant bargaining power? Do buyers have low switching costs? Do buyers have superior market information? Are transaction costs for buyers low? Is the buyer dependent on the product or service? Do buyers need customized products or services? Are buyers sensitive to pressure from their customers? Can buyers integrate upstream? Are buyers price sensitive? Are buyers brand or fad conscience? Are buyer profits too low to sustain their activities? Are buyers open to substitution of products and services?
New Entrants or Substitutes	Are there low barriers to entry? Are switching costs low? Does inadequate capacity currently exist? Are current profit levels likely to attract new entrants? Is the market susceptible to fragmentation? Do potential entrants have superior technology? Do potential entrants have a cost advantage? Are new entrants nimble and flexible?

Figure 5–8   *(continued)*

Category of Risk	Potential Indicators of Risk
Economic	Is the organization susceptible to general economic conditions? Is the organization affected by changes in the money supply and inflation? Is the organization affected by changes in the labor pool and levels of unemployment? Is the organization susceptible to changes in energy costs? How is the organization affected by the economic cycle? Is the organization affected by changes in commodity markets? Is the organization affected by changes in capital markets?
Political	How susceptible is the organization to changes in tax laws or tax jurisdictions? Is the organization affected by international trade regulations? Is the organization affected by domestic regulations, including labor laws, consumer protection, lending rules, or environmental regulation? Is the industry a target for antitrust attention? Is the industry subject to wage or price controls? Does the organization or industry receive favorable regulatory treatment?
Technological	Is the organization dependent on current scientific advancement? Are technology advantages subject to protection from competition? How rapidly is key technology changing? What is the rate of new product introductions? What is the level of automation and prospects for future change? What is the appropriate level of R&D relative to current activity?
Social	Is the organization dependent on the supply of educated and trained skilled labor? Is the organization of interest to non-government organizations? Does the industry have a negative reputation? Is the industry affected by changes in life styles? Do workplace expectations affect labor relations? How do demographic changes affect the organization?

Free Trade of the Americas Summit meeting in Quebec City reflected worldwide differences in attitudes towards environmental concerns, treatment of workers, and human rights. Employee attitudes towards overtime, customers' attitudes towards specific products (such as tobacco), population shifts and demographics, levels of education, and quality of life concerns can all create problems for an organization. For example, General Motors chose to build its Saturn plant in

Tennessee because the employees, although members of the United Auto Workers union, are considerably less militant than workers in other areas of the country. Social problems are complicated when the organization's activities are international. Fur coats may be perfectly acceptable in European countries, but wearing such a coat in some parts of Canada or the United States risks a confrontation with animal rights advocates. Large multinational corporations often face pressure to acknowledge their responsibilities to key societal stakeholders, such as local communities, employees, and environmental concerns.

Example

Attitudes towards employee rights can be particularly tricky for an organization. Americans are accustomed to working overtime and on weekends, whereas Europeans typically work less overtime. In many countries (such as Sweden), employees expect high levels of benefits and management consideration that are less prevalent in the United States (such as in-house day care, vacations, maternity leave, and cafeterias). Canadians have almost double the number of long weekends each year compared to Americans, and have, on average, a week more of paid vacation. A company that wishes to open a factory in another country needs to be very careful to consider local employment practices in the planning of the facility.

Technological

Risk arising from technology typically relates to the rate of innovation in an industry and the risk of being stuck with the wrong or insufficient technology. Technology can affect many facets of an organization, including the manner in which it conducts its basic operations, processes information, markets its products, designs its manufacturing processes, and develops new products. Technology can be used as a source of competitive cost advantage within the manufacturing process.

Example

When Daimler-Chrysler established its plant for producing its M-Class SUV in Alabama, it embedded an enterprise resource planning (ERP) system managed by IBM into its lean manufacturing process that communicates to all of its subassembly suppliers when a car has left the paint process. At that point, the suppliers have approximately 180 minutes to deliver the necessary subassemblies (e.g., seats) for that specific vehicle. This process is termed by Daimler "just-in-time, in-sequence" production.

Example

In 2005, *Fortune* magazine named Internet blogs the most important technological force affecting businesses because bloggers—individuals conveying opinions about companies and the media—were using information technology to quickly spread opinions throughout the marketplace. Examples of how blogger networks may influence an organization include leaking information about new products, serving as a depository for complaints, and even providing CEO-authored blogs about company strategies and products.

INDUSTRY FORCES (PORTER'S FIVE FORCES)

Competitors

The most immediate risk to a business is the threat that competitors will erode or steal a company's market share by offering superior products, better service, or better prices. Most companies are very cognizant of what their competitors are doing, and actively plan strategies for coping with those threats. Competition can take on many forms. One common example is price competition, which may force the organization to adjust its own prices or compete in some other way. Alternatively, an organization can respond to price competition by improving warranties and customer service.

Example

Grocery chains often get into price wars over common purchases (such as bread, milk, and butter). Since much of a grocery chain's costs are fixed, grocers search for ways to reduce employee and distribution costs. Wal-Mart became the largest grocer in the United States in a short time by (1) utilizing the hypermarket format in which grocery products serve as loss leaders for higher margin products in the store and (2) leveraging its efficient distribution processes to keep costs lower than the competition.

Potential Entrants

Another threat is the possibility that new competitors will enter the market. Rapidly growing or highly profitable industries tend to quickly attract new competitors. For example, the online auctions pioneered by eBay have been quickly copied by other online retailers. The threat from potential competitors depends on the level of barriers to entry such as

- Economies of scale in production
- Loyalty to existing brands
- Costs of switching product lines
- Restricted technology and trade secrets
- Low exit barriers (it is easy to get out of a market)
- The diversity of competitors
- The relative lack of excess capacity

Example

The inventor of carry-on wheeled luggage that has a hidden, extractable pull handle enjoyed a short but highly profitable period before other imitators were able to get their own versions to market. The wheeled luggage market had low barriers to entry because the costs of switching production capacity was low for the established manufacturers who already had brand loyalty and established distribution channels. Furthermore, the wheel technology was not sufficiently unique to be legally protected from imitators. Consequently, the original inventor found margins and market share being eroded by cutthroat competition.

Substitutes

Substitute products are also a threat to many companies. Economic history is filled with stories of products that were extremely profitable in their heyday but which were eventually driven off the market due to changes in technology and the introduction of substitutes. This type of threat may be direct (such as the substitution of MP3 files for compact discs or the decline in landline telephones as the world converts to a wireless network) or due to forces affecting other markets (such as the disappearance of buggy whip manufacturers as cars replaced horse-drawn carriages). The extent to which e-commerce will replace traditional retailing is yet to be seen. Determinants of the threat from substitutes include

- The performance quality of the substitutes
- The cost of potential substitutes
- The cost to customers of switching to the substitutes
- Buyer loyalty to the original product (for example, many people use the same brand of toothpaste for almost their entire life!)

Example

SAP is one of the largest suppliers of enterprise resource planning systems based on business processes. Installation of an SAP application is costly, complex, and time consuming, and requires significant internal computing assets. Some analysts now believe that Internet-based software will make SAP-type installations unnecessary. If so, sales of SAP products may be squeezed and organizations with significant SAP-related assets may need to consider whether their value is impaired.

Suppliers

Another threat comes from suppliers, often taking the form of increased costs or restricted access to raw materials. For example, Starbucks or Tim Horton's could be adversely affected by bad weather in coffee-growing countries that creates a shortage of coffee beans. When a computer chip factory in Japan was destroyed by fire in 1993, computer manufacturers around the world were negatively affected by the resulting shortage in chips. The seriousness of potential threats from suppliers will depend on

- The degree of specialization required for inputs (especially complex components)
- The concentration and monopoly power of potential suppliers
- The existence of substitute inputs
- The degree of cooperation among suppliers that could lead to uniform pricing

Example

Beginning in 2004, a number of circumstances combined to cause a significant increase in worldwide oil prices. Businesses dependent on oil, such as utilities and airlines, found their profit margins significantly reduced. To the extent oil is a cost component of a product, the large increase could have a significant impact on production costs and potentially threaten the existence of financially weak organizations.

Example

The so-called Year 2000 (Y2K) threat, in which a defect in legacy computer systems might have caused some computer systems to malfunction by switching to 1900 after December 31, 1999, was particularly problematic for automotive manufacturers utilizing many tiers of suppliers in a just-in-time manufacturing process. Because most of their suppliers helped in designing parts and in many cases possessed required tooling for parts of the car, should one of them have been unable to function because of a Y2K malfunction, no cars could have been produced until the problem was fixed.

Customers

Another source of threats to a business comes from the company's customers. Customers are usually considered a positive element in doing business, but their degree of bargaining power may constitute a threat. Also, customer tastes change rapidly, and failing to adequately gauge the nature and extent of changes can create significant risk. The seriousness of threats from customers will depend on

- The level of individual customer volume in relation to total sales
- The ability of buyers to share pricing and service information that would lead to disclosure of special deals made with one buyer and then demanded by others
- The existence of brand recognition for components sold as inputs to consumer products; for example, the inclusion of an Intel chip and Windows software are probably more important to most computer purchasers than the brand of a computer

Example

In the 1990s, General Electric failed to deliver a sufficient inventory of light bulbs at year end to The Home Depot. Founders Bernie Marcus and Arthur Blank responded by ceasing any business with GE in the future. Although GE developed a significant presence at The Home Depot in other product lines, only Philips light bulbs were sold at The Home Depot during the tenure of Marcus and Blank.

The collective impact of macroenvironmental and industry forces creates a mosaic of risks that an organization must effectively manage if it is to succeed and meet its objectives. The more effective the company is at managing these risks, the fewer problems an auditor can expect to encounter during an engagement. To help further the understanding of the nature of strategic risks, we now discuss how risks originating in the external environment can affect the internal operations of the organization, and ultimately the audit of financial statements.

ANALYZING THE AUDIT IMPLICATIONS OF STRATEGIC RISKS

Several examples of strategic risks an organization might face are presented in Figure 5–9. Although these risks are not specific to any single organization, they illustrate the potential range of strategic risks that can arise from various sources. However, not all risks will be of equal importance to management or the auditor.

Figure 5–9   Strategic Risks and Potential Audit Implications: Some Examples

Strategic Business Risk/Threat	Source of Threat	Potential Audit Implications
SR1: Competitors begin offering extended warranty protection on products.	Competitors	• Audit Risk: Increase in warranty commitments may require that warranty expense estimates be increased above historical patterns. • Comments for client: Implement a system for tracking warranty costs.
SR2: Competitors are rapidly increasing the rate paid to key senior accounting and management personnel.	Competitors	• Control Environment: Reliability of decision making and information processing may decrease with employee turnover. • Audit Risk: Allocations of labor costs may need to be revised based on relative changes in salary levels. • Audit Risk: Accruals for benefits may need to be increased.
SR3: Top-grade raw materials are in extremely short supply due to bad weather conditions in producing regions.	Suppliers	• Audit Risk: Wastage and spoilage rates may need to be increased in standard costing formulas. • Audit Risk: Valuation problems related to purchase commitments may exist. • Control Environment: Pressure to cut corners to meet customer demand.
SR4: Customer industries are in a recession.	Economic, Customers	• Audit Risk: Receivables may not be collectable at historic rate and allowance for uncollectibles may need to be increased. • Viability: Shrinking customer base.
SR5: Consumer tastes have changed, necessitating improved functionality and quality in company products.	Social, Customers	• Viability: Loss of market share. • Audit Risk: Inventory on hand may become obsolete or out of favor so that carrying values may not be realizable. • Control Environment: Pressure to hit sales targets to protect jobs or bonuses.
SR6: The preferred distribution channel for the company's product changes from retail locations to Internet, telemarketing, and home delivery.	Technology, Customers	• Audit Risk: Existing distribution channels may need to be shut down with resulting restructuring cost (layoffs, asset disposal). • Viability: Inability to adapt on a timely basis.
SR7: New entrant to the market is technologically superior to current products.	Technology, New entrants	• Audit Risk: Inventory valuation may need to be reduced to lower of cost or market due to obsolescence or excess quantities. • Viability: Loss of market share.

Figure 5–9   *(continued)*

Strategic Business Risk/Threat	Source of Threat	Potential Audit Implications
SR8: Government imposes new regulations on distribution of a company's product.	Social, Political	• Viability: Loss of market share if not adaptable. • Audit Risk: Inventory valuation may need to be reduced to lower of cost or market due to obsolescence or excess quantities. • Comments for client: Advise client management about need to comply with new regulations. • Control Environment: Efforts to circumvent regulations to meet sales targets.
SR9: Activists protest the company's approach to R&D.	Social	• Audit risk: Valuation of capitalized development costs if associated product demand drops. • Control Environment: Efforts to hide or disguise nature of R&D. • Comments for client: Assurance to outsiders concerning the nature of the R&D process used by the company.
SR10: Foreign currency fluctuations squeeze profit margins on international sales.	Economic	• Audit Risk: Proper treatment of exchange gains and losses. • Audit Risk: Accounting treatment of financial derivatives. • Comments for client: Advise management on risk issues associated with hedging foreign currency exposures.
SR11: Manufacturing facilities become noncompetitive due to age and inability to upgrade processes.	Technological	• Audit Risk: Impairment of fixed assets. • Viability: Tightening margins leading to losses, if prices cannot be increased.

NOTE: All risks create specific expectations about the financial statements. These are not specifically illustrated in this example. Expectations related to risks are discussed in more detail in Chapter 9 on preliminary analytical procedures and in Chapter 14 on business measurement.

A common technique to assess and document the relative importance of a large number of risks is in a *risk map* as illustrated in Figure 5–10. The significance of a business risk can be assessed along two dimensions: (1) the likelihood of the risk causing negative outcomes for the organization, and (2) the magnitude of negative outcomes if the problem actually occurs. Only the first five risks in Figure 5–9 are included to keep the graph manageable in appearance, but all eleven risks would normally be assessed and ranked if they pertain to a specific organization.

Figure 5–10   Using a Risk Map to Prioritize Risks

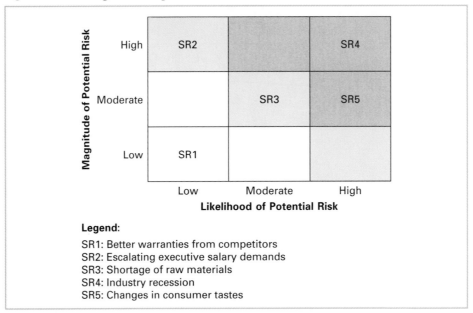

Legend:
SR1: Better warranties from competitors
SR2: Escalating executive salary demands
SR3: Shortage of raw materials
SR4: Industry recession
SR5: Changes in consumer tastes

Risks that are classified in the lower left corner are considered to be less serious because they are unlikely to pose serious problems for an organization. In the diagram, *SR4*, an industry recession, is clearly the most significant, and the one management would likely focus on most. *SR1*, improved warranties from competitors, might be ignored by management (that is, accepted) due to its relative insignificance. The balancing of *SR2* (escalating labor rates) and *SR5* (changing consumer tastes) is challenging to management because they each rate highly on one dimension, and management's responses would depend on the circumstances of each risk. In most organizations, risks with low likelihood and high impacts (*SR2*) are addressed collectively on an exception or crisis basis.[3] Risks that are small in magnitude but may occur frequently (*SR5*) are usually addressed within routine processes and procedures.

Once strategic risks have been prioritized, the auditor should then consider the implications the risks have for planning and conducting the audit. Figure 5–11 illustrates five types of issues that can arise from any given risk:

- *Expectations:* Knowledge of a risk condition will influence what an auditor expects to see in the financial results. For example, knowing that a competitor has triggered a price war would cause the auditor to expect a slowdown in revenue growth and tightening margins. The company may not wish to match price decreases but could respond by increasing service levels, thus increasing costs and squeezing margins from the other side.

- *Client Viability:* If a risk is severe enough, it may indicate that an organization is no longer viable given its current business plan and target market. If the

---

3 For severe risks, crisis management policies and procedures generally consist of a crisis management team dedicated to designing a response plan for most any crisis that heavily involves public and media relations, CEO involvement, formal channels of communication, business continuation processes, customer and supplier interaction, among others.

Figure 5–11 Potential Audit Implications of Business Risks

problem is critical, the company may not be a going concern and the auditor will have to consider the possibility of bankruptcy. Even if the problem is of a long-term nature, the auditor may need to consider whether financial disclosures adequately reflect the situation.

Example

WordPerfect was the largest selling word processing package for personal computers in the early 1990s. It was developed and sold by a relatively small independent company based in Utah, which was purchased by Corel – an Ottawa-based Canadian company. However, WordPerfect was surpassed by Microsoft's Word, not because it was a clearly superior product, but because of the marketing power and installed base of Microsoft. Corel built a suite of software around other independent programs (such as, Quattro spreadsheets). In the end, Microsoft dominated and WordPerfect lost significant market share, resulting in significant losses to Corel.

- *Audit Risks:* Some risks provide evidence that certain financial statement assertions may be inaccurate. For example, threats from competitors or new entrants can result in lost sales. If inventory is obsolete as a result of the threat, there may be a problem with inventory valuation. If entire factories depend on the manufacture of an obsolete product, there may be a broader problem with asset impairments that the auditor should consider.

Example

Automotive workers have their union contract renegotiated every few years and may go on strike to win significant increases in pay and benefits. In such circumstances, the auditor needs to consider the impact of a new contract on pension and post-retirement liabilities, other accrued employee costs, and standard costs for production (due to a higher labor cost content in inventory).

- *Control Environment:* Some threats put pressure on the control environment in such a way that management may feel that the only response is to undertake inappropriate actions. Such stresses and pressures are important to auditors because management may use accounting manipulation to disguise economic failures (as occurred at Enron and WorldCom).

Example

Stock options create a potential incentive for executives to manipulate earnings. The value of the options is tied to the price of a company's stock. Therefore, management will be harmed if bad news causes the price of the stock to drop significantly. This could cause management to try to hide bad results through accounting tricks. During the 2005 trial of Bernie Ebbers, former CEO of WorldCom (now part of Verizon), witness and former CFO Scott Sullivan alleged that Ebbers instructed him to ensure that earnings forecasts were achieved using any trick necessary because of the ramifications to the executive's personal wealth should the price of WorldCom stock fall. Sullivan claimed that this pressure led him to undertake the largest fraud in U.S. history.

- *Comments for Client:* Some threats simply highlight that the client may not have an adequate response for risks from the environment. Auditors may identify and communicate unmet risks to client management and the audit committee so that the organization may take steps to deal with the risk. Such advice is an integral part of the audit and does not imply that the auditor will participate in the correction of the problems.[4]

Figure 5–9 provides a number of examples of the possible implications of the identified strategic risks. To illustrate, consider the risk that buyers will change their preferences for the distribution channel of a product (*SR6*). A product that has been sold through retail outlets may become more attractive if it is sold through the Internet with direct home delivery. This change creates risk for a company because customers may turn to competitors. Computer supplies are a market where this phenomenon is occurring. The effect on internal activities could be extensive: the nature of sales and product delivery will change, shifting to a more technology-based approach. Logistics and distribution will be seriously affected as the company shifts from bulk delivery to retail outlets to small parcel, multiple-destination shipping. Customer service may need to provide dedicated resources to handle customer questions, complaints, and problems that were traditionally handled in-store (such as an 800 phone number and well-designed FAQs online). Technology and tangible resources are also affected because of the equipment and system needs of setting up the new sales and distribution system.

Example

The initial response of Barnes & Noble, a traditional book retailer, to inroads by Amazon into the book market was to set up its own web site for customer sales. However, the new website was rushed and opened before Barnes & Noble was fully prepared to handle Internet transactions. As a result, the company shut down the web site after a few months, redesigned the processes needed to support e-commerce, and then relaunched the web site a year later.

---

4 In audits of non-public companies, such as private company audits and audits of not-for-profit organizations, the audit firm employing personnel not involved in the audit may also be able to assist the company in designing and implementing a response to risk. For public companies the level of assistance, beyond the identification of risks that may be provided by the audit firm, is dependent on national regulations about the nature and type of non-audit services that a public accounting firm can offer its audit clients. For U.S. SEC registrants, there are relatively few such services that can be offered.

The discussion of business risks and management responses is important for auditing because their impact on economic reality needs to be properly reflected in the financial statements. In our example, a change in distribution channels may raise questions about the impairment of assets that are used in the "old" channel. Furthermore, if the changes are radical enough, the organization may need to undertake significant restructuring that may result in the layoff of some personnel, the relocation and retraining of other employees, and the disposal of assets. All of these outcomes will create issues that the auditor must examine in order to assure that they are appropriately reflected in the financial statements.

Many of the audit implications suggested in Figure 5–9 are general in nature. The audit process requires a much more detailed understanding of overall audit risks, but the analysis of business risks tells the auditor a great deal about the nature of a company and the industry in which it operates. By the time the auditor has completed this analysis, he or she should have an extremely deep understanding of the client, its market position, the factors that will determine its success, and the risks it faces. If this were all that was obtained from the analysis, it would be useful. However, the auditor's understanding of a client's risk profile also provides extremely helpful insight into the organization's control environment and the risk of material misstatement in areas affected by significant client business risks. In turn, these insights help the auditor to plan and conduct the audit of the financial statements.

> **Authoritative Guidance & Standards**
> Understanding an entity and its environment through performing a strategic analysis should help auditors in assessing the risk of material misstatement for the entity on an overall basis (SAS 109, ISA 315), particularly in fulfilling the requirement to assess fraud risk (SAS 99, ISA 240).

LINKING STRATEGIC RISKS TO INTERNAL PROCESSES

Most external risks have a predictable link to activities within the organization. Internal processes are designed to facilitate the strategy of the company, to interact with the external elements of the environment, and to minimize the potential impact of threats from external sources. Consider the following examples:

- Threats from competitors and potential entrants are most likely to affect sales, product delivery, branding, and customer service. These threats may create downward price pressure that, in turn, may require the organization to innovate the way it delivers products and develops new brands, and to consider new marketing efforts. For example, competitive pricing and the bundling of service contracts with products may raise issues related to accounting for revenue and inventory.
- Threats from suppliers are most likely to affect supply chain management and production. Supplier threats affecting the quality or supply of raw materials may have an impact on the number of suppliers utilized, the willingness to pay transportation costs for dispersed suppliers, manufacturing changes needed to adjust for changes in the quality of materials (resulting in higher rates of wastage or spoilage during production), or after-market service (resulting in higher warranty costs due to guaranteed repairs).
- Threats from customers are most likely to affect sales, logistics and distribution, and customer service. Telemarketing and direct home delivery may replace retail outlets, changing the nature of distribution and the fixed asset base needed by the company.

The connection between macroenvironmental forces and internal processes can also be important. Social attitudes can affect the public's acceptance of a company's products or affect the way that labor is managed and compensated. Political forces may affect the way an industry is regulated. Consequently, a multinational organization will have internal processes to deal with environmental, legal, and regulatory management. In many ways, investor relations is an internal process that helps ensure that market regulations are properly followed. Economic forces also have a significant impact on most organizations. For example, most banking institutions have economic risk management as a core objective of the organization.

Example

Social: Starbucks' rapid growth in the 1990s can partially be attributed to the social popularity of its hometown, Seattle, as the cultural hot spot in the United States during that time. (Seattle's grunge music scene, the rapid rise of Microsoft, and the proliferation of espresso coffee houses are examples of a thriving popular culture). In fact, the successful television show, *Friends*, was heavily influenced by the 1992 movie, *Singles*—Cameron Crowe's snapshot of Seattle's culture at that time. However, as Starbucks grew and the trends changed, Starbucks adapted by expanding its branding efforts to widen its appeal beyond the so-called Generation X that helped them achieve such rapid growth. Now in some parts of the world, the opening of a new Starbucks is met with resistance from local people protesting globalization, demonstrating how a social phenomenon can be affected by political factors.

Example

Political: Many multinational organizations have formal processes in place for lobbying activities to ensure that their voices are heard by regulators that can significantly impact core operations of their business through restrictions related to business operations, trade restrictions, or taxes.

Example

Economic: Bank of America's board of directors has an asset management committee that focuses exclusively on management's policies and effectiveness for managing economic risks associated with the bank's operations and products. Furthermore, the bank has a chief risk officer responsible for the organization's enterprise risk framework that is heavily driven by the economic risks facing the organization.

Finally, technology forces tend to have a pervasive impact on any organization, particularly those associated with high volumes of transactions or wide geographic reach. As a result, most companies have a chief information officer and an extensive information management process. The most significant technology risk facing many organizations is a lack of sufficient expertise to manage information systems. As a result, many organizations utilize strategic partners to help manage these risks.

Example

The plant established in Alabama in 1996 to manufacture M-Class SUVs for Mercedes-Benz was the first time that Daimler had ever built a vehicle outside of Germany. Because of the number of risks with which the company had to cope, it was decided that technology risks would best be managed by an alliance partner. As a result, IBM was hired to implement and manage the plant's Baan enterprise resource planning information system.

SUMMARY AND CONCLUSION

This chapter introduced a systematic approach to understanding a client's business and industry, strategy, operations and activities, risk, and potential audit implications arising from those conditions and circumstances. The analysis is based on a model that facilitates the identification and summarization of important information about an organization. Organizational Business Models describe the client's role in its industry. External risk analysis identifies the business risks and threats confronting the organization. Analysis of audit implications generates insights into the impact that existing circumstances and conditions are likely to have on the conduct of the audit. The analysis performed in this chapter is a useful starting point for assessing risks and determining their effect on the planning and conduct of the audit. In the next chapter, we discuss internal processes in more detail and expand our analysis of risk to include process risks. In later chapters we will discuss how management copes with risk through the risk management framework and related internal control.

BIBLIOGRAPHY OF RELATED PROFESSIONAL LITERATURE

Research

Ballou, B., C. E. Earley, and J. S. Rich. 2004. The Impact of Strategic-Positioning Information on Auditor Judgments about Business Process Performance. *Auditing: A Journal of Practice & Theory*. 23 (2): 71–88.

Choy, A. K. and R. R. King. 2005. An Experimental Investigation of Approaches to Audit Decision Making: An Evaluation Using Systems-Mediated Mental Models. *Contemporary Accounting Research*. 22 (2): 311–350.

O'Donnell, E. and J. J. Schultz, Jr. 2005. The Halo Effect in Business Risk Audits: Can Strategic Risk Assessment Bias Auditor Judgment about Accounting Details? *The Accounting Review*. 80 (3): 921–940.

Porter, Michael, 1980. *Competitive Strategy: Techniques for Analyzing Industries and Competitors*. The Free Press.

Porter, Michael. 1985. *Competitive Advantage: Creating and Sustaining Superior Performance*. The Free Press.

Porter, Michael and Victor Millar. 1985. How Information Gives You Competitive Advantage. *Harvard Business Review*, July–August: 149–160.

Auditing Standards

AICPA *Statements on Auditing Standard (SAS)* No. 99, "Consideration of Fraud in a Financial Statement Audit."

AICPA *Statements on Auditing Standard (SAS)* No. 109, "Understanding the Entity and Its Environment and Assessing the Risks of Material Misstatement."

Committee of Sponsoring Organizations of the Treadway Commission. *Internal Control/Integrated Framework*. AICPA, 1992.

IAASB *International Standards on Auditing (ISA)* No. 240, "The Auditor's Responsibility to Consider Fraud in a Financial Statement Audit."

IAASB *International Standards on Auditing (ISA)* No. 315, "Understanding the Entity and Its Environment and Assessing the Risks of Material Misstatement."

QUESTIONS

1. What is strategic analysis? Discuss the types of knowledge that auditors strive to obtain from the analysis.

2. What are the elements of an organizational business model? How does this information help an auditor better develop a strategy for conducting an audit?

3. Briefly explain the five audit implications of strategic risks.

4. Describe and discuss the categories of strategic risks, including both macroenvironmental forces and industry forces, that the auditor should consider in strategic risk analysis.

5. Describe the position of strategic analysis in the auditor's knowledge acquisition process and its relationship to the other parts of this process (use Figure 5–2 as a guide).

6. Any given strategic risk can have a number of implications for the audit process. Describe the general audit implications discussed in the chapter.

7. What is a residual risk? What is the primary implication of residual risk for assessing the risk of material misstatement as shown in Figure 5–2?

8. Explain what procedures are involved in strategic analysis, process risk analysis, and residual risk analysis.

9. Give five examples of the potential indications of weak strategic management, and discuss their respective audit implication(s).

10. What is a risk map? What value can an auditor derive from plotting strategic risks on a risk map?

11. What is external risk analysis, and how does it help the auditor to better understand the residual risks associated with the classes of transactions, accounts, and disclosures?

12. Figure 5–2 describes a top-down perspective for understanding a client's business. Consider how an auditor can better understand how to approach testing management assertions for inventory related transactions and accounts by first working through this process (that is, by linking external risks to the inventory management business process to identify residual risks). As part of your answer, compare this perspective to a strategy of addressing each of the management assertions for material inventory related transactions and accounts without first working through this process.

PROBLEMS

1. A business model analysis provides the auditor with a basis for determining the unique issues that the client faces in its operations by identifying and analyzing the firm's suppliers, competitors, buyers, external agents, and so forth. Many companies can say that they are a supplier, a competitor, and a buyer to themselves. One such company is General Motors.
   a. Construct a business model for General Motors by referring to Figure 5–6, which concerns a publishing company.
   b. What is a major implication to the auditor of General Motors of such a high level of integration (that is, being a supplier, competitor, and a buyer all at the same time)? Specifically, what transactions or balance sheet items should the auditor be more concerned with than usual as a result of GM's business model?

2. Suppose you are the auditor of a company which cuts timber and processes logs for export purpose. Construct a plausible organization business model for this company.

3. External risk analysis involving industry forces involves studying five risks common to all businesses. They are as follows:

     a.   Competitive intensity
     b.   Potential entrants
     c.   Substitutes
     d.   Suppliers
     e.   Buyers

     Consider a sole proprietor pizzeria in the food court of a large mall. Identify the five external threats listed here for the pizzeria and discuss the implications of those threats to the pizzeria's auditor.

4. Conduct a strategic analysis using macroeconomic forces (PEST factors) and industry forces (Porter's Five Forces) for British Airways.

5. Starbucks dominates the coffee roasting, distribution, and pouring market. Starbucks owns or licenses over ten thousand stores internationally that sell primarily various coffee-related drinks featuring its gourmet roasts of coffee. To expand its market presence and increase its brand value, Starbucks has created alliances to serve its coffee in prestigious retail and leisure outlets, including distribution agreements with major hotels, booksellers, airlines, and department store organizations. In addition, Starbucks has agreed to supply coffee flavoring for candy and ice cream with leading providers of each product. Starbucks has a well-developed web site that offers a line of coffeehouse-oriented CDs and furniture, both produced by outside (third party) corporations.

     Discuss the impacts of Starbucks' strategic alliances on the organization's business risks. How should the audit be adjusted to account for these risks?

6. Consider Dell Computer Corporation, which markets its products directly from the manufacturing facilities to customers through purchases on the Internet or via telephone.
     a.   Discuss the macroenvironmental forces (PEST factors) that may have an affect on Dell and its ability to meet its business objectives.
     b.   As Dell's auditor, how would you adjust your audit based on developments in any of these factors? Specifically, how would you link these PEST factors to internal processes of Dell? What are the audit implications relating to expectations developed, viability assessments, and audit risks?

7. You are auditing Telezee Limited, a major company in the telecommunications industry in New Zealand. Explain one audit implication for each of the following five issues that you discover during your review of business risk and strategy:
     a.   The revenue of the industry is growing overall, but there are changes. For example, revenue from broadband and mobile phones is growing, whereas revenue from landlines and toll calls is not.
     b.   At present the industry is not heavily regulated, but there is a possibility in future of stronger regulation that could control prices.
     c.   Competitors are expanding. For example there are rival cell phone companies operating, and alternative services such as phone cards.
     d.   The industry is affected by new technologies in areas such as cell phone transmission and computer systems.
     e.   The company has now decided to start using external contractors to provide maintenance services rather than employ its own maintenance staff.

8. New Age Imports is based in India and specializes in exporting clothes from India throughout Asia. New Age handles product design, marketing, and sales. The company has a team of designers in India who develop a new product line for the company every six months. The product design includes specifications related to fabrics, colors, patterns, sizes, and accessories. When the design is completed, manufacturing is outsourced to clothing manufacturers located in Indonesia. The company solicits bids for each new product line, but the contract has been rewarded to Textile, Inc., for the past three years.

     The company also has a team of salesmen in India, China, Japan, and Thailand that contact various regional retail and wholesale stores taking orders for each new product line. Virtually all of New Age's products are sold under store brand names, meaning customers do not know that they are purchasing New Age's products. The brand names are proprietary to each separate retailer. When an order is received, the customer information is transmitted to the manufacturer, who inserts the appropriate brand name (depends on the retailer) and ships the appropriate quantity directly to the retailer. The retailer pays New Age, and New Age pays the supplier.

New Age also undertakes extensive marketing efforts in trade journals, conventions, and by contacting purchasing agents directly.

Required

Identify a strategic risk in each of the following categories that is relevant to the audit of New Age. Also indicate at least one audit implication of each risk.

Type of Risk	Describe Risk	Audit Implication(s)
Political		
Technological		
Social		
Economic		
Competitors		
Customers		
Suppliers		

9. Access the corporate web site for The Gap, Inc., which operates The Gap, Old Navy, Banana Republic, and Forth and Towne. Search the web site for information about its business processes, products, history, and so forth, and construct a business model based on what is contained on the site (use Figures 5–5 and 5–6 as a guide).

10. Use the information in the business model (prepared for question 9) and on the web site for The Gap, Inc., as a basis for identifying the company's strategic objectives and then perform an external risk analysis that addresses key threats to meeting those objectives (use Figure 5–10 as a guide).

11. Use Figure 5–9 as a guide in determining the audit implications for the following possible business risks associated with Loblaw's, the largest food distributor and one of the largest retail grocers in Canada.
    - The grocery industry is in a state of decline, as new competitors not strictly in the business enter the market (such as Wal-Mart).

- Consumer needs are changing to include more demands for ready-prepared meals, premium brands, and private label brands.
- Loblaw's has begun offering financial services to its customers, including banking, a MasterCard, and insurance products.
- Failure to re-engineer distribution processes to include business-to-business electronic commerce could reduce ability to compete with Wal-Mart, which has extensive experience with this distribution process.
- The company is expanding its non-grocery inventory to counterattack market penetration by other types of retailers (for example, drug stores).

12. Identifying residual strategic risks (that is those that are uncontrolled or insufficiently controlled) is important for auditors to understand where the risk of material misstatements might be increased by increasing external pressures on an organization. Consider Apple, which has seen its business rapidly grow in the 1980s, struggle in the 1990s, and thrive in the 2000s. Identify and discuss three residual strategic risks that impact management assertions about specific transactions, accounts, or disclosures that you believe Apple's auditors should factor into its engagement. For each risk, describe why you believe that it may or may not be adequately controlled by the organization.

13. Consider the strategic positioning strategies described in this chapter. Discuss how the auditors might alter their audit approach to account for the company's particular differentiation strategy. Consider both strategic and process issues.
- Signet (which operates under Signet Jewelers in the United Kingdom and Kay Jewelers in the United States) utilizes a differentiation strategy.
- Tiffany & Co. utilizes a differentiation niche strategy.

Case 5–1: Hoosier Cycle

The holiday sales season is around the corner for Hoosier Cycle. But instead of focusing on stores' orders, Hoosier is unsure whether 90,000 bicycles stuck in China are being delivered because they cannot get on a ship. "It's scary," says Dan Heitger, president of the Bloomington, Indiana, distributor of racing bicycles, whose deliveries are running as much as a month late.

For U.S. companies, Asian shipments are moving more slowly than ever. U.S. importers are seeing record numbers of delays and mistakes on shipments of practically all products, most of which are stranded by a shipping jam between Asia and the United States. The problem is turning the pre-holiday shipping season into a transportation comedy of errors, with some shipments lost for days in overloaded ports and other cargo getting loaded onto ships after long delays, only to get bumped off like a standby passenger.

Some frustrated importers are accusing shipping lines of breaking contract agreements to illegally charge higher rates. The Federal Maritime Commission plans on investigating charges that shippers are unfairly treating customers. If the commission finds that shippers broke the law, they could face fines or other penalties.

Different problems await consumers, including higher prices and product shortages. Late deliveries from suppliers have created this problem, which probably will not end before the next holiday shopping season. Transportation costs account for 5 to 10 percent of the price of goods, so delays could justify charging higher prices.

Requirements

1. What strategic risks arise for Hoosier Cycle from the conditions presented in the case description?
2. One possible risk to Hoosier is customer dissatisfaction from late deliveries. What internal processes of Hoosier Cycle are affected by the risk? Explain.
3. How could the company mitigate the risk in the future?
4. What performance indicator(s) should the company monitor related to this risk?
5. What are the audit implications of this risk? Be specific and include potential impacts on management assertions on transactions, accounts, or disclosures.

Case 5–2: The Unfriendly Skies

The airline industry in the United States suffered a difficult year in 2005, when four airline carriers—Delta, Northwest, United, and US Airways—that have traditionally flown the bulk of domestic passengers in the United States all filed or struggled to get out of U.S. bankruptcy protection (only one legacy airline, American, was not involved). As of 2006, all airlines but US Airways continued to make changes to their business model to enable each organization to re-emerge as a successful airline. Only US Airways merged with another airline, America West, to become part of a larger "discounter" airline that would compete with other American discount airlines (such as Southwest, JetBlue, and AirTran).

One aspect leading to the problems associated with the so-called legacy airlines from 2001 to 2005 concerns forces external to the specific airlines largely beyond their control. In fact, American Airlines is the only legacy carrier not to file for US bankruptcy protection during the time period from 2001 to 2005.

However, another possible contributing factor for why these airlines suffered is that they were utilizing flawed business models. This argument is based on the fact that while legacy airlines suffered during the time period, the so-called "discounter" airlines not following the same model were profitable or sustained much fewer losses.

It is important for auditors to effectively assess whether financial statements reflect economic reality. For example, auditors of U.S. legacy airlines should have viewed clients quite differently than auditors of U.S. discounter airlines during the 2001–2005 time period.

Requirements

1. Identify external forces that you believe negatively impacted the airline industry during the time period 2001–2005.
2. Investigate each of the following airlines by researching their web sites, financial reports, regulatory filings, and so forth. For each airline, describe what you believe to have been its strategic positioning within the airline industry during the 2001–2005 time period:
   a. Delta
   b. Southwest
   c. United Airlines
   d. JetBlue
3. Using Figures 5–5 and 5–6 as a guide, prepare business models for Delta Airlines and Southwest Airlines that you believe were likely to be in place during 2005.
4. Explain whether you believe that the business model for Delta was flawed relative to that of Southwest. As part of your argument, explain why you believe that external forces either did or did not impact Delta more than Southwest.

5. Contrast how the auditor for Delta should approach the audit engagement as compared to how the auditor for Southwest should.

6. Describe how an increasingly global economy is likely to impact the U.S. airline industry. For example, the rapidly expanding economy in China has impacted the industry in various ways—a material increase in demand for more of the world's oil supply, a material increase in the demand for airplanes, increase in corporate travel, and so forth.

Case 5–3: Plastic Gizmos, Inc.

Background Information

Plastic Gizmos, Inc., is primarily in the business of manufacturing plastic consumer and industrial products. For a decade, Plastic Gizmos has been among the top ten of *Fortune* magazine's Most Admired companies, as judged by customers, competitors, financial analysts, and others. The company is widely held, and its stock is listed on the New York Stock Exchange. The stock is followed by analysts around the world and is generally considered a "blue chip" security. It broadly trumpets its many-year run of successfully hitting or exceeding its annual growth targets of 15 percent for revenue, profits, and shareholder value. The unaudited financial statements for the 2007 fiscal year end are presented below, along with the audited results for 2006 (amounts are in millions).

The company's mission is "to be the leading producer of plastic products through its world-class product innovation and customer service." The company has the related goal of being a "socially aware" organization in which "all stakeholders needs are considered in decision making and company behavior." Plastic Gizmos (PG) manufactures a wide range of plastic products and is organized into three divisions:

- Housewares: This division manufactures plastic products for the home, kitchen, and bath, including trash cans, food storage containers, mats, kitchen utensils, and related products.
- Toys: This division, which operates under a separate brand name, manufactures a broad range of children's toys, including larger items such as toy kitchens, workbenches, playhouses, and related equipment.
- Industrial: This division specializes in products for outside or business use including large scale storage containers, storage structures, shelving, and benches.

The toy division is the most successful of the three and returns the highest margins. The housewares division is the most competitive, with the lowest margins. Industrial products is by far the smallest division, contributing the least to the Company's profits. The company's brands have very high rates of recognition among customers and consumers and a general reputation for being high quality with a relatively high price point.

The company is widely renowned for its continual innovations in both quality and styling. They are generally considered the industry leader in product development and innovation. The company has a research and development facility located in Michigan, which is staffed by industry-recognized leaders in the technology of plastics. The CEO of PG has frequently commented in public that his goal is to stay two steps ahead of the competition and to get to every new market for plastics at least a year sooner than anyone else. He feels that this allows the company to become entrenched among major customer groups, making it very difficult for competitors to crack the same market.

185

The company operates seven U.S.-based manufacturing plants in five states and has one overseas manufacturing facility in Europe. Products are shipped to a series of regional warehouses located in ten locations in the United States plus one in Canada, two in Europe, two in Asia, and one in Australia. This allows the company to service its wholesale and retail customers quickly and efficiently.

Most of the company's sales go to large corporate customers in the retail, construction, and transportation industries. In retail, major customers for housewares and toy products include large department store chains and specialty retailers around the world. The company does not generally sell its products directly to individual consumers, although the company has started a web site for direct marketing. The company has outsourced the maintenance of the web site, processing of Internet transactions, and related distribution. In construction and transportation, the company sells its industrial products directly to consumers and also to supply chain retailers who market to smaller construction and transportation companies.

Business and Industry Information

Plastic Gizmos sells its retail goods through 100,000 stores, which, it claims, devote more miles of shelf space to its products than to those of any other housewares manufacturer. Industrial products are marketed directly to large customers and through wholesale channels that deal directly with smaller industrial and commercial customers. The company's revenue breaks down approximately as 50 percent housewares, 35 percent toys, and 15 percent industrial products.

The company changes 40 percent of its housewares product line every year. Many changes are cosmetic in nature, including colors, sizes, and dimensions. Toys are changed less predictably because demand for specific products is not easily forecasted. A successful toy product may remain unchanged for a number of years, whereas an unsuccessful product may be discontinued or redesigned after a few months on the market. New ideas for housewares and toy products are generated by the R&D staff based on market and scientific research. The development of industrial products is less systematic, and products are often designed and produced in response to specific opportunities identified by the dedicated industrial sales force. For example, a plastic bench for bus terminals was designed and marketed based on ideas solicited from bus companies.

PG has extensive competition for many of its plastic products. There are a number of large companies around the world, primarily in Korea, Taiwan, and Eastern Europe, that manufacture plastic-based product lines that compete directly with much of PG's product lines. These companies often have competitive advantages due to lower labor costs and government protection in the home market. Furthermore, much of the production for these companies' products is aimed at the U.S. and European markets, areas that generate over 75 percent of PG revenues. There are also a few small U.S. companies with similar product lines which specialize in narrow markets. None of the company's competitors have as extensive an international distribution network as PG.

Primary resources used in the production process include human resources, technology resources, facilities, and materials. Approximately 60 percent of the company's U.S. labor force is unionized, but the company has generally had good relationships with its unions because its compensation and benefits packages tend to be higher than comparative organizations. The company devotes significant resources to R&D-related technology and provides a world-class environment at its product development facility. The company hires the best and brightest from the leading graduate research universities around the world and has a core of highly respected scientists that has been in place and stable for over ten years. The research scientists are generally provided with the best equipment available.

The most important component of the company's supply chain are the manufacturers of resin, an oil-based by-product that is the primary input for plastic products. The company deals with a number of resin suppliers around the world and each factory manages its own supply-chain relationships. Most resin contracts are of short duration and denominated in U.S. dollars, consistent with the underlying oil market. Approximately 3 percent of materials used in production are from recycled plastic. The company would like to increase this proportion but is limited by the cost of technology needed for high quality recycled materials because there is an extremely broad range of chemical compounds used in plastic, each of which has its own requirements for environmentally safe and effective recycling.

The company has opened a new factory or renovated an existing factory every three years on average. During construction/renovation of manufacturing facilities, the company designs each plant considering the most current production technology available at the time. Once a facility is up and running, few changes are made to the production equipment other to adjust for new designs and products (such as new molds for plastic extrusion). The production process includes a few proprietary techniques that reduce costs and are subject to patent protection but few of these serve as barriers to the entry of new competitors because functionality, not product design, is usually the basis for competition.

The company has established key alliances with many organizations. Its toys are featured in many highly visible and trend setting retailers. It maximizes its shelf space by working with retailers to generate efficiencies in the distribution and marketing of products. For example, local advertising for the company's products is managed by retail customers based on a cost-sharing arrangement with PG. Specially designed products are often marketed through exclusive contracts with specific retailers.

The company's internal operations include

- Product portfolio and research: This set of activities focuses on investigation, testing and creation of new products and rationalizing the overall product portfolio. Product style decisions are part of this process.
- Supply chain and production: This set of activities focuses on procurement, storage, and use of resources for production as well as the production process itself. The process includes inventory management and production scheduling.
- Marketing and Sales Management: This set of activities focuses on marketing and advertising, distribution and delivery, and customer service, including managing customer relationships.
- Human resources: Recruiting, hiring, training, compensating, and evaluating employees.
- Facilities: Acquiring, managing, and maintaining production and administration facilities.
- Technology: Acquiring, implementing, and maintaining information systems and related assets.
- Financial management and reporting: Balancing cash flow and capital needs, managing financial structure, reporting and managing investor relations.

Strategic Risks

As is the case with any large and successful organization, PG faces risks from many directions and not all is rosy at Plastic Gizmos as the company looks at its future plans. After years of relatively easy success, one problem seems to have led to another, and they're beginning to add up. Much of the bad news for PG started in the spring of 2007 when the price of resins, the raw material used in almost all of Plastic Gizmos' 5,000 products, began to rise, eventually doubling. Far from taking that blow in stride, Plastic Gizmos tripped up, revealing weaknesses throughout the company. Some particularly worrisome problem areas include

- Customer Relations: Plastic Gizmos angered its most important retail buyers with the heavy-handed way it tried to pass along its ballooning costs. Some became so angry that they have given more shelf space to PG's competitors. Relations with Wal-Mart, its biggest customer, have become arctic.
- Operations: Although it excels in creativity, product quality, and merchandising, PG is showing itself to be a laggard in more mundane areas such as modernizing machinery, eliminating unnecessary jobs, and making deliveries on time.
- Competition: PG has been slow to recognize that other housewares makers— once a bunch of no-names who peddled junk—have greatly improved over the past half-dozen years. The premium prices Plastic Gizmos charges over those rivals are beginning to turn away customers.
- Culture: The company's extraordinary financial targets of 15 percent annual growth in revenues and profits seem unrealistic—and straining to reach them is proving increasingly troublesome. Some of the friction between Plastic Gizmos and its customers can be traced to PG's voracious appetite for growth.
- Overseas: To reach its goal of doubling in size by the year 2010, Plastic Gizmos has to expand its foreign business at a prodigious rate. But it has made an awkward start in Europe and gaining a foothold in Asia has been more difficult than the company anticipated.

Requirements

1. Analyze the strategic environment of Plastic Gizmos.
   a. What is the overall strategy of Plastic Gizmos?
   b. Identify three critical success factors for Plastic Gizmos if it is to establish a sustainable source of competitive advantage. Why are these critical?
   c. Complete an organizational business model.
2. Prepare a strategic risk analysis for Plastic Gizmos.
   a. Identify two potentially important risks for each category of strategic risk.
   b. Evaluate the significance of each risk identified and document in a risk map.
      - Using three categories (high, moderate, low) assign each risk to a category based on likelihood of occurrence. No more than half should be rated as highly likely.
      - Using three categories (substantial, moderate, little) assign each risk to a category based on the magnitude of the impact if the risk occurs. No more than half should be rated as substantial impact.
      - Plot each risk on the two-dimensional risk map.
3. For each risk identify one or more potential risk management and/or audit implications.

Exhibit 3–1   Plastic Gizmos Inc.

Financial Statements
for Year Ended
December 31, 2007

	2007 (unaudited)	2006 (audited)
Income Statement		
Net sales	$ 6,045	$ 5,585
Cost of sales	4,385	3,895
Selling and other expenses	650	690
Administrative expenses	480	420
Other expenses	50	65
Taxes	365	175
Net Income	$ 115	$ 340
Balance Sheet		
Cash	$ 10	$ 312
Market securities	125	120
Accounts receivables (net)	700	350
Inventories	300	310
Prepaid expenses	50	75
Plant, property, & equipment (net)	575	640
Intangible assets	310	300
Total assets	$ 2,070	$ 2,107
Current liabilities	$ 395	$ 377
Long term debt	525	625
Shareholders' equity	1,150	1,105
Total liabilities and equity	$ 2,070	$ 2,107

Note: Intangible assets are almost entirely due to goodwill from acquisitions, which is tested annually for impairment.

6

Business Processes and Internal Risks

INTRODUCTION

In Chapter 5, we examined a client's external environment for the purpose of understanding its source of competitive advantage and identifying potential threats to its success. As we noted in the previous chapter, strategic risks often have a direct effect on a company's internal operations. The execution of a company's strategy and its ability to cope with strategic threats depends critically on the manner in which it organizes its internal operations. Management allocates its available resources (e.g., employees, tangible assets, financial resources) into *business processes*.

Well-designed processes reduce the potential impact of strategic risks by standardizing the organization's response to external stimuli and coordinating operations to manage those risks. Accordingly, key information systems for most organizations are designed to accommodate effective and efficient business processes. There are a large number of processes that are embedded in an organization, and problems occurring within one process can have an adverse effect on other processes. Furthermore, breakdowns within a business process will often have an effect on the organization's financial statements. The challenge to the auditor is to identify the processes that have the most potential impact on the audit.

> **Authoritative Guidance & Standards**
> This chapter incorporates and expands on standards on understanding an entity and its environment and assessing the risk of material misstatement (SAS 109, ISA 315) and internal control over financial reporting (AS 2). Understanding an entity and its environment is required under SAS 109 and ISA 315, particularly for how they impact the risk of material misstatement. Understanding the business processes put in place to implement a company's strategy helps the auditor to assess the risk of material misstatement for financial statement assertions.

Processes pertain to the full scope of activities within the organization, ranging from strategic planning at the level of senior management, to budgeting and accounting by professional staff, to sales and marketing by account managers, to housekeeping by custodial staff. Regardless of the level at which an activity is performed, virtually all processes have a dual purpose: (1) to advance the objectives of the organization and (2) to minimize the risks of not achieving those objectives. The importance of strategic planning, accounting, and marketing may be self-evident, but the potential problems of excess dust in the computer room that could cause system disruptions, or dirty bathrooms in a restaurant that could disgust customers, can elevate a mundane activity such as housekeeping to a level of importance. Process failure can be just as harmful to an organization as poor strategic planning. The purpose of this chapter is to expand our understanding of a client environment and its risk by examining the internal processes of an organization (Figure 6–1).

Example

A small regional burger chain in Western Canada was effectively shut down for 10 days when it was found that its staff at one location was spreading a highly contagious virus. The problem was that the organization had no procedures for monitoring sick employees. The owner-manager voluntarily closed *all* locations until remedial training and disinfection were completed. Hence, the news stories changed from a focus on the illnesses caused by the chain to the "concerned owner" who put the health of customers ahead of the profits of his burger chain. When the chain reopened, customers came back in a rush, and the company avoided repercussions that might have led to bankruptcy if management's response had been less assertive.

INTERNAL OPERATIONS AND BUSINESS PROCESSES

A *value chain* is a collection of processes designed to carry out the operations and activities of an organization in an effective and controlled manner. More specifically, a value chain describes how the organization creates value for all stakeholders, including shareholders, customers, and so forth. A generic value chain for organizations that manufacture, distribute, or sell tangible products is depicted in Figure 6–2. This figure also highlights some of the accounting issues that may arise in the transactions and estimates recorded as part of different processes within the value chain.

There are two dimensions to a value chain: primary processes and support processes. *Primary processes* are those that are performed to directly create value in the form of a product or service. Acquiring raw materials, assembling a product, and delivering the product to a customer are all considered primary processes,

Figure 6–1　Overview of the Audit Process

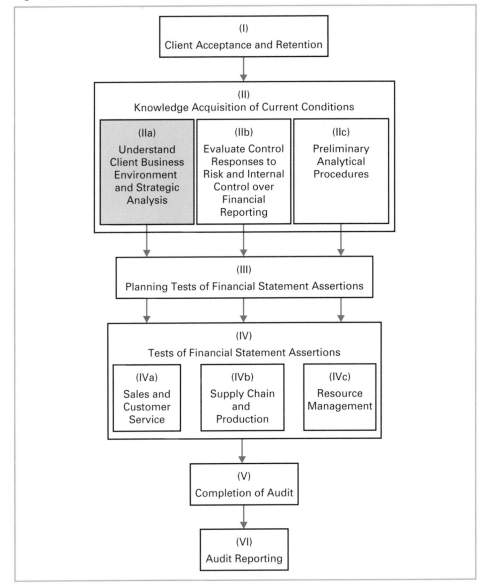

and hence they generate what we call primary transactions in the accounting system. *Support processes* are those that are performed in order for the organization to function properly but have an indirect effect on the creation of product value. The accounting and personnel departments are examples of support processes. Below we describe the elements of a typical value chain in more detail.

Primary Processes

The primary processes for an organization represent its efforts to take a group of inputs and create an output that has value. There are five types of primary processes for organizations that manufacture, distribute, or sell tangible products:

Figure 6–2   Generic Value Chain for Typical Business Organization and Its Impact on Financial Reporting

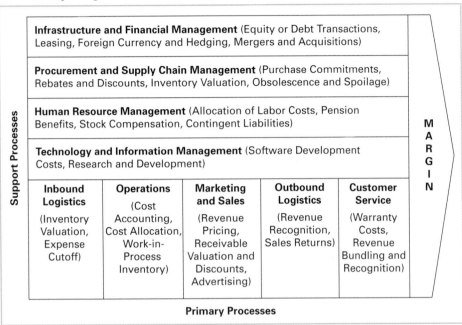

Source: Authors' example using the value chain in Michael Porter's *Competitive Advantage: Creating and Sustaining Superior Performance,* The Free Press (1985).

1. **Inbound Logistics:** These processes consist of the physical activities by which the organization obtains, stores, and manages input to the production, warehousing, or retail process. Examples of activities included as part of inbound logistics are materials handling, warehousing, and purchase returns. The complexity of inbound logistics will depend on
   - The volume and range of inputs needed for production
   - The mode and timing of resource deliveries
   - The need to control resources once they are received
   - The method of inventory management employed (e.g., just-in-time inventory)
   - The process for handling purchase returns

   Accounting and audit issues associated with inbound logistics transactions and estimates include the completeness and valuation of incoming inventory as well as the timing of expenses and liabilities.

Example

The manufacture of a car requires a much larger set of inputs than does the production of a newspaper. An organization that uses small but valuable inputs susceptible to theft (e.g., gold or electronic components) has challenges that are different from one that uses mostly commodities (e.g., lumber or coal).

2. **Operations:** These processes enable the company to transform inputs into a product that can be sold to customers. They include machining, assembly, packaging, and testing. They may also include certain maintenance activities

directly related to the operating process. The complexity of operations will depend on

- The extent resources are transformed by the organization (production)
- The need to control and manage inventory levels
- The complexity of product costing (e.g., large overhead allocations)
- The extent and costs of by-products, waste, rework, and so forth

Accounting and audit issues associated with operations transactions and estimates include the costing of goods and services, which in turn depends on various cost allocations (such as indirect labor, service departments, depreciation, and amortization).

Example

Repackaging and redistributing merchandise manufactured by other producers is significantly less complex than the manufacturing processes used to build an automobile.

3. **Marketing and Sales:** These processes develop brand recognition, create demand for the company's products, manage customer relations, and initiate sales. They include advertising, selecting a distribution channel, maintaining a sales force, and setting prices. The complexity of marketing and sales activities depends on
   - The scope of brand development activities (e.g., international, regional, local)
   - The nature of promotion (e.g., Internet advertising, television/print media, product placement)
   - The extent of differential pricing
   - The form of sales contact with customers (e.g., personal contact, telemarketing, Internet-based)
   - The selection of distribution channel

   Accounting and audit issues associated with marketing and sales transactions and estimates include revenue recognition as affected by the terms of sale (e.g., rights of return) and the collectibility of receivables.

4. **Outbound Logistics:** These processes involve delivering the products and services to customers. They also include activities related to order processing. The complexity of outbound logistics will depend on
   - The nature of the product or service being delivered
   - The form of delivery (e.g., via retail outlet, company-owned trucks, independent shippers, the postal system)
   - Transfer of title of goods (e.g., consignment, FOB-shipping point)
   - The contractual arrangements with customers (e.g., long-term construction contracts, rights of return for unsold merchandise)

   Accounting and audit issues associated with outbound logistics transactions and estimates include the cutoff of sales, the timing of revenue recognition, and the extent of sales returns.

5. **Service:** These processes are performed by the company after goods and services have been delivered, including installation, training of customer personnel, and repairs. The complexity of service activities will depend on
   - The complexity of installation and use of a product
   - The extent and nature of warranty coverage

- The role of customer follow-up in developing repeat customers
- The existence of extended service contracts, often bundled with the product itself
- The process of performing repairs and part replacement (e.g., independent repair shops versus in-house experts)

Accounting and audit issues associated with service activities transactions and estimates include contingent costs (such as warranties) and the timing of revenue recognition under extended service contracts or when service contracts are bundled with product sales.

These processes are important for all organizations that manufacture, distribute, or sell tangible products. However, the relative importance of the primary activities will depend on the company's operations and the many strategic decisions that management has made concerning the way it will conduct business. For example, manufacturing processes are not relevant to a retailer, but choice of distribution and marketing channels may be critical if, for example, the retailer offers merchandise through department stores, mail order catalogs, or the Internet. Two retailers may make very different choices about their distribution channel, which will have a big impact on the nature of outbound logistics. For example, a mail-order retailer must arrange direct shipment to many individual customers, whereas a department store must coordinate large shipments to stores. These choices affect how accounting and control systems are designed and the risks associated with these design choices.

Similar differences can be observed in other types of businesses. For example, marketing and service activities may be critical for a bank, but outbound and inbound logistics are less important given that few tangible items are acquired or delivered. A manufacturer of specialized machine tools may consider operations and service to be the most critical activities while placing less importance on sales and marketing due to the small and specialized market niche it serves. In contrast, a manufacturer of consumer durables (e.g., appliances) may consider sales and marketing and service to be vital to its success.

An important consideration that can affect an organization's primary processes is whether to form strategic alliances to facilitate any of the primary activities. The decision to form an alliance generally occurs when an organization has significant limitations on resources (e.g., insufficient capital or expertise) such that a competitive advantage cannot be sustained unless some of the risks and rewards are shared with an alliance partner.

Example

Pixar Animation Studios is one of the most successful entertainment companies in recent history given the success of each of its theatrical releases *(Toy Story, A Bug's Life, Toy Story 2, Monsters Inc., Finding Nemo, The Incredibles,* and *Cars).* Pixar, which was founded by Apple Computer creator Steve Jobs, has never performed marketing or outbound logistics for any of its movies, instead relying on a strategic alliance with the Walt Disney Company. This alliance generated significant returns for both organizations to the extent that many analysts argue that the failure of Disney to retain the alliance was a core reason the board of directors pressured the CEO, Michael Eisner, to retire. The importance of this strategic relationship was confirmed by their merger after Eisner left Disney.

SUPPORT PROCESSES

There are four basic types of support processes that are considered necessary to the creation of value by the company but are not linked directly to the production, distribution, or sale of a product or service. Some activities for these processes will be performed in support of a specific primary activity. Other support process activities will be pervasive to the organization and not directly linked to other activities. Many of the support processes described below focus on obtaining the resources needed by the organization to keep its primary activities operating effectively and efficiently, such as capital, materials, equipment, labor, and technology. Often these processes result in the creation of capital assets or period expenses.

1. **Infrastructure and Financial Management:** These activities are often referred to as "corporate overhead." They include general management, accounting, corporate governance, treasury, tax planning, and strategic management. These activities can be extremely important to the auditor because many are directly relevant to the conduct of the audit and may result in highly material transactions. Examples of transactions that would be of interest to the auditor include acquiring financing, entering into long-term leases, acquiring other companies, or executing investment and hedging transactions. Perhaps most importantly, the financial statements are generated within the accounting sub-process that has taken on a new importance in public companies registered with the U.S. SEC, which now must provide additional reports about their internal controls over financial reporting (to be discussed in Chapter 8).

2. **Procurement and Supply Chain Management:** These activities relate to the arrangements made to acquire materials, supplies, and other tangible inputs that are used throughout the organization. Most of the inputs will be received through inbound logistics and utilized during operations. Procurement activities tend to be present throughout an organization even though a single official purchasing department may exist for inputs directly related to production. Given that the procurement process often commits the organization to acquiring goods from outsiders, the process is of interest to the auditor in terms of the authorization of transactions and the recognition of liabilities. Audit issues that might arise from procurement include purchase commitments, estimates of asset impairments, and estimates associated with inventory valuation or problems with defective materials. Furthermore, the purchasing process is an area of high risk for fraud or misappropriation of assets because of the ability of purchasing agents to receive kickbacks from vendors in exchange for favorable treatment.

3. **Human Resource Management:** These activities involve the acquisition of human resources, primarily the recruiting, hiring, training, retention, evaluation, and compensation of employees. The acquisition and management of human resources supports the entire value chain. Problems in human resource development will almost always create problems for other primary or support activities. The way that an organization manages its personnel will reveal much about its overall competence and its attitudes towards honest business dealings, accurate and reliable information systems, and the potential for delivering quality goods and services. Audit issues related to human resource activities include allocations of direct and indirect labor costs, liabilities associated with compensation or benefits (e.g., pensions, post-retirement benefits, and stock option plans), or estimates of contingent liabilities that may arise from improper employee policies, procedures, or behavior (e.g., sexual harassment or discrimination).

Example

The Home Depot is one of the fastest growing retailers in history, reaching annual sales of $50 billion in fewer than 25 years. In addition to being an innovator of the category-killer warehouse concept, in which massive economies of scale are used to offer low prices to drive out competition, The Home Depot has grown rapidly because of its reputation for exemplary customer service. Founders Bernie Marcus and Arthur Blank focused on developing individuals' abilities to become do-it-yourselfers for home improvement by having well-trained employees in its stores to answer almost any question customers might raise. When both founders retired and Robert Nardelli became CEO, one challenge faced by the organization was that it had grown to the extent that employees were not as committed or as well trained as during the early years. Nardelli initially responded by committing more resources to human resources, spending more on employee training than any other company in the United States. However, pressure to reduce costs subsequently led to an increase in hiring part-time employees and reductions in profit sharing. As a result, The Home Depot's reputation for customer satisfaction was negatively impacted.

4. **Technology and Information Management:** These activities involve the acquisition of technological or knowledge-based resources. This set of activities can be examined at three levels:
    a. Research and development for new products
    b. Research and development applied to primary activities and related business processes, such as robotic assembly lines developed to replace labor
    c. Research and development applied to support activities, such as the development and analysis of benchmarking databases for strategic planning purposes and improvements in information systems

    Audit issues that may arise from technology development mainly relate to the proper recognition and allocation of costs. In the United States, research and development costs are expensed, but many countries allow development costs to be capitalized and amortized under certain conditions. Technology development can also impact the existence and reliability of information relevant to the audit of the financial statements. Common problems related to technology development include business interruption due to system failure and excess development costs associated with integrating new and existing information systems (or integrating systems when merger and acquisition activities occur). A common example of this situation occurs when organizations implement enterprise resource planning systems that feature organization-wide, integrated systems.

All processes are potentially important to the success of an organization and may be relevant to the conduct of the audit. An auditor's chief concern is determining which processes are critical for an organization in meeting its objectives and managing its most important strategic risks, regardless of whether they are primary or support processes. However, for organizations that are SEC registrants,

Example

Many organizations control production costs by relying heavily on supply chain management. Most automobile manufacturers rely on suppliers to help design and assemble key parts of an automobile. In these cases, auditors should consider the nature of the strategic alliance and related risks when considering the financial reporting issues related to the alliance.

all processes that generate a material amount of transactions are considered critical when reporting on the internal controls over financial reporting.

AN EXAMPLE OF BUSINESS PROCESSES COMPRISING A VALUE CHAIN

The distinction between primary processes and support processes depends upon the type of organization in question. For service organizations or organizations that deal in intangible products, the value chain may vary in that support processes may become primary processes, depending on the core service or product offered by the organization. For example, a public accounting firm relies heavily upon human resource management (including training), research and development, and quality management for effective and efficient delivery of its services.

It should be evident that every organization has a unique set of business processes. An example of the value chain for a manufacturer of copiers is presented in Figure 6–3. Many of the functions included in the primary activities are typical for most manufacturers. For example, most manufacturers will have processes for inbound materials handling, inbound inspection, fabrication, advertising, order processing, and shipping. Note that support services for human resources, procurement, and technology may apply to specific primary activities. For example, inbound and outbound logistics need transportation services, operations needs materials, and marketing needs media services, all of which are arranged through the procurement processes.

To illustrate how processes may be interdependent across activities, consider the set of service activities in Figure 6–3. High-volume, high-quality copiers usually require regular service by a trained technician. Consequently, the training and availability of personnel, technical support, and the availability of parts and supplies are all important for sustaining a competitive advantage in service. Technology development is particularly important for a copier manufacturer because this activity determines if the company's products are technologically competitive, manufactured as efficiently as possible, and easy to service and maintain.

Figure 6–3   Value chain for Copier Manufacturer*

Procurement and Supply Chain Management (Transportation Services, Materials, Energy, Parts & Supplies, Media Services, Supplies, Travel, Computer Services)					
Human Resource Management (Recruiting, Training)					M
Technology and Information Management (Design of Automated Systems, Component Design, Assembly Design, Machine Design, Testing Procedures, Market Research, Sales Materials, Information Systems)					A R G I N
Inbound Logistics (Materials Handling, Inspection, Parts Delivery)	**Operations** (Fabrication, Assembly, Testing, Maintenance)	**Marketing and Sales** (Advertising, Promotion, Sales Force)	**Outbound Logistics** (Order Processing, Shipping, Billing)	**Service** (Service Reps, Spare Parts)	

* As previously noted, internal control cannot be perfect due to the possibility of human failure, collusion between parties in the system, and bypassing of control by senior management.

Source: Authors' example using the value chain in Michael Porter's *Competitive Advantage: Creating and Sustaining Superior Performance,* The Free Press (1985).

Information about the reliability of machines can be obtained from service personnel to assist product designers in their R&D efforts.

Value chain models are also useful for highlighting key strategic decisions that will influence the ultimate success of the company. For example, is it better to be a mail-order retailer than a store-based retailer given the nature of the product being marketed? Should extended service be provided through independent organizations or by in-house experts? Should inbound materials be warehoused or managed on a just-in-time basis? Is research and development activity potentially undermined by problems related to human resource development? Answers to these questions are obviously important to management, but they also increase the auditor's understanding of the client's risks. These choices also have profound implications for the generation of related accounting transactions and estimates as well as the information systems in which these transactions and estimates are made.

AN OVERVIEW OF PROCESS ANALYSIS

From an auditor's perspective, some processes will be more important than others, and the auditor must judiciously select the processes that have the most potential for affecting the audit. We will define an *audit-sensitive process* as a process that is critical to the conduct of the audit and that is likely to have a significant impact on the evidence that an auditor collects during the course of the engagement. Audit-sensitive processes are expected to be the main source of residual risks within the audit. A process can be considered to be audit-sensitive if it meets one or more of the following four conditions:

1. **Process critical to achieving objectives:** Some processes are vital to the success of the organization because they comprise the set of activities that are the source of the organization's competitive advantage. Failure within these processes will generally lead to failure for the organization as a whole. For example, in a biotech company, research drives the organization's overall success and is therefore considered a critical process. The auditor needs to understand these processes because they reflect the organization's ability to respond to external threats, which determines the viability of the organization.
2. **Process with extensive external interactions:** Other processes involve important and sizable interactions with outside parties, and often generate large transactions that are reflected in the financial statements. These processes are significant to the auditor because of the materiality of the individual transactions that can occur. Examples include mergers and acquisitions, capital market activities, financing activities (e.g., leasing), and facility expansion.
3. **Process with high risk:** Processes that are subject to a high degree of risk and where problems are most likely to occur within an organization are also audit-sensitive. A process can be considered high risk because it is highly complex, involves significant management judgment, is expected to exhibit weak internal control, frequently experiences unusual transactions, or has a prior history of problems. High-risk processes are of interest to the auditor because resulting business problems often manifest themselves as accounting or auditing problems.
4. **Process related to a major class of transactions:** This category primarily relates to organizations that have to comply with Section 404 of the Sarbanes-Oxley Act on internal controls over financial reporting. All processes that

generate material transactions or estimates are considered audit-sensitive for purposes of evaluating internal controls over financial reporting.

Often, audit-sensitive business processes meet more than one of these conditions because processes most critical for achieving objectives often involve extensive external interactions and contain high risk. Given that developing a competitive advantage typically involves consciously accepting a certain amount of risk in dealing with customers or capital markets, auditors spend a great deal of time analyzing a relatively small number of business processes that meet all three conditions.

Example

One of the most important competitive advantages for an oil exploration company is its process for identifying and extracting oil reserves. The most serious risk is that it will not find adequate reserves of oil or natural gas to justify the high cost of exploration. The uncertainty surrounding such endeavors raises serious questions about the valuation of assets related to exploration, the potential viability of the company, and the value of discovered reserves. Oil exploration companies strive to minimize the potential impact of these risks with their corporate structure (often forming as limited partnerships rather than corporations), with investments in improved exploration technology, and by lobbying for special tax treatment. An auditor would have a difficult time assessing the financial reporting risks of such a company without evaluating the oil exploration process in detail.

The auditor identifies audit-sensitive processes for the purpose of determining which processes should be examined in detail during the course of the engagement. Once the audit-sensitive processes are identified, the auditor will need to gather a great deal of information about each process, including

- The purpose and objectives of the process
- The activities which comprise the process
- The information flows related to the process (including relevant information systems)
- The accounting transactions and estimates that result from the process
- The key risks that threaten the objectives of the process
- Management's response to process risks (e.g., controls)
- Performance measures related to specific risks

We will use two tools to assist in our analysis of processes. The first tool, referred to as a *process map*, is mainly used to document the facts and circumstances surrounding a specific process. The second tool, *internal threat analysis*, will assist us in analyzing process risks.

Completion of a process map and an internal threat analysis for a specific process will provide the auditor a basis for reaching conclusions about residual risks arising from that process. As we noted before, residual risks can have various implications for the conduct of the audit including helping the auditor to frame expectations about financial results and to identify assertions that may be misstated. These conclusions could lead the auditor to modify the conduct of the audit or perform additional substantive tests of financial statement assertions. After completing the analysis of a process, the auditor can then modify the conclusions about residual risks that were derived from strategic analysis.

PROCESS MAPS

Once an audit-sensitive process is identified, the next step is for the auditor to gather information about the process to help develop a sufficient understanding of how the process affects financial reporting. Accordingly, there is a great deal of information about a process that could be of interest to the auditor. To systematically gather accurate, relevant information, the auditor will conduct interviews with personnel involved in the process, including the managers responsible for the process. We will use a *process map* consisting of four components to document details about a business process: (1) process objectives, (2) process activities, (3) information flows in and out of the process, and (4) the accounting impact of transactions occurring within the process.

We will illustrate process analysis using human resource management. This process includes recruiting and hiring personnel, setting work hours, training, payroll processing, and employee evaluation. It also includes the activities for terminating an employee, which may occur as a result of voluntary departures, layoffs, retirement, death, or disability. The human resource management process is likely to be a critical process in most companies. The process does not include the actual duties assigned to personnel that are performed as part of other processes.

PROCESS OBJECTIVES

The first element of the process map is identification of the objectives relevant to a process. The top panel of Figure 6–4 illustrates the objectives for human resource management. Process objectives represent an explicit statement of what the process is trying to achieve. Ideally, process objectives should link to broader strategic goals and reflect the organization's overall plan for developing and sustaining competitive advantage. For example, if the company has adopted a low-cost strategy, then many processes will have a related objective of minimizing costs within the process.

In general, the objective of human resource management is to assure that the organization has an adequate employee base with the skills that are needed to execute the organization's plans. An organization must identify and recruit appropriate human resources. Once hired, personnel need to be trained and managed. Critical to this objective is the establishment of compensation and benefit policies that are consistent with the desired work force and strategic direction of the company. Poor management of human resources can have a devastating impact on the entire organization because all processes require appropriate personnel. It is also important that information about the process and its outputs be used to improve process efficiency and facilitate effective decision making.

Example

In order to attract high-caliber, creative, and energetic personnel, many companies considering going public routinely issue stock options to new hires. The use of options allows the company to attract people that share the company's vision as well as reducing cash compensation costs. Furthermore, because such companies are usually dynamic, exciting, and challenging, employment opportunities are attractive to many highly talented people. However, recent moves by the FASB and IASB to ensure that these option grants are reflected as compensation expense on the income statement may cause them to be less attractive in the future. Additionally, the SEC in the United States has been requiring organizations to restate financial statements because of a practice of backdating options to points when stocks are trading low so that employees can unfairly profit from them.

Figure 6–4   Process Map: Human Resource Management

Process Objectives
- Identify and acquire adequate human resources
- Attract and hire highly skilled, loyal, and motivated employees
- Provide adequate training for employees
- Establish policies and procedures for managing, evaluating, and compensating employees
- Effectively manage employee turnover
- Comply with workplace health and safety regulations
- Compile, process, and report information necessary for process improvement

Process Activities
- Identify human resource needs
- Authorize hiring
- Recruiting
- Hiring
- Training and motivation
- Payroll processing
- Employee evaluation
- Promotion and changes to compensation
- Employee termination

Process Data Streams

Information Feeds
- Strategic plans and budgets
- Recruitment needs and hiring requests
- Position descriptions
- Workforce regulations
- Tax regulations
- Union contracts
- Labor market statistics and demographics

Information Generation
- Personnel files
- Tax forms
- Employment contracts
- Human resource procedures
- Performance evaluations/reviews
- Contract revisions
- Training schedules
- Payroll data and costs
- Payroll tax remittances

Accounting Impact of Activities

Routine Transactions
- Recruiting and hiring expenses
- Payroll
- Benefits
- Payroll taxes
- Training costs
- Employee retirements

Non-routine Transactions
- Pensions, health care, and other post-retirement costs
- Bonuses
- Employee terminations
- Employee deaths
- Disability claims
- Employment litigation

Accounting Estimates
- Pension accruals
- Post retirement benefit accruals
- Self-insured medical or workers' compensation obligations

PROCESS ACTIVITIES

Process activities reflect the discrete actions and steps that are performed within the process to achieve process objectives. There are numerous types of general activities that can be performed within a process:

- Decision making
- Information gathering

- Information processing and communication
- Process monitoring and improvement
- Accounting for transactions and estimates
- Physical actions (e.g., training employees, converting raw materials).

Most processes involve a large number of activities that, in turn, are comprised of numerous detailed steps. A challenge to the auditor is to decide what level of detail is needed for the analysis. The auditor wants to analyze process actions at a level of detail that allows the identification of key risks related to the objectives of the process. The description of process activities should be adequate to describe how the process starts, how it terminates, and what happens in between. Controls are part of the internal threat analysis and do not need to be specifically identified within the process map.

The second panel of Figure 6–4 illustrates the activities performed as part of the human resource management process. Execution of these activities depends on the various strategic and process decisions that an organization makes, such as where to locate, how much to automate, and how to compensate employees. Key human resource activities for most organizations include

- Identifying human resource needs: The organization continually assesses its personnel needs including number, type, and qualifications of factory workers and service providers, administrative staff, and professional and management personnel. As part of this activity, job descriptions and guidelines for minimum qualifications are developed that can be used to guide the search for appropriate personnel.
- Authorizing the hiring of personnel: Management approves the initiation of a process to fill identified positions that satisfy specific needs. Management also authorizes general guidelines for compensation and benefits for a position.
- Recruiting: The search for employees takes many different forms and depends on the types of skills that are needed. The hiring of entry level factory or service sector workers is different from hiring professional staff or senior management. Negotiation of individual compensation and benefits is also considered part of the recruiting process unless it is predetermined by union contract or legal constraint.
- Hiring: Administratively, adding a new employee to payroll involves a number of detailed steps. An employment agreement that stipulates compensation and benefits must be prepared. Payroll deductions are authorized and processed such as payroll taxes, insurance coverage, and pension contributions. Maintenance of accurate and up-to-date personnel files is an important aspect of this activity.
- Training and motivation: Organizations promote employee competence with training and educational support. They promote appropriate behavior and discourage undesirable behavior with a statement of core values, mission statement, and code of personal conduct, backed up with appropriate enforcement of firm policies.
- Payroll processing: Paying people on a periodic basis is a routine but complex set of activities. Numerous inputs are needed to process payroll including hours worked, pay scales, payroll deductions, and tax withholding. This information is used to compute payroll amounts for the employees in the organization. Disbursements are made by check or electronic funds transfer. Proper accounting for all of this activity is an important part of the process. This step may be outsourced to a third party service provider.

- Employee evaluation: Employee performance should be evaluated periodically. The evaluations can be used to improve performance, justify promotions, warn employees who are not meeting expectations, or terminate poor performers.
- Employee pay and benefit adjustments: Employment arrangements with individuals change over time as they gain more experience and assume more responsibility. Promotions and pay increases should be reviewed and authorized by appropriate levels of management.
- Employee termination: Employees leave an organization for a number of reasons: new jobs, life changes (e.g., new partners), death, disability, and involuntary termination. Each of these situations must be handled in a different fashion. Many forms of employee termination involve employee payments (e.g., pension, severance pay).

Management of human resources can be a very complex and difficult task. Complexity arises for many reasons, including the wide variety of employment opportunities within the organization, the diverse sources of qualified personnel, the terms of employment and compensation, and the variety of reasons for employee terminations. Furthermore, current trends in employment practices only serve to increase this complexity. Temporary employment, telecommuting, flextime, and outsourcing all affect the way in which employees are hired and managed. Compensation arrangements such as stock options and benefits such as on-premises day care and maternity leave affect the cost of labor. Also, changes in employees' attitudes about loyalty and work-life balance affect the relationship between employees and the company. Finally, employment regulations continue to evolve in areas such as employment discrimination, accommodation of disabilities, privacy, workplace harassment, and worker safety. Failure to adequately consider these regulations can leave an organization with an inadequate workforce or exposed to litigation and fines.

Example

Many organizations have begun to outsource more of their noncritical processes and related personnel. Facilities maintenance, delivery and shipping, and transaction processing activities are areas where outsourcing has become common. The organization benefits by gaining more control over its human resources by turning what is often a fixed cost component of operations into a variable cost which can be easily adjusted as personnel needs change. The primary disadvantage is that the company gives up some control over personnel hiring and assignments that could lead to quality problems and additional tax or legal complexities.

INFORMATION FLOWS

Processes use, produce, and transform information. The third panel of Figure 6–4 lists the information needs and outputs of the human resource management process. The accountant needs to understand the nature and reliability of information flows within a process for three reasons:

1. *Information within a process will have a direct impact on the financial statements:* Information about transactions is initially captured within a process and then transformed through various internal systems. If that information is not reliable, the risk of financial statement misstatement is higher.

2. *Information provides the auditor assurance about the quality of a process:* If key information is missing, untimely, or unreliable, actions taken within the process are less likely to be efficient or effective. For example, if a credit manager lacks access to external credit reports, the auditor would conclude that risks associated with credit approval are high. Also, the auditor can analyze where information goes once it is produced, that is, information output from one process is presumably input to another process. Information that is not available to a process that may need it may create problems in other areas of the company.

Example

Transactions executed on the Internet provide a rich and detailed information trail that can be used to improve marketing, advertising, and distribution. Every hit on a web page can reveal a great deal of information about the visitors' identity or demographics, how they got there, what they looked at and for how long, and where they went when they left. Capturing and using this information can lead to significant improvements in process performance. If no one uses the information, an opportunity may be lost to better understand the company's web-based customers. If the information is misused (e.g., through theft of identity), it can create other serious risks for the business.

3. *Information provides the auditor evidence about the significance of process risks:* By tracking key performance measures over time, the auditor (and management) can identify when a process may be inefficient or ineffective. For example, sales managers may monitor on-time delivery statistics to be warned when deliveries are slow, which could lead to a loss of customer goodwill. Such information may provide the auditor with an excellent source of analytical evidence concerning risks that may impact the audit.[1]

Key information used in the human resource management process includes job descriptions and hiring authorizations, legal regulations, personnel data, payroll records, tax information, and training and work schedules. Auditing standards require that the auditor obtain a basic understanding of the flow of transaction data and related internal control so the auditor should consider the reliability of relevant information systems. For example, the auditor will look at information that is processed manually differently from information that is processed electronically. Some information systems will connect directly to accounting and the financial statements (e.g., sales journal entries, inventory changes) whereas others are useful as a potential source of analytical evidence (e.g., customer ratings and satisfaction). Further, some systems operate independently from each other, whereas other systems are linked across processes or even companies. If an important information system is highly automated, it may be necessary for the auditor to use an information technology specialist to evaluate the design and reliability of the system.

ACCOUNTING IMPACT OF PROCESS ACTIVITIES

The final element of the process map is identification of the accounting transactions and estimates that are affected by the activities within the process. This provides a direct link to the financial statements being examined. As a general rule,

1 Chapter 9 discusses process performance measures in detail.

the more effective and efficient a process is on an overall basis, the more likely that transaction processing within the process will be accurate and reliable. Auditors classify transactions into two categories: (1) accounting transactions and (2) accounting estimates. The first category may be broken down into routine and non-routine transactions. This classification is important because each transaction type may have different effects on the financial statements and may exhibit different risks of misstatement.

Routine Transactions: These transactions reflect events and circumstances that occur on a regular and systematic basis. Routine transactions drive most processes because they reflect normal activity that occurs on a daily basis. Most companies invest heavily in controls over routine transactions, and often use automated systems to process routine transactions in a highly reliable manner. Failure on the part of a company to effectively and efficiently control routine transactions likely will lead to process or even business failure. Also, because of the emphasis by management on routine transactions and the presence of automated controls, these transactions are harder to manipulate by individuals wishing to commit fraud. However, the auditor cannot ignore routine transactions because, cumulatively, they usually have a highly material effect on the financial statements. Furthermore, they are often the source of period-end adjustments that can be manipulated for fraudulent purposes. Routine transactions arising from human resource management include the computation and payment of periodic payroll.

Non-routine Transactions: These transactions reflect events or circumstances that do not occur on a regular or frequent basis and may involve complex calculations or require significant judgment on the part of management. Examples might include purchase of new facilities, introduction of new products, or negotiating a new union contract. Because these transactions are infrequent, information systems may not be structured to process them reliably. Furthermore, non-routine transactions often arise when a process does not operate as planned. For example, disposing of underperforming assets, discontinuing product lines, terminating contracts, or repossessing assets are usually non-routine events for an organization. However, these events are often associated with unforeseen developments that management might be tempted to underreport in the financial statements. Because of these conditions, the risks of error and misrepresentation are higher than for routine transactions. Determining whether a specific transaction is routine or non-routine requires judgment by the auditor. Examples of non-routine transactions arising in human resource management include payments for employee termination, disability, or litigation.

Example

For a retail operation, sales returns are probably considered a relatively routine transaction and can be highly automated, even though such transactions are less routine than the initial recording of sales. To compensate for the slightly less routine aspects of sales returns, many retailers may require that they be processed by supervisors rather than clerks. In contrast, many industries have very few sales returns, so they would then constitute a non-routine transaction. Consider the builder of nuclear submarines—the idea of a sales return is probably silly. However, sales adjustments for production deficiencies might be a common transaction in such an environment.

Accounting Estimates: Accounting estimates involve judgment on the part of management and typically pervade the financial statements. Estimates are not transactions in the typical sense because they might not be associated with a specific event. However, estimates may be the most critical accounting aspect of a process because management bases the decision on how to account for estimates primarily on their opinions, hypotheses, and asymmetric knowledge relating to the underlying facts and events. Thus, should management want the financial statements to reflect a specific outcome, the use of estimates is a powerful tool for managing earnings or bolstering the level of performance reported in the financial statements. It is hard to argue with a process manager who asserts that the current recorded level of an estimate is consistent with his extensive industry experience. However, most of the major accounting frauds of the 20th century involved accounting estimates, highlighting to auditors the need to evaluate estimates very carefully.

The financial statements contain numerous estimates related to the realizability of asset values, the market value of investments, the present value of obligations, and the likelihood of loss contingencies. Some important examples of estimates include

- Collectibility of receivables
- Reserves for probable future losses
- Asset impairments
- Warranty costs
- Sales returns and allowances
- Environmental liabilities
- Casualty losses subject to litigation

Such estimates present a challenge to the auditor because their ultimate resolution depends on uncertain future events. Lacking a crystal ball, the auditor must make a best guess about future outcomes and their impact on current financial statements. Further, the best source of information about the resolution about these events is the organization's management, who may be biased toward some desired outcome that may or may not be known by the auditor. Examples of estimates related to human resource management include pension and post-retirement benefit accruals.

The risk of an estimate being misstated is directly affected by its complexity, the availability and reliability of data used to make the estimate, the nature of assumptions used, and the degree of uncertainty surrounding future events. Warranty costs on small appliances that have been manufactured for a long time without significant production changes will be relatively easy to estimate as long as the client accurately records actual warranty costs as they arise. This historical data can be extremely useful for supporting reasonable estimates. In contrast, environmental liabilities arising from the clean up of toxic land sites may be extremely difficult to estimate due to the long lead time of the clean-up process, uncertainty surrounding who pays and how much, the changing nature of clean-up technology, changing trends in regulatory assessment, and potentially biased input from management.

> **Authoritative**
> **Guidance & Standards**
> SAS 109 and ISA 315 indicate that routine transactions generally are best performed using automated systems. However, both standards note that for non-routine transactions and estimates in which judgment is required, manual processes likely will be necessary.

The auditor's objective is to test management assertions associated with estimates. Most of the evidence needed to evaluate accounting estimates is obtained during the review of key processes and related information flows. Typical audit procedures include analysis of significant business risks, inquiry about client procedures for dealing with estimates, analytical procedures applied directly to the results of the estimation process, and evidence obtained from other tests that may be pertinent to the reasonableness of estimates (e.g., evidence of obsolescence from observing the physical condition of inventory). For particularly difficult estimates, internal information may be supplemented with industry statistics or outside experts may be needed (e.g., actuaries, engineers).

INTERNAL THREAT ANALYSIS AND PROCESS RISKS

One of the reasons an auditor prepares a process map is to provide a framework for analyzing the risks associated with a process. In Chapter 5, we discussed strategic risks that arise primarily in the external environment. Many of those risks will have a direct impact on potential risks within individual processes. An economic recession in the external environment may cause customers to be slow in paying their bills, which directly relates to customer service. Problems with suppliers will have an impact on internal operations and procurement. In this section, we will discuss the types of risks that can arise within a process and how they might lead to significant residual risks that affect the audit.

The purpose of *internal threat analysis* is to assess the impact of process risks on the organization, including proper reflection in the financial statements. There are three components to internal threat analysis: (1) risk identification, (2) risk response (e.g., controls), and (3) risk monitoring. Column 1 of Figure 6–5 identifies numerous risks that might occur as part of the human resource management. Process risks can emanate from many internal or external sources. For example, external developments in technology can have a direct impact on the technology of specific processes by making existing systems obsolete. Other process risks will be unique to individual processes, for example the risk of incorrectly processing loan payment transactions is primarily a financial management problem. Our focus in this chapter is to analyze the specific risks that arise in business processes. To facilitate our discussion, we will discuss the eight categories of internal risk identified in Figure 6–6.

PEOPLE RISKS

Managerial Risk: Risk can occur when a process is not adequately managed or clear lines of authority and accountability are lacking. The efficiency and effectiveness of a process is dependent on a proper balance between manager responsibilities, competence, experience, and incentives. Managers who lack appropriate authority, who are not adequately trained for their position, or who lack experience are more likely to make mistakes. For example, union rules often limit the flexibility a manager has in directing subordinates. Performance incentives can work to increase process efficiency, or they can create unforeseen problems if not properly aligned with the objectives of the process. Risk may also arise if there is a lack of procedures, policies, and decision limits within a process. For example, an organization may establish maximum credit limits that can be assigned by a credit manager or maximum price discounts that can be granted by a sales manager.

Figure 6–5   Internal Threat Analysis: Human Resource Management

Process Risks	Potential Audit Implications
PR1: Lack of personnel with appropriate skills	• Expectations: High levels of process errors and related costs • Viability: Risk of failure if critical skills missing • Control environment: Lack of personnel may cause processes to be ineffective or segregation of duties to be bypassed.
PR2: Excess or unneeded personnel	• Expectations: High overhead or administrative costs • Audit risk: Proper allocation of excess labor costs, especially if related to production (standard costs)
PR3: Discriminatory employment practices	• Audit risk: Contingent liabilities due to litigation • Control environment: Attitudes of management and employees towards fellow employees may have implications for financial reporting.
PR4: Excess costs of recruiting and hiring	• Expectations: High overhead or administrative costs • Audit risk: Cost allocation, especially related to production
PR5: Errors in payroll authorizations (pay rates, taxes, time)	• Audit risk: Errors in payroll related transactions and accounts • Control environment: Heightened control risk related to payroll transactions • Comment for Client: Improved procedures for payroll authorizations
PR6: Errors in payroll processing	• Audit risk: Errors in payroll-related transactions and accounts. • Control environment: Heightened control risk related to payroll transactions • Comment for Client: Improved procedures for payroll processing
PR7: Low employee morale	• Expectations: Increased costs related to poor worker performance, e.g., direct labor or product defects. • Control environment: Disgruntled employees may be ineffective or act against interests of company.
PR8: Violations of employment laws	• Audit risk: Contingent liabilities due to fines and penalties • Control environment: May indicate attitudes towards regulation in general (including financial reporting) • Comment for Client: Process improvement to assure compliance with labor laws
PR9: Failure to provide adequate feedback or training for improvement	• Control environment: Disgruntled employees may be ineffective or act against interests of company.
PR10: Unplanned loss of critical personnel or excessive turnover	• Viability: Risk of failure if critical personnel depart. • Control environment: If losses are critical to financial reporting, there may be a pervasive effect on levels of control risk.

Figure 6–6   Analyzing Process Risks

People Risks		
Managerial Risk	**Ethics Risk**	**Human Resource Risk**
Lines of authority	Management fraud	Competence
Performance incentives	Employee theft	Performance incentives
Institutional constraints	Illegal acts	Hiring and retention
Competence	Unethical behavior	Training and development
	Unauthorized actions	Required skills

Direct Process Risks	
Operational Risk	**Information Risk**
Quality of products	Reliability of information
Cost of processes	Quality of performance measurement
Cycle time	Timeliness of information
Efficiency	Relevance
Capacity usage	Completeness
Repairs and maintenance	Dissemination and reporting
Resource utilization and wastage	
Process failure	
Process interruption	

Indirect Process Risks		
Technology Risk	**Planning Risk**	**Regulatory Risk**
System reliability	Budgeting and planning	Labor laws
System adequacy	Incentives	Tax laws
System security	Adequacy of resources	Environmental laws
Process efficiency	Performance measurement	Health and safety regulations
System changes		Product licensing

Example

Netscape was one of the first successful Internet-related companies to go public. Its stock, initially issued at $28, rose to $97 5/8 at the time Netscape merged with AOL in 1999. Marc Andreessen, co-founder of Netscape, revealed in an interview after the merger that he had misunderstood the nature of his company and its ability to generate value from the Internet. He had believed that his company was essentially a software company that would grow and profit from enhancing its web-browser software. However, what he subsequently learned was that his company was a portal to the Internet and that software was just a facilitator of Internet activity. In the long run, he felt that the company could only be profitable by taking advantage of its value as a portal, not as a producer of software. His failure to appreciate his own company's business strategy was one reason the company was unable to continue as an independent entity.

Ethics Risk: The auditor should examine a process for indications that there is a lack of integrity or ethical behavior by individuals. Given that people bring their attitudes about ethical behavior with them from the outside world, this risk follows somewhat from risks associated with social attitudes and the market for labor. The auditor should consider whether the company is alert to potential unethical behavior and whether it actively strives to avoid conflicts of interest and illegal actions by employees. The auditor's evaluation of the organization's control environment is an important predictor of whether individuals at the process level perceive that unethical behavior will be tolerated or come to believe that unethical behavior is necessary to succeed. The auditor should consider conditions that might cause otherwise honest individuals to behave in questionable ways.

Example

Prudential Insurance Co. was subject to an extensive scandal involving sales practices of its agents. Insurance agents are generally paid on commission for writing policies. Commissions on new policies are generally higher than renewed policies. Agents would contact existing policyholders and urge them to cancel their old policies and replace them with new policies with better benefits. In order to make the new policies appear cheaper, the agents would take the accumulated cash value of the old policy and offset it against new premiums. The new policies would look less expensive because agents would disguise or misrepresent the loss of cash value. When the questionable sales practices were revealed, Prudential suffered large fines, extensive class action litigation, and substantial loss of reputation, all because of unethical practices related to the sales process.

Human Resource Risk: The effectiveness and efficiency of most processes will be dependent on the quality of personnel assigned to the activities that comprise the process. The auditor should consider whether individuals have the qualifications, competence, and training to adequately perform their duties. The quality of personnel is directly affected by conditions in the market for labor and is influenced by a company's approach to recruiting, compensation, training, and supervision. If any of those functions are performed poorly, the quality of a process will deteriorate because disgruntled employees can negatively impact a process. Although auditors are often uncomfortable judging individuals, the assessment of employee competence and attitudes is an important element of process risk assessment.

Example

Auditors are often asked by audit committees to comment on the quality of an enterprise's financial management. Auditor responses are often quite positive no matter what the actual auditor experience has been with the client because executives responsible for financial management generally have influence over the appointment and reappointment of the auditor. However, recent events such as the Enron scandal have resulted in auditors paying more attention to their responsibility to the board, via the audit committee, and these discussions are reported to be much more frank in today's environment, particularly when the audit committee hires and fires the auditor.

DIRECT PROCESS RISKS

Operational Risk: This risk category pertains to the execution of the basic activities within a process and encompasses the potentially wide range of things that can wrong within a process. Potential operational risks relate to

- *Quality:* Is the process subject to unacceptable rates of defects, mistakes, or errors?
- *User satisfaction:* Are users of the process unhappy after the process is complete?
- *Cycle time:* Do processes take too long to execute?
- *Obsolescence/impairment:* Does the process depend on obsolete products or practices?
- *Shrinkage:* Is there excess waste in the process (e.g., time, materials)?

- *Capacity:* Does the process exhibit excess or inadequate capacity to handle the work flow demanded?
- *Process failure:* Are there excessive breakdowns or work stoppages in the process?
- *Process linkages:* Are connections to other processes (including external parties) subject to problems?

Operational risks tend to be unique to a specific process. However, many of these risks are dependent on the nature of other process risks, especially people risks. In fact, the visible manifestation of people risks may be in the form of operational risk. For example, if employees are not adequately trained, quality, cycle time, or customer satisfaction may deteriorate.

Example

Many customer service problems are individually minor but can create a backlash from customers if they occur frequently. For example, many fast food restaurants have a drive-through window. Most customers who are served at the window consume their purchase away from the restaurant location. If they discover that the attendant has made an error (e.g., left out the fries), the negative reaction by the customer tends to be severe. The cost of the error may be less than a dollar but the negative impression left with the customer will be large. If this were to happen frequently, the cumulative effect of a bunch of very small mistakes could be to lose a significant portion of the store's customer base.

Information Risk: Numerous problems can arise in the absence of accurate and reliable information about and within a process. Reliable information is needed for decision making, to monitor process activity, and to evaluate performance. Of particular importance to the auditor is the reliability of transaction processing. Given that most accounting transactions are initially identified, captured, and measured during process activities, information risks may have a direct impact on the risk of material misstatements in financial reports. in financial reports. The reliability of information processing will depend on a number of factors, including the design of the system, the reporting structure, the dependence on information technology, reliance on external providers of information technology (software, hardware, and service bureaus[2]), the accessibility of information, and control over changes to information processing.

Example

Control over system changes can be extremely critical. Many large companies have or will adopt enterprise resource planning (ERP) systems that link the information flows across processes. These systems are extremely complex, costly to install, and difficult to maintain. Inadequate resources or expertise can result in a changeover disaster. A hospital decided to undertake the installation of a new patient and revenue system without the use of external consultants—internal computer personnel assured management that they could handle the changeover. The start-up of the new system was scheduled for a weekend when activity was expected to be slow. Due to unforeseen problems, the start-up failed and also destroyed many months of patient transaction data. The hospital had to bring in outside experts (at a high cost) to recover from the disaster, and some information was permanently lost.

---

2 A service bureau is an outside organization that provides computing services to other companies, alleviating the need for the companies to maintain their own computing resources. Payroll is probably the most frequently outsourced computing service. Such services are provided by companies that specialize in computing services, and often by banks.

INDIRECT PROCESS RISKS

Regulatory Risk: Most organizations are subject to a broad variety of external regulations that impact different processes within the organization. Employment laws affect human resource processes; worker safety and environmental laws place boundaries on production practices; consumer protection laws do likewise for sales efforts; and securities regulators monitor and can dictate acceptable financial and accounting practices. The auditor should identify the forms of regulation that affect a process and assess the likelihood that the organization can comply. Lack of compliance with appropriate regulations opens the organization to possible material fines and penalties, and may harm its reputation among important stakeholders.

Example

Most countries have drug regulators (e.g., Health Canada and the Food and Drug Administration in the United States) that establish rules for the manufacture of pharmaceuticals. All aspects of the production process must comply with the the regulators' required manufacturing practices. Failure to follow those regulations can lead to the shut down of the facility by the regulators. For example, one FDA requirement that is particularly important from an accounting perspective is that all production batches must be uniquely identified, including the source and identification of the chemicals used in a specific batch. The batches must be controlled and monitored until delivered to the purchaser. As a result, the quantity, condition, and existence of pharmaceutical inventories are highly controlled.

Technology Risk: Every process has elements of technology, and the role of IT in most processes is increasing rapidly. Technology risks can arise from the external environment, as when new advances render internal systems obsolete, or internally, as when research and development initiatives fail to produce desired results. Within a process, the auditor should consider whether technology has been appropriately utilized and whether a process has the appropriate level of technology investment necessary to achieve its objectives, including sufficient automated controls. The design and installation of new systems creates special challenges to an organization. Technology can affect a process in a number of ways:

- *Execution of a process:* The design of a process is often dictated by the technology available. For example, technology can affect manufacturing (e.g., robots can make welds, apply paint, or install parts in a car) and the execution of transactions (e.g., credit cards can be verified by "swiping" the card through a reader).

Example

The Internet is rapidly changing the way many processes are performed. Web-based procurement is becoming common in many industries. An Internet company can establish a virtual market that lets many sellers list their merchandise, prices, and terms on a web site. Potential buyers can then search the site for what they need and compare prices/terms across suppliers (Orbitz, Amazon). Access to one site allows access to multiple buyers and sellers at the same time. Some sites also support an auction process where potential buyers can enter prices they are willing to pay and suppliers can accept or reject (eBay). Potential buyers can then bid against each other. Auctions sites are particularly useful for degradable or time-sensitive products and services such as airline seats or advertising space. The Internet company receives a small commission on each transaction executed through the site. Buyers' search time and costs are dramatically reduced, and sellers are able to obtain rapid and easy access to their target customers.

- *Information processing:* The manner in which information is captured and processed is dependent on technology. Manual entry of a sale into a cash register is different than scanning bar codes on merchandise. Enterprise resource planning systems allow companies to link data across processes and facilitate the integrated analysis of results for the entire organization.
- *Process monitoring:* The cost of monitoring a process is declining as the power of technology increases. Most cars now have a large number of different sensors for monitoring potential problems ranging from low fuel levels to whether a door is open. Production processes are no less amenable to electronic monitoring, which creates enormous potential for the auditor to assess the effectiveness and efficiency of processes in real time. A sensor in an automotive assembly line that detects that door installations are slightly misaligned helps the company detect such a problem before it has resulted in a number of defective vehicles, and provides evidence to the auditor that routine activities are being effectively performed (e.g., such activities might result in fewer warranty claims).

The accuracy of transaction recording is increased through the use of electronic data entry and processing. However, technology can be either inadequate or too complex. In the former case, the quality of a process may deteriorate because of a breakdown in manual procedures. For example, manual entry of sales data is less reliable than scanning. However, technology can also be too complex leading to process breakdowns or difficulties in integrating systems.

Planning Risk: Issues related to planning that can have a negative impact on a process include budgeting, scheduling, resource and cash needs, and financial reporting. In essence, planning risk reflects the possibility that resource allocations do not match the needs of specific processes. If plans and budgets are unreasonable or unrealistic, they can cause dysfunctional performance. For example, if production demands exceed process capacity, it is likely that quality problems will arise and errors occur as the components (equipment and labor) are pushed beyond their intended endurance levels. If excess attention is devoted to inappropriate performance measures, employees may focus on activities that are reflected in the performance measures at the expense of other important activities. Perhaps even more serious is when too much emphasis is placed on performance measures within a single business process at the expense of performance across business processes in the value chain, leading to better process "performance" but poorer performance for the organization overall.

AN EXAMPLE OF PROCESS ANALYSIS: HUMAN RESOURCE MANAGEMENT

Process maps and internal threat analysis are very useful for identifying residual risks arising from specific processes. To illustrate the use of these techniques in more detail, we will further examine the process of human resource management. Human resource management is usually an important process for an auditor to consider because the success of an organization depends on the quality of its people and there are a large number of routine and non-routine transactions generated by the process. The accounting implications of human resource management range from mundane payroll processing and payments to employees to much more complicated issues related to retirement benefits and incentive compensation.

The key transactions related to human resource management are identified in Figure 6–4. Employees are usually paid on a periodic basis, for example, every two weeks. The emphasis of payroll processing is on the periodic preparation of payroll and the proper classification of the expenditures. The detailed steps for processing payroll are indicated in Figure 6–7. Hourly employees use physical or electronic *time cards* to check in and out of work to record their hours worked. Hourly employees may also complete a *time report* or *job ticket* that describes exactly what they did during a given pay period. This information is needed to

Figure 6–7   Summary of Payroll Activities

PROCESS/Activity	Documents	Journals, Ledgers, and Records Used	Typical Journal Entry
Hiring: Recruiting new employees based on company needs and policies	Employment application (internal)	Job descriptions and guidelines	
Personnel: Maintain accurate records on all personnel including pay rates, deduction authorization, tax information, and fitness reports.	Pay rate authorizations (internal) Tax forms (external) Deduction authorizations (external)	Employee master file	
Employee time reporting: Employees report time spent on job-related activities with frequency and level of detail dependent on nature of employment	*Hourly workers:* Time cards Job tickets (internal) *Salaried workers:* Time report (internal)		
Payroll preparation: Payroll costs are computed and disbursements are prepared	Check (internal) EFT authorization (internal)	Payroll register Labor distribution report	
Payroll distribution: Payroll disbursements are delivered to employees, by check, cash, or direct deposit.		*(Documents may be provided by service organization if payroll processing is outsourced)*	
General accounting: Payroll expenditures and liabilities are recorded in the appropriate accounts.	Journal entry ticket (internal) Tax forms (internal)	General ledger	Dr. Payroll Expenses Dr. Assets (inventory) Cr. Cash Cr. Accrued Liabilities

assure that payroll expenditures can be debited to the appropriate expense or asset account. Salaried employees do not need to complete time cards but are often asked to complete a time report for each pay period.

Payroll computations are based on hours worked, authorized wage and salary scales, and appropriate deductions. Gross payroll reflects total wages earned prior to deductions; net payroll reflects the amount actually paid to an employee after considering all mandatory and voluntary deductions. Employee *paychecks* or direct deposit documents are prepared, approved, and distributed to the employees.[3] Payroll information is summarized in the *payroll register*, including gross pay, taxes, deductions, and net pay, which becomes the basis for making entries to the general ledger and preparing payroll tax returns that are filed with various taxing authorities (e.g., local, state/provincial, and federal/national governments).

The key event of this process is the completion of service by the employees. Each day, hour, and minute that an employee works adds to the amount of the company's liability to that employee. However, because payroll costs are usually recorded when employees are paid (i.e., on a periodic basis), a timing issue can arise when the end of a fiscal period does not coincide with the end of a pay period. This also applies to payroll taxes and other personnel expenses such as vacation time that accrue but that may be paid much later.

Examining the process map for human resource management (Figure 6–4) in more detail, we see that process objectives include assuring an adequate supply of labor with the appropriate skill and training to fulfill key jobs within the organization. Also of importance is the need to evaluate and compensate employees commensurate with their value to the organization. Furthermore, an organization wants to carefully manage turnover, retaining desirable employees but terminating undesirable employees in a fair and legally justifiable manner. Workplace conditions, employee treatment, and wrongful terminations can all cause severe problems for an organization.

Example

Wal-Mart attributes much of its success to a highly motivated and non-unionized work force. Large union groups are continuously trying to organize Wal-Mart employees but have been generally unsuccessful. However, as the company has grown, difficulties with employees have become more severe, often resulting in litigation against the company. In a recent lawsuit, a jury in California ordered Wal-Mart to pay $172 million to approximately 116,000 employees who were forced to work through their lunch breaks without being paid in 2001. Further, in 2006, the company finally acquiesced to some degree by advertising for a director to handle stakeholder relations to help repair its deteriorating reputation related to employee practices. In contrast, Costco has outperformed Wal-Mart's Sam's Club warehouse division. Costco claims this success is due in part to paying its employees the highest average wages and benefits in the retail industry. In the case of Costco, however, investors have placed pressure on the organization for paying its employees too much because it reduces the returns to shareholders. The contrast between Wal-Mart and Costco illustrates how workforce relations can be elevated to the level of a key element of strategic positioning differentiation.

---

3 Direct deposit of payroll into employee bank accounts is becoming more common. In a direct deposit system, paper checks are not needed and payroll distribution is performed electronically. However, employees usually receive a pay advice summarizing the gross pay and deductions used to compute net pay deposited to the employee's bank account.

Poorly trained employees, dishonest employees, and inadequate personnel can have serious ramifications for the effectiveness and efficiency of many parts of the organization. Problems in human resource management may often be revealed by problems in other processes such as sales and customer service, and may be especially important in service organizations where the employees are the main source of value creation. Internal threat analysis for human resource management (Figure 6–5) highlights ten possible risks. These are intended to be representative, and other organizations might have more or different risks. Key risks pertain to hiring the appropriate labor force in a cost effective manner (*PR1, PR2, PR3, PR4*), managing the workforce for best results (*PR7, PR8, PR9, PR10*) and assuring accurate information processing related to payroll (*PR5, PR6*). Although any of these process risks may be relevant to the audit, the last two are most directly significant because they directly affect financial reporting.

The auditor develops a process map and assesses internal threats for the purpose of assessing residual risks that are likely to have a significant impact on the conduct of the audit. Consequently, the last step of process analysis is to assess the significance of the risks. Whether a risk needs to be controlled depends on how it affects the performance of the organization. For our analysis, let's assume that the company is a software company that is owned and managed by a small group of friends who dropped out of their university to start up the business. It has been generally successful and is rapidly growing and evolving in a very competitive environment. Within this context, the small sample of human resource risks is plotted in a risk map (Figure 6–8).

Figure 6–8   Assessment of Inherent Risks for Human Resource Management

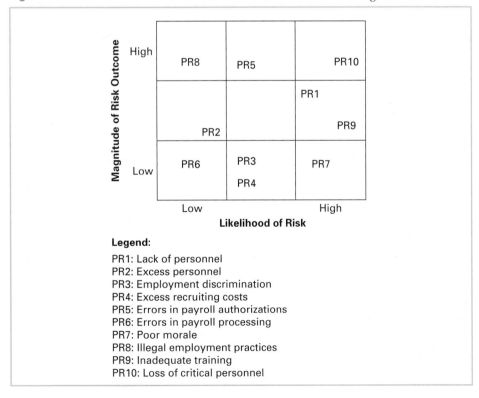

Legend:
PR1: Lack of personnel
PR2: Excess personnel
PR3: Employment discrimination
PR4: Excess recruiting costs
PR5: Errors in payroll authorizations
PR6: Errors in payroll processing
PR7: Poor morale
PR8: Illegal employment practices
PR9: Inadequate training
PR10: Loss of critical personnel

In the example, *PR10,* the risk of unplanned loss of key personnel, is considered the most significant risk. In different ways, *PR5* (risk of errors in payroll authorizations), *PR1* (lack of personnel with appropriate skills), and *PR9* (failure to provide training or feedback) are also very important risks. Risks *PR2, PR3, PR4,* and *PR6* are considered to be relatively insignificant unless subsequent performance indicates a rising problem. Finally, the remaining risks (*PR7, PR8*) have attributes that indicate they could be significant under some conditions. The potential implications of the individual risks are summarized in Figure 6–5 (second column). The relatively high level of significance for *PR10, PR5, PR1,* and *PR9* indicates that they may turn out to be residual risks so their implications take on an increased importance for the auditor.

SUMMARY AND CONCLUSION

The purpose of this chapter was to introduce business processes, their related accounting transaction and estimates, and assessment of internal process risks. A value chain describes the processes within the organization that contribute to its success. Business processes are designed to respond to specific pressures or threats from the external environment. The assessment of process risks and the analysis of their audit implications add to the auditor's understanding of existing circumstances and conditions likely to affect the conduct of the audit. The analyses performed in this and the prior chapter are useful for assessing risks, but whether or not identified risks pose a major concern to the auditor depends on how management responds to the risks. The next two chapters introduce internal control and provide tools for the auditor to extend his or her understanding of risks in the organization.

BIBLIOGRAPHY OF RELATED PROFESSIONAL LITERATURE

Research

Ballou, B., C. E. Earley, and J. S. Rich. 2004. The Impact of Strategic-Positioning Information on Auditor Judgments about Business Process Performance. *Auditing: A Journal of Practice & Theory.* 23(2): 71–88.

Kopp, L. and E. O'Donnell. 2005. The influence of a process focus on category knowledge and internal control evaluation. *Accounting Organizations and Society.* 30(5): 423–434.

Leonard, J. and A. E. Gray. 1999. *Process Fundamentals.* Harvard Business School, HBS No. 9-696-023.

O'Donnell, E. and J. J. Schultz Jr. 2003. The Influence of Business-Process-Focused Audit Support Software on Analytical Procedures Judgments. *Auditing: A Journal of Practice & Theory.* 22(2): 265–281.

Porter, Michael. 1985. *Competitive Advantage: Creating and Sustaining Superior Performance.* The Free Press.

Auditing Standards

AICPA *Statements on Auditing Standard (SAS)* No. 109, "Understanding the Entity and Its Environment and Assessing the Risks of Material Misstatement."

IAASB *International Standards on Auditing (ISA)* No. 315, "Understanding the Entity and Its Environment and Assessing the Risks of Material Misstatement."

PCAOB. Auditing Standard No. 2, "An Audit of Internal Control Over Financial Reporting Performed in Conjunction with an Audit of Financial Statements."

QUESTIONS

1. What is a business process? How do organizations use them as a key part of the strategic management process at an organization?

2. Why should auditors develop an understanding of business processes? What impact does such understanding have on the ability to conduct an effective and efficient audit of the financial statements?

3. Business processes are described as being either primary processes or support processes. Compare and contrast each type of business process. Explain as part of your answer why either type of business process can be critical for an organization for achieving its strategic objectives.

4. What is a value chain? Examine the sample value chain presented in Figure 6–3 and describe how breakdowns in various parts of the value chain can affect management assertions about classes of transactions on the financial statements.

5. Compare and contrast business process risks to strategic risks. When considering both types of risks, consider how management responds to each type of risk.

6. What is the role of business processes for financial reporting? How do information systems impact this role?

7. Describe the importance of understanding process objectives. Who in the organization should an auditor utilize to best understand the process objectives in place for a given business process? How should an auditor evaluate business process objectives?

8. Why should auditors understand and document process activities, inputs, and outputs for a process being analyzed? For example, by documenting process activities, how will the auditor's ability to develop an understanding about transactions generated within the process be impacted?

9. What are the key differences between routine transactions, non-routine transactions, and accounting estimates that are relevant for the auditor. As part of the discussion, consider the likelihood of misstatements across each classification and the client's motivation to develop effective controls for each.

10. When identifying key process risks that could reduce the likelihood of achieving process objectives and impact the likelihood that transactions generated within the process could be misstated, why should the auditor consider both the likelihood and impact of the inherent risk? After assessing the inherent risks (e.g., by plotting them on a graph similar to what is shown in Figure 6–8), how should the auditor determine which risks should be incorporated into the audit?

11. Figure 6–6 provides eight classifications of process risks that should be considered by auditors when analyzing business processes. For each broad category of risks—people risks, direct process risks, and indirect process risks—describe how the transactions generated within business processes might be at a greater risk of misstatement should these risks not be properly addressed.

12. Explain how business processes can reduce risk but also be a source of risk. Illustrate with an example.

13. What is an audit-sensitive process? When is a process considered to be audit-sensitive? Illustrate with examples.

14. Why is technology considered such an important source of risk?

PROBLEMS

1. A value chain dissects the firm into its value-adding components, including primary activities and support processes. The primary activities of the value chain model are as follows:
   a. Inbound logistics
   b. Operations
   c. Marketing and sales
   d. Outbound logistics
   e. Service
   Consider a value chain model of an office equipment manufacturer (e.g., photocopiers). For each of the primary activities, discuss a potential audit risk inherent to it, including any accounts and audit objectives that would likely be affected.

2. For each of the following events in a wholesale auto parts firm, identify its location in the value chain. If it is a support activity, identify the primary activity it is supporting.
   a. Hiring new salespeople
   b. Filling an order for a large retail auto parts distributor
   c. Contract negotiation with auto parts manufacturers
   d. Construction of automated warehouse management system
   e. Study of emerging trends among consumers of auto parts
   f. Purchasing of advertising in trade magazines
   g. Training of new warehouse workers
   h. Signing a new agreement with unionized delivery employees
   i. Issuing equity to add new distribution hubs
   j. Receiving a shipment of air filters from a supplier

3. For each of the following events in a large baked goods manufacturer, identify its location in the value chain. If it is a support activity, identify the primary activity it is supporting.
   a. Production information system development
   b. Deliveries of baked goods to chain supermarkets
   c. Long-term debt refinancing to take advantage of lower interest rates
   d. Deliveries of flour and yeast to factory warehouse
   e. Securing adequate supplies of flour and yeast
   f. Training new salespeople
   g. Preparation of manuals for the production information system
   h. Negotiating favorable rates for power and water
   i. Construction of automated warehouse receiving system
   j. Installing new racks at their convenience customers' locations

4. Research each of the following companies and provide three examples of business processes that are likely to be audit-sensitive processes. For each company, provide one process that is critical to achieving objectives, one that involves extensive external interactions, and one that poses high risk. Explain why you believe that each process is applicable.
   a. PepsiCo, Inc.
   b. Foster's Group
   c. Lloyd's
   d. eBay

5. Process objectives represent an explicit statement of what a business process is trying to achieve. Most processes will have a number of objectives, of which only a few are likely to be most critical. Wal-Mart's strategy is based on offering a wide variety of desirable products at the lowest prices possible. For each of the following processes likely

to be in place at Wal-Mart, list what you believe to be the most critical process objectives (hint: use Figure 6–4 as a starting point):
   a.   Resource Acquisition
   b.   Store Layout and Product Placement
   c.   Vendor Selection
   d.   Materials Handling
   e.   Pricing

6. Starbucks has a strategy to establish its brand name as a universal symbol of quality for premium coffee and products associated with the lifestyles of those who enjoy premium coffee. For each of the following processes likely to be in place at Starbucks, list what you believe to be the most critical process objectives (hint: use Figure 6–4 as a starting point):
   a.   Human Resources
   b.   Resource Acquisition
   c.   Information Technology
   d.   Brand Management
   e.   Alliance Management

7. Because of the reliability of controls included in automated information systems, often routine transactions are not a high-risk area for substantive testing on audit engagements. Furthermore, recent evidence that estimates are often used in managing earnings and committing fraud emphasizes the need to carefully examine all key estimates on audit engagements. Depending on a client's internal control, non-routine transactions will require varying degrees of substantive testing. Thus, identifying transactions as routine, non-routine, or accounting estimates is important. For each of the following transactions likely to occur at Toyota, indicate whether the transaction is routine, non-routine, or an accounting estimate.
   a.   Merger and Acquisition Costs
   b.   Write-off of Existing Assets
   c.   Provision for Future Costs
   d.   Recognition of Intangible Assets
   e.   Reserves for Excess/Obsolete Inventory
   f.   Purchases of Components for Assembly
   g.   Contracts with Licensed Dealers
   h.   Capital Equipment Procurement
   i.   Accruals for Warranties
   j.   Stolen or Damaged Vehicles
   k.   Transportation Costs
   l.   Acquisition of New Product Brand Names
   m.   Advertising Costs for Brand Support
   n.   Sales to Dealerships
   o.   Special Promotion Incentives
   p.   Product Recalls
   q.   Dealer Warranty Claims

8. Internal risks can emanate from a number of different sources. Provide an example for each of the following internal risks for The China Construction Bank, which in 2005 became the first major bank in China to issue an initial public offering (IPO): Use Figure 6–6 to help you in completing this problem.
   a.   Managerial Risk
   b.   Ethics Risk
   c.   Regulatory Risk
   d.   Technology Risk
   e.   Financial Planning Risk

      f.   Human Resource Risk
      g.   Operational Risk
      h.   Information Risk

9. For each of the following business risks/threats, identify the potential audit implications (see Figure 6–5).

Business Risk/Threat	Potential Audit Implications
(1) Widespread recession is decreasing disposable income.	
(2) An exotic animal virus is affecting your ability to get high-quality meat for your restaurant.	
(3) Computer users find your new software difficult to install and use.	
(4) Advances in cable television technology mean that consumers can bypass your video store and order their movies through their cable provider.	
(5) The zoning council recently approved an area near the office building you own for further commercial development.	
(6) A large retail chain locates to your town and offers higher wages for employees.	
(7) Shortly after one of your airliners crashes, the media portrays your airline as unsafe.	
(8) Customers are shifting away from your network operating system product and towards "intranet" products.	

10. Match.com is one of the world's largest online matchmaking (i.e., dating) services. Access the company's web site and perform research to develop an idea of the matchmaking process for organization sufficient to complete the following components of a process map.
    a.   List probable objectives for the matchmaking process.
    b.   Describe the activities performed in the matchmaking process.
    c.   Describe information inflows and outflows related to the matchmaking process.
    d.   What routine and non-routine transactions and accounting estimates are impacted by the matchmaking process?

Case 6–1: Strategic Analysis and Business Processes

The value chain approach to business modeling is useful for developing an understanding of how a client runs its business. It is particularly useful for identifying the critical success factors that have the most impact on the client's ability to succeed by highlighting areas of the organization's operations where operating risks are most severe. Many of a client's operating risks also relate to audit risks that concern the auditor and that must be considered in planning the engagement. As a result, a carefully constructed model of a client's value chain is useful for audit planning.

Requirements

1. Select one of the following business organizations and prepare a general model of its value chain. Base the specification of activities within the value chain on your own experiences and general understanding of each type of business. The value chain does not have to be comprehensive (given the lack of specific information for each business) but should specifically consider the types of activities or business processes that could be expected to comprise each of the nine major components of the value chain.
   - Pizzeria
   - Manufacturer of artistic T-shirts
   - Distributor of soft drink products (soda, flavored teas)
   - Campus bookstore
   - Walk-in medical clinic providing emergency and outpatient services
   - Apartment complex
   - Computer repair shop
2. For each business process identified in the value chain, identify one potential audit risk that the auditor should consider in planning the engagement.
3. For each risk identified in part 2, descibe audit implications associated with the risk.

Case 6–2: Personal Computing Concepts

Personal Computing Concepts is a small computer software company based in Palo Alto, California. The company's main product is a computerized day planner (i.e., personal calendar) and contact manager (i.e., for keeping track of phone numbers and addresses for business contacts) called *Keep Contact*. The software is designed for use on Windows-compatible personal computers. The company markets its products primarily through independent retail stores (computer and business supply stores primarily) and through online retailers. The company also ships directly to customers who place orders through the Internet site. The primary users of the software are individuals (rather than businesses). The software is advertised as an individual productivity enhancer. The software lists for $39.95 but often has a "street" price of less than $30.00.

This niche in the software market is extremely competitive, but the company's products are considered to be the most technologically advanced among its competitors. A number of reasonably good programs are currently available as shareware, however, and can be obtained by downloading from the Internet. These programs usually carry a voluntary price of $10 but do not have many of the fancier features available in *Keep Contact*.

Sales revenue has grown at a rate of about 25 percent per year for the last four years and the company strives to introduce enhanced versions of the software at least once a year. Registered users of *Keep Contact* are allowed to purchase newer versions of the software directly from the company for a token fee of $11.95.

The company primarily advertises the software in major computer magazines and online where its customers typically visit. Finally, the company's home page describes the product in addition to selling it. The software comes with three months of free support for registered users. Support after the initial three-month period may be obtained at a cost of $5.00 per 10 minutes of phone time.

Requirements

Exhibit 2–1 presents a value chain model for Personal Computing Concepts.

1. Explain the nature of each of the activities identified in the value chain model.
2. For each of the identified activities, describe one or more potential threats to the organization that may arise. Identify the source of the threat, describe how the threat could impact the organization, and assess the likelihood of the threat occurring.
3. For each of the threats identified in part 2, identify and describe an audit risk that the auditor should consider in planning the audit of this organization.

Exhibit 2–1   Value Chain Model for Personal Computing Concepts

	Inbound Logistics	Operations	Marketing and Sales	Outbound Logistics	Service
Infrastructure	Financing	Planning / Facilities Management	Planning	Planning / Licensing	Facilities Management
Human Resources	Benefits/ Compensation	Recruiting	Recruiting		Recruiting
Technology	R&D / Design / Engineering	Testing			User Feedback
Procurement	Intellectual Property / Materials	Documentation			
	Materials Handling	Programming	Advertising / Sales Force	Distribution / Packaging	Product Support / User Support

MARGIN

7

Risk Management and Internal Control

Outline

INTRODUCTION

In the previous two chapters, we explored the nature of strategic and process risks that can be relevant to the planning and conduct of the audit. We now turn our attention to the manner in which management responds to risks through the enterprise risk management framework. Enterprise risk management is used by management to reduce the likelihood of risks, the potential magnitude of risks, or both. For the remainder of the book, we will refer to components of an organization's enterprise risk management framework that have audit implications as *internal control*. In this chapter, we focus on the management of business risks in general, and in the next chapter we address managing risk related to financial reporting specifically.

Auditors traditionally have examined internal control as part of the audit in order to determine the reliability of information processing related to transactions and to assess control risk. Consequently, auditors tended to focus on controls over transactions from authorization through to summarization and posting to journals and ledgers. As will be discussed in Chapter 8, auditors need to assess control risk for financial statement assertions, but their perspective on internal control has also broadened dramatically. Now, controls related to decision making, process efficiency, and compliance are considered relevant to the audit process, as they affect the reliability of the controls over financial reporting.

In most cases, management has an incentive to minimize its business risks whenever possible. If management is aware of the risks it faces, a well-run company will have policies, systems, and procedures in place for coping with those risks. Lack of management awareness of a risk is also relevant to the auditor and may represent a significant deficiency in the control environment. Management responses that are effective at reducing risk can also have the impact of reducing risks for the auditor. Consequently, an auditor needs to develop an extensive understanding of how management uses internal control to respond to important risks as this knowledge sets the context for subsequent audit testing (see Figure 7–1).

> **Authoritative Guidance & Standards**
>
> The definition of internal control and the definitions of the components of internal control used in this textbook are based on definitions provided in AS 2, SAS 109, and ISA 315. Neither COSO's "Internal Control—Integrated Framework" or COCO's "Guidance on Control" are required to be used during the audit under GAAS or PCAOB standards. However, SAS 109 and ISA 315 incorporate the elements of internal control described in the COSO framework, and AS requires that internal control over financial reporting be linked to an acceptable framework such as COSO.

USING INTERNAL CONTROL TO MITIGATE RISK

Management has to balance the significance of a risk against the cost of implementing a control response. For some risks, the cost of control is prohibitive, and the company can either choose to accept or avoid the risk (if possible). If cost-effective controls are available, management will choose techniques to reduce the risk or share the risk through insurance or strategic alliances. Management, especially for SEC registrants, may have little choice but to implement controls over material transactions that directly affect financial reporting because failure to do so will result in a qualified audit opinion about the effectiveness of internal control over financial reporting.

INTERNAL CONTROL DEFINED

Control "comprises those elements of an organization (including its resources, systems, processes, culture, structure, and tasks) that, taken together, support people in the achievement of the organizations objectives."[1] Internal controls should be designed to provide reasonable assurance that the organization's objectives are being met. There are three categories of objectives that are relevant to internal control:

1. To improve the effectiveness of management decision making and the efficiency of business processes.
2. To increase the reliability of information (especially financial reporting).
3. To foster compliance with laws, regulations, and contractual obligations.

An organization may use different types of internal control for achieving each of the three objectives—it is the auditor's responsibility to obtain a basic understanding of the controls being used.

---

1 Criteria of Control Committee: Guidance on Control, 1995, paragraph 6.

Figure 7–1   Overview of the Audit Process

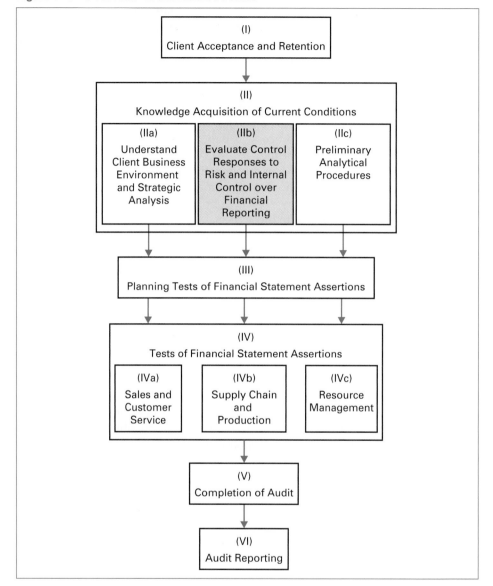

There are a number of important attributes of internal control that need emphasis. First, internal control is a process, meaning it is something the organization does on an ongoing basis. Situations, people, and risks change, suggesting that internal control needs to be a continuous activity. Second, internal control is ultimately part of management's responsibilities, and failure to design effective controls is itself a deficiency and suggests ineffective management. Third, internal controls have inherent limitations that prevent them from eliminating all risks. For example, employees make mistakes, senior management may bypass controls, and individuals may collude to commit fraud. Because some problems may not be prevented or detected by controls, the goal of internal control is to provide *reasonable assurance,* rather than absolute protection, against risks. Internal controls are directly linked to the organization's objectives. Given that a risk is any condition that can cause the organization to not achieve its objectives, internal control can be considered the antidote to risk (i.e., activities that reduce the potential for negative outcomes from risks and increase the ability of the organization to achieve its objectives).

Example

An objective of a pharmaceutical company is to comply with all government regulations on product testing. Not only is this a legal requirement, but it also makes business sense because few companies would like to be known for cutting corners on product testing, especially when consumer safety is affected. Consequently, product safety is probably not a risk that is to be accepted or insured—it must be reduced. The company will institute very stringent controls to minimize the risk that a defective or dangerous product is introduced.

COMPONENTS OF INTERNAL CONTROL

Internal control consists of five components as depicted in Figure 7–2. Each element is important for the effective management of risk. Furthermore, auditors need to understand the various components of internal control in order to conduct the audit effectively. A complete understanding of internal control often provides assurance to the auditor that many risks have been effectively reduced.

Control Environment: The foundation of internal control is the *control environment*, which refers to the organization's integrity, attitudes towards ethical dealings and general competence. Accordingly, the control environment is commonly referred to as the organization's *tone at the top*. The control environment is affected by the way in which management grants authority and assigns responsibility because this will have an impact on how decisions are made and the possibility that individuals can take unilateral action that negatively affects the organization. Without a solid control environment as a foundation, the remaining

Figure 7–2   Elements of Internal Control

Source: COSO, *Internal Control—Integrated Framework*, 1992. Used with permission of COSO.

components are not likely to be effective. The control environment often is described as the most important element of internal control because of its apparent role in a vast majority of material frauds. For example, a study examining U.S. accounting frauds over a 10-year period showed that 84 percent of all frauds involved the CEO, CFO, or both.[2]

The most important aspects of the control environment are management's attitudes and incentives. If management is unconcerned about policies and procedures that effectively mitigate risks, control risk in the audit will probably be very high no matter how good other elements of internal control appear to be. For example, if management is lackadaisical about enforcing controls, lower-level personnel are unlikely to adhere to policies and procedures.

Management's incentives may also shed light on the control environment. If management is evaluated and rewarded on a contingent basis, individual managers may be hesitant to comply with controls that have a negative impact on the evaluation of their performance. For example, if management is to receive a bonus based on sales volume, they may be less willing to deny credit to risky customers.

Example

A number of industries, including software, tobacco, and consumer products, are famous for a sales practice called "channel stuffing." Essentially, channel stuffing involves shipping a large volume of merchandise to regular customers near the end of the fiscal year, even if it has not been ordered or requested. These shipments can then be recorded as sales in the fourth quarter, ensuring that management meets its performance goals. The amount of merchandise that is "stuffed" into the distribution channel will depend on the level of sales needed to reach the sales target. Unfortunately, such shipments may not meet the definition of a sale according to GAAP because much of the merchandise will be returned for credit, often after the end of the audit. The practice reveals a weakness in the control environment. Furthermore, the practice may actually harm the company because the merchandise may have a limited shelf life (e.g., food products) and not be sellable upon return.

A number of organizational factors provide indications of the effectiveness of the control environment. Clear lines of authority, responsibility, and performance evaluation are usually indicative of an effective control environment. Management's use of effective monitoring techniques such as budgets, periodic performance reports, and variance analyses are also indicative of a good control environment. Other factors that are important include the existence of a competent and independent internal audit department, and clearly stated and documented personnel policies (e.g., hiring and firing, training, performance evaluation, job descriptions and requirements). A common element of the control environment of public companies is the quarterly meeting of the board of directors and the related audit committee.

Auditors can also look at outside influences and constraints imposed on the organization which may affect the control environment. External requirements often cause management to be particularly observant about the policies and procedures in certain areas of their operations. For example, a bank is subject to

---

2 Beasley, Carcello, and Hermanson, *Fraudulent Financial Reporting: 1987–1997. An Analysis of US Public Companies.*

strict accounting and reporting requirements imposed by government regulatory authorities. As a result, information systems in banks are highly sophisticated and reliable. This does not mean that risk is low in all areas, however, as evidenced by the problems with bad loans that banks, especially in Western Canada and the United States, experienced in the 1980s. As another example, pharmaceutical companies must operate under very strict inventory control regulations to ensure product safety. This may indicate to the auditor that risks related to inventory are relatively low; however, that does not necessarily translate to a good control environment for other risks the company faces.

Risk Assessment: Management should put in place a set of procedures whose purpose is to identify, analyze, and manage risks of the type discussed in Chapters 5 and 6. Identifying a risk that is likely to affect an organization is the critical first step to reducing or managing the risk—a risk that is unknown cannot be controlled. Consequently, it is important for management and the auditor to continually scan the environment for new risks or changing conditions that could increase risk. Common causes of increased risk include new information systems, employee turnover, changes in product lines or operating systems, or corporate restructuring. Significant and rapid changes in an organization or its environment are particularly troublesome because risks arise quickly in such an environment. Furthermore, a company that is experiencing high growth may find that its information and monitoring systems are inadequate for coping with new conditions. Once risks are identified, management should assess the likelihood of their occurrence and the severity of any negative effects that may be experienced.

Risk assessment is an area of internal control that has not received a great deal of attention relative to other elements of internal control. However, this element is critical for an organization as a necessary condition for identifying appropriate risk responses. To help organizations better understand the critical nature of risk assessment, COSO expanded this element greatly when drafting *Enterprise Risk Management—Integrated Framework*. Under the ERM framework, "risk assessment" is considered to consist of four elements: objective setting, event identification, risk assessment, and risk response.

When evaluating an organization's effectiveness at risk assessment, that is, deciding which risks to include and how to determine their significance, auditors should carefully consider each of the four components of risk assessment specifically as they relate to financial reporting:

1. What are the objectives of the process that have financial reporting implications?
2. What risk events could lead to a failure to achieve those objectives?
3. What is the likely impact of those risks?
4. What response has management taken (i.e., accept, avoid, reduce, or share) to address the risks?

By considering the risk assessment process, auditors are in a much better position to understand how risks may impact the financial statements and when material misstatements are likely to occur.

Control Activities: Management must decide how to respond to risky conditions. Management must first assess whether controlling a risk has a net benefit to the organization. If management believes that it is cost effective to respond to a risk, then control activities are the actual procedures that are performed to reduce the likelihood or potential impact of the risk in question. There are many types of controls that an organization can use. The design and execution of a control activity is affected by numerous considerations, including the level of personnel exercising control, the extent of automation built into the activity (e.g., manual versus computerized), the information system in place, and the subjectivity of the risk condition being monitored. Control activities can serve a preventive role, a detection role, or both. A preventive control primarily reduces the likelihood that a risk will emerge as a problem (e.g., reduces the likelihood of a material misstatement). A detective control reduces the impact of the risk if something bad were to occur. In a sense, detective controls "stop the bleeding" when an actual problem occurs.

Information and Communication: Internal control can rarely be effective unless an organization has adequate information for monitoring potential risks on a timely basis. The fourth component of internal control is communication, which means that important information is identified, captured and made available to the appropriate persons in the organization. Effective communication is critical to high-quality internal control to ensure that all parties clearly understand their role in the system, and that problems are brought to the attention of the proper level of the organization for corrective action. Information must flow throughout the organization if control is to be effective. Information needs to flow *up* so that management can respond to current conditions. Information must also flow *down* so that staff and employees are aware of the policies and decisions that may affect their individual activities. Finally, information needs to flow *across* functional departments so that interconnected processes can function effectively and events and transactions can be processed smoothly.

Monitoring: The final component of internal control is monitoring, the process whereby the organization tracks the effectiveness of internal control. Monitoring activities are designed to provide information to management about potential and actual breakdowns in the control system that could allow risks to become problems. Normal management and supervisory activities may be considered a form of monitoring, such as when management checks with subordinates to see how things are going. Monitoring can also be a specific activity assigned to a group within the organization. In many organizations, the internal audit department is responsible for monitoring the quality of internal control. Monitoring activities can be performed on an ongoing basis, often using technology to provide a continuous check on information processing. In other situations, monitoring can be based on periodic evaluations of performance over a period of time.

Authoritative Guidance & Standards
The Sarbanes-Oxley Act requires all U.S. registered public companies to have an internal audit function that reports to the audit committee. The Act allows companies the option of outsourcing internal audit to other professional accounting firms but precludes the firm that performs the external audit the company from also performing internal audit services.

LEVELS OF CONTROL ACTIVITY

Internal control can be exercised at different levels within an organization, but it is helpful to consider two distinct categories of control: (1) management controls and (2) process controls (including process controls over the financial reporting process). *Management controls* are the activities undertaken by senior management to mitigate strategic risks to the organization, and to promote the effectiveness of decision making and the efficiency of business activities. In general, management controls help to determine the design, implementation, and monitoring of the other components of internal control and include

- Communicating a belief system (including business objectives) throughout the organization
- Setting strategic boundaries (i.e., activities that an organization will not pursue)

- Establishing and enforcing boundaries of behavior (e.g., through formal codes of conduct and acceptable business practices)
- Establishing lines of authority and accountability
- Implementing and executing an enterprise risk management framework to identify, assess, address, communicate, and monitor business risks
- Allocating resources through the design and execution of business processes
- Forming strategic alliances to manage strategic risks

Example

Establishing and enforcing a policy on conflicts of interest for managerial person-nel is a common management control. Such a policy is important for minimizing the self-serving behavior of individuals in positions of authority that might in-crease risks to the organization. A key problem at Enron was that the chief financial officer was also the general partner of many of the entities employed to keep lia-bilities off the books of Enron. Indeed, what is particularly amazing about this is that Enron's board of directors approved this violation of the company's conflict of interest policy.

Process controls refer to the control activities that are performed as part of the various processes within the organization. Process controls are usually performed by staff employees and low-level management, but they are set in the context of the broader management controls and may not be effective if the management controls are not effective. Process controls are generally focused on internal risks within processes and reflect the formal policies and procedures defined by senior management. Also, process controls deal with the reliability of accounting infor-mation and compliance with rules and regulations. Traditionally auditors have examined internal controls over the financial reporting process at this level, but re-cent developments have required the auditor to take a broader perspective when considering internal controls over financial reporting. The topic of controls over financial reporting will be addressed in detail in Chapter 8.

Example

Assigning responsibility for making decisions or authorizing transactions to spe-cific individuals is a form of process control. In this way, responsibility can be as-signed to individual employees in the event of bad decisions or significant errors. Failure to assign responsibility for authorizing transactions creates a void in a busi-ness process that can have a negative impact on its effectiveness. Process out-comes in the absence of assigned authority can be unpredictable. For example, transactions may be approved that don't meet the objectives of the company (e.g., selling to bad credit risks) or potential transactions may be missed because no one has the authority to act in a given situation.

MANAGEMENT CONTROLS

TYPES OF MANAGEMENT CONTROL

Management control systems are "the systems that are used to maintain or alter the pattern in organizational activities."[3] Management controls tend to focus on

3 Robert Simons, "The Strategy of Control," *CA Magazine,* March 1992, p. 44.

overall effectiveness and efficiency within an organization rather than on details of individual activities or transactions, but without such controls it is unlikely that internal controls at the activities or transactions level would be effective in reducing the risk of material misstatement. Most management controls are designed to provide an overall indication that processes and activities are functioning properly, and to provide an effective response to risk in a timely manner. The attention that an organization devotes to managing a business process is a good indicator of its importance and the effectiveness and efficiency with which it will be performed.

Management controls can take many forms and may not always reflect formal procedures. For example, the president may have lunch with the vice president of marketing on a weekly basis to get a feel for what is selling and what is not. Management controls that may be relevant for the audit include:

- Top-level reviews
- Direct activity management
- Performance indicators and benchmarking
- Independent evaluation

Top-Level Reviews: These controls involve senior management periodically reviewing the results of operations against forecasts and budgets and quickly following up on potential problems. The more frequent and insightful these reviews, the less likely it is that large business threats will remain undetected. The quality and effectiveness of top-level reviews will depend on the timeliness, reliability, and relevance of the information used during the review process. Biased or incomplete information will undermine the ability of management to perform such reviews.

Example

> The manager responsible for overseeing production may get a weekly report that details production costs by product line and manufacturing process, including an analysis of cost variances. If costs are going up rapidly, this information may be useful for assessing and countering risks that affect the organization's supply chain.

Direct Activity Management: Managers at various levels (executive, functional, or activity) who are directly responsible for managing specific business processes are often in the best position to quickly identify problems while they are still small. To be effective, managers need to receive performance information on a timely basis. Management's effectiveness will then depend on their ability to spot problem areas and react appropriately to early warning signals. For example, a competent manager of a loan portfolio is in the best position to identify trends that threaten loan collectibility. Information for management analysis should be disaggregated enough to provide details by product line, location, type of customer, or other relevant dimension in order to identify potential problems. For this reason, an auditor should communicate directly with managers to understand how risks are handled within a business process.

Example

Many manufacturing companies have delegated some responsibility for production quality to the people working in the factory. They are closest to the process and in the best position to observe when product quality is deteriorating due to poor materials or equipment failure. At the General Motors–Suzuki joint venture called "CAMI" in Ontario, Canada, all production workers have access to a "stop work" signal that can shut down the production line if a defect is spotted. Identifying defects early can avoid a stockpile of products needing rework at the end of the assembly line and cut overall warranty and service costs in the long run.

Performance Indicators and Benchmarking: The use of diagnostic indicators based on operating and financial data is a potentially powerful tool for monitoring the status of an organization. This tool is made even more powerful if relevant benchmarks are available. A benchmark is simply a target level or standard of comparison for an indicator of interest, such as the delinquency rate on receivables. Benchmarks can be based on an analysis of prior results, predefined best-case results, or competitors' results. A well-designed indicator may be very useful for highlighting problems at an early stage. For example, potential inventory valuation problems arising from competition or new entrants may be indicated by looking at the rate at which inventory is being sold, disaggregated by product line and geographic region (e.g., umbrellas may sell well in Seattle or Vancouver in January whereas snow shovels sell well in Quebec or Maine). The use of benchmarks is discussed in detail in Chapters 9 and 14.

Example

J.D. Power and Associates collects data on customer satisfaction for all major automobiles sold in the United States and Canada. Because the company is independent of the manufacturers, the customer satisfaction ratings they publish are highly respected. A good rating is actively pursued by the car companies. The Canadian Automobile Association also provides independent ratings on dependability, safety, and repairs for most major car companies. These rating agencies provide very important benchmarks for car manufacturers who wish to maintain and enlarge their market share. Significant changes in ratings can alert management to problems with their product and may also provide evidence to the auditor about potential problems in production or design processes.

Independent Evaluations: Control is most effective if exercised by someone who is independent of the operations or activities being controlled. Management is usually in the best position to exercise independent oversight for most activities within the organization. Segregating incompatible duties is one element of establishing independent control within an organization (to be discussed in more detail in Chapter 8). More importantly, however, is the need for managers who are responsible for reviewing and controlling a process or activity to be distinct from the individuals who are charged with executing the process or activity. For example, unfavorable budget variances may not be followed up aggressively unless brought to the attention of someone who is independent of the process creating the variances.

EVALUATING MANAGEMENT CONTROLS

In order to assess the effectiveness of management controls, the auditor must first identify the management controls utilized to mitigate individual risks. The auditor may review procedures manuals, periodic reports, and internal audit testing in order to evaluate how effective management is in identifying, monitoring, and controlling risk. In most situations, a key step is interviewing personnel who are assigned the responsibility of dealing with critical risks. Key personnel responsible for managing risk typically include senior management, such as the CEO, CFO, COO, and senior-level vice presidents (e.g., a senior VP-Strategy). Those charged with risk management responsibility should be able to answer the following questions:

- How do you identify risks that need to be addressed?
- How do you assess and prioritize the significance of risks?
- What information and reports do you use to monitor important risks? Who produces the information? How reliable and timely is the information?
- How do you decide what action to take in response to an identified risk?
- When are superiors or personnel from other areas involved in responding to a risk?
- How responsive are others to risks you identify?
- Are resources adequate (time, budget, qualified personnel) for effectively responding to risks on a timely basis?

An important part of evaluating management control is to identify the appropriate person to question. Upper and middle management in different departments will be responsible for different aspects of managing risk. In addition to interviewing the senior manager ultimately responsible for managing risk, the auditor should discuss controls with the person(s) who are closest to the risk in the process. These people are often referred to as *process owners* because they are responsible for managing a process within the organization. In many cases, the appropriate persons to interview are outside the accounting and finance area and may be in such diverse functions as research and development, personnel, or manufacturing. By talking to many people about the same risks, and obtaining supporting documentation whenever possible, the auditor can develop a relatively complete picture of the quality of management controls.

Example

During the course of the audit of a mid-size European bank, the audit team identified foreign exchange risk as very important to the bank. To control currency risks, the senior management of the bank established a policy limiting the amount of exposure (assets, loans, guarantees) in specific currencies. In assessing this control, the auditor discovered that the information for monitoring currency positions was maintained by a clerk using a personally designed spreadsheet with manual input from currency traders whenever they remembered to notify the clerk of currency trades. The clerk did not really understand the purpose of the procedure, nor did she have authority to influence the bank's day-to-day activities. Consequently, the bank's risk exposure was much larger than believed because senior-level management failed to ensure that management controls were effective.

A common characteristic of effective management control is the need for reliable, timely, and appropriate information. The process of preparing monitoring reports must be reliable. Information used in a monthly budget analysis is more likely to be reliable if generated from the main accounting system by the data processing department than if it is generated by a manager using a desktop spreadsheet of his or her own design. Furthermore, using the wrong information to monitor a process could unknowingly lead to undesirable results.

Example

A telemarketing company implemented a system to monitor telephone sales representatives that emphasized the number of successfully completed calls per work shift. This created an incentive for the salespeople to get on and off a call quickly once they had gotten the details of an order. However, the company discovered that customer satisfaction was deteriorating and revenue growth was below targets. Management soon realized that the performance measure put too much emphasis on speed and not enough on answering customer questions. Furthermore, marketing research has demonstrated that it is easier to get additional revenue from an existing customer than it is to obtain a new customer.[4] The company changed its performance measurement system to emphasize customer satisfaction and revenue per successful call. Sales growth resumed and customers were more satisfied.

For each significant risk identified by the auditor, consideration should be given to any management controls that may exist to mitigate the risk. If a strategic risk has significant implications for the audit, then the related controls are also relevant to the conduct of the audit. The relationship between management controls and audit planning is illustrated in Figure 7–3 for a number of different control activities. Consider the first item, monitoring competitors' actions. This procedure is very important for managing the risk that competitors introduce new products, reduce prices, or improve service without warning. This risk could affect revenue levels, margins, inventory valuation, service costs, and selling expenses, depending on how the company responds. To evaluate whether management is effective, the auditor could examine the periodic reports that management uses and evaluate the nature and timeliness of management's responses. Furthermore, the reports may provide information that is directly relevant to assessing the valuation of inventory.

Numerous controls that management performs on a routine basis may provide useful information for the auditor during the course of the engagement. Particularly strong controls can be tested by the auditor and may serve as a source of audit evidence. For example, management controls that utilize operating or other data may be an important source of analytical evidence for the auditor. For example, management may be concerned that a shortage of raw materials might develop because of weather conditions in certain parts of the country. Management could respond to such risks by entering into long-term supply contracts so that the company has a fixed supply or by diversifying the company's sources of supplies. Similarly, management might be concerned that a competitor offers lower prices to increase market share. Management's response could be to monitor competitors' prices and meet or beat those prices as a matter of policy.

4 Fast food restaurants have this incremental sales approach down to a fine art—they charge an apparently small premium for large servings. Because of the trivial costs of the food, the small premium over the price of medium servings produces more profits than the base price as a percentage of incremental revenue.

Figure 7–3   Management Controls and Implications for the Audit of Financial Statements

Management Control	Audit Evidence Needed to Test Control Effectiveness	Potential Impact on Analytical Evidence	Potential Impact on Tests of Assertions
The company monitors its main competitors to estimate their time-to-market for new products. The effectiveness of marketing is also assessed relative to the competition.	The auditor can obtain and review reports from the marketing department concerning time-to-market and quality of advertising and promotions.	The market data may provide a leading indicator of potential competitive problems and evidence of new product or advertising failures.	Indications of failed products or marketing campaigns may raise questions of asset impairment or inventory obsolescence.
A company prepares annual sales, expense, and expenditure budgets and monitors variances on a monthly basis. Corrective action, when needed, is initiated on a timely basis.	The auditor can obtain copies of the annual budgets and monthly variance reports. Handling of the variances should be discussed with appropriate personnel.	The monthly variance reports identify unusual conditions or developments that may indicate increasing risks or accounting problems.	Minimal, unless results from analytical evidence suggest accounting problems that impact specific financial reporting items.
A company maintains and enforces a policy on management conflicts-of-interest. All management personnel must complete a conflict-of-interest report every year.	The auditor can discuss conflict-of-interest policies with management, review a selection of conflict-of-interest reports and verify follow-up and resolution of apparent conflicts.	Minimal.	The conflict reports may indicate related party or other transactions that should be disclosed. Valuation of such transactions may need to be verified.
The company prepares weekly sales reports that track turnover by product lines and geographic region.	The auditor can obtain the weekly reports (or a sample) and review them for proper review and follow up by appropriate personnel.	The weekly reports provide analytical evidence about the valuation of inventory. Quantities in weekly reports may be used to reconcile inventory counts per perpetual records.	Inventory turnover statistics can indicate items that the auditor should count and examine during the year end testing of inventory assertions.

Figure 7–3   *(continued)*

Management Control	Audit Evidence Needed to Test Control Effectiveness	Potential Impact on Analytical Evidence	Potential Impact on Tests of Assertions
The controller monitors past due receivables on a monthly basis and follows up on any accounts that are 60 days past due. Account write-offs must be approved by both the controller and the CFO.	The auditor can discuss the monitoring process with the controller and review reports used or prepared by him. Also, a sample of past due accounts can be reviewed for proper disposition.	The controller's reports provide analytical evidence about the collectibility of accounts.	The controller's reports identify transactions or accounts that may require in-depth analysis at year end.
The company uses the internal audit department to perform periodic compliance review of key regulations.	The auditor can obtain copies of the internal audit programs, work product, and reports. Documents should be reviewed for unusual conditions.	Minimal.	The internal audit reports may reveal conditions to be disclosed or may lead to the recognition of a contingent liability for fines or penalties

Example

Evidence of "coordinated" price movements is apparent in the retail gasoline market in many communities. Often, one gas chain implements a price cut in a certain region, which is quickly followed by similar cuts by other gasoline companies that are in direct competition. Similarly, one gasoline company may announce price increases, but competitors may not choose to follow, and the company initiating the increase is usually forced to retract the price increase. Collusion is often suspected as a result of this apparent coordination, but, in reality, the commonality of pricing is probably the result of extensive competition. Given the large number of local markets in which a gasoline company may operate, matching competitors' prices requires active and continuous monitoring of the prices charged by competitors. The management response in this situation is dependent on timely, reliable information from the external environment.

EVIDENCE OF INTERNAL CONTROLS MITIGATING RISK

Although management controls may appear to be effective, an auditor must also obtain evidence to support the conclusion that controls are effective. An auditor cannot simply reduce assessments of risk based on the auditor's intuition or management's unsupported claims about the controls the company has in place. The auditor needs to obtain sufficient and appropriate evidence to justify the conclusion that risks are less significant than initially believed. This evidence is often obtained through *tests of controls* and some examples are included in Figure 7–3.

Evidence to support conclusions about the effectiveness of management controls include

- Client inquiries: Although discussions with client personnel are considered a weak form of evidence, by conducting discussions with multiple individuals about similar topics, the auditor may obtain insight into how effective management controls really are. In a sense, multiple interviews can be used to "triangulate" actual conditions.
- Observation: The auditor may be able to observe actual work effort in real time and form an opinion as to the appropriateness, competence, and reliability of management controls. For example, the auditor might attend management meetings to observe how the management team deals with problems.
- Review of documentation: Because many management controls rely on standard, periodic reports, the auditor should obtain copies of any reports or documents that provide evidence about management's efforts to control specific risks. The report should be discussed with appropriate management, and the auditor should obtain evidence that indicates how actual problems were addressed (e.g., what does management actually *do* with the information in the reports?).

AUDIT IMPLICATIONS OF MANAGEMENT CONTROLS

Chapter 5 presented a number of examples of strategic risks from various sources. In this chapter, we add to that analysis by linking the identified risks to specific business processes and management controls. Building on Figure 5–9 from Chapter 5, Figure 7–4 illustrates the relationship among business risks, business processes, management controls, and audit implications for a sample of common strategic risks. For each risk, we identify the processes in the value chain that are most likely to be affected by the risk and management controls that could be used to mitigate the potential threat. Some risks may also be subject to process controls that may reduce their significance even farther.

There is a predictable relationship among the sources of strategic risks and the internal activities, transactions, and accounting estimates that are affected by the risk. For example, threats from suppliers are most likely to affect inbound logistics and procurement. We see an example of this type of risk involving raw materials (*SR3*). Threats from customers are most likely to affect outbound logistics, sales and marketing, and service activities (*SR5*). Threats from substitutes and new entrants are most likely to affect sales and marketing or technology (*SR7*). Finally, although sales and marketing or service are probably the most obvious areas where competitors may impact the company, other areas may also be affected by risks from competitors as illustrated by the competition for human resources (*SR2*).

Management controls for many risks focus on the efficiency and effectiveness with which the company is managed or the reliability and timeliness of information. For some risks, an organization may not have any specific management controls in place, or may lack relevant data with which to anticipate and analyze the risk condition, either of which increases the risk of problems in the future.

The audit implications suggested in Figure 7–4 are the same as presented in the prior chapter. However, with the additional information about management controls, the auditor will be able to make informed judgments about the significance of individual risks. In Chapter 5, we specifically discussed the risk that a

Figure 7–4   Strategic Risks, Management Controls, and Audit Implications: Some Examples

Strategic Risk/Threat	Source of Threat	Activity Likely to be Affected	Potential Management Controls	Potential Audit Implications
SR1: Competitors begin offering extended warranty protection on products.	Competitors	Service	• Policy for responding to competitors' actions. • Established market research procedures for early identification of market trends. • Reliable and timely data on actual warranty costs.	• Audit Risk: Increase in warranty commitments may require that warranty expense estimates be increased above historical patterns. • Comment to Client: System for tracking warranty costs.
SR2: Competitors are rapidly increasing the rate paid to key senior accounting and management personnel.	Competitors	Human resources Infrastructure	• Senior management review of personnel policies. • Hiring, promotion, and compensation processes that are fair and responsive to market conditions. • Reliable and timely data on payroll costs.	• Control Environment: Reliability of decision making and information processing may decrease with employee turnover. • Audit Risk: Allocations of labor costs may need to be revised based on relative changes in salary levels. • Audit Risk: Accruals for benefits may need to be increased.
SR3: Top-grade raw materials are in extremely short supply due to bad weather conditions in producing regions.	Suppliers	Inbound logistics Operations Procurement	• Timely monitoring of long-term sources of supplies. • Reliable and timely data on input costs. • Established long-term supply relationships and commitments.	• Audit Risk: Wastage and spoilage rates may need to be increased in standard costing formulas. • Audit Risk: Valuation problems related to purchase commitments may exist. • Control Environment: Pressure to cut corners to meet customer demand.

(continued)

Figure 7-4 (continued)

Strategic Risk/Threat	Source of Threat	Activity Likely to be Affected	Potential Management Controls	Potential Audit Implications
SR4: Customer industries are in a recession.	Economics, Customers	Sales and marketing Outbound logistics	• Active management of customer accounts. • Reliable and timely data on industry trends, payment history, and problem accounts • Benchmarking of delinquency rates against competitors.	• Audit Risk: Receivables may not be collectible at historic rate and allowance for uncollectibles may need to be increased. • Viability: Shrinking customer base.
SR5: Consumer tastes have changed, necessitating improved functionality and quality in company products.	Social, Customers	Operations Technology Sales and marketing	• Market research. • Consumer focus groups. • Forward-thinking research efforts. • Creating an environment of innovation and risk taking.	• Viability: Loss of market share. • Audit Risk: Inventory on hand may become obsolete or out of favor so that carrying values may not be realizable. • Control Environment: Pressure to hit sales targets to protect jobs or bonuses.
SR6: The preferred distribution channel for the company's product changes from retail locations to Internet, telemarketing, and home delivery.	Technology, Customers	Sales and marketing Outbound logistics Technology	• Market research. • Monitoring of technological developments. • Timely management retreats and creative thinking exercises.	• Audit Risk: Existing distribution channels may need to be shut down with resulting restructuring cost (layoffs, asset disposal). • Audit Risk: Ongoing client viability: Inability to adapt on a timely basis.
SR7: New entrant to the market is technologically superior to current products.	Technology, New entrants	Sales and marketing	• Top-level reviews of market trends by senior marketing managers. • Market surveys. • Reverse engineering of competitor products. • Product innovation and research. • Monitoring technology trends in industry.	• Audit Risk: Inventory valuation may need to be reduced to lower of cost or market due to obsolescence or excess quantities. • Audit Risk: Ongoing client viability due to loss of market share.

Strategic Risk	Category	Value Chain	Management Response	Audit Implications
SR8: Government imposes new regulations on distribution of a company's product.	Social, Political	Sales and marketing; Outbound logistics	• Monitoring and proactive involvement in regulatory activity on a timely basis. • Innovation and research. • Monitoring technology trends affecting industry.	• Audit Risk: Ongoing client viability due to loss of market share if not adaptable. • Audit Risk: Inventory valuation may need to be reduced to lower of cost or market due to obsolescence or excess quantities. • Comment for Client: Develop controls to provide assurance that the organization complies with new regulations. • Control Environment: Efforts to circumvent regulations to meet sales targets.
SR9: Activists protest the company's approach to R&D.	Social	Technology	• Proactive involvement with activist causes. • Charitable work in community. • Monitoring technology trends in industry.	• Audit Risk: Capitalized development costs may not be recovered if product performance suffers. • Control Environment: Efforts to hide or disguise nature of R&D.
SR10: Foreign currency fluctuations squeeze profit margins on international sales.	Economic	Infrastructure; Sales and marketing; Outbound logistics (billing)	• Establish and monitor active hedging program. • Consider setting up subsidiaries in foreign countries. • Reassess transfer pricing policies. • Establish information system to monitor exposure.	• Audit Risk: Proper treatment of exchange gains and losses. • Audit Risk: Accounting treatment of financial derivatives. • Comment for Client: Develop control systems to enable early and accurate identification of risks associated with hedging foreign currency exposures.
SR11: Manufacturing facilities become noncompetitive due to age and inability to upgrade processes	Technological	Operations; Technology	• Monitor current technology trends. • Benchmark production costs against competition. • Establish forward thinking strategic plan.	• Audit Risk: Impairment of fixed assets. • Audit Risk: Client viability if tightening margins leading to losses or if prices cannot be increased.

company will select an inappropriate or ineffective distribution channel. To reduce this risk, management can undertake timely market research and monitor technology trends that might have an impact on the company's distribution chain. Furthermore, tasking specific managers to challenge the accepted wisdom in an organization can be an effective way to protect the company from stale or out-of-date ideas.

If risks are considered less significant due to the presence of effective management controls, the auditor will next develop an approach for testing the controls that will justify the auditor's conclusions about risk. The evidence needed to support the conclusion that management controls are effective will depend on the nature of the control and the information flow relevant to the procedure. After completing the analysis of risks and related controls and obtaining required corroborative evidence, the auditor will be able to determine which risks pose a continuing and significant threat to the organization.

The auditor documents conclusions about the effect of internal control on identified risks using a risk map as illustrated in Figure 7–5. Arrows indicate a reduction in the significance of a risk, with stars indicating the updated assessment of the risk. Risks for which the auditor believes management has an effective response can be downgraded in significance. For example, changes in consumer tastes (SR5) may be effectively addressed through market research and innovation, whereas escalating executive salaries (SR2) may be addressed through proactive personnel policies and industry benchmarking. Although the risk of an industry recession (SR4) is largely beyond the control of management, certain procedures can be taken to minimize the effect of a recession on the company's performance. However, in this case, the auditor has concluded that management's response does not significantly reduce the risk and it remains characterized as a potential residual risk. The auditor must obtain evidence to support reduced risk assessments that will affect the subsequent conduct of the audit.

Figure 7–5   Impact of Management Control Activities on Risk Assessments

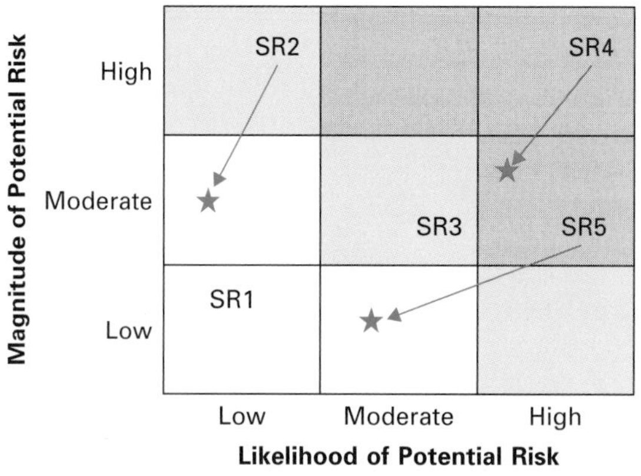

Legend:

SR1: Better warranties from competitors
SR2: Escalating executive salary demands
SR3: Shortage of raw materials
SR4: Industry recession
SR5: Changes in consumer tastes

LIMITATIONS OF MANAGEMENT CONTROL

Although management controls are an effective way to respond to risks from the external environment, there are also a number of conditions that can lead to ineffective application of management control. When such conditions exist, risk may not be reduced and, worse, may be much higher than expected because of management's incorrect (but comforting) belief that effective controls are in place. The effectiveness of management control can be limited by the following:

- **Failure by employees to internalize the organization's mission and objectives:** Individuals responsible for specific functions within the organization can operate effectively only when they fully understand the mission and objectives of the organization and accept their role. Failure to ensure that the message is internalized at all levels can lead to unproductive, and possibly harmful, behavior. For example, some organizations simply post their mission and objectives on the company web site with little follow-up training. An auditor can test for this condition rather easily by randomly quizzing employees in the organization to see whether the mission and objectives have been absorbed by employees.
- **Inaccurate or out-of-date assumptions:** In framing a response to external risks, management often has to make assumptions about the environment. These assumptions may be at odds with actual conditions or may become inflexible in the face of changing conditions. Controls based on flawed assumptions will be less effective than expected. An important challenge for the auditor is to evaluate the accuracy of management's perceptions of its environment; for example, is management's outlook realistic given the current industry conditions?
- **Undue focus on current conditions:** It is very easy for management to get caught up in the pressure of current challenges and fail to adequately consider future plans. Without a clear vision of the future, current actions may turn out to be inadequate or counterproductive in the future.
- **Rigid organizational structure:** External conditions tend to be fluid but internal lines of authority tend to be fixed and slow to change. This mismatch can lead to an organizational structure appropriate for yesterday's challenges but inadequate for the current/future environment.
- **Failure to enforce accountability:** Much of the internal control within an organization is based on the assumption that members of the organization will be held accountable for their actions in accordance with the plan and structure of the organization. Failure to enforce such accountability undermines the performance of responsibilities.
- **Communication breakdowns:** Any significant breakdown in communication is likely to undermine the efficiency and effectiveness of an organization. Although such breakdowns are probably inevitable to some extent, the frequency and severity of the communication failures will have a direct impact on whether management controls are effective.
- **Top management failure:** In most major accounting frauds, it is the top management of a company that is the source of control failure. Indeed, one analysis of the Securities and Exchange Commissions enforcement actions in the United States found that the vast majority of frauds were instigated by the very senior managers who had responsibility for the control system's design and monitoring.

The auditor should discuss these possible conditions with management and the audit committee and determine if any of these problems are likely to occur. If the auditor feels that some or all of these conditions currently exist, the quality of management control could be significantly weakened.

PROCESS CONTROL ACTIVITIES

After evaluating management controls, the auditor will then consider how process controls might affect risks in the organization. Recall that management can choose to accept, avoid, share, or reduce risks. Process control activities tend to focus on specific risks within a process, although one control activity may mitigate multiple risks. Continuing our analysis of the human resource management process from Chapter 6, column 2 of Figure 7–6 indicates a number of process controls that might be used to control risks that were identified in Figure 6–5. Control at the process level should reflect the organization's broader strategic decisions. For example, the control environment at the corporate level will manifest itself in attitudes towards careful performance of assignments, implementation of control procedures, and reporting relationships at the process level. Finally, monitoring procedures for the entire organization, such as the internal audit function, will also affect individual processes.

> **Authoritative Guidance & Standards**
>
> Control activities are described in SAS 109 and ISA 315. Specifically, SAS 109 describes controls as authorization, segregation of duties, safeguarding, and asset accountability. SAS 109 describes information processing controls more specifically according to whether they are general or application controls. ISA 315 similarly describes process controls as authorization, performance reviews, information processing, physical controls, and segregation of duties. Descriptions of control activities in both standards are consistent with descriptions herein. The PCAOB's AS 2 also includes descriptions of control activities consistent with those in this section.

There are a number of common control activities that an organization can use to minimize process risks including:

- Performance reviews
- Processing controls
- Physical controls
- Segregation of duties

However, each process is unique so a variety of control activities might be effective at preventing or reducing process risks. The auditor must assess the impact of controls when determining whether or not any of the process risks represent significant residual risks that may need additional attention. Furthermore, the existence and effectiveness of these controls may be relevant to the auditor's assessment of control risk related to misstatements in accounting information.

PERFORMANCE REVIEWS

Management can compare actual performance within a process to a set of standards that may include prior results, forecasts, budgets, and external benchmarks. A manager watches for signs that a process is out-of-control or failing to meet its objectives. Warning signs can often be captured in a set of performance indicators that measure the level of specific process risks. An analogy can be made to the needles or digital readouts contained in the dashboard of a car: various indicators are monitored by the driver for warnings that fuel is low, speed is too fast, oil needs to be changed, or seatbelts are not buckled. The driver monitors these gauges or indicators for warning signs about specific "risks" associated with the process of driving a car.

Figure 7–6 Internal Threat Analysis: Human Resource Management

Process Risks	Controls Linked to Risks	Performance Measures
PR1: Lack of personnel with appropriate skills.	• Formal job descriptions for all positions. • Systematic approach to recruiting. • Monitor market and demographic conditions. • Establish strategic relationships with potential suppliers of labor (e.g., universities, schools, head hunters).	• Number of unfilled positions. • Time-to-fill vacant positions.
PR2: Excess or unneeded personnel.	• Planning and budgeting procedures. • Formal assessment of labor needs. • New positions approved by appropriate management. • Procedures for reassigning excess personnel to different functions.	• Employee chargeable time. • Employee down time. • Unassigned personnel.
PR3: Discriminatory employment practices.	• Establish and monitor hiring policies and procedures. • Interviews with those who turned down offered positions. • Exit interviews with employees leaving the company. • Establish communication channel for work force complaints.	• Labor force demographics. • Frequency of complaints from recruits. • Frequency of complaints from employees.
PR4: Excess costs of recruiting and hiring.	• Establish budget for recruiting. • Monitor recruiting costs. • Appropriate approval of recruiting functions. • Appropriate approval of hiring bonuses and moving cost allocations.	• Cost per new hire. • Bonuses paid to new hires. • Moving costs per new hire. • Ratio of acceptances to offers.
PR5: Errors in payroll authorizations (pay rates, taxes, time).	• Obtain written authorizations for all payroll adjustments. • Changes in payroll authorizations are properly authorized. • Overtime approved in advance.	• Number of processing errors. • Dollar value of pay discrepancies. • Frequency of discrepancies in employment documents.
PR6: Errors in payroll processing.	• Maintain and update master payroll files on a timely basis. • Process payroll on a timely basis. • Use time cards to report time worked. • Use time reports to allocate labor costs. • Review all time cards, reports, and payroll records. • Use prenumbered payroll documents in sequence. • File tax reports on a timely basis.	• Number of processing errors. • Number of exceptions caught by system. • Size of transaction adjustments.

(continued)

Figure 7–6   *(continued)*

Process Risks	Controls Linked to Risks	Performance Measures
PR7: Low employee morale.	• Monitor employee satisfaction. • Belief systems (e.g., core values, mission statement) • Institute programs for improving morale (e.g., business casual dress codes, special functions, work-life balance programs).	• Employee absenteeism. • Employee satisfaction.
PR8: Violations of employment laws.	• Establish formal policies and procedures for hiring and workplace behavior including acceptable Internet use policies. • Establish appropriate privacy policies with respect to employee information. • Monitor workforce behavior. • Establish communication channel for work force complaints. • Timely and effective response to complaints.	• Number of citations by enforcement agencies. • Percent of labor force completing training on employment laws. • Frequency of employee complaints.
PR9: Failure to provide adequate feedback or training for improvement.	• Establish formal policies and procedures for employee evaluation. • Require employee signoff on evaluations. • Require management to perform evaluations as part of core duties. • Establish formal policies for employee training.	• Training hours per employee. • Frequency of employee evaluations. • Ratings of training programs. • Percent of employees receiving "poor" evaluations. • Timeliness of required evaluations.
PR10: Unplanned loss of critical personnel or excessive turnover.	• Monitor employee satisfaction. • Monitor and maintain competitive compensation and benefit packages. • Monitor and establish procedures for improving employee morale. • Conduct exit interviews with departing employees.	• Employee turnover rates. • Results from exit interviews. • Turnover rates for key personnel.

Example

The risk of late or lost shipments during the sales and delivery process is an important consideration for most retailers. Sales managers will monitor statistics related to on-time delivery to determine if customers are receiving their shipments. Delayed or lost shipments tend to irritate customers, which may lead to a significant drop in customer satisfaction and lost customers. On-time delivery statistics provide an indication whether this particular risk is a problem for the organization.

The effectiveness of performance reviews depends on whether a manager can monitor measures that will provide effective warning when risk levels or conditions have changed significantly. The auditor can use quantitative measures, called *performance indicators*, to assess whether process risks are an immediate threat. The challenge for the auditor is to determine which performance indicators the organization has available and then connect those indicators to specific risks. Column 3 of Figure 7–6 indicates a number of performance indicators that might be used to assess risks arising from the human resource management. The analysis of performance indicators serves as a detective control and provides the auditor evidence about process risks and whether they are likely to be relevant to the audit. No single performance indicator provides a complete picture of a process, and many may pertain to multiple risks, so the auditor needs to examine multiple indicators to develop an overall perspective of the process.

Most of the performance indicators are based on information that is generated internally but some may require external data also. There are two potential problems the auditor can encounter when examining performance indicators. First, auditors have to rely on the organization to provide appropriate data. The auditor is therefore limited to the data maintained by the client and useful measures might not always be available. The lack of appropriate performance indicators provides an indication that management of a process may not be effective. Second, the auditor must have some assurance that the data underlying a performance measure is reliable. If data is unreliable, the auditor will have difficulty using performance data as a source of analytical evidence.

Processing Controls

An organization will have many policies and procedures in place to assure the proper authorization of activities and to verify the accuracy and completeness of transaction processing. There are two broad categories of processing controls: general controls and application controls. *General controls* pertain to the manner in which a process is designed and managed. For example, procedures for defining steps and tasks within a process, authorizing decisions, implementing system changes, establishing processing schedules, updating system documentation, and assuring software and data integrity (i.e., file back-up procedures) are common general controls.[5]

Example

Most organizations recognize that installing new computer software can be complex and difficult. Consequently, they usually follow formal procedures for selecting vendors/consultants, designing applications, installing and testing software, and controlling system use. However, in a distributed data processing environment, much of an organization's computing is performed on desktop machines, and the installation and maintenance of software may be haphazard. Because important decisions are often made using information from desktop applications, this overall weakness in general controls could represent a serious risk to the organization. As an illustration, international public accounting firms consistently reported that one of the most common problems found when first testing internal control effectiveness at public companies in the United States was that many critical spreadsheets throughout an organization were located on individual computers with little supporting documentation.

---

5 The concept of "general controls" was first developed in the context of computerized information systems so many of the examples directly apply to risks associated with computerization of accounting processes. However, the term general controls can be interpreted in a much broader manner and is used in this book to refer to a specific type of control activity occurring within a business process, regardless of whether the actions or steps being addressed relate to computerized information systems.

Organizations should maintain current *procedures and systems documentation* either in manuals or on intranet web sites that describe how the activities and control procedures of a process are to be executed. The documentation should describe the tasks and responsibilities of key individuals in a process, that is, how things are to be done. Procedures documentation should also include a description of the flow of documents and records in the organization, a listing of reports and who receives them, and a chart of accounts. The *chart of accounts* lists and describes the acceptable ledger accounts to be used for recording transactions (a key component of a process map) and is useful for proper classification of transactions occurring with a process.

System documentation for key applications of information technology (IT) is an important form of general control because much of the system's operations are not directly observable by the organization's personnel or the auditor. Because the activities of the automated system are represented by code that may be difficult to decipher, verbal and visual (e.g., flowcharts) descriptions of the system are useful to the auditor. At a minimum, IT documentation should include the following:

- *Systems requirements:* A description of the purpose of the software and the required input and output.
- *Program documentation:* A description of the application logic, computer code, and reliability testing. A particularly important aspect is the description of the procedures for testing, authorizing, and instituting changes to the software.
- *Run instructions:* A description of how the software is to be executed including details on hardware and software configurations, operating schedules, and possible error conditions. The specification of operating schedules is important for computer applications that are run periodically. Also, a computer application should be capable of flagging errors that occur in input or processing and to produce a message (called an *edit listing*) that can be used by management to identify system weaknesses.
- *User instructions:* For mainframe applications, these instructions will primarily be a description of the output and who should receive it. In microcomputer applications, user instructions may be combined with elements of the run instructions.

Application controls pertain to the way in which individual tasks are performed and transactions are handled within a process. For example, procedures for verifying decision authorization and transaction accuracy are common application controls. An auditor will be particularly interested in three types of application controls: (1) *authorization procedures*, (2) *use of documents and records*, and (3) *independent verification procedures*.

Authorization procedures: Control procedures should be established that provide assurance that only authorized activities are performed. Approval of individual transactions should be performed only by authorized personnel. Authorizations may be either general or specific. *General authorization* allows an individual to execute all tasks or transactions that meet certain criteria. For example, a sales clerk may be allowed to accept a customer's check for up to $500 upon presentation of a major credit card and driver's license. As another example, the use of fixed reorder points for inventory purchasing represents a form of general authorization for maintaining inventory levels. *Specific authorization* should be required for any actions that are not subject to general authorization. For example, a check in excess of $500 may need approval by a store manager or purchase orders for new items of inventory may require approval by a senior marketing manager.

Example

Financial institutions that maintain and trade marketable securities, such as bonds, equities, or derivatives, often specify exposure limits for different categories of investments. A bank may wish to hold fewer bonds denominated in Mexican pesos than it would for bonds denominated in Japanese yen. The exposure limits are a form of general authorization and investment levels that exceed the limits for any given category would be identified and referred to appropriate management for rectification. Of course, the ability to monitor actual investment levels across many categories in a highly dynamic trading environment creates challenges for information processing because the market positions of the firm relative to exposure limits need to be measured in real time.

Use of documents and records: The proper design of documents and records is a very important element of internal control and helps assure the reliability of information within a process. The concepts of good document design apply equally to physical documents filled out by hand and to electronic facsimile documents that are viewed on a computer screen and completed with input from a keyboard. Documents should be designed so that all pertinent information is entered at the time that the document is completed (which should be when a transaction is being executed). The appropriate input can be specified by indicating what information is to be entered in a document—blank data fields would indicate missing information. Similarly, data entry fields on a computer screen can be used to provide prompts for the data to be entered.

Documents—paper or electronic—that represent transactions should be sequentially *prenumbered* whenever their use is intended to be sequential (e.g., checks, invoices, vouchers, purchase orders). In that way, the sequence of documents that are actually used can be easily verified. Documents that are generated by the computer can be assigned numbers from a pre-established sequence to facilitate control over the order of transactions. Documents that are not necessarily used in sequence (e.g., discount coupons, remittance advices sent back by customers with their payments) can have identification numbers to facilitate cross-referencing to other documents and records.

Documents should be designed for ease of use. This is accomplished for online documents using specified data fields, pop-up options, and help screens that are embedded in the software. Documents should provide an indication of what types of authorization are needed for an action to occur or a transaction to be executed. An obvious example of this is a check that requires two signatures and thus has two signature lines. Another example is space provided on credit card receipts for credit approval codes. More recent advances in electronic transaction processing allow such authorizations to be performed online and in real time.

An important distinction should be made between boundary documents and processing documents. *Boundary documents* are those that are prepared upon execution of a transaction with an external party and provide evidence that a transaction has occurred. *Processing documents* assist in tracking the internal flow of resources and information within the accounting system. To illustrate, consider payroll processing that occurs as part of human resource management. *Time cards* are the boundary document that demonstrates that an employee has worked a certain number of hours and is owed wages. *Payroll checks* are the boundary documents that demonstrate settlement of payables to employees. *Job tickets* are used to keep track of what employees do with their time and facilitate recording the cost of labor in an appropriate expense or asset account.

The current trend of linking information systems across organizations is changing the way that auditors think about documents and organizational boundaries. Customers and suppliers use electronic data interface (EDI) to improve the efficiency of transaction processing and to reduce the costs of holding and moving inventory. In an EDI system, major suppliers of an organization directly monitor inventory levels at the customer and determines what and when to ship to the customer. Orders are nearly instantaneous, including the electronic transfer of funds (EFT), and avoid traditional (and cumbersome) procurement processes and documents. Although the use of information technology and general authorization of transactions improves the efficiency of a process, electronic linkages make the supplier and customer much more dependent on each other. Integrated systems are one form of a strategic alliance in which information processing risks of one party become information processing risks of the other party, meaning that auditors must consider such risks *for both organizations*.

Example

The use of EDI and newer Internet-based procurement systems has allowed many companies to adopt just-in-time inventory techniques. Instead of maintaining a large stock of parts and supplies, a manufacturer may rely on its suppliers to monitor its inventory levels and send shipments of needed parts based on production orders. Often, the lead time for such deliveries is short: the Mercedes factory in Alabama that makes the M-class sports utility vehicle requires that suppliers deliver appropriate parts within three hours of an order being placed. The parts are immediately used in the manufacturing process, resulting in virtually no parts supplies being maintained at the Mercedes factory. However, the integrated systems extend information processing risks from the suppliers to Mercedes. The Year 2000 (Y2K) fear caused many companies to worry about whether information systems and databases would be adversely affected when computers tried to switch from 1999 to 2000. Although auditors of the Mercedes plant were not concerned about their information system, they had to investigate the situation at their suppliers to ensure that a system breakdown elsewhere would not halt operations at Mercedes.

Independent verification procedures: A common method for maintaining reliable information in a system is through independent verification. One type of verification involves direct examination of individual transactions for accuracy or proper approval. For example, a store manager can review credit card slips for entry of credit verification codes; computations on a customer bill can be manually or electronically checked for accuracy; and shipments can be examined to make sure they match the items ordered. In automated systems, the conversion of data to machine-readable form is a potential problem. Scanning technology has greatly reduced the risk of error during data entry, but manual entry is still common for non-routine tasks. To reduce the risk of errors, the same data may be input twice and then compared. If the two entries do not agree, the item entered will be flagged as an error. This process is referred to as *key verification*.

Example

Changing the password for accessing computer files (e.g., the PIN code for ATM machines) usually requires entering the new password twice to make sure that the code that is entered is the one intended by the user.

Check digits are another type of verification often used for account codes, parts numbers, or customer accounts. Check digits involve embedding special code digits that represent a mathematical combination of the other digits in an identification number. For example, a customer number may be defined to be eight digits long with the first six digits indicating the customer identification and the last two being the check digits. The two check digits could be the simple sum of the other six digits or may be derived using a more complex formula. For example, assume the first six digits of Mr. Smith's account number are 983425. The check digits 31 (9+8+3+4+2+5) could be added to form an eight-digit code (i.e., 98342531). The presence of the check digits provides a mechanism for verifying the accuracy of the customer number that is entered for a transaction.[6]

A final type of independent verification involves comparing and *reconciling data* that should be the same but is taken from two different sources. This type of comparison can be made between internal records and external data sources. The most common example of this is a bank reconciliation that compares the organization's internal records of cash transactions with the records of the bank. Reconciliations can also be made between two or more internal data sources. Due to the nature of most accounting systems, the same data often appears in more than one set of records. For example, sales are chronologically listed in the sales journal but listed by customer in the accounts receivable subsidiary ledger. To verify that the data is included properly in both places, total sales from the sales journal can be reconciled with the debits in the accounts receivable ledger. For human resources, the hours worked by employees that are recorded in a payroll register can be reconciled with the hours charged to specific asset and expense accounts.

Batch controls are used to test sequential processing of data. Typically, a large number of similar transactions are combined and processed as a group. For example, all sales transactions in a day could form a batch. The batch is represented by one or more *control totals* that reflect the summation of a common element in the batch. For sales transactions, the control total could be the total sales for the day, the number of transactions, or the number of items sold. Once the control total is established, it can be compared to subsequent totals that are computed as the group is processed. For example, the control total for sales could be compared to the total sales for the day according to the sales journal or the total debit postings to the accounts receivable subsidiary ledger. The control

---

6 The specification of check digits must be done with care in order to assure that the check digits are unique. Simple summation is not usually the best technique because digits can be transposed—a common mistake—and yield the same check digit, e.g., the computer would accept 98435231 as correct even though 98342531 is the correct code. One way to overcome this problem is to multiply each digit by a unique factor and then add. For example, 983425 could yield check digits of 90 (1*9 + 2*8 + 3*3 + 4*4 + 5*2 + 6*5).

total for the number of transactions could be compared to the number of entries in the sales journal. The control total for items sold could be compared to the number of items removed from perpetual inventory. If any of these comparisons revealed a discrepancy, accounting personnel could investigate the cause and make needed adjustments.[7]

PHYSICAL CONTROLS

Limiting access to assets that are susceptible to defalcation and records that are subject to falsification is an important control. Most people know to keep cash secure, not to allow customers to roam around inventory storerooms, and to keep important documents and securities in a safe place. Locking doors and limiting access to restricted areas within an organization's facilities are often highly effective methods for preventing unauthorized use of assets. Limiting access to documents and records is also important because many documents, when properly completed, provide access to assets. For example, assets may be misappropriated by presenting an authentic, but forged, check at a bank.

Most organizations now realize that two important but traditionally overlooked assets that need physical controls are people and information. For example, many businesses take expensive precautions to protect employees and customers, including hiring guards and limiting access to facilities through the use of complex entry controls (e.g., hologram-encoded passes, fingerprint scanners, metal detectors). Similarly, as hackers have become more sophisticated, companies have invested significantly in mechanisms to encrypt data and protect access from unauthorized users (e.g., firewalls). The media has regaled readers with stories about computer hackers who have gained entry to a computer system and wreaked havoc with computerized records. Consequently, limiting electronic access may be more important and difficult than physical access.

Example

A particularly famous case of employee fraud (emulated in the movie *Office Space*) involved a computer programmer at a bank who rewrote a computer program to deposit all rounding adjustments on interest accruals into his personal account. Deposits of less than a penny may seem small, but the amount can grow rapidly when accumulated over a multitude of accounts and an extended time period. Another infamous case involved a computer hacker who gained entry to a telephone company's materials purchasing system. He ordered the system to place an order for materials that were delivered to him but billed to the phone company. As a result, the hacker was able to steal thousands of dollars of equipment from the company.

SEGREGATION OF DUTIES

Adequate segregation of duties within and across processes is extremely important and can significantly strengthen other control activities that are in place. In

---

7 Control totals do not need to be meaningful on their own. Artificial control totals are referred to as *hash totals* and are useful for verifying account numbers or other identification numbers. For example, a hash total of customer numbers can be computed for all sales transactions in a batch. Then, when the sales are posted to the accounts receivable ledger, a second total of the account numbers posted can be computed. The second total should agree with the control total if the posting process has been performed correctly even though the hash totals do not have any meaning themselves.

concept, the segregation of duties is relatively simple—individuals responsible for operational decisions, transaction authorization, maintaining custody of assets, and handling accounting records should not perform any of the other roles. However, determining if an organization has proper segregation of duties can be difficult because potentially risky combinations of functions may not be easy to discern. Some common problems include

1. *Failure to segregate asset custody from the accounting function:* Access to both assets and accounting records allows an individual to misappropriate assets and then hide the action by changing the accounting records.
2. *Failure to segregate transaction authorization from asset custody:* If a single individual can authorize improper transactions and get access to the related assets, it is possible to misappropriate assets and cover up the theft. A good example of this type of problem is in payroll: the person who authorizes the hiring of employees should not have access to payroll checks so as to avoid payments to fictitious employees.
3. *Failure to segregate operating functions from accounting functions:* If an operating unit maintains its own accounting records, the personnel in that unit may have an incentive to bias the information, especially if current performance is poor.

Example

Consider a situation where a storeroom clerk authorizes inventory acquisitions and also keeps the accounting records related to inventory. The clerk could authorize the acquisition of unnecessary inventory, remove the material from the premises (or simply have it shipped to another address), and alter the accounting records to make it look like the inventory never existed or had been sold. As long as the accounting records agreed with the inventory on hand, the theft would be difficult to detect without a special investigation.

Segregation of duties should also be considered within the data processing function. The use of automated systems often creates ways to electronically obtain access to assets or to authorize transactions that could not be accomplished physically. Improper combinations of functions related to data processing can undermine otherwise good segregation of duties. In general, the following data processing activities should be handled separately:

- Systems analyst (responsible for general design of the system)
- Programmer (responsible for writing computer code and testing of the system)
- Computer operator (responsible for actual running of installed system)
- Troubleshooter (responsible for addressing problems in the system)
- Data librarian (responsible for maintaining computerized files and records)
- Data control group (responsible for internal audit of all computerized functions)

As a result of concerns about segregation of duties, a typical organization creates separate functional groups to perform the accounting function (the controller), handle receipts and disbursements (the treasurer), provide independent monitoring (internal auditing), and design, implement, and maintain computer systems (IT department). However, the proper segregation of duties is much more difficult in a distributed processing environment where accounting records are kept on desktop computers that are not under the control of either accounting or data processing.

AN ILLUSTRATION OF PROCESS CONTROLS: HUMAN RESOURCE MANAGEMENT

discussed in Chapter 6, process maps and internal threat analysis are very for identifying residual risks arising from specific processes. To illustrate the use of these techniques in more detail, we continue our discussion of human resource management. The accounting implications of human resource management range from basic payroll processing to much more complicated issues related to retirement benefits and incentive compensation. Examples of process risks related to human resource management are presented in the first column of Figure 7–6. These risks are intended to be representative rather than comprehensive. As previously discussed, key risks pertain to hiring the appropriate labor force in a cost effective manner (*PR1, PR2, PR3, PR4*), managing the work force for best results (*PR7, PR8, PR9, PR10*), and assuring accurate information processing related to payroll (*PR5, PR6*).

Management's responses to many of these risks involve monitoring labor market conditions; establishing formal procedures for performing activities in the process to assure they are done appropriately and in accordance with firm policies; establishing and maintaining effective communication channels with employees; monitoring employee performance, behavior, and attitudes; and intervening in situations where employee relations deteriorate. Some controls that are relevant to human resource management include

- Establishing codes of conduct: Management should formally establish core values and a code of conduct, invest sufficient resources to ensure that employees are familiar with them, and punish violators when appropriate.
- Performance reviews or monitoring controls: Management should actively monitor labor market conditions, recruiting and training performance, regulatory compliance, personnel needs and labor costs, and employee morale and workloads.
- Segregation of duties: Incompatible functions in personnel payroll include authorization of new positions, hiring, employee supervision and evaluation, payroll processing and payroll authorization.
- Processing controls: Authorization should be required for creating a position, selecting the person to fill the position, establishing the rate of pay, assigning work schedules (including whether there is paid overtime or not), determining appropriate mandatory and voluntary deductions, and generating payroll checks.[8] Appropriate documents and records should be used to assure accurate payroll processing and recordkeeping.
- Physical controls: Physical controls primarily pertain to the accessibility of facilities to personnel and protecting personnel and payroll accounting records.

---

8 Employers must comply with numerous state/provincial and national/federal laws applicable to hiring personnel and in some countries local level regulations (e.g., anti-discrimination laws). Auditors must be alert to possible noncompliance with such laws because of the significant penalties and contingent losses that may be imposed on the organization.

Of particular importance to the auditor are any internal controls over financial reporting that are embedded in the process. Authorizations of employee activities, preparation of paperwork, maintenance of accurate records, reliable processing of payroll related costs and expenditures, and proper handling of payroll taxes and deductions are all important to the auditor because of their direct link to the financial statements. Controls that relate to the valuation of long-term employment obligations (e.g., pensions, health care, and other post-retirement benefits) are also very important, as are controls that minimize potential contingent liabilities due to discrimination, harassment, or wrongful termination.

Once management has decided how to respond to identified risks, it also needs to identify performance indicators that measure the significance of each risk. These indicators can provide an early warning when one or more risks are about to become serious problems. Many key indicators pertain to process efficiency including employee costs (wages, benefits, support, travel, termination) and transaction processing (error rates, processing costs, errors in authorizations). Other performance measures relate to hiring (recruiting costs, unfilled positions), employee utilization (down time, overtime, training, absenteeism), and employee attitudes (morale, turnover).

Example

Many organizations promote the fact that people are their key competitive advantage, either due to superior management practices or the ability to hire the "best and brightest" (e.g., see list of Fortune Top 100 Companies in the United States, the Financial Times Top 100 in the United Kingdom). An auditor would be worried when auditing such a company to find above average turnover, evidence of low employee morale, performance evaluations carried out sporadically, or an inability to find key operational personnel due to unscheduled absences.

INTERNAL CONTROL AND RESIDUAL RISKS

The auditor develops a process map and assesses internal threats for the purpose of assessing residual risks that are likely to have a significant impact on the conduct of the audit. Consequently, the risk map developed in Chapter 6 for human resource management would need to be updated to reflect management's responses to risks. Recall that this example is for a software company that is owned and managed by a small group of university friends and has been rapidly growing. In order to update the initial risk assessments, we add a few more facts related to internal control:

- The company is very active in monitoring competitors and labor markets and is quite successful at attracting talented employees.
- The company has excellent employee training and incentive programs.
- The company uses an outside service organization to process its payroll, and all payments are made electronically.
- Most employees are salaried.
- The company has a legal firm periodically review its hiring, promotion, and termination policies and procedures.

If the auditor considers the affect of these management responses on the identified risks, he or she might conclude that some individual risks should shift

Figure 7–7   Effect of Controls and Performance Indicators on Inherent Risks for Human Resource Management

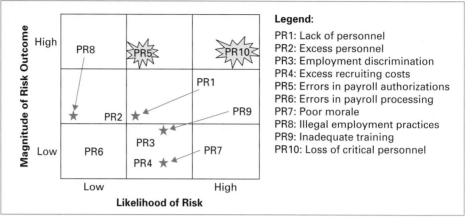

downward on the risk map. Specifically, the auditor might be able to downgrade *PR1* due to the recruiting experience of the firm, *PR8* due to the legal review, and *PR9* due to an evaluation of the company's training practices. These conclusions are documented in Figure 7–7. However, any such shifts would necessitate that the auditor obtain evidence that the identified control responses were effective, such as evidence related to training practices and the quality of the outside service bureau as well as a report on employment practices from the law firm.

The auditor should also consider evidence indicating heightened residual risk. Assume that in the course of discussions with client personnel, it is revealed that there is no systematic approach to promotions and pay raises. Employees are often promoted and given hefty bonuses or raises on the whim of one or two of the members of the management team. Paperwork for these actions is often ignored, delayed, or lost. Even members of the management team admits that they do not always recall what they promised by the time they get around to formalizing the related paperwork. Because changes in pay rates are initiated by the company, they cannot be processed by the outside service center without appropriate supporting documentation; this slipshod approach suggests that there is a significant risk of errors in payroll authorization, at least as pertains to changes in pay levels. Thus, the problems with payroll authorizations would justify maintaining *PR5* at a high level.

As part of the process review, the auditor would also look at the key performance indicators available. Assume the following for our illustration:

- There are few processing exceptions reported by the outside service center.
- Recruiting costs per new employee are in line with industry levels.
- Employee morale consistently ranks high.
- Open or new positions are filled quickly.
- Training hours per employee exceed the industry average by 10 percent.
- Employee turnover is higher than the industry and has increased in the past year.

Some of these indicators support the auditor's conclusions about some of the risks documented in Figure 7–7, notably, the downgrading of *PR1* (positions fill quickly) and *PR9* (adequate training occurs). Furthermore, the performance measures provide evidence to support a downgrade of *PR7* since employee morale is high. However, the increase in employee turnover is a concern and suggests that *PR10* should continue to be considered a potential residual risk.

After considering control responses and performance measures, the auditor is left with two possible residual risks related to human resources: *PR5*, payroll authorizations, and *PR10*, loss of critical personnel. How should the auditor respond to *PR5* and *PR10*? Having identified these residual risks, the auditor then needs to address their impact on the risk of material misstatement and the conduct of the audit. Recall that a residual risk can have up to five types of implications: (1) conditioning expectations about financial results, (2) suggesting financial misstatements, (3) raising concerns about viability, (4) indicating potential threats to the control environment, and (5) highlighting potential comments for client.

Consider *PR5* first. This is a relatively straightforward accounting problem and could well be considered a significant deficiency in internal control over financial reporting. The risk probably does not tell the auditor much about expected financial results given that errors in authorization could lead to overstated or understated pay levels, nor does the risk suggest a going concern problem. However, the nature of the problem does indicate heightened risk of material misstatement because (1) inherent risk is increased by the inaccurate payroll information and (2) control risk is heightened since authorizations are not being properly performed. The auditor would probably use tests of controls and transactions to assess the extent of any errors in the financial statements arising from these risks.

For *PR10*, loss of critical personnel, the auditor's concerns are a bit broader and may even go to the viability of the company. Of most concern is identifying who is leaving the company and understanding why. Although overall indicators suggest a happy and competent workforce, a discernable pattern of employee departures may indicate behavior that could be of concern to the auditor. For example, people may be leaving due to harassment and mistreatment, concern about corporate behavior, or worries about the future of the company, or to seek better economic opportunities. Any of these could be a warning sign of deeper problems that the auditor would want to investigate. Whether the auditor performs any substantive testing related to this risk will depend on the nature of the problem. If it is discovered that employees are leaving because of concern about fraud, the implications to the auditor are quite serious. If departures are due to mistreatment, contingent losses due to litigation may not be far behind.

> **Authoritative Guidance & Standards**
>
> Both SAS 109 and ISA 315 require audit teams to have a discussion regarding the risk of material misstatements of the financial statements, considering both inherent risks and residual risks after considering the presence and likely effectiveness of internal control. By completing a risk map that illustrates inherent risks, controls, and residual risks, audit teams would be in a good position to discuss the risk of material misstatement, particularly when comparing residual risks across all business processes being analyzed.

Example

In August 2001, Jeff Skilling, CEO of Enron announced that he was leaving the company. In a conference call with financial analysts, he and Ken Lay, chairman, explained that the decision was due to family reasons. Skilling was quoted as stating that "the company is in great shape." Lay added: "There are no accounting issues, no trading issues, no reserve issues, no previously unknown problem issues." Although they were not entirely successful in soothing the concerns of the market, the departure would stand as a rather significant warning signal that was not fully appreciated at the time, least of all by the auditor.[9]

---

9 Quotes are found in *Conspiracy of Fools* by Kurt Eichenwald (Broadway Books, 2005), p. 486.

All risk assessments should be supported by appropriate evidence obtained while developing an understanding of the client's business. To support risk reductions based on process controls, the auditor would document tests of the effectiveness of key controls to ensure they are consistently applied. These tests could involve discussions with individuals within the organization who are responsible for various aspects of the process and examination of transaction and control documentation. Also, the auditor would review process documentation and procedures and observe personnel in their duties at a sufficient level to ensure that the controls are consistently applied. Finally, the auditor would need to document the analytical evidence pertaining to performance indicators associated with specific risks.

SUMMARY AND CONCLUSION

In this chapter, we discussed management's approach to dealing with strategic and process risks, referred to as internal control. We defined internal control and described its five basic components: control environment, risk assessment, control activities, information and communication, and monitoring. We then discussed management controls and process controls in more depth. Finally, our example based on human resource management was extended to include a discussion of internal control related to specific risks. We document conclusions about internal control in a risk map, indicating risks that can be downgraded due to the existence of effective internal controls related to specific risks. The conclusion that risks *PR5* and *PR10* are significant residual risks for human resource management has implications for the conduct of the remainder of the audit. There will probably be other residual risks arising in other processes. We defer further discussion of what the auditor does when a significant residual risk has been identified until Chapter 10, and first turn our attention to a more detailed discussion of internal control over financial reporting (Chapter 8).

BIBLIOGRAPHY OF RELATED PROFESSIONAL LITERATURE

Research

Armour, M. 2000. Internal Control: Governance Framework and Business Risk Assessment at Reed Elsevier. *Auditing: A Journal of Practice & Theory*. 19(Supplement): 75–82.

Beasley, M. S., J. V. Carcello, and D. R. Hermanson. 1999. *Fraudulent Financial Reporting: 1987–1997 An Analysis of US Public Companies*. Committee of Sponsoring Organizations of the Treadway Commission. Jersey City, NJ.

Farrell, J. 2004. Internal Controls and Managing Enterprise-Wide Risks. *The CPA Journal*. 74(8): 11–12.

Simons, R. 1992. The Strategy of Control. *CA Magazine*, March, 44–46.

Spira, L. and M. Page. 2003. Risk Management: The Invention of Internal Control and the Changing Role of the Internal Audit. *Accounting, Auditing & Accountability Journal*. 16(4): 640–661.

Professional Reports and Guidance

PCAOB. Policy Statement Regarding Implementation of Auditing Standard No. 2

PCAOB. Report on the Initial Implementation of Auditing Standard No. 2

PCAOB. Staff Questions and Answers on Auditing Standard No. 2

Auditing Standards

AICPA *Statements on Auditing Standard (SAS)* No. 109, "Understanding the Entity and Its Environment and Assessing the Risks of Material Misstatement."

Committee of Sponsoring Organizations of the Treadway Commission (COSO). *Internal Control—Integrated Framework.* AICPA, 1992.

Criteria of Control Committee. 1995. *Guidance on Control.* Toronto: Canadian Institute of Chartered Accountants.

IAASB *International Standards on Auditing (ISA)* No. 315, "Understanding the Entity and Its Environment and Assessing the Risks of Material Misstatement."

PCAOB *Auditing Standard No. 2,* "An Audit of Internal Control Over Financial Reporting Performed in Conjunction with an Audit of Financial Statements."

QUESTIONS

1. Describe the three objectives of internal control and explain how a failure of any of the three objectives could impact the financial statements.

2. The control environment is described as critical for effective internal control at an organization. Describe policies that can be instituted at an organization that would help it reflect a strong tone-at-the-top. Such a tone suggests that issuing fairly stated financial statements is a top priority and that integrity is a core value of the organization.

3. Discuss why risk assessment improves both the effectiveness and efficiency of an organization's internal control.

4. Why is management control important for organizations? As part of your answer, describe how each of the following four types of management controls helps organizations meet strategic objectives by mitigating strategic risks:
   a. Top-level reviews
   b. Direct activity management
   c. Performance indicators and benchmarking
   d. Independent evaluation

5. For each of the following examples of internal control limitations, provide specific examples of how the limitation impedes one of the four management control types ability to effectively mitigate strategic risk:
   a. Failure by employees to internalize the organization's mission and objectives
   b. Inaccurate or out-of-date assumptions
   c. Undue focus on current conditions
   d. Rigid organizational structure
   e. Failure to enforce accountability
   f. Communication breakdowns
   g. Top management failure to achieve objective strategic objectives

6. Describe strengths and weaknesses of each of the tests of management controls described in the chapter—client inquiries, observation, and review of documentation. Offer suggestions for how using combinations of these tests help auditors attain more persuasive evidence that the controls are or are not operating effectively.

7. What are the four options that clients have for responding to process risks? For risks that clients have chosen to reduce, how should the auditor adjust risk assessments based on the perceived effectiveness of the mechanisms utilized to reduce the risk (e.g., if the client implements a control activity, how should the effects of the control be depicted on the risk assessment diagram depicted in Figure 7–7)?

8. After plotting strategic risks and depicting the expected residual process risks after considering any control put in place to reduce the risks, what decision about designing

audit tests can the auditor make based on the perceived effectiveness of controls? In other words, how can the assessment of strategic risks and judgment of perceived effectiveness of controls help auditors to design effective and efficient audits?

9. How can auditors use performance measures that are used to monitor risk as evidence in performing the financial statement audit? What considerations should auditors make in determining which measures should be used and the extent to which they can be relied upon?

10. What is a residual risk? Why should the auditor take residual risks into account in his audit? How can he identify these risks?

11. What is the general relationship between business risks, business processes, management controls, and audit implications? Illustrate with an example.

PROBLEMS

1. Contrast management controls with process controls. Why do management controls (or the lack thereof) carry such heavy implications for audit risk assessment when they don't necessarily concern themselves with accounting numbers? Answer in terms of the model of internal control components in Figure 7–2.

2. The objectives of internal controls include the following:
    - To improve effectiveness and efficiency of operations
    - To increase reliability of accounting information
    - To foster compliance with rules and regulations

    An average retail grocery store, like any other business, uses numerous internal controls to meet these objectives. Consider your local grocery store and list at least two examples of controls for each objective. Discuss how each one of them accomplishes one or more of the objectives for internal controls.

3. Management controls mitigate the strategic risks of the firm and promote efficiency and effectiveness of operations. The four types of management controls are:
    - Top-level reviews
    - Direct activity management
    - Performance indicators and benchmarking
    - Independent evaluation processes

    Consider a large computer network consulting operation, specializing in large-scale systems integration projects. Among their management controls are the following:

    a. Senior management expects expenses (other than payroll) per consultant to be $4,000 per month.

    b. The area managers, looking for unusually large transactions, review payroll disbursements for their hourly employees.

    c. An assistant controller, looking for unusually large transactions, reviews payroll disbursements for hourly employees.

    d. Senior management secludes itself once each quarter to review industry trends and potential threats.

    e. The vice president of marketing reviews the requests from each geographic region for decreases in customers' bills.

    f. The manager of the southeast region expects to see revenue per consultant reach $18,000 per month.

    g. The controller supervises a comprehensive inventory of all computer equipment each year.

    h. The managers of the geographic regions receive copies of all their consultants' time sheets.

    Categorize each of these management controls into one of the four types of management control. For each, discuss the specific ramifications (if any) for audit risk assessment.

4. Franz Ferdinand Corp. is a manufacturer of high-quality electric guitars. As a part of the company's annual survey of its environment, FFC has identified several business risks/threats. Reviewing the list, you realize that the risks/threats could have ramifications for your audit. Complete an analysis of those risks/threats in a manner similar to that shown in Figure 7–4.

Business Risk/Threat	Source of Threat	Activity Likely to Be Affected	Relevant Management Controls	Potential Audit Implications
(1) Musicians are switching to synthesized guitars.				
(2) Blight is reducing availability of wood.				
(3) Competitors are releasing a line of beginner-priced guitars in hopes of securing brand loyalties among the young.				
(4) Union contract is up for review.				
(5) Music stores are consolidating to just a few large chains.				
(6) Chief product spokesman is now endorsing a rival brand.				
(7) Foreign producers improve the manufacturing process and undercut markets.				
(8) Lawsuits arising from accidental electrocution are mounting.				

5. Performance indicators are important for assessing whether any identified process risks are currently a significant problem. These problems can arise because risks are not effectively controlled or controls are not operating effectively. For each of the following process risks associated with a human resources management process at a home improvement retailer, like The Home Depot, provide examples of measures that can be used as performance indicators (Use Figure 7–6 to help in completing this problem):

a.   Poorly motivated employees

b.   Mismatch in employee placement and expertise required

c.   Discriminatory hiring practices

   d.   Noncompetitive compensation practices
   e.   High levels of turnover
   f.   Ineffective training programs

6. Petro-Canada, like any major petroleum company, faces a number of significant process risks associated the extraction of oil from the ground or ocean. Below are several example risks likely impacting extraction of oil for Petro-Canada. Using the same format as provided in Figure 7–6, list controls that might be in place at Petro-Canada for each process risk and possible performance measures that might signal control effectiveness or the level of residual risk.
   a.   Natural disasters disrupt oil production capabilities.
   b.   Employees are seriously injured during production.
   c.   Oil reserves are significantly lower than expected.
   d.   Business disruption caused by public unrest associated with environmental impacts of oil production.
   e.   Oil production equipment breakdowns cause oil production disruptions.

7. Consider a fast food restaurant, such as Burger King (Hungry Jacks in Australia), that hires a large number of unskilled employees, many of whom are relatively young. Accordingly, there is a high turnover rate at most restaurants. Considering the many challenges of a young, transient, unskilled workforce, describe examples for each of the types of control activities likely to be in place for employees in Burger King restaurants.
   a.   Performance reviews
   b.   Processing controls
   c.   Physical controls
   d.   Segregation of duties

8. Listed below are three problems that can occur within the customer service process for Kentucky Fried Chicken (KFC). For each problem, indicate (1) a control activity that could prevent or detect the problem and (2) a performance indicator that could be used to monitor the problem. Be specific.

Description of Problem	Suggested Control Activity	Suggested Performance Indicator
A salesman sold a large order of processed chicken to a local fast food chain at a price below cost because he did not know that the price of chicken parts had increased recently due to international shortages associated with the H5N1 bird flu virus.		
A special sales promotion involving giving away action figures from a new movie failed because the movie was a flop. The expected increase in sales did not occur.		
Several receipts from customers were entered into the accounting system twice because the clerk responsible for data entry took a coffee break and forgot which items had been previously entered.		

9. Consider Figure 7–5, which depicts the impact of controls on risk assessments. For each of the following management controls, describe the extent to which you believe the risk moved down or to the right on the grid. In other words, to what extent is the magnitude of possible misstatement or likelihood of misstatement reduced?

   a. The CEO of the company reviews budget variances for each senior VP on a monthly basis.

   b. The manager in charge of the company's most important product line investigates market reports and production plans for each product on a weekly basis.

   c. A major auto manufacturer's risk committee reviews J.D. Power and Associates and *Consumer Reports* evaluations of their vehicles. Vice presidents of operations, research and development, and marketing are then allowed to respond to the criticisms and accolades provided in the reports.

10. Consider the following two plots of risks and controls.

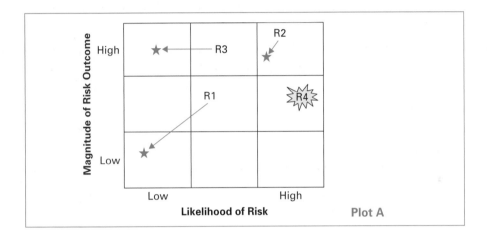

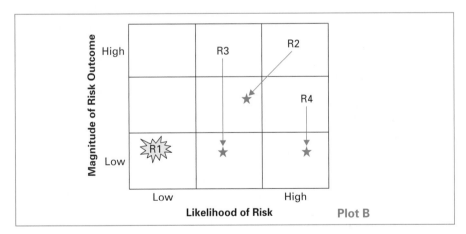

Based on these two plots of risks and controls, explain the audit implications for the different plots for each of the four risks and controls across Plot A and Plot B.

   a. Risk 1
   b. Risk 2
   c. Risk 3
   d. Risk 4

Case 7–1: Alliance Management at Nike

Nike has been highly successful creating marketing alliances with well-known and successful athletes, academic institutions, and professional franchises. This success would be difficult to achieve without a successful alliance management business process. Nike has formed international alliances with athletes in basketball, hockey, football, American football, baseball, and various other sports. To see a list of the athletes that they have as part of their alliance network, access their web site.

Alliances have been an important part of Nike's growth over the past 25 years. The Company's first major success was when an alliance was formed with Michael Jordan in the 1980s. The alliance coupled with an advertising campaign featuring director Spike Lee often is cited as the watershed moment in the company's growth. The alliance with golfer Tiger Woods in the 1990s helped Nike develop as one of the world's premier golf equipment and apparel manufacturers. The company's success has led to a proliferation of competition for alliances with competing athletic and footwear manufacturers. Indeed, these contracts often have been followed by the media and even featured as important elements of movies (e.g., *Jerry Maguire*). For example, Nike's aggressive pursuit of high school basketball star LeBron James was often cited as a key reason that James skipped college and moved directly to the National Basketball Association of the United States.

In addition, Nike has agreements with universities and professional teams in a variety of sports that involves exclusive use of footwear and other athletic apparel in exchange for cash payments and other promotional considerations (e.g., sale of university merchandise at Nike stores, etc.). The Company's aggressive use of promoting its brand, the "swoosh," on apparel of these teams often is discussed by media outlets.

Perform research on Nike sufficient to make logical inferences when completing a process analysis for the alliance management process, which is used to identify alliances, develop contracts with alliance partners, and monitor alliance performance to effectively execute, renegotiate, or terminate the contracts.

Requirements

a. Research Nike to create a process map for the alliance management business process. Refer to Figure 6–4 when creating the process map.
b. Use the process map that you created in requirement (a) as a guide for creating an internal threat analysis for Nike's alliance management process. Refer to Figure 7–6 when creating the internal threat analysis.
c. Use the internal threat analysis that you created in requirement (b) to plot the risks and impact of controls on a graph where the likelihood of risk is the x-axis and the magnitude of risk outcome is the y-axis. Refer to Figures 6–8 and 7–5 when completing the graph.

Case 7–2: Franchise Management at McDonald's

McDonald's has grown to be the largest and most respected chain of fast food restaurants largely due to its franchising business process. By relinquishing control of day-to-day operations at individual locations but at the same time establishing controls for keeping quality high across franchises, McDonald's has set the standard for other franchisers to follow.

However, for McDonald's to maintain in competitive brand strength, the company needs to ensure that only qualified and financially stable franchisees are selected to operate McDonald's locations. Further, upon selecting franchisees, effective contracts need to be designed outlining expectations and financial payments for franchisees. In addition, McDonald's needs to ensure that it is complying with its contractual obligations and that franchisees are monitored for compliance with the franchise agreement.

Requirements

a. Use the information available on McDonald's web site to create a process map for the franchising business process. Refer to Figure 6–4 when creating the process map.
b. Use the process map that you created in Requirement (a) as a guide for creating an internal threat analysis for McDonald's franchising business process. Refer to Figure 7–6 when creating the internal threat analysis.
c. Use the internal threat analysis that you created in Requirement (b) to plot the risks and impact of controls on a graph where the likelihood of risk is the x-axis and magnitude of risk outcome is the y-axis. Refer to Figures 6–8 and 7–5 when completing the graph.

Case 7–3: Duria's Retail

Duria's Inc. is a discount retailer of small home appliances, china and glassware, luggage, electronic equipment, and jewelry. Merchandise is displayed in a showroom located in a small shopping center. Customers browse through the merchandise at their leisure but must obtain help from a floor clerk if they wish to purchase an item. A description of the sales system is provided below.

1. When a customer is ready to make a purchase, a floor clerk will fill out a four-part prenumbered sales invoice for the customer (see Exhibit 3–1). There are usually three to six floor clerks working at a given time and each has his or her

Exhibit 3–1 Duria's Showroom Shopping

NAME: _____

ADDRESS: _____

CITY: _____   STATE: _____

ZIP CODE: _____   PHONE: _____

FORM OF PAYMENT: ___ Cash ___ Visa ___ M/C ___ Other

ORDER FILLED BY: _____   DATE: _____

Catalog Number	Warehouse Use	Qty	Item Description	Unit Cost	Total Cost
_____	_____	___	_____	_____	_____
_____	_____	___	_____	_____	_____
_____	_____	___	_____	_____	_____
_____	_____	___	_____	_____	_____
_____	_____	___	_____	_____	_____
_____	_____	___	_____	_____	_____
_____	_____	___	_____	_____	_____
_____	_____	___	_____	_____	_____

SUBTOTAL   _____

SALES TAX   _____

AMOUNT DUE   _____

All returns must be accompanied by a sales receipt and in their original carton and packing (no returns after 10 days).

own book of blank sales invoices. Each book contains 100 invoices that are sequentially numbered. The invoice numbers in one book begin where the preceding book ended. When a book is empty, the clerk turns it in to the store manager, who gives the clerk a new book of invoices. The store manager is the only person who has access to the books of unused invoices. At the end of a shift, each clerk returns his or her book to the store manager. If a book still has invoices to be used, the manager will issue that book to the clerk's replacement. If there is no replacement, the partially used book is stored with the unused books for later use.

2.   When preparing an invoice, the clerk fills out the eight-digit item number (which has a two-digit check digit embedded in the sequence), a description of the item, the quantity desired, its price as posted on the display, and the customer name and address. The invoice has room for eight items to be entered. Copy 3 of the invoice is given to the customer, who is then directed to the waiting/pickup area. The floor clerk keeps copy 4 of the invoice in the invoice book. Copies 1 and 2 are placed in a plastic container which is sent to the storeroom/warehouse via a pneumatic tube.

3.   The storeroom/warehouse uses the invoice to select the merchandise and place it on a conveyor belt that takes it to the customer pickup area. Copy 1 is initialed by the storeroom clerk who prepares the merchandise. Copy 1 is then firmly attached to the merchandise before it is placed on the conveyor belt. Copy 2 of the invoice is used by a storeroom clerk to update perpetual inventory records. Copy 2 is then filed numerically in the storeroom. If the merchandise is not in stock, the storeroom manager calls the customer waiting area to inform the customer. In this case, both copy 1 and 2 of the invoice are stamped "cancel not in stock" and filed in the numerical file.

4.   There are usually one to four cashiers in the customer pickup area. Cashiers are always supervised by a cashier supervisor. When merchandise comes off the conveyor belt, a cashier identifies the customer and uses Copy 1 of the invoice to ring up the sale on an electronic cash register. Each cashier is assigned to a specific register. The item number, quantity and price are taken off Copy 1 of the invoice and entered into the cash register. All sales are paid for by cash or major credit card. The cashier retains Copy 1 of the invoice in the register drawer, and the customer keeps Copy 3 plus the cash register receipt to indicate payment. At the end of the day, the copies of all the invoices that have accumulated in the drawer are sent to the accounting department where they are filed numerically without further examination.

5.   The cash register is tied into the central computer system, which automatically accumulates total sales, cash receipts, and credit sales. The computer posts these sales to the appropriate acccount and to the inventory control account. When a cashier shift change occurs, a subtotal of sales and receipts is run off the cash register by the cashier supervisor and compared to cash in till while cashier is present. At the close of business (around 10:00 p.m.), the store manager and the cashier supervisor (together) run off a tape of the sales, cash receipts, and credit charges for the day, classified by type of inventory. This tape is initialed by both persons and put in the manager's desk drawer. The next day, after the accounting staff have reported for work, the manager delivers the previous day's tapes to the accounting manager, who files them without examination.

Requirements

1. Prepare a flowchart or a control narrative of the sales/collection system for Duria's.
2. Analyze the strengths and weaknesses of the system as described above. For each weakness, prepare a recommendation to management to remedy the potential problem.
3. What are the audit implications of the weaknesses that you noted? What types of substantive tests of transactions or account details might you use to satisfy yourself that these weaknesses have not resulted in errors in excess of tolerable error being included in the following accounts?
    a. Sales
    b. Inventory (credit entries only)
    c. Cash (debit entries only)
    d. Receivables from credit card companies

Evaluating Internal Control over Financial Reporting

8

Outline

INTRODUCTION

In Chapters 6 and 7 we introduced the basic approach for evaluating risks associated with audit-sensitive business processes. We discussed that a key component of process analysis is the evaluation of internal control activities that mitigate the risks within a process, especially controls over accounting transactions and estimates. This chapter discusses internal controls designed specifically to reduce the risk of errors in the financial reporting process (see Figure 8–1). More specifically, this

Figure 8–1   An Overview of the Audit Process for Financial Statement Audit

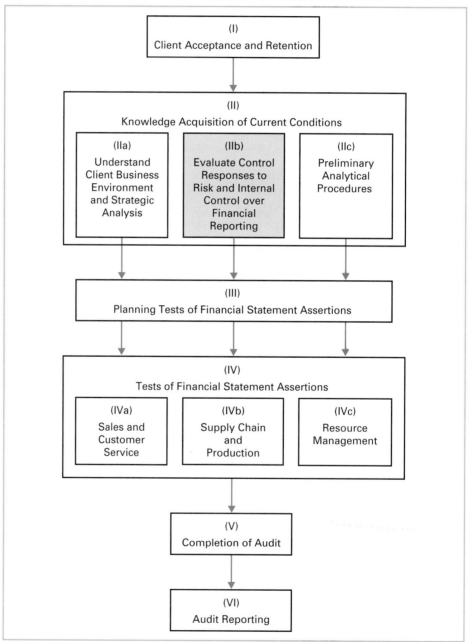

chapter deals with *internal controls over financial reporting (ICOFR)* that are put in place within and across business processes to provide reasonable assurance that the financial statements are fairly presented.

Much of the auditor's analysis of controls focuses on the reliability of information generated within a process since the information will eventually be included in the financial statements or affect auditor judgments about the conduct of the audit. Linking the auditor's conclusions about risks derived from process analysis to the risk of misstatement in the financial statements necessitates that the auditor focus on the controls directly related to financial statement assertions. Furthermore, if the economic context and business purpose of a transaction is not understood, auditors may fixate on whether the transaction meets the precise rules of GAAP but miss the real implications for the financial statements.

> **Authoritative Guidance & Standards**
> This chapter focuses primarily on the guidance provided in AS 2 for companies that are publicly traded in the United States. However, it also builds upon the standards on understanding an entity and its environment and assessing the risk of material misstatement (SAS 109, ISA 315) and describes tests of controls described in standards on performing procedures in response to assessed risks (SAS 110, ISA 330).

Example

In a lawsuit against the auditors of Lincoln Savings and Loan, detailed testimony and working papers were presented to support the auditor's contention that they had carefully considered the revenue recognition policy of Lincoln during the course of the audit. Specifically, they had tested whether Lincoln met the criteria for revenue recognition for real estate transactions according to SFAS 66 (U.S. GAAP). Although the auditors considered the technical requirements of the standard, they failed to question whether the recognition of sizable revenues with profit margins in the hundreds of percent were realistic given the well-publicized real estate slump in Arizona at the time. Apparently, this inconsistency did not cause the auditors to be suspicious of the values placed on transactions.

INTERNAL CONTROL AND FINANCIAL REPORTING

Internal control over financial reporting may involve control activities employed at multiple levels within an organization including all of the following:

- *Management controls* that relate to selecting accounting personnel, planning the installation of information/accounting systems, authorizing access to journals, and specifying the nature and timing of acceptable transactions.
- *Business process controls* that relate to authorizing specific transactions and capturing information at the point that a transaction occurs (e.g., linking the invoicing system to the sales journal).
- *Monitoring controls* that provide periodic performance reports to process owners and can lead to managerial intervention when problems occur.
- *Financial reporting controls* that relate to estimating accruals, making adjusting entries, and preparing disclosures and reports.

No system of internal control is perfect—errors may be made and fraud may occur even in an organization with outstanding process controls and internal control over financial reporting. Controls that appear to be quite rigorous may fail for a number of reasons. Generally, an organization is only as good as its personnel. If personnel are not competent, mistakes may occur and go undetected. If personnel are not trustworthy, individuals may collude (work together) to undermine the financial reporting process, or management may use its power and prerogatives to circumvent (or override) financial reporting controls. With these limitations in mind, the auditors' understanding of internal control over financial reporting is an important factor for assessing the corresponding level of control risk for financial statement assertions.

Auditors differentiate between the many controls addressing strategic and operating risks and controls that relate to how specific transactions and accounting estimates are recorded within a process. Both are important because internal control over financial reporting is less likely to be effective if other types of process risks are not well managed. Furthermore, analysis of process risks beyond those associated with the financial statements provides a context for evaluating the competence of management, the nature of required reporting for a process, and the context in which to evaluate the appropriateness and reasonableness of transactions, accounts, and estimates affected by a process.

In this chapter, we will focus on process controls related to internal control over financial reporting, starting from the point where transactions are initiated and initially recorded and culminating with final presentation of the results in the financial statements. We first review the financial reporting process. Next, we discuss the techniques employed by the auditor to gain an understanding of a client's internal control over financial reporting. We then examine specific auditor planning and testing of internal control over financial reporting. We also present a detailed example of how an auditor may evaluate internal control over financial reporting. Finally, we consider the additional work necessary under an integrated audit framework.

> **Authoritative Guidance & Standards**
>
> AS 2 defines ICOFR as "a process designed by, or under the supervision of, the company's principal executive and principal financial officers, or persons performing similar functions and effected by the company's board of directors, management, and other personnel, to provide reasonable assurance regarding the reliability of financial reporting and the preparation of financial statements for external purposes in accordance with [GAAP]..." All references to and descriptions of ICOFR in this chapter are consistent with this definition.

THE FINANCIAL REPORTING PROCESS

The financial reporting (accounting) process comprises the set of activities used by an organization to capture and communicate financial and other information and to foster accountability within the organization. These processes are usually embedded within the overall processes of the organization. The primary purpose of the accounting system is to identify, record, classify, aggregate, and report transaction information. The quality of the information and communication that occurs will have a direct impact on management's ability to effectively and efficiently manage the resources and activities of the organization.

The financial reporting process generally includes routine (and non-routine transactions) between an organization and external parties, as well as transactions or transfers within an organization. It also includes adjusting entries needed for accounting estimates or to comply with generally accepted accounting principles. Transactions with external parties represent exchanges involving the receipt and distribution of various types of resources (e.g., cash, materials, equipment, and promises to pay). In most organizations, exchange transactions are voluminous and a formal system is required to make sure each is identified and captured by the system. Other events may be less obvious but still need to be captured by the system, for example a decline in the collectibility of receivable balances. Typically, identifying and recording these circumstances is a greater challenge for the accounting system.

Management assertions, discussed in detail in Chapter 3 and summarized in Figure 8–2, reflect the output from the accounting system. Internal control over financial reporting should be designed to provide reasonable assurance that conditions that could lead to material misstatement of these assertions are prevented or

Figure 8–2   Management Assertions about Financial Reporting

MANAGEMENT ASSERTIONS
Transactions
Occurrence
Completeness
Accuracy
Cutoff
Classification
Accounts
Existence
Completeness
Valuation and Allocation
Rights and Obligations
Presentation and Disclosure
Occurrence and Rights and Obligations
Completeness
Classification and Understandability
Accuracy and Valuation

corrected by management. The financial reporting process will vary across companies based on the structure of business processes and the design of the information systems used to process transactions and compile the financial statements. In general, all financial reporting systems are composed of four components:

1. Source documents and transactions.
2. Journals
3. General and subsidiary ledgers
4. Financial statements

In this section, we briefly describe each component as a basis for understanding internal controls over transaction recording and financial reporting.

Source Documents and Transactions

Transactions reflect an exchange, usually with an independent organization. For a sale, a transaction occurs when goods are shipped to another organization or funds are transferred in payment for goods. In an automated system, the accounting process may be triggered by electronic data entry related to these events. For transactions that are not in electronic form, the receipt of documentation indicating a sale or payment may trigger the recognition of a transaction.

Accounting transactions usually generate one or more source documents, whether paper based or electronic. Some examples of documents used to process a sales transaction include:

- *Sales order:* This document represents an order received from a customer and indicates the nature and quantity of items the customer wishes to purchase.

- *Bill of lading:* This document indicates that a shipment has been made and a sale has occurred. Traditionally, this has been a paper document, but transportation companies are increasingly using electronic documents with an electronic signature.
- *Sales invoice:* This document represents a bill to the customer and indicates the quantity of goods shipped, their price, and the payment terms.

Transactions can also arise from internal actions taken by an organization such as asset transfers or internal work effort. Because GAAP requires the use of accrual-based accounting, the accounting system needs to record these activities as part of the financial reporting process. For example, when employees produce work for an organization, there is a corresponding expense and liability for their efforts before payment occurs. Therefore, organizations must develop financial reporting systems that facilitate recognition of payroll accruals at the end of a period (e.g., wages payable).

Auditors should be particularly concerned about non-routine transactions and estimates, such as period-ending adjusting entries, which are typically used to ensure that financial statements comply with generally accepted accounting principles. In many past accounting frauds, perpetrators hid their activities by using adjusting journal entries to move fraudulent entries from accounts where they might be detected to accounts where detection would be more difficult.

E x a m p l e

Cendant—a travel and leisure company—perpetrated an accounting fraud that involved fictitious sales transactions recorded throughout the year. The intent of these transactions was to convey the message that the company's customer base was growing rapidly. However, before the auditors investigated the sales transactions at the end of the year, the company would transfer some of the fictitious sales accounts to other (reserve) accounts created to account for reorganization costs. Although this fraud sounds fairly easy to identify, the complexity of the sales transactions and reorganization process employed by Cendant made the detection of the adjusting entries very difficult.

JOURNALS

Transactions are generally recorded and summarized in either a *general journal* or a specific journal, such as a sales journal, cash disbursements journal, or purchases journal. For example, the *sales journal* represents a chronological listing of all sales transactions. In most companies this journal is generated electronically even if the actual sales invoices are in paper format. Journal entries represent the authorization to increase or decrease an account balance for a specific amount at a specific point in time. In a manual system, the totals of specific journals for a specific period of time (e.g., a day) are entered into the related accounts (e.g., sales) through a journal entry. For an automated system, a journal entry might be a command to change amounts in an accounting database, such as the addition of a new sales record linked to a specific customer.

LEDGERS

Ledgers aggregate the transaction activity on an account basis and indicate the current balance at a point in time. Ledgers include a transaction summary for all authorized accounts. In a manual system, ledgers will indicate the final balance of each account after all current journal entries are posted. For automated systems, ledgers are the summation of master files organized by account balance. The ledger utilized most by auditors is the *general ledger*, which is a summary of the net activity for all accounts contained in the chart of accounts at a point in time (possibly daily). A *trial balance* is a listing of the ending balances for accounts in the general ledger, typically classified by financial statement line item.

Because many accounts contain a tremendous amount of detailed information about a group of transactions, most companies maintain subsidiary ledgers to break down the account into specific categories. For example, accounts receivable can be broken down by customer by using an *accounts receivable subsidiary ledger*, which is a listing of all customers and the balances owed. Sales are entered as debits to this ledger and payments are credits. In most companies this is done electronically. Similarly, payables may be disaggregated using an *accounts payable subsidiary ledger*,[1] and plant, property, and equipment may be disaggregated using a *fixed asset ledger* (essentially a listing of all long-lived assets).

Ledgers are important for auditors because financial reporting misstatements and fraud must be included in one or more the ledgers of the organization in order to affect the financial statements. Careful analysis of ledger activity is needed to understand the nature and effect of a misstatement or fraud in order to correct the problem prior to preparing the financial statements.

Example

One of the problems encountered in the WorldCom fraud was the reclassification of expenses as an asset, thus removing their effect from the income statement. To be able to reclassify expenses, WorldCom used a fictitious account, called "prepaid capacity." Management first had to add this account to the chart of accounts in the general ledger; otherwise, there would be no account in which to place the debit part of the journal entry which reduced expenses. To understand the nature of this fraud, the auditor would need to examine the credit activity in the expense accounts and the debit activity in the account for the nonexistent asset.

FINANCIAL STATEMENTS

Financial statements consist of line items that summarize related account balances conditional on account type, materiality, and GAAP requirements. For example, a company may have a number of different types of long-lived assets such as vehicles, buildings, land, computers, office equipment, and factory equipment. For financial reporting purposes, all these may simply be combined into a single line item: Plant, Property, and Equipment. Accumulated depreciation may be reported separately or netted against the related asset. The process of aggregating accounts into line items may become quite complex for organizations with subsidiaries that must be consolidated with the financial statements of the parent organization. Furthermore, accumulating information to be disclosed in the footnotes can be quite challenging because much of disclosure information is descriptive and may need to be collected manually.

---

1 Payables may also be disaggregated by a voucher ledger, which essentially lists amounts payable by the date the liability was incurred or is due.

Example

A company with ineffective controls related to financial statement preparation may find that it is unable to reconcile accounts at the parent level with accounts at the subsidiary level. This problem is considered to be quite serious because it suggests that the consolidated financial statements may contain undetected misstatements or omissions that may be material.

Impact of Information Technology on Financial Reporting

Every client has a different accounting system, some being manual bookkeeping systems and others being highly computerized. Consequently, the auditor must be familiar with the many types of systems used for financial reporting. Although internal control over financial reporting should be active at many levels of the organization, from the audit committee to clerks in the accounts payable department, the underlying goal is quite simple: all journal entries, ledger amounts, and financial statement presentations should be free of any material misstatements relating to transactions, accounts, estimates, and disclosures.

A significant difference between systems that are primarily manual and those that are highly automated is the degree to which the functioning of the system can be "observed" by the auditor. In manual systems, virtually every step of the financial reporting process can be examined. For example, the auditor can determine the following:

- Documents are filled out with essential information.
- Journal entries are properly prepared and posted to journals and ledgers.
- Account ledgers are accurately totaled.
- Trial balances are accurate.
- Closing entries are complete and accurate.
- Financial statements are prepared properly.

Purely manual systems are becoming relatively rare, however, as even the smallest businesses adopt inexpensive, off-the-shelf accounting software. Highly automated accounting systems may include the following attributes:

- Paper documents (if they exist) are printed by the computer after data is entered at a keyboard (or via scanning).
- Journal entries are generated by the computer.
- Posting and account accumulation is done automatically.
- Reports are printed out by the computer based on pre-programmed formats.

In this type of system, most of the process is unobservable, except data entry and the documents and records that are produced.

Example

Example: Most gasoline in the United States is now sold on a self-service basis. Not only does the customer pump his or her own gasoline, but the customer can also pay for the gasoline by simply inserting a credit card into a reader that is built into the pump. With virtually no human intervention, this relatively simple transaction has a multitude of effects:

- the transaction is recognized as a sale by the gas station by automatically listing the transaction in a computerized sales journal;

- gasoline supplies on hand are automatically updated based on the volume pumped by the customer;
- a receivable is recognized from the credit card company by the gas station;
- the credit card company recognizes a payable to the gas station owner;
- the credit card company charges the customer's account for the credit card transaction; and
- the credit card company recognizes a small fee as revenue based on a percentage of the transaction.

In short, a large number of accounts are affected in two separate organizations almost simultaneously, with no paper trail being produced, except for a small receipt that the customer can print out at the pump.

The nature of errors that can occur in an accounting system will depend on the extent of automation. In a purely manual system, human error can introduce many types of error due to mistakes made by individuals processing transactions. In a complex computerized system, transaction processing is highly accurate so random errors are much less likely to occur. However, because computer systems often lack flexibility, systematic errors may occur if new transactions arise that do not meet the parameters specified by the system. Finally, in a mixed system, transaction processing may be highly accurate, but random errors are likely to occur at the interface between manual and automated systems, typically at the time of data input (e.g., entering payment amounts into a cash register).

Auditors must be comfortable shifting from one type of system to another given that the objective of obtaining reliable information is the same regardless of the form of the system. Routine transactions tend to be highly automated, whereas non-routine transactions and accounting estimates may be processed manually. Systems are becoming more complex, and even small organizations are becoming dependent on information technology. The trend towards enterprise resource planning systems (ERPs) and complex systems that link information flows from all the key processes of an organization is changing the way that organizations look at financial reporting. In turn, this trend creates new challenges for auditors who must increase their understanding of new information technologies.

THE ROLE OF INTERNAL CONTROL OVER FINANCIAL REPORTING

Establishing effective internal control over financial reporting is a basic responsibility of management. The link between internal control and the financial statement audit has been well established in the auditing profession for decades. As noted in Chapter 3, the audit-risk model presumes a relationship between the risk that controls fail to prevent or detect a financial misstatement and the extent of auditor effort needed to gather substantive evidence about financial statement assertions. The extent to which auditors test controls during the course of the audit depends on the auditors' judgments about the quality of internal control, the trade-off between reliance on internal control versus the use of substantive tests to reduce audit risk, and the professional rules applicable to the engagement. The techniques used to evaluate and test controls are essentially the same in all audits.

In the United States, the PCAOB also requires that the auditor of an SEC-registered company evaluate and test the company's control systems. For an integrated audit as defined by the PCAOB, the auditor must test control design and implementation for all public company audits because such companies are presumed to have strong internal control systems that reduce control risk to a low level for all material classes of transactions and account balances. Thus, the primary differences between an integrated audit and a traditional audit are the auditor's planning objectives related to internal control assessment, the nature and extent of control testing, and the internal and external reporting requirements.[2]

MANAGEMENT'S FUNDAMENTAL RESPONSIBILITY FOR INTERNAL CONTROL

As previously noted, management has a fundamental responsibility to establish internal control over the operational and reporting activities of the company. The COSO model identified in Chapter 7 provides a convenient model of how a well designed control system should work. Figure 8–3 summarizes the five components of internal control as defined by COSO: (1) control environment, (2) risk assessment procedures, (3) control activities, (4) monitoring activities, and (5) information and communication. Control environment, risk assessment, and general monitoring activities were discussed as part of the overall strategic planning of the organization. We now focus on control activities and process-oriented monitoring activities, which are the major component of internal control over financial reporting.

A weakness in internal control is referred to as a *control deficiency*, and is defined as a design flaw or operational breakdown in any part of the system of internal control over financial reporting such that errors or misstatements may not be prevented or may go undetected. Management's responsibility includes designing

Figure 8–3   Elements of Internal Control

Source: COSO, *Internal Control – Integrated Framework*, 1992. Used with permission of COSO.

2 Note, at the time this text was written other countries were considering adopting regulations similar to those in the United States for some or all of their domestic regulated public companies. To the extent that other countries decide to adopt an integrated audit reporting requirement, a broader set of companies in those countries would be affected by these requirements than just the companies registered for trading in the United States. We note that depending on the country, at the present time, many significant non-U.S. companies are subject to the integrated audit, including over 170 large public companies in Canada such as the Royal Bank of Canada, many of the large industrial companies in Europe such as DaimlerChrysler and Mercedes, as well as Asian and Australian companies.

an effective system of internal control over financial reporting so that control deficiencies are minimized. To do so, management designs internal control to:

- *Initiate, authorize, record, process, and report significant accounts and disclosures and related assertions about the financial statements:* The significance of control deficiencies within a process depends on the value, volume, and financial reporting risk associated with process transactions.

- *Enable selection and application of accounting policies in conformity with generally accepted accounting principles:* Control deficiencies might occur if management fails to properly review and apply new accounting pronouncements in a timely manner.

- *Prevent fraud:* Control deficiencies might occur if management fails to set a proper control environment to prevent and detect fraud.

- *Serve as general controls over information technology or those upon which other significant controls are dependent:* Control deficiencies might occur if management fails to design controls over program development and changes, computer operations, or access to programs or data.

- *Facilitate significant non-routine or non-systematic transactions:* Control deficiencies might occur if there is a lack of documentation for complex accounting estimates.

- *Facilitate period-end financial reporting, including preparing financial statements and disclosures:* Control deficiencies might occur if management fails to ensure that the use of journals, ledgers, and financial statements is appropriate.

THE AUDITOR'S ROLE IN EVALUATING INTERNAL CONTROL OVER FINANCIAL REPORTING

When evaluating internal control over financial reporting, the auditor must understand and evaluate the effectiveness of internal control itself and identify any control deficiencies that might have implications for the conduct of the audit. Figure 8–4 summarizes the elements of internal control over financial reporting that are of direct interest to the auditor and the types of information the auditor should consider in evaluating each element. To effectively conduct the audit, the auditor must determine the effectiveness of these elements of internal control. The basic steps for evaluating internal control are summarized in Figure 8–5.

Plan the Evaluation: Planning the evaluation of internal control over financial reporting is important in order to identify critical controls to be considered by the auditor. In making planning decisions, the auditor considers the complexity of the system, materiality, and the risk of fraud. The assessment of materiality will help the auditor to assess the significance of identified control deficiencies. An assessment of the controls in place to prevent or detect fraud, including the control environment, are also important in planning because the presence of fraud-related control deficiencies will have a significant

Authoritative Guidance & Standards
The description of the auditor's role in evaluating ICOFR described in this chapter is consistent with the requirements contained in AS 2. For U.S. public companies, auditors must perform each of the steps described.[3] Guidance in SAS 109 and ISA 315 require auditors to develop a sufficient understanding of the entity and its environment sufficient to assess the risk of material misstatement, including being able to determine the design effectiveness of internal controls. For controls that the auditor wishes to rely upon, tests of operating effectiveness, described as tests of controls, should be performed according to SAS 110 and ISA 330.

---

3 To help smaller public companies in the United States better comply with the requirements of COSO's 1992 internal control framework, COSO issued *Guidance for Smaller Public Companies Reporting on Internal Control over Financial Reporting* in 2005. The final document is scheduled for release during 2006. Further, the SEC has been deliberating during 2006 on the extent to which smaller registrants must comply with AS 2. As of the publication of this text, the SEC had yet to issue a final ruling.

Figure 8–4   Elements of Internal Control over Financial Reporting Relevant to the Conduct of the Audit

Control Environment	Risk Assessment	Control Activities	Information and Communication	Monitoring Activities
• Management philosophy and operating style • Organizational structure • Corporate governance • Board committees • Proper lines of communication, authorization, and responsibility • Management control methods • Internal auditing • Personnel policies • External constraints	• Changes in environment • Changes in personnel • Changes in information systems • Rapid growth • New technology • Changes in product lines or operations • Corporate restructuring • Accounting changes	• Performance reviews • Processing controls • Physical controls • Segregation of duties	• Define classes of transactions and events to be captured • Initiate events and transactions • Record events and transactions • Summarize and classify events and transactions • Reporting (financial statements and other)	• Attitudes and competence of senior management and the board • Real time monitoring of ongoing activities • Periodic performance evaluations • Periodic process reviews • Performance of internal auditors

effect on the eventual testing of the financial statements. Auditors should also keep in mind that the evaluation and testing of internal control may require different assessments and tests when an organization has multiple locations, especially if some locations are individually important.

Evaluate Management's Control Documentation and Testing: Understanding how management assesses and monitors the accounting system enhances the auditors' understanding of the entity's internal control over financial reporting. Auditors will usually evaluate the documentation of internal control that is available from management to ensure that the company has identified critical controls related to transactions, accounts, and disclosures. A lack of such documentation would suggest that the control environment of the organization is weak. The auditor also evaluates internal controls to assess the likelihood that control deficiencies could result in a misstatement. This evaluation should include the impact of any *compensating controls*—controls that might help in addressing apparent deficiencies in the system. Auditors will also consider how management communicates deficiencies to affected parties and the nature of corrective actions that may have been taken to address such deficiencies. Finally, auditors should consider the results of tests of controls performed by company personnel (e.g., internal auditors) and third parties working under the direction of management.

Obtain an Understanding of Internal Control: A critical step in evaluating internal control over financial reporting is to determine what controls are in place to ensure that transactions, accounts, and disclosures are not materially misstated. As part of this process, auditors use a number of approaches for documenting

Figure 8–5   Steps for Evaluating Internal Control Design and Effectiveness

Plan the Evaluation
• Materiality considerations • Fraud considerations • Multi-location testing considerations

Evaluate Management's Control Documentation and Testing
• Obtain an understanding of management's control documentation. • Obtain an understanding of management's control assessment process.* • Evaluate how management determines the controls to be tested (if any).* • Evaluate the completeness of management's documentation and the effectiveness of the control as designed. • Evaluate the likelihood that control failures could result in a misstatement. • Obtain an understanding of the results of testing performed by company personnel or third parties. • Evaluate whether management's documentation supports its assessment.* • Evaluate audit committee effectiveness*

Obtain an Understanding of Internal Control
• Identify significant account balances and disclosures. • Identify significant processes and major classes of transactions. • Identify relevant assertions for transactions, accounts, and disclosures. • Understand the financial reporting process. • Perform walkthroughs. • Evaluate design of controls for effectiveness in preventing material misstatements.** • Identify controls to test, if any.

Assess Control Risk for Financial Reporting Assertions

• For each significant financial statement assertion for each material class of transaction or balance, assess control risk as
  • Maximum
  • Slightly reduced from maximum (high)
  • Moderate
  • Low***

Test the Effectiveness of Internal Control
• Consider use of the work of others (when allowed). • Establish timing of tests of controls. • Perform tests of controls.

Assess Operational Effectiveness of Internal Controls over Financial Reporting
• Based on control design effectiveness and tests of operating effectiveness, conclude whether preliminary control risk assessments are reasonable. • If control risk assessments are reasonable, continue with audit plan. • If control risk assessments are not reasonable, consider the nature and extent of changes to be made to the planned substantive tests in the audit plan (or in the extreme, consider whether the entity is auditable).

* Indicates procedures required in an integrated audit. However, these procedures can also be used when an integrated audit is not required.
** New requirement in 2006 for all entities that are not SEC registrants reporting under SOX 404 per SAS 109 and ISA 315.
*** An implicit assumption in an integrated audit is that control risk should be evaluated at low in all public company audits, hence tests of controls are required.

the financial reporting process of an organization. The three primary techniques are:

- *Written narrative:* A narrative is simply a written description of the organization's processes and controls. At a minimum, the narrative should include a description of the key processing steps that occur, identification of all documents and records used in the accounting system, and the identification of relevant control activities that provide assurance that the process is reliable. This information may be included in a process map for particularly important processes. Copies of documents (or key computer screens) may be included as exhibits to the narrative. The description should include discussion of the control environment, risk-assessment process, and specific control activities.

- *Flowchart:* A flowchart is a diagram of a process describing the key sequential steps in the process. A very simple flowchart can be used to describe the activities in a process map. An example of a system flowchart appears in Figure 8–6 and is discussed in detail later in the chapter. The flowchart should show the source, handling and disposition of transactions within a process using standardized symbols. The flowchart can be supplemented by brief descriptions where further detail may be needed. Flowcharts have the advantage of providing a general overview of a system.

- *Control questionnaire:* A control questionnaire is a series of questions, usually in a yes/no format, about the control activities that could be performed within a specific process. In most cases, a "yes" answer indicates that a control procedure is performed and that a deficiency does not exist. A "no" answer implies that there is no control of the indicated type and that a deficiency may exist depending on whether there are compensating controls. Questionnaires are useful for quickly identifying the control procedures that an organization has in place in key processes. Because a good questionnaire is comprehensive, the auditor is unlikely to overlook any control procedures that might have an impact on the audit. However, a questionnaire rarely provides a coherent picture of internal control and should be used as a supplement to a written narrative or flowchart. Furthermore, since questionnaires are general in nature, it is the auditor's responsibility to consider the unique circumstances of the client being audited.

Authoritative Guidance & Standards

Under AS 2, auditors are required to perform walkthroughs as part of their testing of the design of internal controls. SAS 109 and ISA 315 also describe a walkthrough as a procedure that an auditor can perform to gain a sufficient understanding of an entity's internal control design. In some cases, a walkthrough can also serve as a test of control effectiveness (e.g., an automated control of an information processing system).

One procedure that is particularly useful for developing an understanding of the controls in a process is a *walkthrough*. This procedure involves tracing one (or a few) transaction(s) from origination through the entire information system of the organization, including manual and automated activities, culminating in inclusion in the financial statements. Though extremely useful in virtually all audits, walkthroughs are required for all major classes of transactions in an integrated audit. One common misconception about walkthroughs is their role as evidence for an auditor. Because a walkthrough only consists of one test item, it is a very weak test of control effectiveness. Rather, walkthroughs are used to develop a better understanding on how controls are designed and whether they appear to be in operation.

A particularly challenging aspect of evaluating internal control is assessing the effectiveness of the audit committee, which is responsible for hiring and terminating the auditor. This assessment is

Figure 8–6   Sales Order Entry and Billing Functions

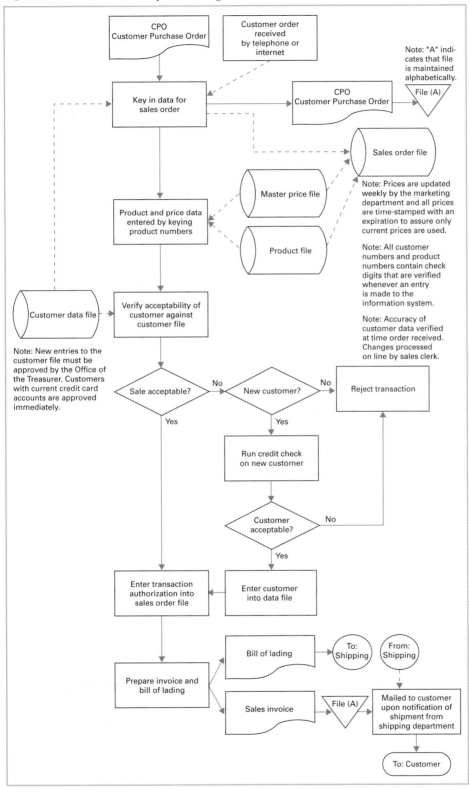

(continued)

Figure 8–6   *(continued)*

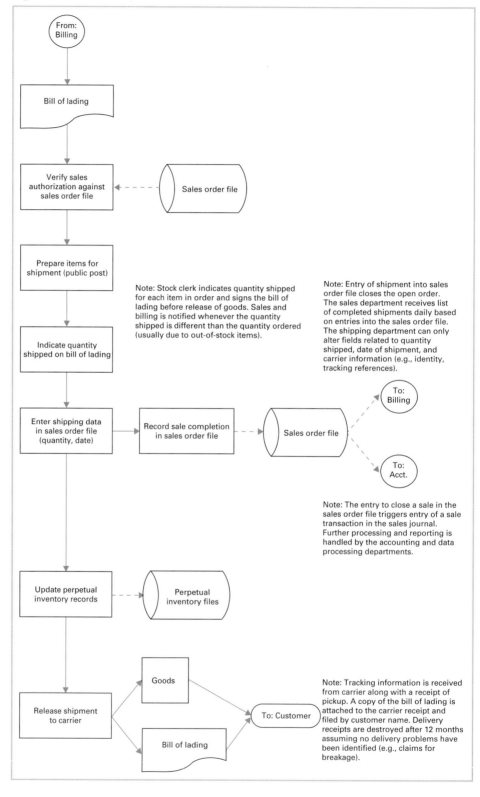

Figure 8–6   *(continued)*

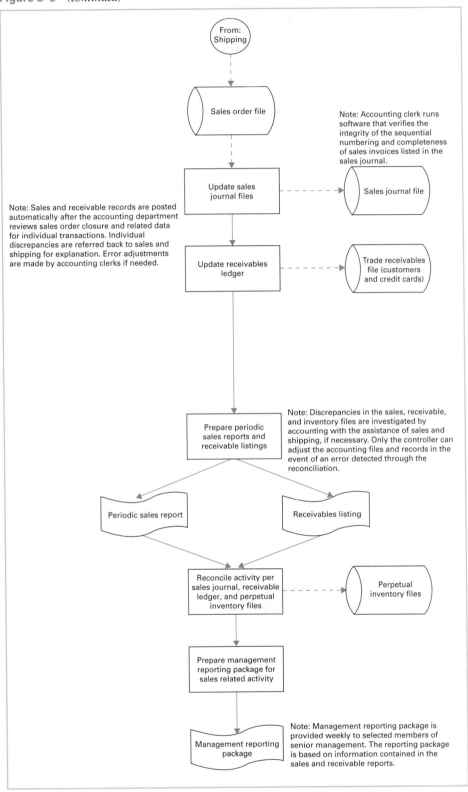

important because of the critical role that the audit committee serves in establishing and maintaining an effective overall control environment. Factors that are considered during the evaluation of the audit committee include the independence of committee members from management, the clarity with which the audit committee's responsibilities are articulated and understood, the level of involvement and interaction with the independent auditor and internal auditors, consideration as to whether relevant questions related to financial reporting are raised by the audit committee, and the committee's responsiveness to issues raised by the independent auditor.

Assess Control Risk for Financial Statement Assertions: The auditor will next link his or her understanding of internal control over financial reporting to the risk that material misstatements may not be prevented or may go undetected in specific financial statement assertions. Thus, the auditor makes a preliminary assessment of *control risk* for significant management assertions. If internal control over financial reporting appears to be reliable, the auditor's control risk assessment can be reduced. Control deficiencies related to specific management assertions may lead to inaccurate information processing and result in misstatements in the financial reports. If the auditor thinks that such occurrences are likely, control risk would be increased for specific assertions, leading to adjustments in the conduct of the audit and subsequent audit testing. In general, there are three possible levels at which control risk can be assessed:

1. Control risk is maximum: The auditor will not use evidence about internal control to reduce audit risk; therefore, detection risk will need to be reduced using very extensive substantive tests. However, the auditor is still required to gain sufficient knowledge of internal control to evaluate the design effectiveness of the control system.
2. Control risk is slightly reduced from maximum: Internal control reduces audit risk slightly, but the auditor will perform extensive substantive tests to adequately reduce detection risk.
3. Control risk is reduced to a moderate or low level: The auditor will rely heavily on the quality of internal control to reduce audit risk and perform minimal substantive tests to reduce detection risk.

It is implicit under PCAOB rules that an organization should establish and maintain a system of internal control over financial reporting such that control risk for all material transactions and balances is low. Hence, the auditor must extensively test internal controls over financial reporting except in the rare case where serious control deficiencies exist. When not subject to PCAOB regulations, the auditor can choose whether or not to test controls as long as the subsequent substantive audit tests reduce all significant residual risks to an appropriately low level as discussed later in this chapter.

Test the Effectiveness of Internal Control: Auditors perform procedures to test and evaluate the effectiveness of internal controls. In evaluating operating effectiveness, auditors consider whether a control is operating as designed and whether the person performing the control possesses the necessary authority and qualifications to perform the control appropriately. The auditor will perform a variety of procedures to test controls, including inquiry, inspection of records, observation, and re-performance to ascertain whether control activities are consistently and appropriately applied. Inquiry alone (as is common in a walkthrough) is itself not sufficient to conclude whether internal control is effective due to the possibility that management has made inaccurate or biased representations about the internal control system.

Example

> For a retail client, an auditor may perform a number of tests to determine if there is adequate control over cash that is kept in the cash drawers used by cashiers who operate the checkout registers in a store. First, the auditor might review the software that controls access to the cash drawers. For example, the auditor could review who can get into the drawers (clerks, supervisors) and under what conditions (at time of a transaction or to correct an error). Second, the auditor could observe how cashiers handle their cash drawers (e.g., Are they left open? Are unauthorized personnel allowed access?). Third, the auditors could review documentation related to the pick up of cash drawers by individual cashiers at the start of shift and their return to safekeeping at the end of a shift. Fourth, the removal of excess cash can be observed or verified by reviewing documentation and authorizations by cashiers and supervisors. Finally, documentation related to the reconciliation of cash on hand to automatically generated transaction totals (e.g., sales per shift) can be reviewed for accuracy and proper handling.

The auditor should perform sufficient testing to justify a conclusion about the effectiveness of internal control over financial reporting consistent with the objectives of the audit. The level of evidence obtained in order to plan a traditional audit will generally be significantly lower than the level of evidence needed in an integrated audit. The auditor may rely to some extent on the work of others, including company personnel, internal auditors, and third parties working under the direction of management or the audit committee (e.g., an inventory count service). In determining the extent to which the work of others is used, the auditor should evaluate the nature of the controls tested, evaluate the competence and objectivity of the individuals who performed the work, and test some of the work performed by others. Two areas in which auditors are generally *not* allowed to use the work of others include (1) testing controls that are part of the control environment, including controls specifically established to prevent and detect fraud and (2) walkthroughs used to develop a sufficient understanding of internal control over financial reporting.

Assess Operational Effectiveness of Internal Control over Financial Reporting: After completing the planning, walkthroughs, and tests of controls, the auditor should be able to reach a conclusion about the effectiveness of internal control. The culmination of this work is reflected in the final assessments of control risk, which may need to be revised based on the outcomes of testing. As will be discussed in Chapter 10, when internal controls are found to be ineffective, or less effective than originally expected, the auditor may need to adjust the nature and extent of planned substantive audit procedures incorporated in the audit plan.

ASSESSING CONTROL RISK

After assessing the effectiveness of internal control over financial reporting, the auditor's next step is to link those assessments to the risk of material misstatements within the financial statements. Auditors use control risk to provide this link. The evidence from process analysis and system walkthroughs can be used to justify some reduction in control risk even if other tests of controls are not used. Consequently, control risk for many assertions may be reduced from the maximum level based on the procedures that the auditor has performed during strategic and process analysis. The evidence to support this conclusion will consist of client inquiries about the design of the system, observation of client personnel performing their duties, and limited examination of documentation as part of the system walkthroughs.

An auditor may set control risk at a maximum level if the auditor concludes that substantive tests will be so effective that no reliance on controls is necessary to form an opinion about the financial statements, even if internal controls are designed effectively and could be tested. In this case, the auditor is essentially ignoring internal control as a source of evidence and completely relying on substantive tests of transactions and accounts. Consequently, an auditor should document why substantive procedures alone reduce audit risk to an appropriately low level before setting control risk at the maximum level by choice.[4] This approach is becoming less acceptable in practice as international and U.S. auditing standards presume that some testing of controls is necessary to reduce audit risk to an acceptable level. Internal controls are an important element of reducing misstatement risk in any organization; hence, they should not be ignored by auditors simply in the name of perceived audit efficiency. However, it is also possible that some systems of internal control are so weak as to justify a maximum level of control risk. The primary procedures needed to support an assessment of maximum control risk are client inquiries, observations, and documentation of client activity performed as part of strategic and process analysis and an assessment of whether the controls are designed to effectively reduce risk of material misstatement, even if they are not being tested for reliance.

One other issue the auditor must consider is how internal control may have changed during the course of the year. Management might be aware of a serious control deficiency early in the year and correct it sufficiently to conclude that the deficiency no longer exists at the end of the year. However, the fact that some portion of transactions for the year were processed when a serious control deficiency existed means that misstatements may have occurred. This possibility must be considered when the auditor assesses control risks for the purpose of planning substantive procedures to cover all transactions from the period.

CONTROL RISK AND TESTS OF FINANCIAL STATEMENT ASSERTIONS

When control risk is assessed at a relatively high level, there is an increased likelihood that there are undetected misstatements in financial reports. When control risk is assessed at a relatively low level, the auditor believes that there is less risk of material undetected misstatements in transactions, accounts, estimates, or disclosures. In essence, to achieve a given level of audit risk, auditors need to choose whether to rely on a client's controls or substantive tests of specific assertions. This decision is driven by the effectiveness of the client's accounting system in preventing and detecting material misstatements that might affect the financial statements.

---

4 The emphasis on requiring that controls normally be tested as part of the audit of financial statements is a change from previous audit practice. Until recently, it was assumed that control risk could be set at maximum for any or all assertions and account classes because substantive procedures alone could efficiently provide all necessary audit evidence. The choice was often justified as a more cost-efficient approach even though testing of internal controls has been encouraged by professional standards for over three decades but has never been required.

Figure 8–7   Summary of Combinations of Evidence to Achieve the Same Level of Audit Risk

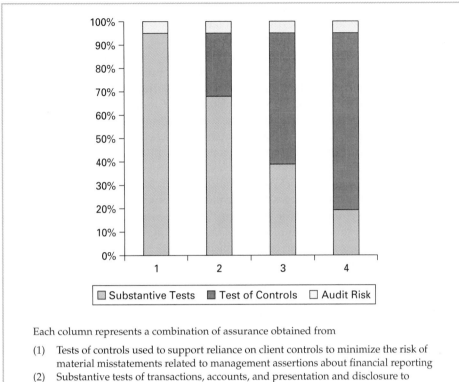

Each column represents a combination of assurance obtained from

(1)   Tests of controls used to support reliance on client controls to minimize the risk of material misstatements related to management assertions about financial reporting

(2)   Substantive tests of transactions, accounts, and presentation and disclosure to identify material misstatements related to management assertions about financial reporting

In each scenario, 95% assurance is obtained such that there is a 5% level of audit risk of issuing an unqualified opinion when a material misstatement exists.

Figure 8–7 illustrates several examples of the trade-offs between reliance on internal control and substantive testing that an auditor can make for a given level of audit risk. Moving from left to right, we see that auditors are willing to rely more and more on evidence concerning internal control over financial reporting that supports a low assessment of control risk, and less and less on direct evidence about transactions, accounts, and presentation and disclosure. Although the same level of overall audit risk (e.g., 5 percent) is achieved in each scenario, the mix of tests an auditor performs can vary a great deal. In cases where a client has relatively weak internal control (such as the left-most scenario in Figure 8–7), the auditor must document that substantive evidence alone can support the auditor's opinion.

The Auditor's Reporting Responsibilities in a Traditional Audit

Although no formal report is issued on internal control in a traditional financial statement audit, some matters related to internal control should be communicated to the audit committee of the client (or closest equivalent). More specifically, the auditor should communicate to the client the nature of any *reportable conditions* that were discovered during the course of the audit. A reportable condition is a deficiency in internal control that adversely affects its ability to generate accurate and reliable accounting information. The auditor is not required to plan the financial statement audit engagement to uncover all possible reportable conditions, but the auditor's process analysis, especially related to process risks and controls, may reveal reportable conditions. These are the matters that should be communicated to the client, preferably in a written report.

Among the set of reportable conditions, the auditor may observe a *material weakness* in internal control that may allow an assertion in the financial statements to be materially misstated. An auditor is not required to distinguish between reportable conditions and material weaknesses in the report to the audit committee. The reportable conditions/material weaknesses letter sent by the auditor to the audit committee is separate from the audit report and can be sent at any time in the audit process.

The auditor should also note other situations that do not constitute reportable conditions or control deficiencies but should be brought to the attention of the client as part of the comments for the client. These circumstances are usually communicated in the form of a *management letter* and often include suggestions on

> **Authoritative Guidance & Standards**
> The auditor's responsibility to communicate reportable conditions, including material weaknesses, for companies other than registered pubic companies is described in SAS 60 and ISA 260.

how business processes can be improved. Many of the situations discussed in the management letter will not have an effect on the reliability of the financial statements, but such communications can be an effective method of adding value to the audit and assisting the client in process improvement. The management letter is an excellent opportunity for auditors to demonstrate their expertise as both an accounting and an industry expert. At a minimum, a thoughtful management letter conveys that the auditors are offering more than simply a commodity service.

AN EXAMPLE OF INTERNAL CONTROL EVALUATION AND CONTROL RISK ASSESSMENT

An example of a portion of the sales and distribution process of J.J. Mean Company, a privately owned mail-order bookseller (e.g., book of the month club), is depicted in flowchart form in Figure 8–6. The sales process consists of three separate activities: sales order entry and billing, shipping, and accounting/data processing. This example does not include marketing and promotions, cash collections, sales returns or customer service, all of which can are also considered to be part of the sales and distribution process in most companies. This example assumes that the management of information resources (e.g., system design, system programming, and data librarian functions) is independent of the data processing depicted in the flowchart.

EVALUATING INTERNAL CONTROL OVER FINANCIAL REPORTING

Processing of transactions is relatively simple in this example. Sales orders are received from potential customers (by phone, mail, or Internet), goods are shipped if they are in stock, customers are billed, and accounting records are updated. The accounts affected by this process are primarily Sales Revenue and Trade Accounts Receivable. The primary documents and records used in the system include (1) sales orders, (2) sales invoices, (3) bills of lading, (4) a sales journal, and (5) the accounts receivable subsidiary ledger. Sales orders are electronic documents, whereas invoices and bills of lading are both paper (sent to customers) and electronic. The accounting records (sales journal and accounts receivable subsidiary ledger) are electronic but are printed on a periodic basis for review by the controller.

The auditor's task is to analyze the process and related controls and assess the control risk for the financial assertions affected by the process. Figure 8–6 provides documentation of the process and control activities. Additional documentation of control activities can be provided by completing an appropriate control questionnaire as illustrated in Figure 8–8. Close examination of the flowchart and the questionnaire reveals a number of control strengths and a few potential deficiencies.

Segregation of Duties: The company seems to have very good segregation of duties. Sales and billing, shipping, and accounting are all independent. Also, there is good segregation within accounting/data processing, which allows independent verification of data entry. However, we can observe one potential deficiency related to the approval of customers:

D1: There is a lack of segregation in the approval of credit. There should be an independent credit check to make sure that sales are made only to credit-worthy customers and that the pre-authorized credit limits are enforced. This is especially important for new customers.

Although this deficiency is potentially important, it would only be relevant to customers who maintain a personal account with the company. If the deficiency is serious enough, it could lead the auditor to increase the risk of material misstatement for the valuation of receivables. The fact that many customers have credit cards on file has the impact of transferring some collection risk to the credit card companies, which is an example of a compensating control.

Authorization Procedures: Clear procedures exist for authorizing transactions. General authorization is established for customer credit and prices. Shipments are only allowed when independent approval has been provided.

Use of Documents and Records: Reasonable documents and records are used in order to facilitate accurate transaction processing. Key documents are sequentially numbered to control their use. Electronic links within the process add assurance that routine transactions will be properly processed. However, the system is less well-suited for situations where quantities shipped do not agree with the initial order, as in the case of out-of-stock items.

D2: A problem may arise when an order is not filled completely. The shipping department adjusts the bill of lading to reflect the amount of the actual shipment and notifies billing of the change. However, this process is informal and may omit some of the changes. This could result in billing for items not shipped.

This deficiency could lead to an increase in the risk of material misstatement for the assertions of occurrence and accuracy as they relate to sales transactions.

Independent Verifications: Several important independent verifications are performed:

- Electronic data processing facilitates accurate processing and verification of transaction information.
- Customer number check digits are automatically verified upon entry to assure posting to the correct customer balance.
- Data entry into the sales journal, accounts receivable ledger, and perpetual inventory file is performed independently and reconciled daily.
- The sequence of sales invoices used is reviewed for completeness.

Figure 8–8   Control Questionnaire for Sales Transactions—J.J. Mean Company

Management Assertion	Yes	No	N/A	Comments
Occurrence, Completeness, and Accuracy				
1. Customer credit is approved by an appropriate official who is independent of the sales function.		X		Approval is performed by the sales department and is not independent.
2. Proper procedures exist for approving credit for new customers and changing credit limits for existing customers.	X			The treasurer's department does credit checks on customers to set credit limits. Many customers have credit card data on file.
3. A master price list is maintained and current prices are entered on sales documents. Standard discount and payment terms are used.	X			Master price data file is time-stamped so that expired prices are less likely to be used.
4. Proper procedures exist for periodically revising the master price list and assuring the current list is in use.	X			Master price data file is reviewed and updated weekly by the marketing department, which is independent of sales processing.
5. Shipments can only be made with evidence of proper authorization and access to shipping is limited to prevent unauthorized shipments.	X			Shipments only occur upon receipt of a completed and approved bill of lading and sales invoice that is verified against approved sales orders.
6. Shipping personnel are segregated from other aspects of sales transaction processing.	X			
7. Billing personnel are segregated from other aspects of sales transaction processing.		X		Billings are prepared at the same time as sales order is taken by sales clerks. Invoice and pricing is generated electronically. Only potential problem is failure to send invoice to customer.
8. Sales transactions are supported by appropriate documents that indicate approval of the transaction.	X			The company uses a sales order, sales invoice, and bill of lading, all of which are in electronic form and must be approved for a transaction to be processed.
9. Sales order documents are prenumbered and accounted for on a periodic basis to assure that all approved sales are executed.		X		Sales order documents are prenumbered but approved sales are *not* reviewed for completion.

Figure 8–8   *(continued)*

Management Assertion	Yes	No	N/A	Comments
Occurrence, Completeness and Accuracy				
10. Sales invoice documents are prenumbered and accounted for on a periodic basis to assure that all sales are included in summary records.	X			The sequence of sales invoices is independently verified by the accounting department.
11. Shipping documents are prenumbered and accounted for on a periodic basis to assure that all shipments are billed.		X		Bills of lading are prenumbered but the sequence is *not* reviewed. Simultaneous preparation of invoice and bill of lading mitigates against unrecorded shipments, however.
12. Shipping and billing documents are matched to properly approved sales orders and reviewed for accuracy.	X			Computer software prepares all documents based on shared information reducing the risk of inconsistencies across documents and files.
13. Sales documents are processed in the proper time period.		X		There is a potential delay between shipment and recording of a sale because accounting doesn't post the sale until notified by shipping. Entry is supposed to be daily, but no independent verification is done to make sure that posting is timely.
14. Quantities shipped are independently verified, e.g., by double counting.		X		Quantities that are shipped are indicated on the bill of lading. If quantities shipped differ from the initial order (which is the basis of the invoice), excess quantities may be billed if such changes go unnoticed by the billing department.
Cutoff and Classification				
1. Accounting personnel handling sales transactions are independent of other aspects of sales transaction processing.	X			There is good segregation of duties in the accounting/data processing area.
2. Monthly statements are sent to customers.			X	Mailing the invoice separately from the shipment of goods should cause customers to notify the company when shipments go astray.

(continued)

Figure 8–8   *(continued)*

Management Assertion	Yes	No	N/A	Comments
Cutoff and Classification				
3. Procedures exist to assure that receivables are posted to the correct customer.	X			Customer numbers include a check digit that is electronically verified.
4. Sales data posted to sales records is reconciled with sales data posted to receivables records.	X			Reconciliation performed by accounting and data processing.
5. Summary records for sales (e.g., sales journal) and receivables (e.g., accounts receivable ledger) are footed and reconciled with the general ledger.	X			All significant records and files are computerized and internally reconciled on a regular basis.

One independent verification is missing that could affect the reliability of processing of sales transactions, however:

D3: Sales orders are not reviewed to make sure that all approved sales have actually been filled. Failure to follow up open orders could result in lost revenues.

This deficiency could lead the auditor to increase the risk of material misstatement related to the completeness or cutoff assertions as they relate to sales transactions.

Physical Controls: Access to inventory is limited to shipping personnel and documents and records are stored and filed in the locations that they are used.

Assessing Control Risk

The auditor would analyze the implications of internal control over financial reporting for each management assertion and evaluate the effect of the identified deficiencies on control risk assessments. At this point, control risk assessments about control design effectiveness are tentative based on basic process analysis. Tests of controls are used to confirm or adjust these assessments. In order to justify a control risk assessment of low or very low, the auditor must plan and perform extended tests of controls to obtain evidence that justifies reduction of control risk. It may be possible to justify a moderate control risk assessment based on strategic and process analysis and system walkthroughs, but the auditor needs to exercise care that such a conclusion is truly warranted based on the procedures performed. Figure 8–9 illustrates the control risk assessments related to our example.

There are three control deficiencies evident in the example which may lead to moderate or high risk of material misstatement for some assertions. Specifically, these deficiencies could cause the auditor to undertake direct tests of the following management assertions:

1.   Valuation (collectibility) of customer receivables.
2.   Accuracy (quantity of inventory) of sales transactions.
3.   Cutoff of sales transactions.

Figure 8–9   Analysis of Control Risk and Audit Planning

Assertion	Control Risk (H/M/L/VL)	Basis of Conclusions about Control Risk	Audit Implications
Occurrence: Recorded Sales transactions (including details such as credit approval, items shipped prices, and payment terms) are authorized and actually occurred.	Low	1. Proper authorizations are required, but a problem may arise due to poor segregation of duties for the credit check of customers not using credit cards. 2. Proper use of documents and records makes it unlikely that a fictitious sale can be entered into the system. A problem may occur when quantities shipped are different from the quantities initially entered on the sales invoice.	1. Rely on internal control for most transaction attributes (e.g., payment terms and shipping authorization). 2. Perform substantive analytical procedures to verify collectibility of receivable balances of non-credit card customers. 3. Perform some tests of transactions to verify that correct quantities are billed to customers.
Completeness: All transactions that have occurred have been recorded.	Very Low	1. Pre-numbering the bill of lading and simultaneous preparation of the invoice makes it unlikely that sales will be omitted.	1. Test controls. 2. No direct tests of completeness needed.
Accuracy: Sales transactions are recorded at the proper amount and are correctly summarized and aggregated.	Moderate	1. Lack of independent credit approval may results in sales to high-risk customers. 2. Errors could occur when quantity shipped is different from the quantity ordered. 3. Independent processing of sales and receivable data, use of pre-numbered documents, and independent reconciliation of posting reduce errors in summarization. 4. Aggregations done by computer.	1. Heavy reliance on internal control. 2. See audit implications related to "occurrence." Items (2) and (3) also apply to "accuracy." 3. Review a sample of daily activity reconciliations and trace totals to inclusion in the general ledger. (Note: There is no need to foot the sales journal or accounts receivable ledger if tests of controls are acceptable.)

(continued)

Figure 8–9   *(continued)*

Assertion	Control Risk (H/M/L/VL)	Basis of Conclusions about Control Risk	Audit Implications
Cutoff: Sales transactions are recorded in the proper period.	Low	1. There is a delay in recording transactions until accounting is notified of transactions and there is no independent verification that sales are recorded on the day of shipment.	1. Perform cutoff tests on a sample of sales transactions. Compare the posting date per the sales journal to date on the shipping document. If there is a significant number of delays, test transactions at year end for recognition in the proper period.
Classification: Sales transactions are recorded in the proper accounts, ledgers, and journals.	Very Low	1. Check digits facilitate proper classification of transactions.	1. Test controls. 2. No tests of classification needed.

The final decision regarding the significance of these risks will depend on the evidence from the tests of controls and the availability of performance indicators related to critical risks. For example, strategic analysis may have suggested that the company faces an economic risk from recession, suggesting increased rates of customer defaults and valuation problems for receivables. Internal performance measures such as rate of customer delinquency and percentage of sales on account may provide an indication as to whether the valuation of receivables is a significant residual audit risk.

CONTROL RISK ASSESSMENTS AND PLANNED AUDIT PROCEDURES

The extent of substantive testing of financial assertions that will be performed by the auditor depends on the final assessments of control risk. Based on these conclusions, the auditor adjusts the conduct and scope of the audit in various ways. Some adjustments an auditor might make to substantive testing include

- **Selecting different audit procedures:** The auditor has a portfolio of procedures to use to obtain direct substantive evidence about financial statement assertions. If control risk is assessed at a relatively low level, the auditor can choose less time-consuming and less diagnostic procedures. For example, confirmations and physical examination tend to be more reliable audit evidence, but much more costly and time consuming, than documentation and analytical procedures.
- **Adjusting the timing of audit work:** The auditor often has an option as to when to perform audit tests. Substantive tests after the end of the year are usually considered more effective because more evidence is potentially available to the auditor. For example, confirmation of accounts receivable might normally

be performed as of December 31 but could be done earlier (rather than year end) if control risk is low.

- **Adjusting the extent of testing:** Many audit procedures are performed on a sample basis—that is, not all transactions are examined. When control risk is assessed at a relatively low level, the auditor may be justified in examining fewer transactions related to a process.

As these options illustrate, an auditor has a great deal of flexibility in specifying the procedures to be performed, the number of transactions to examine, the timing of the tests, and the evidence to be gathered. For example, the risk related to quantities shipped may appear to be high. The auditor might test quantities shipped for individual transactions by examining a number of transactions and comparing the quantities shipped per the various documents and records that are affected by the transaction. The auditor could examine 50, 100, or 500 transactions. Obviously, the more transactions that the auditor looks at, the more confident he or she can be that management's assertions about the accuracy of sales are not materially misstated.[5]

Every organization will have different processes, control activities, and control risks. The auditor must conduct the audit in accordance with the actual conditions observed in the organization and its processes. Figure 8–10 illustrates how the auditor's approach to understanding internal control and assessing control risk might be different for two different clients, one small and family-owned and one large and publicly traded. This illustration emphasizes the need to consider the unique circumstances of each client because those circumstances can affect the auditor's understanding and evaluation of internal control over financial reporting.

CONSIDERATION OF INTERNAL CONTROL OVER FINANCIAL REPORTING IN AN INTEGRATED AUDIT

As previously noted, an integrated audit as defined by the PCAOB imposes additional requirements on the auditor regarding the testing and reporting on internal control over financial reporting. We now turn our attention to a more detailed discussion of those requirements. Although the techniques for documenting, assessing, and testing internal controls over financial reporting are the same in all audits, the introduction of the integrated audit has resulted in changes to the way that the audit is planned and conducted, and has increased the focus on the nature and extent of internal control testing. Furthermore, the integrated audit has introduced additional reporting requirements for the auditor.

MANAGEMENT'S RESPONSIBILITY TO FORMALLY ASSESS AND TEST INTERNAL CONTROL

An important premise underlying the integrated audit is that management is formally responsible for establishing, implementing, and

> **Authoritative Guidance & Standards**
> The relative responsibilities of management and the auditor for performing an audit of ICOFR are described in AS 2. For registered public companies, management must perform each of the steps described. Furthermore, the use of the terms significant deficiency and material weakness are consistent with AS 2. The distinction between classifications of deficiencies requires extensive judgment by both management and the auditor. Nine large U.S.-based public accounting firms have issued *A Framework for Evaluating Control Exceptions and Deficiencies Version 3*, but they explicitly note this cannot substitute for professional judgment.[6]

---

5 An unstated assumption about the performance of audit testing is that the company will correct any mistakes that the auditor detects. This is now required for U.S.-registered public companies under SOX rules.

6 BDO Seidman et al, *A Framework for Evaluating Control Exceptions and Deficiencies Version 3*.

Figure 8–10   Effect of Client Characteristics on the Auditor's Approach to Assessing Control Risk

	Small, Family-Owned Client	*Large Publicly Traded Client Registered with US SEC*
Internal Control Environment	*Nature of Management:* The owner is often an active manager in the enterprise.	*Nature of Management:* The management typically has little direct ownership interest in the enterprise other than in the form of stock incentive plans (and possible incentive compensation).
	Auditability: May be a question if documents and records are not available.	*Auditability:* May be a question if management integrity is in serious question.
	Client Goals: The owner/ manager is usually more concerned with reducing tax liabilities than maximizing reported profits.	*Client Goals:* The management is usually concerned with maximizing reported profits.
Risk-Assessment Procedures	Risk assessment may be informal, relying mainly on the firsthand knowledge of the owner/manager.	Formal assessment procedures will be used to identify and measure potential risks. This analysis may be performed by internal auditors.
Control Activities	Procedures and segregation of duties may be lacking, due to small number of personnel. Owner involvement may compensate for some control weaknesses.	Procedures tend to be many, formal, and complex. Many independent verifications may be performed within a computerized system.
Information and Communication (Accounting system)	Tends to be relatively simple with heavy use of manual procedures and independent microcomputer applications.	Tends to be highly sophisticated with heavy use of mainframe computing and networked microcomputer applications.
Monitoring Activities	Monitoring will often be informal due to the direct involvement of the owner/manager.	Formal and sophisticated monitoring procedures on a continuous basis using technology or separate evaluations by internal auditors.
Auditor Documentation	Documentation using a narrative will often be adequate due to simplicity of system(s).	Documentation using flowcharts and questionnaires is advised due to complexity and number of systems.

monitoring internal control over financial reporting. In order to fulfill this formal responsibility, management must

- Explicitly acknowledge responsibility for the effectiveness of internal control over financial reporting
- Explicitly evaluate the effectiveness of internal control over financial reporting using suitable control criteria (e.g., the COSO criteria discussed in Chapter 7)
- Support the evaluation with sufficient evidence, including documentation of the design of controls related to all relevant assertions
- Present a written assessment of the effectiveness of internal control over financial reporting as of the end of the most recent fiscal year

Following procedures similar to those described earlier in this chapter, management must analyze the significance of any control deficiencies that are identified during the course of their evaluation of internal control over financial reporting as of the end of the year. A control deficiency occurs when the design or operation of any part of the system of internal control over financial reporting is insufficient to prevent or detect significant errors or misstatements. Control deficiencies are classified into three categories, as indicated in Figure 8–11, depending on the likelihood of a deficiency leading to material misstatement and the magnitude of misstatement that would occur:

1. *Insignificant Deficiency.* The control deficiency has either a remote likelihood of leading to a misstatement or the misstatement resulting from the deficiency is inconsequential.
2. *Significant Deficiency.* The control deficiency has a more than a remote likelihood of leading to a misstatement that is consequential but not material. Significant deficiencies often occur when a control is not operating effectively but compensating controls exist and no material misstatements are likely to occur.
3. *Material Weakness.* The control deficiency has more than a remote likelihood of leading to a material misstatement. Material weaknesses often occur when a control is not operating effectively and there are no compensating controls or there is evidence of actual misstatements arising from the deficiency.

Figure 8–11   Control Deficiencies in Internal Control over Financial Reporting

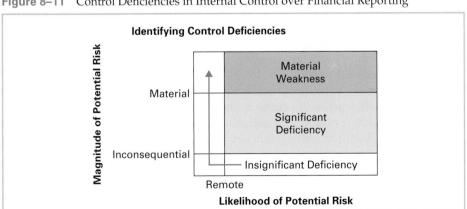

REQUIREMENT FOR THE AUDITOR TO PLAN INTERNAL CONTROL TESTS

In an integrated audit, the auditor must plan the audit to directly evaluate and test internal control over financial reporting for all major accounts and classes of transactions as of year end. Thus, the auditor's focus on internal control is significantly more extensive than might occur in a more traditional audit, yet also more limited in that it focuses on the control system only at year end and does not consider changes that may have taken place during the year. The auditor's process of documenting, evaluating effectiveness, and testing controls follows the steps illustrated previously in this chapter. However, there are three key considerations that have a direct effect on the planning of an integrated audit:

1.   The auditor must document and consider the effectiveness of internal controls over financial reporting for all material classes of transactions and balances, even if substantive testing can provide excellent evidence to support the reported financial statement amounts.
2.   The auditor must test the operating effectiveness of the controls unless there exists a material weakness in the design of the control so that, even if it was implemented as designed, the control would not prevent material misstatements.
3.   The auditor must take into account the length of time a control that has been in place if changes were made to the internal control system during the year.

ASSESSMENT OF CONTROL RISK: IMPLICATIONS FOR TESTS OF FINANCIAL STATEMENT ASSERTIONS

In an integrated audit, conclusions about control risk follow logically from the existence of one or more material weaknesses or significant deficiencies. Furthermore, the evidence needed to support conclusions about control risk is collected as part of the auditor's evaluation and testing of internal control over financial reporting. If a material weakness exists, then control risk is likely to be set at a maximum level for one or more assertions. If a significant deficiency exists (but there are no material weaknesses), then some assertions may have slightly reduced control risk.

To reduce control risk substantially below maximum, there must be no material weaknesses or significant deficiencies. However, the auditor must also consider the possibility that there may have been deficiencies in internal control at other times during the year that have been remedied by management prior to year end. Although the auditor's conclusions about significant deficiencies are based on year-end conditions, assessments of control risk related to management assertions must also consider significant deficiencies that may have existed at other times. If the auditor does not identify any material weaknesses or significant deficiencies during the evaluation of internal control over financial reporting, it is likely that the auditors will have performed sufficient tests of controls to justify a significant reduction in control risk for many assertions. Even if one or more material weaknesses are identified, there may be many assertions that are unaffected by the control deficiencies. For these assertions, the extensive control testing performed by the auditor may justify reduction of control risk for those assertions unaffected by the identified control deficiencies.

THE AUDITOR'S REPORTING RESPONSIBILITIES IN AN INTEGRATED AUDIT

In an integrated audit, the auditor will issue two formal reports: (1) an opinion on management's assessment of internal control over financial reporting and (2) the auditor's own opinion on the effectiveness of internal control over financial

Figure 8-12   Possible Auditor Reports on Internal Control over Financial Reporting in an Integrated Audit

Management's assessment of controls	Auditor's test of effectiveness show:	Report to be issued on management's assertions about the effectiveness of internal control	Report to be issued concerning auditor's opinion of actual effectiveness of internal control
No Material Weakness	No Material Weakness	Unqualified	Unqualified
No Material Weakness	Material Weakness	Adverse	Adverse
Material Weakness	Material Weakness	Unqualified	Adverse

reporting. These reports are in addition to the required opinion on the financial statements. As discussed in Chapter 4, auditors can issue one of two opinions: unqualified or adverse. For management's assessment of internal control over financial reporting, an *unqualified opinion* may be issued when the auditor feels that management assertions about internal control are fairly stated in all material respects, otherwise the auditor will issue an *adverse opinion*. The auditor's own opinion of internal control may be either unqualified, if he or she concluded that internal control over financial reporting is effective in all material respects, or adverse, if the auditor concludes that internal control over financial reporting is not effective due to one or more material weaknesses. Figure 8–12 illustrates the possible combinations of reports that might be issued by the auditor given what is contained in management's report.

The auditor's opinion might be modified if a *scope limitation* exists, meaning that auditors are unable to gather sufficient evidence to make an informed assessment on internal control due to a lack of sufficient evidence concerning the internal control system. If the reason for the scope limitation is beyond the control of the client or auditor, the possible reports are either a *qualified opinion* (i.e., an unqualified opinion "except for" the aspect of internal control over financial reporting that could not be evaluated) or a *disclaimer of opinion* (i.e., no opinion). In some cases, the auditor may withdraw from the engagement. The choice of which course of action to take depends on the severity of the scope limitation. Should the scope limitation be imposed by management, the auditor generally should issue a disclaimer of opinion or withdraw from the engagement.

> **Authoritative**
> **Guidance & Standards**
> The auditor's responsibilities for reporting on management's assessment of ICOFR effectiveness and on the auditor's own assessment of ICOFR are explicitly described in AS 2.

SUMMARY AND CONCLUSION

In this chapter, we have discussed the role of internal control in financial reporting in both traditional audits, where the auditor evaluates internal control over financial reporting for the sole purpose of assessing control risk, and the newer integrated audit required by the PCAOB, where the auditor must issue two reports regarding the effectiveness of a company's internal control over financial reporting. The auditor's evaluation of internal control over financial reporting is illustrated and summarized in Figure 8–13.

Figure 8–13   Relating Conclusions about Internal Control over Financial Reporting to Substantive Testing

	Control Risk = 100% (Maximum))
Conditions Necessary in an Integrated Audit	The auditor's assessment and testing of internal control over financial reporting reveals the existence of one or more *material weaknesses.*
Conditions Necessary in a Financial Statement Audit	The auditor assesses that controls are lacking, or tests of internal control over financial reporting reveal one or more *material weaknesses.* **OR** The auditor can justify that substantive tests alone are effective for reducing achieved audit risk to an acceptable level. *(Such circumstances would be considered to be rare under current international audit standards.)*
Nature of Evidence Required to be Documented in order to Support Conclusions about Internal Control over Financial Reporting and Resulting Assessments of Control Risk	• Client Inquiry: Extensively used to obtain details of control activities. • Observation: Performed to obtain details of control activities.
Implications for Planning Substantive Tests of Transactions, Accounts, Estimates and Disclosures	Reliance on Internal Control to reduce audit risk: *None* Use of Substantive testing to reduce control risk: *Very Extensive* 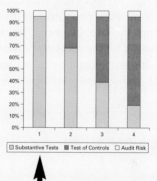

Control Risk < 100% *(Slightly Reduced)*	*Control Risk ≪ 100%* *(Greatly Reduced)*
The auditor's assessment and testing of internal control over financial reporting reveals the existence of one or more *significant deficiencies* (but no material weaknesses).	The auditor's assessment and testing of internal control over financial reporting reveals no significant deficiencies or material weaknesses.
The auditor assesses that some key controls are lacking, or tests of internal control over financial reporting reveals one or more *significant deficiencies* (but no material weaknesses).	The auditor's assessment and testing of internal control over financial reporting reveals no significant deficiencies or material weaknesses.

OR

Procedures are limited to basic process analysis, client inquiry, walkthroughs, and limited observation. Additional tests of controls are not considered appropriate based on the auditor's preliminary assessment of internal control over financial reporting

- Client Inquiry: Extensively used to obtain details of control activities.
- Observation: Performed to obtain details of control activities and repeated during different time periods to check for changes.
- Documentation: Reviewed on a walkthrough basis to clarify control activities performed.

- Client Inquiry: Extensively used to obtain details of control activities.
- Observation: Performed to obtain details of control activities and repeated during different time periods to check for changes.

Plus: Tests of Controls
- Client Inquiry and Observation: Used to *verify* control activities.
- Documentation: Extensively used to see if appropriate control activities were performed.
- Accuracy: To test whether reconciliations have been effectively performed and reviewed.

Reliance on Internal Control to reduce audit risk:
None/Limited

Use of Substantive testing to reduce control risk:
Extensive

Reliance on Internal Control to reduce audit risk:
Extensive

Use of Substantive testing to reduce control risk:
Minimal

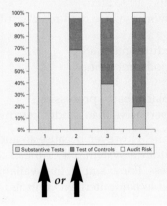

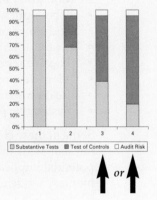

Regardless of the type of audit being performed, the techniques and procedures used to evaluate internal control are essentially the same for all audits. What differs between an integrated audit and a financial statement audit are the objectives of control assessment, the extent and nature of control testing, and reporting requirements to internal and external users of the financial statements. In either case, the auditor will assess control risk for management assertions as high, moderate, or low based in the evaluation of internal control, perform tests of controls where necessary (or mandated), and adjust substantive tests of assertions so as to reduce audit risk to the desired level. In general, the better the internal control over financial reporting, meaning the fewer deficiencies and material weaknesses, the less substantive testing the auditor will perform. We will re-examine the trade-off of internal control testing and substantive testing in more detail in Chapter 10 after examining in more detail how inquiry and analysis (analytical procedures) are used in the audit.

APPENDIX A: INFORMATION TECHNOLOGY AND INTERNAL CONTROL[7]

The objective of an audit and the need to assess risks and understand control are not affected by the extent and nature of information technology used by an organization—the same basic auditing standards and financial reporting objectives apply in all situations. However, the auditor must be aware of the nature of an organization's information technology because the design and operation of systems will have a direct impact on audit risk, the conduct of the audit, the evaluation of processes and the nature of audit evidence to be gathered.

IMPACT OF INFORMATION TECHNOLOGY

A number of differences can be observed in an organization's processes when it is highly computerized and automated. Some of the more significant changes include

- Computer input/output devices (keyboard, mouse, and printer) replace manual devices (typewriter, pencils, and document imprinting machines).
- Computer screens and electronic images replace paper documents.
- Computer files replace paper journals and ledgers.
- Fiber optics, cable connections, networks, and e-mail replace interoffice mail and fax communications.
- Application software replaces procedures manuals.
- Flexible reporting replaces fixed periodic reporting.
- More data replaces less data.
- Real-time transaction processing replaces batch processing.
- Systematic problems become more pervasive than random errors.

Some of these changes may seem mundane. However, because an auditor must be familiar with the risks and controls within a system, all of these changes have potential implications for the audit process. For example, the availability of documentary evidence, the existence of reliable computerized controls, variations in

---

7 There are several excellent textbooks that provide extensive coverage of this topic. For example, R. Weber, *Information Systems Controls and Audit* (Upper Saddle River NJ: Prentice Hall, 1999) gives over 1,000 pages of guidance in this area. The Information Systems Audit and Control Association that grants the Certified Information Systems Auditor (CISA) Designation is another resource in this area. See http://www.isaca.org/.

reporting, and the ability to access large volumes of online data all have implications for conducting the audit and the nature of evidence that will be available to the auditor for testing specific management assertions.

Probably the most relevant distinction is the last one—the nature of errors that can occur. Prior to extensive computerization, manual processing of individual transactions meant that every single transaction was at risk of improper handling. With computerization, consistency across transactions is increased. If the system is properly programmed to handle a specific type of transaction, it will be handled in essentially the same way every time. Thus, routine transactions are typically low risk. Problems arise when a transaction falls outside the normal parameters of the system. For example, a transaction may be for an amount larger than the system allows or involve nonstandard terms. In these cases, the system will repeatedly mishandle the transaction. Consequently, the risk of random errors in routine transactions is reduced but the risk of systematic errors in unusual transactions may be increased.

MYTHS CONCERNING INFORMATION TECHNOLOGY AND INTERNAL CONTROL

A number of myths have evolved over time concerning the relationship between information technology and internal control. In many cases, these myths result from a serious misunderstanding on the part of auditors of the strengths and limitations of information technology. Often these myths have resulted in the auditor treating computer systems as being unfathomable, causing the auditors to "audit around" the computer. Such an approach forces the auditor to consider only paper-based evidence of transactions and may lead to ineffective or inefficient audits.

The biggest myth is that control objectives change when an information system is automated. This is not true because the basic definition of internal control makes no reference to technology; it simply refers to the three basic objectives of good internal control:

1. To improve the effectiveness of management decision making and the efficiency of business processes.
2. To increase the reliability of accounting information.
3. To foster compliance with rules and regulations.

These objectives apply regardless of the extent of computerization. Other myths concerning internal control in automated systems include the following:

Myth 1—Information technology is primarily a risk to be controlled: Many auditors perceive that computerized systems increase risk. This perspective fails to consider the increase in control that may be achieved through computerized controls and the processing consistency that can be achieved across transactions. Complex systems may create some new risks for the organization, but the auditor should not overlook the extensive control advantage that can be achieved through computerization of information processes. IT is often a facilitator of control, not a threat to control.

Myth 2—The more complex a technology-based system, the greater the risks: Complexity may tend to increase certain kinds of risks, especially related to interactions between subsystems, networks, data files, and program code, but manual systems or mixed systems are not necessarily of lower risk. Information manipulation and transfer that is performed manually is always subject to corruption; mixed manual-computerized systems often involve manual interfaces where human error can be introduced. Spreadsheets are an area where the use of technology can be both an aid to control and a threat to reliability.

Myth 3—Automated information processing destroys the audit trail: This myth focuses narrowly on a paper-based audit trail. Computerization can actually increase the audit trail for a transaction by using internal references to connect transactions across subsystems in a network. For example, the use of scanning technology to keep track of the location of packages in the Federal Express shipping system enhances the ability to follow transaction processing. Similarly, reference numbers can be used to keep track of transactions or events in progress (e.g., confirmation numbers for hotel reservations and cancellations).

Myth 4—Weaknesses observed on an anecdotal basis prove the inability to control complex systems: A few well-publicized system failures are often used as an argument for minimizing system complexity. This perspective reveals more about the fear of technology than actual system reliability. When a large bank fraud is perpetrated using computer technology, or the phone system in a major city fails due to a software glitch, the popular media tends to overstate the risk and extent of such problems, leading to the myth that complex systems are inherently unstable. In fact, given the pervasiveness of such systems, the relative lack of problems is notable and creates an expectation of perfection that results in overreaction to the rare failure that does occur.

Myth 5—Small organizations cannot have good automated controls: A few years ago, computerized systems were synonymous with large mainframe computers and complex application codes. With the increase in computing power now available on the desktop, as well as the related advances in software, even the smallest organization can use technology to establish and operate an automated information system. For a relatively small investment, fairly sophisticated accounting systems can be put in place that provide much of the analytical power and control over processing that was only available in large applications a decade ago.

These myths, when taken together, highlight the fact that the introduction of technology is a double-edged sword. It does create some new risks for the organization but often alleviates many other, more significant risks. In general, the introduction of technology in an information system results in improved quantity, quality, and availability of information for use in the organization.

ILLUSTRATIVE CONTROLS IN A COMPUTERIZED INFORMATION SYSTEM

The nature of specific control activities change in a highly computerized information environment. These changes arise due to new activities and processes, which lead to new risk concerns as well as new opportunities for exercising control over transactions. The following provides some illustrations of control activities in a computerized environment. The details of individual control activities will differ across systems.[8]

Processing Controls

Authorization. There are two aspects of authorization that can be affected by technology. First, technology can lead to standardization of authorization within a

---

8 This overview is not intended to be comprehensive or technical.

process. For example, a grocery store can use scanning technology to link its cash registers directly to the product price database, providing increased consistency and easy modification of current prices. Similarly, online approvals of credit card purchases decreases the risk of fraudulent use of credit cards. Second, the design and implementation of the system raises numerous authorization issues. System parameters and changes need to be authorized, often requiring significant design, development, and testing, before systems are allowed to come online.

Use of Documents and Records. Documents and records are more and more frequently becoming digital, often with no paper existence at all. Computer screen images are used for data input/output (documents) and computerized data files contain all evidence of transaction processing (records). Consequently, the basic design principles for documents and records apply to digital images as much as paper documents. Data input screens should be well-designed to minimize entry errors, transactions should be prenumbered and cross-referenced to related "documents," and the integrity of data files must be maintained against improper changes or usage.

Controls over file revision and destruction are very important in a computerized environment, especially when master files are periodically updated using data from transaction files. Multiple generations of master files need to be maintained to assure processing accuracy and to protect against hardware or software failures that might corrupt or destroy data, necessitating expensive file reconstruction. File controls such as external and internal labels, the use of read-only files, and file protection rings on tapes are all useful for preventing accidental destruction or corruption of data.

Independent Verifications. Probably the most numerous of computerized controls fall in the area of independent verification, especially as relates to data entry. The range and nature of data entry and transaction controls is quite large and depends on the method of processing being used. Manual data entry, such as keypunching, presents problems that are different from scanning entry or direct data download from an external party (e.g., electronic connections to suppliers). Electronic edit checks tend to replace manual data checks when systems are computerized. Some of the more common verifications are described in Figure 8–14.

Other controls include the use of batch control totals, exception reporting, and process controls. Batch controls use summary data over a group of related transactions to verify that the group was accurately processed *in total*. Exception reporting triggers human intervention when a transaction fails some test condition embedded in the system. Processing controls tend to focus on the revision of data included in the organization databases so as to assure long-term reliability and data integrity.

Physical Controls

Access controls in a computerized system take on new meaning, but this is one area where the popular media has properly sensitized people to potential risks. Increased use of the Internet for credit transactions has highlighted the potential dangers of transmitting sensitive economic data electronically. Data encryption reduces the risk of unauthorized interception and use of information that is being transmitted over the Internet. However, the Internet is an open medium and the problems of misuse of data, invasion of privacy, theft of identity, and outright fraud are very real when dealing in a world of electronic commerce (e-commerce).

Figure 8–14   Common Edit Checks in Automated Systems

Edit Check	Description
Key verification	Duplicate processing of input to identify discrepancies in data entry
Verification of check digits	Embedding digits into an account code that reflect the numerical combination of other digits in the code, which can be tested for internal consistency by the computer
Completeness check	Verification that all required data has been entered
Use of default values	Substitution of default values for key data fields unless explicitly replaced by the user. An example is automated entry of the sales tax percentage during billing processing.
Range check	Verification of a value against maximum and minimum limits (e.g., credit limits)
Validity check	Verification of new data against previously entered data maintained in a master file. For example, when new shipments are being entered into the perpetual inventory records the computer can verify that specific part numbers are included in the master database
Sign check	Verification that proper positive or negative values are entered
Referential integrity check	Verification that two data sets that share a common data field have the same items included. For example, if a payroll register includes a specific employee, the inclusion of that person could be tested in related files such as the master payroll file, insurance coverage file, and pay rate authorization file.
Reasonableness check	Verification that summary totals for a transaction fall within specified guidelines
Sequence check	Verification that transaction identification numbers are used in the proper sequence
Transaction type check	Verification that a transaction is being entered into the proper records. For example, an attempt to improperly enter a payroll transaction into the purchases journal could be prevented

Access controls can help with both network security and unauthorized entry by outside parties (hackers). Limitations on access can be improved with physical controls such as securing the facilities where computers, data files, and system documentation are maintained, as well as electronic controls, which forestall unauthorized access to the system. Electronic access controls can include the use of passwords and user identifications, scheduled processing that allows access to certain files only at specified times, and dedicated communication channels not accessible to outsiders.

Segregation of Duties

Introduction of technology into information systems tends to result in the need for two-dimensional segregation of duties. Not only must an organization segregate across traditional dimensions (access to assets, accounting for assets, and authorization of assets) but also across the data processing function itself. The segregation within data processing should, at a minimum, provide adequate separation of the system analyst, programmer, computer operator, data librarian, and data control group.

SUMMARY

System computerization is often a mixed blessing to an organization. The fear that computerization of information systems will induce increased risk is usually based on a lack of understanding of the benefits that can accrue from proper utilization of system automation. The objectives of the audit process are not affected by the existence of extensive computerization within an accounting system, but the auditor must be aware that computerization will have a tremendous impact on how a system is designed and operated. Consequently, different risks may become important to the auditor, and the audit plan will be modified to reflect those risks and the evidence available to support management's assertions.

APPENDIX B: FLOWCHARTING TECHNIQUES

OVERVIEW OF FLOWCHARTING

Flowcharting is an extremely useful technique for documenting activities and transaction processing within an organization. When combined with a narrative description of the system and a completed internal control questionnaire, the auditor can obtain a thorough understanding of how a system operates, which provides a good foundation for making initial assessments of control risk. An example of a simple system flowchart was presented in Figure 8–6.

There are many variations in the way flowcharts are prepared. The purpose of this appendix is to introduce a few of the more common techniques and guidelines for preparing flowcharts. The level of detail to include in the flowchart depends on the objectives of the exercise and the preferences of the preparer. At one extreme, flowcharts can be very broad and general, especially when applied to organization-wide systems. These types of flowcharts are useful when preparing a process map and for identifying the key activities in an organization, the personnel associated with each activity, and the connections among the activities. At the other extreme, flowcharts can be very detailed, depicting the tiniest steps in the process. These flowcharts may be prepared from the perspective of a single department or even a single individual. The example in Figure 8–6 can be considered to be at the moderate level of detail because it encompasses a perspective across departments with some departmental details included.

KEY ELEMENTS OF A FLOWCHART

All flowcharts consist of three basic components: (1) symbols to represent activities and objects in the system, (2) discrete sections to demarcate responsibilities across departments and individuals, and (3) lines and arrows to represent movement within the system.

Figure 8–15 displays some of the most common symbols used in flowcharts. The definition of flowchart symbols is not completely standardized, and different auditors, firms, and systems analysts may have different variations. Most of the symbols depicted in Figure 8–15 are used in the example documented in Figure 8–6.

Figure 8–15   Selected Flowchart Symbols

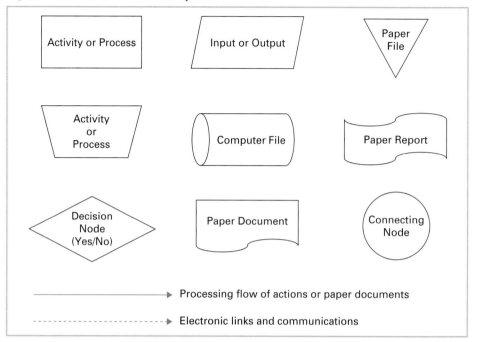

The boundaries between areas of responsibility are key elements of a flow-chart. Symbols for actions should pertain to a specific department or individual that can be easily identified with a glance at the flowchart. For example, Figure 8–6 depicts three areas of responsibility: sales order entry and billing, shipping, and data processing. By placing the flowchart symbols within a clearly defined area, the flowchart identifies who is performing the activity.

Lines and arrows are used to indicate the connections between various objects within the flowchart and the flow of information, documents, and authority. Most commonly, a line with an arrow indicates that paperwork is being sent from one place to another, but lines and arrows can be used to indicate the electronic flow of data as well (e.g., dotted lines). Occasionally, a line/arrow will connect to an object that appears on another page of the flowchart. In that case, the line is taken to the edge of the page and terminated in a circle. The circle indicates an inter-page connection, and the reader should be able to find another circle with the same code on another page of the flowchart where the information flow resumes.

GUIDELINES FOR FLOWCHART PREPARATION

All well-prepared flowcharts follow a few simple rules which improve interpretation of the flowchart in spite of personal variations in style.

- **Flows should go from left to right and top to bottom:** Flowcharts, like books, are easiest to interpret if they are presented from left to right and from top to bottom. Connections going up or to the left are allowed but should be used sparingly. Such "reverse" flows generally mean that a transaction is being recycled or reprocessed.

- **Origination of all actions and documents should be clearly indicated:** Documents may arrive from outside the organization, be created by someone depicted in the flowchart, or arrive from a part of the organization that is not presented in the flowchart.

- **Termination of all actions and documents should be clearly indicated:** Documents should terminate by leaving the organization, being permanently filed in a department depicted in the flowchart, or being forwarded to a part of the organization that is not presented in the flowchart.

- **Keep it simple:** Flowcharts should be presented in as streamlined a manner as possible to retain the information that needs to be presented. An excessively "busy" or cluttered flowchart can create confusion rather than clarity. The appropriate level of detail is a matter of judgment, but it should be detailed enough to present the activities that are important to the reader. However, it is critical that each step of the process be easily understood by someone who is not familiar with the underlying process.

- **Check for completeness:** A final review should be made to make sure that no significant elements, activities, or connections have been omitted. The preparation of a flowchart tends to be an iterative process, resulting in frequent changes and revisions as more information becomes available and is selected for inclusion in the flowchart.

Auditors use flowcharts to enhance their understanding of the accounting system, transaction processing, and internal control. Although there is no single proper way to prepare a flowchart, the use of the techniques described above will increase the effectiveness and efficiency of preparing flowcharts and understanding the information contained therein.

BIBLIOGRAPHY OF RELATED PROFESSIONAL LITERATURE

Research

Ashton, R. H. 1974. An Experimental Study of Internal Control Judgments. *Journal of Accounting Research.* 12(1):143–157.

Biggs, S. and T. J. Mock, 1983. An Investigation of Auditor Decision Processes in The Evaluation of Internal Controls and Audit Scope Decisions. *Journal of Accounting Research.* 21(1): 234–255.

Kreutzfeldt, R. W. and W. A. Wallace. 1990. Control Risk Assessments: Do They Relate to Errors? *Auditing: A Journal of Practice and Theory.* 9(Supplement): 1–48.

Mayper, A. G. 1982. Consensus of Auditors' Materiality Judgments of Internal Accounting Control Weaknesses. *Journal of Accounting Research.* 20(2 Part II): 773–783.

Mock, T. J. and J. L. Turner. 1981. *Internal Accounting Control Evaluation and Auditor Judgment.* Auditing Research Monograph No. 3, New York: AICPA.

Trotman, K. T. and R. Wood. 1991. A Meta-Analysis of Studies on Internal Control Judgment. *Journal of Accounting Research.* 29(1): 180–192.

Willingham, J. J. and W. F. Wright. 1985. Financial Statement Errors and Internal Control Judgments. *Auditing: A Journal of Practice and Theory.* 5(1): 57–70.

Professional Reports and Guidance

BDO Seidman LLP, Crowe Chizek and Company LLC, Deloitte & Touche LLP, Ernst & Young LLP, Grant Thornton LLP, Harbinger PLC, KPMG LLP, McGladrey & Pullen LLP, PricewaterhouseCoopers LLP and W. F. Messier Jr. 2004. *A Framework for Evaluating Control*

Exceptions and Deficiencies Version 3. December 20. Available online at http://www.granthornton.com/portal/site/gtcom/menuitem.91c078ed5c0ef4ca80cd8710033841ca/?vgnextoid=506aa3e0aec36010VgnVCM100000308314acRCRD&vgnextfmt=default. (accessed March 21, 2006).

PCAOB. Policy Statement Regarding Implementation of Auditing Standard No. 2

PCAOB. Report on the Initial Implementation of Auditing Standard No. 2

PCAOB. Staff Questions and Answers on Auditing Standard No. 2

Auditing Standards

AICPA *Statements on Auditing Standard (SAS)* No. 60, "Communications of Internal Control Related Matters Noted in an Audit."

AICPA *Statements on Auditing Standard (SAS)* No. 109, "Understanding the Entity and Its Environment and Assessing the Risks of Material Misstatement."

AICPA *Statements on Auditing Standard (SAS)* No. 110, "Performing Audit Procedures in Response to Assessed Risks and Evaluating the Audit Evidence Obtained."

Criteria of Control Board. 1995. *Guidance on Control.* Canadian Institute of Chartered Accountants.

Committee of Sponsoring Organizations. 1992. *Internal Control: An Integrated Framework.*

IAASB *International Standards on Auditing (ISA)* No. 315, "Understanding the Entity and Its Environment and Assessing the Risks of Material Misstatement."

IAASB *International Standards on Auditing (ISA)* No. 330, "Performing Procedures in Response to Assessed Risks."

PCAOB. *Auditing Standard No. 2*, "An Audit of Internal Control Over Financial Reporting Performed in Conjunction with an Audit of Financial Statements."

QUESTIONS

1. Distinguish between internal controls and internal controls over financial reporting. Under what circumstances does this distinction matter for auditors?

2. Distinguish between each of the following types of controls and given an example of each that makes the difference clear.
   a. Management controls
   b. Business process controls
   c. Monitoring controls
   d. Financial reporting controls

3. Distinguish between the following management assertions about transactions and give an example of each that makes the difference clear.
   a. Classification vs. Accuracy
   b. Occurrence vs. Completeness
   c. Occurrence vs. Accuracy
   d. Occurrence vs. Cutoff

4. For each of the four components of a financial reporting process, provide an example for how a control weakness within that component could result in materially misstated financial statements.
   a. Source documents and transactions
   b. Journals
   c. General and subsidiary ledgers
   d. Trial balances

5. For each of the four components of a financial reporting process, discuss how information technology can be used to reduce the likelihood or impact of a material misstatement.

Also, describe how using information technology could increase the likelihood or impact of a material misstatement without effective automated controls.

   a.   Source documents and transactions

   b.   Journals

   c.   General and subsidiary ledgers

   d.   Financial statements

6. Compare and contrast the merits and drawbacks associated with the requirement for U.S. registered companies and auditors to perform assessments of the effectiveness of internal control over financial reporting. Conclude by arguing either for this requirement to be discontinued for U.S. registered companies or that these opinions should be required for all companies and auditors worldwide.

7. Define a *walkthrough*. As part of the definition, describe how the procedure is used to develop an understanding of internal control over financial reporting. Also, describe the conditions, if any, under which a walkthrough can serve as a test of operating effectiveness of a control for purposes of forming an opinion on ICOFR or financial statements.

8. Why is the assessment of control risk a critical part of any financial statement audit? What is the impact on an auditor's financial statement audit strategy if control risk is set at a high level versus being set at a low level? What is the impact on the financial statement audit if an auditor sets control risk too low, tests controls for operating effectiveness to justify the risk, and then learns that controls are not operating effectively?

9. Compare and contrast a material weakness discovered during an assessment of internal control over financial reporting for a U.S. registered public company and a reportable condition identified during any other type of audit engagement. As part of the comparison, describe whether there can be reportable conditions that would not be considered material weaknesses for a U.S. registered public company internal control over financial reporting audit.

10. What are compensating controls? When would an auditor need to identify compensating controls, and how can the auditor determine whether they serve their intended purpose? For example, what would be possible compensating controls for not having separate personnel collect cash from customers and record that a sale has occurred for a fashion retailer?

11. The chapter emphasizes accounting informations systems in ensuring internal control over financial reporting. What is the role of financial reporting personnel in internal control over financial reporting?

12. What is a control deficiency in an integrated audit (i.e., an audit that includes opinions related to ICOFR)? What are the three categories of control deficiencies? How does the presence of these deficiencies affect auditor testing of financial statement assertions?

PROBLEMS

1. Suppose that as an audit staff associate of an accounting firm, you are asked to perform a complete walkthough of two financial reporting processes at a retailer that specializes in selling athletic equipment for winter sports (e.g., skis, hockey equipment, ice skating apparel). For each of the following financial reporting subprocesses, describe your expectation for the audit trail associated with performing a walkthrough of one transaction.

   a.   A manual process for sales returns

   b.   An automated process for ordering inventory from an equipment supplier

2. In its first Assessment of Internal Control over Financial Reporting (for the fiscal year ended December 31, 2004), General Electric identified a material weakness in internal control and concluded that its internal control over financial reporting was not effective as of that date. General Electric's auditor, KPMG, agreed with General Electric's assessment that internal control over financial reporting was not effective as of December 31, 2004 and hence issued an adverse opinion over the effectiveness of internal control over financial reporting. Below is the sole material weakness as stated in both reports:

> A failure to ensure the correct application of SFAS 133 when certain derivative transactions were entered into at [GE Capital Corporation] prior to August 2003 and failure to correct that error subsequently.

Describe whether or not you concur that this one material weakness is sufficient to conclude that General Electric's internal control over financial reporting was not effective. In other words, describe whether you concur that the presence of one material weakness is sufficient to make such a strong conclusion. If you believe that this opinion is too harsh, offer an alternative that you believe is more justifiable.

3. As an audit manager, you have been given charge of assessing risk management for two business processes of The Solas Co., a privately owned wholesaler of textbooks (hence not subject to PCAOB AS 2).

    The first process, sales collection, processes high-volume payments from many small, independent bookstores and a few large-dollar payments from large chain bookstores. In past audits, it has scored poorly on its tests of controls that impact financial reporting, but management has instituted a program to correct that situation.

    The second process, human resources management, processes a large volume of small-dollar transactions. This process supports all of the other business processes. Many of the top managers and all of the salespeople are on incentive compensation plans. The remaining employees for the organization, including administrative personnel are paid hourly wages at rates consistent with organizations of similar size.

    a. Discuss conditions under which you would choose whether or not to perform tests of controls when analyzing these two business processes. Specifically, what characteristics of each process would suggest that the audit would be appropriate for performing tests of controls and what characteristics would argue against performing them?

    b. What are the implications for the financial statement audit if tests of controls for each business process are not performed?

4. For each of the following, state the financial reporting process control activity that is being followed and which management assertion for associated transactions is strengthened if a company actually performs it.

    a. Only certain employees are allowed into the central computer room. Those employees have "cardkeys" to gain access to the area.

    b. Once every week, open (unfilled) sales orders are compared to inventory lists.

    c. Checks are prepared by accounts payable clerks and then given to a corporate officer for signing.

    d. An inventory clerk prepares a picking ticket from the sales order and then gives it to a warehouse worker so that the inventory can be prepared for shipping.

    e. A receiving clerk fills out a receiving form from the purchases department that does not include the amount ordered on it.

    f. Before shipping any goods, the shipping department compares a copy of the original sales order to the picking ticket.

    g. The head of information systems receives a report each day of unsuccessful log-on attempts.

    h. All checks received at the receivables processing area are clearly date stamped.

    i. An internal auditor reconciles the purchases journal to the inventory received register at least once per month.

    j.   A salesperson may not depart from a master price list without approval from the vice president of marketing.

    k.   Before taking the daily deposit to the bank, a clerk compares the deposit ticket amount to the totals from the lockbox area.

    l.   To gain entry into the cash vault, an employee must submit to a retina scan to determine his identity.

    m.   Hash totals from a batch process are compared at each step of payables posting.

    n.   Accounting clerks rely on a chart of accounts for journalizing transactions.

5. In preparing to conduct the audit of the O'Farrell Corp, a manufacturer of fine Irish apparel, you have prepared the following narrative description of the process internal controls over financial reporting related to the materials acquisition process. The narrative is based on conversations with various department heads and the responses to a questionnaire passed out to the operating personnel.

    The foreman of the production line completes a requisition for raw materials and forwards it to the purchasing business process. Purchasing uses the request to determine who is the best vendor for the materials from among their approved vendors carried on a master file. A prenumbered purchase order is then prepared in triplicate with one copy sent to the vendor, the second copy sent to receiving personnel in inventory management, and the third copy filed along with the requisition.

    When the materials are received by inventory management, they are reconciled to the purchase order, a receiving report is completed in four parts (including date of arrival) and, if the goods are approved, they are sent to the factory floor. The first copy of the receiving report goes to payables personnel, the second copy goes along with the goods to the factory floor, the third copy is filed in receiving, and the fourth copy is sent to accounting in the financial management process for updating the general ledger.

    Once the goods arrive at the factory floor, a receiving clerk is required to reconcile the goods received to the receiving report. From there, the goods are placed in service or are stored in a locked warehouse that adjoins the shop floor.

    Personnel in payables file its copy of incoming receiving reports under the vendor number while they await the invoice. When the invoice arrives from the vendor, payables personnel reconcile the invoice to the receiving report and approves the invoice for payment. They then review the terms of the invoice to determine whether they may take advantage of any purchase discounts. If so, the invoice is marked for payment at the next weekly check run. If not, it is filed by date for payment no later than the due date (but not much earlier). Upon payment, a voucher is created and sent to accounting.

    Accounting personnel reconcile the voucher to the original receiving report and update the appropriate ledger accounts on a batch basis once each week. Control totals and hash totals are kept.

Required

    a.   Prepare a flowchart that depicts the materials acquisition process for O'Farrell Corp.

    b.   List the process controls evident in this process and state which financial reporting control objective the control is designed to achieve.

    c.   List the most important process control weaknesses and strengths of the materials acquisition process for O'Farrell Corp.

6. You are analyzing the control plans of a new client, McGriff Co., a publicly traded U.S. airline specializing in long-distance cargo shipping. Its receivables processing business subprocess is your special concern as its operations affect such a large part of their financial statements. In analyzing the process and talking to the workers, you develop the following (rudimentary) narrative of its operations:

    Mail clerks open the incoming mail, remove the checks and remittance advices, and prepare a schedule of payments for other clerks to use to post to the accounts receivable subsidiary ledger. They include the remittance advices with the schedule. Other clerks then prepare a deposit slip from the checks themselves. An armored car picks up the deposit each day at 1:00 p.m.

The posting clerks use the schedule to post to a batch file of transactions using the terminals connected to the corporate accounting database. Once completed, the remittance advices and schedules are filed by day of receipt.

Required

a. List possible risks associated with this process as described.
b. Describe whether you believe there are any potential significant deficiencies or material weaknesses.
c. Should the problems that were identified in Requirement b be material weaknesses, how would they affect the results of the integrated audit?
d. Identify possible process controls that can be put into place to manage the identified risks that would mitigate any significant deficiencies or material weaknesses identified.

7. USBB, an Australian property and casualty insurer, actively seeks to maintain a paperless office. Toward that end, it has invested in optical character recognition scanning technology so that incoming paperwork (e.g., an insurance application) can be immediately scanned into an electronic file. From there, its image or the data on it can be sent to whomever needs it via the company's vast computer network that connects offices throughout its nationwide operations. A copy is also stored in USBB's centralized database.

a. Discuss the implications USBB's system (i.e., optical character recognition scanning technology) may have on your audit of the company.
b. How will this level of sophistication in use of information technology affect your assessment of the organization's ability to mitigate its risks and reduce the risk of misstatements in the financial statements? In other words, what types of errors or fraud will be more prevalent in this setting as opposed to the more traditional paper-based one?

8. Consider the following control weaknesses revealed by your tests of controls on a publicly held U.S. mail-order computer peripheral retailing company.

a. Clerks do not compare daily sales orders to credit limits until after the day's business has been transacted and the orders shipped.
b. Warehouse workers make direct entries into the inventory accounting system.
c. Open sales orders are not reviewed periodically.
d. Checks written require only an assistant treasurer's signature.
e. Copies of receiving reports are often not given to the accounting clerks until a week has passed.
f. Sales return documents are not prenumbered.
g. Neither control totals or hash totals are kept by the clerks who post to the general ledgers.

For each of these control weaknesses (considered independently),

a. What risk exposures result from the lack of control?
b. What types of misstatements may occur as a result of the weakness?
c. What information is necessary to distinguish whether the control weakness constitutes a significant deficiency or material weakness?
d. What is the impact on the audit if management's assessment of internal control identified these weaknesses versus if the auditors are the first to identify them?

9. Consider the following situations for each of the privately owned organizations independently. For each situation, identify the risk exposures and any possible controls.

a. In your observation of the payables posting function of a construction firm, you notice that a payables clerk prepares a check, obtains the signature of a corporate officer on it, then posts the transaction to the general ledger using the check and supporting documents as source data. The same clerk then prepares the check for mailing to the vendor. An accounts payable manager will reconcile the bank account to the appropriate subsidiary journal when the statement comes the next month. The statement is sent to the clerk's office.

b. During your review of the documentation flow of a warehouse for an audio equipment retailer, you see that the warehouse workers get a copy of the original purchase order whenever they complete a receiving report on an incoming shipment. Upon walking through the warehouse itself, you see that if work backs up, just-arrived goods are often left in the warehouse for several hours before the receiving report is completed.

c. Your client, a multinational manufacturer of personal communications devices, convenes a board of directors meeting each quarter. At that meeting, the controller makes a report on any control deficiencies her staff of internal auditors has identified. The board consists primarily of the senior managers of the firm and a few outside directors appointed mostly for their status in the political community.

d. The sales return procedure for your client, a large retailer of housewares, goes as follows: A sales clerk removes a sales return form from a pad, fills it out with the customer's personal information, accepts the merchandise back, and refunds the money listed on the receipt. The sales return form is then given to an accounting clerk while the original clerk returns the merchandise to the shelf or places it in a bin for repair.

e. The sales order process for your client, a mail-order software firm, is as follows: Clerks discuss the order over the telephone, input a customer number (if a repeat customer) into sales-order system, enter the goods ordered into a batch file, and secure the customer's commitment to the sale. The batch file from yesterday's sales is downloaded to the warehouse each morning where an automated system generates picking tickets and invoices. Warehouse workers find the software package, affix the invoice, ship the goods, and update the accounting records accordingly.

f. On observing the incoming receipts process of a regional newspaper, you notice the following: Checks and remittance advices are received along with the rest of the newspaper's mail. Clerks open the mail, remove the contents, mark the remittance advice with the customer's payment, prepare the deposit slip, and give it to the armored courier each afternoon. The remittance advices are then forwarded to the data processing area for entry into the subsidiary ledger.

10. Consider the following independent assessments of the level of control risk for a class of transactions the following publicly traded U.S. companies.

a. The control plans for the accounts payable function of a real estate management firm are very poorly conceived.

b. The deferred tax accounting controls for a chain of hair styling salons appear to be well designed.

c. Based on your walkthrough of the raw materials inventory control procedures for a packaged food processor, you believe that the controls give you some assurance against misstatement.

d. The loan loss management control procedures for a regional bank are well documented and conceived, but the level of compliance with those plans is unclear.

e. The controls over the accounts receivable function for a retail clothing store appear to be applied effectively based on your observation of the workers in the area.

f. Your interview with the chief financial officer of a large sporting goods manufacturer revealed that the company requires board approval for borrowings or equity sales in excess of one million dollars.

For each of the preceding:

1. Would you perform tests of controls beyond those already performed for the preliminary assessment? Justify your choice.

2. If you choose not to perform further tests of controls, what implications does that have for your audit planning?

3. If you perform more extensive tests of controls, discuss the implications for your audit plan if your tests support a conclusion that control is effective.

4. Discuss the implications for audit planning if the tests support a conclusion that control is ineffective.

11. Explain the following internal control procedures classified under "Independent Verifications." Give an example where a newspaper subscription processing department might use each of them.
    a. Key verification
    b. Check digits
    c. Reconciliations
    d. Batch controls
    e. Control totals
    f. Customer acknowledgements

Case 8–1: The City of Smallville

The city of Smallville, Kansas, has a population of approximately 100,000 and has adopted a commission form of government. The city commission consists of five elected commissioners, one of whom is appointed to be mayor (primarily a figure-head position). The city provides services that are typical for a municipality of its size: police and fire protection, traffic control, parks and recreation, social services, trash collection, and so forth.

The city approves separate revenue and expenditure budgets every year. The revenue budget indicates the sources of funds that will be available for expenditure during the fiscal year. The expenditure budget indicates approved uses for the city's funds during the fiscal year. The expenditure budget is classified by service or activity (e.g., fire, police, parks) and function (e.g., wages, equipment, supplies). The city has a centralized purchasing and disbursement system that is depicted in the flowcharts provided at the end of this case. The city has a separate payroll system. Additional system information is provided below.

1. The following items are prenumbered and used in sequence:
   - Purchase orders
   - Vouchers
   - Checks
2. All purchases are originated by a requisitioning department (i.e., the department that will ultimately use the items to be acquired). All requests for purchases must be supported by a completed purchase requisition that indicates the quantity and quality of the items needed as well as the reason for the purchase. This form must be approved by the department head of the requisitioning department before the purchasing department will act upon the request.
3. If purchases are expected to exceed $20,000, public notices must be printed in the local newspaper in order to solicit bids. After publication of the notice, the purchasing department identifies qualified suppliers from respondents to the solicitation or from previously used suppliers. If the purchase will exceed $3,000, at least three possible vendors must be identified. The qualified vendors are asked to submit bids and the lowest bid is typically selected.
4. Purchases are approved by the purchasing department supervisor. Purchases in excess of $20,000 must also be reviewed and approved by the city commission.
5. Purchase orders (POs) are batched before being sent to the data processing department. A control total is computed for the estimated total cost of each PO. The estimated cost per the POs is used to record an "encumbrance" in accordance with accounting standards for governmental organizations. This encumbrance is not a liability but represents a commitment of funds that has been made by the organization. At any point in time, total expenditures and encumbrances to date should be less than the amount that has been budgeted for a given function and activity.

321

6. The receiving department checks all incoming supplies against the amounts and descriptions that are included on the purchase order in their files. Discrepancies are noted on the receiving report. Shipments for which the receiving department lacks a PO are not accepted without the express authorization of the city manager's office.

7. The accounts payable department holds all documents until a vendor's invoice is received, typically by mail. Then, all appropriate documents are retrieved and compared and a voucher is prepared. The voucher is the basis for an entry to the liability account.

8. Entries to the accounting records to record encumbrances and liabilities are keypunched by clerks in data processing using the appropriate source documents as references. All account codes include a check digit that is automatically verified by the computer upon entry by the clerk.

9. Disbursement checks are prepared in the accounts payable department based on the due dates by which the vouchers are filed. Vouchers are stamped "PAID" immediately after a check is prepared. A clerk in accounts payable keypunches the data for the check register from the data on the prepared check.

10. The city manager signs all checks on a weekly basis (on Friday of each week) after reviewing the supporting documentation. The signed checks are eventually returned to accounts payable for actual mailing. If the city manager is not available for check signing, the prepared checks are held until his return.

Notes about the format of the flowchart

1. When multiple documents are combined into a batch, documents that are conditional or optional are indicated in parentheses.

2. Documents are identified by shorthand initials indicated at the bottom of the document when it first appears in the system.

3. Files are indicated as alphabetical ("A") or numerical ("N").

4. Individual documents that are batched and processed together are indicated in the same way as other documents with the additional notation "batched."

Requirements

1. What transactions and accounts are affected by these business processes?

2. In general, what would be the primary business risks of a municipality as related to these processes?

3. What key performance indicators would you wish to examine related to these business processes? Explain.

4. Identify control strengths that would have an impact on the planning of your audit of this municipality. For each control, answer the following questions:
   a. Which risks identified in Requirement 2 are addressed by the control?
   b. Which transactions and accounts identified in Requirement 1 are less likely to be misstated based should the control be effective?
   c. How would you test the control's effectiveness?
   d. How would you modify your substantive testing of the impacted transactions and accounts if the control was effective?

5. Identify control weaknesses, either missing controls for an associated risk or ineffective controls, that would have an impact on the planning of your audit of this municipality. For each weakness, answer the following questions:

    a. Which risks identified in Requirement 2 are impacted by the weak or missing control?

    b. Which transactions and accounts identified in Requirement 1 are more likely to be misstated based on the control weaknesses?

    c. How would you modify your audit program in response to the weakness?

6. Prepare an audit program for the tests of transactions for the purchasing process.

Originating Department

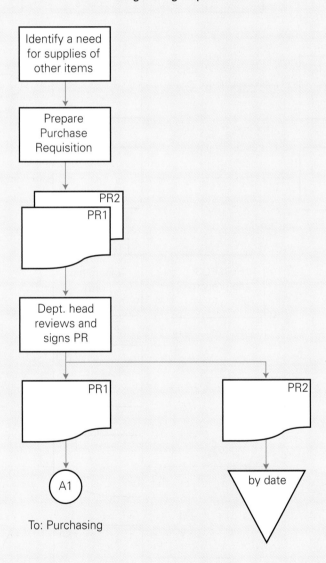

Purchasing

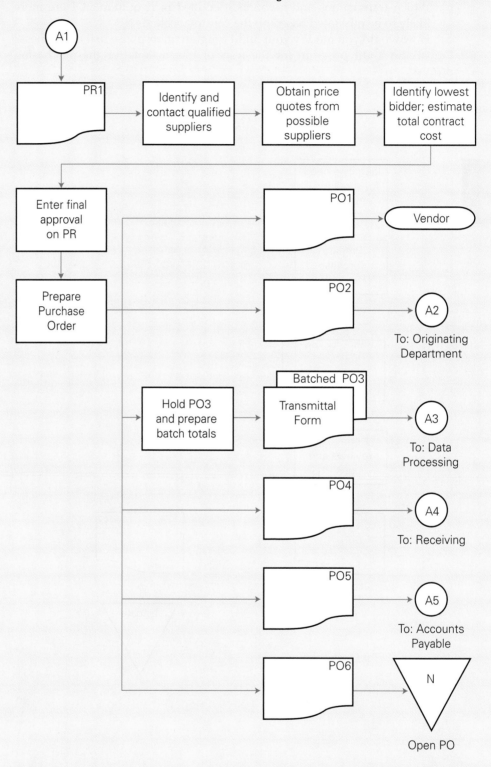

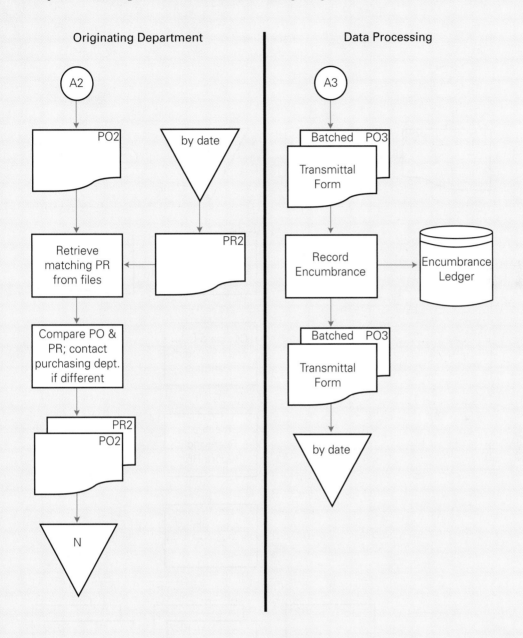

Receiving

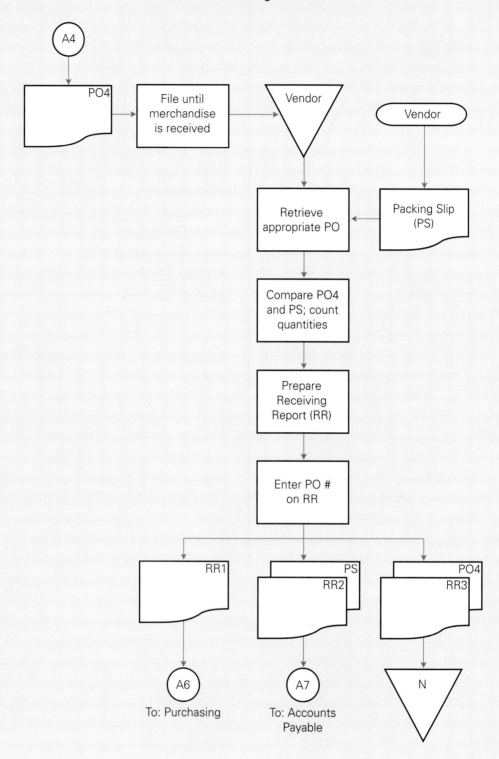

Purchasing

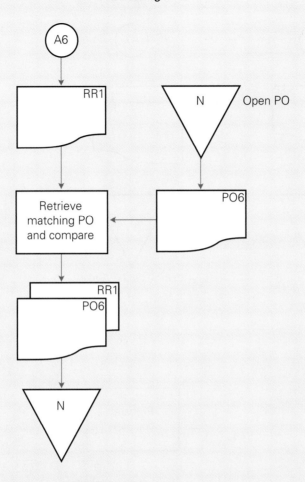

Accounts Payable

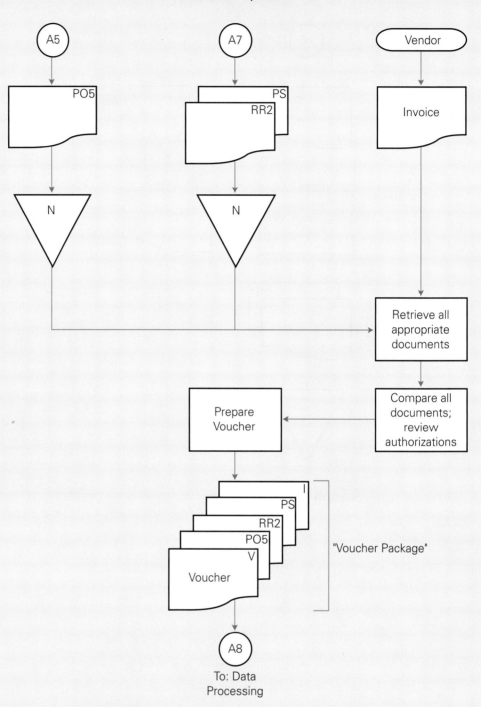

Data Processing

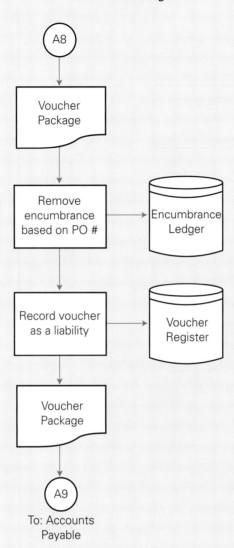

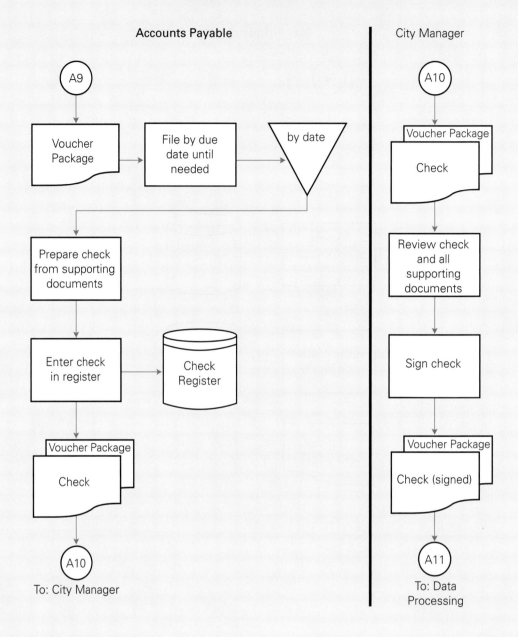

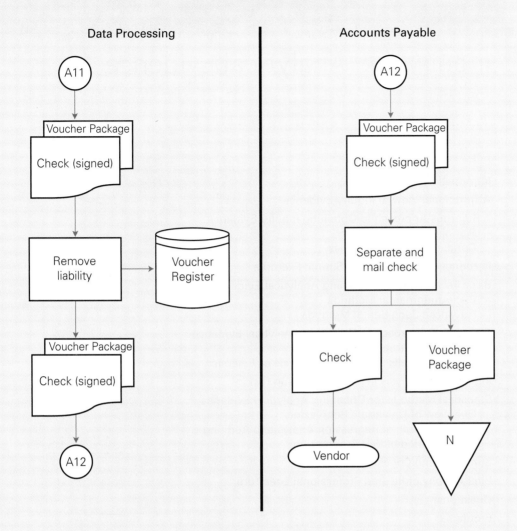

9

Inquiry and Analytical Evidence

Outline

INTRODUCTION

One of the things that auditors do is ask lots of questions. In fact, almost everything the auditor does during the course of an audit involves formulating questions and then searching out answers. We have already discussed a number of general categories of questions an auditor asks in an audit: What risks threaten an organization? How does the company respond to risk? Is internal control reliable? Are the numbers accurate? The answers to these questions may be available in the documents and records of a client but, more often than not, the auditor will need to obtain information, clarification, insight, and explanations from client personnel or others who hold the required information. In short, client inquiries are an integral and crucial part of the auditor's audit tool kit.

Commonly linked to inquiry are various forms of auditor *analysis* (also referred to as *analytical procedures* or *analytical review*). Analysis refers to the examination of preliminary performance results for indications of potential risk or problems within the financial statements. Analysis may indicate areas of the financial statements where more in-depth audit testing is needed. Inquiry is intrinsically linked to analysis because numbers usually mean little without an explanation of what they represent. Auditors often turn to management to obtain these explanations.

A classic example of the interplay between analysis and inquiry occurs when the auditor asks management to explain some observed performance result. For example, the auditor may have noted that sales in a specific time period have experienced an unusual increase or decrease. A thoughtful auditor may be curious as to why that has happened. Although nothing untoward may have occurred, the unusual sales pattern catches the attention of the auditor because of the possibility that the results may indicate accounting problems or misstatements. The obvious place to start to obtain an explanation is the management of the company. By discussing the result with management, the auditor can begin to discern the cause of the performance results. However, the manager who is approached may be in a hurry, distracted, or misinformed, so the explanation that is offered may be incorrect or incomplete. It is then up to the auditor to determine if such responses have any value as evidence in the conduct of the audit.

The purpose of this chapter is to assist an auditor in the conduct of analysis and inquiry in an efficient and effective manner. The information provided in the scenario just described will not always be reliable audit evidence, so the auditor needs to develop appropriate skills for sorting out the true and important from the biased and trivial in client inquiries. In this chapter, we introduce an integrated approach for understanding basic relationships among financial statement and nonfinancial data to facilitate analysis and inquiry. *Preliminary analytical procedures* performed at the level of the overall financial statements, or significant business segments, are an important part of the auditor's risk assessment procedures. In essence, an auditor examines financial and other data in order to identify risks and account relationships that seem inconsistent with known economic circumstances (see Figure 9–1). Auditors are generally required to perform preliminary analytical procedures as part of audit planning. Furthermore, analytical procedures may be performed at other stages of the audit, including the testing of account balances (i.e., substantive analytical procedures). Finally, analytical procedures are required as part of the final overview of the audit results (see Chapter 14 for details).

> **Authoritative Guidance & Standards**
> This chapter emphasizes two commonly used types of evidence gathering: inquiry and analytical procedures. Standards on audit evidence (SAS 106, ISA 500) cover both types of evidence; however, separate standards (SAS 56, ISA 520) provide additional guidance on analytical procedures.

A TRADITIONAL VIEW OF INQUIRY EVIDENCE

Formally, *inquiry* involves seeking appropriate information from knowledgeable persons located within or outside the entity. There has never been an audit performed that did not incorporate extensive inquiries of management and others. However, in recent years, inquiry has taken on a greater importance to auditors for a number of reasons. For example, risk analysis is most effectively performed by

Figure 9–1   Overview of the Audit Process

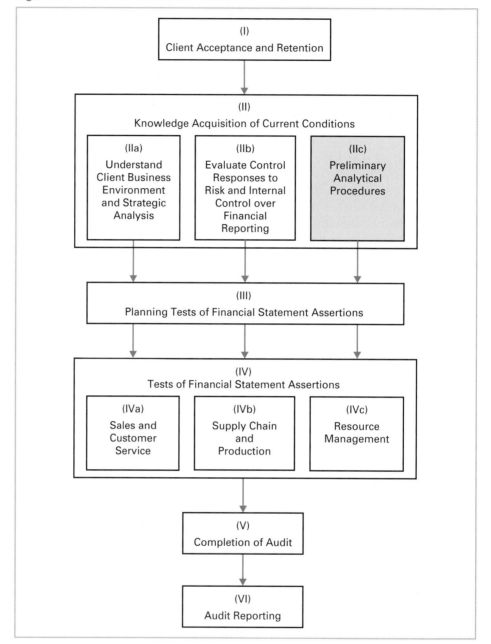

talking to a large number of people with insight about the organization. Second, much of the information needed in an audit is the personal knowledge of individuals and is often not documented in any formal or systematic manner. Third, tangible evidence about events, circumstances, and decisions may be lacking, especially in a computerized environment. Although these are but a few examples, they illustrate the importance of inquiry as a source of information during the course of the audit.

Inquiry, however, is rarely an adequate source of evidence by itself. This point is critical to keep in mind because management responses to inquiries may be naïve, overly optimistic, or misinformed. In extreme situations, management may even lie to the auditor. Consequently, the responses to client inquiries should rarely be taken at face value. Rather, the answers to inquiries, especially of management, often point to other aspects of a client that the auditor should examine. The auditor needs to gather other evidence to corroborate explanations provided by management that are critical for evaluating whether the financial statements are free of material misstatements.

Overreliance on evidence from inquiry or gullible acceptance of management responses to inquiries have created problems for auditors in the past, often leading to severe audit problems, exposure to litigation, and damage to auditor reputations. When an auditor fails to challenge critical but unsupported management responses to inquiries, the risk of audit failure increases if the issues later turn out to be linked to fraudulent behavior or other sources of material misstatements. Although inquiry is the most common source of *information* in an audit, professional standards make it clear that inquiry is the least reliable source of audit *evidence*, especially if the responses to inquiries come from members of management.

Example

In the ZZZZ Best fraud, entrepreneur Barry Minkow created a carpet cleaning and insurance restoration company in which almost every client was fraudulent. Virtually all information in the financial statements was fraudulent, resulting in unreasonable financial ratios and unrealistic business process measures. However, Minkow was able to fool the auditors on the engagement mostly through his slick ability to persuade the auditors with his clever answers to inquires, many of which were not followed up by the auditors (or were followed up with limited corroborative evidence).

Inquiry is not a discrete step in the auditor's process of collecting evidence like other audit procedures, such as examining a specific transaction's documentation or confirming customer accounts. Rather, inquiry permeates the audit and is reflected in both formal interviews that are planned in advance and informal discussions with management. Indeed, a rigorous auditor is never "off-duty" when in the presence of client personnel. The auditor should always be alert for the opportunity to gain additional insights from client management or other personnel through informal or, even, accidental conversations.

Professional standards have always recommended that information obtained from management inquiries be corroborated by other evidence due to the inherent unreliability of management inquiry. As a result, auditors normally supplement and corroborate evidence from inquiry with evidence obtained through observation, documentation, or confirmation procedures. Although inquiries are not usually corroborated with additional inquiries of client personnel, there are situations in which information obtained from multiple sources within the organization can be compared for consistency. However, unless inquiries are conducted as part of a rigorous plan for collecting evidence, the reliability of individual responses should be viewed skeptically.

A RIGOROUS APPROACH TO OBTAINING INQUIRY EVIDENCE

Figure 9–2 illustrates the five major elements that may affect the quality of inquiry evidence. The planning and conduct of client inquiries should consider all five attributes to obtain the best possible evidence:

1. Attributes of the interviewee: Does the interviewee have the appropriate knowledge, and can he or she be expected to be honest in providing information?
2. Attributes of the interviewer: Does the interviewer have an appropriate attitude, knowledge of the area to be discussed, and appreciation for the context of the discussion?
3. Conduct of the interview: Is the discussion scheduled at an appropriate time with well-thought-out objectives and issues to discuss?

Figure 9–2   A Rigorous Approach to Inquiry

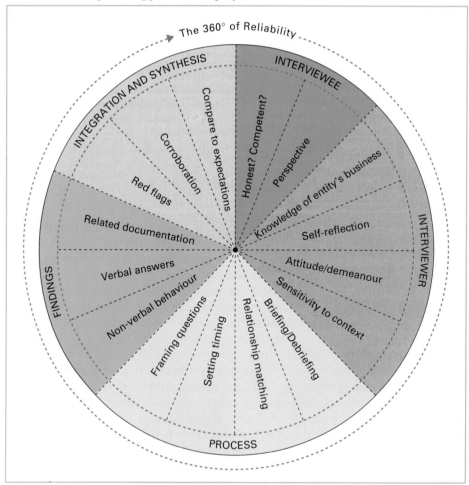

Source: CICA Research Report "Audit Inquiry: Seeking More Reliable Evidence from Audit Inquiry," Canadian Institute of Chartered Accountants, 2000. p. 30. Used with permission.

4. Documenting findings: Have interviewee responses (verbal and nonverbal) been evaluated and adequately captured in the audit documentation?
5. Integrating and synthesizing the meaning of inquiry evidence: Does the information confirm expectations, corroborate other audit evidence, or raise red flags about the issues discussed?

Each of these steps should be given consideration when developing a rigorous interview program for obtaining inquiry evidence and are discussed in more depth below.

PLANNING CLIENT INQUIRIES

Before inquiries occur (and probably before fieldwork begins), the audit team should identify situations in the audit where rigorous inquiry evidence will be needed and develop an interview plan for the *formal* inquiry phase of the audit. Some examples where formal inquiries are encountered in the audit include

- Obtaining an understanding of a client's environment and activities
- Discussing the design and operation of processes with client personnel
- Identifying important changes in the client's internal or external environment
- Discussing risks and controls with client personnel
- Evaluating the nature of performance results with management
- Identifying key accounting policies, assumptions, and estimates
- Discussing possible future plans of the organization

An important audit decision is determining the appropriate client personnel to interview. If the questions to be discussed involve the financial reporting process, interviews with accounting personnel are appropriate. However, when trying to understand the reasonableness of transactions and balances, auditors should find client personnel who are responsible for conducting the underlying activities. Although finding and interviewing operating personnel can be intimidating, these employees will have a better understanding of the business than accounting personnel because they are directly involved in executing transactions. Further, they usually have less accounting knowledge and are less likely to bias their answers in a way to make results appear better than they really are. To the extent possible, auditors should speak with operating personnel without accounting personnel present. Interviews with operating managers need to use terms and jargon with which they are comfortable—that is, "talk their language." Hence, it is important that auditors have a sufficient understanding of the business and industry before conducting detailed interviews with operating personnel.

Example

A senior manager from an international accounting firm shared this actual encounter with one of the co-authors recently. He was touring the central warehouse of his bed and bath products retailer client with the warehouse manager. The controller insisted on accompanying the senior manager and warehouse manager on the tour. During the tour, the accounting senior manager asked about the layout of the warehouse, causes of bottlenecks, additional activities when deliveries were late, and so forth. The warehouse manager provided much information about the need for extra employees and expensive costs associated with overnight deliveries using alternate carriers, among other things. The controller acted as if he were unaware of all of these additional costs and tried to blame the manager for not ensuring that these costs were properly recorded. Finally, near the end of the tour, the senior manager asked the warehouse manager about the room off to the side of the warehouse full of inventory. The warehouse manager commented that it was full of inventory that was never going to be sold, so they found a place to get it out of the way. The controller, without missing a beat, reached up and slapped the warehouse manager on the back of the head. The inventory in that room was listed on the books at full cost.

Planning considerations include matching the appropriate members of the audit team with client personnel to be interviewed and ensuring that interviewers have the appropriate background knowledge of the client to conduct the interview effectively. In general, audit partners will conduct interviews with the audit committee, CEO, and CFO; audit managers will interview senior managers, especially those in charge of key business units; and junior auditors will interview client accounting personnel and lower-level operational managers. To enhance learning and the effectiveness of the interview process, a more junior auditor should accompany a more senior auditor and act as a note taker if the interview is to be lengthy or broad-ranging. This mentoring arrangement allows the more experienced auditor to focus on the meaning of client responses, manage the flow of the interview, note and interpret the non-verbal reactions of client personnel, and draw out nuances of client's responses without the distraction of taking notes of the conversation. In addition, inexperienced auditors can learn to conduct effective interviews themselves by observing others.

Although it can and should be preplanned, an interview should not consist of a list of standardized questions. An auditor may schedule an interview with a set of generic questions in mind, but every attempt should be made to customize the interview to the client's particular situation, drawing on knowledge from previous audits and knowledge of the client's industry. Furthermore, the auditor must consider the language to be employed in the interview. Approaching the interviewee with a view to understanding his or her world is one of the keys to establishing effective rapport and in eliciting meaningful responses. Figure 9–3 provides some guidance on how questions should be prepared prior to an interview.

CONDUCTING CLIENT INQUIRIES

When conducting a formal interview, the auditor should be clear about what is to be discussed, stay on topic (unless follow-up is needed or important tangential issues arise), and respect the interviewee's time. To the extent possible, the audit team should plan interviews to take place at a time convenient to client personnel when they are not under unusual time pressure. Interviews should be planned so they take place at separate times with a manager's supervisors, colleagues, and subordinates with little chance that the manager has time to coordinate responses. The auditor should also consider interviews with other client employees in different parts of the organization to corroborate responses from multiple sources. Consistency of client responses enhances the reliability of evidence obtained through inquiry. If one finds puzzling contradictions or implausible responses, this should alert a sceptical auditor to delve deeper into the area in question, often through the use of other audit procedures.

Figure 9–3   Preparing Interview Questions

- Use terminology the interviewee understands.
- Stay within the area of the interviewee's work responsibilities (formally or informally).
- Have the interviewee tell "a story" about what you want to know, instead of using a formal question and answer structure:
  - Tell me about your system for receiving goods?

      ≪ *instead of* ≫

  - Does the shipper sign the receiving report?
- Phrase questions to elicit information, not suggest an answer:
  - What do you think is causing the decrease in inventory turnover this year?

      ≪ *instead of* ≫

  - Inventory turnover decreased this year. Is it due to {interviewer suggestion}?
- Always be neutral in wording your questions:
  - What happens if a sales order does not get input into the system?

      ≪ *instead of* ≫

  - What happens when your people lose a sale because they are not paying attention?
- Don't show off your own expertise/knowledge:
  - What causes your inventory turnover to be lower in the summer?

      ≪ *instead of* ≫

  - Based on my experience at other car dealerships I assume that inventory turnover is generally lower in the summer, right?

The information gleaned from interviews should be documented in a manner that captures the key points in an understandable fashion so that the information can be shared with other members of the audit team. Furthermore, regular audit team meetings should be scheduled to discuss what has been learned through inquiry in an open and candid environment. Audit partners benefit from this debriefing process because they may grasp the significance of some information that may have eluded less experienced personnel. Also, these discussions can help inexperienced auditors to understand potentially worrisome information by putting it in the broader context of the audit and client. Often it is only through discussion among members of the team that patterns of inconsistent responses emerge or non-verbal cues can be meaningfully interpreted.

An excellent opportunity for discussion among team members is during the mandatory brainstorming session when the risk of material misstatement and fraud are discussed by the audit team. If team members observe that company personnel provide contradictory or inconsistent answers to critical questions, the audit team should consider increasing its assessment of the risk of fraud or material misstatement. At a minimum, the auditor should gather enough evidence to reconcile the apparent inconsistencies, possibly with evidence obtained from procedures other than inquiry. If the contradictions are severe enough, more formal interviews may be conducted, possibly by specialists in forensic auditing, or other rigorous procedures may be used to gather additional evidence. For all interviews, the auditor should consider possible sources of evidence

Authoritative Guidance & Standards

SAS 106 and ISA 500 are very clear about the need to corroborate inquires. The standards note that "the auditor should perform audit procedures in addition to the use of inquiry to obtain sufficient appropriate audit evidence. Inquiry alone ordinarily does not provide sufficient appropriate audit evidence to detect a material misstatement at the relevant assertion level."

that might be used to corroborate the evidence from inquiry. Some examples include

- Viewing documentary evidence maintained by the interviewee or other personnel that supports the inquiry evidence.
- Examining third-party documents or data that reinforces the information obtained through inquiry.
- Consulting industry experts who provide context about information and evaluate the reasonableness of evidence from inquiry.

Example

In the Enron fraud, one of the allegations about Arthur Andersen's audit work was that the firm did not properly follow up on answers to inquiries related to the special purpose entities (SPEs) that were established to move debt off on Enron's books, while simultaneously enabling key officers to profit from the transactions (through the receipt of Enron stock to cover any losses associated with the SPEs). Although there were several partners at Andersen who were uncomfortable with the SPEs, the auditors would have had a better chance of unraveling the fraud had they utilized more third party documents and outside financial experts to follow up on these issues.

INTRODUCTION TO ANALYSIS: A SIMPLE EXAMPLE

The complement to inquiry evidence is analysis. Analysis encompasses the use of quantitative tools and analytical procedures to facilitate decisions, evaluate performance, and signal risk conditions affecting an organization. Analysis is frequently utilized as part of the strategic and process analyses performed during the engagement but can also be used for substantive testing of transactions, accounts, and presentation and disclosure. Management itself uses many forms of analysis to monitor and assess its success and the extent of risks it faces. An auditor's analysis can be used to corroborate evidence from inquiries about the client's operations and activities.

The process of performing analytical procedures is relatively simple in concept but complex in practice. The level of judgment that is needed to perform effective analytical procedures necessitates that auditors obtain a great deal of training and experience. The auditor selects a measurement of interest (e.g., concerning

Authoritative Guidance & Standards
SAS 56 and ISA 520 require auditors to perform analytical procedures at the beginning of the audit to identify issues and at the end of the engagement as a last big-picture look. Although analytical procedures are not required to be used as substantive evidence, they are frequently used for this purpose.

a risk, account balance, or process attribute), generates an expectation about the item, and compares that expectation to actual results. If the expectation and the actual outcome are significantly different, the auditor needs to obtain an explanation of the unusual variation. If unexpected results cannot be adequately explained, the auditor could conclude there may be significant residual risks associated with the performance measure being examined, which would affect the subsequent conduct of the audit.

We will introduce several analysis techniques that are used by auditors to obtain analytical evidence about risks, processes, and accounts. The computation of numbers is not the purpose of the analysis: the purpose is to obtain a better understanding of what is happening to the company and to highlight areas where risks are significant or financial results are unexpected, unusual, or possibly erroneous. Although very useful, none of these techniques are sufficient if used in isolation and should be combined with effective client inquiries. To illustrate the basic approach to preliminary analytical procedures, consider the following descriptive data for accounts receivable and sales:

Example

	20x7	20x8
Accounts Receivable (net)	$ 6,000	$ 8,000
Receivables/Assets	18.5%	17.9%
Sales Revenue	$50,000	$65,000
Sales growth	19%	30%

This illustration shows sales have increased significantly. Receivables also have increased but not at a pace commensurate with sales. We can compute an interesting ratio using the above data called Days-to-Collect, which indicates how long it takes for the company to turn receivables into cash receipts:[1]

Days-to-Collect	43.8 days	44.8 days

We see that the speed of collection has slowed down slightly, that is, customers are not paying their bills as fast in 20x8 as they did in 20x7. This could be the result of natural fluctuations in the company's operations or could occur for a number of specific reasons:

• The company has loosened its credit standards and is selling to riskier customers.
• The industry is in a recession, and all customers are paying more slowly.
• The company has changed its policy of writing off bad debts.
• There is an error or fraud in receivables.

The first explanation is unlikely because we expect that loosening sales credit in a period of rapid sales growth would lead to proportionally more rapid growth in receivables—the opposite of what is suggested by the raw data. The rapid sales growth also seems to belie the recession explanation. Regarding the third possible explanation, the auditor may inquire about the company's policy for writing off bad debts but must keep in mind that it is possible the receivable balance is incorrect. The audit should be conducted to provide reasonable assurance for eliminating the last possibility.

Consider an additional fact to this example: the allowance for bad debts was $1,000 at the end of 20x7 but is $800 at the end of 20x8. Typically, an auditor would expect an inverse relationship between the receivable turnover and the allowance for bad debts. When customers are paying more slowly or other factors affect the recoverability of receivables, the company bears a greater risk that receivables will not be collected. This risk should be translated into a higher estimate of bad debts. In other words, given that the receivable turnover has decreased, an auditor would find it *unusual* that the allowance for bad debts has decreased. This is an example of the type of integrated analysis that an auditor should perform during

Authoritative Guidance & Standards

SAS 56 and ISA 520 specify that analysis involve comparing financial reporting information to auditor expectations. Even when auditors use basic analytical procedures, they should base them on expectations established by the auditor. For example, comparing current and prior year results is only appropriate when there is an expectation that the numbers will be the same, which is rarely the case.

---

1 Exact formulas for Days-to-Collect and other ratios are discussed later in this chapter.

preliminary analytical procedures. The next section illustrates techniques used for obtaining a broad base of analytical evidence for a client.

BASIC TECHNIQUES FOR OBTAINING ANALYTICAL EVIDENCE

Auditors have traditionally relied on extensive review of financial statement balances when performing analytical procedures. However, analytical evidence from nonfinancial performance measures is becoming more common and is particularly useful for assessing the performance of processes. There are six basic approaches for performing analytical procedures:

- Basic judgmental methods

    Comparative financial statement analysis
    Common size financial statement analysis[2]
    Ratio analysis

- Advanced judgmental methods

    Cash flow analysis
    Nonfinancial performance measurement
    Competitive benchmarking

Although each method is individually useful, the auditor cannot interpret a single number or set of numbers in isolation and without a basis for evaluating observed results. The appropriate standard of comparison may take many forms: prior-year results, management's budgeted results, an auditor's industry expertise, or results from other companies. Furthermore, unique facts known about the company must be considered in determining whether a specific performance measure is unusual or not. Thus, much of the interpretation of analytical evidence involves extensive client inquiries.

BASIC JUDGMENTAL METHODS

Comparative financial statement analysis: The comparison of financial statement balances across time is one of the oldest and most common analytical procedures used by auditors. In general, an auditor is interested in understanding why significant accounts have increased or decreased over time, especially if the change in account balances is extreme or unusual. Accounts that fluctuate in dramatic steps are of most interest. However, although steady growth of revenues by 5 percent per year may not raise many questions, it is not necessarily indicative of low risk.

An example of comparative financial statements is presented in the first four columns of Figure 9–4 for a hypothetical company called AMA Autoparts Inc. A few dramatic account changes can be noted immediately:

- The wild swings in the cash balance
- The doubling of accounts receivable in 20x8
- The reduction in plant assets in 20x8
- The reduction in retained earnings in spite of increasing profits
- The dramatic growth in revenue
- The unusual level of dividends

Tentative explanations for some of the changes in account balances may already be apparent, such as the large dividend explains the drop in retained

2 Also known as *percentage analysis*.

Figure 9–4   An Example of Comparative and Common Size Analysis: Basic Financial Data for AMA Autoparts Inc.

Balance Sheet

	Audited 20x6	Audited 20x7	Unaudited 20x8	Percentage Analysis 20x6	20x7	20x8
Cash	$ 26,000	$ 312,000	$ 10,000	1.47%	14.81%	0.48%
Marketable Securities	100,000	120,000	125,000	5.66%	5.70%	6.04%
Accounts Receivable	525,000	350,000	700,000	29.73%	16.61%	33.82%
Inventory	310,000	310,000	300,000	17.55%	14.71%	14.49%
Prepaid Expenses	60,000	75,000	50,000	3.40%	3.56%	2.42%
Current Assets	1,021,000	1,167,000	1,185,000	57.81%	55.39%	57.25%
Long-Term Investments	275,000	300,000	310,000	15.57%	14.24%	14.98%
Plant and Property Accumulated	555,000	740,000	640,000	31.43%	35.12%	30.92%
Depreciation	(85,000)	(100,000)	(65,000)	−4.81%	−4.75%	−3.14%
Total Assets	1,766,000	2,107,000	2,070,000	100.00%	100.00%	100.00%
Accounts Payable	32,000	110,000	85,000	1.81%	5.22%	4.11%
Wages Payable	28,000	32,000	18,000	1.59%	1.52%	0.87%
Dividends Payable	0	5,000	130,000	0.00%	0.24%	6.28%
Taxes Payable	36,000	55,000	62,000	2.04%	2.61%	3.00%
Current Portion of Debt	150,000	175,000	100,000	8.49%	8.31%	4.83%
Current Liabilities	246,000	377,000	395,000	13.93%	17.89%	19.08%
Mortgage Payable	800,000	625,000	525,000	45.30%	29.66%	25.36%
Total Liabilities	1,046,000	1,002,000	920,000	59.23%	47.56%	44.44%
Common Stock ($10 par)	110,000	150,000	225,000	6.23%	7.12%	10.87%
Additional Paid-In Capital	260,000	345,000	425,000	14.72%	16.37%	20.53%
Retained Earnings	350,000	610,000	500,000	19.82%	28.95%	24.15%
Total Equity	720,000	1,105,000	1,150,000	40.77%	52.44%	55.56%
Total Liability and Equity	1,766,000	2,107,000	2,070,000	100.00%	100.00%	100.00%

Income Statement

	Audited 20x7	Unaudited 20x8	Percentage Analysis 20x7	20x8
Sales	4,185,000	6,045,000	100.00%	100.00%
Cost of goods sold	(2,565,000)	(4,015,000)	−61.29%	−66.42%
Gross margin	1,620,000	2,030,000	38.71%	33.58%
Depreciation expense	(90,000)	(75,000)	−2.15%	−1.24%
Selling expense	(600,000)	(575,000)	−14.34%	−9.51%
Administrative expense	(420,000)	(480,000)	−10.04%	−7.94%
Net operating income	510,000	900,000	12.19%	14.89%
Interest expense	(65,000)	(50,000)	−1.55%	−0.83%
Net income before taxes	445,000	850,000	10.63%	14.06%
Income tax expense	(175,000)	(365,000)	−4.18%	−6.04%
Net income	270,000	485,000	6.45%	8.02%

earnings, but at this point our explanations will be incomplete and mere guess-work without additional information and analysis (and inquiry).

Common-size financial statement analysis: Common-size financial statement analysis is based on the premise that the relationships among accounts in the balance sheet and income statement are predictable. For example, a typical manufacturing company will have relatively minor cash balances whereas inventory and plant assets will be a large proportion of total assets. Common-size analysis entails transforming all of the data in the balance sheet and income statement into percentages relative to a common denominator. This is accomplished for the balance sheet by dividing each account balance by total assets, yielding the percentage of total assets that is accounted for by each account or group of accounts. A similar transformation is obtained for the income statement by dividing each nominal account by total sales (or total revenues). An example of this type of transformation is provided in the last three columns of Figure 9–4 for AMA Autoparts Inc.

Simply noting that a company has more receivables or inventory is not very meaningful given that a successful company grows over time. The more important question pertains to which assets have grown fastest (or slowest) and why. In our example, building and equipment has decreased as a percentage of total assets (35.12 to 30.92 percent). In most businesses, plant assets will increase because new facilities are needed as the company grows. At the same time, older equipment may be retired and replaced by newer equipment, which is typically more expensive. These two trends would tend to cause plant assets to grow at a rate commensurate with total asset growth. In our example, we have already seen that plant assets decreased in 20x8. Such an outcome may be the natural result of conditions within the organization (e.g., the company has changed its operations), the result of accounting changes, or an indication that the company has made an accounting error (e.g., failed to capitalize some expenditures that should be treated as assets).

Ratio analysis: Auditors and financial analysts have traditionally used a number of common ratios to assess the financial performance of a company. These ratios fall into five broad categories:

- **Profitability ratios:** These ratios measure the profitability of the company relative to its asset base and revenue stream.
- **Asset management ratios:** These ratios measure the company's effectiveness and efficiency at managing various types of assets.
- **Liquidity ratios:** These ratios measure the ability of the company to satisfy its obligations in the near term (usually considered to be the next 12 months).
- **Debt management ratios:** These ratios measure the ability of the company to manage its capital financing and to satisfy its obligations in the long run.
- **Market value ratios:** These ratios measure the company's standing in the eyes of outside investors.

An advantage of using ratios as a source of analytical evidence is that they allow the auditor to look at performance results in a manner different than traditional financial statements. Often, ratios allow an auditor to link information from the balance sheet to activity in the income statement in order to identify unusual relationships across the financial statements. Thus, ratios may tell an auditor something about an organization that is not apparent from the raw accounting data used in comparative or common-size financial analysis.

The formulas for some commonly used ratios in each of these categories are presented in Figure 9–5. Before discussing these ratios, two points should be

Figure 9–5   Ratios Used for Analysis of Financial Statements

Liquidity Ratios:

Quick Ratio
$$\frac{\text{Cash} + \text{Marketable Securities} + \text{Net Receivables}}{\text{Current Liabilities}}$$

Current Ratio
$$\frac{\text{Current Assets}}{\text{Current Liabilities}}$$

Debt Management Ratios:

Payable Turnover
$$\frac{\text{Cost of Goods Sold}}{\text{Accounts Payable}}$$

Debt Ratio
$$\frac{\text{Total Liabilities}}{\text{Total Assets}}$$

Interest Coverage Ratio
(Times Interest Earned)
$$\frac{\text{Earnings before Interest \& Taxes}}{\text{Interest Expense}}$$

Interest Rate Ratio
$$\frac{\text{Interest Expense}}{\text{Average Total Debt}}$$

Asset Management Ratios:

Inventory Turnover
$$\frac{\text{Cost of Goods Sold}}{\text{Inventory}}$$

Receivable Turnover
$$\frac{\text{Net Sales or Revenue}}{\text{Net Receivables}}$$

Fixed Asset Turnover
$$\frac{\text{Net Sales or Revenue}}{\text{Net Fixed Assets}}$$

Total Asset Turnover
$$\frac{\text{Net Sales or Revenue}}{\text{Total Assets}}$$

Average Days to Collect   365/Receivable Turnover

Average Days to Sell   365/Inventory Turnover

Average Operating Cycle   Average Days to Sell + Average Days to Collect

Depreciation Rate
$$\frac{\text{Depreciation Expense}}{\text{Net Fixed Assets}}$$

Profitability Ratios:

Return on Assets
$$\frac{\text{Net Income} + \text{Interest Expense} \times (1 - \text{Avg Tax Rate})}{\text{Total Assets}}$$

Return on Equity
$$\frac{\text{Net Income} - \text{Preferred Stock Dividends}}{\text{Total Common Equity}}$$

Profit Margin
$$\frac{\text{Net Income}}{\text{Net Sales}}$$

Market Value Ratios:

Price/Earnings
$$\frac{\text{Common Stock Price}}{\text{Earnings per Share}}$$

Earnings per Share
$$\frac{\text{Net Income for the Current Period}}{\text{Number of Common Stock Shares}}$$

(continued)

Figure 9–5   *(continued)*

Market Value Ratios:	
Market/Book	$\dfrac{\text{Common Stock Share Price}}{\text{Common Stock Book Value}}$
Dividend Payout	$\dfrac{\text{Dividends Paid Out}}{\text{Net Income}}$
Book Value per Share	$\dfrac{\text{Total Equity Attributable to Common Stock}}{\text{Number of Common Stock Shares}}$

noted. First, this list is not intended to be comprehensive. There are many different ratios that may be relevant and important for the evaluation of any given company. For example, additional ratios may be needed to evaluate a company that has a heavy commitment to research and development. Other specialized industries (e.g., banking, insurance, health care) may require an entirely new set of ratios. The second point is that the formulas for computing ratios are intended to be flexible. Data may not be available to compute some of the ratios exactly as stated in Figure 9–5. In these cases, the ratios may need to be slightly modified.

Figure 9–6 presents some key ratios for AMA Autoparts Inc. Profitability ratios reveal that the company was significantly more profitable in 20x8 than in 20x7. Profit margin, which indicates the percentage of each dollar of revenue that is profit, increased from 6.45 percent to 8.02 percent. The return on assets (usually abbreviated ROA) indicates the magnitude of profits relative to total assets and increased from 15.98 percent to 24.59 percent. ROA is independent of the forms of financing used by the company and is not affected by the extent of debt that a company has issued. The return on equity (abbreviated ROE) measures the profit relative to the amount of equity invested by common shareholders—that is, it factors out the cost of debt. ROE increased from 29.59 percent to 43.02 percent.

Asset management ratios provide an indication of how well a company is utilizing various types of assets. Higher asset management ratios indicate more efficient management of assets; for example, a high inventory turnover may indicate that the company makes effective use of just-in-time inventory techniques. However, it is also possible that very high values may indicate problems; in some cases, high inventory turnover may occur because the company maintains too little inventory and loses revenues due to stock-outs or shortages. In our example, the inventory turnover has increased substantially from 8.27 to 13.16. The company may have improved its marketing, it may be experiencing inventory shortages, or an error may have occurred in the recording of the inventory balance at year-end. The auditor must conduct the audit to have reasonable assurance that the cause is not an error or fraudulent transaction.

Liquidity and debt ratios show that the company is more liquid in 20x8 than it was in 20x7. The company is paying its bills faster (i.e., payable turnover went from 36.13 to 41.18), has better interest coverage (18.00 versus 7.85), and lower levels of debt relative to assets (44.44 percent versus 47.56 percent). These results indicate that the company has a stronger financial position than in the prior year.

Figure 9–6 An Example of Ratio Analysis

Ratio Analysis	20x8	20x7
Liquidity Ratios:		
Quick Ratio	2.11	2.07
Current Ratio	3.00	3.10
Asset Management Ratios:		
Inventory Turnover	13.16	8.27
Receivable Turnover	11.51	9.57
Fixed Asset Turnover	9.95	7.54
Asset Turnover	2.89	2.16
Average Days to Collect	31.71	38.14
Average Days to Sell	27.74	152.08
Averaging Operating Cycle	59.45	190.22
Depreciation Expense/Plant Assets	1.24%	2.15%
Debt Management Ratios:		
Payable Turnover	41.18	36.13
Debt/Assets	44.44%	47.56%
Interest Coverage	18.00	7.85
Profitability Ratios:		
Return on Assets	24.59%	15.98%
Return on Equity	43.02%	29.59%
Return on Sales (Profit Margin)	8.02%	6.45%
Earnings per Share	$ 2.16	$ 1.80
Market Value Ratios:		
Price/Earnings	8.93	12.08
Book Value of Equity	5.11	7.37
Dividend Payout	122.68%	3.70%
Effective Tax Rate	42.94%	39.33%

ADVANCED JUDGMENTAL METHODS

Cash flow analysis: Most financial statement and ratio analysis is based on accrual accounting numbers. However, a company must also generate positive cash flow over a reasonable period of time, or it will not be able to pay its obligations or satisfy its investors. Companies are required to prepare a Statement of Cash Flows as part of the annual financial report. Accountants usually analyze three components of cash flow: cash from operations, cash from investing activities, and cash from financing activities. Cash from operations refers to the net cash flows generated from the day-to-day activities of the company such as producing and selling inventory. Cash from investing activities reflects the purchase (and sale) of long-lived assets such as plant assets and investments. Cash from financing reflects the sources of financing (debt, equity) and payments to investors and creditors.

Cash flow is not expected to be positive from all three components, but over an extended period the company needs to generate a positive cash flow. The cash flow profile of an organization will generally follow a predictable pattern based on its life cycle. In the early growth stages, most companies will have negative cash flow from operations and significant cash inflows from financing and outflows for investments. In a mature, stable period, the company should have relatively balanced cash flow from all three sources with new financing activity mainly being used to fund replacement of productive assets. In the decline stage, cash flow from operations may still be positive (but reduced), investing activity will slow down and possibly create a positive cash flow as productive assets are sold, and cash will flow out to investors and creditors as the company winds down its operations.

Example

> Companies in the biotech industry burn cash at a high rate in the early, but lengthy, period during which they are undertaking research and development. Such a company may have very little cash inflows from operations and may be totally dependent on positive cash infusions from grants or investments from venture capitalists or large corporate allies. In this situation, accounting earnings are less important for the valuation of the company than is its ability to obtain sustainable sources of cash to underwrite R&D activities, which will hopefully lead to the discovery and marketing of successful products.

Many traditional accounting ratios can be recast as cash flow ratios if desired. For example, many Internet companies report cash flow per share (usually positive) along with earnings per share (almost always negative) in order to communicate their financial health. Similarly, interest coverage can be calculated based on net cash flow rather than earnings. An important cash flow indicator is *free cash flow*. This is usually defined as cash flow from operations less dividends and any capital expenditures needed to maintain *current* capacity.[3] Free cash flow reflects the amount of money the organization has available for expansion, new product development, and to absorb the impact of risk or shocks within the industry. A company with negative free cash flow will need to shrink or shut down eventually.

Nonfinancial performance measurement: Many risks, especially within processes, are more effectively measured using nonfinancial measures than traditional accounting results. Financial analysts frequently use nonfinancial indicators when evaluating potential investments. For example, the value of a professional sports franchise is driven more by its win-loss record and the size of local market than it is by any traditional accounting measures. Common nonfinancial measures that apply to most organizations include:

- Market share: This is the percentage of total market consumption that is filled by a specific company or product. A successful company will have a larger market share. An interesting aspect of defining market share is to define the relevant market. Coca-Cola controls a dominant portion of the "cola" market or even "soft drink" market. However, if the market is defined as "thirsty people," Coke comes in a distant second to water.
- Customer satisfaction: Long-term success for most organizations depends on providing satisfying experiences to their customers. A drop in customer satisfaction generally leads to reduced revenue and profits.
- Time-to-market for new products: This is the length of time it takes a company to conceive a new product and begin to sell it. The longer it takes to get a new idea to market, the more risk there is that a competitor will get there first, or external developments will cause early obsolescence. The software and media industries are particularly sensitive to time-to-market issues.

---

3 Free cash flow also reflects the effect of debt financing. Under current accounting rules, interest payments are subtracted directly from cash flow from operations.

- New product success rates: Companies may introduce many new products and multiple product introductions maximize the chance that some of the products will prove successful and profitable. Movie studios, record companies, book publishers, and consumer products manufacturers (e.g., Proctor & Gamble) all use this approach, and improvement in the success rate of new products can have a very positive effect on the company.

Example

The rate of success for developing new pharmaceuticals is very low, and those that are successful take a long time to bring to the market. On average, the pharmaceutical industry must identify and test 5,000 new compounds in order to obtain a single viable product. Although the success rate is very low, the potential rewards can be huge when success is achieved, especially if the drug is effective against a broad-based disease. The time-to-market can be as long as 13 years because of the approval process used by government agencies that often requires years of testing for new drugs. In such an environment, small gains in success rates or time-to-market can yield a significant competitive advantage to a pharmaceutical company.

Because nonfinancial measures are not limited by the same constraints as traditional accounting, the use of such measures is dependent on the availability of systematic and reliable data. The need for reliable data has created opportunities for organizations to develop and sell the output of proprietary measurement systems (J.D. Power & Associates report customer satisfaction for automobiles) and independent ratings for products and service (e.g., *Consumer Reports* provides quality assessments for a wide variety of consumer products). Nonfinancial performance measures tend to be industry specific. Some examples of nonfinancial measures include

- Airlines: On-time percentages
- Automobiles: Reliability ratings and number of recalls
- Hotels: Average occupancy rates
- Internet sites: Number of hits by web surfers
- Internet service providers (e.g., AOL): Account renewal rates
- Universities: Student performance statistics, such as graduation rates

Competitive benchmarking: The evaluation of performance measures is a complex process. In general, some standard of comparison is needed in order to determine if a specific measurement indicates good or bad news. Internal comparisons over time or comparisons with forecasted results (such as budgets) are very useful. Another common approach is to compare a company's performance to outside organizations. This technique is referred to as *competitive benchmarking*. For example, General Motors may compare itself to Toyota to determine its relative time-to-market.

Example

General Motors could also analyze how long it takes to fill a customer order by considering its competitors' strategy. At some time in the near future, Toyota wants to be able to deliver a newly manufactured car in five days from receipt of customer order. If the company is able to accomplish this goal, it would be a dramatic improvement over the current 6–8 week delivery time, and would give Toyota a significant competitive advantage over other automobile manufacturers.

The two challenges for effective competitive benchmarking are (1) identifying the appropriate external organization to use as a comparison and (2) obtaining meaningful data for comparison. Organizations in the same industry provide an obvious starting point because they will often have processes that are similar to the client. However, the auditor must be careful to consider differences across companies in the same industry. For example, distribution processes for Amazon are significantly different from Barnes & Noble, and one can not realistically be used as a benchmark for the other. Sometimes, the appropriate benchmark for a process is found in an entirely different industry. For example, LL Bean, a mail-order retailer, has a world class telemarketing operation that could be used as a competitive benchmark for the telemarketing activity in other industries such as insurance or telecommunications.

The problem of obtaining meaningful data is aggravated by the efforts of most organizations to keep information about their internal processes secret. Proprietary internal information is seen as a source of competitive advantage, so that organizations are often unwilling to share data on performance measures. This obstacle is sometimes overcome by using independent third parties such as trade associations and not-for-profit rating agencies to compile sensitive data and then disguise actual results from individual organizations. Nevertheless, acquiring meaningful external benchmarks is a serious challenge for the auditor and management.

A RIGOROUS APPROACH TO OBTAINING ANALYTICAL EVIDENCE

Analysis can be used in numerous phases of the audit: as a planning tool or a risk assessment procedure to guide the audit or to allocate resources to potentially problematic areas, as a substantive test (substantive analytical procedure) that signals potential material misstatements, as an overall test of reasonableness of the financial statements near the end of the audit, and to inform the overall going concern judgment the auditor must make. There are a number of differences in the use of analysis among these stages: (1) the level of detail utilized in the analysis, (2) the precision of the expectations developed prior to carrying out the analysis, and (3) the nature and extent of the follow-up work carried out by the auditor when there is a difference from expectation. Figure 9–7 summarizes the differences in using analysis at each of the various stages of the audit.

PERFORMING STRUCTURED ANALYSIS

Given the huge volume of performance measures, accounts, ratios, and percentages that an auditor could consider during the course of an audit, it is vital that the auditor adopt a systematic approach to evaluating analytical evidence. Effective and efficient use of analytical evidence requires training and experience. The interpretation of the results from analytical procedures is more an art form than a mechanical process. Nevertheless, the auditor can follow a systematic process that makes the interpretation more effective, as illustrated in Figure 9–8.

Step 1 is to identify the attribute that the auditor wishes to evaluate. The attribute of interest can be a specific risk, an account balance, or the effectiveness of a process. The auditor may choose to measure a risk because it is potentially significant to the conduct of the audit. A specific account may be selected because it is material to the financial statements, or because the auditor feels that it is significantly affected by current risks and conditions. Process attributes may be selected in order

Figure 9–7 Analysis at Various Audit Phases

Audit stage	Level of analysis and precision of expectations	Follow-up when expectations are not met
Preliminary or planning analytical procedures (also known as risk assessment procedures)	**Level of analysis** • Financial statement level. • Significant operating segments level. • Legal entity level. **Precision of expectation** • Tends to be more general such as "increasing trend" or "same as last year".	• Seek explanations from client management. • Plan additional audit tests to corroborate those explanations. • Note differences for follow-up at later in the audit.
Substantive analytical procedures	**Level of analysis** • At a segment or sub-segment level often focused on a particular account or set of accounts. • Could be product line, geographic area, individual store, or factory. **Precision of expectation** • Must be able to quantify in advance a level of tolerance for variation from expectation that is relatively precise.	• Seek explanations from client management, especially client operations management. • Plan additional substantive tests of details to support both the direction of observed discrepancies and the amount of the discrepancies based on the client's explanations. • Consider alternative reasons for the expectation not being met, including possibility of deliberate misstatement, and carry out tests with added professional skepticism.
Overall or end-of-audit analytical procedures (including evaluating going concern issues)	**Level of analysis** • Financial statements taken as a whole and perhaps all reportable operating segments as per the notes to the financial statements. **Precision of expectation** • Assessment of reasonableness in light of knowledge gathered to date in audit. • Consider further whether anything at this stage suggests a "going concern" issue.	• Obtain additional explanations from client management if needed. • Maintain professional skepticism about management's responses. • Conduct additional testing if unable to resolve inconsistency based on the reasonableness of the available evidence.

to verify the effectiveness of process controls for mitigating risks at the process level (e.g., as part of the review of internal control over financial reporting).

Step 2, gathering relevant facts, is an important but often overlooked step. The interpretation of analytical evidence can only be effective when the auditor factors

Figure 9–8 A Systematic Process for Conducting Analytical Procedures

PURPOSE: To use analytical evidence to identify accounts, risks, or process attributes where observed outcomes are inconsistent with the auditors' expectations, requiring further investigation during the course of the audit.

STEP 1: Identify a process attribute, risk, or account to be subject to analysis: The focus of the analysis needs to be specified. An account balance can be examined to determine if it may contain material misstatement, a specific risk can be measured to determine if it was significant, or nonfinancial process attributes can be examined to see if they are consistent with reported financial results.

STEP 2: Gather facts relevant to the analysis: Identify key events, situations, or other facts that may have an impact on the interpretation of performance indicators.

STEP 3: Identify relevant performance measures: The auditor must decide what attributes to measure. The selection may be self-evident in the case of accounts, but less obvious for risks or process performance indicators.

STEP 4: Obtain data and perform computations: Performance measures should be based on reliable data and computational procedures. Hence, steps must be taken to examine controls over data collection and computation prior to carrying out substantive analytical procedures.

STEP 5: Impose structure: Organize the numerical data into logical segments or audit areas that can be separately analyzed for unusual results, events, or patterns.[4]

STEP 6: Analyze: Analyze each performance measure for deviations from expectations. Reactions to unexpected deviations depend on the nature of the measure and the size of the deviation (i.e., quantitative and qualitative materiality).

STEP 7: Conclude: Construct a cohesive explanation of the numerical data, which incorporates all of the data, facts, and circumstances that are known about the company and determine the implications for the conduct of the audit.

in what he or she already knows about the company, often as a result of client inquiries. Strategic and process analysis provides much of the information needed to interpret performance measures. If the company has undertaken major or unusual transactions, the results from the current year may be quite different from prior years for legitimate reasons. If unaware of these facts, the auditor may conclude that reported results appear unusual or erroneous when the problem really lies with the auditor's lack of knowledge. Alternatively, the industry may have gone through significant change in the current year, so an auditor who bases his or her expectations on "no change" would reach inappropriate conclusions as to the meaning of performance data.

Example

The WorldCom auditors are alleged to have done a great deal of analysis based on the expectation that results would be similar to prior years. The problem was that the worldwide telecommunications industry was undergoing a rapid transformation due to excess capacity, and hence expectations that results would be the same as last year were inappropriate. The fact that the auditor observed that important financial items were close to the levels of the prior year should have triggered additional investigation, NOT provided the auditor with comfort about the reported results.

---

4 Step 5 will be discussed in more detail in Chapter 14.

Step 3, identifying the appropriate performance measures, may be trivial in the case of an account balance, but may be difficult when the attribute of interest is the company's current conditions. First, the attribute or risk may not have an obvious performance measure or the appropriate performance measure may be nonfinancial. Selection of an inappropriate performance measure may yield confusing or inaccurate results. Second, accurate and complete data must be available to determine the value of the performance measure.

Step 4 is computational, and can be facilitated using computer software. Development of a spreadsheet to compute common-size financial statements and ratios is relatively straightforward. Many commercial software accounting packages also generate such statistics. The key concern for the auditor is making certain that the data being used and the computational procedures are reliable. It is also vital that the auditor not rely on the software's default features to flag problems and that the auditor carefully set the parameters of the program when the program generates a list of unexpected fluctuations.

Step 5, imposing structure, is helpful for developing an integrated understanding of the company's operations and results. The organization of data into logically related categories helps bring together disjointed data that relates to the same attribute or activity. This topic will be discussed in more detail in Chapter 14.

Step 6 of the analysis is where the auditor's skill, experience, and expertise have the most impact. The ability to integrate a large volume of information into a coherent picture of a client's situation is obtained with training and experience. Probably the hardest part of this process is deciding when the reported results do not meet expectations. Such a decision must draw upon the auditor's knowledge of the company, industry, and specific facts.

As a final step, the auditor should be able to reconcile all the facts that are available, and explain why some performance indicators went up, some went down, and others were stable. In particular, the auditor needs to focus carefully on facts that do not fit the expected pattern. It is these facts that may often be a clue to something far more important. The auditor should be able to reach conclusions about specific risks that are potentially significant, processes that may not be operating effectively, and account balances that may not be in line with expectations. When expectations are met, the auditor has strong evidence about risk levels, process effectiveness, and information reliability. When expectations are not met, additional effort is usually needed for the auditor to determine how these circumstances affect the audit. Unexplained changes in performance measures indicate a potential residual risk.

The analysis process described above is summarized as a decision flowchart in Figure 9–9. The evaluation of analytical evidence is iterative in nature since the auditor can never know if their expectations are completely reasonable. As new information becomes available, an auditor may revise his or her expectations. At some point, however, the auditor will reach a conclusion as to whether actual conditions and results confirm the expectations, suggesting that the assertion being examined is acceptable, or will identify a discrepancy that will influence the conduct of the audit.

POTENTIAL PITFALLS FROM USING ANALYSIS AS EVIDENCE

Analytical procedures can be an extremely useful technique for identifying areas of high risk in the audit. However, the auditor must be careful to avoid some

Figure 9–9   Evaluation of Analytical Evidence

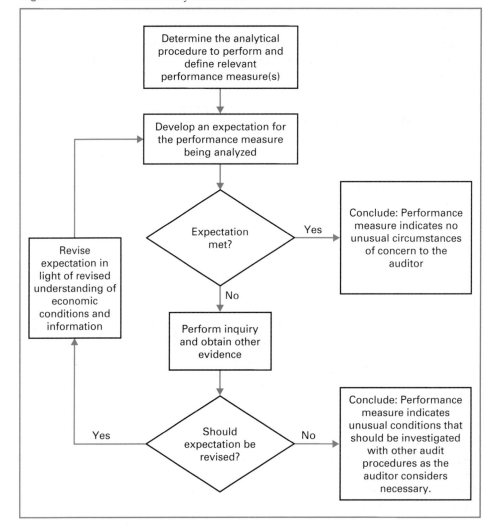

common pitfalls that could lead to a reduction in their usefulness. The most common mistakes made in applying analytical procedures include

- **Simplistic or ill-defined expectations:** Analytical procedures are most effective when the auditor generates an independent expectation about an attribute being evaluated (risk, process, or account). Unfortunately, in many situations the auditor may not have a good basis for generating an expectation. For example, auditors may oversimplify their expectations about accounts by using the prior-year balance as the current-year expectation. If the auditor cannot generate a reasonable and logical expectation, the benefit of performing the analytical procedure will be reduced.

- **Lack of precision:** All expectations involve a range of values that are reasonably likely to occur—the auditor's expectation is just one point in that range. The range of reasonable expectations reflects the margin of error of the estimate and can be quite large. The larger the margin of error, the less accurate will be the analytical procedure. Unfortunately, the auditor rarely knows the true margin of error for a specific performance measure and may end up questioning fluctuations that are normal fluctuations, rather than indicative of an underlying problem, risk, or error.

- **Lack of reliable data:** Auditor expectations will not be reliable if they are based on inaccurate or unreliable data. Misleading data will often cause the auditor to develop unreasonable expectations and decrease the precision of the estimation. This problem is potentially compounded whenever an analytical procedure uses data from outside the organization or data which is not controlled effectively within the organization (e.g., nonfinancial information that is processed outside the accounting system).

- **Influence of reported outcomes:** The auditor often knows the reported outcome for an attribute before performing an analytical procedure. Knowledge of the reported outcome has the tendency to bias the auditor's expectation in the direction of the known value and can potentially reduce the effectiveness of an analytical procedure. This problem commonly arises when the auditor is aware of the unaudited book value for an account that is being analyzed. Unfortunately, professional standards reinforce this issue by requiring that preliminary analytical procedures be performed early in the audit, causing an auditor to fixate on the reported values.

- **Incomplete or inconsistent explanation of fluctuations:** When an auditor identifies an attribute where expectations diverge from reported outcomes, he or she should generate possible explanations for that fluctuation. Fluctuations can occur because of natural business conditions, increased risks, process breakdowns, or accounting errors. An auditor may not be aware of many of the possible conditions that could explain the fluctuation. The auditor will only investigate explanations that come to his or her attention; therefore, failure to recognize possible explanations for the fluctuation may lead the auditor to overlook the underlying problem. Furthermore, even when a potential explanation is recognized, the auditor may not realize that it only partially explains the fluctuation.

- **Poor pattern recognition:** Many performance indicators interact in predictable patterns—that is, they are correlated. Analytical procedures are most effective when the changes in different attributes are recognized as forming a pattern indicative of underlying conditions. Unfortunately, recognizing patterns in a diverse set of data is very difficult for most people.

Example

Accounting records are built on double-entry bookkeeping. Consequently, when an account has a significant discrepancy, there must be some other account that is also affected by the discrepancy; for example, improperly recording selling expenses as part of inventory results in an overstatement of inventory and an understatement of selling expense.

- **Undue reliance on management inquiry:** Auditors have a natural tendency to ask management to provide an explanation for any unusual fluctuations observed while performing analytical procedures. As discussed earlier in this chapter, client inquiry is a legitimate source of audit evidence, but the auditor must be careful not to be overly swayed by management's explanations. First, there is always the possibility that the explanation is not accurate or does not explain the entire fluctuation. The auditor should consider other possible explanations for the fluctuations, especially those that might indicate an error or problem. Second, the auditor should obtain independent corroboration of the explanation if possible.

In spite of the potential pitfalls in analytical procedures, they are extremely useful and powerful techniques for the auditor to evaluate the level of strategic and process risks present in the various areas of the audit. Familiarity with the potential pitfalls will help the auditor to perform the procedures effectively and efficiently.

INQUIRY AND ANALYSIS IN ASSESSING FRAUD RISK

One area of the audit where analysis and inquiry are particularly important is in assessing the risk of accounting fraud. Although outright fraud is a relatively rare situation for an auditor to encounter, many of the hints or clues that fraud may be a problem initially arise during analysis and inquiry. Suspicion of fraud makes an innocuous pattern of financial results appear suspicious, and innocent sounding client explanations sound furtive. An auditor must always be alert to indications of fraud and should process all evidence from analysis and inquiry with an appropriate degree of skepticism.

When performing analytical procedures, an auditor may encounter a number of circumstances that might be a prelude to fraud. Almost any unusual fluctuation in performance results could be a warning of a deeper problem. In some cases, the lack of a fluctuations may be even more important. Some examples of circumstances that might alert an auditor to a risk of fraud include

- Unexplained shortages or adjustments to asset accounts which could be indicative of theft or embezzlement
- Excessive costs of materials which could be indicative of bribes or kickbacks
- Unusually high number of debit or credit entries, which could indicate fictitious accounting entries
- Unreasonable expenses, expenditures, or reimbursements, which could indicate improper use of corporate assets or improper rebates
- Unusual relationships among expense and revenues, which could indicate manipulation of the elements of net income

Some examples of unusual account relationships that might indicate a heightened fraud risk include increased revenue when receivables, inventory, cash flows, or marketing expenses are declining; increased inventory when payables, warehousing, or employee costs are declining; increased inventory activity when unit costs of production are increasing or scrap, waste, or overhead is declining; and increased profits when revenues are stagnant or declining or costs are rising. If the auditor observes these conditions, a full explanation is needed to be sure that client personnel or management are not manipulating accounting results or otherwise behaving in a fraudulent manner.

Example

Two of the most widely documented frauds of the late 1980s could have been identified through careful analysis and inquiry. For example, the ZZZZ Best Fraud involved false insurance restoration contracts. Evidence was presented during congressional hearings that the market share data that ZZZZ Best offered to the auditors suggested that the company possessed more than 100 percent of the worldwide market for insurance restoration contracts. Further, the Lincoln Savings and Loan fraud in Arizona in the late 1980s was conducted in part by the company recording market values for land transactions well in excess of the average market values of any land transaction in the area at the time of the transactions. In both frauds, inquiries made by the auditors were met with fraudulent representations by management (and even third parties in the case of Lincoln Savings and Loan). Only with careful analysis comparing data received from the client with industry data could the auditors have been able to detect the inconsistencies in the data.

The conduct of client interviews will be affected if an auditor is suspicious of a client's actions and motivations. The auditor will probably adjust the approach to the interview including adjusting the type of questions asked, the personnel interviewed, and the degree to which statements are corroborated. The key for the auditor is to place an interviewee in a situation where manifestations of discomfort can appear. Most people will become uncomfortable if they have something to hide but are not sure what the auditor knows, what questions will be asked, and how the interview will be conducted. This makes it difficult for a person with something to hide to prepare completely for the interview. Although the auditor will want to establish rapport with the interviewee so as to foster communication, the auditor should not signal too much to the interviewee. Often, important information will be revealed because an interviewee is led to assume that the auditor knows it already and tries to explain it or put the information into a context that makes it seem innocuous.

Client personnel with something to hide will usually exhibit any of a number of verbal and non-verbal indications of discomfort. The way a person answers a question may be more revealing of a potential problem than the actual information that is provided. For example, people being less than honest with an auditor may tell less complex stories, use fewer self-references, and use more negative emotion-laden words.[5] Individuals under stress and faced with difficult questions may try to stall the interview by repeating the questions asked, making gratuitous comments about the circumstances of the interview, fawning over the interviewer or feigning interest in his family, or answering a question with a question. The interviewee may also try to bolster his or her own believability by emphasizing his or her own general honesty, implying that others will vouch for them, and denying any knowledge or involvement with questionable activity before such possibilities are raised. Furthermore, a person who is particularly uncomfortable in an interview situation may make excuses for hypothetical behavior, exhibit a selective memory about important information, pretend to be uninterested in the issues at hand, and be reluctant (or in an extreme hurry) to have an interview end.

A skilled interviewer with forensic experience can also obtain a great deal of insight from the non-verbal behavior of an interviewee. Body motions, squirming, and use of hands and arms may all provide clues about whether a person is trying to hide something during the course of an interview.[6] In the extreme, the interviewee may become agitated and, possibly, volatile. In general, an effective interview

5 Newman et al., "Lying Words: Predicting Deception from Linguistic Styles."
6 DePaulo et al., "Cues to Deception."

will keep the interviewee engaged, talking, and helpful. Creating a situation where an interviewee can shut down, justifiably disagree with the interviewer, or end the interview on his or her own terms is unlikely to be helpful to the auditor. Rather, the auditor gains most by having the interviewee speak freely and in a non-confrontational manner.

Routine questions can be used to establish a cordial framework for the discussion. Questions should not be leading in nature, where the appropriate answer is implied in the question, but should encourage open-ended responses. Sensitive questions should be transitioned to carefully, but an auditor can also use a surprise question to elicit an unguarded response. Although a general auditor will never be as skilled at forensic auditing as a fraud expert or criminal investigator, all auditors can be alert to suspicious information that is obtained through analysis and inquiry.

Example

> Staff auditors are rarely in a position to ascertain whether an interviewee is lying because interview and interrogation techniques used by forensic auditors require specialized training and experience. However, auditors should be careful to document answers based on representations by management. When answers appear inconsistent, interviewers should carefully document inconsistencies and ask interviewees to reconcile such inconsistencies—being careful not to imply that the interviewee is lying. Interviewers should also carefully note any non-verbal reactions to these requests and subsequent explanations and document them to the best of their abilities. At that point, the manager or partner of the engagement team can consider whether it makes sense to seek further advice from a forensic accountant.

There is no one indicator that has been found to be diagnostic of lying, hence the trained interviewer is looking for a pattern of behaviors and does not focus on just one behavior. Furthermore, research has shown that behaviors such as eye contact, blinking, and shrugs are not reliably diagnostic of lying. Indeed, it has been very difficult to identify classes of trained investigators that can detect deception, exceptions being well-trained and experienced members of some law enforcement agencies. Thus, relying only on inquiry, indicators of discomfort, and non-verbal behavior is unlikely to be effective in detecting fraudulent misrepresentation by a determined person. Indeed, many of the non-verbal behaviors that some investigators appear to rely on in isolation consistently lead to incorrect identification of responses as being deceptive when they are not.

STATISTICAL METHODS FOR OBTAINING ANALYTICAL EVIDENCE

An auditor has two significant problems to consider when using the judgmental analysis techniques discussed above: (1) generating an expectation about an account of interest and (2) deciding when a fluctuation from that expectation is important enough to require adjustments to risk assessments. The first problem arises because the auditor does not necessarily know what to expect about any given account or variable. Should the account increase? If so, how much should the increase be? The second problem arises because there is no good definition of what constitutes an unusual variation. Is a five percent fluctuation important? Ten percent? Statistical regression has been used in recent years to systematize the analysis, reduce these problems, and add rigor to the analytical review process.

OVERVIEW OF UNIVARIATE REGRESSION

Regression is a method of statistical analysis that facilitates the rigorous comparison of data for two or more variables. The primary logic underlying regression is that the value of one variable can be used to predict the value of another variable based on past history and a theoretically sound computational procedure. For example, weather forecasters know that when the barometric pressure changes in certain ways, rain is likely to follow. This relationship is based on observation of weather patterns over many years. Regression can be used to measure the increased likelihood of rain in terms of specific changes in barometric pressure. Such a model improves the quality of weather predictions. However, regression models, like the weather, have a random element that makes it impossible to predict future events with certainty—there is always a margin of error in regression models.

We will use regression to capture the benefit of prior knowledge about a client in a systematic manner. Regression analysis is an effective tool to use in the audit process because analytical procedures often involve comparisons of results over many variables and an extended period of time. Regression analysis is based on a theoretical, linear relationship between two variables as depicted in the following equation:

$$y_i = \alpha + \beta x_i + \varepsilon_i$$

In this equation, y_i is the variable that we wish to estimate, x_i is the variable that we can observe to assist us in developing our expectations, α and β are regression parameters which define the relationship between x_i and y_i and ε_l is a random error term which reflects that the relationship is not perfectly predictable.[7] By deriving values for α and β, we can predict the value of y_i given any value of x_i.

An example of the type of linear relationship underlying regression analysis is depicted in Figure 9–10. The straight line shows the relationship between y_i and x_i. Given the random nature of the relationship, the actual data for a given model are scattered around the line. The vertical distance between any single point and the regression line is ε_i. Regression analysis is based on a formula that determines the line that best "fits" a set of observed data.

AN APPLICATION OF REGRESSION ANALYSIS TO AUDITING

We will use the following six-step process to develop a regression model, develop expectations about an account of interest, and evaluate the results in terms of the audit.

- Identify the model to be estimated.
- Obtain the appropriate data.
- Calculate the regression model.
- Assess the quality of the regression model.
- Generate expectations for the variable of interest for the period being audited.
- Compare regression expectations to actual results.

Identify the Model to be Estimated: The first step in the process is to decide what variable the auditor is going to estimate (y_i, the dependent variable) and the

---

7 The random error in the regression equation (ε_i) is expected to have an average of zero.

Figure 9–10   Assumed Linear Relationship for Regression Models

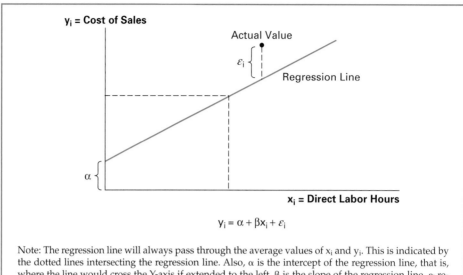

Note: The regression line will always pass through the average values of x_i and y_i. This is indicated by the dotted lines intersecting the regression line. Also, α is the intercept of the regression line, that is, where the line would cross the Y-axis if extended to the left. β is the slope of the regression line. ε_i reflects the dispersion of the scattered points from the regression line.

variable that will serve as the basis for generating our expectation (x_i, the independent variable).[8] The context in which regression is to be used is important. First, because of the difficulty of obtaining data to support the regression model, the method is best used for material accounts that have an expected relationship with another variable. Second, a model that is based on logical relationships is easier to understand and interpret. An auditor might believe that sales revenue is related to the phases of the moon, but it would be difficult to make a logical argument that such a relationship exists. Finally, the auditor must be careful to assure that the model being estimated is stable, meaning that it does not change over time. Most applications of regression require the auditor to use historical data from prior periods. If the underlying relationship between x_i and y_i has changed, expectations based on the prior relationship will not be appropriate for the current period.

To illustrate the use of regression analysis, we will look at the hypothetical relationship between cost of goods sold (y_i) and direct labor hours (x_i) in a manufacturing company because they have a predictable relationship, especially if the production process is labor intensive. Other independent variables could be tried if direct labor hours was not expected to have a relationship with cost of goods sold. Examples of other possible independent variables include raw material prices, quantity of raw material, or hours of machine time used in production.

Obtain the appropriate data: Once the auditor has decided what variables to include in the model, the next step is to obtain adequate data on which to base the

8 Regression analysis can be applied in situations where there is more than one independent variable. That is, the dependent variable of interest may be related to a number of independent variables that could be included in the regression model if adequate data is available. A regression model with more than one independent variable is called a multivariate model. The underlying computations and checks for assumption appropriateness for multivariate models are more complex than the univariate model we use in this book, but the process and interpretation of the results are essentially the same.

Figure 9–11 Data Used to Estimate Regression Model Used in a Preliminary Analytical Procedure

Month	Cost of Sales (Y) (in 000's)	Direct Labor Hours (X) (in 000's)
20x6:		
January	160.31	9.99
February	156.59	8.71
March	170.73	10.54
April	161.33	9.57
May	155.27	8.25
June	145.44	7.18
July	156.95	8.28
August	139.37	6.15
September	130.84	5.73
October	189.88	11.53
November	183.29	11.23
December	162.07	9.38
20x7:		
January	153.52	8.64
February	150.77	8.56
March	178.27	8.93
April	190.25	10.28
May	167.71	7.21
June	181.63	7.06
July	173.46	8.11
August	195.08	11.18
September	169.63	7.22
October	151.87	6.13
November	142.84	5.51
December	183.66	10.97

estimates of α and β. We will denote our estimate of α as a and β as b. The more data that is available, the more robust will be the model's predictions (meaning, there will be smaller margin for error). The data for our example is presented in Figure 9–11. We will base our estimate of the regression model on data from the 24 months that precede our audit period (20x6 and 20x7). A sample size of 24 data points is the minimum that should be used to estimate a regression model. In many industries, data are collected on a daily or weekly basis, thus allowing a larger sample on which to base the model, which will increase its reliability. Shortly, we will use the results of our analysis to form an expectation about the level of costs of goods sold for the months in the period under audit (20x8). It is important to base the estimates of α and β on data from the period prior to the audit because we want to be able to use the estimated model to *independently* test the current-year results.

The quality of the data used in the estimation model will have a direct impact on the quality of the expectations developed from the model. The input data should be reliable and, ideally, would have been audited in a prior period. The user must be careful not to select data that is inappropriate for the model. Very old data may have been generated when production processes were significantly

Figure 9–12   Excel Output of Regression Results for Cost of Sales Regressed on Direct
Labor Hours

Correlation Coefficient (r)	0.747
Variance Explained (r^2)	0.558
Standard Error (S)	11.776
Observations (n)	24.000

	df	SS	MS	F	P-Value
Regression	1.000	3853.805	3853.805	27.789	0.001
Residual	22.000	3050.971	138.681		
Total	23.000	6904.776			

		Coefficients	Standard Error	t Stat	P-value
Intercept	a	103.611	11.819	8.766	0.001
Direct Labor Hours	b	7.096	1.346	5.272	0.001

different and may not be appropriate for the current model. Also, data from multiple factories or locations, even if from the same time period, may not be appropriate if the separate locations have different production processes.

Calculate the regression model: Software is generally available to perform the computations needed to derive a regression model. Simple spreadsheet packages like Microsoft Excel include a data analysis package that supports various statistical techniques including linear regression. An example of the output from regression software is depicted in Figure 9–12. The first issue related to the regression results is whether the expected relationship between x_i and y_i actually exists. The analysis is not of much use if this relationship is not statistically significant as measured by the value and significance level of the F-statistic reported in Figure 9–12. In our example, the F-value of 27.789 can only occur in less than one in a thousand chances (as indicated by a p-value less than 0.001). Furthermore, both a and b are significant in the model, with p-values less than 0.001.

Assess the quality of the regression model: Next, the auditor should assess how well the model explains the variation in the historical data. There are four primary measures of the quality of the model. Such measures are often referred to as *goodness-of-fit tests* because they measure how well the linear model represents the underlying data.

- **Coefficient of correlation (r):** The higher the value of *r*, the better the model captures the relationship between x_i and y_i. There is no absolute threshold for evaluating *r*. A reasonable rule of thumb is that a value of *r* in excess of 0.50 is an acceptable model on which to develop expectations about y_i. Values of *r* in excess of 0.90 are considered to be excellent. In our example, the *r*-value of 0.747 is acceptable.

- **Variation explained (r^2):** An alternative way to look at the goodness of fit is to consider r^2 (often referred to as "r squared") as a measure of the amount of variation in the linear regression that is captured by the model. In our example, 55.8 percent of the variation in the data is explained by the relationship between cost of goods sold and direct labor hours. Again, this appears to be acceptable.

- **Standard error (S):** Standardized errors are useful for measuring the dispersion of the actual results around the predicted values. The smaller these values, the better the model fits the data. A large standard error indicates that the data naturally varies over a very wide range, and may mean that the model will have limited use for making predictions; that is, the margin of error will be large. The standard error in our example is 11.776.
- **Standard error of the estimate (S'):** S' is calculated by dividing S by the square root of the number of observations. In our example, $S' = 11.776$ is divided by the square root of 24, which yields 2.41. One way to judge whether S' is small enough to be useful is to compare it to materiality for the account being examined. If S' is no more than half of materiality, the regression model is probably adequate for audit testing purposes. If S' is larger than half of materiality, then the model could identify random errors that would appear to be significant to the auditor but which are simply random deviations inherent in the model, in which case, the model will not be able to distinguish between possible accounting misstatements and random deviations.

Generate expectations for the dependent variable: Given that the regression model fits the data well enough, the values of a and b can then be used to generate expectations of y_i for the audit period as long as we know the corresponding values of x_i. The equation used to estimate current year values for costs of goods sold based on the results reported in Figure 9–12 is

Cost of Sales = 103.61 + 7.096 (Direct Labor Hours)

The expectations generated from this equation are presented in Figure 9–13, Column (3) "Projected Costs." Care must be exercised to limit expectations from the model to the general range of values that are present in the estimation period. For example, the most extreme values for x_i during the estimation period are 5.51 and 11.53. Expectations will be most accurate as long as the values of x_i stay within or close to that range. Using a value of 100 for x_i would probably

Figure 9–13 Results of Regression Predictions

20x9 Month	(1) Cost of Sales(Y) (in 000's)	(2) Direct Labor Hours (X) (in 000's)	(3) Projected Cost (Y') (in 000's)	(4) = (1) − (3) Residual (in 000's)	(5) = (4)/S' Standardized Deviation
January	206.61	14.05	203.33	3.28	1.36
February	152.61	7.02	153.41	(0.80)	(0.33)
March	167.50	8.84	166.33	1.17	0.49
April	145.68	5.62	143.47	2.21	0.92
May	153.23	6.92	152.70	0.53	0.22
June	153.80	6.78	151.71	2.09	0.87
July	158.41	7.51	156.89	1.52	0.63
August	194.73	12.89	195.09	(0.36)	(0.15)
September	202.83	13.99	202.90	(0.07)	(0.03)
October	191.82	12.09	189.41	2.41	1.00
November	186.57	9.58	171.59	14.98	6.22
December	215.66	15.75	215.40	0.26	0.11

lead to a meaningless prediction since that level of labor has not been previously observed.

Compare regression expectations to actual results: The expectations of the regression model will rarely, if ever, come out exactly equal to the observed values for y_i. The difference between predicted and actual values should be computed and inspected for any unusual results that the auditor might wish to investigate. In the example, all but one of the residuals fall below 3.28 (see column (4), "Residual"). The November residual is rather large at 14.98; hence, it seems so unusual that it heightens the inherent risk of the account, and requires further investigation. At this point, the auditor can take advantage of the regression results to make statements about the likelihood that residuals are the result of random errors (as embodied in ε) or are possible misstatements. Before doing this, it is important to understand that regression analysis is based on the assumption that random errors (ε) are *normally distributed* (the so-called bell shaped curve) with a mean of zero and constant variance, which we can infer from the data. Furthermore, auditors should assume that the error terms across time are uncorrelated, meaning that the value of ε in one month does not influence the value in another month.

We start by "standardizing" the residuals by dividing each by S'. By dividing S' into the residuals based on our current year data, we get a number called the standardized deviation. We know from basic probability theory that approximately 95 percent of the random deviations will fall within about two standard deviations of zero.[9] At 95 percent probability, cost of goods sold can have standardized deviations that range as high as 2.0 just by random chance, without the account having any misstatements or other problems. Similarly, 80 percent of the random deviations will fall within about 1.3 standard deviations of zero. The last column reports the standardized deviation from zero for each of our predictions. Only November has a standardized deviation in excess of 2.00.

The result for November may be explained by unusual circumstances. For example, a labor strike or extreme weather conditions may have affected operations, causing cost of goods sold to be much higher than would have been expected given the observed level of direct labor hours. Another possibility is that the company has made an error in the accounting records in that month that is disrupting the expected relationship captured in the regression model. At this point, the auditor will need to decide what to do to follow up on the unexplained deviation. Until the deviation is adequately explained, residual risk is considered significant and the auditor should consider increasing risk assessments for assertions related to the cost of goods sold. The auditor may obtain additional evidence for cost of goods sold in November to be sure that the deviation is not the result of an error. The regression model provides a powerful signal of unusual conditions, but ultimately, it is up to the auditor to investigate and resolve the uncertainty of the conditions.

---

9 The number of standard deviations is called a *t-statistic*, and its value depends on the size of the sample used to estimate the regression model. If the sample is very large, then the distribution of random deviations will approximate the *normal distribution*, in which case 95 percent of the random deviations will fall within 1.96 standard deviations of zero. The smaller the sample, the larger the t-value becomes. For our sample of 24, 95 percent of the random deviations will fall within 2.074 standard deviations of zero. If the sample size was only 12, the corresponding t-value would be 2.228. Standardized tables exist that provide the t-statistic for any sample size and for any probability level.

CONSIDERATION OF KEY ASSUMPTIONS

The previous discussion illustrated how regression analysis can be used to facilitate audit planning by signaling conditions that may not be consistent with the auditor's expectations as captured in a regression model. However, the auditor must be aware of the potential problems that can arise when using regression:

- **Too few data points:** The size of the standard error is a direct function of the sample size (n) used to estimate a and b. If there are too few observations, S and S' may be too large to allow for accurate predictions. Also, this may result in a small value for r and a corresponding lower value for r^2, which does not seem to happen in this case even though we have a relatively small number of observations (24).

- **Non-normal error term:** The interpretation of the standardized deviations in Figure 9–13 is based on the assumption that ε is normally distributed. If this is not the case, then the results could be biased. Regression software generally tests for this potential problem and provides a warning message if the normality assumption is violated. There are numerous techniques for fixing this problem if necessary. Normally, this would involve a consultation with a specialist in the firm trained in statistics.

- **Nonconstant variance:** Regression analysis assumes that the variables in the sample have constant variance over the period of estimation. Violation of this assumption will lead to biased results. Regression software generally tests for this potential problem, and there are numerous techniques for fixing this problem. Again, this problem would lead the auditor to consult with a specialist in statistics. As a first test, we examine the plotted predicted versus actual data (see Figure 9–14).

- **Autocorrelation:** This problem occurs when ε has a drift or pattern that emerges over time. For example, ε may tend to grow, in which case the error terms are not considered to be independent. This is a difficult problem to deal with and will definitely require consultation with an expert statistician.

Regression analysis can be a powerful tool for the auditor to gather evidence and assist in assessing risks. However, regression should only be used when it is

Figure 9–14 Linearity and Nonconstant Variance Assumption Tested

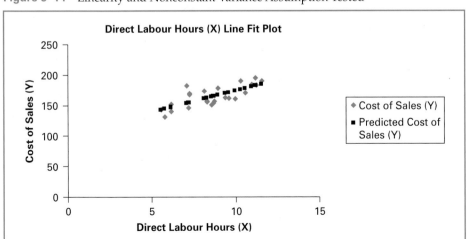

appropriate and the auditor must be careful that the underlying assumptions are not violated. If used properly, however, the analysis of the residuals or the standardized deviations can improve the effectiveness and efficiency of the audit.

SUMMARY AND CONCLUSION

Inquiry and analysis are common audit procedures that are used throughout the audit. In this chapter, we introduced systematic approaches for obtaining both inquiry and analysis evidence. Although relatively common and easy to perform, inquiry and analysis procedures often require additional corroboration in order to be useful as meaningful audit evidence. This chapter discussed how auditors can improve the quality of inquiry and analysis evidence during the course of the audit. In either case, the quality of the evidence obtained from a client depends on the experience and expertise of the auditor conducting the inquiry or analysis. The strength of such evidence can be improved in conjunction with thorough strategic and process analysis during the early stages of the audit. However, auditors must always be aware of the possibility that inquiry and analysis may produce confusing, incomplete, or misleading evidence and maintain appropriate professional skepticism whenever they conduct such audit procedures.

BIBLIOGRAPHY OF RELATED PROFESSIONAL LITERATURE

Research

Anderson, U., K. Kadous, and L. Koonce. 2004. The Role of Incentives to Manage Earnings and Quantification in Auditors' Evaluations of Management-Provided Information. *Auditing: A Journal of Practice & Theory.* 23(1): 11–28.

Ballou, B. and D. Heitger. 2005. A Cognitive Characterization of Audit Analytical Procedures under Strategic-Systems Auditing. *Journal of Theoretical Accounting Research.* 1(Fall): 1–37.

Beasley, M. S., J. V. Carcello, D. R. Hermanson, and P. D. Lapides. 2000. Fraudulent financial reporting: Consideration of industry traits and corporate governance mechanism. *Accounting Horizons* 14(4): 441–454.

Cohen, J. R., G. Krishnamoorthy, and A. M. Wright. 2000. Evidence on the Effect of Financial and Nonfinancial Trends on Analytical Review. *Auditing: A Journal of Practice & Theory.* 19(1): 27–48.

DePaulo, B. M., J. J. Lindsay, B. E. Malone, L. Muhlenbruck, K. Charlton, and H. Cooper, 2003. Cues to Deception. *Psychological Bulletin.* 129(1), 74–118.

Glover, S. M., J. Jiambalvo, and J. Kennedy. 2000. Analytical Procedures and Audit-Planning Decisions. *Auditing: A Journal of Practice & Theory.* 19(2): 27–46.

Green, W. and K. T. Trotman. 2003. An Examination of Different Performance Outcomes in an Analytical Procedures Task. *Auditing: A Journal of Practice & Theory.* 22(2): 219–238.

Hirst, E. and L. Koonce. 1996. Audit Analytical Procedures: A Field Investigation. *Contemporary Accounting Research.* 13(2): 457–487.

Knapp, C. A. and M. C. Knapp. 2001. The Effects of Experience and Explicit Fraud Risk Assessment in Detecting Fraud with Analytical Procedures. *Accounting Organizations and Society.* 26(1): 25–37.

Leitch, R. A. and Y. Chen. 2003. The Effectiveness of Expectation Models in Recognizing Error Patterns and Generating and Eliminating Hypotheses While Conducting Analytical Procedures. *Auditing: A Journal of Practice & Theory.* 22(2): 147–170.

Newman, M. L., J. W. Pennebaker, D. S. Berry, and J. M. Richards. 2004. Lying Words: Predicting Deception from Linguistic Styles. *Personality and Social Psychology Bulletin.* 29(5): 665–675.

Wilks, T. J. and M. F. Zimbelman. 2004. Using Game Theory and Strategic Reasoning Concepts to Prevent and Detect Fraud. *Accounting Horizons* 18(3): 139–153.

Professional Reports and Guidance

CICA Research Report. 2000. *Audit Inquiry: Seeking More Reliable Evidence from Audit Inquiry.* Canadian Institute of Chartered Accountants.

Auditing Standards

AICPA *Statements on Auditing Standard (SAS)* No. 56, "Analytical Procedures."

AICPA *Statements on Auditing Standard (SAS)* No. 106, "Audit Evidence."

IAASB *International Standards on Auditing (ISA)* No. 500, "Audit Evidence."

IAASB *International Standards on Auditing (ISA)* No. 520, "Analytical Procedures."

QUESTIONS

1. Why do you believe that auditors traditionally have been required to perform preliminary analytical procedures? What role does these procedures help achieve in the risk assessment process?

2. Inquiry has long been considered one of the most controversial forms of audit evidence. Describe the strengths for the audit if an auditor effectively utilizes inquiry as a key source of audit evidence. Also, describe the weaknesses associated with that strategy and discuss how an auditor can overcome such weaknesses.

3. Three considerations provided in the chapter when conducting inquiries include
   • Being clear to the interviewer and the interviewee as to what is to be discussed
   • Staying on topic unless follow-up is needed or important tangential issues arise in the conversation
   • Respecting the interviewee's time

   Discuss why these considerations are important elements for an inquiry strategy. As part of your answer, describe potential consequences of not effectively adhering to these considerations.

4. The chapter discusses the need to compare and contrast answers to inquires made across different aspects of the audit (e.g., this discussion can occur during engagement brainstorming sessions). For example, why might operations personnel provide different answers than accounting personnel to questions about factors contributing to increases in gross margin? How can an auditor reconcile different answers to reach appropriate conclusions?

5. Consider each of the basic judgmental methods for obtaining analytical evidence:
   • Comparative financial statement analysis
   • Common-size financial statement analysis
   • Ratio analysis

   Describe strengths of using these methods for gathering analytical methods and the limitations associated with using them instead of more advanced methods.

6. Describe the strengths and weaknesses associated with using nonfinancial performance measures. How can auditors ensure that they are properly utilizing nonfinancial

performance measures as analytical evidence? As part of you answer, illustrate your suggestion using an example nonfinancial measure (e.g., time-to-market for a new product, customer satisfaction measures).

7. Use the systematic process for conducting analytical procedures provided in Figure 9–8 to design an approach for developing an expectation for the commissions expense account for an electronics retailer that pays its employees based in part on pre-established commission rates.

8. Developing expectations independent of the client is critical for effective use of analytical evidence. Figure 9–9 presents a process for evaluating analytical evidence. Examine the figure and apply it to an example situation in which an auditor develops an expectation that the allowance for uncollectible accounts should be approximately 4 percent of the ending balance of gross accounts receivable. Suppose that the recorded allowance for uncollectible accounts is actually 2 percent. What types of information could the auditor gather that might enable his or her expectation to be adjusted to re-evaluate whether the 2 percent allowance is reasonable?

9. Regression can help the auditor develop fairly precise expectations for financial reporting. However, auditors should use regression carefully. For example, consider the following scenario:

> The relationship depicted in the model is not valid; rather, the relationship in the model exists because a third variable not depicted in the model is driving the regression coefficient.

What impact would this result have on the auditor's use of regression in developing financial statement expectations? How can auditors reduce the likelihood that this scenario is present?

10. When using regression, interpreting the output is very important for carefully using the results as analytical evidence. Discuss each of the following regression terms and describe how they can be used to evaluate regression results as analytical evidence for the auditor:
   - Correlation coefficient
   - Variance explained (r-squared)
   - P-value of a statistical result (e.g., F, t-statistic)

11. What aspects should be taken into account when planning client inquiries? How can evidence collected by means of inquiry be supplemented with other types of evidence? Give examples.

12. One of the techniques that auditors can use when obtaining analytical evidence is ratio analysis across a number of categories. Describe these categories and provide examples of ratios in each category.

13. Analytical review evidence is required during two stages of the audit and allowable in another. Identify all three stages and describe how the use of analysis differs among these stages?

14. Although analysis can be a very helpful tool for the auditor in identifying risks, there are a number of common mistakes made when performing these procedures. Describe the most common mistakes and provide an example of each.

PROBLEMS

1. Assume that as an audit manager of a large multinational manufacturer of athletic apparel (e.g., Adidas, Nike, Reebok), you perform high-level preliminary analytical procedures on the unaudited financial statements at the beginning of the audit engagement and discover the following fluctuations:

a. Inventory turnover increased from 2.5 times to 3.75 times.
b. Depreciation expense has been about 2 percent of total assets for several years. This year it was only 1 percent of total assets.
c. Interest expense has been about 6 percent of total debt; this year it was 8 percent.
d. The quick ratio has decreased from 1.45 to 0.95.
e. Average days payable decreased from 35 days to 29 days.
f. Average days receivable increased from 28 days to 35 days.
g. Return on assets increased from 2.5 percent to 4 percent.

Assuming that each of these is considered material to the audit risk assessment, generate two hypotheses that might explain each change in the client's ratios: one that suggests a normal consequence of business; and one that would suggest increased audit risk.

2. For each of the items in Problem 1 above, discuss what procedure you would follow to investigate whether the change in the ratio resulted from the normal business event you hypothesized. What other ratios may give you some clues to aid your investigation?

3. Consider the following comparative balance sheet and income statement for HOC Enterprises, a Canadian wholesaler of automotive parts.

	Balance Sheet HOC Enterprises (000's omitted)	
	Audited 12-31-06	Unaudited 12-31-07
Cash	$ 8,000	$7,000
Accounts Receivable (net)	18,000	21,000
Inventory	111,000	130,000
Other Current Assets	11,000	17,000
Total Current Assets	$148,000	$175,000
Land	$ 50,000	$ 50,000
Building and Equipment	65,000	92,000
Accumulated Depreciation	(10,000)	(12,000)
Total Assets	$253,000	$305,000
Accounts Payable	$ 37,000	$85,000
Total Current Liabilities	37,000	85,000
Long-Term Debt	10,000	11,000
Total Liabilities	47,000	96,000
Contributed Capital	189,000	189,000
Retained Earnings	17,000	20,000
Total Liabilities and Owner's Equity	$253,000	$305,000

	Income Statement HOC Enterprises (000's omitted)	
Sales	$98,000	$112,000
Cost of Goods Sold	24,000	37,000
Gross Profit	$74,000	$ 75,000
SG&A Expenses	$69,000	$ 70,000
Interest Expense	1,000	1,500
Net Income	$ 4,000	$ 3,500

Required

a. Using the above data, "common-size" the income statement and balance sheet. (You may find a spreadsheet software package helpful.)

b. Generate some ratios you may find useful in identifying audit risk for this company.

c. Comment on the result of your analyses. What specific cycles do you think will require more audit effort? Are there any areas where you can probably reduce your risk assessment?

4. The results of the preliminary analytical review for Monk, Inc. include the following:

	12-31-06	12-31-07
Days receivables outstanding	31.4	32.2
Inventory turnover	2.7X	2.5X
Depreciation expense (as a % of fixed assets)	12%	13%

The ratios have not changed significantly over the past year. Does this finding suggest that risk in these areas is assumed to be lower than if the ratios had changed dramatically? Give an example for each ratio where its lack of change would be cause for concern.

5. Market value ratios, such as the market-to-book ratio or dividend payout ratio, are helpful to the auditor in assessing risk for an engagement. For example, assume that you are the partner in charge of the audit of Clary Co., a publicly traded cable television company serving several medium-sized cities in the United States. The senior management of Clary Co. is well respected in the industry and your audit firm has enjoyed a good relationship with management in that few conflicts have arisen over misstatements and those that have were quickly resolved to your satisfaction. However, with the latest deregulation moves by the U.S. government and the ensuing volatility in the telecommunications industry, Clary's position in this formerly stodgy marketplace is not clear.

Your audit staff hands you the following market value ratios on Clary Co. using the most recent audited financial statements and up-to-date market information:

Price-earnings ratio	8.40
Market-to-book ratio	1.45

a. What steps should you take to determine whether these ratios have any implications for the audit?

b. Assuming that the ratios indicate that the capital markets are undervaluing Clary's stock, what implications does that fact have for your audit of Clary Co.?

6. Describe the effect of adding debt to a company's balance sheet has on the company's ROA versus its ROE. Specifically, why does ROE vary more widely for any given change in performance when the company acquires more debt? (Hint: Use as an example an all-equity firm with total assets of $100,000 and net income of $10,000 compared to a 50 percent equity-financed firm with the same income and a 5 percent cost of debt. Then do the same analysis with a $2,000 net income. Ignore taxes.)

7. You are planning the audit of Ruta Corp., a privately held publisher of comic books. Step 1 of the preliminary analytical procedures requires you to gather as many facts as possible on the company's activities in the past year that may affect the financial statements. Among those facts are the following:

a. The company has switched to a "just-in-time" inventory system whereby input factors, such as pulp paper and ink, are ordered so that they arrive just before they are needed in the production process.

b. The company recently sold its old fleet of delivery trucks and now uses contracted carriers.

c. In an attempt to increase sales and spread its distribution, the company loosened credit terms.

d.   The company refinanced its mortgage on the factory in such a way that, although its interest rate is lower, it had to pay the bank a large up-front fee.

e.   Negotiations with the printers' union left the company agreeing to higher pension benefits.

f.   Although the company has used the double-declining-balance method for depreciation, it changed to the straight-line method for many of its fixed assets this year to mirror its tax depreciation method. (The relevant tax authority allows a switch to straight-line depreciation when doing so increases depreciation expense over accelerated methods.)

g.   The company acquired a small rival for cash in a purchase combination.

h.   Its marketing department has been successful at introducing a higher-end, higher-margin product designed to appeal to aging baby boomers and collectors.

For each of the above, discuss the accounts and ratios that you expect will be affected in your preliminary analytical procedures. Include the direction and probable magnitude of the change (if any) and remember the effect on the overall profitability ratios. Then comment briefly on your ability to draw any firm conclusions from the analytical procedures given these facts.

8.   Once you have completed the preliminary analytical review stage of the audit, you will next determine the implications for audit planning from the risks identified in the analysis. Suppose you are the audit manager for McNulty Co., a large New Zealand canner of fruit and nuts sold through grocery stores. The preliminary analytical procedures reveal the following items that peak your interest:

Account/Area	Problem and Associated Impact on Account in Question or Other Accounts	Management Assertion at Risk of Misstatement
(a) Long-Term Debt	Interest expense as a percentage of long-term debt decreased	
(b) Operating Margins	Sales returns as a percentage of gross sales has decreased	
(c) Fixed Assets	Net account balances steady despite closing some unprofitable operations	
(d) Revenue Recognition	Large increase in accounts receivable at end of year	
(e) Accruals	Prepaid assets as a percentage of total assets decreases	
(f) Deferred taxes	Liability remained steady despite taking on some new long-term assets	
(g) Inventory	Inventory turnover has decreased	
(h) Accounts Receivable	Days receivable has increased	

For each of the items above, describe the accounts and management assertions that are at increased risk.

9. Examine the following data from the preliminary analytical procedures for Hammer-Head Company, a Canadian tool manufacturer, that relates manufacturing costs of a socket wrench to units manufactured.

Month	Production Costs (in thousands of dollars)	Units Manufactured (in thousands)
January 2006	$114	20
February	921	196
March	560	115
April	245	50
May	575	122
June	475	100
July	138	33
August	727	154
September	375	80
October	670	147
November	828	182
December	762	160

Required

a. Estimate a univariate regression where units of production predict production costs. (Hint: An electronic spreadsheet can calculate the model parameters and will report many of the following values.)

b. Calculate the coefficient of correlation. How well does units manufactured predict manufacturing costs?

c. Calculate a prediction for January 2007's production costs if production was 75,000 wrenches. If the actual production costs were $375,000, would you attribute it to error or to randomness in the process?

d. Interpret the "slope" and "intercept" term of the regression. Do they represent "variable" and "fixed" costs, respectively? Why or why not?

10. Below you will find the financial statements for nine companies in different industries. Match each financial statement to the corresponding company:

1. Clothing Retailer   4. Commercial Bank 7. Computer Manufacturer
2. Electric Utility   5. Grocery Retailer 8. Pharmaceutical Manufacturer
3. Machinery Manufacturer   6. Liquor Distiller 9. Specialty Paper Manufacturer

Balance Sheet, End of Year	A	B	C	D	E	F	G	H	I
Assets									
Cash & Marketable Sec.	323.1%	5.3%	9.6%	0.1%	1.9%	0.2%	0.5%	4.1%	16.7%
Current Receivables	734.3%	16.5%	25.5%	1.5%	8.5%	7.0%	11.7%	14.6%	21.9%
Inventories	4.4%	28.0%	11.6%	13.1%	13.8%	5.9%	11.6%	22.7%	11.2%
Property, Plant, & Equipment									
Cost	15.1%	35.5%	55.2%	16.1%	90.9%	214.5%	26.4%	62.2%	53.2%
Accumulated Depreciation	0.0%	15.2%	29.5%	6.1%	26.6%	65.5%	12.7%	31.4%	20.1%
Net	15.1%	19.3%	25.7%	16.1%	64.3%	149.0%	26.4%	30.5%	33.1%
Other Assets	53.0%	26.6%	8.4%	0.1%	48.5%	44.8%	4.2%	6.5%	4.8%
Total Assets	1129.9%	94.7%	81.1%	30.9%	137.0%	208.0%	54.4%	78.7%	87.7%
Liabilities & Equities									
Current Liabilities	1019.6%	17.0%	36.7%	10.7%	15.5%	30.7%	8.3%	14.7%	51.0%
Long-Term Debt	17.2%	9.1%	0.3%	3.8%	38.5%	57.7%	11.4%	18.3%	5.4%
Other Noncurrent Liabilities	N/A	10.3%	8.7%	3.6%	26.6%	40.2%	4.9%	7.4%	15.5%
Owners Equity	93.1%	58.3%	35.4%	12.8%	56.5%	79.4%	29.9%	38.3%	16.9%
Total Liabilities & Equities	1129.9%	94.7%	81.1%	30.9%	137.0%	208.0%	54.4%	78.7%	87.7%
Income Statement for Year									
Revenue	100.0%	100.0%	100.0%	100.0%	100.0%	100.0%	100.0%	100.0%	100.0%
Cost of Revenue (w/o Depn)	31.2%	41.0%	46.8%	79.3%	71.5%	39.9%	69.4%	77.0%	32.0%
Depreciation	1.9%	3.0%	5.6%	1.6%	6.4%	9.0%	3.5%	4.1%	3.2%
Interest Expense	6.4%	1.1%	0.3%	0.5%	3.7%	5.2%	1.0%	2.4%	3.4%
SG&A	44.7%	40.5%	44.0%	13.3%	16.8%	36.8%	19.3%	11.9%	42.3%
R&D	0.0%	0.0%	11.9%	0.0%	1.0%	0.0%	0.0%	0.9%	9.2%
Income Taxes	4.3%	6.1%	0.7%	2.1%	1.2%	2.9%	4.1%	1.8%	7.0%
All Other Items (net)	-1.4%	-3.2%	-4.8%	0.0%	-2.3%	-2.4%	-3.7%	-0.5%	-1.0%
Total Expenses	87.1%	88.4%	104.4%	96.8%	96.3%	91.3%	93.6%	97.6%	96.1%
Net Income	12.9%	11.6%	-4.4%	3.2%	1.7%	8.7%	6.4%	2.4%	3.9%

Case 9–1: Stripenburn Construction Company

Stripenburn Construction Company is a new audit client of your firm. They have never been audited but did have another accountant perform a "review" of their financial statements as of December 31, 2005 and before. You will be auditing the December 31, 2006 financial statements. Stripenburn primarily constructs apartment and condominium complexes in South Florida. The company had four projects in progress during 2006. Three had also been in progress in 2005 and two are complete by the end of 2006. The company is considered to be a highly successful construction company that is in high demand among developers who are involved in multi-unit projects.

The company is privately owned by the Stripen family. The president, vice president, secretary/treasurer, and three project managers are all family members. Also, the chief architect, the controller, and the equipment manager are all related to the family by marriage. All management employees who must travel to job sites (including the nine family members mentioned above) are assigned company-owned cars for their personal use. The company has a total of 80 company cars. Employees have access to these cars at all times, and the cars are not expected to be returned to the company parking yard except for periodic servicing. The company also owns a number of vans and trucks that are used by various company employees to transport equipment, supplies, labor, and materials to and from job sites. These vehicles are stored at the company facilities when not in use and are never available for personal use. Finally, the company has a number of special-use heavy vehicles that are used at job sites and stored at the job site or in the parking yard of the company.

As part of the 2006 audit, you have been assigned the task of auditing fuel expense. The balance of fuel expense according to the general ledger is $317,224. According to the client, last year's balance was $375,542. After you complete your testing of fuel expense, the total will be allocated between different construction projects as direct production costs or will be recorded as selling, general, and administrative expense.

At this point, your supervisor has not told you how to go about testing this balance, and she will not be available for guidance until late in the day. You need to get started, and you think that she would like you to use some form of analytical procedure, if possible. By checking certain company records and asking management and motor pool personnel, Jane Nohelp has gathered the following information for you:

Type of Vehicle	No.	Fuel Usage	Miles or Usage
Small autos	60	20 mpg	21,000/each
Large autos	20	10 mpg	25,000/each
Pickup trucks	45	8 mpg	19,000/each
Vans	35	7 mpg	9,500/each
Flatbed trucks	6	4 mpg	6,500/each
Dump trucks	5	3 mpg	7,300/each
Loaders	3	3 gal/hr	Unknown**
Bulldozers	4	6 gal/hr	Unknown**
Graders	2	5 gal/hr	69 person-days*
Scrapers	1	6 gal/hr	80 person-days*

Other information:

* 1 person-day equals 8 hours

** According to the construction foreman, these generally are in continual usage every day a job is in progress. The company has been extremely busy and has a backlog of jobs but does not have its crews work overtime or weekends.

Jane has also determined that the autos and pickup trucks run on gas and the larger trucks and equipment use diesel. The price of gasoline has been relatively stable during 2006 and averaged $3.05/gallon. The price of diesel has gone up significantly during the year and you determine the following typical prices:

1/1/06	$2.90
3/1/06	2.94
6/1/06	2.99
11/1/06	3.05

Requirements

1. What management assertions are relevant to the audit of fuel expense?
2. How would you test fuel expense if you were not able to use analytical procedures?
3. Using the information provided, develop an estimate of what you think fuel expense should be for 2006.
4. Compare your estimate of fuel expense to the recorded balance. What do you conclude? What would you do now?
5. What other information would you like to have available to refine the accuracy of your analytical procedure? Explain.
6. Suggest some reasons why your analytical procedure might produce a result that was significantly different than the recorded value for the account. How would you determine if any of those explanations were applicable to the current situation?
7. How do you think Jane obtained the various items of information that you used for your estimate? What types of tests should you perform to verify this data?
8. How would you test the allocation of fuel expense to various accounts (e.g., construction in progress, administrative expense, or other accounts)?

Case 9–2: The Cleaning Company

Audit Senior Information

As a newly promoted audit senior, you are assigned to evaluate the control environment as a basis for planning your audit. Your goal is to obtain an "Understanding of Control Environment and Control Systems" via your upcoming interview with one of the company owners. As this is a new client, the partner's description of the company is rather vague, and, of course, there is no file from last year to rely on.

Partner's Description of The Cleaning Company

- The Cleaning Company has been in business for five years.
- The company provides industrial and domestic carpet steam-cleaning services.
- The Cleaning Company is a new client for your firm that has been required by its bank to have an audit for the first time as a requirement of it being able to continue its line of credit. The Company has never been audited before, as the bank considered a monthly listing of accounts receivable to be sufficient. As the loan grew larger, the bank decided it wanted audited financial statements.
- The company's gross revenue is $1,650,000.
- The company is owned by two brothers, Doug and Dave Dosio. The board of directors is composed of the brothers and their spouses.
- The company is run with low overhead, has a lot of part-time help, and employee turnover is probably high given the partner's experience with other cleaning companies.
- The company's office manager, Joe Knight, acts as the accountant in his spare time supplemented by a part-time staff of several university students who are majoring in accounting.
- There is a rudimentary computerized accounting system that CC is considering replacing. The partner hopes that you can convince Doug to buy the software system and support services from your firm's related computer consulting company.
- The time budget will be tight on this job as the owners are extremely price sensitive. Essentially, there is no money in the budget for more senior staff involvement except at the review stage. You get the strong impression you are on your own with junior staff on this engagement.

Requirements

1. Your task is to prepare for the interview with Doug Dosio to gain an understanding of his business sufficient to plan the audit. Please compile a series of

Source: Adapted from "Steam-Vac, Inc." in Ronald E. Marden, Sandra L. Schneider, Gary L. Holstrum, "Instructional Case: Using Professional Judgment in Control Environment Evaluation," Issues in Accounting Education. May 1996, pp. 419–431. Copyright the American Accounting Association, Sarasota, FL. Reprinted by permission. Full text of articles is available online at http://aaahq.org/pubs/electpubs.htm. This case has been prepared as the basis for class discussion only. It is not intended to be illustrative of either effective or ineffective handling of an administrative situation.

questions that allows you to cover this matter in the minimum possible time but with the maximum reliability of information.

2. After the 20 minutes preparation time you will interview Doug Dosio, Company co-owner. As Doug is very busy, you will have a maximum interview time of 20 minutes. (Calls for a role play by instructor or classmate—your instructor has a briefing memo in the solutions manual.)

3. Once the interview is completed, you have 20 minutes to complete your memo to the file summarizing your understanding of the client's business and to consider your preliminary assessments of the strength of the control environment. You must also document a "To Do" list for yourself to indicate what other steps you need to take in order to ensure that your control environment assessment is accurate and complete.

Case 9–3: UDUB Limited

UDUB Limited is a small, privately held manufacturing client for which your firm has provided financial statement audits during the last two years (i.e., 2005 and 2006). You are an audit senior about to begin planning-stage analytical procedures for the year ending December 31, 2007.

For this relatively small audit, audit planning involves a plant visit one month subsequent to year end. Before visiting UDUB's headquarters, you received the financial statements illustrated in Exhibits 3–1 and 3–2 and the production information listed in Exhibit 3–3.

Exhibit 3–1

<table>
<tr><td colspan="3" align="center">UDUB Limited
Comparative Balance Sheets
as of December 31, 2007 and 2006</td></tr>
<tr><td colspan="3" align="center">Assets</td></tr>
<tr><td></td><td align="center">*2007*</td><td align="center">*2006*</td></tr>
<tr><td>Current Assets:</td><td></td><td></td></tr>
<tr><td>Cash</td><td>$ 5,000</td><td>$ 5,000</td></tr>
<tr><td>Accounts Receivable (gross)</td><td>430,000</td><td>379,000</td></tr>
<tr><td>Less Allowance for Uncollectibles</td><td>10,000</td><td>9,000</td></tr>
<tr><td>Accounts Receivable (net)</td><td>420,000</td><td>370,000</td></tr>
<tr><td>Inventories</td><td>185,000</td><td>165,000</td></tr>
<tr><td>Total Current Assets</td><td>$ 610,000</td><td>$540,000</td></tr>
<tr><td>Fixed Assets:</td><td></td><td></td></tr>
<tr><td>Property, Plant, and Equipment</td><td>$1,000,000</td><td>$900,000</td></tr>
<tr><td>Less Accumulated Depreciation</td><td>(650,000)</td><td>(560,000)</td></tr>
<tr><td>Net Fixed Assets</td><td>350,000</td><td>340,000</td></tr>
<tr><td>Total Assets</td><td>$960,000</td><td>$880,000</td></tr>
<tr><td colspan="3" align="center">Liabilities and Shareholder's Equity</td></tr>
<tr><td>Current Liabilities:</td><td></td><td></td></tr>
<tr><td>Bank Loan</td><td>$ 100,000</td><td>$ 70,000</td></tr>
<tr><td>Accounts Payable</td><td>314,300</td><td>332,000</td></tr>
<tr><td>Payroll Withholdings</td><td>30,000</td><td>28,000</td></tr>
<tr><td>Income Tax Payable</td><td>10,000</td><td>20,000</td></tr>
<tr><td>Total Current Liabilities</td><td>$ 454,300</td><td>$450,000</td></tr>
<tr><td>Shareholder's Equity:</td><td></td><td></td></tr>
<tr><td>Capital Stock</td><td>$ 10,000</td><td>$10,000</td></tr>
<tr><td>Retained Earnings</td><td>495,700</td><td>420,000</td></tr>
<tr><td>Total Shareholder's Equity</td><td>$ 505,700</td><td>$430,000</td></tr>
<tr><td>Total Liabilities and Shareholder's Equity</td><td>$ 960,000</td><td>$880,000</td></tr>
</table>

Exhibit 3–2

UDUB Limited Comparative Statements of Income and Retained Earnings for the Years Ending December 31, 2007 and 2006	2007	2006
Net Sales	$2,824,900	$2,593,600
Cost of Sales	1,584,600	1,426,500
Gross Profit	$1,240,300	$1,167,100
Operating Expenses		
Selling Expenses	$1,007,800	$908,300
Administrative Expenses	136,700	135,500
Total Operating Expenses	$1,144,500	$1,043,800
Income before Income Taxes	$ 95,800	$ 123,300
Provision for Income Taxes (21% rate)	20,100	25,900
Net Income	$ 75,700	$ 97,400
Beginning Retained Earnings	420,000	322,600
Ending Retained Earnings	$ 495,700	$ 420,000

The audits of UDUB have not presented any notable problems in the past, and their internal control structure is reasonable for a firm of their size.

You decide to conduct some planning-stage analytical procedures. To help formulate expectations about the nature of any changes in this year's financial statements, you hold the following conversation with UDUB's controller, Ms. Cardinal. The first thing you inquire about is whether there have been any significant changes in pricing or cost of sales. Ms. Cardinal replies:

"This year has been another profitable year here at UDUB. We launched a credit initiative that resulted in selling more products, but, of course, we had to finance our receivables a little longer. Also, our costs of production increased since we updated our manufacturing machinery. The depreciation of our new machines significantly increased the overhead that we attach to our product as it's produced."

After absorbing this information you inquire specifically about whether UDUB could pass such costs to consumers. Ms. Cardinal's reply:

"Unfortunately, we're not yet the market leader in our industry. As you might surmise, we were not in a position to pass the increase in cost to our consumers. So while our gross margin is down from historical levels, we hope to make up the difference in volume."

Ms. Cardinal then politely excuses herself for an important conference call that undoubtedly will take the rest of day. You decide to think through the ramifications of Ms. Cardinal's remarks. What sorts of changes, if any, do you expect to see in this year's financial data relative to the previous two years? A few ratios come immediately to your mind, but you wonder if there is anything else that should be examined. You start to examine the comparative balance sheets and income statements for the last two years as well as the production history for UDUB's last three years. If everything in these data seems to fit Ms. Cardinal's story, then there's no reason to alter this year's approach to auditing UDUB Limited, you reason. You then begin your analysis.

Exhibit 3–3

<td colspan="8" align="center">UDUB Limited Production History (All Figures in 00s)</td>
Year	Month	Sales	Cost of Goods Sold	Selling Expenses	Units Shipped	Units Produced	Ending Inventory
2001	Jan.	$ 1,239	$ 689	$ 430	50	55	5
	Feb.	1,335	737	466	53	58	10
	March	1,610	886	560	64	69	15
	April	1,405	768	495	56	61	20
	May	1,511	828	528	60	65	25
	June	1,600	878	568	64	69	30
	July	1,750	962	614	70	75	35
	Aug.	1,910	1,052	669	76	81	40
	Sept.	2,011	1,104	700	80	70	30
	Oct.	2,230	1,224	786	89	79	20
	Nov.	2,300	1,261	807	92	82	10
	Dec.	1,849	1,020	643	74	70	6
2005 Totals		$20,750	$11,409	$7,266	828	834	6
2002	Jan.	1,549	850	540	62	67	11
	Feb.	1,669	916	586	67	72	16
	March	2,012	1,107	706	80	85	21
	April	1,756	968	615	70	75	26
	May	1,889	1,037	660	76	81	31
	June	2,000	1,103	707	80	85	36
	July	2,187	1,208	766	87	92	41
	Aug.	2,387	1,310	836	95	100	46
	Sept.	2,514	1,380	881	101	91	36
	Oct.	2,787	1,536	970	111	101	26
	Nov.	2,875	1,580	1,008	115	105	16
	Dec.	2,311	1,270	808	92	88	12
2006 Totals		$25,936	$14,265	$ 9,083	1,036	1,042	12
2003	Jan.	$ 1,704	$ 1,000	$ 598	68	73	17
	Feb.	1,835	1,100	640	73	78	22
	March	2,213	1,216	774	88	93	27
	April	1,756	1,068	767	77	82	32
	May	1,902	1,148	729	83	88	37
	June	2,095	1,218	770	88	93	42
	July	2,406	1,320	844	96	101	47
	Aug.	2,626	1,440	916	121	109	35
	Sept.	2,765	1,520	966	111	108	32
	Oct.	3,066	1,683	1,074	130	112	14
	Nov.	3,162	1,737	1,109	126	116	4
	Dec.	2,719	1,396	891	102	111	13
2007 Totals		$28,249	$15,846	$10,078	1,163	1,164	13

Requirements

1. Point out any unusual signs of misstatement with UDUB's sales.
2. Point out any unusual signs of misstatement with UDUB's cost of sales.
3. Employing regression analysis and using the Excel data file for Exhibit 3–3 supplied by your instructor, determine which month is most likely to have an overstatement of gross margin in it that requires follow-up. Three sets of relationships are necessary to determine the month in question and to rule out alternative explanations.
4. Recommend any changes in how substantive testing efforts for UDUB's sales and/or cost of sales transactions should be allocated. Historically, these transactions have been randomly sampled and, to ensure broad coverage, the sampling is stratified so about 15 transactions from each month are sampled, except for January and December. For those two months an additional 20 transactions are sampled to guard against cutoff concerns.

10

Evidence about Management Assertions: Linking Residual Risks to Substantive Tests

INTRODUCTION

In previous chapters, we discussed how understanding an organization's strategic position, plans, risks, controls, and processes is critical for the performance of an effective audit of financial statements and internal controls over financial reporting. In this chapter, we link our previous risk analysis to the auditor's tests of management assertions that comprise the financial statements (Figure 10–1). These tests are conditional on the current strategic and process risks, including financial reporting risks, an organization faces. In essence, information gathered during the knowledge acquisition stage of the audit provides assurance about business and audit risks, especially about the risk of material misstatement. The auditor relies

Figure 10–1   Overview of the Audit Process

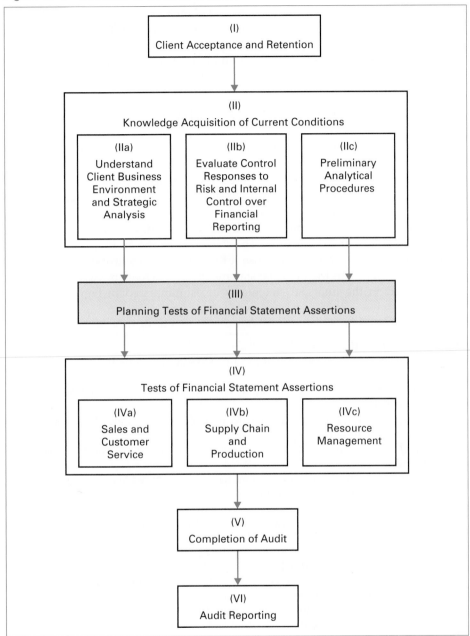

on this assurance when deciding what direct tests of transactions, accounts, and presentation and disclosures are needed.

The purpose of this chapter is to describe the planning of *substantive audit tests* that are needed to obtain sufficient evidence to support an opinion about the financial statements. At this point in the process, the auditor possesses a substantial set of evidence about conditions within the organization and has identified residual strategic risks, process risks, and any significant deficiencies or material weaknesses in internal control over financial reporting that are relevant to the financial statement audit, including assessment of the risk of material misstatement. The auditor's assessments of residual risks guide the auditor in designing tests of specific financial information. Decisions concerning the evidence to be gathered about specific assertions and the allocation of audit resources across segments of the financial statements are reflected in an *audit program* for substantive testing.

ASSERTIONS, RISKS, AND EVIDENCE REVISITED

The general concepts underlying the auditor's decision process were described in Chapter 3, including the concepts of management assertions, audit procedures, and audit evidence. Ultimately, the auditor must issue an opinion about the fairness of the financial statements and related disclosures in accordance with generally accepted accounting principles. However, most of the evidence obtained during knowledge acquisition, including tests of controls, is indirectly linked to financial statement assertions and disclosures. The challenge for the auditor is to take his or her accumulated knowledge and to use it to formulate conclusions about specific information included in the financial statements. The management assertions that are embedded in the financial statements are summarized in Figure 10–2. The

Figure 10–2   Overview of Management Assertions Comprising the Financial Statements

---

Management Assertions about Transactions
- *Occurrence*—Transactions and events that have been recorded have occurred and pertain to the entity.
- *Completeness*—All transactions and events that should have been recorded have been recorded.
- *Accuracy*—Amounts and other data relating to recorded transactions and events have been recorded appropriately.
- *Cutoff*—Transactions and events have been recorded in the correct accounting period.
- *Classification*—Transactions and events have been recorded in the proper accounts.

Management Assertions about Accounts
- *Existence*—Assets, liabilities, and equity interests exist.
- *Rights and obligations*—The entity holds or controls the rights to assets, and liabilities are the obligations of the entity.
- *Completeness*—All assets, liabilities, and equity interests that should have been recorded have been recorded.
- *Valuation and allocation*—Assets, liabilities, and equity interests are included in the financial statements at appropriate amounts and any resulting valuation or allocation adjustments are appropriately recorded.

Management Assertions about Presentation and Disclosure*
- *Occurrence and rights and obligations*—Disclosed events and transactions have occurred and pertain to the entity.
- *Completeness*—All disclosures that should have been included in the financial statements have been included.
- *Classification and understandability*—Financial information is appropriately presented and described and information in disclosures is clearly expressed.
- *Accuracy and valuation*—Financial and other information is disclosed fairly and at appropriate amounts.

---

* Some countries do not explicitly break out presentation and disclosure assertions, leaving them implicit in the assertion of "proper presentation and disclosure."

auditor may determine that some assertions are more significant than others for specific transactions, accounts, financial statement items, or disclosures. Furthermore, the auditor may have reached different conclusions about the risk of material misstatements affecting specific assertions based on the information available from strategic and process analysis.

Ultimately, the auditor needs to obtain sufficient appropriate evidence to support a conclusion that these assertions have been satisfied. The auditor has already performed procedures to understand the client's environment, assess its internal control, and measure its performance (i.e., preliminary analytical procedures). Residual risk assessments reflect the auditor's judgment based on the evidence that was obtained from these procedures. Additional evidence will be needed to verify specific assertions or disclosures, but the nature and extent of that evidence varies based on the level of residual risk.

> **Authoritative &
> Guidance & Standards**
> This chapter re-examines many of the standards discussed in earlier chapters associated with the risk assessment process. The main standards discussed in the chapter include audit evidence (SAS 106, ISA 500), audit risk and materiality (SAS 107, SAS 109, ISA 320, ISA 315), and performing audit procedures (SAS 110, SAS 330).

At this point, the auditor has a variety of substantive procedures from which to choose: (1) detailed analytical procedures, (2) tests of transactions, and (3) tests of accounts including presentation and disclosure. The auditor must consider both the costs and quality of the evidence needed; however, audit scandals such as WorldCom and Parmalat highlight why the auditor should not place undue emphasis on minimizing the cost of evidence. The selection and mix of tests will vary across segments of the audit due to different residual risks. In general, the more significant and risky an assertion, the more important it is that the auditor obtain high quality evidence.

ANALYZING RESIDUAL RISKS IDENTIFIED FROM STRATEGIC AND PROCESS ANALYSIS

Figure 10–3 summarizes the process the auditor used to acquire an understanding of the client's business environment, risks, and controls. The output of this process is a set of residual risks that the auditor believes are potentially significant to the organization. A residual risk can be significant if the potential likelihood or magnitude of a negative outcome is high and the organization has failed to effectively mitigate the risk. As we discussed in Chapter 5, a residual risk can impact an audit in five ways:

1. **Condition expectations:** A residual risk can condition the auditor's expectations about financial results that can then be compared against actual outcomes to determine if financial reports are consistent with underlying economic circumstances (e.g., develop expectations for analytical procedures).
2. **Raise concerns about viability:** A residual risk can raise concerns about the ability of an organization to continue in operation (i.e., going concern issues).
3. **Increase risk of material misstatement:** A residual risk may provide evidence that specific management assertions are misstated (i.e., suggesting that extensive substantive tests are necessary).
4. **Increase control risk:** A residual risk can indicate that there are stresses within the control environment that may negatively impact individual behavior (i.e., increasing the organization's susceptibility to employee or financial reporting fraud).
5. **Comment for client improvement:** A residual risk may highlight areas where additional control efforts may be appropriate (both as advice to the board and management and as a basis for more extensive audit work).

Figure 10–3   Identifying Residual Risks

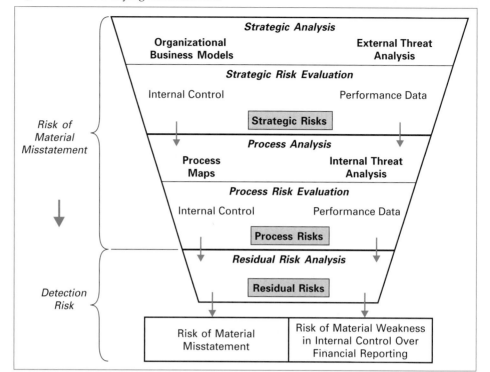

Of particular interest in this chapter is the third implication, namely, whether there are indications that management assertions are misstated that should be subject to substantive tests.

To illustrate, consider the analysis of human resource management discussed in Chapter 7. In that analysis, we concluded that there were two risks that could qualify as significant residual risks. Referring to Figure 10–4 (see also Chapter 7), we see that eight of the ten risks were either assessed as being low initially, or were reduced to an acceptable level by controls and positive performance indicators (indicated in the figure with arrows and stars). The remaining residual risks, errors in payroll authorizations (*R5*) and loss of critical employees (*R10*), remain in the high risk area of the risk map, implying that they are likely to have a significant negative impact on the company. The auditor should analyze the implications of each of these risks as they relate to the conduct of the audit. Some of the possible implications of these risks are summarized in Figure 10–5.

Notice that the implications of the two risks are quite different. The risk of errors in payroll authorization is primarily a process risk and has a direct effect both on internal control over financial reporting and on the risks of material misstatement for related transactions. The auditor will probably increase tests of internal control and payroll transactions in response to this risk. The auditor can only assess whether the effect is material with additional testing, but there is a good chance that any resulting errors will be small, offsetting, and immaterial.

The other risk, loss of personnel, is more strategic in nature, so its implications are less directly related to the financial statements. The risk may mean little in the course of the audit, or it could have a pervasive effect on the audit, especially if the

Figure 10–4   Residual Risk Assessment for Human Resource Management

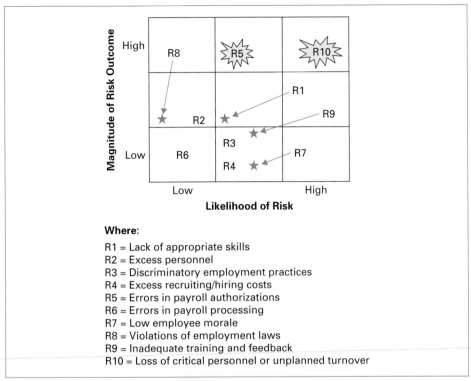

Where:
R1 = Lack of appropriate skills
R2 = Excess personnel
R3 = Discriminatory employment practices
R4 = Excess recruiting/hiring costs
R5 = Errors in payroll authorizations
R6 = Errors in payroll processing
R7 = Low employee morale
R8 = Violations of employment laws
R9 = Inadequate training and feedback
R10 = Loss of critical personnel or unplanned turnover

control environment is undermined by employee turnover. In the extreme, if the client's success is dependent on the personnel who depart, various assets may need to be evaluated for impairment and the question of whether the company is a going concern could become important.

Example

Nortel Networks Inc. is one of the world's largest providers of telecommunications systems. It has had to delay regulatory filings every year since 2003 and has had to restate its financial statements in the period 2003 to 2006 three times with the potential for further restatements. One of the key causes identified for these ongoing problems was "lack of sufficient personnel with appropriate knowledge, experience and training."

THE AUDIT RISK MODEL

The selection of tests of management assertions about financial reporting is affected by residual strategic and process risks. The auditor's approach to planning the tests of assertions is embodied in the *audit risk model*, which is a method for decomposing the concept of audit risk into its constituent parts. We have previously defined the term audit risk as "the likelihood or probability that the auditor will conclude that all material assertions made by management are true when, in

Figure 10–5   Example: Audit Implications of Human Resource Risks

Implication	R5: Risk of errors in payroll authorizations	R10: Risk of loss of critical personnel or unplanned turnover
Expectations	Unclear since direction of potential errors is unknown.	(1) Increased payroll costs due to an increase in recruiting and hiring activity, as well as increases in personnel costs due to hiring new personnel. (2) If personnel critical to the strategy of the organization leave (e.g., in R&D, sales, production), overall performance may be negatively affected, which could affect one of more areas of the financial statements.
Going concern	Minimal	Likelihood of failure may increase if personnel critical to the strategy and processes of the organization leave unexpectedly.
Risk of material misstatement	Errors in pay rates, withholding, or benefits can lead to errors in wage-related expenses and liabilities (*accuracy of transactions*).	Probably minimal, however, if overall performance is affected, valuation issues may arise related to inventory and other assets (*valuation and allocation of accounts*).
Control environment	Indicates that internal control over financial reporting related to payroll may be ineffective (i.e., significant deficiency or material weakness).	Overall control environment of the organization might be negatively affected depending on the personnel who depart (e.g., executives in the accounting or financial area). If loss results in turnover of key accounting personnel who are not readily replaceable or a change in the "tone at the top," this could substantially increase risk of material misstatement.
Comments for client	Improved internal control over payroll-related record-keeping and authorizations.	Client may need to look into succession planning, training or morale development, or compensation arrangements.*

* The auditor can point this out to the client, typically in the form of a management letter. Indeed, it may be required in an integrated audit if the "tone at the top" or the qualifications of the accounting personnel are changed due to turnover. In most audits it would be inappropriate for the auditor to directly assist the client in improving these areas of operations because such work would be considered a potential violation of auditor independence.

fact, at least one assertion is incorrect." Auditing standards actually present a slightly more formal definition:

> *Audit risk:* The risk that the auditor may unknowingly fail to appropriately modify his or her opinion on financial statements that are materially misstated.

Two attributes of this definition should be emphasized. First is the idea that the auditor has reached an incorrect conclusion about the financial statements. Saying that the statements are presented fairly when they are not could cause the auditor to suffer losses from litigation, fines, or reputation damage, particularly if the auditor was negligent in not finding the misstatement(s). Second, the concept of materiality, which was defined in Chapter 3, is an integral part of the definition. The auditor is concerned only with misstatements that would influence the decisions of potential readers of the financial statements. However, determining materiality within an engagement is a significant challenge to auditors.

In theory, audit risk can vary from 0 percent (complete certainty that financial statements do not contain material misstatements) to 100 percent (complete certainty that financial statements contain material misstatements). However, auditors design engagements to provide a reasonable level of assurance that financial statements are free of material misstatement. Given that *reasonable assurance* implies a high level of assurance, and a low probability of misstatement, most auditing firms require that engagements are conducted at relatively low audit risk percentages, usually no higher than 5 percent. Because an auditor cannot perform tests on all transactions and accounts, and because significant judgment is required for many financial statement measures, conventional wisdom suggests that an audit cannot be performed with an audit risk level below 1 percent. Thus, for most firms, audit risk is established somewhere along the following continuum.

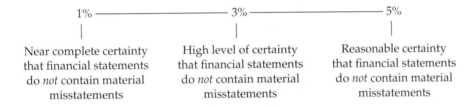

In practice, the costs associated with moving below 1 percent typically are quite high relative to the reduction in audit risk. Conversely, 5 percent is probably the highest probability that can or should be accepted while still providing a high level of assurance.

RISK OF MATERIAL MISSTATEMENT

Risk of material misstatement is the risk that the financial statements are misstated prior to audit. Risk of material misstatement can also be phrased at the assertion level: the risk that an assertion contains a material error prior to carrying out the audit procedures. Risk of material misstatement at the assertion level can be separated into two highly interrelated parts: inherent risk and control risk.

Inherent risk is defined as the likelihood that a management assertion may be misstated before considering the effect of internal controls. Inherent risk is affected by a number of factors. Some of the more important factors are described in Figure 10–6. Many of these risk factors are explicitly considered during the strategic and process analysis performed by the auditor. In general, the presence of a risk factor does not mean that the related assertion(s) and account(s) are misstated; rather, the presence of a risk factor means that the risk of misstatement is higher than it would be if the factor was not present. Some of these risk factors are pervasive to the entire engagement (e.g., honesty of management), whereas others may only affect a small subset of assertions or accounts.

Figure 10–6   Factors Affecting Risk of Assertions Being Materially Misstated

	Effect on Risk of Material Misstatement	
Factor	*Higher Risk Condition*	*Lower Risk Condition*
Nature of client's business and industry	Cyclical, evolving, declining, overly competitive, recent frauds uncovered, threatened regulation.	Stable or mature.
Integrity of management	Dubious (especially if there is a prior record of accounting manipulation).	Respected. Trustworthy.
Client ownership and/or management motivations	Need to satisfy budget goals, existence of contingent bonus or option plans, undue emphasis on reducing tax liabilities.	Budgets are readily met, management compensation is not highly contingent on results, lack of prior IRS sanctions.
Results of prior-year audits	Frequent errors found in prior-year engagements.	Few errors found in prior-year engagements.
Tenure of auditor	Initial audit engagement with new client and little client-specific knowledge.	Repeat and ongoing audit engagement with extensive client specific knowledge.
Existence of related parties	Many related party transactions that raise valuation and disclosure problems.	Few related party transactions.
Frequency of transactions	Unusual transactions for which the client lacks the expertise or accounting system to record the transactions accurately.	Frequent homogeneous transactions whose handling is automated and electronic, and where a well designed system handles transactions efficiently on a regular basis.
Subjectivity of transaction values	Transaction requiring judgment to assign a value.	Easily determined exchange price for transaction.
Susceptibility to defalcation	Assets easily stolen or misdirected.	Assets that cannot be easily moved or misappropriated.
Size of balance/ Number of transactions	Many separate small transactions.	Few large transactions.

Some of the risk factors listed in Figure 10–6 may be counterbalancing. For example, a large account with frequent transactions is more likely to have mistakes because the volume of transactions implies that there is more opportunity for something to go wrong. At the same time, the client will have a great deal of experience handling a transaction that occurs frequently and will devote signifi-cant internal control resources to ensuring that mistakes are not made in that process. This latter point highlights the interrelatedness of inherent risk and con-trol risk.

The client motivation factor listed in Figure 10–6 deserves further discussion. A critical element of assessing inherent risk is determining the potential motiva-tions of management, which may wish to increase profits so that the market value of the company's stock increases, making management's stock options more valu-able. The mere presence of a stock option plan is not bad; indeed, most public com-panies have them, but the risks deepen if an inappropriate mix of compensation is offered such that management is induced to artificially overstate profits. This risk factor requires a deeper understanding of management's attitudes towards artifi-cially boosting profits and the inherent risk of the engagement depends on whether management attempts to cash in on the options by manipulating ac-counting results. In a similar vein, if a company is small and family-owned, the owners may be interested in keeping profits low so that the company can mini-mize its tax bill. In this situation, the auditor must then be aware of the potential motivation to intentionally understate income.

Example

The explosion of initial public offerings (IPOs) of Internet-related stocks in the 1990s (so-called dotcom companies) highlighted the risks and incentives associ-ated with new issues of securities. For most dot com companies, the road to wealth for owners and managers was through a successful IPO. Obviously, the auditor of such firms had to be very careful that the information provided to potential in-vestors was accurate. A company about to go public could have tremendous incentive to hide accounting problems, shift costs and revenues, and manipulate earnings in the short term to provide the best possible image to the investing public.

Control Risk is defined as the likelihood that internal control will not pre-vent or detect a misstatement in a management assertion. Factors affecting con-trol risk are examined during the auditor's strategic and process analysis, and many of the factors that affect inherent risk also affect control risk, as was illus-trated in the previous discussion of inherent risk. Management integrity and the control environment are particularly important for assessing control risk, over and above the factors discussed in inherent risk. If the auditor suspects that man-agement is less than completely honest, the risk of material misstatement be-comes extremely high.

A significant deficiency or material weakness in internal control over financial reporting is likely to have a significant influence on control risk. Consequently, the evaluation of internal control over financial reporting is integrated with the audit of financial statements. This approach is required for public companies that are SEC registrants. However, in audits where such an integrated approach is not required, auditors may set control risk at maximum if they can justify that sub-stantive procedures alone will result in audit risk being reduced to an appropri-ately low level. New U.S. (SAS 109) and international auditing (ISA 330) stan-dards emphasize that some control testing is likely to be necessary to reduce audit risk to an appropriately low level (e.g., paragraphs 117–120 of SAS 109 describe aspects of the audit—such as when routine transactions rely heavily on automated systems—in which reliance on substantive testing alone likely will not be sufficient).

DETECTION RISK

Detection Risk is the risk that the auditor will not detect a material misstatement that exists in the financial statements or more specifically in a financial statement assertion. This risk can be traced to the failure of substantive tests. An auditor may fail to detect an existing misstatement in the financial statements for a number of reasons. The level of detection risk for any specific assertion is related to four potential problems:

1. **Inadequate planning:** An auditor may not plan or perform the audit procedure(s) necessary to detect an existing misstatement.
2. **Sampling omissions:** Auditors cannot look at every transaction; thus, an existing misstatement may not be discovered because it is not among the sample of transactions that are examined.
3. **Procedural errors:** An auditor may not apply a procedure correctly or may not recognize an error even when an erroneous transaction is selected for testing. This problem may result from poor supervision and review of work of junior auditors, but can occur at any level in the audit firm.
4. **Improper corrective actions:** Even when an auditor identifies an erroneous transaction, there is a possibility that the auditor's response will be inappropriate (intentionally or unintentionally) and not result in the removal of the misstatement.

Example

In the past, a common practice among auditors was not to correct a detected misstatement because the amount in question was not considered "material." In one infamous case investigated by the SEC, an intentional manipulation of earnings amounting to $60 million was not corrected in the financial statements because the auditor felt that it was not material. Regardless of the magnitude of the number, however small or incidental, the fact that the misstatement emanated from an intentional action by management should have been enough to make the matter material to the auditor.[1] Indeed, this allegedly immaterial misstatement allowed the company to meet forecasted earnings for the quarter, thus maintaining the value of the stock which would most likely have dropped if the EPS target was not met.

Inadequate planning, procedural errors or improper corrective actions are potentially severe problems for auditors because they represent a breakdown in the auditor's planning or judgment. The auditor tries to control these problems through compliance with GAAS, training and supervision of personnel, and careful review of work by experienced auditors. The auditor attempts to control sampling risk through careful selection of transactions to be tested.[2] While sampling omissions are an inherent part of the audit process and can never be avoided entirely, they have rarely been the primary cause of an audit failure.

---

1 W. R. Grace was accused of hiding profits in the early 1990's so that they could be deferred to later years when financial results were not so robust.

2 Statistical sampling of transactions will be discussed in more detail in Chapter 16.

Figure 10–7   Illustration of Audit Risk Model

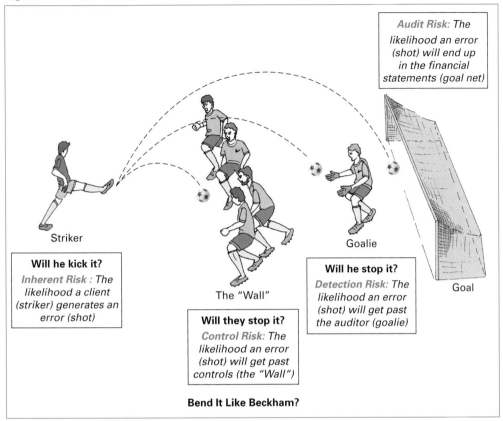

Audit Risk: The likelihood an error (shot) will end up in the financial statements (goal net)

Striker

Will he kick it?

Inherent Risk : The likelihood a client (striker) generates an error (shot)

The "Wall"

Will they stop it?

Control Risk: The likelihood an error (shot) will get past controls (the "Wall")

Goalie

Will he stop it?

Detection Risk: The likelihood an error (shot) will get past the auditor (goalie)

Goal

Bend It Like Beckham?

APPLYING THE AUDIT RISK MODEL

Taken together, the components of audit risk indicate that three events must happen for a material misstatement to affect the financial statements. First, a misstatement (error or fraud) must be generated. Second, internal controls fail to prevent or detect the misstatement once it has occurred. Third, the misstatement remains undiscovered or uncorrected after the auditor performs substantive tests. If all three of these events occur, a material misstatement will infect the financial statements and an auditor issuing a standard unqualified opinion may issue the wrong opinion.

Figure 10–7 illustrates the interaction between inherent, control, detection, and audit risks using the example of a soccer match (known as football in much of Europe). The objective of the game is to score goals, but the opponent constructs defenses to inhibit the ability of the other team to do so. Very few kicks are actually shots on goal and most balls that are kicked are stopped by either players on the other team or the goalie. Very few balls find their way into the net. In this analogy, the ability of a striker to get off a shot on goal reflects inherent risk; in other words, the ability of the attacker affects the likelihood of a shot heading towards the goal. Defensemen reflect the concept of control risk; that is, most kicked balls are turned aside by the defenders. However, a few balls do get past the defensive "wall," and then the goalie tries to stop the ball from entering the net. The goalie represents the auditor, the last line of defense before a ball (misstatement) enters the goal (financial statements). The likelihood of the auditor (goalie) detecting a misstatement (stopping the ball) is detection risk. Taken together, these separate risks compose overall audit risk.

Another way to look at these relationships is with the audit risk model. The audit risk model should be thought of as an aid to understanding how various factors affect the amount of substantive testing done in an audit. Although the audit risk model is a mathematical formula, its use is more conceptual than computational, and auditors would generally not try to apply it as tool for calculating risk. Rather, the model provides guidance as to a general level of substantive testing that is needed given the conditions of a client. Specifically, the model relates the components to overall audit risk as follows:

$$AR = RMM \times DR \tag{1}$$

where AR refers to audit risk, RMM refers to risk of material misstatement, and DR refers to detection risk. Although newer audit standards increasingly suggest that inherent and control risk should be considered jointly, the two interrelated components of RMM can be substituted into the model:

$$AR = (IR \times CR) \times DR \tag{2}$$

where IR refers to inherent risk and CR refers to control risk. The components of audit risk focus on management assertions; therefore, this equation helps us understand how RMM impacts DR because the nature and extent of substantive tests performed by the auditor are driven by assessments of IR and CR.

Looking at the individual components of the audit risk model, we know that RMM is not controlled by the auditor and must be assessed as part of strategic and process analysis. The auditor's understanding of current conditions, risks, controls, and performance indicators provides a solid foundation for making such assessments as they relate to specific management assertions included in the financial statements. That is, the auditor must analyze the strategic and process risks of the organization, evaluate the accounting system that the client is using, and determine the risk that the system will generate material misstatements that go undetected by the internal controls.

DR is the only risk that is under the direct control of the auditor. If the auditor wishes to have a low detection risk, he or she must conduct extensive substantive tests of specific management assertions (normally tests of transactions, accounts, and presentation and disclosure). If the auditor decides that a higher level of DR is acceptable, then the auditor is willing to reach a conclusion about the fairness of financial statement based upon less substantive evidence, possibly substituting substantive analytical evidence for other substantive tests.

The terms of the risk model can be rearranged to emphasize the role of detection risk in planning substantive testing:

$$DR = \frac{AR}{RMM} \tag{3}$$

Substituting the components of RRM:

$$DR = \frac{AR}{(IR \times CR)} \tag{4}$$

The revised form of the model tells us that DR will be lower when AR is lower or RMM is higher. The opposite is also true—DR will be higher when AR is higher or RMM is lower. Given that higher DR implies the need for less evidence about financial assertions, and lower DR implies a need for more evidence, different values for detection risk translate into different sets of substantive audit procedures. This relationship is illustrated in Figure 10–8. Examining the curve labeled with points A and B, we see that the amount of substantive evidence

Figure 10–8   Materiality, Detection Risk, and Substantive Audit Tests

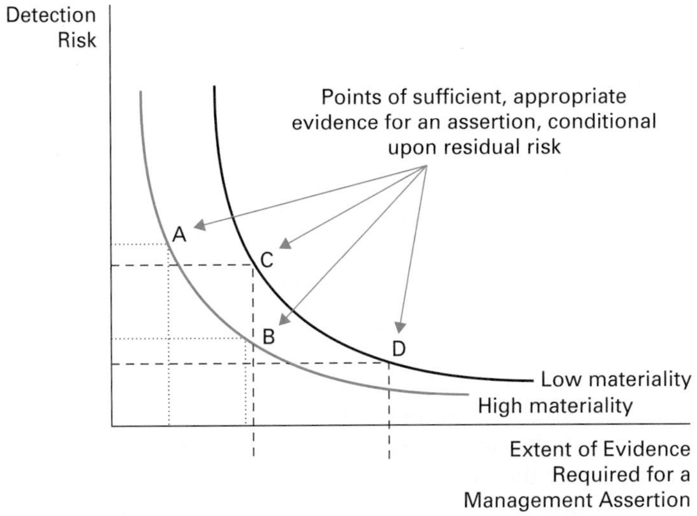

needed depends on DR and materiality. For example, points A and B could occur under the following conditions:

	Point A	Point B
Audit Risk (AR)—assumed	5%	1%
Risk of Material Misstatement (RMM)—assessed	50%	75%
Detection Risk (DR)—computed	10%	1.33%

Because the required detection risk is much lower for Case B, substantive evidence will be more extensive for the assertion being examined.[3]

In analyzing the two examples, keep in mind that this guidance is extremely general. There is no formal rule to compute the exact amount of evidence that is required to achieve the desired detection risk for any specific management assertion. In fact, audit evidence is often not quantifiable. What the model does tell us, however, is that there should be more and better substantive evidence gathered in Case B so as to convince the auditor that the level of detection risk (and therefore audit risk) is as low as desired. We will discuss what attributes make evidence "better" later in this chapter.

We can further examine the relationship of detection risk and audit evidence by considering the impact of materiality. The location of the AB curve in Figure 10–8 is dependent on a given level of materiality. If materiality is changed, the curve will shift and the trade-off of risk and audit effort will change. This relationship is shown in Figure 10–8 by comparing the two curves: The curve with points A and B reflects high materiality, whereas the curve with points C and D reflects low materiality. In general, all points on curve CD require more substantive testing than those on curve AB. However, all four points represent potentially acceptable levels for testing depending on the risk and materiality judgments made by the auditor.

---

3 The use of specific probabilities in the audit risk model is intended for illustration only. The auditor can rarely refine risk assessments to the level where specific probabilities can be assigned to the components of the audit risk model. In practice, the components of the risk model are usually assessed categorically as being high, moderate, or low. The relationship embedded in the audit risk model is then used to infer whether detection risk should be high, moderate, or low.

Authoritative Guidance & Standards

U.S. audit standards (SAS 107) include all components of the audit risk as described in this chapter—the international standards (ISAs 315, 330) do not include the explicit model but refer to the breakdown of risk of material misstatement in the standard's footnote. SAS 107 does not explicitly require the use of the audit risk model. Rather, the standard requires auditors to assess the risk of material misstatement and perform a combination of procedures (e.g., SAS 110, ISA 330) to achieve an appropriate level of audit risk.

The benefit of using the audit risk model for planning substantive tests is that it provides guidance about the appropriate level of detection risk given the established level of AR and the assessed level of RMM. It also allows the auditor to focus on specific management assertions where risk of misstatement is most severe. However, auditors must also be aware that the guidance from the model is only as good as the auditor's risk assessments. Assessing the risk of material misstatement as low can justify a higher level of detection risk and less substantive testing, so it is critical that the assessment of RMM be based on firm and defensible evidence from strategic, process, and internal control analysis.[4]

Setting Audit Risk

Should an auditor perform the audit to a 5 percent risk level? A 3 percent risk level? One percent? A number of factors will influence the auditor's decision. In general, the auditor will prefer lower audit risk whenever the potential cost of issuing an incorrect opinion is large.

An incorrect opinion may lead to lost engagements, negative publicity, or litigation. Loss of even one lawsuit can expose auditors to millions of dollars of claims. Thus, the more likely the auditor is to face such sanctions in the event of audit errors, the lower the desired audit risk will be. As a result, many auditing firms have a formal policy of setting audit risk the same for all engagements.[5]

One factor the auditor should consider in setting desired audit risk is the number of external users who will be relying on the financial statements. The more external users there are, the larger the number of people who will be adversely affected if the auditor issues an incorrect opinion. The number of potential users of the financial statements is related to the size of the client, the distribution of its ownership's interests, whether the stock is publicly traded, and the nature and extent of its debt financing. The desired audit risk used to plan an audit will usually be much lower for a large publicly traded company than for a small single-owner retail store because the auditor's exposure is much greater.

Another factor to consider when setting desired audit risk is the likelihood that the client organization will suffer financial difficulties in the near future. A company that goes bankrupt shortly after the auditor issues an opinion on the financial statements exposes the auditor to potential litigation. In assessing this possibility, the auditor should examine the client's financial status, its methods of financing, the competence of management, and the nature of the industry. Other factors that may have an impact on the desired audit risk are the auditor's professional attitudes about the level of assurance to be obtained during the engagement, the auditor's attitudes towards risk, and the overall experience and competence of the auditor.

A factor that may affect assessment of audit risk, but should not, is the extent of competition among auditors. There have been cases in the past where an auditor has cut back on the amount of audit work performed, and thus the amount of

4 The problem of auditor's underestimating risk is well described by J. Weil in a *Wall Street Journal* article entitled "Missing Numbers—Behind the Wave of Corporate Fraud: A Change in How Auditors Work—'Risk Based' Model Narrowed Focus of Their Procedures, Leaving Room for Trouble—A $239 Million Sticky Note" (March 25, 2004).

5 Firms that alter the acceptable level for audit risk justify their decision by considering the business risk of the engagement.

evidence obtained, because competition among auditing firms decreased the fee for the engagement to a point where a reasonable profit could not be earned by performing the needed work. In these cases, a greater risk level was accepted by the auditor in order to justify less evidence gathering, resulting in a reduction of the engagement cost. Such strategies are not consistent with professional standards and are potentially costly to the auditor in the long run (e.g., lost clients or litigation). In the current post-Enron environment, these competitive pressures have been reduced due to the new regulatory regime in the United States and enhanced regulation in many other countries. In the end, it is the auditor's high level of commitment to being a professional, including the willingness to embrace strong ethical values, that provides the best protection for users of audited financial statements.

MATERIALITY

OVERALL PLANNING MATERIALITY

A key concept underlying the audit of financial statements and the audit risk model is materiality, which was defined in Chapter 3 as "the magnitude of an omission or misstatement of accounting information that, in light of surrounding circumstances, makes it probable that the judgment of a reasonable person relying on the information would have been changed or influenced by the omission or misstatement." The concept of materiality is important to auditors because it has a direct impact on the amount of effort auditors must expend during the course of an engagement. Remember, the smaller the magnitude of misstatement that is considered to be important, the harder the auditor will have to look in order to be sure that no such misstatements exist. Finding a needle in the proverbial haystack is harder than finding a broom.

As discussed in Chapter 3, the materiality threshold is subject to a great deal of judgment, and auditors have developed numerous rules of thumb for setting an initial quantitative materiality level. The challenge for auditors is that the definition of materiality is necessarily vague as it depends on client-specific risks and does not provide a strict formula for quantifying the size of misstatement that is important. Virtually every reader of financial statements will have a different idea as to what constitutes a material misstatement. Generally, standard setters suggest net income or net assets as the base for establishing quantitative materiality, with percentages between 5 and 10 percent for net income and 1 and 3 percent of net assets.

Auditors may select some other justifiable basis for establishing materiality, however. For example, an auditor who believes that readers of the financial statements focus on revenues or gross margin may use 3 percent of revenues or 10 percent of gross margin for materiality. For biotech companies that generate little or no profits or revenues in the conventional sense, gross research and development expenditures may be a more appropriate base for planning purposes. Other bases that might be appropriate in specific circumstances include current assets, net working capital, total assets, total revenues, gross profit, total equity, and cash flows from operations. Auditors have also developed industry-specific measures of materiality such as

(a) Not-for-profit organizations: ½–2 percent of total expenses or total revenues; 3 percent of net assets.

<table>
<tr><td>

**Authoritative &
Guidance & Standards**

Standards (SAS 107, ISA 320) note that materiality for specific items in the financial statements that could impact decisions made by users might be lower than planning materiality. Two examples provided in the standards are research and development expenses for a pharmaceutical manufacturer and financial performance of a newly acquired subsidiary.

</td></tr>
</table>

(b) Mutual fund industry: ½–1 percent of net asset value.

(c) Real estate industry when an entity owns income-producing properties: 1 percent of revenue.

To illustrate the auditor's challenge in setting quantitative materiality, consider two companies with the following financial results:

	ABC Company	XYZ Company
Net income (loss)	$ 600,000	$ 20,000
Total assets	3,000,000	3,000,000
Net assets	750,000	750,000
Sales	3,000,000	1,000,000

What would be considered a material misstatement for each of the companies? As noted, a common rule of thumb is to set materiality equal to 5 percent of net income. This would result in a materiality level of $30,000 for ABC and $1,000 for XYZ. Do these results seem reasonable? For ABC, $30,000 may be about right since that represents 1 percent of total assets and 4 percent of net assets. Most auditors would probably agree that materiality would not normally be any smaller than $30,000 given the circumstances of ABC Company.

For XYZ, $1,000 seems quite small and represents only 0.03 percent of total assets. Most auditors would conclude that this value is too low given the general concerns of the readers of the financial statements. So what materiality level is appropriate for XYZ Company? One possibility is to use $30,000, as was done for ABC Company, as this represents 1 percent of total assets. This choice may not be wise, however, because a $30,000 misstatement, if it remained undetected, would change a small loss into a small profit. Knowing that a company actually has a net loss (albeit small) would be important to most readers of the financial statements and should be taken into consideration by the auditor independent of the quantitative level of materiality. Therefore, materiality should be no larger than $20,000 for XYZ Company and may be set at as low as $10,000 by many auditors, especially if XYZ is a public company.

QUALITATIVE CONSIDERATIONS IN SETTING MATERIALITY

Possibly more important than the level of quantitative materiality are the qualitative factors that surround a potential misstatement of financial results. In judging an actual misstatement, context matters very much. Qualitative factors that may be important when setting the overall level for planning materiality include

- **Misstatements relative to segment or interim results:** An error may not seem significant when compared to overall financial results for a fiscal year. However, investors also look closely at segment data and interim results. If a misstatement has a significant impact on such information, it should be considered material in spite of its small impact on the annual results.
- **Nature of misstatements:** Fraudulent transactions are considered extremely significant regardless of the amount of the misstatement. Auditors often adopt a "where there's smoke there's fire" view when dealing with potential fraud, which makes the discovery of a single fraudulent transaction extremely important, even if it is immaterial in amount.

Example

Many instances of fraudulent financial reporting start relatively small. For example, a company may hold open the sales journal for a day or two at the end of the year in order to record a few more dollars of sales to meet its sales targets. However, such situations tend to become more serious over time. Furthermore, managers that are detected committing a small fraud are often willing or forced to escalate their fraudulent activity in future periods.

- **Nature of contractual constraints:** The auditor should be aware of any contractual or legal limits that may be affected by the financial results of the company. Misstatements that cause violations of debt covenants, or that disguise actual violations of such covenants, are important even if small in amount.

Example

Debt covenants may require a minimum level of working capital or a maximum debt/equity ratio, or regulators may require a certain minimum level of equity capital (e.g., for banks or insurance companies). Misstatements that allow a company to appear to be in compliance should be considered material.

- **Trends are important:** Reported results that indicate a significant change in the trend of results over time are important. A small decrease in sales or net income may be considered to be important. Misstatements that alter the direction of trends in the financial results of the company, or change a loss to a gain or vice versa, are important even if the amounts are small.
- **Meeting or exceeding incentive goals:** If management or employees have incentive-based contracts, misstatements that allow them to achieve their goals should be considered material.
- **External expectations:** If the broad market expects certain outcomes, misstatements that confirm or refute those expectations may have a significant impact on the market.

Example

The valuation of equities is very sensitive to the ability of a company to meet or exceed the consensus earnings forecasts that are published by analysts. Failure to meet earnings forecasts by even a penny can have a dramatic impact on the price of a stock. Consequently, management is very much aware of the level of forecasted earnings. A misstatement that allows a company to meet such forecasts could be considered material even if the amount is small.

In the past, securities regulators have raised serious concerns about the materiality judgments made by auditors when evaluating potentially material misstatements. Although not establishing any new standards, recent statements by securities regulators have highlighted the importance of considering qualitative factors in assessing materiality, including the importance to investors of the matter being evaluated, the impact of misstatements on management compensation, and the impact of a misstatement on trends and earnings levels. Furthermore, materiality is not an appropriate justification for failing to correct a discovered misstatement of any magnitude—even though most accounting pronouncements explicitly note that the suggested or required standards do not apply to immaterial transactions. Indeed, for U.S.-registered public companies all auditor-proposed adjustments to correct errors must be posted by the client management irrespective of materiality except in the case where they are clearly inconsequential.[6] To conclude, setting materiality requires careful analysis and sound judgment because the auditor's decisions concerning materiality early in the audit have a direct impact on subsequent testing.

TOLERABLE ERROR: ALLOCATION OF MATERIALITY TO ACCOUNTS

Many auditors decompose materiality into smaller pieces applicable to specific audit areas or accounts. The amount of materiality assigned to individual accounts is called *tolerable error*, which refers to the amount of error that an auditor can tolerate in a specific account before it is considered to be materially misstated. Tolerable error can differ for each account because some accounts are more susceptible to error or are more significant to the overall financial results of the organization. The profession does not have formal rules for determining tolerable error for account balances, but two generally accepted guidelines are often used:

- Tolerable error should be less than the overall materiality level.[7]
- The sum of tolerable error across all accounts may equal materiality or may exceed materiality.

These guidelines reflect the most conservative (i.e., lowest) risk approach for an engagement. There are many situations where the auditor may wish to have the sum of tolerable error exceed planning materiality. In general, increasing the sum of allocated tolerable error means that the auditor is willing to tolerate larger errors in some accounts, which would increase the overall risk that a material misstatement will remain undetected. However, this need not increase *overall* audit risk if one of the following two conditions is met:

1. **Offsetting errors affecting net income:** Errors in different accounts may be offsetting, meaning that the error in one account increases net income while the error in another account decreases net income. The net error is not material so the use of higher tolerable error levels does not increase overall audit risk.
2. **"Unused" tolerable error:** Error equal to or in excess of tolerable error is unlikely to occur in all accounts. Increasing tolerable error may not increase audit risk as long as actual error in some accounts is less than the tolerable error. In such a case, the sum of *actual* errors would be less than overall materiality even though the sum of tolerable errors exceeds materiality.

Overall, tolerable error is a mechanism for planning and conducting an audit performed by a team of auditors who are simultaneously examining multiple accounts. If tolerable error is not defined by an auditor, audit differences in different accounts may be deemed to be individually immaterial but, when added to other immaterial misstatements, could result in the financial statement being materially misstated on an overall basis. By utilizing a careful process for establishing and allocating tolerable misstatement, auditors decompose materiality to an account

---

6 "Clearly inconsequential" is generally accepted as being a small fraction of materiality in a quantitative sense. See BDO et al., 2004. *A Framework for Evaluating Control Exceptions and Deficiencies Version 3.*

7 Even this rule is not universally followed. As some auditors do not distinguish between materiality and tolerable error, they are essentially setting them equal.

level. Regardless of the amount of tolerable error utilized, total audit differences across all accounts must be combined and the net effect on earnings must be less than overall materiality in order for the auditor to conclude that the financial statements are free of material misstatement.

DETERMINING THE NATURE, EXTENT, AND TIMING OF SUBSTANTIVE TESTING

Once the auditor has made all the necessary risk and materiality assessments, he or she is ready to design the substantive audit program that will guide the testing of assertions regarding transactions, accounts, and presentation and disclosures. At this point, the auditor must make a number of decisions for each significant management assertion:

- What audit procedures should be performed?
- When should the procedures be performed?
- If sample-based testing is used, how many transactions or what percentage of the account balance should be examined?
- If sample-based testing is used, which transactions in the account should be examined?

These questions refer to the *nature, extent, and timing* of substantive testing. The answers to the four questions for all significant management assertions will serve as the basis for the audit program for substantive testing of transactions, accounts, and presentation and disclosure. The structure of the audit program will be discussed in more detail below. Suffice it to say that the final audit program for substantive testing must provide adequate evidence concerning all material assertions in the financial statements conditional on the risks and assurance derived during strategic and process analysis. However, the audit program is continually subject to revision as new information comes to the auditor's attention.

APPROPRIATENESS OF AUDIT EVIDENCE

When selecting procedures to address specific management assertions, the auditor will consider the risk assessments related to the assertion and its materiality relative to the overall financial statements. With this in mind, the auditor will then determine how strong or persuasive the evidence needs to be in order to satisfy the auditor's goal for detection risk. If the desired detection risk is low, the auditor will want a great deal of sound substantive evidence; if desired detection risk is high, the auditor may utilize smaller samples with the same procedures or substitute substantive analytical procedures for some substantive tests of transactions or accounts. We use the term *appropriateness* to describe the strength or persuasiveness of audit evidence.

Recall from Chapter 3 that there are seven basic types of audit evidence that an auditor can obtain:

- Inspection (also known as physical examination) of tangible assets
- Confirmation
- Inspection (also known as vouching) of records or documents
- Observation

- Recalculation or reperformance
- Analytical evidence (also known as analytical procedures or more generally, analysis)
- Client inquiry

How does an auditor know the appropriateness or quality of the evidence obtained from a specific audit procedure? There are a number of characteristics that the auditor can consider in order to understand the appropriateness of evidence.

- **Degree of relevance:** Is the evidence relevant to the assertion being examined? If the auditor wishes to know if year-end inventory exists, the best way to find out is to inspect the tangible inventory on hand and count the items. Of course, inspection of the tangible inventory will not tell the auditor whether or not the items in the warehouse are actually owned by the client, nor will it help the auditor to know if inventory is properly valued at historic cost.
- **Independence of the provider:** Is the source of the evidence independent of the company, or is it subject to possible manipulation? Information obtained from a person outside the client is usually considered to be superior to that received from an insider. An outsider is assumed to have no vested interest in the outcome of the audit, whereas an insider may try to sway the auditor's opinion in order to advance his or her own goals.
- **Degree of auditor's direct knowledge:** Is the evidence directly observable at its source by the auditor? The adage "seeing is believing" clearly applies to auditors. Again, the best way to determine if inventory is present is to look at it—this process is often called the "kick test." Supplier invoices may indicate how many items of inventory the client acquired, but this type of documentary evidence is only second-best to direct physical examination.

Example

A famous audit fraud was perpetrated by a manufacturer of disk drives for personal computers who was able to fool the auditors into thinking that the warehouse was full of inventory by placing bricks into disk-drive boxes, shrink-wrapping the boxes, and stacking them in the warehouse. The auditor failed to realize the charade when physically examining the inventory. "Seeing is believing" only when the auditor knows what he or she is looking at!

- **Qualifications of the provider:** Is the source of the evidence qualified to provide reliable evidence? When receiving evidence, the auditor should consider the competence of the provider. For example, the best person to provide information to the auditor about a pension plan is probably an actuary. Similarly, the best person to provide information about the value of real estate is an appraiser.
- **Degree of objectivity:** Is the evidence open to interpretation so that support for an assertion is ambiguous? Audit evidence is rarely clear-cut in its support of an assertion; this is especially true for the valuation assertion. For example, a company may provide extensive evidence concerning sales debits and cash credits to a customer's account. How does the auditor determine if the net balance is actually collectible? Does the evidence that a customer has paid his or her bill in the past imply that he or she will continue to pay his bill? The evaluation of such evidence bears directly on the recorded value of receivables but is potentially ambiguous.

- **Quality of internal control:** How reliable is evidence generated from the company's accounting system? Auditors make great use of the client's internal recordkeeping system. In every audit, vouching is a common audit procedure performed for many classes of transactions, especially as related to the validity and completeness assertions. However, the use of internal company documents as audit evidence presumes that those documents are accurate. If internal control is weak and internal documents are potentially inaccurate, the auditor may need to obtain other forms of evidence.

- **Specificity of Evidence**: Given that analytical procedures and client inquiry are heavily utilized by auditors, the care with which these procedures are planned impacts the appropriateness of the evidence. Analytical procedures are based upon client data and communications and are used to assess whether results confirm the auditor's expectations. Thus, the more specific the foundation for the expectation and the more precise the computations, the more appropriate the evidence. Also, conducting client inquiry without carefully considering the incentives of the client increases the auditor's susceptibility to being fooled by self-serving information.

Figure 10–9 illustrates the typical hierarchy of evidence based on the above attributes. In general, the auditor will try to obtain more appropriate evidence (the "best" evidence) when desired detection risk for an assertion is low. When detection risk is moderate or high, the auditor will usually be satisfied with evidence considered "good." However, the auditor will rarely be totally satisfied

Figure 10–9   Hierarchy of Evidence Reliability

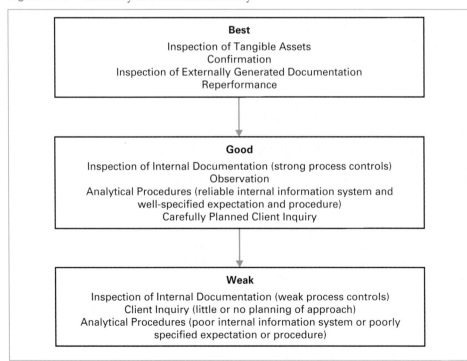

Best
Inspection of Tangible Assets
Confirmation
Inspection of Externally Generated Documentation
Reperformance

Good
Inspection of Internal Documentation (strong process controls)
Observation
Analytical Procedures (reliable internal information system and
well-specified expectation and procedure)
Carefully Planned Client Inquiry

Weak
Inspection of Internal Documentation (weak process controls)
Client Inquiry (little or no planning of approach)
Analytical Procedures (poor internal information system or poorly
specified expectation or procedure)

Figure 10–10   Trade-Off of Detection Risk and Audit Evidence

Low Detection Risk/High Audit Effort	*High Detection Risk/Low Audit Effort*
Audit Procedures Performed for Client B (See Figure 10–8)	Audit Procedures Performed for Client A(See Figure 10–8)
Client Conditions	
Low detection risk results from a high assessed risk of material misstatement due either to high inherent risk that controls cannot reduce to a low level, to ineffective controls, or to the decision to set control risk as maximum. Hence, there is the need for a high level of substantive audit tests.	High detection risk results from the low assessed risk of material misstatement due to having effective internal controls that reduce the assessed level of inherent risk and control risk to a low level. The assessment must be supported by appropriate control tests. Hence, there can be fewer substantive audit tests.
Effect on Substantive Testing	
Aged trial balance for receivables prepared by the auditor.	Aged trial balance for receivables prepared by the client's personnel and reviewed by auditor.
25 largest customer accounts plus 100 customer accounts.	50 customer accounts judgmentally selected (e.g., large balances, small balances).
No client restrictions placed on population of accounts to confirm.	A few accounts omitted from confirmation by request of the client.
Accounts to be confirmed pertain to other businesses.	Accounts to be confirmed pertain to retail consumers.
Customer accounts confirmed as of 12/31 (for fiscal year end of 12/31).	Customer accounts confirmed as of 11/1 (for fiscal year end of 12/31).

with evidence classified as "weak" except to corroborate other "good" or "strong" evidence.

To illustrate the trade-off of the quality of evidence and risk, consider the procedures to test accounts receivable for different levels of risk as described in Figure 10–10. The preparation of the aged trial balance by the client personnel is higher risk because the preparer is not independent. Selecting 125 accounts to confirm is better than selecting 50 accounts because the sample has a greater chance of detecting existing errors. Client management's restriction on the selection of customer accounts interferes with the independence of the evidence and reduces its appropriateness. Confirmations sent to businesses will usually be more reliable than those sent to retail customers because businesses are likely to have accounting systems that allow them to respond accurately to the confirmation request. Companies utilizing electronic data interchange with suppliers often have the capability to send electronic confirmations that can be routed back directly to the auditor. Finally, confirming accounts before year end provides weaker evidence because it is less timely than direct year-end confirmation.

AN EXAMPLE: LINKING RESIDUAL RISK ASSESSMENTS TO TESTS OF MANAGEMENT ASSERTIONS

To illustrate the links between strategic and process risks and tests of management assertions, let's consider the example of an electronics company that specializes in high performance sound equipment. The company's strategy is to differentiate its product based on quality. In order to succeed, the company needs to develop and manufacture products that are of higher quality and superior reliability than its competitors, and for which they can charge a premium price. Given the company's strategy, significant threats can arise from its supply chain if vendors are unable to provide components and raw materials that are of sufficiently high quality to meet the company's performance specifications. The company might try to mitigate this risk at the strategic level by establishing alternative sources of supply, vertically integrating, or forming alliances with key suppliers.

Failure to obtain an adequate supply of high-quality inputs will have an impact on the products and processes of the electronic company. The manufacturing process could be affected by problems in the supply chain for a number of reasons:

- Disruptions in deliveries (especially if the process operates on a just-in-time basis)
- Down time or retooling of equipment originally designed to utilize higher quality inputs than currently available
- Waste due to the disposal of unacceptable units or materials
- Defects and rework due to deterioration of the quality of outputs

The company normally will try to mitigate each of these risks through various controls and procedures. For example, on-site inspections can occur at the supplier for materials utilized on a just-in-time basis, penalty clauses in performance contracts with suppliers can be enforced, assembly and production processes can be adjusted to compensate for lower quality inputs, and new suppliers can be obtained when specialized tooling is not involved. Furthermore, the level of these risks should be measured through the use of several performance indicators, including on-site inspection ratings, delivery statistics, factory operating statistics, production waste and defect rates, customer complaints, and warranty claims.

For the purposes of our illustration, assume that the company has implemented all of the controls indicated above and is monitoring the indicated performance measures. The controls seem to be operating effectively except for deliveries from one specific supplier of a complex component. This supplier has recently been late with deliveries and on-site inspection ratings have been lower than past periods. As a result, the electronics company has suffered delays and been forced to reconfigure some assembly processes. In general, performance measures indicate that deliveries are occurring on time from all other suppliers, there is no indication of increased rejection of deliveries, and the supply chain has not been disrupted. Other performance measures indicate an increased rate of defects, customer complaints, and warranty claims, however. These facts, taken together, could cause the auditor to conclude that there is an increased residual risk of delayed and inferior components.

The auditor would next link the conclusions about residual risks to specific audit implications and assertions that may exhibit an elevated risk of misstatement.

Assertions in at least two account areas could be affected by the residual risk described above, one obvious and one not so apparent:

1. Warranty Expense: The increased level of customer complaints, warranty claims, and defects indicates that the supply chain problems are negatively affecting product quality. This suggests that the completeness and valuation of warranty expenses and the associated liability may have high risk of material misstatement.
2. Inventory: Due to production delays and reconfiguration of the assembly process, the valuation of work-in-process and finished goods inventory may be inaccurate. Because the costs of delays and changing production processes are considered an indirect manufacturing cost, the company's overhead allocations and standard costs may be inaccurate, causing the valuation of inventory to have high risk of material misstatement.

Given that these assertions have high risk of misstatement, the auditor selects appropriate tests of transactions and accounts to achieve a suitably low detection risk for each assertion. For testing the completeness and valuation of warranty expense and liability, the auditor could undertake some or all of the following *substantive* tests:

*   Obtain listings of warranty claims for the quarters during the prior year (or two) to benchmark current performance results.
*   Obtain historical data on warranty claims and develop a projection of future claims based on changes in current conditions. Compare the projection to the recorded balance of claims and determine if it is adequate.
*   Review warranty claims being filed after the end of the fiscal year and verify that the pattern of claims is consistent with recorded balances.
*   Compare company claims history to industry trends and patterns.
*   Test the recognition and valuation of a sample of actual claims to determine if they are accounted for properly.

For testing the valuation of inventory, the auditor could use some or all of the following substantive tests:

*   Review production cycle times (or variances) and determine if unusual patterns or trends are apparent. Increased cycle times could be associated with increased production costs—both labor and overhead.
*   Review the overhead allocation and standard cost computations for products affected by the supplier in question.
*   Obtain documentation in support of the data used in the standard cost computations (for example, vendor invoices and receiving reports).
*   Trace the cost of process down time and reconfiguration into the overhead allocations and standard cost calculations.

Not all of these substantive tests may be needed in order to obtain sufficient evidence. The actual selection of procedures will depend on the level of detection risk for the assertions. In general, the auditor should obtain enough evidence to be assured that the high residual process risk that was identified is not resulting in material misstatements in the related management assertions.

DEVELOPING THE AUDIT PLAN FOR TESTS
OF MANAGEMENT ASSERTIONS

The preparation of an audit plan for substantive testing requires that the auditor judgmentally select the best set of procedures to be performed in order to obtain sufficient, appropriate evidence that the financial statements are fairly presented. Recall that the auditor can use substantive analytical procedures or tests of transactions, accounts, and disclosure details. An important part of the *audit program* is the list of the substantive procedures that the auditor has decided to perform, typically classified by account area (e.g., transactions cycle or business process) and assertion. The relationship among audit procedures and types of audit evidence is summarized in Figure 10–11. Different procedures provide evidence of different quality so the auditor must carefully match the quality of the evidence to the detection risk for an assertion.

Figure 10–11   Relationship Between Audit Procedures and Audit Evidence When Planning Tests of Financial Statement Assertions

Type of Audit Procedure	Type of Audit Evidence Obtained	Relationship of Evidence to Possible Financial Statement Errors
Substantive Analytical Procedures	Client Inquiries Analytical Procedures	Indirect: Unusual results may be due to error or non-error causes. The actual cause of an unusual discrepancy must be determined using other procedures.
Tests of Transactions	Client Inquiries Observation Inspection of Documents Recalculation/Recomputation	Direct and Indirect: Actual errors can be detected in the transactions that have been examined. Actual errors indicate the likelihood that errors may have occurred in other transactions not examined.
Tests of Account Balance Details	Client Inquiries Inspection of Documents Recalculation/Recomputation Confirmation Inspection of Tangible Assets	Direct: Actual errors can be detected in year-end balances.
Tests of Presentation & Disclosure Details	Client Inquiries Inspection of Documents Recalculation/Recomputation Confirmation	Direct: Actual errors can be detected in financial statement line items or footnote disclosures.

SELECTING EFFECTIVE AND EFFICIENT AUDIT PROCEDURES TO TEST ASSERTIONS

Recognizing that an auditor will try to follow the basic strategy of obtaining sufficient, appropriate evidence, in the most efficient and least costly manner, Figure 10–12 depicts the various approaches that the auditor can adopt for preparing the audit program. The process depicted in Figure 10–12 starts at the point where the auditor has assessed risk of material misstatement for material assertions. At this point, the auditor has three alternatives:

1. Assess risk of misstatement for an assertion as high based on a high level of inherent risk and a high or maximum level of control risk. Under this option, the auditor performs the engagement assuming that inherent risk is too high to

Figure 10–12   Alternative Audit Planning Strategies

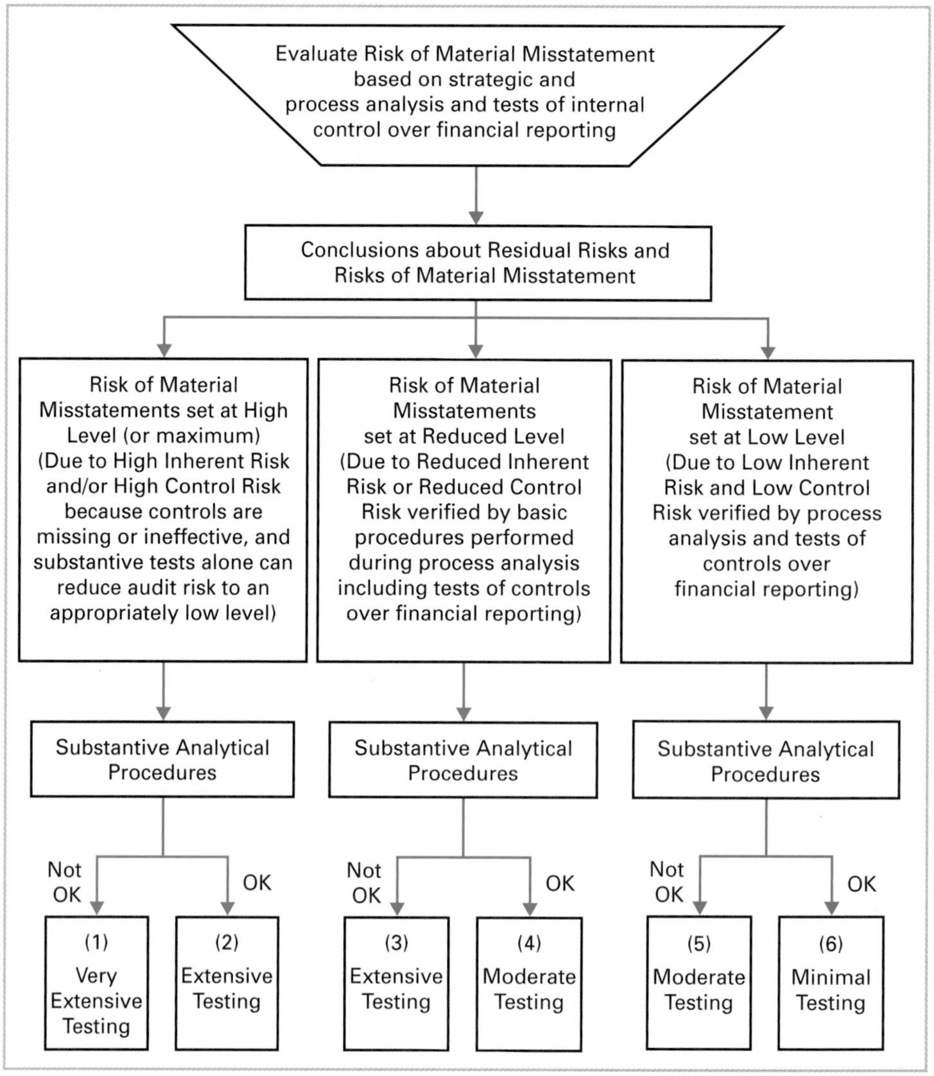

allow reliance on internal control or that no assurance can be obtained from internal control (note that this option should be utilized only in exceptional cases when testing internal control is deemed too costly relative to benefits or the client has no effective controls).

2. Assess risk of misstatement for an assertion at a reduced level based on the procedures performed during strategic and process analysis including the testing of controls over the financial reporting process. To justify this risk reduction, the auditor should conduct walkthroughs and limited tests of controls as part of process analysis.

3. Assess risk of misstatement for an assertion at a low level based on low inherent risk and low control risk. To justify this risk reduction, the auditor should conduct extensive walkthroughs and tests of controls as part of process analysis, including testing controls over the financial reporting process.

The analysis in Figure 10–12 highlights the conditional nature of substantive tests. After establishing risk of material misstatement for significant assertions, the auditor will perform substantive analytical procedures based on fairly precise expectations about appropriate performance measurements derived during strategic and process analysis. Finally, the auditor will perform adequate tests of transactions, accounts, and disclosures to complete the engagement and obtain the remaining evidence that is required to render an opinion on the financial statements. Depending on existing evidence, the extent of substantive tests of transactions or accounts can range from extensive to minimal. Six possible outcomes to the auditor's planning process are summarized in Figure 10–13. Each set of conditions is a unique combination of control risk, analytical evidence, and tests of details of transactions or accounts.

SEGMENTING THE AUDIT PLAN

The auditor needs to divide the audit into manageable segments given that different processes affect different assertions in different ways. Indeed, in large multinational organizations the auditor begins this process by dividing the client organization into a series of auditable entities as a precursor to auditing the consolidated entity. One efficient way to segment the auditable entity into smaller pieces is by business process, although many auditors will divide the audit by transaction cycle or account type. We adopt the approach of segmenting the audit by business process and then identifying the accounts affected by a given process.

Figure 10–13   Summary of Alternative Audit Planning Outcomes (Assuming a Given Level of Audit Risk)

Outcome from Fig. 10–11	Extent of Tests of Account Details	Desired Detection Risk	Reliance on Analytical Procedures	Reliance on Tests of Details
(1)	Very extensive substantive tests	Very Low	Low	Very High
(2)	Extensive substantive tests	Low	Moderate	High
(3)	Extensive substantive tests	Low	Low	High
(4)	Moderate substantive tests	Moderate	Moderate	Moderate
(5)	Moderate substantive tests	Moderate	Low	Moderate
(6)	Minimal substantive tests	High	Moderate	Low

In this book, we will discuss the following processes, all of which typically are further broken down into subprocesses for conducting an audit:[8]

- **Sales and Customer Service:** This process deals with customers. It includes activities such as marketing, sales order entry, product delivery, pricing, billing, and cash receipts. The accounts affected by this process include cash, receivables, inventory, cost of goods sold, and selling expenses.
- **Supply Chain Management and Manufacturing Conversion:** This process deals with acquiring the resources needed for production and converting them into a product or service. It includes activities such as purchasing, receiving, manufacturing, and cash disbursements. The accounts affected by this process include inventory, accounts payable, and cost of goods sold.
- **Human Resource Management:** This process acquires, manages, and compensates human resources. The accounts affected include production costs, accrued liabilities, employee benefits, and equity (e.g., stock options).
- **Facilities Management:** This process acquires, utilizes, and maintains fixed physical assets such as factories, vehicles, and retail locations. The accounts affected include most fixed assets, depreciation, production costs (for cost allocation), accounts payable, and asset-based obligations (such as mortgages or leases).
- **Financial Resource Management:** This process obtains capital for the organization, makes financial investments (other than mergers and acquisitions), and manages cash flow. The accounts affected include long-term debt, equity, long-term investments, financing expenses, and investment revenue.

Each process has its own objectives, risks, controls, and performance measures that the auditor should evaluate as part of strategic and process analysis. Each process interfaces with different accounts in the financial statements. The auditor needs to understand which processes can affect which accounts, link residual risks from the process to management assertions, and plan substantive tests based on the assessments of risk and materiality and the availability of evidence. Figure 10–14 provides an overview of how significant business processes link to specific elements of the financial statements. Segmentation of the audit in this way provides complete coverage of the information in the financial statements and becomes the basis for finalizing the plan for testing assertions of transactions, accounts, and disclosures.

THE SUBSTANTIVE AUDIT PROGRAM

The preparation of the plan for testing management assertions requires the auditor to draw upon all of his or her knowledge of the client organization. This knowledge includes the auditor's own prior experiences, as well as the risk assessments and other facts derived from the analysis of the client's environment and activities. Before an audit commences, the auditor will have some expectations of where problems are likely to occur and which accounts are most important based on a general understanding of the client's industry and prior-year audits. As a result, auditors often follow general guidelines when planning substantive testing, which

---

8 Different organizations have different processes. The ones we discuss here include the most common processes found in most organizations. Other processes that could be important to an organization include research and development, brand management, or mergers and acquisitions.

Figure 10–14   Relationships Among Accounts and Processes

Account Area or Class of Transactions	Core Processes		Resources Management Processes		
	Sales and Customer Service (1) [Chapter 11]	Supply Chain and Production [Chapter 12]	Facilities [Chapter 13]	Human Resources [Chapter 7, 13]	Capital and Investment [Chapter 13]
Assets					
Cash and short-term investments	Cash receipts	Cash payments	Cash payments	Cash payments	Cash receipts, Cash payments, Trading securities
Receivables	Sales, Receipts, Returns, Bad debts				Investment income
Inventory	Cost of goods sold	Purchases, Production, Inventory valuation	Depreciation (product cost)	Direct labor costs	
Plant, property, and equipment, including accumulated depreciation			Purchases of tangible assets, Asset disposals, Depreciation, Leased assets		
Investments					Purchase investments, Sell investments
Liabilities					
Accounts payable		Vendor payables			
Accrued liabilities (2)	Commissions	Indirect overhead costs	Maintenance, Utilities, Leases	Wages, Benefits, Payroll taxes,	Interest, Dividends, Income taxes, Deferred taxes
Debt and borrowed funds			Mortgage payable		Borrow funds, Repay debt
Paid in equity capital					Sales of equity, Repurchase of equity
Retained earnings					Dividends, Net income

(continued)

Figure 10–14 *(continued)*

Account Area or Class of Transactions	Core Processes		Resources Management Processes		
	Sales and Customer Service (1) [Chapter 11]	Supply Chain and Production [Chapter 12]	Facilities [Chapter 13]	Human Resources [Chapter 7, 13]	Capital and Investment [Chapter 13]
Income and Expense					
Sales, revenue, and gains	Sales		Asset disposals		Investment income and gains
Cost of goods sold	Cost of goods sold	Costs of production, Cost allocation	Depreciation (product cost)	Direct labor costs	
Depreciation expense			Depreciation (period cost)		
Selling, general, and administrative expenses			Maintenance, Utilities, Operating leases	Wages and related expenses	Interest expense
Tax expense (3)	Sales taxes		Property taxes	Payroll taxes	
Other Disclosures/Accounts					
Other (4)	Vendor rebates	Purchase commitments, Waste and spoilage	Interest capitalization, Impairments, Leasehold improvements	Stock options, Pensions and post-retirement benefits	Off balance sheet items, Investment impairments

Notes: (1) Shaded cells indicate accounts and processes that have no direct link under normal circumstances.

(2) Most prepaid current assets arise from the same sources as accrued liabilities.

(3) Income tax expense, Income taxes payable, and Deferred taxes would be determined in a separate process.

(4) Most intangible assets are related to "other" business process such as "research and development" (patents), "brand management" (trademarks), or "mergers and acquisitions" (goodwill).

are modified based on the actual results obtained during strategic and process analysis and the resulting residual risks.

Figure 10–15 illustrates some of the common planning guidelines used for the accounts of a merchandising or manufacturing engagement. Accounts receivable and inventory are usually accounts with high risk of material misstatement. In

Figure 10–15   Relationships Among Tolerable Error, Risk, and Substantive Tests for Specific Balance Sheet Accounts

Account	Key Management Assertions for Account	Risk of Misstatement	Typical Level of Substantive Tests
Cash	Existence Valuation	Low	Low
Accounts Receivable	Existence Valuation	Moderate	High
Inventory	Existence Completeness Rights Valuation	High	High
Land	Valuation Rights	Low	Low
Building	Valuation Rights	Moderate	Moderate
Accumulated Depreciation	Valuation	Low	Low
Investments	Existence Valuation Rights	Moderate	High
Accounts Payable	Completeness Valuation	Moderate	Moderate
Accrued Liabilities	Completeness Valuation	Moderate	Low
Common Stock Equity	Valuation	Low	Low

both cases, the auditor is concerned with the occurrence of transactions and valuation of accounts so the amount of audit effort expended in those areas will be extensive. Other accounts have varying risks of misstatement. Cash, fixed assets, accounts payable, and accrued liabilities usually are assessed as having a moderate risk of material misstatement. Cash is rarely a material account balance, but it is important because of the volume of transactions that flow through the account and the need to strictly control access to cash. Accounts payable and accrued liabilities are often subject to cutoff problems and unrecorded obligations. Fixed assets are usually highly material but may have only a few large transactions in a given period. Land and equity are usually subject to minimal testing since they usually have very few transactions in a given period. Accumulated depreciation often requires only that the appropriate amount has been allocated to expense in the current period. Some investments (especially financial instruments) may have a high risk of material misstatement due to the complexity of transactions, the valuation of securities, and specific disclosure requirements.

The embodiment of the risk assessments and selection of the nature, extent, and timing of audit procedures is the audit program. An example of an audit program for one account, cash and cash equivalents, is presented in Figure 10–16

Figure 10–16   An Illustrative Audit Program: Cash Accounts

Step	Workpaper Reference where Results Documented	Audit Procedure	Relevant Management Assertion	Performed by whom?	Performed when?
1	A	Conduct a surprise count of cash and receipts on hand in the petty cash fund. Reconcile receipts to proper imprest balance.	Existence Completeness	WRK	12/30/x7
2	A-1-1	Arrange to obtain a bank confirmation as of 12/31/x7 and a bank cutoff statement as of 1/10/x8 for each of the primary disbursement accounts used by the company.	Rights	WRK	12/23/x7
3	A-1 A-2	Obtain a client-prepared bank reconciliation for each bank account as of 12/31/x7. Test each bank reconciliation using the following procedures: • Trace balance per bank to bank confirmation. • Trace balance per books to the general ledger and the cash lead sheet included in the workpapers. • Test the accuracy of the bank reconciliation. • Trace a sample of outstanding checks to the bank cutoff statement for proper clearance and to the cash disbursements journal. Verify that all items are recorded in the proper period. • Trace deposits in transit to the bank cutoff statement for proper clearance and to the cash receipts journal. Verify that all items are recorded in the proper period.	Existence Completeness Valuation	WRK	1/15/x8

#	Ref	Procedure	Assertions		
		• Trace other reconciling items to the appropriate supporting documentation and proper inclusion in the general ledger. • Obtain first and last check numbers used in 19x7 and perform cash disbursement cutoff test. • Prepare adjusting entries for any items requiring correction on the books of the company.			
4	A-2-2	Prepare a proof of cash for the main disbursement account used by the company.	Existence Completeness Valuation	WRK	1/15/x8
5		Select a sample of cash disbursements and trace to supporting documentation to verify proper processing.	Valuation Existence/ Validity		
6		Select a sample of cash receipts and trace to supporting documentation to verify proper processing.	Valuation Completeness		
7	A-1-1 A-2-1	Review minutes for meetings of the Board of Directors and other management committees for indications of restrictions on cash which should be disclosed. Also review loan agreements and other contracts.	Valuation	WRK	1/15/x8
8	AJE	Review the cash lead schedule and bank reconciliations for any items requiring disclosure, adjustment or reclassification.	Valuation	WRK	1/15/x8
9		Other procedures deemed necessary due to current circumstances: Describe.			

(details will be discussed in Chapter 11). This particular audit program is probably appropriate for management assertions associated with low detection risk, meaning that extensive substantive evidence is needed for the account details, financial statement presentation, and disclosures associated with the cash and cash equivalent accounts. Many clients would probably require much less substantive testing of cash and cash equivalents.

Substantive audit programs across multiple engagements often have a great deal of similarities. As a result, many firms use automated and standardized programs that are adaptable to specific client conditions, often by means of menudriven inputs. Of course, the auditor must be watchful for circumstances where these programs are not appropriate, especially considering client specific factors that might not be captured in the standard set of planning inputs, and modify the audit approach accordingly. A high-quality audit program for substantive testing has a number of features:

- The audit program for substantive tests should include a comprehensive list of all substantive procedures to be performed, when they are to be performed, and guidelines for selecting the transactions, account balance details, or presentation and disclosure items to examine.
- The audit program for substantive tests should match procedures with management assertions to ensure that all assertions are adequately addressed conditional on residual risk assessments. The matching of processes and accounts depicted in Figure 10–14 helps assure complete coverage of the financial statements.
- The audit program should be easy to revise if new information or evidence becomes available that indicates that the risk assessments or other assumptions underlying the program are not accurate.
- The audit program should provide a mechanism to document the performance of procedures. As the audit program is a comprehensive list of procedures, there should be an indication made on the program as to whether each procedure has been performed, when it was performed, where the procedure is documented, and who did the work.

A comprehensive and accurate audit program provides a record of the audit work performed on the engagement and is an effective control to ensure that all procedures are completed before the audit opinion is issued. Indeed, the latest documentation standards require that the audit program and the results of audit testing be sufficiently documented such that another auditor could reperform the procedures, including selection of the same individual audited items, and arrive at the same conclusions.

SUMMARY AND CONCLUSION

We have described the basic approach to substantive testing of financial statements in this chapter. The auditor's strategy is simple in concept: select audit procedures that provide sufficient appropriate evidence on which to base an opinion of the fairness of management's assertions about transactions, accounts, and presentation and disclosure, both individually and for the financial statements taken as a whole. The audit program is dependent on the auditor's knowledge of current conditions and risk assessments for various components of audit risk, and reflects the auditor's materiality and tolerable error estimates, so as to provide an effective and cost-efficient method for gathering sufficient and appropriate audit evidence to support the auditor's opinion over the financial statements. Given that many of the elements of this process are subjective in nature, and new information is continuously being made available to the auditor, the audit program should be flexible so that the auditor can readily revise the program while producing a record of decisions made during the course of the audit.

In future chapters we will consider gathering and interpreting audit evidence for specific segments of the audit. Chapter 11 discusses the audit of the sales and customer service process, Chapter 12 discusses the audit of the supply chain and conversion process, and Chapter 13 discusses various resources management processes (including human resources, facilities, and financial management). For each process, we will prepare a process map; look at the significant management assertions that comprise affected transactions, accounts, and presentation and disclosure; and discuss sources and control of risks in the process. We will also discuss the types of testing decisions and choices that are described in this chapter in more detail. A key thought to keep in mind while studying future chapters is that the selection of substantive audit procedures, sample sizes, and transactions to test is risk-driven. The auditor's ultimate goal is to determine if the financial statements are free of material misstatements conditional on the knowledge obtained from strategic and process analysis.

BIBLIOGRAPHY OF RELATED PROFESSIONAL LITERATURE

Research

Aasmund, E., W. R. Knechel, and P. Wallage. 2001. Application of the Business Risk Audit Model: A Field Study. *Accounting Horizons.* 15(3): 193–207.

Asare, S. K. and A. M. Wright. 2004. The Effectiveness of Alternative Risk Assessment and Program Planning Tools in a Fraud Setting. *Contemporary Accounting Research.* 21(2): 325–352.

Bedard, J. C. and L. E. Graham. 2002. The Effects of Decision Aid Orientation on Risk Factor Identification and Audit Test Planning. *Auditing: A Journal of Practice & Theory.* 21(2): 39–56.

Bedard, J. C. and K. M. Johnstone. 2004. Earnings Manipulation Risk, Corporate Governance Risk and Auditors' Planning and Pricing Decisions. *The Accounting Review.* 79(2): 277–304.

Braun, K. W. 2001. The Disposition of Audit-Detected Misstatements: An Examination of Risk and Reward Factors and Aggregation Effects. *Contemporary Accounting Research.* 18(1): 71–100.

Glover, S. M., J. Jiambalvo, and J. Kennedy. 2000. Analytical Procedures and Audit-Planning Decisions. *Auditing: A Journal of Practice & Theory.* 19(2): 27–46.

Joyce, E. J. 1976. Expert Judgment in Audit Program Planning. *Journal of Accounting Research.* 140(Supplement): 29–60.

Messier, W. F., Jr. and L. A. Austen. 2000. Inherent Risk and Control Risk Assessments: Evidence on the Effect of Pervasive and Specific Risk Factors. *Auditing: A Journal of Practice & Theory.* 19(2): 119–132.

Kizirian, T. G., B. W. Mayhew, and L. D. Sneathen, Jr. 2005. The Impact of Management Integrity on Audit Planning and Evidence. *Auditing: A Journal of Practice & Theory.* 24(2): 49–68.

Low, K-Y. 2004. The Effects of Industry Specialization on Audit Risk Assessments and Audit Planning Decisions. *The Accounting Review.* 79(1): 201–219.

Smith, J. R., S. L. Tiras, and S. S. Vichitlekarn. 2000. The Interaction Between Internal Control Risk Assessments and Substantive Testing in Audits for Fraud. *Contemporary Accounting Research.* 17(2): 327–356.

Wright, A. M. and J. C. Bedard. 2000. Decision Processes in Audit Evidential Planning: A Multi-stage Investigation. *Auditing: A Journal of Practice & Theory.* 19(1): 123–144.

Professional Reports and Guidance

BDO Seidman LLP, Crowe Chizek and Company LLC, Deloitte & Touche LLP, Ernst & Young LLP, Grant Thornton LLP, Harbinger PLC, KPMG LLP, McGladrey & Pullen LLP, PricewaterhouseCoopers LLP, and W. F. Messier, Jr. 2004. *A Framework for Evaluating Control Exceptions and Deficiencies Version 3.* December 20. 22 pages. Located online at http://www.grantthornton.com/portal/site/gtcom/menuitem.91c078ed5c0ef4ca80cd8710033841ca/?vgnextoid=506aa3e0aec36010VgnVCM100000308314acRCRD&vgnextfmt=default. Accessed March 21, 2006.

Auditing Standards

AICPA *Statements on Auditing Standard (SAS)* No. 106, "Audit Evidence."

AICPA *Statements on Auditing Standard (SAS)* No. 107, "Audit Risk and Materiality in Conducting an Audit."

AICPA *Statements on Auditing Standard (SAS)* No. 109, "Understanding the Entity and Its Environment and Assessing the Risks of Material Misstatement."

AICPA *Statements on Auditing Standard (SAS)* No. 110, "Performing Procedures in Response to Assessed Risks and Evaluating the Audit Evidence Obtained."

IAASB *International Standards on Auditing (ISA)* No. 315, "Understanding the Entity and Its Environment and Assessing the Risks of Material Misstatement."

IAASB *International Standards on Auditing (ISA)* No. 320, "Audit Materiality."

IAASB *International Standards on Auditing (ISA)* No. 330, "The Auditor's Procedures in Response to Assessed Risks."

IAASB *International Standards on Auditing (ISA)* No. 500, "Audit Evidence."

QUESTIONS

1. The risk model from the chapter can be restated as follows:

$$DR = \frac{AR}{(IR \times CR)}$$

   where   DR = detection risk
             IR = inherent risk
             AR = audit risk
             CR = control risk

   This representation illustrates that an increase in either inherent risk or control risk or a decrease in audit risk will decrease detection risk (all else being equal). Using the definitions of the risks, how do you explain this result? How does an increase in either of two types of risk (IR or CR) decrease another type of risk (DR)?

2. In 1999, the U.S. Securities and Exchange Commission issued SAB 99-3, which essentially established that no level of materiality is acceptable for intentional misstatements involving any registered public U.S. company (e.g., a company opts not to value its

marketable securities at market (as required by U.S. GAAP), even if they only constitute two percent of net assets). In contrast, accounting standards issued by standards-setters (including the FASB) contain a disclaimer that "this standard does not apply to immaterial items." Why would the SEC require that companies follow GAAP for immaterial items when the actual standards do not require GAAP to be followed (i.e., there is no GAAP for immaterial items)?

3. Explain the benefit of setting tolerable misstatement for individual accounts. Argue for or against using the same level of tolerable misstatement for each account.

4. Misstatements that are not corrected in a given year because they are not deemed material likely will affect the financial statements in the following year. This impact might be in the form of a reversal of the amount (i.e., an overstatement of inventory in year 0 results in an understatement in year 1—effectively canceling each other out) or the same level of misstatement may persist (valuing assets at cost overstates them across multiple years when depressed market values persist). Thus, auditors should consider this "rollover" effect of materiality when assessing the following year's financial statements. However, auditors also consider the absolute level of misstatement for any given year by drawing an "iron curtain" between each year. Determining whether auditors should consider misstatements from both a "rollover" and "iron curtain" perspective has been controversial for auditors. Argue whether auditors should consider misstatement strictly within a given year, across multiple years, or both.

5. Consider each of the qualitative considerations in setting materiality listed below. For each, describe why it could lead to users being more impacted by smaller levels of misstatements (i.e., why it could lead auditors to set materiality at lower levels).
- Materially significant segments
- Fraudulent misstatements
- Existence of contractual constraints
- Negative industry trends
- Incentives tied to goals
- Earnings expectations generated by market analysts

6. Three of the most important decisions that auditors make concern the nature, timing, and extent of evidence. Describe each of these decisions, carefully describing how each decision impacts the other decisions as part of your answer.

7. Describe how residual business process risks impact management assertions about transactions and accounts. As part of your answer, consider the risk that management fails to properly store and label perishable inventory for a grocery store.

8. Consider the factors described in Figure 10–6 that affect the risk of assertions being materially misstated. For each of the following factors from that table, describe how the high-risk condition could impact a management assertion related to sales transactions.

Factor:	Nature of client's business and industry
High Risk Condition:	Threatened litigation

Factor:	Integrity of management
High Risk Condition:	Prior restatements of financial statements

Factor:	Frequency of transactions
High Risk Condition:	Unusual transactions based on complex sales contracts

Factor:	Management motivation
High Risk Condition:	Existence of contingent bonus plan

9. Consider the alternative audit planning strategies depicted in Figures 10–12 and 10–13 and answer each of the following questions.
  a. Why would a strategy of performing moderate substantive tests of details not be acceptable, regardless of the outcome of substantive analytical procedures when the risk of material misstatements is set at a high level?

b. Why would an auditor only be required to perform moderate substantive tests of accounts when substantive analytical procedures do not result in finding outcomes that meet auditor expectations?

10. Describe how an auditor is able to achieve a given level of audit risk through different combinations of tests of controls and substantive tests (hint: consider the soccer/football analogy provided in Figure 10–7).

11. Risk of material misstatement can be decomposed into two highly interrelated risks. Discuss these risks and indicate how they are related.

12. What factors should the auditor consider in setting the level of audit risk? How do these factors affect the level of audit risk?

13. What is materiality? Why is it an important concept for auditors to consider in the conduct of their audits?

14. How do auditors establish a materiality level? What factors affect the level of materiality set by the auditor?

15. What characteristics can be considered by the auditor to assess the appropriateness of audit evidence? Define these characteristics and illustrate each with an example.

16. What is an audit program? How does the auditor compose the audit program?

PROBLEMS

1. Using the audit risk model, compute the detection risk for the following values of audit risk, inherent risk, and control risk. Then answer the questions below.

	Point A	Point B	Point C
Audit risk	10%	5%	1%
Inherent risk	25%	40%	50%
Control risk	50%	75%	5%

a. Which of the "points" yields the highest required detection risk? What does this imply for evidence gathering by the auditor?
b. Which of the "points" yields the lowest required detection risk? What does this imply for evidence gathering by the auditor?
c. Which point would require more audit effort (i.e., has the higher required detection risk)—Point B or Point C? Explain.
d. What factors affect the interpretation of these results?

2. Consider a manufacturing operation with the following balance sheet and income statement:

Manny Corp.
Balance Sheet
12-31-06
(000's omitted)

Cash	$ 8,000	Accounts Payable	$ 33,000
Accounts Receivable	21,000	Long-Term Debt	141,000
Inventories	86,000	Capital Stock	82,000
Fixed Assets	147,000	Retained Earnings	6,000
Total Assets	$262,000	Total Equities	$262,000

Manny Corp.
Income Statement
For Period Ending 12-31-06
(000's omitted)

Sales	$110,000
Cost of goods sold	80,000
Gross profit	$ 30,000
Selling, general, & admin	31,000
Net income (Loss)	($ 1,000)

   a. At what level would you set materiality for an audit of Manny Corp.? Explain.

   b. How would your answer change if Manny were in a highly regulated industry such as banking or insurance?

   c. How would your answer change if sales for Manny were $150,000 and cost of goods sold was $90,000?

   d. What other information would help us make the materiality judgment in this case?

3. Assume that a client has materiality of $10 million for financial statements that has accounts receivable (net) of $20 million and inventory of $80 million.

   a. What amount of tolerable misstatement would you establish for accounts receivable? Justify your answer.

   b. What amount of tolerable misstatement would you establish for inventory? Justify your answer.

4. Armour Inc. has been in the defense contracting business for about 22 years. From its small factory in Wales, it manufactures boots, belts, ammo holders, and assorted accessories for foot soldiers in the British Army. Raw materials are obtained from sources around the world. Armour bids on a few dozen contracts a year, winning about six. Each contract requires a certain number of items built to a well-established minimum standard. Government inspectors reserve the right to return any lot they feel does not live up to standards, at which time they may assess penalties for non-performance.

Senior management consists primarily of retired army noncommissioned officers who performed these same operations, from the military's side, when they were in the service. Although they have always enjoyed a good reputation with the military, they have expressed considerable alarm at the lack of profitability on the contracts. This is your second year as their auditor.

Discuss the factors that would affect your assessment of inherent risk for Armour Inc.

5. In practice, the auditor frequently sets tolerable error on individual accounts so that the sum of those errors is greater than the level of materiality for the engagement. For example, the audit manager on the Mary Sue Co. audit set tolerable error on its accounts as follows:

Cash	$ 20,000
Accounts receivable	35,000
Inventory	20,000
Current liabilities	15,000
Long-term debt	5,000

The overall materiality level for the audit is $40,000. How can the auditor justify this practice and still maintain the appropriate level of audit risk?

6. For each of the following independent scenarios, state whether detection risk is higher or lower. If detection risk is higher, select the reason for the increase from the following four: inadequate planning, sampling omissions, non-sampling errors, or improper corrective actions.

a. The auditor fails to notice that an accounts payable payment (selected at random) was made to an unauthorized vendor.

b. The auditor assumes that tracing a randomly chosen sample of accounts receivable transactions from source documents to the accounting records will be sufficient to establish the account's accuracy. A confirmation of the largest accounts receivable balances would show that the accounts were misstated.

c. The auditor chooses to ignore the warning from an internal auditor that control procedures are not always followed in the shipping department.

d. A company has several hundred bank accounts (e.g., remote locations, payroll, payables, etc.). The auditor reconciles about one-half of them and, finding no errors, concludes that the cash balance is fairly stated. One of the other accounts is materially misstated.

e. An auditor performs preliminary analytical procedures on the fixed assets account and concludes that it can be safely ignored for auditing purposes. Several of the assets are obsolete.

f. In performing test counts of inventory during an inventory observation, an auditor fails to open some boxes purported to contain expensive electronic components. Many of the boxes contain bricks.

g. In confirming inventory existence, an auditor opens most of the boxes in a large electronic components warehouse. Although all the boxes the auditor opened contained the proper components, several of the other boxes contained bricks.

h. Although a sales clerk has unknowingly lost several large orders, the auditor fails to identify missing prenumbered sales order forms during substantive testing.

7. For each of the following situations, discuss the competence of the evidence gathered to support the assertion being audited. Where possible, suggest a more competent procedure. Why might your suggested procedure not be performed?

a. In her audit of the cash balances of a very large wholesaler, an auditor employs a sophisticated analytical procedures program that uses activity in other accounts such as purchases and payables to predict cash activity. The auditor is the in-house expert on such programs.

b. To help determine the pension liability for a large manufacturer, the auditor reviews documentation on pension investment and payout activity provided by the senior vice president for human resources.

c. On the audit of inventory for a computer manufacturer, an auditor relies on the services of an independent inventory-taking firm for the physical count.

d. An auditor makes extensive use of confirmations to audit the balance in short-term notes payable.

e. The sales manager of a large office supply retailer provides an auditor with an aging of accounts receivable to help audit the balance in the allowance for doubtful accounts account. The sales manager is partially paid via a bonus program based on net income.

f. An audit staff member is building a regression model to predict depreciation expense for a fast-food chain.

8. Consider the following three independent scenarios:

a. Chieftain's, Inc.: A chain of finer men's clothing shops with locations in malls throughout the country.

Account	Tolerable Error	Risk of Misstatement	Planned Audit Effort	Evidence to Be Gathered
Inventory	Moderate	High		
Accrued Liabilities	High	Moderate		
Cash	High	Low		

b.   Sunnystuff Inc.: A bottler of juice-based beverages and teas.

Account	Tolerable Error	Risk of Misstatement	Planned Audit Effort	Evidence to be Gathered
Fixed Assets	Low	Moderate		
Accounts Payable	Low	High		
Common Stock	Low	Low		

c.   Sarah Co.: A manufacturer of high-tech hospital equipment (e.g., MRI scanners).

Account	Tolerable Error	Risk of Misstatement	Planned Audit Effort	Evidence to be Gathered
R&D	Moderate	High		
Compensation Accruals	High	High		
Deferred Taxes	High	High		

Complete the last two columns of the worksheet for each of the three scenarios. Discuss the reasoning behind each choice, including the interaction of materiality with the risks identified and the industry's characteristics.

9. McGuffin Corp. is a manufacturer of aircraft parts for government-owned and commercial planes. The company's government contracts are usually performed on a "cost-plus" basis whereas its private contracts are competitively bid for a fixed amount. During your annual audit of the company's financial statements, you discover that it has been paying a related party for "consulting fees" out of the funds for a division that provides parts to the government. The related party then endorses the check back to McGuffin, who records the funds as "Donated Capital" in the stockholder's equity section of the balance sheet. The total of all these transactions is well under the threshold for overall materiality set for the engagement.

Describe the implications of this discovery for the audit.

10. In planning the audit of Tralfaz Co., a manufacturer of animal feeds and fertilizers, a staff member prepares the following audit program for the substantive test of the accounts receivable balance:

Step	Audit Procedure
1	Trace a sample of transactions from the sales journal through the general ledger.
2	Review minutes of board of directors meetings for evidence of factoring or other restrictions.
3	Confirm several accounts.
4	Observe receiving clerks for evidence of pilfering and non-compliance with control procedures.

a.   For each step in the audit program identify
   • The audit objective(s) being addressed
   • The type of audit procedure being performed
   • The nature of the evidence to be obtained
b.   Identify the deficiencies in the audit program.

11. Assume that materiality was set for Barclay's Bank at 5 percent of net income. Research Barclay's Bank and describe qualitative reasons for why an auditor of Barclay's might assess materiality lower than this amount.

Case 10–1: Bigbox Home Improvement Incorporated

BigBox Home Improvement is a fast-growing warehouse home improvement retailer that builds approximately 100 new warehouse stores each year. As a result, the company places a great deal of emphasis on the site selection business process. In fact, there is so much emphasis on new store construction and new store openings that construction-in-progress is a line item on the balance sheet and store opening expenses is a line item on the income statement, because each represents a material amount on the financial statements.

Suppose that the audit team performed a process analysis, identifying risks that might impact the extent to which these two accounts are likely to be misstated. The analysis of the process resulted in identifying the following risks and controls.

Risk 1: Lack of adequate market and customer research
Control: Formal market and customer research process, including post-launch

Risk 2: Cost overruns
Control: Capital expenditure approval procedures and project management procedures

Risk 3: Community rejects a new store site
Control: Careful site selection, including zoning research and proactive community intervention

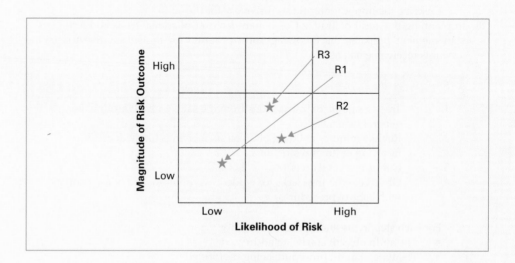

Assuming that tests of controls and assessments of residual risks utilizing performance measures justifies these residual risk plots, complete the following requirements:

Requirements

1. Describe how each risk might impact the two accounts, construction-in-progress and store opening expenses. Be sure to include the management assertions about the accounts that are most likely to be affected.
2. Based on your concerns, describe the nature, extent, and timing of substantive testing for the assertions of construction-in-progress and store opening expenses impacted by the three residual risks.
3. How would the answers to Requirements 1 and 2 change if tests of controls resulted in the finding that all three of the controls were not operating effectively?

Case 10–2: Rubba-Dub-Dub Tub and Commode Company

Rubba-Dub-Dub Tub and Commode Company (RTCC) is a manufacturer of ceramic bathroom and kitchen fixtures located in Cornwall, Ontario. The president and owner of the company is "Bubbles" McClean. McClean started his career as a plumbing contractor. The plumbing company grew substantially over a 10-year period. McClean sold his interest in that company in 1984 for an enormous profit. Shortly thereafter, and because of a noncompete clause in the sales contract for the plumbing company, McClean decided to take over a floundering manufacturer of bathroom and kitchen fixtures, which he renamed RTCC. This occurred in 1990.

McClean is a down-to-earth individual who believes in the sanctity of his word and his handshake. He claims that "he would never cheat a man 'lessen he had it comin'." He has no formal business education, tends to jump to quick conclusions about people, makes seat-of-the-pants business decisions, and can be rude and obnoxious to people he perceives as lazy or incompetent. In spite of this, he has succeeded at all his business ventures.

The takeover of RTCC was originally financed by the proceeds from the sale of his plumbing business and a small loan from the government's Canadian Business Development Bank. He is the only producer of kitchen and bathroom fixtures in Eastern Ontario. The company has expanded continuously since McClean took over and is always in need of working capital and additions to the fixed asset base. This has occasionally created a cash flow problem for the company, but the company currently has a substantial unused line of credit with a major Canadian bank.

McClean has not been involved with the day-to-day operations of RTCC for at least eight years, preferring to spend his "golden" years working on his golf handicap. He has three people who take care of most of the business for him, and he checks in with them on an irregular basis.

John Flushing (General Manager): Flushing has been running the day-to-day operations of RTCC for over ten years. McClean admits that Flushing's energy, devotion, and salesmanship are the main reasons why RTCC has been so successful and grown so rapidly. He is the sole "salesman" for the company and also supervises the manufacturing operations. He has no accounting responsibilities but does sign checks (general and payroll) based on the documentation prepared by the bookkeeper. He also distributes bi-weekly paychecks. He and his crew take an annual year-end physical inventory under your firm's supervision. He is extremely well paid (over $100,000), but the company has no profit-sharing plan. You consider him to be competent, honest, and loyal to McClean.

Donna Draine (Receptionist and clerk): Besides answering the phone and typing letters, Donna also takes phone orders from customers, prepares and mails monthly statements to customers (based on the accounts receivable sub-ledger), and prepares and makes daily bank deposits.

Headley Tubbs (Bookkeeper): Headley performs most of the accounting functions for the company. Sales are recorded in a sales journal based on shipping documents and disbursements are prepared based on vendors' invoices when they are due. Headley prepares payroll and general checks. He reconciles the bank account monthly. Headley has been with the company for 10 years and is dedicated and hardworking. The company does not maintain a subsidiary ledger for accounts payable or an inventory of fixed assets.

In the past, RTCC has hired a small local accounting firm to provide write-up services on a monthly basis. These include posting general ledger accounts and preparing rudimentary financial statements (without footnotes). These statements are reviewed by McClean. On an annual basis, the accounting has also helped the company prepare inventory adjustments based on their physical inventory and the application of lower of cost or market.

Your firm has been engaged to audit RTCC because the bank providing the line of credit is requiring RTCC to be audited annually. You are currently getting ready to audit the financial statements for 2007 (see Exhibits 2–1 and 2–2).

Exhibit 2–1

	2007	2006
Rubba-Dub-Dub Tub and Commode Company Balance Sheet December 31, 2007 and 2006		
Cash and cash equivalents	71,600	33,560
Trade receivables	240,560	175,600
Allowance for doubtful accounts	(24,560)	(22,560)
Raw materials inventory	75,860	108,750
Work in progress inventory	98,745	68,755
Finished goods inventory	145,890	124,355
Prepaid expenses	2,450	3,200
Land	76,000	76,000
Buildings and improvements	456,230	407,230
Machinery and equipment	178,650	152,050
Vehicles	145,785	150,650
Accumulated depreciation	(149,780)	(124,560)
	1,317,430	1,153,030
Notes payable	100,000	45,000
Accounts payable	134,555	94,560
Accruals	15,600	23,500
Current portion of long-term debt	50,000	50,000
Long-term debt	250,000	300,000
Common stock	350,000	350,000
Retained earnings	417,275	289,970
	1,317,430	1,153,030

Exhibit 2–2

Rubba-Dub-Dub Tub and Commode Company Statement of Earnings December 31, 2007 and 2006		
	2007	*2006*
Sales: Bathroom division	1,022,500	980,125
Sales: Kitchen division	1,418,550	1,045,600
	2,441,050	2,025,725
Cost of goods sold: Materials	(341,500)	(339,560)
Cost of goods sold: Labor	(752,050)	(748,560)
	(1,093,550)	(1,088,120)
Gross margin	1,347,500	937,605
Manufacturing overhead:		
Depreciation	(45,000)	(41,320)
Insurance	(10,500)	(9,000)
Utilities	(37,860)	(35,640)
Repairs and maintenance	(35,600)	(12,650)
Other	(47,890)	(42,500)
General expenses:		
Wages and salaries	(298,650)	(274,780)
Office supplies	(11,125)	(9,985)
Bad debts	(8,450)	(3,450)
Professional services	(23,345)	(14,235)
Taxes and licenses	(28,750)	(26,780)
Advertising	(12,300)	(14,560)
Interest	(43,560)	(39,500)
Depreciation	(7,860)	(6,475)
Payroll taxes	(19,785)	(15,460)
Insurance	(3,000)	(2,500)
Income before taxes	713,825	388,770
Income taxes	(242,701)	(132,182)
Net income	471,124	256,588
Beginning retained earnings	289,970	225,640
Dividends	(343,820)	(192,258)
Ending retained earnings	417,274	289,970

Requirements

1. Do you consider this engagement to be high, moderate, or low risk? Translate that assessment into an assessment of acceptable audit risk. Explain.
2. What conditions are you aware of that would increase or reduce the risk of material misstatement in certain accounts? Indicate the condition and the account(s) affected, and explain.
3. What level would you set for overall planning materiality? Explain.

4.   Rate the risk of potential material errors for this engagement as low, moderate, or high for each of the following audit areas. Also indicate the level of tolerable error you would use for each account. Justify your conclusions.

	Low	Moderate	High	Tolerable Error
Accounts receivable	_____	_____	_____	_____
Inventory quantities	_____	_____	_____	_____
Inventory pricing	_____	_____	_____	_____
Fixed assets	_____	_____	_____	_____
Accounts payable	_____	_____	_____	_____
Expenses	_____	_____	_____	_____
Revenues	_____	_____	_____	_____
Contingencies	_____	_____	_____	_____

5.   Given your prior responses, indicate the nature and extent of testing that you would perform in each of the following areas.

E = Extensive
M = Moderate
L = Little
N = None
* = Not applicable

	TOC	TT	AP	TD
Accounts receivable	_____	_____	_____	_____
Inventory quantities	_____	_____	_____	_____
Inventory pricing	_____	_____	_____	_____
Fixed assets	_____	_____	_____	_____
Accounts payable	_____	_____	_____	_____
Expenses	_____	_____	_____	_____
Revenues	_____	_____	_____	_____
Contingencies	_____	_____	_____	_____

Where: TOC = Tests of Controls
TT = Substantive Tests of Transactions
AP = Analytical procedures
TD = Tests of Detailed account balances

6.   Identify the account that will have the highest likelihood of material misstatement and document, in a memo to the file, your approach to testing that account.

7.   Do you have any suggestions to include in a management letter to RTCC? Consider cost-effective and practical changes to the control system and operation.

11

Audit Testing for the Sales and Customer Service Process

Outline

430

INTRODUCTION

Having completed our discussion of risk assessment and planning substantive procedures, we now turn to the audit of specific processes within an organization. We will decompose the audit into core processes and then discuss the risks, controls, audit issues, and evidence pertinent to each process. Given that all significant transactions are affected by at least one major process, cumulative audit consideration of the processes within an organization should provide sufficient appropriate evidence on which to base an opinion about the financial statements.

We will first consider the audit of sales and customer service in a typical manufacturing or merchandising company (see Figure 11–1). We start with this set of processes for a number of reasons. First, the activity in this process represents the "earning process" of most companies. Second, this process has a heavy volume of routine transactions, so internal control considerations, including internal control over financial reporting, and the assessment of control risk are important. Finally, a relatively small number of account balances are affected by the transactions (e.g., sales, receivables, cash, inventory), so we can concentrate our discussion on the residual risks and tests of controls and transactions, accounts and disclosures associated with the activity in this process. Figure 11–2 presents a summary of the accounts affected by the sales process.[1]

To facilitate our discussion, we will use a process map and internal threat analysis to highlight the important characteristics of sales and customer service that could have an impact on the conduct of the audit. In the next section, we will discuss the basic objectives and activities of sales and customer service. We will then discuss the specific transactions that occur within these processes, the nature of process risks, types of internal control, and metrics for performance measurement. Finally, we will use our understanding of the process to illustrate how the auditor reaches conclusions about residual risks and designs specific tests of financial statement assertions that are related to sales and customer service.

> **Authoritative Guidance & Standards**
> This chapter applies standards covered in previous chapters to a specific business process—sales and customer service. Several observations from auditing standards are included throughout the chapter (e.g., SAS 106, SAS 107, SAS 109, SAS 110, ISA 315, ISA 320, ISA 330, ISA 500). The AICPA has issued an Auditing Guide, *Auditing Revenue in Certain Industries,* to aid U.S. auditors in dealing with specific industry issues.

AN OVERVIEW OF OBJECTIVES AND ACTIVITIES RELATED TO SALES AND CUSTOMER SERVICE

The sales and customer service process make up the set of activities by which goods and services are sold and delivered to customers in return for immediate or future payments. This process includes customer service activities in support of

---

1 The material in this chapter could also be applied to a service organization such as an accounting firm.

Figure 11–1   An Overview of the Audit Process

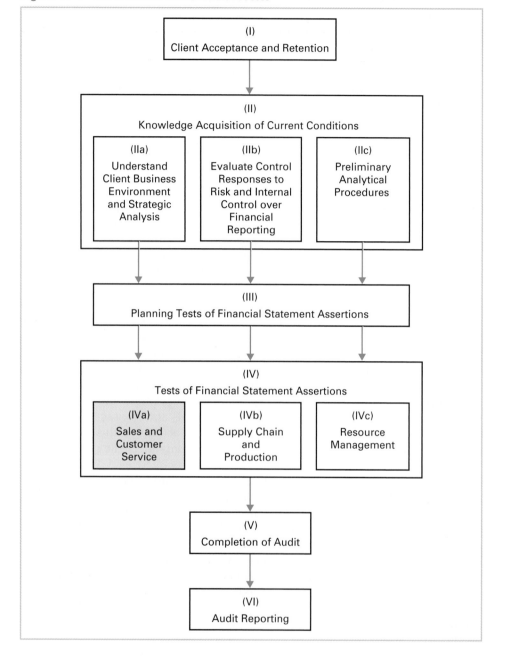

sales or after sales have occurred (e.g., sales returns or warranty claims). This process does not include the acquisition or manufacture of goods and services, although sales activities can have important implications for supply chain management and manufacturing.

PROCESS OBJECTIVES

Figure 11–3 depicts a general process map for sales and customer service. In order to meet its sales targets, a company must design the sales and customer service

Figure 11–2   Relationships Among Accounts and Processes

Account Area or Class of Transactions	Core Processes		Resources Management Processes		
	Sales and Customer Service [Chapter 11]	Supply Chain and Production [Chapter 12]	Facilities [Chapter 13]	Human Resources [Chapter 7, 13]	Capital and Investment [Chapter 13]
Assets					
Cash and short term investments	Cash receipts	Cash payments	Cash payments	Cash payments	Cash receipts, Cash payments, Trading securities
Receivables	Sales, Receipts, Returns, Bad debts				Investment income
Inventory	Cost of goods sold	Purchases, Production, Inventory valuation	Depreciation (product cost)	Direct labor costs	
Plant, property, and equipment including accumulated depreciation			Purchases of tangible assets, Asset disposals, Depreciation, Leased assets		
Investments					Purchase investments, Sell investments
Liabilities					
Accounts payable		Vendor payables			
Accrued liabilities	Commissions	Indirect overhead costs	Maintenance, Utilities, Leases	Wages, Benefits, Payroll taxes	Interest, Dividends, Income taxes, Deferred taxes
Debt and borrowed funds			Mortgage payable		Borrow funds, Repay debt
Paid in equity capital					Sales of equity, Repurchase of equity
Retained earnings					Dividends, Net income

(continued)

Figure 11–2   *(continued)*

Account Area or Class of Transactions	Core Processes		Resources Management Processes		
	Sales and Customer Service [Chapter 11]	Supply Chain and Production [Chapter 12]	Facilities [Chapter 13]	Human Resources [Chapter 7, 13]	Capital and Investment [Chapter 13]
Income and Expense					
Sales, revenues, and gains	Sales		Asset disposals		Investment income and gains
Cost of goods sold	Cost of goods sold	Costs of production, Cost allocation	Depreciation (product cost)	Direct labor costs	
Depreciation expense			Depreciation (period cost)		
Selling, general, and administrative expenses			Maintenance, Utilities, Operating leases	Wages and related expenses	Interest expense
Tax expense	Sales taxes		Property taxes	Payroll taxes	
Other Disclosures/Accounts					
Other	Vendor rebates	Purchase commitments, Waste and spoilage	Interest capitalization, Impairments, Leasehold Improvements	Stock options, Pensions and post-retirement benefits	Off balance sheet items, Investment impairments

process to carry out the strategy adopted by the company. Objectives mostly pertain to maximizing revenue by creating products and services that match price and quality to those demanded by customers, building a reputation for high quality or low prices, meeting or exceeding customer expectations, and delivering appropriate products or services on a timely basis. Failure to meet one or more of these objectives could lead to increased risk for the organization, and might eventually result in organizational failure.

PROCESS ACTIVITIES

The typical activities that make up sales and customer service are indicated in Figure 11–3, although organizations design processes that are unique to their own strategy and objectives:

- Marketing and brand awareness: A company must deliver a message to prospective customers that attracts them to its products and services. Market

Figure 11–3   Process Map: Sales and Customer Service

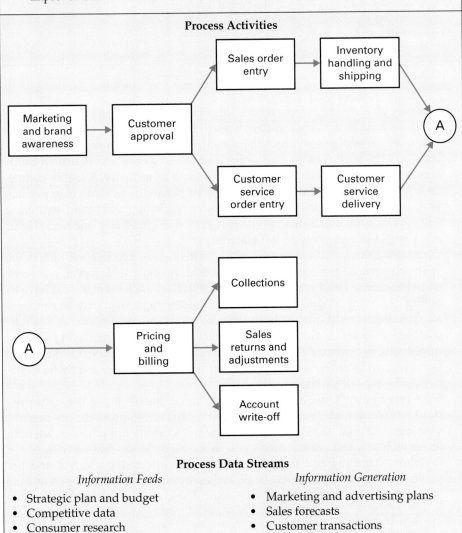

Process Objectives
- Create product awareness within target market and enhance brand images.
- Increase customer base and the proportion of repeat customers.
- Match price and quality to achieve desired share of target market.
- Maximize revenue opportunities.
- Minimize sales returns.
- Minimize customer credit problems and collect cash on a timely basis.
- Minimize transactions costs for sales, collections, and returns
- Continually improve customer satisfaction.
- Deliver goods and services on a timely basis.
- Minimize loss of assets due to theft or misuse.
- Capture and effectively utilize customer information.
- Capture, process, and report information necessary for process improvement.

Process Activities

Process Data Streams

Information Feeds
- Strategic plan and budget
- Competitive data
- Consumer research
- Marketing and promotion programs

Information Generation
- Marketing and advertising plans
- Sales forecasts
- Customer transactions
- Revisions to customer files

(continued)

Figure 11–3   *(continued)*

- Customer data
- Product attributes and specifications
- Inventory levels
- Delivery options and times
- Payment options
- Pricing and discount policies
- Customer service policies

- Changes in inventory levels
- Customer satisfaction and retention
- Customer complaints and resolution
- Collections, returns, write-offs
- Market share and related statistics

Accounting Impact of Activities

Routine Transactions	*Non-routine Transactions*	*Accounting Estimates*
• Sales and revenue	• Bad debt write-offs	• Bad debt expense
• Cash receipts	• Price adjustments and promotions	• Warranty claims
• Sales returns	• Valuation of returned inventory	
• Cost of goods sold	• Vendor allowances or rebates	
• Sales-related expenses		
• Advertising and marketing costs		

research, advertising, telemarketing, special promotions, and brand development are ways in which a company tries to get its message to target customers. The more recognized a brand, the easier it is to get customers to consider a product. The emphasis on marketing and brand awareness is driven by the competitiveness and customer make-up within an industry. A highly competitive industry (e.g., commercial banking) or highly dispersed customer base (e.g., consumer products) requires extensive marketing and brand awareness. Conversely, a smaller industry with few customers (e.g., airplane manufacturers) places less emphasis on these activities.[2]

- Customer approval: If marketing and advertising are effective, customers will wish to purchase the company's products and services. However, customers must be screened and approved to assure that they are legitimate and have the ability to pay for products and services. Customer approval may be simple, as in obtaining a credit card authorization, or can be more complex, as when the company extends credit directly to the customer. Minimizing credit risks is an important objective of this activity. Customer screening becomes even more important in an Internet environment, where credit card fraud and theft of identity can be serious problems.
- Sales order entry: Once a customer is approved, the details of the transaction must be determined. The customer's desires can be communicated by personal visit (e.g., to a retail store), letter, telephone call, customer purchase order, or Internet web site, and are matched to the available products and services.
- Inventory handling and shipping: Inventory is selected, packaged, and prepared for shipment. Items may be picked up by customers, or shipped by mail, parcel post, or company delivery vehicles. The choice of distribution channel

---

2 Two other processes could be incorporated into our discussion of marketing and sales: brand management and product development. These processes are beyond the scope of this text.

will impact the actual steps performed in the process. Timely and error-free shipments are an important objective of this activity.

- Customer service order entry: In the case of services, schedules must be assigned and arrangements made for performance of the service. If the service involves repairs, parts need to be obtained. For warranty work, authorization is needed to perform the service at no charge to the customer.
- Customer service delivery: The timely provision of quality customer service can greatly influence customer satisfaction. Given that customer service requires the interaction of company personnel with customers, the staff's professionalism, training, and general demeanor can have a direct impact on achieving organizational objectives.
- Pricing and billing: Appropriate prices must be assigned to goods and services and communicated to customers. Pricing can range from quite simple to very complex. Most grocery stores, convenience stores, bookshops, and electronics stores set prices based on manufacturer suggestions and local competition. More complicated is pricing of airline or insurance services, situations in which every individual customer may receive a different price based on sophisticated analysis by the company.
- Collection: Payments from customers are received in various forms, including cash, checks, gift certificates, credit memos, in-house credit, and payments from third parties (e.g., bank credit cards, PayPal). These payments must be captured, protected from theft, credited to the appropriate customer, and sometimes refunded (e.g., when a fraudulent credit card sale must be refunded to the bank).
- Sales adjustments: Sales returns are the most common form of adjustment. Incoming merchandise must be processed and inspected, and proper refunds or credits issued to customers. Another example of a sales adjustment is a retroactive price change.
- Account write-offs: In the event that a customer is unable to pay amounts owed, a process should exist to attempt collection and to authorize removal of receivables in the event that collection is impossible.

The complexity of these processes will depend on the strategic and process decisions of the organization. Some of the decisions that could affect these activities include

- The marketing strategy of the company
- The method of delivery of goods or services
- The timing and form of customers' payments
- Policies on sales returns and adjustments
- The extent of computerization in transaction processing

For example, organizations can adopt different strategies for marketing products, ranging from subtle media exposure to print advertising and from direct mail campaigns to televised infomercials. Similarly, distribution channels can differ across companies; for example, the delivery of merchandise is much different for a retail company with physical stores than it is for an Internet-based retailer. At the same time, the handling of customer payments is different for cash purchases, credit card charges, and direct company credit. Returns may require significant inventory handling and repackaging. Finally, the extent to which computers automate transaction processing affects how a process is performed.

Example

Many retailers have both a physical location and an Internet site, but in some cases retailers may only exist on the Internet without a physical retail location. The extent to which technology is used to process orders can vary dramatically across such organizations. Some retailers use the Internet to provide product information but not to accept customer orders (e.g., car manufacturers). Others accept online order entry, but they do not allow Internet activity to link to internal systems so that on-line orders must be transferred (often manually) to the internal sales system. The most sophisticated online retailers link Internet activity directly to internal systems to control product movement, order processing, and supply chain activity. The complexity of these different approaches varies significantly and can affect the auditor's evaluation of process risks.

The information flows associated with sales and customer service are also illustrated in Figure 11–3. Information requirements focus on competitor, customer, and product data as well as on pricing, payment, and delivery policies. Information outputs from the process include marketing activities, transaction data, and changes to customer and product records. Feeding information from marketing and sales into planning and production activities is particularly important to facilitate the organization's response to changed market and competitive conditions.

Example

A drop in demand for a product may necessitate a change in restocking procedures. The sooner information related to a change in demand can be communicated along the supply chain, the less likely excess inventory will build up in the company or the supplier. In a similar vein, the better the ability to capture pricing information from competitors and feed it into its marketing efforts, the better able the company is to nimbly respond to competitive pressures. Airlines, booksellers, and consumer electronics retailers are particular effective at tracking competitor pricing.

TRANSACTIONS ARISING FROM SALES AND CUSTOMER SERVICE

A number of accounts and transactions are affected by the sales and customer service process, as indicated in Figure 11–3. The most common transactions in this process are sales, receipts, returns, and bad debts. The key steps in handling sales, collections, and related transactions are described in Figure 11–4 and discussed below.[3]

SALES

A *sales* transaction for a manufacturer typically starts with sales order entry, which produces a *sales order* that is forwarded to the credit department for

---

3 The acquisition of advertising and marketing resources, such as television time, newspaper space, advertising graphics, and so on, can be considered to be part of the company's supply chain (see Chapter 12).

Figure 11–4   Summary of Sales and Customer Service Activities

Process/Activity	Documents	Journals, Ledgers, and Records Used	Typical Journal Entry
Sale Transaction			
Sales order entry: An incoming communication from a prospective customer begins the sales process.	Customer purchase order (external) Sales order (internal)		
Credit approval: The customer is investigated to determine if sale on credit is appropriate.		Approved customer list	
Shipping: Items to be purchased are prepared for delivery or pickup	Bill of lading (internal)		
Pricing/ Billing: Appropriate pricing assigned and total billing amount computed.	Sales invoice (internal)	Price list Sales journal	
Receivable posting: Credit sales are posted to appropriate receivable accounts (e.g., customer or credit card agency).		Accounts receivable subsidiary ledger	
General accounting: The sale, receivable, and reduction of inventory is recorded in the appropriate accounts.	Journal entry ticket (internal)	General ledger	Dr. Accounts Receivable Cr. Sales
Collection Transaction			
Receipt capture: Payments are opened, identified, and separated from other documents. A cash prelist is prepared.	Customer check (external) Remittance advice (internal)	Cash prelist	
Receipt processing: Customer and payment information is verified and receipts are deposited.	Deposit slip (internal)	Cash receipts journal	
Receivable posting: Payments are posted to the payer's account.		Accounts receivable subsidiary ledger	
General accounting: Payments are recorded in the appropriate accounts.	Journal entry ticket (internal)	General ledger	Dr. Cash Cr. Accounts Receivable

(continued)

Figure 11–4   *(continued)*

Process/Activity	Documents	Journals, Ledgers, and Records Used	Typical Journal Entry
Sales Return Transaction			
Returns processing: Returned goods are processed and an appropriate refund or credit issued to the customer.	Credit memo (internal) Inventory ticket (internal)	Sales returns journal	
Receivable posting: Credit is entered into payer's account (e.g., customer or credit card agency).		Accounts receivable subsidiary ledger	
General accounting: The return of goods and the refund are recorded in the appropriate accounts.	Journal Entry ticket (internal)	General ledger	Dr. Sales Returns Cr. Accounts Receivable
Bad Debt Write-Off			
Uncollectible account processing: Overdue accounts are reviewed and uncollectible accounts removed.	Write-off authorization (internal)		
Receivable posting: Amounts to be written off are removed from customer balances.		Accounts receivable subsidiary ledger	
General accounting: Write-offs of account balances are recorded in the appropriate accounts.	Journal entry ticket (internal)	General ledger	Dr. Bad Debt Allowance Cr. Accounts Receivable
Bad Debt Estimation			
Estimation: Future bad debts are estimated from payment history and financial status of customers.	Worksheet (internal)	Aged receivables trial balance	
General accounting: Estimated bad debt expense is recorded in the appropriate accounts.	Journal entry ticket (internal)	General ledger	Dr. Bad Debt Expense Cr. Bad Debt Allowance

approval. The approved sales order then serves as an authorization for shipping. The shipping department will release the requested items and prepare a *shipping document* (often called a *bill of lading*) as evidence of the shipment. The shipping document becomes the basis for billing the customer, via a *sales invoice*, after prices and terms have been determined. Sales invoices are separately posted to the *accounts receivable ledger* and accumulated in the *sales journal* (which is usually the basis for recording sales).

The key event in the sales process is the delivery of the goods to the customer. At this point, the earnings process is substantially complete and the company should recognize the occurrence of a sale transaction. The shipping document (or bill of lading) is the boundary document for the transaction. In many systems, however, the invoice is used to recognize sales because prices are not usually entered on shipping documents.

Organizations that primarily sell goods and services to other businesses, or that sell to customers via the Internet, primarily conduct sales through automated processes, including *electronic data interchange (EDI) systems*. These systems link sales and inventory systems together so that suppliers of goods are authorized to ship new inventory to a customer when certain conditions occur (a low level of inventory on hand) rather than having to wait to receive a formal sales order. Furthermore, the shipment of goods triggers the subsequent cash collection process without separate sales invoices being sent (although for Internet sales, customers are usually sent e-mail notification of shipments).

Example

Wal-Mart requires all of its suppliers worldwide to be part of its extensive EDI system. The company's sales system is linked to its ordering and collections systems so that when goods are sold to consumers in stores, suppliers are notified electronically that Wal-Mart has made a sale and that the supplier should ship new goods to replace what has been sold (i.e., the sales order for the supplier is generated automatically based on Wal-Mart's sales records).

COLLECTIONS

Cash receipts encompass all payments received from customers. Incoming payments in the form of cash or checks must be captured by the system, credited to the proper account, and deposited in a bank. Most companies use *remittance advices* for customers to send with their payments to facilitate proper processing. Returned remittance advices are the boundary documents proving the receipt of a payment. Incoming payments are accumulated on a *cash prelist* by the mailroom (or other recipient) and then passed on for further processing. Checks are separated from remittance advices and deposited. Payments are entered in the *cash receipts journal*—the basis for recognition of receipts in the general ledger— and are posted to customers' accounts. Posting of customer balances and preparation of the cash receipts journal is often computerized, whereas the initial processing of incoming receipts is done manually.

Organizations that primarily sell goods and services to other businesses or that sell to customers via the Internet primarily receive payments electronically through *electronic funds transfers (EFTs)*. For business-to-business (B2B) transactions, such transfers typically involve the customer's bank sending a cash payment electronically to the seller's bank. A confirmation of the transfer is also sent directly to the company receiving the payment (also electronically). When utilized as part of an EDI system, the transfer occurs based on pre-specified terms that have been built into the system (e.g., payment upon presentment). Overall, automated systems that involve both the sales and collections process can dramatically reduce the cost of each transaction for both the seller and buyer.

SALES RETURNS

The key activities in the sales return process are refunding customer payments or granting customer credit, and restocking returned goods in inventory (if they can be resold). Typically, a sales return will be evidenced by a *credit memo* and, possibly, a separate *inventory ticket* to show receipt of merchandise.

BAD DEBT ESTIMATION

On a periodic basis, typically when financial statements are prepared, a company will assess the realizable value of all existing receivables. Based on previous experience and current economic conditions, the company will attempt to predict what portion of receivables will become uncollectible even though they may not be overdue at the moment. An estimate of uncollectible accounts is usually developed based on a review of different categories of accounts included in the *accounts receivable subsidiary ledger*. Typically, accounts are classified by the time that has passed since a sale was made using an *accounts receivable aging schedule*. For example, a retailer might estimate that 2 percent of all current accounts are uncollectible, but estimate that 10 percent of accounts more than 30 days past due are uncollectible, 40 percent of accounts more than 60 days past due are uncollectible, and so on. The financial statements are then adjusted to reflect the resulting estimate of bad debts.

BAD DEBT WRITE-OFFS

Delinquent customer accounts should be periodically reviewed and removed from the receivables ledger if they are deemed to be uncollectible. The write-off of an account is evidenced by a *write-off authorization*. The write-off of an account does not mean that collection efforts cease, only that the accounts receivable balance should be adjusted to reflect its realizable value. Accounts that are subsequently collected can be reinstated as the need arises. This process is different from bad debt estimation in that direct write-offs are non-routine transactions that require specific investigation and authorization. This process is meant to ensure that proper measures are taken to collect overdue accounts, whereas bad debt estimation is performed to ensure that expenses are properly matched with revenues in each reporting period.

VENDOR ALLOWANCES AND REBATES

Retailers often have a choice of products to sell and may have concerns about whether products that are selected will be sold at a price that provides an adequate margin to justify the decision to stock the product. To encourage retailers to carry their product, manufacturers will often provide vendor allowances or rebates.

These allowances or rebates may serve as an incentive for a retailer to sell an item or to allocate it prominent display space. They may also be used to share any loss that arises from discounting slow-moving inventory. Vendor allowances and rebates may take many forms: (1) a direct reduction in the amount owed by the retailer to the manufacturer, (2) a discount on future purchases from the manufacturer, or (3) vendor payments for joint vendor–retailer advertising. Regardless of the form of the rebate, accounting rules require that these allowances be recorded as a reduction in costs of goods sold in the period in which the deal is negotiated.

Example

In 2005, the U.S. retailer Saks Fifth Avenue was fined by the Securities and Exchange Commission for failing to properly account for vendor allowances. Improper accounting related to vendor allowances from 1996 through 2003 resulted in Saks collecting more than $34 million in inappropriate allowances by falsifying information provided to vendors. Discovery of this fraud resulted in the termination of Saks' chief accounting officer and repayments to vendors of $48 million (including interest).

INTERNAL THREAT ANALYSIS FOR SALES AND CUSTOMER SERVICE

An internal threat analysis for sales and customer service is illustrated in Figure 11–5. A number of potential process risks are identified in the first column and then linked to possible controls for mitigating the risk and performance measures that could be used to monitor the risks. The list of risks is not intended to be comprehensive and could vary for many organizations depending on the design of their sales and customer service activities. Furthermore, the controls and performance measures are intended to be illustrative.

IDENTIFICATION OF PROCESS RISKS

The existence and significance of process risks will depend on the design of specific processes. A significant risk for one company may not be relevant to the comparable process within another company.

Example

The choice of an IT system can be a source of both risk and competitive advantage for a retailer. During the Christmas shopping season in 2003, Sobeys (a large Canadian grocery chain) experienced difficulty delivering its products to some of its stores because of problems related to the company's enterprise resource planning (ERP) system. These problems highlighted the need for a reliable and efficient IT system that could respond to heavier than usual order flows. Although competitors were acknowledged to have older technology, they achieved a competitive advantage over Sobeys during the period in which the ERP software was being implemented and debugged. It is not uncommon for the transition process of installing an ERP system to take more than a year.

Figure 11–5   Internal Threat Analysis: Sales and Customer Service

Process Risks	Controls Linked to Risks	Performance Measures
(1) Weak portfolio of brands and products.	• Adequate investment into product research and development. • Investment program to acquire existing brands and trademarks. • Systematic promotion and marketing plan. • Consumer research.	• Market share by product line. • Customer brand awareness. • Age of products.
(2) Failure to provide unique product value.	• Consumer research. • Research on competition. • Clear strategy and goals. • Effective capital budgeting procedures. • Specific guidelines for product introduction and evaluation.	• Market share by product line. • Price point relative to competition. • New customer acquisition rate.
(3) Ineffective or inappropriate marketing, advertising, or promotions	• Monitor rate of exposure and market penetration of marketing and advertising campaigns. • Adequate marketing research.	• Customer brand awareness. • New customer acquisition rates. • Percentage of sales due to promotions. • Marketing/advertising as a percentage of sales. • Transaction closure rates. • Sales per salesperson.
(4) Inappropriate incentive programs.	• Monitor success rate of specific promotions. • Monitor competitor programs and offers.	• Average realized markdowns. • Transaction closure rates. • Average transaction size relative to costs of promotions.
(5) Failure to respond to customer needs.	• Send monthly statements to customers. • Establish system for obtaining satisfaction ratings and feedback from customers.	• Customer satisfaction ratings. • Customer retention rates. • Transaction cycle time. • Processing time.
(6) Excessive credit risk.	• Segregate credit approval from sales processing. • Maintain and monitor current credit limits for approved customers. • Perform credit checks on new customers. • Review existing accounts for potential collection problems. • Maintain history of bad debt experiences.	• Delinquency rates. • Percent of receivables written off. • Receivable turnover and time-to-collect. • Average age of customer balances. • Average customer balances.

Figure 11–5 *(continued)*

Process Risks	Controls Linked to Risks	Performance Measures
(7) Failure to deliver product or service on a timely basis.	• Maintain a file of open orders and review for completion. • Utilize alternative shipping channels.	• Transaction cycle time. • Shipping and on-time delivery statistics. • Frequency of product shortages or partial shipments.
(8) Failure to achieve sales targets.	• Establish strategic plans and goals and review progress on a periodic basis. • Link product development, marketing, pricing, and service processes to strategic objectives.	• Market share by product line. • Sales versus target.
(9) Inadequate profit margins.	• Establish policies on price reductions and mark-downs. • Control shrinkage and fraud. • Maintain cost discipline in customer service.	• Profit margins by product line. • Selling expenses as a percentage of sales. • Sales commission rates. • Marketing costs as a percentage of sales. • Sales relative to asset base.
(10) Unsatisfactory customer experiences and loss of customers.	• Timely response to customer questions and complaints. • Monitor customer satisfaction. • Staff training and scheduling. • Monitor and meet offers by the competition.	• Customer satisfaction ratings. • Customer retention rates. • Order fill rate. • Customer complaints
(11) Excessive inventory carrying and handling costs.	• Forecast capacity and location needs. • Invest in appropriate technology for monitoring inventory. • Automate stock replenishment systems. • Review actual-to-expected inventory levels.	• Inventory turnover by product line. • Cost of carrying inventory. • Costs of obsolescence.
(12) Unauthorized, incorrect, or inappropriate shipments.	• Shipment authorized by credit and sales departments. • Shipments verified against supporting documentation.	• Number of incorrect shipments. • Merchandise returns. • Customer complaints related to delivery.

(continued)

Figure 11–5 *(continued)*

Process Risks	Controls Linked to Risks	Performance Measures
(13) Inaccurate or unauthorized pricing.	• Maintain master price list. • Establish standard payment terms. • Automate pricing and billing information.	• Percentage of transactions with price adjustments. • Average size of price adjustments. • Number of pricing errors.
(14) Excessive returns or price adjustments.	• Establish clear policy and procedures for accepting returns. • Monitor competitor offers.	• Merchandise returns as a percentage of sales. • Average cost per return.
(15) Excessive fraud, inventory shrinkage or theft.	• Control access to inventory. • Establish clear lines of responsibilities and authority over transaction processing. • Segregate incompatible activities. • Establish procedures for handling cash receipts. • Independent authorization of unusual transactions or account write-offs.	• Shrinkage statistics. • Differences between perpetual inventory records and actual counts. • Time-to-collect statistics. • Delinquency rates.
(16) Inaccurate information processing.	• Proper completion and verification of supporting documents. • Appropriate segregation of duties across activities. • Use of standard control numbers for accounts, products, etc. • Update files and accounting records on a timely basis.	• Percent of transactions subject to processing errors. • Size of transaction adjustments. • Number of transaction adjustments.
(17) Failure to capture desired information.	• Use and verify prenumbered documents for transactions. • Record all events and transactions on a timely basis.	• Number of missing documents from sequence. • Number of missing fields in customer records.
(18) Inadequate or unsatisfactory customer service.	• Proper training of customer service personnel. • Effective and convenient scheduling of customer service calls.	• Customer satisfaction ratings. • Number of repeat service efforts. • Customer wait time. • Customer service time.

Figure 11–5   *(continued)*

Process Risks	Controls Linked to Risks	Performance Measures
(19) Excessive customer service costs.	• Proper training of customer service personnel. • Establish policies on appropriate customer service levels and monitor performance.	• Service costs as a percentage of sales. • Service costs per customer. • Merchandise return rates. • Warranty claims.
(20) Failure to link supply chain and production to sales activity.	• Supply chain integration and information sharing. • Sales forecasting and joint marketing/production planning. • Establish standards for supplier qualifications.	• Percent of product shortages. • Length of product backlog • Time delay in filling backlog.
(21) Failure to innovate.	• Monitor competition and customer needs. • Adequate product research and development.	• New product introduction rate. • Time-to-market for new products. • Age of product lines.
(22) Inadequate training/staffing.	• Monitor employee training. • Establish appropriate compensation and promotion policies. • Adopt flexible staffing and work rules.	• Employee satisfaction. • Time spent in training per employee. • Training budget.
(23) Improper accounting for vendor allowances or rebates.	• Document and monitor vendor allowance agreements. • Establish vendor allowance policies (e.g., discounts, advertising).	• Vendor allowances per buyer. • Total vendor allowances compared to competitors.

Column 1 of Figure 11–5 lists a number of risks that could arise within sales and customer service. Examples of specific process risks relevant to sales and customer service include

People Risks

• Managerial Risk: Incompetent management or management that lacks authority can lead to poor decision making within a process. A weak brand portfolio (risk 1), failure to deliver adequate product value (risk 2), ineffective marketing (risk 3), and failure to innovate (risk 21) can all arise due to problems in process leadership. Furthermore, a failure to monitor and respond to changes in external forces can lead to poor process performance. For example, the ability to adjust marketing, pricing, and sales-mix strategies to respond to dramatic increases in energy costs is expected to be a key factor for succeeding in various industries, such as retailing, manufacturing, and transportation.

- Ethical Risk: Dishonest or unethical employees can lead to misuse of assets or inaccurate information processing. Excessive inventory shrinkage (risk 15) or inappropriate shipments (risk 12) may occur when distribution employees are dishonest and not subject to adequate control.
- Human Resource Risk: All processes involve human effort to some degree. Failure to adequately train, manage, and supervise personnel can create many problems within a process. For example, human resource risks can affect sales and customer service through poor customer service (risks 5 and 18), poor evaluation of credit risks (risk 6), and inadequately trained personnel (22).

Direct Process Risks

- Operational Risk: Operational risks encompass a broad variety of performance problems within a process. Late deliveries (risk 7), low customer satisfaction (risk 10), excessive inventory costs (risk 11), inaccurate pricing (risk 13), excessive sales returns (risk 14), and excessive service costs (19) could all be attributable to inefficient or ineffective operations.
- Information Risk: The absence of reliable information about a process and the emphasis on internal control over financial reporting makes information risk a potentially critical concern to the auditor. Consequently, the auditor may devote more time to evaluating the completeness and reliability of information flows than might be devoted to other process risks. A process characterized by inaccurate information processing (risk 16) or omitted information (risk 17) would lead to higher risk assessments by the auditor.

Indirect Process Risks

- Technology Risk: Technology can affect the overall performance of a process, the reliability of information within the process, or the ability of management to monitor the process. The pervasive presence of technology and potential weaknesses in an information system create risks including failure to identify and respond to customer needs (risk 5), inefficient inventory handling (risk 11), inaccurate information processing (risk 16), failure to capture required information (risk 17), and failure to link sales activity to supply-chain activity (risk 20).
- Planning Risk: Risks often arise because of ineffective planning and budgeting or a failure to provide adequate resources for process activities. Such problems could result in risks related to inadequate marketing (risk 3), failure to achieve sales targets and profit margins (risks 8 and 9) or failure to respond to customer needs (risks 5 and 18).
- Regulatory Risk: Failure to comply with regulations pertinent to a process can lead to significant fines and penalties. If inventory is required to be strictly controlled (e.g., pharmaceuticals), risk can arise when inventory control systems are inadequate or break down. Similarly, marketing or sales incentives based on false or deceptive sales practices can run afoul of consumer protection laws (risks 3 and 4).

As we can see from the examples above, potential sources of risk can interact to influence the existence and significance of actual risks within a process. Some risks may affect multiple areas of an organization. Furthermore, strengths in one area may offset weaknesses in other areas. For example, effective process design and use of technology could partially compensate for weak or unethical employees. Similarly, regulatory attention can offset a tendency toward operational inefficiency or ineffectiveness. In the case that management is incompetent, employees are poorly trained and motivated, process technology is inadequate, or operations are poorly structured, the level of process risk would be significantly heightened. Of particular importance to the auditor is the interaction of technology and information risks, especially as it affects the flow of information within the process and the links to financial reporting.

ANALYSIS OF PROCESS CONTROLS

Different types of controls may be used to mitigate different risks. Recall from our earlier discussions that the company has four options for responding to a specific risk: accept, avoid, share, or reduce.

Example

Accepting credit cards (e.g., Visa) is one way to share credit risk with another party. Implementing strict guidelines for granting credit to a customer and placing limits on the amount of credit awarded to individual customers are ways to reduce or control credit risk internally.

Column 2 of Figure 11–5 describes numerous controls that might be effective for reducing the risks related to sales and customer service. These controls fall into four basic categories:

1. Performance reviews or monitoring controls: Active monitoring of risk conditions and timely responses to increased risk are important for establishing control within a process. Within sales and customer service processes, the auditor should expect to see effective monitoring of the following:
   * Competition (e.g., new products and marketing efforts)
   * Customer attributes (e.g., tastes)
   * Technological advances
   * Operational effectiveness (e.g., risks affecting delivery performance, employee morale, customer returns, and processing errors)
   * Overall performance (e.g., sales and profitability relative to targets)
2. Segregation of duties: Some duties within a process are likely to be incompatible, and failure to achieve adequate separation of these activities could create opportunities to commit fraud or allow processing errors to go undetected. For sales and customer service, we should see a number of duties separated: (1) credit approval and sales entry, (2) cash receipt handling and receivable posting, and (3) data processing and transaction authorization.
3. Processing controls: These controls reflect a broad range of procedures including required authorizations, use of adequate documents and records, and independent verification of information. For sales and customer service, appropriate authorization procedures should be specified for granting credit, setting prices, releasing shipments, and accepting sales returns. Appropriate documents should be used within the process including order entry forms, shipping documents, invoices and remittance advices, all of which should be prenumbered and used in sequence (see Figure 11–4). Finally, there are numerous aspects of the process that may be subject to independent verification including reviewing and comparing documents for discrepancies, checking batch and control totals, monitoring open transactions, and investigating customer complaints or discrepancies. Many of these procedures are directly relevant to the auditor's evaluation of internal control over financial reporting.

4.   Physical controls: Limiting access to tangible assets, cash, and accounting records is helpful for minimizing risks arising from unauthorized decisions or actions. The receipt of cash is an area where physical control is particularly critical.

Many of the controls described in Figure 11–5 may be either manual or automated. Controls related to transaction documentation and verification are especially amenable to computerization. The selection of control procedures for a process depends on the structure of the process, the significance of the various risks, and the cost of implementing specific controls. Given that every company has a slightly different set of activities and risks, each will have a slightly different set of controls. Many controls may be adapted to different risks. The controls listed in Figure 11–5 provide a good starting point for an auditor's analysis, although not all procedures will be applicable to, or needed by, all companies.

ANALYSIS OF INTERNAL CONTROL OVER FINANCIAL REPORTING

Of particular concern to most auditors are process controls affecting financial reporting. Because most audit-sensitive processes generate transactions that are included in the financial statements, the auditor must be concerned that transaction processing is accurate. Figure 11–6 lists a number of controls specifically related to financial reporting that would be appropriate for sales and customer service processes:

Sales: The critical controls for sales are those related to shipping, pricing, and billing. The utmost concern to the auditor is that all sales are recorded and that the valuation of transactions accurately reflects the quantity shipped, the prices charged, and the payment terms. Other controls address the creditworthiness of customers and the accuracy and timeliness of transaction posting. Because sales transactions tend to be routine for many organizations, auditors should expect the presence of many automated controls for sales. In fact, auditors should be wary of any system that contains material manual journal entries for sales. At a minimum, the organization should have well-designed controls to prevent and detect any unauthorized or unreasonable adjusting entries to sales.

Example

Many previous accounting frauds involve fictitious sales throughout the year that are "hidden" by creating adjusting journal entries to write-off fictitious sales or transfer them to other accounts. Another common accounting problem arises when an organization sells service contracts that extend over a period of time at the same time a product is sold. It is then important that the sales price of the bundled products and services be properly allocated to current and future revenue.

Receipts: The most critical concern for receipts is control over cash and checks upon taking possession and prior to deposit in order to minimize the chance that receipts may be lost or misappropriated. The immediate creation of a cash list by the cashier or mailroom clerk opening the mail is essential for capturing transactions. After the list is prepared, misappropriation of cash or checks is difficult because missing funds will create a discrepancy between the receipt list and subsequent processing. Additionally, customers are encouraged to return a remittance advice with a payment to minimize the risk of incorrect processing or posting.

An alternative to direct handling of cash receipts by the company is use of a third party receipt service, such as a bank, or online transfer of funds. The former

Figure 11–6   Financial Reporting Controls for Sales-Related Transactions

Transaction	Typical Financial Reporting Controls
Sales	Maintain a list of approved customers. Segregate credit approval from sales activity. Maintain up-to-date approved credit limits for existing customers. Use prenumbered sales, shipping, and billing documents in sequence. Utilize automated systems (e.g., point-of-sale system) to track all sales by operations personnel, including any discounts offered, etc. Provide indication of credit approval in documentation. Verify quantities shipped against the shipping document and sales order. Provide indication of shipment in documentation. Verify prices charged for items shipped. Verify extensions and totals on invoice. Post transactions on a timely basis. Use control and hash totals to verify accuracy of postings. Customer account numbers and product numbers should contain check digits. Match and verify all documents. Maintain up-to-date chart of accounts. Reconcile general ledger totals and activity with subsidiary ledger and supporting journals. Utilize automated systems to post all routine sales transactions. Use proper access controls to enable adjusting entries. Review all adjusting journal entries prior to entering. Investigate unusual entries to accounts.
Cash receipts	Automate receipts through use of electronic funds transfers handled by qualified third-parties (e.g., banks, PayPal). Separate initial handling of receipts from other accounting functions and sales-related activities. Obtain item counts of incoming payments. Prepare list of all cash receipts immediately. Do not accept cash payments through mail. Use prenumbered receipts for cash transactions. Restrictively endorse all checks received as "for deposit only." Use lockbox system. Compare amount received to amount per remittance advice. Separate checks from remittance advices and prepare timely bank deposit. Verify that payments agree with quoted terms (e.g., discounts, time period, interest). Post transactions on a timely basis. Use control and hash totals to verify accuracy of postings. Reconcile bank accounts independently of receipt processing and posting. Reconcile general ledger totals and activity with subsidiary ledger and supporting journals and records (e.g., bank deposits, cash listing). Send monthly statements to customers.

(continued)

Figure 11–6   *(continued)*

Transaction	Typical Financial Reporting Controls
Sales return processing	Use prenumbered credit memos.
	Record credit memos on a timely basis.
	Require approval of sales returns by operations personnel not directly interacting with customers.
	Segregate preparation of credit memos from cash receipt processing.
	Prepare receiving reports (prenumbered) of returned goods on a timely basis.
	Reconcile amounts per credit memo with documentation of original sale.
	"Cancel" original sales documents to prevent duplicate returns.
Write-off processing	Prepare an aged receivables trial balance on a regular basis.
	Review overdue accounts periodically.
	Keep customer correspondence files related to overdue amounts current.
	Approve write-offs by someone independent of the sales and cash receipt functions.
	Use prenumbered documents to evidence write-offs.
Bad debt estimation	Maintain bad debt historical data.
	Review assumptions underlying estimation procedures for appropriateness.
	Review calculation procedures for deriving estimates.

system requires customers to mail payments directly to the company's bank. The processing of receipts becomes the bank's responsibility and many of the control procedures listed for receipts then become unnecessary. The bank provides a report to the company listing the customers and the amounts of the receipts, which the company can use to post its accounts. Of course, the bank charges a fee for this service, and the cost of using the bank has to be weighed against the improvement in control that is gained.

Sales adjustments and bad debts: Still other controls pertain to the risks arising from sales adjustments and bad debts. Proper authorization procedures are particularly important for sales adjustments and bad debts. Additionally, accurate processing of adjustments and write-offs is fostered through the use of appropriate documents and records (e.g., credit memos) and independent verification of individual transactions and transaction batches.

A company may have different systems and controls to respond to different situations and events. One type of transaction may be well controlled (e.g., mail orders), whereas another may be subject to significant processing errors (e.g., cash sales with immediate delivery). It is the responsibility of the auditor to develop an adequate understanding of processing controls and controls over financial reporting to support an assessment of control risk for key assertions affected by a process. When assessing control risk, the auditor must consider all possible circumstances, not just the most common. An organization implementing a large number of the procedures listed in Figures 11–5 and 11–6 would probably have moderate-to-low control risk for most assertions related to sales and customer service, especially if many of the controls are embedded in a well-designed, automated information system. Absence of such controls may indicate the existence of a significant deficiency in internal control over financial reporting.

EVALUATION OF PROCESS PERFORMANCE INDICATORS

The auditor should also examine performance indicators and monitoring controls used to monitor process risks. A systematic review of a range of performance indicators can be useful for identifying risk conditions that may need further attention. Appropriate performance indicators for the identified process risks are listed in Figure 11–5. These measures cover a number of areas including

- Financial performance: Sales levels and profitability provide an indication of the overall success of sales and customer service. Therefore, the auditor should examine growth in sales, trends in profitability, and profit margin ratios.
- Market performance: Statistics on market share and customer satisfaction provide direct measures of how the market views the company's sales and service efforts. Customer acquisition and retention rates can be particularly useful in gauging market reactions.
- Process performance: In general, financial and market performance are driven by process performance. Consequently, statistics for delivery time, transaction closure rates, costs per transaction, and delivery error rates are particularly helpful.

In deciding which performance indicators to examine and evaluate, the auditor must consider both the cost of obtaining the information and the reliability of the information. Unless a company has a well-developed and fully integrated information system, such as an ERP system, some of the measures identified in Figure 11–5 may be difficult to obtain. Financial results extracted from the basic accounting system are likely to be the most reliable performance measures, whereas operating statistics that are generated from other systems or using desktop technology may be less reliable. Performance measures that are subjective in nature (e.g., customer satisfaction and employee morale) are also potentially unreliable unless gathered in a systematic and rigorous manner.

An auditor would examine the key performance measures for specific risks that are of concern (i.e., potential residual risks). For example, declining market share, deteriorating customer satisfaction, and increased delivery and service delays could indicate heightened process risk. To illustrate, consider the situation where the rate of customer delinquency is increasing, receivable turnover is decreasing, sales adjustments are increasing, and customer complaints are on the rise. This pattern of results would suggest weaknesses in the collection of receivables that have been billed to customers. The auditor would need to consider the implications of high residual credit risk. Presumably, the auditor would then expect that bad debt expense should increase and the percentage of receivables reserved against future losses should be growing. These expectations could be compared to actual results to evaluate the risk of material misstatement for relevant financial statement assertions, e.g. the valuation of receivables.

Negative performance indicators can also put stress on credit managers to improve performance by becoming overly aggressive with customers or imposing overly strict conditions on customer credit. Worse still, managers may attempt to disguise actual results. These behavior patterns are not in the best interests of the company and could have important implications for the auditor's assessment of the control environment. In short, a pattern of negative performance measures would lead to increased risk assessments for some aspects of sales and customer service.

Figure 11–7   Residual Risk Map for Sales and Customer Service*

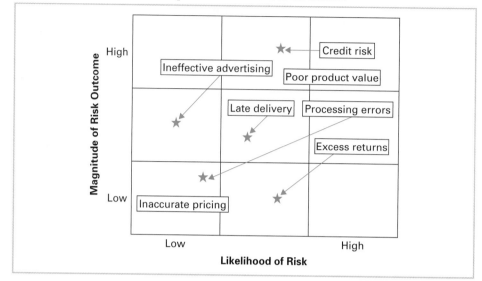

*For ease of exposition, not all risks identified in Figure 11–5 have been included in the risk map. This does not imply that omitted risks are less important. The risks that are included were chosen for illustrative purposes only.

CONCLUSIONS ABOUT RESIDUAL RISKS FROM SALES AND CUSTOMER SERVICE

After completing a process map and internal threat analysis, the auditor should have adequate knowledge and evidence to assess the residual risks in a process that are potentially significant. Risk assessments are documented in a risk map as illustrated in Figure 11–7 for a few of the risks we have discussed related to sales and customer service. The initial assessment of a risk is indicated by a box. Risks that are located in the upper right of the graph are considered to be potentially significant residual risks. Risk reduction due to internal control is indicated by shifting a risk down and to the left. Final risk assessments, after consideration of controls and performance indicators, are indicated with a star. When risks may be reduced due to controls, especially controls related to financial reporting, the auditor must gather evidence to support the risk reduction using *tests of controls*.

TESTING PROCESS CONTROL AND INTERNAL CONTROL OVER FINANCIAL REPORTING

The purpose of tests of controls is for the auditor to obtain evidence that important internal controls are effective, especially those over financial reporting. Not all controls need to be tested by the auditor. The controls of primary importance for all audits are those that shift risk from a significant level to an acceptable level. For an integrated audit of U.S. registered public companies, all important internal controls over financial reporting must be tested by the auditor, even if they have not been identified as shifting risk significantly. Some examples of tests of controls for sales and customer service are described in Figure 11–8. Tests of controls related to sales and customer service tend to emphasize proper authorization of

Figure 11–8   Testing Internal Controls Related to Sales and Customer Service

Performance Reviews and Overall Process Management
- Review policies for establishing strategy, goals, and budgets for marketing, product innovation, customer service, and sales activity.
- Evaluate whether policies and decisions related to sales and customer service are consistent with the overall strategy and objectives of the organization.
- Review and evaluate internal analyses related to competitors, customers, marketing efforts, and market conditions.
- Examine documentation in support of key decisions related to sales and customer service.
- Review sales and marketing plans and budgets and verify that variances have been investigated.
- Review receivables reports and verify timely handling of adjustments and bad debts.
- Evaluate competence and training of key individuals within the process.
- Discuss performance measures and process evaluation with appropriate management and evaluate whether process oversight is effective.
- Identify and review appropriate performance indicators relevant to key process risks.

Information Processing Controls
Proper Authorization Procedures
- Verify existence and use of general authorization related to prices (master price list), credit approval (approved customer lists and credit limits), shipping and payment terms, and account classifications (chart of accounts).
- Review the process for revising general authorizations.
- Obtain a sample of sales documents and verify that all required approvals are properly noted on the documents.

Use of Adequate Documents and Records
- Verify that documents are prenumbered and used in sequence including shipping documents, sales invoices, and receipt lists.

Independent Verification of Employee Responsibilities
- Verify that all exception reports and computer edit listings are followed up and cleared on a timely basis.
- Obtain a sample of sales documents and verify that all required verifications are properly noted on the documents, including evidence of posting.
- Obtain sample of receipt lists and remittance advices and verify that all required verifications are properly noted on the documents, including evidence of posting.
- Verify that proper reconciliations are performed on a timely basis for (1) sales journal and receivable postings, (2) receipts journal and receivable postings, and (3) bank reconciliations and receipts journal.

Physical Controls
- Observe facilities and client personnel for control over access to assets, documents and records.

Segregation of Duties and Process Design
- Verify that appropriate segregation of duties exists for sales activities.
- Discuss work responsibilities with employees assigned to transaction processing, and evaluate effectiveness and consistency of individual responsibilities and authority.
- Examine procedures manuals, personnel policies, organization charts, the chart of accounts, and other documents and records used in the system.
- Identify and evaluate significant changes within the process occurring in the past year.

transactions, including the establishment of credit, the release of inventory, the pricing of inventory, the billing of customers, and the timing of payment. The auditor would also want to know how the company initiates, approves, and implements changes to these authorization policies.

Many of the control tests involve interviewing individuals within the process. The auditor needs to clearly understand what each person does, how he or she fits into the overall structure of the process, and whether he or she has the training and expertise to effectively perform his or her tasks. Obtaining this information usually involves interviewing numerous staff, line, and low-level managerial personnel as part of a walkthrough of the process. Although individual responses do not provide strong evidence of process effectiveness, the overall consistency of the information can provide some assurance about the effectiveness of controls.

Where possible, the auditor should obtain documentation to further support conclusions about control. Auditors commonly examine a sample of transactions for tangible evidence of proper approval and processing. For example, the auditor could look at the credit manager's sign-off on a sales order to verify that credit has been approved. Proper release of goods for shipment may be evidenced by the warehouse supervisor's signature on the shipping document. This type of evidence must be interpreted carefully, however, because signatures and initials do not guarantee that the transaction was actually processed correctly. That is, a credit manager may sign off on a sale without actually doing a credit check.

Other forms of documentation include obtaining exception reports (especially if generated by an automated system) and determining whether problems are handled promptly and appropriately, reviewing official policies and comparing them for consistency with information obtained from process personnel, and examining internal reports used for monitoring process performance. The last form of documentation is particularly important because it highlights that performance measures, if effectively monitored and acted upon by management, can be a strong source of evidence about the effectiveness of internal control.

In some situations, it is possible to observe process personnel in the performance of their duties. Observation should be as unobtrusive as possible to obtain an accurate impression of the seriousness and reliability of the personnel responsible for a key control. Also, observation may need to be repeated under different conditions and at different times, especially if the client has a change in personnel related to important controls.

For automated systems, it may not be possible to test controls without involving a computer expert. Most large accounting firms have a specialized group of information systems experts who are qualified to examine technical documentation and analyze program code to determine whether automated controls are well designed and operating effectively. For public company audits, it is now expected that at least one member of the engagement team will have such specialized expertise.

Our example in Figure 11–7 indicates that risks from ineffective advertising (risk 3) and excess returns (risk 14) are reduced to an acceptable level by internal control. To test controls over ineffective marketing, the auditor would review and evaluate the company's procedures for monitoring the competitive environment and the impact of its marketing efforts. Tests of controls for excess returns would be performed by reviewing the company's returns policy and interviewing appropriate process personnel to verify that it is applied effectively. Also, documents could be examined for a sample of unusual sales returns. Figure 11–7 indicates that controls over information processing are particularly important (e.g., see risk 16 in

Figure 11–5). Since these controls are likely to pertain to financial reporting, the auditor would test the most important procedures, including verifying documentation and observing segregation of duties if necessary.

It is also important to note when controls do not need to be tested. Controls over poor product value would not be tested because they are either absent or the auditor has concluded that they would not be effective. Unless the engagement is for an integrated audit under PCAOB rules, controls over inaccurate pricing may not be tested because the risk is considered low regardless of controls. Controls over credit risk do not need to be tested because their impact is not adequate to reduce the risk to an acceptable level and there will be significant residual credit risk in any event. If credit risk is material to the financial statements, this could be considered a significant deficiency or a material weakness in internal control over financial reporting.

IDENTIFYING SIGNIFICANT RESIDUAL RISKS

The risk map depicted in Figure 11–7 provides the support necessary to reach conclusions about residual risks related to sales and customer service. In this example, two risks would be classified as significant residual risks upon completion of risk assessment: credit risk and poor product value. The auditor must analyze the implications of these risks for the conduct of the audit and subsequent tests of financial statement assertions. As previously noted, residual risks can affect the auditor's assessment of expected financial results, the quality of the control environment, the viability of the company, or the likelihood of accounting misstatements.

A high level of credit risk suggests that receivables and bad debts could have high inherent or control risk related to the valuation assertion. Poor product value would suggest that the company's products may not sell well and that the valuation of inventory could have high risk of material misstatement. This analysis conditions the auditor's expectations about the collectibility of receivables and the valuation of inventory. Furthermore, these risks would cause the auditor to design tests of the affected financial statement assertions to gather enough evidence to conclude that the assertions in question were not materially misstated. In the remainder of this chapter, we will discuss substantive tests that can be used if specific financial statement assertions related to cash and receivables have a high risk of material misstatement. Given that different substantive tests are used for different assertions, the auditor will select the substantive tests that are relevant for the specific high-risk assertions.

PLANNING TESTS OF FINANCIAL STATEMENT ASSERTIONS: REVENUE AND ACCOUNTS RECEIVABLE

The purpose of substantive tests of financial statement assertions is to provide direct evidence that an account is not materially misstated, especially if it is considered a residual risk after tests of controls and evaluation of relevant performance indicators. A comprehensive approach for substantive testing of accounts receivable is summarized in Figure 11–9. Substantive audit procedures for revenue and receivables include

- Tests of sales transactions
- Substantive analytical procedures

Figure 11–9   Substantive Tests for Accounts Receivable Account Assertions

Audit Assertion	Typical Substantive Audit Procedures
Existence: All recorded transactions related to receivables occurred and recorded receivables exist.	• Confirm accounts receivable and follow up on exceptions and non-responses. • Vouch a sample of sales and collection transactions from the period.
Completeness: All receivable transactions and balances have been recorded.	• Confirm accounts receivable and follow up on exceptions and non-responses. • Vouch a sample of sales and collection transactions from the period.
Valuation: Transaction detail included in subsidiary journals and ledgers agrees with the general ledger balances related to receivables.	• Obtain an aged receivable trial balance as of the close of business on the last day of the fiscal period. • Test the accuracy of the aged trial balance. • Reconcile the total per the aged trial balance with the receivable balance per the general ledger. • Select a sample of accounts in the aged trial balance and test the aging by examining the appropriate supporting documentation. • Reconcile activity per the sales journal, cash receipts journal, and postings to the accounts receivable subsidiary ledger with recorded activity in the general ledger receivables account.
Valuation: Transactions have been recorded in the proper period.	• Vouch transactions (sales, receipts, returns) prior to and after the fiscal year end and determine if they have been recorded in the proper period.
Valuation: Receivables are recorded at the appropriate gross amount and uncollectible amounts have been properly estimated.	• Confirm accounts receivable and follow up on exceptions and non-responses. • Examine supporting documentation of delinquent accounts and make an assessment of the likelihood of collection. • Develop an estimate of future uncollectible amounts. • Vouch a sample of sales and collection transactions from the period. • Vouch cash receipts subsequent to year end for indications of collectibility of delinquent accounts.
Valuation: Receivables are properly classified.	• Examine aged trial balance for unusual accounts that should be reclassified (credit balances, related parties, notes receivable).
Ownership: Receivable balances are owned by the company.	• Review board of directors minutes, bank confirmations, attorney letters, and other correspondence to identify receivables that have been factored. • Obtain representations from management about ownership of receivables.

- Tests of accuracy of the aged receivables trial balance
- Confirmations
- Cutoff tests
- Tests of revenue recognition
- Tests of receivable valuation

This list of procedures is intended to be very broad and few engagements would require the use of all of these tests unless the risk of material misstatement was considered to be high for a large number of assertions. Also, the extent of the procedures (i.e., sample size) would be adjusted for assessed risk levels. Some of the identified audit procedures provide evidence relevant to multiple assertions (e.g., confirmations test existence *and* valuation), whereas other procedures pertain to a single assertion (e.g., testing the accuracy of the aged trial balance).

TESTS OF SALES TRANSACTIONS

Typical tests of sales transactions are described in Figure 11–10. Most of these tests rely heavily on the documents and records produced during transaction processing. These tests provide direct documentary evidence as to whether individual transactions are misstated. In a highly computerized environment, these tests may require specialized software to trace and compare various attributes of a transaction.

There are two approaches to performing tests of transactions for sales and collections. One approach is to select a sample of transactions from those listed in the primary transaction journals (e.g., the sales journal or the cash receipts journal). The auditor then examines all supporting documentation for the transactions selected. This approach is particularly useful for testing occurrence, accuracy, classification, and cutoff. The second approach is to select a sample from the boundary documents used for a transaction (e.g., shipping documents or receipt lists) and trace the items to proper inclusion in the appropriate transaction journal. This approach is particularly useful—and often the best way—to test completeness. The auditor must be confident that he or she has identified the appropriate population to examine and that the sample is representative of the entire population. For example, if the auditor is selecting sales from the sales journal, he or she would want to be assured that the entire sales journal is available for sample selection.[4]

The auditor may be able to combine selected tests of transactions and tests of controls. For example, the auditor can verify approvals on documents (test of controls) at the same time that sales prices, quantities, and extensions are being verified (substantive test of transactions). These tests are referred to as *dual-purpose tests* because they facilitate simultaneous testing of the effectiveness of controls and the accuracy of transactions.

> **Authoritative**
> **Guidance & Standards**
> Dual-purpose tests are discussed as part of the standard on performing procedures in response to assessed risks (SAS 110, ISA 330).

SUBSTANTIVE ANALYTICAL PROCEDURES

Expectations of many sales and collection-related accounts can be reasonably estimated using the client's financial and operating data. For example, if the company is able to provide reliable data for the number of units sold, the auditor can

---

4 In general, samples can be obtained randomly or judgmentally (which is discussed in more detail in Chapter 16). A random sample requires the auditor to generate a set of random numbers that correspond to the numerical sequence of the transactions being examined. A judgmental sample emphasizes transactions that are of specific interest to the auditor, such as large transactions or transactions near year end.

Figure 11–10   Testing Assertions Related to Sales and Receipts Transactions

---

Sales Processing

Occurrence, Accuracy, Timing, Classification: Select a sample of sales transactions from the sales journal. Obtain the related invoices along with all supporting documentation. Perform the following tests and note any exceptions found:

- Trace customer to approved customer list and compare to approved credit limits.
- Compare quantities per sales order, shipping document, and invoice.
- Trace price to appropriate master price list.
- Recompute extensions and footing of invoice.
- Trace invoice to proper inclusion in the sales journal.
- Compare date shipped per shipping document to date posted to the sales journal.
- Trace invoice to proper posting in the accounts receivable subsidiary ledger.
- Test accuracy of customer record in the subsidiary ledger.
- Vouch subsequent payment of invoice including validity of discounts taken and interest charged (if any).
- Test the accuracy of the sales journal. This may be done on a sample basis by selecting a few days and testing the daily totals and then aggregating the daily totals to test the period totals.*

Completeness: Select a sample of shipping documents from the prenumbered sequence and trace to proper inclusion in the sales journal, noting the existence of an invoice and the date of posting.

Receipt Processing

Occurrence, Accuracy, Timing, Classification: Select a sample of receipt transactions from the cash receipts journal and obtain the related remittance advices and other supporting documentation. Perform the following tests and note any exceptions found:

- Trace the remittance advice to proper inclusion in the appropriate receipt listing.
- Trace the remittance advice to proper inclusion in the appropriate duplicate deposit slip.
- Trace the remittance advice to proper and timely posting to the accounts receivable subsidiary ledger.

Completeness, Accuracy: Test the accuracy of the cash receipts journal. This may be done on a sample basis. Compare daily totals to totals per the receipt listing and deposit slip.

---

*Note that this test could also be performed as a substantive test of account balances if the test is performed after year end and the entire period is included in the test.

develop an estimate of sales revenue by multiplying the units sold by average prices. The reasonableness of revenues can then be tested by comparing this estimate to recorded sales.

Consider sales commissions as an example: If the company pays a 10 percent commission on sales (as verified against published employment policies) and total sales are $125,000, the auditor would estimate commission expense to be $12,500. If the company has recorded commission expense of approximately $12,500, the auditor could conclude that the account balance is reasonably accurate and perform no further testing. What does the auditor do if the recorded commission expense is much lower, perhaps $8,500? In that situation, further investigation is needed to determine the cause of the discrepancy.

To gather additional evidence, the first step should be to determine if the estimation method is reasonable. For example, the auditor may not know that there are actually two commission rates, with a lower rate of 5 percent being used for some products. With that new information, the auditor could re-estimate commission expense:

	10% rate	5% rate
Sales revenue subject to commission	$70,000	$55,000
Commission rate	x 10%	x 5%
	$ 7,000	$ 2,750

The total estimated commission is now $9,750, which is closer to the recorded balance of $8,500. This result may or may not be acceptable to the auditor; however, the fact that the estimate still exceeds the actual balance by 14.7 percent could concern the auditor since the difference may be due to unrecorded commissions. If the auditor is aware that the client records commissions when they are paid at the time of the bi-weekly or monthly payroll, the results may suggest that the year end accrual of commissions payable has not yet been recorded.

Further refinement of the estimate could be obtained by breaking sales down by location or product line. A well-accepted principle underlying substantive analytical procedures is that the finer the level of detail that is analyzed, the more likely the auditor is to spot any problems or misstatements that may exist. However, the auditor must keep in mind that each refinement of the computation requires more information. Additionally, the reliability of the information used as input must be considered. As the level of detail of the computation increases, so does the amount of effort needed to perform the analytical procedure.[5]

TESTS OF THE AGED RECEIVABLES TRIAL BALANCE

The purpose of testing the aged trial balance is to assure the auditor that all receivables have been identified and that the details in the subsidiary ledger agree with the general ledger. The auditor could test the subtotals per the aged trial balance and reconcile those totals with summary totals in the general ledger. Additionally, the auditor might test the aging of individual customer accounts in order to determine if the client has accurately identified accounts that are overdue, as this information is also important for the auditor's assessment of the allowance for uncollectible accounts. These types of tests are becoming less common since such accounting operations are generally performed by computer. However, auditors should always use professional judgment to assess the reasonableness of assumptions used to estimate bad debts.

CONFIRMATIONS

A general presumption held by auditors is that receivables should be directly confirmed with the company's customers. Confirmations are considered to provide

---

5 Another analytical technique is the use of regression analysis as discussed in Chapter 9. For example, a regression model could be developed that predicts the level of a company's sales as a function of various economic variables which are external to the company (e.g., interest rates, unemployment rates, inflation rates, number of housing starts). Such models have the advantage of being theoretically sound and free of potential bias that might arise from using the company's internal information (which may not be accurate). One potential drawback of such models is that their level of precision may not be adequate to generate truly meaningful estimates (i.e., the margin of error may be large). Another potential drawback is that the cost and effort of acquiring the data and building the model may be large, although most computer audit programs provide this facility as a standard feature in their software.

high-quality evidence because they are obtained from sources outside the company. Confirmation of receivables is expected in all engagements but is not required if (1) receivables are not material to the financial statements, (2) the use of confirmations would not be effective, or (3) the auditor has assessed risk of material misstatements related to receivables at a low enough level that sufficient appropriate evidence can be obtained from other tests and procedures. The use of confirmations is often a time-consuming and costly process and the reliability of the evidence may not be as good as hoped. Key decisions by the auditor about the confirmation process can have a significant impact on the quality and cost of evidence from confirmations.

The first decision that an auditor makes is whether to use the positive or negative form of confirmation. When the auditor uses a *positive confirmation*, he or she expects an answer from a customer and will evaluate the evidence received based on the nature of the response (i.e., agreement or disagreement with the existence of a receivable or the amount of a balance). The auditor must use alternative procedures when a customer fails to respond to a positive confirmation request. When the auditor uses a *negative confirmation*, he or she expects a response only when the customer *disagrees* with the reported balance. No response from a customer is considered to be evidence that the balance is valid but does not imply that the account is correctly stated. Positive confirmations are considered more reliable than negative confirmations and are preferred by auditors when large balances are being confirmed, risk of material misstatements are considered to be high, or there is a question about the recipient's willingness or ability to respond.

Once the decision is made to use positive or negative confirmations, or a combination of both,[6] the auditor (or the client under the auditor's direction) prepares the confirmation requests. A sample request to positively confirm an account balance is presented in Figure 11–11. A confirmation request should originate from the client but the response should be returned to the auditor. The recorded balance (e.g., $5,237) is indicated in the request. An alternative method that is occasionally used, especially with very large balances, is to leave the amount blank and have the customer enter the balance according to his or her records. If the auditor uses the negative form, the bottom of the request would direct the recipient to respond only if he or she disagreed with the indicated balance (thus, a negative confirmation cannot be blank).

Next, the auditor chooses the customers to whom to send confirmation requests. The selection of accounts to confirm should be made by the auditor, not management. The size and selection of the sample will depend on residual risk, the materiality of receivables (in total and individually), the number of accounts, the number of sales personnel handling customer accounts, the level of desired detection risk, the results of other audit tests, and results obtained in prior years. For example, if there are a few large accounts that make up most of the receivables balance, a few positive confirmations may suffice.

After the auditor has made the relevant decisions concerning the use of confirmations, a number of practical considerations must be taken into account. It is critical that the auditor maintain control over the confirmations at all times. Confirmations that are accessible to client personnel are of questionable value as audit evidence because the auditor cannot be assured that the responses have not been improperly altered. The auditor can have the client prepare the confirmations but must check

---

6 For example, an auditor may decide to use positive confirmations for large balances and negative confirmations for a sample of small accounts.

Figure 11–11   Example of Accounts Receivable Positive Confirmation

Jones Manufacturing Inc.
Gainesville, Florida

January 6, 20x8

Brown & Son
2020 N. Market Street
Gainesville, FL 32602

Dear Sirs:

Our financial statements are currently being examined by the auditing firm of Smith & Company, CPAs (Gainesville, Florida). In connection with this examination, we ask that you examine the information provided below related to your account with us. Please confirm directly to our auditors whether you agree or disagree with the correctness of this information.

This is not a request for payment. Please do not send payment to our auditors. Your prompt attention to this request is greatly appreciated. A stamped, self-addressed envelope is enclosed for your reply.

Edgar Jones

Edgar Jones, Controller

Smith and Company, CPAs
Gainesville, Florida

Please check one of the following:

_____ The balance of **$5,237** owed by us to Jones Manufacturing as of December 31, 20x7 is correct.

_____ The balance of **$5,237** is not correct for the reasons noted below:

_____

_____

_____

_____   Signed: _____

each request for accuracy and maintain strict control over them thereafter. This means that the auditor should personally mail the requests outside the client's facilities. Also, confirmations should be returned directly to the auditor's office.

The auditor should maintain a control list of mailed confirmation requests, including the date sent and date returned. For positive confirmations, the auditor should send second and third requests if no response is received. The control list should document the nature of the response (i.e., agreement or disagreement with the reported balance). Finally, the control list is used to compute the percentage of accounts receivable that are actually confirmed.

If the auditor is unable to obtain a response to a positive confirmation request, alternative procedures should be performed to determine if the customer's balance is correctly stated. The alternative procedures typically involve examining supporting documentation of sales (similar to tests of transactions), customer correspondence (for evidence of disputes), and receipts subsequent to year end that indicate the customer has paid the balance. Requests that are returned by the post office as being undeliverable may indicate that the client's billing system is out-of-date or the customer does not exist. In either case, the auditor must be concerned with the implications of such evidence as it relates to the existence and valuation of receivables.

Finally, the auditor must follow up on every response that indicates possible disagreement between the client and the customer. Many of these disagreements will be due to timing differences (e.g., the customer's check is in the mail or a shipment is in transit). The explanations for these differences must be clearly documented but they are not considered misstatements. Some differences may reflect actual errors in the client's records, e.g., a sale recorded at an incorrect amount or a payment received that was not posted to the customer's account. The accounting records should be adjusted for these errors and the auditor should consider the impact of errors on the overall risk of material misstatement.

For example, if the auditor sent positive confirmations to 20 percent of large accounts and negative confirmations to 5 percent of small accounts, the auditor's assessment of potential misstatement must consider the results obtained for each group. To illustrate, if there were errors detected totaling $25,000 in the large balances and $1,000 in the small balances, the auditor could estimate the total misstatement of accounts receivable as follows:

Large balances	$125,000	($25,000/0.2; sample is 20% of large balances)
Small balances	20,000	($1,000/0.05; sample is 5% of small balances)
Total A/R Misstatement	$145,000	(3% of $5 million balance)

However, because the auditor did not look at all items in the account, there may be a range for the possible misstatement in an account. Consequently, the auditor must use professional judgment in projecting identified misstatements to the entire account.[7]

CUTOFF TESTS

The purpose of cutoff tests is to determine if the client has recorded transactions in the correct period. The general approach for cutoff tests is to examine documentation for transactions (sales, receipts, or returns) that occur just before and just after the end of the fiscal year. Auditors should observe the last shipping document(s) sent on the last day of the fiscal year—often this procedure is performed in conjunction with year-end inventory observation since shipping occurs at the warehouse where inventory is counted. This type of test is facilitated if the company uses prenumbered documents in sequence and can readily determine the last document number used in the period. The auditor will almost always test the timing of the largest transactions around the end of the year, but the auditor may perform more extensive cutoff tests when risk of material misstatement related to timing is high. Cutoff tests for sales returns can be particularly important because they may indicate fictitious sales or sales that should not be recognized due to a customer's right to return the merchandise.

---

7 Alternatively, the auditor might compute an average dollar misstatement per customer confirmation sent and multiply that amount by the total number of customers in each sample to arrive at an expected misstatement.

Example

> Companies in high-tech industries are notorious for shipping a great deal of merchandise at the end of the fiscal year in order to pump up recorded sales—a procedure commonly known as channel stuffing. The returns of that merchandise are often significant and may not occur until two or three months after year end.

TESTS OF REVENUE RECOGNITION

One of the most important and common risks of significant misstatement involves improper revenue recognition. Because no other class of transactions on the income statement receives more attention by users of financial statements, organizations face a great deal of pressure to conform to expectations about revenues, and in many cases, appropriately recognizing revenue can be a fairly complex process. Accordingly, the timing of and procedures employed to recognize revenue are very important for auditors to test when conducting the audit of the sales process. The issue of revenue recognition will become increasingly challenging for auditors as more organizations develop innovative ways to foster customer loyalty (e.g., frequent shopper clubs) and customer sales and service become more dependent on strategic alliances (e.g., airline code sharing).

Because of an organization's motivation to fraudulently recognize revenue— revenue recognition frauds have been among the most prevalent form of material fraud over the past 50 years—auditors should generally consider the risk of material misstatement associated with revenue recognition during the mandatory brainstorming session required for all audits. To assess fraud risk, auditors should develop a sufficient understanding of the revenue generating process for clients and the accounting policies and procedures employed for recognizing revenue. For organizations in which revenues are generated via routine transactions, auditors should expect to find highly automated systems in place that capture revenue (e.g., an integrated ERP sales process that links together a network of point-of-sales systems at retail outlets). These systems should have well-documented and effective automated controls ensuring that sales are recorded at the point in time when title transfers and at the correct sales price. It should prevent unauthorized users from accessing sales data and should facilitate recording the sale of the right items at the right prices. Furthermore, the organization should have effective controls in place restricting the creation of adjusting journal entries used to supplement the automated process for recording sales.

Example

> Major warehouse retailers, such as Costco, have an automated point-of-sales system that tracks all sales across all warehouse locations on a real-time basis. Prices for goods are input into the system at the corporate level to ensure that all consumers receive the same prices, reducing the risk of price discrimination. Further, should adjustments to sales prices need to occur, for example to satisfy a customer, the system tracks the employee who overrides the system to ensure that no unusual transactions are recorded. Often, only a supervisor can access the point-of-sales system to enable an override (e.g., a key must be inserted in the system or a password entered). To test the effectiveness of the system, an auditor could test the controls of the system to ensure that they are operating effectively. Also, the auditor could examine all adjustments to the system for a sample of days throughout the year and at the end of the reporting period, noting any unusual adjustments.

Auditors should be concerned about errors (and even fraud) when revenue recognition is difficult to calculate. This condition can occur for transactions that are not common within an industry of for non-routine sales transactions that involve complex issues, such as difficult decisions determining when title transfers. For example, many organizations in a highly competitive marketplace use various strategies to develop customer loyalty. Costco generates a material portion of its revenues by charging customers annual membership fees for the right to shop in the store. These membership fees are collected up-front, but the revenue should not be recognized until they are earned; that is, one-twelfth of the fee should be recognized each month following collection. Accordingly, auditors should gather sufficient evidence related to complex revenue recognition transactions to adequately assess whether conditions exist to recognize revenue.

Example

Several U.S. retailers, including Best Buy, were forced to restate reported earnings because they had been improperly recognizing revenue associated with fees received for joining "rewards" programs, in which customers pay a fee to receive future discounts on items when purchases reach certain levels. Organizations like Best Buy were recognizing the fees as revenue when they were collected, instead of deferring the revenue and recognizing it evenly throughout the period of time covered by the fees.

Tests of Uncollectible Amounts

The auditor should determine if recorded receivables have been adequately adjusted to reflect potentially uncollectible amounts. Because the auditor cannot predict the future, the identification of uncollectible accounts requires careful analysis and judgment. The auditor will typically undertake two types of substantive tests for assessing uncollectible balances.

One procedure is to examine the documentation of large balances, especially those that are already delinquent, to determine if the amounts will ultimately be paid by the customer. Transactions that are in dispute or customers that are in fiscal distress (e.g., bankruptcy) indicate a lower likelihood of collection. Also, the auditor can vouch cash receipts occurring after year end to determine if the customer has made any payments on the account because an actual payment is the best evidence that the receivable is collectible. Based on the review of the files, the auditor may judge that a portion of some accounts will not be paid. The amounts would be aggregated for all customers and compared to the recorded value of allowance for bad debts.

Another way to test bad debts is to directly estimate the level of bad debts using the information included in the aged trial balance. The longer an account is overdue, the less likely it is that the amount will be collected and the higher the percentage of an account that should be reserved against future losses. The percentage of accounts deemed uncollectible should be based on historical experience modified for current economic circumstances and changes in the company's credit policies. To facilitate this process, the auditor often keeps year-to-year records about the client's collection history.

To illustrate, consider the following computation of expected bad debts based on the age of receivables and historical delinquency rates:

Aging Category	Receivable Amounts	Delinquency Rate	Potential Bad Debts
Current Balances (less than 30 days since date of sale)	$ 100,000	2%	$ 2,000
30 days past due (less than 60 days since date of sale)	40,000	4%	1,600
60 days past due (less than 90 days since date of sale)	20,000	15%	3,000
90 days past due (less than 120 days since date of sale)	10,000	50%	5,000
Auditor's estimate of uncollectible amounts			$ 11,600

The auditor's estimate would be compared to the recorded value of the allowance for uncollectible accounts to assess whether the allowance is adequate. If we assume that the client has a credit balance of $8,000 in the allowance, the auditor might suggest an adjustment of $3,600. However, because the auditor's estimate is subject to uncertainty, it is not possible to conclude beyond doubt that the company has a $3,600 error. The best arguments that an auditor can use when challenging estimated uncollectible accounts are: (1) determining whether the client's procedures are consistent from year-to-year and (2) evaluating whether the reported results are consistent with the auditor's understanding of the current economic conditions of the client and industry.

SUMMARY AND CONCLUSION

We have discussed a broad approach for auditing sales and customer service in this chapter. We used a process map and internal threat analysis to evaluate process objectives, activities, risks, controls, and performance indicators. We used the results of the process analysis to assess residual risks and analyze how residual risks would affect the conduct of the audit, especially the tests of financial statement assertions affected by sales and customer service. Finally, we discussed specific substantive tests that could be performed when the risk of material misstatement is considered high for assertions related to sales and receivables.

A common theme presented in this book is that the tests of financial statement assertions should follow directly from the auditor's residual risk assessments and their impact on specific assertions related to transactions, accounts, and disclosures.

The extent of testing applied to receivable balances depends on the risk of material misstatement assessments made by the auditor. When risk is low for the majority of receivable assertions, the auditor might disregard most of the tests listed in Figure 11–9. Testing would be focused on a few large or unusual items. When inherent or control risk is high for a significant number of the receivable assertions, the auditor would increase the nature and extent testing. Consequently, the selection of substantive testing procedures will vary across clients. Auditors can adjust their substantive audit testing by choosing to perform certain procedures but not

Figure 11–12   Tests of Financial Statement Assertions Related to Accounts Receivable for Different Levels of Risk of Material Misstatement

Type of Procedure	High Detection Risk Case (Low risk of material misstatement)	Low Detection Risk Case (High risk of material misstatement)
Tests of transactions	Moderate tests as described in Figure 11–10, mostly performed prior to year end.	Extensive tests as described in Figure 11–10, many performed after year end.
Test of accuracy of aged trial balance	Minimal or no testing. Totals traced to the general ledger.	Summary totals tested in detail. Some accounts traced to supporting documentation to test aging.
Confirmations	Small sample of positive confirmations; moderate sample of negative confirmations; may be done at interim date rather than year end.	Large sample of positive confirmations as of year end.
	Reduced testing of non-responses to positive confirmations	Extensive testing of non-responses to positive confirmations.
Cutoff tests	Minimal or no testing.	Tests of year-end transactions on a sample basis.
Estimation of bad debt expense	Substantive analytical procedures performed using data from aged trial balance and historical loss rates.	Substantive analytical procedures supported by detailed examination of customer files related to large accounts that are at risk of loss.

others, by increasing or decreasing the sample size of items examined, or by adjusting the timing of the performance of procedures.[8] These types of choices are illustrated for assertions related to receivables in Figure 11–12 for two levels of risk of material misstatement. Regardless of the level of substantive testing deemed necessary, the auditor will need to fully document the process analysis, the conclusions about residual risks, and the results of substantive testing.

APPENDIX A: PLANNING TESTS OF FINANCIAL STATEMENT ASSERTIONS RELATED TO CASH BALANCES

The sales and customer service process also has a significant effect on the cash balances of a company, mainly through cash receipts. A company may have "cash" in different forms: coins and currency, general checking accounts, imprest checking accounts, and money market accounts. Most companies maintain a general disbursement account for processing receipts and disbursements. Payroll disbursements are

---

8 The timing of audit procedures has a direct impact on the detection risk achieved through those procedures. For example, confirmation of receivables usually occurs at year end because those are the balances that are of direct interest to the auditor. However, if risk of material misstatement is considered to be low, the auditor could choose to perform confirmation work at an earlier date as a matter of convenience (i.e., there is one less thing to do after year end when there is a great deal of time pressure to complete the audit).

usually made from an imprest account that is maintained at a constant level and replenished each time payroll checks are issued. A company may have petty cash at multiple locations, but the amounts tend to be small. Finally, a company may maintain a savings or money market account for temporary investment of excess cash.

Cash is usually a relatively small portion of a company's balance sheet but takes on greater importance because of the large volume of transactions that flow through the account. Although internal control over cash is usually quite effective in most organizations, there are a number of procedures that are traditionally used to audit cash. Cash is a relatively easy account to audit, and the auditor can easily achieve very low detection risk. A general approach for the substantive testing of cash balances is outlined in Figure 11–13. The primary procedures to test financial assertions related to cash include

- Test of cash receipts
- Bank confirmations
- Bank reconciliations
- Proof of cash
- Tests of interfund transfers

TESTS OF CASH RECEIPTS

The primary transactions affecting the cash account are cash receipts and disbursements. Cash receipts arise naturally as part of sales and customer service processes and can be tested using the procedures listed in Figure 11–10. Tests of cash receipts focus on proper identification, processing, and deposit of receipts on a timely basis.[9]

BANK CONFIRMATIONS

A *bank confirmation* is a standardized request from an auditor to a client's bankers for the confirmation of checking or other deposit accounts. The confirmation may also provide information concerning loans or lines of credit to the client, loans guaranteed by the client (a contingent liability), and assets pledged as collateral. A sample of a bank confirmation request is presented in Figure 11–14. As is the case with all confirmations, the request comes from the client but is returned to the auditor. Bank confirmations are usually sent out blank.

BANK RECONCILIATIONS

The purpose of a *bank reconciliation* is to identify any discrepancies between the cash balance recorded on the books at a point in time and the balance according to the bank as of the same point in time, as illustrated in Figure 11–15. The auditor obtains reconciliations for bank accounts that have heavy activity or large balances. Bank reconciliations may be prepared by the auditor, or prepared by the client's personnel and checked by the auditor.

Reconciling items represent transactions that have been recorded by either the bank or the company, but not both. For example, checks issued by the company that have not yet cleared the bank will cause the book balance to be lower than the bank balance. Similarly, if the bank has added interest to the company's account,

---

9 Tests of cash disbursements are discussed in Chapter 12 as part of supply-chain management.

Figure 11–13   Substantive Tests for Cash Account Assertions

Audit Assertion	Typical Substantive Audit Procedures
Existence: Cash on hand and cash in bank exists.	• Count cash on hand. • Review and test bank reconciliations. • Prepare and verify an interfund transfer schedule. • Test cash receipt and disbursement transactions.
Completeness: All cash assets of the company are included in the general ledger.	• Review board minutes for indications of new or closed accounts. • Review cash disbursements to identify accounts used. • Obtain representation from management concerning the existence of bank accounts and locations that cash is stored. • Prepare and verify an interfund transfer schedule. • Test cash receipt and disbursement transactions.
Valuation: Cash balances reconcile with cash on hand and cash in bank.	• Obtain and foot bank reconciliations for all bank accounts. • Trace balance per bank to the bank statement and bank confirmation. • Trace balance per books to the general ledger. • Count cash on hand and compare the total to the general ledger.
Valuation: Cash balances are correctly valued.	• Obtain and verify bank reconciliations. • Obtain and verify proof of cash. • Test cash receipt and disbursement transactions. • Vouch selected reconciling items in the bank reconciliations.
Valuation: Cash balances are correctly classified.	• Review bank reconciliations and confirmations for items requiring reclassification (e.g., credit balances, compensating balances).
Valuation: Cash receipts and disbursements are recorded in the proper period.	• Obtain bank cutoff statement. • Obtain and verify bank reconciliations. • Obtain and verify proof of cash. • Perform cash receipt and disbursement cutoff tests. • Vouch selected reconciling items in the bank reconciliations.
Ownership: Cash balances are owned by the company.	• Obtain and review bank confirmation for pledged balances or compensating balances. • Prepare and verify an interfund transfer schedule. • Obtain representation from management concerning potential commitments, claims, or liens on bank accounts.

but the company is unaware of the amount, the bank balance will exceed the book balance. There are four types of reconciling items:

Reconciling items to the book balance:

Debits to books not recorded by bank	*Ex: Deposits in transit not yet received by bank*
Credits to books not recorded by bank	*Ex: Outstanding checks not yet paid by bank*

Reconciling items to the bank balance:

Debits by bank not recorded on books	*Ex: Bank fees* *Ex: Deposits returned due to insufficient funds*
Credits by bank not recorded on books	*Ex: Interest earned* *Ex: Collections by bank on behalf of company*

Figure 11–14   Example of a Standard Bank Confirmation

STANDARD FORM TO CONFIRM ACCOUNT
BALANCE INFORMATION WITH FINANCIAL INSTITUTIONS

_____

Customer Name

We have provided to our accountants the following
information as of the close of business on _____,
20___, regarding our deposit and loan balances.
Please confirm the accuracy of the information,
noting any exceptions to the information provided.

Financial   [   ]
Institution's   [   ]
Name and   [   ]
Address   [   ]

If the balances have been left blank, please complete
this form by furnishing the balance in the appropriate
space below. Although we do not request nor expect
you to conduct a comprehensive, detailed search of
your records, if during the process of completing this
confirmation additional information about other
deposit and loan accounts we may have with you
comes to your attention, please include such information below. Please use the enclosed envelope to return
the form directly to our auditors.

1. At the close of business on the date listed above, our records indicated the
    following deposit balance(s):

Account Name	Account No.	Interest Rate	Balance

2. We were directly liable to the financial institution for loans at the close of business
   on the date listed above as follows:

Account No./ Description	Balance	Date Due	Interest Rate	Date Through Which Interest Paid	Description of Collateral

_____   _____
(Customer's Authorized Signature)   (Date)

The information presented above by the customer is in agreement with our records.
Although we have not conducted a comprehensive, detailed search of our records, no
other deposit or loan accounts have come to our attention except as noted below.

_____   _____
(Financial Institution Authorized Signature)   (Date)

_____
(Title)

Exceptions and/or Comments

Please return this form directly to our auditor:	

Figure 11–15   Example of Bank Reconciliation

			A-1
Jones Manufacturing, Inc.			
Bank Reconciliation—Sunshine Bank			*WRK*
12/31/x7			*PBC 1/24/x8*
Balance per Bank, 12/31/x7		2,000	*A-1-1*
Deduct: Outstanding checks			
#126, 12/26	800 ✓		
#129, 12/30	200 ✓		
#130, 12/30	1,200 ✓		
#131, 12/30	1,250 ✓		
	3,450		*T*
Adjusted Bank Balance		(1,450)	*T*
Balance per Books, 12/31/x7		(1,500)	*A*
Unrecorded adjustments:			
Interest credited by bank		50	*~ AJE1*
Adjusted Book Balance		(1,450)	*T AJE2*

T   Footed and total agrees.

✓   Traced outstanding checks to cash disbursements journal for 12/x7 and bank cutoff statement for 1/10/x8 received directly from bank. Amounts agree.

~   Traced bank adjustments to bank statement as of 12/31/x7. Amounts agree.

Note: Check #131 was the last check issued in December 20x7.

Reconciling items to the bank balance represent transactions that have not been recorded by the company and may necessitate an adjusting entry to correct the cash balances of the company.

Bank reconciliations may be prepared in various formats. The format used in Figure 11–15 reconciles both the book and bank balance to an adjusted balance that is "correct" in the sense that it represents the amount that should be reported on the balance sheet. An alternative is to start with the bank balance and reconcile it to the book balance. The format used in Figure 11–15 has the advantage of highlighting the items that may not have been recorded by the company.

Auditors verify the accuracy of bank reconciliations by performing a number of relatively simple tests. First, the auditor tests the accuracy of the schedule. The auditor then compares the reconciling items for the books to internal supporting documents and records. Finally, the reconciling items for the bank are compared to supporting documentation from the bank. Properly prepared and verified bank reconciliations result in a very low detection risk for cash assertions.

PROOF OF CASH

In situations where control risk for cash is high, the auditor may also wish to prepare a *proof of cash* for one or more of the company's bank accounts. A proof of cash can be prepared for any period of time, such as a month or year. A proof of cash starts

Figure 11–16   Example of Proof of Cash

```
                                                                        A-1-2
                         Jones Manufacturing, Inc.
                       Proof of Cash—Sunshine Bank                      WRK
                               12/31/x7                            PBC 1/24/x8

                          12/31/x6      Cash-In       Cash-Out     12/31/x7

Balance per bank            5,000 ✓     939,000 ~     942,000 ~     2,000 R
Deposit in transit        10,000 ✓     (10,000)
Outstanding checks: 20x6  (13,200) ✓                 (13,200)
Outstanding checks: 20x7                                3,450      (3,450) R
Other reconciling items                    (50)                      (50) R
                          _____      _____      _____     _____
Balance per books          1,800 ✓     928,950 ✗     932,250 ✗    (1,500) R

                            T            T             T             T
```

T	Footed and total agrees.
R	Traced to and agrees with 20x7 bank reconciliation (see *A-1*) and cross-footings verified.
✓	Traced to and agrees with bank reconciliation in prior year's working papers.
✗	Traced to and agrees with cash receipts journal (Cash in) or cash disbursements journal (Cash out).
~	Traced to and agrees with totals per bank statements.

with normal bank reconciliations at two points in time and then reconciles the receipts and disbursements across time. A simple proof of cash for Jones Manufacturing is illustrated in Figure 11–16. The last column of the schedule contains the same information as the bank reconciliation presented in Figure 11–15 but in a slightly different form. To facilitate the example, the bank reconciliation for the beginning of the period (12/31/x6) is also presented. The middle two columns include detailed information about cash receipts and disbursements affecting the account.

To see how the proof of cash works, consider the $10,000 deposit in transit included in the 20x6 reconciliation. This is added to the bank balance in order to reconcile with the book balance on 12/31/x6. However, when we examine the second column, we are looking at the receipts for 20x7. This $10,000 would be listed as a receipt by the bank in 20x7, but the company recorded it in 20x6. Therefore, the $10,000 must be subtracted from the receipts per the bank in order to reconcile with the receipts per the books.[10] Next, consider the $3,450 in outstanding checks on 12/31/x7 (the last column). Here we see the item subtracted from the bank balance to reconcile with the book balance. Because the disbursement is recorded in 20x7 by the company, but after 12/31/x7 by the bank, the $3,450 must be added to the disbursements per the bank in order to reconcile with the disbursements per the books.

The receipts and disbursements according to the bank can be traced to the bank statements for the period under consideration and the receipts and disbursements per the books can be traced to the appropriate transaction journals. Every

10 The analysis could also start with the receipts per the books and work to the receipts per the bank. In that case, the $10,000 would be added to the receipts per the books.

reconciling item in the first and last columns (the point-in-time reconciliations) has a complementary item in the receipt or disbursement columns. If cash balances are correct, the receipts and disbursement columns should balance, providing evidence that cash transactions have been properly recorded by the company.

TESTS OF INTERFUND TRANSFERS

Another significant concern the auditor has related to cash is the transfer of funds between bank accounts near the end of the year. Such transfers, called *interfund transfers*, represent a deposit to one account of the company and a withdrawal from another account. Both sides of the transfer affect accounts held by the company, so that if the transaction is not properly recorded, the same money may be accidentally recorded in two different accounts at the same time, or in no accounts. The problem of double-counting transfers is called *kiting*, and can occur when the deposit in one account is recorded earlier than the withdrawal from the other account.

Interfund transfers are tested using an *interfund transfer schedule* as illustrated in Figure 11–17. This schedule illustrates five interfund transfers at or near year end. The schedule lists the date of deposit per the books (column B) and per the bank (column D), and the date of withdrawal per the books (column A) and per the bank (column C). If the dates in all four columns fall in the same fiscal period, the transfer is correctly recorded.

Transfer errors arise when the dates in the various columns fall in different fiscal periods. Four possible problems are summarized under the "Rules of Analysis" in Figure 11–17. For a transfer to be correctly recorded, A and B must be in the same period and at the same time or earlier than C and D. Some of the potential problems would be revealed by a well-prepared bank reconciliation alone. However, the interfund transfer schedule reveals two problems not detectable with a standard bank reconciliation: kiting and unrecorded cash. Kiting occurs when the date in column B is in an earlier period than the date in column A. This occurs for the $20,000 transfer from Bank 3 to Bank 4. Because the deposit is recorded for Bank 4 in 20x7 but the withdrawal is not recorded for Bank 3 until 20x8, the $20,000 is included in both accounts as of 12/31/x7. If A is in a period earlier than B, cash will not be recorded in any account, which is also an error.

Example

Kiting, if done intentionally by the client, is an illegal act, and the auditor should consider the implications for the entire audit. In the late 1970s, the brokerage firm of E. F. Hutton was discovered to be running a giant kiting scheme involving hundreds of banks and hundreds of millions of dollars, resulting in the receipt of millions of dollars in interest income they did not deserve.

Cash is an area where most companies have excellent internal control, so many of the procedures listed in Figure 11–13 would probably be unnecessary for most clients. The cash tests described in this chapter are used less and less as information systems improve and the cash disbursements process is increasingly automated. However, confirmations should almost always be obtained from the client's primary financial institutions. In the cases where inherent or control risk is high for a number of cash assertions, or there is a concern about the risk of fraud related to cash balances, other procedures can be performed to obtain evidence that cash is not materially misstated.

Figure 11–17   Example of Test of Interfund Transfers

Description	Amount	(A) Date per Books: Cash Out	(B) Date per Books: Cash In	(C) Date per Bank: Cash Out	(D) Date per Bank: Cash In	Implications
Bank 1 to Bank 2	$100,000	12/31/x7	12/31/x7	1/2/x8	1/3/x8	Payout Bank: Outstanding check Deposit Bank: Deposit in transit Books: None
Bank 2 to Bank 3	50,000	12/31/x7	1/3/x8	12/31/x7	1/3/x8	Payout Bank: None Deposit Bank: None Books: Error (Unrecorded transfer)
Bank 3 to Bank 4	20,000	1/3/x8	12/31/x7	1/3/x8	12/31/x7	Payout Bank: None Deposit Bank: None Books: Error (Kiting)
Bank 4 to Bank 5	120,000	1/3/x8	1/3/x8	12/31/x7	1/3/x8	Payout Bank: None Deposit Bank: None Books: Error (Unrecorded payment)
Bank 5 to Bank 6	70,000	1/3/x8	1/3/x8	1/3/x8	12/31/x7	Payout Bank: None Deposit Bank: None Books: Error (Unrecorded deposit)

Rules of Analysis:

Difference between A and C: Reconciling Item for Disbursing Bank
- If A is sooner than C: Outstanding check
- If C is sooner than A: Unrecorded disbursement (error)

Difference between B and D: Reconciling Item for Receiving Bank
- If B is sooner than D: Deposit in transit
- If D is sooner than B: Unrecorded deposit (error)

Difference between A and B: Error to books
- If A is sooner than B: Unrecorded transfer (error)
- If B is sooner than A: Duplicate cash—kiting (error)

APPENDIX B: AN OVERVIEW OF WORKING PAPER DOCUMENTATION TECHNIQUES

THE NEED FOR DOCUMENTATION

The auditor is required to prepare *audit documentation* that indicates that he or she has complied with all appropriate elements of generally accepted auditing standards. One purpose of preparing documentation of audit work is to demonstrate that the auditor has obtained sufficient, appropriate evidence upon which to base an opinion about the financial statements. Each and every audit working paper prepared by an auditor will be unique, depending on the assertions being tested and the nature of the evidence obtained. Accounting firms vary in terms of how they utilize audit documentation, ranging from fully automated systems of files (including scanned documents) to folders containing *working papers* (consisting of schedules, memos, and copies of client documents).

Audit documentation is typically organized into *files* or binders classified by audit area (e.g., process or account). Auditors generally use two types of files: current files and permanent files. *Current files* contain the documentation of the work that has been performed during the current audit. For example, the documentation of receivables confirmation may be in one current file, whereas bank reconciliations and confirmations for cash may be in another.

A current file usually includes a *lead sheet* that lists all of the accounts in the general ledger that relate to a specific line in the financial statements. For example, there may be many different inventory accounts used by a company for control purposes. The lead sheet for inventory lists the different types of inventory that appear as separate accounts in the general ledger but that are added together and reported as a single line item in the balance sheet. Following the lead sheet will be other working papers that contain the evidence in support of the balances. For example, the documentation illustrated in Figures 11–15 and 11–16 would be in the current file for cash.

Permanent files contain information that is of ongoing interest to the auditor from one year to the next. This set of files will contain information about the client's accounting and control system, various legal documents (e.g., leases, notes payable), minutes from board of directors meetings, organization charts for the client, a chart of accounts, and results from prior-year audits. The prior-year results will include summary information on errors found, as well as the final financial statements and data needed for evaluating historical trends (e.g., bad debt history for receivables).

AUDIT DOCUMENTATION IDENTIFICATION

Individual files (or working papers) are used to document the work performed in an audit engagement based on a few general guidelines that most auditors follow. First, every document should be clearly identified, including the identity of the client, the year being audited, and the purpose of the document. This information usually appears in the heading of the document. Referring again to Figures 11–15 and 11–16, we see two illustrations of the basic format of audit documentation. Both contain a clear statement of the nature of the audit test, the client, and the period under examination. The top of the documents also includes an indication of who performed the audit work. In these two cases, the auditor has initialed the upper right corner "WRK" and indicated the date that the work was performed (1/24/x8 in both cases).

The letters "PBC" at the left of the "WRK" notation stand for "Prepared By Client," which means that the client, rather than the auditor, has initially prepared this schedule. Of course, the auditor is responsible for verifying that the information contained in the schedule is accurate. However, it is usually more efficient to have the client search out the relevant information and prepare the schedule for the auditor's examination.

Paperless Audits

Many public accounting firms have converted all or at least part of their audit documentation to automated working papers. There are a wide number of alternatives for firms to select from when designing an automated audit documentation system, but there are several features that are common across systems used in audit practice. Typically, files are stored on centralized servers that can be accessed by multiple engagement team members at the same time. Auditors who work on information can choose to synchronize their updates with the information stored in the master file. That way, if two individuals are working on the same file, the system can force individuals to reconcile information that might become inconsistent. The primary benefit of having working papers stored on a centralized server is that engagement team members can be in different locations when working on the same engagement.

Another important benefit of most automated audit documentation systems is that the system can be designed as a decision aid for ensuring that engagement team members adequately follow the firm's audit approach while conducting the audit. For example, if the firm's audit approach dictates that auditors conduct substantive tests of details for any account in which there is a high level of residual risk, the system can require that audit documentation for a substantive test of details be completed before allowing an auditor who has assessed residual risk for the account as high to sign off on the account. Furthermore, many auditing firms have designed pop-up screens to enable auditors to seek guidance while they are performing audit procedures in case they are not be quite sure of what to do next.

Automated audit documentation also greatly enhances the review process, both for detail review of working papers and for general review by partners. Checking to see which areas have been completed and cross-referencing audit areas is much easier when the reviewer is able to gain quick access to other areas of an audit (as opposed to having to search through multiple working papers stored in various binders). The review process is further expedited because the reviewer can access the files from offsite locations.

Documentation Referencing

Another feature of audit documentation is the letter-number code in the upper right corner. These codes are called *indices* or *references*. Every document should be identified by a unique index so that they can be maintained in a logical order. In our example, the bank reconciliation is indexed as A-1 and the proof of cash is indexed as A-1-2. Indices are often specified as a letter followed by one or more numbers. The letter indicates the general area of audit work (e.g., "A" indicates cash in this case), and the numbers indicate the intended order of pages. Different letters would be used for other areas in the audit (e.g., the letter B could be used to indicate receivables, C to indicate inventory, and so on).

Figure 11–18   Structure of the Current File for Cash

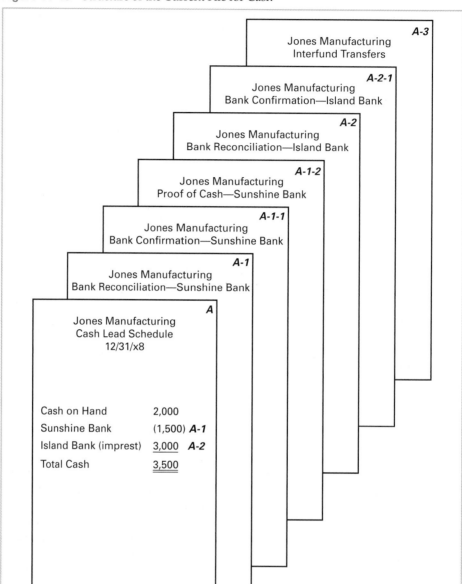

The structure of a current file for cash is depicted in Figure 11–18. In our example, the cash lead sheet would be placed in the front of the current file for cash and indexed as *A*. An index may have one or more numbers appended to the first letter. The bank reconciliation for Sunshine Bank is indexed as A-1 followed by the related bank confirmation, which is indexed as A-1-1. This tells the auditor that schedule A-1-1 relates to, and follows, schedule A-1 and precedes A-2 (which contains the bank reconciliation for Island Bank). This method of indexing is quite flexible and allows the insertion of additional documents without renumbering all the pages in the file.

CROSS REFERENCES

A significant advantage of indexing documents is that information that appears on more than one schedule can be easily cross-referenced. That is, the auditor, when reading one schedule, can be alerted that certain information on that schedule also relates to, and appears on, another schedule. Returning to Figure 11–15, we see the index A-1-1 entered next to the $2,000 balance per bank as of 12/31/x7. This tells the reader that further information related to that number appears on schedule A-1-1, which would be the bank's confirmation of the account balance (not presented here). We also see the index A entered next to the balance per books. This would be a cross-reference to the lead schedule for cash that lists all of the bank accounts and other forms of cash that the company owns. Cross-references should be circular. That is, the auditor should also see cross-references to schedule A-1 on schedules A (the lead sheet, see Figure 11–18) and A-1-1 (the bank confirmation, not presented).

Another form of cross-reference is illustrated with the letters AJE1 and AJE2 in Figure 11–15. These references refer to adjusting entries to correct the company's records. All adjusting entries identified during the course of an engagement should be summarized on a single schedule. In our example, we see that AJE1 is necessary to correct for the unrecorded interest income and AJE2 is necessary to reclassify the net credit balance as a payable. The full details of both adjusting entries would appear on the summary listing of adjusting entries.

TICKMARKS

The auditor uses *tickmarks* to indicate the tests that were used to verify the information contained in an audit document. For example, in Figure 11–15 we see the symbol ✓. This symbol appears next to the amounts of outstanding checks listed and again at the bottom of the schedule. Reading the explanation at the bottom, we see that the symbol means that the outstanding checks have been compared to the disbursements journal and the bank cutoff statement. If these comparisons had revealed any discrepancies, the auditor would have made a note of the problem and proposed an adjusting entry if necessary. Two other tickmarks—$\mathcal{T}$ and ~ —are used on A-1 and explain other tests that were performed. Turning to Figure 11–16 (A-1-2), we see the same symbols as on A-1 but the interpretation for ✓ is different than on the prior schedule. We also see two other tickmarks that were not used before—$\mathcal{R}$ and ✘. Tickmarks can be of various shapes and sizes, but they should be easy to distinguish one from another so as to avoid undue confusion. In addition, every tickmark used on a page should be explained by a note somewhere on the same page (usually at the bottom).[11]

CONCLUSION

The documentation of audit work and testing performed by an auditor is extremely important. Audit documentation is intended to be the written record of

---

11 Standardized tickmarks are occasionally used when a tickmark is specified as meaning the same thing on every document.

the auditor's efforts. The tests performed, evidence gathered, and conclusions reached should be documented in such a way that other readers have no trouble understanding the work performed. Audit documentation is intended to be flexible so as to be easily adapted to many diverse situations. Finally, audit documentation should be neat, complete, and clear. Audit documentation is increasingly becoming electronic. This makes it easier to prepare, correct, and store audit documentation. It also makes it easier for different people to work on the same schedule, even if separated geographically. As electronic audit documentation becomes the norm in the profession, the organization, cross-referencing, and handling of files will change accordingly.

BIBLIOGRAPHY OF PROFESSIONAL LITERATURE

Research

Asare, S. E., G. M. Trompeter, and A. M. Wright. 2000. The Effect of Accountability and Time Budgets on Auditors' Testing Strategies. *Contemporary Accounting Research.* 17(4): 539–560.

Engle, T. J. and J. E. Hunton. 2001. The Effects of Small Monetary Incentives on Response Quality and Rates in Positive Confirmation of Account Receivable Balances. *Auditing; A Journal of Practice & Theory.* 20(1): 157–168.

Professional Reports and Guidance

AICPA *Auditing Revenue in Certain Industries—AICPA Audit Guide.*

Auditing Standards

AICPA *Statements on Auditing Standard (SAS) No. 67*, "The Confirmation Process."

AICPA *Statements on Auditing Standard (SAS) No. 106*, "Audit Evidence."

AICPA *Statements on Auditing Standard (SAS) No. 107*, "Audit Risk and Materiality in Conducting an Audit."

AICPA *Statements on Auditing Standard (SAS) No. 109*, "Understanding the Entity and Its Environment and Assessing the Risks of Material Misstatement."

AICPA *Statements on Auditing Standard (SAS) No. 110*, "Performing Procedures in Response to Assessed Risks and Evaluating the Audit Evidence Obtained."

Emerging Issues Task Force (EITF). Issue No. 02-16, *Accounting by a Customer (Including a Reseller) for Certain Consideration Received by a Vendor.*

IAASB *International Standards on Auditing (ISA) No. 315*, "Understanding the Entity and Its Environment and Assessing the Risks of Material Misstatement."

IAASB *International Standards on Auditing (ISA) No. 320*, "Audit Materiality."

IAASB *International Standards on Auditing (ISA) No. 330*, "The Auditor's Procedures in Response to Assessed Risks."

IAASB *International Standards on Auditing (ISA) No. 500*, "Audit Evidence."

IAASB *International Standards on Auditing (ISA) No. 505*, "External Confirmations."

QUESTIONS

1. Explain how creating a process map and internal threat analysis helps in determining the extent to which substantive testing is to be performed on the accounts associated with the marketing, sales, and distribution process.

2. One of the most common forms of fraudulent financial reporting is recording sales that never occurred. Examine the examples of financial reporting controls for sales-related transactions in Figure 11–5. Identify relevant controls that can be used to help prevent or detect fraudulent sales from being recorded and explain how they help reduce the likelihood of such fraudulent financial reporting.

3. Reconciliation is an important control for helping to test the management assertions of completeness, occurrence, and accuracy of cash receipts transactions. Describe how a reconciliation helps test all three assertions for cash receipts.

4. Examine the inherent risk, impact of controls, and residual risk plots in Figure 11–6 for the sales and customer service process. Based on this plot, what conclusions should an auditor reach for each of the risks regarding whether to test controls and the extent to which substantive testing should be performed?

5. Figure 11–7 contains a listing of tests of operating effectiveness for internal controls related to the sales and customer service process. For each type of control activity (performance reviews and overall process management, information processing controls, physical controls, and segregation of duties and process design), describe the impact on the audit for each of the following results of controls testing.
   a. Controls are found to be operating effectively
   b. Controls are found to be operating ineffectively

6. Among the tools the auditor may employ to determine the reasonableness of the sales amount for a company during a given accounting period is regression analysis, whereby the company's sales are predicted using various economic factors such as interest rates and unemployment.
   a. Discuss the advantages and disadvantages of using this technique on a large automobile company, such as Ford.
   b. Discuss the advantages and disadvantages of using this technique on a smaller firm, such as a regional distributor of photographic equipment and supplies.

7. Discuss the utility of using confirmations to test the valuation of accounts receivable. Assuming that the auditor has decided to employ confirmations, discuss the possible ways the auditor may use them (i.e., positive vs. negative, to whom they should be sent, and so on). How should the auditor treat a request for confirmation that is not returned?

8. Many organizations are moving to automated processes for performing the sales and customer service process, using such processes as electronic data interchange, in which order placing, product tracking, invoicing, and collecting activities occurring electronically through systems connecting the buyer and seller of merchandise. Describe the challenge auditors face in identifying and testing controls of these real-time, integrated systems when gathering evidence supporting management assertions associated with sales and cash receipts transactions.

9. Evidence gathering procedures for the cash account have been de-emphasized by many auditors in recent years. As described in Appendix 11A, there is a large volume of transactions that flow through the account. Describe whether you believe that this reduction in emphasis is appropriate and defend you answer.

10. Audit documentation, described in detail in Appendix 11B, has received attention during the past several years, with standards being issued emphasizing its importance by international standards setters (including the IAASB and PCAOB). Describe the role that audit documentation plays for the auditor and why you believe that there has been renewed interest in ensuring proper audit documentation supporting auditor opinions.

11. What process objectives and activities typically are associated with the sales and customer service process? Why is understanding them important for the auditor?

12. What key accounts and transactions are affected by the sales and customer service process? Discuss and illustrate with examples.

13. As part of his or her internal threat analysis of the sales and customer services process, the auditor will pay special attention to internal control over financial reporting. In the context of the sales and customer service process, what controls specifically relate to financial reporting and will therefore be the focus of the auditor's attention?

PROBLEMS

1. For each of the following process activities for sales and customer service, discuss management assertions related to transactions or accounts that are impacted by the specific activity:
   a.   Marketing and brand awareness
   b.   Customer approval
   c.   Customer service order entry
   d.   Sales order entry
   e.   Customer service delivery
   f.   Inventory handling and shipping
   g.   Pricing and billing
   h.   Collections
   i.   Sales returns and adjustments
   j.   Account write-offs

2. Consider Apple's sales process for selling iPods to customers via the company's web site. To investigate the process, access the company's web site and walk through the sales process for an item. Stop short of completing the order, but note how the process works. Read other information on the site relating to sales and returns.
   a.   Use Figure 11–3 as a guide and complete a process map.
   b.   Use Figure 11–5 as a guide and complete an internal threat analysis.
   c.   Use Figure 11–7 as a guide and complete a residual risk map.
   d.   Use Figure 11–6 as a guide and complete a description of financial reporting controls that you would expect to see present.
   e.   Describe tests of controls that you would perform to satisfy yourself that the business risk and financial reporting controls are in place and operating effectively.

3. For each of the following internal controls in the sales order processing function, state the management assertion related to sales and receipts transactions that the control helps meet. Then list a test that would give the auditor assurance that the control procedure was effectively performed.
   a.   All sales orders at an Internet and mail-order clothing company are first given to the credit department for approval.
   b.   Cashiers at a retail grocery store must enter a personal identification code before they may ring up a purchase.
   c.   Every Friday afternoon, a clerk at an electronic components distributor compares all open sales orders with shipping documents.
   d.   All electronic payments utilizing a credit card number and expiration date are verified with a clearinghouse for available credit before they are processed further.
   e.   Any account that goes more than 90 days without payment at an office supply distributor is automatically sent to the collections department with a memo to the accounting department that it be written down to 10 percent of its original value.
   f.   Sales return forms are prenumbered and accounted for.
   g.   Incoming cash receipts are date-stamped in the mailroom.
   h.   Sales above a certain amount must be approved by the controller.

4. Examine the following questions from an internal control questionnaire for the sales process of a large home improvement retailer that extends credit to small contractors. Assume that the answer to each of these is "no" (which means that the control is weak in that area). For each of the following questions, identify the accounts that might be affected, state the management assertion that might be compromised for those accounts, and suggest a substantive audit procedure to test for misstatement in the accounts.

   a. Is an accounts receivable aging schedule prepared and reviewed periodically?

   b. Are the totals in the accounts receivable subsidiary ledger reconciled to the master account balance?

   c. Are cashiers' registers verified by a person independent of the accounting function?

   d. Are validated deposit slips compared to the cash receipts journal regularly?

   e. Are sales returns recorded on prenumbered documents and are those documents accounted for periodically?

   f. Are invoices for credit sales independently compared with customer orders to verify prices, quantities, accuracy, and so on?

   g. Is the collection function separated from normal sales and marketing activities?

   h. Is credit approved by someone independent of the marketing/sales function?

5. The following are routine procedures for the audit of revenue processes. For each procedure, state whether it is a test of controls or a substantive test of transactions, state which management assertion the procedure is designed to fulfill, and state the type of evidence used in the procedure.

   a. Review minutes from meetings of the board of directors for evidence that accounts receivable have been factored—sold to a third party.

   b. Gather a sample of sales invoices and ensure that a copy of the sales order and the shipping document has been attached.

   c. Reconcile a sample of deposit slips to entries in the cash receipts journal.

   d. Observe the incoming receivables processing area to ensure that checks are immediately separated from remittance advices.

   e. Confirm accounts receivable with follow-up on exceptions.

   f. Obtain an accounts receivable aging schedule and assess the likelihood of collection.

   g. Review a sample of sales orders for evidence that they have received proper approval from the credit department.

   h. Vouch those transactions that occur at year end and shortly after the year end and reconcile them to the general ledger.

6. High-tech manufacturers are notorious for practicing "channel stuffing," whereby they ship to their distributors a great deal of merchandise shortly before the end of the accounting period, knowing full well that most of it will be returned—but not until after the beginning of the new accounting period. In the meantime, the manufacturer counts the shipments as sales. In fact, this practice has occurred, to one extent or another, in many industries. Regarding such practices, answer the following questions:

   a. What management assertion(s) for what account(s) will be affected if the client engages in channel stuffing?

   b. What elements of the control environment could alert the auditor that the client may be prone to engage in such activity?

   c. What tests of controls will give the auditor some assurance that the client has not engaged in channel stuffing?

   d. What substantive audit procedures might help uncover the practice?

7. Your assignment as an auditor is to reconcile the general disbursement account at the Green Dolphin Bank for Monk, Miles, and Trane Co. as of 12-31-06. Your analysis of its cash activity for the month of December 2006 is as follows:

Balance per bank, 12-31-06	$22,800
Balance per books, 12-31-06	14,200
Checks written during December	98,000
Deposits made during December	91,500

In addition, your study of the 12-31-06 bank statement yields the following:

Checks cleared during December	$93,500
Deposits credited during December	93,900
Deposited item returned NSF	600
Bank service charge	100
Collection of bond interest	5,000

Finally, the 11-30-06 bank reconciliation yielded the following:

Balance per bank, 11-30-06	$18,100
Add: Deposits in transit	5,100
Less: Checks outstanding	(2,500)
Correct cash balance, 11-30-06	$20,700

   a. Starting from both the bank and book balance, prepare a reconciliation of cash to find the correct cash balance as of 12-31-06. You may assume that all checks written by Monk, Miles, and Trane will clear the bank within a week. What items from the above will you test most thoroughly?
   b. How would you audit the bank reconciliation if it had been prepared by the client?
   c. Prepare a proof of cash in good form for 12-31-06. What management assertions are addressed by a proof of cash?

8. In preparation for your audit of the accounts receivable of Stern Co., you compose a confirmation letter to send to several of their largest customers. Your effort looks like the following:

Whattsamatta, Yew, CPAs
Gainesville, FL

Large Customer
Street Address
City, State Zip

Dear Sir or Madam:

To help us audit the financial statements of Stern Co., we ask that you provide us with some information related to their open account with you. Specifically, please tell us directly what your accounts payable balance to Stern Co. was as of December 31, 2006.

   This is not a request for payment. Please do not send us any money. We appreciate your prompt attention to this matter.

Yours sincerely,

Offwit Yew, Managing Partner

Discuss the deficiencies in this confirmation. Then discuss alternative ways it can be written.

9. In your audit of the allowance for uncollectible accounts for Patrick Co., a wholesaler of hospital supplies, you prepare the following aging schedule:

Age	Amount Owed	% Uncollectible	Potential Bad Debt
< 30 days	$400,000	3%	$12,000
30–60 days	260,000	6%	15,600
60–90 days	100,000	15%	15,000
> 90 days	25,000	50%	12,500
Estimate of uncollectible amounts	$785,000		$55,100

a.   What type of audit evidence is this schedule?

b.   If the beginning balance in allowance for uncollectible accounts was $51,000, what amount would this schedule suggest should be the bad debt expense for the year?

c.   Suppose the client declined to accrue any additional bad debt expense for the year (and you considered your answer in part b to be a material amount). What reasonable arguments might the client advance to support his position?

d.   What assumptions about the aging schedule are likely to have a large impact on the estimate?

e.   What other evidence might the auditor gather to support his or her contention that additional bad debt expense should be accrued?

10. Discuss the deficiencies in the following audit program for the tests of controls over the sales order process of Skylark, a cable TV home shopping channel.

Step	Working Paper Reference	Audit Procedure	Performed by?
1		Observe telephone operators for compliance with control procedures related to credit card entry.	
2		Trace sample of daily totals in sales journal to the general ledger.	
3		Review a sample of transactions for amounts which exceed established customer limits for the credit manager's initials.	
4		Review system documentation for effectiveness of computer security over transaction data and credit card numbers.	
5		Input dummy sales data into the sales order system to review the computation of the proper sales tax.	
6		Input invalid customer numbers and inventory control numbers to test check digit routines.	
7		Verify a sample of initials on reconciliations of batch control tickets that require exception processing.	
8		Perform analytical procedures on reasonableness of sales return estimates.	

Case 11–1: LowMaxx Retail

LowMaxx (LM) is a chain of discount "outlet" type retail stores that specializes in deep discount selling of merchandise (mostly clothing) acquired from mainstream department stores. Generally, LM is able to purchase leftover merchandise from other retailers in bulk at a price that averages about 30 percent of original cost and 15 percent of full retail. LM uses a complex pricing algorithm to set prices for its merchandise. Initially, merchandise is marked up 100 percent from the price LM pays for it. However, in order to move the merchandise out of stores as fast as possible, it has an aggressive system of markdowns that systematically reduces prices over a six-week period to cost plus 10 percent. Any merchandise not sold after six weeks is given to charity.

Furthermore, LM offers a price guarantee—the store will refund to customers who ask the difference between the price they paid for an item and any discounts that are made within seven days of the customer's purchase. Although this results in a net loss of revenue, customers have to come to the store for the refund, often resulting in additional impulse purchases. Consequently, core customers become accustomed to visiting LM stores every week or so. This has resulted in an impressive level of loyalty from LM's regular customers.

It is also LM's policy to match the price of any other retailer within 25 miles of its location. If customer's bring in evidence that an item can be purchased cheaper at another retail store, LM will either match the price or issue a refund for the difference if the customer has already purchased the item from LM. There is a seven day time limit on matching prices.

LM also offers an in-house credit card at no charge to customers. To qualify, a potential customer simply has to produce two other credit cards and a photo identification. Credit is granted instantly and can be arranged at the point of checkout by the cashier operating the register. New credit accounts are granted an instant 10 percent discount on all merchandise purchased on the day the credit card is issued (if done in the store) or receive a coupon for 10 percent discounts at a future date (if done by mail or phone).

Customers may return merchandise within 21 days for full refund if they have a receipt. The company's return policy is flexible and favors the customers, even when the customer's behavior may be questionable (e.g., returning clothing after it has been worn). Product exchanges are allowed, or in-store credit issued, if the customer does not have a receipt. In the absence of a receipt, customers are granted credit reflecting the lowest price of the item returned for the past 21 days.

In order to keep costs low, LM's stores are considered to be "no frills." Few services are offered by clerks other than checkout and assistance with changing rooms. The store ambiance can best be described as "1980's industrial warehouse" with glaring lighting and minimal decorations or amenities. Most clothes are hung on wheeled metal racks to ease the process of reorganizing and restocking merchandise.

You are assigned to the audit of the customer service and revenue process of LM. The senior of the engagement has identified four risks related to customer service that she believes reflect significant residual risk:

1. LM's pricing strategy will not be effectively implemented and will result in lost revenues and reduced margins.
2. Holders of in-house credit cards may cause bad debts that undermine profit margins.
3. Excessive sales returns may result in overstocked merchandise and reduced margins.
4. Customers' tastes may change such that the company's deep discount strategy becomes unappealing.

For each risk:

1. Explain why the senior might feel the risk is a significant residual risk.
2. Identify the account(s) and assertion(s) that are likely to reflect high risk of material misstatement. Be specific.
3. Describe a strategy for performing substantive tests related to the accounts/ assertions. Be sure to consider the nature, extent, and timing of the tests you propose.

Case 11–2: Compuville Computers

[Author's Note: The following facts are based on a true story. The names have been changed to protect the parties involved but the equipment is accurately identified so as to promote realism (and because the problems were not the fault of the equipment manufacturer). The dates were also retained because computer equipment cost much more at the time, especially high-quality printers, and connectivity between Apple and IBM-based machines was extremely problematic. At the time of this transaction, Windows was not available for desktop computers, and the Apple graphical user interface was widely believed to be a superior operating system for new and novice users.]

In the summer of 1992, Joe Hardluck decided to take the plunge into the computer revolution and purchase a fancy computer from a reputable mail-order retailer, Compuville Computers Inc. Because of its reputation for being easy to use, Joe selected a top-of-the-line Apple computer called a Quadra. Joe estimated that the computer would cost him about $7,000. Unfortunately, that left Joe without much money to buy a printer. One of Joe's friends volunteered to let Joe have an older model Hewlett-Packard laser printer that he had sitting in his attic. After talking to the representative of the computer retailer, Joe decided to take the friend up on his offer. In order to connect the printer to his computer, Joe also needed to purchase network and printer accessories (including a computer card to control the fonts) for about $700 (which was significantly lower than a comparable quality new printer would have cost).

In early June 1992, Joe placed the order for the computer and the printer accessories with Compuville. The computer arrived safely on June 24 and the printer accessories on July 9. Joe paid for the equipment by using his Visa and MasterCard credit cards (neither had a credit limit high enough to handle the entire purchase). When Joe received his June credit card bills, he found the following charges related to these purchases:

Visa	6/16/92	$3,430.75
Visa	6/29/92	32.12
Visa	6/30/92	654.10
Mastercard	6/16/92	3,387.60

Joe was happy with his new purchases until he tried to connect the old printer to the new computer. After weeks of effort and repeated calls to the retailer's technical support line, Joe finally decided to give up the challenge as a lost cause. Joe then called the computer retailer to get authorization to return all of the printer accessories and to order a new Apple laser printer that would work with his computer. Joe packed up and returned the printer accessories in late September, and the new laser printer was delivered on October 11, 1992.

Unfortunately, when Joe unpacked the new printer, he found that it had been damaged in shipment and would not work properly. Somewhat angry at this point, Joe again called Compuville and asked for shipment of a replacement. The company agreed to send out a new unit immediately and have the delivery agent pick up the defective printer at the same time. The retailer billed Joe's Mastercard $2,624.90 on October 7, 1992 for the first printer.

At this point, Joe was reasonably satisfied because he had a working computer system and everything was settled with the retailer (or at least he thought). However, after anxiously examining both his October and November credit card statements, he realized that the company had failed to issue any credits for the returned merchandise. Joe once again called the company to find out the status of his returns. The company admitted that they had failed to process the credits and immediately issued four credit memos for all of the returned merchandise (see attached documents).

Joe again thought everything was settled until he received his December MasterCard statement, which, to his surprise, revealed a credit from Compuville in the amount of $2,624.90!

Joe has now come to you for help in clearing up this mess. He has provided you with the following relevant documents (listed chronologically):

Document	Number	Date	Description
Invoice	80053685	6/22/92	Invoice for initial computer purchase
Invoice	80062648	7/6/92	Invoice for accessories to connect old printer
Invoice	80067970	7/10/92	Invoice for additional printer accessories
Return slip	57419	10/5/92	Return authorization for accessories
Invoice	80135148	10/9/92	Invoice for new laser printer and accessories
Invoice	80136950	10/13/92	Invoice for second printer
Return slip	54416	10/13/92	Return authorization for defective printer
Return slip	57420	10/16/92	Return authorization for accessories
Return slip	54932	10/20/92	Return authorization for accessories
Credit memo	947470	12/14/92	Credit for printer accessories
Credit memo	947473	12/14/92	Credit for printer accessories
Credit memo	947630	12/15/92	Credit for defective printer
Credit memo	948105	12/22/92	Credit for printer accessories

Requirements

1. List all identifiable processing errors committed by Compuville related to this sequence of events. Indicate the dollar value associated with each processing error, if any.

2. Analyze the sequence of transactions and determine whether Joe owes Compuville money, or vice versa, and the amount owed. Document how you arrived at the amount.

3. Assume that you are the auditor of Compuville, and you detect this and similar problems from routine tests of transactions. Which management assertions would be affected by these problems? Explain.

4. Prepare a preliminary audit program to test sales returns, assuming that you feel the relevant management assertions have high risk of material misstatement.

5. Prepare one or more management letter comments that you would provide to Compuville Computers as a result of analyzing these events.

Exhibit 2–1

Compuville Computers, Inc.

	INVOICE	
Number	Date	Page
80053685	06/22/92	1

PPS NO. 337186
ORDER NO. 285468

S O L D	T O	Joe Hardluck 123 North Main Street Anywhere, FL 32333	S H I P	T O	Joe Hardluck 123 North Main Street Anywhere, FL 32333

P.O. Number	P.O. Release #	Terms	Ship Date	Carrier
VISA		Visa Charge	06/22/92	337186-26

Customer #	Reference #	Sales Representative	Request Date	Dept.	Rep Code	
000019706	26021218		06/16/92	26	63	no tm

Quantity			Item	Manufacturer		Item	Unit	Extended
Order	Ship	B/O	Number	Code	Part Number	Description	Price	Total
memo: EXPANDED RAM TO 20MB, INC. OF 4MB.								
			MUST BE DELIVERED BY TUES 6/16/92					
			SPC. OR=					
			PART#SMA-16MB-Q900 SPECIAL ORDER SKU(S) ORDERED					
PLEASE DISREGARD THIS INVOICE IF PAYMENT HAS BEEN MADE								
1	1	0	073490	APP	M5724LL/A		4959.72	4959.72
						Mac Quadra 700 4MB/400		
					F1219594C84			
1	1	0	050823	APP	M0401ll/b		613.83	613.83
						App Hi-Res RGB Monitor (Mac II)		
					7101004M0401LL"			
1	1	0	050693	APP	M0312		141.00	141.00
						App SE, Mac II Ext Keyboard (New)		
1	1	0	051413	PSD	051413		50.00	50.00
						Configuration Apple & Addl Hardware		
1	1	0	088154	SLD	SMA-16MB-Q900		599.00	599.00
						SLD Expanded RAM to 20MB w/4MB		
						Subtotal		6,363.55

REMIT TO: **DUE:**   Continued: 2

Exhibit 2–1   *(continued)*

Compuville Computers, Inc.

	INVOICE		
	Number	**Date**	**Page**
	80053685	06/22/92	2

PPS NO. 337186
ORDER NO. 285468

S	Joe Hardluck	S	Joe Hardluck
O T	123 North Main Street	H T	123 North Main Street
L O	Anywhere, FL 32333	I O	Anywhere, FL 32333
D		P	

P.O. Number	P.O. Release #	Terms	Ship Date	Carrier
VISA		Visa Charge	06/22/92	337186-26

Customer #	Reference #	Sales Representative	Request Date	Dept.	Rep Code	
000019706	26021218		06/16/92	26	63	no tm

Quantity			Item Number	Manufacturer		Item Description	Unit Price	Extended Total
Order	Ship	B/O		Code	Part Number			
1	1	0	032202	FRT		Actual Freight	25.00	25.00
						Actual Freight		

Tax rate % 7.00   445.45

REMIT TO: **DUE:**   6,834.00

Exhibit 2–2

Compuville Computers, Inc.

INVOICE		
Number	Date	Page
80062648	07/06/92	1

PPS NO. 347279
ORDER NO. 295063

S O L D T O	Joe Hardluck 123 North Main Street Anywhere, FL 32333		S H I P T O	Joe Hardluck 123 North Main Street Anywhere, FL 32333

P.O. Number	P.O. Release #	Terms	Ship Date	Carrier
VISA		Visa Charge	07/06/92	B356

Customer #	Reference #	Sales Representative	Request Date	Dept.	Rep Code	
000019706	26021626		06/30/92	26	63	no pk

Quantity			Item Number	Manufacturer		Item Description	Unit Price	Extended Total
Order	Ship	B/O		Code	Part Number			

memo: SPECIAL ORDER SKU(S) ORDERED

PLEASE DISREGARD THIS INVOICE IF PAYMENT HAS BEEN MADE

Order	Ship	B/O	Item Number	Code	Part Number	Description	Unit Price	Extended Total
1	1	0	089014	ABL	0996-75	ABL PVC Silver Satin Cbl for RJII	25.00	25.00
2	2	0	089015	ABL	0710	ABL RJII Crimp Modular Connector	1.50	3.00
						Subtotal		28.00
1	1	0	032202	FRT		Actual Freight Actual Freight	2.13	2.13
						Tax rate % 6.00		1.68

REMIT TO:	DUE:	31.81

IMPORTANT: The reverse side of this document contains the additional terms and conditions under which the products and/or services described on this invoice are being sold or licensed to you, including Compuville's disclaimer for liability for any special, indirect, incidental or consequential damages. By using the products and/or services you expressly agree to and accept these terms and conditions. All accounts past due are subject to a 1 1/2% per month service charge (18% per annum). Returns: 15% restocking charge on stock items only, non-stock items are not returnable. No goods will be accepted for credit without our return material authorization number.

Exhibit 2–3

Compuville Computers, Inc.

INVOICE		
Number	Date	Page
80067970	07/10/92	1

PPS NO. 351439
ORDER NO. 295062

S O L D	T O	Joe Hardluck
		123 North Main Street
		Anywhere, FL 32333

S H I P	T O	Joe Hardluck
		123 North Main Street
		Anywhere, FL 32333

P.O. Number	P.O. Release #	Terms	Ship Date	Carrier
VISA		Visa Charge	07/10/92	B322

Customer #	Reference #	Sales Representative	Request Date	Dept.	Rep Code	
000019706	26021625		06/30/92	26	63	no pk

Quantity			Item	Manufacturer		Item	Unit	Extended
Order	Ship	B/O	Number	Code	Part Number	Description	Price	Total
PLEASE DISREGARD THIS INVOICE IF PAYMENT HAS BEEN MADE								
1	1	0	075296	HP	33416B	#ABA	168.23	168.23
						HP LJ III/D Appletalk I/F		
1	1	0	029000	ABL	0001-10		20.00	20.00
						ABL Cbl Par Std 10'		
1	1	0	051979	HP	33439Q		302.93	302.93
						HP LJ IID/P/P+ Postscript Font		
2	2	0	072798	HP	92215N		30.59	61.18
						HP Apple Lan Conn to Deskwriter		
1	1	0	050625	APP	M0403		55.78	55.78
						APP Universal Mtr Stand (Hi-Res)		
						Subtotal		608.12
1	1	0	032202	FRT	Actual Freight		6.76	6.76
						Actual Freight		
						Tax rate % 6.00		36.49

REMIT TO: **DUE:**   651.37

Exhibit 2–4

Compuville Computers, Inc.

	INVOICE		
Number	Date		Page
80135148	10/09/92		1

PPS NO. 421933
ORDER NO. 364792

S		Joe Hardluck		S		Joe Hardluck
O	T	123 North Main Street		H	T	123 North Main Street
L	O	Anywhere, FL 32333		I	O	Anywhere, FL 32333
D				P		

P.O. Number	P.O. Release #	Terms	Ship Date	Carrier
VISA		Visa Charge	10/09/92	SB 7012075287-296

Customer #	Reference #	Sales Representative	Request Date	Dept.	Rep Code	
000019706	26023883		10/12/92	26	63	no fs

Quantity			Item Number	Manufacturer		Item Description	Unit Price	Extended Total
Order	Ship	B/O		Code	Part Number			
PLEASE DISREGARD THIS INVOICE IF PAYMENT HAS BEEN MADE								
1	1	0	050805	APP	M6000		1333.64	1333.64
						APP Laserwriter II (Engine only)		
						CA2313EC]6000		
1	1	0	073423	APP	M6504LL/B		860.82	860.82
						Laserwriter IIF Controller Card		
1	1	0	050682	APP	M6002		79.53	79.53
						APP Laserwriter II Toner		
1	1	0	050689	APP	M2068		75.00	75.00
						APP Mac-Laser Localtalk 8Pin Connec		
2	2	0	048087	FAR	PN308		27.39	54.78
						Phonenet + Connector		
1	1	0	029888	PSD	29888		15.00	15.00
						Config-Printer Upgrade		
						Subtotal		2,418.77

REMIT TO: **DUE:**   Continued: 2

Exhibit 2–4 *(continued)*

Compuville Computers, Inc.

INVOICE		
Number	Date	Page
80135148	10/09/92	2

PPS NO. 421933
ORDER NO. 364792

S O L D	T O	Joe Hardluck 123 North Main Street Anywhere, FL 32333

S H I P	T O	Joe Hardluck 123 North Main Street Anywhere, FL 32333

P.O. Number	P.O. Release #	Terms	Ship Date	Carrier
VISA		Visa Charge	10/09/92	SB 7012075287-296

Customer #	Reference #	Sales Representative	Request Date	Dept.	Rep Code	
000019706	26023883		10/12/92	26	63	no fs

Quantity			Item Number	Manufacturer		Item Description	Unit Price	Extended Total
Order	Ship	B/O		Code	Part Number			
1	1	0	010286	FRT	Freight		61.00	61.00
						Freight Misc.		
						Tax rate % 6.00		148.79

REMIT TO: **DUE:**   2,628.56

IMPORTANT: The reverse side of this document contains the additional terms and conditions under which the products and/or services described on this invoice are being sold or licensed to you, including Compuville's disclaimer for liability for any special, indirect, incidental or consequential damages. By using the products and/or services you expressly agree to and accept these terms and conditions. All accounts past due are subject to a 1 1/2% per month service charge (18% per annum). Returns: 15% restocking charge on stock items only, non-stock items are not returnable. No goods will be accepted for credit without our return material authorization number.

Exhibit 2–5

Compuville Computers, Inc.

INVOICE		
Number	Date	Page
80136950	10/13/92	1

PPS NO. 424119
ORDER NO. 366426

S	Joe Hardluck		S	Joe Hardluck
O T	123 North Main Street		H T	123 North Main Street
L O	Anywhere, FL 32333		I O	Anywhere, FL 32333
D			P	

P.O. Number	P.O. Release #	Terms	Ship Date	Carrier
VISA		Visa Charge	10/13/92	F1 7012079776

Customer #	Reference #	Sales Representative	Request Date	Dept.	Rep Code	
000019706	26024267		10/14/92	26	63	no fs

Quantity			Item Number	Manufacturer		Item Description	Unit Price	Extended Total
Order	Ship	B/O		Code	Part Number			
memo:								
memo: RMA #54416								
PLEASE DISREGARD THIS INVOICE IF PAYMENT HAS BEEN MADE								
1	1	0	050805	APP	M6000		1333.64	1333.64
						APP Laserwriter II (Engine Only)		
						CA223PC8]6000		
1	1	0	073423	APP	M6504LL/B		860.82	860.82
						Laserwriter IIF Controller Card		
						Subtotal		2,194.46
1	1	0	010286	FRT	Freight		0.00	0.00
						Freight Misc.		
						Tax rate % 6.00		131.67

REMIT TO: DUE: 2,326.13

IMPORTANT:

The reverse side of this document contains the additional terms and conditions under which the products and/or services described on this invoice are being sold or licensed to you, including Compuville's disclaimer for liability for any special, indirect, incidental or consequential damages. By using the products and/or services you expressly agree to and accept these terms and conditions. All accounts past due are subject to a 1 1/2% per month service charge (18% per annum). Returns: 15% restocking charge on stock items only, non-stock items are not returnable. No goods will be accepted for credit without our return material authorization number.

Exhibit 2–6

Compuville Computers, Inc.   **RMA REQUEST**   RMA #: _57419_

Customer Information:

Acct#: _000019706_   PO#: _Visa_

Ship to: _Joe Hardluck_

Address: _123 N. Main St._

City: _Anywhere_   St: _FL_   Zip: _32333_

Contact: _Joe Hardluck_

Branch Information:

Request Date: _10/5/92_

Branch: _26_   Admin: _Jane Johnson_

Rep Name: _—_   Rep Code: _63_

Invoice #: _80067970_   Invoice Date: _7/10/92_

Approved by: _TL_

Qty	SKU No.	Vendor Code	Stock Code	Description	Unit Price	Total Price	Reason for Return
1	029000	ABL	01	ABL Cbl Par Std 10'	20.00	20.00	35
1	051979	HP	02	HP LJ IIISI/PIP+ Postscript	302.93	302.93	35
1	072798	HP	04	HP Apple Lan Conn	30.59	30.59	35
1	075296	HP	03	HP LJ IIISI/D Appletalk	168.23	168.23	35

Stocking Charges: _-0-_   *No replacement order*

Exhibit 2–7

Compuville Computers, Inc.   **RMA REQUEST**   RMA #: _54416_

Customer Information:

Acct#: _000019706_   PO#: _Visa_

Ship to: _Joe Hardluck_

Address: _123 N. Main St._

City: _Anywhere_   St: _FL_   Zip: _32333_

Contact: _Joe Hardluck_

Branch Information:

Request Date: _10/13/92_

Branch: _26_   Admin: _Jane Johnson_

Rep Name: _—_   Rep Code: _63_

Invoice #: _80135148_   Invoice Date: _10/9/92_

Approved by: _TL_

Qty	SKU No.	Vendor Code	Stock Code	Description	Unit Price	Total Price	Reason for Return
1	050805	APP	01	Laserwriter II (engine only)	1333.64	1333.64	10
1	073423	APP	02	Laserwriter IIf (card)	860.82	860.82	10

Stocking Charges: _-0-_   *Replacement 26024267*

Exhibit 2–8

Compuville Computers, Inc.   **RMA REQUEST**   RMA #: _57420_

Customer Information:

Acct#: _000019706_   PO#: _Visa_

Ship to: _Joe Hardluck_

Address: _123 N. Main St._

City: _Anywhere_   St: _FL_   Zip: _32333_

Contact: _Joe Hardluck_

Branch Information:

Request Date: _10/16/92_

Branch: _26_   Admin: _Jane Johnson_

Rep Name: _—_   Rep Code: _63_

Invoice #: _80062648_   Invoice Date: _7/6/92_

Approved by: _TL_

Qty	SKU No.	Vendor Code	Stock Code	Description	Unit Price	Total Price	Reason for Return
1	089014	ABL	04	ABL PVC Silver Satin Cbl	25.00	25.00	35
2	089015	ABL	04	ABL RJ11 Crimp Mod Con	1.50	3.00	35

Stocking Charges: ___-0-___   *No replacement*

Exhibit 2–9

Compuville Computers, Inc.   **RMA REQUEST**   RMA #: _54932_

Customer Information:

Acct#: _000019706_   PO#: _Visa_

Ship to: _Joe Hardluck_

Address: _123 N. Main St._

City: _Anywhere_   St: _FL_   Zip: _32333_

Contact: _Joe Hardluck_

Branch Information:

Request Date: _10/20/92_

Branch: _26_   Admin: _Jane Johnson_

Rep Name: _—_   Rep Code: _63_

Invoice #: _80135148_   Invoice Date: _10/9/92_

Approved by: _TL_

Qty	SKU No.	Vendor Code	Stock Code	Description	Unit Price	Total Price	Reason for Return
1	050689	APP	02	APP Mac Laser 8 Pin	75.00	75.00	30

Stocking Charges: ___-0-___   *No replacement*

Exhibit 2–10

Compuville Computers, Inc.

INVOICE		
Number	Date	Page
947470	12/14/92	1

PPS NO. 0
ORDER NO. 0

CREDIT MEMO

S O L D	T O	Joe Hardluck
		123 North Main Street
		Anywhere, FL 32333

S H I P	T O	Joe Hardluck
		123 North Main Street
		Anywhere, FL 32333

P.O. Number	P.O. Release #	Terms	Ship Date	Carrier
VISA		Visa Charge	12/14/92	

Customer #	Reference #	Sales Representative	Request Date	Dept.	Rep Code	
000019706			12/14/92	26	63	no jb

Quantity			Item	Manufacturer		Item	Unit	Extended
Order	Ship	B/O	Number	Code	Part Number	Description	Price	Total
memo: R-54932 I-80135148 12-11-92 30R								
-1	-1	0	050689	APP	M2068		75.00	-75.00
						APP Mac-Laser Localtalk 8Pin Connec		
-2	-2	0	048087	FAR	PN308		27.39	-54.78
						Phonenet + Connector		
1	1	0	051971	ADM	051971		0.00	0.00
						7.5% Restocking Fee		
						Subtotal		-129.78
						Tax rate % 6.00		-7.79

REMIT TO: **DUE:**   -137.57

IMPORTANT: The reverse side of this document contains the additional terms and conditions under which the products and/or services described on this invoice are being sold or licensed to you, including Compuville's disclaimer for liability for any special, indirect, incidental or consequential damages. By using the products and/or services you expressly agree to and accept these terms and conditions. All accounts past due are subject to a 1 1/2% per month service charge (18% per annum). Returns: 15% restocking charge on stock items only, non-stock items are not returnable. No goods will be accepted for credit without our return material authorization number.

Exhibit 2–11

Compuville Computers, Inc.

INVOICE		
Number	Date	Page
947473	12/14/92	1

PPS NO. 0
ORDER NO. 0

CREDIT MEMO

S	Joe Hardluck		S	Joe Hardluck
O T	123 North Main Street		H T	123 North Main Street
L O	Anywhere, FL 32333		I O	Anywhere, FL 32333
D			P	

P.O. Number	P.O. Release #	Terms	Ship Date	Carrier
VISA		Visa Charge	12/14/92	

Customer #	Reference #	Sales Representative	Request Date	Dept.	Rep Code	
000019706			12/14/92	26	63	no jb

Quantity			Item	Manufacturer		Item		Unit	Extended
Order	Ship	B/O	Number	Code	Part Number	Description		Price	Total
memo: R-57420 I-80062648 12-11-92 35R									
-1	-1	0	089014	ABL	0996-75			25.00	-25.00
						ABL PVC Silver Satin Cbl for RJII			
-2	-2	0	089015	ABL	0710			1.50	-3.00
						ABL RJII Crimp Modular Connector			
							Subtotal		-28.00
-1	-1	0	032202	FRT	Actual Freight			2.13	-2.13
						Actual Freight			
							Tax rate % 6.00		-1.68

REMIT TO: **DUE:**   -31.81

IMPORTANT: The reverse side of this document contains the additional terms and conditions under which the products and/or services described on this invoice are being sold or licensed to you, including Compuville's disclaimer for liability for any special, indirect, incidental or consequential damages. By using the products and/or services you expressly agree to and accept these terms and conditions. All accounts past due are subject to a 1 1/2% per month service charge (18% per annum). Returns: 15% restocking charge on stock items only, non-stock items are not returnable. No goods will be accepted for credit without our return material authorization number.

Exhibit 2–12

Compuville Computers, Inc.

INVOICE		
Number	Date	Page
947630	12/15/92	1

PPS NO. 0
ORDER NO. 0

CREDIT MEMO

S		Joe Hardluck	S		Joe Hardluck
O	T	123 North Main Street	H	T	123 North Main Street
L	O	Anywhere, FL 32333	I	O	Anywhere, FL 32333
D			P		

P.O. Number	P.O. Release #	Terms	Ship Date	Carrier
VISA		Visa Charge	12/15/92	

Customer #	Reference #	Sales Representative	Request Date	Dept.	Rep Code	
000019706			12/15/92	26	63	no jb

Quantity			Item Number	Manufacturer		Item Description	Unit Price	Extended Total
Order	Ship	B/O		Code	Part Number			

memo: R-54416   I-80135148 121492 10D

Order	Ship	B/O	Item Number	Code	Part Number	Description	Unit Price	Extended Total
-1	-1	0	073423	APP	M6504LL/B	Laserwriter IIF Controller Card	860.82	-860.82
-1	-1	0	050805	APP	M6000	APP Laserwriter II (Engine Only)	1333.64	-1333.64
					CA2313EC			

Subtotal	-2,194.46
Tax rate % 6.00	-131.67

REMIT TO: **DUE:**   -2,326.13

IMPORTANT: The reverse side of this document contains the additional terms and conditions under which the products and/or services described on this invoice are being sold or licensed to you, including Compuville's disclaimer for liability for any special, indirect, incidental or consequential damages. By using the products and/or services you expressly agree to and accept these terms and conditions. All accounts past due are subject to a 1 1/2% per month service charge (18% per annum). Returns: 15% restocking charge on stock items only, non-stock items are not returnable. No goods will be accepted for credit without our return material authorization number.

Exhibit 2–13

Compuville Computers, Inc.

	INVOICE	
Number	Date	Page
948105	12/22/92	1

PPS NO. 0
ORDER NO. 0

CREDIT MEMO

S O L D	T O	Joe Hardluck 123 North Main Street Anywhere, FL 32333

S H I P	T O	Joe Hardluck 123 North Main Street Anywhere, FL 32333

P.O. Number	P.O. Release #	Terms	Ship Date	Carrier
VISA		Visa Charge	12/22/92	

Customer #	Reference #	Sales Representative	Request Date	Dept.	Rep Code	
000019706			12/22/92	26	63	no ph

Quantity			Item Number	Manufacturer		Item Description	Unit Price	Extended Total
Order	Ship	B/O		Code	Part Number			
memo: R-57419 I-80067970 12/11/92*35R								
-1	-1	0	029000	ABL	0001-10		20.00	-20.00
						ABL CBL Par Std 10'		
-1	-1	0	051979	HP	33439Q		302.93	-302.93
						HP LJ IID/P/P+ Postscript Font		
-1	-1	0	075296	HP	33416B	#ABA	168.23	-168.23
						HP LJ III/D Appletalk I/F		
1	1	0	051970	ADM	051970		0.00	0.00
						5% Restocking Fee		
1	1	0	051971	ADM	051971		0.00	0.00
						7.5% Restocking Fee		
						Subtotal		-491.16
						Tax rate % 6.00		-29.47

REMIT TO: **DUE:**   -520.63

IMPORTANT: The reverse side of this document contains the additional terms and conditions under which the products and/or services described on this invoice are being sold or licensed to you, including Compuville's disclaimer for liability for any special, indirect, incidental or consequential damages. By using the products and/or services you expressly agree to and accept these terms and conditions. All accounts past due are subject to a 1 1/2% per month service charge (18% per annum). Returns: 15% restocking charge on stock items only, non-stock items are not returnable. No goods will be accepted for credit without our return material authorization number.

Case 11–3: IOU A-Lot Inc.

After graduation, the lure of Florida proved to be too strong for you, and you joined a small CPA firm near the University of Florida. You are auditing IOU A-Lot Inc. for the year ended December 31, 2006. The company is a web-based discount retailer of electronic equipment. One of the company's main marketing advantages is that it is willing to finance sales to customers for up to 90 days without interest charges. However, for customers with poor credit ratings, the company requires an advance deposit of 30 percent of the purchase price before it will deliver. The credit manager determines the appropriate financing arrangement that can be offered to a specific customer. Of course, the company also accepts cash and credit card payments, but approximately 40 percent of its sales are financed internally.

Total sales for the year were $400,000. Customers typically make payments in three separate installments based on monthly billings. Failure to make a payment on time makes the entire balance due and payable immediately. At the point that any single scheduled payment is past due, the entire account is classified as delinquent, even amounts that have not yet been billed. In addition, the company begins to charge interest on the entire balance due at a rate of 22.5 percent per annum. For the purpose of aging receivables, a balance is considered past due if a scheduled payment is missed by more than 30 days.

The confirmation control schedule for the audit of receivables is shown in Exhibit 3. This has been prepared and audited by an intern working on the audit. Your audit senior has asked you to review the intern's work. Assume that the receivable working papers have the following indices:

B	Receivables lead schedule (Exhibit 3–1)
B-1	Aged trial balance (Exhibit 3–2)
B-2	Confirmation control schedule (Exhibit 3–3)
B-3	Confirmation responses (Exhibit 3–4)

Exhibit 3–1

IOU A-Lot Inc.
Receivables Lead Schedule
December 31, 2006

	2006	2005
Trade receivables	$33,494.54	$27,888.60
Advances from customers	(1,200.56)	(867.40)
Due from employees	2,345.78	2,134.90
Allowance for doubtful accounts	(1,654.76)	(1,538.95)
	$32,985.00	$27,617.15

Exhibit 3–2

IOU A-Lot Inc.
Aged Trial Balance
December 31, 2006

Customer	0–30	30–60	60–90	>90	Total
Jane Smith	3,245.23	0.00	0.00	0.00	3,245.23
John Hunt	0.00	89.50	0.00	0.00	89.50
Roy Schafer	79.37	198.63	0.00	0.00	278.00
Tom McDonald	945.63	0.00	0.00	0.00	945.63
John Doe	441.62	0.00	125.60	0.00	567.22
Joe Cruz	0.00	0.00	0.00	23.00	23.00
Gary Brown	1,133.55	222.65	0.00	0.00	1,356.20
Mark Brown	0.00	0.00	0.00	1,078.45	1,078.45
David Summers	158.90	0.00	0.00	0.00	158.90
Dawn Stewart	1,463.67	612.34	704.55	0.00	2,780.56
Dan Kim	244.16	0.00	456.80	678.90	1,379.86
Linda Johnson	723.00	0.00	0.00	0.00	723.00
Frank Reeves	975.00	0.00	0.00	0.00	975.00
Abigail Palmer	558.00	300.00	300.00	300.00	1,458.00
Bill Fleet	236.30	208.00	0.00	0.00	444.30
Joann Smart	125.56	112.00	0.00	0.00	237.56
Sam Murphy	97.43	0.00	0.00	0.00	97.43
David White	145.99	0.00	0.00	0.00	145.99
Jennifer Murphy	921.18	309.00	1,115.80	0.00	2,345.98
Eleanor Ricks	54.63	0.00	0.00	0.00	54.63
Sara McPherson	1,005.60	0.00	0.00	0.00	1,005.60
Mary Reed	567.67	289.30	0.00	0.00	856.97
William Collins	537.88	675.46	0.00	0.00	1,213.34
Liz Horne	302.45	0.00	0.00	0.00	302.45
Rob Hendricks	131.71	145.96	56.00	0.00	333.67
Alan Hill	367.69	478.00	0.00	0.00	845.69
Lynn Jenkins	0.00	245.60	0.00	0.00	245.60
James Dixon	1,852.90	0.00	0.00	0.00	1,852.90
Joseph McCray	1,465.89	0.00	0.00	0.00	1,465.89
Robert Palmer	448.00	0.00	0.00	0.00	448.00
Robert Mason	3,391.55	985.40	0.00	0.00	4,376.95
John McGill	0.00	0.00	56.36	0.00	56.36
Albert Martin	375.74	178.96	109.80	0.00	664.50
Paul Bunyan	916.88	0.00	60.00	465.30	1,442.18
Totals	22,913.18	5,050.80	2,984.91	2,545.65	33,494.54

Exhibit 3–3

IOU A-Lot Inc.
Confirmation Control Schedule

Customer Number	Customer Name	Amount	Date Requests Sent			Date Returned	Amount Confirmed	Amount of Error
			First	Second	Third			
1012	Jane Smith	$3,245.23	1/7/07	1/24/07		2/2/07	2,956.20	
1116	John Doe	567.22	1/7/07			1/16/07	567.22	
1356	Gary Brown	1,356.20	1/7/07	1/24/07		1/31/07	1056.20	300.07
1426	Linda Johnson	723.00	1/7/07	1/24/07				
1589	David White	145.99	1/7/07			1/14/07	145.99	
1605	Jennifer Murphy	2,345.98	1/7/07			1/22/07	2345.98	
1770	William Collins	1,213.34	1/7/07	1/24/07	2/4/07			
1835	James Dixon	1,852.90	1/7/07			1/21/07	1852.90	
1935	Robert Mason	4,376.95	1/7/07			1/14/07	2000.00	
1978	Albert Martin	664.50	1/7/07	1/24/07		2/2/07	664.50	
Total confirmed		$16,491.31						
Total not confirmed		$17,003.23						
Total Receivables		$33,494.54						

Customer
Number Explanations:

1012	Customer omitted interest accrued on account.
1356	Customer omitted sale on 12/30/07.
1770	All returned by Post Office.
1925	Customer paid difference on 12/1/06.

Notes:

1. First requests were mailed from our CPA office. Second and third requests were mailed by client.
2. All replies were sent direct to our CPA office.

Exhibit 3–4   Confirmation Responses

IOU A-Lot Inc.
1 S.E. 1st Street
Gainesville, FL 32601

January 7, 2007

Ms. Jane Smith
945 Carolina Avenue
Ft. Lauderdale, FL 33312

Dear Ms. Smith:

Our financial statements are currently being examined by the auditing firm of Smith & Company, CPAs (Gainesville, Florida). In connection with this examination, we ask that you examine the information provided below related to your account with us. Please confirm directly to our auditors whether you agree or disagree with the correctness of this information.

   This is not a request for payment. Please do not send payment to our auditors. Your prompt attention to this request is greatly appreciated. A stamped, self-addressed envelope is enclosed for your reply.

Brian A. Monbourne, Controller

Smith & Company, CPAs
Gainesville, Florida

Please check one of the following:

_____ The balance of **$3,245.23** owed by us to IOU-A-Lot Inc., as of December 31, 2006, is correct.

___X___ The balance of **$3,245.23** is not correct for the reasons noted below:
My records show a balance of $2951.20, but I do not know how much interest I owe.

Date: 1/26/07   Signed: Jane Smith

Exhibit 3–4   *(continued)*

IOU A-Lot Inc.
1 S.E. 1st Street
Gainesville, FL 32601

January 7, 2007

Mr. John Doe
200 Dryden Place, Suite 1
Jacksonville, FL 32202

Dear Mr. Doe:

Our financial statements are currently being examined by the auditing firm of
Smith & Company, CPAs (Gainesville, Florida). In connection with this
examination, we ask that you examine the information provided below related to
your account with us. Please confirm directly to our auditors whether you agree
or disagree with the correctness of this information.

This is not a request for payment. Please do not send payment to our
auditors. Your prompt attention to this request is greatly appreciated. A stamped,
self-addressed envelope is enclosed for your reply.

Brian A. Monbourne, Controller

Smith & Company, CPAs
Gainesville, Florida

Please check one of the following:

_____X_____ The balance of **$567.22** owed by us to IOU-A-Lot Inc., as of
December 31, 2006, is correct.

_____ The balance of **$567.22** is not correct for the reasons noted below:

Date: 1/11/07   Signed: John Doe

Exhibit 3–4   *(continued)*

IOU A-Lot Inc.
1 S.E. 1st Street
Gainesville, FL 32601

January 7, 2007

Mr. Gary Brown
175 Hickory Crest Drive
Orlando, FL 32802

Dear Mr. Brown:

Our financial statements are currently being examined by the auditing firm of Smith & Company, CPAs (Gainesville, Florida). In connection with this examination, we ask that you examine the information provided below related to your account with us. Please confirm directly to our auditors whether you agree or disagree with the correctness of this information.

   This is not a request for payment. Please do not send payment to our auditors. Your prompt attention to this request is greatly appreciated. A stamped, self-addressed envelope is enclosed for your reply.

Brian A. Monbourne, Controller

Smith & Company, CPAs
Gainesville, Florida

Please check one of the following:

_____ The balance of **$1,356.20** owed by us to IOU-A-Lot Inc., as of December 31, 2006, is correct.

____*X*____ The balance of **$1,356.20** is not correct for the reasons noted below:

I think I only owe you guys $1056.20.

Date: 1/29/07   Signed: Gary Brown

Exhibit 3–4   *(continued)*

IOU A-Lot Inc.
1 S.E. 1st Street
Gainesville, FL 32601

COPY – NO response

January 7, 2007

Ms. Linda Johnson
2001 Space Odyssey Parkway
Cocoa Beach, FL 32931

Dear Ms. Johnson:

Our financial statements are currently being examined by the auditing firm of
Smith & Company, CPAs (Gainesville, Florida). In connection with this
examination, we ask that you examine the information provided below related to
your account with us. Please confirm directly to our auditors whether you agree
or disagree with the correctness of this information.

   This is not a request for payment. Please do not send payment to our
auditors. Your prompt attention to this request is greatly appreciated. A stamped,
self-addressed envelope is enclosed for your reply.

Brian A. Monbourne, Controller

Smith & Company, CPAs
Gainesville, Florida

Please check one of the following:

_____ The balance of **$723.00** owed by us to IOU-A-Lot Inc., as of December
31, 2006, is correct.

_____ The balance of **$723.00** is not correct for the reasons noted below:

Date: Signed:

Exhibit 3–4   *(continued)*

IOU A-Lot Inc.
1 S.E. 1st Street
Gainesville, FL 32601

January 7, 2007

Mr. David White
21042 Dandy Road
Arlington, TX 76010

Dear Mr. White

Our financial statements are currently being examined by the auditing firm of Smith & Company, CPAs (Gainesville, Florida). In connection with this examination, we ask that you examine the information provided below related to your account with us. Please confirm directly to our auditors whether you agree or disagree with the correctness of this information.

     This is not a request for payment. Please do not send payment to our auditors. Your prompt attention to this request is greatly appreciated. A stamped, self-addressed envelope is enclosed for your reply.

Brian A. Monbourne, Controller

Smith & Company, CPAs
Gainesville, Florida

Please check one of the following:

_____*X*_____ The balance of **$145.99** owed by us to IOU-A-Lot Inc., as of December 31, 2006, is correct.

_____ The balance of **$145.99** is not correct for the reasons noted below:

Date: 1/10/07   Signed: D. White

Exhibit 3–4 *(continued)*

IOU A-Lot Inc.
1 S.E. 1st Street
Gainesville, FL 32601

January 7, 2007

Mrs. Jennifer Murphy
6112 Braden Run
Bradenton, FL 34202

Dear Mrs. Murphy

Our financial statements are currently being examined by the auditing firm of Smith & Company, CPAs (Gainesville, Florida). In connection with this examination, we ask that you examine the information provided below related to your account with us. Please confirm directly to our auditors whether you agree or disagree with the correctness of this information.

This is not a request for payment. Please do not send payment to our auditors. Your prompt attention to this request is greatly appreciated. A stamped, self-addressed envelope is enclosed for your reply.

Brian A. Monbourne, Controller

Smith & Company, CPAs
Gainesville, Florida

Please check one of the following:

___X___ The balance of **$2,345.98** owed by us to IOU-A-Lot Inc., as of December 31, 2006, is correct.

_____ The balance of **$2,345.98** is not correct for the reasons noted below:

I sent a payment on 12/29/06 but they must not have got it yet.

Date: 1/20/07   Signed: Mrs. Jennifer Murphy

Exhibit 3–4   *(continued)*

IOU A-Lot Inc.
1 S.E. 1st Street
Gainesville, FL 32601

COPY returned by Post Office.

January 7, 2007

Mr. William Collins
519 SE 6th Avenue
Lexington, NC 27292

Dear Mr. Collins:

Our financial statements are currently being examined by the auditing firm of Smith & Company, CPAs (Gainesville, Florida). In connection with this examination, we ask that you examine the information provided below related to your account with us. Please confirm directly to our auditors whether you agree or disagree with the correctness of this information.

    This is not a request for payment. Please do not send payment to our auditors. Your prompt attention to this request is greatly appreciated. A stamped, self-addressed envelope is enclosed for your reply.

Brian A. Monbourne, Controller

Smith & Company, CPAs
Gainesville, Florida

Please check one of the following:

_____ The balance of **$1,213.34** owed by us to IOU-A-Lot Inc., as of December 31, 2006, is correct.

_____ The balance of **$1,213.34** is not correct for the reasons noted below:

Date: Signed:

Exhibit 3–4   *(continued)*

IOU A-Lot Inc.
1 S.E. 1st Street
Gainesville, FL 32601

January 7, 2007

Mr. James Dixon
510 Grey Street
Tampa, FL 33680

Dear Mr. Dixon:

Our financial statements are currently being examined by the auditing firm of
Smith & Company, CPAs (Gainesville, Florida). In connection with this
examination, we ask that you examine the information provided below related to
your account with us. Please confirm directly to our auditors whether you agree
or disagree with the correctness of this information.

   This is not a request for payment. Please do not send payment to our
auditors. Your prompt attention to this request is greatly appreciated. A stamped,
self-addressed envelope is enclosed for your reply.

Brian A. Monbourne, Controller

Smith & Company, CPAs
Gainesville, Florida

Please check one of the following:

_____X_____ The balance of **$1,852.90** owed by us to IOU-A-Lot Inc., as of
December 31, 2006, is correct.

_____ The balance of **$1,852.90** is not correct for the reasons noted below:

I am still waiting to receive an order placed in November.

Date: 1/31/07   Signed: J. Dixon

Exhibit 3–4   *(continued)*

IOU A-Lot Inc.
1 S.E. 1st Street
Gainesville, FL 32601

January 7, 2007

Mr. Robert Mason
16061 Cherokee Road
St. Paul, MN 55116

Dear Mr. Mason:

Our financial statements are currently being examined by the auditing firm of
Smith & Company, CPAs (Gainesville, Florida). In connection with this
examination, we ask that you examine the information provided below related to
your account with us. Please confirm directly to our auditors whether you agree
or disagree with the correctness of this information.

This is not a request for payment. Please do not send payment to our
auditors. Your prompt attention to this request is greatly appreciated. A stamped,
self-addressed envelope is enclosed for your reply.

Brian A. Monbourne, Controller

Smith & Company, CPAs
Gainesville, Florida

Please check one of the following:

_____ The balance of **$4,376.95** owed by us to IOU-A-Lot Inc., as of
December 31, 2006, is correct.

___*X*___ The balance of **$4,376.95** is not correct for the reasons noted below:

*My balance is no more than $2000 since I paid the rest off in early December. These guys
keep losing my payments.*

Date: 1/11/07   Signed: Robert Mason

Exhibit 3–4   *(continued)*

IOU A-Lot Inc.
1 S.E. 1st Street
Gainesville, FL 32601

January 7, 2007

Mr. Albert Martin
1716 Verde Drive
Clearwater, FL 34625

Dear Mr. Martin:

Our financial statements are currently being examined by the auditing firm of
Smith & Company, CPAs (Gainesville, Florida). In connection with this
examination, we ask that you examine the information provided below related to
your account with us. Please confirm directly to our auditors whether you agree
or disagree with the correctness of this information.

This is not a request for payment. Please do not send payment to our
auditors. Your prompt attention to this request is greatly appreciated. A stamped,
self-addressed envelope is enclosed for your reply.

Brian A. Monbourne, Controller

Smith & Company, CPAs
Gainesville, Florida

Please check one of the following:

_____*X*_____ The balance of **$664.50** owed by us to IOU-A-Lot Inc., as of
December 31, 2006, is correct.

_____ The balance of **$664.50** is not correct for the reasons noted below:

OK

Date: 1/25/07   Signed: Albert Martin

Requirements

1. What are the relevant management assertions being addressed by the confirmation of receivables?
2. Evaluate the sample selection for confirmations. Do you feel that the selection of accounts to confirm is appropriate? What would you have done differently? Explain.
3. Review the working papers and note any deficiencies. Use a format that would be appropriate for reviewing a subordinate's work.
4. How would you follow up on any exceptions noted in the confirmation responses?
5. Prepare a summary memo of the confirmation results and disposition of exceptions.
6. Do you think the allowance for doubtful accounts is adequate? Explain and provide evidence to support your opinion.

12

Audit Testing for the Supply Chain and Production Process

Outline

INTRODUCTION

Most organizations create value by obtaining resources from suppliers and transforming those resources into goods and services that are demanded by customers. An organization can develop and sustain a competitive advantage over its competition by managing supply and production in ways that are difficult for others to duplicate. For example, a company could develop proprietary production technology (e.g., high-tech manufacturers). Additionally, a company can use innovative ways to manage its supply chain by identifying and managing effective alliances with suppliers. In fact, supply chain integration and management is widely regarded as one of the most important aspects of sustaining competitive advantages in today's interconnected, global economy. Due to the importance of supply chain management to the success of most organizations, we make it the focus of this chapter (see Figure 12–1).

Example

United Parcel Service (UPS) has developed into one of the world's largest global supply chain managers. To help companies become more efficient and improve customer service, UPS now performs portions of an organization's supply chain that are sensitive to delivery and turnaround times. For example, UPS picks up, services, and redelivers all Toshiba laptops from customers; receives orders, picks, inspects, packs, and delivers products for Nike orders placed over the Internet; and performs all on-site repairs for HP printers in Europe and South America.

This chapter is similar in structure to the last chapter. We will use a process map and internal threat analysis to highlight the important characteristics of supply chain and production management that could have an impact on the conduct of the audit. In the next section, we will discuss the basic objectives and activities of the supply chain and production. We will then discuss the transactions that occur within these processes, the nature of process risks, types of process (internal) control, and metrics for performance measurement. Figure 12–2 presents a summary of the accounts affected by the supply chain and production process. Finally, we will use the process knowledge to illustrate how the auditor reaches conclusions about residual risks and designs specific tests of financial statement assertions that are related to supply chain and production management.

> **Authoritative Guidance & Standards**
> This chapter applies standards covered in previous chapters to a specific business process—the supply chain and production process. Several observations from auditing standards are included throughout the chapter (e.g., SAS 106, SAS 107, SAS 109, SAS 110, ISA 315, ISA 320, ISA 330, ISA 500).

AN OVERVIEW OF OBJECTIVES AND ACTIVITIES RELATED TO SUPPLY CHAIN AND PRODUCTION MANAGEMENT

The supply chain and production management process consists of the set of activities by which resources used in production are obtained and transformed into products and services to be sold to customers. This process includes design, procurement, purchasing, materials handling, and storage of raw materials and components. It also includes the myriad aspects of production—fabrication, assembly, finishing, and packaging. The process does not include the acquisition or

Figure 12–1   An Overview of the Audit Process

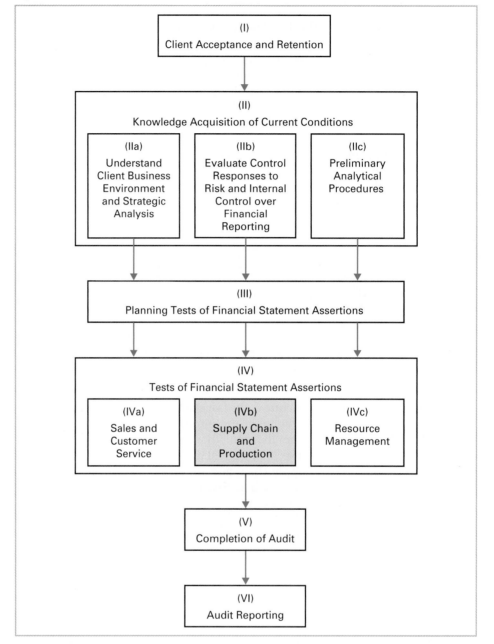

maintenance of physical plant or management of the labor force (both are re-source management processes to be discussed in Chapter 13). The process links directly to the marketing, sales, and distribution process discussed in Chapter 11. In fact, supply chain management and production can have a direct effect on mar-keting and sales because production problems may lead to inventory shortages (affecting delivery) or product quality (affecting customer service). In service firms, while the acquisition of human resources is done via resource management processes, the management of professionals is considered to be part of the

Figure 12–2   Relationships among Accounts and Processes

Account Area or Class of Transactions	Core Processes		Resources Management Processes		
	Sales and Customer Service [Chapter 11]	Supply Chain and Production [Chapter 12]	Facilities [Chapter 13]	Human Resources [Chapter 7, 13]	Capital and Investment [Chapter 13]
Assets					
Cash and short-term investments	Cash receipts	Cash payments	Cash payments	Cash payments	Cash receipts, Cash payments, Trading securities
Receivables	Sales, Receipts, Returns, Bad debts				Investment income
Inventory	Cost of goods sold	Purchases, Production, Inventory valuation	Depreciation (product cost)	Direct labor costs	
Plant, property, and equipment including accumulated depreciation			Purchases of tangible assets, Asset disposals, Depreciation, Leased assets		
Investments					Purchase investments, Sell investments
Liabilities					
Accounts payable		Vendor payables			
Accrued liabilities	Commissions	Indirect overhead costs	Maintenance, Utilities, Leases	Wages, Benefits, Payroll taxes	Interest, Dividends, Income taxes, Deferred taxes
Debt and borrowed funds			Mortgage payable		Borrow funds, Repay debt
Paid in equity capital					Sales of equity, Repurchase of equity
Retained earnings					Dividends, Net income

(continued)

Figure 12–2 *(continued)*

Account Area or Class of Transactions	Core Processes		Resources Management Processes		
	Sales and Customer Service [Chapter 11]	Supply Chain and Production [Chapter 12]	Facilities [Chapter 13]	Human Resources [Chapter 7, 13]	Capital and Investment [Chapter 13]
Income and Expense					
Sales, revenue, and gains	Sales		Asset disposals		Investment income and gains
Cost of goods sold	Cost of goods sold	Costs of production, Cost allocation	Depreciation (product cost)	Direct labor costs	
Depreciation expense			Depreciation (period cost)		
Selling, general, and administrative expenses			Maintenance, Utilities, Operating leases	Wages and related expenses	Interest expense
Tax expense	Sales taxes		Property taxes	Payroll taxes	
Other Disclosures/Accounts					
Other	Vendor rebates	Purchase commitments, Waste and spoilage	Interest capitalization, Impairments, Leasehold Improvements	Stock options, Pensions and post-retirement benefits	Off balance sheet items, Investment impairments

production process. Indeed, failure to adequately manage the time of professionals may result in lost opportunities in much the same way that an empty seat on a plane represents lost revenue to an airline.

PROCESS OBJECTIVES

Figure 12–3 depicts the general process map for the supply chain and production process. The overall objective of supply chain and production management is to assure that the organization can manufacture products as efficiently and effectively as possible. This overall objective can be decomposed into a number of very specific concerns related to procurement, materials handling, assembly, and packaging. Particularly important is ensuring the availability of materials, achieving efficiency of communications within the supply chain, facilitating efficient material handling and production, maintaining quality, and minimizing costs. These objectives will also facilitate marketing and sales objectives, and should result in achieving profitability goals. It is also important that information about the process be used to improve process efficiency and facilitate effective decision making.

Figure 12–3   Process Map: Supply Chain and Production Management

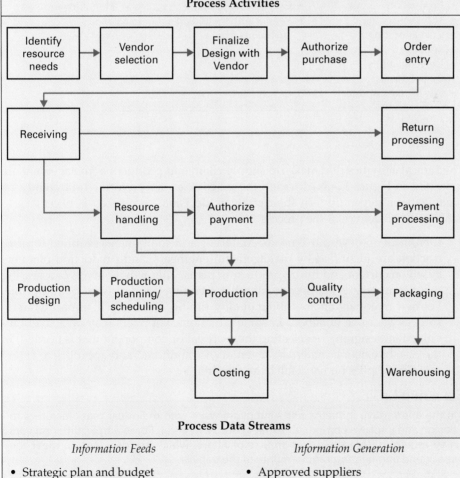

Process Objectives

- Identify legitimate resource needs.
- Establish reliable supply chain meeting quality, cost, and delivery needs.
- Obtain resources at the best price given quality and other constraints.
- Minimize production costs, using vendors as part of the design process
- Ensure availability of resources at time and place needed.
- Minimize procurement and transaction costs.
- Minimize storage and handling costs.
- Protect resources and inventory from loss or unauthorized use.
- Make payments for legitimate obligations only.
- Produce goods and services that meet cost and quality targets.
- Maximize use of capacity.
- Minimize and control spoiled and defective units and properly handle by-products.
- Minimize and control waste.
- Capture and effectively utilize supplier and production information.
- Capture, process, and report information necessary for process improvement.

Process Activities

Identify resource needs → Vendor selection → Finalize Design with Vendor → Authorize purchase → Order entry

Receiving → Return processing

Resource handling → Authorize payment → Payment processing

Production design → Production planning/scheduling → Production → Quality control → Packaging

Production → Costing

Packaging → Warehousing

Process Data Streams

Information Feeds	*Information Generation*
- Strategic plan and budget	- Approved suppliers
- Material and component requirements	- Material requisitions
- Cost targets and procurement policies	- Material and component acquisitions

(continued)

Figure 12–3   *(continued)*

Process Data Streams (continued)	
Information Feeds	*Information Generation*
• Quality standards • Manufacturing specifications • Vendor history and profiles • Sales forecasts and customer orders • Capacity parameters • Inventory levels	• Contract terms and negotiated prices • Supplier performance measures • Standard cost schedules • Production plan and schedule • Production statistics • Payments • Delivery schedules • Changes in inventory levels and costs

Accounting Impact of Activities		
Routine Transactions	*Non-routine Transactions*	*Accounting Estimates*
• Purchases • Material receipts • Disbursements • Production • Transfer pricing • Cost allocation • Spoilage • Defective units • By-products • Waste and disposal	• Long-term supplier contracts • Standard cost revisions • Commodity hedging • Vendor returns and adjustments	• Inventory valuation • Environmental cleanup costs • Vendor allowances or rebates

PROCESS ACTIVITIES

The typical activities that make up supply chain and production management are indicated in Figure 12–3. Although these activities are performed differently by organizations depending on their strategic decisions, each step is necessary to achieve the objectives of the process.

- Identification of resource needs: Materials and components required for production are identified by management, engineers, and production planners based on current and future production plans. This activity involves assessing what components are needed, in what quantities, and at what point in time. For new materials, choices about quality, timing, and cost will impact what resources are to be obtained. In some situations, suppliers may be actively involved in designing or selecting the material or component that is needed. In the case of existing materials, inventory is monitored and appropriate action taken if supplies on hand fall below desired levels.

Example

In the automotive industry, parts suppliers work with major car manufacturers to design and improve components that go into a new car. For example, different cars may require different sizes or shapes of filters, which are designed to meet the space and engineering requirements of the vehicle.

- Vendor selection: Potential suppliers are identified and screened to determine those that potentially meet the quality, cost, payment, and delivery requirements of the company. Reliability and prior experience may have a significant impact on the acceptability of a specific vendor. Once selected, vendors may collaborate with the company on the specifications and design of materials to be supplied by the vendor.

- Purchase authorization: The quantity, price, payment terms, and delivery schedule must be negotiated with the supplier. In many cases, purchase authorization will result in a long term contract to provide a steady supply of materials or components. One-time or infrequent purchases may be handled differently each time.

- Order entry: Specific transaction details are prepared and transmitted to the vendor for a purchase. Purchase orders can be prepared internally and sent to the supplier on a periodic basis. Alternatively, in the case of a long-term agreement, vendors can use technology to monitor inventory levels at the company and automatically ship materials when inventory falls below a specified level.

- Receiving: Incoming shipments are inspected, verified against internal documents, and accepted (or rejected). Shipments can arrive by public post or vendor shipping, or can be picked up by the organization's own personnel. In a just-in-time inventory system, inspection may be minimal due to the trust placed in the underlying relationship with the supplier.

- Resource handling: Incoming shipments are prepared for movement or storage within the organization. Materials are often received at a central location, at which point they may be placed into general warehouse storage or moved to other company locations (e.g., retail locations). In a just-in-time environment, materials and components may go directly from receiving into production.

- Authorize payment: Payments for shipments received are authorized according to organizational policies (e.g., taking discounts, avoiding interest or late fees).

- Payment processing: Payments are prepared, approved, and forwarded to the vendor. Payments can be made by check or electronic funds transfer. In an integrated supply chain, payments may be tendered electronically upon delivery from the supplier.

- Return processing: If incoming shipments are not acceptable (e.g., they do not meet quality specifications), they are returned to the vendor rather than placed in storage. Vendors should make appropriate billing adjustments for returned materials.

- Production design: The arrangement of the factory and the production specifications of machinery will impact the materials and components needed for the production process. Size, shape, and packaging of materials and components can influence the way production is organized and impact the efficiency of the production process.

Example

A bakery was able to reduce its production costs by arranging with a supplier to deliver powdered cocoa rather than chocolate bars, which needed to be melted before use in baking. This arrangement allowed the bakery to redesign its production layout, eliminating some steps in the production process.

- Production planning: Not all products are exactly the same, and similar products may vary in size, shape, or color (e.g., consumer products like toothpaste). Production of different versions of products needs to be scheduled and may require changes to the assembly line. Changing an assembly line from one version of a product to another may be time consuming and costly. This activity is even more critical in a job order environment where each product or group of products is different and frequent changes are needed in the production process (e.g., furniture).

- Production: The fabrication, assembly, and completion of products and services are often the core activities in supply chain and production management. Production is the activity where resource inputs are transformed into new products. A main concern of production is tracking the stage of completion of work-in-process or the location of inventory as it moves throughout the supply chain. This allows the organization to monitor cycle time within the process.

- Quality control: Quality testing and inspection is often a necessary step in the production process to assure that quality standards are consistently achieved. Quality rejects can be reworked or treated as waste. Failure to assure product quality can have a negative impact on customer service.

- Packaging: This activity includes boxing, shrink-wrapping, and bundling finished goods for sale, shipment to customers, or storage in company facilities. Protection from accidental damage during movement and shipping is an important concern of packaging activities.

- Warehousing: Finished goods are stored until delivered to customers or shipped to retail outlets. Inventory in the warehouse should be protected from unauthorized use or accidental damage. Information systems should be able to track the location of inventory as it is moved through and around storage facilities.

- Costing: Tracking the costs of production is the purpose of cost accounting and can be a complex challenge for accountants. Allocating overhead costs, estimating labor costs, tracking material usage, and computing standard costs are part of this activity. The primary concern of costing is to assign a reasonable cost to specific units of production. There are many different ways to perform product costing depending on the objectives of management (e.g., direct costing, ABC costing, absorption costing).

The complexity of these activities will depend on the various strategic and process decisions made by the organization. Some of the decisions and circumstances that could affect these activities include:

- The nature of materials and components being purchased
- The use of technology to integrate the supply chain
- The method of delivery
- The complexity of the production process (including extent of automation)
- The frequency of production changes
- The complexity of standard costs
- The nature of regulations in countries where products are produced or transferred as components to be included in finished products
- The nature and volume of waste, defective units, and by-products

For example, hazardous or perishable materials may require special handling arrangements. Deliveries made by third parties or the vendor can be handled on the loading dock, but materials to be picked up by the company necessitate acquisition of transportation services. Obviously, the more complex production and costing, the more challenging the process will be to manage. Managing waste can also be challenging, especially if it can have a negative impact on the environment. By-products and reworked units are potentially valuable to the company and also must be handled appropriately.

Of particular importance to the supply chain is the degree of integration with vendors. Current technology is allowing more and more companies to link information systems across the supply chain to improve the flow of information between

Example

A trend in consumer product manufacturing, especially clothing, is to send slightly defective units or products that do not quite meet quality standards to "outlet" stores, usually located in special shopping centers or malls. This is one way that a company obtains maximum value for its products. These products are usually labeled as "irregular" to avoid conflicts with local stores selling the same products at full retail prices. Outlet stores are also used to dispose of slow moving or outdated merchandise that retailers wish to remove to make space for newer products. By bringing this merchandise together into an outlet store, a manufacturer or retailer is able to efficiently dispose of excess inventory while minimizing the impact on its primary retail sales.

suppliers and customers. These links can be made through proprietary networks (so-called electronic data interfaces or EDI) or across the Internet by establishing an electronic market where vendors and customers can interact. One advantage of supply chain integration is that it reduces transaction costs since paper flows are reduced and redundant procedures are eliminated. Integration also facilitates a just-in-time approach to inventory flows and reduces the level of excess inventory held across the entire supply chain, thus cutting storage and carrying costs. The primary disadvantage of supply chain integration is that it reduces the flexibility of a company to change suppliers when performance, quality, or price become unacceptable. This inflexibility is exacerbated when suppliers have designed the components being supplied. Often, manufacturers are unable to switch suppliers until new designs replace current products, allowing a change in suppliers (e.g., automotive companies typically introduce new or redesigned models every three to four years).

The information requirements and output of supply chain and production management are described in Figure 12–3. Key information requirements include production specifications, inventory levels, supply channels, and sales forecasts. Production planning and material acquisitions are critically dependent on accurate sales forecasting if the company wishes to avoid either material shortages or excesses. Information output includes purchase and transaction data, production schedules, and supplier statistics. Production schedules may affect marketing and sales activities. Supplier statistics can be used to renegotiate contracts and alter the relationships in the supply chain, including dropping poorly performing vendors.

TRANSACTIONS ARISING FROM SUPPLY CHAIN AND PRODUCTION MANAGEMENT

The supply chain and production process potentially affects a broad range of accounts and transactions, as indicated in Figure 12–3. In general, the key transactions arising in this process are purchasing, disbursements, and production. The execution of these transactions is illustrated in Figure 12–4 and discussed below.

PURCHASES

Material purchases may be initiated by a *purchase requisition* from the production department or because inventory reaches a restocking point that triggers an automatic reorder. The placement of an order is usually evidenced by the completion of a *purchase order*, although standing orders for some resources (e.g., long term purchase contracts, utilities, or other monthly services) may obviate the need for a

Figure 12–4   Summary Supply Chain and Production Activities

Process/Activity	Documents	Journals, Ledgers, and Records Used	Typical Journal Entry
Purchases			
Requisitioning: Request for material or component purchase.	Purchase requisition (internal)		
Purchasing: Order transmitted to appropriate supplier based on open contracts or new supplier selection.	Purchase order (internal) Contract (external)	Approved vendor list	
Receiving: Resources are received and placed in storage or delivered to the requisitioning department.	Receiving report (internal) Bill of lading (external)	Receiving report journal	
Payable recognition: Liability recognized based on receipt of shipment and vendor invoice.	Vendor's invoice or statement (external) Voucher (internal)	Purchases journal **or** Voucher register	
Payable posting: The liability is posted to the appropriate vendor account.*		Accounts payable subsidiary ledger	
General accounting: The purchase, payable, and asset or expense is recorded in the appropriate accounts.	Journal entry ticket (internal)	General ledger	Dr. Expenses Dr. Purchases (inventory) Dr. Assets Cr. Accounts Payable
Disbursements			
Check preparation: Liability identified for payment and a disbursement is prepared.	Check (internal) EFT authorization (internal)	Cash disbursements journal Check register	
Payment authorization: The payment is reviewed, authorized, and transmitted to the vendor.			

* A company that uses a voucher system may not maintain an accounts payable subsidiary ledger. Instead, the voucher register is used as the summary record of liabilities.

Figure 12–4 *(continued)*

Process/Activity	*Documents*	*Journals, Ledgers, and Records Used*	*Typical Journal Entry*
Disbursements			
Payable posting: The payment is debited to the appropriate vendor account.		Accounts payable subsidiary ledger	
General accounting: The payment is recorded in the appropriate accounts.	Journal entry ticket (internal)	General ledger	Dr. Accounts Payable Dr. Accrued Liabilities Cr. Cash
Production			
Start of production: Materials and components are placed into the manufacturing process.	Materials requisition (internal)	Raw materials perpetual inventory	Dr. Work-in-Process Cr. Raw Materials
Production: Machining and assembly of products.	Job-cost ticket (internal) Work ticket (internal)		
Cost assignment: Costs of goods are determined and assigned to units.	Job-cost ticket (internal)	Standard cost computations Overhead cost records	Dr. Work-in-Process Cr. Direct Labor Applied** Dr. Work-in-Process Cr. Overhead Applied***
Finished Goods: Transfer of inventory to storage.			Dr. Finished Goods Cr. Work-in-Process

** The amount of labor assigned to work-in-process is usually based on standard cost computations but may be based on actual costs (as in a job-cost system). In either case, a separate account is used to record direct labor costs that have been incurred. The balance of direct labor applied can be compared to the balance of actual direct labor on a periodic basis to determine if the company is assigning too much or too little direct labor to the units of production. If direct labor applied is significantly different from direct labor incurred, standard costs may not be reasonable under current economic conditions.

*** The amount of overhead assigned to work-in-process is usually based on standard cost computations. A separate account is used to record overhead costs that have been incurred. The balance of overhead applied can be compared to the balance of actual overhead on a periodic basis to determine if the company is assigning too much or too little overhead to the units of production. If overhead applied is significantly different from overhead incurred, standard costs may not be reasonable under current economic conditions.

purchase order. Subsequent delivery of materials is evidenced by a *receiving report*. The *vendor's invoice* (and the receiving report) is the basis for recognizing a liability via the preparation of a *voucher*.[1] The voucher and the appropriate supporting documents (e.g., purchase requisition, purchase order, receiving report, and the vendor's invoice/statement) are together referred to as a *voucher package*, which forms the basis for posting to the *voucher register*, *accounts payable subsidiary ledger*, and general ledger. The voucher register lists all vouchers in numerical order and the subsidiary ledger lists liabilities by vendor. A given vendor may have multiple vouchers outstanding at any point in time. The purchase process can be readily automated if both the supplier and the buyer allow electronic orders to flow between the computer systems of the respective organizations.

The key event in the purchasing process is the delivery (or, in some cases, shipment) of resources to the company. At this point, a liability exists that is owed to the supplier (vendor). This means that the receiving report (or shipping notification) is the boundary document representing a liability. In many systems, however, the vendor's invoice or monthly statement is used to record the liability because it contains complete information about prices and totals. This situation could lead to a delay in the recognition of liabilities and represents a potential timing problem for the auditor. This delay could be extensive, especially if liabilities are posted only on receipt of vendors' monthly statements. Again, with electronic data interchange all of this can be set up so that most of these handling steps can be eliminated from the buyer's system.

DISBURSEMENTS

The disbursement process comprises the activities for paying vendors for goods and services. Payment terms and the availability of cash will determine when checks are prepared or funds transferred. A *check register* lists the checks issued on a specific account in sequence of issue. A *cash disbursements journal* is used to list all payments in chronological order. Once a check is prepared, the supporting documents (e.g., the voucher package) and the unsigned check are sent to an appropriate corporate official (typically the treasurer) for approval (signature) and mailing. Information contained in the cash disbursements journal is used to update the accounts payable subsidiary ledger and the general ledger. The key event in the process is the delivery of a check to the vendor, usually by mail, but increasingly through electronic funds transfer, which can be automated using electronic data interchange. At that point the liability is satisfied.[2]

> **Authoritative Guidance & Standards**
>
> Because cash disbursements can be paid in response to fictitious purchases or based on inappropriate dealings with vendors (SAS 107, ISA 320), auditors focus on the existence assertion when examining disbursements.

PRODUCTION

Production involves the internal movement and transformation of materials and components to produce goods and services for sale. Production activities do not usually generate transactions with outside parties once the raw materials or

---

1 The preparation of a voucher is a common method for recording liabilities but there are other systems also used in practice.

2 A company will occasionally cut a check and hold on to it because funds are not immediately available to cover the amount. In these situations, the liability should remain on the books until the check is mailed or delivered to the vendor.

Figure 12–5   Perpetual Inventory Record

PRODUCT: K3456, Gasket Cover

Date	Document Reference	Unit Cost In	Unit Cost Out	Number In	Number Out	Balance (units)	Balance (cost)
1/1/x7	Balance					120	$1,218
1/15/x7	RR 10292	10.40		1000		1120	11,618
1/25/x7	SI 90927		10.37		320	800	8,300
2/3/x7	RR 10333	10.67		800		1600	16,836
2/27/x7	SI 91233		10.52		440	1160	12,207
3/15/x7	SI 91444		10.52		235	925	9,735
3/22/x7	RR 10568	10.95		750		1675	17,948

components have been supplied.[3] Inventory related accounts include Supplies Inventory, Raw Materials Inventory, Work-In-Process Inventory, Finished Goods Inventory, and Cost of Goods Sold. In order to effectively manage inventory, however, a company will typically use other accounts for accumulating costs to be assigned to individual units of inventory. Acounts used for cost assignment include Raw Materials Used, Direct Labor Applied, Direct Labor Incurred, Factory Overhead Applied, Factory Overhead Incurred, and Cost of Goods Manufactured. Other accounts may be needed to record waste, defective units, or by-products or variances from standard costs.

Of importance to the accounting function is the point at which inventory is transformed from raw materials to work-in-process, and from work-in-process to finished goods. Also of importance is the way in which the cost accounting system assigns labor and overhead costs to work-in-process. A company may use a job cost system, a process cost system, or an activity-based cost system, but the issue is essentially the same from the auditor's point of view—determining the appropriate cost of inventory as it is transformed by the manufacturing process. The system should provide a reasonable basis to track the physical movement of inventory, the assignment of labor and overhead costs to units, and the proper classification of units at each stage of the process. Central to the process is the *perpetual inventory system*. An example of a traditional perpetual inventory record to track inventory levels is shown in Figure 12–5.

INTERNAL THREAT ANALYSIS FOR SUPPLY CHAIN AND PRODUCTION MANAGEMENT

An internal threat analysis for supply chain and production management is illustrated in Figure 12–6. A number of potential risks are identified in the first column and then linked to potentially mitigating controls and relevant performance indicators that could be used to monitor the risks. This list is not intended to be exhaustive, and process risks could vary across organizations due to differences in the activities within the process. Furthermore, the controls and performance indicators are not intended to be comprehensive.

---

3 Exceptions include waste or by-products, both of which may involve exchanges with outside parties.

Figure 12–6   Internal Threat Analysis: Supply Chain and Production Management

Process Risks	Controls Linked to Risks	Performance Measures
(1) Failing to select an appropriate supplier or obtain an adequate supply of appropriate resources.	• Forecast resource needs based on sales and link to procurement activities • Investigate suppliers • Long term contracts covering supply of key materials and components • Electronic interface with suppliers • Establish back-up suppliers • Periodically review open purchase orders • Just-in-time inventory system	• Financial ratios of suppliers • Number of suppliers • Supplier on-time performance • Frequency of material outages • Days lost to material shortages • Production versus forecast
(2) Acquiring unneeded or excess resources.	• Monitor inventory levels • Automated replenishment system • Segregate purchase authorization from other activities • Independent verification of purchases • Just-in-time inventory system	• Material turnover • Rate of material spoilage or obsolescence • Production versus forecast
(3) Purchases that do not meet quality, price, payment, or delivery specifications.	• General authorization for routine purchases • Specific authorization procedures for unusual or high-value resources • Long-term contracts covering supply of key materials and components • Independent verification of purchases • Quality inspection prior to acceptance of shipment	• Supplier reject or defect rates • Supplier on-time delivery statistics • Material costs • Purchase order error rates • Material price and usage variances • External quality ratings • Customer complaints
(4) Excess transaction processing costs.	• Electronic processing of purchase transactions • Establish process for routine purchases • Monitor process performance	• Processing cost per purchase transaction • Percentage of purchases in electronic form • Percentage of payments in electronic form
(5) Damage or spoilage of materials after receipt.	• Adequate personnel training • Schedule deliveries to allow time for proper handling • Establish proper handling procedures by type of material • Well-designed layout for receiving area	• Material usage variances • Value of purchase returns • Costs of material spoilage

Figure 12–6   *(continued)*

Process Risks	Controls Linked to Risks	Performance Measures
(6) Unauthorized use or loss of resources including inventory shrinkage.	• Physical security • Movement of inventory only upon appropriate authorization • Periodic book-to-physical inventory reconciliation • Background checks of personnel	• Inventory shrinkage • Book-to-physical discrepancies in inventory
(7) Acceptance of unauthorized or inappropriate shipments.	• Quality inspection at time of receipt • Do not accept unknown shipments	• Value of purchase returns • Frequency of rejected deliveries
(8) Unauthorized or inappropriate payments.	• Payments generated upon completion of appropriate documentation • Cancel supporting documentation upon payment to avoid duplication • Security over checks, check-writing equipment, and check-signing plates • Independent handling and verification of payments.	• Frequency and number of payments without full documentation • Frequency and number of vendor complaints • Cash losses • Percentage of payments made electronically
(9) Inaccurate information processing.	• Proper completion and verification of supporting documents • Appropriate segregation of duties across activities • Use of standard control numbers for parts, vendors, products, etc. • Update files and accounting records on a timely basis	• Percent of transactions subject to processing errors • Size of transaction adjustments • Number of transaction adjustments
(10) Failure to capture desired information.	• Use and verify prenumbered documents for transactions • Record all events and transactions on a timely basis	• Number of missing documents from sequence • Number of missing fields in purchase, vendor, or inventory record
(11) Inaccurate valuation of liabilities.	• Verify recorded liabilities and vendor's invoice against supporting documentation • Use of voucher system for obligations • Prenumbered vouchers used in sequence	• Number and amount of billing adjustments • Frequency and resolution of billing disputes • Missing voucher numbers • Number of warranty claims/recalls

(continued)

Figure 12–6   *(continued)*

Process Risks	Controls Linked to Risks	Performance Measures
(12) Failure to pay obligations on a timely basis.	• Use automated payment timing system • Pay bills upon presentment • Follow up on vendor correspondence or complaints	• Value of lost discounts • Vendor finance charges • Payable turnover rate
(13) Inefficient production design resulting in increased long term costs.	• Research into production best practices • Competitive research • Adequate internal R&D • Effective capital budgeting procedures	• Production variances • Changeover times • Production cycle time per production stage • Material usage versus planned • Time lost to maintenance and equipment failure
(14) Inefficient production planning resulting in increased costs.	• Use of materials resource planning technology • Use of production scheduling technology • Monitoring of frequency and efficiency of production changeovers	• Percent of capacity used • Frequency of changeover • Changeover times
(15) Poor quality products due to production problems.	• Monitor defect and rework rates • Timely intervention upon detection of quality problems	• Product reject rates • Product rework rates • Cost of rework
(16) Excess spoilage or waste.	• Monitor spoilage and waste rates against targets • Timely intervention in process	• Cost of waste and spoilage • Volume of waste and spoilage
(17) Improper handling of spoilage and waste.	• Establish procedures and guidelines for disposal of wastes • Long-term contract with reputable waste disposal company	• Cost of waste disposal • Fines or citations for improper waste disposal
(18) Inappropriate or inaccurate cost allocation and standard costing.	• Cost allocations verified against supporting documentation • Review and authorization of standard costs • Monitoring of standard cost variances for systematic discrepancies	• Production costs actual versus budget • Production cost variances
(19) Excess storage or transportation costs.	• Monitor turnover statistics • Link sales forecasts to materials orders • Just-in-time inventory systems • Use of material resource planning technology	• Finished goods turnover • Days supply on hand • Warehousing and shipping costs

IDENTIFICATION OF PROCESS RISKS

Process risks affecting supply chain and production management can come from a number of sources. Examples of specific process risks relevant to supply chain and production management include

People Risks

- Managerial risk: Problems with management within a process can have a significant impact on the type and extent of process risks. Failure to obtain adequate supplies or selecting poor quality, inefficient, or insolvent suppliers (risk 1); acquiring excess supplies (risk 2); failing to obtain resources consistent with production specifications (risk 3); and inefficient production design and scheduling (risks 13 and 14) may all be due to weak or ineffective management.
- Ethical risk: Theft or misuse of assets arises because some employees may be dishonest or unethical. The risk of inventory shrinkage (risk 6) or inappropriate disbursements (risk 8) can be due to improper actions by employees who are not subject to an adequate level of control or oversight.
- Human resource risk: As in all processes, people can make mistakes that cause problems within the process. Risks that are particularly sensitive to human error include damage to materials (risk 5), acceptance of unauthorized shipments (risk 8), inaccurate information processing (risk 9), inaccurate valuation of liabilities (risk 11), and inefficient production design or scheduling (risks 13 and 14).

Direct Process Risks

- Operational risk: There are numerous operational risks that affect efficiency and effectiveness of the supply chain and production in an organization. Some of the more significant risks are excess transaction processing costs (risk 4), damage to materials (risk 5), acceptance of unauthorized shipments (risk 7), production problems (risk 15), excess spoilage or waste (risk 16), and excess storage or transportation costs (risk 19). Also, ineffective communication with suppliers regarding important supply chain issues can be an important operational risk.
- Information risk: In order to effectively manage a process, management needs timely and reliable information about the activities and risks within the process. The auditor also needs process information in order to identify and evaluate risks that might impact the conduct of the audit. Consequently, the risks of inaccurate information processing (risk 9), omitted information (risk 10), or inaccurate valuation of liabilities (risk 11) are particularly relevant information risks to both management and the auditor.

Indirect Process Risks

- Technology risk: Technology can have a pervasive effect on the design of the production process, the nature of communications within the supply chain, the scheduling of materials and production, and the reliability of information within the process. Technology problems may lead to delays in receiving materials (risk 1), inaccurate information processing (risk 8), omission of key information (risk 9), inefficient production design (risk 13), inefficient production scheduling (risk 14), and inaccurate cost allocations (risk 18).
- Planning risk: Many risks may increase if planning is ineffective or resources are inadequate to carry out the activities of a process. Poor planning and resource allocation can lead to inadequate sources of supply (risk 1), delays in paying vendors (risk 12), or inefficient production scheduling (risk 14).

- Regulatory risk: Many organizations face numerous regulations for handling materials (especially if hazardous or perishable), controlling production, and disposing of wastes. Failure to comply with these regulations can result in significant penalties. Improper handling of toxic wastes (risk 17) can be a particularly significant risk in the production process.

Notice that a specific risk can be associated with many different causes. The more causes that can interact to affect a risk within a process, the more likely that the risk will become a problem. For example, the risk that the company fails to obtain an adequate supply of materials delivered on a timely basis could be due to weak management (leadership), poor planning, inadequate information systems, or human error. As is the case in most processes, technology, human resource, and information risks are of particular importance to the auditor because their interaction has a direct impact on the quality of information that is generated within a process.

ANALYSIS OF PROCESS CONTROLS

As in prior examples, different types of controls can be used to mitigate different risks. The decision to accept, avoid, transfer, or reduce a risk is part of the overall design of the process and should follow from the strategy and objectives adopted by the organization. For example, the use of technology to integrate the supply chain may reduce many risks but also creates other information processing and security risks that are not present in an isolated internal system. Furthermore, the controls that are available in a complex technology environment are different than those that can be used in a simpler, partially manual, system.

Example

> As part of supply chain management, many companies have adopted a policy of immediate electronic funds transfer to suppliers upon electronic presentation of an invoice. Because billing and payment are fully automated, many of the normal steps in a traditional disbursement process are eliminated. This approach may increase some risks (unauthorized payments) but reduce other risks (e.g., billing errors and late payments). The net reduction in administrative costs and the increased predictability of cash flows result in savings to both the vendor and the customer.

Column 2 of Figure 12–6 describes numerous controls that might be effective for reducing risks related to supply chain and production management:

- Performance reviews/monitoring controls: Many risks can be effectively mitigated through active monitoring of conditions and timely intervention by management. For the supply chain and production, management should actively monitor
  - Inventory levels
  - Supplier performance (quality, service, processing errors, and timeliness)
  - Levels of waste and spoilage
  - Product quality
  - Technological developments impacting the supply chain and production
  - Production efficiency and operational effectiveness
- Segregation of duties: Incompatible duties that are important to segregate within the supply chain and production process include (1) production design and planning; (2) soliciting and selecting potential suppliers; (3) authorizing

purchases, handling inventory, accounting for inventory activity; and (4) authorizing disbursements and processing disbursements.

- Processing controls: There is a broad range of processing controls that can be implemented in the supply chain or as part of production depending on the specific activities and steps of the process. Important authorization steps include selecting suppliers, ordering inventory, accepting shipments, controlling production, warehousing finished goods, handling waste and spoilage, and processing disbursements. Appropriate documents that should be used within the process include purchase orders, receiving reports, vouchers, checks, inventory movement documents, and job tickets (see Figure 12–4). Most of these documents should be prenumbered and used in sequence. Key journals and ledgers include the payable ledger or voucher register, the cash disbursement journal, standard cost schedules, and perpetual inventory records. Numerous independent verifications can be performed within the process, including periodic physical inventories, checking documents for discrepancies, comparing batch and control totals, and investigating unusual events. Many of these procedures are directly relevant to the auditor's evaluation of internal control over financial reporting.

- Physical controls: Limiting access to inventory and cash are obvious controls. It is also important to limit access to documents, records, and computerized systems that could be used to authorize inappropriate movement of inventory or access to cash (e.g., blank checks).

The extent to which these controls are used, how frequently they are used, and whether they are automated depends on the specific design of the process. Not all organizations will need to use all controls as some may be redundant or a specific risk may not be significant to the organization.

ANALYSIS OF INTERNAL CONTROL OVER FINANCIAL REPORTING

Controls over the reliability of information are particularly important to the auditor's analysis. Figure 12–7 identifies a number of accounting controls, discussed below, that could be potentially relevant to purchases, disbursements, and inventory.

Purchases: The most critical controls for supply chain management focus on the proper selection of suppliers, authorization of purchases, and completeness of liabilities. Key internal controls related to financial reporting include the following:

- Suppliers should be selected only after careful review of operational and financial historical performance of alternative potential suppliers. Supplier evaluation should be segregated from supplier selection. Only appropriate purchases of materials should be made, and disbursements should be in accordance with the terms of an approved acquisition.

- Existence or validity is less a concern because recognition of fictitious liabilities is not common except in the case of related party transactions (see Chapter 4).

- Proper valuation is facilitated by timely completion of a prenumbered receiving report. Verification of the vendor's invoice by comparison with receiving reports and other supporting documents is also helpful.

- Timing is important because liabilities may not be recorded until a vendor's invoice is received. The most important control in this respect is the timely preparation of a voucher. In electronic data interchange systems the opposite might occur, goods are not yet received yet the supplier triggers an electronic payment.

Figure 12–7   Financial Reporting Controls for Purchases and Production

Activity	Typical Internal Controls
Purchases	Segregate purchase accounting from purchasing and production.
	Maintain an up-to-date list of approved vendors and parts/supplies to be acquired.
	Use prenumbered requisitions, purchase orders, and receiving reports.
	Independently review and provide indication of approval of purchase orders.
	Verify incoming shipments against purchase orders and document discrepancies.
	Have vendor invoices and vendor statements sent directly to payable department.
	Verify prices, quantities, payment terms, extensions, and totals per the vendor's invoice against other transaction documents and company policies.
	Review expense or asset classification for each expenditure.
	Reconcile monthly vendor statements against individual transaction activity (purchases and payments).
	Maintain a file of unpaid liabilities arranged by due date.
	Post transactions on a timely basis.
	Use control and hash totals to verify accuracy of postings.
	Maintain an up-to-date chart of accounts.
	Maintain policy on expense recognition for assets of small value.
	Reconcile general ledger totals and activity with the subsidiary ledger and supporting journals.
	Review all journal entries prior to posting.
	Investigate unusual entries to accounts.
Disbursements	Separate disbursement accounting from check preparation (treasury), purchasing, payable recognition, and posting.
	Use prenumbered checks or electronic funds transfers for payments.
	Cancel supporting documents related to disbursements to avoid duplicate payment.
	Use check-writing machine or computer-generated checks with appropriate safeguards.
	Immediately void spoiled checks.
	Verify amount and detail of checks against supporting documents.
	Post transactions on a timely basis.
	Use control and hash totals to verify accuracy of postings.
	Reconcile bank accounts independently of the cash disbursement process.
	Account for the sequence of checks used and follow up on stale checks outstanding.
	Reconcile general ledger totals and activity with subsidiary ledger and supporting journals with special attention to unpaid balances.

Figure 12–7   *(continued)*

Activity	Typical Internal Controls
Production	Segregate inventory accounting from purchase authorization and handling of inventory.
	Track costs by product (including materials, labor, and overhead costs).
	Establish standard costs based on analysis of product design, resource needs, and the production process.
	Evaluate standard costs against actual costs.
	Monitor cost variances and investigate on a timely basis.
	Monitor slow-moving inventory and assess its realizability.
	Monitor and properly account for disposal of waste, scrap, and by-products.
	Maintain adequate perpetual records.
	Maintain a comprehensive chart of accounts for production-related activity.
	Use prenumbered transfer/work documents to account for conversion of materials into finished goods and related movement through the production process.
	Periodically reconcile perpetual records with general ledger activity and physical counts.
	Reconcile and adjust actual versus applied overhead as needed.

- Classification is also important because of the large number of expense and asset accounts that can be affected by procurement. A formal policy to separate assets from expenses assists in proper classification of expenditures.
- Independent review of account classifications for reasonableness, the use of check digits or hash totals, and the use of computerized posting tend to increase the reliability of transaction processing.

Disbursements: Cash payments should be tightly controlled to avoid improper use of cash and to assure that liabilities are paid at the proper amount. Key internal controls related to financial reporting include the following:

- The most critical control element for disbursements is authorization, with separation of check preparation from purchasing and payment authorization. This separation facilitates the independent review of payments to assure that they are proper and accurate. Checks are often prepared electronically and signed using a check-signing machine. The current trend toward electronic funds transfer is reducing the need for manual controls over check preparation but creates a need for other types of controls (e.g., security and data integrity) that often will require evaluation by an IT specialist.
- Payable postings should be verified.
- Documents supporting disbursements should be canceled after payment to assure that the same liability is not paid twice.

Inventory: Controls over inventory emphasize the flow and cost of inventory in the system because management needs to know who has what inventory, and for what purpose, at each stage of processing. Key internal controls related to financial reporting include the following:

- The perpetual inventory system is the key element for establishing control over inventory.

- A periodic physical verification is also an important source of control over inventory.
- Internal control is also needed in the area of waste and scrap (and possibly byproducts). Scrap usually has a positive market value and should be processed and sold to a recycler. Waste is more problematic because its disposal may require compliance with complex environmental laws.

Not all controls within an audit-sensitive process are of interest to the auditor—only those that contribute to a reduction of significant residual risks or control risk related to specific financial reporting assertions. It is the auditor's responsibility to obtain an adequate understanding of process controls and controls over financial reporting so as to have a basis for his or her conclusions about control risk for specific audit objectives. Important controls that contribute to significant risk reduction will be subject to additional testing to obtain evidence that they are effective.

EVALUATION OF PROCESS PERFORMANCE INDICATORS

The fourth column of Figure 12–6 identifies numerous performance indicators that can be used to monitor risks arising in the supply chain or production. The listed performance indicators fall into four broad categories including measures of

- Supplier performance: quality, timeliness, cost, shortages
- Inventory handling and usage: inventory levels, damage, waste, spoilage, defects
- Inventory costs: standard costs, variances, production efficiency, cycle times
- Transaction processing: error rates, processing costs

Given the relative importance of measuring inventory costs, most manufacturers have relatively well-developed cost data on production and inventory that the auditor can use to evaluate process risks. However, nonfinancial data on supplier performance may not be integrated into the accounting system and may be difficult to obtain unless an organization has a highly integrated ERP system. The auditor must consider the reliability of information generated outside the accounting system (or alternatively perform procedures to reconcile this information to that contained in the accounting system) before placing weight on it as evidence about process risks.

The interpretation of performance indicators may require that the auditor consider a number of measures jointly in order to identify patterns or trends in process performance. For example, a decrease in the quality of materials delivered by suppliers could be evidenced by higher delivery reject rates, discrepancies between materials ordered and delivered, material usage variances, external reports on product quality, or customer complaints. At the same time, the deterioration in quality of materials or components can also show up in higher rates of defects, increased material waste, or more frequent production stops to adjust machinery to handle the material.

If the auditor sees evidence of such a problem, then the residual risk would be rated high and a number of potential implications would need to be considered. High residual risk of poor quality materials would cause the auditor to adjust expectations about costs, margins, and cost variances. The risk could also impact assertions related to the valuation of inventory or the valuation of warranty reserves. Finally, the residual risk might create stress or pressure on management to compensate in ways that are inappropriate or not in the best interests of the

Figure 12–8   Residual Risk Map for Supply Chain and Production Management*

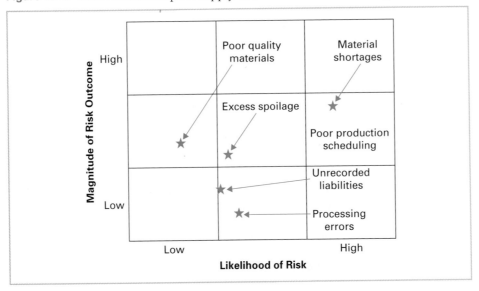

* For ease of exposition, not all risks identified in Figure 12–8 have been included in the risk map. This does not imply that omitted risks are less important. The risks that are included were chosen for illustrative purposes only.

organization, including the possibility of manipulating performance measures to disguise the problem. The auditor's next step would be to analyze these implications and decide how they should impact the conduct of further audit testing.

CONCLUSIONS ABOUT RESIDUAL RISKS FROM SUPPLY CHAIN AND PRODUCTION MANAGEMENT

The auditor's assessments of residual risks are documented in a risk map as illustrated in Figure 12–8. Seven of the risks identified in Figure 12–6 are included for illustrative purposes. Risks in the upper right-hand portion of the chart are considered to be significant residual risks, but we see that many of these risks have been reduced to an acceptable level (lower left portion) due to mitigating controls and monitoring with performance measures. Before analyzing the implications of the residual risks that remain, the auditor should test controls to verify that risk reductions are justified.

TESTING PROCESS CONTROLS AND INTERNAL CONTROL OVER FINANCIAL REPORTING

Tests of controls that could be used for the supply chain and production management process are described in Figure 12–9. These tests may not apply to all organizations and need to be adapted to the specific circumstances of a system and the auditor's risk assessments. Tests of controls related to the supply chain and production tend to emphasize proper authorization of transactions, evidence that transaction amounts have been properly verified, and evidence that production

Figure 12–9   Testing Internal Controls Related to Supply Chain and Production Management

---

Performance Reviews and Overall Process Management

- Review policies for establishing strategy, goals, and budgets for supply chain management and production.
- Evaluate whether policies and decisions related to supply chain management and production are consistent with the overall strategy and objectives of the organization.
- Review and evaluate internal analyses on competitors, production trends, and technology.
- Examine documentation in support of key decisions related to supply chain management and production.
- Review acquisitions, expense, and cash budgets, and verify that variances have been investigated.
- Review payables reports and verify proper and timely handling of adjustments.
- Review standard costs are developed based on analysis of product design, resource needs, and the production process.
- Verify that cost accounting variances are monitored and resolved on a timely basis.
- Verify that slow-moving inventory is monitored and realizability is periodically assessed.
- Verify that waste, scrap, and by-products are monitored for disposal.
- Evaluate the competence and training of key individuals within the process.
- Discuss performance measures and process evaluation with appropriate management personnel and evaluate whether process oversight is effective.
- Identify and review appropriate process performance indicators relevant to key risks.

Information Processing Controls

Proper Authorization Procedures

- Verify existence of general authorization for purchasing goods and services (e.g., purchasing policy manuals, purchasing limits, standardized quality requirements, standardized payment terms).
- Review the process for revising general purchasing authorizations.
- Reperform information systems commands associated with automated controls to ensure that they are operating effectively
- Obtain a sample of vouchers, and verify that all required approvals are present.
- Obtain a sample of disbursement checks, and verify that all required approvals are present.
- Verify that the movement/transformation of inventory is properly authorized (including new acquisitions, materials placed in process, and sales).
- Verify that standard costs are properly authorized.
- Verify that dispositions of obsolete inventory are properly authorized and recorded.
- Verify that dispositions of waste, scrap, and by-products are properly authorized.

Use of Adequate Documents and Records

- Verify that documents are prenumbered and used in sequence including purchase orders, receiving reports, vouchers, checks, time cards, job tickets, and inventory movement documents.
- Observe that master inventory files are maintained on a perpetual basis.

Independent Verification of Employee Responsibilities

- Verify that all exception reports and computer edit listings are investigated and cleared on a timely basis.

Figure 12–9   *(continued)*

- Obtain a sample of vouchers and verify that all supporting documents are present and that verifications are noted on supporting documents.*
- Obtain a sample of general disbursement checks, and verify that all supporting documents are present and that verifications are noted on supporting documents.
- Verify that the proper reconciliations are performed on a timely basis and exceptions fully investigated, including (1) bank reconciliations with the check register, (2) voucher journal with payable postings, (3) perpetual records with physical counts and general ledger activity, and (4) standard cost calculations and overhead allocations with actual results.

Physical Controls
- Observe facilities and client personnel for proper physical controls over assets, documents, and records.

Segregation of Duties
- Verify that proper segregation of duties exists for purchasing, production, and accounting activities.
- Discuss work responsibilities with employees assigned to transaction processing, and evaluate effectiveness and consistency of individual responsibilities.
- Examine procedures manuals, personnel policies, organization charts, the chart of accounts and other documents, and records used in the system.
- Identify and evaluate significant changes within the process occurring during the year.
- Observe personnel in the performance of their duties related to the approval and verification of transactions, including
  - Review and follow-up on open orders
  - Preparation of receiving reports and verification of incoming shipments
  - Movement of goods out of receiving to storage or other departments
  - Check preparation and approval
  - Cancellation of supporting documents upon payment to vendor
  - Check distribution

---

* The same samples of vouchers and checks can be used to test both authorization and various independent verifications.

costs are properly tracked and estimated. The auditor should first determine that the company has appropriate policies regarding purchasing, including assessing the need for goods and services, the selection of vendors, the negotiation of prices and terms, and the receipt of goods and services. The organization should also have clear-cut policies regarding the preparation and authorization of disbursements. Furthermore, the organization should have a well-designed information system for tracking production and allocating overhead costs. Finally, the auditor should examine the process by which these policies are updated.

The auditor has three basic approaches for determining if existing policies are being properly applied. The first is to interview company employees and observe them in the performance of their duties. Observation may be particularly useful for assessing the handling and movement of inventory during receiving and production. Observation should be as unobtrusive as possible and may need to be repeated under different conditions and at different times, especially if the client has a change in personnel or procedures.

The second approach is to obtain documentary evidence of the performance of control procedures. Documentation can include internal analyses, exception reports, internal memos and communications, procedures manuals, programming codes for production and inventory management systems, and transaction documents. The auditor will usually verify that prenumbered documents are being properly used in sequence. The auditor may then select a sample of acquisitions and disbursements and examine evidence that the appropriate authorizations are present and that required reviews have been performed by responsible personnel. For example, the auditor could look at the purchasing department's sign-off on a purchase order to verify that appropriate quality, prices, and terms have been obtained. Proper receipt of goods may be evidenced by the warehouse supervisor's signature or initials on the receiving report. For disbursements, the auditor may examine canceled checks and supporting documents to ascertain that all proper authorizations are present. The results from vouching tests must be interpreted carefully, however, because signatures and initials do not guarantee that a transaction was processed correctly.

The third approach is to reperform controls to see that they are operating properly. Reperformance is used to test automated controls embedded in complex inventory systems, electronic data interchange (EDI) systems, or integrated enterprise resource planning systems. To test automated controls, auditors will send test items through the system to ensure that controls are operating effectively. Basically, automated controls should prevent commands from being performed that are outside limits established within the system (e.g., fictitious vendor numbers, product costing outside of standard costing amounts). These tests are often performed by computer specialists.

Perpetual inventory records are a critical element for controlling the movement of materials and the production of inventory. Accurate accounting for and control over inventory requires that perpetual inventory records be accurate. Such control is becoming even more critical as manufacturers move to just-in-time inventory systems, establish computerized data links with suppliers, and try to minimize the carrying costs of inventory on hand. The client (and the auditor) will periodically observe inventory to determine if the perpetual records are accurate. The more reliable the perpetual records are, the more comfort the auditor has that inventory balances are correctly stated.

Figure 12–8 illustrates that a number of process risks have been substantially reduced by process controls, including the risk of receiving poor quality materials, excess spoilage, unrecorded liabilities, and processing errors. The latter two risks are particularly important because they directly impact the reliability of financial information. To test controls over material quality, the auditor could review the vendor approval and purchase authorization process by conducting interviews with key personnel, examining long-term purchase contracts, and documenting and understanding inspection processes during receipt of shipments at the client.[4] To test controls over information processing and recognition of liabilities, the auditor could test individual purchase transactions using the procedures described in Figure 12–9. Additional tests would be performed for controls over excess spoilage. Controls related to poor production design would not be needed since the risk is not significant. Figure 12–8 suggests that the auditor believes there are no effective controls over production scheduling and the controls for avoiding

4 Under sole-sourcing contracts or many just-in-time inventory environments, inspections occur at the supplier prior to shipment to the client, and no inspections occur at the client's production facility. This process occurs because many just-in-time environments are designed such that supplier deliveries go straight from the delivery vehicle to the assembly line, with no ability for inspection ahead of time.

material shortages are not effective enough to justify further examination (i.e., the risk remains high in spite of the control assessment).

IDENTIFYING SIGNIFICANT RESIDUAL RISKS

Figure 12–8 indicates that the risk of errors in information processing, unrecorded liabilities, or lost inventory appear to be low. However, these areas are often the focus of a great deal of an auditor's substantive testing. In our example, it is short-ages of material and poor production scheduling that represent significant resid-ual risks. These are the risks the auditor should consider in further detail.

The risk of inadequate materials will condition the auditor's expectations about a number of performance measures. Costs would be higher (due to the allo-cation of fixed costs over fewer units produced), inventory turnover would be higher due to lower levels of inventory, and order backlogs would be longer. Mate-rial shortages may impact the valuation of long-term contracts that would necessi-tate additional substantive testing or disclosures. If the company decided to use forward contracts or other forms of derivatives to manage the risks associated with obtaining a steady supply of materials, the auditor would need to consider testing the financial reporting and disclosure impact of such arrangements. Furthermore, problems associated with an inadequate supply of materials could cause deteriora-tion in the control environment. Procurement managers might choose to deal with less reputable or reliable suppliers in order to obtain adequate supplies, or might accept lower quality materials. In the worse case, managers might manipulate in-ventory and production information in order to hide the problems.

Although poor production scheduling is considered to be highly likely as in-dicated in Figure 12–8, the magnitude of its impact is considered to be relatively low. Consequently, the auditor would devote moderate attention to this risk. The risk will probably affect the auditor's expectations about costs, margins, and plant utilization, but probably will not have a significant impact on material financial statement assertions. The auditor's testing related to this risk could be limited to substantive analytical procedures and would not involve either tests of transac-tions or other substantive tests.

In the remainder of this chapter, we will discuss substantive tests that can be used if specific financial statement assertions related to the supply chain or pro-duction are considered to have high inherent or control risk. These tests specifi-cally apply to accounts payable and inventory. Different substantive tests are used for different assertions, so the auditor will select the substantive tests that are rele-vant for the specific assertions that have high risk.

PLANNING TESTS OF FINANCIAL STATEMENT ASSERTIONS: PURCHASES AND ACCOUNTS PAYABLE

Supply chain activities generate purchase transactions, which usually create liabil-ities that are reported on the balance sheet. The purpose of substantive tests of accounts payable is to verify the completeness and valuation of the company's obligations. Auditors are also concerned about completeness and understandabil-ity assertions related to presentation and disclosure. A comprehensive approach for testing accounts payable is presented in Figure 12–10. The primary substantive tests for purchases and payables include:

- Tests of purchase and disbursement transactions
- Substantive analytical procedures

Figure 12–10   Substantive Tests of Accounts Payable Account*

Management Assertion	Typical Substantive Audit Procedures
Existence: All recorded transactions related to accounts payable occurred and recorded payables exist.	• Confirm payable balances with vendors and follow up on exceptions and non-responses. • Vouch a sample of purchases and disbursements from the period
Completeness: All existing accounts payable transactions and balances have been recorded.	• Confirm payable balances (including some zero-balance accounts) with vendors and follow up on exceptions and non-responses. • Select a sample of receiving reports prepared shortly before and after year end and trace to proper inclusion in the voucher register and accounts payable subsidiary ledger. • Vouch payments made shortly before and after year end to determine if liabilities and payments have been recorded in the proper period. • Vouch a sample of purchases and disbursements from the period.
Valuation: Transaction detail included in subsidiary journals and ledgers agrees with the general ledger balances for accounts payable.	• Obtain an accounts payable trial balance as of the end of the fiscal period. • Test the accuracy of the trial balance. • Reconcile the totals per the trial balance with the balance per the general ledger and the accounts payable subsidiary ledger. • Select a sample of accounts in the trial balance and trace to the accounts payable subsidiary ledger. • Reconcile activity per the purchases journal, cash disbursements journal, and accounts payable subsidiary ledger with recorded activity in the general ledger
Valuation: Accounts payable are recorded at the appropriate amounts.	• Select a sample of recorded liabilities from the trial balance and trace to appropriate supporting documentation, including vendors' statements. • Confirm payable balances with vendors and follow up on exceptions and non-responses. • Vouch a sample of purchases and disbursements from the period.
Valuation: Accounts payable are properly classified.	• Examine the accounts payable trial balance for items to be reclassified (e.g., debit balances, notes payable).
Valuation: Transactions affecting accounts payable have been recorded in the proper period.	• Vouch payments made shortly before and after year end to determine if liabilities and payments have been recorded in the proper period. • Perform inventory cutoff tests and physical observation of inventory at year end (see Figure 12–15).

* The auditor would also use a disclosures checklist and management representation letter to help ensure that assertions related to presentation and disclosure of purchases transactions and accounts payable are fairly stated.

- Tests of the Accounts Payable Trial Balance
- Tests for unrecorded liabilities
- Confirmation of payables

Most of these audit procedures will provide evidence for more than one assertion. Very few clients would need all these tests unless they had very high risk of material misstatement for numerous assertions related to purchases and accounts payable.

Tests of Purchase and Disbursement Transactions

An illustration of the appropriate tests of transactions for purchases and disbursements is provided in Figure 12–11. The assertions of occurrence, accuracy, timing, and classification are tested using a sample taken from the population of recorded documents supporting each type of transaction. The appropriate sample for purchases is selected from recorded vouchers; for disbursements, the sample is selected from recorded checks. The sample for tests of transactions can be the same as that used for tests of controls (i.e., dual-purpose tests). For transactions to be tested, the supporting documentation is reviewed to make sure that all information is consistent and recorded properly at the correct amount, in the right account, and in the correct time period. Accuracy is verified by testing the summary journals and ledgers, that is, the voucher register or purchases journal, and the cash disbursements journal or check register. Key totals should also be traced to the appropriate accounts in the general ledger. Completeness of accounts payable is tested by selecting a sample of receiving reports from the period, with specific focus on the time around the end of the fiscal year, verifying supporting documentation, and tracing the transactions to proper inclusion in the voucher register.

Substantive Analytical Procedures

Substantive analytical procedures are especially useful for testing expense accounts that result from procurement activities. For some accounts, substantive analytical procedures may be the only tests that are necessary. Different analytical approaches are used for different accounts depending on the nature of the account balance and the level of precision desired. The more detailed the information used, the better the evidence that can be obtained from substantive analytical procedures. When available, auditors should analyze significant expenses by time period, by location, or by product line. Analytical approaches that are frequently used by an auditor include

- Trend Analysis of Expenses: Expenses can be analyzed in absolute amount or relative to a logical base such as sales revenue. Expenses that are essentially fixed and invariant to volume can be expected to change little over time. Other expenses can be expected to be stable relative to some base. For example, expenses such as utilities and materials or supplies can be expected to increase as production activity increases.
- Direct Estimation of Expenses: Some expenses may be directly estimated using client operating data about units, time, or volume of transactions. For example, if the auditor knows that a company received 1,000 shipments and the average shipping cost of a purchase is $25 (both numbers are process-related performance indicators), an estimate of total shipping costs can be

Figure 12–11   Tests of Transactions Related to Supply Chain and Production Management

---

Purchases

Occurrence, Accuracy, Timing, Classification

- Review the voucher register or purchases journal for large or unusual transactions to be examined in detail.
- Select a sample of purchase transactions from the voucher register.* Obtain the related vouchers and all appropriate supporting documents (purchase requisition, purchase order, contract, receiving report, vendor invoice and vendor statement). Perform the following tests and note any exceptions found:
  - Trace vendor to the approved vendor list.
  - Compare quantities per the purchase requisition, purchase order, receiving report, and vendor's invoice.
  - Review price per vendor's invoice for accuracy (e.g., by reference to published price list or contract terms).
  - Recompute extensions and footings on vendor invoice or statement.
  - Compare totals per vendor's invoice or statement to the voucher.
  - Trace voucher to proper inclusion in the voucher register.
  - Compare receiving date per receiving report to posting date per the voucher register.
  - Trace voucher to proper posting in the accounts payable subsidiary ledger.
  - Review asset/expense classification for reasonableness.
  - Trace inventory items and quantities to proper inclusion in the perpetual inventory records.
  - Test accuracy of vendor account in the subsidiary ledger.
  - Vouch subsequent payment to vendor noting validity of discounts taken and interest paid (if any).

Accuracy: Test the accuracy of the voucher register (or purchases journal). This may be done on a sample basis by selecting a few days (or other distinct subsection of the journal) and testing daily totals and then aggregating daily totals to test the period totals. Trace totals to proper inclusion in the general ledger.

Completeness: Select a sample of receiving documents from the prenumbered sequence and trace to proper inclusion in the voucher register, noting the existence of a corresponding voucher and other supporting documentation and the date of posting (as compared to the date on the receiving report).

Disbursements

Occurrence, Accuracy, Timing, Classification

- Review the cash disbursements journal or check register for large or unusual transactions to be examined in detail.
- Select a sample of disbursement transactions from the cash disbursements journal.** Obtain the voucher package in support of the disbursement. Perform the following tests and note any exceptions:
  - Review and compare the information in the supporting documents.
  - Verify that the amount of payment is consistent with vendor billings and payment terms (e.g., discounts, interest).
  - Examine the canceled check for payee, proper signature, vendor endorsement, and bank stamp.

---

* Alternatively, the sample can be selected from the purchases journal as long as the documents are prenumbered, used in sequence, and traceable to inclusion in the accounts payable subsidiary ledger.

** Alternatively, the sample can be taken from the check register if the company uses only one general disbursement account.

Figure 12–11   *(continued)*

> - Compare date on check to cancellation date for possible indications of held checks.
> - Trace check to proper posting in the accounts payable subsidiary ledger.
>
> *Completeness, Accuracy:* Test the accuracy of the cash disbursements journal (and check register if desired). This may be done on a sample basis. Trace totals to proper inclusion in the general ledger.***

*** The preparation of bank reconciliations for the audit of cash (see Chapter 11) also provides evidence concerning the completeness of disbursements.

computed, in this case, $25,000. If this result is close to the recorded balance, it represents reasonable evidence that the account is correctly stated.

- Ratio Analysis: A number of ratios based on financial and operating data can be examined to identify unusual changes in operating patterns that might indicate the existence of a misstatement in an account balance. For example, actual production costs per unit can be compared to standard costs to evaluate the accuracy of reported inventory balances.

Regardless of the method(s) used, the auditor ultimately has to make a judgment as to whether differences between recorded account balances and the auditor's expectations are important. The auditor's expectation should be conditioned on the knowledge obtained about strategic and process risks obtained during the risk assessment phase of the audit. The auditor's response to an apparent discrepancy between expected and actual results will depend on the size, direction, and possible explanations of the difference. Divergence from expectations may indicate a change in operations (e.g., adding productive capacity), a change in accounting method (e.g., FIFO to LIFO), or a misstatement in an account balance. If a difference seems significant, the auditor will need to further investigate the account.[5]

Tests of Accounts Payable Trial Balance

The primary test of accuracy involves obtaining a trial balance listing recorded accounts payable by vendor or voucher. This schedule should be footed and reconciled with the general ledger payable balance. This schedule should also be reviewed for unusual items that may need to be reclassified or that require further explanation.

Tests for Unrecorded Liabilities

A common substantive test for accounts payable is the search for unrecorded liabilities. This test is really a form of cutoff test. Typically, the auditor will select a sample of disbursements that have been made since the end of the fiscal year, examine the supporting documentation, determine if the payment is for a liability that existed at year end, and then determine if an actual liability had been recorded for the item. The auditor would propose adjustments to the account balance for

5 Regression analysis can also be used for expenses. For example, utility expense could be estimated based on the number of days worked, the volume of production, the average weather conditions (which affect heating and cooling), the average price per kilowatt, and so on. The primary challenge for building such an expectation model is the availability of reliable data to use as input to the estimation process.

Figure 12–12   Sample Confirmation for Accounts Payable

Jones Manufacturing, Inc.
Gainesville, Florida

January 6, 20x6

Brown & Son
2020 N. Market Street
Gainesville, FL 32602

Dear Sirs:

Our financial statements are currently being examined by the auditing firm of Smith
& Company, CPAs (Gainesville, Florida). In connection with this examination, we
ask that you provide them with the following information:

- An itemized statement of accounts payable owed to you by our company as of
  December 31, 20x5.
- An itemized list of notes payable, acceptance, or any other obligations owed to
  you by our company as of December 31, 20x5.
- An itemized list of merchandise that is in our possession on consignment from
  you as of December 31, 20x5.

Please reply directly to Smith & Company. An addressed return envelope has been
enclosed for your convenience. Thank you for your assistance with this request.

Sincerely,

Edgar Jones

Edgar Jones, Controller

any unrecorded liabilities that are detected. The size of the transactions tested after
year end will depend on the auditor's assessment of the risk of material misstatement for liability assertions.[6]

CONFIRMATION OF PAYABLES

Auditors may also confirm accounts payable balances with vendors. The use of
confirmations for payables is not required by auditing standards, however, and
is much less common than the confirmation of receivables. Confirmations for
payables are almost always sent out in the positive or blank form (i.e., negative
confirmations are not used). A sample payable confirmation is presented in Figure 12–12. The confirmation also asks for information on formal financing arrangements (notes and acceptances) and inventory on consignment. This information
is useful for auditing other assertions but is not directly pertinent to accounts
payable.

The confirmation of payables presents a unique challenge to the auditor since
the use of the payables trial balance as the population of accounts to be sampled is
problematic. In general, the auditor is looking for unrecorded or understated liabilities, and selecting accounts to confirm from among those already recorded is
not likely to produce adequate evidence to satisfy the completeness objective.

---

6 The results from the vouching of subsequent cash disbursements can be supplemented with the cutoff tests
performed for inventory given that the presence of many errors related to unrecorded inventory may also indicate the existence of an unrecorded account payable.

However, the trial balance is often the only alternative for selecting the sample. As a result, the auditor will supplement the selection of accounts from the trial balance with a selection of vendors that have a zero (or small) balance at year end but with which the company does business on a regular basis. Non-responses, and responses that indicate disagreement with the client's records, should be investigated by the auditor. Typically the auditor examines documentation supporting the recorded liabilities and cross-references confirmation results to the vouching tests for unrecorded liabilities.

The extent of testing applied to liability assertions depends on the risk of material misstatement as assessed by the auditor. When risk is low for the majority of payable assertions, the auditor might avoid most of the tests described in Figure 12–10 and limit testing to a few large purchase transactions and payments made after the end of the year. When the risk of material misstatement is high for most payable assertions, the auditor will perform more of these substantive tests, and use larger sample sizes for the tests of transactions and unrecorded liabilities.

PLANNING TESTS OF FINANCIAL STATEMENT ASSERTIONS: INVENTORY

Inventory is usually a highly material element in the financial statements of a manufacturing or merchandising company. Furthermore, inventory is often considered to be high risk because of the inherent complexity of the activities related to production and the direct control that management can exercise over inventory transactions and valuations. When a company is going through a rough period, inventory manipulations often become an easy way to boost earnings and present a good appearance on the financial statements. Brief consideration of two infamous cases of inventory fraud helps illustrate the auditor's concern:

- MiniScribe Corp.: This defunct company was a manufacturer of computer disk drives that was accused of "perpetrating a massive fraud" to improperly boost net income by manipulating inventory balances. In 1986 alone, the company was forced to record a $10 million reduction in income when fraudulent activity related to sales and inventory was detected by the auditor. One fraudulent technique used by the company was to ship bricks disguised in computer boxes and record the shipments as sales. Another deception was facilitated by creating a computer program, called "Cook Book," to inflate the year-end inventory data. (*The Wall Street Journal*, May 14, 1992.)
- Phar-Mor, Inc.: This national chain of discount drugstores maintained impressive earnings growth by inflating the value of its inventory, resulting in an accounting charge of $350 million when the fraud was uncovered. The company was able to disguise the overstatement by spreading nonexistent inventory over many store locations. Company executives made arrangements for inventory to be accurate in stores visited by the auditors. At other times, inventory numbers prepared by outside inventory specialists were simply increased by company management. (*The Wall Street Journal*, August 28, 1992.)

These cases are illustrative of an unfortunately large number of cases where auditors have been fooled about the levels of inventory held by a company. The common lesson from cases of this type is that inventory is an area where the auditor must be skeptical. The complexity of inventory and the potential for management override of control systems increases the risk that material misstatements and fraud can occur in inventory transactions.

The auditor's key concerns related to inventory are that inventory exists, is properly valued at the lower of cost or market, is recorded in the proper period, and is accurately summarized in the accounts. Completeness is usually less of a concern unless inventory is stored at distant or independent locations, or has been shipped on consignment. Classification can also be an important issue for auditors to consider when there is significant work-in-process, in which case the stage of completion can significantly affect the carrying value of inventory (and thus the cost of goods sold and reported earnings).

Example

Fashion retailers like Federated Department Stores (e.g., Macy's, Bloomingdales) must deal with difficult valuation issues for much of their inventory. Buyers for a department store often negotiate revised payment terms with vendors after merchandise has been sold based on the prices that the store was actually able to obtain when merchandise was sold to end-customers. Further complicating the process is that the cost associated with "suggested retail price" rarely is the market cost when products are sold. As goods continually are marked down (i.e., as items go "on sale"), lower of cost or market accounting requires that retailers realize markdown losses in conjunction with the markdowns. As a result, the auditors of a fashion retailer will devote significant time to the valuation assertion associated with inventory and cost of goods sold.

A comprehensive set of substantive tests for inventory are described in Figure 12–13. The primary procedures to test assertions related to inventory include

Authoritative Guidance & Standards
Standards (SAS 106, ISA 500) state that auditors generally should perform an inspection of physical inventory to test its existence and completeness. Generally this evidence is gathered at that same time that the auditor performs an observation of the client's periodic inventory count.

- Tests of inventory purchases, conversion, and movement
- Substantive analytical procedures
- Inspection of inventory
- Inventory price tests
- Tests of inventory compilation
- Cutoff tests

Auditing standards include a presumption of inventory inspection by the auditor. As a result, the physical observation of inventory is performed for virtually all clients that possess a material amount of inventory.

TESTS OF INVENTORY PURCHASES, CONVERSION, AND MOVEMENT

There are few tests of transactions that are routinely performed for inventory movement and conversion because production does not involve an exchange with external parties. The results from sales and purchase tests, however, are relevant to inventory management given that they usually increase or decrease inventory levels. If the auditors wishes, sales and purchase tests can be augmented with tests of internal movement and conversion of inventory. For example, movement of materials into production can be tested for proper inclusion in work-in-process, and job tickets can be tested for appropriate standard costs.

SUBSTANTIVE ANALYTICAL PROCEDURES

Substantive analytical procedures can be useful for testing the valuation of inventory, especially if there is a question about potential impairment of value. Sales can be analyzed by location or branch to identify those that are experiencing problems.

Figure 12–13   Substantive Tests of Inventory*

Management Assertion	Typical Audit Procedures
Existence: All recorded transactions related to inventory occurred; recorded inventory exists and properly reflect inventory in transit or held on consignment from other parties.	• Observe periodic inventory (see Figure 12–15). • Confirm the existence of inventory in the hands of third parties (e.g., consignments, independent warehouses). • Perform substantive analytical procedures. • Perform tests of sales (Chapter 11) and purchases (Figure 12–11).
Completeness: All existing inventory transactions and balances have been recorded and properly reflect inventory in transit, held on consignment by other parties, or stored in independent warehouses.	• Observe periodic inventory (see Figure 12–15). • Confirm the existence of inventory in the hands of third parties (e.g., consignments, independent warehouses). • Review consignment and purchase commitments or other inventory arrangements. • Perform substantive analytical procedures. • Perform tests of sales (Chapter 11) and purchases (Figure 12–11).
Ownership: Inventory balances are owned by the company.	• Confirm the existence of inventory in the hands of third parties (e.g., consignments, independent warehouses). • Obtain a representation letter from management regarding ownership of inventory. • Review board of directors minutes, legal letters, contracts, etc., for evidence of pledging or other potential claims of ownership on inventory.
Valuation: Inventory balances are recorded at the proper amounts using an appropriate accounting method with proper allocation of indirect manufacturing costs, and considering possible reductions in the realizable value of inventory on hand.	• Observe periodic inventory (see Figure 12–15). • Perform substantive analytical procedures. • Perform price tests on items in inventory (e.g., purchase prices, standard costs). • Test the computation and application of overhead allocations and standard costs. • Test the realizability of recorded inventory values. • Perform tests of sales (Chapter 11) and purchases (Figure 12–11).
Valuation: Transaction detail included in subsidiary journals and ledgers agrees with the general ledger balances related to inventory.	• Test accuracy of inventory listing and trace items to proper inclusion in the perpetual inventory records. • Test the accuracy of perpetual inventory records. • Reconcile totals per inventory listing to balance of inventory per the general ledger. • Trace test counts from inventory observation to proper inclusion in the inventory listing.
Valuation: Inventory balances and related costs are properly classified.	• Review consignment and purchase commitments or other inventory arrangements. • Review production variances for proper disposition. • Perform substantive analytical procedures. • Verify stage of completion for work-in-process.
Valuation Transactions affecting inventory have been recorded in the proper period.	• Observe periodic inventory (see Figure 12–15). • Perform cutoff tests for receipt and shipment of goods.

* To test assertions associated with presentation and disclosure related to inventory, auditors review consignment and purchase commitments or other inventory arrangements, complete disclosure checklist for inventory, obtain a representation letter from management regarding disclosure of inventory, and review proposed disclosures for accuracy.

For example, if the client is able to track performance results by product line, then analysis of sales, costs of sales, gross margins, and inventory turnover ratios for each product can be very useful for assessing the realizability of inventory balances. Items that have very low margins or turnover rates are candidates for write-down to the lower of cost or market. If capitalized inventory costs exceed the revenue generated for a reasonable period of time, the auditor could suggest the write-off of excess cost. An example of this type of analysis is presented in Figure 12–14. In this example, the auditor uses a simple rule of thumb to write off any inventory exceeding one year's sales. A more complex analysis might be used to generate a more precise estimate of the amount of obsolete inventory if the auditor felt that the risk of material misstatement was high for inventory valuation.

Substantive analytical procedures are also useful for assessing the reasonableness of overhead allocations and standard costs. Overhead and labor allocated to individual units of production can be estimated using aggregate costs incurred and total production data by product line to determine if the labor and overhead components of standard costs are reasonable. Furthermore, the company's own variances for over- and underapplied overhead can be reviewed by the auditor for disposition and adjustment of inventory carrying costs.

A third possible substantive procedure is the comparison of quantities on hand between the current and prior year by product line. Such a comparison may reveal unexplained inventory build-ups that may indicate problems with the existence or validity of inventory or cutoff problems related to inventory receipts and shipments. Alternatively, inventory levels that are unusually low or nonexistent may indicate problems with the completeness of inventory.

Figure 12–14   Substantive Analytical Procedure to Test Inventory Obsolescence

C-4

Jones Manufacturing, Inc.
Substantive Analysis of Inventory Turnover
For Year Ended 12/31/x6

WRK
PBC   1/24/x7

Item No.	Current-Year Sales		Year-End Inventory		Turnover Ratio		Proposed Adjustment	
X445	$121,345	✓	$ 86,376	✗	1.40	R	0	T
Y357	354,435	✓	110,888	✗	3.20	R	0	T
J665	12,478	✓	32,688	✗	0.38	R	20,000	T
D112	659,999	✓	186,974	✗	3.53	R	0	T
F145	634	✓	25,487	✗	0.02	R	25,487	T
A129	175,886	✓	121,456	✗	1.45	R	0	T
L089	76,479	✓	27,599	✗	2.77	R	0	T
			Total proposed adjustment				45,487	AJE 8
							T	

Note: Per discussion with controller, the company agrees to write off any inventory costs in excess of one year's supply. See *AJE #8* for effect of $45,487 adjustment to inventory.

T   Footed and cross-footed without exception.

✓   Traced to and agrees with sales report classified by product line.

✗   Traced to and agrees with year-end perpetual inventory records.

R   Recomputed without exception.

INSPECTION OF INVENTORY

The process for inventory inspection is described in Figure 12–15. Although inventory is physically inspected in most engagements, the nature and extent of the inspection can vary a great deal. At one extreme is the situation where client controls are weak and the auditor is very concerned about the existence and valuation of inventory. In these cases, the auditor will primarily conduct substantive tests by

Figure 12–15   Inventory Inspection Procedures

Preliminary
1. Review client's inventory procedures prior to the date of the inventory. Tour facilities where inventory is stored. Determine if all inventory locations are to be counted. Be sure that the following controls are used during the conduct of the inventory count:
   - Count teams should consist of two people to ensure accurate counts.
   - Count teams should have clearly delimited areas of responsibility.
   - Prenumbered, two-part tags for entering counts should be used and attached to inventory that has been counted.
   - A separate review (by supervisor) should be performed to ensure that all inventory is counted and tagged.
   - Movement of inventory and personnel should be limited during counts.
   - Arrangements should be made for specific handling of shipments made or received during the count process.

Conduct of Inventory Inspection
2. Observe the client's personnel in the execution of the inventory counts. By observing the client perform inventory counts—a test of control—the auditor can justify performing less inspection of actual inventory—a substantive test.
3. Randomly select a sample of completed tags and verify the accuracy of the item description and quantities. (These tags should be noted for follow-up when the inventory listing is prepared.)
4. Inspect inventory on hand and note any indications that inventory is obsolete, to be scrapped or on consignment.
5. Assess reasonableness of percentage completed or stage of completion assigned to work-in-process.
6. Survey areas where counts have been completed to ensure that all inventory has been counted and tagged. Only then does the client personnel return to pull the tags.
7. After tag pulling is complete, survey areas to ensure that all tags have been pulled.
8. Note the sequence numbers of all tags used in the count process at each location.
9. Note the number of the last receiving and shipping reports used for subsequent follow-up in cutoff tests.

Test of Inventory Compilation
10. Obtain a complete list of inventory quantities listed by tag number and test its accuracy.
11. Trace inventory tags observed during test counts to proper inclusion in the inventory listing.
12. Verify completeness and validity of tags listed in the compilation report against tag numbers used in actual observation.
13. Compare quantities per inventory listing to quantities per perpetual inventory records and note disposition of any inconsistencies.
14. Perform price tests on items in inventory.
15. Test the accuracy of the compilation and reconcile with the general ledger accounts.

performing a large number of test counts (inventory inspections) and personally visit all significant inventory locations. At the other extreme is the situation where client controls are strong or inventory is inspected by internal auditors or a third party inventory service. Under these conditions, the auditor will perform mainly tests of controls over the client's inventory inspection with minimal test counts, a few visits to selected locations, and observation that client personnel are adhering to approved inventory instructions.

During inventory observation, it is important that the auditor obtain assurance that all items are accurately counted and included in the overall compilation. To facilitate this objective, the auditor should make sure inventory is not moved around during the count, that all storage areas are counted, that newly arriving shipments are properly included in the count, that outgoing shipments are not included, and that the actual counts are carefully conducted. The use of prenumbered inventory tags and auditor oversight of count teams are extremely important to achieving an accurate and complete count. Test counts should be traced to the inventory compilation that is prepared based on the inventory observation. The compilation should be tested for accuracy and reconciled with the general ledger. An example of the type of documentation that might be used for testing the compilation of inventory quantities and inventory test counts is presented in Figure 12–16.

Finally, auditors should be alert for valuation issues associated with inventory when conducting an inventory inspection. Typically, auditors test the existence of inventory by tracing inventory from accounting records to its location in the warehouse, and test completeness by tracing inventory from the warehouse to accounting records. Auditors should open boxes, make sure that there are no "holes" (i.e., missing boxes in the middle) for large quantities of boxes stacked on large skids, and make sure that the inventory being counted is saleable. Further, auditors should be alert for inventory that is segregated or has a large amount of dust accumulated on it. These conditions suggest that the associated inventory might not be ready for sale. This so-called "white glove test" helps auditors assess the presence of obsolete inventory that might need to be marked down to lower of cost or market.

INVENTORY PRICE TESTS AND OBSOLESCENCE

Once the auditor is satisfied that the accounting records accurately report the quantity of inventory on hand, the next step is to determine what cost should be assigned to the units. This process depends on three key factors: the inventory method being used for purchased inventory, the existence of manufactured inventory, and the possibility of obsolescence.

- Purchased Inventory: Costs for purchased inventory (including raw materials used in production) should be traced to appropriate vendor invoices consistent with the accounting method being used. If the company uses FIFO, inventory on hand should be priced using the most recent vendor invoices. The auditor must be careful to examine enough invoices to cover all units on hand. For example, if there are 100 units but the most recent invoice was for only 60 units, older invoice(s) must also be examined to determine the cost of the other 40 units.
- Manufactured Inventory: Costs for manufactured inventory must be traced to the appropriate standard costs for each product. The computation and reasonableness of standard costs should be tested and the level of actual versus absorbed overhead should be reviewed to ensure that all proper product costs

Figure 12–16   Inventory Count List*

<table>
<tr><td colspan="6" align="right">C-3</td></tr>
<tr><td colspan="6" align="center">Jones Manufacturing, Inc.
Inventory Count List
For Year Ended 12/31/x6</td></tr>
</table>

Inventory Item No.	Item Description	Tag No.	Count per Physical Inventory	Count per Perpetual Inventory	Difference
X3467	Sheet metal	1345	232 ✓		
		1346	145 ✓		
		1349	155		
			532 T	542 ✗	(10) T a
V33356	Copper tubing	1093	987	988 ✗	(1) T a
R34347	Gaskets	0567	57		
		0577	94		
			151 T	151 ✗	0 T
D41123	Clamps	2112	1046 ✓		
		2133	1077		
		2134	845		
			2968 T	2710 ✗	258 T a
F49990	Porcelain fixtures	1856	124		
		1876	324 ✓		
			448 T	443 ✗	5 T b

T Footed and cross-footed without exception.

✓ Traced to and agrees with test counts performed by Joe Smith at time of physical inventory observation on 12/31/x6.

✗ Traced to and agrees with perpetual inventory as of 12/31/x6.

a Perpetual inventory records adjusted to reflect this difference.

b Difference due to inventory count error. Perpetual inventory records are correct.

WRK
PBC 1/24/x7

* This facsimile working paper assumes that the lead schedule for inventory is indexed as C.

have been included in the unit cost. The stage or percentage of completion for work-in-process must also be verified to ensure that the proper portion of finished cost is assigned to those units.

- Tests for Obsolescence: If there is a question of the realizability of inventory due to price declines, the auditor should examine the unit costs in relation to the potential selling price of the inventory. If the selling price of a product minus selling expenses and a reasonable profit margin is less than its carrying cost, the auditor should suggest that inventory be written down to its net realizable value.[7]

7 Preferably, the test for lower-of-cost-or-market should be applied to each product in inventory. However, many companies apply the test to overall inventory, which allows gains and losses across units to offset. This is allowed by GAAP but makes it easier to manipulate inventory as an anomalous test for any individual product can be explained away as not being representative of the category tested.

TESTS OF INVENTORY COMPILATION

If the auditor is satisfied that inventory quantities and unit costs are reasonable, the next step is to test the accuracy of the compilation of the final balance by footing and cross-footing the inventory listing. This test can be performed manually or by using computer-assisted techniques. The total per the inventory listing should be tied to the perpetual inventory records and reconciled with the inventory accounts included in the general ledger. The auditor should also verify that inventory is properly classified and disclosed in categories such as raw material, work-in-process, finished goods, and supplies (which is not manufacturing inventory).

CUTOFF TESTS

The auditor should test the cutoff of inventory. These tests can usually be performed in conjunction with the inspection (or observation) of inventory and the cutoff tests for sales and purchases. The critical issue is to determine whether the company has properly included or excluded inventory on hand, in transit, or stored at independent warehouses. If inventory is observed at year end, the auditor can observe whether inventory is included or not included in the counts as is appropriate under the circumstances. The auditor should also identify the number of the last shipping and receiving documents used in order to facilitate the vouching cutoff tests for sales and purchases.

Although inventory is typically observed and price tests are usually performed on most engagements involving a material amount of inventory, the auditor has a great deal of flexibility in the scope of these tests. When the client's information system for inventory is reliable and provides highly detailed inventory data by product line, substantive analytical procedures become a viable and effective method for obtaining evidence about the accuracy of inventory balances. When control risk is low or high-quality substantive analytical procedures are available, the auditor can use smaller sample sizes for price tests or can perform the inventory observation and price tests at an interim date. Price tests are particularly problematic in companies selling large numbers of different products because the projection of small discrepancies to the entire population of transactions may indicate a material misstatement. As a result, auditors must carefully consider the sample size for these tests in order to obtain the needed degree of assurance.

SUMMARY AND CONCLUSION

We have discussed a broad range of issues related to the audit of the supply chain and production management process. We used a process map to identify objectives, activities, and transactions, and internal threat analysis to consider process risks, controls, and performance indicators. The results of the process analysis are used by the auditor to identify and evaluate residual risks that might impact the conduct of the audit.

The most common transactions occurring in the supply chain and production will affect either accounts payable or inventory, or both. An auditor can select among numerous substantive tests to examine assertions related to these accounts. The nature and extent of substantive testing for payables and inventory depends on the assessed level of the risk of material misstatement for each assertion. Figure 12–17 illustrates how the various substantive tests described in this chapter might be adapted under different risk conditions. Ultimately, the auditor must

Figure 12–17   Tests of Financial Statement Assertions for Different Levels of Risk of Material Misstatement

Type of Procedure	High Detection Risk Case (Low Risk of Material Misstatement)	Low Detection Risk Case (High Risk of Material Misstatement)
Accounts Payable		
Tests of transactions	Moderate tests as described in Figure 12–11, mostly performed at interim dates.	Extensive tests as described in Figure 12–11, many performed after year end.
Test of accuracy of the accounts payable trial balance	Minimal or no testing. Totals traced to general ledger.	Trial balance footed and reconciled with the general ledger with some accounts traced to the subsidiary ledger.
Confirmations	Few (if any) confirmations used.	Many confirmations used at year end.
Tests for unrecorded liabilities	Moderate vouching tests of cash disbursements after year end.	Extensive vouching tests of cash disbursements after year end.
Inventory		
Tests of transactions	Minimal to no testing.	Moderate testing of inventory movements and cost assignment.
Observation of inventory	Performed as a test of controls with minimal test counts performed by auditor.	Extensive test counts performed by auditor.
Inventory price tests	Moderate testing of purchase prices and standard costs.	Extensive testing of purchase prices and standard costs. Detailed testing of standard costs for a sample of products.
Tests of inventory compilation	Minimal tests. Reconciliation of total inventory with inventory compilation, perpetual inventory records and general ledger.	Moderate to extensive tests of footings and cross-footings. Reconciliation of individual products with perpetual records and total inventory with general ledger.
Cutoff tests	Minimal testing. Transactions tested based on size.	Moderate to extensive sample of transactions tested.

decide which of these tests to perform on a given client and the extent of testing needed to gather adequate evidence to support the audit opinion.

BIBLIOGRAPHY OF PROFESSIONAL LITERATURE

Research

Johnston, H., W. D. Lindsay and F. Phillips. 2003. Undetected Deviations in Tests of Controls: Experimental Evidence of Nonsampling Risk. *Canadian Accounting Perspectives.* 2(2): 113–134.

Auditing Standards

AICPA *Statements on Auditing Standard (SAS)* No. 106, "Audit Evidence."

AICPA *Statements on Auditing Standard (SAS)* No. 107, "Audit Risk and Materiality in Conducting an Audit."

AICPA *Statements on Auditing Standard (SAS)* No. 109, "Understanding the Entity and Its Environment and Assessing the Risks of Material Misstatement."

AICPA *Statements on Auditing Standard (SAS)* No. 110, "Performing Procedures in Response to Assessed Risks and Evaluating the Audit Evidence Obtained."

IAASB *International Standards on Auditing (ISA)* No. 315, "Understanding the Entity and Its Environment and Assessing the Risks of Material Misstatement."

IAASB *International Standards on Auditing (ISA)* No. 320, "Audit Materiality."

IAASB *International Standards on Auditing (ISA)* No. 330, "The Auditor's Procedures in Response to Assessed Risks."

IAASB *International Standards on Auditing (ISA)* No. 500, "Audit Evidence."

QUESTIONS

1. Explain how creating a process map and internal threat analysis helps in determining the extent to which substantive testing is to be performed on the accounts associated with the supply chain and production management process.

2. Testing for unrecorded liabilities involves vouching a sample of disbursements made after fiscal year end to determine whether the underlying liabilities for the disbursements were recorded at the balance sheet date.
   a. Discuss some sampling strategies for the test of unrecorded liabilities.
   b. How might an unrecorded liability elude a well-conceived and executed sampling strategy (other than through ordinary sampling risk)?
   c. What are the implications for the audit if an unrecorded liability is found?

3. Examine the process activities and transactions for the supply chain and production management process shown in Figure 12–3.
   a. Using the example transactions listed in the same figure, describe which transactions or estimates are impacted by the different activities listed in the process.
   b. Describe which accounts are impacted by each of the transactions.

4. Examine the inherent risk, impact of controls, and residual risk plots in Figure 12–8 for the supply chain and production management process. Based on this plot, what conclusions should an auditor reach for each of the risks regarding whether to test controls and the extent to which substantive testing should be performed?

5. Figure 12–9 contains a listing of tests of operating effectiveness for internal controls related to the supply chain and production management process. For each type of control activity (performance reviews and overall process management, information processing controls, physical controls, and segregation of duties and process design), describe the impact on the audit for each of the following results of controls testing.
   a. Controls are found to be operating effectively
   b. Controls are found to be operating ineffectively

6. Describe the similarities and differences between periodic and perpetual inventory accounting information systems. Include in your discussion the impacts on the types of tests performed and audit evidence gathered to test management assertions about transactions and accounts.

7. Describe why using confirmations for testing completeness of accounts payable is more challenging than using confirmations for testing existence of accounts receivable? How can auditors address this challenge (e.g., what is a search for unrecorded liabilities)?

8. Observing the client's physical inventory is required for all audits in which inventory is a material item. Using Figure 12–15 as a guide, describe why the auditor's key responsibilities for inspecting inventory are important for auditing inventory-related transactions and accounts (e.g., what management assertions do they help test?).

9. Describe the inventory price test, explicitly separating how the auditor collects evidence to support that the appropriate cost of inventory and to support the appropriate market value of inventory. Argue why you believe this to be one of the more or less difficult substantive tests of balances that auditors perform.

10. Many organizations are implementing production process innovations designed to move more to a just-in-time (JIT) systems emphasizing lean manufacturing. One of the goals of this process is to minimize inventory storage costs for production inputs and outputs. Describe the impact of the production environment on the balance sheets of companies that use JIT compared to companies that do not utilize this approach.

11. What key accounts and transactions are affected by the supply chain and production process? Discuss and illustrate with examples.

PROBLEMS

1. Consider the purchases function of a manufacturing company. To overcome a downward profitability trend, management recently instituted a "just-in-time" system of acquiring raw materials for its manufacturing operations. Under this system, raw materials are inventoried in real time—through a bar-coding tracking system—so that orders can be generated to their suppliers automatically whenever the inventories reach a specific point. The best approach is to order the materials at just the right time to ensure an adequate stock for manufacturing operations but without tying up scarce capital in inventory.

   Discuss how the new just-in-time inventory system will affect the predictive power of preliminary and substantive analytical procedures on the receiving function (e.g., the purchases account). Will it make analytical procedures more or less effective at identifying risk and potential misstatement in the purchases process? Why?

2. The following are routine procedures for the audit of the purchases process. For each procedure, (1) state whether it is a test of controls or a substantive test of transactions or balances, (2) state which management assertion the procedure is designed to fulfill, and (3) state the type of evidence used in the procedure.
   a. Compare totals from a sample of purchase documents to canceled checks.
   b. Perform analytical procedures on expenses to determine unexpected fluctuations.
   c. Confirm accounts payable balances of the customers with whom the company purchases its highest volume.
   d. Examine a sample of checks written for more than a certain amount for proper signatures.
   e. Vouch a sample of purchase orders to receiving documents.
   f. Confirm that the master vendor list is up to date and contains only valid vendors.
   g. Ensure that all appropriate documents and approvals are present for a sample of payments.
   h. Vouch all payables paid on the last few days of the fiscal year.

3. In your audit of Faye Co., management gives you the following (partial) list of internal controls over accounts payable:
   • The check approving and preparation duties are performed by separate individuals.
   • Checks of more than $1,000 require the treasurer's signature whereas those for less are produced mechanically using a signature plate stored in the treasurer's safe.
   • Before a check is prepared, the purchase order/check request is matched against the invoice.

- Control totals from the check register are compared to those from the cash disbursements journal after every batch of transactions is completed.
- Management maintains a master vendor list. No check may be written to a vendor not on the list without approval from the controller.
- All disbursement accounts are independently reconciled with exceptions followed up promptly.
- Faye Co. uses hash totals to ensure that expenditures are charged to the proper accounts.
- All checks and purchase orders are prenumbered.

In your test of controls, you find the following:

a.   Upon vouching some of the canceled checks with their supporting documents, you find that one $1,800 check matches the invoice amount but is $100 more than the purchase order listed.

b.   A large number of the checks were written to vendors who required special approval as they were not on the approved list.

c.   Four checks written for more than $1,000 did not carry the treasurer's signature. All were written for less than $1,500, and no other problems were identified.

d.   One invoice had been paid twice.

e.   Two checks were missing from the listing of checks cleared. Upon investigation, they were found to have been destroyed in the check-writing machine.

f.   One expenditure was posted to the wrong expense account.

For each of the above:

1.   State which management assertions are in question.

2.   Discuss whether you believe that an ineffective control represents a significant deficiency or material weakness.

3.   Discuss the ramifications of the items for an assessment of control risk for this function.

4.   When applicable, suggest a more effective control.

4. In her audit of disbursements at a recycling operation, Trudy Jackson, CPA, performs the following procedures. Prior to testing, she had assessed audit risk as high and control risk and inherent risk as low; therefore, she appropriately established a high level of detection risk by her choices of procedures, timing, and sample sizes.

a.   She vouches a small sample of canceled checks (chosen at random) to the appropriate supporting documentation and traces the vendor to the approved list, foots the invoice and the purchasing order, traces the transaction to the appropriate journal and ledger, and reviews the transaction for reasonableness.

b.   She samples a group of timecards for a given payroll cycle (chosen at random) and checks the withholdings for accuracy.

c.   She reconciles the larger disbursement accounts and traces their adjusted balances to the general ledger.

d.   She obtains representations from management regarding the existence and valuation of notes payable.

e.   She samples some receiving reports (chosen at random) and traces the inventory to the accounts payable and inventory accounts in the general ledger.

Now assume that Trudy Jackson has determined that control risk and inherent risk are high and that detection risk must be set lower. For each of the above, discuss how her audit techniques would change and, where applicable, discuss any additional procedures she might perform.

5. For each of the following internal controls in the conversion/warehousing process of a consumer goods wholesaling firm, state the management assertion that the control helps meet and suggest a test of controls that would give the auditor some assurance that the control procedure was effectively performed.

a. The handling of physical inventory is separated from the accounting function.

b. Management periodically reviews slow-moving inventory for evidence of obsolescence.

c. Shipping documents are compared to sales orders and picking tickets before goods are shipped.

d. Using bar-coding technology, inventory clerks update perpetual inventory records in real time as goods are received or shipped.

e. At least once each quarter, a physical inventory is performed and the results are compared to the perpetual inventory records.

6. The CEO of Textrala Petroleum, a crude oil wholesaler, is on an incentive compensation plan that weighs accounting net income heavily when awarding compensation. For 2003, Textrala has done so well that the CEO's bonus has reached its maximum under the compensation contract. Shortly before year end, the CEO is informed that a large oil tanker is sitting off the coast of Texas waiting to discharge its load at the company's terminals. Once it does, the oil will be counted in Textrala's ending inventory for 2003. The CEO asks that the ship be held off for a few days, at some expense, until after the beginning of the new accounting year.

a. Why did the CEO make this request?

b. As Textrala's auditor, can you say that the financial statements for the fiscal year 2003 are misstated?

c. Discuss the ramifications of the CEO's action for your audit.

7. Examine the following questions from an internal control questionnaire for the assembly process of a yacht manufacturer. Assume that the answer to each of these is "no" (which means that the control is weak in that area). For each of the questions, identify the accounts that might be affected, state the management assertion that might be compromised for those accounts, and suggest a substantive audit procedure to perform on the accounts.

a. Are variances from standard costs investigated promptly?

b. Is a comprehensive chart of accounts kept for recording various inputs to and transfers of manufactured inventory?

c. Are the duties of those who handle inventory separated from those who handle the records of inventory?

d. Are adequate records kept for and periodic inspections made of inventory kept offsite?

e. When raw materials inventory arrives, do the receiving department employees have blank forms to fill out (i.e., are the quantities and qualities of the products ordered *not* on the form)?

f. Are control totals reconciled to reflect when inventory arrives or moves between accounts?

g. Does management make periodic reviews of slow-moving inventory for determining obsolescence?

h. Does the requisitioning of raw materials from inventory require a supervisor's initials before materials are released?

8. The following are routine procedures for auditors of the supply chain management and production processes to perform. For each procedure, state whether it is a test of controls or a substantive test of transactions, state which management assertion the procedure is designed to fulfill, and state the type of evidence used in the procedure.

a. Observe how employees gain access to the warehouse.

b. Trace the entries on a batch of job-costing documents to the appropriate journals.

c. Review receiving documents for evidence of inventory held on-site for other entities.

d. Review the receiving and shipping documents for goods transferred in or out of finished goods inventory around the end of the fiscal period. Examine the shipping terms carefully (e.g., FOB Destination).

    e.   Enter phony product identification codes into the inventory master file server and observe what happens.

    f.   Trace a sample of the entries in the control account journals to the general ledger.

    g.   Select a sample of batch cards (e.g., number of boxes, number of items per box, totals) from the internally taken inventory and check them for accuracy.

    h.   Examine actual costs incurred to standard costs applied throughout the cost accounting system.

9. Consider the following two independent situations:

    a.   Company Alpha supplies women's clothes from its seven regional warehouses to small retail stores in shopping malls and roadside mini-malls throughout the country. By employing a sophisticated bar-coding scheme, Company Alpha tracks each article of clothing from the moment it is received at the receiving department to the time it is placed on board the trucks that leave its warehouses early each morning. The inventory tracking mechanism was instituted primarily to provide sales and marketing managers with nearly real-time data on what products are moving and which are not, and when stocks require reordering. However, the system interfaces with the accounting system to provide the controller with information on inventory levels for financial statement preparation purposes.

    b.   Company Beta is a large retail women's clothing store located in a regional shopping mall. Their inventory tracking scheme consists primarily of a document-based system of purchase orders, receiving reports, and sales receipts. A periodic physical inventory is taken each year by the store personnel.

For each of these two companies, discuss a general strategy for testing management assertions for the inventory account.

10. United States accounting rules (Accounting Research Bulletin No. 43) require that inventory be carried on the financial statements at the lower of its cost or market value with the market value of the inventory bounded on the upper end by net realizable value and on its lower end by net realizable value less a normal profit margin. In your audit of Jones Company that manufactures microchips for high-end workstations and mini-computers, you determine that a material quantity of the company's chips are currently valued (per the company's costing system) at an amount higher than their net realizable value.

    a.   Define *net realizable value.*

    b.   What types of evidence would the auditor gather to determine that the microchips are overvalued?

    c.   What arguments could Jones Manufacturing's management advance to defend against a write-down?

11. Consider Figure 12–13, where a substantive analysis of inventory turnover was performed during the audit of Jones Manufacturing Company to determine whether inventory should be written down due to obsolescence.

    a.   Is the total proposed adjustment material? What factors go into your judgment?

    b.   What factors may need further consideration before the auditor argues for a write-down on item no. J665?

    c.   What arguments could Jones Manufacturing's management advance to defend against an obsolescence write-down?

12. For each of the following internal controls in the payables department, state the management assertion that the control helps meet. Then describe a test of controls to obtain assurance that each procedure was effectively performed.

    a.   The signature plate for the check-writing machine is kept in a locked safe that requires two keys to open.

    b.   Hash totals of account numbers are prepared and verified after the cash disbursements journal is used to post to the accounts payable ledger.

    c.   Control totals of posting amounts are prepared and verified whenever payroll is posted to the general ledger.

- d. Details from all accounts payable outstanding at year end are automatically reported to the controller for comparison to the cash disbursements register.
- e. Open purchase orders are compared to the accounts payable ledger periodically with exceptions followed up on promptly.
- f. Employees are issued their time cards only when they show up for work, and they must surrender them upon leaving.
- g. All purchases over $1,000 require the signature of the departmental vice president.
- h. Keying transactions into the electronic database/accounts payable journal requires two entries. If not matched, the transaction is rejected.

Case 12–1: Wal-Mart Suppliers

Consider the supplier development portion of the supply chain management process for Wal-Mart, which is generally believed to be the best in the retail industry. Access the Company's Supplier Proposal Packet on its web site—click on suppliers tab. Read the requirements of suppliers, including issues such as

- supplier agreements
- product supplier web site (termed Retail Link)
- electronic data interchange requirements
- lead-time requirements
- timely shipping
- quality assurance and testing
- industry knowledge and integrity
- transportation logistics
- security source tagging

Requirements

Based on this information (or other information obtained from the Company's web site), Complete the following:

1. Use Figure 12–3 as a guide and complete a process map.
2. Use Figure 12–6 as a guide and complete an internal threat analysis.
3. Use Figure 12–7 as a guide and describe the financial reporting controls that you would expect to see present for supplier development and describe a possible test of each control.
4. Use Figure 12–8 as a guide and complete a residual risk map.

Case 12–2: Global Crossing

Global Crossing Ltd was one of the largest corporate bankruptcies in the history of the USA. Global Crossing (GC) was a telecom with a huge investment in its fiber-optic communication network. The telecom and fiber-optic industry is very competitive, with many large and small organizations controlling different pieces of the worldwide network for fiber-optic communications.

GC would invest in developing a fiber-optic network in an area and then sell access to that network to other networks that did not have service in the area. Once built, the network is essentially a fixed cost, so GC had the incentive to sell as much access to other parties as it could, subject to its overall capacity. At the same time, GC would purchase access to other networks in order to weave a broad network covering as much area as economically possible. The buying/selling of network access was often in the form of swaps, where both the sale and purchase would be with the same partner.

To illustrate, GC might have a fiber-optic cable between Miami and Mexico City (see Exhibit 2–1). At the same time, Little Telecom, Inc (LT) might have a link between Atlanta and Miami. In order for GC to get access to Atlanta, they would purchase capacity from LT. At the same time, LT would purchase access to GC's Miami-Mexico link. If both transactions were for $100 million, this would constitute a swap. Both companies would record the $100 million as revenue on the sale and an asset on the purchase. Cash may or may not actually be exchanged, but the net effect on cash would be zero for both companies. This swap would be considered a legitimate business transaction and it increases the efficiency of the global telecom market, enabling steadily dropping prices of communications.

However, the salutary effect of the accounting for the transaction also makes it an enticing area for manipulation by management wishing to increase its revenues. Note that the transaction makes business sense as long as the value of the access to both companies is really $100 million. What happens if the value of either part of the transaction is much less than indicated? The company still receives the boost to its financial statement, even though the transaction may not reflect

Exhibit 2–1   Example of Fiber-Optic Swap between Telecoms

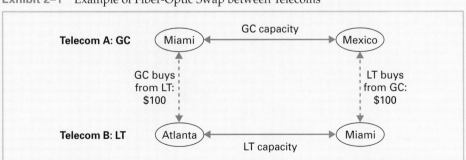

565

economic reality. If desperate enough, management might undertake such transactions simply to obtain the accounting benefit—such transactions are referred to as *hollow swaps*. Even worse, management might give up a valuable asset (e.g., access to its Miami-Mexico link) for something that it did not really need or value (e.g., access to LT's Atlanta-Miami link). This swap is representative of the poor transactions that GC is alleged to have executed prior to going bankrupt, often to maintain the appearance of growth and success in a period of rapidly declining prices for fiber-optic access. The combination of hollow swaps and dropping market prices for fiber-optic access was economically unsustainable for the company.

Requirements

Given your understanding of swaps and hollow swaps in the telecom industry, how would the following aspects of an integrated audit facilitate the auditor's understanding and testing of these transactions?

1. Strategic risks: What strategic risks does the organization face that create the need for legitimate swaps? What strategic risks create the pressure to undertake hollow swaps?
2. Management controls: How can the organization manage the risk associated with an improper or ineffective swap strategy?
3. Performance measurement: How can the organization measure swap-related risks? How can the auditor use these measurements as audit evidence?
4. Process controls: How can properly designed process controls help mitigate the risks associated with an improper or ineffective swap strategy?
5. Residual risks: What are the implications to the conduct of the audit if the risk of an improper and ineffective swap strategy is considered to be a residual risk? Consider the following five implications: (1) expectations about current performance results, (2) corporate viability, (3) control environment, (4) financial statement assertions, and (5) client's need for assistance.
6. Substantive audit tests: What substantive test might an auditor use to test swap transactions that are considered to be associated with high residual risk?

Auditing Resource Management Processes

13

Outline

INTRODUCTION

Sales and customer service, as well as supply chain management and production, are often considered the core or primary processes of most organizations. However, to be successful, all organizations need to mobilize and manage a broad variety of resources such as people, property, and capital. This chapter deals with how an organization would manage two of these important resources: facilities and capital (see Figure 13–1). Few organizations could succeed without effective management of these resources, and risks arising in these areas can have a significant impact on the conduct of the audit.

We first discuss the property management process. This process comprises the activities of acquiring, utilizing, and maintaining the organization's base of capital assets. We then discuss the financial resource management process, which consists of activities for obtaining and managing cash flow and financial capital such as

Figure 13–1   Overview of the Audit Process

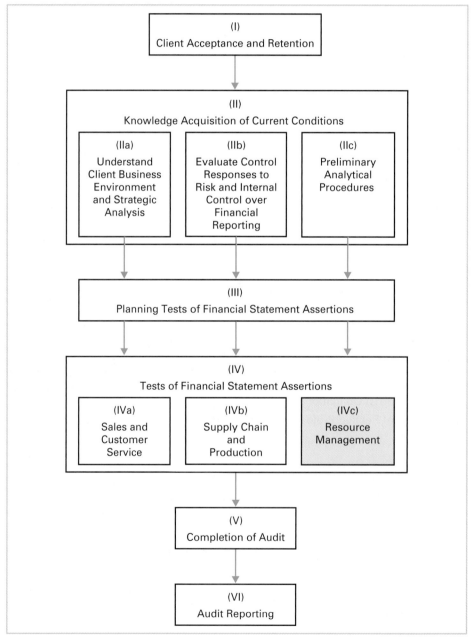

debt and equity. For each process, we will present a process map and prepare an internal threat analysis. After analyzing risks, controls, and performance indicators for each process, we will then discuss substantive tests that can be used to test financial statement assertions that are affected by the process.[1]

PART A: AUDITING THE PROPERTY MANAGEMENT PROCESS

PROCESS MAP

The property management process is the set of activities related to acquiring, preparing, and maintaining the organization's physical assets. Facilities include factories, warehouses, administrative offices, retail locations, equipment, computers, and vehicles. Maintenance and repair of assets is also part of this process. The wide range of assets included in this process creates a number of challenges because acquisition and maintenance may vary greatly depending on the type of asset. Scheduling and use of the assets in operations is not part of this process and would pertain to the specific processes where the assets are used (e.g., production scheduling).

> **Authoritative Guidance & Standards**
>
> This chapter applies standards covered in previous chapters to specific business processes—the property management and financial management processes. Several observations from auditing standards are included throughout the chapter (e.g., SAS 106, SAS 107, SAS 109, SAS 110, ISA 315, ISA 320, ISA 330, ISA 500).

Example

> The now infamous fraud involving WorldCom, which was the final blow leading the U.S. Congress to pass the Sarbanes-Oxley Act of 2002, was driven by a massive fraud involving property management. The fraud involved capitalization of $5 billion worth of expenses as a property account entitled prepaid capacity. All of these amounts should have been expensed as incurred but were instead capitalized as a capital asset to be expensed over time.

Objectives

A process map for property management is presented in Figure 13–2. The primary objective of property management is to assure that the organization has the productive capacity and facilities it needs to pursue its objectives and plans. In more precise terms, property management involves forecasting resource needs, acquiring appropriate resources at a reasonable cost, and maintaining facilities in appropriate working condition. Maintenance is particularly important because it is an ongoing activity and can directly affect the productivity, and even the safety, of personnel within the organization. Effective and reliable information processing is also important to facilitate process improvement and to assist in the forecasting of future needs.

Activities

The physical assets of an organization provide the productive base for its operations. Even "virtual" companies need some physical facilities and equipment. The activities necessary to manage these resources effectively include

- Assessing needs: The first step in the process is to identify the asset needs of the organization. The need for new factories, retail locations, vehicles, and

---

1 Human resource management is another important resource management process. We introduced the process map for human resource management in Chapter 6. In the appendix to this chapter, we discuss the nature of testing for transactions and accounts related to human resource management.

Figure 13–2   Process Map: Property Management

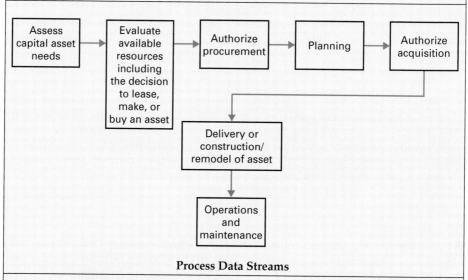

Process Objectives
- Effectively forecast and plan for current and future resource needs.
- Obtain capital resources that meet the technology and capacity needs of the organization.
- Maximize value of capital expenditures, including construction/remodeling.
- Establish efficient procedures for effective maintenance.
- Minimize operating costs.
- Minimize risk of asset losses or safety problems.
- Develop and implement contingency plans should major loss of property occur due to natural disaster or acts of terrorism.
- Maintain effective insurance coverage.
- Capture, process, and report information necessary for process improvement.

Process Activities

Assess capital asset needs → Evaluate available resources including the decision to lease, make, or buy an asset → Authorize procurement → Planning → Authorize acquisition → Delivery or construction/remodel of asset → Operations and maintenance

Process Data Streams

Information Feeds	*Information Generation*
- Strategic plans and budgets	- Acquisition decisions
- Capital budgets	- Building plans and schedules
- Capacity requirements	- Acquisition schedules
- Production specifications	- Acquisition budgets
- Suppliers/builders	- Asset acquisitions
- Location and infrastructure data	- Maintenance schedule
- Market data (e.g., costs, availability)	- Operating plans and procedures

Accounting Impact of Activities

Routine Transactions	*Non-routine Transactions*	*Accounting Estimates*
- Asset purchases*	- Asset construction/remodeling*	- Asset impairment
- Insurance expense	- Leases*	- Self-insured losses
- Utilities expense	- Asset disposals*	- Depreciation parameters
- Maintenance expense	- Cost abatements	
- Taxes	- Interest capitalization	
- Depreciation		

* Could be either routine or non-routine depending on organization's normal activities.

computers must be evaluated. Asset needs will usually be based on forecasts, future plans, and overall strategy. Effective strategic planning is critical for this step of the process.

- Evaluating available resources: There are often many alternatives available once a resource need is identified. Factories can be located in different cities, states/provinces, and countries depending on factors such as logistical infrastructure, employee base, and governmental incentives. Retail locations will depend on customer traffic, accessibility, and land costs. Options also exist for more mundane assets, such as trucks or computers. Effective property management requires a full analysis of the advantages and disadvantages of the various alternatives for acquiring assets including the decision to lease, make, or buy assets.

- Authorization of procurement: Once options have been specified and evaluated, senior management needs to make decisions concerning which options to pursue. Should a new factory be built in Tennessee or Tasmania? Should new trucks come from Volvo or General Motors? Should computers be supplied by Dell or Lenovo? These decisions will be based on preliminary information and tentative negotiations with potential suppliers.

- Planning: Formal negotiations with suppliers will determine contract prices and terms (including financing), delivery schedules or milestones, and service or warranty arrangements. Final selection of suppliers and specific models/versions/designs/floor plans will occur at this point in the process.

- Authorization of acquisition: Given the extensive details to be considered for most asset acquisitions, it is important that there be a separate review and approval of final plans for an acquisition. Significant asset acquisitions may involve approval by the board of directors. This step generally results in a signed contract with a chosen supplier and commitment to a delivery or construction schedule.

- Acquisition or construction/remodeling: For most assets, this step of the process involves taking delivery of the asset (e.g., vehicles, computers, furniture), physical set-up, and testing. For land or buildings, the acquisition process may be quite complex and time consuming, especially if the asset is to be constructed.

- Operations and maintenance: After delivery, all assets require continuous maintenance and upkeep, and occasional repairs. This is an ongoing activity in most organizations.

Execution of these activities may be relatively straightforward, as in the case of vehicle purchases, or may be very complex, as in the case of building a new factory. In general, the more unique the asset and the longer the lead time necessary to arrange for the acquisition, the more complex this process will be and the more things that can go wrong. Acquiring new computers usually involves no more than contacting a vendor, explaining the organization's needs, and negotiating the terms of a contract (including price, delivery and set-up, and service). Construction of a new building will involve complex planning with architects, attorneys, contractors, local government, and lenders. The tracking of costs on such a project can be a challenge, especially if construction uses internal resources (people, equipment) and funds (interest capitalization).

Transactions

The information flows associated with property management are described in Figure 13–2. Information for planning and control are particularly important to this process. Effective management of property and acquisitions is dependent on the availability of appropriate information. Although the occurrence of recordable transactions is less frequent than in many processes, accounting for plant, property, and equipment requires a number of accounts, including accumulated depreciation.

Most companies maintain separate accounts for different types of depreciable assets. For example, separate accounts may be used for tools, equipment, buildings, and land. Assets may be further classified as manufacturing, whose depreciation is capitalized as part of the inventory, or administrative, whose depreciation is charged off as a period cost. Finally, separate accounts may be used for assets that are acquired through capital lease arrangements. In general, asset accounts are used to record additions and disposals of physical assets at cost. Accumulated depreciation is used to record periodic depreciation expense and must also be adjusted when an asset disposal occurs. Depreciation expense and gains or losses on asset disposals are included in the income statement.

A number of different types of transactions occur within the property management process including

- Purchase of equipment or other facilities assets (e.g., shelving for a warehouse)
- Construction/remodeling of facilities (including interest capitalization)
- Operating expenses
- Maintenance and repairs
- Sale of assets
- Leasing

Transaction documentation will vary depending on the nature of the acquisition. Routine purchases of equipment and machinery may be very similar to acquisitions of material discussed in Chapter 12. Recurring operating expenses are handled in a similar manner. Other transactions, such as purchase of real estate or leasing arrangements, may involve complex legal documents and contracts. Periodic adjustments to asset accounts (e.g., depreciation) may be supported by a journal entry ticket alone. Repairs and maintenance involve the additional concern that they be properly classified as assets or expenses depending on the nature of the repair.

INTERNAL THREAT ANALYSIS

Analysis of Process Risks

Internal threat analysis for property management is illustrated in Figure 13–3. Potential risks are described in the first column. Mitigating controls and relevant performance measures are also identified for each risk. Examples of process risks arising from property management include

People Risk

- Managerial risk: Many decisions related to the acquisition of physical assets can be critical to the organization's success as they often involve a significant investment of funds and can be very difficult to retract or fix. Poor decision making and management can lead to insufficient capacity (risk 1), excess

Figure 13–3   Internal Threat Analysis: Property Management

Process Risks	Controls Linked to Risks	Performance Measures
(1) Insufficient capacity.	• Long-term planning and budgeting • Monitor current usage • Adequate lead time for new facilities • Establish appropriate maintenance program • Establish back-up sources for peak loads	• Total capacity measures • Space utilization statistics • Space shortages • Revenue per square foot • Repair costs
(2) Excess capacity.	• Long-term planning and budgeting • Procedures for authorizing and disposing of property • Utilize flexible resources when possible (e.g., employee-shared space)	• Space utilization statistics • Time-in-use measures • Revenue per square foot • Value received for asset disposals
(3) Impaired asset values.	• Periodic review of asset portfolio • Independent appraisals	• Market value of assets • Market value per square foot • Time-to-sell property assets • Percent markdown on disposed assets
(4) Excess deterioration due to poor maintenance.	• Appropriate maintenance schedules • Outsourcing of maintenance activities • Monitor technology and competition for possible improvements • Provide appropriate training to personnel	• Maintenance budgets • Cleanliness ratings • Equipment breakdowns • Repair costs • Days lost to equipment failures • Rate of production defects due to equipment problems
(5) Inefficient space utilization.	• Systematic plans for space usage • Long term plans for acquisitions • Monitor current usage • Flexible space-usage designs	• Space utilization statistics • Frequency and cost of reconfigurations • Cost per square foot • Revenue per square foot • Square feet per employee
(6) Casualty losses including loss of use of significant physical facilities due to natural disaster or terrorism.	• Periodic safety inspections • Adequate insurance or self-insurance • Crisis management and contingency plans • Disaster recovery plans	• Value of casualty losses • Insurance claims • Uninsured losses • Days lost to crisis or damage conditions • Insurance premiums and deductibles • Tests of disaster recovery plans

(continued)

Figure 13–3   *(continued)*

Process Risks	Controls Linked to Risks	Performance Measures
(7) Lack of resources to acquire assets.	• Effective capital budgeting • Access to financial resources • Effective management of cash flow • Creative financing (e.g., leasing)	• Cost of borrowed funds for project • Percentage of funds from outside sources • Amount of debt service relative to cash flow from project • Internal rate of return
(8) Poor location selection.	• Investigate all acquisitions and location characteristics • Negotiate arrangements with local officials • Evaluate transportation and infrastructure of area • Evaluate quality of local human resources	• Cost to acquire property • Local demographics • Travel time to primary customers or from key suppliers • Travel or transportation costs • Value of incentives or abatements from local authorities
(9) Cost overruns or delays.	• Obtain bids for acquisitions • Establish acquisition plan and timing of milestones for completion • Monitor acquisition costs on a timely basis	• Actual cost compared to budget • Days late on acquisitions • Project progress relative to milestones
(10) Inaccurate information processing.	• Proper completion and verification of supporting documents • Appropriate segregation of duties across activities • Use of standard control numbers for parts, vendors, products, etc. • Update files and accounting records on a timely basis	• Percent of transactions subject to processing errors • Size of transaction adjustments • Number of transaction adjustments
(11) Inaccurate cost measurement.	• Establish procedures and policies for determining asset cost • Adequate documentation of acquisitions • Proper allocation of internal costs for acquisitions	• Actual costs compared to budget • Percentage of internal costs allocated to capital assets (e.g., interest) • Asset costs relative to appraised value
(12) Improper or unauthorized usage.	• Physical security • Proper authorization procedures • Maintain inventory of physical assets including location information • Periodic physical inventory observation	• Value of lost assets • Book to physical adjustments for physical assets

Figure 13–3 *(continued)*

Process Risks	Controls Linked to Risks	Performance Measures
(13) Lack of compliance with regulations (e.g., zoning, environmental)	• Monitor appropriate property regulations and environmental laws • Periodic inspections • Long-term planning to assure compliance with changes in regulations • Adequate capital budgeting	• Number of known violations • Fines and penalties for violations • Days lost due to violations • Cost of environmental clean-up
(14) Inaccurate or unreasonable amortization.	• Establish amortization policies and procedures by asset type • Monitor economic and technology trends that may impact assets • Comparative analysis with other organizations and competitors	• Useful life of assets by type • Useful lives relative to tax standards • Useful lives relative to competitors • Percentage of assets in use that are fully depreciated • Average gain/loss on asset disposals
(15) Safety hazards.	• Monitor safety and health regulations • Perform periodic safety inspections	• Number of worker injuries • Cost of time lost to worker injuries • Worker's compensation costs • Regulatory (e.g. OSHA in United States citations)

capacity (risk 2), poor maintenance (risk 4), lack of resources (risk 7), poor locations (risk 8), and cost overruns (risk 10).

• Ethics risk: The integrity of employees pertains to their work ethic as well as their honesty. For property management, slipshod efforts could lead to sloppy maintenance (risk 4), casualty losses (risk 6), lack of regulatory compliance (risk 14), or safety hazards (risk 16). Outright employee fraud such as kick-backs from contractors could be associated with cost overruns (risk 10) or improper usage of assets (risk 13).

• Human resource risk: In the context of property management, human resource risk refers to how well people fulfill their duties. Consequently, poor performance by personnel can contribute to the risk of poor maintenance (risk 4), cost overruns (risk 10), or improper usage (risk 13).

Direct Process Risks

• Operational risk: Ineffective or inefficient property management can result in excess capacity (risk 2), impaired asset values (risk 3), poor maintenance (risk 4), inefficient space utilization (risk 5), cost overruns or delays (risk 10), and safety hazards (risk 16).

• Information risk: Problems with information systems will have the most direct effect on the risk of inaccurate information processing (risk 11), inaccurate cost measurement (risk 12), and inaccurate amortization (risk 15).

Indirect Process Risks

- Technology risk: The design of facilities will depend on current construction and manufacturing technology. Tracking of costs will also depend on the reliability of technology used in information systems (risk 11). Technology risks related to construction can affect the rate of deterioration of the facility (risk 4) and the potential for cost overruns (risk 10).
- Planning risk: Property management is particularly dependent on financial, budgeting, and contingency planning decisions. Insufficient resources or poor planning can lead to insufficient capacity (risk 1), poor maintenance (risk 4), loss of use of significant physical facilities due to natural disaster or terrorism (risk 6), and a lack of resources to fund acquisitions (risk 7).
- Regulatory risk: The location, design, construction, and maintenance of facilities are all subject to extensive regulation. In the case of constructed assets, regulations can be as detailed as dictating the number and width of doorways and the accessibility of the premises to disabled employees and patrons. Regulatory risk could lead to noncompliance with zoning (risk 14) or safety hazards (risk 16).

Example

Loblaws, a large Canadian grocery chain, expanded into a French speaking part of Canada where the legal system was more similar to France's Civil Code than to English speaking countries' common law. Loblaws did not follow local zoning laws carefully in constructing a large state-of-the-art retail grocery store and found itself facing a court ordered demolition of the building as that was the only penalty the Civil Code provided for such a violation.

The sources of process risks interact to influence the overall level of risks. For example, poor maintenance leading to deterioration of facilities, and possible impairment of value, can be caused by weak planning, lazy employees, or insufficient maintenance resources. The auditor should consider the interaction of risks when assessing the residual risks of a process.

ANALYSIS OF PROCESS CONTROLS AND INTERNAL CONTROL OVER FINANCIAL REPORTING

Figure 13–3 identifies a number of controls that might be used to mitigate various property management process risks including

- Performance reviews and monitoring: Assessment of needs and long-term planning are critical to effective property management. To facilitate this process, management should actively monitor and react to
  - Strategic and contingency plans
  - Forecasts of resource needs
  - Acquisition planning and identification of alternatives
  - Acquisitions in process, including construction
  - Contract negotiations
  - Maintenance planning and activities
  - Asset values and amortization
  - Regulatory compliance and safety records
- Segregation of duties: The appropriate segregation of duties for acquisitions is similar to those specified for acquisitions of material: namely, there should be

separation among need assessment, procurement and contract negotiation, acquisition authorization, asset delivery, payment authorization, and asset accounting.

- Processing controls: Authorizations are needed for planning, to begin procurement and negotiations, to identify alternatives, to execute a transaction, to accept delivery, and to make payments. Adequate records and documents are needed to assure accurate accounting and are similar to those used for materials procurement and production. Some examples include procurement and purchase documents, receiving reports, vendor's invoices and statements, checks for disbursements, contracts, and internal documents for cost allocations of labor, materials, and overhead. Most companies will also maintain a ledger of long-lived assets that summarizes the date they were acquired, the cost, and related depreciation information. Independent verifications and reconciliations over purchases, disbursements, and general ledger accounts can be used to verify accurate transaction processing.

- Physical controls: Important physical controls relate to taking possession and utilizing acquired assets. Controls should be designed to limit access and the use of assets for legitimate purposes, and to minimize the risk of casualty losses or safety hazards. Additionally, records and documents related to asset acquisitions should be properly handled and protected.

Bad decisions related to capital assets can impair the competitive position of an organization. Consequently, controls related to planning and authorization are critical for successful and efficient property management. Given that most asset acquisitions are high value and occur infrequently, controls may be unevenly applied and adapted for each transaction. This uneven application of controls may be problematic for organizations subject to the integrated audit where all material processes are expected to have adequate internal controls over financial reporting. Such inconsistent controls could be considered a control deficiency that might be significant or material.

EVALUATION OF PROCESS PERFORMANCE INDICATORS

Relevant process indicators for property management are listed in Figure 13–3. These indicators can provide a source of evidence concerning risks in the property management process. However, many of these measures may not be available within the basic accounting system, so data availability and reliability may impact the auditor's ability to evaluate the performance measures. For example, measures of capacity utilization may indicate if a company has excess capacity that may need to be written off. The rate of defects in production may indicate that equipment is old and needs to be repaired or replaced, or could indicate that the equipment is being improperly utilized. In either event, the auditor would need to consider whether the observed defect rates are consistent with the standard costs of units being produced.

TESTS OF FINANCIAL STATEMENT ASSERTIONS: PROPERTY, EQUIPMENT, AND DEPRECIATION

Typical substantive tests for plant, property, and equipment are summarized in Figure 13–4. The approach to testing property assertions is based on the assumption that beginning asset balances were previously audited. The testing of assets

Figure 13–4   Substantive Tests of Plant and Equipment Transactions, Accounts, and Disclosures

Management Assertion	Typical Substantive Audit Procedures
Accuracy/Valuation: Plant, property, and equipment balances reconcile with subsidiary ledgers and the general ledger.	• Obtain schedules of additions and disposals of plant and equipment assets for the fiscal period and test for mechanical accuracy (including the computation of gains and losses for disposals). • Reconcile total additions and disposals with activity in the general ledger. • Tie in opening asset balances with prior-year audit results.* • Recompute balances in plant and equipment assets and accumulated depreciation using prior-year balances and current-year activity.
Existence: Recorded plant, property, and equipment exist.	• Vouch a sample of acquisitions selected from the additions schedule. • Physically observe the existence of a sample of plant and equipment assets. • Vouch a sample of disposals selected from the disposals schedule and verify supporting documentation.
Completeness: All existing plant, property, and equipment assets of the company are recorded.	• Select a sample of repairs and maintenance charges and review supporting documentation to determine that payments have been correctly recorded. • Physically observe the existence of a sample of plant and equipment assets. • Review lease agreements for possible capital leases.
Rights and obligations: Plant, property, and equipment are owned by the company.	• Examine vendors' invoices related to additions. • Obtain a representation letter from management pertaining to the ownership of assets. • Review minutes from board of directors and other management meetings to identify significant asset disposals.
Accuracy/Valuation: Plant, property, and equipment are correctly valued with reasonable allowance for depreciation.	• Vouch asset additions for accuracy. • Vouch disposals for accuracy, including relief of accumulated depreciation. • Test depreciation expense and accumulated depreciation using substantive analytical procedures. • Test the computation of capitalized interest for self-constructed assets. • Inquire as to unused assets or assets with permanent impairment of value to be written off. • Confirm terms of contracts or leases.

* If prior-year financial statements are unaudited or unavailable, the auditor will need to extend the tests of additions to include all assets held at year end.

Figure 13-4   *(continued)*

Management Assertion	Typical Substantive Audit Procedures
Classification: Plant, property, and equipment balances are correctly classified.	• Vouch asset additions for accuracy of classification. • Select a sample of repairs and maintenance charges and review supporting documentation to determine that payments have been correctly classified.
Cutoff: Plant, property, and equipment transactions are recorded in the proper period.	• Perform cutoff tests for acquisitions and disbursements and vouch transactions near year end.
Completeness/Existence/ Valuation: All required disclosures pertaining to plant, property, and equipment are included in the financial statements.	• Complete a disclosure checklist for plant and equipment assets. • Review board of directors' minutes, bank confirmations, attorney letters, and other correspondence for indications that assets have been pledged or leased. • Obtain representations from management about disclosures related to plant and equipment assets.

then focuses on verifying current-year additions and disposals only.[2] Accumulated depreciation is verified by examining current-year disposals and performing substantive analytical procedures on current-year depreciation expense. Gains and losses on disposals are tested as part of the testing of asset disposals. Lease arrangements are also examined to determine that their treatment as capital or operating leases is appropriate. The primary substantive tests for property include

> **Authoritative Guidance & Standards**
> Held property must be tested for impairment by assessing fair values. Authoritative guidance for gathering auditing evidence to assess management's assessment of fair values and to assess fair values is found in SAS 101 and ISA 545.

- Substantive analytical procedures
- Tests of valuation and allocation
- Tests of transactions

SUBSTANTIVE ANALYTICAL PROCEDURES

Substantive analytical procedures can be very useful for testing depreciation. Most companies use a single depreciation method and classify assets into categories with a single useful life (e.g., 5, 10, or 25 years), so that the auditor can usually generate a relatively precise estimate for depreciation expense. To illustrate, assume that the client has two types of depreciable assets: buildings and equipment. The buildings are assumed to have a useful life of 30 years and the equipment has a useful life of 10 years. The auditor can estimate depreciation expense based on the average recorded cost of the assets, the useful life, and the depreciation method used by the client (assumed to be straight line in this example):

---

2 If the opening balance for plant, property, and equipment has not been audited, the auditor would probably need to obtain a trial balance of all assets included in the account(s). This schedule would need to be tested for accuracy and individual assets would be tested using vouching (valuation) and physical examination (existence).

	Buildings	Equipment
Average balance of depreciable assets	$150,000	$80,000
Useful life	÷ 30 yrs	÷ 10 yrs
Estimated depreciation expense	$ 5,000	$ 8,000

The auditor estimates that depreciation should total about $13,000. If the client's records indicate depreciation that is close to that amount, the auditor would probably conclude that depreciation was properly recorded unless other evidence of a problem became available. However, if the client's records show an amount that is significantly different, the auditor would investigate the discrepancy. In such cases, the auditor would probably start by refining the estimate. For example, the auditor might need to consider additional categories of assets with different useful lives.[3] If that does not close the gap, other substantive tests of depreciation may be required (e.g., testing depreciation for specific material assets).

Other accounts where substantive analytical procedures could be useful include insurance expense, property taxes, and utilities. Repairs and maintenance expense relative to gross plant assets is also a useful measure and provides an indication of proper classification of asset-related expenditures. The strength of analytical evidence will depend on the precision of the estimate, the reliability of the information used as input to the estimation, and the size of the discrepancy between the estimate and the actual recorded value. Again, if the unexplained discrepancy is large, the auditor will need to follow up until satisfied that there is no material misstatement in the account in question.

TESTS OF VALUATION AND ALLOCATION

The auditor should obtain schedules of asset additions and disposals for each material asset account. These schedules should be tested for accuracy and the activity included in the schedules should be reconciled with what is recorded in the general ledger. An example of a schedule of additions for equipment is presented in Figure 13–5. The schedule of additions and disposals should provide the information needed to roll the balance of plant, property and equipment forward from the beginning to the end of the year.

Auditors should also test property, plant, and equipment for impairment. For example, auditors should consider whether there are any capital assets associated with any products that have been discontinued (or for which production has been significantly reduced). In many cases, new versions of products or different products require different capital assets, resulting in impairments in assets currently in place. Furthermore, decisions to move physical administration, manufacturing, distribution, or retail operations likely will result in impairments to buildings, capital leases, and even land in some cases.

Example

During the early 2000s, Wal-Mart underwent a major shift in its stores, moving from discount stores to Supercenter hypermarkets that include grocery in addition to its previous product offerings. Accordingly, as Wal-Mart builds new Supercenters in the same general locations as existing discount stores, the old buildings may be impaired in an accounting sense while awaiting sale to other retailers or real estate companies.

---

3 Estimated depreciation expense may need to be computed separately for each category of asset. The auditor would also have to include depreciation charged to inventory and cost of goods sold when assessing the reasonableness of the estimate.

Figure 13–5   Audit of Plant and Equipment Additions*

			F-1
	Jones Manufacturing, Inc.		
	Analysis of Equipment Additions		*WRK*
	For Year Ended 12/31/x6		*PBC 1/24/x7*
Date	Description of Transaction	Amount	
1/31/x6	Purchase of furniture for factory personnel from Walnut Office Furniture.	400,000 ✓	
2/20/x6	Purchase of heavy duty drill presses from Morgan Tool Co.	350,000 ✓	
3/15/x6	Purchase of production control computer equipment from IBM including terminals and network software.	845,000 ✓	
7/20/x6	Purchase and installation of conveyor belt for moving completed inventory from Hanover Systems Inc.	554,000 ✓	
10/6/x6	Purchase of 30 delivery trucks from Johnson's Heavy Truck Sales and Service.	1,456,000 ✓	
	Other additions (less than $100,000 each)	418,000	
	Total additions to Equipment	4,023,000	*F*
		T	

T Footed and agrees.

✓ Traced to supporting documentation (voucher package). Verified amount of transaction and classification of asset. Examined supporting documentation for proper authorizations. No exceptions noted.

* This facsimile working paper assumes that the lead schedule for plant, property, and equipment is indexed as *F*.

TESTS OF TRANSACTIONS

Property management typically has relatively few routine transactions except for maintenance and basic operations, and testing for those transactions is usually minimal because the biggest cost of maintenance is payroll, which is considered in the human resource process (see Appendix and Chapters 6, 7 and 10). Smaller acquisitions for equipment and furniture may be common and subject to an over-all contract so a small sample of such transactions may be tested. However, many asset acquisitions are large and infrequent. The auditor will often vouch the largest asset acquisitions because they may be individually material to the financial statements. Vouching individual additions involves examining supporting documentation to verify the valuation of the asset (see notations in Figure 13–5). Confirmations for contracts and leases may be obtained and some assets may be physically examined. For assets that are self-constructed, the auditor will need to examine evidence of the materials (inventory), labor (payroll), and administrative oversight used in production, as well as the possibility that interest should be capitalized as part of the cost of the asset.

Asset disposals would be tested by examining supporting documentation and vouching receipts, with the added steps of verifying the relief of accumulated depreciation and the computation of a gain or loss on the transaction. For assets that were traded for new assets, the auditor will need to verify the proper accounting for exchanges of nonmonetary assets and cross-reference the disposal with the asset addition.

PART B: AUDITING THE FINANCIAL MANAGEMENT PROCESS

PROCESS MAP

The purpose of the financial management process is to forecast and control the timing and nature of the company's cash flow stream so as to provide adequate support for ongoing operations. The key to financial management is balancing cash inflows from operations and sources of capital against the outflows needed for operations and long-term investments. Companies raise capital by issuing equity and borrowing from diverse creditors (banks, bond holders, vendors), and make short-term investments with funds not needed immediately.

Objectives

A process map for financial management is presented in Figure 13–6. The primary objective of financial management is to manage financial resources to allow the organization to achieve its desired goals. More specifically, financial planning has the objective of effectively planning for the cash flow needs of the organization and making arrangements to assure that adequate financial resources are available. This process involves identifying potential sources of capital, minimizing the cost of the organization's capital structure, and making sure obligations can be paid on time. Another objective is to maximize the earnings on invested funds subject to a board or management determined tolerable level of risk.

Activities

The key activities that comprise financial management are depicted in Figure 13–6. The importance of these activities is conditional on the strategic decisions that the organization makes concerning its capital structure, such as whether to borrow extensively or maintain a relatively debt-free balance sheet. Financial management activities include

- Planning and budgeting: Projecting cash flows from operations is the starting point for financial planning. Strategic goals and long-term plans dictate how much free cash flow the organization needs at any point in time. If cash flow is inadequate, either plans need to change or other sources of financing must be arranged. Accurate forecasting becomes the basis for critical decisions about financial structure and the need for additional capital.
- Evaluating financing options: An organization can raise funds externally by borrowing or issuing equity. Borrowed funds can come from bank loans, publicly issued bonds, commercial paper, leases, or even vendors. Equity financing usually involves issuing common or preferred stock. A key concern of this activity is monitoring the cost of capital and assessing the most reasonable source of funds.
- Borrowing funds: The key elements of this activity are identifying sources of credit and arranging acceptable terms. This activity results in the inflow of financial resources.

Figure 13–6   Process Map: Financial Management

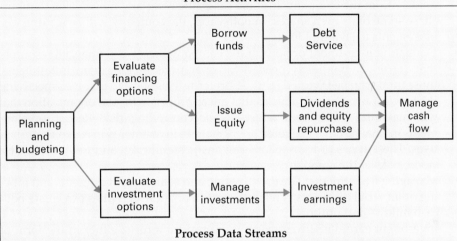

Process Objectives
- Prepare accurate budgets and financial reports on a timely basis.
- Optimize capital structure given current economic environment.
- Minimize cost of capital over long term.
- Maximize return from investments for a given level of risk tolerance.
- Manage cash flows to meet obligations on a timely basis.
- Comply with obligations and terms of financing contracts.
- Capture, process, and report information necessary for process improvement.

Process Activities

Process Data Streams

Information Feeds
- Strategic plan and budgets
- Financing sources and potential lenders
- Financial market data including stock prices, bond yields, and derivative product availability
- Capital budgets
- Cash flow requirements
- Financial asset levels
- Stock compensation plans

Information Generation
- Budgets and forecasts
- Investment transactions
- Borrowing transactions
- Risk assessments associated with investing and borrowing especially related to derivative transactions
- Equity transactions
- Investment performance
- Cost of capital
- Debt contracts and covenants
- Financial reports

Accounting Impact of Activities

Routine Transactions
- Line of credit
- Notes payable
- Debt payments
- Interest
- Dividends
- Investments*
- Sale of investments
- Investment earnings
- Exercise of options

Non-routine Transactions
- Bonds payable
- Debt retirement
- Equity issues
- Equity repurchase
- Option grants
- Mergers and acquisitions

Accounting Estimates
- Impairment of investments
- Stock compensation
- Cost allocation for mergers.

* Many companies are attempting to employ derivatives to manage risks in a way that they have not before. Hence, while some investments might be routine, others may be non-routine until sufficient organizational learning has taken place.

- Debt service: This activity involves the routine handling of periodic interest and principle payments.
- Issuing equity: Equity financing is usually more complex than borrowing because of the need to engage underwriters and other financial professionals. Also, public stock offerings are subject to extensive examination and regulation by government agencies, especially securities market regulators like the SEC. In addition to straight stock issues, new securities can be issued as part of stock option or employee stock purchase plans. This activity creates a cash inflow for the organization.
- Returns to shareholders: Dividends constitute the primary return to shareholders from the company. In some cases, the company may decide to repurchase some of its own shares. In both cases, the company will be making disbursements to shareholders.
- Evaluating investment options: If the company has excess financial resources that are not immediately needed for operations or long-term investments, those funds can be invested in the short term. This activity involves specifying the types of investment vehicles that are appropriate for the organization that will maximize investment returns while controlling risk. Recent developments in finance have triggered an increase in investments in complex derivatives. These types of transactions can create significant, and often misunderstood, risks to the company.
- Managing investments: The daily buying and selling of investments and moving of financial resources is relatively routine. These activities can create both cash inflows and outflows.
- Investment earnings: Investments will produce returns either in the form of interest and dividends or capital gains. This activity focuses on realizing and recording investment earnings, which generally will produce a cash inflow for the company.
- Manage cash flow: The combined effect of operations, financing transactions, and investment activities determines net cash flow to the company at any point in time. Minimizing the amount of idle financial resources while satisfying all operating and capital obligations is the purpose of cash flow management.

The complexity of financial management will primarily depend on the capital structure of the organization and the predictability of cash flows. A company that is highly leveraged may have more difficult challenges related to financial management than one that is equity financed, especially if cash flow from operations is weak or deteriorating. Financing with bank loans and basic equity is relatively easy to manage. Financing with publicly traded debt, leases, derivatives, and hybrid securities (such as convertible bonds) increase the challenges of financial management.

Transactions

Financial resource management involves a broad range of potential transactions affecting numerous accounts including

- Cash and cash equivalents
- Short term investments (marketable securities)
- Long term investments
- Notes payable
- Debt obligations

- Capitalized lease obligations
- Shareholder's equity (and related accounts)

Most large financial transactions are unique and occur relatively infrequently (e.g., issuing stock). Proper processing of these transactions receives extensive scrutiny from senior management and the board of directors. Routine transactions such as the receipt of dividends or payment of interest are often highly automated. Proper processing and accounting for routine transactions is similar to the cash receipt and cash disbursement activities that have been discussed in earlier chapters.

Investments can be either short or long term in duration. Short-term investments are usually made with excess cash that is not needed for operations. Due to their short duration, these investments will be structured to avoid downside market risk and maximize cash earnings (e.g., interest). Long-term investments are usually undertaken for strategic purposes, for example, as a precursor to acquiring another company. These investments are probably less concerned with downside market risk and focus more on the underlying benefits of the securities acquired. Regardless of the form of the investment, the basic events are the same: buy an investment, collect periodic earnings, sell the investment.

An organization can borrow funds in a number of ways. Common forms of borrowed funds are bank loans (i.e., notes payable) and bonds that are issued to the public. Other forms of borrowed funds include lines of credit, leases, and specialized financial instruments. Although there is a wide disparity across types of borrowings, the basic elements of the transactions are essentially the same: funds are received, interest is paid, funds are returned. For example, principal repayments may be periodic or in a lump sum. Interest may be explicit and periodic, or may be implicit (as in the case of zero coupon bonds). The obligation may allow either the borrower or the lender to terminate the arrangement (e.g., through a call or prepayment provision). Some obligations may not appear on the financial statements at all as a result of specialized accounting treatment (e.g., operating leases).

A company can issue two general types of equity: common stock and preferred stock. Most equity transactions involve large amounts and must comply with complex regulations but are relatively simple from an accounting perspective (e.g., the issuance of common stock and the payment of dividends). Stock options, stock rights, and acquisitions funded with stock and convertible securities can raise some difficult accounting issues, however. The basic elements of all equity transactions are the issuance of an equity security (and the receipt of consideration), the payment of dividends and, occasionally, the repurchase/retirement of equity. Most companies maintain a *stock book*, or similar ledger, to keep track of who owns the stock of the company at any point in time. Publicly traded companies in many countries must have an independent stock transfer agent that handles all transactions related to who owns the stock of the company at any given time.

As financial management has grown in sophistication over the past decade, financial managers have taken advantage of complex financial derivatives that change the risk profile of a debt or equity instrument. For example, a company's fixed rate long-term mortgage on a building can be converted into a variable rate demand loan via the creative use of derivative contracts. Here the auditor needs to identify the resulting risks and determine whether a specialist level assistance is needed to determine proper accounting and disclosure. Additionally, *hybrid* instruments are frequently found that have aspects of debt and equity rolled into one security. The classification of this type of instrument is problematic, as the financial accounting rules are complex in this area, and regulatory scrutiny tends to be high, as these instruments are often traded on public markets.

INTERNAL THREAT ANALYSIS

Analysis of Process Risks

Internal threat analysis for financial management is illustrated in Figure 13–7. A broad set of potential process risks are listed in the first column including

People Risks

- Managerial risk: Determining capital structure and investment policies are key responsibilities of management. Poor analysis and decision making can lead to ineffective planning (risk 1), inappropriate debt or equity transactions (risk 4), weak capital structure (risk 6), unintended risk exposures (risk 7), and poor investment decisions (risk 9).
- Ethics risk: The control environment of an organization has a direct impact on financial resource management because of the liquidity of the assets that these managers deal with. Consequently, unethical or dishonest employees may make inappropriate investment decisions (risk 8), undertake inappropriate actions as a result of misaligned incentives for financial managers (risk 1), or incur violations of securities laws (risk 10).
- Human resource risk: Because financial transactions tend to be complex, the effectiveness and efficiency of financial management is dependent on the competence and expertise of personnel. Weak personnel can contribute to ineffective planning (risk 1), excess risk exposures (risks 7 and 9), inappropriate transactions (risk 8), and violations of securities laws (risk 10).

Direct Process Risks

- Operational risk: The operations of financial management pertain primarily to planning, processing, and accounting for investment and capital transactions. Consequently, operational weaknesses are most likely to lead to inadequate cash flow (risk 2) or an imbalance of financial resources and obligations (risk 5).
- Information risk: Given the importance of information to effective and efficient financial resource management, the impact of inaccurate or incomplete information can be critical. Unreliable information can lead to poor planning (risk 1), violations of debt covenants (risk 3), and exposure to excess risk levels (7).

Indirect Process Risks

- Technology risk: Recent years have seen tremendous innovations in cash management and financing structures. These trends are often complex and difficult to implement. Technology problems in financial management can lead to an imbalance of investments and obligations (risk 5), inadequate cash flows for operational purposes (risk 2), and excessive risks (risks 7 and 9).
- Planning risk: The effectiveness of planning depends on having adequate competent staff and resources available to perform the diverse activities that comprise the process. Inadequate resources can contribute to ineffective planning

Figure 13–7   Internal Threat Analysis: Financial Management

Process Risks	Controls Linked to Risks	Performance Measures
(1) Ineffective planning and budgeting including inappropriate incentives to financial resource management.	• Establish strong financial information systems • Establish independent budgeting and forecasting group • Senior management actively involved in planning and budgeting • Have budget and plans reviewed by line managers • Establish policies for compensation of financial resources managers that does not give them incentives to invest in riskier investments than firm policy allows	• Extent and nature of budget variances • Number of budget amendments • Cycle time for budget preparation • Finance and budgeting department head count • Cost of budgeting and planning department • Compensation contracts for financial resource managers
(2) Inadequate cash flow.	• Effective cash flow budgeting • Establish adequate lines of credit • Optimize timing of disbursements • Optimize use of cash float	• Cash balances • Average draws on lines of credit • Receivable turnover relative to payable turnover • Amount of free cash flow • Interest or fixed charge coverage ratio • Level of short-term borrowings • Bond ratings • Market valuation of debt
(3) Violations of debt or other agreements.	• Monitor compliance with debt covenants on timely basis • Effective and independent internal audit group • Proactive involvement with creditor groups	• Number of violations • Frequency of violations • Level of working capital • Interest coverage ratio • Dividend payout rate • Bond ratings
(4) Inappropriate debt or equity transactions.	• Establish policies concerning acceptable terms for borrowings and equity transactions • All debt and equity transactions approved at Board level • Engage outside experts to assist on new issues. • Monitor debt and equity position on a timely basis	• Cost of capital • Cost of debt • Amount of free cash flow • Leverage ratios • Return on equity • Market valuation of debt and equity • Market "beta"

(continued)

Figure 13–7   *(continued)*

Process Risks	Controls Linked to Risks	Performance Measures
(5) Imbalance between investments and obligations or cash flow.	• Establish formal investment policies for excess cash • Match investments to timing of cash needs • Establish lines of credit to provide financing flexibility	• Time-to-maturity of investments • Yield on investments • Cash flow from investing activities
(6) Suboptimal capital structure.	• Effective financial planning and budgeting • Engage outside experts to assist in planning • Establish lines of credit to provide financing flexibility	• Cost of capital • Cost of debt • Market valuation of debt and equity • Market return on common shares
(7) Excessive or unknown risk exposures (e.g., derivatives, guarantees).	• Establish formal policy on acceptable derivative investments • Monitor derivative and value at risk on a timely basis • Senior-level approval of derivative transactions • Independent appraisal of riskiness and value of derivative investments • Effective and independent internal audit group	• Losses due to derivatives • Value at risk for derivatives • Volume of hedging activity • Yield on derivative investments • Yield on investments
(8) Unauthorized or inappropriate investment transactions.	• Engage outside experts to assist with investment planning • Establish formal policies on acceptable investment strategies • Monitor investments on a timely basis. • Senior-level approval of all non-routine investments • Effective and independent internal audit group	• Violations of investment guidelines • Value at risk in investments • Yield on investments
(9) Unforeseen changes in market conditions that cause losses.	• Establish process to monitor and react to market changes • Engage outside experts to assist with investment planning • Establish policies and procedures for risk- hedging activities	• Unrealized losses • Realized losses • Insider trading activity • Yield on investments

Figure 13–7   *(continued)*

Process Risks	Controls Linked to Risks	Performance Measures
(10) Violations of security regulations.	• Effective board and senior management oversight • Establish formal policies and procedures for financial reporting and accounting choices • Engage outside experts to assist with investment planning • Effective and independent internal audit group	• Citations from regulatory bodies • Timeliness of required filings

(risk 1), inadequate cash flows for operational purposes (risk 2), and poor control over risk exposures (risks 7 and 9).

- Regulatory risk: Many of the individual transactions generated by financial management are subject to significant regulatory oversight, especially the issuance of bonds or equity securities. Failure to comply with regulations can lead to inappropriate investments (risk 8) and violations of security laws (risk 10).

There is a great deal of overlap among the various sources of risk. The effectiveness of planning may be particularly problematic given that performance depends on the quality of management, personnel, technology, and the process used to develop plans and budgets.

ANALYSIS OF PROCESS CONTROLS AND INTERNAL CONTROL OVER FINANCIAL REPORTING

Figure 13–7 also identifies numerous controls that might mitigate the risks of financial management. Key controls may include

- Performance reviews and monitoring: Effective financial management will be facilitated if management monitors and reacts to
  - Market conditions especially changes in the economic environment
  - Trends in financing structure and financial transactions
  - Cash flow budgets and forecasts
  - Compliance with debt covenants and regulations
  - Cost of capital
  - Investment policies and the nature of acceptable investments
  - Investment performance
- Segregation of duties: Incompatible duties related to financial management include authorization of capital structure and investment policies, authorization of investment transactions, processing of receipt and disbursement transactions, physical access to financial assets, and information processing for financial activities.
- Processing controls: Authorizations are critical to financial management because transactions are often sizable and involve financial resources that are highly liquid. Individual investment and financing transactions should be

subject to appropriate high-level authorization. Transaction processing procedures should be established for investments, investment income, debt, debt service, equity, and dividends. The broad range of transactions may require a diverse set of procedures. Processing controls would focus on cash receipts and disbursements, as well as on the valuation of investment and financing transactions. The company should maintain a complete inventory of all investments, whether held by a third party (e.g., broker) or in their own possession. These should be reviewed to determine if the investments are still appropriate and that related income is being properly recognized. For debt, special considerations should be given to retiring obligations and amortizing discounts or premiums when the effective interest rate on debt differs from the stated rate. Tracking of equity interests (e.g., to determine the owner of record for payment of a dividend) is usually facilitated by employing a *registrar* or *stock transfer agent* to monitor shareholder transactions.

- Physical controls: Limitations on access to investments, cash, and accounting records for these assets and liabilities are important in the financial management process.

Routine transactions such as disbursements and receipts are subject to the same controls as similar transactions in other processes. Non-routine transactions tend to be scrutinized by senior management and the board of directors, and controls focus on detailed valuation and authorization of such transactions.

EVALUATION OF PROCESS PERFORMANCE INDICATORS

Relevant performance indicators for financial management are listed in the last column of Figure 13–7. Because most of the important indicators involve financial information, the measures are generally available and reliable. These performance measures can provide the auditor with a wealth of evidence about the financial management process. For example, many companies carefully monitor their external bond ratings to make sure that they can obtain the best possible terms when borrowing money. The downgrade of a company's bond rating can have a serious impact on its cost of capital and its profitability.

TESTS OF FINANCIAL STATEMENT ASSERTIONS: INVESTMENTS, BORROWED FUNDS, AND EQUITY

SUBSTANTIVE TESTS FOR INVESTMENTS

The audit procedures that are appropriate for testing investment balances are summarized in Figure 13–8. The primary substantive audit tests that are performed are

- Confirmation or physical observation to establish validity of investments.
- Tests of market value for possible unrealized losses.
- Vouching tests for current-period acquisitions or dispositions.
- Substantive analytical procedures to test the reasonableness of interest and dividend income.

The actual scope of the substantive tests will depend on the risk of material misstatement for investments and the materiality of investment balances to the financial statements.

Figure 13–8   Substantive Tests About Investments

Management Assertion	Typical Audit Procedures
Valuation and Allocation/ Accuracy: Transaction detail included in subsidiary journals and ledgers agrees with the general ledger balances related to investments.	• Reconcile detailed investment listings with the general ledger. • Reconcile brokerage statements (or other independent investment listings) with detailed investment listings and the general ledger. • Test accuracy of detailed investment listings, including related income.
Existence/Occurrence: All recorded transactions related to investments occurred and recorded investments exist.	• Confirm securities held by broker or other fiduciary. • Physically inspect securities on hand. • Perform substantive analytical procedures to test investment income.
Completeness: All existing investment transactions and balances have been recorded.	• Review bank confirmations, brokerage confirmations, board of directors minutes, attorney letters, etc., for indications of unrecorded investments especially for derivative products. • Perform substantive analytical procedures to test balance of investments relative to investment income. • Obtain representation letter concerning completeness of detailed investment listings.
Rights and obligations: Investment balances are owned by the company.	• Confirm the existence of investments in the hands of third parties. • Obtain a representation letter from management regarding ownership of investments. • Review board of directors' minutes, legal letters, contracts, etc., for evidence of pledging or other potential claims of ownership on investments.
Accuracy and Valuation: Investment balances are recorded at amounts properly reflecting their realizable value.	• Vouch a sample of investment purchases. • Vouch a sample of investment sales. • Recompute gains and losses on investment sales. • Review accounting methods used for handling investment securities (e.g., lower-of-cost-or-market vs. equity methods). • Assess realizability of securities held at year end. • Perform substantive analytical procedures to test investment income.
Valuation and Allocation/Classification: Investment balances and related costs are properly classified.	• Review investment listings for unusual items that should be reclassified. • Review and test management policy for classifying securities as short-term, long-term, or held for sale. • Obtain representation letter concerning classification policy.

(continued)

Figure 13–8   *(continued)*

Management Assertion	Typical Audit Procedures
Cutoff: Transactions affecting investments have been recorded in the proper period.	• Perform cash receipt cutoff tests for investment sales and investment income. • Perform cash disbursement cutoff tests for investment purchases. • Perform substantive analytical procedures to test investment income.
Completeness/Classification and Understandability: All required disclosures pertaining to investment balances are included in the financial statements.	• Complete disclosure checklist for investments. • Obtain representation letter from management regarding disclosure of investments. • Review proposed disclosures for accuracy.

The key assertions related to investments are existence/occurrence and valuation. Existence can be determined via physical examination of actual securities or via confirmation with independent fiduciaries (e.g., brokers). Valuation of investments is particularly important because of the accounting treatment of unrealized losses. Verification of valuation may present problems to the auditor if market values are not readily determinable for some investments. Classification of investments is also critical due to the different accounting treatment allowed for different types of investment securities.[4] Cutoff is usually a concern only in regard to the accrual of investment income. Finally, disclosure requirements are extensive for financial instruments, and some derivatives that involve material amounts can readily be hidden for substantial periods of time if proper authorization controls are not in place.[5]

> **Authoritative Guidance & Standards**
>
> Investments that are available for sale are recorded at fair values. Authoritative guidance for gathering auditing evidence to assess management's assessment of fair values and to assess fair values, including financial instruments for which there is an active market, is found in SAS 101 and ISA 545.

SUBSTANTIVE TESTS FOR BORROWED FUNDS

In general, transactions related to borrowed funds are infrequent but large. Typical audit procedures related to borrowed funds are described in Figure 13–9. The primary substantive tests for borrowed funds are

- Confirmations from banks and known creditors to establish validity and completeness of obligations.
- Examination of legal documents to test valuation and disclosure of obligations.
- Cutoff tests for unrecorded liabilities (especially interest accruals and derivative transactions).

---

4 FASB Statement No. 115, "Accounting for Certain Investments in Debt and Equity Securities," requires different accounting treatments for investments classified as "held to maturity," "trading securities," or "available for sale," which is similar to the treatment prescribed in IAS 39, "Financial Instruments: Recognition and Measurement."

5 For example, see FASB Statement No. 107, "Disclosures About the Fair Value of Financial Instruments" and IAS 32, "Financial Instruments: Disclosure and Presentation."

Figure 13–9   Substantive Tests About Borrowed Funds

Management Assertion	Typical Audit Procedures
Valuation and Allocation/ Accuracy: Transaction detail included in subsidiary journals and ledgers agrees with the general ledger balances related to borrowed funds (debt, lines of credit, and notes payable).	• Obtain a listing of all known obligations (notes payable, capital leases, lines of credit, bonds, etc.) and tie into the general ledger. • Reconcile subsidiary records (e.g., for notes payable) with the general ledger.
Existence/Occurrence: All recorded transactions related to borrowed funds occurred and recorded obligations exist.	• Examine the supporting documentation for a sample of recorded obligations. • Confirm obligations and terms with creditors. • Examine board of directors' minutes for authorization of borrowings.
Completeness: All existing borrowed funds and obligations have been recorded.	• Examine payments subsequent to year end for indication of obligations not recorded at year end. • Obtain and review a standard bank confirmation for indications of unrecorded obligations. • Confirm zero-balance accounts with known creditors. • Obtain representation letter from management regarding the completeness of borrowed funds.
Rights and Obligations/Valuation and allocation: Borrowed funds are owed by the company and recorded at the proper amounts.	• Examine supporting documentation for recorded obligations and determine that interest expense, interest payable, current balance of principal, and long-term balance of principal are correctly recorded. • Perform substantive analytical procedures to test interest expense. • Recompute balances for obligations that are issued at a discount, have non-market interest rates, or do not have a stated face value (e.g., capital leases). • Recompute actual interest expense using interest rates and balances of borrowed funds for a sample of obligations. • Confirm obligations and terms with creditors.
Valuation and Allocation/Classification: Borrowed funds are properly classified.	• Scan the list of obligations for items that are unusual and may require reclassification. • Examine supporting documentation for recorded obligations and determine that current and long-term portions of principal are correctly classified.

(continued)

Figure 13–9 *(continued)*

Management Assertion	Typical Audit Procedures
Cutoff: Transactions related to borrowed funds (including interest expense and payments) have been recorded in the proper period.	• Examine payments subsequent to year end for indication of obligations not recorded at year end. • Perform substantive analytical procedures to test interest expense. • Recompute actual interest expense using interest rates and balances of borrowed funds for a sample of obligations.
Completeness/Classification and Understandability: All required disclosures pertaining to borrowed funds are included in the financial statements.	• Complete a disclosure checklist related to borrowed funds. • Obtain representation letter from management regarding disclosure of borrowed funds. • Review proposed disclosures for accuracy.

- Substantive analytical procedures to test interest expense.
- Assessment of the reasonableness and extent of disclosures.

The auditor must also test for compliance with debt covenants, violations of which may create contingent liabilities for the company or affect the timing (and classification) of obligations.[6] Finally, off-balance sheet obligations must be reviewed to assure proper disclosure in the financial statements. The extent and nature of substantive tests performed for borrowed funds will be related primarily to the complexity of financing arrangements.

Authoritative Guidance & Standards

SAS 67 and ISA 505 provide guidance on confirmations of all types, including debt. These standards note that the requests for confirmation related to debt should be directed to those within the organization expected to have knowledge about the information. For example, to confirm information about waivers related to debt covenants, the confirmation should be directed to an official of the creditor with the knowledge and authority to respond to the confirmation.

The auditor's primary concerns related to borrowed funds are that all such arrangements are recorded (completeness) on a timely basis (cutoff) at a proper amount (valuation and allocation) and fully disclosed in accordance with appropriate accounting principles (presentation and disclosure). Completeness and cutoff are usually tested with confirmations and as part of the general search for unrecorded and contingent liabilities (see Chapter 15). Valuation is usually determined via examination of supporting documentation, especially related legal documents. Proper disclosure is achieved through a careful examination of confirmations and legal documents, and consideration of appropriate reporting standards.

SUBSTANTIVE TESTS FOR EQUITY

Equity transactions also tend to be infrequent but large. Typical substantive tests related to equity are summarized in Figure 13–10. The primary audit tests are

- Confirmation of existence, completeness, and valuation of equity with the independent registrar or transfer agent.

---

6 Violation of a covenant in a loan agreement could result in the obligation being due and payable immediately. Lenders do not often enforce such contract provisions but the potential contingent liability arising from acceleration of loans is important to the disclosure and classification audit objectives.

Figure 13–10   Substantive Tests About Equity

Management Assertion	Typical Audit Procedures
Valuation and Allocation/Accuracy: Transaction detail included in subsidiary journals and ledgers agrees with the general ledger balances related to equity.	• Reconcile the type and number of shares issued per the stock book with the general ledger. • Analyze current-year stock activity and trace to proper inclusion in the general ledger. • Confirm details of outstanding equity with outside parties (e.g., registrars, stock transfer agents, trustee for employee stock ownership plans).
Existence/Occurrence: All recorded transactions related to equity occurred and recorded equity balances exist.	• Perform substantive analytical procedures. • Analyze current-year equity activity. • Confirm details of current-year activity with outside parties (e.g., underwriters, stock transfer agents, trustee for employee stock ownership plans). • Review board of directors' minutes for date and amount of dividend declarations, stock splits, stock dividends, option grants, and treasury stock acquisitions. • Vouch selected equity transactions.
Completeness: All existing equity transactions and balances have been recorded.	
Rights and Obligations/ Valuation and Allocation: Equity balances reflect investments made by shareholders and are recorded at the proper amounts.	
Valuation and Allocation/ Classification: Equity balances are properly classified.	
Cutoff: Equity transactions (including dividend declarations) have been recorded in the proper period.	
Completeness/Classification and Understandability: All required disclosures pertaining to equity balances are included in the financial statements.	• Complete a disclosure checklist related to equity. • Obtain representation letter from management regarding disclosure of equity, especially stock compensation arrangements. • Review proposed disclosures for accuracy.

- Examination of board of directors' minutes for authorization and details about current-period transactions.
- Substantive analytical procedures to test dividend accruals and totals.
- Assessment of the reasonableness and extent of disclosures.

In general, the audit of equity is usually a minor portion of the audit unless there have been complex transactions, such as a merger or the company uses esoteric equity arrangements.

The auditor's primary concerns related to equity are completeness and cutoff of equity transactions, such as new issues, splits, and dividends. Given the divergence between the date of record and the date of execution/clearing for many equity transactions, auditors must be careful to determine that equity transactions are recorded in the proper period. It is important to remember that the buying and selling of stock between investors does not affect the accounts of the company. Such transactions are of interest to the company only in regard to who actually owns stock at a point in time and should receive dividends upon the date of record. The valuation of equity transactions is also of concern to the auditor, especially for complex transactions that involve deferred compensation, hybrid securities, or derivatives. Finally, disclosure requirements for equity are extensive and must be evaluated by the auditor.

SUMMARY AND CONCLUSION

In this chapter, we discussed the audit of the facilities and financial management processes. These are considered critical resource management processes in most organizations. In each case, we discussed a process map for the process and analyzed the internal threats to the process. Residual risks identified during process analysis would be linked to financial statement assertions with high risk of material misstatement and appropriate substantive procedures selected to test high-risk assertions. Potential substantive tests for assertions affected by each process were discussed in detail.

The most common transactions occurring in facilities management would affect property and equipment assets and related depreciation; and in financial resource management, they would affect long-term debt, equity, and investments. These processes are generally characterized by large and infrequent transactions where controls may be performed on an ad hoc basis. Under the integrated audit, however, the auditor needs to consider the controls over financial reporting for all material processes, and as these transactions tend to be material, the auditor needs to examine the controls over the various resource management processes.

Traditionally, because many of the facilities and financial management transactions are large and material, the auditor has focused on refining substantive tests to be used to examine assertions related to these accounts. Figure 13–11 illustrates how the various substantive tests described in this chapter might be adapted under different risk conditions. Substantive testing related to facilities and financial management tends to focus on year-end balances and activity such as acquisitions and disposals and issuances of debt and equity in financial management. Ultimately, the auditor must decide which of these tests to perform on a given client and the extent of testing needed to gather adequate evidence to support the audit opinion.

APPENDIX: SUBSTANTIVE TESTS FOR TRANSACTIONS AND ACCOUNTS IN HUMAN RESOURCE MANAGEMENT

The human resource management process is likely to be a critical process in most service firms as people are the key to delivering services. We previously presented a process map and internal threat analysis for human resource management (see

Figure 13–11   Tests of Financial Statement Assertions at Different Levels of Risk of
Material Misstatement for Resource Management Processes

Type of Procedure	High Detection Risk Case (Low risk of material misstatement)	Low Detection Risk Case (High risk of material misstatement)
Plant, Property, and Equipment		
Tests of additions	Vouch a small sample of additions (stratified by size) with few or no physical inspections of assets.	Vouch large sample of additions and physically examine significant new assets.
Tests of disposals	Vouch small sample of disposals.	Vouch large sample of disposals.
Tests of repairs expense	Tested by review of repairs expense account.	Tested by review and vouching of repairs expense account.
Tests of depreciation	Tested with substantive analytical procedure.	Tested with substantive analytical procedure and supplemented with tests of depreciation for individual assets.
Investments, Borrowed Funds, and Equity		
Investments	Vouch large purchases or sales. Obtain confirmations from external parties pertaining to assets held. Test overall market value of investment portfolio. Use substantive analytical procedures to test investment income.	Vouch numerous sales and disposal transactions. Obtain confirmations from external parties pertaining to assets held. Physically examine investments on hand. Test overall market value of investment portfolio and vouch market value of specific items. Use substantive analytical procedures supplemented by tests of transactions to test investment income.
Borrowed Funds	Minimal vouching of large borrowings and payoffs. Confirm obligations with outside parties. Scan post-year–end disbursements journal for unrecorded liabilities. Use substantive analytical procedures to test interest expense and accruals.	Moderate to extensive vouching of borrowings, interest, and payoffs. Confirm many obligations with outside parties. Perform extensive search for unrecorded liabilities. Use substantive analytical procedures to test interest expense and accruals supplemented by extensive tests of transactions.

(continued)

Figure 13–11   *(continued)*

Investments, Borrowed Funds, and Equity		
Equity	Verify authorization of equity transactions. Review proper accounting for equity transactions. Vouch a few large transactions.	Verify authorization of all equity transactions. Perform tests of transactions on all significant transactions. Confirm all equity positions with appropriate outside parties.

Chapters 6 and 7). The human resource management process comprises the set of activities that an organization uses to recruit and coordinate its employees from the newest hire in the proverbial "mailroom" to the chief executive officer hired from outside the company. This process includes recruiting and hiring, setting work hours, training, payroll processing, and employee evaluation. It also includes the activities for terminating an employee, which may occur as a result of voluntary departures, layoffs, retirement, death, or disability. We can now discuss the nature of substantive tests that may be applied to transactions and accounts affected by the human resource process.

HUMAN RESOURCE TRANSACTIONS

As previously discussed in Chapter 6, the key transactions related to human resource management include hiring, managing, and compensating employees. The emphasis of payroll processing is on the periodic preparation of payroll and the proper classification of the resulting expenditures. The steps for processing payroll are indicated in Figure 13–12 (previously presented in Figure 6–7). Hourly employees traditionally use *time cards* to check in and out of work, but electronic swipe cards are increasingly used to track employee work hours. The time recorded using these cards becomes the basis for computing an employee's gross pay. Hourly employees may also complete a manual or electronic *time report* or *job ticket* that describes exactly what they did during a given pay period. This information is needed to assure that payroll expenditures can be debited to the appropriate expense or asset account. Salaried employees do not need to complete time cards but are often asked to complete a time report for each pay period.

Payroll computations are based on authorized wage and salary scales and appropriate deductions. Gross payroll reflects total wages earned prior to deductions; net payroll reflects the amount actually paid to an employee after considering all mandatory and voluntary deductions. Employee *paychecks* or other pay records (i.e., direct deposit documents) are prepared, approved and distributed to the employees.[7] Payroll information is summarized in the *payroll register*, including gross pay, taxes, deductions, and net pay, which becomes the basis for making entries to the general ledger and preparing payroll tax returns that are filed with

---

7 Direct deposit of payroll into employee bank accounts is becoming more common. In a direct deposit system, paper checks are not needed and payroll distribution is performed electronically. However, most countries still require that employers provide some form of written "pay advice" to their employees summarizing the gross pay and various deductions to arrive at net pay deposited to bank account.

Figure 13–12   Summary of Payroll Activities

Process/Activity	Documents	Journals, Ledgers, and Records Used	Typical Journal Entry
Hiring: Recruiting new employees based on company needs and policies.	Employment application (internal)	Job descriptions and guidelines	
Personnel: Maintain accurate records on all personnel including pay rates, deduction authorization, tax information, and fitness reports.	Pay rate authorizations (internal) Tax forms (external) Deduction authorizations (external)	Employee master file	
Employee time reporting: Employees report time spent on job-related activities with frequency and level of detail dependent on nature of employment	*Hourly workers:* Time cards (internal) Job tickets (internal) *Salaried workers:* Time report (internal)		
Payroll preparation: Payroll costs are computed and disbursements are prepared	Check (internal) EFT authorization (internal)	Payroll register Labor distribution report *(Documents may be provided by service organization if payroll processing is outsourced)*	
Payroll distribution: Payroll disbursements are delivered to employees by check, cash, or direct deposit.			
General accounting: Payroll expenditures and liabilities are recorded in the appropriate accounts.	Journal entry ticket (internal) Tax forms (internal)	General ledger	Dr. Payroll Expenses Dr. Assets (inventory) Cr. Cash Cr. Accrued Liabilities

various taxing authorities (e.g., local, state/provincial, and federal/national governments).

The key event of this process is the completion of service by the employees. Each day, hour, and minute that an employee works adds to the amount of the company's liability to that employee. However, because payroll costs are usually recorded when employees are paid (i.e., on a periodic basis), a timing issue can arise when the end of a fiscal period does not coincide with the end of a pay period. This also applies to payroll taxes and other personnel expenses, such as vacation time, that accrue but that may be paid much later. As with other disbursements, the key event for satisfaction of the liability is the delivery of a check.

TESTS OF FINANCIAL STATEMENT ASSERTIONS: PAYROLL AND ACCRUED LIABILITIES

As with all processes, the auditor considers the results of strategic and process analysis, evaluating and testing controls, and monitoring performance indicators in order to assess the residual risks related to human resources that have an impact on the conduct of the audit. As seen in earlier chapters, the auditor would assess the frequency and magnitude of the risks and summarize the results using a risk map with supporting documentation. In the event that residual risks result in high risk of material misstatement for one or more financial statement assertions, the auditor would perform substantive testing relevant to the assertion.

For example, the auditor might conclude that controls over authorization of overtime were not adequate leading to excess overtime payments to employees. This might be revealed by performance measures of overtime hours worked and could lead to a drop in employee morale and increased employee turnover. Some employees could take advantage of the poor controls to inflate their paychecks by working unnecessary hours. Furthermore, the organization might conclude from all the overtime that it needs to expand the workforce, ultimately leading to increased personnel costs and underutilization of the workforce.

The auditor would analyze the implications of this residual risk and could come to a number of conclusions. First, the risk would condition the auditor's expectations about labor costs, margins, administrative expenses, benefit costs, and payroll taxes. Second, if the problem is severe and compounds through the addition of excess labor, the long-term fiscal health of the company may be threatened as its cost structure becomes noncompetitive. The pressure on costs and margins could also create problems in the control environment as management takes steps to cope with the problem, possibly creating a discriminatory or threatening environment. The pressure could also result in a confrontational relationship between management and labor. Finally, the high residual risk could have an impact on specific financial statement assertions, such as benefit accruals, standard cost estimates, or termination payouts. If financial statement assertions are deemed to have high risk of material misstatement, substantive tests will be used to minimize detection risk for the affected assertion. Basic substantive tests for payroll and related liabilities are summarized in Figure 13–13 and include

- Tests of transactions
- Substantive analytical procedures
- Cutoff tests
- Confirmation of obligations

TESTS OF TRANSACTIONS

Payroll transactions are generally routine but voluminous. Furthermore, except for certain pension, health, and post-retirement obligations, and accrued vacation time, liabilities related to payroll tend to be small and very short term. Consequently, payroll testing tends to focus on transactions rather than balances. Figure 13–14 describes general procedures for testing payroll transactions, which

Figure 13–13   Audit Objectives and Related Evidence for Payroll*

Management Assertion	Typical Audit Procedures
Accuracy/Valuation: Payroll registers and related liability records agree with balances in the general ledger.	• Verify the accuracy of a sample of payroll registers and trace payroll totals to proper inclusion in general ledger accounts. • Verify the accuracy of general ledger balances. • Reconcile subsidiary records with general ledger including records provided by third party service providers.
Existence/Occurrence: Payroll-related obligations are for work rendered by actual employees.	• Perform tests of transactions on payroll disbursements including records provided by third party service providers. • Vouch payments to taxing authorities and other entities for payroll-related expenditures (e.g., health insurance premiums)
Completeness: All payroll-related obligations are recorded.	• Perform tests of transactions on time cards and time reports. • Perform search for unrecorded payroll liabilities (e.g., year-end bonuses, unrecorded commissions)
Accuracy/Valuation: Payroll-related obligations are recorded at the proper amounts including authorized and mandated deductions.	• Perform tests of transactions on payroll disbursements. • Verify and vouch amounts included in payroll tax returns. • Perform substantive analytical procedures on payroll expenses and obligations. • Obtain actuarial report for pension, health, or post-retirement benefits. • Recompute pension, benefit, and vacation/sick leave expenses and obligations.
Cutoff/Valuation: All payroll related obligations have been recorded including vacation accruals.	• Review end-of-year payroll and determine if appropriate accruals have been made. • Perform substantive analytical procedures on year-end balances.
Classification/Valuation: Personnel costs and obligations are recorded in the proper accounts.	• Verify classification of accrued liabilities and labor costs as part of tests of transactions. • Review year-end accrual balances for proper classification.
Completeness/ Understandability: All disclosures related to personnel and payroll obligations are properly included in the financial statements.	• Complete a disclosure checklist for payroll and benefit costs and obligations. • Review board of directors' minutes, bank confirmations, attorney letters, and other correspondence for indications that compensation plans have changed or other payroll-related information. • Obtain representations from management about disclosures related to payroll and benefits.

* The ownership objective does not apply to payroll-related liabilities.

Figure 13–14   Tests of Transactions for Payroll Processing

Occurrence and Accuracy,
- Review the payroll register(s) for large and unusual transactions to be examined via vouching to source documents.
- Select a sample of payroll disbursement transactions from the payroll register. Obtain the supporting documentation for the disbursements. Perform the following tests and note any exceptions:
  - Compare time cards to compensated time per the payroll register.
  - Trace pay rates and deductions to proper authorizations in personnel files.
  - Test accuracy of gross pay, deductions, and net pay per employee.
  - Examine canceled checks for payee, amount, proper signature, employee endorsement, bank cancellation, and date of deposit.
  - Reconcile hours per the time card and hours per the job ticket/time report.
  - Trace cost allocation to the labor distribution report.

Note: Salaried workers would be vouched to an approved salary contract or agreement.

Completeness and Accuracy
- Test the accuracy of the payroll register (all tests apply whether this is generated internally or by a third party service provider). This may be done on a sample basis. Trace totals to proper inclusion in the general ledger.
- Test the accuracy of the labor distribution report. This may be done on a sample basis. Trace totals to proper inclusion in the general ledger.
- Reconcile totals per the labor distribution report with totals per the payroll register.

emphasize authorization and valuation of payroll expenditures. In situations where payroll is prepared by a third party service organization, these tests may be unnecessary or impossible to perform, in which case the auditor would obtain a report on internal control within the service organization prepared by that organization's auditor.[8]

Substantive Analytical Procedures

Many payroll expenses are amenable to estimation using substantive analytical procedures. Given the easy accessibility of information on the number of employees, workloads, pay scales, authorized deductions, and tax rates, many expenses may be computed directly by the auditor. For example, payroll tax expense can be estimated by multiplying the statutory rate for social security and unemployment taxes times the total payroll for the period. Substantive analytical procedures could also be used to calculate year-end balances for accumulated sick leave or vacation pay that might not be paid out until future periods. Accrued payroll taxes may also be tested in this way.

---

8 There are specific auditing standards applicable to the audit of a data processing service organization. See Section AU 324, also known as SAS 70. Other countries have similar standards (e.g. Canada 5970, Audit Reports on Controls at a Service Organization) but to date there are no International Standards on Auditing in this area, although ISA 402 recognizes the need to use such a report when third party service organizations carry out material activities on behalf of the organization.

Figure 13–15   Substantive Testing for Accrued Payroll Liabilities

	Accrued Payroll Liabilities
	Beginning Balance (A)
Payments (C)	Expenses (B)
	Ending Balance (D)

Tests of Account Details

(A) Trace to prior-year financial statements or audit results.*

(B) Expenses are usually recomputed or estimated using substantive analytical procedures. Expenses may be tested through examination of transactions included in the related expense account (e.g., Payroll Tax Expense).

(C) Tests of transactions can be used to test payments throughout the period.

(D) Test accuracy of account balance. Vouch and review individually significant transactions that are included in the year-end balance. Payroll information for the last pay period in the fiscal year can be traced to proper inclusion in the liability account. Given that pay periods rarely coincide with the fiscal year end, the amounts reported in the payroll register and payroll tax returns may need to be pro-rated to obtain the proper cutoff.

* If the prior-year financial statements were not audited or were audited by some other firm, additional audit testing (e.g., vouching) may be needed to verify the opening balance.

Cutoff Tests

Cutoff tests are particularly effective for accrued liabilities related to payroll because either the end of the fiscal year corresponds with the end of a pay period or the payroll period ends shortly after the end of the year. The analysis of accrued liabilities is illustrated in Figure 13–15. Given that the beginning balance is known, payments can be verified with tests of transactions, and expenses can be estimated using substantive analytical procedures, it is relatively easy to compute the year-end balance. Additionally, the year-end balance can be subject to a cutoff test based on the payroll data for the period which includes the fiscal year end. To illustrate, assume that the fiscal year end is December 31 and the payroll covers the two-week period ending January 8. By implication, 8 days of the payroll period pertain to the new year and 6 days to the prior year. Therefore, the balance sheet as of December 31 should include a liability for six-fourteenths of the payroll computed for January 8. If the total payroll is $100,000, the accrued liability on 12/31 would be $42,857.[9]

Confirmation of Obligations

Some obligations arising from payroll are effectively tested by obtaining confirmations from outside parties. Pension liabilities and obligations related to post-retirement benefits should be confirmed with an actuary or insurance company, depending on the structure of the plan. If the company maintains a pension fund

9 The liability would need to be classified into appropriate accounts related to taxes, wages, and deductions, but the separate accounts would likely be aggregated for financial statement presentation.

for its employees, the current balance of obligations and related disclosures should be confirmed with the administrator of the plan. Similarly, obligations for health insurance or other employee benefits can be confirmed directly with the providers of the coverage or benefit.

The selection of appropriate substantive tests depends on the linkage between residual risk from the process and inherent and control risks for specific assertions. However, payroll costs and liabilities are generally considered to be routine transactions so issues related to validity, completeness, and valuation of basic payroll usually have low inherent or control risk. However, audit risk often arises related to the valuation of long-term liabilities such as pensions and the related disclosures that are required for financial reporting.

BIBLIOGRAPHY OF PROFESSIONAL LITERATURE

Research

Ashton, R. H. 1974. An Experimental Study of Internal Control Judgments. *Journal of Accounting Research.* 12(1): 143–157.

Bradshaw, M. T., S. A. Richardson, and R. G. Sloan. 2001. Do Analysts and Auditors Use Information in Accruals? *Journal of Accounting Research.* 39(1): 45–74.

Bulter, M., A. J. Leone and M. Willenborg. 2004. An Empirical Analysis of Auditor Reporting and its Association with Abnormal Accruals. *Journal of Accounting & Economics.* 37(2): 139–160.

Dietrich, J. R., M. S. Harris, and K. A. Muller III. 2000. The Reliability of Investment Property Fair Value Estimates. *Journal of Accounting & Economics.* 30(2): 125–158.

Earley, C. E. 2001. Knowledge Acquisition in Auditing: Training Novice Auditors to Recognize Cue Relationships in Real Estate Valuation. *The Accounting Review.* 76(1): 81–97.

Earley, C. E. 2002. The Differential Use of Information By Experienced and Novice Auditors in the Performance Of Ill-Structured Audit Tasks. *Contemporary Accounting Research.* 19(4): 595–614.

Francis, J. R. and J. Krishnan. Accounting Accruals and Auditor Reporting Conservatism. *Contemporary Accounting Research.* 16(1): 135–165.

Gordon, T. P. and M. S. Niles. 2005. Lucent Loses its Luster: Accounting for Investments Turned Bad. *Issues in Accounting Education.* 20(2): 183–194.

Hitzig, N. B. 2004. The Hidden Risk in Analytical Procedures: What WorldCom Revealed. *The CPA Journal.* 74(2): 32–36.

Menelaides, S. L., L. E. Graham, and G. Fischbach. 2003. The Auditor's Approach To Fair Value. *Journal of Accountancy.* 195(6): 73.

Muller III, K. A. and E. J. Riedl. 2002. External Monitoring of Property Appraisal Estimates and Information Asymmetry. *Journal of Accounting Research.* 40(3): 865–282.

Taylor, M. 2000. The Effects of Industry Specialization on Auditors' Inherent Risk Assessments and Confidence Judgements. *Contemporary Accounting Research.* 17(4): 693–712.

Zekany, K. E., L. W. Braun, and Z. T. Warder. 2004. Behind Closed Doors at WorldCom: 2001. *Issues in Accounting Education.* 19(1): 101–118.

Auditing Standards

AICPA *Statements on Auditing Standard (SAS)* No. 67, "The Confirmation Process."

AICPA *Statements on Auditing Standard (SAS)* No. 101, "Auditing Fair Value Measurements and Disclosures."

AICPA *Statements on Auditing Standard (SAS)* No. 106, "Audit Evidence."

AICPA *Statements on Auditing Standard (SAS)* No. 107, "Audit Risk and Materiality in Conducting an Audit."

AICPA *Statements on Auditing Standard (SAS)* No. 109, "Understanding the Entity and Its Environment and Assessing the Risks of Material Misstatement."

AICPA *Statements on Auditing Standard (SAS)* No. 110, "Performing Procedures in Response to Assessed Risks and Evaluating the Audit Evidence Obtained."

IAASB *International Standards on Auditing (ISA)* No. 315, "Understanding the Entity and Its Environment and Assessing the Risks of Material Misstatement."

IAASB *International Standards on Auditing (ISA)* No. 320, "Audit Materiality."

IAASB *International Standards on Auditing (ISA)* No. 330, "The Auditor's Procedures in Response to Assessed Risks."

IAASB *International Standards on Auditing (ISA)* No. 500, "Audit Evidence."

IAASB *International Standards on Auditing (ISA)* No. 505, "External Confirmations."

IAASB *International Standards on Auditing (ISA)* No. 545, "Auditing Fair Value Measurements and Disclosures."

QUESTIONS

1. Explain how creating a process map and internal threat analysis helps in determining the extent to which substantive testing is to be performed on the accounts associated with each of the following processes:
    a.   Human resource management
    b.   Property management
    c.   Financial resource management

2. Examine the process activities and transactions for the property management process shown in Figure 13–2.
    a.   Using the example transactions listed in the same figure, describe which transactions or estimates are impacted by the different activities listed in the process.
    b.   Describe which accounts are impacted by the each of the transactions.

3. Examine the process activities and transactions for the financial management process shown in Figure 13–6.
    a.   Using the example transactions listed in the same figure, describe which transactions or estimates are impacted by the different activities listed in the process.
    b.   Describe which accounts are impacted by the each of the transactions.

4. The internal threat analysis shown in Figure 13–3 contains a listing of controls linked to risks related to the property management process. For each process risk, describe the impact on the audit for each of the following results of controls testing.
    a.   Controls are found to be operating effectively
    b.   Controls are found to be operating ineffectively

5. The internal threat analysis shown in Figure 13–7 contains a listing of controls linked to risks related to the financial resource management process. For each process risk, describe the impact on the audit for each of the following results of controls testing.
    a.   Controls are found to be operating effectively
    b.   Controls are found to be operating ineffectively

6. The financial management process is important for auditors because of its role in helping to form expectations about financial statement results. To illustrate this concept, explain how an understanding of the controls and performance measures in place to manage the following risks impacts expectations about financial statement results (use Figures 13–6 and 13–7 to help answer this question):

Risks

a.   Inadequate cash flow
b.   Excessive or unknown financial exposures
c.   Unforeseen changes in market conditions which cause losses
d.   Manipulation of financial reporting
e.   Errors in financial reporting

7.   After an analysis of the borrowed funds portion of the financial management process, an auditor might choose not to perform many tests of controls but will instead concentrate on substantive tests of account balance details.
    a.   What unique characteristics of borrowed funds motivate an auditor to bypass such tests of controls?
    b.   Argue why an auditor might be better off testing controls and suggest some tests and the evidence needed to perform them.

8.   Based on this chapter and the result of answering the previous questions, offer an explanation for why performing a detailed analysis of resource management is an important part of the auditing engagement. As part of your answer, provide several specific examples for when failing to properly understanding the business or financial reporting risks associated with resource management processes could lead to an increased risk of materially misstated financial statements.

PROBLEMS

1.   The property management process is important for gasoline retailers like Chevron. Access Chevron's web site and research the descriptions of its service stations through its learning center link. Use this information and Figures 13–2 and 13–3 to create an internal threat analysis for Chevron's service station property management process.

2.   Site selection and property development is an important property management subprocess for many organizations. Consider The Home Depot, which opened at least 100 stores per year for more than 15 years consecutively, making it the fastest growing retailer in U.S. history. Its growth rate is evidenced by construction-in-progress and store opening expenses—two accounts that are significant enough to appear as line items on the company's financial statements. Access The Home Depot's web site and research the company's growth rate over its relatively young history. Use this information and Figures 13–2 and 13–3 to create an internal threat analysis for The Home Depot's site selection and property development process.

3.   Consider an internal threat analysis for the property management of a food chain specializing in donuts and coffee (e.g., Dunkin' Donuts, Tim Horton's, etc.). Using Figure 13–3 as a guide:
    a.   Describe the people risks, direct process risks, and indirect process risks associated with a move to expand the chain more heavily into geographic locations not previously penetrated the organization.
    b.   For each risk, describe a control that might be put in place to address the risk. Consider performance reviews and monitoring, segregation of duties, processing controls, and physical controls.

4.   Organizations often will utilize third parties to perform their resource management processes. For example, organizations can utilize investment banks to perform financial asset management to conduct many of the activities shown in Figure 13–6. Access Credit Suisse's web site and research the descriptions and product offerings under asset management. Use this information and Figures 13–6 and Figure 13–7 to create an internal threat analysis for organizations that opt to use Credit Suisse to perform financial resource management.

5. Consider an internal threat analysis for the loan management process for the commercial bank segment of a large financial banking institution (e.g., Bank of America, Deutsche Bank, etc.). Using Figure 13–7 as a guide:

   a. Describe the people risks, direct process risks, and indirect process risks associated with a move to shift the bank's loan portfolio to include businesses and individuals with lower credit ratings but the potential for earning higher rates of return.

   b. For each risk, describe a control that might be put in place to address the risk. Consider performance reviews and monitoring, segregation of duties, processing controls, and physical controls.

6. Following are some routine procedures for the audit of payroll (discussed in the Appendix). For each procedure, (1) state whether it is a test of controls or a substantive test, (2) state which management assertion the procedure is designed to fulfill, and (3) state the type of evidence used in the procedure.

   a. Observe employees clocking in for a few shifts.

   b. Sample some payroll check stubs and manually calculate the withholding allowances for taxes.

   c. Sample some time cards for proper management approvals.

   d. Enter some dummy data into the automated payroll system to ensure proper withholding is done and proper accruals are made.

   e. Compare a sample of employees from the master payroll file with actual personnel files.

   f. Trace footings of payroll journals to entries in general ledger.

   g. Estimate accruals for end-of-period salaries payable using production and sales data.

   h. Study minutes of board of directors' meetings for evidence of new executive compensation plans.

7. Consider Manny Corp., our military outfitting operation from Chapter 10. Its financial data is reprinted here for convenience.

Manny Corp.
Balance Sheet
12-31-06
(000's omitted)

Cash	$ 8,000	Accounts Payable	$ 33,000
Accounts Receivable	21,000	Long-Term Debt	141,000
Inventories	86,000	Capital Stock	82,000
Fixed Assets	147,000	Retained Earnings	6,000
Total Assets	$ 262,000	Total Equities	$262,000

Manny Corp.
Income Statement
For Period Ending 12-31-06
(000's omitted)

Sales	$110,000
Cost of Goods Sold	80,000
Gross Profit	$ 30,000
Selling, General, & Admin.	31,000
Net Income (Loss)	($ 1,000)

   a. If you were the auditor assigned to perform substantive analytical procedures on expenses, describe the management assertions you would be hoping to support and for which accounts.

    b.   What techniques and variables would you employ in your analysis?

    c.   Suppose your analysis indicated that depreciation expense was reported to be lower than your prediction. What implications would this have for your audit?

8. The controller of Mingus & Mingus Inc., a construction company, provides you with the following schedule of additions and disposals to fixed assets for the past year:

Disposals	Original Cost	Accumulated Depreciation Taken	Amount Received
Crane #8	$470,000	$310,000	$180,000
Bulldozer #20	140,000	60,000	50,000
Bulldozer #11	170,000	100,000	Bulldozer (FMV = $80,000)

Acquisitions	Cost	Estimated Life
Backhoe #19	$90,000	10 yrs.
Backhoe #20	80,000	10 yrs.

The following account balances were obtained from the financial statements from last year and the trial balance (unaudited) from this year:

	12-31-06 Audited Balance	12-31-07 Unaudited Balance
Fixed assets	$14,000,000	$13,470,000
Accumulated depreciation	6,000,000	6,430,000
Depreciation expense	N/A	900,000

Assuming that the depreciation expense for 2007 does not include any depreciation taken on the assets listed above, and that Mingus & Mingus Inc. uses the straight-line method of depreciation with no salvage values, do you have evidence of misstatement here? If so, where? Restate the balances to correctly reflect the activity shown.

9. The disclosure objective for the equity portion of the audit is said to be critical. Examine the partial balance sheet of Barron Co., a large, diversified financial services firm with 22,000 employees worldwide:

Stockholder's Equity
(000's omitted)

Preferred Stock 6%, $100 par	$ 42,000
Add'l. Paid-in-Capital—Preferred	31,000
Common Stock, $1 par	40,000
Add'l. Paid-in-Capital—Common	118,000
Retained Earnings	442,000
Treasury Shares	(9,000)
Receivable from Exercise of Stock Options	(1,000)
	$663,000

    a.   What are the deficiencies in this disclosure?

    b.   What further disclosures should be made in the footnotes?

    c.   How does the auditor go about auditing these disclosures for accuracy and completeness?

Case 13–1: OPM Leasing Inc.

OPM Leasing Inc. is one of the largest clients in your office. The company is in the business of leasing computers to small businesses. OPM Leasing is a publicly traded company that is subject to the reporting requirements of the U.S. SEC. Many small investors own about 40 percent of the stock of OPM Leasing. The remainder of the stock is owned by OPM Consulting Company, which is a closely held, unaudited corporation that is not publicly traded. OPM Consulting is owned by the key managers of OPM Leasing.

OPM Consulting provides information system design services to many small and family-owned businesses. Based on the consultant's recommendations, OPM Leasing purchases computer equipment from major vendors (e.g., Lenovo, Dell, Compaq) for installation in the offices of the consulting clients. The money to acquire the computer equipment is borrowed by OPM Leasing from financial institutions and limited partnership arrangements are set up for the express purpose of financing computer leases. All debt raised in this manner is secured by the computer equipment. The equipment is then leased to the consulting clients, with OPM Leasing serving as the lessor, using long-term lease arrangements that typically include a bargain purchase option at the end of the lease term. OPM Leasing earns an 8 percent return on its leases and remits a significant portion of their net cash flow to OPM Consulting in the form of consulting fees, referral fees (for the lease transactions), maintenance fees (for ongoing service of the computers in operation), and dividends. Dividends, of course, are also paid to the minority shareholders of OPM Leasing.

You have audited OPM Leasing for the last five years and have always issued an unqualified opinion. You have not audited OPM Consulting, which is not subject to public disclosure requirements. Your previous audits have been planned based on your interpretation of GAAS and you have never uncovered any questionable activity. One of the procedures that you routinely perform as part of your audit is to confirm with the lessees the lease arrangements and the existence of the equipment. You have never physically examined any of the computer equipment since it is located at many distant locations. Your last audit report was dated March 2, 2004, for the year ended December 31, 2003.

You are now reviewing the second quarter (ending June 30) interim financial statements for 2004 that are to be filed with the SEC. One of OPM Leasing's newly hired employees informs you that she suspects that the company has been executing fraudulent transactions for quite awhile. Her main suspicion is that many of the "leased" computers are nonexistent and the companies that supposedly lease the equipment are shell corporations set up by the managers of OPM Leasing (who are also the owners of OPM Consulting). The money that was borrowed to purchase these nonexistent computers has been misappropriated by these managers. Until now, the fraud has been concealed by having the managers return the auditor's confirmations without exception. Cash flow was "managed" by "lapping" lease payments from actual leases. The managers also were able to make payments on some of the fake leases using funds that were obtained from their ownership interest in OPM Consulting. As the fake leases age, they are written off as uncollectible due to "technological obsolescence" of the equipment. This employee thinks that this scheme has been underway for at least three years.

You discretely follow up on this information and find that it is probably true, and you estimate that as many as 30 percent of the computer leases may be fraudulent. The total recorded value of fraudulent leases appears to be about twice the amount of recorded equity on December 31, 2003. Based on these revelations, you feel that OPM Leasing will collapse immediately if the information is publicly disclosed. OPM Leasing may be bankrupt by the end of 2004, anyway, even if the information is not disclosed, due to the difficulty of "managing" the cash flows.

Requirements

1. Prepare a diagram of key components of the scheme and the cash flows related to the scheme. Explain how this scheme could work without the auditor detecting the problem.
2. Do you feel that the auditor complied with GAAS prior to the discovery of the problem? Explain.
3. What audit procedures would have been effective at discovering the problem?
4. Discuss the auditor's responsibilities now that the problem has been discovered. Consider professional, ethical, and reporting requirements.
5. Identify the stakeholders in this situation and describe their interest in the auditor's ultimate actions.
6. What would you do? Explain and justify.
7. Discuss the legal ramifications to the auditor if OPM Leasing collapses. What arguments would the plaintiff's attorneys use in a suit against the auditor? What are the auditor's defenses and how good are they?

Case 13–2: WorldCom

The largest fraud and bankruptcy in U.S. history was discovered at WorldCom in the spring of 2002 and was widely considered to be the deciding factor in moving forward the Sarbanes-Oxley Act of 2002. Interestingly, the most significant part of the fraud involved the property management business processes and the decision to capitalize $2.5 billion of costs in 2001 and 2002 associated with excess capacity relating to the communications network at the telecommunications company. Under GAAP, the amounts should have been expensed, thus reducing reported net income; however, management at WorldCom capitalized the amounts to defer the expenses. The internal audit department, under the leadership of Cynthia Cooper (one of *Time* Magazine's 2002 Persons of the Year), discovered the fraud and persisted with the audit committee and KPMG (the auditing firm succeeding Arthur Andersen on the engagement) until the amounts were publicly disclosed and the fraud exposed.

Requirements

1. Use the Internet or library resources to conduct additional research on the widely documented WorldCom fraud. Prepare a bibliography of the resources accessed and analyzed.
2. Based on your research, prepare a process analysis for property management at WorldCom, along with the risks and controls that should exist.
3. What were the control weaknesses in the propoerty management business process at WorldCom that allowed the improper captialization of line costs at WorldCom?
4. Based on your understanding of this aspect of the WorldCom, argue for or against the following statement:

   "The external auditors (Arthur Andersen) failed to detect the improper capitalization of line costs because they failed to properly conduct their analysis of the property management process as opposed to failing to conduct sufficient substantive testing on the related asset and expense accounts."

14

Completing the Integrated Audit I: Business Measurement Analysis

Outline

INTRODUCTION

In this chapter, we begin our discussion of the final phase of the audit process. During the final stages of an engagement, the auditor evaluates the evidence he or she has collected and compares it to the set of financial statements and related disclosures prepared by management (see Figure 14–1). This process reflects all of the

Figure 14–1   Overview of the Audit Process

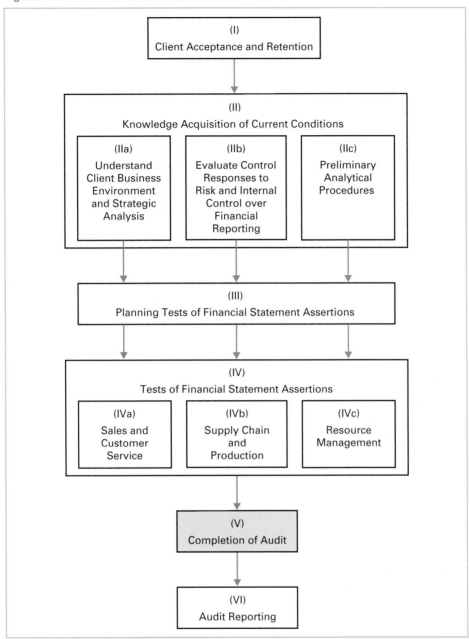

auditor's judgments and decisions about residual risks, the effectiveness of internal controls, the risk of material misstatement, and the evidence gathered to test management's assertions about transactions, accounts, and presentation and disclosure. At this stage the auditor has to consider the appropriateness of the client's accounting policies and choices and evaluate the overall quality of the information contained in the financial statements.

One of the key procedures an auditor uses at this stage of the audit is final review of all financial information. This process is similar to that discussed in

Authoritative Guidance & Standards
This chapter focuses on key assessments of overall performance by examining analytical information about performance to better understand whether financial statements reflect economic reality. The key audit standards addressed in this chapter are for analytical procedures (SAS 56, ISA 520).

Chapter 9 but with the focus now on overall financial reporting quality. At this point in the engagement, the auditor should be able to explain all of the significant results and relationships reported in the financial statements. Any open questions that remain should be cleared as part of this final review.

AN OVERVIEW OF FINAL EVIDENCE AGGREGATION AND PREPARATION OF THE FINANCIAL STATEMENTS

After an auditor completes the strategic and business process analyses, including evaluating the financial reporting process, the next step is to aggregate all of the evidence gathered about management assertions for specific classes of transactions. The purpose of this effort is to assess whether the auditor's individual conclusions are supported by the evidence and are consistent across classes of transactions and accounts. The aggregation of evidence is particularly important when the audit is conducted by a large number of auditors or involves different audit teams in different locations.

There are a number of basic procedures that an auditor will use during the aggregation process (some of which are discussed in detail in the next chapter):

- Obtain audit workpapers and audit evidence from multiple locations and multiple audit teams.
- Review the workpapers for accuracy of testing and completeness of evidence according to the audit plan.
- Reconcile the line items in the financial statements to the underlying account detail.
- Test consolidated financial statements provided by the client.
- Review the appropriateness of accounting policies used by the client.
- Perform final audit wrap-up procedures (see Chapter 15 for details)
- Evaluate the overall reasonableness of reported earnings (often referred to as *earnings quality*).
- Verify the accuracy of information included in footnote disclosures and review the wording of disclosures for understandability and reasonableness.

A particularly important element of the process is to test the grouping of individual accounts into line items to be reported in the financial statements. Most companies of any size are structured as a set of strategic business units that are managed separately and are treated as separate units for the purpose of financial reporting. Hence, the preparation of the final financial statements that are publicly released is a two-stage process: (1) finalize the financial statements for each operating unit and (2) compile the final financial statements for the entity as a whole (including consolidating subsidiary or division statements). The second step of this process occurs near the reporting deadline and is often done under time pressure. The process may involve significant manual entry and re-entry of data that could result in the introduction of errors. More importantly, the pressure and dynamic nature of this process may provide unprincipled management with an opportunity to manipulate the results.

The process of testing management's compilation of financial statements is relatively straightforward but a necessary step in the audit. For example, recomputing the total of all accounts that comprise a line item and then checking the accuracy of any rounding (e.g., to the nearest million dollars) assures that the client has not misclassified accounts or introduced an erroneous or fraudulent component to the line item. Although this process seems rather basic, auditors occasionally encounter clients where this last step of the accounting process is performed manually or in a sloppy manner. For example, the final aggregation of accounts and business units may be accomplished with a spreadsheet that is susceptible to error due to the manual input of a large volume of data. Thus, while the transactions and accounts may be free of material error, the final tally of line items can introduce error into the financial statements.

Example

The aggregation process can be particularly challenging for auditors of a multinational organization with multiple subsidiaries in a multitude of countries. In such companies, the consolidated financial statements should be reconciled to the subsidiary financial statements and the auditor needs to carefully test the translation and aggregation process that management employs. Failure by management to have such a reconciliation process and related controls would be considered a material weakness in an integrated audit. More importantly, it highlights that errors in the consolidation process could go undetected and uncorrected, resulting in a material misstatement in the financial statements.

BUSINESS MEASUREMENT ANALYSIS: ANALYZING THE COMPILED FINANCIAL STATEMENTS

Once the financial statements have been compiled, auditors are required to perform a final analytical review. To facilitate this review, we will elaborate on our approach for analytical procedures that was presented in Chapter 9. We refer to this review as *business measurement analysis*, which constitutes the use of financial and nonfinancial performance measures to evaluate the status and performance of an organization. Auditors use business measurement techniques to compare the performance of a company with what the auditor expects based on previous strategic analysis, process analysis, and the detailed audit testing that has been carried out. After completing risk assessment, control testing, and substantive procedures, the auditor must address whether the financial statements capture the underlying business reality of the organization consistent with what the auditor knows about its activities and circumstances. That is, the auditor should give careful consideration to whether his or her analysis of business performance is consistent with the performance portrayed in the financial statements under generally accepted accounting principles.

Business measurement analysis helps the auditor to integrate the evidence from all the procedures performed during the course of the audit to provide a final test of whether the financial statements are misleading. Furthermore, this review may reveal results that are still unexplained or inconsistent with the auditor's understanding of the firm's economic reality and should be subject to further review and inquiry by the auditor.

> **Authoritative Guidance & Standards**
> A final review of the financial statements is required by auditing standards (SAS 56, ISA 520). The review described here is more in-depth than required by current standards, but is consistent with current best practice, as it helps auditors to understand whether findings and expectations hold across business processes.

Evaluating Performance: Financial Performance Measures

Business measurement analysis usually starts with measures of financial performance for the period being examined. However, before examining specific financial measures of performance, it is important for the auditor to understand the significant accounting policies and practices that the client used during the period and the accounting methods generally used within the industry. The auditor should consider the degree of aggressiveness or conservatism reflected in management's choices of accounting policies and practices. In particular, the auditor should consider revenue recognition as this is an area of frequent abuse by high-flying companies.

Once the auditor understands the key accounting policies in use, the next step is to examine an extensive set of financial measures and ratios that are typically available for a client. Most large public accounting firms have databases that allow very detailed ratio analyses within and between industries to benchmark a client's performance. Should the accounting policies of the client diverge significantly from industry norms, the auditor may need to adjust the client's financial results to be on a comparative basis with the accounting policies that are typical for the industry. The pro forma results can then be compared with industry benchmarks. Of course, the auditor must also consider why the company is at variance with industry practice and make sure that this is clear to the readers of the financial statements.

Example

Most fashion retailers value inventory using the retail form of last-in, first-out (LIFO). However, U.S. fashion retailer Nordstrom utilizes the retail first-in, first-out (FIFO) method. Although in many years there might be no difference, users will be unsure whether differences in key ratios are due to different accounting methods for inventory. For example, Nordstrom reported gross margin percentages of 36.1 percent, 34.6 percent, and 33.2 percent for fiscal years 2004, 2003, and 2002 respectively. Federated Department Stores (i.e., Macy's), which uses retail LIFO, reported gross margin percentages of 40.5 percent, 40.4 percent, and 40 percent for the same three years. Accordingly, users cannot tell whether Federated was more profitable because of better operations or because the retail LIFO method resulted in more favorable results.

Financial analysis may reveal areas where the company's results are inconsistent or suspicious, even after all audit tests have been conducted. In such cases, the auditor needs to follow up with management about the unexpected results and possibly revisit some substantive testing to verify the accuracy of the numbers (and any explanation provided by management). These issues, arising late in the audit process, should also be discussed with the audit committee when the draft auditor's report is discussed.

Evaluating Performance: Nonfinancial Performance Measures

Auditors also obtain a great deal of nonfinancial performance data during the course of the audit. Much of this data will originate in key business processes. Nonfinancial performance measures provide additional support for the financial results and allow the auditor to develop a deeper understanding of the conditions that underlie the company's performance. That is, the auditor can gain deeper insight into the relationship between the financial and nonfinancial performance measures to better assess the reasonableness of the financial statement amounts and related disclosures. Nonfinancial performance measures are usually related to specific processes within a company. Thus, the auditor needs to capture nonfinancial performance data as part of business process analysis (Chapter 6). An auditor is usually constrained in the analysis of nonfinancial data by the accounting system of the client—the auditor cannot analyze data that is not available.

Example

Consider a client that has limited financial resources and therefore has not invested heavily in new production capability. The company is producing its products with the same technology that the company employed ten years ago. An analysis of the nonfinancial performance measures is consistent with these limited resources (e.g., measures of machine down time are increasing each year). The financial statements, however, show a lower percentage of repairs and maintenance expense to gross fixed assets than in previous years. This scenario indicates an inconsistency that needs to be resolved, possibly including the use of additional substantive audit procedures, in order to ensure that repair and maintenance expenditures were not being capitalized as fixed assets.

The auditor must also be aware of the possibility that nonfinancial data is unreliable, especially if it comes from a source other than the client's accounting system. On the other hand, management is much less likely to manipulate nonfinancial data than financial data since much of the data is handled by individuals outside of the accounting area. Hence, the auditor needs to make a tradeoff of financial and nonfinancial data based on the perceived reliability of each. The auditor's ultimate goal is to link the nonfinancial performance measures to the financial performance measures with the following question in mind: Are the nonfinancial performance measures consistent with the reported financial results?

BUSINESS MEASUREMENT ANALYSIS BASED ON THE BALANCED SCORECARD

Business measurement analysis produces a lot of data that must be interpreted and analyzed by the auditor. Accountants are accustomed to using financial statements to organize financial data into a coherent picture. A similar technique would be useful for auditors who analyze a great deal of nonfinancial data along with the financial data. We use a variation of the balanced scorecard as presented in Figure 14–2.

Figure 14–2   The Balanced Scorecard Model

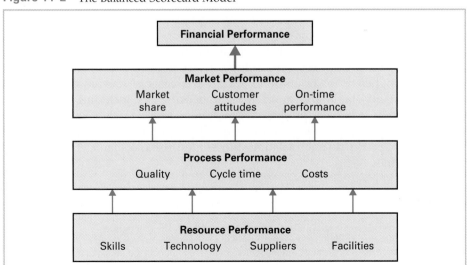

The following four perspectives comprise the balanced scorecard we use for business measurement analysis:

1. Financial: This perspective reflects the investors' viewpoint and measures the overall financial performance of the organization.
2. Market: This perspective reflects customers' viewpoints and measures the success of the organization in obtaining and satisfying its customer base.
3. Core processes: This perspective reflects an internal viewpoint, focusing on the performance of the core processes that create value (e.g., products and services).
4. Resource management processes: This perspective reflects a combined external/internal viewpoint, focusing on the performance of resource management processes and interactions with external resource providers (e.g., labor, vendors).[1]

The auditor's use of a scorecard to organize his or her audit evidence does not require that the client management have a balanced scorecard system in place, just that the client has enough performance-related data to facilitate a comprehensive and meaningful analysis.

A balanced scorecard approach highlights to the auditor that performance in one area of the client can affect or relate to outcomes in other areas. For example, employee problems may be revealed by performance indicators related to human resource management (e.g., a drop in training statistics or deteriorating employee morale). These indicators could be leading warnings of problems in core processes (e.g., decreased quality as employees are less careful in their jobs) or market performance (e.g., customer satisfaction can be dragged down by interactions with unhappy or surly employees). Eventually, problems in resource or core processes are likely to show up as negative financial results, such as decreased revenue, slower growth, higher sales returns and allowances, and increased warranty claims. Within each of the four dimensions, the auditor will identify a mix of financial and nonfinancial performance measures to measure and monitor over time, normally based on the set of measures that the client has available or has agreed to collect for the auditor.

Process and Resource Performance: Figure 14–3 identifies a number of possible performance indicators that might be appropriate for core and resource processes. Performance measurement for core processes tends to focus on the quality, timeliness, and cost of process activities. In general, deterioration in any one attribute of a process could lead to poor market performance and weak financial results. Common cost measurement problems include determining the factors that actually drive costs higher or lower and allocating those costs to specific activities and products. Quality can be measured in a number of ways, including defect rates, product yields, waste rates, product returns, and warranty costs. Cycle time is important for assessing process performance. Although traditional financial reporting systems typically do not track time, most enterprise risk management systems track cycle times.

---

1 The four-fold classification of the balanced scorecard is not a formal requirement. The number of categories to be analyzed depends on the facts and circumstances of the client. The four perspectives included in a balanced scorecard development for management purposes are financial, customer-focused, internal processes, and learning and growth (Kaplan and Norton 1996).

Figure 14–3   Measuring Process and Resource Performance

Core Processes	Resource Management Processes
Process Time: • Time to market • Operating cycle • Turnover	**Human Resources:** • Employee productivity • Employee attitudes • Employee turnover • Employee competencies
Process Cost: • Cost drivers • Cost allocations • Cost per activity	**Information Technology:** • Reliability of information • Timeliness of information • System development
Process Quality: • Defect rates • Product yields • Scrap/waste rates • Product returns • Warranty costs	**Property:** • Facility acquisition • Facility utilization • Facility maintenance • Facility reliability
	Supply Chain: • Delivery performance • Service performance • Quality • Costs
	Financial: • Cost of capital • Cash reserves • Cash float • Taxes • Cost of transaction processing

Example

Appropriate performance measures for human resource management include employee productivity, morale, turnover, and competencies. These attributes would be particularly important for assessing the risks and potential for success of a professional services firm. The historical level of employee turnover in major accounting firms and the increasing cost of developing experienced personnel have created challenges for firms as they manage their most critical knowledge assets—people.

Market Performance: Figure 14–4 summarizes the relationship between key measures of market success. Market performance and customer attitudes are reflected in total market share. Better products and services (which depend on the core and resource processes) usually lead to a larger market share. Market share is the net result of the rate at which customers are acquired and retained (or lost). Generally, the acquisition and retention of customers is driven by customer satisfaction, which can be a critical leading indicator of future problems. Highly sophisticated companies can track the profitability of individual customers in order to guide future sales and marketing efforts. Other market performance measures that might be of interest to a client include brand awareness, the rate of

Figure 14–4   Measuring Market Performance

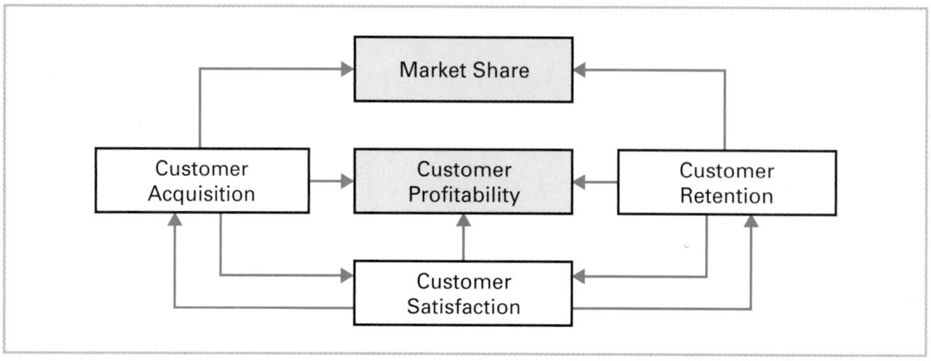

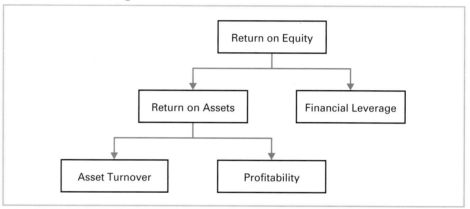

Figure 14–5   Measuring Financial Performance

success at introducing new products, and revenue growth (total and by product line).

Example

Most large banks track the profitability of individual customers by monitoring the fees an individual generates across a wide range of services (e.g., checking accounts, credit cards, loans, safe deposit boxes). By monitoring customer profitability, the bank knows when to offer a good customer some extra incentives. For example, the average customer may need to pay a fee for a credit card or whenever he or she bounces a check. A customer with a very large loan that is profitable to the bank may have fees waived on credit cards or overdrafts. This is one way the bank can maintain customer loyalty.

Financial Performance: Figure 14–5 provides an overview of the financial perspective, listing the relationships among standard financial ratios that have been previously discussed in Chapter 9. Return on equity can be decomposed into two components: (1) return on assets, which measures the profit generated given the asset base of the company and (2) financial leverage (debt/assets), which measures the extent of debt financing used by the company. Return on assets can be further decomposed into various asset turnover ratios (e.g., receivables, inventory, PPE) and profit measures (e.g., net income/sales).

The relationship between ROA and ROE is particularly important for many clients. This relationship is directly affected by the amount of debt that a company has issued. When a highly leveraged company has a good year, shareholders benefit. When it has a bad year, however, the leveraged company has trouble and the shareholders suffer. This pattern of results occurs because the debt holders must be paid regardless of whether the client has a good or bad year. If ROA is greater than the fixed rate paid to debt holders, ROE will exceed ROA. On the other hand, if ROA is less than the fixed rate, ROE will be less than ROA.[2]

FINAL REVIEW OF FINANCIAL RESULTS: AN INTEGRATED EXAMPLE

We will now discuss a comprehensive application of business measurement as applied to a fictitious company: AMA Autoparts Inc. This company was previously introduced in Chapter 9 when we discussed analytical procedures for planning. Appendix A at the end of this chapter provides further descriptive data about AMA Autoparts that would be known by the end of the audit. Basic financial statement data for three years (20x8, 20x7, and 20x6) is presented in Figure 14–6 and Figure 14–7. This information should be reviewed before proceeding with our analysis. The current audit engagement pertains to 20x8, and we will assume that the prior-year results have been previously audited. We will also introduce numerous nonfinancial performance measures as we work our way through the illustration. Our goal is to use this data to finalize our understanding of the financial statements and to identify any lingering audit issues that need to be resolved that have not been dealt with in the current audit files. We adapt the approach introduced in Chapter 9 for evaluating analytical evidence for the final review of the financial statements (see Figure 14–8).

Step 1 of our analysis is to identify the aspects of financial reporting that the auditor wishes to review in detail. We will follow our variant of the balanced scorecard approach and assume that the auditor is interested in the following aspects of AMA's performance:

1. Financial performance
2. Market performance
3. Process performance (Product design and development, Customer sales and distribution, Production management)
4. Resource performance (Human resources, Supply chain management, Property management, Financial management)

The second step is to identify the facts, both from the final financial statements and the audit files, that may be pertinent to our interpretation of the financial statements. Reading the appendix (which, in the auditor's files, would be in the

---

2 The relationship between ROA and ROE was the motivating factor behind many of the highly leveraged takeovers of the early 1980s. In many takeovers, the raider could borrow money (often at a high interest rate in the form of "junk bonds"), purchase the company, reorganize the company so as to increase its ROA and, finally, if the ROA exceeded the interest rates paid on the borrowed money, keep the difference. In this way, the raider was able to make large profits with a very small investment in the takeover company.

Figure 14–6   An Example of Comparative and Common size Analysis: Basic Financial Data for AMA Autoparts inc.

Balance Sheet

	Audited 20x6	Audited 20x7	Unaudited 20x8	Percentage Analysis 20x6	20x7	20x8
Cash	$ 26,000	$ 312,000	$ 10,000	1.47%	14.81%	0.48%
Marketable Securities	100,000	120,000	125,000	5.66%	5.70%	6.04%
Accounts Receivable	525,000	350,000	700,000	29.73%	16.61%	33.82%
Inventory	310,000	310,000	300,000	17.55%	14.71%	14.49%
Prepaid Expenses	60,000	75,000	50,000	3.40%	3.56%	2.42%
Current Assets	1,021,000	1,167,000	1,185,000	57.81%	55.39%	57.25%
Long-Term Investments	275,000	300,000	310,000	15.57%	14.24%	14.98%
Plant and Property	555,000	740,000	640,000	31.43%	35.12%	30.92%
Accumulated Depreciation	(85,000)	(100,000)	(65,000)	−4.81%	−4.75%	−3.14%
Total Assets	1,766,000	2,107,000	2,070,000	100.00%	100.00%	100.00%
Accounts Payable	32,000	110,000	85,000	1.81%	5.22%	4.11%
Wages Payable	28,000	32,000	18,000	1.59%	1.52%	0.87%
Dividends Payable	0	5,000	130,000	0.00%	0.24%	6.28%
Taxes Payable	36,000	55,000	62,000	2.04%	2.61%	3.00%
Current Portion of Debt	150,000	175,000	100,000	8.49%	8.31%	4.83%
Current Liabilities	246,000	377,000	395,000	13.93%	17.89%	19.08%
Mortgage Payable	800,000	625,000	525,000	45.30%	29.66%	25.36%
Total Liabilities	1,046,000	1,002,000	920,000	59.23%	47.56%	44.44%
Common Stock ($10 par)	110,000	150,000	225,000	6.23%	7.12%	10.87%
Additional Paid-In Capital	260,000	345,000	425,000	14.72%	16.37%	20.53%
Retained Earnings	350,000	610,000	500,000	19.82%	28.95%	24.15%
Total Equity	720,000	1,105,000	1,150,000	40.77%	52.44%	55.56%
Total Liability and Equity	1,766,000	2,107,000	2,070,000	100.00%	100.00%	100.00%

Income Statement

	Audited 20x7	Unaudited 20x8	Percentage Analysis 20x7	20x8
Sales	4,185,000	6,045,000	100.00%	100.00%
Cost of Goods Sold	(2,565,000)	(4,015,000)	−61.29%	−66.42%
Gross Margin	1,620,000	2,030,000	38.71%	33.58%
Depreciation Expense	(90,000)	(75,000)	−2.15%	−1.24%
Selling Expense	(600,000)	(575,000)	−14.34%	−9.51%
Administrative Expense	(420,000)	(480,000)	−10.04%	−7.94%
Net Operating Income	510,000	900,000	12.19%	14.89%
Interest Expense	(65,000)	(50,000)	−1.55%	−0.83%
Net Income Before Taxes	445,000	850,000	10.63%	14.06%
Income Tax Expense	(175,000)	(365,000)	−4.18%	−6.04%
Net Income	270,000	485,000	6.45%	8.02%

Figure 14–7   An Example of Ratio Analysis

Ratio Analysis	20x8	20x7
Liquidity Ratios:		
Quick ratio	2.11	2.07
Current ratio	3.00	3.10
Asset Management Ratios:		
Inventory turnover	13.16	8.27
Receivable turnover	11.51	9.57
Fixed asset turnover	9.95	7.54
Asset turnover	2.89	2.16
Average days to collect	31.71	38.14
Average days to sell	27.74	152.08
Averaging operating cycle	59.45	190.22
Depreciation expense/plant assets	1.24%	2.15%
Debt Management Ratios:		
Payable turnover	41.18	36.13
Debt/assets	44.44%	47.56%
Interest coverage	18.00	7.85
Profitability Ratios:		
Return on assets	24.59%	15.98%
Return on equity	43.02%	29.59%
Return on sales (Profit margin)	8.02%	6.45%
Earnings per share	$ 2.16	$ 1.80
Market Value Ratios:		
Price/earnings	8.93	12.08
Book value of equity	5.11	7.37
Dividend payout	122.68%	3.70%
Effective tax rate	42.94%	39.33%

Figure 14–8   Business Measurement Analysis: A Seven-Step Process for Reviewing the Compiled Financial Statements

PURPOSE: To use business measurement analysis as a final review of the compiled financial statements to assure that reported results are consistent with the auditor's understanding of the organization's environments, risks, processes, and activities, and economic events.

STEP 1: Identify aspects of performance to be evaluated.

STEP 2: Review the facts relevant to the analysis: This information comes from the auditor's review of the client's environment, strategic analysis, process analysis, and audit testing.

STEP 3: Identify relevant business measurement: The auditor must decide what attributes to measure. These are the financial and nonfinancial results included in the balanced scorecard.

STEP 4: Obtain data and perform computations.

STEP 5: Impose structure: The Balanced Scorecard is a useful technique for organizing results.

STEP 6: Analyze: Analyze each of the business measurements for deviations from expectations.

STEP 7: Conclude: Construct a cohesive explanation of the numerical data, which incorporates all of the numerical data, facts, and circumstances that are known about the company, and determine the implications for the audit, including the potential need for additional testing or inquiry.

format of a strategic analysis and process analysis) brings the following key facts to light:

1. The company's products are of high quality, which implies that its cost of production should be higher than its competitors', as should its sales prices. About 25 percent of its product line was designed and developed internally.
2. The company sells more to autoparts stores than original equipment manufacturers (60:40 mix). If these markets have different profit margins, the company's results will be affected by the sales mix. Note that other companies in the industry sell more to manufacturers (40:60 mix). Customers are serviced by a small group of salespeople with specific geographic responsibilities.
3. The company uses LIFO, which typically lowers inventory balances and increases cost of goods sold in times when there is cost or price inflation.
4. The dollar amount of the company's bad debt allowance has slowly increased over the last three years.
5. The company uses technology to maximize the efficiency of its supply chain and interactions with suppliers.
6. The company is young, which means that its fixed asset costs may be higher than its competitors'. The company uses straight-line depreciation.
7. The company had a major transaction involving the sale and leaseback of two warehouses. The sale and leaseback of the warehouses is being treated as an operating lease by the client.
8. The company recently entered into a new union contract that raises the wages and benefits of factory employees.
9. The company's accounting for joint ventures is unusual. Investments in joint ventures are usually accounted for using either the cost or equity method, depending on the degree of control exercised over the venture.
10. The company's mortgage is standard and is being systematically paid down over time. The stated interest rate is 9 percent with year-end payments.
11. The company is closely held and had relatively few shareholders prior to its public offering in 20x7. The company has a stock option plan for senior employees. The company issued a large number of new shares during the year and paid a huge dividend prior to issuing the new stock.[3]

The next three steps involve identifying the appropriate business measurements to analyze, gathering the data and computing the performance measures, and imposing structure on the diverse set of data that is to be obtained. The results of these steps are presented in Figures 14–9 through 14–17. These tables contain numerous nonfinancial indicators and a few industry benchmarks when such comparisons would be reasonably available. Lack of comparable industry benchmarks is one of the key challenges of performing business measurement analysis. As a result, most audit firms invest in databases about industries where they have a number of clients. Nonetheless, an auditor will frequently encounter situations where only limited industry data is available. We will assume that all nonfinancial performance measures have been collected from data systems that either have been reconciled to the financial reporting system or have been determined to be reliable during process analysis and control testing.

---

3 The public offering in 20x8 should have caused the auditor to heighten concern for the accuracy of the 20x7 financial statements because they would have been the basis for selling new shares to the public.

Figure 14–9   An Example of Integrated Analysis: Financial Performance

Financial Performance	20x8	20x7	Industry
Net income	$485,000	$270,000	
Earnings per share	$2.16	$1.80	
Return on assets	24.59%	15.98%	19.40%
Return on equity	43.02%	29.59%	32.00%
Return on sales	8.02%	6.45%	6.85%
Asset turnover	2.89	2.16	
Share price	$19.25	$21.75	
Price/earnings	8.93	12.08	14.22

Figure 14–10   An Example of Integrated Analysis: Market Performance

Market Performance	20x8	20x7	Industry
Gross revenues	$6,045,000	$4,185,000	
Revenue growth	44.44%	32.40%	11.30%
Customer satisfaction rating (of 5)	4.63	4.85	
Customer acquisition rate/year	12%	16%	
Customer retention rate/year	87%	92%	
Brand awareness (of 5)	4.75	4.52	

FINANCIAL PERFORMANCE

The financial performance of AMA Autoparts is summarized in Figure 14–9. Profitability statistics reveal that that the company has had an outstanding year. Income ($485,000) and earnings per share ($2.16) are up significantly. All measures of profitability have increased a great deal, and are significantly higher than the rest of the industry. Hence, superior performance should also be apparent in key processes as documented in the audit files. The only signs of weakness are the market price of the stock and the ratio of price to earnings. If the company had maintained its P/E ratio into 20x8, its stock would likely be trading in excess of $24 (at least 25 percent higher than it is). This discrepancy suggests that market investors are concerned about this company in some way that is not reflected in its reported earnings or that some other change in the overall economy has changed the relationship. The auditor should keep these competing explanations in mind during subsequent analyses.

MARKET PERFORMANCE

The market performance of AMA Autoparts and the attitudes of its customers are summarized in Figure 14–10. The good news is that the company's sales are growing rapidly (44.44 percent in 20x8), and the company has a growth rate far higher than the rest of the industry. However, some of the customer statistics are worrisome, at least for the longer run. Although the changes are small, customer satisfaction (4.63), customer acquisition rates (12 percent), and customer retention rates (87 percent) are all deteriorating, suggesting that customers are less happy with the company than they were in the past. This could indicate that the company's rapid growth has begun to outstrip its ability to effectively service its customers. Most significantly, it is not consistent with the financial performance reported

Figure 14–11   An Example of Integrated Analysis: Process Performance—Product Design and Development

Product design	20x8	20x7	Industry
Time to market (years)	2.3	2.4	1.9
Product introduction success rate	64%	83%	
Years to recover development costs	1.60	1.30	
Product recalls	3	1	

above and may indicate difficulties ahead for the company. The only performance indicator consistent with superior future performance is that brand awareness improved (to 4.75).

PROCESS PERFORMANCE: PRODUCT DESIGN AND DEVELOPMENT

AMA Autoparts's recent product development experience is summarized in Figure 14–11. First, we see that the company is slow to get new products to market when compared to the industry (2.3 versus 1.9 years). This suggests that AMA may be lagging behind its competitors in the development of a new generation of products. Although this problem would only affect the 25 percent of the products that are developed internally, the problem is compounded by the observation that fewer new products are succeeding (64 percent versus 83 percent) and that it is taking longer for AMA to recover the development costs of new products (1.6 versus 1.3 years). Most worrisome are the three product recalls, which suggest the company is having quality problems. Given the company's strategy of being a high quality/high price supplier, the trends reported could be crippling to its future prospects, a potential warning sign for future audits when considering the going concern assumption. Furthermore, these trends are inconsistent with sustaining superior financial performance in future periods, and may place pressure on management to hit earnings targets that would affect the control environment of the client in the future.

PROCESS PERFORMANCE: CUSTOMER SALES AND SERVICE

Figure 14–12 provides insight into customer service and distribution. Sales per customer have increased ($18,039 to $26,283), and selling expenses relative to revenue (9.51 percent) and per salesperson ($143,750) have dropped, which suggests that the sales force is becoming more effective. The ability to control selling expenses, while increasing sales, is consistent with past superior performance. However, after the initial sales contract is obtained, on-time delivery has declined (98 percent to 93 percent) as has the company's ability to fill orders on a timely basis (order fill rates dropped from 85 percent to 80 percent). This pattern of performance has occurred during the same time that customer complaints have risen (to 49). These indicators may indicate that the company will have difficulty sustaining their industry-leading profits in the future.

An analysis of selling and administrative expenses raises an important issue concerning the difference between fixed and variable costs. Costs that are essentially variable can be expected to increase, in absolute terms, as sales increase, but remain relatively stable as a percentage of sales. Costs that are essentially fixed would be expected to remain stable in absolute terms but to decrease as a percentage of sales as sales increase. This pattern holds for administrative costs that do not fluctuate much

Figure 14–12   An Example of Integrated Analysis: Process Performance—Customer Sales and Service

Customer Sales and Distribution	20x8	20x7	Industry
Inventory turnover	13.16	8.27	12.15
Inventory/assets	14.49%	14.71%	17.20%
Gross profit margin	33.58%	38.71%	42.20%
Receivable turnover	11.51	9.57	15.78
Receivable/assets	33.82%	16.61%	28.15%
Bad debt percentage	1.10%	1.80%	
Selling expense/sales	9.51%	14.34%	21.23%
Cost of returns/sales	2.24%	2.09%	
Selling expenses/salesperson	$143,750	$200,000	
Sales per customer	$26,283	$18,039	
On-time delivery percentage	93%	98%	
Order fill percentage	80%	85%	
Volume of customer complaints	49	32	
Percent sales to retail	60.00%	59.00%	40.00%

since they are composed of salaried administrative employees and fixed assets used for administrative activities. On the other hand, selling expenses are often considered to be variable and a drop in selling expense as a percentage of sales could indicate that the company has not properly accrued selling expenses. If noted during planning, this pattern might cause the auditor to adjust the audit program to investigate selling expenses in detail. At the end of the audit, the auditor would consider evidence related to sales expenses obtained from tests of controls and transactions, as well as any direct tests of sales expenses performed during substantive testing, in determining if the reported balance was materially misstated.

The data on receivables shows the balance has increased significantly during the current year (consistent with the growth of sales), and the turnover is improving but is still significantly below the industry. The company's bad debt reserves have declined as a percentage of receivables (1.8 percent to 1.1 percent). If observed during planning, this pattern of results might cause the auditor to adjust the audit program related to the valuation of receivables. As the audit is being wrapped up, the auditor would consider whether adequate evidence had been gathered to support the conclusion that the valuation assertion for receivables is free of material misstatement. For example, the auditor knows from strategic analysis that auto supply stores pay more slowly than large car manufacturers so the company's customer mix justifies the slower rate of collections to some extent. Other evidence that could be relevant to the final conclusions about receivable valuation would include:

- The results of tests of controls performed during the analysis of customer sales processes, especially related to credit authorization and approval
- Tests of transactions for sales and cash receipts
- Review of the aged trial balance and analysis of the pattern of bad debts over time
- Tests of receipts from customers after year end

If the results of these tests support the reported balance for receivables, the auditor can then conclude that there is no material misstatement in spite of the unusual performance results.

Inventory balances are relatively stable, which is not uncommon with the use of LIFO. Cost of goods sold is high and gross margin is low (33.58 percent) relative to sales, especially compared to the rest of the industry. Given that the company specializes in high-quality parts, one would expect cost of goods sold per unit to be relatively higher than the industry, but this should be offset by higher prices. The fact that the majority of sales are made to supply stores would also imply that the margin should probably be higher, because large manufacturers of automobiles could be expected to negotiate quantity discounts that would not be available to small supply store chains. The accounting treatment of the income from the joint venture violates GAAP and should be corrected in the financial statements. This adjustment would increase the cost of goods sold by $34,000, causing gross margin to decrease even further, to 33.02 percent for 20x8.

The low margins on the company's sales would be considered a serious issue during the planning of the audit and the auditor would probably undertake extensive audit testing to determine if inventory and costs of goods sold is free of material error. Some of the evidence that the auditor would consider includes the following:

- Strategic analysis would provide insight into the competitiveness of the market for autoparts, including the impact of any industry forces that affect the relative bargaining power of parts stores and parts manufacturers (e.g., consolidation or new entrants).
- Business process analysis of production would provide insight into the reliability and efficiency of the production process.
- Business process analysis of customer sales would provide insight into the pricing and marketing strategy of the company.
- Tests of sales transactions would determine if product pricing is accurate.
- Tests of standard costs would determine if unit costs are accurate.
- Tests of ending inventories would determine if year end balances are accurate (which would have a carry on effect on costs of goods sold).

Depending on the evidence available from these tests, the auditor could conclude that the affected accounts are free of material misstatements. However, the performance results suggest that the espoused and actual strategies of this company are diverging, and this may have longer run implications for the future viability of the company.

PROCESS PERFORMANCE: PRODUCTION MANAGEMENT

Performance measures for production management are presented in Figure 14–13. Although production costs are higher than in the past (66.42 percent versus

Figure 14–13   An Example of Integrated Analysis: Process Performance—Production Management

Production Management	20x8	20x7	Industry
Inventory/assets	14.49%	14.71%	17.20%
Cost of goods sold/sales	66.42%	61.29%	
Cost of waste and spoilage/sales	0.71%	0.92%	
Cost of defects/sales	0.86%	1.13%	
Warranty costs/sales	4.71%	3.41%	

Figure 14–14   An Example of Integrated Analysis: Resource Performance—Human Resources

Human Resource Management	20x8	20x7	Industry
Employee morale (of 5 pts)	4.63	4.85	
Employee turnover	16%	8%	
Size of work force	31	26	
Days lost to absenteeism	119	79	
Labor cost per employee	$52,100	$49,330	$47,540
Fringe benefit per employee	$7,530	$7,300	$7,800

61.29 percent), inventory balances are stable and the costs of defects (0.86 percent) and waste (0.71 percent) have declined. This suggests that the company's supply chain management has become more effective, consistent with the firm earning industry leading profits. Better quality inputs, delivered on an as-needed basis, would cause this pattern of results (higher costs, less waste) and indicate that the company's production processes are improving. Rising warranty claims (from 3.41 percent to 4.71 percent) may be due to the incidence of product recalls that was previously mentioned, rather than production problems per se. At this point, the auditor would specifically consider whether evidence from tests of transactions, substantive analytical procedures, or other substantive tests supports the level of warranty expenses accrued by the company.

RESOURCE PERFORMANCE: HUMAN RESOURCES

Figure 14–14 presents various statistics related to the management of human resources. Costs have increased as expected given the new labor contract which recently took effect. The company's labor costs are higher than the industry because competitors are operating under an older contract. The work force has increased by almost 20 percent (26 to 31) as expected given the rapid growth of the company. The increase in employee turnover (to 16 percent) and the days lost to employee absenteeism (to 119), as well as the direct measure of employee morale (4.63 percent), all indicate that the company may be pushed to the limit to cope with its aggressive growth and are consistent with the quality issues and customer satisfaction issues noted above. These results hint at future problems that might negatively affect the performance of the company, undermining the sustainability of superior performance and, possibly, putting pressure on management to achieve performance targets. Such pressure could lead to a deterioration of the control environment and the auditor should review current year evidence to assess whether this has happened already.

RESOURCE PERFORMANCE: SUPPLY CHAIN

The company's supply chain statistics are summarized in Figure 14–15. Supply chain management would be considered a key business process for this client and subject to extensive process analysis. Consistent with strategic analysis (e.g., the company is an industry leader), the company appears to be quite effective in managing its supply chain relationships with a sophisticated information system for coordinating orders to suppliers and minimizing the carrying costs of inventory. Supplier deliveries are generally on time (87 percent) and improving, and there are very few returns to vendors (only 0.16 percent). Furthermore, the electronic links

Figure 14–15   An Example of Integrated Analysis: Resource Performance—Supply Chain

Supply Chain Management	20x8	20x7	Industry
Supplier on-time percentage	87%	82%	
Returns to suppliers/COGS	0.16%	0.20%	
Payable turnover	41.18	36.13	21.50

Figure 14–16   An Example of Integrated Analysis: Resource Performance—Property

Property Management	20x8	20x7	Industry
Plant assets/assets	27.78%	30.37%	
Accum. depreciation/plant assets	10.16%	13.51%	
Depreciation expense/plant assets	11.72%	12.16%	
Fixed asset turnover	9.95	7.54	11.21
Cost per square foot	$183	$211	
Plant maintenance costs/sales	4.05%	5.10%	

with suppliers allow for rapid invoice presentation and payment, as evidenced by the high payable turnover ratio (41.18 in 20x8).

RESOURCE PERFORMANCE: PROPERTY

Performance statistics for property and facility management are presented in Figure 14–16. The company's fixed asset turnover (9.95), cost per square foot ($183) and maintenance costs (4.05 percent of sales) have improved, but its asset base is shrinking. We know that the company removed two large assets from the balance sheet through the sale and leaseback of two warehouses. The impact of this transaction was to remove the warehouses from the balance sheet *but not from usage*; that is, the company's operating assets have not changed. We also know that the company charged a $30,000 gain on asset disposal against depreciation expense, explaining the slight decline in depreciation as a percentage of plant assets from 12.16 percent in 20x7 to 11.72 percent in 20x8. Although this change is small, the auditor would expect the average depreciable life of the remaining plant assets to decrease and depreciation to increase given that the company disposed of two significant long-lived assets (the warehouses).[4]

The auditor would have tested the sale and leaseback transaction during the substantive testing phase of the audit because it is individually significant to the financial statements. Also, since the accounting for the gain is incorrect, the auditor would also propose to management a $30,000 adjustment to depreciation expense. Finally, the auditor would consider if there is adequate evidence to support the recorded level of depreciation (after adjusting for the known error). If the $30,000 is added back to depreciation expense, the amount for 20x8 increases to $105,000, which is more reasonable given the activities of the organization. Although the revised analysis of depreciation is consistent with expectations, the auditor would

---

4 To see this, consider a group of assets with a useful life of 5 years—the depreciation percentage should then be about 20 percent. For assets with a longer useful life of 10 years, the depreciation percentage would be about 10 percent. It is possible that the removal of the warehouses would not reduce the average of the remaining asset lives if the warehouses were close to being fully depreciated. Given that the company is young, this is an extremely unlikely explanation for the results.

Figure 14–17   An Example of Integrated Analysis: Resource Performance—Financial Management

Financial Management	20x8	20x7	Industry
Quick ratio	2.11	2.07	
Current ratio	3.00	3.10	
Cash + Securities/assets	6.52%	20.51%	
Payables/assets	19.08%	17.89%	
Effective tax rate	42.94%	39.33%	33.50%
Interest expense/debt	7.02%	7.43%	
Interest coverage	18.00	7.85	
Debt/assets	44.44%	47.56%	65.00%
Dividend payout	122.68%	3.70%	45.00%
Book value of equity	$5.11	$7.37	

also consider the results of business process analysis for facilities management and any related tests of controls or transactions (primarily additions and disposals).[5]

RESOURCE PERFORMANCE: FINANCIAL MANAGEMENT

The current financial condition of AMA Autoparts is summarized in Figure 14–17. The company has several strong indicators of fiscal health, both short term and long term. Working capital, as measured by the quick (2.11) and current (3.00) ratios, appears adequate and consistent with the past. The company's debt is being paid off systematically and on time, and is low by industry standards (44.44 versus 65.00 percent). The interest coverage ratio is improving (to 18.0) and the average interest rate paid is stable, as would be expected since the largest component of interest expense comes from a fixed rate mortgage. The computed average interest rate of 7.02 percent seems low given the stated rate of 9 percent on the mortgage but is consistent with the previous year's 7.43 percent. The auditor would then consider the following evidence to assess whether interest is likely to be misstated:

- Strategic analysis related to economic conditions and market rates of interest
- Business process analysis related to financial management and the terms of financing that carry interest charges (e.g., are rates fixed or variable?)
- Analysis of balance levels and payment patterns throughout the year to refine the estimate of interest expense
- Reconciliation of interest payment information contained in bank confirmation(s) with recorded financial results

OVERALL AUDIT CONCLUSION IMPLICATIONS

Figure 14–18 summarizes the questions, potential problems, and issues that were raised in the preceding discussion. The most critical observations for 20x8 are:

- Problems associated with rapid growth: Due to its rapid growth, the company appears to have difficulties related to quality, development, and human resources. If these issues are not addressed by management in the near future,

---

5 The large increase in return on assets (15.98 percent to 24.59 percent) must be viewed carefully given that the base of accounting assets has shrunk dramatically.

Figure 14–18   Summary of Results from Business Measurement Analysis

Process/ Area	Potential Concerns	Possible Audit Implications	Possible Additional Substantive Procedures
Financial overview	Drop in P/E ratio in spite of rapid growth and record profits.	• Viability: The market may feel that there are internal problems that will limit the company in the future. • Control Environment: Inconsistency between reported earnings and market valuation might indicate potential for earnings manipulation as management attempts to improve the company's market standing.*	• Complete going concern review. • Note going concern and pressure on control environment as concerns for future audits. • Examine year end closing and adjusting entries to ensure they are legitimate.
Market performance	Customer attitude statistics are deteriorating.	• Control Environment: The company's processes may not be able to keep pace with rapid growth, leaving customers dissatisfied due to errors and service problems. This problem could also affect information processing.	• Additional detailed review by senior audit staff of the results from tests of controls to ensure that there is sufficient evidence to support the level of reliance on controls.
Product design	Slow to get new products to market. Declining rate of success for introducing new products. Increased rate of product recalls.	• Viability: For a company whose strategy is based on being high quality, loss of reputation could significantly reduce its chance of success in the longer term. • Valuation of warranty expenses and accruals • Valuation and disclosure related to failed and recalled products in inventory.	• Consider the possibility of asset impairments that may need to be adjusted. • Note risk of material misstatement due to asset impairments in future audits. • Consider post-year end and last quarter trend in warranty claims and product returns to determine if additional allowances are needed.
Customer sales and distribution	On-time delivery and order fill statistics have declined.	• Viability: Failure to deliver appropriate products on time can cause loss of customer satisfaction and erosion of market share in a competitive market in future periods.	• Complete going concern review. • Note risk of material misstatement in future audits.

* Management's incentives would be affected by the existence of contingent compensation such as stock options.

Figure 14–18 *(continued)*

Process/ Area	Potential Concerns	Possible Audit Implications	Possible Additional Substantive Procedures
Customer sales and distribution	Significant drop in selling expenses.	• Valuation, completeness, and classification of selling expenses.	• Inquire of management about this pattern. • Review relevant evidence obtained during strategic and process analysis and substantive testing. • Consider additional substantive tests in this area to determine if an adjustment is needed.
Human resources	Deterioration in absenteeism and employee turnover statistics.	• Control Environment: Personnel problems could result in low-skilled, inexperienced personnel handling critical tasks, increasing the likelihood of problems and errors in information processing. Frequent process breakdowns may compound other problems (e.g., customer relations and product development).	• Additional detailed review by senior audit staff of the results from tests of controls to ensure that there is sufficient evidence to support reliance on controls. • Review relevant evidence obtained during strategic and process analysis and substantive testing.
Property resources	Average depreciation rates indicate that the company may not have correctly computed current year expense.	• Valuation of fixed assets and depreciation expense.	• Review relevant evidence obtained during strategic and process analysis and substantive testing. • Request additional internal audit testing in this area. • Consider additional substantive tests in this area to determine if an adjustment is needed.
Property resources	Unusual sale-leaseback transaction.	• Valuation and disclosure of property and obligations related to the sale and leaseback.	• Quantify and propose adjustments to bring in compliance with GAAP. • Discuss with audit committee.
Financial management	Unacceptable accounting method used for income from joint venture.	• Valuation, classification, and disclosure of the joint venture. • Difference is immaterial to point of being insignificant	• Quantify and propose adjustments to bring in compliance with GAAP. • Discuss with audit committee.

the auditor will need to carefully consider the effect on client viability, the control environment, and the risk of material misstatement in future audits.

- Financial performance: The superior performance reported in the financial statements rests mainly on its ability to acquire new customers and manage its supply chain. Issues in several key business processes, although not reducing this year's financial performance, raise issues about whether this level of earnings is sustainable in the future (see the discussion of earnings quality in the next chapter).

- Pressures from the equity market: Market valuations appear to be out of line with accounting results, putting pressure on management to meet market expectations. Although there is no evidence that suggests any accounting manipulation has occurred, given the conclusions that short term financial performance may not be sustainable, the pressure on management could be quite intense in the coming year, possibly leading to higher engagement risk for the auditor.

- Potential misstatements: The available audit evidence and the results of business measurement analysis reveal some known errors (e.g., accounting for the joint venture, treatment of gain on sale-leaseback of warehouses) and a few areas where the auditor would need to determine if the available evidence was adequate to conclude there were no material misstatements (valuation of inventory/cost of goods sold, valuation of bad debts, completeness of interest expense). Any actual misstatements would be documented and brought to the attention of management for correction. We discuss the process of correcting accounting errors in the next chapter in more detail.

This section has illustrated the use of a structured approach for analyzing a complex set of performance measurements. Although the analysis has been done in the context of a final review of compiled financial results, a similar approach could be used as part of preliminary planning. If performed early in the audit, the auditor will have less information available to evaluate unusual results or trends. However, such an analysis would facilitate the identification of risks that should be considered by the auditor in the planning and conduct of the audit. As a final wrap-up review, this analysis highlights any unanswered questions that the auditor may face, facilitates overall evaluation of the audit evidence gathered in the course of the audit, and highlights possible concerns for next year's audit.

EVALUATION OF POTENTIAL GOING CONCERN PROBLEMS

One of the most difficult judgments that an auditor must deal with in the course of the audit is to identify when an organization is in sufficient danger of going bankrupt or experiencing financial distress such that an explanatory paragraph should be added to an otherwise unqualified audit report. The auditor is often confronted with a dilemma: if the opinion is not modified and the organization subsequently fails, the auditor will be subject to criticism and possible litigation. If the auditor does modify the opinion, investors and creditors may be so sensitized to the possible risk that they become leery of dealing with the organization, triggering the failure that was feared. Maintaining a balance between conservatism and fairness to the client is a difficult challenge to the auditor. Unfortunately, there have been a number of infamous cases in the past where an auditor gave a clean opinion to a company only to have the company declare bankruptcy shortly after the release of the financial statements. As a result of these cases, auditing standards require the auditor to evaluate whether there is substantial doubt about an organization continuing as a going concern for twelve months after the date of the financial statements being audited.[6]

Example

Subsequent to the events of September 11, 2001, most U.S. airline companies struggled due to rising fuel costs and general economic recession. Within a four-year period, four legacy air carriers—United, USAir, Northwest, and Delta—all filed for bankruptcy protection in the U.S. courts system (Chapter 11). Subsequent to initial bankruptcy filings, accounting firms for most U.S. airlines included an explanatory paragraph in their opinions that substantial doubt existed about the entity's ability to continue as a going concern. In some cases, the airlines did not file for bankruptcy protection in the following year(s); however, in other cases, the airlines did file for bankruptcy protection.

Business measurement analysis provides an excellent foundation on which to base an assessment of the likelihood of a company failing in the near term. The auditor uses a three-step process for assessing whether there is substantial doubt about whether an organization will be able to continue as a going concern:

1. Consider evidence that indicates that a going concern problem *may* exist.
2. Evaluate management's plan to mitigate the identified conditions.
3. Determine if management's plan is adequate and appropriate for the circumstances and assess the likelihood that the company will suffer financial distress.

> **Authoritative Guidance & Standards**
> Auditing standards (e.g., SAS 96, ISA 570) require auditors to perform the procedures described herein to assess an entity's ability to continue as a going concern. Should an auditor have substantial doubt about an entity's ability to continue as a going concern, an explanatory paragraph is added to the auditor's report conveying such doubt as discussed in Chapter 15.

ASSESSING THE RISK OF FINANCIAL FAILURE

During the course of the audit—strategic analysis, process analysis, business measurement analysis—the auditor may observe warning signals of potential financial problems for the client. Some of the more common signals of financial distress include negative information about (1) asset composition, (2) debt levels, (3) cost structure, and (4) equity position. Examples of these warning signs include

1. **Asset composition:**
   - Existence of significant underperforming assets
   - Limited ability to dispose of assets (e.g., no secondary market, environmental concerns)
   - Failures related to new product research, development, or introduction
   - Loss of major contracts or customers
   - Loss of patent protection or legal monopoly
   - Loss of critical human capital
   - Inability to modernize or expand facilities in response to growing market opportunities

---

6 The period of the auditor's responsibility for evaluating going concern may differ depending on the laws of the country involved or the regulations by stock regulators and others.

2. **Debt levels:**
   - Excessive debt incurred
   - Inability to meet current obligations
   - Lack of new sources of debt financing
   - Excessive debt service costs (e.g., interest or principal payments)
3. **Cost structure:**
   - Negative cash flows
   - Noncompetitive production processes and production costs
   - Excessive overhead and administrative costs
   - Inflexible union contracts
   - Overly generous fringe benefits (e.g., health care, pension)
   - Unfavorable tax treatment of transactions
   - Losses from litigation
4. **Equity position:**
   - Inability to maintain dividend payout
   - Inability to obtain additional equity financing
   - Excessive cash drains related to investments in affiliates

The presence of any single condition may not be a strong signal of problems, but multiple signals across two or more categories suggest that the auditor should seriously consider the issue of potential financial distress.

In addition to the above warning signs, an auditor can also use the results of business measurement analysis to obtain a broader understanding of the financial status of an organization. An organization that is not profitable and has serious cash flow problems is a likely candidate for financial distress. Consequently, auditors often look at profitability, leverage, and solvency ratios in order to identify conditions that may indicate current or future financial distress. Many of the ratios that are useful for this purpose were discussed in Chapter 9 and include[7]

- Current or quick ratio
- Debt ratio
- Interest coverage ratio
- Total asset turnover
- Return on assets
- Profit margin

The fact that some ratios may have values that are worrisome does not automatically imply financial distress, however. All ratios and facts must be considered together by the auditor. Such a judgment is highly subjective, requires extensive experience, and should be made with utmost care.

CONSIDERING MANAGEMENT RESPONSES TO GOING CONCERN THREATS

If an auditor believes that there is substantial doubt about the company continuing as a going concern, the situation should be discussed with management to determine its intentions for dealing with the underlying problems. Circumstances that might mitigate a perceived going concern problem include

- Plans for disposal of extraneous assets
- Restructuring of financing

---

7 Refer to Chapter 9 for the formulas to compute these ratios.

- Acquisition of new financing
- Reduction or deferral of expenditures

The auditor should evaluate management's plans to determine the likelihood that it will rectify the organization's problems. Not all management plans will be successful. Furthermore, asset disposals may be a good source of cash but cannot be repeated and may have a negative impact on operations by reducing capacity that could be needed in the future. Cost and expenditure deferrals must also be considered with care. The reduction of costs without serious evaluation of the underlying activities of the organization may create problems in the future as the organization tries to cope with new challenges with fewer resources. Finally, acquisition of new financing, or restructuring of existing financing arrangements, may be possible, but the auditor must evaluate whether the company will be able to meet its new obligations. Ultimately, if survival is in serious question and management plans seem to be inadequate or unlikely to be effective, then the auditor will need to modify his or her audit report accordingly.

SUMMARY AND CONCLUSION

In this chapter, we discussed the process of aggregating audit evidence and preparing the financial statements based on the results of the audit. We also introduced a rigorous approach to business measurement analysis that can be used during the final review of the compiled financial statements. If there are unresolved issues, unanswered questions, or unclear results, the auditor should consider additional testing and inquiry to resolve these remaining issues. The additional audit work might include more extensive review by senior audit personnel of the results of procedures conducted to date or more extensive substantive procedures in order to collect additional evidence to determine whether an account or balance is correctly stated. In the next chapter, we conclude our discussion of the procedures used by an auditor to complete the audit. We will also discuss the nature of auditor reports that are generated once the audit is complete.

APPENDIX A: BACKGROUND INFORMATION FOR AMA AUTOPARTS INC.

COMPANY BACKGROUND

AMA Autoparts Inc. is a manufacturer of autoparts that are sold to retail car outlets (such as Pep Boys and Sears). The balance sheets for 20x6, 20x7, and 20x8 and income statements for 20x7 and 20x8 were originally presented in Figure 9–4 and are repeated in Figure 14–6. Selected ratios were reported in Figure 9–6, and are repeated in Figure 14–7. The company was formed in 20x1 and first "went public" in 20x2.

The company is the newest entrant into a business that is considered to be highly competitive. It has captured about 12 percent of the market (based on sales volume) for the past few years. Most of the company's competition comes from autopart subsidiaries of the Big Three U.S. auto manufacturers and numerous foreign (Japanese, Korean) companies that also supply their domestic auto manufacturers.

The company's parts are considered to be high-quality compared to other replacement (and some original equipment) autoparts, and sell at a price premium.

Most sales in this industry are made to auto manufacturers (about 40 percent for AMA Autoparts) or retail outlets. Sales terms are typically "net 30." The company develops its own products as well as manufacturing parts based on plans and specifications provided by the major automotive manufacturers. About 25 percent of the company's products are designed and developed in-house. Selected results for the industry for 20x8 are as follows:

Gross profit percentage	42.20%
Inventory turnover	12.15
Inventory as a percentage of assets	17.20%
Receivable turnover	15.78
Receivables as a percentage of assets	28.15%
Growth in revenue	11.30%
Dividends/Net income	45.00%
Return on assets	19.40%
Return on equity	32.00%
Return on sales (after tax)	6.85%
Fixed asset turnover	11.21
Debt/Assets	65.00%
Percent of sales to retail outlets	40.00%
Effective tax rate	33.50%
Selling and administrative expense/Sales	21.23%
Payable turnover	21.50
Labor cost per employee	$47,540
Fringe benefits per employee	$ 7,800
Time to market	1.90 years
Price/Earnings	14.22

SUMMARY OF KEY ACCOUNTING POLICIES AND PROCEDURES

Inventory: The company values all inventory using the LIFO method.

Receivables: The company maintains a reserve for potentially uncollectible accounts amounting to $7,500, $6,400, and $6,100 in 20x8, 20x7, and 20x6, respectively.

Plant, Property, and Equipment: The company's plant assets consist of land, manufacturing facilities, warehouses, office facilities, and equipment. Long-lived assets are depreciated using the straight-line method with useful lives ranging from 5 to 30 years. In 20x8, the company disposed of two warehouses in a sale-leaseback transaction (see below). A gain of $30,000 on the transaction has been included in depreciation expense.

Long-Term Investments: The company uses the equity method to account for long-term investments. All long-term investments represent joint ventures in enterprises that provide raw materials and components to the company. The income from such investments is treated as a reduction of cost of goods sold. Net investment income was $34,000, $28,000, and $25,000 in 20x8, 20x7, and 20x6, respectively.

Income Taxes: The company paid income taxes of $358,000 and $156,000 in 20x8 and 20x7, respectively. The average tax rates were 42.94 percent and 39.32 percent in 20x8 and 20x7, respectively. The company has no deferred taxes as of 20x8.

PRODUCTION AND SALES

The company has a small sales force. Each salesperson is assigned a large geographic region but deals mostly with the centralized purchasing departments of the larger autoparts stores and automotive manufacturers. Servicing customer accounts requires significant travel by salespeople. Orders are actually placed through a secure Internet site, although a salesperson may occasionally write up a transaction if he or she is visiting a store or autopart retailer.

The company's production processes are highly automated and environmentally friendly, an advantage of being a young company given that the factory was designed to utilize state of the art production techniques. The company's goal is to keep waste, scrap, and defects to the absolute minimum that current technology will allow. The company coordinates its supply chain through the use of highly sophisticated materials planning software. Orders are transmitted to suppliers electronically whenever the production software identifies an inadequate level of parts or materials.

The company's labor force is 80 percent unionized. The union is especially strong among factory employees, who won a new contract during 20x8. Although a strike was averted, the compensation and benefits of AMA Autoparts are higher than the union was able to win from other companies in the industry during negotiations conducted in 20x7.

All of the company's products are backed by one of the best warranty programs in the industry. Generally, defective parts are returned to the point of purchase and then returned by the store to AMA Autoparts. The company honors all warranty claims regardless of whether the part is defective or simply misused. Unfortunately, during 20x8, the company also had three recalls for internally developed products that were discovered to contain design flaws.

FINANCING ARRANGEMENTS

Lease Commitments: On May 1, 20x8, the company disposed of two warehouses in a sale-leaseback transaction. The warehouses had an original cost of $195,000 and were 40 percent depreciated at the time of the sale. The company also entered into a lease commitment to rent the warehouses for a 10-year period beginning May 1, 20x8. Annual payments of $12,500/warehouse are due on May 1 of each year. At the end of ten years, the company has the option to repurchase the warehouses at their current market value. This lease is treated as an operating lease by the company.

Mortgage Payable: The company has a 9 percent mortgage outstanding, which is secured by the main manufacturing facility. Payments of $100,000 are due on December 31, 20x6 and 20x7, followed by five annual payments of $85,000 due on December 31 of each year.

Equity Transactions: The company is closely held and, until recently, had fewer than 300 shareholders. Common stock has a par value of $10. The company has 100,000 shares authorized and there were 22,500 shares, 15,000 shares, and 11,000 shares outstanding in 20x8, 20x7, and 20x6, respectively. The company offers an incentive stock option plan to senior managers. In 20x8, options on 1,000 shares were granted to eligible executives. The exercise price is equal to the market price on the date of grant. During 20x8, 2,000 previously issued stock options were exercised at an average price of $17. The overall option activity is summarized below:

	20x7	20x8
Options outstanding, January 1	1,200	1,900
Granted	1,500	1,000
Exercised	(800)	(2,000)
	1,900	900
Average exercise price	$17.50	$18.95

In July, common stock totaling 5,500 shares was issued to the public for $22/share. Dividends of $470,000 and $5,000 were paid in 20x8 and 20x7, respectively. The large dividend in 20x8 (paid in June) is partially attributable to the cash proceeds received from the sale of the warehouses discussed above. The remainder of the large dividend reflects a one-time decision by the board of directors to return profits not needed for future expansion to the shareholders.

APPENDIX B: IDENTIFYING GOING CONCERN PROBLEMS USING STATISTICAL ANALYSIS

The use of statistical techniques to predict the failure of a business organization is well established. Statistical analysis allows the simultaneous consideration of multiple indicators of financial distress. It is also a powerful technique for identifying patterns in data that may indicate potential failure conditions.

Most of the statistical models used for bankruptcy prediction have been developed and tested by academic researchers using large databases of failed and healthy companies. Their approach is to identify potentially useful indicators of financial distress, measure those variables for a large sample of healthy and unhealthy companies, and run regression analysis that can combine the information from multiple variables into a single assessment of the probability of failure for a given organization.[8] By examining a large number of cases involving both failed and healthy organizations, regression analysis can be used to combine data from many variables in an effective manner. There are a number of published prediction models that are based on different time periods, different indicator variables, and different samples. Many of these statistical measures are at least 85 percent effective at correctly separating firms that will fail within two years from those that will not fail.

The most frequently used statistical measure of potential for failure is referred to as the Altman Z-score. This model was shown to be 95 percent effective in correctly identifying failed and healthy firms in the sample used in the original research. The Z-score is computed for any organization from the following equation:

$$Z = 0.717 \times X_1 + 0.847 \times X_2 + 3.11 \times X_3 + 0.420 \times X_4 + 0.998 \times X_5 \qquad (14.1)$$

where:

X_1 = net working capital ÷ total assets
X_2 = retained earnings ÷ total assets
X_3 = earnings before interest and taxes ÷ total assets
X_4 = shareholders' equity ÷ total liabilities
X_5 = sales ÷ total assets

---

8 The form of regression analysis that is most frequently used is called LOGIT analysis and provides a measure of the probability of failure based on the analysis of actual cases of healthy and failed organizations.

A Z-score less than 1.20 is considered a strong signal of financial distress while a score in excess of 2.90 is believed to indicate a solid, healthy organization. A score in the 1.20 to 2.90 range is unclear and should be further investigated by the auditor given the possibility that such a company could fall into the "distress" category in the near future.

To illustrate the use of the Z-score, consider data taken from the financial statements of Lucent Technologies Inc. for the year ended September 30, 1999. The ratios are computed as follows (dollar-denominated numbers in millions):

$$\text{Net working capital} = \$10,153$$
$$\text{Total assets} = \$38,775$$
$$X_1 = 10,153 \div 38,775 = 0.262$$

$$\text{Retained earnings} = \$6,099$$
$$X_2 = 6,099 \div 38,775 = 0.157$$

$$\text{Earnings before interest and taxes} = \$7,157$$
$$X_3 = 7,157 \div 38,775 = 0.185$$

$$\text{Shareholders' equity} = \$13,584$$
$$\text{Total liabilities} = \$25,191$$
$$X_4 = 13,584 \div 25,191 = 0.539$$

$$\text{Sales} = \$38,303$$
$$X_5 = 38,303 \div 38,775 = 0.988$$

Therefore, $Z = 0.717 \times 0.262 + 0.847 \times 0.157 + 3.11 \times 0.185 + 0.420 \times 0.539 + 0.998 \times 0.988 = 2.108$. As would be expected for a large successful company, the Z-score tends towards the safe zone.

Statistical measures such as the Z-score should be used with care. The predictions from such methods are not perfect and unusual conditions can occur in which the statistical measure indicates that the organization is healthy while it is on the way to failure. In reality, Lucent nearly went into bankruptcy in 2002 in spite of the positive Z-score in 1999. Furthermore, if the input data is subject to management manipulation or if an organization being examined is significantly different from those used to estimate equation 14.1, the value of the Z-score may not be meaningful. Auditors should always use common sense when applying statistical measures and not forget to consider both warning signs and other ratios that may give a picture that is different from the statistical estimation of the likelihood of failure.

BIBLIOGRAPHY OF RELATED PROFESSIONAL LITERATURE

Research

Barrett, M., D. J. Cooper, and K. Jamal. 2005. Globalization and the Coordinating of Work in a Multinational Audit. *Accounting Organizations and Society.* 30(1): 1–24.

Gillett, P. R. and N. Uddin. 2005. CFO Intentions of Fraudulent Financial Reporting. *Auditing: A Journal of Practice & Theory.* 24(1): 55–76.

Joe, J. R. 2003. Why press coverage of a client influences the audit opinion. *Journal of Accounting Research.* 41(1): 109–133.

Johnstone, K. M., J. C. Bedard, and S. F. Biggs. 2002. Aggressive Client Reporting: Factors Affecting Auditors' Generation of Financial Reporting Alternatives. *Auditing: A Journal of Practice & Theory.* 21(1): 47–66.

Wilkens, M. S. 1997. Technical Default, Auditor's Decisions and Future Financial Distress. *Accounting Horizons.* 11(4): 40–48.

Yip-Ow, J. and H. T. Tan. 2000. Effects of Preparer's Justification on the Reviewer's Hypothesis Generation and Judgment in Analytical Procedures. *Accounting Organizations and Society.* 25(2): 203–215.

Professional Reports and Guidance

Boritz, J. E. 1990. *Approaches to Dealing with Risk and Uncertainity.* Toronto: CICA: Research Report.

Boritz, J. E. 1991. *The Going Concern Assumption: Accounting and Auditing Implications.* Toronto: CICA: Research Report.

Neely, A., ed. 2002. *Business Performance Measurement: Theory and Practice.* Cambridge: Cambridge University Press.

Auditing Standards

AICPA *Statements on Auditing Standard (SAS)* No. 96, "The Auditor's Consideration of an Entity's Ability to Continue as a Going Concern."

AICPA *Statements on Auditing Standard (SAS)* No. 506, "Analytical Procedures."

IAASB *International Standards on Auditing (ISA)* No. 520, "Analytical Procedures."

IAASB *International Standards on Auditing (ISA)* No. 570, "Going Concern."

QUESTIONS

1. Aggregating audit evidence across business processes is an important auditing issue that has received relatively little emphasis by auditing standard setters and auditing researchers (other than to consider total misstatements identified). Describe what you believe are the most imporant benefits associated with properly aggregating audit evidence and the implications for the audit if evidence is not properly aggregated.

2. Why should auditors be diligent in ensuring that different business segments' financial statements properly reconcile to the consolidated financial statements? As part of your answer, describe reasons why errors might occur in this activity and why management would choose this aspect of financial reporting for perpetrating fraud.

3. Final analytical review is required by auditing standards for all auditing engagements and, in practice, generally is performed by the partner on the engagement. What is the purpose of conducting a general analytical review of this nature? What are the limitations associated with this type of analysis (i.e., why is it not likely to be effective for its intended purpose)?

4. What is meant by business measurement analysis as described in this chapter? How should the auditor perform such an analysis? If performed properly, why should it help address the limitations associated with general analytical review performed by a partner at the end of an engagement?

5. Financial performance measures have traditionally been used to assess the reasonableness of the overall financial statements. Financial ratios and comparisons with other organizations in the same industry have been heavily used for this purpose. List financial

ratios and financial metrics that can be used for this purpose and describe how auditors can use them to assess the overall reasonableness of financial statements.

6. This chapter argues that nonfinancial measures are useful in assessing whether reported financial results are reasonable. Offer an explanation for why this argument should be valid for most auditing engagements and provide conditions under which it might not be valid.

7. Describe what is meant by a balanced scorecard approach for business measurement analysis. As part of your explanation, describe each of the four perspectives utilized in this chapter (see Figure 14–2). How can an auditor use this approach to help assess the overall reasonableness of the financial statements?

8. As part of the audit evidence aggregation process, auditors should consider the relationship across business processes performance. Describe how an auditor could assess the overall reasonableness of reported financial performance by considering business process performance for the following business processes: brand and image delivery, pricing and sales, and customer service.

9. Why do you believe that auditors must assess the risk of an organization being able to continue as a going concern, given that auditors perform no other procedures regarding future performance of an organization? Do you believe that auditors should have to perform this assessment and inform users when they believe that there is substantial doubt about the entity's ability to continue as a going concern?

10. Describe signals of financial distress offered in the chapter for assessing asset composition, debt levels, cost structure, and equity levels. What are the strengths and weaknesses associated with these signals?

PROBLEMS

1. Consider the following information gathered by several auditors on the same engagement team performing an audit of the financial statements of a home improvement center.

Business Process:	Site Selection and Development
Balance Sheet Account:	Construction-in-Progress
Recorded Balance:	$125 million
Tolerable Misstatement:	$6 million

Suppose the audit team gathered the following subtantive evidence when testing existence and valuation account:

- Of the 100 new locations under construction as of the balance sheet date, the audit team visit five sites on a random basis to inspect the reasonableness of the percentage of completion compared to the amount recorded. The auditors found for the five sites that records indicated that projects were, on average, one percent less completed in reality as compared to the recorded completion costs.
- Based on inspection of 20 randomly selected construction files (which represented 40 percent of the total balance), the audit team identified that total recorded costs for the projects were approximately two percent higher than the amount recorded for these sites.
- Based on review of the contracts included in each file, amounts are paid to the managing contractor on an ongoing basis, and the property belongs to the retailer, who hires the contractor to manage the project.

Based on this evidence, what conclusions can the auditor reach, if any, about the assertions associated with the construction-in-progress account?

2. Consider the following financial statement line items reported from three subsidiary locations of a manufacturer:

British Manufacturing Operation	
Cash	15 million British pounds
Accounts Receivable	225 million British pounds
Inventory	450 million British pounds
Other Current Assets	40 million British pounds
Total Current Assets	730 million British pounds

Canadian Manufacturing Operation	
Cash	30 million Canadian dollars
Accounts Receivable	190 million Canadian dollars
Inventory	500 million Canadian dollars
Other Current Assets	20 million Canadian dollars
Total Current Assets	740 million Canadian dollars

U.S. Manufacturing Operation	
Cash	60 million U.S. dollars
Accounts Receivable	180 million U.S. dollars
Inventory	565 million U.S. dollars
Other Current Assets	65 million U.S. dollars
Total Current Assets	870 million U.S. dollars

Assume the following exchange rates:

1 U.S. dollar = 0.57 British pounds
1 U.S. dollar = 1.15 Canadian dollars
1 British pound = 2.016 Canadian dollars

Explain the audit issues that arise in the translation, aggregation, and consolidation of the three subsidiaries.

3. Consider the following analytical procedures performed as of the end of the audit:

Red Hawk Apparel
Final Analytical Procedures
For year ended 12/31/08

	12/31/08	12/31/07	% Change
Cash	$ 5,500	$ 5,000	10%
Accounts Receivable, net	12,000	8,000	50%
Inventory	14,000	10,000	40%
Property, Plant, Equipment, net	21,000	20,000	5%
Payables	$ 5,500	$ 6,000	(8%)
Long-Term Debt	22,000	20,000	10%
Stockholders' Equity	25,000	17,000	47%
	10/31/08	10/31/07	
Sales	$ 50,000	$ 45,000	11%
Cost of Goods Sold	(28,000)	(25,000)	12%
Gross Margin	22,000	20,000	
Bad Debt Expense	5,000	4,500	11%
Operating Expenses	5,000	5,000	0%
Tax Expense	2,200	2,000	10%
Net Income	9,800	8,500	

Suppose the working papers include a summary document indicating that

- Sales have increased because of an increase in sales price.
- Ten new employees were added to the production line.
- A new storage facility was added to property, plant, and equipment.
- Loan of $3 million was taken out during the year.

a. What evidence would you expect to find in the detailed working papers to support these conclusions?

b. Do you have any concerns regarding the ability of this organization to continue as a going concern based on this analysis?

c. Are there any other issues that you believe need additional attention based on these overall analytical procedures?

4. Consider the department store example provided in the chapter regarding gross margin percentages under different inventory methods:

	2004	2003	2002
Nordstrom (FIFO)	36.1%	34.6%	33.2%
Federated (Macy's) (retail LIFO)	40.5%	40.4%	40.0%

How might an auditor approach developing a pro forma version of this data to enable a comparison between both retailers?

5. Consider the following information about an international luxury hotel chain:

Industry Growth:	Projection over next 5 years, 2.7% increase in demand for rooms
Recent Changes:	2005—room demand in World was 10.1 million rooms 2004—room demand in World was 9.3 million rooms 2003—room demand in World was 7.5 million rooms 2002—room demand in World was 7.2 million rooms 2001—room demand in World was 7.9 million rooms
Hotel Rooms Owned:	2005—1.9 million rooms 2004—1.6 million rooms 2003—1.3 million rooms 2002—1.0 million rooms 2001—0.9 million rooms
Occupancy Rate:	2005—75% occupied 2004—70% occupied 2003—70% occupied 2002—69% occupied 2001—73% occupied

Based on this information, what are some general, relative expectations that can be inferred from this information for 2003, 2004, and 2005 for revenues, operating costs, and depreciation? Furthermore, given that there has been little activity related to equity transactions, what expectations do you have regarding financing transactions during this period?

6. The Balanced Scorecard is a business measurement tool that enables an auditor to better understand whether financial measures reported by an organization are consistent with measures about the organization's market, core processes, and resource management processes. Assume that you are auditing Google. Research the company by examining its web site and other available information about the company. Based on your findings, provide example measures for each of the four categories of the balanced scorecard that should provide auditors with key pieces of financial information and indicators of Google's performance in its market, core processes, and resource management processes. These measures should help assess whether its customer, innovative, and other key influences are suggest that such financial performance is reasonable.

7. Consider the following measures taken from product design and development, customer sales and service, production management, and human resource management business processes for the manufacturer of parts for the appliance industry:

	2008	2007	Industry
Time to market (years)	2.9	2.1	2.4
Product introduction success rate	79%	68%	
Years to recover development costs	2.50	2.30	
Inventory turnover	11.36	10.27	11.85
Gross profit margin	26.8%	25.47%	30.7%
Receivable turnover	10.51	11.57	10.33
Bad debt percentage	0.90%	1.20%	
Selling expense/sales	11.55%	12.23%	12.13%
Selling expenses/salesperson	$166,350	$142,433	
Sales per customer	$44,283	$ 38,539	
On-time delivery percentage	88%	84%	
Inventory/assets	16.74%	14.07%	15.90%
Cost of waste and spoilage/sales	0.88%	0.89%	
Employee morale (of 5 pts)	4.88	4.15	
Employee turnover	11%	18%	
Size of work force	41	39	
Days lost to absenteeism	78	90	
Labor cost per employee	$72,990	$ 68,873	$68,654

Based on this information, what concerns do you have for each of the following when comparing the performance of the manufacturer from 2007 to 2008 and compared to the industry?

- Financial performance
- Market performance
- Core business process performance
- Resource management process performance

To document these concerns and integrate them into your audit strategy, prepare a Summary of Results from Business Measurement Analysis using Figure 14–18 as a guide.

8. The Altman Z-score (see Appendix B) predicts bankruptcy using commonly available financial accounting information (e.g., EBIT and total assets). Suppose you are studying a company (whose primary business is produce wholesaling) for purposes of making the going concern determination and its Altman Z-score comes to 2.68, indicating that there is not an immediate threat of bankruptcy but that they deserve watching. Further suppose that the ratio analysis of the company yields the following:

Current ratio	0.54
Inventory turnover	41.9 times
Debt/Equity	7.1
Times interest earned	2.6 times
Gross margin	22%

Finally, suppose that you know the following about the company:
- Although its bank requires them to pay off their line of credit for at least 30 days per year, it frequently does so only by extending its trade payables significantly.
- Its suppliers (e.g., the farmers) are beginning to favor marketing their crops through a nonprofit co-op.
- Management has been in the fruit and vegetable business for many years but no plans for an orderly management succession have been made.
- A major competitor just installed an inventory control system that makes extensive use of bar-coding. As a result, the competitor's losses on spoilage have decreased significantly.
- Due solely to poor weather, operating margins have been squeezed between farmers demanding more for their crops and the company's customers' ability to obtain supplies from foreign sources.

Although the picture looks bleak for your client, discuss several mitigating factors that, if present, would likely moderate any inkling you may have to give the company a modified audit report with a going concern qualification. What would be the likely affect of an unfavorable going concern opinion on its ability to operate?

9. This chapter uses the Balanced Scorecard as an mechansim for conducting business measurement analysis. An increasingly used approach for tracking performance measurement is the use of dashboard software. Conduct research on the use of dashboards for tracking and reporting on performance measurement within an organization. How are dashboards typically utilized in organizations? What are the primary arguments offered for why they are used by a large number of the world's largest companies? What considerations should organizations make to ensure that they are not met with resistance by employees? How can auditors utilize dashboard measures to help assess the overall reasonableness of the financial statements?

Case 14–1: Video Replay

Video Replay Inc. is a chain of DVD/video rental stores located in Alberta and British Columbia, Canada. The stock of the company is publicly traded on the TSX Venture Exchange (formerly listed on the Alberta Stock Exchange prior to the Exchange mergers). The chain currently has 28 outlets and six more are under construction. Until recently, the company was content to be a small participant in the video market. However, the founder of the company, Buddy Shuster, decided to take the company public about five years ago and immediately undertook an aggressive expansion using the proceeds of the stock offering. Buddy is still the largest shareholder (at 40 percent) and the chief executive officer of the company. The company hopes to grow by at least 20 locations a year and branch into other western provinces and indeed maybe into Ontario. Buddy also has plans to enter into a joint venture with a major pizza chain (BP Pizza) in order to offer pizza sales through small takeout only stores that are adjacent to the video store.

The company has been an audit client of your firm since its inception in 1995, but this is your first year on the engagement. The company's primary assets are its DVDs/videotapes, fixtures, and equipment (including computers in the stores). It leases all of its retail locations, most of which are located in strip shopping malls. The company hires a full-time manager for each location and staffs the stores with college-age, part-time employees. The company runs little advertising and rarely deviates from its fixed pricing schedule (that is, there are few if any price promotions or special discounts). The company uses simple software to manage its rental revenue and to keep track of tapes in the possession of customers. This software was designed by a local Chartered Accounting (CA) firm about four years ago and has not been updated.

The primary problem for the company is that it operates fairly small stores with a relatively small selection of DVD/videos at each location. Most of the existing stores are at least six years old and date from when video rentals were just becoming popular. The new stores under construction will be much larger with four times the number of titles available. Many of the company's stores now compete directly against bigger chains (e.g., Blockbuster) or chains that also sell other products (e.g., Rogers). The company is also confronted with a number of other challenges that may affect its future success such as pay-per-view, digital cable networks, direct disk broadcasting, and Internet broadcasting.

A secondary problem that faces the company is the relatively low level of turnover on many DVDs/videos. In the past, the company would buy a few copies of most DVDs/videos that came to market. The company would then hold on to the DVDs/videos for as long as they were of sufficiently good condition to rent out. DVDs/videos were removed from stock only when they wore out from use. This strategy worked well in the early years because there were few titles available for rental and customers were willing to wait for the opportunity to rent the big name films. In recent years, this strategy has not worked well, often resulting in lost revenues as customers decided to go to video stores that had larger quantities of popular titles. The company is currently re-examining its system for acquiring new titles and managing DVDs/videos in stock.

Buddy is contemplating a new marketing plan based on the concept of generating loyal customers. His idea is to set up his computer system so as to identify customers who are frequent renters. Customers would be awarded points for each rental, and once they accumulated a certain number of points, they would receive special bonuses such as coupons for free rentals and priority for new popular titles. However, such an initiative would require a large capital infusion to cover the development and start-up costs associated with a new computer system.

Last year the company showed a loss equal to 15 percent of shareholders' equity and had net negative cash flows from operations and investing activity amounting to $200,000. In order to meet operating costs, Buddy Shuster made a personal loan to the company totaling $525,000. This loan was made two weeks after the prior year's audit report was issued. Last year's audit report was unqualified with no mention of going concern issues either in the notes to the financial statements or in the auditor's report. This year the loss looks to be as much as 35 percent of equity with negative net operating and investing cash flows close to $400,000. This year, Buddy has promised to advance another $500,000 to the company on March 1. He has signed a representation letter to that effect. Unfortunately, due to covenants on a loan with a local bank, your report must be issued by February 15. It is highly unlikely that the company would be able to issue more equity or obtain bank financing at this point, and Buddy is likely to be the only source of working capital for the foreseeable future.

Requirements

1. What are the auditor's responsibilities for assessing whether an organization is a going concern?
2. Do you feel there is any doubt as to Video Replay's ability to continue operations? Explain.
3. Do the intentions of Buddy Shuster provide sufficient mitigation of any going concern questions? Which facts and plans are relevant for your evaluation of mitigating circumstances and what evidence would you obtain in making your evaluation?
4. What type of opinion would you issue? Explain. Draft the opinion.
5. How would your answers change if Buddy presented a check for $500,000 to the company on February 1? Explain.
6. What other circumstances might make you feel more comfortable that the company will continue as a going concern?

15

Completing the Integrated Audit II: Audit Reporting

Outline

INTRODUCTION

The final step in the audit process involves reaching an overall conclusion about the fairness of the financial statements and communicating the results to interested parties. The purpose of this, and the prior, chapter is to describe the steps needed to complete the audit (see Figure 15–1). Wrap-up procedures are designed to

Figure 15–1   An Overview of the Audit Process

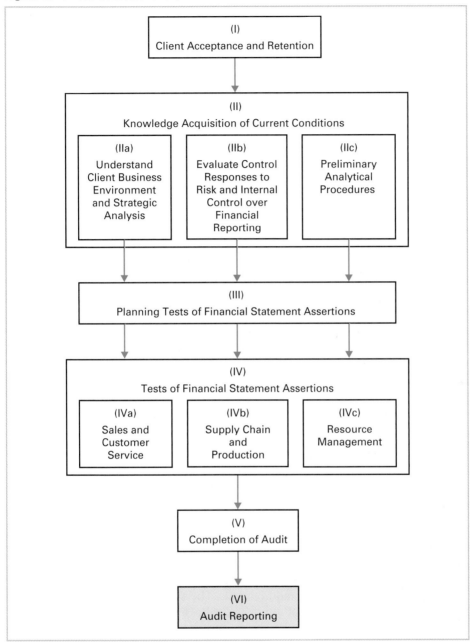

assure that the conclusions are appropriate and based on a full understanding of all available information. This chapter also discusses the various ways in which the auditor communicates the results of the examination to interested parties. The primary form of external communication is the auditor's report, which is distributed along with the financial statements to external stakeholders. In addition, companies that are publicly registered in the United States also issue two reports related to internal control over financial reporting, one from management and one from the auditor. Other communications are intended for internal parties, including a report to the audit committee and a management letter.

COMPLETION PROCEDURES

Authoritative Guidance & Standards
This chapter examines the audit procedures associated with ensuring that sufficient, competent evidence has been gathered in order to issue an opinion, which is addressed by several auditing standards (e.g., SAS 12, SAS 85, ISA 560, ISA 580, etc.). This chapter also covers external communications, including audit reports (SAS 58, ISA 700, AS 2).

After all necessary risk assessments and tests of management assertions have been completed, the auditor performs a final set of procedures designed to eliminate open items and assure that all available information has been appropriately considered. The auditor also wishes to make sure that all professional standards have been followed and that the financial statements are complete. A number of procedures facilitate the completion process. The key procedures are

- Review contingent losses
- Obtain an attorney (legal) confirmation letter
- Review subsequent events
- Obtain a representation letter from management
- Complete final evaluation of evidence and prepare financial statements

REVIEW FOR CONTINGENT LIABILITIES

Near the end of the engagement, the auditor should identify and evaluate potential contingent liabilities that may have an impact on the financial statements. Virtually all organizations are exposed to potential losses that are contingent on future events. An extreme example is an insurance company that is in the business of assessing and measuring future losses arising from insured risks. More typical are contingent losses arising from uncollectible customer accounts. Contingent liabilities that impact most organizations include

- Losses associated with litigation
- Losses associated with disputes with regulatory bodies
- Income tax liabilities in dispute
- Warranty expenses
- Guarantees of third-party debt
- Losses on purchase commitments
- Compensated absences (e.g., vacation or sick leave)
- Losses on receivables sold with recourse

Management has the ultimate responsibility to prepare and present any estimates required for full and fair disclosure of contingent liabilities. Consistent with its responsibilities, management is expected to identify needed estimates and develop an estimation technique that considers appropriate assumptions, data, computational models, and GAAP requirements. The auditor has the responsibility to identify potential contingent liabilities, assess the likelihood and manner in which they will be resolved, evaluate the proper accounting treatment, and test the reasonableness of resulting estimates.

The accounting standards for contingent losses identify three possible treatments for contingencies depending on the likelihood of occurrence and the measurability of the impact on the financial statements:

- **Accrue the loss:** A contingent loss must be accrued if the loss is *probable* and *reasonably estimable*. A loss is considered probable if it is likely to occur. The loss is reasonably estimable if a specific value or range of values can be determined. If the loss is likely to fall within a range of values, the lower end of the range is used.

- **Disclose the loss:** If a contingency is probable but cannot reasonably be estimated, the nature of the contingency should be disclosed in the financial statements. Disclosure is also appropriate if the contingency is considered to be *reasonably possible*, which is defined as less than probable.
- **No accounting recognition:** Contingencies considered to be *remote* need not be mentioned at all.

The auditor's primary objective in the area of contingent losses is to verify that the client has properly disclosed and accounted for all contingent losses. As a result, the completeness and valuation assertions are considered most important. The auditor performs the following procedures to search for and assess contingent losses:

- Inquire of management about the existence of contingent losses
- Review prior-year working papers for previously existing contingencies and follow up on their resolution in the current year
- Review regulatory and tax filings for potential claims
- Review the minutes of meetings of the board of directors for indications of potential contingent losses (e.g., purchase commitments)
- Analyze legal expenditures and review legal invoices for ongoing or unasserted legal claims
- Obtain attorney confirmations from all attorneys providing services to the organization
- Review estimates related to identified contingencies in accordance with the appropriate auditing standards
- Review other company disclosures, including corporate sustainability reports or other press releases

The risk of a contingent loss estimate being misstated is directly affected by the complexity of the estimate being made, the availability and reliability of data used to make the estimate, the nature of assumptions used, and the degree of uncertainty surrounding future events. For example, environmental liabilities arising from the clean-up of toxic land sites may be extremely difficult to estimate due to the long lead time of the clean-up process, the uncertainty surrounding who pays, and the changing nature of clean-up technology.

ATTORNEY (LEGAL) CONFIRMATIONS

One of the best but most problematic sources of evidence related to contingent losses are *attorney confirmations*, also referred to as *legal letters*. An attorney confirmation can be an excellent source of evidence because it comes from a party who is intimately involved with existing and *unasserted claims* against the company.[1] On the other hand, the evidence is often difficult to interpret because attorneys are hesitant to reveal facts or conditions they feel are covered by confidentiality rules. Attorneys generally resist making precise estimates about the amount or likelihood of potential losses that may result from litigation.

In order to overcome some of these problems, attorney associations and national auditing standard setters have agreed to policies concerning attorneys' responses to requests for information from auditors. An example of an attorney confirmation is presented in Figure 15–2. The auditor is primarily interested

---

1 Unasserted claims are potential losses arising from events which have already occurred and are *expected* to result in a lawsuit against the organization. For example, many tort injuries have a three-year statute of limitations, so a lawsuit could be filed up to three years after an event has occurred.

Figure 15–2   Example of Legal Inquiry Letter

Johnson Pharmaceuticals Inc.

Mr. Jonathan Orwell   (Date)
Orwell, Orwell & Hatchburg, Attorneys at Law
45 N. Main Street

Dear Mr. Orwell:

In connection with the audit of our annual financial statements as of December 31, 20x7, management has prepared a description and evaluation of certain contingencies. This list has been furnished to our auditors, Smith & Company. Included on the list are the following matters with which you have been engaged and to which you have devoted substantive attention on behalf of Johnson Pharmaceuticals in the form of legal consultation or representation. These contingencies are considered to be material to the fair presentation of our financial statements. Your response should include matters that existed at December 31, 20x7 and during the period from that date to the date of the completion of your response.

Pending or Threatened Litigation: The following litigation has been identified as pending or threatened:

> [A list of pending or threatened matters would be provided including the nature of litigation, the current status and progress of the case, management's actual or intended response (e.g., vigorous defense or out-of-court settlement), and an estimate of the likelihood and amount (if possible) of an unfavorable outcome.]

Please furnish our auditors such explanation, if any, that you consider necessary to supplement the foregoing information, including an explanation of those matters as to which your views may differ from those stated and an identification of the omission of any pending or threatened litigation, claims, and assessments or a statement that the list of such matters is complete.

Unasserted Claims and Assessments: The following matters have been identified as giving rise to possible unasserted claims or assessments:

> [A list of unasserted matters would be provided including the nature of the matter, management's actual or intended response, and an estimate of the likelihood and amount (if possible) of an unfavorable outcome.]

Please furnish our auditors such explanation, if any, that you consider necessary to supplement the foregoing information, including an explanation of those matters as to which your views may differ from those stated.

We understand that whenever, in the course of performing legal services for us with respect to a matter recognized to involve an unasserted possible claim or assessment that may call for financial statement disclosure, you have formed a professional opinion that we should disclose or consider disclosure concerning such possible claim or assessment, as a matter of professional responsibility to us, you will so advise us and will consult with us. Please specifically confirm to our auditors that our understanding is correct.

Please specifically identify any limitations to your response and the nature of those limitations.

Respectfully,

Samuel Johnson
President, Johnson Pharmaceuticals Inc.

in the existence of conditions giving rise to a contingent loss, the period in which the event(s) occurred, the probability of ultimate loss, and the amount (or range) of potential losses that may be incurred. To obtain this information, management prepares a list of potential claims which is then forwarded to the company's law firms for confirmation and evaluation. The formal request asks the attorney to provide the following, and because the request comes from management, it enables the attorney to provide information without violating confidentiality concerns:

- Information about *pending* claims identified by management and confirmation of relevant facts including
  - Nature of the claim against the company
  - Status of the case
  - Planned client actions
  - Assessment of the likelihood and amount of unfavorable outcomes
- Information about *unasserted* claims identified by management including confirmation of relevant facts
- Information about *omitted* claims that are pending or unasserted of which the attorney is aware but that have not been specifically identified by management in the confirmation request. If the attorney knows of no omitted claims, he is asked for a specific statement to that effect.

Under the commonly agreed upon guidelines between the accounting and legal profession, the attorney may provide the requested information subject to some limitations: (1) the information is limited to those cases for which the law firm has been substantively consulted and (2) the response may also emphasize the inherent uncertainties related to facts and conclusions subject to adjudication. If a law firm that is substantively involved in a case does not respond to the request for information, the auditor should consider this a potential scope limitation. A lawyer is required by legal professional ethics to withdraw from providing services to a client if the client will not fully disclose all material lawsuits to the auditor. Thus, the auditor should be extremely suspicious if the law firm withdraws from a client engagement after the legal letter has been sent.

REVIEW OF SUBSEQUENT EVENTS

The auditor must consider any events, conditions, or information that arise after year end that may have implications for the reporting of financial results as of the end of the fiscal year. For example, the bankruptcy of a major customer in January indicates that the customer's receivable balance as of December 31 may not be collectible and should be considered a potential bad debt. Such an event provides evidence on the valuation of receivables. Similarly, much of the testing for unrecorded liabilities involves examining disbursements that occur after the end of the year. The auditor should explicitly consider evidence about subsequent events as part of the substantive testing of financial statement assertions and disclosures.

> **Authoritative Guidance & Standards**
> Auditing standards for ensuring that subsequent events are properly accounted for and disclosed are contained in SAS 98 and ISA 560.

Figure 15–3 depicts the period subsequent to year end during which events are potentially significant to the auditor. Auditors are responsible for evaluating events that occur before the end of fieldwork, which is also the report date on the

Figure 15–3   Subsequent Events Period

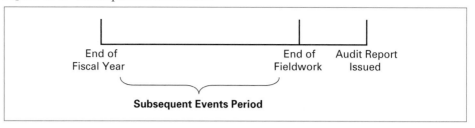

auditors' report. In general, two types of subsequent events are of interest to the auditor:

1. **Events requiring an adjustment to the financial statements:** These are events that provide information about circumstances that existed as of the fiscal year end, for example, the bankruptcy of a major customer suggests that any receivables from that customer may be uncollectible. Other examples include settlement of litigation, which provides evidence about the amount of loss related to a contingent liability, and the disposal of assets at a significant loss, which provides evidence about the impairment of those assets at year end.[2]

2. **Events requiring disclosure in the financial statements:** These are events that have occurred since the end of the year but do not directly relate to the year-end balances. A presumption is made that knowledge of these events has a strong influence on how the financial statements are interpreted and that the readers of the financial statements would be adversely affected if they were not told about these events. Examples include business acquisitions or large casualty losses occurring after year end.

E x a m p l e

To distinguish between events requiring an adjustment to the financial statements versus events requiring disclosure, consider companies impacted by the severe earthquakes in California and Japan in the mid-1990s and the tsunami in Southeast Asia in 2004. Both earthquakes occurred in January, which was subsequent to year end for those companies with a calendar fiscal year. Thus, losses associated with the earthquakes would have been disclosed as a subsequent event for the prior fiscal year. Conversely, the tsunami occurred in late December, which would require affected organizations to adjust the financial statements for any losses relating to the disaster.

Because the annual report is issued after the end of fieldwork, companies sometimes have a subsequent event that occurs after fieldwork but prior to the release of the financial statements. In this scenario, auditors will re-open the audit for the subsequent event only and issue the audit report as a *dual date report*. The report will be signed and dated with the fieldwork date, but a second date will be indicated that relates to the disclosure describing the subsequent event that occurred after the end of fieldwork.

After the annual report is issued, the auditor is under no further obligation to monitor the subsequent events of the company. However, new information may

2 The assumption made in the case of assets sold at a loss is that the loss existed as of the fiscal year end, but the existence or amount of the loss was uncertain at that time. The actual sale after year end therefore provides evidence about the loss that had already occurred.

come to the attention of the auditor that a misstatement was contained in the financial statements as of year end. In this case, the auditor would ask management to *recall* the financial statements and if not, to take actions necessary to dissociate the audit firm from the financial statements. If management has not recalled the financial statements, the auditor needs to seek legal advice as to his or her responsibilities, especially for public companies and when the auditor knows that users are still relying on the audited financial statements. The only exception to this requirement is if the information is received during the subsequent audit. Because the auditor is in the process of issuing a new report that covers both the subsequent year end and the year end containing the misstatement, the auditor can issue a report in the subsequent year based on the corrected financial statements.

REPRESENTATION LETTERS

The auditor should obtain a *representation letter* from management at the end of the audit. The purpose of the representation letter is to document management's responses to a number of critical inquiries (e.g., the nature of related parties, commitments and contingencies, asset valuations), ensure that those inquiries have been correctly understood, and impress on management its responsibility for all information included in the financial statements. A representation letter does not replace other forms of audit testing but does provide an effective method for avoiding misunderstandings about management's responsibilities or the meaning of important information provided by management to the auditor. In addition, because the letter forces management to document the information provided to the auditor, the letter provides a written record of any misrepresentations that management may have made, giving the auditor some defense against charges of negligence in the event of an audit failure.

> **Authoritative Guidance & Standards**
> Auditing standards on management representation letters are found in SAS 12 and ISA 580. Further, the Sarbanes-Oxley Act (Section 302) requires the CEO and CFO of U.S.-registered public companies to sign a certification that they have read and concur with the financial statements.

A simple representation letter is presented in Figure 15–4. The letter is addressed to the auditor and dated as of the end of fieldwork. The CEO or CFO sign the letter. Management refusal to provide a representation letter represents a scope limitation that may justify a disclaimer of opinion or withdrawal from the engagement. The letter should include a specific reference to management's responsibilities for the financial statements and a statement that management believes the financial statements to be free of material misstatement. The following items should also be covered in the representation letter:

- The completeness of financial records, documents, minutes of board meetings, and regulatory reports made available to the auditor
- The absence of unrecorded errors or transactions related to the financial statements and management's belief that the effect of any uncorrected errors is immaterial
- The completeness of information pertaining to related party transactions
- The completeness of information pertaining to subsequent events and uncertainties
- Information about fraud that may have occurred
- Management plans that might have an impact on the valuation or classification of transactions
- Legal title of assets and liens against assets

Figure 15–4   Example of Representation Letter

Johnson Pharmaceuticals Inc.

Ms. Roberta Smith, CA   Date
333 E. University Avenue

Dear Ms. Smith:

In connection with your audit of the financial statements for Johnson Pharmaceutical
Inc. as of December 31, 20x7 and the period then ended for the purpose of expressing
an opinion as to whether the financial statements present fairly, in all material respects,
the financial position, results of operations and cash flows of Johnson Pharmaceuticals
Inc. in conformity with generally accepted accounting principles, we confirm, to the
best of our knowledge and belief, the following representations made to you during
your audit.

- We are responsible for the fair presentation in the financial statements of financial
  position, results of operations, and cash flows in conformity with generally accepted
  accounting principles.
- We have made available to you (1) all financial records and related data and
  (2) complete minutes for meetings of directors, shareholders, and committees of
  directors.
- There has been no (1) fraud involving management or employees who have a significant role in internal control of the company, (2) fraud involving employees that
  could have a material effect on the financial statements, or (3) communications from
  regulatory agencies concerning noncompliance with, or deficiencies in, financial reporting practices that could have a material effect on the financial statements.
- The effect of any uncorrected misstatements identified during the audit is not material to the latest period, either individually or in the aggregate.
- We have no plans or intentions that may materially affect the carrying value or classification of assets. [Details can be added for specific items such as intent to hold
  noncurrent investments to maturity or intent to dispose of idle property.]
- The following have been properly recorded and disclosed in the financial statements:
  1. Related party transactions and related amounts receivable or payable, including
     sales, purchases, loans, transfers, leasing arrangements, and guarantees
  2. Capital stock repurchase options or agreements or capital stock reserved for
     options, warrants, conversions, or other requirements
  3. Arrangements with financial institutions involving compensating balances or
     other arrangements involving restrictions on cash balances and line-of-credit or
     similar arrangements
  4. Agreements to repurchase assets previously sold
  5. Guarantees under which the company is contingently liable
  6. Significant estimates and material concentrations known to management
- There are neither (1) violations or possible violations of laws or regulations whose
  effects should be considered for disclosure in the financial statements or as a basis
  for recording a loss contingency, nor (2) other material liabilities or gain or loss contingencies that are required to be accrued or disclosed by accounting standards.
- There are no unasserted claims or assessments that our lawyer has advised us are
  probable of assertion and must be disclosed in accordance with accounting standards.
- There are no material transactions that have not been properly recorded in the
  accounting records underlying the financial statements.
- Provision, when material, has been made to reduce excess or obsolete inventories to
  their estimated net realizable value.

Figure 15–4   *(continued)*

- The company has satisfactory title to all owned assets, and there are no undisclosed liens or encumbrances on such assets, nor has any asset been pledged.
- Provision has been made for any material loss to be sustained in the fulfillment of, or from the inability to fulfill, any sales commitments.
- Provision has been made for any material loss to be sustained as a result of purchase commitments for inventory quantities in excess of normal requirements or at prices in excess of the prevailing market prices.
- We have complied with all aspects of contractual agreements that would have a material effect on the financial statements in the event of noncompliance. [Specific debt covenants may be addressed if particularly important.]
- No events have occurred subsequent to the balance sheet date that would require adjustments to, or disclosure in, the financial statements.

Respectfully,

_____   _____
Samuel Smith, President   Victoria Rose, Controller

- Information about issues that may require disclosure or accounting recognition including significant estimates, risk and uncertainties, regulatory noncompliance, unasserted claims, and contingent losses

In a large, multinational organization, there may be representation letters for separate business units within the corporation. Auditors should be alert to situations where a financial manager at the business unit level refuses to sign a representation letter even though senior management is willing. This may indicate that the business unit manager has concerns about senior management's representations. This possibility should be considered a serious problem for the auditor. Furthermore, the auditor should not simply accept that it is corporate policy to only have senior management sign representation letters.

Example

In 2004, Deloitte & Touche resigned from the audit of Molex, a global electronic components company based in Illinois, because Molex's audit committee and board of directors unanimously rejected Deloitte's demand that both the CEO and CFO be removed as officers of the company. This demand was based on two issues. First, the CFO had knowledge of misstatements in the financial statements yet indicated in the management representation letter (which she signed) that no misstatements existed. Second, the CEO signed the management representation letter but admitted that he had not read the letter before signing it. Ernst & Young later accepted the client, but only after the audit committee and board of directors reversed their earlier decision and removed both individuals as officers of Molex.

FINAL EVALUATION OF AUDIT EVIDENCE

The final evaluation of audit evidence is designed to provide a last check on the work of the auditor, to make sure that all pieces of the audit lead to the same conclusion, and to assure that no important matters have been overlooked.

EVALUATION OF PRESENTATION AND DISCLOSURE ASSERTIONS

Although the audit steps associated with management assertions about transactions and accounts take most of the time required in the audit, auditors also have the responsibility of evaluating the final presentation and disclosure of the information in the financial statements. Given that the information included in the financial statements is often highly aggregated and involves a great deal of textual information, the auditor must evaluate each financial statement line item and disclosure, and the financial statements as a whole, to ensure that the presentation and disclosure assertions are valid.

Occurrence and Rights and Obligations: Most of the testing of ownership and rights and obligations is completed as part of the tests of transactions and accounts. As a consequence, the evaluation of the disclosure of occurrence and rights and obligations usually entails a review of the textual disclosures to make sure they do not contradict the results of the other audit tests and that there are no disclosures that have been overlooked by management. If management has added new disclosures that were not previously examined, the auditor must undertake additional procedures to ensure that the presentation and disclosure assertions are valid for these items.

Completeness and the Use of a Disclosure Checklist: A particularly challenging aspect of the presentation and disclosure assertions is the need to evaluate whether the disclosures in the financial statements are complete, that is, all required disclosures are included. To help ensure that all necessary disclosures are complete, auditors often utilize a *disclosure checklist* that includes all required disclosures, including specific requirements for public companies or companies in an industry that has specialized practices. Completion of such a checklist helps the auditor identify any disclosures that may have been overlooked in the preparation of the financial statements.

Example

Many industries have complex and unusual accounting rules for reporting transactions that are unique to the industry. In the United States, the AICPA publishes a series of industry guidebooks in areas such as banking, insurance, and health care due to the unique financial reporting practices in those industries. For example, in the insurance industry, customers pay for an insurance policy when it is issued but may not make a claim against that policy for many years (if ever). This creates a unique accounting challenge for the insurance company because the premiums collected are a form of deferred revenue and the "cost" of the services rendered to the customers may not be known for a very long time. As a result, the insurance industry has developed specialized techniques for estimating the portion of premiums that are "earned" in any given year and the matching "losses" that might occur in the future as a result of issuing the policy.

Accuracy, Valuation, Classification, and Understandability: Another important consideration for auditors is that management might use the final financial statements to alter transaction or account information that has been audited by the auditors. For example, management might accidentally or intentionally alter otherwise accurate transaction and account data when aggregating it for financial statement presentation, especially when consolidated accounts are drawn up after the individual corporate accounts are audited. Thus, as previously noted, the auditor must test the accuracy of the management's process for producing the final financial statements.

Furthermore, management may try to influence the interpretation of reported results through misleading, vague, or intentionally complex descriptions in the footnotes. Auditors must carefully read all financial statement disclosures to ensure that they can be understood by reasonably astute financial statement users, especially when disclosures involve complex business transactions combined with complicated reporting regulations. For example, financial derivatives are highly complex transactions in their own right; the accounting for such transactions is just as complex and requires significant expertise by the auditor to evaluate and verify.

Example

One of the primary problems with the financial reporting by Enron was the incredibly complex disclosures found in the company's footnotes surrounding the accounting treatment of off balance sheet special purpose entities (SPEs) where the company was able to hide much of its accumulated financial loss and funnel cash to corporate executives. Many analysts (and possibly auditors) were hard-pressed to interpret the information contained in these disclosures, which may have been intentionally written to disguise financial and operating activities that the company did not want external readers to know about.

REVIEW OF AUDIT DOCUMENTATION AND CONCLUSIONS

As we noted in Chapter 14, one of the most prevalent quality control techniques used by auditors is the review of the documentation of audit evidence obtained during the engagement by senior members of the audit team. Audit documentation may be reviewed two or three times during the course of the audit. Work initially performed by staff accountants is usually reviewed on a detailed basis by senior accountants and on a general basis by managers. Work performed by senior accountants is usually reviewed on a detailed basis by managers and possibly on a general basis by partners. Ultimately, the responsibility for the overall quality of the work in the engagement rests with the partner in charge of the engagement team; however, partners often focus their reviews on key accounting issues and highly material transactions, accounts, or disclosures. If the reviewer has a question about the evidence contained in the documentation, an effort must be made to resolve the issue. Questions raised during reviews may cause the auditor to gather additional evidence, as was pointed out in the AMA example in Chapter 14. The audit report should not be issued until all questions raised during the review have been appropriately addressed by the members of the audit team.

CLIENT NEGOTIATION AND RESOLUTION OF KNOWN MISSTATEMENTS

As a result of audit testing, the auditor may discover misstatements of financial information. These misstatements will differ on a number of dimensions:

- Size relative to materiality
- Degree of objectivity (e.g., objective error in a transaction versus subjective difference in opinion about the valuation of an account)
- Impact on financial statements (e.g., increase or decrease of net income)
- Implications for overall audit risk (e.g., unintentional errors versus fraudulent behavior)

Figure 15–5 Example of Error Summary Worksheet

						X-1
	Jones Manufacturing Inc.					WRK
	Summary of Unadjusted Audit Differences					1/24/x7
	12/31/x6					

W/P Ref	Description	Total	*Effect on Accounts: Debit (Credit)* Assets	Liability	Revenue	Expense
C-2	To restate inventory for inventory on hand per physical observation	10,000	(10,000)			10,000 ✓
B-3	To reflect expected bad debts	8,000	(8,000)			8,000
I-4	To accrue investment income	5,500	5,500		(5,500)	
L-3	To accrue unrecorded liabilities	20,000		(20,000)		20,000 ✓
F-2	To record repairs that should be capitalized	3,500	3,500			(3,500)
	Total effect of audit differences		(9,000)	(20,000)	(5,500)	34,500
			T	T	T	T
	Total unadjusted audit differences		(9,000)	0	(5,500)	15,500
			T	T	T	T

✓ Adjustment booked by client and reflected in financial statements

T Footed without exception

Conclusion:
After booking all individually material adjustments (denoted with a ✓), the net effect of all other unadjusted differences is deemed to be immaterial. Adjustment of further items is passed.

As the audit is executed, proposed audit adjustments for known errors should be accumulated for disposition at the end of the engagement. An example of an error summary worksheet is presented in Figure 15–5.

Auditors typically consult with management about which proposed adjustments will be made to the financial statements. Ultimately, the financial statements are the responsibility of management and the auditor cannot make adjustments unless management agrees. Adjustments that are material and objective will likely be posted to the financial statements with a minimum of argument from management. However, management may debate adjustments that are immaterial, have offsetting effects, or involve subjective estimates. If management is unwilling to correct the financial statements for adjustments that the auditor deems to be material misstatements, the auditor can issue a qualified audit opinion or resign. Before resorting to such options, however, most auditors try to resolve the issues through negotiation.

The process of negotiating financial adjustments with management can be complex and difficult. There may be audit differences where the auditor and management can honestly disagree because they are subjective in nature or based on predictions about the future. In these cases, there may be a number of alternative resolutions that are equally defensible. Both the auditor and management have their own interests in the outcome of the audit process and are entitled to their own position on an issue, but this will influence each side's willingness to resolve audit differences. Understanding the position and views of the other side in a negotiation process increases the likelihood of a positive outcome from the process. More specifically, the likelihood of a mutually satisfactory outcome to the negotiation process will depend on:

- Commitment to principles or objectives relevant to the issue in question: Both management and the auditor have legitimate goals and principles driving their behavior that can cause them to disagree over specific matters. For example, the auditor will have a strong commitment to professional standards and the more that an audit difference is perceived to be in violation of those standards, the more firm the auditor's position will be regarding making an adjustment. Management may be committed to organizational success, and the more that an audit difference reflects weak performance, the more management may resist making the adjustment.
- Perceived fairness: The more that each side perceives that it has been treated fairly, the more understanding it will be of the other side's position. Compromise may be appropriate for audit differences that are subjective and uncertain, especially if management's assumptions are reasonable, albeit different, from those of the auditor.
- Effectiveness of communication: The better each party is able to communicate its objectives, principles, needs, desires, and potential areas for compromise, the more likely the groups are to reach a mutually agreeable solution. Knowing the potential limits of the other side's position helps to avoid unproductive ultimatums and a collapse of the negotiation process. For example, trying to force an auditor to accept an accounting treatment that is clearly in violation of GAAP and for which objective evidence exists increases the likelihood that the auditor will be forced to resign or issue a qualified opinion.
- Strength of relationship: If the auditor and management have mutual respect and do not wish to jeopardize an ongoing professional relationship, they will be more likely to achieve a cooperative solution. However, the auditor should be careful to not allow the relationship with the client to undermine the auditor's compliance with professional standards relating to objectivity and independence.

In the example presented in Figure 15–5, the adjustments for inventory and unrecorded liabilities have been recorded in the financial statements, probably because they are large and objectively determined. The adjustment for bad debt expense is subjective and may be difficult to justify to management if the estimation is based on assumptions that are debatable. Furthermore, when netted against the two other errors, the net result is an immaterial amount. Consequently, three adjustments are *waived* by the auditor, meaning that the auditor does not insist on their correction in the financial statements.

For audits of registered public companies in the United States, the Sarbanes-Oxley Act is believed to have strengthened the auditor's negotiation power with management. Under the law, auditors are required to discuss with the audit com-

> **Authoritative Guidance & Standards**
>
> For U.S.-registered public companies, the Sarbanes-Oxley Act requires that auditors meet with the Audit Committee to discuss all disagreements with management related to accounting policies or application of principles. The audit committee must then decide how to resolve the issues. However, the auditor always has the final say as to the opinion provided in the audit reports.

mittee any disagreements with management regarding accounting policies or application of principles. Thus, should management not agree to a proposed audit adjustment and be unable to convince the auditor that it has valid reasons for doing so, the auditor will provide this information to the audit committee, which then must decide whether or not to force management to make the adjustment. Should the audit committee agree with management, the auditor could then choose to issue a qualified opinion or to resign.[3] Because the Sarbanes-Oxley Act makes audit committee members individually liable for misstated financial statements, audit committees are expected to be reluctant to side with management in such disputes. Nevertheless, negotiation can still be expected to occur, even though the bargaining power has shifted towards the auditor in these situations.

FINAL TECHNICAL REVIEW

As one last check on the accuracy of the financial statements, an audit partner who has not been involved in the engagement, often referred to as the *concurring (or review) partner*, will perform a review of the statements, supporting documentation, and audit conclusions. The primary purpose of this review is to determine if the engagement complies with all relevant auditing standards. Because the individual performing the review is not close to the engagement, the documentation must present the sole basis for reaching a conclusion. In this way, the audit firm has assurance that the workpapers adequately support the conclusion that generally accepted accounting principles (GAAP) have been correctly applied and that the data in the financial statements has been subjected to adequate audit verification. Absent any problems arising from the final technical review, the audit is essentially complete and the audit report can be issued.

ACCOUNTING CHOICES AND THE QUALITY OF EARNINGS

The financial statements are a set of complex documents intended to communicate the financial performance and status of the organization to interested readers. However, even after all the numbers and disclosures have been audited, a final question may arise as to the general quality of the information included in a financial report. *Earnings quality* is much debated in accounting, as is its inverse, *earnings management*. Figure 15–6 presents three separate definitions of earnings

---

3 In some countries, an auditor cannot resign without issuing a report.

Figure 15–6   Alternative Definitions for Earnings Management

1. Managing earnings is "the process of taking deliberate steps within the constraints of generally accepted accounting principles to bring about a desired level of reported earnings." Davidson, Stickney, and Weil (1987), cited in Schipper (1989) p. 92
2. Managing earnings is "a purposeful intervention in the external financial reporting process, with the intent of obtaining some private gain (as opposed to say, merely facilitating the neutral operation of the process) . . . . A minor extension of this definition would encompass "real" earnings management, accomplished by timing investment or financing decisions to alter reported earnings or some subset of it." Schipper (1989) p. 92
3. "Earnings management occurs when managers use judgment in financial reporting and in structuring transactions to alter financial reports to either mislead some stakeholders about the underlying economic performance of the company or to influence contractual outcomes that depend on reported accounting numbers." Healy and Wahlen (1999) p. 368

management. A simple definition of earnings is "the amount that can be consumed during the period, while leaving the firm equally well off at the beginning and end of the period." All three earnings management definitions are consistent with this definition of earnings, as all three imply some deviation in reported earnings from the amount that can be consumed leaving the entity as well off at the end of the period as at the beginning.

At least three major groups care about earnings quality. First, the company's shareholders make judgments about management and whether to continue to invest in the company. Second, potential shareholders may purchase stock in the company based on their expectations of future earnings, which they forecast based on current earnings. Third, other stakeholders may enter into contracts with the entity. These stakeholders include managers (who are frequently compensated based on reported earnings) and creditors (who evaluate their credit risk based on earnings). Finally, in the big picture there are losses to society based on the inefficient allocation of scarce capital to firms whose poor performance is masked via earnings management. This behavior results in losses to investors and lending institutions, which can have a dampening effect on the entire economy.

THE IMPACT OF ACCOUNTING CHOICES, POLICIES, AND PROCEDURES

Although accounting is viewed as a technical topic, in which computational measurement is an important part of effective accounting (and auditing), there also is a judgmental aspect of accounting involving the way that management interprets the economics underlying a transaction and the wording of accounting standards. For this aspect, accounting becomes a judgment exercise full of choices that affect the numbers reported in financial statements. Generally accepted accounting principles (GAAP) often provide options for reporting a specific type of transaction; for example, inventory can be accounted for using LIFO (which generally reduces earnings), FIFO (which usually yields higher earnings), or some other accounting method. Furthermore, management can often structure transactions to achieve a desired accounting result and to portray transactions in the best possible light.

Example

Leases are complex transactions that can be structured in different ways in order to arrive at a desired accounting result. Many leases are long term in nature and are, in substance, purchase transactions. However, leases can often be structured such that the underlying asset and debt are not recorded on the balance sheet of the lessee, relieving the company of the need to compute depreciation on the asset while hiding the debt off the balance sheet. Accounting rules and regulations attempt to separate such capital leases from short-term operating leases, but companies can be very creative in getting around the rules. Consequently, management can usually obtain an arrangement with a seller/lessor such that a transaction is structured in the most advantageous manner.

Financial statements are the responsibility of management, and management makes the decisions about how to structure transactions and account for them. Given the flexibility of many accounting standards and the control of the underlying transactions, management may be able to manipulate financial results using accounting legerdemain. Auditors have the responsibility to provide an objective evaluation of the reasonableness of accounting choices made by management. If a client's accounting choices are excessively aggressive in maximizing reported earnings, the auditor must consider whether management is behaving appropriately, and whether some of the accounting choices cross the line from acceptable to inappropriate. Furthermore, just because a selected accounting treatment is acceptable within the standards does not mean that it is fair or desirable. Many abuses of financial reporting in the past few years were technically "correct" but ethically indefensible, as they did not portray the underlying economics of a transaction or events appropriately. Consequently, the auditor must maintain his or her skepticism when considering the appropriateness of management's accounting choices.

Auditors should pay careful attention to the current environment and conditions in which an organization operates when evaluating the accounting policies and procedures chosen by management. For example, when investors and market analysts place pressure on management to improve earnings, there is a heightened probability that the organization will structure transactions to achieve a desired accounting result. This issue becomes even more important when management decides to change accounting methods for previously existing transactions. In that case, the auditor should be clear as to the reason for the change.

Example

In 2005, gasoline prices increased dramatically in the United States during the summer and fall. During the summer, increased demand in Asia often was cited as driving the changes. During the fall, shortages resulting from Hurricanes Katrina and Rita were cited as driving the changes. Consumers and some regulators hypothesized that petroleum companies were exaggerating conditions and charging excessive prices in response to these problems. Several petroleum companies announced significant increases in earnings during this period, causing a number of politicians and commentators to investigate the behavior of the oil companies. Given this type of attention, oil companies might be motivated to structure transactions and make accounting choices that would reduce their short-term profits so as to avoid intervention from regulators. Indeed, the companies probably had a reasonable fear of such intervention because the Federal government did impose a "windfall profits" tax on the oil industry when a similar market phenomenon occurred in the 1970s.

Figure 15–7   Financial "Shenanigans" that Produce Lower Quality Earnings*

1. Recording revenue too soon or of questionable quality
   a. Recording revenue when material future services remain to be provided
   b. Recording revenue when the customer is not obligated to pay for goods or services received
2. Recording fictitious revenue
   a. Recording cash received in lending transactions as revenue
   b. Recording as revenue supplier rebates tied to future required purchases
3. Boosting income with one-time gains
   a. Selling assets valued at historical cost to produce accounting gains
   b. Using investment income to increase operating revenue or decrease operating expenses
4. Shifting current expenses to a later or earlier period
   a. Capitalizing normal operating costs
   b. Amortizing costs too slowly
   c. Failing to write-down or write-off impaired assets
5. Failing to record or improperly reducing liabilities
   a. Reducing liabilities by changing accounting assumptions
   b. Failing to record expenses and related liabilities when future obligations remain
6. Shifting current revenue to a later period
   a. Creating reserves around times of infrequent activity (e.g. mergers) and releasing them into income in a later period
7. Shifting future expenses to the current period as a special charge.
   a. Improperly inflating a write-down or write-off so that future expenses will be understated
   b. Accelerating discretionary expenses that will benefit future period's performance to current period

*Drawn from Howard Schilit, *Financial Shenanigans*, 2nd ed. (New York: McGraw-Hill, 2002), 24–25. Reprinted with permission of The McGraw-Hill Companies.

SEVEN WAYS ACCOUNTING CHOICES CAN LOWER EARNINGS QUALITY

Figure 15–7 illustrates seven ways that the accrual accounting system can be used to manage earnings. Indeed, some market observers go as far as to call these techniques "financial shenanigans." Although all these techniques reduce the information quality of reported results, many of them do not cross the line into fraudulent behavior unless they are a blatant and deceptive misrepresentation of economic facts. For example, recording nonexistent revenue is fraudulent, but shifting real revenue between periods may not be because it may be a legitimate use of management discretion under GAAP. Even if the auditor wishes to challenge these behaviors, management can often hide behind the technical rules of GAAP. By first considering whether management's proposed accounting treatment of a transaction reflects its economic reality, the auditor shifts the focus of the discussion from technical accounting requirements to whether compliance with formal requirements is appropriate.

Section 204 of the Sarbanes-Oxley Act of 2002 addresses this issue by focusing on the practice of structuring transactions simply to enable preferred GAAP accounting. In the wake of Enron and other frauds, the Sarbanes-Oxley Act now requires auditors of U.S. public company registrants to discuss disagreements about accounting for transactions with the audit committee. Should auditors believe that the form of the transaction does not correspond appropriately with its substance, they should document their concerns and present them to the audit committee. Because the audit committee is accountable for financial reporting for the company (i.e., it can be held personally liable), auditors now have more leverage in convincing clients to account for transactions in ways that are less aggressive and more transparent than the extreme limits of GAAP might allow.

ASSESSING EARNINGS QUALITY

Earnings quality is most often associated with conservative accounting policies, that is, recognizing expenses and losses as soon as they are identified and delaying revenue recognition and gains until realization is certain. However, the nature of double entry accounting means that what is conservative in one period may reverse and become aggressive in a subsequent period; for example, increasing depreciation expense in the early years of an asset's life using an accelerated method results in larger earnings being reported in later years. To help evaluate the appropriateness of a company's accounting choices, the auditor should evaluate the client's *quality of earnings* based on the following circumstances:

- Correlation with underlying economic activity: Financial results should relate to the underlying condition of the industry. Record profits in a time of recession are suspicious and may indicate potential earnings manipulation.
- Permanence and sustainability: Companies may recognize one-time transactions to achieve certain financial goals or to maintain trends in a consistent direction, such as recording a gain on the sale of plant assets. Earnings quality is decreased in such cases because results do not reflect underlying operating patterns and the transactions may not be repeatable in the future.
- Relationship with market valuation: Inconsistency between the valuation of a company's stock and its underlying performance could indicate low-quality earnings. The auditor should question whether the market is reacting to information outside the context of the financial statements that might be relevant to financial reporting.[4]
- Extent and impact of discretionary accruals: As noted above, management's decisions regarding accounting methods, estimates, and accruals will have an impact on the quality of the company's earnings. To the extent that aggressive choices are used to artificially inflate financial results, earnings quality will be reduced.
- Transparency and completeness of disclosures: The openness and understandability of financial disclosures provides an indication of management's willingness to communicate effectively with shareholders and analysts.
- Impact on corporate image: Management often considers how financial information reflects on the company in a broader sense. A company earning monopoly profits may wish to use very conservative accounting techniques to reduce reported income and minimize the notice that apparently unconscionable earnings would draw from the media, tax authorities, and regulatory agencies.

4 Toward the end of the 1990s, the stock market experienced amazing market valuations placed on technology companies that had no reported profits, and no expectation of profits in the near term. Such valuations would seem to be a bet that some IT companies would eventually be enormously profitable.

- Handling of "bad" news: The way that management communicates bad news about the organization can be revealing of its attitudes towards financial reporting. Attempts to sugarcoat the news or to compound losses with unnecessary write-offs, both indicate potentially poorer earnings quality.

The auditor will need to take these considerations into account when the financial statements are compiled and subject to final review. Although these indicators of earnings quality are useful for auditors, economic circumstances in an industry do not always foster smooth accounting results. In those cases, the auditor must also be aware of the possibility that management may use accounting tricks to mask volatile conditions to present an illusion of high quality earnings.

Example

A recent article about General Electric noted: "GE also has a long-standing reputation for 'managing' its earnings, by taking money from one pocket and putting it into another. Depending on your sympathies, GE does this either to help smooth reported earnings (and therefore to disguise all that hidden riskiness), or to demonstrate more clearly to investors the growth of the company's underlying businesses."[5] A common perception of financial reporting is that management first decides on the final earnings to report and then undertakes accounting manipulations to achieve that result.

EXTERNAL COMMUNICATION OF AUDIT RESULTS

The primary external communication prepared by the auditor is the formal auditor's report(s). If a traditional audit of the financial statements has been performed, the form of report will depend on the outcome of that audit; the completeness, credibility, and persuasiveness of the evidence obtained; the compliance (or lack thereof) with GAAP and GAAS; and management's willingness to adjust the financial statements for known errors. If an integrated audit is performed, the auditor will also provide reports on management's assessment of the effectiveness of internal controls over financial reporting and the auditor's own assessment of the effectiveness of internal controls over financial reporting.

> **Authoritative Guidance & Standards**
> Auditing standards for preparing auditor's reports for financial statement audits of all companies except U.S.-registered public companies are found in SAS 58 and ISA 700. For U.S.-registered public companies, auditing standards associated with management's assessment of the effectiveness of internal control over financial reporting and the auditor's assessment of the effectiveness of internal control over financial reporting are found in AS 2.

STANDARD UNQUALIFIED AUDITOR'S REPORT

After completing all planned audit work, the auditor should be able to conclude whether material management assertions are reasonable. If all material assertions related to transactions, accounts, disclosures, and the financial statements as a whole have been evaluated, the auditor can conclude that the financial statements are fairly presented. If any significant management assertion is not reasonable such that a material misstatement has been identified, the auditor cannot conclude that the financial statements are fairly presented. In either case, the auditor issues a formal report stating the nature of his or her

---

5 "The Jack and Jeff Show Loses its Lustre," *The Economist*, May 2, 2002.

Figure 15–8 Standard (Unqualified) Auditor's Report

Title	Auditor's Report (or Report of Independent Public Accountant)
Addressee	To the Shareholders of Pizzeria Inc.
Intro	We have audited the accompanying balance sheet of Pizzeria Inc. as of December 31, 20xx, and the related statements of income, retained earnings, and cash flows for the year then ended. These financial statements are the responsibility of the Company's management. Our responsibility is to express an opinion on these financial statements based on our audit.
Scope	We conducted our audit in accordance with generally accepted auditing standards.* Those standards require that we plan and perform the audit to obtain reasonable assurance whether the financial statements are free of material misstatement. An audit includes examining, on a test basis, evidence supporting the amounts and disclosures in the financial statements. An audit also includes assessing the accounting principles used and significant estimates made by management, as well as evaluating the overall financial statement presentation.
Opinion	In our opinion, the financial statements present fairly, in all material respects, the financial position of Pizzeria Inc. as of December 31, 20xx, and the results of its operations and its cash flows for the year then ended in accordance with generally accepted accounting principles.
Signer	[Name of the accounting firm]
Date	[Date]

* For publicly listed companies in the United States, "generally accepted auditing standards" would be replaced in the auditor's report with "standards promulgated by the Public Company Accounting Oversight Board."

conclusions. The auditing standards for auditor's reports are very specific and depend on national and international regulations.

In most engagements, the auditor will conclude that the financial statements are fairly presented and can then issue a *standard unqualified report* sometimes called a "clean opinion." The nature of this report was discussed in Chapter 3 and is illustrated in Figure 15–8. There are seven parts to the standard unqualified report:

- **Title:** The title of the report is "Independent Accountant's (or Auditor's) Report."
- **Addressee:** The addressee is the shareholders or the board of directors.
- **Introductory paragraph:** The introductory paragraph specifies the assertions that were examined (i.e., the financial statements) and the relative responsibilities of the auditor and management.
- **Scope paragraph:** The scope paragraph provides a brief description of what the auditor has performed, including the type of assurance provided and limitations associated with the audit.
- **Opinion paragraph:** The opinion paragraph indicates the auditor's conclusion based on established criteria.
- **Signature:** The report is "signed" by the auditing/public accounting firm.
- **Report Date:** The date of the report is the date on which the auditor completes the audit fieldwork.

The key terms in the report are "reasonable assurance" in the scope paragraph and "present fairly" in the opinion paragraph. By specifying reasonable assurance, the auditor is conveying that users on the financial statements can rely on the financial statements to the extent that the auditors are providing high, but not absolute, assurance about the financial statements. The criteria used for reaching the conclusion that the financial statements are fairly presented are based on generally accepted accounting principles. As should be obvious from prior discussions concerning audit risk, complete certainty cannot be achieved in any engagement.

Unqualified Auditor Reports with an Explanatory Paragraph

There are a number of circumstances or conditions when the auditor wishes to emphasize something to the readers of the financial statements without indicating a problem in the overall fairness of the report. Typically, the auditor will then depart from the standard unqualified report by adding a fourth paragraph just before or just after the opinion paragraph. This paragraph is used to describe the reasons for the departure from the standard unqualified report and will often refer to a specific note in the financial statements that presents relevant facts.

Going Concern Problem: If the auditor has concluded that there exists a substantial doubt about a client's ability to survive as a going concern for the next year, and the client has clearly disclosed these circumstances in the financial statements or the notes, the auditor should issue a modified unqualified report. An additional paragraph should be added to the auditor's report that there is substantial doubt about the entity's ability to continue as a going concern.[6] The facts related to the doubt should be presented in a note to the financial statements to which the auditor refers in the explanatory paragraph.[7] An illustration of a report modified for a going concern is presented in Figure 15–9. An auditor should not use conditional language that might undermine the communication of substantial doubt.[8]

Example

During fall 2005, both Northwest Airlines and Delta Airlines filed for Chapter 11 bankruptcy protection under U.S. bankruptcy law. Accordingly, both organizations automatically would receive opinions containing a going concern explanatory paragraph, even though the financial statements receive an unqualified opinion because there are no material misstatements in the financial statements.

Emphasis of a Matter: An auditor will occasionally wish to emphasize certain facts or conditions that may influence how a reader interprets the financial statements. The auditor might decide to emphasize that the company had significant related party transactions or that the prior year's financial statements were audited by another public accounting firm. The auditor may emphasize such a matter by adding an explanatory paragraph to the audit report. Another common matter that

6 Canada is currently alone among major auditing standard-setting nations in not requiring the addition of an explanatory paragraph after the opinion paragraph describing the going concern. There is a project under way to bring Canadian audit practice into conformity with U.S. and international auditing standards in this area.

7 Failure to adequately disclose the conditions leading to the going concern problem may cause the auditor to issue a qualified report due to inadequate disclosure.

8 For example, the auditor should not use language such as "*If the company does not obtain new sources of financing*, then there may be substantial doubt . . ."

Figure 15–9   Auditor's Report Modified For Going Concern*

Title	Auditor's Report (or Report of Independent Public Accountant)
Addressee	To the Shareholders, ABC Company Inc.
Introduction	We have audited the accompanying balance sheets of ABC Company Inc. as of December 31, 20x7 and 20x6, and the related statements of income, retained earnings, and cash flows for the years then ended. These financial statements are the responsibility of the Company's management. Our responsibility is to express an opinion on these financial statements based on our audit.
Scope	We conducted our audit in accordance with generally accepted auditing standards. Those standards require that we plan and perform the audit to obtain reasonable assurance whether the financial statements are free of material misstatement. An audit includes examining, on a test basis, evidence supporting the amounts and disclosures in the financial statements. An audit also includes assessing the accounting principles used and significant estimates made by management, as well as evaluating the overall financial statement presentation.
Opinion	In our opinion, the financial statements referred to above present fairly, in all material respects, the financial position of ABC Company Inc. as of December 31, 20x7 and 20x6, and the results of its operations and its cash flows for the years then ended in conformity with generally accepted accounting principles.
Emphasis	*Without qualifying our opinion, we draw attention to Note X in the financial statements which indicates that the company incurred a net loss of ZZZ during the year ended December 31, 20X7 and, as of that date, the company's current liabilities exceeded its total assets by ZZZ. These conditions, along with other matters as set forth in Note X, indicate the existence of a material uncertainty that may cast significant doubt about the company's ability to continue as a going concern.*
Signer	[Name of the public accounting firm]
Date	[Date]

* Based on IAASB ISA 570.

might be emphasized involves significant litigation. In addition, auditors should consider the information included in the unaudited portion of a document that also contains audited financial statements to determine if it is inconsistent with information contained in the financial statements, in which case the auditor should draw attention to any inconsistencies in an explanatory paragraph.

Example

In concluding an audit, an engagement team member typically will review the management discussion and analysis section of the annual report. Should management include an evaluation of litigation that suggests that lawsuits have little merit when the footnote disclosure suggests that an unfavorable judgment is reasonably possible, the auditor should note this inconsistency in an explanatory paragraph as an emphasis of a matter.

Consistency Exception: Financial statements typically are presented on a comparative basis. For example, U.S. public companies must present the prior-year balance sheet and two prior years' income statements, and statements of retained earnings and cash flows. Accordingly, the auditor will insert an explanatory paragraph so that users understand when financial statements from prior years are inconsistent with current year statements. Two common consistency exceptions are changes involving GAAP that do not require restatements of prior year financial statements and corrections of errors in prior year financial statements.

Example

When an accounting standard-setter, such as the FASB or IASB, issues a new accounting standard changing the method in which a company accounts for the way it values intangible assets, companies may make the accounting change for the current year financial statements but not necessarily for prior year financial statements. Accordingly, companies that are affected by the new pronouncement will receive an auditor's report that includes an explanatory paragraph describing this inconsistency.

Auditor Agrees with GAAP Departure: In extremely rare cases, management of an organization might decide that following GAAP will mislead investors. Generally, an auditor will require the client to make adjustments to ensure conformance to GAAP or change the opinion in the auditor's report. However, to ensure that auditors remember that the main purpose of GAAP is to provide information that is reliable and relevant to users, auditing standards allow for deviations from GAAP in situations in which auditors agree with management that the strict application of GAAP would mislead users. In such cases, the auditor's report must contain an explanatory paragraph describing the departure from GAAP, including an explanation of why following GAAP could mislead users.

Part of an Audit Performed by a Different Auditor: Often auditors utilize other auditing firms to conduct a significant portion of the audit. This typically occurs in large, multinational audit engagements, particularly when the primary auditor does not have a presence in a country where the client has significant operations that need to be examined. When one accounting firm uses another firm to conduct part of the audit, there are several options for allocating responsibility among the firms, two of which require that the auditor's report be modified.

First, auditors can assume full responsibility for the engagement and make no reference to the other firm in its auditor's report—resulting in a standard unqualified report. Second, auditors can choose to share responsibility. In this case, the auditor's report mentions in the introductory opinion that part of the audit was performed by another firm. Then, in the opinion paragraph, the opinion is provided on behalf of both firms. The signature, however, is only provided for the primary accounting firm (and no explicit name of the other firm is contained in the auditor's report). Third, the auditor can accept no responsibility for the work of the other auditor. This scenario often applies when an accounting firm has not audited prior-year financial statements. In this case, the introductory opinion mentions the part of the audit performed by the other firm and refers users to the report of the other firm. In the opinion paragraph, only the part of the audit for which the primary auditor is taking responsibility is referenced.

Example

When the accounting firm Arthur Andersen was dissolved in 2002, many of the ensuing engagements taken on by other existing firms referred to the work performed by "another auditor" for prior-year financial statements. In these cases, the auditor's report was modified based on the work of another auditor. Ernst & Young noted in its 2002 Audit Report for Waste Management (signed in 2003) that the 2001 financial statements were audited by other auditors who have ceased operations but who expressed an unqualified opinion before restated adjustments contained later in the audit report.

Subsequent Events and Dual Dating: As was previously discussed, the auditor is generally not responsible for examining events or transactions that occur after the end of fieldwork. However, in the case where a significant event comes to the attention of the auditor after fieldwork has been completed but before the financial statements are released, the auditor should consider the ramifications of the event in relation to the financial statements being issued. If there is a significant issue requiring accrual or disclosure, the auditor should obtain evidence in order to evaluate the fairness of the recording and disclosure of the event. However, because such an approach involves audit work after the end of fieldwork, the rest of the audit does not need to be updated. This situation usually leads to *dual dating* of the audit report, meaning that the auditor's report is dated as of the original end of fieldwork with a notation of the later work that was performed on the isolated event. The later date pertains only to the verification of the subsequent event and related accounts and does not apply to any other events, transactions, or accounts. This distinction is usually noted by indicating that the audit report is dated "February 20, 20x7, except for Note X, as to which the date is March 4, 20x7."

Example

A common condition that leads to a dual dating scenario occurs when an organization enters into a major acquisition, such as the acquisition of another organization, subsequent to the end of fieldwork but prior to issuing the financial statements. In these cases, the acquirer will include a footnote to the prior financial statements detailing the specifics of the transaction and any information regarding its impact on prior period financial statements. The auditor's report would include an explanatory paragraph directing users to the footnote and include a second date in the opinion restricted to only the information contained within the footnote.

AUDITOR'S REPORTS OTHER THAN UNQUALIFIED

One of three alternative report forms may be used if an auditor cannot issue an unqualified opinion. Under international standards, this situation is referred to as a "reservation of opinion." If the auditor is aware of misstatements in the financial statements, the auditor can issue a qualified or adverse opinion depending on the seriousness of the problem. If the auditor is unable to obtain adequate evidence about the fairness of the financial statements, the auditor can issue a qualified opinion or a denial (disclaimer) depending on the significance of the limitation.

Qualified Reports: A qualified report is issued when the auditor believes that the financial statements are mostly, but not completely, fairly presented. This can occur when there are scope limitations affecting the availability of evidence or violations of GAAP (e.g., a departure from GAAP, inadequate disclosure). In either

Figure 15–10   Auditor's Report Qualified for Scope Limitation

Intro	*(No change)*
Scope	*Except as discussed in the following paragraph,* we conducted our audit in accordance with generally accepted auditing standards. . . . (continues with standard wording)
Explanatory	*We were unable to obtain audited financial statements supporting the Company's investment in a foreign subsidiary, the carrying value of which was stated at $1,000,000 and $1,200,000 at December 31, 20x7 and 20x6, respectively, and the equity in earnings of which was $400,000 and $200,000, which is included in the net income for 20x7 and 20x6, respectively, as described in Note X to the financial statements; nor were we able to satisfy ourselves as to the carrying value of the investment in the foreign subsidiary or the equity in its earnings by other auditing procedures.*
Opinion	In our opinion, *except for the effects of such adjustments, if any, as might have been determined to be necessary had we been able to examine evidence regarding the investment and earnings related to the foreign subsidiary discussed in the preceding paragraph,* . . . (continues with unqualified opinion wording)

case, the condition creating the problem must be sufficiently narrow and constrained so that most of the information in the financial statements is fairly presented; that is, the problem can be isolated among a few accounts in the financial statements and does not have a pervasive impact. Each of the conditions discussed below has a more extreme counterpart if the conditions causing the problem are severe and pervasive to the financial statements.

- **Scope limitation:** A scope limitation occurs when the auditor is unable to obtain sufficient, competent evidence on which to base an opinion. Scope limitations may be caused by the circumstances of the audit, such as an inability to observe inventory at year end or when there is inadequate evidence available to support accounting estimates involving future uncertainties. Other scope limitations may be client-imposed, such as when the client forbids communications with some customers about its receivable balance.[9] An illustration of the changes that the auditor would make for a qualified opinion that is issued due to a scope limitation is presented in Figure 15–10.

- **Departure from GAAP:** A departure from GAAP occurs when an improper accounting method is used. A departure from GAAP can also occur if a company is using unrealistic estimates. Examples of departures that are significant but not pervasive include failure to capitalize lease obligations, improper capitalization of R&D costs, or inadequate allowance for bad debts. An illustration of the changes that the auditor would make to the auditor's report for a qualified opinion due to a departure from GAAP is presented in Figure 15–11. Notice that the auditor should describe the effect of the departure from GAAP if it can be reasonably determined.

- **Inadequate disclosure:** Inadequate disclosure is another form of departure from GAAP in that the financial statements do not include all information required by appropriate authoritative accounting standards, including information about

---

9 A client-imposed scope limitation should be evaluated in the broader context of the engagement, including implications for the auditor's assessment of management integrity.

Figure 15–11   Auditor's Report Qualified for Departure from GAAP

Intro	*(No change)*
Scope	*(No change)*
Explanatory	*The Company has excluded certain lease obligations from property and debt in the accompanying financial statements that, in our opinion, should be capitalized in order to conform with generally accepted accounting principles. If these lease obligations were capitalized, property would be increased by $3,000,000 and $3,500,000, long-term debt would be increased by $3,400,000 and $3,950,000 and retained earnings would be decreased by $400,000 and $450,000 as of December 31, 20x7 and 20x6, respectively. Additionally, net income would be increased (decreased) by $400,000 and ($50,000), and earnings per share would be increased (decreased) by $0.40 and ($0.05) for the years ended December 31, 20x7 and 20x6, respectively.*
Opinion	In our opinion, *except for the effects of not capitalizing certain lease obligations as discussed in the preceding paragraph,* . . . (continues with unqualified opinion wording)

Figure 15–12   Auditor's Adverse Report

Intro	*(No change)*
Scope	*(No change)*
Explanatory	*As discussed in Note X of the financial statements, the Company reports its financial status and results of operations on a modified cash basis. Further, the company does not capitalize most assets with long lives and, as a result, does not compute depreciation on such assets. Nor does the company accrue liabilities that may have been incurred as of year end. Generally accepted accounting principles require that financial statements be prepared on an accrual basis with capitalization and depreciation of long-lived assets and timely accrual of incurred liabilities. Due to the pervasive nature of these violations of generally accepted accounting principles, we are unable to assess the effect of adjustments that would be needed to restate the Company's financial position and the results of operations to conform with generally accepted accounting principles.*
Opinion	In our opinion, *because of the effects of the matters discussed in the preceding paragraph,* the financial statements referred to above ***do not*** present fairly, in conformity with generally accepted accounting principles, the financial position of ABC Company as of December 31, 20x7 and 20x6, or the results of operations or its cash flows for the years then ended.

future uncertainties that should be reported in the financial statements. The auditor's report in these situations is similar to that used for other departures from GAAP. The missing information should be provided by the auditor in the explanatory paragraph if it is reasonable to do so.

Adverse Reports: When the auditor concludes that the financial statements are pervasively misstated, an adverse report should be issued. This form of report might be used when the company is using the cash basis of accounting or uses other non-GAAP accounting methods that have an impact on most of the accounts in the financial statements. An example of the changes needed for an adverse auditor's report is presented in Figure 15–12. The opinion paragraph makes an assertive declaration that the financial statements are *not* fairly presented. Although

Figure 15–13   Auditor's Denial of Opinion Due to Scope Limitation

Intro	We were engaged to audit the accompanying balance sheets of ABC Company Inc. as of December 31, 20x7 and 20x6, and the related statements of income, retained earnings and cash flows for the years then ended. These financial statements are the responsibility of the company's management.
Scope	*(No change)*
Explanatory	The Company did not make a count of its physical inventory and we were not able to apply other auditing procedures to satisfy ourselves as to inventory quantities and costs. As a result, we are unable to determine whether adjustments were required in respect of recorded or unrecorded assets, recorded or unrecorded liabilities, and the components making up the statements of income, retained earnings, and cash flows.
Opinion	In view of the possible material effects on the financial statements of the matters described in the preceding paragraph, we are unable to express an opinion whether these financial statements are presented fairly in accordance with generally accepted accounting principles.

rarely used by auditors, the possibility of issuing an adverse report represents one of the auditor's strongest tools for encouraging management to prepare fair financial statements in accordance with generally accepted accounting principles.

Denial of Opinion (Disclaimer) Reports: A final type of report that an auditor can issue is a denial of opinion, also referred to as a disclaimer, which is used when the auditor is either unable or unwilling to make any statement about the fairness of the financial statements. One situation where a denial is used is when there are pervasive scope limitations that preclude obtaining adequate evidence about the fairness of the financial statements. A denial should not be used in lieu of an adverse report. If the auditor has evidence that the financial statements are not presented fairly, he or she cannot avoid expressing that opinion by issuing a denial. An illustration of the changes needed to the auditor's report for a denial due to a scope limitation is presented in Figure 15–13. This report indicates that the auditor has been engaged to perform an audit but is unable to do so due to lack of evidence. A common situation where this may occur is when the auditor is unable to verify the opening or ending inventory balance for the period. Two scope limitations that generally should result in the auditor disclaiming an opinion occur when the client does not allow the auditor access to minutes of the board of directors meetings or when the auditor is unable to receive a confirmation from the client's outside attorney regarding threatened and actual litigation matters.[10]

Subsequent Discovery of a Misstatement in the Financial Statements

The auditor has no responsibility to continue to monitor a client after the completion of fieldwork. However, if information comes to the attention of the auditor that affects the reliability or interpretation of the audited financial statements, the auditor has the responsibility to determine if readers will be adversely affected by

10 A disclaimer opinion should also be used when the auditor is not independent of the client.

reliance on the previously released statements. In doing so, the auditor must answer "yes" to each of the following four conditions:

1. The facts were available at or before the date of the auditor's report;
2. The facts are based on reliable information;
3. The effect of the facts is material to the financial statements and hence to the auditor's report;
4. Users are still relying on the auditor's report.

If the auditor determines that readers will be adversely affected, the auditor should have management modify the statements as appropriate and publicize the change to readers who may still be using the financial statements.[11] The auditor then issues an updated report consistent with the new information.

AUDIT REPORT FOR INTERNAL CONTROL OVER FINANCIAL REPORTING

As previously discussed, an audit of internal control over financial reporting (ICOFR) is mandated for all registrants of the U.S. Securities and Exchange Commission.[12] The evaluation and testing of internal control over financial reporting by either management or the auditor may reveal one or more control deficiencies that indicate that the design or operation of internal control may not prevent or detect misstatements on a timely basis.

A *significant deficiency* occurs when "a control deficiency, or combination of control deficiencies, adversely affects the company's ability to initiate, authorize, record, process, or report external financial data reliably in accordance with generally accepted accounting principles such that there is more than a remote likelihood that a misstatement of the company's annual or interim financial statements that is more than inconsequential will not be prevented or detected." A *material weakness* is "a significant deficiency, or combination of significant deficiencies, that results in more than a remote likelihood that a material misstatement of the annual or interim financial statements will not be prevented or detected" in its assessment. The initial implementation of Auditing Standard No. 2 resulted in many companies reporting material weaknesses in internal control.

The auditor issues two reports related to internal control over financial reporting (ICOFR). One report pertains to management's assessment of the effectiveness of its own ICOFR and the other report reflects the auditor's direct assessment of the effectiveness of the control system. Figure 15–14 shows the possible combinations of reports that might be issued by the auditor given what is contained in the management assessment of internal control. If a company has one or more material weaknesses in internal control, the auditor's direct report should be adverse (e.g., internal control is not effective). If management appropriately reports the same material weakness(es), the auditor's report pertaining to management's assessment will be unqualified (e.g., management correctly reports internal control as ineffective). However, if management asserts that internal control over financial reporting is effective but the auditor disagrees, the auditor will then issue an adverse opinion on management's report. Note, there is no option for a qualified opinion related to internal control except in the case of a

---

11 The publication of adjusted results can be done in later annual or quarterly reports if their release is imminent and available to essentially the same audience as the original report.

12 See PCAOB Auditing Standard No. 2. At the time of the writing of this book, the SEC was considering whether to exempt smaller registrants from some of the requirements of Section 404.

Figure 15–14   Possible Auditor Reports on Internal Control Over Financial Reporting

Management's assessment of controls	Results of auditor's tests of internal control effectiveness	Report to be issued on management's assertions about the effectiveness of internal control	Report to be issued concerning auditor's opinion of actual effectiveness of internal control
No Material Weakness	No Material Weakness	Unqualified	Unqualified
No Material Weakness	Material Weakness	Adverse	Adverse
Material Weakness	Material Weakness	Unqualified	Adverse
	Inconclusive (Scope Limitation)	Qualified	Qualified

scope limitation. Figure 15–15 shows an unqualified opinion for both management's assessment and the auditor's direct evaluation of ICOFR.

COMMUNICATIONS OF AUDIT RESULTS TO MANAGEMENT AND THOSE CHARGED WITH GOVERNANCE

In addition to the formal report issued to accompany the financial statements, an auditor may also issue internal communications directly to the client's management or board of directors. These communications are not intended for distribution to outside parties. The three most common forms of internal communications are (1) reports to a board subcommittee–the audit committee, (2) reports on internal control issues discovered as part of the financial statement audit, and (3) management letters.

FORMAL REPORTING TO THE AUDIT COMMITTEE

Publicly traded companies usually have an audit committee that is charged with overseeing the financial reporting process. Ideally, members of the audit committee should not hold management positions with the company and this is required for public companies in many countries including the U.S., Canada, and the U.K. Auditors are required to communicate certain matters directly to the audit committee (or equivalent group) of the client. Typical matters to be communicated directly to the audit committee include

- That the audit firm is independent of client management and the client firm with a description of how this was determined
- The nature of significant accounting policies and procedures used in preparing financial statements
- Management judgments related to significant accounting estimates
- The nature and resolution of significant adjustments found during the audit, including immaterial differences that were not corrected by management

Figure 15–15   Report Expressing an Unqualified Opinion on Management's Assessment of the Effectiveness of Internal Control Over Financial Reporting and an Unqualified Opinion on the Effectiveness of Internal Control Over Financial Reporting Employing PCAOB Audit Standard #2

Report of Independent Registered Public Accounting Firm
(or Registered Auditor's Report)

[Introductory paragraph]

We have audited management's assessment, included in the accompanying [title of management's report], that W Company maintained effective internal control over financial reporting as of December 31, 20X3, based on [identify control criteria, for example, "criteria established in *Internal Control—Integrated Framework* issued by the Committee of Sponsoring Organizations of the Treadway Commission (COSO)"]. W Company's management is responsible for maintaining effective internal control over financial reporting and for its assessment of the effectiveness of internal control over financial reporting. Our responsibility is to express an opinion on management's assessment and an opinion on the effectiveness of the company's internal control over financial reporting based on our audit.

[Scope paragraph]

We conducted our audit in accordance with the standards of the Public Company Accounting Oversight Board (United States). Those standards require that we plan and perform the audit to obtain reasonable assurance about whether effective internal control over financial reporting was maintained in all material respects. Our audit included obtaining an understanding of internal control over financial reporting, evaluating management's assessment, testing and evaluating the design and operating effectiveness of internal control, and performing such other procedures as we considered necessary in the circumstances. We believe that our audit provides a reasonable basis for our opinion.

[Definition paragraph]

A company's internal control over financial reporting is a process designed to provide reasonable assurance regarding the reliability of financial reporting and the preparation of financial statements for external purposes in accordance with generally accepted accounting principles. A company's internal control over financial reporting includes those policies and procedures that (1) pertain to the maintenance of records that, in reasonable detail, accurately and fairly reflect the transactions and dispositions of the assets of the company; (2) provide reasonable assurance that transactions are recorded as necessary to permit preparation of financial statements in accordance with generally accepted accounting principles, and that receipts and expenditures of the company are being made only in accordance with authorizations of management and directors of the company; and (3) provide reasonable assurance regarding prevention or timely detection of unauthorized acquisition, use, or disposition of the company's assets that could have a material effect on the financial statements.

[Inherent limitations paragraph]

Because of its inherent limitations, internal control over financial reporting may not prevent or detect misstatements. Also, projections of any evaluation of effectiveness to future periods are subject to the risk that controls may become inadequate because of changes in conditions, or that the degree of compliance with the policies or procedures may deteriorate.

[Opinion paragraph]

In our opinion, management's assessment that W Company maintained effective internal control over financial reporting as of December 31, 20X3, is fairly stated, in all material respects, based on [identify control criteria, for example, "criteria established in

Figure 15–15 *(continued)*

Internal Control—Integrated Framework issued by the Committee of Sponsoring Organizations of the Treadway Commission (COSO)"]. Also in our opinion, W Company maintained, in all material respects, effective internal control over financial reporting as of December 31, 20X3, based on [identify control criteria, for example, "criteria established in *Internal Control—Integrated Framework* issued by the Committee of Sponsoring Organizations of the Treadway Commission (COSO)"].

[Explanatory paragraph]

We have also audited, in accordance with the standards of the Public Company Accounting Oversight Board (United States), the [identify financial statements] of W Company and our report dated [date of report, which should be the same as the date of the report on the effectiveness of internal control over financial reporting] expressed [include nature of opinion].

[Signature]

[City and Country]

[Date]

- The auditor's responsibility relative to supplemental information included with the basic financial statements (e.g., management discussion and analysis)
- The nature and resolution of disagreements with management concerning accounting issues, estimates, and the scope of audit evidence
- The nature of management's consultations with other accountants
- Major issues discussed with management prior to being retained for the engagement
- Difficulties encountered during the engagement, such as delays in providing information, missing documents and records, unreasonable timetables, lack of access to documents and records, or lack of expected assistance by client personnel

If the company is subject to securities regulators in the United States or Canada, the auditor is also required to discuss the quality of the organization's accounting choices, not just their acceptability.

The primary purpose of this communication is to assure that the audit committee is informed of problems encountered during the audit. Conflicts with management or difficulties resolving auditing issues can be communicated directly to the committee in this way. Regulatory bodies (e.g., the SEC) have begun calling for the auditors to discuss the quality of earnings with the audit committee when presenting their draft audit report.[13] In addition, if management threatens to fire the auditor or goes fishing for preferable treatment from other accounting firms, the current auditor has recourse to the audit committee. Such communications may be oral or written and must be documented in the working papers. The communication may occur after the release of the financial statements, but timely communication is desirable.

---

13 To see more about the movement to require auditors to discuss earning quality with those charged with governance, see Bellovary, Giacomino, and Akers, "Earnings Quality: It's Time to Measure and Report," *CPA Journal*, November 2005.

REPORTS ON INTERNAL CONTROL ISSUES DISCOVERED AS PART OF THE FINANCIAL STATEMENT AUDIT

Even when the auditor is not required to audit internal control over financial reporting (e.g., private companies, not-for-profit organizations, and public companies not registered in the United States), the auditor may come across matters related to internal control that should be communicated to the client's audit committee. More specifically, the auditor should communicate to the client the nature of any *reportable conditions* that were discovered during the course of the audit. A reportable condition is a deficiency in internal control that adversely affects the client's ability to generate accurate and reliable accounting information.[14] The auditor is not required to plan the engagement to uncover possible reportable conditions, but the execution of the auditor's procedures, especially process analysis and obtaining an understanding of internal control, may bring reportable conditions to his or her attention.

The auditor may make his or her report either orally or in writing. If oral communication is used, the nature of the communication should be documented in the working papers. However, standard-setters prefer the auditor issue a written report. The report should indicate that it is based on an audit whose purpose was to report on the financial statements and not provide assurance about internal control. The report should include a definition of reportable conditions. Additionally, the report should contain a statement limiting the distribution within the client's organization. Generally, a separate paragraph is used to describe each reportable condition, and the auditor may state that none of the reportable conditions were material. If no reportable conditions are noted during the audit, the auditor should *not* issue a report stating no reportable conditions were found.

MANAGEMENT LETTERS

The auditor may wish to bring other issues to the attention of management or the board of directors, such as inconsequential control issues that the auditor observed that did not impact internal control reporting or the financial statements. During strategic and process analysis, numerous client comments may have been identified as a result of analyzing risks, controls, and performance indicators. Such matters are usually communicated via a *management letter*. Because auditors are not being paid specifically for the advice contained in the management letter, these suggestions are not considered consulting services. Rather, they are suggestions to management that are meant to enable the company to improve performance in some way. In general, such issues relate to ways in which the company can more effectively or efficiently run its operations. Topics can range from operational and administrative procedures to strategic policies. There is no required format for communicating these issues, but the letter should clearly state the purpose, the fact that no assurance is provided on the included matters, and the limitations on distribution.

---

14 The auditor may also observe *material weaknesses* in internal control. A material weakness is a reportable condition that may allow material misstatements to be included in the financial statements. An auditor is not required to distinguish between reportable conditions and material weaknesses in the report to the audit committee.

SUMMARY AND CONCLUSION

The purpose of this chapter was to discuss the wrap-up procedures performed by the auditor that are necessary to complete the engagement and the nature of communications that are used to report the results of the audit to interested parties. A primary objective of wrap-up procedures is to bring together and integrate the vast amount of audit evidence obtained by the auditor in order to reach an overall conclusion about the fairness of the financial statements taken as a whole. In performing these procedures, the auditor is making sure that the evidence is consistent and complete, and fully supports the overall conclusions. Based on these conclusions, the auditor will prepare the appropriate formal report to external users of the financial statements. The extent of the communication, generally a three-paragraph document, may seem minor given the extensive effort that went into the acquisition and evaluation of evidence, but this does not reduce the importance of the reporting process. The formal auditor's report can take various forms under different conditions. Finally, we discussed the internal communications that may be needed as a result of completing the engagement.

BIBLIOGRAPHY OF RELATED PROFESSIONAL LITERATURE

Research

Agoglia, C. P., T. Kida, and D. M. Hano. 2003. The Effects of Alternative Justification Memos on Judgments of Audit Reviewees and Reviewers. *Journal of Accounting Research*. 41(1): 33–46.

Braun, K. W. 2001. The Disposition of Audit-detected Misstatement: An Examination of Risk and Reward Factors and Aggregation Effects. *Contemporary Accounting Research*. 18(1): 71–99.

Carcello, J. V. and T. L. Neal. 2000. Audit Committee Composition and Auditor Reporting. *The Accounting Review*. 75(4): 453–467.

Carcello, J. V. and T. L. Neal. 2003. Audit Committee Characteristics and Auditor Dismissals Following "New" Going Concern Reports. *The Accounting Review*. 78(1): 95–117.

Chen, C. J. P., X. Su, and R. Zhao. 2000. An Emerging Market's Reaction to Initial Modified Audit Opinions: Evidence from the Shanghai Stock Exchange. *Contemporary Accounting Research*. 17(3): 429–455.

Citron, D. B. and R. J. Taffler. 2004. The Comparative Impact of an Audit Report Standard and an Audit Going Concern Standard on Going-Concern Disclosure Rates. *Auditing: A Journal of Practice & Theory*. 23(2): 119–130.

Favere-Marchesi, M. and C. E. N. Emby. 2005. The Impact of Continuity on Concurring Partner Reviews: An Exploratory Study. *Accounting Horizons*. 19(1): 1–10.

Gibbins, M., S. McCracken, and S. Salterio. 2005. Negotiations over Accounting Issues: The Congruency of Audit Partner and Chief Financial Officer Recalls. *Auditing: A Journal of Practice & Theory*. 24(supplement): 171–194.

Gibbins, M., S. Salterio, and A. Webb. 2001. Evidence About Auditor-Client Management Negotiation Concerning Client's Financial Reporting. *Journal of Accounting Research*. 39(3): 535–563.

Gibbins, M. and K. T. Trotman. 2002. Audit Review: Managers' Interpersonal Expectations and Conduct of The Review. *Contemporary Accounting Research*. 19(3): 411–444.

Gieger, M. A., K. Raghunandan, and D. V. Rama. 2005. Recent Changes in The Association Between Bankruptcies and Prior Audit Opinions. *Auditing: A Journal of Practice & Theory.* 24(1): 21–37.

Krogstad, J. L., M. H. Taylor, and M. J. Stock. 2002. An Experimental Investigation of the Efficacy Of Lawyers' Letters. *Auditing: A Journal of Practice & Theory.* 21(1): 79–94.

Nelson, M., J. Elliott and R. Tarpley. 2003. How Are Earnings Managed? Examples from Auditors. *Accounting Horizons.* 17–35.

Ng, T. B-P. and H.T. Tan. 2003. Effects of Authoritative Guidance Availability and Audit Committee Effectiveness on Auditors' Judgments in Auditor-Client Negotiation Context. *The Accounting Review.* 78(3): 801–818.

Tan, H.T. and J. Yip-Ow. 2001. Are Reviewers' Judgments Influenced by Memo Structure and Conclusions Documented in Audit Workingpapers? *Contemporary Accounting Research.* 18(4): 663–678.

Tuttle, B., M. Coller, and R. D. Plumlee. 2002. The Effect of Misstatements On Decisions Of Financial Statement Users: An Experimental Investigation Of Auditor Materiality Thresholds. *Auditing: A Journal of Practice & Theory.* 21(1): 11–28.

Wilks, T. J. 2002. Predecisional Distortion of Evidence as a Consequence of Real-Time Review. *The Accounting Review.* 77(1): 51–71.

Accounting Standards

FASB *Statement* No. 5, "Accounting for Contingencies."

SEC *Staff Accounting Bulletin* No. 99, "Materiality."

Auditing Standards

AICPA *Statements on Auditing Standard (SAS)* No. 12, "Inquiry of a Client's Lawyer Concerning Litigation, Claims, and Assessments."

AICPA *Statements on Auditing Standard (SAS)* No. 58, "Reports on Audited Financial Statements."

AICPA *Statements on Auditing Standard (SAS)* No. 85, "Management Representations."

AICPA *Statements on Auditing Standard (SAS)* No. 98, "Omnibus Statement on Auditing Standards."

AICPA *Statements on Auditing Standard (SAS)* No. 106, "Audit Evidence."

AICPA *Statements on Auditing Standard (SAS)* No. 107, "Audit Risk and Materiality in Conducting an Audit."

AICPA *Statements on Auditing Standard (SAS)* No. 109, "Understanding the Entity and Its Environment and Assessing the Risks of Material Misstatement."

AICPA *Statements on Auditing Standard (SAS)* No. 110, "Performing Procedures in Response to Assessed Risks and Evaluating the Audit Evidence Obtained."

IAASB *International Standards on Auditing (ISA)* No. 315, "Understanding the Entity and Its Environment and Assessing the Risks of Material Misstatement."

IAASB *International Standards on Auditing (ISA)* No. 320, "Audit Materiality."

IAASB *International Standards on Auditing (ISA)* No. 330, "The Auditor's Procedures in Response to Assessed Risks."

IAASB *International Standards on Auditing (ISA)* No. 500, "Audit Evidence."

IAASB *International Standards on Auditing (ISA)* No. 560, "Subsequent Events."

IAASB *International Standards on Auditing (ISA)* No. 580, "Management Representations."

IAASB *International Standards on Auditing (ISA)* No. 700, "The Auditor's Report on Financial Statements."

QUESTIONS

1. Contingent liabilities often are one of the most serious issues for an auditor to audit because a single contingent liability can be highly material. Further, clients are hesitant to establish accruals or make related disclosures about contingent liabilities. Thus, assessing attorney confirmations and determining whether to classify items as probable, reasonably possible, or remote is an important activity for the auditor. Discuss the difference between these issues, including the types of evidence that might lead the auditor to classify a contingency under each classification.

2. Determining whether a subsequent event requires an adjustment to the financial statements is difficult in many circumstances. Discuss the primary difference between subsequent events that require adjustment and those that only require disclsoure. As part of your explanation, include examples of subsequent events that would fall under each categorization.

3. Argue whether you agree or not that a representation letter is a critical part of an audit engagement. Consider in your argument that the letter itself can only serve as minimal evidence because it is an inquiry, but also that auditors have been known to resign when a letter has not been properly read by those who have signed it.

4. Many auditors rely on a disclosure checklist when evaluating presentation and disclosure assertions. Describe the benefits of using a checklist to help in performing this evaluation. In addition, describe the drawbacks to using a checklist and your suggestions for overcoming such drawbacks.

5. Describe the difference between a known and a likely misstatement. As part of your explanation, describe the roles of each of the following:
   - Materiality
   - Degree of objectivity
   - Impact on financial statements
   - Implications for overall audit risk

   Also, under what conditions would the auditor negotiate with a client in deciding whether to require the client to correct the financial statements for either type of misstatement?

6. Describe how a client with *high* quality of earnings likely should appear under each of the following circumstances:
   - Correlation with underlying economic activity
   - Permanence and sustainability
   - Relationship with market valuation
   - Extent and impact of discretionary accruals
   - Transparency and completeness of disclosures
   - Impact on corporate image
   - Handling of "bad" news

7. Public accounting firms and regulators have long been concerned with the notion of the "expectations gap," which describes an accounting firm's understanding of the assertions provided in an auditor's report compared to the users' understanding of those assertions. Consider the form and content of a standard unqualified auditor's report (e.g., Figure 15–8). Surveys regarding what users believe is conveyed in an opinion suggest that an expectations gap exists. The most serious gap found is a consistent belief by users that they are receiving a guarantee against fraud and errors from the auditor. Based on your review of the standard unqualified report, describe why you believe that this gap persists.

8. Auditors typically are not responsible for evaluating the performance of an organization or its prospects for future performance; however, they are required to include an explanatory paragraph when they believe that there is substantial doubt regarding the

ability of an organization to continue as a going concern. Describe why you believe that auditors are required to make this evaluation and whether you agree or disagree with this requirement.

9. In practice, auditors who are unable to convince clients to adjust for known or likely misstatements often resign from an engagement instead of issuing a qualified or adverse opinion. Argue for or against this practice as being acceptable given the duty of the auditor to serve the public's best interests.

10. Compare and contrast the reporting requirements for the presence of a significant deficiency and material weakness under an integrated audit under AS 2. Why, in your opinion, do these reporting differences exist?

11. For each of the following situations, indicate which type of audit report you would issue if you were the partner in charge of the engagement and explain why.
    a. Although the audit of Coltrane Enterprises occurred without incident and you are prepared to issue an unqualified opinion, you discover after the engagement that one of the partners in your firm (who did not have any direct ties to the engagement) holds a material investment in its common stock.
    b. This is the first year you have audited Monk & Co.'s financial statements. The previous auditors have gone out of business and their level of cooperation with your auditors is negligible. A few of your conclusions rest on the old auditors' work.
    c. Due to a conflict of interest discovered between another audit firm and Jamal Corp., your firm was brought in to audit the financial statements well after the end of the fiscal year. The old firm is cooperating fully with your auditors and you are prepared to issue an unqualified opinion except that you could not physically count the ending inventory. You have, however, satisfied yourself through other audit procedures that the inventory balance is fairly presented.
    d. Despite your urgings, the management of Parker Co., an arms dealer, refuses to allow you to examine some details on its customer base. As a result, you cannot be sure of the value of its receivables.
    e. In the course of your audit of Rollins and Gordon, Ltd., you discover that the company recorded its office building purchase in a land account and, therefore, does not depreciate it. The land account makes up about 10 percent of the total assets of the firm.
    f. Abigail Co.'s largest asset, a portfolio of mortgage-based securities that makes up about 60 percent of the assets of the company, is carried at cost although a substantial market for the securities exists. The difference between the carrying value and the market value is currently immaterial.
    g. Holiday Co.'s audit went without incident except that you are convinced that its deteriorating cash position and its poor position in a declining industry will make it highly unlikely to be in business this time next year.

12. Consider the following standard unqualified report issued by your audit firm for Adderly Brothers, Inc., a publicly held company based in New York:

Auditor's Report

To the management of Adderly Brothers, Inc.:

We have audited the accompanying balance sheet of Adderly Brothers, Inc. and the related statements of income, retained earnings and cash flows. Our audit opinion is based on this audit.

We conducted our audit in accordance with generally accepted accounting standards. Those standards require that we plan and conduct the audit in such a way as to assure interested parties that the financial statements are free from material misstatement and that no material fraud exists within the company's operations. An audit includes gathering and examining test evidence supporting the amounts and disclosures in the financial statements. We believe that our audit provides a reasonable basis for our opinion.

In our opinion, the financial statements herein present fairly Adderly Brothers, Inc.'s financial position, the results of its operations and its cash flows for the year in conformance with generally accepted auditing principles.

Your Accounting Firm, P.A.
April 22, 2006
New York, NY

Discuss the deficiencies in this report. Be sure to identify the location of the errors or deficiencies by the name of the paragraph in which they reside.

PROBLEMS

1. Consider the following letter from the managing partner of Cooney & Associates, CPAs, to the legal counsel for their client, The Chartreuse Catfish Restaurant Group, requesting information on potential contingent liabilities:

June 10, 2007

Ms. Betty Barrister
The Firm, LLP
104 Business Row
Gainesville, FL 32601

Dear Ms. Barrister:

We have nearly completed our audit of the financial statements of our mutual client, The Chartreuse Catfish Restaurant Group, for the fiscal year ending 3/31/07, and we thought we might ask you a few questions about the current status of their legal problems.

1. A customer recently slipped in the bathroom of one of the restaurants and has sued the Group for $50,000. The customer has shown no indications he is willing to settle. Management does not feel they are liable given the risks of the environment in the bathroom.
2. The chain has recently come under attack from some civil rights groups for the costumes its service personnel is forced to wear. For now, they appear to be happy with boycotts and protests and the like, but they have not ruled out a class-action lawsuit on behalf of the "victims."

Any help you may give us with proper disclosure of these matters would be appreciated. If we may be of service to you, please don't hesitate to ask.

Yours sincerely,

H. O'Donnell Cooney, CPA
Managing Partner, Cooney & Associates, CPAs, LLP

Describe all the elements of this letter that make it unsatisfactory for its stated purpose.

2. For each of the following events concerning disclosure of events that took place after year end, discuss the manner in which it should be disclosed in the financial statements or the audit report. Assume that all items are material.

    a. Shortly after the audit report has been issued, your client announces a major merger with a competitor. Although the talks had been going on at the time of the audit report's issue, the merger was not considered likely enough to disclose in the financial statements or the audit report.

    b. During fieldwork for the fiscal year-end audit, you discover a material error in the mechanical part of the inventory calculations. Such errors are routine in this industry where profitability limitations do not allow sophisticated inventory control systems.

    c. A few months after the issue of the audit report, your client settles a lawsuit for about twice the amount accrued in the financial statements as a contingent liability.

    d. During the fiscal year, management had written down an investment in a bio-technology based on their belief that approval by regulatory authorities (essential to its marketability) was unlikely. During fieldwork, regulatory approval is given.

    e. Reconsider part d. Would your answer change if the approval came after the audit report was issued?

    f. During the fieldwork portion of the audit, your client announces that it is marketing a new type of microprocessor. Industry analysts are unanimous in their belief that the chip will revolutionize microcomputing and will bring in substantial profits for your client.

3. Each of the following techniques for managing earnings was described in the chapter:
    *   "Big Bath" charges
    *   Write-off of acquired assets
    *   "Cookie Jar" reserves
    *   Abuse of materiality
    *   Questionable revenue recognition

    For each of the following examples of earnings management, state which technique is being used and suggest a method of resolving the issue with management:

    a. A tire manufacturer has produced record earnings in this fiscal year. Management accrues $10 million of loss for anticipated inventory write-downs in the next year. Your review of the market suggests that all inventory should be marketable at or above its recorded cost.

    b. A software manufacturer places its product on retailers' shelves for sale to the public. The retailer keeps 10 percent of the retail sales and sends the rest of the revenue to the manufacturer upon sale. Unsold software is returned to the manufacturer. The company recorded $10 million in sales for its final shipment of software sent to retailers at the end of the fiscal year.

    c. An e-business bookseller merged with an ebusiness DVD/video seller to expand its product base and change its image to an entertainment provider. The bookseller added the DVD/video seller's $100 million inventory to its inventory base and expensed the remainder of the acquired company, other than a small amount of property, plant, and equipment. The bookseller justified this decision because it argued that the merger was, in reality, a purchase of inventory.

    d. A large consumer products manufacturer placed some excess cash in trading securities that dropped in value by $1.5 million. Because purchasing short-term securities is unusual for the company, management valued the securites at cost and decided to hold on to the securities until the values increased. The company had $40 million net income for the fiscal year.

    e. An airline suffered an operating loss of $30 million this fiscal year, largely due to increases in fuel prices. The company had been struggling with the auditors for several years concerning the realizeable value of its airplane fleet. The auditors had been concerned that the fleet might be overvalued by $15 to $30 million. The company informed the auditors that it was willing to write-off $30 million of the value of its airplane fleet.

4. For each of the following scenarios, indicate whether earnings quality is likely to be high, moderate, or low. Based on your assessment, how might an auditor adjust the nature or extent of audit testing, including investigations into possible earnings manipulation?

   a. A drug manufacturer has exceeded analyst forecasted earnings for five consecutive years. During that period, the company has received FDA approval for four major drugs, all of which have six or more years of patent protection against competition.

   b. A clothing retailer has increased its net income in each of the past four years. During this profitable period, the company has continually decreased the percentage of accounts receivable that are reserved as uncollectible.

   c. A paper manufacturer has been slightly underperforming against analyst expectations but generating small profits over the past two years. However, the manufacturer is outperforming its three main competitors, all of which have been generating significant losses during the same period.

   d. A home improvement retailer that has a dominant market share utilizes conservative accounting policies and discloses timely information about its performance— both good and bad—to the analysts who follow the company.

5. For each of the following situations that require an audit report: (1) determine what type of audit report is called for and (2) for reports other than standard unqualified, state where in the audit report changes would have to be made and make the changes. Be specific.

   a. The accountant merely compiles the financial statements based on management's representations. No audit work is performed at all.

   b. The auditor has no reason to believe that the financial statements are prepared differently from GAAP but wants to call attention to management's continuing relationship with a company whose management substantially overlaps with the client's.

   c. In performing the audit, you do not believe you had adequate access to important records on the company's cash wire transfer activity.

   d. Management no longer estimates its uncollectible receivables each fiscal year end, preferring instead the direct write-off method. They argue that it is not material. You believe otherwise.

   e. A material portion of the work on the audit of the inventory value was performed by another audit firm (whose work you believe you can trust).

   f. In the second year of your audit relationship, the client has decided to disclose an ongoing contingent liability in its financial statements for the first time. The company's failure to do so last year caused you to issue a qualified audit report.

   g. A material portion of the audit work was performed by a firm whose work you cannot obtain and whose partners are unwilling to discuss your client.

   h. Your client is currently subject to material legal claims under strict consumer product liability law.

   i. You are convinced that your client's business will not likely survive for another year.

   j. Due to substantial difficulty in estimating its uncollectible accounts and given the relatively small amount of receivables on your client's financial statements, you concur with its use of the direct write-off method for accounting for bad debt.

6. A study of the Los Angeles police department by management consultants (as reported in *The Wall Street Journal*, June 11, 1996) uncovered numerous practices that tended to decrease the efficiency and effectiveness of the force. Among the practices the report criticized and the costs it estimated were the following:

   a. At shift change time, officers have to go through an elaborate sign-out procedure for their weapons, radios, and other equipment that takes about 30 minutes. The consultants estimated that the department-wide personnel costs for the procedure were the equivalent of 236 full-time officers.

    b.   Every four weeks, each officer is expected to complete forms requesting his or her desired time off for the following month. Then, several supervisory level officers manually create the deployment schedule. From there, the schedule is transcribed manually into the timebooks for all layers of management and into the city's payroll department. The line officers' time alone approached the equivalent of 51 full-time officers, to say nothing of the clerical and supervisory time.

    c.   All arrests have to be approved by the watch commander, meaning that arresting officers must drive the suspect to the station, locate the watch commander, get his or her approval, and then drive the suspect to the jail. Approval is automatic in virtually every case.

    d.   The paperwork involved in arresting a juvenile drunk-driving suspect requires the officer to enter the suspect's name 70 separate times. Those papers are then filed in several separate locations.

Assume that you are the auditor for the Los Angeles police department and that you uncovered all of the preceding in your audit. For each of the "production problems," write a paragraph that could be a part of a "management letter" to the chief of police for Los Angeles. Discuss the costs of the problems in terms of personnel costs and in less tangible terms, such as morale of the officers. Suggest at least one solution to the production problem for inclusion in the management letter. Remember that the solution must be palatable to the chief. In addition, anticipate and address the objections to changing the procedure. Be specific.

7. In your audit of the Strangelove Group, a privately-held company based in Great Britain, you encountered the following situations:

    a.   The internal control plans in the payables processing area are poorly designed or are not well executed. However, your audit of the area failed to turn up any evidence of misstatement either from error or fraud.

    b.   Management employs a sophisticated model of its receivables collection patterns in its estimate of uncollectible accounts.

    c.   Several material errors were found in the inventory calculations, the interest expense accruals, and the proofs of cash. Your negotiations with management on correcting the errors were concluded satisfactorily such that you do not believe any remaining misstatements are material.

    d.   The order processing department is chronically understaffed and the computer network into which sales orders are entered is antiquated. As a result, customers spend a great deal of time getting through, and many hang up.

    e.   Although you have no reason to issue an audit report other than the standard unqualified one, you are disappointed in Strangelove's internal auditors, who were frequently uncooperative and preoccupied with other projects.

    f.   Strangelove employs no unusual accounting methods.

    g.   Although the audit turned up no evidence of misstatement, the security in the inventory processing/warehouse area probably allows for significant defalcation.

(1) Discuss the manner in which you would communicate any pertinent information to Strangelove, if necessary. Specifically, to whom would the communication be directed, under what heading (e.g., management letter) and to what extent would the item be discussed?

(2) Also, how would your answer be different if Strangelove was a U.S.-registered public company subject to PCAOB AS 2?

8. Consider the following summary of unadjusted audit differences for Avni Co., a privately-held importer of fine wines with total assets of $1.5 million.

    a.   Which items do you think management will accept without much argument? Why?

    b.   Which items do you think management will be less willing to accept? Why?

    c.   What strategies might you employ to convince management to make the changes?

Avni Co.
Summary of Unadjusted Audit Differences
12/31/07

Effect on Accounts: Debit (Credit)

Description	Total	Assets	Liability	Revenue	Expense
(1) To accrue additional pension expense	$84,500		($84,500)		$84,500
(2) To adjust inventory to reflect late-arriving goods shipped FOB shipping point	47,200	$47,200			(47,200)
(3) To adjust prepaid assets to reflect expiration of private club dues	700	(700)			700
(4) To adjust revenue, cost of goods sold, inventory, and accounts receivable to reflect proper sales cutoff	20,000	(49,990) 20,000		$49,990	(20,000)
(5) To post unrecognized trade payables	18,045		(18,045)		18,045
Totals		($16,510)	($102,545)	$49,990	$36,045

9. Consider the following auditor's report that refers to a shared engagement of a privately-held organization:

Independent Auditor's Report

To the Board of Directors of Martin Co.

We have audited the accompanying balance sheets of Martin Co. as of December 31, 2007 and 2006, and the related statements of income, retained earnings, and cash flows for the years then ended. These financial statements are the responsibility of Martin Co.'s management. Our responsibility is to express an opinion on these financial statements based on our audit. However, another audit firm, with more expertise in this area, performed the substantive tests on the inventory balances.

We conducted our audit in accordance with generally accepted auditing standards. Those standards require that we plan and perform the audit to obtain reasonable assurance that the financial statements are free of material misstatement. An audit includes examining, on a test basis, evidence supporting the amounts and disclosures in the financial statements. An audit also includes assessing the accounting principles used and significant estimates made by management, as well as evaluating the overall financial statement presentation. We believe that our audit provides a reasonable basis for our opinion.

In our opinion, based on our audit, the financial statements referred to above present fairly, in all material respects, the financial position of Martin Co. as of December 31, 2005 and 2004, and the results of its operations and its cash flows for the years then ended in conformity with generally accepted accounting principles.

Ed's Accounting Firm and Wash-a-Teria

April 1, 2008

Discuss the deficiencies with this audit report.

10. Consider the report that refers to an integrated audit under AS 2.

Report of Registered Public Accounting Firm

We have audited management's assessment, included in the accompanying Management's ICOFR Report, that Charlie Company maintained effective internal control over financial reporting as of December 31, 2006, based on Internal Control—Integrated Framework issued by the Committee of Sponsoring Organizations of the Treadway Commission (COSO). Charlie Company's management is responsible for maintaining effective internal control over financial reporting and for its assessment of the effectiveness of internal control over financial reporting.

We conducted our audit in accordance with the standards of the Public Company Accounting Oversight Board (PCAOB) (United States). Those standards require that we plan and perform the audit to obtain reasonable assurance about whether effective internal control over financial reporting was maintained. Our audit included obtaining an understanding of internal control over financial reporting, evaluating management's assessment, testing and evaluating the design and operating effectiveness of internal control, and performing such other procedures as we considered necessary in the circumstances. We believe that our audit provides a reasonable basis for our opinion.

A company's internal control over financial reporting includes those policies and procedures that (1) pertain to the maintenance of records that, in reasonable detail, accurately and fairly reflect the transactions and dispositions of the assets of the company; (2) provide reasonable assurance that transactions are recorded as necessary to permit preparation of financial statements in accordance with generally accepted accounting principles, and that receipts and expenditures of the company are being made only in accordance with authorizations of management and directors of the company; and (3) provide reasonable assurance regarding prevention or timely detection of unauthorized acquisition, use, or disposition of the company's assets that could have a material effect on the financial statements.

In our opinion, management's assessment that Charlie Company maintained effective internal control over financial reporting as of December 31, 2006, is fairly stated based on criteria established in Internal Control—Integrated Framework issued by the Committee of Sponsoring Organizations of the Treadway Commission (COSO). Also in our opinion, Charlie Company maintained effective internal control over financial reporting as of December 31, 2006, based on criteria established in Internal Control—Integrated Framework issued by the Committee of Sponsoring Organizations of the Treadway Commission (COSO).

We have also audited, in accordance with the standards of the Public Company Accounting Oversight Board (PCAOB)(United States), the balance sheet, income statement, statement of cash flows, and statement of retained earnings of Charlie Company and our report dated February 21, 2007, expressed an unqualified opinion.

Tick-n-Tie Partners LLP

February 14, 2007

Discuss the deficiencies with this report.

Case 15–1: Auditor's Reports

Use online research databases and other sources of information to find examples of each of the following reports for actual companies.

- Standard unqualified independent auditor's report for the financial statements
- Standard unqualified registered auditor's report for internal control over financial reporting
- Qualified independent auditor's report for the financial statements
- Qualified independent auditor's report for internal control over financial reporting
- Standard unqualified auditor's report for financial statements with an explanatory paragraph related to uncertainty about the organization's ability to continue as a going concern

Based on your research, answer each of the following questions:

1. How difficult was locating an example for each report? Why do you believe that it is more difficult to find qualified reports than unqualified reports?
2. For each report, examine the auditor's report for the prior year. Describe any differences from one year to the next.
3. For the qualified reports and the unqualified report with an explanatory paragraph, describe any mention of actions by management to eliminate the need for the same opinion in the following year. If there is a report available for the following year, was management successful in its efforts?
4. Based on your research and evaluation of the reports, what observations can you make that might suggest why an expectations gap exists between what users believe that they are being provided in an auditor's report and what auditors believe they are communicating in an auditor's report?

16

Interpreting Sample-Based Audit Evidence

Outline

INTRODUCTION

Auditors can never examine every risk, event, or transaction that may affect the financial statements of a company, nor can they use substantive tests to verify every entry to every account in the financial statements. For companies such as Wal-Mart or The Home Depot, which experience millions of sales transactions, auditors may examine only a small portion of the actual recorded transactions. Auditors need to prioritize their audit efforts and focus their attention on areas where risks are most significant to the company and the risk of material misstatements is highest. The phrase "nature, extent, and timing of audit evidence" implicitly recognizes that the auditor must make tradeoffs in the type and volume of evidence obtained during the audit.

When considering tests of controls or substantive tests, an auditor will obtain *sample* evidence concerning risks, controls, transactions, or assertions being examined. *Sampling risk* is the portion of detection risk that arises because the auditor does not examine all items in a population of transactions or accounts. A well-designed approach to audit sampling can help the auditor to accurately assess and manage sampling risk. The other component of detection risk is *non-sampling risk*, which is best managed with a careful selection of audit procedures to be performed.

> **Authoritative Guidance & Standards**
> This chapter covers audit sampling, which is described in SAS 39/SAS 111 and ISA 530.

THE ROLE OF SAMPLING IN AN AUDIT

The nature and extent of sampling used by an auditor depends on the assertions being tested, the nature of the population from which the items are to be selected, and the auditor's assessment of the risk of material misstatement. Examples of common audit procedures that involve sampling include

- Select a *sample* of weekly sales reports and review management's response to potential problems in the process (test of management controls)
- Select a *sample* of purchase requisitions and verify proper authorizations (test of process or internal controls)
- Select a *sample* of locations and observe inventory count procedures executed by client personnel (test of process or internal controls)
- Select a *sample* of shift changes within the factory and observe employees clocking in and out (test of process or internal controls)
- Select a *sample* of sales invoices and test the accuracy of individual transactions by verifying quantities and prices against appropriate supporting documentation (substantive test of transactions)
- Select a *sample* of accounts receivable to be confirmed with customers (substantive test of account details)

Although the increased use of computer-assisted audit techniques (CAATs) that enable an auditor to examine all items in a population reduces the need for sample-based tests, there are many process controls that cannot be tested by using CAATs. For example, a CAAT test can ensure that the system produces the weekly sales reports and compares it to budget or standard, but it cannot tell if the manager actually reviewed the report, noticed a discrepancy, and acted on it to assure that the sales system system is under control.

Sampling is not an end unto itself; it is the means of collecting audit evidence that is then evaluated to determine if various assertions are accurate and, in the aggregate, whether the financial statements are in accordance with GAAP. There are two ways to implement sampling once the decision to sample has been made:

- **Statistical:** The factors that are important to collecting the sample are quantified and used as input to the sampling process. As a result, the auditor can interpret the evidence collected using established statistical principles that consider the margin of error in the resulting evidence.
- **Non-statistical (judgmental):** This approach relies on the auditor's experience and judgment to determine how many sample items to select and how to interpret the sample evidence.

Many large public accounting firms have chosen to use judgmental sampling on many clients, and often use standardized sample sizes such as 25, 50, or 100 items, with the larger samples being used where the risk of material misstatement is considered to be the greatest.[1] Where do these numbers come from? Are they reasonable? Are they big enough or too big? How much can the auditor rely on the evidence from such samples? How do auditors project the evidence from a handful of transactions to the entire population of transactions? These questions can only be answered by having a good understanding of the concepts and theory that provide the foundation on which sampling methods are based, be they statistical or judgmental.

Many audit tests are activity-dependent or transaction-dependent, meaning that a sample of items to be tested should be selected from the full set of activities or transactions that have taken place to provide evidence that the activity or recorded transaction occurred or exists (this is especially important for assets and revenue). For example, an auditor can select a sample from the sequence of prenumbered sales invoices to test that each sale was authorized, valued correctly, and made to a real customer. Other procedures are time-dependent, requiring the auditor to select periods of time to test (i.e., times to observe employee behavior or dates to test transaction totals). Still other procedures may be dependent on tangible characteristics, for example, store locations, items of inventory, or physical but movable fixed assets (furniture and fixtures).

Regardless of the actual audit procedures being performed, well-established techniques exist for improving the quality of evidence the auditor obtains through sampling. No matter how an auditor obtains a sample, it is vital that he or she interpet the results in a consistent and logical manner. The auditor should consider three issues when obtaining evidence using a sample-based audit procedure:

1. **The number of transactions or items to examine:** This decision will often be based on the risk associated with the account being audited, with larger samples being used in higher risk situations.
2. **The actual transactions or items to examine:** The selection of items to be examined can be accomplished in a number of ways depending on the composition of the activity, account balance, or nature of transaction.

---

1 Survey research shows that roughly 85 percent of auditors (government, public accounting, and internal audit) employed rules of thumb to choose the sample size. See "Sampling Practices of Auditors in Public Accounting, Industry and Government," by T. W. Hall, J. E. Hunton, and B. J. Pierce, *Accounting Horizons.* 16(2): 125–136.

3. **Interpreting the results of the sample:** The auditor makes inferences about the entire population based on the sample results. This process depends on the nature of the procedure being performed, the sampling process, and the results of the examination.

In the remainder of the chapter, we will first consider the sample selection process. We will then consider two specialized applications of statistical sampling: (1) sampling used for tests of internal controls and tests of transactions and (2) sampling used for substantive tests of account details. For each of these approaches, we will address the questions of sample size and sample evaluation from a statistical viewpoint. We conclude the chapter with a discussion of non-statistical or judgmental sampling as well as common errors made by auditors when using sample-based evidence.

SELECTING A SAMPLE FOR AUDIT TESTING

The first question an auditor must address is the size of a sample to use when gathering evidence from a larger population. The sample size for a given audit procedure will depend on two main factors:

1. **The assertion(s) being tested:** A sample-based test can be used to examine a number of attributes that might be of interest to an auditor including whether a transaction is properly authorized, meets appropriate control requirements, and is correctly valued and processed. The more significant the assertion(s) is to the overall audit, the larger the sample will be.
2. **Assessment of risk:** The higher the level of risk associated with the assertion, the larger the sample size will be for testing the attributes associated with that assertion. That is, the higher the likelihood that an audit procedure will reveal significant problems, the more items the auditor will wish to examine to have a better basis to quantify potential problems.

Once the sample size has been determined, the auditor chooses the actual items or transactions that are to be examined from the population.

POPULATION OF PRENUMBERED DOCUMENTS

The most common application of sampling is when there are a large number of documents from which to choose. In many cases, documents are prenumbered (either preprinted on a form or numbered by the computer system), used in sequence, and the auditor knows the first and last document used in the period being audited. Then, selecting a sample to test simply involves choosing numbers that uniquely identify documents within the period. The overall goal of sample selection is to obtain a sample that is *representative* of the underlying population. If 5 percent of the transactions in the underlying population have errors, a good sample would reveal a 5 percent error rate. Of course, the auditor can never know the error rate in the population, which is why sampling is needed in the first place.

The auditor's understanding of the risk, either process- or strategic-based, and the nature of the processes and management controls that seek to reduce that risk, provide the basis for evaluating the likelihood of error. A representative sample allows the

> **Authoritative Guidance & Standards**
> SAS 39 and ISA 530 state that sample items should be selected in such a way that they are representative of the population, regardless of the method chosen to select the sample.

auditor to accurately evaluate the amount of sampling risk implicit in a sampling plan. Furthermore, different approaches to sampling affect the likelihood the auditor will obtain a representative sample. The following five sampling techniques are commonly used by auditors, but the first two are most likely to result in a representative sample:

1. Random sampling
2. Systematic sampling
3. Block sampling
4. Haphazard sampling
5. Judgmental sampling

For our discussion, assume we wish to generate a sample of 10 invoices from a total population of 65 invoices that were prepared during one month.[2] Figure 16–1 presents information on each transaction including the invoice number, the date, and the amount. This summary provides us with enough information to use any of our sampling techniques, each of which is explained next.

Random Sampling: *Random sampling* is based on the assumption that every item in the population has an equal probability of selection regardless of its individual attributes. Random sample selection is performed by obtaining a series of random numbers that uniquely identify specific items in the population. Random numbers can be generated using a computer program. For example, random numbers can be generated easily using Microsoft Office Excel (e.g., see Figure 16–2).[3] In our example, we want to select 10 items selected from 65 invoices that are sequentially numbered from 10394 to 10458. Employing MS Excel "random number generation" data analysis program found under the "Tools" menu bar, we would select 10 as the number of random numbers to generate, over a uniform distribution (equal likelihood of selecting each invoice) for items 10394 to 10458. After sorting (and possibly removing duplicate numbers), we might get the 10 numbers indicated under "Random Sampling" in the second column of Figure 16–3 for testing. Of course, given this is a *random* number generator, if you carry out this exercise you should obtain a different set of random numbers (if you do not, then Excel is not really generating random numbers!).

Systematic Sampling: An alternative to random sample is referred to as *systematic sampling*. This approach starts with one randomly selected transaction and then uses a predetermined selection interval to identify the rest of the sample. In our example, our selection interval should be 7. This was determined by dividing the population size by the sample size and then rounding to the next larger integer (i.e., $65/10 = 6.5$, rounded up to 7). The selection interval must be determined by rounding up to the nearest integer in order to assure that every item in the population has a chance of selection. We then select a starting point that falls within the first seven transactions (the interval size). An interval of six would not result in a representative sample because the last item in the sequence (10458) could never be chosen regardless of the starting point.

If we select the second invoice (10395) as our starting point (and this should be determined randomly), we will then select every seventh invoice thereafter until

2 To keep our example manageable, we use a small population and sample, but the same techniques can apply when the population being audited numbers in the thousands or even millions of documents. In fact, in such large scale situations, sampling is a necessity.

3 Random number generation appears under the "Tools" command under the "data analysis" heading. The user must then fill in the dialogue box for "random number generation."

Figure 16–1   Sampling from a Population of Prenumbered Documents: Sales Journal Example

Item Count	Sales Invoice Number	Date of Sale	Transaction Total	Cumulative Total
1	10394	1/2	422.28	422.28
2	10395	1/2	2,982.13	3,404.41
3	10396	1/2	1,854.92	5,259.33
4	10397	1/3	778.70	6,038.03
5	10398	1/4	2,989.73	9,027.76
6	10399	1/4	994.86	10,022.62
7	10400	1/5	1,157.55	11,180.17
8	10401	1/5	504.33	11,684.50
9	10402	1/5	2,301.01	13,985.51
10	10403	1/5	1,953.77	15,939.28
11	10404	1/5	901.86	16,841.14
12	10405	1/7	97.37	16,938.51
13	10406	1/8	2,886.61	19,825.12
14	10407	1/8	4,384.24	24,209.36
15	10408	1/8	2,863.38	27,072.74
16	10409	1/8	869.77	27,942.51
17	10410	1/8	2,414.72	30,357.23
18	10411	1/8	1,579.92	31,937.15
19	10412	1/9	770.19	32,707.34
20	10413	1/11	660.04	33,367.38
21	10414	1/12	2,683.15	36,050.53
22	10415	1/12	934.81	36,985.34
23	10416	1/12	1,177.98	38,163.32
24	10417	1/12	1,872.47	40,035.79
25	10418	1/12	317.66	40,353.45
26	10419	1/14	1,157.45	41,510.90
27	10420	1/14	4,288.68	45,799.58
28	10421	1/15	289.35	46,088.93
29	10422	1/17	441.17	46,530.10
30	10423	1/17	178.61	46,708.71
31	10424	1/18	374.78	47,083.49
32	10425	1/18	151.07	47,234.56
33	10426	1/18	1,550.34	48,784.90
34	10427	1/18	268.64	49,053.54
35	10428	1/18	2,826.96	51,880.50
36	10429	1/18	513.93	52,394.43
37	10430	1/20	1,521.21	53,915.64
38	10431	1/20	588.92	54,504.56
39	10432	1/20	2,311.14	56,815.70
40	10433	1/21	1,072.78	57,888.48
41	10434	1/22	114.83	58,003.31
42	10435	1/23	2,467.88	60,471.19
43	10436	1/23	891.82	61,363.01
44	10437	1/23	1,257.52	62,620.53
45	10438	1/23	2,171.68	64,792.21
46	10439	1/24	88.23	64,880.44
47	10440	1/24	1,382.15	66,262.59
48	10441	1/25	2,936.26	69,198.85

(continued)

Figure 16–1   *(continued)*

Item Count	Sales Invoice Number	Date of Sale	Transaction Total	Cumulative Total
49	10442	1/25	858.11	70,056.96
50	10443	1/25	1,145.88	71,202.84
51	10444	1/26	5,250.50	76,453.34
52	10445	1/28	630.16	77,083.50
53	10446	1/29	2,312.04	79,395.54
54	10447	1/29	1,740.13	81,135.67
55	10448	1/29	701.74	81,837.41
56	10449	1/30	1,187.52	83,024.93
57	10450	1/30	297.67	83,322.60
58	10451	1/30	1,192.97	84,515.57
59	10452	1/30	330.40	84,845.97
60	10453	1/30	9,639.16	94,485.13
61	10454	1/30	183.47	94,668.60
62	10455	1/30	2,230.97	96,899.57
63	10456	1/30	489.71	97,389.28
64	10457	1/30	83.63	97,472.91
65	10458	1/30	879.26	98,352.17
	Total Sales	January	98,352.17	

we get our sample of 10. The result of this sampling process is summarized in the third column of Figure 16–3 under the heading "Systematic Sampling." A complication that can occur is that the end of the population is reached before the entire sample is selected. Whether this will happen depends on the size of the interval and the starting point. This is not a problem, however, because the auditor can simply cycle back to the beginning of the population. It should be noted that the systematic approach results in an approximately random sample due to the use of the random number as the starting point.

Block Sampling: Another way to simplify the selection process and still maintain a degree of randomness is through the use of *block sampling*. This approach assumes that the auditor will examine groups (blocks) of sequential transactions but the selection of each block will be random. The auditor must determine how many blocks to test and select as many random numbers as there are blocks. Each block consists of a randomly selected start point and the items that follow it in sequence. The block sample approach is simpler than pure random sampling but does not result in a true random sample. The more blocks that are selected, the more closely the sample will approximate a random sample. Block sampling may be appropriate in some situations where the auditor is interested in testing a sequence of transactions. The results of this selection process are summarized in the fourth column of Figure 16–3 under the heading "Block Sampling."

Haphazard Sampling: *Haphazard sampling* is the most commonly used approach by auditors.[4] Instead of formally generating random numbers, the auditor mentally generates a set of random numbers to use as a sample by making up

4 This is according to survey research of government auditors, public accounting auditors, and internal auditors. See "Sampling Practices of Auditors in Public Accounting, Industry and Government," by T. W. Hall, J. E. Hunton, and B. J. Pierce, *Accounting Horizons*. 16(2): 125–136.

Figure 16–2   Random Dollars Selected by Excel Random Number Generator

238 numbers were required based on the textbook example between 1 and 600,000 with a uniform (equal likelihood of selection) distribution. After sorting from lowest to highest, here are the sample units (dollars) selected to identify accounts for confirmation.

1685	104190	210889	320389	407166	485464	580828
2985	106772	213361	320591	407788	486489	580902
3095	108695	214423	324491	412165	489914	582165
8698	110727	215009	324656	417658	490738	583502
9577	111185	219349	326926	419819	497531	585424
10254	113950	221162	326981	420185	510257	586120
19428	117063	223103	327311	421979	510385	591540
22779	119059	224073	329032	423023	511411	591778
23475	120286	225501	331394	423646	515293	594745
24427	123472	226691	332182	424433	515421	598627
25489	126658	229200	333097	425422	517948	
27284	130650	231800	334233	426905	520054	
32063	131767	240864	334599	427363	523844	
35707	138432	242879	335350	433241	529868	
37172	138487	244435	344707	434449	530766	
38435	147020	244453	345549	434596	535307	
39405	150462	248518	347673	438716	536827	
44606	153374	255696	348021	439009	538072	
49367	153758	259047	350713	443037	538420	
51033	153923	261043	350951	444282	539463	
51582	154015	264632	352031	450124	542320	
57222	155077	271059	353862	453200	542430	
57479	157329	272231	355821	453694	545158	
60189	162566	279611	356590	456935	546184	
60408	162896	279794	357891	459114	547282	
65133	168206	289810	361132	464461	555358	
66305	171026	292227	362047	465395	555687	
66616	171319	293893	370562	465413	556163	
68905	174780	295743	371642	466585	557299	
79232	176739	297629	375909	470138	558031	
79360	180126	298215	394110	473415	568853	
83151	180126	300467	399438	477755	569109	
87472	182342	306729	399640	478011	570611	
91336	195087	309989	400867	481289	571014	
97397	197815	310886	402936	481307	572588	
98477	198053	313669	404987	483395	575079	
100858	200378	314072	405573	483999	578576	
103934	205853	317277	406708	484402	580480	

numbers within the range of interest. For example, the auditor could select 10 invoices from those in Figure 16–1 which "approximates" a random sample. Another approach to haphazard sampling is used when the documents are physically available to the auditor. For example, if all the invoices are in a single file, the auditor may simply reach in and pull out 10 invoices without looking at them or considering any attributes about the invoices. Finally, for tests of process controls that involve observing employee actions, the auditor might choose to perform

Figure 16–3   Alternative Samples Using Different Sampling Techniques

Sampling Technique	Random Sampling	Systematic Sampling	Block Sampling
Description	Random number generation from Excel for a uniform distribution from invoice number 10394 to 10458	Starting with the second invoice, select every seventh invoice thereafter. The starting point should be randomly selected from the first seven invoices.	Select two blocks of five invoices each. Use the random number table to select the first invoice of each block in a manner similar to random sampling. Blocks start at 10424 and 10448.
Items Selected	10398 10400 10401 10406 10407 10422 10427 10441 10447 10454	10395 10402 10409 10416 10423 10430 10437 10444 10451 10458	10424 10425 10426 10427 10428 10448 10449 10450 10451 10452

Sampling Technique	Judgmental Sampling (size)	Judgmental Sampling (time)	Haphazard Sampling
Description	Select the invoices for the 10 largest sales during the period. This results in the examination of all transactions over $2,800.	Select the 10 transactions that occur on or near the first and last day of the period. This results in the selection of the first five and last five invoices.	Select any 10 invoices that attract the attention of the auditor.
Items Selected	10395 10398 10406 10407 10408 10420 10428 10441 10444 10453	10394 10395 10396 10397 10398 10454 10455 10456 10457 10458	Not determinable. The actual sample will vary for every auditor.

haphazard sampling when visiting the client's facilities for other reasons (a meeting) rather than on a random basis.

Judgmental Sampling: There are many situations where the auditor wishes to consider the attributes of the items in the population when determining which ones to examine. The consideration of transaction attributes negates the possibility of random sampling and is commonly referred to as *judgmental sampling*. This approach does not necessarily result in a representative sample, but its use is often justified because it allows the auditor to focus on items that are more likely to have problems or have a material impact on the financial statements. Common attributes that the auditor might consider when judgmentally selecting a sample include

- **Magnitude of a transaction:** The auditor will usually care more about large transactions than about small ones because large transactions are more likely to have a material effect on the financial statements.
- **Date of a transaction:** The auditor may be concerned that transactions at the beginning and end of a period may be subject to cutoff problems and concentrate testing on those transactions.
- **Parties to the transaction:** The auditor will usually be interested in related party transactions and may select a large proportion of such transactions to test.
- **Nature of underlying assets and liabilities:** The assets obtained or liabilities incurred as a result of the transaction may be of concern to the auditor (e.g., sales to failing companies may be more likely to be uncollectible).

To illustrate the use of judgmental sampling, Figure 16–3 presents two possibilities. The first sample is based on size and selects the 10 largest transactions in the population. The second approach is based on time and selects the first five transactions of the period as well as the last five. Judgmental sampling can also be based on multiple attributes. For example, the auditor might select the first two transactions, the last two transactions, and the six largest transactions.

Statistical sampling had its heyday in the 1980s, but then auditors turned to judgmental sampling based on the belief that it is costly to train audit staff in the proper use of statistical sampling techniques or that it is time-consuming to rigorously select a random sample from a very large population. In addition, auditors argue that they get more competent evidence from examining transactions that are selected for specific reasons, such as their large size or susceptibility to material misstatement. Although these arguments have some merit, the combination of mandatory ongoing training for practicing auditors and the rapid increase in the availability and decrease in the cost of computer-assisted audit tools means that they can be used to facilitate rigorous sample selection in many audits. Suggestions have recently arisen among some auditors that the Public Company Accounting Oversight Board (PCAOB) recognize the superiority of statistical sampling in situations where the auditor has no specific knowledge on which to base informed judgmental sample selection.

A TECHNIQUE FOR REFINING SAMPLE SELECTION: STRATIFIED SAMPLING

In some situations, an auditor may wish to split a population into smaller groups and use different sampling approaches for each group. Separating a population into subgroups for sampling purposes is referred to as *stratified sampling*. For example, the auditor may separate large transactions from small transactions and use judgmental sampling for the large transactions and random sampling for the small transactions. A similar size distinction could be made for confirmation of receivables or audits of selected branch offices. Another reason to use stratified sampling is because one subgroup of a population may be considered high risk, and the auditor will wish to sample from it very heavily, whereas another subgroup is considered low risk and will be subject to light sampling. In general, stratified sampling allows the auditor to tailor his or her sampling strategy to the characteristics of the population so as to obtain the most effective and efficient evidence. Stratified sampling can be used in conjunction with all of the sampling techniques discussed above.

OTHER TYPES OF POPULATIONS

Sampling from populations consisting of items other than documents can be complicated. If no other approach is reasonable, the auditor can always use haphazard sampling. In most cases, however, the auditor may be able to assign a sequence of unique, individual reference numbers to each item in the population and then use random or systematic sampling to choose the sample items. If an auditor wishes to draw a sample of days from a specific time period, calendar dates can easily be transformed into a four-digit code that is amenable to random number generation: April 27 becomes 0427 while December 8 becomes 1208. Similarly, weeks can be represented with two-digit numbers ranging from 01 to 52.

Samples based on pages or lines within a journal or ledger are also easy to obtain because each page in the document of interest can be assigned a unique number. If transactions are listed in a book, then a numbering scheme based on page numbers and line numbers is feasible. For example, assume that warranty claims are listed in a journal that has 22 pages, and each page has 45 lines. Sampling could be performed by forming four-digit numbers based on page and line numbers. Line 10 on page 18 becomes 1810, whereas line 42 on page 7 becomes 0742. Alternatively, each page may reflect a separate date so that days can be randomly selected and then lines on the page can be selected separately.

Populations of physical items such as parts or locations are more difficult to sample because existing numbers may not be sequential. Obtaining a sample from transactions or documents that are not numbered is the most difficult. Even in these cases, though, a logical sampling approach can usually be developed. For example, if the documents are loosely gathered into a physical file, a systematic process can be used where the auditor chooses documents based on a prespecified interval.

TESTS OF PROCESS CONTROLS AND TRANSACTIONS: ATTRIBUTE SAMPLING AND SAMPLE EVALUATION

Some of the most common applications of sampling are for tests of internal controls and substantive tests of individual transactions. The sampling approach used for these audit procedures is designed to determine if a specific attribute of interest is present in a transaction. In general, the auditor is searching for violations of some prespecified condition that is of interest. For example, an auditor can examine a sales invoice to see if it is approved by the credit manager. Similarly, the auditor can test to see if the price on an invoice is correct when compared to a master price list. In both cases, the presence or absence of a specific condition is of interest to the auditor: the sale is either authorized or it is not; the price is either correct or it is not. Auditors refer to violations of the specified conditions as *deviations* and use *attribute sampling* to perform these types of tests. The following 12-step process facilitates the use of attribute sampling:

1. Identify the audit procedure and the purpose of the test.
2. Define the population and sample unit.

3. Define the deviation conditions.
4. Specify the tolerable deviation rate.
5. Specify the acceptable risk that the auditor's conclusion will be incorrect.
6. Estimate the expected population deviation rate.
7. Determine the sample size.
8. Select the sample.
9. Perform the audit procedure and document the results.
10. Generalize the sample results to the population.
11. Analyze individual deviations.
12. Conclude whether the assertion tested is acceptable or not.

Some of these steps may be handled by computer support software where the auditor only provides the inputs necessary for the analysis; for example, the software calculates the required sample size given inputs from the audit team.

Step 1: Identify the Audit Procedure and the Purpose of the Test

The first step in any sampling process is to clearly state the purpose of the procedure and provide clear guidelines on how the test is to be performed. Failure to clearly state the purpose and nature of the audit procedure can result in an ineffective or inefficient sampling plan and inadequate or misleading evidence. For example, the purpose of the audit procedure may be to determine if sales have been recorded, classified, and summarized in accordance with management's general authorization. The following combined or dual purpose audit procedure could be used to examine both internal control attributes (a, b, c) and substantive attributes (d, e, f) of sales transactions:

Example

Obtain a random sample of invoices from the invoices included in the sales journal along with the related supporting documents. The invoices should be selected using a random sample from the sequence of sales invoices for the year. Each invoice should be examined as follows:

(a) Verify that the sales order, bill of lading, and customer purchase order exist and are attached.
(b) Examine the documents for proper authorization by the credit manager.
(c) Verify that the correct price was used on the invoice by tracing unit prices to the master price list.
(d) Test the computational accuracy of the invoice.
(e) Test that the sales invoice has been properly included in the sales journal.
(f) Verify that the transaction is posted on a timely basis.

Step 2: Define the Population and Sample Unit

In our example, the *population* is the set of "recorded sales invoices." The *sample unit* is an individual sales invoice. Defining the population or sample unit may be more difficult in other situations. For example, if the auditor is interested in testing for completeness, he or she must determine what population to use as the basis for the sample. The population of recorded invoices would not be appropriate because they represent *recorded* transactions, and the auditor is interested in what has been *omitted*. As an alternative, completed sales orders might be used as the population for testing completeness, with the sales order being the sample unit. This approach would be effective since the population includes all potential sales, but it may be inefficient because the auditor would also have to look at sales orders that were canceled or rejected. A better sample population for testing completeness would be shipping documents because each one represents an actual delivery to a customer and a sale that should have been recorded.

Another problem with defining the population may occur when time-dependent or location-dependent samples are used. For example, if the auditor wishes to observe employees on a sample basis as they open mail containing incoming receipts, the population would be all time periods in which this activity occurs and the sample unit could be a block of time, such as one hour. Another example is testing process controls over warehouse goods handling procedures in a just-in-time (JIT) environment. Here both the selection of locations and the time are critical for determining the sample.

STEP 3: DEFINE THE DEVIATION CONDITIONS

After clearly specifying the audit procedure to be performed, the auditor then defines the deviation conditions that are being tested. *Deviations* indicate that a process or control has failed but do not mean that the transaction is necessarily misstated. For example, failure of the credit manager to approve a sale does not mean the sale is invalid or incorrect or has been sold to someone who cannot pay. *Transaction errors* are situations where a transaction is processed improperly and may or may not result in a monetary misstatement. For example, charging a customer an incorrect low price on a sale is unfortunate, but it does not mean that the recorded amount of revenue is incorrect (i.e., the amount of revenue per the general ledger agrees with the amount per the invoice, even though the wrong price was used). Some transaction errors may cause account misstatements, for example, omission of a sales invoice from the sales journal would directly lead to an understatement of sales revenue.

Returning to our example, the auditor might identify the following conditions as being deviations or errors:

Attribute	Test for Following Condition	Negative Outcome
(a)	Missing document	deviation
(b)	Absence of initials	deviation
(c)	Prices do not agree	deviation
(d)	Extensions are incorrect	transaction error
(e)	Invoice not included in journal	transaction error
(f)	Posting in wrong period	transaction error

The distinction between deviations and errors relates to the likelihood that an account will be misstated as a result of the condition.

STEP 4: SPECIFY THE TOLERABLE DEVIATION RATE (TDR)

The *tolerable deviation rate* (TDR) is a measure of how many deviations or errors the auditor can willingly accept before concluding that the process or control is not effective. The auditor specifies a tolerable deviation rate for each of the attributes being tested. If the auditor thinks that credit approval is not an important source of audit assurance, he or she may set TDR to be high for that attribute, say 8 percent. If the auditor feels that entering incorrect prices is very significant to the audit, the TDR may be set low (e.g., 2 percent). We will see that the auditor's subsequent actions will be dictated by whether the tests reveal an actual deviation rate above or below the tolerable deviation rate. If actual deviation rates are below TDR, the auditor will then be able to conclude that the process or activity being tested is reliable consistent with the auditor's assessment of risk.

STEP 5: SPECIFY THE ACCEPTABLE RISK OF OVERRELIANCE (ARO) ON CONTROLS

The *acceptable risk of overreliance* (ARO) on controls is a measure of the risk that the auditor will conclude that the actual deviation rate is below TDR when, in fact, it is higher. This situation implies that an auditor has reached an incorrect conclusion. As a practical matter, ARO measures the risk that the auditor will conclude that a given residual risk for a process or control risk for an assertion is less severe than is appropriate. Such an erroneous decision will ultimately affect the quality of the audit, as the auditor would plan the audit based on an understated assessment of the client's risks. This would probably lead to inadequate substantive testing, higher detection risk than desired, and an unknown increase in the audit risk. In practice, common values for ARO are 10, 5, and 1 percent.

STEP 6: ESTIMATE THE EXPECTED DEVIATION RATE (EDR)

The auditor also needs to generate a tentative estimate of the *expected deviation rate* (EDR) for the population being tested in order to calculate the desirable sample size in Step 7. One possible source of the estimate is the results from a prior audit. If similar tests were performed in the past, the actual deviation rate from those tests could be used as the estimate of the deviation rate for the current year after adjusting for any process changes (improvements) that may have been made. Another approach that may be used is to audit a small preliminary sample of transactions and use those results to estimate the EDR for the main sample to be taken later. In some cases, the auditor may simply specify the expected deviation rate as zero.

STEP 7: DETERMINE THE SAMPLE SIZE (n)

The sample size an auditor should use to test a specific attribute is calculated from the tolerable deviation rate (TDR), the expected deviation rate (EDR), and the acceptable risk of overreliance (ARO). Returning to our example, let's assume that the six attributes being tested have the values for TDR, EDR, and ARO described in Figure 16–4. The appropriate sample size for each attribute is calculated as

$n = R/P$

where: n = sample size
           R = Risk factor based on ARO and the expected number of errors in the sample
           P = TDR − EDR (the precision gap is the difference between tolerable deviations and expected deviations)

The R-factor is based on the assumption that most audit populations will be found to be in compliance and follows a specific form of probability distribution called a

Figure 16–4   Calculating an Attribute Sample Size

Attribute	TDR	EDR	P (= TDR – EDR)	ARO (Risk level)	R Factor (Figure 16–5 for 1 error)	n = R/P*
(a)	5.0%	2.00%	3.0%	10.0%	3.89	130
(b)	6.0%	2.00%	4.0%	10.0%	3.89	98
(c)	5.0%	2.00%	3.0%	5.0%	4.75	159
(d)	6.0%	3.00%	3.0%	10.0%	3.89	130
(e)	3.0%	0.25%	2.75%	5.0%	4.75	173
(f)	3.0%	0.50%	2.5%	5.0%	4.75	190

* Rounding up to the next largest whole number

Figure 16–5   Determination of Factors Used for Sample Size and Error Projection Computations*

No. of Errors	Risk Level = 10% (90% confidence)		Risk Level = 5% (95% confidence)		Risk Level = 1% (99% confidence)	
	R factor	PGW factor	R factor	PGW factor	R factor	PGW factor
0	2.31	–	3.00	–	4.61	–
1	3.89	0.58	4.75	0.75	6.64	1.03
2	5.33	0.44	6.30	0.55	8.41	0.77
3	6.69	0.36	7.76	0.46	10.05	0.64
4	8.00	0.31	9.16	0.40	11.61	0.56
5	9.28	0.28	10.52	0.36	13.11	0.50
6	10.54	0.26	11.85	0.33	14.58	0.47
7	11.78	0.24	13.15	0.30	16.00	0.42
8	13.00	0.22	14.44	0.29	17.41	0.41
9	14.21	0.21	15.71	0.27	18.79	0.38
10	15.41	0.20	16.97	0.26	20.15	0.36
11	16.60	0.19	18.21	0.24	21.49	0.34
12	17.79	0.19	19.45	0.24	22.83	0.34
13	18.96	0.17	20.67	0.22	24.14	0.31
14	20.13	0.17	21.89	0.22	25.45	0.31
15	21.30	0.17	23.10	0.21	26.75	0.30

* Guy, D. M., D. R. Carmichael, and O. R. Whittington, *Audit Sampling: An Introduction*. 5th ed. (New York: Wiley, 2001).

"Poisson" distribution.[5] Figure 16–5 presents the appropriate R-factor for various combinations of ARO (denoted "risk level" in Figure 16–5) and the expected number of errors to be found in a sample. For our example, we will assume that the auditor expects one error or deviation for each test performed. Note that this is only an assumption for our example's purposes and other expectations for deviation numbers may be appropriate depending on the purpose of the test.

We see in Figure 16–4 that, all other things held constant, increasing ARO yields smaller sample sizes. Similarly, increasing TDR or reducing EDR yields smaller

5 The Poisson distribution is often used to represent random events which are dichotomous, meaning they can either happen or not happen. The Poisson distribution is skewed and peaked to the right, unlike the Normal distribution (sometimes called the Bell curve), which is symmetric and peaked in the middle.

sample sizes. Less obvious may be the fact that the difference between TDR and EDR directly impacts the size of the sample. This can be seen by comparing attributes (a) and (d)—the difference between EDR and TDR is the same for each (3 percent), resulting in the same sample size (130). Given that the various attributes have different values for TDR, EDR, or ARO, the sample sizes for each attribute are different. However, all the tests are focused on the same sample unit (invoice), so the auditor could use the largest value of n (190) and apply all tests to all invoices.[6]

STEP 8: SELECT THE SAMPLE

After determining the sample size, the auditor then selects the items that are to be examined. Although random sampling or systematic sampling (with a random start point) are much preferred sampling methods, the auditor might also use haphazard or judgmental sampling. However, the use of judgmental or haphazard sampling makes it harder to generalize the sample results to the population. Furthermore, the use of judgmental or haphazard sampling explicitly precludes the use of the statistical evaluation methods for generalizing the sample results described in Step 10.

STEP 9: PERFORM THE AUDIT PROCEDURE AND DOCUMENT THE RESULTS

Once the sample is selected, the auditor then obtains the documents needed to perform the specified tests and notes any deviations or errors that are detected. The auditor's documentation of this step can vary based on individual firm practices, but it should fully describe the nature of all deviations and errors that are detected, including an explanation of the problem. For a sample size of n, the results of the procedures can be summarized by the *sample deviation rate* (SDR):

SDR = Number of deviations found/n

To continue with our example, we will assume that the auditor finds seven deviations: two deviations for attribute (a), three deviations for attribute (b), one deviation each for (d) and (f), and no deviations for (c) and (e). These deviations are summarized in Figure 16–6.

> **Authoritative Guidance & Standards**
> SAS 39 and ISA 530 state that the deviation rate in the sample is the auditor's best estimate of the deviation rate in the population and should be compared to the tolerable rate for the population.

STEP 10: GENERALIZE THE SAMPLE RESULTS TO THE POPULATION

After the auditor has performed the audit procedure and tabulated the observed deviations (e.g., where the internal control has not been correctly applied or where there is a numerical error in a sales invoice), the next step is to generalize the results to the entire population.[7] Assuming a random sample and the results reported in Figure 16–6, the auditor next determines if sample deviation rate (SDR) is *tolerable;*

---

6 If the number of invoices in the sequence is less than 1000, a slightly smaller sample may be employed by reducing the computed number by the finite correction factor. The **finite correction factor** is computed as

$$n' = \frac{n}{(1 + n/N)}$$

where N is the number of items in the entire population, n is the sample size computed using $n = R/(TDR - EDR)$, and n' is the final sample size.

7 The generalization procedure described is only appropriate when the auditor uses random sampling, systematic sampling with a random start point, or a large number of randomly selected blocks. It is not appropriate when using judgmental or haphazard sampling as these are not *statistical* methods.

Figure 16–6   Documenting Deviations Found via Attribute Sampling

				M-1
	Johnson Pharmaceuticals Attribute Deviations for Tests of Controls and Transactions: Sales Transactions for the Year Ended 12/31/x7			*WRK*
				1/24/x7
				PBC
Attribute Tested	Deviation Number	Description of Deviation Found	UDR vs. TDR	Comments: Implications for the Audit
(a)	1	Customer purchase order was not attached to the sales invoice because the order was received by phone.	OK*	No special audit concern. The company is not set up to handle phone orders. Suggest that management consider this in the system design.
(a)	2	The sales order was not attached. Sales clerk remembers that it was destroyed when a cup of coffee spilled on it.	OK	No special audit concern. Suggest that duplicate copies of destroyed documents be included in the files.
(b)	1	The sales transaction was not approved by the credit manager because he was on vacation at the time. There is no alternative procedure in this situation.	Too high	Indicates that the control procedure is not being applied in all cases. May result in increased problems of collection.
(b)	2	The sales transaction was not approved by the credit manager because of accidental oversight.	Too high	Indicates that the control procedure is not being applied in all cases. May result in increased problems of collection.
(b)	3	The credit manager reviewed this transaction but neglected to sign the proper place on the form.	Too high	Indicates carelessness in applying the authorization procedure. Suggest to management increasing the reliability of this process.
(d)	1	An incorrect amount of sales tax was computed on a sale made to an out-of-state customer.	OK	No special significance because this type of sale is rare and the amounts of error are small.

* See Figure 16–7.

Figure 16–6 *(continued)*

Attribute Tested	Deviation Number	Description of Deviation Found	UDR vs. TDR	Comments: Implications for the Audit
(f)	1	The transaction was posted to the sales journal three days later than normal because the transaction occurred at the end of business on a Friday before a holiday weekend.	OK	No special significance because this situation is a rare occurrence.

that is, is the sample deviation rate low enough to be acceptable? We rearrange our formula for sample size in order to help us evaluate the results:

$$n = R/P \quad \text{becomes} \quad P = R/n$$

where, as before, n is the actual sample size and R is the risk factor based on ARO and the number of deviations found in the sample. Figure 16–5 presents the R-value for the number of deviations discovered and the planned level of ARO (denoted as "risk level" in the figure).

P captures the precision of the estimate and will be referred to as the *upper deviation limit* (UDL). The UDL is the maximum (or upper) deviation rate that an auditor can expect given the observed deviations and the auditor's acceptable risk. In other words, it includes what is more generally called the "margin for error." This means that when ARO is 5 percent, there is no more than a 5 percent chance that the true value of a deviation rate for an attribute will exceed the UDL. For example, if an auditor observes one deviation in a sample of 100 items, the sample deviation rate is 1 percent (1/100). Based on the R-factors in Figure 16–5, the upper deviation rate would be 4.75 percent (R/n = 4.75/100) for an ARO of 5 percent (R-value for one deviation in the column headed "Risk Level = 5%"). This is the same as saying that there is a 95 percent chance that the true deviation rate is less than 4.75 percent. If our TDR is 5 percent then the control is considered effective at its assessed level (UDL < TDR).

The tolerable deviation rate is a matter of judgment by the auditor. It reflects how effective the control must be in order to reduce the risk of material misstatement to an acceptable level for the particular assertion(s) related to the test being performed. If the auditor had determined when planning the test that the acceptable TDR is 4.5 percent, then the control would *not* be considered effective at its assessed level (UDL > TDR). This difference in interpretation reinforces our earlier caution that sampling is no more than a means to an end, and what an auditor concludes depends on the level of error that is acceptable to still conclude that a control is effective or a transaction is correctly stated.

Returning to our example, the outcomes of the six attributes tests are summarized in Figure 16–7.[8] For example, we see that attribute (a) had two observed

8 Our remaining discussion will be based on the sample sizes computed for each individual attribute, not the maximum sample.

Figure 16–7   Evaluating Results from Attribute Sampling

Attribute	n from Figure 16–4	ARO (Risk level)	Deviations (D) found in sample	SDR = D/n	R*	UDL = R/n X 100	TDR	Conclusion
(a)	130	10.0%	2	1.52%	5.33	4.1%	5.0%	Acceptable**
(b)	98	10.0%	3	3.41%	6.69	6.8%	6.0%	Unacceptable
(c)	159	5.0%	0	0.00%	3.00	1.9%	5.0%	Acceptable
(d)	130	10.0%	1	0.76%	3.89	3.0%	6.0%	Acceptable
(e)	173	5.0%	0	0.00%	3.00	1.7%	2.0%	Acceptable
(f)	190	5.0%	1	0.64%	4.75	2.5%	3.0%	Acceptable

* See Figure 16–5 for ARO (risk level) and actual number of deviations (D) found in sample.
** TDR > UDL means assertion is acceptable.

deviations in a sample of 130 at an ARO level of 10 percent, resulting in a UDL of 4.1 percent. Given that the UDL is less than the TDR of 5 percent, we can conclude that the control is effective at the planned level. The tests of attributes (c), (d), (e), and (f) are also within the acceptable TDR. However, we also see that attribute (b) has a UDL of 6.8 percent, which is greater then the TDR of 6 percent. Hence, we would conclude that the control is not effective at the planned level of reliability that was assessed during audit planning.

The auditor has a number of alternatives when the UDL exceeds TDR. One possibility is to revise either TDR or ARO upward. Such a revision after a test has been performed makes it easier to obtain a result that is acceptable to the auditor, meaning that the auditor can conclude no problems exist for a given attribute. However, this approach is highly inadvisable because the original estimates of TDR and ARO were the auditor's best judgment at the time, and revision of those values in order to obtain more acceptable test results suggests that the audit procedures may be biased. Another possibility is to increase the size of the sample used in the test, looking at additional items from the population. This approach is best employed when the UDL is very close to the TDR. If the additional items do not have any deviations, the UDL will get lower as *n* increases. This approach is acceptable when additional testing can be performed but the auditor must also be aware that additional deviations may be found which could lead to a higher value of UDL.

STEP 11: ANALYZE INDIVIDUAL DEVIATIONS

The computation of UDL is only one aspect of the auditor's evaluation of the results from sample-based tests. Even if the UDL is less than TDR for all attributes, the auditor should still examine the nature of the actual deviations in the sample. One characteristic the auditor will consider is whether any of the deviations indicate fraudulent activity. A deviation that hints at possible employee or management fraud is always significant because it raises questions about the integrity of the people in the organization. Another type of deviation that is of interest indicates a systemic problem within a process or information system. Even though a process works fine for most transactions, there may be a type or class of transactions that are routinely mishandled. For example, a company that deals primarily with credit card sales may not have a good system for handling cash receipts.

Therefore, the cash sales may have a higher incidence of errors and mistakes than credit sales, and could be examined in more detail.

STEP 12: CONCLUDE WHETHER THE ASSERTION TESTED IS ACCEPTABLE

The final step of attribute sampling is to reach an overall conclusion about the population being tested based on the sample results. For tests of internal controls, the auditor's conclusions may relate to residual risks in a process or the control risks related to financial statement assertions. For substantive tests of transactions, the conclusions drawn from sample-based tests pertain to the detection risk of specific financial statement assertions. There are three possible outcomes for a sample-based attributes test:

> **Authoritative Guidance & Standards**
>
> SAS 39 and ISA 530 state that auditors should consider the qualitative aspect of deviations, including (a) the nature and cause of the deviations, such as whether they are errors or fraud or are due to misunderstanding or carelessness, and (b) the possible relationship of the deviations to other phases of the audit.

1.   The upper deviation rate is less than the tolerable deviation rates for all attributes tested, and the individual deviations do not reveal any significant or systemic problems within the system. In this situation, the auditor would conclude that the initial risk assessments made during audit planning are correct.

2.   The upper deviation rate is more than the tolerable deviation rate for one (or a few) attributes tested, or the analysis of individual deviations indicates some systemic problems. In this situation, the auditor might increase residual risk assessments for the affected attributes. As a result, the auditor would increase the amount of substantive testing in selected areas to reflect that some of the initial assessments of control effectiveness were not supported by the tests of controls.

3.   A large number of unacceptable deviation rates are found or there are many indications of significant or systemic problems. In this situation, the auditor is likely to conclude that residual process risks are significant and not adequately controlled. This will lead the auditor to increase detection risk for specific assertions and significantly increase the use of substantive audit procedures. In addition, in an integrated audit (i.e., SOX Section 404), the auditor needs to consider whether the control problems constitute significant deficiencies or material weaknesses in internal control over financial reporting as of the end of the year.[9]

In our example (Figure 16–7), we see generally good results with five of the six attributes having acceptably low deviation rates. Only attribute (b) has a deviation rate that would be considered unacceptable. Consequently, the auditor confirms his or her initial assessment of the risk of material misstatement for the assertions affected by the attributes with low deviation rates. For example, given the low incidence of unrecorded sales (attribute e), the auditor may conclude that the risk of material misstatement for the completeness of sales transactions is very low. Similarly, because there are few missing documents (attribute a), validity of sales would appear to support an assessment of low risk of material misstatement.

---

9 This is an example of a situation where reliance on controls for the audit of financial statement purposes can be inconsistent with the internal control audit requirement of SOX Section 404. To reduce the number of substantive tests in the audit of financial statements, the controls need to be effective for the *entire* period under audit. Under the internal control audit requirement the controls only need to be effective as of *year end*. Thus, it is an interesting question as to how long before year end the controls have to be put in place in order for the client to test the new controls and the auditor to opine on the client tests and satisfy himself or herself that the redesigned system will detect material errors beyond a remote likelihood.

Finally, since attribute (f) has a tolerably low deviation rate, the auditor could conclude that the timing of sales transactions is at or below the assessed risk of material misstatement.

Valuation of sales transactions is more difficult to assess since more than one attribute affects the assertion. The low incidence of pricing errors (attribute c) indicates low valuation risk. However, at the same time, the failure of the credit manager to check transactions (attribute b) indicates that there may be a high risk of collection problems in the future. In this situation, the auditor would probably conclude that risks associated with pricing of sales are low, but additional substantive evidence will be needed to determine the appropriate level of bad debt expense for the period.

Completion of the 12-step process for attribute sampling highlights how evidence from tests of controls and individual transactions supports the auditor's assessment of residual risk. Attribute sampling is a methodical approach for testing the presence or absence of certain conditions within transactions. By relying on random sampling, a single table of computational factors, and some straightforward computations, the auditor is able to compute the best sample size consistent with the auditor's understanding of the population being tested and to generalize observed deviation rates from the sample to the entire population. Consequently, the auditor has a rigorous basis for reaching conclusions about the risks related to a process or assertion.

TESTS OF ACCOUNT BALANCE DETAILS: DOLLAR UNIT SAMPLING

The second major area where an auditor can apply sampling is for substantive tests of account balances. For example, an auditor may decide to confirm selected receivable balances or verify quantities for selected items in inventory. In general, these tests are designed to detect dollar-denominated errors that may exist in a recorded account balance. The sampling approach used most often by auditors is referred to as *dollar unit sampling* or *DUS*.[10] Dollar unit sampling is so-named because each dollar included in an account is considered a sample unit that can be uniquely identified and audited. Dollar unit sampling involves a 12-step process similar to attribute sampling:

1. Identify the audit procedure and purpose of the test.
2. Define the population and sample unit.
3. Define the error conditions applicable to the audit procedure.
4. Specify the tolerable error rate.
5. Specify the acceptable risk of inappropriately accepting an account as correct.
6. Estimate the expected error level and the expected tainting factor.
7. Determine the sample size.
8. Select the sample.
9. Perform the audit procedure and document the results.
10. Generalize the sample results to the population.

10 The term *monetary unit sampling* is occasionally used synonymously with dollar unit sampling. A more general term that is used is *sampling proportionate to size* because the application of DUS results in large items being more likely to be selected than small items. A different approach to sampling for tests of account details is called *variables sampling*. Variables sampling is based on the number of items in a population rather than dollars. It includes approaches to sampling that are often referred to as *classical sampling*, which differ significantly from the sampling methods described in this chapter.

11. Analyze individual errors.
12. Conclude whether the account balance tested is acceptable or not.

STEP 1: IDENTIFY THE AUDIT PROCEDURE AND PURPOSE OF THE TEST

The first step is to clearly identify the audit objective(s) being addressed and the audit procedure to be performed. For example, the auditor may use confirmations to test the validity and valuation of accounts receivable as discussed in Chapter 11. The auditor will rarely be able to confirm every customer's account balance. In fact, the auditor is probably most interested in the largest account balances because an overstatement of a receivable balance would probably cause an overstatement in net income. We will use the following audit procedure to illustrate the application of dollar unit sampling:

Example

Select a random sample of customer accounts to be confirmed. Prepare positive confirmations of account balances as of 12/31/x5 and mail out confirmations on 1/3/x6. Confirmations should be prepared by the client but reviewed and mailed by the auditor. Responses should be directed to the auditor's office address. Perform the following related procedures:

a. Prepare a confirmation control list to facilitate documentation of the confirmation process.
b. Maintain a confirmation log to record when confirmations are sent and received.
c. Send second and third requests, if necessary.
d. Investigate all discrepancies identified in returned confirmations.
e. Prepare adjusting entries to propose to client for any detected errors.

STEP 2: DEFINE THE POPULATION AND SAMPLE UNIT

The sample unit for dollar unit sampling is a single dollar and the entire "set" of dollars that comprise an account balance is the population. An account with a balance of $1,000 consists of 1,000 sample units; an account that has a balance of $10,000 has 10,000 sample units. Any individual dollar can be selected during the sampling process, so a customer account with a large balance contains more sample units and is more likely to be selected than a small account.

This approach to defining the population and sample unit has a number of advantages. First, large accounts are more likely to be selected since they consist of more sample units. Second, any individual dollar that is sampled can be in one of two conditions, either correct or incorrect. This allows the auditor to use a sampling method similar to that used for attribute sampling. Third, this approach does not require the auditor to make any assumptions about the distribution of the errors in accounts. This advantage may not be readily apparent, but alternative approaches usually require that errors adhere to a normal distribution (bell-shaped curve).

DUS also has some disadvantages that the auditor must consider. DUS ignores accounts with a zero or credit balance. A customer who usually carries a balance may have a low balance at year end (or even a credit balance) due to an error that understates sales or overstates cash receipts. Such errors are unlikely to be detected using DUS because an account with a zero or negative balance has no sample units. This also implies that understatement errors in general are less likely to be detected. An account with a balance of $1,000 that is overstated by $400 (correct balance is $600) is more likely to be selected than an account with a balance of $600 that is understated by $400 (correct balance is $1,000) even though both accounts contain a $400 error. The auditor will normally use separate procedures to test for understated receivables if deemed necessary by risk conditions.[11]

STEP 3: DEFINE THE ERROR CONDITIONS APPLICABLE TO THE AUDIT PROCEDURE

The error condition for tests of account details is usually easy to specify—the account is either correct or not. However, the sample unit is a dollar, not an account, making interpretation of the error condition more subtle. When a dollar is selected for confirmation, it is "associated" with a specific customer. In order to confirm the selected dollar, the entire customer account needs to be confirmed. That means that the actual confirmation applies to the entire account balance, for example $1,000, and the audit procedure provides evidence about more than just the sample unit selected. If an error exists in the $1,000 balance, then 1000 sample units are considered to be in error, that is, the selected sample unit is incorrect as well as the other 999 sample units that were not selected but were covered by the confirmation.

STEP 4: SPECIFY THE TOLERABLE ERROR LEVEL (TEL)

Based on our previous discussion of materiality and tolerable error (Chapter 10), we can specify the *tolerable error level* (TEL) for the account being examined, in this case accounts receivable. The tolerable error level for an account reflects the maximum size of a misstatement that could exist before the auditor would conclude that the account is materially misstated. Auditors can set tolerable errors in one of two ways: (1) by directly allocating a portion of overall materiality to the account in dollar terms or (2) by calculating TEL as a specified percentage of the account (e.g., 5 percent, 2 percent, or 1 percent are common). Smaller values of TEL are associated with lower detection risk.

STEP 5: SPECIFY THE ACCEPTABLE RISK OF INCORRECT ACCEPTANCE (ARIA)

The *acceptable risk of incorrect acceptance* (ARIA) reflects the maximum likelihood the auditor is willing to accept that he or she will reach an incorrect conclusion about an account that is materially misstated. ARIA is similar to detection risk but applied to a single account. Common values for ARIA are 10 percent, 5 percent, and 1 percent. When using Figure 16–5, the ARIA is denoted as the "risk level."

STEP 6: ESTIMATE THE EXPECTED ERROR LEVEL (EEL) AND THE EXPECTED TAINTING FACTOR (ETF)

The auditor must also generate an estimate of the *expected error level* (EEL), the auditor's best guess of the expected misstatement for the account prior to being

---

11 Another advantage of DUS that is not obvious from the exposition so far is that it usually results in smaller sample sizes than alternative approaches. Another disadvantage is that the computations for DUS can become quite complex if the population is very large.

tested. This estimate is needed in order to calculate the sample size in Step 7. One possible source of the estimate are the results from last year's audit. If similar tests were performed in the past, the actual dollar error from those tests could be used as the estimate of the dollar error for the current year. Another approach is to take a small preliminary sample, perform some audit testing, and use those results to estimate the EEL for the main sample to be taken later. In some cases, there may be little basis for estimating EEL but the auditor should be aware that higher levels of EEL increase sample sizes.

As noted above, the sample unit for DUS is an individual dollar but the actual audit procedures must be applied to some other unit, such as a customer account. That means that when an error is discovered it pertains to the entire account, both the dollars that were selected in the sample as well as those that were not. This raises the question of whether an error is attributable to the specific dollar sampled, some other dollar(s) not selected, or all dollars in the account. As a matter of simplicity, auditors assume that a discovered error in an account is equally applicable to all sample units (dollars) that comprise that account. For example, assume that a customer's account is recorded at $1,000 but is discovered to be overstated by $200. Because the overstatement represents 20 percent of the account balance, every individual dollar is assumed to be overstated by 20 percent. To look at it differently, the $200 error in an account is translated into a 20 cent error in each sample unit (dollar). The rate of misstatement (20 percent) is referred to as the *tainting factor* (TF), calculated as follows:

$$\text{Tainting Factor (TF)} = \frac{\text{Book value (BV)} - \text{Correct Audited Value}}{\text{Book value (BV)}}$$

In order to compute the appropriate sample size for DUS, the auditor must specify the *expected tainting factor* (ETF) for the account as a whole. This reflects the auditor's conditional expectation of how large an error is likely to be, if one is discovered through an audit procedure. The value of 50 or 100 percent is often used for ETF as they are relatively conservative and result in larger sample sizes and more accurate estimates of potential misstatements.

STEP 7: DETERMINE THE SAMPLE SIZE (n)

The appropriate sample size for DUS depends on the TEL, ARIA, EEL, and ETF. Because the auditor is sampling individual dollars and each dollar is correct or incorrect, a variation of attributes sampling can be used for dollar unit sampling. The main challenge is to determine an equivalent for the R-factor that can be applied to a dollar unit sample. In general, R is based on the specified level of ARIA (denoted the "risk level" in the Figure 16–5) and an assumption of either zero or one or more expected errors (with zero errors being the most conservative, leading to larger sample sizes). The sample size is then computed as:

$$n = \frac{\text{BV} * \text{R} * \text{ETF}}{(\text{TEL} - \text{EEL})}$$

where BV is the book value (balance) of the account being audited. In general, sample sizes increase when ARIA is lower, ETF is larger, or TEL is smaller. A value of EEL in excess of zero will also cause sample size to increase.

For an illustration of this computation, consider the following facts for our confirmation procedure to be performed:

Book Value (BV) of accounts receivable	$600,000
Number of customers	545 individual accounts
Tolerable Error Level (TEL)	$24,000 (4%)
Expected Error Level (EEL)	$0
Expected Tainting Factor (ETF)	100%
Acceptable risk of incorrect acceptance (ARIA)	5%

We will also assume an error level of one for determining the R-factor to use in the calculation, yielding R = 4.75 based on ARIA set at 5 percent (see Figure 16–5, under column entitled "Risk level = 5%" and row with one error). We can then calculate the sample size as 119 sample units as follows:

$$n = (BV * R * ETF)/(TEL - EEL) = (\$600{,}000 \times 4.75 \times 1.00)/(\$24{,}000 - \$0) = 119$$

If the expected tainting factor was 50 percent, the sample size would be half as large.

STEP 8: SELECT THE SAMPLE

After determining the appropriate sample size, the auditor must then select the sample. Using random sampling or systematic sampling with a random start point will allow the auditor to quantify sampling risk. The use of any form of judgmental or haphazard sampling precludes the application of statistical methods for generalizing the results from a sample-based test to the population (as in Step 10). For either random or systematic sampling, the items in the population must be logically ordered, usually by account number, and a running total determined after the addition of each item. This is illustrated in Figure 16–8 for the first 15 customers in the accounts receivable ledger.

The auditor must document which accounts are selected and prepare a confirmation control sheet indicating when confirmations are sent and received. The auditor can take a random sample for the confirmation of receivables simply by generating 119 random numbers between 1 and 600,000, and then mapping them to the cumulative totals in Figure 16–8.

Alternatively, the auditor can take a systematic sample with a random start point. The sample interval would be BV/$(n - 1)$ = $600,000/118 = 5085. This means that the auditor would randomly select a dollar between 1 and 5085 as the random start point and then every 5,085th dollar after that. If the start point is less than 4118, the first item selected will be the first account (132409). If the start point is larger than 4118, the first item will not be selected. Assume the auditor selects 4338 as the start point. The first account selected would be 136861 since 4338 exceeds the cumulative total of the first account but is less than the cumulative total of the second account. The second dollar selected would be 9423 (4338 + 5085), which also pertains to customer 136861. The third dollar selected would be 14508 (9423 + 5085), falling in account number 136895. The first 11 sample units (and 9 selected accounts) are illustrated in Figure 16–8. The selection process would continue in this manner until all 119 sample units (dollars) are selected.

Although the sample size is 119, the auditor would actually send out fewer than 119 confirmations because some accounts are selected more than once. We see this for items 2 and 4, but it could occur for other accounts in the population. Any account that is larger than the sample interval will always contain at least one

Figure 16–8   Extracts from Dollar Unit Sampling for Selecting Receivable Accounts to Confirm

Item No.	Customer Number	Balance	Cumulative Total	Systematic Sample		Balances to be Confirmed
1	132409	4,118.85	4,118.85			–
2	**136861**	9,717.34	13,836.19	4338	9423	9,717.34
3	136871	445.21	14,281.40			–
4	**136895**	7,683.03	21,964.43	14508	19593	7,683.03
5	**137127**	2,793.39	24,757.82	24678		2,793.39
6	**137472**	9,044.62	33,802.44	29763		9,044.62
7	137743	1,471.44	35,273.88	34848		1,471.44
8	137854	4,939.33	40,213.21	39933		4,939.33
9	**138651**	2,906.08	43,119.29			–
10	**138846**	1,433.63	44,552.92			–
11	**138988**	4,914.56	49,467.48	45018		4,914.56
12	139124	869.72	50,337.20	50103		869.72
13	**139319**	1,762.02	52,099.22			–
14	**139707**	2,738.36	54,837.58			–
15	139754	923.09	55,760.67	55188		923.09
⋮	⋮	⋮	⋮	⋮	⋮	⋮
	Total	**$600.000**				**$150.000**

Figure 16–9   Summary of Confirmation Results Obtained from Dollar Unit Sampling

Customer Number	Book Value (BV)	Corrected Audited Value (AV)	Difference = BV-AV	Tainting Percentage = Difference/BV
139834	$1,000	$ 500	$ 500	50%
140102	3,000	2,100	900	30%
140367	2,000	1,600	400	20%
Total known misstatements			**$1,800**	

sample unit and will be selected for confirmation no matter what the starting point for sample selection. Any account that is more than twice the sample interval will contain at least two sample units, any account larger than three times the sample interval will contain at least three sample units, and so on. The counting of the same account as multiple samples is based on the underlying theory that it is the individual dollar in the account that we are sampling, not the account itself.

STEP 9: PERFORM THE AUDIT PROCEDURE AND DOCUMENT THE RESULTS

Regardless of the sample selection method, the auditor then sends confirmations to the individual customers within which each selected dollar is included. The auditor will keep a log of customers who respond and investigate any discrepancies noted in the confirmations. The auditor will also document if alternative procedures are performed for non-responses and prepare a summary of any errors that are detected by the audit test (see Chapter 11 for more detail). Figure 16–9 describes

Figure 16–10   Projection to the Population

	(a) PGW Factor (see Figure 16–5)	(b) Tainting Factor	(c) Average Sampling Interval	Subtotal (a) × (b) × (c)	Dollar value of error
Basic error margin	3.00	100%	5,085		**$15,255**
Most likely error					
Customer 139834	1.00	50%	5,085	2,543	
Customer 140102	1.00	30%	5,085	1,526	
Customer 140367	1.00	20%	5,085	1,017	5,086
Most likely error					**$20,341**
Precision Interval					
Customer 139834	0.75	50%	5,085	1,907	
Customer 140102	0.55	30%	5,085	839	
Customer 140367	0.46	20%	5,085	468	3,214
Upper error limit (UEL)					**$23,555**

three errors that were discovered through the confirmation of accounts receivable in our sample. The total discovered error is $1,800. Some discrepancies will not be errors from the point of view of the client. For example, a common discrepancy that occurs in receivables that is not an error is when the client adds interest to a customer's balance but the customer does not consider the interest when confirming the amount owed. Errors and non-errors must be clearly separated prior to the next step of the process.

STEP 10: GENERALIZE THE SAMPLE RESULTS TO THE POPULATION

One of the main advantages of employing statistical sampling is the ability to quantify sampling risk and calculate an upper bound on the maximum error in the population for a given level of ARIA.[12] This allows the auditor to project the detected amount of error to the population as a whole. Figure 16–10 illustrates the error calculations for the example.

1. **Basic Margin of Error:** Even when an audit procedure reveals no errors, the fact that the auditor only tests a sample instead of the entire population creates a margin of error in the results. The basic margin of error in all sampling plans is always less that the tolerable error level (TEL) because the structure of the sampling plan. The calculation of the basic margin of error is based on the R-factor for zero errors for a given level of ARIA as indicated in Figure 16–5. For our example, the R-factor for zero errors is 3.00 (zero errors in column headed "Risk level = 5%"). We also assume a tainting factor of 100 percent for the basic margin of error. The basic margin of error is $15,255, which is well below the TEL of $24,000. Thus, if the auditor had detected NO errors, the account balance would be accepted as free of material misstatement.

2. **Most likely error:** Errors detected during the audit procedures are used to calculate the most likely (or average) error. This calculation quantifies the mean

---

12 For samples that are selected judgmentally, the generalization of sample results to the population should be based on the techniques described in the section "Judgmental Approaches to Sampling" later in this chapter.

amount of error in the population based on errors discovered in our sample. We list these errors from largest tainting factor to the smallest tainting factor.[13] In Figure 16–10, we find the most likely amount of error due to overstatements is $5,086.

3. **Precision interval:** The final component of the error projection is the precision interval, which reflects the sampling risk associated with the known errors. The computation of the precision interval is based on the precision gap widening (PGW) factors in Table 16–5.[14] Each error detected in the sample is assigned a different PGW-factor. By convention, the first error is considered the one with the largest tainting factor (50 percent). Ordering the errors based on the tainting factor is conservative because it yields the largest precision interval. The precision interval for our example is $3,214.

> **Authoritative Guidance & Standards**
> SAS 39 and ISA 530 require the auditor to project monetary errors found in the sample to the population, regardless of the sampling method selected The projected error should be compared to tolerable error.

STEP 11: ANALYZE INDIVIDUAL ERRORS

In addition to generalizing the error results to the entire population, the auditor must also analyze each error to see if it has implications for the risk of material misstatement, including the risk of fraud. The auditor must be comfortable with the explanation obtained for each of the discovered errors. Errors can fall into one of three categories: random unintentional errors, systematic unintentional errors, and fraud. For errors that are considered to be unintentional and random, it is safe to draw conclusions about the entire account based on the results of the sample. Errors that are systematic mean that there is a basic flaw in the system that will lead to an error whenever certain conditions occur. These errors should be separated from the random errors and subject to separate audit testing. The remaining random errors can then be analyzed using the statistical evaluation approach described above. If the analysis reveals potential fraud, the auditor must carefully assess the extent of the problem, evaluate the implications for completing the audit, and communicate with the appropriate levels of management. The use of statistical evidence should be re-evaluated in the presence of fraud because of the intentional manipulation of the data that is the basis of the sampling plan.

STEP 12: CONCLUDE WHETHER THE ACCOUNT BALANCE TESTED IS ACCEPTABLE

The final step in the process is to reach an overall conclusion about the account balance being examined. As indicated, the overall **Upper Error Limit** (UEL) is $23,555. Because this is less than the TEL of $24,000, the auditor can conclude that accounts receivable is not materially overstated with a 95 percent confidence level

---

13 It is necessary to separate overstatement errors from understatement errors in doing the computation of most likely error and upper error limit.

14 The PGW factors are based on the assumption that each error in the sample increases the aggregate R-factor for the sample. Because our example revealed three errors, the upper value of the R-factor is 7.76, and each error contributes to the increase in the R-factor from 3.0 (no errors) to 7.76. The PGW-factor is computed by taking the change in R-factor for a specific error, less 1.0. For example, the first error increases the R-factor from 3.00 to 4.75. Thus, the first error contributes a PGW increment of 0.75 (4.75 − 3.0 − 1.0). The second error increases the R-factor from 4.75 to 6.30 and the PGW increment is 0.55 (6.30 − 4.75 − 1.0). Similarly, the incremental PGW-factor for the third error is 0.46 (7.76 − 6.30 − 1.0).

(i.e., ARIA = 5 percent). Although understatements are usually of less concern to auditors when testing accounts receivable, a *Lower Error Limit* (LEL) should also be computed. Given that there were no understatement errors, the most likely error for understatements is 0. Therefore, the lower error limit is simply the basic margin of error, $15,255. Based on the UEL and LEL, the auditor can be 95 percent confident that the true account balance falls between $564,745 (BV – LEL) and $623,555 (BV + UEL). Because both error limits fall within the acceptable range (BV ± TEL), the auditor will conclude that accounts receivable are free of material misstatement. However, the known misstatement of $1,800 should be brought to management's attention for further action and correction.

If either UEL or LEL exceeds TEL, there exists an unacceptable risk that the account is misstated in an amount that exceeds tolerable error. If this occurs, the auditor has a number of possible responses:

- **Increase ARIA or TEL:** Either of these two actions will result in more tolerance for error, but this approach is NOT recommended on an *ex post facto* basis because it appears that the auditor is biasing the results of the tests towards accepting the client's book values.

- **Expand the sample size for the audit procedure:** If additional items can be selected and tested, the UEL may be reduced as long as no other errors are detected. This approach has two drawbacks: (1) it may not work if additional errors are detected and (2) it may not be possible to audit additional items in the population. For example, if confirmations are being obtained as of December 31, the auditor will not know until February that there is a problem in the account. At that time, it is probably too late to obtain additional confirmations.

- **Adjust the account balance for discovered (or known) errors:** This should be suggested to client management regardless of the TEL. The adjustment for known overstatement errors has the effect of reducing the UEL by the amount of the adjustment. In our example, the auditor can reduce UEL by $1,800 by requesting client management correct the three accounts that were found to contain errors. This reduces UEL to $21,755 ($23,555 – $1,800).

- **Adjust the account balance for projected error:** The auditor might recommend that the client reduce the balance of accounts receivable by the UEL or some portion of UEL. Such a recommendation would probably only be made when UEL exceeds TEL by an amount that is greater than the known misstatements. Making this proposal to client management has at least two drawbacks: (1) client management may balk at the idea of a large adjustment because the support for the adjustment is based on a statistical, rather than actual, measure of error, and (2) the adjustment may over-correct the problem and cause a material understatement of the account.

- **Expand audit testing that focuses on specific problems identified in the sample:** The auditor might choose to perform additional tests that are focused specifically on the risks revealed by the confirmation procedures. This would provide additional evidence to the auditor as to whether the problems are universal or isolated. If the additional evidence shows that the errors in the sample are isolated and not likely to be repeated on a large scale, those errors can be removed from the statistical analysis and simply adjusted in the accounts. This approach is probably the most common approach used by auditors.

Example

> For an illustration of the use of expanded testing, consider the three errors included in our example. Assume that two of the errors relate to the pricing of inventory and one is due to a cutoff problem. The auditor could design and perform additional tests related to cutoff and pricing in order to determine if the discovered errors are unique or occur frequently. If no additional problems are detected by the expanded testing of transactions, the auditor would be justified in concluding that accounts receivable is not misstated, after making appropriate adjustments for known errors.[15]

- **Get the client to check the entire population:** Once the nature of the problem is diagnosed, the auditor can request that the client test the entire population to ensure all mistakes are found. If client management carries out the procedures then the auditor must take a sample and determine if management carried out the procedures correctly. The advantage of this approach is that it reduces management's reluctance to make an adjustment as the adjustment is based on known errors, not projections or sampling risks. The disadvantage of this approach is its cost, either in auditor or client time.

JUDGMENTAL APPROACHES TO SAMPLING

Auditors are not always willing to use formal statistical methods of sampling and sample evaluation. The auditor should consider the following characteristics when determining sample size in a judgmental approach:

- **Individually significant items:** Transactions that are considered to be material or significant on their own should be selected for testing. Any transaction that exceeds half of tolerable error is usually considered to be individually significant.
- **Variation of the population:** The more variation there is in the population of items, the larger the sample should be. Variation can come in terms of size or other attributes of interest (timing, nature of transactions). The sample should be large enough to be representative of all conditions typically encountered in the population.
- **Tolerable error level (TEL) and acceptable risk of incorrect acceptance (ARIA):** Although these terms are not used in their statistical sense, the concepts apply for judgmental sampling. In general, smaller TEL and lower ARIA lead to larger samples.
- **Extent of expected error:** This concept is similar to EEL but is less formally stated. The more expected error there is the larger sample sizes should be.

Based on these concepts, the American Institute of Certified Public Accountants provides the following formula for determining sample size:

$n = (\text{BV} \times \text{Assurance Factor})/\text{TEL}$

---

15 An auditor might also decide not to expand tests and wait to see what the entire set of detected and projected errors looks like for the financial statements taken as a whole. See Chapter 15 for a discussion of evaluating potential adjustments at the end of the audit. The auditor might expect that the problems that are suggested by the confirmations of receivables may be offset by other facts discovered in the course of the audit and that no adjustment may be necessary in spite of UEL exceeding TEL for a single account.

Figure 16–11   Using Judgmental Samples in Auditing

Panel A: Assurance Factors for Judgmental Sampling*

Desired degree of audit assurance from the test sample	Little or no error expected in the account	Some error expected in the account
Substantial	3.0	6.0
Moderate	2.3	4.0
Little	1.5	3.0

Panel B: Calculation of Most Likely Error for a Judgmental Sample

Total Accounts Receivable (from Figure 16–8)	$600,000
Total Accounts Receivable confirmed	150,000
Total known misstatement (from Figure 16–9)	1,800

Average sample misstatement:

$$\frac{\text{Total known misstatement}}{\text{Total accounts confirmed}} = \frac{1,800}{150,000} = 0.012\ (1.2\%)$$

Most likely error in entire population:
$$= \text{Average Sample Misstatement} \times \text{Book Value}$$
$$= 1.2\% \times \$600,000$$
$$= \$7,200$$

* American Institute of Certified Public Accountants, *Audit Sampling—An AICPA Audit Guide* (New York: AICPA., 2001).

© 2001 by AICPA, reproduced with permission.

where the *assurance factor* is selected from the possible combinations of expected error and the degree of desired assurance depicted in Panel A of Figure 16–11. The appropriate assurance factor must be judgmentally selected by the auditor based on his or her experience and the factors mentioned above. Assuming the auditor believed there was some risk of error and wanted moderate assurance about the account, the judgmental sample size for our previous example would be 100 items ($600,000 × 4.0/$24,000).

Auditors may calculate a sample size using a statistical approach but then decide to evaluate sample results employing non-statistical or judgmental means. This situation will occur when the auditor employs a judgmental or haphazard sample selection method to select the items to be tested. Although the sample is not selected randomly, the discovered errors must be projected to the entire population. Panel B of Figure 16–11 illustrates one way to project the $1,800 of errors detected by the confirmation procedures. Because the confirmed portion of the population has a 1.2 percent error rate, it is reasonable to project this error rate to the remainder of the population. The most likely error found in the population is $7,200 (1.2% × $600,000).

Another way to project the error from a judgmental sample is to compute the average error per confirmed account and then to apply that to accounts that have not been confirmed. In our example, the average error per account confirmed is $15.12 ($1,800 in known errors divided by 119 confirmed accounts). Projecting the error to the entire account yields a most likely error of $8,240 (545 total accounts × $15.12 per account). Although either of these estimates is reasonable, neither takes into account sampling risk. Consequently, the auditor must rely on professional judgment to determine if the estimated error is close enough to TEL to warrant additional substantive procedures.

COMMON ERRORS IN SAMPLING

Sampling as a source of audit evidence presents the auditor with a number of difficult judgments, and there are many ways in which an auditor can bias the choice of sample size, sample selection, or interpretation of test results. Some of the more common pitfalls in acquiring and interpreting sample evidence include

- **Sample size is too small given reliance placed on the sample results:** Average sample sizes for substantive audit procedures such as accounts receivable confirmations and inventory test counts have been steadily declining in recent years while clients have become larger and more complex.[16] The quest for efficiency in audit testing may have caused a drop in the effectiveness of sample-based testing as a result of this shrinkage.
- **Misuse of decision aids:** Many firms use decision aids to guide auditors in the determination of sample sizes for substantive testing. However, researchers have found that auditors who are given a decision aid may manipulate the input parameters in order to get the sample size they want.[17]
- **Influence of irrelevant transaction attributes:** Research has shown that auditors reveal very subtle biases when called upon to draw a haphazard sample. Irrelevant characteristics of a transaction, such as the size, color, and location of documents, often influence the selection of items to be included in a sample. For example, the selection of accounts payable documents to be tested can be influenced by the size of the voucher package supporting a payment or the compactness of the storage space, which affects the ease with which the auditor can remove a set of documents from a cabinet. Furthermore, the physical placement of documents can influence the selection process because documents in the back of a file drawer or in a low-level file drawer are less likely to be selected than documents that are front and center in a waist-level file drawer.[18]
- **Use of statistical evaluation on the results from a judgmental sample:** Another common error is for an auditor to evaluate the results from a judgmental sample by employing statistical methods. This approach is inappropriate and has the appearance of rigor while lacking an adequate foundation on which to justify the projection.
- **Failure to project known errors to the population:** Failure to project known errors or an inappropriate projection method are also common problems encountered in interpreting sample evidence.[19]

16 See "A Longitudinal Field Investigation of Auditor Risk Assessments and Sample Size Decisions," by R. J. Elder and R. D. Allen, (*The Accounting Review.* 78(4): 983–1002).

17 See "An Experimental Assessment of Recent Professional Developments in Nonstatistical Audit Sampling Guidance, " by W. F. Messier, Jr., S. J. Kachelmeier, and K. L. Jensen, *Auditing: A Journal of Practice & Theory.* 20(1): 81–96.

18 See "Sampling Practices of Auditors in Public Accounting, Industry and Government," by T. W. Hall, J. E. Hunton, and B. J. Pierce, *Accounting Horizons.* 16(2): 125–136.

19 Researchers have found that audit seniors with more than three years of experience tend to underestimate the most likely error in the population when evaluating sample results as well as under-adjusting for the added risk that comes with any sample. See "Error Projection and Uncertainty in Evaluation of Aggregate Error," by D. Burgstahler, S. Glover, and J. Jiambalvo, *Auditing: A Journal of Practice & Theory.* 19(1): 79–100.

Example

> In the fall of 2004, the Public Company Accounting Oversight Board (PCAOB) reported on its initial review of Big 4 audit clients, including consideration of audit sampling. The PCAOB made the following observation about one audit it examined: "In one instance, the engagement team used non-statistical audit sampling in testing the valuation of the materials inventory balance. The engagement team did not, however, project a known misstatement to the untested portion of the materials inventory balance. Such projection is necessary to evaluate whether the aggregate misstatement, which is the known misstatement plus the projected misstatement, exceeded the {tolerable error} . . . In response to this comment, the engagement team projected the known misstatement to the untested portion of the materials inventory balance and determined that the aggregate misstatement exceeded the {tolerable error}."

- **Improper omission of isolated or unique errors from a projection:** Another strategy that auditors use when evaluating individual sample errors is to show that the error is isolated to a "well defined" subpopulation so as to limit the auditor's additional testing to that subpopulation, and to justify not projecting the error to the population as a whole.[20]

SUMMARY AND CONCLUSION

Auditors can rarely examine every risk, event, or transaction that can affect the financial statements. Consequently, auditors are forced to rely on evidence obtained from sample-based audit procedures, be they tests of process controls, substantive tests of transactions, or tests of account details. In order to assure that the sampling evidence is properly obtained and evaluated, auditors have developed preferred methods for performing audit procedures that generate sample-based evidence. There are a number of techniques for selecting transactions from a large population of transactions or accounts. Random sampling or systematic sampling with a random start point is preferable in most situations, but auditors can also use random block sampling, haphazard sampling, or judgmental sampling. Different approaches are used for determining the proper sample size and evaluating the results of tests of process controls and individual transactions (attribute sampling) and tests of account balance details (dollar unit sampling). In general, the use of attribute sampling and dollar unit sampling is preferable to the use of judgmental methods when the goal is to quantify the sampling risk of an audit procedure.

BIBLIOGRAPHY OF RELATED PROFESSIONAL LITERATURE

Research

Burgstahler, D., S. Glover, and J. Jiambalvo. 2000. Error Projection and Uncertainty In Evaluation of Aggregrate Error. *Auditing: A Journal of Practice & Theory.* 19(1): 79–100.

Cleary, R. and J. C. Thibodeau. 2005. Applying Digital Analysis Using Benford's Law to Detect Fraud: The Dangers of Type I Errors. *Auditing: A Journal of Practice & Theory.* 24(1): 77–81.

---

20 See "The Effect of Containment Information and Error Frequency on Projection of Sample Errors to Audit Populations," by R. B. Dusenbury, J. L. Reimers, and S. W. Wheeler, *The Accounting Review.* 69(1): 257–264.

Dusenbury, R. B., J. L. Reimers, and S. W. Wheeler. 1994. The Effect of Containment Information and Error Frequency on Projection of Sample Errors to Audit Populations. *The Accounting Review.* 69(1): 257–264.

Elder, R. J. and R. D. Allen. 2003. A Longitudinal Field Investigation of Auditor Risk Assessments and Sample Size Decisions. *The Accounting Review.* 78(4): 983–1002.

Gillett, P. R. and R. P. Srivastava. 2000. Attribute Sampling: A Belief Function Approach to Statistical Audit Evidence. *Auditing: A Journal of Practice & Theory.* 19(1): 145–156.

Hall, T. W., T. L. Herron, B. J. Pierce, and T. J. Witt. 2001. The Effectiveness of Increasing Sample Size to Mitigate The Influence Of Population Characteristics in Haphazard Sampling. *Auditing: A Journal of Practice & Theory.* 20(1): 169–186.

Hall, T. W., J. E. Hunton, and B. J. Pierce. 2002. Sampling Practices of Auditors in Public Accounting, Industry and Government. *Accounting Horizons.* 16(2): 125–136.

Messier, Jr, W. F., S. J. Kachelmeier, and K. L. Jensen. 2001. An Experimental Assessment of Recent Professional Developments in Nonstatistical Audit Sampling Guidance. *Auditing: A Journal of Practice & Theory.* 20(1): 81–96.

Professional Reports and Guidance

American Institute of Certified Public Accountants. 2001. *Audit Sampling: An AICPA Audit Guide.* New York: AICPA.

Guy, D. M., D. R. Carmichael, and O. R. Whittington. 2001. *Audit Sampling: An Introduction,* 5th ed. New York: Wiley.

Auditing Standards

AICPA *Statements on Auditing Standard (SAS)* No. 39, "Audit Sampling."

AICPA *Statements on Auditing Standard (SAS)* No. 111, "Amendment to Statement on Auditing Standards No. 39, Audit Sampling."

IAASB *International Standards on Auditing (ISA)* No. 530, "Audit Sampling and Other Means of Testing."

QUESTIONS

1. Compare and contrast statistical and non-statistical (judgmental) sampling. Include in your discussion conditions that might make one approach to sampling more desirable than the other.

2. The chapter discussed three issues to consider when obtaining evidence using a sample-based audit procedure:
   a.   The number of transactions or items to examine
   b.   The actual transactions or items to examine
   c.   Interpreting the results of the sample
   Discuss the how the presence of a misstatement couuld go undetected should any of the three issues fail to be considered appropriately.

3. For each of the five sampling techniques commonly used by auditors, discuss an audit test using the sampling technique that should enable to auditor to conduct an effective and efficient audit test.
   • Random sampling
   • Systematic sampling
   • Block sampling
   • Haphazard sampling
   • Judgmental sampling

4. Suppose that an auditor chooses to use a random sampling technique to test additions to fixed assets for the fiscal year for manufacturing company. Walk through the key steps the auditor should consider to make sure that the random sample audited is representative of the population of fixed asset additions for the year.

5. Suppose that an auditor is interested in stratifying a sample of accounts receivable customers and then using a judgmental sampling approach. Suggest a strategy for stratifying the sample of accounts receivable so that the judgmental sampling approach will result in an effective means for testing assertions for the account.

6. Consider the formula for selecting a sample size when performing attribute sampling:

$$n = R/P$$

where: n = sample size
   R = Risk factor based on ARO and the expected number of errors
   P = TDR – EDR

Explain why this formula should be effective for determing a sufficient sample size to enable conclusions to be drawn based on the results. As part of your discussion, consider the roles of ARO, TDR, and EDR.

7. Consider the example provided in the chapter for selecting a sample for dollar unit sampling application, where sample size is computed as

$$n = \frac{BV * R * ETF}{(TEL - EEL)}$$

Where:

Book Value (BV) of accounts receivable	$600,000
Number of customers	545 individual accounts
Tolerable Error Level (TEL)	$24,000 (4%)
Expected Error Level (EEL)	$ 0
Expected Tainting Factor (ETF)	100%
Acceptable risk of incorrect acceptance (ARIA)	5%

and:

$$n = (BV*R*ETF)/(TEL - EEL) = (\$600,000 \times 4.75 \times 1.00)/(\$24,000 - \$0) = 119$$

Explain the rationale for why 119 "sample units" should be sufficient for the auditor to draw statistical conclusions about accounts receivable based on the results of the test(s) performed. As part of your discussion, consider the roles of TEL, EEL, ETF, and ARIA.

8. Compare and contrast the implications of deviations found when testing process controls and misstatements found when performing substantive tests. Include in your discussion the rationale behind the implications of finding sample deviation rates and sample misstatements.

9. Consider the following findings from the test of accounts receivable using DUS:

An auditor determines that the most likely error based on a sample is 4 percent of the total accounts receivable balance. By projecting the 4 percent error rate on the entire population, the UEL is $3 million. However, TEL for accounts receivable is $3.1 million. The auditor requires the client to adjust the accounts receivable balance.
Even though UEL < TEL, explain why the auditor made a prudent decision in requiring the client to adjust this balance.

10. For each of the common errors in sampling provided below, describe steps that the auditor can take to avoid the errors whenever possible.
   • Sample size is too small given reliance placed on the sample results
   • Misuse of decision aids
   • Influence of irrelevant transaction attributes
   • Failure to project known errors to the population

- Use of statistical evaluation on the results from a judgmental sample
- Improper omission of isolated or unique errors from a projection

PROBLEMS

1. Sampling risk is the probability that a misstatement exists in the population but is not selected in an auditor's sample. Non-sampling risk is the probability that a misstatement exists in an auditor's sample, but the auditor fails to identify it. Do you believe that either of these scenarios can be defensible against claims of auditor negligence? If so, why? How can auditors protect themselves against both of these risks?

2. You have been assigned to audit the accounts payable of Slamtastic, a small recording company specializing in alternative music. Following is a portion of their accounts payable journal for the month of December:

Item	Purchase Order Number	Date	Transaction Total	Cumulative Total
1	04142	12-08	$1,447.85	$125,777.55
2	04143	12-08	354.67	126,132.22
3	04144	12-08	64.28	126,196.50
4	04145	12-09	6,500.00	132,696.50
5	04146	12-09	12,428.99	145,125.49
6	04147	12-09	552.81	145,678.30
7	04148	12-09	8,988.46	154,666.76
8	04149	12-10	580.03	155,246.79
9	04150	12-10	6,431.82	161,678.61
10	04151	12-10	311.00	161,989.61
11	04152	12-13	9,597.82	171,587.43
12	04153	12-13	51.31	171,638.74
13	04154	12-13	4,720.90	176,359.64
14*	04155	12-13	2,847.63	179,207.27
15	04156	12-14	8,992.22	188,199.49
16	04157	12-14	59.34	188,258.83
17	04158	12-14	7,571.61	195,830.44
18	04159	12-14	98,523.00	294,353.44
19*	04160	12-15	689.79	295,043.23
20	04161	12-15	99.60	295,142.83
21	04162	12-15	4,465.01	299,607.84
22	04163	12-15	8,836.70	308,444.54
23	04164	12-15	722.30	309,166.84

* Check made to a related party.

Generate a sample of eight transactions under the following sampling methods using the random number table from Figure 16–2 when necessary:
   a. Random sampling
   b. Systematic sampling
   c. Block sampling
   d. Judgmental sampling
   e. Haphazard sampling

3. Consider the data from the previous problem. For each of the sampling methods named:
   a. Compute the total amount of the transactions sampled and the proportion of the cumulative total the sample represents.
   b. Discuss the advantages and risks of each sampling method assuming that it would be applied to the entire accounts payable ledger.

    c.   Suggest and defend an optimal combination of methods for the audit sample in this case.

4. Suppose you are the audit manager on the audit of a large computer peripherals Internet business and you are attempting to test the controls of its processes. Members of the audit staff have brought you samples of the following items:

    a.   Credit approvals from a file cabinet drawer in the credit manager's office sampled haphazardly

    b.   Remittance advices and deposit slips filed by date sampled randomly

    c.   Purchase orders filed by vendor number in an electronic medium, such as a computer database, sampled haphazardly

    d.   A report on employees' timecard maintenance for a shift change (chosen haphazardly) including observations of their clocking-in and clocking-out

    e.   Invoices filed by customer number sampled randomly

    f.   Sales orders filed by an internally generated code sampled in blocks

    g.   Physical examinations of inventory sampled haphazardly

    h.   Batch headers from the automated payables posting area sampled judgmentally on the size of the batch

For each of these items: (1) discuss the risks associated with the sample generation method (including the potential biases associated with a haphazard sample) and (2) suggest and discuss the details of a sampling method that would more accurately reflect the characteristics of the underlying population but would still be efficient with respect to the task.

5. In your audit of the accounts payable function of Gorgon Inc., you notice the following:

    a.   Several checks do not bear the appropriate signature for the nature or amount of the payment.

    b.   The prices paid on the invoice do not match those on the purchase order on several transactions.

    c.   Due to delays in computer repairs, a few batches of transactions from the payables journal were improperly posted in the next accounting period.

    d.   Some purchase orders were incorrectly footed.

    e.   Supporting documents for a few payables transactions were missing.

    f.   The initials signifying that the manager of the area compared the check with the supporting documentation were missing from several transactions.

    g.   A few transactions were never posted to the account payable ledger.

    h.   Although Gorgon's policy is to take advantage of purchase discounts if offered, many payments missed the deadlines by just a few days.

For each of the items above, state whether it is a deviation or a misstatement. If it is a deviation, what implications does it have for the audit? Specifically, does the deviation mean that control in this area is weak? If not, what other explanation might be offered?

6. For the sample size calculation described in Figure 16–4, explain the following statements:

    a.   The required sample sizes are larger (all else held equal) the lower the tolerable deviation rate (TDR).

    b.   The required sample sizes are larger the lower the acceptable risk of overreliance (ARO).

    c.   The required sample sizes are larger the higher the expected deviation rate.

    d.   The required sample sizes get larger when the difference between EDR and TDR increases (e.g., an EDR of 1 percent and TDR of 5 percent requires a sample size of 77 [10 percent ARO] whereas an EDR of 2 percent and TDR of 6 percent requires a sample of 88). What does this imply for your estimate of EDR?

    e.   The finite correction factor lowers the necessary sample size.

7. You are auditing the sales order processing department at Joe Henderson & Co., a high-end book publisher. You are attempting to determine whether you can rely on the control procedure that stipulates that all sales invoices will bear the prices from a master price list.

    a.   Find the sample size necessary to determine (with a 5 percent acceptable risk of overreliance) whether you can rely on the prices for a population of 800 sales invoices. Last year's deviation was 0.75 percent, and you are willing to tolerate up to 4 percent of the invoices as incorrectly priced before you conclude that the pricing process is poorly controlled.

b. Now assume that you can make do with a 10 percent acceptable risk of overreliance, but you assume that the company is not assigning prices to the invoices as well as it did last year, so you increase the expected deviation rate to 1.25. What sample size would you draw now?

c. Suppose that you found four deviations in the sample you took based on your calculations from Part a. Can you conclude that the pricing process is reliable? Why or why not?

d. Suppose you had already chosen a random sample of invoices to test another attribute. Could you use those same items to test the pricing attribute? Under what circumstances could you use them? Under what circumstances should you select a new sample?

8. You are conducting dollar unit sampling (DUS) of the accounts receivable balances of an agricultural co-op. You are willing to accept a 5 percent risk of incorrect acceptance, the book value of the account is $2,500,000 and your sample size (based on a tolerable error limit of $125,000, an expected tainting factor of 100 percent and an expected deviation rate of zero) is 59. The results of your sample are as follows:

Error Number	Book Value	Correct Value	Error	Tainting Factor	Explanation
1	$71,330	$60,631	$10,699	15.0%	Incorrect amount entered from a remittance (valuation)
2	18,996	17,096	1,900	10.0%	Cash receipt recorded in wrong period (cutoff)
3	30,081	21,057	9,024	30.0%	Incorrect price used (valuation)
4	3,555	1,422	2,133	60.0%	Posting to wrong subsidiary account (classification)

a. Using the results of your sample and an assumed tainting factor of 100 percent, calculate the upper error limit (UEL). Interpret the result.

b. Repeat Part a but with actual tainting factors. Interpret the difference between that result and the result from Part a.

c. Calculate the UEL (using actual tainting factors) assuming a 10 percent acceptable risk of incorrect acceptance as opposed to a 5 percent level. Why is the result different from your result in Part b?

9. Regarding the facts in problem 8:

a. If your tolerable error limit (TEL) is $250,000 (10 percent of the account balance), are you satisfied that accounts receivable are fairly stated? Why or why not?

b. If your tolerable error limit (TEL) is $175,000 (7 percent of the account balance), are you satisfied that accounts receivable are fairly stated? Why or why not?

c. Assuming that the answer in Part b is no (you cannot accept the hypothesis that the account is fairly stated), discuss the various alternatives you have available to satisfy yourself that the account is not materially misstated.

10. Typically, sampling for tests of transactions occur when the client stores transaction files from which the auditor selects a sample. For some automated systems (e.g., electronic data interchange, point-of-sales systems), clients do not save transaction data beyond a month or so (or the transaction files are stored off site and inconvenient to retrieve). Discuss options available to the auditor for overcoming the lack of available transaction data?

17

The Ethical Auditor: Factors Affecting Auditor Decision Making

INTRODUCTION

> *Auditors are professionals*
> *Professionals are people*
> *People make mistakes*
> *Therefore, auditors make mistakes*

This compound syllogism reflects a core element of the audit process: it is grounded in the judgment of fallible humans who are subject to errors and mistakes. At its core, auditing is a process of making professional judgments. Auditors, as members of a profession, are expected to serve a role in society that is unique and transcends the individual. What an auditor does, and how he or she behaves as a professional, is

732

generally governed by the ethical and legal precepts of the profession. The role, expectations, and governance of a profession may be based on long-standing custom or may emanate from legal requirements imposed by government. In this chapter, we start by discussing the nature of the professional environment in which an auditor fulfills his or her responsibilities. It is the existence of this professional environment that defines the nature of ethical decision making within the context of the audit.

As noted, auditors can make mistakes. Although auditors undergo extensive training and are subject to a high degree of quality control, mistakes can still happen in the audit process. The audit process includes a high degree of formal structure and, increasingly, utilizes sophisticated computer technology to reduce the possibility of auditor error. However, the reality of even the most sophisticated audit technology is that the design and use of any process or system is governed by the judgments of auditors, meaning people. Numerous institutional elements of the audit profession are aimed at improving the judgment and decision making of the auditor. Indeed, one of the principle functions of an audit firm is to implement an audit process that overcomes deficiencies in individual auditor judgment. However, as events of the last few years have shown, audit firms are also subject to forces that undermine the quality of their decisions.

Beyond the audit firm, there are other institutions that motivate auditors toward making ethical decisions. These include professional codes of conduct, independence rules, auditing standards, quality control standards, and inspections of audit work. Furthermore, regulatory and legal structures can be used to punish auditors who fail to live up to the precepts of the profession. Figure 17–1 illustrates the interaction of the various forces constraining auditor judgment and decision making. The purpose of this chapter is to discuss the personal attributes and institutional forces that affect the quality of auditor judgment and decisions.

Figure 17–1   Auditor Judgment: Personal and Institutional Constraints on Auditor Choices

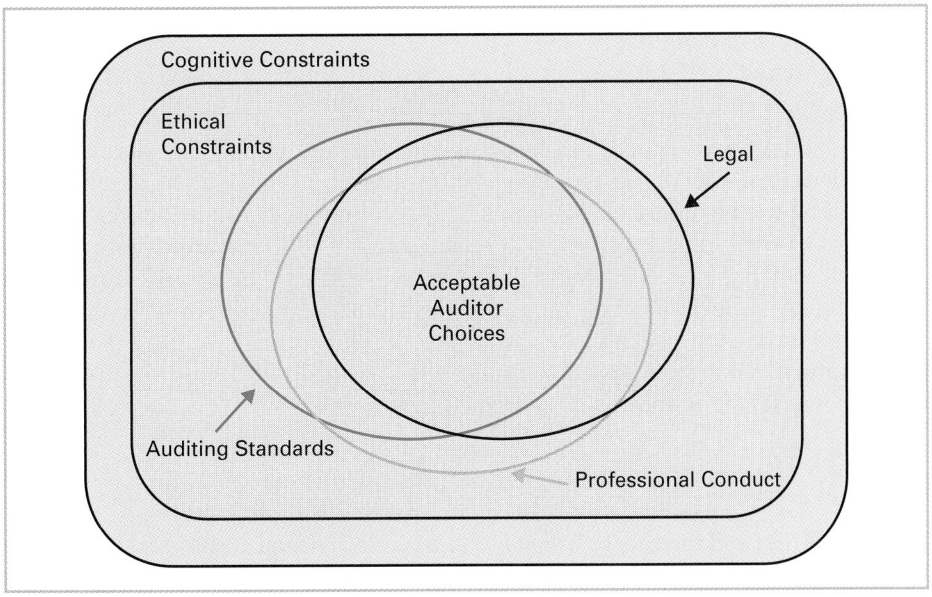

Source: W. R. Knechel, "Behavioral Research in Auditing and Its Impact on Audit Education," Issues in Accounting Education, November 2000, pp. 695–712. Copyright the American Accounting Association, Sarasota, FL. Reprinted by permission. Full text of articles is available online at http://aaahq.org/pubs/electpubs.htm.

AUDITING AS A PROFESSION

Accountants and auditors are members of a *profession*. Although widespread use has diluted the meaning of the word "profession" in recent years, the ideal of a being a member of a profession has some very specific consequences. The International Federation of Accountants *Code of Ethics for Professional Accountants* notes the following attributes that are the hallmark of a profession:

6. A profession is distinguished by certain characteristics including:

- *Mastery of a particular intellectual skill, acquired by training and education;*
- *Adherence by its members to a common code of values and conduct . . . . , including maintaining an outlook which is essentially objective; and*
- *Acceptance of a duty to society as a whole . . . .*

7. Members' duty to their profession and to society may at times seem to conflict with their immediate self interest or their duty of loyalty to their employer.

The latter point highlights that a competent auditor must also be ethical when making the various judgments that comprise an audit because there may be times when audit decisions conflict with the individual's immediate self-interest. At the heart of ethical decision making is consideration of others, and it normally reflects considerations broader than strict self-interest. As we noted in Chapter 1, there are various philosophical frameworks for evaluating ethical behavior:

- **Utilitarianism** involves making decisions that will provide the maximum benefit to a well defined group of people.
- **The Golden Rule** involves making decisions that result in treating others in a manner in which the individual making the decision would like to be treated.
- **Theory of Rights** suggests that the rights of a decision maker and other parties should be equally balanced in making a decision.
- **Theory of Justice** suggests that decisions should treat all stakeholders fairly, impartially, and equitably.
- **Enlightened Self-Interest** involves pursuing long term self-interests and avoiding a short-term focus that might harm others.

Although these views differ in the aspects of ethics they emphasize, all can lead to ethical decisions. One of the key aspects of a profession is to foster a shared ethical code among the members of the profession such that individuals will reach similar decisions when presented with a similar set of facts. Many commentators argue that such a shared ethical framework is impossible in a diverse multicultural and multireligion society that has moved away from a consensus about universal rights and wrongs to a relativist approach for judging what is "right." An opposing argument is that such diversity underscores the need for an agreed upon ethical framework among those belonging to a profession.

AUDITING AS AN ETHICAL JUDGMENT PROCESS

Auditing is first and foremost a *judgment process*. Individual auditors must exercise judgment throughout the audit process, often aided by extensive audit tools and techniques. Some examples of important judgments in the audit process include

- Evaluating a prospective client or deciding to retain an existing client
- Establishing materiality

- Assessing various types of risk
- Allocating audit effort between tests of controls and substantive testing
- Evaluating the effectiveness of controls
- Evaluating fluctuations in performance indicators
- Selecting audit procedures
- Evaluating the competence of evidence

ETHICS AND JUDGMENT

A common thread that runs through many of the judgments made by auditors is the acquisition and evaluation of evidence. Much of the activity of an audit focuses on deciding what evidence to obtain, acquiring the evidence, and evaluating the evidence. Auditors may fail to collect appropriate evidence or misinterpret evidence because of a breakdown in judgment. This can occur by mistake and may be due to an auditor's cognitive limitations. However, if the auditor makes good decisions about obtaining and interpreting audit evidence, what the auditor does with the evidence enters the realm of ethical reasoning. If an auditor chooses to ignore evidence of problems within a client, the auditor is breaching precepts of ethical conduct.

Auditor judgments become ethical in nature when they result in a conflict between the auditor's own self-interest and the auditor's duty to society as a whole. Consider the following situation: an auditor collects compelling evidence that suggests he or she failed to identify a material misstatement in the previous year's financial statements. This oversight may arise from overlooking or misinterpreting evidence due to an auditor's individual cognitive limitations. Now that the auditor is aware of the problem, the auditor's choice of action creates a potential ethical dilemma. Management might point out that revelation of the problem at this time would lead to dismissal of the audit firm, hurt the auditor's career, and might trigger lawsuits against the audit firm. Furthermore, management may offer to correct this misstatement in the future if the auditor keeps quiet about the problem. Because no one knows about the problem, the auditor can easily delete the information from the file without his or her colleagues at the audit firm detecting it. What should the auditor do?

As this example indicates, what starts as a typical audit decision involving a series of professional judgments about collecting and interpreting audit evidence can turn into an ethical quandary for the auditor. The "right" action for the auditor to take may be readily apparent, but the auditor's choice of action could be influenced by the conflict between the auditor's short-term self-interest and his or her duty to society.

Example

In the case of Arthur Andersen and Enron, evidence obtained through e-mails sent among team members suggests that certain personnel at Andersen believed that the firm should resign from the Enron engagement because of discomfort with accounting policies related to off-balance-sheet special purpose entities (SPEs). However, others in the firm pointed to the $50 million in annual fees being earned from contracts with Enron, and the potential for the firm to earn $100 million in annual fees, as justification for retaining the high-risk client.

PROFESSIONAL AUDIT JUDGMENT AND ETHICAL DECISION MAKING

Decision making is a process, whether applied by an auditor to a professional problem or applied by an individual to a personal choice. What all decisions have in common is the need to make a selection from a set of alternatives in order to achieve some desired result. Decisions come in many shapes and forms: "What car should I buy?", "What should I eat for dinner?", and "What audit opinion should I issue?" are all examples of decision problems. *Judgment* is the process by which the individual thinks about the relevant aspects of the decision problem. Errors in judgment often reveal themselves as erroneous decisions. To the extent that judgment errors can be understood and minimized, decision making can be improved.

Deliberate decisions follow a sequential process whether the decision context is an audit or purchase of a new car. New alternatives may become available or decision criteria may change as more information becomes available, and it is common to revise judgments several times before making final decisions in an audit. An individual's decision process for deciding among multiple alternatives broadly follows six steps:

1. Define the decision problem: In an audit, the essential decision is whether financial statements are fairly presented. However, there are a multitude of decisions made during the execution of the audit, the cumulative effect of which will be reflected in the final opinion about the financial statements. Decisions concerning materiality, risk, and evidence are all important to the final opinion and are subject to errors in judgment.

2. Identify the evaluation criteria: For a financial statement audit, the evaluation criteria are embodied in GAAP and GAAS. Other decisions may be made based on assessments of materiality, risk, and the competence of evidence. Implicit in the choice of evaluation criteria is the auditor's belief that if one applies these criteria carefully, one will arrive at an ethical judgment.

3. Weigh the relevant criteria: Not all criteria are equally important to the decision maker. Reducing audit risk may be more important than obtaining evidence quickly, suggesting that a decision to obtain additional evidence may be more affected by the level of the achieved audit risk than by audit deadlines. Similarly, due to materiality concerns, certain aspects of GAAP may be more important than others. These judgments have an implicit ethical dimension in that there is a trade-off between the auditor's self-interest (i.e. performing the audit engagement faster, keeping client management happy by not asking difficult questions) and his or her duty of care to the public.

4. Generate alternatives: In the audit process, the alternatives for most decisions are well understood by accountants. At the highest level, the alternatives reflect the different types of audit reports that could be issued, each of which is used under fairly clear conditions. However, a decision to issue a report other than an unqualified opinion is bound to result in conflict with client management, and a conflict between the auditor's short-run self-interest and his or her duty to society.

5. Rate the alternatives: Once the alternatives are identified, the decision maker must rate each of them using the defined criteria. For example, some procedures may provide more competent evidence but are costly to perform. Other procedures may be time-sensitive (e.g., confirmations of receivables). These decisions implicitly include an ethical dimension in the trade-off of costs and auditor effort.

6. Select the "best" alternative: The selection of the best alternative follows from weighing the alternatives. In an audit, the auditor selects the best mix of evidence to achieve the desired level of audit risk. Tests of controls that mitigate risk can be an efficient source of evidence about a process; account confirmations may be used because they are considered a competent source of evidence; or a qualified opinion may be issued because the client has failed to comply with GAAP. In the end, the auditor decides whether to base decisions on self-interest or professional duty.

In complex environments, a decision maker may not have sufficient information available to choose among alternatives or may lack experience with the decision context. In such cases, the decision maker may search for the first viable solution that is consistent with prior experience, adjusting for obvious differences in the context. For example, an auditor who has a great deal of experience in the retail industry may conclude that lower-than-expected sales during the holiday shopping season are due to a slowdown in the economy. To determine if this explanation is reasonable, the auditor will consider general economic conditions and experiences from past years. The auditor will probably not generate a comprehensive list of alternative explanations but will rely on how well available evidence confirms the auditor's understanding of the client and the conditions surrounding the decision context.

Figure 17–2 illustrates two decisions in the audit process: selection of an audit procedure and issuance of the audit opinion. Both require extensive professional judgment. Failures in judgment, especially if the auditor resolves judgment issues in ways that are in his or her short-term self-interest, can lead to incorrect decisions, often with a negative impact on the auditor, the client, and parties relying on the financial statements. If judgment failures are widespread in the profession, they may cause a loss of confidence among users of financial information. If that happens, auditors will be subject to a backlash from the public. In the extreme, the value of auditing as a professional service may be undermined, essentially destroying the ability of auditors to consider themselves as members of a profession.

THREATS TO THE QUALITY OF INDIVIDUAL AUDITOR JUDGMENT

Detection risk arises in an engagement because auditors can make mistakes during the collection and evaluation of evidence that allow material misstatements to go undetected. Some misstatements may be overlooked due to sampling risk, such as not including a misstated transaction in the sample of items to be examined. However, a more significant component of detection risk is non-sampling risk, which may arise due to

- Failure to select the appropriate audit procedures
- Failure to properly perform the selected audit procedures
- Failure to recognize that a transaction being tested is misstated
- Failure to act on a detected misstatement

Any of the above errors can be due to errors in judgment, that is, to unintentional breakdowns in auditor judgment. However, some of the errors could also occur as the result of ethical lapses on the part of the auditor. For example, failure to properly perform an audit procedure (or to not perform it at all) may be a willful choice

Figure 17–2   Audit Judgment and Decision Making: Two Examples

Step	Audit Evidence Decision	Audit Opinion Decision
Define the choice context	What type and quantity of substantive evidence should an auditor obtain to verify the valuation assertion for accounts receivable?	What form of audit report should an auditor issue after completing the acquisition and evaluation of evidence?
Identify the evaluation criteria	(1) Time and effort to obtain evidence (2) Relevance of evidence (3) Availability of evidence (4) Level of sampling risk (5) Ease of interpretation of evidence (6) Quality of client internal control	(1) Compliance with GAAP (2) Materiality (3) Risk of undetected misstatements (4) Risk of going concern problems (5) Potential costs of incorrect opinion (6) Duty to society to identify and correct misstatements
Weight the criteria	An auditor may consider criteria (1) to be the most important consideration, with (2) a close second, but all six can be relevant to the auditor's decision. Criteria (5) may depend on the experience of the audit personnel. Criteria (4) will depend on whether a sampling approach is being used. Criteria (6) will affect the reliability of internally generated evidence.	An auditor may consider criteria (5) and (6) to be the most important consideration but all six have relevance to the auditor's decision. Criteria (1) and (2) are always important. The importance of criterias (3) and (4) will depend on whether there is any evidence to indicate that those problems may exist.
Generate alternatives	• Send confirmations (positive or negative) • Vouch sales and receipt transactions • Perform analytical procedures	• Standard unqualified opinion • Modified unqualified opinion • Qualified opinion • Disclaimer
Rate each alternative	• Confirmations: Costly to obtain, of minimal value for valuation, time sensitive (done after year end), good when controls are poor, subject to sampling risk. • Vouching: Moderately easy to perform, not time sensitive (can be performed any time), acceptable when controls are poor, some sampling risk. • Analytical procedures: Easy to perform, good when controls are good, no sampling risk, may be difficult to interpret and require other tests as follow-up, most useful after year end but can be used anytime.	• The choice of audit opinion depends on the conditions described in Chapter 15. Other than the standard unqualified opinion, each of the other alternatives will normally involve an ethical balancing of management's desires and the auditor's responsibility to foster accurate financial reporting.

Figure 17–2   *(continued)*

Step	Audit Evidence Decision	Audit Opinion Decision
Select an alternative	The auditor may choose to send some positive confirmations, test a few transactions, and perform extensive analytical procedures if detection risk is moderate to high.	The auditor may select the standard unqualified opinion because there is no evidence of misstatement or going concern problems, GAAP is correctly applied, and the auditor has enough evidence to alleviate his or her worry about reaching the wrong conclusion.

by the auditor due to time pressure. Similarly, the auditor might be pressured by management to overlook known errors in the financial statements.

Concerns about Bias in Individual Professional Judgment

Although auditors are generally considered to be rational decision makers, extensive psychological research has shown that people make common mistakes when processing information and analyzing a specific decision. Some of the reasons why even well-intentioned auditors may make mistakes in professional judgment include the following:

1. Auditors may not be able to define their decision problem clearly: The purpose of the audit is relatively clear-cut—to issue an opinion on the financial statements—but not all decisions are easy to specify so rigorously. How does the auditor know when enough evidence has been obtained?
2. Auditors may not be able to consider all relevant evidence and alternatives: evidence needed for the audit may not always be available to the auditor. Information may be difficult to evaluate because it is subjective or the auditor may not have the perceptive ability to make an accurate evaluation of the evidence. Auditors may also become fatigued or run out of time in the course of the audit.
3. Auditors may act in a biased manner: Auditors are expected to be objective in gathering and evaluating evidence. Unfortunately, auditors, like others, often jump to conclusions based on intuition and presumptions rather than sound reasoning.
4. Auditors may not select the "best" alternative: an auditor should make decisions that are consistent with available evidence. However, auditors may not be able to identify or recall all reasonable alternatives or the related evidence in a given situation.
5. Auditors may fail to understand the dynamic nature of their clients. Organizations are constantly changing as a result of external forces, new strategies, employee turnover, new technologies, and so on. Too often, auditors expect performance to be consistent over time in spite of these changes.

All people employ, whether they know it or not, three basic heuristics or ways of simplifying complex information processing tasks. These heuristics, although normally leading to acceptable decisions and judgments, can result in a number of decision biases. As auditors are people, these heuristics may also affect an auditor's professional judgment.

Availability Heuristic: An individual's ability to identify options and evaluate likely outcomes is often affected by his or her own prior experiences. A situation that is similar to something the auditor has previously encountered is likely to influence an auditor's judgment, even if the situations are not really similar. The *availability heuristic* reflects this tendency and can manifest in the audit in a number of ways: Auditors tend to search for similar errors to those encountered in previous audits, use the same audit procedures from one year to the next, and interpret responses to management inquiries in light of previous conversations. Figure 17–3 illustrates specific ways in which the availability heuristic may affect the audit process. In all cases, the essence of this heuristic is that the auditor can think of some outcomes or conditions more easily than others, and this affects the consideration of alternatives in the audit process.

Example

The quality of analytical procedures depends on the auditor's ability to accurately identify the cause of unusual variations in account balances or other data. Researchers have shown that auditor's often have trouble identifying error-related causes, and often focus more heavily on explanations provided by management or explanations that do not suggest errors in the underlying data. Because most fluctuations are due to normal operating conditions and do not reflect errors, the easy availability of non-error explanations provided by management may distract the auditor from more serious underlying causes of a fluctuation.[1]

Representativeness Heuristic: Individuals often use stereotypes for evaluating new situations. Similarities between familiar and unfamiliar situations may cause an individual to judge that an unfamiliar situation is similar to a situation that has been previously encountered, and should be handled in a similar manner. This is akin to reasoning by analogy, where knowledge of one set of facts is used to interpret a different set of facts. However, this approach can lead to judgment errors when differences between the two situations are not noticed by the auditor. The *representativeness heuristic* may lead an auditor to use similar audit programs across multiple clients or to use a fixed formula to establish materiality for all engagements. Figure 17–3 provides a number of illustrations of how representativeness may affect the audit process. The essence of this heuristic is that the auditor places undue weight on similarities across decision contexts and conditions and does not adequately consider the unique characteristics of each audit client.

Example

Research has demonstrated that auditors are sensitive to the reliability of the source of evidence.[2] One study had auditors review workpapers with known errors included in the documentation. The study found that auditors reviewing audit evidence gathered by others on an engagement team tended to be more careful and thorough when they were unfamiliar with the work of the person who initially gathered the evidence. However, this increased care did not lead to the discovery of more errors in the audit work when compared to review of audit evidence prepared by people familiar to the reviewer. This suggests that although the reviewers were sensitive to the source of the audit work, they were not more effective in the audit.[3]

1 Among the first to identify this in auditing was Lisa Koonce in her 1992 article "Explanation and Counter-Explanation during Analytical Review" (*The Accounting Review,* 68(1), pp. 59–76).

2 Although many others have studied this issue, the first article on this topic was "Are Auditors' Judgments Sufficiently Regressive?" by E. J. Joyce and G. C. Biddle (*Journal of Accounting Research,* Autumn 1981, pp. 323–349).

3 See "The Effects of Familiarity with the Preparer and Task Complexity on the Effectiveness of the Audit Review Process" by S. Asare and L. S. McDaniel (*The Accounting Review,* April 1995, pp. 139–160).

Figure 17–3   Examples of Judgment Biases Applied to Auditing

Nature of Bias	Description of Bias	Example: Possible Impact on Auditing
Examples of the Availability Heuristic		
Ease of recall	Experiences that are vivid or recent are easier to remember and may be deemed to occur more frequently than those that are less vivid or recent.	An auditor who experiences a fraud at one client may think fraud is more likely to occur at all clients, even though it is a fairly rare event.
Retrievability	An individual's ability to remember specific facts may cause those facts to be perceived as more likely than those that can't be recalled.	Recalling that a client had a problem with inventory shrinkage last year may cause the auditor to concentrate on that problem and fail to consider other inventory problems that may exist.
Presumed associations	Experiencing certain facts in combination may cause a person to overestimate the likelihood that they will always occur together.	An auditor who has observed in the past that gross margin goes down when unionized employees get a raise may not adequately consider the possibility that gross margin could go down for other reasons.
Examples of the Representativeness Heuristic		
Insensitivity to base rates	Ignoring the relative frequency of a condition occurring in the general population may cause misestimation of the likelihood of that condition occurring in a specific situation.	An auditor may overestimate the risk that a client will go bankrupt because he or she fails to appreciate the relatively low frequency of bankruptcies in the entire economy.
Insensitivity to sample size	People tend to ignore the size of a sample and the fact that larger samples are generally more accurate.	When performing substantive tests of transactions, an auditor may consider a small sample to be more competent than it really is, leading to systematic undersampling of transactions.
Misconceptions of chance	People mistakenly expect that chance will cause conditions to even out over time, that is, people think that a random sequence will always look random.	When examining a series of sales figures, an auditor may expect to see random fluctuations that go up-down-up-down, even though such a pattern is not random.
Regression to mean	Individuals tend to overestimate the likelihood that extreme conditions will repeat rather than return to something more "normal."	A client that has a large increase in sales in one period may be expected to repeat that performance in the future. This could have a negative impact on the evaluation of analytical evidence.

(continued)

Figure 17–3   *(continued)*

Nature of Bias	*Description of Bias*	*Example: Possible Impact on Auditing*
Conjunction fallacy	People may think that two conditions occurring together are more likely than one of the conditions occurring alone.	An auditor may believe that the combined occurrence of management fraud and contingent compensation is more likely than the occurrence of fraud irrespective of compensation arrangements.*

Examples of the Anchoring and Adjustment Heuristic

Insufficient anchor adjustment	Initial information becomes a starting point for a decision and additional information is not adequate to compensate for the effect of the initial anchor.	An auditor uses the prior-year sample size as a starting point for performing substantive tests of transactions and fails to adequately adjust for changes in risk conditions in the current year.
Conjunctive and disjunctive events	Events that occur together are often considered to be more frequent than they actually are, whereas events that happen independently are considered to be less frequent than they are.	In sampling transactions, an auditor may mistakenly believe that the probability of selecting 25 correct transactions in a row is higher than selecting one erroneous transaction out of 25.**
Overconfidence	Most people have unjustified faith in their ability to make accurate estimates.	An auditor may not gather enough evidence in support of an assertion or account because he or she places excessive confidence on the competence of the evidence that is already available.

Examples of Other Biases

Confirmation	An individual tends to search for information that supports his or her opinion and neglect or avoid information to the contrary.	If an auditor believes that the risk of misstatement for an assertion is low, he or she may search only for evidence that supports that perspective and disregard evidence to the contrary.

* In terms of probability, the conjunction fallacy states that the probability of events A and B occurring together is higher than the probability of A occurring (with or without B) or the probability of B occurring (with or without A). In the auditing example, A would be the statement "management has committed a fraud" and B would be the statement "management has contingent compensation." Obviously the probability of "management committing fraud AND management having contingent compensation" cannot be higher than the probability of "management committing fraud," because the latter statement includes all conditions in which contingent compensation is present and not present.

** If the error rate in the population is 5 percent, the probability of selecting 25 error-free transactions is 27.7 percent (0.95^{25}) whereas the probability of selecting one erroneous transaction out of 25 is 36.5 percent ($25 \times 0.95^{24} \times 0.05$).

Figure 17–3   *(continued)*

Nature of Bias	Description of Bias	Example: Possible Impact on Auditing
Examples of Other Biases		
Hindsight ("Curse of Knowledge")	Individuals will assign a higher likelihood to the occurrence of an event after the fact than they would have before the event has occurred.	When evaluating an accounting estimate, the auditor may conclude that a client's estimate is wrong this year because it turned out to be wrong last year, even though the estimate was deemed reasonable at the time.

Anchoring and Adjustment Heuristic: In many decision contexts, an individual approaches a decision with a preconceived notion or prior expectation of the appropriate choice to make. People often use preconceived notions as a starting point when making a decision and slowly adjust their opinion as more information is obtained. However, the strength of an individual's preconceived notions may cause them to not fully appreciate the meaning of new information. The *anchoring and adjustment heuristic* reflects the tendency of an individual to inadequately revise his or her opinion in the face of new information. This tendency can be seen in auditing when an auditor bases decisions about sample size on the prior audit and underestimates the effect of new conditions in the current year (e.g., changes to the accounting system or the competitiveness of the industry). Figure 17–3 provides a number of examples of the anchoring and adjustment heuristic applied to audit judgments. The essence of this heuristic is an auditor's unwillingness to adequately adjust prior decisions in the face of new information.

Example

Auditors typically analyze evidence in the sequence it is received rather than waiting for all evidence to be available and then analyzing the evidence simultaneously. Numerous research studies have demonstrated that auditors are susceptible to a "recency" effect, in which the most recent evidence received has the most impact on an auditor's judgment. In fact, evidence received early in the audit process will not have the same impact on auditor's judgments as the same evidence received late in the process. This finding can have serious implications for the audit because it suggests why two auditors can look at the same set of evidence but reach different conclusions.[4] In a separate line of research, auditors have been observed to inappropriately anchor on the unaudited book value of an account when performing analytical procedures.[5]

Other Biases: There are two other individual judgment biases that are applicable to audit decisions: (1) the confirmation bias and (2) the hindsight bias (also referred to as the "curse of knowledge"). They are defined and illustrated

4 The first article to document this in auditing was "Sequential Belief Revision in Auditing" by R. H. Ashton and A. H. Ashton (*The Accounting Review*, October 1988, pp. 623–641).

5 See "Mitigating the Consequences of Anchoring in Auditor Judgments" by W. R. Kinney Jr. and W. Uecker (*The Accounting Review*, January 1982, pp. 55–69).

in Figure 17–3. The confirmation bias is particularly important to auditors because it implies that auditors may favor evidence that supports a preconceived opinion about the financial statements. This could lead the auditor to disregard evidence that might be important.

CONCERNS ABOUT ETHICAL REASONING IN INDIVIDUAL PROFESSIONAL JUDGMENT

> **Authoritative Guidance & Standards**
> The AICPA *Code of Professional Conduct* and IFAC *Code of Ethics for Professional Accountants* both establish a minimum level of acceptable ethical conduct by professional accountants (e.g. CPAs, CAs CGAs, CMAs and so on).

Ethics is a set of moral values or principles upon which an individual bases decisions about his or her behavior. Because of ethics, an individual will place boundaries on what is acceptable behavior. Elements of ethics include honesty, integrity, fairness, respect for others, loyalty, steadfastness, and personal responsibility. These virtues are universal and most people would acknowledge the desirability of using them as a guide for one's behavior, whether in personal life or business.

Unfortunately, people are often placed in situations where their actions are inconsistent with personal or societal ethical standards.

Why do good people do questionable things? This can occur because one person's ethics may be significantly different from the norms of general society or because the person chooses to disregard ethics and make decisions that are self-centered and selfish. In other situations, competing ethical principles can come into conflict resulting in a trade-off among desirable virtues; for example, does one tattle on a friend who has broken a rule (loyalty versus honesty)?

There are many excuses for unethical behavior in business: "my boss told me to," "it's not my job," "it's company policy," "nobody told me not to do it," and "life is not fair" are some of the excuses one might hear when questionable behavior is revealed. In general, there are at least four reasons why an individual may choose to act in an unethical manner:

1. The "everybody does it" rationalization: In some situations, the fact that many other people are acting in a specific manner, or at least the belief that they are acting that way, is often used to rationalize unethical behavior. In an audit context, the fact that some staff accountants fail to report their total time spent on an audit may be considered justification for others not to report their time accurately.

2. The "legal equals ethical" fallacy: Many difficult personal decisions come down to a person's sense of right and wrong, not an interpretation of formal laws and regulations. In an audit context, the fact that a disclosure complies with the formal requirements of GAAP does not mean that it is adequate or accurate.

3. The "no one will ever know" delusion: Perhaps the strongest motivation for behaving unethically is the belief that no one will ever know, that the truth will not be detected. In an audit context, an auditor may sign off on an audit procedure without doing the work because he or she does not expect that anyone will ever find out.

4. The "slap on the wrist" syndrome: Even if ethical misbehavior may be detected, individuals may feel safe to act in inappropriate ways if the perceived consequences are minimal. If auditors are not punished for ethical lapses (e.g., reduced performance evaluations, slower advancement), they are less likely to consider the ethical dimensions to their decisions.

The forces against ethical behavior can be quite powerful in some situations, and often lead to serious internal conflict within people. Most business relationships are built on trust; when trust is destroyed, so is the business relationship. If this is not obvious, then consider the poor reputations associated with used car dealers. In other words, because trust is a foundation for business, ethical behavior is good for building and maintaining business relationships. This is especially true in a profession such as accounting where the quality of the product is difficult to perceive and the main characteristic that makes professional accountants valuable to their clients is that they are trusted. Nevertheless, in spite of the common sense that supports ethical behavior and decisions, many situations are ethically unclear and individuals may need assistance to maintain an ethical approach to decision making.

Because auditing is a profession, there is also an institutional aspect to ethical conduct. Even a well-intentioned auditor may be susceptible to institutional forces that create a potential tension between individual ethics and organizational actions. Two important and universal forces in auditing compound this potential tension: (1) the contracting arrangement with the client and (2) the reward system of the audit firm.

1. Contracting with the client: The quality of auditor judgment may be influenced by who hires, fires, and compensates the auditor. Management often has a great deal of influence over hiring the auditor, although the arrangement must be ratified by the board of directors. Management may use its contracting power to try to influence the conduct and outcome of an audit, undermining the objectivity and judgment of the auditors, as their personal self-interest may be served by keeping management happy. Recent audit scandals have focused public attention on the relationship between management and the auditor. The Sarbanes-Oxley Act placed the authority of hiring and compensating the auditor with the audit committee for U.S. SEC registrants. Nevertheless, management will continue to influence auditor contracting because the audit committee will look to management for information about the auditor.

2. Firm reward systems: The individual auditor's progression in the audit firm depends on at least two things: (a) perceived technical ability and (b) ability to manage client relationships. Regarding (a), no one wants to be perceived as incompetent, so an auditor may not be forthcoming in revealing an error in the conduct of an audit (especially a prior audit he or she was involved with) for fear of punishment, loss of professional status, or dismissal. Regarding (b), the loss of a significant audit client by an audit partner may be interpreted as a sign that the auditor cannot manage client relationships. Hence, the auditor has a self-interest in not raising contentious issues with client management that may lead to complaints that the auditor is "hard to get along with."

Figure 17–4 illustrates a classic ethical issue encountered by auditors where personal self-interest comes into conflict with the requirements of GAAP and GAAS. The combination of these two forces, in the absence of countervailing forces, could result in the auditor acquiescing to all but the most blatant violations of GAAP. Other common ethical dilemmas that an auditor may encounter include (1) inappropriate pressure to sell non-audit services that could undermine the objectivity of the audit, (2) alignment of interests with management rather than other stakeholders, and (3) violation of audit firm policies in order to placate client management.

Figure 17–4   Example: Ethical Decision Making in an Audit Context

Scenario: Jane Yardley is a senior accountant in the firm of Varnish & Co. Jane is considered a rising star in the firm and has been privately assured that she will be promoted to manager in the next two months and will receive a hefty raise. Based on this knowledge, Jane has recently acquired some of the trappings of a successful professional—a new house, an expensive car, and a membership to a prestigious local country club. Jeff Smalley is a partner in the firm of Varnish & Co. and has been in charge of many of the engagements on which Jane has worked. He has a tremendous respect for Jane's capabilities and has recently requested that she be assigned to his newest client, Brown Brothers Inc.

Brown Brothers is a manufacturer of women's clothing that is sold through moderate-to low-price department stores, mostly under house brands. The company has been audited by another firm for a number of years and always received a standard unqualified opinion. The company has been profitable in the past but last year the company incurred a small loss. Due to changing fashions and an incorrect guess that miniskirts would be big sellers, the company has accumulated a significant amount of inventory in its warehouses. As a result, the company realizes it may have to report a large loss this year.

Jane has been assigned to the audit of inventory for the current year. Upon completion of the planned audit work, Jane concludes that inventory should be written down by as much as 50 percent to reflect lower of cost or market. She has prepared a memo with documentation and included it in the workpapers. Jeff, upon reviewing the inventory work, calls Jane to his office and states that he disagrees with her conclusions and does not think that a write-down is necessary; he tells Jane to replace her memo with a more upbeat memo which concludes that the inventory is properly valued at cost. In support of his position, Jeff points out that the company has always been able to dispose of inventory with minimal loss and that a discounter is likely to purchase the inventory in bulk. Furthermore, the company has indicated that it will change auditors rather than record the write-down.

What should Jane do?

REDUCING ETHICAL DILEMMAS AND JUDGMENT BIASES AMONG PROFESSIONALS

The long list of potential judgment errors and ethical pressures could be disconcerting to auditors if there was no way to offset these limitations on auditor judgment. An audit firm will use its training, support tools, and internal structure to reduce the potential effect ethical dilemmas and judgment biases may have on the audit process. Some of the most common techniques that are used include

- Improving expertise: One of the most common ways to avoid judgment errors is to rely on highly educated and trained professionals. Audit firms and the accounting profession invest a huge amount of money into training audit professionals. The more familiarity an individual has with a decision situation, the more effective the auditor will be. In an audit firm, managers generally have more expertise than seniors, and seniors more expertise than staff.
- Training: Audit firms often use case-based training to improve an auditor's judgment process and to sensitize individual auditors to potential judgment biases and ethical dilemmas they may encounter. Training is an especially important element of instilling the firm's ethical values into the conduct of individual auditors.

- Framing and perspective: Changing the way an auditor looks at a decision problem may help alleviate some judgment biases. Audit firms design and structure the audit process to reduce judgment errors. For example, strategic and process analyses may reveal conditions that suggest weaknesses in the strategy, management, or financial reporting before the auditor looks at the preliminary results. A particular concern for auditors is to not start the audit thinking that the accounts are fairly stated.

- Group decision making and review of individual decisions: Almost all decisions made by auditors in the audit process are made in coordination with other members of the audit team. Group decision making has the benefit of compensating for judgment errors made by individuals. Furthermore, one auditor reviews the work of another in order to identify faulty judgments.

- Justification of decisions: Research suggests that individuals are more conscientious and less susceptible to judgment errors when they are asked to justify decisions. Audit firms and auditing standards require that auditors document their judgments about a client in writing, reducing the risk of judgment errors.

- Use of decision aids: Audit firms also develop and use decision aids that direct the gathering and evaluation of evidence in such a way that common judgment errors are avoided. For example, the use of internal control questionnaires or disclosure checklists helps the auditor to consider all relevant information. Formulas for computing materiality or sample sizes assist in the specification of information to use for a decision as well as the appropriate method for arriving at a conclusion.

- Consultations with other experts: When an auditor encounters complex or difficult issues in an audit, an expert can be brought in to provide guidance on how to handle the situation. Because the expert does not usually have any other links to the client, the auditor can use the outcome of the consultation to resist the demands of the client.

- Internal quality review: Most audit firms have an internal review process whereby specific audit decisions are evaluated with hindsight to see if they meet firm and professional standards. An auditor who knows that key audit judgments will be reviewed later will probably be less willing to succumb to client pressure, especially if such reviews affect personal rewards and advancement in the firm.

- Rewarding ethical conduct: Audit firms can reduce the likelihood of the auditor giving into client pressure by not basing partner earnings solely on his or her current client fees, not creating incentives for audit partners to sell non-audit services, having a culture that recognizes that there can be "good" losses of clients, and by rewarding—not punishing—auditors who report their own mistakes or those of others.

All decision processes are subject to potential judgment errors and erroneous conclusions. No single technique is completely effective at eliminating such problems, but the combined effect of these compensating techniques serves to significantly reduce the possibility that individual auditor judgment biases and ethical lapses will affect the outcome of the audit. Indeed, auditing research has shown when there is an appropriate match between the audit task and a properly trained, properly equipped, and properly supervised auditor, the incidence of judgmental biases and ethical lapses by individual auditors is significantly reduced.

Figure 17–5 illustrates how an ethical dilemma may be addressed given the example in Figure 17–4. Jane would try to settle the situation to the satisfaction of all

Figure 17–5   An Ethical Decision Process

Step	Jane's Ethical Judgment Problem
Define the problem	Jane believes that the company should record the 50 percent write-down but is concerned that her decision will have an adverse effect on her career and the firm.
Identify the evaluation criteria	GAAP, GAAS, Professional Codes of Conduct, Legal responsibilities.
Weigh the criteria	Obviously not being involved in a fraudulent situation would be paramount for Jane hence legal responsibilities and the code of ethical conduct would be important to Jane. Professional technical standards like GAAP and GAAS will heavily influence her judgment. On the other hand, keeping the client and fellow professionals happy is also a concern.
Generate alternatives	(1) Refuse to change or remove her memo (2) Comply with Jeff Smalley's instructions (3) Learn about and follow the firm's policy for resolving differences among members of an engagement team (4) Go to the board of directors and/or audit committee with the story (5) Search for alternative solutions (a compromise) (6) If a public company, consider whether to report problem to relevant regulator (e.g., the SEC) (7) Resign from the firm
Rate each alternative Select a course of action	These alternatives are not mutually exclusive but may be pursued in sequence, with re-evaluation of the situation after each step. Alternative (3) is likely her starting point after ensuring that she has fully understood all that GAAP and GAAS has to say about the issue and considering whether the financial statements would be materially misstated if the adjustment is not made. If she gets nowhere with alternative (3) she can follow alternative (1) and have Jeff overrule her in the audit file. If that occurs then Jane should consider alternative (4) if there is an effective board/audit committee or alternative (6) if it a public company. In all these cases, except where alternative (3) works or Jane is convinced that Jeff is right because of alternative (5), then Jane should consider alternative (7), resign from the firm. Indeed, if the issue is not resolved to her satisfaction, why would Jane want to remain with an unethical firm or at least a firm that condones unethical conduct on behalf of one of its partners to retain a client?

parties as much as possible, but keeping everyone happy may not be possible. Of particular relevance to this situation would be the ability to bring the issue to the entire audit team (group decision making and review), consultations with experts on inventory valuation issues, and an environment that rewards ethical conduct. In addition, putting the issue in writing that will be subject to review at a later date will probably influence the extent to which her supervisor is willing to force the issue. However, it is always possible that Jane will be backed into a corner and will have to choose between what is "right" and what is expedient.

INSTITUTIONAL FORCES THAT REINFORCE ETHICAL AUDITOR JUDGMENT

Beyond the audit firm, there are a number of professional, regulatory, and other institutional forces that provide guidance on acceptable auditor judgment and conduct, and reinforce society's desire for ethical auditor judgment. Specifically, ethical conduct by an auditor is supported through a code of conduct, rules regarding auditor independence, auditing standards, quality control standards, and external inspection of audit engagements.

CODES OF PROFESSIONAL CONDUCT

Auditors throughout the world must follow a code of conduct that defines unacceptable ethical behavior. The International Federation of Accountants (IFAC) requires that all member bodies adopt, except where prohibited by local law, the intent of the provisions of its "Code of Ethics for Professional Accountants." IFAC recognizes that national differences of culture, language, legal, and social systems results in each member body or country developing its own detailed ethical requirements as well as enforcement mechanisms. For example, the U.S. representative to IFAC, the American Institute of CPAs, promulgates the *Code of Professional Conduct* that applies to all members of the AICPA including special provisions for those who are in public practice. The purpose of the AICPA Code is to define the minimum levels of professional responsibility and behavior that are expected of a certified public accountant in the United States.

The AICPA Code consists of three components: (1) Principles, (2) Rules of Conduct, and (3) Interpretations. The *Principles* reflect the guiding philosophy of the profession and provide a framework for the Rules (i.e., if members are striving to meet principles, they are exhibiting the most desired ethical behavior as auditors). The *Rules of Conduct* reflect the enforceable portion of the code and dictate, in broad terms, the types of actions by an accountant that are forbidden or encouraged/ required. *Interpretations* provide guidelines for applying the Rules, but are not intended to limit the scope of the Rules.

The fundamental principles in a code of ethical conduct as defined by IFAC should incorporate rules of professional behavior in the following areas:

- **Integrity:** A professional accountant should be straightforward and honest in performing professional services.
- **Objectivity:** A professional accountant should be fair and should not allow prejudice or bias, conflict of interest, or influence of others to override objectivity.
- **Professional Competence and Due Care:** A professional accountant should perform professional services with due care, competence, and diligence, and maintain professional knowledge and skill at a level required to ensure that a client receives competent, up-to-date, professional service.
- **Confidentiality:** A professional accountant should respect the confidentiality of information acquired during the course of an engagement and should not use or disclose any such information without proper and specific authority or unless there is a legal or professional right or duty to disclose.

- **Professional Behavior:** A professional accountant should act in a manner consistent with the good reputation of the profession and refrain from conduct that might discredit the profession.
- **Technical Standards:** A professional accountant should provide professional services in accordance with the relevant technical and professional standards and should exercise due care and skill. The auditor should also comply with the instructions of the client insofar as they are compatible with the requirements of integrity, objectivity, and independence.

A summary of the AICPA Code of Professional Conduct is presented in Figure 17–6. The Code covers the above topics in a series of general rules, supplemented with detailed interpretations. Rule 101 on independence is the most voluminous and will be discussed in the next section. Other important rules are discussed below.

Integrity and Objectivity (Rule 102): Integrity implies maintaining high moral and ethical standards. Objectivity implies that the auditor will maintain a high level of impartiality when evaluating evidence and reaching a conclusion about the fairness of financial statements. In general, the twin goals of integrity and objectivity imply that an auditor should not knowingly misrepresent information related to the financial statements, should avoid conflicts of interest with the client, and should not subordinate his or her professional judgment to any other party. The essence of professional judgment is developing an honest and objective opinion of the facts in question and taking appropriate action based on those facts. In an audit, that means obtaining adequate evidence on which to base an opinion and reaching an unbiased opinion about the fairness of the financial statements. The question of integrity and objectivity is critical when an auditor accepts an engagement to serve as a client's advocate, such as on a tax matter. Accountants must comply with the rules of conduct in advocacy engagements and must be careful to not risk the loss of credibility by pushing advocacy beyond sound and reasonable professional practice.

Competence (Rule 201): A professional accountant is expected to accept only engagements for which he or she has (or can readily obtain) an adequate degree of competence as evidenced by the exercise of due professional care in providing services, undertaking effective planning and supervision, and using sufficient evidence as a basis for rendering an opinion.

Confidentiality (Rule 301): An independent accountant has a responsibility to maintain client information in utmost confidentiality even after the end of the professional relationship. However, there is no legal right to confidentiality for auditor-client communications as exists in the case of attorney-client privilege under the laws of many countries. Furthermore, confidentiality is not applicable when:

- Disclosure of information is required under technical accounting or ethical standards.
- Information is subject to a legal subpoena or other legally required disclosure.
- Information is needed for a peer or quality review by an authorized body.
- Information is relevant to a legal, regulatory or ethical inquiry.

Professional Behavior: Professional accountants also have responsibilities to the public and to other professionals. These responsibilities fall into the following categories:

- Advertising (Rule 502)
- Form of business practice (Rule 505)

Figure 17-6 Overview of the AICPA Code of Professional Conduct

Rule of Conduct	General Rule	Interpretations*	Impact on Audit Behavior

Rule 101: Independence	A member should be independent in the performance of professional services.	101-1: Conditions impairing independence
		
		101-2: Applicability to former practitioners
		
		101-3: Performance of other services
		
		101-4: Honorary positions with nonprofit organizations
		
		101-5: Loans from clients
		101-6: Impact of litigation
		101-8: Impact of indirect financial interest in a client
		
		101-9: Effect of family relationships
		101-10: Independence from government organizations
		
		101-11: Attestation engagements
		101-12: Cooperative arrangements with clients
		101-13: Extended audit services
		101-14: Alternative practice structures
			• An auditor may not have a direct or material indirect financial interest in a client.
			• An auditor may not serve as trustee of an estate with a financial interest in a client.
			• An auditor cannot serve as a promoter, underwriter, director or employee of the client, nor be a trustee of its pension plan.
			• Non-attest services may impair independence depending on the circumstances (see Figure 17-7 for examples).
			• Loans from client to auditor are not allowed except for car loans, loans collateralized with cash or securities, credit cards up to $5,000, and some preexisting secured loans.
			• Actual or threatened litigation with client impairs independence.
			• Financial interest rules apply to firm personnel as follows:
			  • All partners or shareholders
			  • All managerial personnel in the office conducting the audit
			  • All engagement team personnel
			Family members are bound by the financial interest rules. Furthermore, family members may not hold influential or audit-sensitive positions in the client. Family members include
			  • Spouses and dependent persons
			  • Nondependent children, step-children, siblings, grandparents, parents, in-laws, and spouses

(continued)

* Missing sequence numbers reflect interpretations that have been repealed or deleted.

Figure 17–6 *(continued)*

Rule of Conduct	General Rule	Interpretations	Impact on Audit Behavior
			• A cooperative or business arrangement with a client impairs independence if it is material to the member's firm or the client. • An auditor may perform internal audit activities under some conditions but should not perform ongoing control activities. • Alternative practice structures are allowed (e.g., corporate ownership of a firm performing attest services) but independence rules apply to auditors providing services and their superiors.*
Rule 102: Integrity and Objectivity	Members shall maintain objectivity and integrity, avoid conflicts of interest, and not knowingly misrepresent facts or subordinate own judgment to others.	102-1: Knowing misrepresentations 102-2: Conflicts of interest 102-3: Obligations to an external accountant 102-4: Subordination of judgment 102-5: Applicability of Rule 102 to educators 102-6: Professional services involving client advocacy	• An auditor should not knowingly enter or allow false financial information in documents with which they are associated. • A CPA should avoid the appearance of a conflict of interest but may perform an engagement with a potential conflict as long as objectivity is maintained and consent obtained from client. • Members should exercise care in accepting advocacy engagements that may go beyond the bounds of sound and reasonable professional practice.
Rule 201: General Standards	Members shall comply with general standards of practice.	201-1: Competence	• An auditor should possess adequate professional competence. • An auditor should exercise due care. • An auditor should perform adequate planning and supervision. • An auditor should obtain sufficient evidence on which to base conclusions.

Rule	Description	Interpretations	Notes
Rule 202: Compliance with Standards	Members must comply with standards promulgated by authoritative organizations.	None at this time.	Professional standards include rules promulgated by • FASB • GASB • SEC • Auditing Standards Board • Accounting and Review Services Committee
Rule 203: Accounting Principles	Members should not knowingly provide assurance on statements containing departures from GAAP.	203-1: Departures from GAAP 203-2: Status of FASB and GASB interpretations 203-4: Employee responsibility for GAAP compliance	• Departures from GAAP that are necessary to avoid misleading readers of financial statements should be fully disclosed. • Rules also apply to CPAs not in public practice (e.g., working in a corporate role).
Rule 301: Confidential Client Information	Members must not disclose confidential client information.	301-3: Sales of accounting practice	Exceptions to confidentiality rules include • Information needed for compliance with Rule 202 or 203. • Information requested by subpoena • During AICPA peer review • Information needed for legal or regulatory inquiry
Rule 302: Contingent Fees	Members may not accept contingent fees for an audit, review, compilation, examination of prospective information, or preparation of tax returns.	302-1: Tax matters and contingent fees	• Fees set by a court or public authority after performance of an engagement are allowed.
Rule 501: Acts Discreditable	Members should not commit an act that is discreditable to the profession.	501-1: Retention of client records 501-2: Discrimination or harassment in employment 501-3: Failure to comply with governmental audit standards 501-4: Negligence	Discreditable acts include • Retaining client records after engagement completed • Discriminatory employment practices • Harassment in the work place

(continued)

* An example of an alternative practice structure is when CPAs own a firm but the equipment and employees are owned/controlled by another organization. The fees collected on attest work are paid to the other organization in order to lease equipment and personnel necessary to provide service to clients.

Figure 17-6 *(continued)*

Rule of Conduct	General Rule	Interpretations	Impact on Audit Behavior
		501-5: Failure to follow standards in attest engagements. 501-6: Disclosure of CPA questions or answers 501-7: Failure to file a tax return	• Failure to follow standards during the conduct of an engagement for a governmental organization • Negligently making or facilitating false accounting • Disclosing questions or answers related to the CPA exam • Failing to file a tax return or pay legally due taxes
Rule 502: Advertising and Other Forms of Solicitation	Members shall not obtain clients by using false, deceptive, or misleading advertising.	502-2: False or deceptive advertising 502-5: Referrals	• Auditors should not provide unrealistic fee estimates • Auditors should not imply an ability to influence a court or public official to obtain a desired outcome
Rule 503: Commissions and Referral Fees	Members are not allowed to receive commissions for recommending a product to a client when engaged to perform an audit, review, or compilation or to report on prospective information.	None at this time.	• When not prohibited, commissions must be fully disclosed to the client • Referral fees paid or received shall be disclosed to the client
Rule 505: Form of Organization and Name	Members may practice in any form of organization allowed by state law and consistent with rules of the AICPA. The name of the firm may not be misleading.	505-2: Applicability of rules to members who own a separate business 505-3: Applicability of Rule 505 to alternative practice structures	• A firm may designate itself as a member of the AICPA only if all owners are members of the institute. • CPAs maintaining a separate business must comply with the regulations appropriate for that business. • CPAs who own an alternative practice structure are financially and personally responsible for all attest work in the organization.

- Contingent fees (Rule 302)
- Acceptance of commissions (Rule 503)
- Discreditable acts (Rule 501)

Auditors are allowed to advertise their services but must not do so in a manner that is false, misleading, or deceptive. Practices that are prohibited include creating unjustified expectations about favorable outcomes from an examination, suggesting the ability to unduly influence an authoritative body, or intentionally understating fee estimates. Furthermore, accountants typically offer their services to the public through a partnership or limited liability organization with the idea that partners are personally responsible for the quality of services rendered.

Auditors also have to careful about the types of fee arrangements they enter. In general, auditors are not allowed to accept fees that are contingent on the outcome of the audit (e.g., the auditor can not charge more for an unqualified opinion). In some circumstances, auditors may be offered a fee to recommend a third party's services or products to a client. For example, if a client needs to acquire computer equipment, a manufacturer may be willing to pay the accountant to endorse its products. Similarly, when a client needs professional services that the firm cannot provide, the firm may refer the client to another professional. Normally, auditors are not allowed to accept commissions for recommending another professional or someone's products to the client when the professional accountant is engaged for an audit. In the few non-attest situations where an accountant may be allowed to accept a commission or referral fee, he or she is obligated to fully disclose the commission arrangement to the client.

Auditors are also expected to conduct themselves and their business practices in a respectable manner. For example, auditors cannot retain client records to force the client to pay the auditor. They should avoid discriminatory and harassing behavior in their employment practices. On a professional level, they should do their best to satisfy all legal filing requirements (e.g., for tax returns) and avoid negligent performance of services. Further, they cannot knowingly solicit or distribute CPA exam test questions and answers and must maintain compliance with governmental bodies, commissions, or other regulatory bodies. However, personal failures in behavior are not covered by the Code unless they have an impact on the auditor's professional responsibilities.

Example

A professional who has a substance abuse problem is in an unfortunate situation and probably needs professional help. This is a personal problem, however. It would not be subject to the Code of Conduct unless the substance abuse caused the auditor to violate professional responsibilities. For example, if an auditor steals money from a client or is negligent in conducting an audit, then the auditor would be acting in a manner that is discreditable to the profession. An auditor who is convicted of a felony would probably be investigated for discreditable behavior but may not be found guilty unless the crime has a professional aspect such as committing financial statement fraud. Maurice Stans, a CPA associated with the presidential campaign of Richard Nixon, was involved in the Watergate scandal but not found to have acted discreditably to the profession because his actions were not directly linked to his responsibilities as an accountant.

Rules Regarding Auditor Independence

Auditors are expected to maintain independence from their clients. An auditor must be concerned with both independence in fact and independence in appearance. *Independence in appearance* means that an auditor should do nothing that creates a perception that he or she has a vested interest in the outcome of an audit. The perception that an auditor is not independent, or has a potential conflict of interest in providing audit services of the highest quality, undermines the value of those services even if the auditor is completely unbiased and objective. An auditor who does not possess *independence in fact* may be tempted to bias the execution of the audit, which could manifest itself in poor decisions related to the gathering and evaluation of evidence or the nature and extent of disclosures in the financial statements.

Given the importance of independence, the topic is covered by a large portion of the *Code of Professional Conduct* but is also an area of extensive legal and regulatory attention. The Sarbanes-Oxley Act of 2002 included an extensive set of legal requirements related to independence that are far more restrictive than imposed by the Code. Key independence concerns are summarized in Figure 17–7 considering the various sources of authority governing independence.

Threats to Independence: There are a number of situations that clearly undermine an auditor's independence to conduct an audit. The most obvious examples include having a financial interest in the client (i.e., owning shares or owing the client money), being part of client management (directly or indirectly via making management decisions), having a close family member who is an executive or financial reporting employee, and providing services that are of an advocacy nature (e.g., corporate financial services). Other less obvious conditions that might undermine independence include charging artificially low fees (e.g., "*lowballing*," performing the audit at a below market fee in order to obtain or retain a client), accepting expensive gifts or hospitality, or having a separate business relationship with the client (e.g., marketing joint services together). In general, threats to independence fall into five categories:

- *Self-interest:* An audit firm or individual auditor should not economically benefit from the outcome of the audit (other than a non-contingent fee). Forbidding an auditor to have an ownership interest in a client or to loan money to a client are obvious examples. Other concerns may include borrowing money from a client, investing in a mutual fund that invests in a client's securities, or entering into a partnership with a client to sell products or services.
- *Self-review:* An audit firm or individual auditor should not audit their own work. For example, an auditor should not be engaged to develop and implement a client's accounting system. Nor should the auditor be involved with the valuation of potential acquisitions if those valuations may eventually be included in the financial statements.
- *Advocacy:* An auditor should not be engaged to represent a specific accounting, tax, or legal position of the company that could have an effect on the financial statements. For example, an auditor should not serve as a financial advisor or executive recruiter to a client.
- *Familiarity:* The auditor should not become so close to a client that the ability to be skeptical is undermined. For example, this may occur if the auditor stays on

Figure 17–7   Rules and Standards Regarding Auditor Independence: Combined Analysis of IFAC *Code of Ethics for Professional Accountants* and U.S. SEC and PCAOB Rules

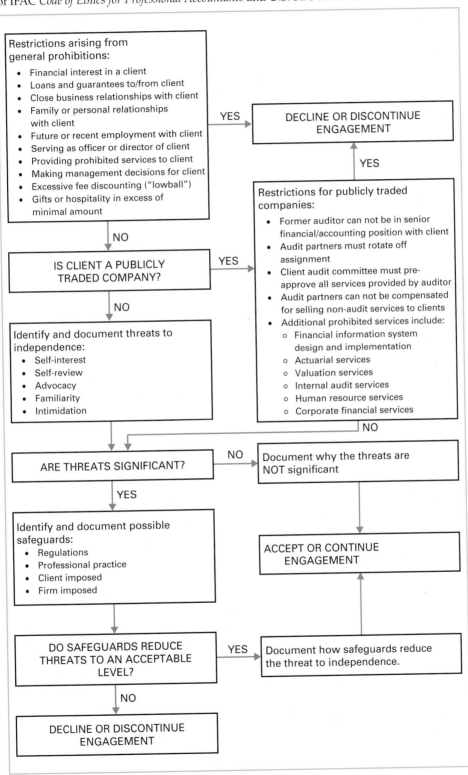

the engagement too long. Similarly, members of the audit firm or engagement team should not have close relatives that work for the client in key accounting, financial, or data processing positions.

- *Intimidation:* An auditor should not feel threatened by the relationship with the client. For example, the auditor may lose objectivity if subject to threats (actual or perceived) by board members, officers, or employees. Such conditions may include a threat to replace the auditor if he or she does not support a specific outcome or position favored by the client. Similarly, existing litigation between a client and an auditor makes them adversaries and undermines independence.

Safeguards against threats: An auditor must be highly alert to possible threats to independence, especially for situations that are not quite as obvious as those that are generally or specifically prohibited by ethical or legal concerns. For example, the audit firm is paid by the client, be it management or the board of directors. This is not a prohibited relationship or service, but it does create a potential for bias due to self-interest or intimidation. Hence, the auditor must consider safeguards against allowing such a relationship to undermine auditor objectivity and skepticism. In practice, there are a number of safeguards to independence:

- Regulation: The establishment of specific rules as described above plus periodic inspection of an auditor's engagements to determine compliance with formal rules.
- Professional practice: Education, training/continuing professional education, and practical experience requirements.
- Client safeguards: Approval of non-audit services by the audit committee and presence of competent client management who are financially literate.
- Firm safeguards: Firm-wide standards, policies, and procedures, such as monitoring of up-to-date databases of firm clients and internal quality review inspections, as well as engagement level policies, such as second partner review and mandatory rotation of audit team personnel.

Service prohibited by the SEC: The SEC independence rules issued in 2000 and the Sarbanes-Oxley Act independence rules from 2002 prohibit a number of other relationships and services for public companies registered with the SEC. Other countries have or are in the process of passing similar, but generally less extensive, rules. Examples of the types of relationships and services that are now prohibited include the following:

- A senior member of an audit team must wait at least a year before going to work for a client in an accounting or financial management position.
- Audit partners must periodically rotate off an engagement, typically after five years, and cannot be reassigned to the engagement for a certain amount of time.
- The audit committee must preapprove all services rendered by auditors that are not part of the financial statement audit.
- Audit partners cannot be directly compensated for selling non-audit services to their audit clients.

EFFECT OF AUDITING STANDARDS ON JUDGMENT

One of the roles of auditing standards is to define the process for conducting an audit. Depending on the country, auditing standards are promulgated by the profession or enacted through legislative or regulatory action (e.g., Germany). Most English-speaking countries have allowed auditors to be self-regulating subject to public oversight. However, events such as Enron and WorldCom led to the passage in the United States of the Sarbanes-Oxley Act of 2002, which established the Public Company Accounting Oversight Board (PCAOB). The PCAOB was given the option by Congress of either directly setting public company auditing standards for all registrants with the SEC or delegating that power while retaining oversight responsibility.

The initial Board decided that it would directly set the auditing standards and as an interim measure adopted existing U.S. GAAS as promulgated by the AICPA's Auditing Standards Board. The PCAOB quickly started to set its own standards (e.g., requiring audit reports on internal control over financial reporting) and required all auditors of U.S.-traded public companies to issue auditor's reports "in accordance with the standards of the PCAOB." The PCAOB required that auditors drop the term "generally accepted auditing standards" from their reports on public companies.

Most other common law countries (e.g., the United Kingdom, New Zealand, and Canada) have not gone as far as the United States, but have enhanced the oversight powers of stock exchange regulators and other oversight bodies that are independent of the profession. Hence, although self-regulation by the profession is still the norm in most English-speaking countries, the United States has joined other countries that codify auditing standards into law. These code law countries (e.g., most members of the European Union) codify the standards such as those from the International Auditing and Assurance Standards Board (IAASB). Even with this level of acceptance and scrutiny by lawmakers, the IAASB has found it necessary to have its parent organization, the International Federation of Accountants (IFAC), establish a public-oversight board that has a majority of members who are not professional accountants or auditors.

AUDIT FIRM QUALITY CONTROL STANDARDS

One response of professional accounting bodies to concerns about audit failure attributable to poor auditor judgment has been the establishment of standards to ensure that independent audits are of high quality. *Quality control standards* address issues related to the management of an accounting practice so as to maximize the quality of the service that a firm delivers to its clients in compliance with all other applicable professional standards. Quality control standards require that an accounting firm have a system of quality control for its accounting, auditing, attest, and related services. Good quality control has the following elements, as described in Figure 17–8:

- Independence
- Human resources
- Acceptance and continuance of clients
- Engagement performance
- Monitoring of performance

Authoritative Guidance & Standards
Standards for quality control are contained within the AICPA *Statements on Quality Control Standards* and the IAASB *International Standards on Quality Control*.

Figure 17–8   Statements on Quality Control Standards: Basic Elements

Elements of Quality Control	Requirements*
Independence	Policies and procedures should be established to provide the firm with reasonable assurance that persons at all organizational levels maintain independence and perform all professional responsibilities with integrity and objectivity.
Human resources	Policies and procedures for assigning personnel to engagements should be established to provide the firm with reasonable assurance that the firm hires personnel with the appropriate skills, that work is performed by persons having the technical training and proficiency required by the circumstances, that personnel receive adequate continuing training, and that the advancement of personnel reflect appropriate qualifications.
Acceptance and continuance of clients	Policies and procedures should be established for deciding whether to accept or continue a client in order to provide reasonable assurance that the firm will not associate with a client whose management lacks integrity, that the required professional services can be competently provided, that the risks of the engagement are appropriately considered, and that a full understanding of the services to be provided is agreed to with the client.
Engagement performance	Policies and procedures should be established to provide reasonable assurance that the work performed meets all appropriate professional standards, including reference to authoritative literature and consultations with experts.
Monitoring	Policies and procedures for inspection should be established to provide the firm with reasonable assurance that the procedures relating to the other elements of quality control are being effectively applied.

* AICPA *Standards on Quality Control*. The *International Standards on Quality Control* also include categories for "leadership," which refers to the responsibility of firm leadership to establish an ethical culture within the firm, and "adherence to ethical requirements," which refers to internal policies and procedures to encourage compliance with appropriate ethical standards.

The emphasis of these standards is on maintaining the reputation of the profession by setting minimum standards of professional behavior. In a sense, quality control standards represent the profession's attempt to self-police the activities of firms and individuals practicing auditing. Although it has not done so yet, many observers believe that the U.S. PCAOB will promulgate quality control standards for auditors of SEC registrants. As an interim measure, it adopted the AICPA's *Statements on Quality Control Standards* which are similar to, but more detailed than, international quality control standards.

Peer Reviews and Practice Inspections

Peer reviews were originally established as a self-regulatory device by the U.S. accounting profession in response to the wave of alleged audit failures occurring in the 1970s. In the 1980s, the SEC required that an auditor of a public company be a member of the AICPA's SEC Practice Section and have a peer review every three years based on the AICPA's *Statements on Quality Control Standards*. This approach created some potential problems for the largest accounting firms because the set of potential reviewers consisted of the other large firms with which they competed. Furthermore, the SEC became concerned that the manner in which peer reviews were conducted was not rigorous, being mostly focused on descriptions of formal processes with relatively little inspection of actual audits.

Example

Just days before it disclosed that it shredded thousands of pages of Enron-related documents, Andersen touted a newly completed peer review of its operations by Deloitte & Touche LLP. That review concluded that Andersen's system of accounting and auditing quality provided reasonable assurance of compliance with professional standards following what Andersen called the most extensive peer review in the firm's history.

Other countries pioneered the concept of practice inspection in the 1980s. Professional accounting bodies would hire practicing auditors as full-time or part-time inspectors to examine the audit engagements of a public accounting firm. Deficiencies could be subject to a variety of sanctions ranging from additional professional training and development to expulsion from membership in the professional body and loss of professional certifications. Like the U.S. peer review system, this worked well for inspections of small and medium-sized audit firms, but the general consensus was that the practice inspectors did not have the resources to carry out meaningful inspections of international firms.

Practice inspections are now required for all firms that audit U.S. SEC registrants. Section 104 of the Sarbanes-Oxley Act requires the PCAOB to conduct a continuing program of inspections of registered public accounting firms. In these inspections, the Board assesses compliance with the Act, the rules of the Board, the rules of the Securities and Exchange Commission, and professional standards, in connection with the firm's performance of audits. The Board issues a report for each firm after completing the inspection. The Act requires annual inspections for firms that provide audit reports for more than 100 SEC registrants and at least triennially for firms with fewer SEC clients. Public versions of the PCAOB reports and the audit firm's responses are posted on the PCAOB web site. The PCAOB also inspects auditing firms located outside the United States that audit U.S. SEC registrants (over 1,200 such registrants existed as of last count by the SEC in 2004) often in cooperation with a local oversight body (e.g. the Canadian Public Accountability Board).

Institutional Forces That Punish Lapses in Auditor Judgment

Regulatory Intervention

A key factor in determining the effectiveness of any regulatory rules or codes of conduct is the extent to which the specific body actively polices these rules. Professional bodies often are reactive, in that they only carry out investigations of members after a complaint is filed. In some countries, like the United States, professional bodies are hesitant to take any actions before related legal cases have been settled. Regulatory agencies vary as well in the extent of their policing. Some regulators are involved in or carry out inspections of audit firms, whereas others do not investigate auditors until there is a reason to do so (e.g., a material restatement of a public company's financial statement or an allegation of fraud from a reputable person).

The existence of regulations and codes of conduct encourage auditors to behave in a professional and ethical manner. However, evaluation and punishment mechanisms are needed to enforce the rules when auditors violate regulations or the code of conduct. Professional sanctions for miscreants may be as simple as a written reprimand, or may involve fines for costs, imposition of educational and professional development requirements, or expulsion as a member from the body of professionals. Regulators can usually impose similar sanctions as well as assess punitive fines, enter the enforcement action onto the public record, have the auditor or audit firm agree not to engage in the behavior again, stop the audit firm from accepting new clients for a period of time, or stop an individual auditor from carrying out all or certain types of audits. In the extreme, regulators can refer a matter to the criminal justice system when fraud is suspected, or can file suit on a civil basis through the court system or a quasi-judicial administrative process.

LEGAL LIABILITY—COMMON LAW

In today's professional environment, an auditor is subject to potential litigation from many sources, including the client and its management, third party users of the audited financial statements, and government agencies. Many estimates place the cost of litigation in the United States at between 10 and 15 percent of audit firm revenues, including insurance, defense costs, and settlement payments. In reality, the largest firms are essentially self-insured and all costs of litigation are born by the partners of the firm. Although insurance is usually available for small and medium audit firms, the rate of increase in insurance costs has been as high as 100 percent per year in recent years.

In many major lawsuits, assessed damages can dwarf the audit fee realized on the engagement, rendering even a single adverse judgment potentially devastating to an accounting firm. Furthermore, the actual damages may be less significant than the threat of *punitive damages*, which are not based on the actual damages incurred by the parties involved and can be assessed against an audit firm when its behavior is considered egregious. The potential assessment of punitive damages makes litigation for professional malpractice a high-stakes game for all parties involved.

Example

Deloitte & Touche carried out the audit of a North Carolina reinsurance firm, Fortress Re. Fortress Re was used by four Japanese insurance companies to manage risks involving aircraft that they insured. The four planes involved in the attacks of September 11, 2001 were all insured by these four Japanese companies. When they went to recover their losses from Fortress, it was found that the owners had pocketed over $400 million in premiums instead of maintaining the reinsurance fund. The Deloitte audit fee never exceeded $100,000, but Deloitte & Touche settled the case out of court for what *The Wall Street Journal* estimated to be $250 million.

In many cases, the auditors are thought of as a deep pocket from which to draw compensation for parties who are damaged by misstated financial reports. This reality is a simple application of economics: by the time a case is litigated, most potential defendants are bereft of financial resources to pay a judgment except the auditor, who is usually "insured" against malpractice losses. Furthermore, because of the concept of *joint and several liability*, the auditor can be held responsible for the entire amount of an adverse judgment even though the he or she may have been only partially responsible for the losses incurred by the plaintiff.[6] Even when an audit firm is successful in defending itself, the costs may be exorbitant.

Example

Ernst & Young in the United Kingdom spent £30 million pounds ($53 million U.S.) plus thousands of hours of the firm's staff time over three years to defend itself against a £2.6 billon claim by its former client, Equitable Life, for audit work carried out in 1998 and 1999. Allegations against Ernst & Young did not surface until 2003 and numerous leaks to news organizations suggested that Equitable's board was open to a settlement offer from the firm to avoid a trial. Ernst & Young proceeded to trial in early 2005, but in September Equitable Life's board withdrew the lawsuit apparently worried that under British law it would be ordered to pay the costs of the firm's defense if the case was decided in Ernst & Young's favor. Equitable Life's former directors are still being sued by the new board, but the claim against the auditors was dropped.

Common Law: The consensus of reasoned judicial decisions and precedents that have been formalized over many years and many cases is referred to as *common law*. This body of law exists as a result of judicial, rather than legislative, actions. Lawsuits against auditors brought under common law typically draw upon either the law of contracts or the law of torts. Common law countries include most English-speaking countries. Consequently, the case law in these countries is similar, although there may be specific points of difference. In the United States, most common law has developed at the state level, whereas in other countries (e.g., the United Kingdom), it developed at the national level.

Under the *law of contracts*, auditors who are engaged to deliver audit services are expected to comply with the terms of the contract established with the client, that is, to deliver an audit that complies with appropriate professional standards. Failure to fulfill the terms of a contract is referred to as a *breach of contract* and may be actionable in court. A client who is unhappy with the performance of the auditor can file suit claiming that the auditor has breached the contract by failing to deliver the appropriate service. In addition, a *third-party beneficiary* who is named in the contract may be able to bring suit against an auditor under contract law. For example, an engagement to audit financial statements in support of a loan application with a specific bank may establish the bank as a third-party beneficiary under contract law. The suing party is referred to as the *plaintiff* and the party being sued (the auditor) is the *defendant*.

Under the *law of torts*, an auditor can be sued by someone who is damaged by the production of an inferior audit. Financial institutions and vendors that lend

---

6 Although less common, some U.S. states allow for *separate and proportional liability*, which has the effect of sharing a judgment among all guilty parties in proportion to their culpability. This is a position that is adopted in other common law countries such as the United Kingdom.

money to a company based on audited financial statements that turn out to be materially misstated may be able to sue the auditor if balances become uncollectible, claiming that the auditor conducted a substandard audit. Similarly, equity investors who suffer a financial loss when relying on misstated financial statements may bring suit against the auditor. In these suits, the plaintiff is arguing that the auditor is the *proximate cause* of the financial loss and, therefore, should compensate the damaged parties for their losses. Cases brought under tort law usually claim that the auditor was grossly negligent, or that the auditor has committed fraud by knowingly making (or allowing) materially false misstatements in an audited financial report.

Plaintiff's keys to winning: To win a case against an auditor under common law, a plaintiff must prove that four conditions have been satisfied:

1. The financial statements of an organization were materially misleading.
2. The misstatement occurred because the auditor was negligent, grossly negligent, or intentionally deceitful (the standard depends on the party bringing suit and the legal basis for the case).
3. The plaintiff used and relied on the financial statements.
4. A loss was suffered by the plaintiff as the result of reliance on the information.

The legal basis for a suit has implications for the degree of audit misconduct that a plaintiff must demonstrate in order to win the case, as well as the defenses that an auditor can use as defendant. There are four possible standards of accountability that can be applied to the conduct of an audit in support of a plaintiff's case:

1. Negligence: A lack of reasonable care in the conduct of the audit, either through accident or the exercise of poor judgment. The standard of comparison for determining negligence is what a *competent* auditor would do given a similar situation. Failure to comply with GAAS is often construed as negligence.
2. Gross negligence: A reckless violation or disregard of auditing standards. In these situations, an auditor has made little effort to comply with appropriate professional standards.
3. Constructive fraud: An intentional violation of auditing standards in order to avoid discovering facts that may be disagreeable is considered tantamount to fraud. Intentionally ignoring potentially questionable activity may be constructive fraud even if the auditor had no intent to deceive the users of financial statements or lacked explicit knowledge of fraud.[7]
4. Fraud: The knowing and intentional misrepresentation of the financial statements with the complicity of the auditor.

In general, cases brought under contract law are judged against a negligence standard, while cases brought under tort law are judgment against a gross negligence or constructive fraud standard. Negligence is the easiest for a plaintiff to prove and the hardest for the auditor to defend against.

Auditor Defenses: The auditor has a number of defenses that can be used to counter charges of professional malpractice. The following five defenses are the most commonly used by auditors but not all defenses apply to all cases:

1. No responsibility to plaintiff: The auditor can claim that there is no "duty of care" or responsibility to the plaintiff, either because the plaintiff was not a

---

7 Many courts in various countries make no distinction between gross negligence and constructive fraud.

party to the contract for services (referred to as a lack of *privity of contract*) or because the level of service agreed to in the engagement letter was less than what is claimed in the lawsuit (e.g., the engagement was not an audit).

2. Lack of reliance by the plaintiff: The auditor can argue that the plaintiff was not aware of, or did not rely on, the information that is claimed to be misstated in the financial statements so the auditor is not responsible for losses incurred by the plaintiff.

3. Auditor exercise of due diligence: The auditor can claim that the conduct of the audit was effective and in compliance with all appropriate professional standards. The basis of this defense is that the audit was not substandard, notwithstanding the subsequent revelation of fraud or financial failure. This defense is most often used to counter an accusation of negligence.

4. Lack of auditor intent to defraud: The auditor can claim that even though some mistakes were made during the course of an audit engagement, they were "honest" mistakes and the auditor did not intentionally set out to perform a substandard audit or to defraud any parties using the financial statements. This defense can be effective against charges of gross negligence or constructive fraud.

5. Contributory negligence by management: This defense is based on the argument that the auditor should not be held liable for losses that are the plaintiff's own fault, that is, losses due to the action (or lack of action) of management. In these cases, the auditor claims a lack of liability because the management could have avoided the problem through appropriate behavior. For example, an auditor can claim contributory negligence when the auditor alerts the company to potential problems but management fails to take corrective action, or when management intentionally deceives the auditor so as to cover up its own improper actions. This defense is useful for cases when the client firm is the plaintiff, or in jurisdictions that embrace the concept of separate and proportional liability.

The most commonly used defenses are no duty of care, lack of reliance by the plaintiff, and the exercise of due diligence by the auditor. However, due diligence may be difficult to demonstrate when an actual fraudulent condition has been discovered or a company has suffered significant financial distress (e.g., recall the hindsight bias).

U.S. common law cases: Figure 17–9 highlights several prominent common law cases against auditors in the United States (see Appendix for cases from other common law countries). Case law in this area was first defined by the *Ultramares* case, which found that a plaintiff must have privity of contract or be a primary beneficiary under the contract in order to sue the auditor for breach of contract. In general, a case based on contract law requires the plaintiff to demonstrate that the auditor was negligent. The court also ruled that a broader class of parties can sue under common law, but the standard of performance used in those cases would be gross negligence or constructive fraud. Although not a judicial decision as the auditor agreed to a large out-of-court settlement, the *McKesson-Robbins* case provides insight into what gross negligence means in the context of auditing malpractice. In this case the auditor failed to confirm receivables or inspect inventory, two procedures that are required to be done by auditors today.

Case law has continuously wrestled with the issue of who can sue an auditor under a negligence standard. Plaintiffs prefer the negligence standard because it is

Figure 17–9   Summary of Significant Litigation Against Auditors Under U.S. Common Law

Case Name	Facts	Finding of Court	Significance to Audit Profession
Ultramares v. Touche, Niven & Co. (1933)	The auditor gave an unqualified opinion on the financial statements even though receivables turned out to be overstated by $1.2 million due to the recording of fictitious customers. The plaintiff lent money to the company based on the misstated financial reports.	• A third-party plaintiff cannot sue an auditor under contract law because they lack privity of contract, so no breach of contract can occur relative to the third party. • A third-party plaintiff can sue the accountant using the standard of gross negligence (constructive fraud) under tort law.	• The auditing profession reworded the standard auditor's report, dropping words such as "certify" and "correct" from the opinion in the United States.
McKesson-Robbins v. Price Waterhouse (1938)	An auditor gave an unqualified opinion on financial statements that included overstated assets of at least $19 million due to the recording of a nonexistent subsidiary supposedly located in Canada. The auditor did not confirm receivables nor observe inventory in Canada.	• Settled out of court.	• New audit standards were developed requiring the confirmation of receivables and the observation of inventory. • Affirmation that the auditor is hired by the shareholders of the company to protect their interests.
Rusch Factors v. Levin (1968)	The auditor was engaged at the request of a lender to audit the financial statements of a prospective borrower. A loan was granted based on the unqualified report of the auditor. The borrower subsequently was determined to be insolvent.	• The lender could be considered a primary beneficiary under the *Ultramares* precedent. • In addition, under tort law, members of a *foreseen and limited class of persons* may be able to sue for ordinary negligence (rather than just gross negligence).	• Reduced the standard of evidence for some classes of plaintiffs, making it harder for auditors to defend against some cases brought under common law.

(continued)

1136 Tenants Corporation v. Max Rothenberg and Company (1972)	An accountant was hired by an apartment co-operative to draft (not audit) financial statements and other reports for the co-op. There was no engagement letter. It was later discovered that management of the co-op was embezzling significant funds which probably would have been discovered using normal audit procedures. The accountant was aware of missing documentation for many transactions. The co-op claimed it believed it was receiving an audit.	• The auditor had performed some tests that would constitute audit procedures. • The auditor was aware of the potential problems but did not report the problems. • The accountant did not issue a disclaimer. • Auditor was held liable.	• Auditors encouraged to always obtain a clear engagement letter. • Auditors required to bring evidence of irregularities to the attention of appropriate personnel within the organization. • Accountants required to issue a disclaimer report whenever they are "associated" with financial statements (see Standards on Compilation and Review Services in Chapter 18).
Cenco v. Seidman & Seidman (1982)	Management of the company systematically overstated inventory balances in order to inflate assets. This allowed the company to file overstated fire insurance claims and to borrow money at favorable interest rates. After the fraud was discovered, the accountants settled a class action suit out of court with shareholders. New management then sued the accountant for breach of contract and gross negligence.	• The pervasive and active role of prior management in perpetrating the fraud was a valid defense against the suit filed by new management.	• Clarified the concept of contributory negligence under common law.

Figure 17-9 *(continued)*

Case Name	Facts	Finding of Court	Significance to Audit Profession
Rosenblum v. Adler (1983)	Giant Stores acquired H. Rosenblum in exchange for stock in Giant. When the financial statements were later discovered to be materially misstated, the stock received by the owners of Rosenblum was virtually worthless. Suit was brought against the auditors of Giant for not discovering the fraud.	• Court rejected the *Ultramares* defense of no privity of contract. • Determined that the auditor has a responsibility to all parties that they could *reasonably foresee* as using and relying on the financial statements for business purposes.	• Extended the concept of foreseeable users who can use the negligence standard under tort law.
National Medical Transportation Network v. Deloitte & Touche (1998)	The auditor was sued by the client after withdrawing from an engagement on the grounds that the CFO resigned rather than sign a representation letter and the company resisted making required adjustments to the financial statements. The company claimed that the auditor's withdrawal damaged the company's prospects for obtaining favorable financing.	• Jury found for company but California Court of Appeals overturned the decision. • Court ruled that judges should instruct juries about the professional standards applicable to an issue.	• Upheld auditor's professional rights and obligations to disassociate for cause from a client of questionable character.

easier to prove; defendants prefer the more lenient gross negligence standard. Two cases were instrumental in broadening the class of potential litigants that could use the negligence standard. In *Rusch Factors v. Levin,* the court concluded that a primary beneficiary who is identified in the audit service contract (the engagement letter) is entitled to sue using the negligence standard even though not an official party to the contract. This decision applies to a class of parties the court described as foreseen and limited. In *Rosenblum v. Adler,* however, a New Jersey court broadened the class to include all reasonably *foreseeable users* of the financial statements whether identified or not. The precedent does not apply to all states, however, many of which follow the *Restatement (Second) of Torts.* However, because the restatement is unclear about distinguishing types of plaintiffs, states cover the full range from *Ultramares* to *Rosenblum*[8] to somewhere in between.

The other three common law cases discussed in Figure 17–9 are notable because of their significance to the practice of auditing. First, the *1136 Tenants* case established the need for clear contractual arrangements with clients (engagement letters) in order to avoid misunderstandings about the level of service being provided. The second case, *Cenco v. Seidman & Seidman,* clarified the concept of contributory negligence on the part of management and emphasized that a client cannot sue the auditor for damages caused by their own actions (or inaction), especially if management was intentionally deceiving the auditor. Finally, in *National Medical Transportation Network v. Deloitte & Touche,* a California court upheld the right and obligation of an auditor to disassociate from a client of questionable integrity and emphasized that professional standards are relevant to determining the merits of a case.

To summarize the current status of auditors' legal liability under common law in the United States: Parties that have privity of contract with an auditor can readily sue for damages using the negligence standard in all U.S. states. Parties that do not have privity or are not primary beneficiaries or foreseeable users may be required to demonstrate gross negligence in order to recover damages depending on the specifics of the individual state. In either case, potentially effective defenses include lack of responsibility, lack of reliance, or contributory negligence.[9] Common law and its applications to specific cases in other English speaking countries are discussed in the Appendix.

Legal Liability—Statutory Law

Auditors are also subject to the requirements embedded in statutory law promulgated by legislative bodies. In common law countries, these laws may supplement rights and obligations established by court precedent, often expanding or limiting the rights of persons to sue an auditor. In code law countries, lawsuits are only possible when expressively permitted by statutory law. Although few countries have a basis for auditor litigation in statutory law, the United States has extensive experience in using civil statute law to pursue and penalize auditors who fail to meet their professional obligations. Most auditor litigation in the United States falls within three sets of statutes: (1) 1933 SEC Act, (2) 1934 SEC Act, and (3) the 1970 Racketeer Influenced and Corrupt Organizations Act (RICO).

---

8 Other cases related to the foreseeable party precedent are *Citizen's State Bank v. Timm, Schmidt & Co.,* Wisconsin, 1983 and *Credit Alliance Corp. v. Arthur Andersen & Co.,* 1985.

9 Whether an auditor can use the contributory negligence defense against *new* management is subject to variations across jurisdictions.

SEC Acts of 1933 and 1934: These statutes provide for either civil lawsuits by third parties for damages or criminal prosecutions of individuals charged with violating the statutes. The *SEC Act of 1933* applies to companies that issue new securities for public trading. Section 11 of the Act imposes liability on parties, including underwriters and auditors, who are associated with misstatements or omissions in a registration statement prepared in conjunction with an initial public offering of securities. Section 12 imposes liabilities if a prospectus is omitted or contains incorrect information and Sections 17 and 24 cover fraudulent actions occurring in conjunction with an initial public offering.

In general, the burden of proof on the plaintiff is relatively low in cases brought under the 1933 Act. In order to win such a case, the plaintiff has to demonstrate that the financial statements were materially misstated at the time the securities were offered to the public, that the auditor was negligent, and that the plaintiff acquired the securities and suffered a loss. The plaintiff does not have to show actual reliance on the financial statements. This standard established a virtual strict liability approach to financial reporting for new issues of securities—if the statements are wrong, the auditor is likely to be held responsible. However, the auditor can use a due diligence defense in such cases.

The *SEC Act of 1934* extends the auditor's liability to any information that is required to be filed with the SEC, most importantly, annual financial statements. From the auditor's perspective, the key part of the statute is Rule 10b-5:

It shall be unlawful for any person directly or indirectly, by the use of any means or instrumentality of interstate commerce, or the mails or any facility of any national securities exchange, (a) to employ any device, scheme, or artifice to defraud, (b) to make any untrue statement of a material fact or omit to state a material fact necessary in order to make the statements made, in the light of circumstances under which they were made, not misleading, or (c) to engage in any act, practice, or course of business which operates or would operate as a fraud or deceit upon any person in connection with the purchase or sale of any security.

Misstatements in the annual financial statements which cause damage to investors can become the basis for a cause of action against the auditor. However, plaintiffs must demonstrate reliance on the information to recover under the 1934 Act. The primary defenses available for civil cases against an auditor under the 1934 Act are due diligence and lack of reliance.

Illustrative cases: Cases related to the statutory law are summarized in Figure 17–10. The *Yale Express* case clarified that Rule 10b-5 applies to information contained in the annual financial statements and placed a burden on the auditor to act upon information that indicates that financial statements are misstated, even if obtained after the end of fieldwork. The *BarChris* case established that compliance with professional standards is not an adequate defense to all claims of negligence and that the auditor must also look to the general fairness of the financial statements when conducting the audit.

The *Hochfelder* case is important to auditors because it represented a judicial swing in their favor. The U.S. Supreme Court concluded that auditors can be held liable under Rule 10b-5 only when they have an intent to deceive readers of the financial statements. Absent intent, a plaintiff cannot recover under securities law. However, the Court went on to hint that reckless behavior by an auditor may be a basis for plaintiff relief, but the Court did not make an explicit finding on the issue. This issue was further resolved a few years later in *Howard Sirota v. Solitron Devices,*

Figure 17–10   Summary of Significant Litigation Against Auditors Under U.S. Statutory Law: Civil Actions

Case Name	Legal Basis	Facts	Finding of Court	Significance to Audit Profession
Fischer v. Kletz "Yale Express" (1967)	SEC Act of 1934	An accountant who was involved in a consulting engagement found evidence of material misstatements in financial statements that were examined by the firm three months previously. The information was not brought to the attention of the audit team or followed up in any way.	The court ruled that Rule 10b-5 of the SEC Act of 1934 applies to annual financial statements. • The auditor has the duty to bring irregularities to the attention of appropriate personnel. • The auditor has the duty to inform parties relying on the previous audit report of the new information.	• Clarified the application of Rule 10b-5 to the audit of financial statements. • Events subsequent to the date of the financial statements should be considered when rendering an opinion on the financial statements.
Escott v. BarChris Construction (1968)	SEC Act of 1933	The company issued convertible bonds shortly after the completion of an audit. The audit failed to detect gross overstatements in earnings due to mistreatment of sale-leaseback transactions. The company went bankrupt and the accountant was sued based on its review of the information in the proxy statements.	• Compliance with current generally accepted auditing standards is not a complete defense against charges of negligence.	• Auditors should emphasize fairness as well as GAAP in evaluating the financial statements.

(continued)

Figure 17–10   *(continued)*

Case Name	Legal Basis	Facts	Finding of Court	Significance to Audit Profession
Hochfelder v. Ernst & Ernst (1976)	SEC Act of 1934	Customers of an investment company were swindled by the president of the organization who misdirected certain deposits to his own use. The funds were not recorded on the books of the investment company. When the fraud was discovered, the investors sued the auditor. The trial court dismissed the action, ruling that negligence is not enough to find the auditor liable. The Court of Appeals reversed the trial court.	• The Supreme Court ruled that the application of Rule 10b-5 requires intent to deceive for the plaintiff to recover, which was absent from the case against the auditors.	• Auditors can be held liable under Rule 10b-5 of the 1934 SEC Act only when they have *scienter* ("the intent to deceive"). • The case left open the issue of reckless behavior which is tantamount to fraud.
Howard Sirota v. Solitron Devices (1982)	SEC Act of 1934	The auditor failed to detect overstatements of inventory balances that resulted in inflated earnings. A jury found the auditor guilty of "reckless behavior" but the judge overturned the decision.	• The Court of Appeals determined that the auditor should have had knowledge of the fraud. • The Court of Appeals concluded that reckless behavior constitutes intent under Rule 10b-5.	• Clarified concept of constructive fraud without intent as applied to reckless behavior of auditors.
Reves v. Ernst & Young (1993)	RICO	The auditor failed to detect behavior by management that was potentially fraudulent and led to the bankruptcy of the client (a farm co-op). Plaintiffs claimed that the firm had misvalued the company and assisted in the perpetration of a fraud.	• The Court found that the auditor must be directly and actively involved in perpetrating fraudulent activity to be accountable under RICO. Mere performance of an attest engagement does not make an auditor liable under RICO.	• Removed the overhanging threat of prosecution under RICO for mere negligence or errors in auditor judgment.

where the Court of Appeals decided that reckless behavior was tantamount to constructive fraud.

Racketeer Influenced and Corrupt Organizations Act (RICO): *Racketeer Influenced and Corrupt Organizations Act (RICO)* identifies a large number of illegal activities that come under the umbrella of the act, including mail fraud and wire fraud, and plaintiffs have attempted to apply this law to instances of financial statement fraud or misstatement. In the case of outright fraud, auditors may be sued under the RICO act for treble damages. However, in *Reves v. Ernst & Young*, the U.S. Supreme Court held that RICO does not apply to auditors unless they are actively involved in the fraudulent activity. Mere negligence, or even gross negligence, does not constitute a sustainable cause of action under RICO. Prior to this decision, the threat of treble damages was a significant incentive for auditors to settle even trivial cases out of court.

LEGAL PROSECUTION—CRIMINAL LAW

Although relatively rare, auditors may be criminally prosecuted if their actions are in violation of criminal statutes. There are three sets of criminal statutes that are relevant to auditors: (1) SEC Acts of 1933 and 1934, (2) obstruction of justice laws, and (3) the Sarbanes-Oxley Act of 2002. The Appendix discusses the use of criminal law to discipline auditors in other English-speaking countries.

SEC Acts of 1933 and 1934: Although rarely used, the SEC Acts of 1933 and 1934 specifically allow for criminal prosecution of auditors who are intentionally culpable in fraudulent misrepresentation of financial statements. Figure 17–11 summarizes legal cases related to criminal prosecutions in the United States. The first case where an auditor was criminally prosecuted was *Continental Vending*. In this case, three auditors were found guilty of constructive fraud because they wantonly ignored evidence of misrepresented related party transactions, even though there were no generally accepted reporting standards for such transactions at the time. In *National Student Marketing*, the auditors were guilty of aiding and abetting the client in executing a fraud and ended up serving prison sentences for their role in violating securities laws. These criminal prosecutions always focused on individual auditors and not the firm as a whole.

Obstruction of justice laws: The infamous criminal prosecution of the firm of Arthur Andersen that followed from the Enron accounting fraud was the first time that the U.S. Department of Justice decided to prosecute more than just the individual partners engaged in the alleged wrongdoing. Furthermore, it was not based on the SEC Acts but rather on an obstruction of justice statute that states in part:

Sec. 1512. Tampering with a witness, victim or an informant . . . . . .

(b) Whoever knowingly uses intimidation or physical force, threatens, or corruptly persuades another person, or attempts to do so, or engages in misleading conduct toward another person, with intent to - . . . . .

(2) cause or induce any person to - . . . . .

(B) Alter, destroy, mutilate, or conceal an object with intent to impair the object's integrity or availability for use in an official proceeding, ...

shall be fined under this title or imprisoned for not more than ten years, or both.

Figure 17–11   Summary of Significant Litigation Against Auditors Under U.S. Statutory Law: Criminal Actions

Case Name	Legal Basis	Facts	Finding of Court	Significance to Audit Profession
United States v. Simon "Continental Vending" (1969)	SEC Act of 1934	The auditor was aware of a number of problems at the client including improper recognition of related party loans and loans that were secured by company stock with an inflated value. At the time, there were no generally accepted accounting principles for reporting related party transactions.	• The Court emphasized the auditor should evaluate fairness of financial reporting, not just compliance with GAAP. • Three auditors were found criminally guilty and sentenced to prison.	• Gave impetus for the development of FASB No. 57 on related party transactions. • Established the threat of criminal prosecution against auditors guilty of constructive or actual fraud.
United States v. Natelli "National Student Marketing" (1975)	SEC Act of 1934	The auditor failed to detect fictitious sales and receivables at the time of an audit. When discovered at a later date, the auditors were persuaded by the client to not reveal the information. No disclosures or adjustments were made to the financial statements in spite of the auditors' knowledge.	• The auditors were criminally guilty of constructive fraud and two individuals were sentenced to prison.	• Emphasized the threat of criminal prosecution in cases of auditor culpability in securities fraud cases.
United States vs. Arthur Andersen (2002)	US Criminal Code Section 1512	The Houston office of Andersen as well as other offices involved in the Enron audit shredded documents and destroyed electronic files that might have been pertinent to an imminent SEC investigation of Enron's accounting.	• The audit firm was found guilty of obstruction of justice in the jury trial and was ordered to pay a fine of $500,0000 • As a convicted felon cannot practice before the SEC, Andersen shutdown operations as of August 31, 2002 • The case was overturned on appeal in 2005 by the unanimous decision of the US Supreme Court based on the judge's instructions to the jury.	• The first criminal prosecution of an entire firm, not just the partners directly involved in the audit. • Demonstrated that audit firms (and auditors) could be criminally prosecuted for actions not directly related to the audit in question but rather how it managed its response to the potential for a government investigation.

Hence, Andersen was not charged with fraud or any illegal act directly related to its audit of Enron but, rather, of destroying documents in anticipation of an SEC investigation into the Andersen audit of Enron. Although the U.S. Supreme Court overturned the guilty verdict on the technical issue of the wording of the judge's instructions to the jury, the guilty verdict meant that Andersen could not continue its audit practice and effectively shut down operations as of August 31, 2002.

Sarbanes-Oxley Act of 2002 (SOX): The provisions of SOX have been mentioned in numerous places throughout the text. This recently enacted law increased the criminal penalties under the SEC Acts from a maximum of 5 to 10 years for most securities offenses. Furthermore, SOX made clear that actions like those taken by Andersen to shred documents in light of the imminent investigation by the SEC were illegal and could result in up to 20 years of imprisonment. Section 303 of SOX also makes it a crime "for any officer or director of an issuer to take any action to fraudulently influence, coerce, manipulate, or mislead any auditor engaged in the performance of an audit for the purpose of rendering the financial statements materially misleading."

SUMMARY AND CONCLUSION

In this chapter, we discussed how the audit process can be viewed as an ethically based decision process carried out by a trained professional accountant as a member of the auditing profession. We documented how the unaided judgment of an auditor can be biased by a variety of information processing heuristics and biases and the conflicts caused by ethical dilemmas. We then examined how auditors constantly strive to get better at what they do. Indeed, one of the principle functions of audit firms is to put processes in place that aid individual auditors in overcoming these judgment deficiencies, although firm incentives may sometimes seem to reward questionable auditor behavior.

We also examined the institutional forces that support the auditor in making ethical decisions, whether they are based on professional rules or mandated by government regulation: codes of professional conduct, rules of auditor independence, auditing standards, quality control standards, and peer reviews or practice inspections. Finally, we examined the institutions that exist to discourage and sanction inappropriate auditor behavior, including regulatory intervention and legal actions of either a civil or criminal nature. The Sarbanes-Oxley Act of 2002 is the most recent development in this area and the Act will continue to influence the behavior of auditors as regulators implement rules and regulations derived from the Act.

APPENDIX

English-speaking countries like the United Kingdom, Ireland, Canada, Australia, and New Zealand tend to refer to precedents in each other's courts. Significant cases in the United Kingdom and other English-speaking countries are described in Figure 17–12.

The key case in the United Kingdom that led to the expansion of the ability of third parties to sue the auditor for negligence was *Hedley Byrne v. Heller & Partners* (1961). The case did not actually involve an auditor but was brought against a

Figure 17-12 Summary of Significant Litigation Against Auditors Under Common Law in Other English Speaking Countries

U.K. Case Name	Facts	Audit Application	Analogous Cases in Other English Speaking Countries
Hedley Bryne v. Heller & Partners	Heller & Partners, a merchant banking firm, provided incorrect data in response to a request from National Provincial Bank for credit information on Easipower Ltd. Heller & Partners knew that National would pass this information on to an unidentified customer. That customer, Hedley Bryne, employed that erroneous information to decide to extend credit to Easipower who subsequently went into liquidation.	Gave rise to the principle of forseen third parties such that even if the auditor did not know the exact identity of the party, the auditor could be reasonably certain of knowing that such a specific party existed to whom a duty of care was owed.	Canada: *Haig v. Bamford*
JEB Fasteners v. Marks Bloom & Co.	JEB Fasteners acquired 100% of the shares of a privately held company relying, at least in part, on the unqualified audit opinion of Marks Bloom. The financial statements contained numerous errors including a material overstatement of inventory. When the auditor did the audit, he was not aware of any takeover, although later he learned of it and cooperated with JEB by providing requested information.	Gave rise to the foreseeable class of third parties such that all potential users of financial statements that could be reasonably inferred to exist would be owed a duty of care by the auditor.	Canada: *Surrey Credit Union v. Willson* Australia: *Columbia Coffee & Tea Party v. Churchill* New Zealand: *Scott Group v. Macfarlane*
Caparo Industries v. Dickman	Existing shareholder and investor bought additional shares based on audited statements that contained clear error (reported profits when company was in loss position).	Established the concept that the forseeable user test should be balanced against the policy implications of an auditor being subject to an indeterminate liability for an indeterminate amount of time to an indeterminate number of parties, negating the possibility of a lawsuit against the auditor in this case.	Canada: *Hercules Management v. Ernst & Young* Australia: *Esanda Finance v. Peat Marwick Hungerfords* New Zealand: *Boyd Knight v. Purdue*

merchant bank, Heller & Partners, that provided credit information about one of its clients to another bank that Heller knew would then be passed on to an unidentified customer. The House of Lords (the United Kingdom's highest court) ruled that the customer, Hedley Byrne, could sue Heller as they had a "special relationship" much like the foreseen person in U.S. common law. This doctrine was immediately applied in auditing cases both in the United Kingdom and in other English-speaking countries. Over time, as litigation continued in other cases, the "special relationship" term was refined to the point that in *Anns vs. London Borough* (1981), the term was given almost the same meaning as the U.S. foreseeability test (see *Rosenblum*). Although the case involved no public accountants, the precedent was cited extensively in litigation against auditors (see *JEB Fasteners v. Marks Bloom & Co.*)

Unlike the United States, other English-speaking countries have seen judicial decisions move away from expanding the common law based duty of care to third parties who do not fit into the categories of primary beneficiaries or foreseen users. *Caparo Industries PLC v. Dickman* decided by the U.K. House of Lords involved Caparo Industries making a takeover bid for Fidelity PLC. After completing the takeover, Caparo found that instead of a profit of £1.3 million, Fidelity had actually lost almost £0.5 million. The House of Lords devised a two part test that has been adopted by Canadian, Australian, and New Zealand courts:

STEP ONE: *Is there a relationship of proximity between the parties? Put another way, are the parties' neighbours? Put another way still, is it reasonably foreseeable that carelessness by one party would adversely affect the other? If the answer is yes, then a duty of care is owed, subject to Step Two.*

STEP TWO: *Are there any considerations which should limit the duty owed or eliminate it entirely?*

Step one depends on the forseeability of use and the nature of the professional relationship. In the case of a public company, the auditor knows that the results of his or her work will be communicated to known third parties or classes of third parties (e.g., potential investors). Assuming the third party can show they had a relationship—in other words, the third party relied on the auditor's work and suffers a loss as a result, and that the audit is being used for the purposes for which it was prepared—then this test is readily met. Hence, for most public company auditors, the "Step One" test is met and the auditor owes a duty of care to these third parties.

The second step involves "policy considerations." In other words, is it good public policy for there to be an indeterminate amount of liability for an indeterminate amount of time to an indeterminate number of parties for auditors of public companies? The House of Lords concluded that this would likely drive audit firms out of business or to charge rates so high that only the largest client companies could afford to be publicly listed. The Lords suggested that this was not in accordance with the best interests of society and hence negated the auditor's duty of care to third parties that would lead to unbounded liability for auditors. Hence, Caparo was not allowed to sue the auditors of Fidelity. Overall, the conclusion across most other English speaking countries is that an auditor may be sued for negligence associated with his or her work by foreseeable third parties but only when there is NOT an indeterminate amount of liability for an indeterminate amount of time to an indeterminate number of parties.

Most countries have the ability to charge auditors under their criminal code using laws that exist against fraud. For example, one possible area of prosecution under the Canadian Criminal Code is the following:

Section 380 (2) Every one who, by deceit, falsehood or other fraudulent means, whether or not it is a false pretence within the meaning of this Act, with intent to defraud, affects the public market price of stocks, shares, merchandise or anything that is offered for sale to the public is guilty of an indictable offence and liable to imprisonment for a term not exceeding ten years.

However, there are no records in Canada of the auditor of a public company being charged with criminal fraud or other criminal offenses related to his or her actions as an auditor.

The only non-U.S. criminal prosecution of an auditor in connection with a public company audit is the Australian case of *Carter v. the Queen*. Carter, an audit partner in a predecessor firm of KPMG, was convicted in 1996 of conspiracy to defraud the public and concurring in publishing false reports in connection with the audit of Rothwells Limited, a clothing retailer turned merchant bank. Although even the prosecutor noted that Carter was not motivated by greed or personal gain, the audit was so poorly carried out that it constituted criminal fraud. The court concluded that the auditor had no chance of detecting material misstatements because he relied almost entirely on management representations and obtained little or no independent evidence to verify those representations. Carter was sentenced to four years and three months in prison for his part in the fraud, and served a year.

BIBLIOGRAPHY OF RELATED PROFESSIONAL LITERATURE

Research

Bell, T. B., J. C. Bedard, K. M Johnstone, and E. F. Smith. KRisk[SM]: A Computerized Decision Aid for Client Acceptance and Continuance Risk Assessments. *Auditing: A Journal of Practice & Theory.* 21(2): 97–113.

Blay, A. D. 2005. Independence Threats, Litigation Risk and the Auditor's Decision Process. *Contemporary Accounting Research.* 22(4): 759–789.

Chaney, P. K. 2002. Shredded Reputation: The Cost of Audit Failure. *Journal of Accounting Research.* 40(4): 1221–1245.

Clarkson, P. M., C. Emby, and V. W-S Watt. 2002. Debiasing the Outcome Effect: The Role of Instructions in an Audit Litigation Setting. *Auditing: A Journal of Practice & Theory.* 21(2): 7–20.

Copeland, J. E. 2005. Ethics as an Imperative. *Accounting Horizons.* 19(1): 35–43.

Cushing, B. E. and D. L. Gilbertson. 2002. Strategic Analysis of Securities Litigation Against Independent Auditors. *Auditing: A Journal of Practice & Theory.* 21(2): 57–80.

Donaldson, I. 2000. The Carter Case: Falling into "The Audit Gap." *Australian CPA.* 70(1): 36–39.

Erickson, M., B. W. Mayhew, and W. L. Felix Jr. 2000. Why Do Audits Fail? Evidence from Lincoln Savings and Loan. *Journal of Accounting Research.* 38(1): 165–194.

Geiger, M. A. and K. Raghunandan. 2002. Going-Concern Opinions in the "New" Legal Environment. *Accounting Horizons.* 16(1): 17–26.

Gunz, S. and S. Salterio. 2004. What if Andersen Had Shredded in Toronto or Calgary? The Potential Criminal Liability of Canadian Public Accounting Firms. *Canadian Accounting Perspectives.* 3(1): 59–84.

Hoffman, V. B., J. R. Joe, and D. V. Moser. 2003. The Effect of Constrained Processing on Auditors' Judgments. *Accounting, Organizations and Society.* 28(7/8): 699–714.

Kadous, K. 2001. Improving Jurors' Evaluations of Auditors in Negligence Cases. *Contemporary Accounting Research.* 18(3): 425–444.

Kaplan, S. E. and S. M. Whitecotton. 2001. An Examination of Auditors' Reporting Intentions When Another Auditor Is Offered Client Employment. *Auditing: A Journal of Practice & Theory.* 20(1): 45–64.

King, R. R. 2002. An Experimental Investigation of Self-Serving Biases in an Auditing Trust Game: The Effect of Group Affiliation. *The Accounting Review.* 77(2): 265–284.

King, R. R. and R. Schwartz. 2000. An Experimental Investigation of Auditors' Liability: Implications for Social Welfare and Exploration of Deviation from Theoretical Predictions. *The Accounting Review.* 75(4): 429–451.

Khurana, I. K. and K. K. Raman. 2004. Litigation Risk and Financial Reporting Credibility of Big 4 versus Non-Big 4 Audits: Evidence from Anglo-American Countries. *The Accounting Review.* 79(2): 473–495.

Krishnan, J. and Y. Zhang. 2005. Auditor Litigation Risk and Corporate Disclosure of Quarterly Review Report. *Auditing: A Journal of Practice & Theory.* 24 (Supplement): 115–138.

Larsson, B. 2005. Auditor Regulation and Economic Crime Policy in Sweden 1986–2000. *Accounting, Organizations and Society.* 30(2): 127–144.

McCracken, S. A. 2003. Auditors' Strategies to Protect Their Litigation Reputation: A Research Note. *Auditing: A Journal of Practice & Theory.* 22(1): 165–180.

Pacini, C., M. J. Martin, and L. Hamilton. 2000. At the Interface of Law and Accounting: An Examination of a Trend to a Reduction in the Scope of Auditor Liability To Third Parties in Common Law Countries. *American Business Law Journal.* 37(2): 171–235.

Ricchiute, D. N. 2004. Effects of an Attorney's Line of Argument on Accountants' Expert Witness Testimony. *The Accounting Review.* 79(1): 221–245.

Thomas, C. W., C. E. Davis, and S. S. Seaman. 1998. Quality Review, Continuing Professional Education, Experience and Substandard Performance: An Empirical Study. *Accounting Horizons.* 12(4): 340–362.

Thorne, L. and J. Hartwick. 2001. The Directional Effects of Discussion on Auditors' Moral Reasoning. *Contemporary Accounting Research.* 18(2): 337–367.

Professional Reports and Guidance

Institute of Chartered Accountants in England & Wales Audit and Assurance Faculty. 2003. *The Audit Report and the Auditors' Duty of Care to Third Parties.* Technical Release.

Library of Congress. 2002. House Resolution Number 3763, An Act to Protect Investors by Improving the Accuracy and Reliability of Corporate Disclosures Made Pursuant to the Securities Laws, and for Other Purposes (*The Sarbanes-Oxley Act of 2002*). http://www.libraryofcongress.gov.

Auditing Standards

AICPA *Code of Professional Conduct*

AICPA *Statements on Quality Control Standards*

IAASB *International Standards on Quality Control*

IFAC *Code of Ethics for Professional Accountants*

IFAC *Handbook Glossary of Terms*

QUESTIONS

1. For each of the following audit judgments, provide one example of a behavior that you believe would be unethical.
- Client acceptance
- Establishing materiality
- Evaluating the effectiveness of controls
- Evaluating client explanations
- Selecting audit procedures

2. Consider the following example of ethical misconduct:

An audit staff member is asked to work extra hours on an engagement and not report the hours worked so that the engagement will report being completed within the budgeted amount of time. The manager who asked the staff to work the hours is trying to be promoted to partner and wants to demonstrate the ability to manage profitable engagements—the fees for the engagement are fixed and were established before the audit commenced.

Explain why the manager's behavior was unethical by discussing which of the six sequential decision-making steps discussed in the chapter were not properly followed and how the manager might have avoided this situation.

3. Consider each of the five examples provided in the chapter for why auditors might demonstrate mistakes in professional judgment:
- Auditors may not be able to define their decision problem clearly
- Auditors may not be able to consider all relevant evidence and alternatives
- Auditors may act in a biased manner
- Auditors may not select the "best" alternative
- Auditors fail to understand the dynamic nature of their clients

Describe ways that you plan to try to avoid each of the mistakes in professional judgment in your career—keeping in mind that avoiding them may prove to be very difficult.

4. Evidence from audit research shows that the anchoring and adjustment heuristic occurs when auditors begin their audit of a financial statement account assertions by first obtaining the unaudited ending balances from the client's management. Consider the following example of this situation.

The auditor receives the unaudited ending balance of accounts receivable of $1 million and begins with the belief that the actual balance likely is between $800,000 and $1.2 million. However, the actual balance should have been $250,000. Thus, the auditor has anchored on $1 million and fails to appropriately consider the likelihood that the actual balance should be much, much lower.

Provide suggestions based on the approach to auditing discussed in this textbook for how an auditor might reduce the likelihood of being placed in this situation.

5. Below are common techniques generally used by an audit firm to reduce the chance that ethical dilemmas will result in auditors making poor decisions. For each technique, describe how you think that it might help you avoid making an unethical decision at your employer.
- Expertise in a subject area
- Training of ethical conduct at the employer
- Structure of the audit approach to follow
- Group decision making and the review process
- Documentation to support decisions
- Utilization of decision aids (e.g., sample-size selection)
- Consulting with other personnel
- Knowledge of a review by a peer firm or regulator
- Understanding that ethical conduct will be rewarded

6. Compare and contrast the concepts of *independence in fact* and *independence in appearance*. Explain why you agree or disagree with the notion that independence in appearance is equally as important as independence in fact, keeping in mind that this argument has been the subject of many heated debates by those who feel strongly about each position.

7. For each of the following threats to independence discussed in the chapter, provide an example of a breakdown of independence in fact or appearance to illustrate why auditors should take the threat seriously.
- Self-interest threat
- Self-review threat
- Advocacy threat
- Familiarity threat
- Intimidation threat

8. Five common auditor defenses when charges of negilence are brought against auditors include
- No responsibility to plaintiff
- Lack of reliance by the plaintiff
- Auditor exercise of due diligence
- Lack of auditor intent to defraud
- Contributory negligence by management

In actuality, most lawsuits brought against auditors are settled out of court because of the difficulties associated with winning a case using one of these defenses (and the high costs of taking a case to trial—both in terms of actual costs and reputational loss). Help auditors overcome this problem by arguing how they might be more successful in winning lawsuits using each of the defenses.

9. The U.S. SEC Acts of 1933 and 1934 established the SEC, in part, to help prevent the business practices, including financial reporting, that worsened the impact of the 1929 depression in the United States. There was not another major piece of congressional legislation to affect public accountants until the Sarbanes-Oxley Act of 2002. Argue for or against the following statement: "The massive frauds and auditor practices that led to the Sarbanes-Oxley Act could have been avoided had there been more legislation involving accounting and auditing between 1934 and 2002." Justify your answer.

10. Consider the following situation. A group of investors who specialize in investing in high-technology IPOs files suit against the auditors of one of those firms when the stock loses 50 percent of its value shortly after issue. Analysts attribute the steep decline to the firm losing a major contract. The investors, however, are basing their claim on the revelation that much of the firm's inventory was carried at a value well above its fair market value.

In fact, the auditors had been negligent in their audit of management's estimate of the market value of inventory. The audit firm failed to hire appropriate specialists to price the goods, instead relying on in-house expertise developed through the firm's extensive experience auditing high-technology firms.

If you were the senior partner of the audit firm for this high-technology IPO, how would you defend against the lawsuit? Specifically, discuss the merits of the defense strategies available to your firm that are noted in the text. Suggest a new defense.

11. Answer each of the following independent questions, based on your understanding of the AICPA Code of Professional Conduct or IFAC Code of Ethics for Professional Accountants. Justify your answer.
- a. May an auditor refer business to a client in exchange for commissions?
- b. May an auditor allow clients to knowingly misstate financial misstatements?
- c. May an audit firm charge a contingent fee for an audit client?
- d. May an auditor ever disclose confidential client information?

e.   What can happen to an auditor who cheats on a filed tax return?

f.   Under what conditions does an auditor in a limited liability partnership face unlimited liability?

g.   May an audit firm collect a "finder's fee" for referring business to another audit firm?

PROBLEMS

1. For each of the following routine audit decisions, use Figure 17–2 as a guide and apply each step of the decision process to the audit decision.

a.   The business process that will require the most attention/resources for a retail clothing chain

b.   The type of specialists to employ on an audit of a diversified manufacturing firm

c.   The level of materiality to set for an engagement

d.   How many staff auditors to assign to an engagement

2. Although the use of heuristics may lead to biased audit decisions in some cases, all humans make use of them. However, it is important to recognize when an auditor is employing a heuristic so that he or she can be cognizant of the biases and can minimize their effect on decision making.

For each of the following situations in which an auditor's decision making may be affected by a bias, (1) identify the heuristic (if any) employed and the bias that results, (2) describe the resulting implications for the audit, and (3) suggest a technique to rectify the bias.

a.   An auditor spends an inordinate amount of time looking for management fraud on an engagement, even though the incidence of management fraud is actually quite low for this type of client.

b.   Believing that the sales order/receivables process is well controlled, an auditor disregards evidence from his sample that the process is not well controlled.

c.   Having just finished an engagement characterized by numerous material inventory misstatements, an auditor pays unwarranted attention to that account on the current engagement.

d.   An auditor believes that the presence of errors in the receivables *and* the inventory is more probable than finding an error in just the inventory.

e.   When conducting attribute sampling for the tests of controls over payables, the auditor sets an initial expectation of error of 3 percent (last year's actual error rate), even though that process saw a great deal of turnover since last year's audit.

f.   When deciding the initial expectation of error for an attribute sample for a test of controls over payroll, the auditor sets a rate higher than last year's actual error rate because that rate exceeded the expectation.

g.   The auditor argues for higher accruals of pension expense based on the executive bonuses given out the previous year in which the company saw unexpectedly large sales and profit increases.

h.   In deciding where to set the control risk for the sales order process, the auditor relies on a sample of just 30 of the 10,000 transactions the client recorded for the period.

3. Auditors employ numerous methods to alleviate the potential biases that may result from the use of judgment heuristics. These include

• Improving expertise
• Debiasing techniques
• Framing and perspective
• Group decision making and review
• Justification
• Decision aids

Examine each of the following incidences of biased audit judgment. Discuss how one or more of these methods may be employed to improve audit judgment.

a. An auditor believes that a sample size of 10 items from a population of several hundred thousand items is enough to judge the quality of compliance with controls over the accounts receivable posting process.

b. Having completed audits for several years on a certain client without incident, an auditor's substantive tests are designed with the perspective that the possibility of misstatement is remote.

c. The auditor who discovered a small fraud related to the prepaid assets account writes a qualified audit report.

d. The auditor who performs preliminary analytical procedures on the reasonability of various sales expenses fails to notice that the client recently instituted a compensation scheme more heavily weighted toward commissions and away from fixed salaries (each of which are recorded in different expense accounts).

e. An auditor argues for a lower risk of material misstatement for a process based solely on the results of her experience with such clients and her walkthrough of the area.

f. Not fully understanding the ramifications of the newly issued financial accounting standard on stock-based compensation, an auditor trusts management's estimates without further testing.

g. An audit manager notices that her new and eager-to-please staff is prone to overestimating the probabilities of certain events that are, in fact, very unusual.

h. An audit senior notices that his staff's interviews with clients during the evaluation of controls are rarely adequate to get a good understanding of the process.

4. Audit decisions sometimes come down to a trade-off between satisfying one set of stakeholders at the expense of others. In the example in Figure 17–4 and 17–5, an auditor is forced to choose between making her superiors and the client happy or doing what she feels is appropriate to the goal of an audit: to attest to the fairness of management's assertions.

Consider each of the following brief situations:

a. An auditor discovers a small employee fraud involving theft of power tools in the service department of a TV/VCR repair operation.

b. An audit manager knows that client management expects all auditors assigned to their engagement to be CPAs, but because of short staffing the manager is considering assigning to the engagement a new hire who has not passed the CPA exam.

c. An auditor discovers that one of his friends and co-workers on an engagement has been using the client's equipment for personal business (i.e., long-distance telephone calls, photocopying).

d. While reviewing the workpapers of an audit on which he worked several years ago, a senior auditor discovers several procedures had been recorded as completed, although he knows they were not. The person who completed the workpapers is now his superior.

e. An auditor knows for a fact that a friend of hers who works for another firm and who represents himself as a CPA has not completed the appropriate mandated continuing education for his CPA certification.

f. The senior partner in charge of an audit engagement is told that his firm will be fired from the audit if he goes forward with his plan to give the company a qualified audit report.

g. An audit manager discovers that controls over the payables process of her client are poor and cannot be relied on. In fact, the controls have been that way for several years, but the manager approved them in years past based on inadequate tests of controls.

h. A junior member of an audit firm discovers that a senior partner in the firm has been adding billable hours to the client bills in an attempt to boost revenue.

For each of the preceding situations, (1) identify the major stakeholders (besides the individual making the decision), (2) identify and discuss the alternatives the subject faces, paying special attention to the ethics involved in the decision, and (3) choose and defend a course of action.

5. Answer each of the following independent questions, based on your understanding of the AICPA Code of Professional Conduct or IFAC Code of Ethics for Professional Accountants. Cite support for your answer.

a. May an auditor refer business to a client in exchange for commissions?

b. Under what conditions may an auditor allow a departure from GAAP to appear in the financial statements?

c. May an audit firm charge a contingent fee for a client who is attempting to secure a refund from a tax authority (e.g., the U.S. IRS)?

d. Does the auditor have to justify his or her independence to a client's audit committee under any conditions?

e. May a former partner of an audit firm accept a position on the board of directors of a client of that audit firm?

f. May the name of the audit firm include a reference to its specialty?

g. May an audit firm collect a "finder's fee" for referring business to another audit firm?

h. To whom may an auditor reveal information relevant to a regulatory investigation on a client?

6. Auditors typically rely on the following legal defenses when parties bring suit against them:

- No responsibility to plaintiff
- Lack of reliance by the plaintiff
- Auditor exercise of due diligence
- Lack of auditor intent to defraud
- Contributory negligence by management

Consider each of the following independent situations:

a. The shareholders of a large, multinational firm bring a class-action lawsuit under common law against the audit firm. They charge that the audit firm was grossly negligent in its responsibilities in that it failed to detect a material management fraud that ended up pushing the firm into Chapter 11 bankruptcy.

b. The shareholders of a retail women's clothing chain bring a lawsuit against the audit firm charging that the audit firm was negligent in not making a large write-down of some obsolete inventory. When the need for the write-down later became public, the company's stock lost 25 percent of its value in one day.

c. The creditors of an aerospace concern that has defaulted on its secured debt file suit against the accounting firm that performed a review and some tax work for it.

d. The shareholders of a large retail drugstore chain file suit against the auditors when it comes to light that the managers have been embezzling large amounts of money from the company treasury. The audit firm had substantially complied with professional standards in its audit, but the managers had colluded in such a way that detection of such a fraud would have been difficult in any circumstances.

e. A large software company files suit against the audit firm of its largest rival when its needless rushing to put out a comparable product jeopardizes its good reputation in the software market. The rival firm went bankrupt shortly after the product's release, but its auditors had not made a going concern qualification in the last audit report. The software company argues that it relied on the rival firm's audit report in its decision to rush its own product to market.

f. The shareholders of a large carpet cleaning chain file suit against the auditors when it comes to light that the firm had far fewer bona fide sales than was alleged in the financial statements. The owner of the firm had entered the false sales in an attempt to puff up the financial statements to attract investors and franchisers. The audit team had sampled the sales transactions as part of its substantive tests of account balance details and had found, correctly, that the sampled sales were legitimate.

For each of the preceding, suggest a defense that the audit firm may employ against the plaintiffs. Note where the defense might be different if the case was litigated outside the U.S.

7. It is important that auditors understand the legal precedents that apply to their profession. Common law applicable to auditors has arisen from court cases spanning back to the 1930s. Several of the most important cases are summarized in Figure 17-9 and internationally in Figure 17–12.

   For each of the following issues, identify the court case(s), under U.S. or international common law, that offer the auditor guidance on his or her responsibilities and summarize the findings.

   a. What classes of plaintiffs may sue an auditor under tort law?
   b. What classes of plaintiffs may be considered privy to the auditing contract?
   c. What are the precedents for defending against a lawsuit on the basis of management's contributory negligence?
   d. What are the legal precedents for the wording in audit reports?
   e. What are the legal precedents for the wording in engagements letters?

8. Securities law applies to auditors engaged in audits of firms that issue shares to the general public. It is important that auditors understand the court cases that have interpreted their liability for fair reporting under the U.S. SEC Acts of 1933 and 1934. Figures 17–10 and 17–11 list the most important of those cases.

   For each of the following issues, identify the court case that offers the auditor some guidance on his or her responsibilities and summarize the findings.

   a. What are the auditor's duties when the client conducts financial transactions that may seem significant but are not required to be disclosed under GAAP?
   b. To what extent does lack of criminal intent protect the auditor when his or her actions are deemed to be reckless?
   c. To what extent is the auditor liable under security law when his or her actions are neither reckless nor intended to deceive?
   d. What are the responsibilities of the auditor when he discovers evidence of material misstatement after fieldwork has been conducted?
   e. Is the auditor criminally liable when he or she colludes with management to defraud investors?

9. Auditors must maintain both the fact and appearance of independence if they are to maintain their respected role in the business community. Consider each of the following independent situations. Using the material in the text, comment on whether the subject is within professional guidelines for maintaining independence. Discuss whether you believe the auditor is within guidelines for independence on those for which there is no clear precedent.

   a. A firm audits a small business client for whom it also provides data processing services.
   b. Trish & Co. audits Robert and David Co., a large, publicly held client for whom it also provides data processing services and tax work.
   c. An audit staffer who works for Danny and Doug's Audit Firm owns a small amount of stock in one of the firm's clients, Susan Corp. The staffer is not assigned to the audit.
   d. An audit manager who reviews some of the work on the Billy Co. engagement owns a small amount of stock in Billy Co.
   e. A senior partner occasionally makes appearances at board of directors' meetings for one of his clients to discuss management strategies.
   f. The audit manager for the Harriet Bank engagement carries a credit card issued by that bank with a $5,000 credit limit. The card has been borrowed against up to its limit. The audit manager is in some financial distress.
   g. Both Maureen & Co., CPAs and one of their clients, Carolyn Corp., a tennis ball manufacturer, are involved in a suit where both are named as defendants in an investment fraud. Neither the audit firm nor the manufacturer plan on coordinating its defense with the other.

h. Graeme Jones, a senior partner of a local accounting firm, serves on the board of directors of Margaret Co. Although no audit relationship exists between the accounting firm and Margaret Co., most of Margaret Co.'s major competitors are audited by Graeme's firm.

i. Heitger and Godwin, CPAs, perform auditing services and consulting services for Tabor Corp. There are no members of the audit engagement team who work on the consulting engagement.

10. Consider the following situation. The board of directors of a major airline promotes one of its marketing vice presidents to the position of president and CEO. Included in the compensation package is a large salary increase and a bonus based on accounting ratios such as return on equity. Before accepting the job, the vice president consults the audited financial statements of the company to determine the prospects for bonuses. Seeing a reasonably well-performing company, the vice president accepts the job and promptly puts a down payment on a large home in a wealthy part of town and signs a hefty mortgage for the remainder.

About nine months into the new president's tenure, the airline undergoes a severe cash shortage due to soaring fuel prices and cutthroat competition at its major hub airports. Having already missed one interest payment, the bondholders are threatening to force the company into liquidation if it misses another. The executives face the following dilemma: Reduce fares and operate the airline at an accounting loss to preserve cash flow and to keep the airline afloat until conditions improve (even though doing so means they will see no bonus), or keep fares high and stretch payables (including the bond interest payments) to the limit so that they will get a bonus but will run the risk of bankrupting the airline.

The new president now realizes that buying an expensive home at this particular time may not have been a wise decision. In fact, when the board overrules the president and votes to lower fares, the president loses the bonus for the year and is forced to sell the new home at a large loss. However, on the advice of an attorney, the president sues the airline's auditors for not disclosing the extent of the company's vulnerability in the last set of financial statements and for allowing misleading financial data—the airline's supposed profitability—to appear in the company's annual report.

If you were the senior partner of the audit firm for this airline, how would you defend against the lawsuit? Specifically, discuss the merits of the defense strategies available to your firm that are noted in the text. Suggest a new defense.

Case 17–1: First Securities

Jane Anderson is a recent graduate of an accounting program that devoted a section of the auditing course to the topic of ethics. As she prepared for the CPA exam, much to her surprise she learned that her state board of accountancy required that she pass a test on ethics before she received her license. Although the test was a take-home one, she wanted to do well and had begun to prepare when she became a staff member at the regional public accounting firm of Andrews & Olds, CPAs. Her initial assignment was to audit the marketable securities account of First Securities, a public company with shares listed on the American Stock Exchange and a large client of Andrews & Olds.

During fieldwork, Jane discovered certain facts to cause her to question management's handling of trading securities. The audit senior disagrees with Jane and has documented some negative comments in the staff review. As the engagement partner began the performance evaluation for those staff members who worked on the First Securities audit, he became quite concerned over the poor rating that Jane received from the audit senior as to her disagreement with First Securities' handling of its trading securities. Jane is to meet with the partner on Monday and is attempting to get her thoughts together to defend her actions.

Client Background

First Securities, a publicly held financial institution, had weathered poorly the economic recession of the early 1990s and 2000s. Its battered portfolio of investment securities survived, but just barely. Only an eleventh hour lobbying effort to Congress delayed a proposed regulatory change by the Federal Deposit Insurance Corporation (FDIC) that would have resulted in additional write-downs to reflect market values in the securities portfolio of First Securities. Such write-downs would have placed the institution's capital base in jeopardy.

Currently, First Securities' capital to debt ratio is 0.75 to 1. Federal requirements consider a financial institution to be capital deficient, and therefore a potential takeover by a regulatory agency, if the capital to debt ratio is below 0.5 to 1. The current proposed regulatory rules would have resulted in a capital to debt ratio of 0.44 to 1. In order to minimize any future legislation, First Securities has banded together with its fellow institutions to fight any additional threats to the historical cost concept in recording their investment securities.

Jane has consulted a recently released audit guide issued by the American Institute of CPAs entitled *Audits of Savings Institutions*. This guide addresses the method of measurement for investments in venture capital divisions of financial institutions. The required method of valuation for such activities is market value—not lower of cost or market.

Source: Case prepared by Robert R. Rouse, PhD, CPA (Professor and Chair, Department of Accounting, College of Charleston) and Thomas R. Weirich, PhD, CPA (Arthur Andersen & Co. Alumni, Professor and Chair, School of Accounting, Central Michigan University).

Much to the delight of First Securities, the market value of the investments for its venture capital division had appreciated millions of dollars above the cost basis previously used. The income from the appreciation totaled $7.2 million and flowed directly to the combined financial statements of First Securities, which proudly disclosed the results in the annual report. First Securities, the once mighty defender of historical cost, threatened with valuation of its investment of its bond portfolio at lower of cost or market, had quickly and quietly succumbed to market valuation—obviously when it benefited the bottom line. Although she did not want to appear too aggressive to the staff and too challenging to the client, Jane was very concerned that an ethical problem may have arisen.

A faithful reader of the daily financial section of the local paper, she remembered that the Securities and Exchange Commission (SEC) had admonished several registrants for their accounting for securities in their registrations filings. She conducted some research in the firm's library and located the SEC's Accounting and Auditing Enforcement Releases Nos. 309 and 316. These two enforcement releases summarized the actions taken by the SEC against Fleet/Norstar Financial Group Inc. and Excel Bankcorp Inc. In both cases, the Commission determined that the entities failed to write down the cost bases of certain of its marketable equity securities to their realizable values and therefore failed to recognize the corresponding losses as required by generally accepted accounting principles.

Jane also finds that the SEC had recognized a third state of reporting of debt securities. In the SEC's *Staff Accounting Bulletin No. 59*, the staff recognized both a temporary and an "other than temporary" decline in aggregate market values. The SEC, in acknowledging this third state of "other than temporary," quickly proposed that an other than temporary decline could occur long before a permanent decline in value occurs. In an attempt to address the concerns of the SEC, the Financial Accounting Standards Board issued SFAS No. 115, *Accounting for Certain Investments in Debt and Equity Securities*, which states that if the decline in fair value is judged to be other than temporary, the cost of the individual security shall be written down to fair value and the amount of the write-down included in current earnings. However, First Securities had equated an other than temporary decline with permanent decline and, therefore, had charged the declines in its unclassified portfolio of marketable securities against the equity section of the balance sheet with no recognition on the income statement.

Jane discussed this issue of "other than temporary" decline with the staff of her firm in their monthly continuing professional education sessions, with particular emphasis on the SEC's developments and the potential impact upon clients' statements. The managing partner was quite impressed with Jane's awareness and decided to have a member of the faculty of her alma mater make a formal presentation on the topic to the audit staff.

Jane's Dilemma

After the presentation, Jane decided to review the portfolio of First Securities and became convinced that although the declines in the portfolio had indeed not become permanent, the declines were certainly not temporary. The value of many of these depressed securities were readily available in the newspaper, and after a thorough review of the past eight quarters, she concluded that the write-downs were in fact other than temporary and should be reported as a charge on the income statement. Such write-downs would result in First Securities charging a

$10.4 million loss to current earnings. She quickly remembered the euphoria of First Securities when it was able to recognize the appreciated market values of the venture capital division and realized it now would be most upset at any suggestion that write-downs through the income statement were forthcoming.

First Securities was the only publicly held client of her firm, and although it had cost the firm a considerable amount of money and effort to become capable of servicing a registrant, the firm took great pride in the association. In addition, First Securities had recently informed the firm that unsolicited serious overtures were being made to the company by the newly opened office of a major public accounting firm. The managing partner of the new office had every intention of proving that a major firm could prosper in the local community, which had rejected several past attempts by other firms.

Jane successfully completed the CPA exam, and she had just returned the ethics part to the state board. She now had more reservations as to the situation at First Securities. The time between her initial recognition of the situation and the present had only confirmed that her concerns regarding the valuation of the securities portfolio were well grounded. She decided to discuss the situation with the managing partner, who had just returned from a retreat with First Securities. He had participated in lengthy discussions with top management about the future and was satisfied that First Securities would remain a client. He was ever more aware of the need to remain very attentive to the client's needs and announced that he had just accepted a free membership in the country club owned by First Securities. Now if he could only improve his golf swing.

Jane is most concerned about her perceived image with her firm. She had recently talked to her former college roommate who had taken a job with a major firm in the state capital. The roommate had called to tell her that she had just received two weeks' notice. Because of a merger involving a client within the office, she was no longer needed.

Jane just received a call that the partner would see her at 8:00 a.m. on Monday morning to review her performance evaluation concerning the First Securities audit. All these issues were swirling in her head. The partner had allocated an hour for the meeting, and she did not want to appear disorganized. As she drove home in anticipation of tomorrow's football game with her alma mater's rival, she decided to spend Sunday afternoon collecting her thoughts.

Requirements

1. Prepare a list of issues that Jane should discuss with the partner.
2. Are there any ethical issues involved or has Jane confused aggressive accounting positions with encroachments upon ethics?

18

Audit and Assurance Services

Outline

INTRODUCTION

The accounting profession provides a variety of services to business organizations, predominantly in three areas: auditing (assurance services), tax support, or consulting services, although the combination of consulting and auditing is limited by law and professional ethics. As discussed in Chapter 2, there is a very broad range of audit-related assurance services that public accountants may provide to clients. Many of the techniques discussed in preceding chapters apply to other assurance services, and the same set of skills can be utilized to attest to assertions other than those embodied in the annual financial statements. Some forms of assurance that are closely related to financial statements include:

- *Reviews:* This service focuses on the plausibility of the financial statements based on a limited amount of testing that is much less extensive than used in an audit. Reviews can be carried out on either annual or interim financial statements.
- *Compilation engagements:* This service focuses on the preparation of the financial statements (i.e., income statement and balance sheet). The accountant provides no assurance about the compliance of these financial statements with GAAP only that they are drawn from the client's records. The accountant performs no tests of the information provided by the client that is used to prepare the financial statements.
- *Agreed-upon procedures engagements:* This service involves the performance of a specified set of audit procedures on specified assertions or elements of the financial statements. No attempt is made to expand testing beyond the procedures agreed to by the parties involved.

In an *audit* (sometimes referred to as an *examination*), an auditor expresses *positive assurance* about an assertion being examined, that is, the assertion is presented in accordance with established criteria (i.e., GAAP) in all material respects. A *review* (sometimes referred to as a *moderate assurance engagement*) provides less assurance than an examination because the auditor only expresses *negative assurance* about the information, that is, the public accountant is not aware of any reasons to conclude the financial statements are not in conformity with established criteria (i.e., GAAP). Finally, an *agreed-upon procedures engagement* involves issuing a report on specific findings obtained by performing specific procedures agreed to by all parties prior to the start of the engagement. The first part of the chapter focuses on assurance services related to financial information.

In a more general sense, assurance services have become a broad umbrella for a large range of services that go far beyond financial information. *Assurance services* are defined as "independent professional services that improve the quality of information, or its context, for decision makers."[1] Although new assurance service development has received less emphasis in the post-Enron environment, professional accounting organizations worldwide, led by a partnership of the AICPA in the United States and the CICA in Canada developed cooperative initiatives such as *WebTrust*[SM] and *SysTrust*[SM] that have laid the foundation for future expansion of assurance services. The second part of this chapter introduces this broader set of assurance services.

> **Authoritative Guidance & Standards**
>
> Standards for assurance services other than financial statements are contained in AICPA Statements on Standards for Attestation Engagements (SSAEs) or Statements on Standards for Accounting and Review Services (SSARSs) and IAASB International Standards on Assurance Engagements (ISAEs), International Standards on Review Engagements (ISREs), or International Standards on Related Services (ISRSs).

FINANCIAL INFORMATION ASSURANCE SERVICES

Public accountants offer numerous assurance services related to the quality of financial information. The audit of financial statements is the most rigorous form of assurance about financial information. As technology expands information available

---

1 AICPA *Special Committee on Assurance Services* 1996.

to investors and makes it more accessible and easy to use, the range of potential assurance services related to financial information also expands. Public accountants offer a broad range of assurance services related to the quality of financial information suited to the dynamic environment of business. These services do not constitute an audit and often are subject to specialized rules and guidelines. In this section we will discuss the following assurance services related to financial information:

- Review of annual financial statements
- Review of interim financial statements
- Compilation of financial statements
- Engagements applying agreed-upon procedures
- Examination of prospective data and forecasts
- Letters to underwriters

REVIEW OF ANNUAL FINANCIAL STATEMENTS

A review engagement provides *moderate assurance* about the quality of information included in a financial report but does not provide as much assurance as an audit because it entails much less effort and evidence than an audit. Reviews may only be performed for privately held or not-for-profit organizations, and typically are performed when organizations have less need of an audit, or possess a sufficient level of confidence in financial reporting, such that the costs of paying for an audit do not result in sufficient benefits to justify an audit. Local and regional public accounting firms perform a majority of review engagements in the United States, where they are typically an important source of revenues for these organizations, although all public accounting firms, no matter what their size, routinely perform review engagements in other countries.

The public accountant gathers evidence about financial information using inquiry of the client firm's personnel and analysis of the client's accounting records.

Authoritative Guidance & Standards
Standards for reviews of financial statements are contained in SSARS 8/SSARS 1 and ISRE 2400.

Figures 18–1 and 18–2 illustrate the types of procedures that would be performed for a review engagement based on the IAASB's *International Standards on Review Engagements* and the AICPA's *Statements on Standards for Accounting and Review Services*. As in all professional engagements, it is strongly recommended that an engagement letter be obtained from the client so as to clearly state the degree of assurance that will be provided by the review.

In general, public accountants performing review engagements are required to be objective and independent, be professionally proficient, exercise due care, and maintain the confidentiality of client information. For a review, a public accountant must possess an adequate level of knowledge of the industry, appropriate accounting standards, and the organization's basic activities. Knowledge of the organization includes a general understanding of its products, production methods, distribution channels, compensation schemes, operating locations, transactions with related parties, and asset/liability base. The public accountant should determine materiality using the same guidelines as an audit.

Public accountants are expected to exercise professional skepticism about the management's assertions and statements and not ignore the possibility that the financial statements are materially misstated subject to the standard of evidence used in a review. The principle sources of evidence are inquiry and analytical procedures, resulting in substantially less evidence than in an audit of financial statements. The analytical procedures used in a review are similar to those discussed in

Figure 18–1   Illustrative Procedures for a Review Engagement Based on International Standards

Inquiries
- Inquiries to obtain an understanding of the entity's business and the industry in which it operates
- Inquiries concerning the entity's accounting principles and practices
- Inquiries concerning the entity's procedures for recording, classifying, and summarizing transactions, accumulating information for disclosure in the financial statements, and preparing financial statements
- Inquiries concerning all material assertions in the financial statements
- Inquiries of persons having responsibility for financial and accounting matters concerning, for example:
  - Whether all transactions have been recorded
  - Whether the financial statements have been prepared in accordance with the basis of accounting indicated
  - Changes in the entity's business activities and accounting principles and practices
  - Matters as to which questions have arisen in the course of applying the above procedures

Analytical procedures
- Analytical procedures designed to identify relationships and individual items that appear unusual. Such procedures would include
  - Comparison of the financial statements with statements for prior periods
  - Comparison of the financial statements with anticipated results and financial position
  - Study of the relationships of the elements of the financial statements that would be expected to conform to a predictable pattern based on the entity's experience or industry norm
  - In applying these procedures, the auditor would consider the types of matters that required accounting adjustments in prior periods

Other information
- Inquiries concerning actions taken at meetings of shareholders, the board of directors, committees of the board of directors, and other meetings that may affect the financial statements
- Reading the financial statements to consider, on the basis of information coming to the public accountant's attention, whether the financial statements appear to conform with the basis of accounting indicated
- Obtaining reports from other public accountants, if any and if considered necessary, who have been engaged to audit or review the financial statements of components of the entity
- Obtain a representation letter from appropriate organization personnel covering
  - Whether the financial statements have been prepared in conformity with generally accepted accounting principles
  - Significant changes to the organization's activities or accounting policies and procedures
  - Information obtained related to matters arising from other review procedures
  - Events subsequent to the date of the financial statements that would have a material impact on the statements

Figure 18–2   Illustrative Procedures for a Review Engagement Based on U.S. Standards

- Inquire about the organization's accounting practices and methods of application.
- Inquire about the organization's procedures for recording, classifying, and summarizing transactions; also inquire about the organization's methods for accumulating information required for relevant disclosures.
- Perform analytical procedures on the data in the financial statements, which will identify relationships or accounts that appear to be unusual or do not meet expectations:
  - Compare current-year amounts with prior-year balances.
  - Compare current-year results with anticipated outcomes such as budgets.
  - Evaluate relationships in the data that would be expected to conform to identifiable patterns.
  - Consider matters related to adjustments required in prior years.
- Inquire as to actions taken at meetings of key management and owner groups (e.g., shareholder meetings, board of directors meetings, and audit committee meetings), and ascertain their implications for the financial statements.
- Read the financial statements to ascertain whether they comply with generally accepted accounting principles based on the accountant's understanding of the organization, its operations, key actions, and analytical results.
- Obtain appropriate reports from accountants who provided audit or review services related to any significant components of the financial statements being reviewed.
- Obtain a representation letter from appropriate organization personnel covering:
  - Whether the financial statements have been prepared in conformity with generally accepted accounting principles.
  - Significant changes to the organization's activities or accounting policies and procedures.
  - Information obtained related to matters arising from other review procedures.
  - Events subsequent to the date of the financial statements that would have a material impact on the statements.

Chapters 9 and 14 but limited to low and moderate levels of analysis. Client inquiries should cover all major asset, liability, and equity classifications on the balance sheet, as well as related income statement accounts. The extent of the inquiries that are necessary will increase when:

- Financial transactions and accounts are complex or material
- The likelihood of misstatement of an account is high
- Knowledge of the client indicates potential problems with some accounts
- Competence of the client's accounting personnel is low
- The value of an account is subjectively determined
- There are observed inadequacies in the organization's financial data or disclosures

The accountant is not required to obtain an understanding of internal control. Substantive evidence for individual transactions is rarely obtained but can be used to clarify issues identified by other procedures. However, legal counsel often advises against performing such substantive tests as they may raise an expectation that an audit is being performed. Furthermore, once an accountant has started a substantive test, he or she has a legal duty to complete the test and evaluate the possibility of material misstatements based on that evidence.

If the public accountant has reason to believe that the information subject to review may be materially misstated, additional testing should be performed to

Figure 18–3   Examples of Review Report on Financial Statements

---

Panel A: Standard Review Report (§AR100.35) under U.S. Standards

We have reviewed the accompanying balance sheet of XYZ Company as of December 31, 20XX, and the related statements of income, retained earnings, and cash flows for the year then ended, in accordance with Statements on Standards for Accounting and Review Services issued by the American Institute of Certified Public Accountants. All information included in these financial statements is the representation of the management of XYZ Company.

A review consists principally of inquiries of company personnel and analytical procedures applied to financial data. It is substantially less in scope than an audit in accordance with generally accepted auditing standards, the objective of which is the expression of an opinion regarding the financial statements taken as a whole. Accordingly, we do not express such an opinion.

Based on our review, we are not aware of any material modifications that should be made to the accompanying financial statements in order for them to be in conformity with generally accepted accounting principles.

Panel B. Unqualified Report under International Standards

We have reviewed the accompanying balance sheet of ABC Company at December 31, 20XX, and the income statement, statement of changes in equity, and cash flow statement for the year then ended. These financial statements are the responsibility of the company's management. Our responsibility is to issue a report on these financial statements based on our review.

We conducted our review in accordance with the International Standard on Review Engagements 2400 *[or refer to relevant national standards or practices applicable to review engagements]*. This Standard requires that we plan and perform the review to obtain moderate assurance as to whether the financial statements are free of material misstatement. A review is limited primarily to inquiries of company personnel and analytical procedures applied to financial data and thus provides less assurance than an audit. We have not performed an audit and, accordingly, we do not express an audit opinion.

Based on our review, nothing has come to our attention that causes us to believe that the accompanying financial statements do not give a true and fair view *[or are not presented fairly, in all material respects]* in accordance with International Accounting Standards *[or indicate relevant national standards]*.

---

conclude that either the information is accurate and supports the issuance of a standard report, or to support the issuance of a modified report if the misstatements are not corrected by management. Hence, in spite of the limited evidence available, a positive responsibility exists to correct or disclose any known errors, omissions or violations of GAAP that come to the attention of the accountant. Figures 18–3 and 18–4 present examples of the public accountant's report for a review engagement: (1) under normal conditions and (2) when departures from GAAP are discovered by the accountant. The opinion is in the form of *negative assurance*, meaning that the accountant states that he or she is unaware of any errors or omissions based on the required procedures.[2]

---

2 Reporting formats frequently differ, especially on minor details, hence each example contains both U.S. and international formats. In areas where no international standards exist, we feature U.S. standards. There has been relatively little attention to international harmonization of these types of services or reports.

Figure 18–4   Examples of Review Reports—GAAP Departures

Panel A: Review Report with Departure from GAAP (§AR100.40) under U.S. Standards

We have reviewed the accompanying balance sheet of XYZ Company as of December 31, 20XX, and the related statements of income, retained earnings, and cash flows for the year then ended, in accordance with Statements on Standards for Accounting and Review Services issued by the American Institute of Certified Public Accountants. All information included in these financial statements is the representation of the management of XYZ Company.

A review consists principally of inquiries of company personnel and analytical procedures applied to financial data. It is substantially less in scope than an audit in accordance with generally accepted auditing standards, the objective of which is the expression of an opinion regarding the financial statements taken as a whole. Accordingly, we do not express such an opinion.

Based on our review, with the exception of the matter described in the following paragraph, we are not aware of any material modifications that should be made to the accompanying financial statements in order for them to be in conformity with generally accepted accounting principles.

As disclosed in note X to the financial statements, generally accepted accounting principles require that inventory cost consist of material, labor, and overhead. Management has informed us that the inventory of finished goods and work-in-process is stated in the accompanying financial statements at material and labor cost only, and that the effect of this departure from generally accepted accounting principles on financial position, results of operations and cash flows has not been determined.

Panel B. Qualification for a Departure from International Accounting Standards

We have reviewed the accompanying balance sheet of ABC Company at December 31, 20XX, and the income statement, statement of changes in equity and cash flow statement for the year then ended. These financial statements are the responsibility of the company's management. Our responsibility is to issue a report on these financial statements based on our review.

We conducted our review in accordance with the International Standard on Review Engagements 2400 *[or refer to relevant national standards or practices applicable to review engagements]*. This Standard requires that we plan and perform the review to obtain moderate assurance as to whether the financial statements are free of material misstatement. A review is limited primarily to inquiries of company personnel and analytical procedures applied to financial data and thus provides less assurance than an audit. We have not performed an audit, and, accordingly, we do not express an audit opinion.

Management has informed us that inventory has been stated at its cost which is in excess of its net realizable value. Management's computation, which we have reviewed, shows that inventory, if valued at the lower of cost and net realizable value as required by International Accounting Standards *[or indicate relevant national standards]*, would have been decreased by $X, and net income and shareholders' equity would have been decreased by $Y.

Based on our review, except for the effects of the overstatement of inventory described in the previous paragraph, nothing has come to our attention that causes us to believe that the accompanying financial statements do not give a true and fair view *[or are not presented fairly, in all material respects]* in accordance with International Accounting Standards *[or indicate relevant national standards]*.

REVIEW OF INTERIM FINANCIAL STATEMENTS

Companies that issue publicly traded securities are required to prepare interim financial statements on a quarterly basis in North America and semi-annually in most of the rest of the world. These statements are not audited, but much of the information will be included in the audited annual financial statements. The quarterly information may be reviewed by the client firm's auditor, whether at year end or when each interim report is prepared. Public companies registered with the SEC are required to have their quarterly financial statements reviewed by their audit firms. In the United States, interim reviews for public companies are subject to specific standards, e.g., SAS 71, "Interim Financial Information," whereas internationally they are incorporated in the standard on the general review of annual financial statements.[3]

The principal difference between a general annual review and an interim review is that the auditor must obtain an understanding of internal control as it applies to the preparation of interim financial information, similar to the second fieldwork of GAAS. Hence, the auditor must consider his or her understanding of the accounting system and the control systems. Also, an interim financial statement review may incorporate some substantive tests of transactions and account balances to gather evidence pertinent to the year end audit, something that would not be done in a general annual review. Because many audit tests can be performed on an interim basis, they may also be relevant to the review of the quarterly statements. Furthermore, auditors should read the minutes of board of directors' meetings in order to assess the impact of actions taken on interim statements.

The standard interim review report used by an independent public accountant is presented in Figure 18–5. There is very little difference between this report and the one used for a general annual review. The report provides an explicit statement of the work performed by the independent accountant and disclaims an audit opinion. The opinion is in the form of negative assurance. The standard report could be qualified due to (1) a departure from generally accepted accounting principles or (2) inadequate disclosures.

COMPILATION OF FINANCIAL STATEMENTS

Public accountants may be hired to draft financial statements based on information provided by the organization. A compilation involves collecting, classifying, and summarizing financial information, that is, basic bookkeeping and financial report preparation. This type of engagement is technically not an assurance engagement because the public accountant does not provide an opinion on the quality of the information. No audit procedures are performed—the client is engaging the accountant's accounting expertise rather than his or her audit expertise. The accountant always disclaims an opinion on compiled financial statements. An engagement letter should be used to clarify the terms of the engagement. Also, the accountant should obtain a representation letter from management stating it is responsible for the financial information.

The standards applicable to compilation engagements are covered in the AICPA's *Statements on Standards for Accounting and Review Services* and international standards are covered in the IAASB's *International Standard on Related*

---

3 Canada also has specific rules for interim reviews (see the CICA Handbook Section 7050, *The Auditor's Review of Interim Financial Statements*).

Figure 18–5   Examples of Review Report on Interim Financial Statements

---

Panel A: Independent Accountant's Report (§AU722.28) under U.S. Standards

We have reviewed the accompanying balance sheet of XYZ Company as of September 30, 20XX, and the related statements of income, retained earnings and cash flows for the three-month period then ended. These financial statements are the responsibility of the management of XYZ Company.

We conducted our review in accordance with standards established by the American Institute of Certified Public Accountants. A review of interim financial information consists principally of applying analytical procedures to financial data and making inquiries of persons responsible for financial and accounting matters. It is substantially less in scope than an audit in accordance with generally accepted auditing standards, the objective of which is the expression of an opinion regarding the financial statements taken as a whole. Accordingly, we do not express such an opinion.

Based on our review, we are not aware of any material modifications that should be made to the accompanying financial statements in order for them to be in conformity with generally accepted accounting principles.

Panel B: Auditor's Report under International Standards

Introduction

We have reviewed the accompanying balance sheet of XYZ Company as of March 31, 20XX and the related statements of income, changes in equity and cash flows for the three-month period then ended, and a summary of significant accounting policies and other explanatory notes. Management is responsible for the preparation and fair presentation of this interim financial information in accordance with *[indicate applicable financial reporting framework]*. Our responsibility is to express a conclusion on this interim financial information based on our review.

Scope of Review

We conducted our review in accordance with International Standard on Review Engagements 2410, "Review of Interim Financial Information Performed by the Independent Auditor of the Entity." A review of interim financial information consists of making inquiries, primarily of persons responsible for financial and accounting matters, and applying analytical and other review procedures. A review is substantially less in scope than an audit conducted in accordance with International Standards on Auditing and consequently does not enable us to obtain assurance that we would become aware of all significant matters that might be identified in an audit. Accordingly, we do not express such an opinion.

Conclusion

Based on our review, nothing has come to our attention that causes us to believe that the accompanying interim financial information does not give a true and fair view of *[or "does not present fairly, in all material respects,"]* the financial position of the entity as at March 31, 20XX, and of its financial performance and its cash flows for the three month period then ended in accordance with *[applicable financial reporting framework, including a reference to the jurisdiction or country of origin of the financial reporting framework when the financial reporting framework used is not International Financial Reporting Standards]*.

Services Engagements to Compile Financial Statements. The accountant must be familiar with the client and its business, as well as the appropriate accounting standards, especially if the organization is subject to industry-specific variations in GAAP. The accountant should discuss the content of the statements with the client

Figure 18–6   Examples of Compilation Report

Panel A: Compilation with Full Disclosures (§AR100.17) under U.S. Standards

We have compiled the accompanying balance sheet of XYZ Company as of December 31, 20XX, and the related statements of income, retained earnings, and cash flows for the year then ended, in accordance with Statements on Standards for Accounting and Review Services issued by the American Institute of Certified Public Accountants.

A compilation is limited to presenting in the form of financial statements information that is the representation of management. We have not audited or reviewed the accompanying financial statements and, accordingly, do not express an opinion or any form of assurance on them.

Panel B: Compilation with Full Disclosure under International Standards

On the basis of information provided by management we have compiled, in accordance with the International Standard on Related Services *[or refer to relevant national standards or practices]* applicable to compilation engagements, the balance sheet of ABC Company as of December 31, 20XX and statements of income and cash flows for the year then ended. Management is responsible for these financial statements. We have not audited or reviewed these financial statements and accordingly express no assurance thereon.

---

to determine that the information is satisfactory. Finally, the accountant should read the statements and note any errors or omissions in the data or in applying GAAP. The public accountant is required to disclose errors or omissions that come to his or her attention but is not under any duty to search for such problems.

> **Authoritative Guidance & Standards**
> Standards for compilations of financial statements are contained in SSARS 8/SSARS 1 and ISRS 4410.

One important and controversial issue relating to compilations is the prohibition of auditors to perform any management functions as part of the compilation engagement. Many regional and local public accounting firms depend on compilation engagements to generate a significant amount of the firm's revenues. Likewise, many small organizations possess very little accounting knowledge and depend upon their auditors to serve as the accounting expert for the organization. Although management is expected to understand the financial reports that are produced, the public accountant often finds himself in the situation of essentially making accounting decisions for the company. Probably the issue that is most problematic is that auditors often approve journal entries for their compilation clients, which constitutes a managerial function.

The accountant will use a form of disclaimer report that indicates that the financial statements have been compiled but not audited. Consequently, the accountant cannot express an opinion or provide any assurance about compliance with generally accepted accounting principles. Figure 18–6 presents the public accountant's standard compilation report. An accountant does not need to be independent of the client to perform a compilation, in which case, the accountant should also disclose the lack of independence. Furthermore, the client may wish to omit most or all of the disclosures that would normally be included in the financial statements under GAAP. The public accountant can still compile the basic financial statements as long as there is no suspicion that the disclosures are being omitted in order to mislead readers. The accountant's report should then indicate that disclosures have been omitted (see Figure 18–7). Finally, should the public accountant become aware of a material departure from GAAP, the circumstances

Figure 18–7   Examples of Compilation Report—Omitted Disclosures

---

Panel A: Compilation with Omitted Disclosures (§AR100.21) under U.S. Standards

We have compiled the accompanying balance sheet of XYZ Company as of December 31, 20XX, and the related statements of income, retained earnings, and cash flows for the year then ended, in accordance with Statements on Standards for Accounting and Review Services issued by the American Institute of Certified Public Accountants.

A compilation is limited to presenting in the form of financial statements information that is the representation of management. We have not audited or reviewed the accompanying financial statements and, accordingly, do not express an opinion or any form of assurance on them.

Management has elected to omit substantially all of the disclosures required by generally accepted accounting principles. If the omitted disclosures were included in the financial statements, they might influence the user's conclusions about the company's financial position, results of operations, and cash flows. Accordingly, these financial statements are not designed for those who are not informed about such matters.

Panel B: Compilation with Omitted Disclosures under International Standards

On the basis of information provided by management we have compiled, in accordance with the International Standard on Related Services *[or refer to relevant national standards or practices]* applicable to compilation engagements, the balance sheet of XYZ Company as of December 31, 20XX and the related statements of income and cash flows for the year then ended. Management is responsible for these financial statements. We have not audited or reviewed these financial statements and accordingly express no assurance thereon.

We draw attention to Note X to the financial statements because management has elected not to capitalize the leases on plant and machinery which is a departure from the applicable financial reporting framework.

---

should be discussed in an explanatory paragraph.[4] If the public accountant believes that the departures from GAAP are misleading, and if the client will not amend the information as requested by the public accountant, then the public accountant should withdraw from the engagement and not let his or her name be associated with this client's financial statements.

Some countries go further and suggest "A Notice to Reader" be put on every page of the financial statements in place of or in conjunction with a separate report. The Canadian standards (CICA Handbook Section 9200) provide an example of this approach and recommend that the following be put on each page of the financial statements:

> *Notice to Reader:* We have compiled the balance sheet of Client Limited as at December 31, 20XX and the statements of income, retained earnings, and cash flows for the (period) then ended from information provided by management (the proprietor). We have not audited, reviewed, or otherwise attempted to verify the accuracy or completeness of such information. Readers are cautioned that these statements may not be appropriate for their purposes.

---

4 It should be emphasized that an accountant has no professional responsibility to search for errors, omissions, or departures from GAAP when performing a compilation. Furthermore, the accountant should be careful not to take actions that could be construed by the client as constituting assurance beyond the level of a compilation.

ENGAGEMENTS APPLYING AGREED-UPON PROCEDURES

Public accountants are often asked to examine one or more specified accounts or elements of the financial statements using limited but specific audit procedures without conducting an audit of the entire financial statements. Examples of specific financial information that could be the subject of such an engagement include:

- Cash balances on a specified date
- Detailed accounts receivable data used for loan collateral
- Detailed analysis of property and equipment for insurance purposes
- Gross income or other components of the income statement
- Retail sales to calculate rent for retail space in a shopping mall

This type of engagement is referred to as an *agreed-upon procedures examination* (also known as "specified audit procedures") and focuses on specific financial assertions or elements of a broader financial report.[5] There are three parties to such an engagement: the *reporting party*, the *specified user*, and the public accountant. The reporting party prepares the information (assertions) to be reported to the specified user. All three parties must agree on the assertion(s) to be examined and the procedures to be performed by the auditor as reflected in a formal engagement letter. A key difference between an audit or review and this type of engagement is that the intended user is specifically identified in the engagement letter and the accountant's report.

In general, the following conditions and requirements must be met in order for an independent public accountant to undertake an agreed-upon procedures engagement:

> **Authoritative Guidance & Standards**
> Standards for agreed upon procedures are found in SSAE No. 4 and ISRS No. 4400.

- The practitioner must be independent of the parties involved.
- The practitioner and the specified users of the final report must agree on the procedures to be performed.
- The specified users of the report are willing to take full responsibility for the sufficiency of the procedures that are performed.
- The procedures will provide consistent, measurable, and objective evidence about the assertions being examined.
- The basis of accounting for transactions covered by the report is clearly specified and evident to all parties.
- Adequate evidence is believed to exist to support the assertions.
- Materiality levels are agreed to by all parties (when applicable).

In short, all parties to the arrangement must understand and agree with the limited scope of the engagement. The distribution of the report is limited to parties who have agreed to the procedures being performed.

Agreed-upon procedures are highly dependent on the exact wording of the engagement letter because there is no typical set of procedures for such an engagement. The public accountant's responsibility in an agreed-upon procedures engagement is to carry out the tests that are identified in the engagement letter and produce a detailed report of the findings, normally with all exceptions identified except when there are agreed upon materiality levels. The auditor has the

---

5 There are two types of agreed-upon procedures engagements: those conducted on elements of the financial statements and those pertaining to other types of assertions. The two engagements are covered by separate standards, but the professional requirements are essentially the same. The primary difference is the identification of the subject matter of the assertion being examined.

responsibility to ensure that the parties involved have a clear understanding of the procedures being performed. The public accountant is not responsible for assessing whether the procedures meet the needs of the parties. Examples of tests that might be performed include:

- Execute sample-based tests of a specific population (e.g., test counts of inventory)
- Inspect documents for prespecified attributes (e.g., test of controls)
- Confirm transactions, balances, or events with third parties
- Compare specified information in individual documents with general accounting records
- Verify the accuracy of computations
- Review and evaluate of tests performed by others (e.g., review of internal audit tests)[6]

Due to the unique nature of an agreed-upon procedures engagement, the accountant's report can be quite cumbersome. At a minimum, the independent public accountant's report for an agreed-upon procedures engagement should:

- Include a title indicating that it is the report of an independent public accountant
- Identify the intended specific users of the report who have agreed to the scope of the engagement
- Refer to the assertion, specified elements, accounts, or items to be examined
- Describe the basis of accounting in general or specific terms (as necessary)
- State that the procedures performed were those that were agreed to by the specified user
- Refer to compliance with applicable standards
- State that the sufficiency of the procedures performed is the responsibility of the specified user
- Provide a list of the procedures performed and the related findings
- Identify materiality limits (if applicable)
- Disclaim an opinion on the financial statements as a whole
- Restrict the use of the statement to identified users
- Disclaim an opinion on the effectiveness of internal control over financial reporting[7]

It is particularly important that the report disclaim an opinion on the financial statements taken as a whole, as the accountant was not engaged to do an audit. Examples of the report for agreed upon procedures are presented in Figure 18–8.

Agreed-upon procedures engagements are increasingly common in practice. There are three primary reasons for this trend. First, this type of engagement allows the auditor to tailor the scope of the engagement to meet the needs of the client while minimizing the cost of the service. Second, by agreeing in advance on the procedures to be performed, the public accountant's potential liability is reduced in the event that material misstatements go undetected. However, public accountants should be careful not to accept an agreed-upon procedures engagement when a standard audit

---

6 The accountant should avoid some types of procedures, however, because they do not represent independent tests of assertions. Examples of procedures that would not be acceptable include: (1) Reading the results of tests performed by others without critical review or evaluation, (2) evaluating the reputation of another party, and (3) interpreting documents outside the accountant's area of expertise.

7 This requirement is unique to the United States.

Figure 18–8   Example Reports: Agreed-Upon Procedures Applied to Specific Elements, Accounts, or Items in the Financial Statements

---

Panel A: Independent Accountant's Report on Applying Agreed-Upon Procedures (§AU622.34) under U.S. Standards

We have performed the procedures enumerated below, which were agreed to by *[list specified users]*, solely to assist you with respect to *[refer to the specified elements, accounts or items of a financial statement of an identified entity and the character of the engagement]*. This engagement to apply agreed-upon procedures was performed in accordance with standards established by the American Institute of Certified Public Accountants. The sufficiency of the procedures is solely the responsibility of the specified users of the report. Consequently, we make no representation regarding the sufficiency of the procedures described below either for the purpose for which this report has been requested or for any other purpose.

[Include paragraphs to enumerate the procedures performed and the findings.]

We were not engaged to, and did not, perform an audit, the objective of which would be the expression of an opinion on the specified financial elements, accounts, or items. Accordingly, we do not express such an opinion. Had we performed additional procedures, other matters might have come to our attention that would have been reported to you.

This report is intended solely for the information and use of *[the specified parties]* and is not intended to be and should not be used by anyone other than these specified users.

Panel B: Auditor's Report on Applying Agreed-Upon Procedures (or Specified Audit Procedures) under International Standards

We have performed the procedures agreed with you and enumerated below with respect to the *[specify specific elements, accounts or items of a financial statement]* of ABC Company as at *[date]*, set forth in the accompanying schedules (not shown in this example). Our engagement was undertaken in accordance with the International Standard on Related Services *[or refer to relevant national standards or practices]* applicable to agreed-upon procedures engagements. The procedures were performed solely to assist you in evaluating the validity of *[specify specific elements, accounts or items of a financial statement]* and are summarized as follows:

[include paragraph to enumerate the procedures performed]

We report our findings below:

[include paragraph to enumerate the findings]

Because the above procedures do not constitute either an audit or a review made in accordance with International Standards on Auditing or International Standards on Review Engagements *[or relevant national standards or practices]*, we do not express any assurance on the *[specify specific elements, accounts or items of a financial statement]* as of *[date]*.

Had we performed additional procedures or had we performed an audit or review of the financial statements in accordance with International Standards on Auditing or International Standards on Review Engagements *[or relevant national standards or practices]*, other matters might have come to our attention that would have been reported to you.

Our report is solely for the purpose set forth in the first paragraph of this report and for your information and is not to be used for any other purpose or to be distributed to any other parties. This report relates only to the accounts and items specified above and does not extend to any financial statements of ABC Company, taken as a whole.

of financial statements is appropriate. In other words, this service should not be employed to avoid issuing a full audit report when the audit shows that the financial statements taken as a whole are materially misstated. Third, this type of engagement has broad usage for assertions other than financial information, specifically, assertions related to financial forecasts and compliance with laws and regulations.

EXAMINATION OF PROSPECTIVE DATA AND FORECASTS

An auditor may be asked to render an opinion on financial statements which consist of projected future financial results. This type of document is sometimes called a *prospective financial statement*. Many managers and investors like to have prospective information available for decision making but are rightly concerned about the reliability of such information and the potential for intentional bias on the part of the preparer. Assurance standards define two types of prospective financial statements:

1. **Financial forecasts:** Prospective financial statements derived based on the *most likely* future outcomes, using assumptions that reflect expected conditions and actions.
2. **Financial projections:** Prospective financial statements derived based on *specific assumptions* about future conditions, actions, or outcomes and not necessarily representative of the most likely outcomes that would occur if current plans and policies are continued.

Prospective financial statements may be prepared for either general distribution or can be limited to management or specific parties. The engagement letter should clearly indicate the extent of distribution allowed for the prospective financial statements. Financial forecasts can be subject to either an examination, compilation, or agreed-upon procedures engagement. Public accountants can also provide assurance about *limited use financial projections*. However, accountants are prohibited from being associated with *general purpose financial projections*

<table>
<tr><td>

Authoritative
Guidance & Standards
Standards for review of prospective financial information are found in SSARS 14 and ISAE 3400.

</td><td>

because potential readers are not in a position to request clarification regarding specific assumptions being made in support of the reported outcomes. Regardless of the nature of the engagement, an auditor cannot attest to the predictive accuracy of the prospective financial statements. Rather, the auditor provides assurance concerning the assumptions used in deriving the statements and the accuracy of the computations on which forecasts are based.

</td></tr>
</table>

The nature of the engagement determines the scope of the public accountant's work, the type of report to be issued, the degree of assurance being provided, and, ultimately, the auditor's responsibility if the forecasts are inaccurate. An auditor hired to perform an examination of prospective information should obtain an understanding of the client's business and industry, significant transactions, and other matters that might materially impact the future financial results. At a minimum, the public accountant should:

- Evaluate the preparation of the prospective information
- Evaluate the underlying assumptions
- Evaluate the presentation of the information in accordance with appropriate guidelines
- Issue a report

The auditor primarily focuses on the completeness and reasonableness of the assumptions concerning current and future conditions, actions, and outcomes. If the

Figure 18–9   Example Reports on Prospective Financial Statements

---

Panel A: Independent Accountant's Report (§AT200.32) under U.S. Standards

We have examined the accompanying forecasted balance sheet, statements of income, retained earnings, and cash flows of XYZ Company as of December 31, 20X6, and for the year then ended. Our examination was made in accordance with standards for examination of a forecast established by the American Institute of Certified Public Accountants and, accordingly, included such procedures as we considered necessary to evaluate both the assumptions used by management and the preparation and presentation of the forecast.

In our opinion, the accompanying forecast is presented in conformity with guidelines for presentation of a forecast established by the American Institute of Certified Public Accountants, and the underlying assumptions provide a reasonable basis for management's forecast. However, there will usually be differences between the forecasted and actual results, because events and circumstances frequently do not occur as expected, and those differences may be material. We have no responsibility to update this report for events and circumstances occurring after the date of this report.

Panel B: Auditor's Report under International Standards

We have examined the forecast *[include name of the entity, the period covered by the forecast and provide suitable identification, such as by reference to page numbers or by identifying the individual statements]* in accordance with the International Standard on Assurance Engagements applicable to the examination of prospective financial information. Management is responsible for the forecast including the assumptions set out in Note X on which it is based.

Based on our examination of the evidence supporting the assumptions, nothing has come to our attention which causes us to believe that these assumptions do not provide a reasonable basis for the forecast.* Further, in our opinion the forecast is properly prepared on the basis of the assumptions and is presented in accordance with *[indicate the relevant financial reporting framework]*.

Actual results are likely to be different from the forecast since anticipated events frequently do not occur as expected and the variation may be material.**

---

* Some countries standards require a more detailed description. For example in Canada, the following is required:
  - as of the date of this report, the assumptions developed by management are suitably supported and consistent with the plans of the Company, and provide a reasonable basis for the forecast;
  - this forecast reflects such assumptions; and
  - the financial forecast complies with the presentation and disclosure standards for forecasts established by The Canadian Institute of Chartered Accountants.

** In Canada the requirement is even blunter: "Accordingly, we express no opinion as to whether this forecast will be achieved."

public accountant is comfortable that the assumptions are reasonable, then the computational process should be examined to determine if the reported results are consistent with the assumptions.

The independent public accountant's standard report for an examination of forecasted financial statements is presented in Figure 18–9. The primary reasons for departing from the standard form of report are (1) violations of appropriate guidelines in presenting prospective financial statements, or (2) the use of assumptions that do not support the reported results. In these situations, the accountant's responsibility is to fully describe the nature of the problem in his or her report.

LETTERS TO UNDERWRITERS

The U.S. Securities and Exchange Commission (and many other international stock exchange regulators) requires a company to prepare a *registration statement*, including financial statements and related information, whenever a company wishes to offer new securities to the public. Because underwriters can be held liable for any misleading information contained in the registration statement, they usually request that the company's auditor provide some assurance that the financial information is accurate. Auditors are also responsible for much of the information contained in the registration statement, so they are usually willing or required to provide a *comfort letter* to the underwriter that indicates that the auditor is not aware of any errors, omissions, or misleading information related to the financial statements. The actual content and wording of the letter is usually negotiated among the underwriter, the auditor, and the company. Such letters tend to be lengthy and address the following issues:[8]

*   The independence of the auditor
*   Whether the audited financial statements comply with the rules of the SEC or other relevant regulatory or legal authority
*   Agreed-upon procedures performed for unaudited information, including financial statements covering the period since the last audit
*   Other financial information subject to agreed-upon procedures and subject to controls over financial reporting
*   Negative assurance whether nonfinancial information complies with SEC or other regulatory rules

GENERAL CHARACTERISTICS OF ASSURANCE ENGAGEMENTS

Every organization has a large number of stakeholders who have their own interests in the activities, risks, and performance of the organization. Some of the key stakeholders for a business include shareholders, creditors, management, employees, customers, suppliers, regulators, taxing authorities, and the general public. All stakeholders are potentially affected by the way in which management identifies and addresses its risks, runs its operations, and reports information to interested parties. The audit of financial statements is just one mechanism for external stakeholders to obtain reliable information with which to inform their decisions. Although prohibitions in the Sarbanes-Oxley Act limit the scope of services that a public accounting firm can offer to an audit client, there are no similar restrictions for clients who are not an audit client. Consequently, there may be many opportunities for accountants to provide valuable assurance services to non-audit clients.

ASSURANCE SERVICES

Public accounting firms are continuously looking for new ways to use their skills to deliver value-added services. Exploring new areas where assurance services and attestation can be provided is one strategy for expanding and improving client

8 See Section AU634 in U.S. standards for more detail on letters to underwriters. Due to the legal nature of such letters, the relevant professional standards in the United States are voluminous and very detailed. Discussing letters to underwriters in more detail is beyond the scope of this text. Canadian standards, while extensive (CICA Handbook Sections 7110, 7115 and 7200), are not as detailed. The International Auditing and Assurance Standards Board is expected to issue a standard on comfort letters sometime after 2006.

service. Assurance engagements are considered to be unique from consulting engagements because of the nature of the service delivered and the professional standards that exist for performing many types of assurance engagements. The AICPA defines *assurance services* as:

Independent professional services that improve the quality of information, or its context, for decision makers.

No authoritative body has endorsed this particular definition, in part because it covers a broad range of potential services. Conceptually, assurance services encompass the basic financial statement audit and services more generally described as attestation. Assurance services also apply to elements of decision making that do not relate to a specific assertion. For example, assurance providers can address questions about the relevance of information, the viability of a company's business plan, the appropriateness of its business processes, the effectiveness of its controls, and the quality of its decision processes.

Any situation that entails risk presents an opportunity for assurance services. Risks that can be addressed with appropriately designed assurance services include the risk of unreliable information, the risk of failing to comply with legal or contractual requirements, and the risk of ineffective or inefficient operations. To illustrate the pervasiveness of opportunities for assurance, consider the risk management process depicted in Figure 18–10 (adapted from Figure 2–4 in Chapter 2). The management of risk involves: (1) identifying risks, (2) preparing a response to

Figure 18–10   The Risk Management Process and Opportunities for Assurance Services

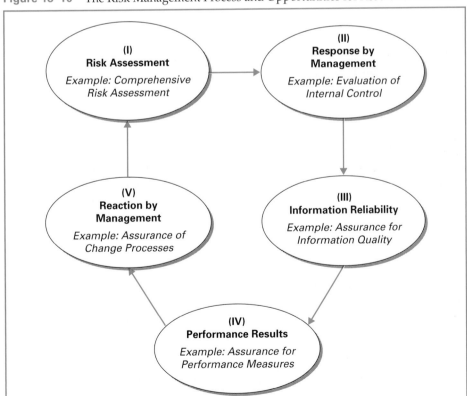

identified risks, (3) obtaining reliable information pertaining to risks, (4) evaluating performance results, and (5) making adjustments to reflect changed conditions or ineffective actions.

The external assurance provider can assist in all phases of risk management. First, public accountants can provide assurance that key risks have been effectively identified and prioritized. Second, accountants can evaluate management's responses to specific risks. Third, the public accountant can evaluate controls over information processing and financial reporting. The second standard of fieldwork (also known as the second examination standard) in GAAS pertain to this area of assurance as it applies to financial reporting, but auditors can also expand their service to nonfinancial areas of a client's information system. Fourth, the reliability of information generated by internal reporting systems can be examined. Finally, accountants can provide assurance about the effectiveness and efficiency of management's responses to risk and changing conditions.

Figure 18–11 highlights how different stakeholders may benefit from expanded assurance opportunities. Traditionally, the auditor has focused on financial reports to shareholders prepared in accordance with generally accepted accounting principles. However, the expanding information needs of stakeholders and the complexity of the risk management process combine to highlight numerous areas where external assurance can be beneficial to many parties. For example, senior management can benefit by receiving assurance over strategic plans, business risks, performance measures, process quality, and regulatory compliance. Similarly, employees benefit when assurance is obtained related to product and process quality and information used to evaluate their performance. It is interesting to note that the

Figure 18–11   Examples of the Potential Increased Role of External Assurance Providers*

Information Need	Potential User
Information about business risk	Board of Directors Senior Management Investors
Information about product quality	Consumers/Customers Employees Investors
Performance measures	Senior Management Employees
Quality of processes and controls	Board of Directors Senior Management Employees Investors
Information about strategic plans	Board of Directors Senior Management Investors
Information on regulatory compliance	Regulators General Public Board of Directors Senior Management

* Adapted from the AICPA's *Report of the Special Committee on Assurance Services*. Similar conclusions have been reached in other countries' studies of assurance service opportunities including Australia, New Zealand, Canada, England, Scotland, Wales, and several continental European countries, such as the Netherlands.

interests of management and employees are often aligned, that is, they both benefit when information related to their individual objectives is reliable.

ASSURANCE ENGAGEMENTS

General concepts for assurance engagements have been under development for a number of years but, other than standards for a few specific types of engagements, there is no authoritative U.S. definition of an assurance engagement. The International Auditing and Assurance Standards Board defines an assurance engagement as "an engagement in which a practitioner expresses a conclusion designed to enhance the degree of confidence of the intended users other than the responsible party about the outcome of the evaluation or measurement of a subject matter against criteria."[9] In general, any engagement that improves the quality of information or the context in which the information is used can be considered an assurance engagement. An assurance provider should only undertake an assurance engagement when six conditions exist:

1. The subject matter must be such that it is reasonable to provide assurance about it.
2. The assurance provider has adequate knowledge of the context in which assurance is to be given.[10]
3. The assurance provider must be independent and objective.
4. Criteria are available that are suitable to the intended users.
5. The subject matter of the assurance can be examined with an objective evaluation process and sufficient appropriate evidence can be collected to support the practitioner's written conclusion.
6. The provision of the assurance service does not conflict with regulatory prescriptions (e.g., violate independence rules applicable to audit clients).

Assurance engagements can be provided at two levels: "reasonable assurance" (i.e., assurance comparable to an audit of financial statements) and "limited assurance" (i.e., assurance comparable to a review of financial statements).

To illustrate the concepts of an assurance engagement, consider the case of measuring business performance. More and more organizations are adopting performance evaluation systems that rely on data other than financial accounting numbers, some of which may be produced independently of the traditional accounting system. The balanced scorecard discussed in Chapter 15 provided a number of examples of such measures. One of the major reasons for broadening performance measurement beyond financial statements is that management can analyze leading indicators to identify problems before they become severe. For example, measures of the skills and motivation of the workforce are often leading indicators of potential problems within processes, which in turn provide warning signals about product quality, customer satisfaction, sales, and cash flow. Although no professional standards yet exist for verifying performance measures specifically, an accountant can undertake an assurance engagement provided the six conditions listed above are met.

9 *International Framework for Assurance Engagements.* Other countries have developed definitions such as the CICA's Handbook Section 5025 that defines an assurance engagement as "an engagement where, pursuant to an accountability relationship between two or more parties, a practitioner is engaged to issue a written communication expressing a conclusion concerning a subject matter for which the accountable party is responsible."

10 It is common for an accounting firm to hire subject matter specialists (i.e. experts) to fill in any gaps in technical knowledge of accounting personnel, such as medical professionals, engineers, architects, and so on.

AN EXAMPLE: CORPORATE SUSTAINABILITY REPORTING

There is a growing trend of providing information about business measures through a separate report, typically called a *corporate sustainability report (CSR)*—also referred to as triple bottom-line reporting, corporate citizenship reports, and so forth. These reports contain summary business measures of concern to a broad set of corporate stakeholders (e.g., customers, suppliers, communities, regulators, governments, employees, etc.). Currently, there are no universally accepted criteria for these reports. The Global Reporting Initiative has established a set of CSR reporting guidelines to which over 800 international companies (including more than 100 U.S. companies) have committed.[11]

Generally, little assurance is provided on these reports, but a handful of European companies have been leaders in exploring the role of assurance related to CSR reporting. To address this growing trend, the IAASB formed a Task Force to develop a set of assurance guidelines on this issue. In addition, the AICPA formed the Enhanced Business Reporting Consortium in 2005, which includes several organizations concerned about business reporting (e.g., NASDAQ, the Business Roundtable). Public accountants have an important opportunity to provide assurance on these documents, which are receiving increased media coverage. For example, *The Wall Street Journal* covered the release of The Gap's CSR report in July 2005, noting that a number of supplier relationships were severed in China due to violations of the Company's Supplier Code of Conduct. Other organizations not in public accounting have begun to provide assurance services related to CSR reports. However, the auditing profession's experience with financial misstatements and fraud suggests an obvious role for auditors in providing such assurance.

To provide assurance about a CSR report, the public accountant needs to collect sufficient appropriate evidence given the objectives of the engagement and the level of assurance. For example, to evaluate the reliability of performance measures contained in a CSR report, the public accountant would examine the process of generating the information and any supporting documentation related to the results, much like the testing in a traditional audit. The public accountant might also survey relevant parties, have discussions with key personnel, and verify computations and tabulations of data. Evaluating the quality of the information system generating the measurements is an important element of verifying the reliability of the results. In essence, testing the reliability of performance measures is similar to testing financial assertions.

A challenge for auditors in performing assurance services such as for a CSR report is that some quantitative measures may be very difficult to audit because they involve non-financial measures outside an auditor's area of expertise (e.g., pollution emissions in the air or water). This problem is further complicated when the information is of a qualitative nature. There are some practices being developed to overcome these problems. For example, Figure 18–12 presents the Independent Assurance Report for Royal Dutch Shell's 2003 CSR Report (two auditing firms conducted the engagement). In that report, the firms used a globe symbol throughout the CSR report to indicate that a business measure was associated with a reasonable level of assurance. Other examples of assurance opinions that have been used include negative assurance that nothing came to the auditor's attention suggesting that a firm did not follow its internal policies for compiling and

---

11 In 2006, the GRI plans to release a new set of reporting guidelines that allow for XBRL report submissions in an effort to increase standardization of reporting (at least within industries).

Figure 18–12   Assurance Report for Shell's 2003 Corporate Sustainability Report

Assurance report

To: Royal Dutch Petroleum Company and the "Shell" Transport and Trading Company, p.l.c.

Introduction

We have been asked to provide assurance on selected data, graphs and statements of the Royal Dutch/Shell Group of Companies (the "Group") contained in The Shell Report 2003. The Shell Report is the responsibility of management. Our responsibility is to express an opinion on the selected data, graphs and statements indicated below based on our assurance work performed.

Assurance work performed

For the safety and environmental parameters identified with the symbol ⊕ on pages 22 to 26, we obtained an understanding of the systems used to generate, aggregate and report the data for these parameters at Group, Business, Zone and Operating Unit level. We assessed the completeness and accuracy of the data reported in respect of 2003 by visiting Operating Units to test systems and review data. We assessed data trends in discussion with management. We tested the calculations made at Group level. We also completed assurance procedures on the Refinery Energy Index and reported our findings to management.

For the Sakhalin Location Report on pages 16 and 17 we visited the location to inspect documentary evidence and held interviews with Business and in-country management and with three major Russian contracting companies to understand and test the systems, procedures, and evidence in place supporting the assertions and matters discussed within this Location Report. We also performed assurance procedures in relation to China West-East pipeline project and reported our findings to management.

We read the whole Report to confirm that there are no material inconsistencies based on the work we have performed.

Basis of opinion

There are no generally accepted international environmental, social and economic reporting standards. This engagement was conducted in accordance with the International Standards for Assurance Engagements. Therefore, we planned and carried out our work to provide reasonable, rather than absolute, assurance on the reliability of the selected data, graphs and statements that were subject to assurance. We believe our work provides a reasonable basis for our opinion.

Considerations and limitations

It is important to read the data and statements in the context of the basis of reporting provided by the management as set out below and the notes below the graphs. Environmental and social data and assertions are subject to more inherent limitations than financial data, given both their nature and the methods used for determining, calculating or estimating such data.

Our assurance scope is limited to those specific matters mentioned in our opinion below. We have not provided assurance over the contents of the entire Shell Report 2003, nor have we undertaken work to confirm that all relevant issues are included. In addition, we have not carried out any work on financial and economic performance data and data reported in respect of future projections and targets. Accordingly, no opinion is given in respect of them. Where we have not provided assurance over previous years' data this is clearly disclosed. We have not performed work on the maintenance and integrity of information from The Shell Report published on the Group's website.

To obtain a thorough understanding of the financial results and financial position of the Group, the reader should consult the Group's audited Financial Statements for the year ended 31 December 2003.

In our opinion:

– The safety and environmental historical data and graphs (together with the notes) on pages 22 to 26, marked with the symbol ⊕, properly reflect the performance of the reporting entities for each of these parameters;

– The assertions and matters discussed in the Sakhalin Location Report, on pages 16 and 17, are fairly described and supported by underlying documentary or other evidence.

22 May 2004

KPMG Accountants N.V.   PricewaterhouseCoopers LLP

The Hague   London

KPMG   PRICEWATERHOUSECOOPERS

Source: Royal Dutch Petroleum Company, The Shell Report 2003, "Assurance and basis of reporting," p. 28. Reprinted by permission.

reporting a CSR report; for example, Starbucks issues CSR reports with this type of assurance from a regional public accounting firm.

ATTESTATION SERVICES

Attestation is a special form of assurance engagement for which numerous professional standards have been developed in the United States. The U.S. AICPA defines an *attest engagement* as one in which

. . . a practitioner is engaged to issue or does issue a written communication that expresses a conclusion about the reliability of a written assertion that is the responsibility of another party.[12]

This definition implies four basic conditions that distinguish an attest engagement from other assurance services:

1. There must be an assertion being made by one party, the accuracy of which is of interest to another party. This assertion may be quantitative or qualitative in nature.

12 See *Attestation Standards*; §AT100.01.

Figure 18–13   Defining the Universe of Assurance Services*

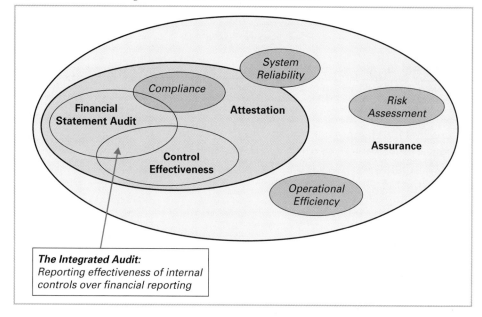

* Adapted from the *Report of the Special Committee on Assurance Services* of the AICPA.

2. There must exist objective criteria that can be utilized to assess the accuracy of the assertion. All parties must agree as to how the assertion is to be evaluated using a common unit of measure and measurement technology.
3. The assertion must be amenable to verification by an independent party. That is, the accountant must be able to obtain adequate, diagnostic evidence to support or refute the assertion being made.
4. The public accountant should prepare a written conclusion about the accuracy of the assertion(s).

An attest engagement is a subset of the broader set of assurance engagements previously discussed. Figure 18–13 illustrates the universe of potential assurance services that a public accountant can offer clients, ranging from the traditional financial statement audit, to more general forms of attestation, to the broadest category of assurance. Note that the Integrated Audit envisioned by the PCAOB actually reflects the combination of two different types of attestation: (1) the audit of the information contained in the financial statements and (2) the examination of the effectiveness of internal control over financial reporting that produces the information.

In order to meet the criteria of an attest engagement, the reporting party has to make a written assertion about the subject matter of interest, the attestation report must apply only to the reliability of the written assertion (not the relevance), and the report must be in writing. An attestation engagement can take the form of an examination (audit or high assurance), review (moderate assurance), or agreed-upon procedures engagement. In an *examination*, the accountant expresses positive assurance that the assertion being examined is presented in accordance with established criteria in all material respects. A *review* provides less assurance than an examination because the accountant only expresses negative assurance that he is unaware of any evidence that the assertions are not in conformity with the established criteria. Finally, an *agreed-upon procedures engagement* involves issuing a report on specific findings obtained by performing specific procedures agreed to by all parties prior to the start of the engagement.

STANDARDS APPLICABLE TO ALL ATTEST ENGAGEMENTS

Professional standards for attestation are established by the Auditing Standards Board, which is part of the American Institute of Certified Public Accountants, and are referred to as *attestation standards (AS)*. There is a great deal of similarity between GAAS and attestation standards. Both sets of standards are presented in Figure 18–14. U.S. attestation standards are divided into three categories: general standards, standards of fieldwork, and reporting standards.

The general standards dictate the minimum qualifications that a professional should have in order to accept an attest engagement. These standards include technical competence, independence, and the ability to exercise due care. The general attest standards also require adequate knowledge of the subject matter and identification of an assertion amenable to estimation. These are critical because they place a practical limitation on the types of assertions that may be subject to attestation by a public accountant.

The standards of fieldwork dictate how an engagement should be performed. The key requirements are adequate planning and supervision of the engagement as well as acquisition of sufficient evidence to support the conclusions reached.

The reporting standards provide guidelines for reporting to interested parties. Reporting standards require communication of the assertion(s) examined, the standard of comparison used, and the overall conclusions reached about the assertions examined. For an examination, a public accountant will give a general opinion based on the outcomes of testing (similar to the opinion given on the audit of financial statements). In other engagements, the public accountant will describe the nature of the tests performed and describe the results such as how many errors or exceptions were discovered.

ATTEST ENGAGEMENTS RELATED TO COMPLIANCE

Most organizations are confronted with a vast sea of laws, rules, and regulations with which they must comply. Management often lacks the expertise to assess compliance in all relevant areas, so it turns to the company's public accountants for assistance in making such determinations. One common type of attestation engagement is *compliance auditing*. In these engagements, public accountants are hired to determine whether an organization has complied with specified laws, rules, regulations, or contractual provisions. The public accountant should obtain a formal engagement letter from the client that clearly defines the purpose and nature of the service to be rendered, the relative responsibilities of management and the accountant, and the acceptable use of any report prepared by the accountant. The focus of a compliance audit may be on past compliance with a specified set of rules, or it may focus on the general effectiveness of the organization's internal controls that foster compliance.

A compliance engagement may take the form of an examination or be limited to agreed-upon procedures.[13] Review (moderate assurance) engagements are not

13 Standards related to compliance engagements are discussed in Section AT500. One common type of compliance engagement is referred to as a *debt letter*, in which an auditor provides assurance that a company has complied with the provisions of its loan covenants. Provision of a debt letter usually requires that the accountant has performed an audit of the financial statements.

Figure 18–14   A Comparison of U.S. Attestation Standards and U.S. Generally Accepted Auditing Standards

Attestation Standards	*Generally Accepted Auditing Standards*
General Standards	
1. The engagement shall be performed by a practitioner . . . having adequate technical training and proficiency in the attest function.	1. The examination is to be performed by a person or persons having adequate technical training and proficiency as an auditor.
2. The engagement shall be performed by a practitioner . . . having adequate knowledge in the subject matter of the assertion.	(Implied by CPA certification)
3. The practitioner shall perform an engagement only if he or she has reason to believe that the following two conditions exist: a. The assertion is capable of evaluation against reasonable criteria . . . b. The assertion is capable of reasonably consistent estimation or measurement using such criteria.	(Defined by GAAP)
4. In all matters relating to the engagement, an independence in mental attitude shall be maintained by the practitioner.	2. In all matters relating to the assignment, an independence in mental attitude is to be maintained by the auditor.
5. Due professional care shall be exercised in the performance of the engagement.	3. Due professional care is to be exercised in the performance of the audit and the preparation of the report.
Standards of Fieldwork	
1. The work shall be adequately planned and assistants, if any, shall be properly supervised.	1. The work is to be adequately planned and assistants, if any, are to be properly supervised.
(Not applicable)	2. A sufficient understanding of internal control is to be obtained to plan the audit and to determine the nature, timing, and extent of tests to be performed.
2. Sufficient evidence shall be obtained to provide a reasonable basis for the conclusion that is expressed in the report.	3. Sufficient competent evidential matter is to be obtained through inspection, observation, inquiries, and confirmations to afford a reasonable basis for an opinion regarding the financial statements under audit.
Standards of Reporting	
1. The report shall identify the assertion being reported on and state the character of the engagement.	(Implied reliance on GAAP)

Figure 18–14   *(continued)*

Attestation Standards	*Generally Accepted Auditing Standards*
Standards of Reporting	
2. The report shall state the practitioner's conclusion about whether the assertion is presented in conformity with the established or stated criteria against which it was measured.	1. The report shall state whether the financial statements are presented in accordance with generally accepted accounting principles.
(Not applicable)	2. The report shall identify those circumstances in which such principles have not been consistently observed in the current period in relation to the preceding period.
(Not applicable)	3. Informative disclosures in the financial statements are to be regarded as reasonably adequate unless otherwise stated in the report.
3. The report shall state all of the practitioner's significant reservations about the engagement and the presentation of the assertion.	4. The report shall either contain an expression of opinion regarding the financial statements, taken as a whole, or an assertion to the effect that an opinion cannot be expressed. When an overall opinion cannot be expressed, the reasons therefore should be stated. In all cases where the auditor's name is associated with financial statements, the report should contain a clear-cut indication of the character of the auditor's work, if any, and the degree of responsibility the auditor is taking.
4. The report on an engagement to evaluate an assertion that has been prepared in conformity with agreed-upon criteria or on an engagement to apply agreed-upon procedures should contain a statement limiting its use to the parties who have agreed upon such criteria or procedures.	

allowed for compliance in the United States, but other countries permit them (e.g., Canada CICA Handbook Section 8600). A public accountant can provide assurance about compliance if the following conditions are satisfied:

- Management accepts responsibility for compliance with applicable rules and regulations.
- Management evaluates compliance with the specified requirements to be examined.
- Management provides a written assertion about the organization's compliance.
- The assertion of compliance must be susceptible to evaluation by the public accountant against a set of criteria that are clear, reasonable, and objective.
- The measurement criteria can be consistently applied.
- Sufficient evidence can be obtained to support or refute the assertion of compliance.

However, the public accountant must be careful to accept only those engagements where he or she has the necessary expertise to assess compliance.

When planning a compliance engagement, the public accountant should consider the desired engagement (attestation) risk that is to be achieved as well as the inherent, control, and detection risks associated with the assertion. Inherent risk will be high when the rules and regulations in question are complex, the organization's prior experience with compliance has been poor, and the potential impact of noncompliance is significant. Control risk depends on the organization's internal control. If the organization does not have an effective system in place to foster compliance with the specific rules or regulations being examined, control risk will be considered to be high. Detection risk depends on the nature, extent, and timing of procedures that are performed. The public accountant should consider the concept of materiality as applied to noncompliance because some forms of noncompliance will bear more significant costs to the organization than others. For example, an organization can be subject to fines and penalties for noncompliance with federal laws (e.g., discrimination, environmental control).

A critical step in a compliance engagement is to obtain a thorough understanding of the applicable rules and regulations and the related criteria being used to assess compliance. Such an understanding can be obtained by reviewing published requirements, reviewing regulatory reports, holding discussions with appropriate organization personnel, and holding discussions with specialists (if needed). The existence of an internal audit department may have a bearing on the engagement as well. Most evidence will be obtained from client inquiries, tests of process controls, and substantive tests of transactions.

An example of a public accountant's standard report on compliance is presented in Figure 18–15. It should include

- A title that includes "independent accountant's (or auditor's) report."
- Reference to management's assertion of compliance (including the applicable time period)

Figure 18–15   Report on Compliance with Rules and Regulations

Independent Accountant's Report (§AU500.58)

We have examined management's assertion about XYZ Company's compliance with *[provide a list of specified compliance requirements]* during the year ended December 31, 20XX included in the accompanying report entitled "Management's Report on Compliance with *[specified regulations].*" Management is responsible for XYZ Company's compliance with those regulations. Our responsibility is to express an opinion on management's assertion about the company's compliance based on our examination.

Our examination was conducted in accordance with attestation standards established by the American Institute of Certified Public Accountants and, accordingly, included examining, on a test basis, evidence about XYZ Company's compliance with those requirements and performing such other procedures as we considered necessary in the circumstances. We believe that our examination provides a reasonable basis for our opinion. Our examination does not provide a legal determination on XYZ Company's compliance with specified requirements.

In our opinion, management's assertion that XYZ Company complied with the aforementioned requirements during the year ended December 31, 20XX, is fairly stated, in all material respects.

This report is intended solely for the information and use of *[specified parties]* and is not intended to be and should not be used by anyone other than those specified parties.

- An acknowledgment that compliance is the responsibility of management
- A statement of the accountant's responsibility
- A statement that the examination was in accordance with appropriate standards
- A statement that the examination provides a reasonable basis for the opinion rendered
- A statement that the examination is not a legal determination of compliance
- An opinion as to whether the organization was in compliance with specified requirements in all material respects
- A restriction on the intended use of the report in most cases (but this is not required)

The public accountant's report may be modified when (1) material noncompliance is discovered, (2) material uncertainties about compliance exist, or (3) the engagement has a significant scope limitation.

A public accountant may also provide a summary of his or her findings to management that describes the nature and significance of individual problems that are detected, even if they are not material to the overall conclusion about the assertion of compliance. This report may be required in some engagements subject to governmental audit standards.[14] An example of a report of findings for a U.S. federal government compliance audit is presented in Figure 18–16.

> **Authoritative Guidance & Standards**
> Standards for compliance auditing are found in SSAE 3 and ISAE 3000R.

Figure 18–16   Example: Report of Findings in a Compliance Audit of US Federal Government Assistance*

Program Being Audited	Finding of Noncompliance	Questioned Costs
Public Housing Improvement Assistance Program: Grant B80MC140009	Of 36 projects examined, monies were expended on two projects that were not approved by HUD because appropriate environmental review procedures were not followed. The city intends to repay these funds.	$49,843
Work Incentive Plan: Grant 189046847	Of 30 employee files examined, wages from two participants were paid at an hourly rate in excess of that allowed by the grant.	1,320
Urban Mass Transit Administration: Grant 872-819041	Quarterly financial reports for certain grant projects were filed more than 30 days after the end of each quarter in violation of timely filing requirements of Circular A102.	0
	Total	$51,163

* See *Audits of State and Local Governmental Units*, AICPA. © 2006 by AICPA, reproduced with permission.

14 Audits of U.S. governmental entities and funding programs are governed by the Single Audit Act of 1984 and OMB Circular A128. See SAS No. 63, "Compliance Auditing Applicable to Governmental Entities and Other Recipients of Governmental Financial Assistance" (§AU801). Other countries adapt generally accepted auditing standards to perform government audits in accordance with applicable legistation.

OTHER ASSURANCE SERVICES

Individuals within an organization often lack perspective in assessing the performance of their own organization, so independent observers can provide a valuable service by evaluating the efficiency and effectiveness of key activities and processes within an organization. Public accountants are uniquely positioned to provide such services, especially as they relate to information systems, and can draw on their familiarity with diverse practices to bring an independent perspective to such an evaluation. These assurance services may or may not lead to an opinion but often meet the definition of an assurance service "that improve the quality of information, or its context, for decision makers." Subject to the independence rules for an external audit, large public accounting firms have well established assurance practices in the areas of

- Enterprise risk management.
- Evaluation of systems reliability: *Trust Services*
- Privacy assurance

Enterprise Risk Management (ERM)

Given the focus on risk assessment, evaluation, and control that is pervasive to an audit, assurance over an organization's identification, measurement, and prioritization of risks (e.g., enterprise risk management) is an obvious extension of services provided by public accounting firms. Trends in technology and business practices contribute to the potential for risk-related assurance services. The growing role of technology and its impact on processes mitigates some risks but also creates new risks, increases the complexity of operations, and raises new challenges for management and accountants. In addition, trends in corporate organization such as downsizing, outsourcing, and strategic partnering give rise to new and challenging risks that can be subject to assurance by accountants. Because a wide and extensive range of risks are routinely examined as part of the audit, public accountants are uniquely positioned to provide additional assurance about the management of business risk. Even in the absence of an audit engagement, public accountants can be directly engaged to examine and provide assurance about the organization's approach to risk assessment and management.

Guidance provided in COSO's *Enterprise Risk Management—Integrated Framework* can be helpful to the auditor when addressing either a comprehensive entity-wide risk assessment or a more limited focus on risk assessment and management.[15] The COSO ERM framework is the first ERM framework that is available for standardizing the ERM process, mainly so that organizations can develop risk-management best practices. Because the framework, which was first discussed in Chapter 2, has discrete phases as depicted in Figure 18–17, auditors should be able to perform services related to enterprise risk management that help organizations understand the extent to which they are effectively and efficiently implementing the model.

Risk assessment and management services can include (1) assessing the extent to which the elements of the COSO framework have been implemented (e.g., has the risk appetite been properly identified as part of the Internal Environment element),

---

15 COSO. 2004. *Enterprise Risk Management—Integrated Framework*. www.coso.org

Figure 18–17   COSO'S 2004 Enterprise Risk Management—Integrated Framework

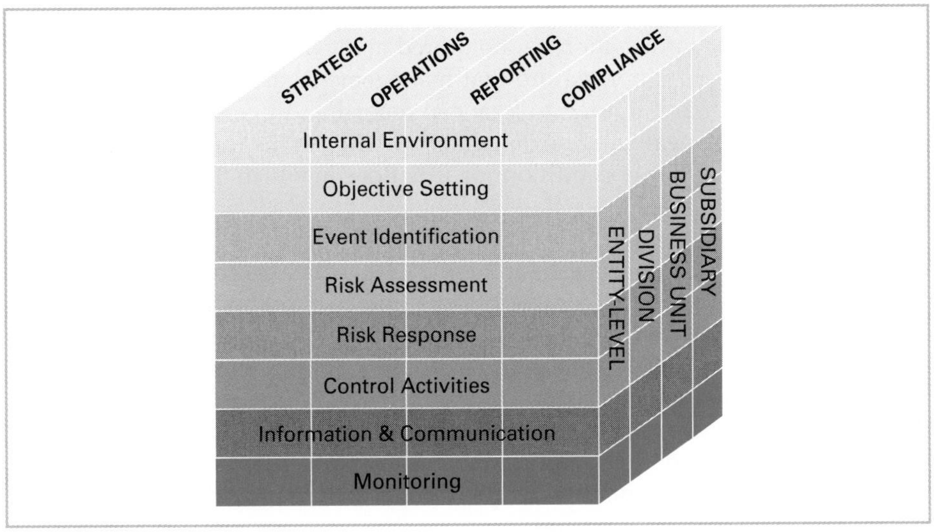

From: *Enterprise Risk Management—Integrated Framework,* Committee of Sponsoring Organizations of the Treadway Commission. 2004, AICPA, Jersey City, NJ. Used with permission of COSO.

(2) proper integration and linking of risks, (3) application of the COSO ERM framework across various risk categories including strategic, operations, reporting, and compliance, and (4) integration of the COSO framework across the business and reporting units of the organizations (i.e., applying the framework properly to all sides of the cube in Figure 18–17).

Example

A common risk affecting many organizations is the risk that a disruption in the company's supply chain will leave it without adequate materials and components to keep its just-in-time inventory system operating efficiently. Public accountants can provide assurance related to management's assessment and handling of this risk. Specific elements of assurance could cover
- The completeness of the identification of sources of potential disruption
- The reliability of management's assessments of the likelihood and magnitude of supply disruption
- The reasonableness of management's prioritization of potential causes of supply disruption
- The effectiveness of the monitoring of current supply conditions
- The effectiveness of management's response to supply disruptions

EVALUATION OF SYSTEMS RELIABILITY: *TRUST SERVICES*

Public accountants can test the reliability of information systems other than those that generate financial reports. One specific area of risk management where assurance services have been developed is in the area of online trust. As discussed previously, SAS 70 discusses reporting on internal control, including information systems, at service organizations or other third-party data processing providers.

Because much of the information that affects decisions within a company is obtained outside the traditional financial reporting system, it is important that the reliability of the information be monitored and evaluated on a regular basis. Systems assurance does not require that management make a specific assertion about reliability nor is it limited to financial reporting. In general, the public accountant engaged to evaluate system reliability will test the integrity of the information system and identify conditions or situations in which the system could be unreliable.

Systems assurance can be of benefit to both internal and external users. The importance of reliable information for internal use is obvious and follows from the needs of management to set strategic goals and to monitor the organization's progress. The trend toward virtual integration across strategic partners is increasing the need for external assurance that internal systems are reliable, especially if internal systems are linked to outside organizations. The issue of system reliability becomes particularly crucial when independent organizations become dependent on information from another's information system. The Internet has spurred this trend and the public accountant is uniquely positioned to provide assurance about system reliability to various parties.

Example

In a virtually integrated supply chain where independent organizations share information about inventory levels, procurement, and delivery of supplies, the various participants have legitimate concerns about the integrity and security of the information flows between the organizations. How does one company know that the other company's information is reliable and secure? How does a company know that sensitive information is not being leaked to outsiders by other participants, either intentionally or accidentally? In 2000, DoubleClick, an Internet marketing and advertising company, admitted that the software supporting interactive banner ads on client web sites was also capturing sensitive information about visitors to the web site and transmitting that data to DoubleClick. The company claimed that this was an unfortunate programming error and that the information was destroyed. However, the problem highlights concerns about the security of information in the complex world of Internet technology.

The AICPA, in partnership with the Canadian Institute of Chartered Accountants (CICA), has developed guidelines for attestation engagements involving the reliability of information systems under the overall banner of *Trust Services*. There are currently two types of trust services: *SysTrust*^SM and *WebTrust*^SM. A public accountant can be engaged to examine the security, availability, processing integrity, online privacy, and confidentiality of an information system. The process of certifying that systems are reliable is depicted in Figure 18–18. Accountants must be licensed by the AICPA/CICA to provide these services. However, unlike in other assurance services, public accounting firms do not have the exclusive right to perform these types of services. In fact, Verisign is the largest provider of web security services in the e-commerce business-to-consumer online world, and many organizations opt to rely strictly on the Verisign seal to provide assurance to customers about the security of their personal information. However, it is interesting to note that Verisign itself reports that it has been audited under the guidelines of *WebTrust* and SAS 70.

Figure 18–18 Trust Services: the Audit Report and *SysTrust*[SM] or *WebTrust*[SM] Seals

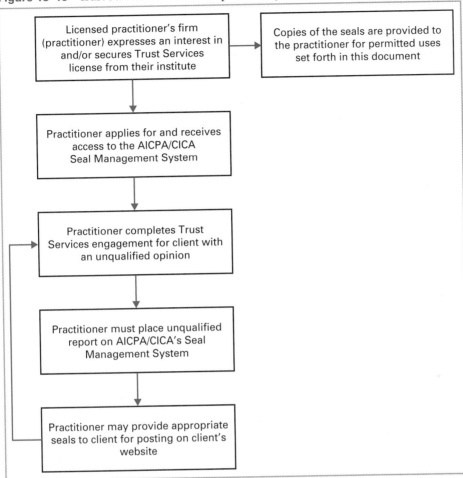

Trust Services are based on the five principles and related criteria as described in Figure 18–19. *Security* is concerned with whether the systems are protected against unauthorized access. *Privacy* deals with whether the customers' private information is handled appropriately. *Processing integrity* considers if transactions are processed properly. *Availability* addresses whether systems are available for operation and use. *Confidentiality* deals with the handling of customers' confidential information.

Figure 18–20 illustrates how various combinations of the five principles are combined into either a *SysTrust*[SM] or *WebTrust*[SM] engagement by a public accountant. The key difference between the two product sets is that *SysTrust*[SM] is aimed at information systems, particularly for business-to-business activity, whereas *WebTrust*[SM] is focused on electronic commerce between sellers and consumers. *WebTrust*[SM] never really caught on as a consumer-oriented product since it competes with a number of other sources of consumer assurance, such as *TRUSTe* and *BBB online* web seals (often available at a much lower cost to online retailers) and the general protection offered by a customer's own credit card. *SysTrust*[SM], with its focus on information systems, has found a much larger market among sophisticated IT

Figure 18–19   Principles and Criteria for Trust Services

Principles	Criteria
Security: The system is protected against unauthorized physical and logical access.	• The entity has defined and documented policies for the security of its system. • The entity communicates its defined system security policies to authorized users. • The entity utilizes procedures to achieve its documented system security objectives in accordance with defined policies. • The entity monitors the system and takes action to maintain compliance with its defined system security policies.
Availability: The system is available for operation and use as committed or agreed.	• The entity has defined and documented its policies for the availability of its system. • The entity communicates its defined system availability policies to authorized users. • The entity utilizes procedures to achieve its documented system availability objectives in accordance with defined policies. • The entity monitors the system and takes action to maintain compliance with its defined system availability policies.
Processing Integrity: System processing is complete, accurate, timely, and authorized.	• The entity has defined and documented its policies for the processing integrity of its system. • The entity communicates its documented system processing integrity policies to authorized users. • The entity utilizes procedures to achieve its documented system processing integrity objectives in accordance with defined policies. • The entity monitors the system and takes action to maintain compliance with defined system processing integrity policies.
Online Privacy: Personal information obtained as a result of e-commerce is collected, used, disclosed, and retained as committed or agreed.	• The entity has defined and documented its policies for the protection of personal information obtained as a result of e-commerce. • The entity communicates its defined policies regarding the protection of personal information to internal and external users. • The entity utilizes procedures to achieve its documented privacy objectives in accordance with defined policies. • The entity monitors the system and takes action to maintain compliance with its defined policies regarding the protection of personal information.
Confidentiality: Information designated as confidential is protected as committed or agreed.	• The entity has defined and documented its policies related to the protection of confidential information. • The entity communicates its policies related to the protection of confidential information to internal and external users. • The entity utilizes procedures to achieve its documented confidentiality objectives in accordance with defined policies. • The entity monitors the system and takes action to maintain compliance with its confidentiality policies.

Figure 18–20   Types of Trust Engagements: *SysTrust*[SM] and *WebTrust*[SM]

	SysTrust[SM]	*WebTrust*[SM]
Primary focus of assurance	IT systems (emphasis on security, processing integrity, and availability)	e-commerce systems (emphasis of privacy and processing integrity)
Application of Trust criteria:		
Security	Yes	Yes
Privacy	No	Yes
Processing integrity	Yes	Yes
Availability	Yes	Yes
Confidentiality	Yes	Yes
Web-based Certification	No	Yes

managers within businesses. An example of a *SysTrust*[SM] report over systems availability and security is found in Figure 18–21.

PRIVACY ASSURANCE

Privacy is defined as "the rights and obligations of individuals and organizations with respect to the collection, use, retention, and disclosure of personal information."[16] Personal information is any data that can be associated with a specific person such as name, home or e-mail address, identification number, physical characteristics, or purchase history. Sensitive information, such as financial, racial, sexual preference, and criminal records, generally requires a high level of protection against unauthorized access and use.

The public accountant can help an organization address privacy issues in several ways including providing assurance about whether an organization has complied with the 10 privacy components developed in the AICPA/CICA *Privacy Framework* that is described in Figure 18–22. Potential services include assisting with the development of a privacy strategy and plan, preparing or evaluating privacy policies and procedures, and assessing privacy risk. Audit-level attest services can be provided for the privacy criteria listed in Figure 18–22.

OTHER NEW ASSURANCE SERVICES

Interest in assurance services like *Trust Services* has waned as the emphasis on financial statements has increased following the accounting scandals of Enron, WorldCom, and Parmalat, and the passage of the Sarbanes-Oxley Act of 2002. The AICPA/CICA partnership that facilitated the development of *Trust Services* continues, but little new development has taken place in recent years. One service that has been actively promoted is *PrimePlus*, a re-branded version of an older service, *Eldercare*. The target clients are older wealthy individuals and their families. The purpose of the service is to provide assurance that elderly persons are cared for properly and their financial assets preserved when family members are distant or otherwise unable to monitor the individual themselves. *PrimePlus* is an example of an assurance service where there is no attestation report. *PrimePlus* builds off the public accountants' expertise in taxation, accounting, and bookkeeping, as well as the accountant's ability to gather evidence about specified criteria. This service is

16 AICPA/CICA Privacy Framework (revised March 22, 2004).

Figure 18–21   Example of a *SysTrust*^{SM} Report for System Availability and Security

≡IJ ERNST & YOUNG

        ≡IJ Emst & Young LLP   ≡IJ Phone: (703) 747-1000
         8484 Westpark Drive   Fax: (703) 747-0100
         McLean, Virginia 22102   www.ey.com

Report of Independent Accountants

To the Management of MCI Enterprise Hosting Operations:

We have examined management's assertion included in the accompanying "Report by Management on the Effectiveness of Its Controls for the MCI Enterprise Hosting Operations Production Environment based on the AICPA/CICA Trust Services Principles and Criteria" (Management's Report) that MCI Enterprise Hosting Operations, during the period November 1, 2003 through October 31, 2004 maintained effective controls over the MCI Enterprise Hosting Operations Production Environment to provide reasonable assurance that the MCI Enterprise Hosting Operations Production Environment was:

- protected against unauthorized access (both physical and logical), and
- available for operation and use, as committed and agreed

based on the AICPA/CICA Trust Services Availability and Security Principles and Criteria. This assertion is the responsibility of MCI Enterprise Hosting Operations management. Our responsibility is to express an opinion based on our examination.

Our examination was conducted in accordance with attestation standards established by the American Institute of Certified Public Accountants and, accordingly, included (1) obtaining an understanding of MCI Enterprise Hosting Operations' relevant security and availability controls over the MCI Enterprise Hosting Operations Production Environment, (2) testing and evaluating the operating effectiveness of the controls over the MCI Enterprise Hosting Operations Production Environment; and (3) performing such other procedures as we considered necessary in the circumstances. We believe that our examination provides a reasonable basis for our opinion.

Because of inherent limitations in controls, error or fraud may occur and not be detected. Furthermore, the projection of any conclusions, based on our findings, to future periods is subject to the risk that the validity of such conclusions may be altered because of changes made to the system or controls, the failure to make needed changes to the system or controls, or a deterioration in the degree of effectiveness of the controls.

In our opinion, MCI Enterprise Hosting Operations' management's assertion referred to above is fairly stated, in all material respects, based on the AICPA/CICA Trust Services Availability and Security Principles and Criteria.

The SysTrust Seal on MCI Enterprise Hosting Operations' Web site constitutes a symbolic representation of the contents of this report and it is not intended, nor should it be construed, to update this report or provide any additional assurance.

Ernst & Young LLP

December 20, 2004

Source: Reprinted by permission of Ernst & Young LLP.

ideal for small and medium-sized practitioners who have an aging and wealthy client base.

OPERATIONAL AND COMPREHENSIVE AUDITS

Operational auditing is often referred to as *management auditing* or *performance auditing* in the private sector, and as *comprehensive auditing*, *value-for-money auditing*, *systems auditing*, or *efficiency auditing* in the public sector. Operational

Figure 18–22 Privacy Components of AICPA/CICA Privacy Framework

---

AICPA/ CICA Trust Services Privacy Principle

Personal information is collected, used, retained, and disclosed in conformity with the commit-ments in entity's privacy notice . . . .

Components

1. *Management:* The entity defines, documents, communicates, and assigns responsi-bility for its privacy policies and procedures.
2. *Notice:* The entity provides notice about its privacy policies and procedures.
3. *Choice and consent:* The entity describes its implicit or explicit consent procedures for collecting, using, and disclosing private information.
4. *Collected information* is only used for the purposes identified in the notice.
5. *Use and retention:* Information after use for identified purposes is not retained longer than needed for that purpose.
6. *Access* must be provided so individuals can review and update their information.
7. *Disclosure to third parties* is only allowed when notice is provided when informa-tion is collected and with implicit or explicit consent.
8. *Security:* Private information is protected against unauthorized access (both physi-cal and logical).
9. *Quality:* The information is not corrupted after collection.
10. *Monitoring and enforcement:* The entity monitors its own compliance with privacy policies and has procedures to address privacy-related complaints and disputes.

---

auditing examines the general effectiveness and efficiency of processes in an or-ganization. There is a great deal of diversity in the subject matter of these audits. Operational audits can focus on either activities within an organization (e.g., pay-roll processing or plant maintenance) or separately identifiable divisions or locations (e.g., a branch office or manufacturing plant). The potential diversity of operational audits is illustrated by the following examples:[17]

- A hospital contracts for cleaning services from a local janitorial company, agreeing to pay the actual personnel costs of the janitors assigned to the hos-pital plus a percentage markup to cover administration and management time. During a routine audit, it was discovered that the hospital was being charged for fringe benefits on all janitors assigned to the hospital even though at least half of the janitors were temporary employees not eligible for fringe benefits. The overstatement of labor costs resulted in extra profit for the jani-torial company as well as an unjustified increase in administrative fees.
- Review of a company's disbursement cycle revealed that clerks were prepar-ing checks to pay vendors the day after an invoice was received, even if pay-ment was not due until a future date. By slowing the payments to vendors, the company was able to keep cash in interest-bearing accounts for a longer pe-riod of time, resulting in a need for smaller cash reserves and an increase in interest income for the period.
- A company produced voluminous reports every morning that were distrib-uted to over 100 managers in the organization. A survey of the recipients re-vealed that only a few needed the information on a daily basis and that many

---

17 *The Internal Auditor*, a monthly periodical published by the Institute of Internal Auditors, has a regular col-umn describing interesting findings from various types of operational audits.

didn't need it at all. The reduction of unnecessary reports reduced the costs of paper, duplicating, and employee time.

- A government program is supposed to provide funding for not-for profit entities to create training opportunities for individuals on unemployment insurance or welfare. An auditor examined whether the program spent the funds for the authorized purposes and discovered a large number of inappropriate expenditures that drained funds from the program, undermining the overall mission of the program.

Planning the engagement involves obtaining an understanding of the client's industry and relevant activities, as well as internal control which pertains to the activities being examined. An operational audit requires clear criteria for assessing efficiency and effectiveness. Because every engagement is unique, the criteria must be developed for each situation, usually in consultation with client personnel. In general, effectiveness criteria deal with whether an organization has achieved its goal(s), whereas efficiency criteria deal with the relationship between outcomes and resources consumed in the process. For example, an effectiveness criterion may take the form of "the reject rate for defects will not exceed 2 percent of completed units." An efficiency criterion may be stated as "the man-hours per unit of production should be no more than 100." Common sources of effectiveness and efficiency criteria include

- Historical standards: A process or organizational unit can be evaluated relative to its prior performance. Nonfinancial performance measures may be useful for evaluating prior performance. Historical standards can only measure relative changes, not absolute levels, of effectiveness or efficiency.
- Peer group standards: There may be identifiable "best practices" for a specific activity within an organization. The performance of these activities can be measured and used as criteria for other parts of the organization. Peer group measures may also be obtained from outside organizations that are considered excellent or "world-class."

Example

Telemarketers such as L.L. Bean, a U.S.-based mail order retailer, are considered to have world class processes for handling telephone communications with customers. Their processes can serve as benchmarks for other industries or companies that have similar processes even if they are in a different line of business. For example, telephone companies have studied L.L. Bean's techniques in order to improve the efficiency and effectiveness of their operators.

- Absolute standards: Fixed measures of performance may sometimes be appropriate if obtained from scientific or engineering studies. For example, the optimal time to perform a task may be estimated using time and motion studies or published production ratings may be available (e.g., energy ratings on appliances or mileage ratings on tires). Measures can also be obtained from internal studies, but these are more costly. All parties should keep in mind that an absolute standard for effectiveness and efficiency may be considered an idealized goal that is rarely achieved within the organization.
- Negotiated standards: In some situations, clear-cut measures may not be available or may involve some subjectivity to evaluate. The criteria used in these situations should be negotiated and agreed to by all parties affected by the examination.

Figure 18–23   Illustrative Report for an Operational Audit of a Business Entity

Independent Accountant's Report

We have completed the audit of the claims processing department for automobile casualty policies. We examined 150 claims files randomly selected from the period January 1, 20XX through June 30, 20XX. We tested the claims files using the following criteria:

- All claims should be settled for amounts consistent with policy and company guidelines.
- All settled claims should be supported by adequate documentation.
- All property-related claims should be settled within 90 days of the report of the accident.
- All personal-injury claims should be subject to medical review.

We noted a number of errors and processing mistakes during the source of our examination, the most significant of which were:

(1) Ten claims were settled for amounts that exceeded the guidelines of the company or the applicable policy.
(2) Eighteen claims files had missing information which might materially affect the proper amount of settlement.
(3) Five claims for property damage were settled beyond the 90-day limit.

Based on our findings and our understanding of claims processing, we recommend that the following changes be implemented so as to improve the efficiency, effectiveness and reliability of the process:

[A discussion of specific control weaknesses and suggested remedies would be presented at this point.]

Evidence gathering and evaluation in an operational audit depends on the nature and complexity of the activities being examined, the criteria being measured, the measurement technology that is available, and the difficulty of obtaining evidence in support of the desired measurement. The most commonly used tests involve documentation, observation, or analysis. The report that is issued will depend on the specific requirements of the engagement and the results that are obtained. Reporting on operational audits is very diverse and no standard report applies to many engagements. In general, a report for an operational audit will provide an overall conclusion about the efficiency and effectiveness of the process being examined, as well as specific suggestions on how to respond to problems that were detected during the course of the examination. A sample report for an operational audit is presented in Figure 18–23.

PUBLIC ACCOUNTING AND THE FUTURE OF ASSURANCE SERVICES

Of all the skills that public accountants possess, the two that are probably most critical to assurance services are objectivity and technical knowledge. Objectivity is critical because assurance is only valuable if it comes from an objective and credible source. If the user thinks the public accountant performing an assurance engagement is biased, either due to a lack of independence or some other impairment, the opinion expressed by the accountant will not be valued by the user. The closer a public accountant gets to being the source of information, the less objective he or she is perceived to be. For example, if a public accountant designs and implements an information system for a client, his or her objectivity for evaluating the reliability of the system may be questionable.

Example

Many accounting firms now provide services that historically have been provided by the client's own internal audit department. Such **outsourcing** allows the organization to reduce or disband its internal audit department. A question of objectivity arises, however, if a public accountant performs the functions of both an external and an internal auditor. In such situations, a layer of potential control has been removed, and the external auditor may become biased in the execution of the audit as a result of performing internal audit functions (e.g., operational audits). Consequently, this combined service has been prohibited for public companies that are registrants of the U.S. SEC.

The other primary skill that a public accountant possesses is his or her technical knowledge. Public accountants are usually perceived as being technical experts on managerial, financial, and taxation accounting topics. This knowledge is clearly relevant to the financial statement audit or other attest engagements related to financial information. The further the public accountant moves from accounting information, however, the less useful that traditional knowledge is for providing service to a client. A public accountant may be competent to provide assurance over many types of assertions, but, if the assertions deal with areas other than basic accounting or business, there may be other professionals who have superior technical knowledge. Hence, the need for accounting firms either to hire the needed expertise or to develop alliances with those that have the technical knowledge but not the assurance skills. This increases the competitive difficulties for the accountant and makes it more difficult to convince potential clients about the value of the accountant's services.

On the other hand, it is difficult to name another profession that has a history of being independent and objective in the collection of evidence. The public accountant's audit skills honed over more than a hundred years of GAAS audits make the public accountant's expertise in planning, collection, and evaluation of evidence a clear competitive advantage for many services. As a result, an accountant may be able to effectively market assurance services that are beyond the core technical knowledge of a public accountant as long as the appropriate technical expertise backs up the accountant, often in the form of multidisciplinary teams consisting of subject matter specialists.

As noted above, audit scandals of the past few years have focused the profession on increasing the quality of the financial statement audit. At the time this text was written, public accountants had their hands quite full dealing with new requirements for documenting and testing internal control over financial reporting and performing audits under new U.S. PCAOB standards that affect auditors on a worldwide basis who deal with U.S.-registered public companies. Nonetheless, assurance services that range beyond the basic financial statement audit continue to be offered by accounting firms. In some cases, assurance services can be carried out in conjunction with the new requirements to evaluate and report on internal control (e.g., *SysTrust*^{SM} services on information systems) or as separate lines of business (e.g., *PrimePlus* in small-to-medium-sized firms). It remains to be seen how assurance services will survive and thrive in the new professional environment.

SUMMARY AND CONCLUSION

In this chapter, we discussed some of the different types of assurance and attestation services that a public accountant can provide. Assurance engagements come in many variations with standards being available from the very broad perspective of assurance engagements, to specific attest standards, to the extremely detailed standards for assurance services related to financial information. Knowledge of the appropriate standards and guidelines for an assurance engagement is critical for a public accountant to maintain a professional approach to such engagements. No assurance engagement should be accepted that cannot be conducted in accordance with professional standards or for which the public accountant lacks appropriate knowledge or expertise. Nevertheless, the world of opportunities for assurance services delivered by public accountants is vast and constrained only by the technical competence of the accountant and the regulatory restrictions of the profession.

BIBLIOGRAPHY OF RELATED PROFESSIONAL LITERATURE

Research

Alles, M. G., A. Kogan, and M. A. Vasarhelyi. 2002. Feasibility and Economics of Continuous Assurance. *Auditing: A Journal of Practice & Theory.* 21(1): 125–138.

American Accounting Association Audit Section. 1998. University of Waterloo Symposium on Auditing Research. *Auditing: A Journal of Practice & Theory.* 17(Supplement). Volume devoted to new assurance services.

Delfgaauw, T. 2000. Reporting on Sustainable Development: A Preparer's View. *Auditing: A Journal of Practice & Theory.* 19 (Supplement): 67–74.

Elliott, R. K. 1995. The Future of Assurance Services: Implications for Academia. *Accounting Horizons.* 9(4): 118–134.

Elliott, R. K. 2002. Twenty-First Century Assurance. *Auditing: A Journal of Practice & Theory.* 21(1): 139–146.

Fogarty, T. J., V. S. Radcliffe, and D. R. Campbell. 2006. Accountancy before The Fall: The AICPA Vision Project and Related Professional Enterprises. *Accounting, Organizations and Society.* 31(1): 1–25.

Gendron, Y. and M. Barrett. 2004. Professionalization in Action: Accountants' Attempt at Building a Network of Support for the WebTrust Seal of Assurance. *Contemporary Accounting Research.* 21(3): 563–602.

Hasan, M., P. J. Roebuck, and R. Simnet. 2003. An Investigation of Alternative Reporting Formats for Communicating Moderate Levels of Assurance. *Auditing: A Journal of Practice & Theory.* 22(2): 171–188.

Hunton, J. E., T. Benford, V. Arnold, and S. G. Sutton. 2000. The Impact of Electronic Commerce Assurance on Financial Analysts' Earnings Forecasts and Stock Price Estimates. *Auditing: A Journal of Practice & Theory.* 19 (Supplement): 5–22.

Jamal, K., M. Maier, and S. Sunder. 2003. Privacy in E-Commerce: Development of Reporting Standards, Disclosure, and Assurance Services in an Unregulated Market. *Journal of Accounting Research.* 41(2): 285–316.

Libby, T., S. Salterio and A. Webb. 2004. The Balanced Scorecard: The Effects of Assurance and Process Accountability on Managerial Judgment. *The Accounting Review.* 1075–1094.

Manry, D., S. L. Tiras, and C. M. Wheatley. 2003. The Influence of Interim Auditor Reviews on the Association of Returns with Earnings. *The Accounting Review.* 78(1): 251–274.

Wallage, P. 2000. Assurance On Sustainability Reporting: An Auditor's View. *Auditing: A Journal of Practice & Theory.* 19 (Supplement): 53–66.

Professional Reports and Guidance

AICPA/CICA. 1999. *Continuous Auditing* Research Report. Toronto: AICPA/CICA.

Committee of Sponsoring Organizations of the Treadway Commissions (COSO). 2004. *Enterprise Risk Management-Integrated Framework.* New York: COSO.

Auditing Standards

AICPA *Statements on Auditing Standard (SAS)* No. 70, "Audits of Service Organizations."

AICPA *Statements on Standards on Auditing Standards* No. 71., "Interim Financial Information."

AICPA *Statements on Standards for Attestation Engagements* No. 3., "Compliance Attestation."

AICPA *Statements on Standards for Attestation Engagements* No. 4., "Agreed-Upon Procedure Engagements."

AICPA *Statements on Standards for Accounting and Review Services* No. 1., "Compilation and Review of Financial Statements."

AICPA *Statements on Standards for Accounting and Review Services* No. 14., "Compilation of Pro Forma Financial Information."

AICPA *Statements on Standards for Accounting and Review Services* No. 8., "Amendment to *Statements on Standards for Accounting and Review Services* No. 1., Compilation and Review of Financial Statements."

IAASB *International Standards on Assurance Engagements* No. 3000R, "Assurance Engagement other than Audits or Reviews of Historical Financial Information."

IAASB *International Standards on Assurance Engagements* No. 3400, "The Examination of Prospective Financial Information."

IAASB *International Standards on Related Services* No. 4400, "Engagements to Perform Agreed-Upon Procedures Regarding Financial Information."

IAASB *International Standards on Related Services* No. 4410, "Engagements to Compile Financial Information."

IAASB *International Standards on Review Engagements* No. 2400, "Engagements to Review Financial Statements."

QUESTIONS

1. Compare and contrast the different levels of assurance provided by assurers who conduct reviews, compilation engagements, and agreed-upon procedures engagements. As part of your answer, describe why an organization would opt to hire assurers to provide each type of service.

2. Why do you believe that the SEC requires that quarterly financial statements be issued and subject to a review? Describe the procedures that an auditor performs when conducting a review of interim financial statements. Describe the risks that investors take when relying on information contained in quarterly financial statements as compared to audited year-end financial statements.

3. Given that a compilation does not involve providing any assurance and the auditor does not need to be independent to conduct the engagement, why do you believe that

auditing standards (for example, the AICPA) prohibits the performance of management functions, such as approving journal entries?

4. Assume that a hotel audit client owned by a consortium of investors is not satisfied with the hotel management company that performs most of its operations. The hotel hires a public accounting firm to go to the hotel management company to perform agreed-upon procedures to make sure that the hotel management company is properly performing all operations (e.g., reservations, housekeeping management, and so forth) for the hotel. Draft an agreed-upon procedures engagement letter based on the information contained in the chapter.

5. Describe why you believe that many auditors are reluctant to issue reports on prospective information and financial forecasts. How do the restrictions associated with these reports help address these risks?

6. What are some risks and barriers associated with providing independent assurance for corporate sustainability reports? What are the possible ramifications of not providing assurance for these reports? How can auditors address the risks and barriers to avoid such ramifications?

7. Compare and contrast an attestation engagement and an audit of financial statements. Provide examples of attestation engagements that are not audits of financial statements and describe how they are different.

8. You are the senior partner of a large, local audit firm. In reviewing the work of a junior staff member on a compilation engagement for Greasemonkey's Delight Inc., a local autoparts store (in which your brother-in-law is the CFO), you notice that she has written the following rough draft for an engagement report:

Audit Report

We have compiled the accompanying balance sheet of Greasemonkey's Delight Inc. as of December 31, 2007, and the related statements of income, retained earnings, and cash flows for the year then ended, in accordance with generally accepted accounting standards.

To the best of our knowledge, the compilation was done faithfully according to Statements on Standards for Accounting and Review Services issued by the AICPA. A significant amount of effort was expended on the engagement and, as such, we believe that the financial statements match what we were given.

Discuss the potentially misleading or deficient statements in this report. What other information do you need to know before issuing a compilation report?

9. Assume the same facts as in the preceding problem except that your junior staff auditors performed a review, instead of a compilation. The rough draft of the engagement report looks like this:

Audit Report

We have reviewed the accompanying balance sheet of Greasemonkey's Delight as of December 31, 2007, and the related statements of income, retained earnings, and cash flows for the year then ended, in accordance with generally accepted auditing standards.

A review is not as reliable for passing judgment on the financial statements as an audit is, but we have no reason to believe that the financial statements herein are stated unfairly. Accordingly, we express the opinion that, up to the point that a review can uncover any misstatements, the financial statements are stated fairly and were prepared in accordance with generally accepted accounting principles consistently applied.

Discuss the deficiencies, omissions, and errors in this report. What other information would be necessary before signing the report?

PROBLEMS

1. Assertions are amenable to attestation when the measures used to make them are objective and the data to support the assertion are available. In that light, consider the following assertions:
   a. Nine out of ten dentists recommend Bleegum toothpaste.
   b. Cholesterol is the leading cause of heart disease among males aged 60 and over.
   c. *Data* magazine tested all major computer operating systems and found that the Peachpit computer operating system outperforms them all.
   d. Latveria University has the best department of accounting in the United States.
   e. Profits at Grintell Semiconductors increased 13 percent over the same quarter last year.
   f. Emissions at the Pelican Point electrical generating plant are down 2 percent.
   g. We average three days on order fulfillment.
   h. The best actress for 2008 is Julia Roberts.

   For each of the assertions, (1) discuss the deficiencies in the assertion that would make it difficult to attest to, (2) discuss the deficiencies in the assertion that would make the intended target of it be able to question its utility, and (3) reword the assertion so that it is more easily interpreted.

2. In reviewing the interim financial statements of Lady Day Enterprises, a publicly traded electronic components wholesaler, your audit firm (which also conducts the annual audit) performs the following procedures:
   - Analytical procedures on the overall reasonableness of most of the account balances on the balance sheet.
   - Client inquiries on the methods used to obtain estimates of bad debts, inventory write-downs, and so on.
   - Analytical procedures on the largest expense categories (i.e., cost of goods sold, selling expenses).
   - Substantive tests on transactions in the inventory account balance where fraud is expected.

   Discuss any deficiencies in the procedures and any special disclosures in your interim review report that will differ from the annual audit report. Assume you found that some inventory is not carried at the lower of cost or market.

3. Your audit firm has been called in to examine the financial forecasts of Martin Corp., a multinational commercial building contractor. Toward that end, your firm conducted the following procedures:
   - Studied the reliability of the statistical models used to predict the economic environment in the countries in which they operate.
   - Evaluated the potential profitability of the projects on which they are now working.
   - Passed judgment on the presentation of the forecasts (e.g., compliance with AICPA or international standards).
   - Studied their competitive position in their industry.

   Using the above information, (1) suggest some other procedures they may want to perform and (2) discuss what kind of assurance your firm would include in the report on the forecast.

4. As part of your audit engagement of Walter's Bank N.A., you have been asked to provide a letter assuring the Office of the Comptroller of the Currency (OCC) that the bank has maintained adequate capital and loan loss provisions against a downturn in their area's economy. Having completed the task, you submit a few drafts of the letter to the partner in charge of the audit for her review. The pertinent sections follow.
   a. "... Walter's Bank N.A. has adequately reserved against adverse economic conditions in its local lending area through its loan loss provisions and its capital position."

b. "... We have audited the financial statements of Walter's Bank, N.A., and can assure the OCC that it has adequately reserved against downturns in their local economy through their loan loss provisions and their capital position."

c. "... Having audited the financial statements of Walter's Bank N.A., we can say that it has substantially complied with the loan loss provisions and the capital requirements of the OCC for these circumstances."

Using the above information, (1) discuss the deficiencies in each of these reports and (2) write the pertinent part of a letter of assurance to the OCC so that it meets the appropriate reporting standards.

5. Flappers, a restaurant located in Birmingville, has hired their auditors, Bud's Accounting Firm, to attest to the following assertion: *"Our chicken wings are world famous!"* Bud's Accounting Firm accepted the engagement mostly because their partners believe that Flappers might use the attestation to increase their sales of chicken wings and, consequently, Bud's will eventually see a higher audit fee.

Given the ease with which Bud's felt they could establish the reach of Flappers' chicken wing fame, and to save money, Bud's skipped over the majority of the planning phase and proceeded directly to their substantive tests. Those tests are as follows:

• Using high school students who needed the summer work, Bud's conducted a telephone poll of randomly selected names from a database provided by the Chamber of Commerce that lists people who have visited Birmingville within the past several months. The question was, "Have you ever heard of Flappers' chicken wings?"

• The daughter of one of the partners asked people coming out of a shopping mall in the nearby city of Mums whether they had ever heard of Flappers' chicken wings.

• Hotel clerks were offered $1.00 per person for signed statements from their out-of-town guests stating that they had heard of Flappers' chicken wings.

Once all the data was collected, the partners of Bud's Accounting Firm found, not surprisingly, that many people from all over the world had heard of Flappers' chicken wings. Based on the criterion that at least one person from 25 states and five foreign nations had to have responded affirmatively to the poll, the partners concluded that Flappers' chicken wings were, in fact, "world famous." Their report follows:

Bud's Accounting Firm

To whom it may concern:

We hereby attest to the assertion that Flappers' chicken wings are "world famous."

Bud Hammer, CPA

Discuss the primary ways that this engagement violates attestation standards. Be specific.

6. Barbara and Bill Hoehn have engaged A. Local Accounting Firm to conduct an audit of the cash accounts of their diamond mining business. The mines are not publicly owned, so a full-fledged audit is neither necessary nor desired, but the Hoehn's are concerned with the possibility that embezzlement has been going on in the area and they also want a clear idea of the current cash on hand. Therefore, the primary focus of the agreed-upon procedures will be a reconciliation of all cash accounts.

Having completed the reconciliations, A. Local is satisfied that the cash on hand as of fiscal year end 2008 matches the amount from their internally generated financial statements.

A. Local's report on the engagement follows:

A. Local Accounting Firm

To whom it may concern:

In order to establish the amount of cash on hand for the Hoehn Diamond Mines, we have reconciled all material cash accounts to the general ledger. Based on those reconciliations, we believe that the accounts are fairly stated.

Sid Dithers, CPA

Discuss the deficiencies in this report and suggest the wording for a proper report.

7. The Buddy Guy Co., a moving and storage firm with operations throughout the Midwest, has contracted with the Memphis Slim Accounting and Consulting Group to evaluate the adequacy of the controls associated with their accounts payable and to test the extent of compliance with them. Memphis Slim received the following letter from Buddy Guy that served as the guide to the engagement:

Dear Mr. Slim,

We hereby engage your firm to evaluate the internal controls in our accounts payable function. Such evaluations should include a comprehensive study of the controls with a view toward finding deficiencies in the internal control that could allow material misstatement into the financial statements. In addition, the evaluation should include tests of the controls in place to determine whether the procedures are followed adequately.

Attached you will find a brief narrative of the accounts payable process highlighted with the inherent controls. Further information will be provided, of course, at your request.

We look forward to your report.

Yours sincerely,

Buddy Guy
President

Buddy Guy Co. has never been audited as they are privately held. However, rapid growth in their business—from a small, 20-employee, two-location operation to one with more than 200 employees in 17 locations in just a few years—concerns the owners and directors enough to ask for Memphis Slim's help in ensuring that its payables operations are not subject to defalcation and misstatement.

   a. Discuss the deficiencies in the engagement letter.

   b. Discuss the steps Memphis Slim must take to form a proper conclusion on the effectiveness and completeness of its control plans. What effects will Buddy Guy's rapid growth have on Memphis Slim's testing?

   c. Draft an engagement report assuming that no material weaknesses are found.

   d. Give an example of a reportable condition that might arise from the testing. How might that condition become a material weakness?

8. Public accounting firms are sometimes called on to perform operational audits, where the operational effectiveness and efficiency of some process of an organization is studied. Consider the following independent situations where a public accounting firm might be asked to perform an operational audit.

   a. A not-for-profit agency wants to gain more productivity from its telemarketers.

   b. A large automobile service operation wants to improve its customer service by improving turnaround times on repairs and by formalizing its customer contact procedures and protocols.

c.   A regional snack food firm wants to improve the efficiency of its rack jobbers, who stock the shelves of thousands of small convenience and grocery stores, but without increasing the number of times that stock is unavailable to consumers.

d.   A large automotive manufacturer wants to decrease the number of people who perform the accounts payable function from 50 to 15 but without compromising control or missing purchase discounts.

e.   An insurance company wants to decrease the average time it takes to underwrite an application for life insurance from 30 days to 15 days without adding staff.

f.   In an attempt to gain market share, a fast-food restaurant chain wants to improve the time it takes to serve an average customer.

g.   The athletic association of a major university wants to improve the efficiency of its ticket operations both to save money and to decrease the incidence of alumni complaints.

h.   The police department of a major metropolitan area wants to decrease the resources it dedicates to procedures for recording arrests and to improve the accessibility of information on open investigations to officers in the field.

For each of the preceding, (1) discuss which procedures the public accountant might perform and (2) discuss whether there are more appropriate benchmarks available (for example, existing standards or standards issued by peer organizations).

9.   The chapter describes five principles that are evaluated during a *WebTrust*^{SM} engagement:

- Availability
- Security
- Processing Integrity
- Privacy
- Confidentiality

Suppose that you are performing a *WebTrust*^{SM} engagement for the order processing system for an online retailer. Classify each of the following controls to one of the above principles and discuss whether the control suggests that the corresponding principle is reliable for the system.

a.   Consumers are able to place orders electronically 24 hours a day, 7 days a week.

b.   Error logs suggest that customer addresses sometimes are not updated appropriately when customers input address changes.

c.   Web site updates in appearance or functionality occur periodically and consumers must update any data previously stored on the web site.

d.   Upon entering the "check-out" area of the web site, consumers must enter their user name and password to access stored information data. If consumers forget their passwords, they can enter a previously saved piece of personal data (e.g., mother's maiden name).

e.   Consumers are not told upon placing orders that goods will be shipped within 2–3 business days. However, they are told that an e-mail will be sent upon shipment. Consumers also are not told that they will be responsible for all costs associated with returning goods.

f.   The online retailer has outsourced the development of access controls for its information system to a consulting firm with an outstanding reputation in the industry.

g.   The system has a control mechanism such that all transactions for which errors are detected are automatically sent to a suspense database. No master records can be updated for the transaction until all problems are corrected.

10. Examine the following report for a *WebTrust*^{SM} engagement for an online retailer of pet supplies:

Independent Certified Public Accountant's Report

We have examined the assertion (www.luvapet.com/consumer_confidentiality.htm) by management of luvapet.com regarding the disclosure of its e-commerce business and information privacy practices on its web site and the effectiveness of its controls over transaction integrity and information protection for e-commerce based on the AICPA/CICA WebTrust Criteria during the period November 1, 2006 through December 31, 2006.

Our examination was conducted in accordance with the attestation standards established by the American Institute of Certified Public Accountants and, accordingly, included (1) obtaining an understanding of luvapet.com Company's e-commerce business and information privacy practices and its controls over the processing of e-commerce transactions and the protection of related private customer information, (2) testing and evaluating the operating effectiveness of the controls, and (3) performing such other procedures as we considered necessary in the circumstances. We believe that our examination provides a reasonable basis for our opinion.

Because of inherent limitations in controls, error or fraud may occur and not be detected.

In our opinion, during the period November 1, 2006 through December 31, 2001, luvapet.com Company, in all material respects:

- *Disclosed its business and information privacy practices for e-commerce transactions and executed transactions in accordance with disclosed practices*
- *Maintained effective controls to provide reasonable assurance that customers' orders placed using e-commerce were completed and billed as agreed*
- *Maintained effective controls to provide reasonable assurance that private customer information obtained as a result of e-commerce was protected from uses not related to luvapet.com's business*

Based on the AICPA/CICA WebTrust Criteria.

Knuckle and Blue, CPAs

Discuss the deficiencies with this report and comment why it is so important for the CPA firm to correct each problem.

Case 18–1: Assurance of Corporate Sustainability Reports

Currently, large companies throughout the world are continuing to issue corporate sustainability reports that report on a so-called triple bottom-line of economic, environmental, and social performance. Although there are several organizations offering reporting standards, some universal for the reports (e.g., the Global Reporting Initiative), and others tailored for specific components of the report (e.g., the Rainforest Alliance for environmental practices), there has yet to be any established standards for performing independent assurance for the reports. The International Accounting and Auditing Standards Board (IAASB) has established a task force to discuss standards for providing assurance but as of 2006, no formal standards exist.

Corporate sustainability reports contain a wide variety of information and formats, but essentially report on an organization's ability to manage economic, environmental, and social risks associated with the organization. Currently, organizations issue reports with varying levels of assurance, ranging from none to limited assurance based on internal policies to assurance based on audit procedures applied to specific quantitative measures contained within the reports.

For this case, access the most recent corporate sustainability reports for each of the following companies from the companies' web sites:

- Royal Dutch Shell (The Shell Report)
- Starbucks (Corporate Social Responsibility Annual Report)
- Nike (Corporate Responsibility Report)

Requirements

1. Examine each report and compare and contrast the approaches that each company has taken to provide assurance on the reports. (For example, a copy of Shell's assurance report is contained in Figure 18–9.)
2. What are the benefits and risks for providing assurance for explicit quantitative measures included in the CSR reports? Explain whether or not providing assurance based on consistent application of internal reporting policies effectively address the weaknesses.
3. What are the benefits and risks for eschewing independent public accountants and instead opting to use assurers associated with other organizations?
4. Some organizations do not address external assurance anywhere within their CSR reports. What are the risks associated with issuing reports containing no external assurance?

Case 18–2: Assurance of Enterprise Risk Management

In 2004, the Committee of Sponsoring Organizations of the Treadway Commission (COSO) issued its *Enterprise Risk Management—Integrated Framework*, which evolves the framework developed for internal controls over financial reporting to cover enterprise risk management.

The framework contains the following elements (which are illustrated in Figure 18–14):

- Internal Environment
- Objective Setting
- Event Identification
- Risk Assessment
- Risk Response
- Control Activities
- Information & Communication
- Monitoring

In the COSO framework, the definition of enterprise risk management is as follows:

Enterprise Risk Management: A process, effected by an entity's board of directors, management, and other personnel, applied in a strategy setting and across the enterprise, designed to identify potential events that may affect the entity, and manage risks to be within its risk appetite, to provide reasonable assurance regarding the achievement of entity objectives.[18]

This definition should enable assurers to provide assurance regarding the effectiveness of an organization's enterprise risk management framework for enabling an organization to provide reasonable assurance that an organization is able to achieve its overall business objectives, particularly because the framework should address strategic, operations, reporting, and compliance objectives of an organization (as shown in Figure 18–17).

Requirements

1. Compare and contrast an assurance approach for an engagement to assess the effectiveness of an organization's implementation of COSO's ERM framework as compared to an engagement to assess the operating effectiveness of an organization's internal control over financial reporting using COSO's 1992 internal control framework (see Chapter 2 for further description of both frameworks).

2. Based on the concepts of auditing and assurance discussed throughout this textbook, describe the most significant challenges that assurers have in planning and performing an engagement to support a reasonable (e..g., high) level

Used with permission of COSO.

18 COSO 2004.

of assurance that an enterprise risk management framework will enable an organization to achieve its objectives.

3. Select the elements of the COSO ERM framework that you believe will be the most difficult to evaluate for effectiveness based on evidence gathering techniques (e.g., procedures for understanding the entity, tests of controls, analytical procedures, substantive tests, etc.) discussed throughout this textbook.

4. Argue a position for or against the importance of providing assurance services regarding the effectiveness of an organization's enterprise risk management framework for providing reasonable assurance for meeting an organization's business objectives.

Index